Driving Global Health and Sustainable Development Goals With Smart Technology

Mohit Kukreti
University of Technology and Applied Sceinces, Oman

Sabina Sehajpal
Chandigarh University, India

Rajesh Tiwari
Graphic Era University, India

Kiran Sood
Chitkara Business School, Chitkara University, Punjab, India

Vice President of Editorial	Melissa Wagner
Managing Editor of Acquisitions	Mikaela Felty
Managing Editor of Book Development	Jocelynn Hessler
Production Manager	Mike Brehm
Cover Design	Phillip Shickler

Published in the United States of America by
IGI Global Scientific Publishing
701 East Chocolate Avenue
Hershey, PA, 17033, USA
Tel: 717-533-8845
Fax: 717-533-8661
E-mail: cust@igi-global.com
Website: https://www.igi-global.com

Copyright © 2025 by IGI Global Scientific Publishing. All rights reserved. No part of this publication may be reproduced, stored or distributed in any form or by any means, electronic or mechanical, including photocopying, without written permission from the publisher.
Product or company names used in this set are for identification purposes only. Inclusion of the names of the products or companies does not indicate a claim of ownership by IGI Global Scientific Publishing of the trademark or registered trademark.

Library of Congress Cataloging-in-Publication Data

CIP Data Pending
ISBN:979-8-3373-0240-9
eISBN:979-8-3373-0242-3

British Cataloguing in Publication Data
A Cataloguing in Publication record for this book is available from the British Library.

ll work contributed to this book is new, previously-unpublished material.
he views expressed in this book are those of the authors, but not necessarily of the publisher.
This book contains information sourced from authentic and highly regarded references, with reasonable efforts made to ensure the reliability of the data and information presented. The authors, editors, and publisher believe the information in this book to be accurate and true as of the date of publication. Every effort has been made to trace and credit the copyright holders of all materials included. However, the authors, editors, and publisher cannot assume responsibility for the validity of all materials or the consequences of their use. Should any copyright material be found unacknowledged, please inform the publisher so that corrections may be made in future reprints.

Table of Contents

Foreword xix

Preface xxi

Introduction xxvii

Chapter 1
Impact of Digital Health Interventions on Healthcare Access in Developing Countries 1
    Anupama Singh, Graphic Era University, India

Chapter 2
Innovating Global Health With Smart Technology to Achieve Sustainable Development 11
    Harshi Garg, IIMT University, India
    Mohammad Kashif, Graphic Era University, India
    Priyank Sharma, IIMT University, India
    Nikita Singhal, IIMT University, India

Chapter 3
Harnessing the Power of Precision Medicine and AI: Success Stories and Ethical Considerations 37
    Latika Sahni, NDIM, India
    Rishi Prakash Shukla, Jaipuria Institute of Management, India

Chapter 4
Ethical, Privacy, and Security Issues in Smart Healthcare 83
    Swati Gupta, Chitkara University, Punjab, India

Chapter 5
Escalating Artificial Intelligence-Enabled Clinical Decision Support Systems to Enhance Home-Based Care: A Study on Healthcare Supply Chains 99
    Manu Sharna, Graphic Era University, India
    Priyanka Gupta, Graphic Era University, India
    Janmejai Shah, Graphic Era University, India
    Sudhanshu Joshi, Doon University, India

Chapter 6
Application of Artificial Intelligence in Healthcare Sector: A Multidimensional Perspective............ 115
  Anu Sayal, Taylor's University, Malaysia
  Ashulekha Gupta, Graphic Era University, India
  Janhvi Jha, Jain University, India
  N. Chaithra, Jain University, India
  Allagari Nithin, Jain University, India

Chapter 7
An Exhaustive Inference of Machine Learning Applications in Healthcare: Analyzing Research Studies on Diagnosis and Prevention............ 139
  Manas Kumar Swain, Siksha O Anusandhan University, India
  Narendra Kumar Kamila, GITA College, India
  Lambodar Jena, Siksha O Anusandhan University, India
  Nilamadhab Mishra, VIT Bhopal University, India

Chapter 8
AI, IoT, and Blockchain in Healthcare: Bridging Technology and Patient Wellbeing............ 161
  Krishnaveni Subramani, SR University, India
  Geetha Manoharan, SR University, India

Chapter 9
AI and Language: Transforming Communication in Health and Wellness............ 181
  Preeti Tushar Joshi, Sri Balaji Vidyapeeth University, India
  Eldad Tsabary, Concordia University, Canada
  Isanka P. Gamage, University of Kelaniya, Sri Lanka

Chapter 10
Exploiting Image Processing and AI for Neurological Disorder Diagnosis: A Focus on Alzheimer's and Parkinson's Diseases............ 213
  Jyoti Kumari, Veer Surendra Sai University of Technology, India
  Santi Kumari Behera, Veer Surendra Sai University of Technology, India
  Prabira Kumar Sethy, Guru Ghasidas Vishwavidyalaya, India

Chapter 11
Health Economics and Sustainability in the Era of Digital Transformation: Addressing Digital Stress and Sustainable Development Goals............ 241
  Priyanka Gupta, Graphic Era University, India
  Girish Lakhera, Graphic Era University, India
  Manu Sharma, Graphic Era University, India
  Sudhanshu Joshi, Doon University, India

Chapter 12
Innovative Financing Models and Future Directions in Healthcare: Evaluating the Impact of Financial Strategies on Digital Health Outcomes and Innovation 267
    Bhupinder Pal Singh Chahal, Yorkville University, Canada
    Umang Sharma, Chandigarh Business School, CGC, Jhanjeri, India
    Bhumika Bansal, NDIM, India

Chapter 13
Navigating Challenges and Innovations in Global Healthcare 303
    Malkeet Singh, Chaudhary Devi Lal University, India
    Khem Chand, Lovely Professional University, India
    Mandeep Singh, Chandigarh University, India

Chapter 14
Pandemic Preparedness and the Economics of Global Health Crises 339
    Larisa Mistrean, Academy of Economic Studies of Moldova, Moldova
    Azad Singh, Mangalmay Institute of Management and Technology, India
    Tripti Desai, New Delhi Institute of Management, India

Chapter 15
Policy and Regulatory Frameworks for Financing Smart Healthcare 367
    Anuradha Jain, Vivekananda Institute of Professional Studies, India
    Raj Kumar Singh, Graphic Era Hill University, India
    Padam Bhushan, Chandigarh University, India

Chapter 16
Precision and Performance: Smart Healthcare Technologies in Sports Medicine Wellness 389
    S. C. Dileepkumar , Kuvempu University, India
    Ravindra Gouda, Kuvempu University, India
    Basavaraj Kumasi, Sri Balaji Vidyapeeth University, India

Chapter 17
Predicting Novel Coronavirus Trends Using Machine Learning 411
    Anamika Ahirwar, Compucom Institute of Technology and Management, Jaipur, India
    Mahendra Singh Panwar, Compucom Institute of Technology and Management, Jaipur, India

Chapter 18
Revolutionizing Finance: The Synergy of Smart Cards and FinTech in Process and Product Innovations 439
    Reepu, Chandigarh University, India
    Sanjay Taneja, Graphic Era University, India
    Luan Vardari, University "Ukshin Hoti", Kosovo

Chapter 19
The Future of the Healthcare Workforce in the Age of Automation 453
    Varinderjeet Singh, Sant Baba Bhag Singh University, India
    Gurinderpal Singh, Chandigarh University, India
    Gajendra Sharma, New Delhi Institute of Management, India

Chapter 20
Transforming Global Health Outcomes Through Smart Technology and the SGD Framework 473
    Vishwajit K. Barbudhe, Sandip Foundation, India
    Shraddha N. Zanjat, SOET, Sandip University, India
    Bhavana S. Karmore, Raisoni Group of Institutions, India

Chapter 21
Unleashing Operational Mastery and Patient-Centric Innovation Through Robotic Process
Automation in Healthcare 491
    Nikhil Yadav, Jaypee Institute of Information Technology, India
    Rinku Taneja, Axis Bank, India

Chapter 22
Use of Artificial Intelligence for Health Insurance: A Bibliometric Exploration............................. 509
    Saurabh Bhatt, Graphic Era University, India
    Rajesh Tiwari, Graphic Era University, India
    Chandra Prakash, Graphic Era University, India
    Bijesh Dhyani, Graphic Era University, India
    Bhanu Sharma, Graphic Era University, India
    Kapil Ahalawat, Graphic Era University, India

Chapter 23
Work From Home and Sustainable Development Goals: A Framework for Healthcare Sector 521
    Ridhima Goel, Maharshi Dayanand Univesity, India
    Jagdeep Singla, Maharshi Dayanand University, India
    Sanjeet Kumar, Chaudhary Devi Lal University, India

Chapter 24
Impact of the Russian Invasion of Ukraine on the Indian Pharmaceutical Sector 543
    Rajesh Tiwari, Graphic Era University, India
    Vivek Verma, Graphic Era University, India
    Vibhuti Jain, Graphic Era University, India
    Vanshika Kakkar, Graphic Era University, India

Compilation of References 557

About the Contributors 633

Index 643

Detailed Table of Contents

Foreword xix

Preface xxi

Introduction xxvii

Chapter 1
Impact of Digital Health Interventions on Healthcare Access in Developing Countries 1
    Anupama Singh, Graphic Era University, India

Technology has permeated all aspects of the healthcare system. The growth and easy availability of internet and smart mobile devices, health monitoring is possible by individuals also. Healthcare systems in developing countries are using technology in many ways to ease access and delivery of health-related services. Developing countries are slowly adapting these technologies, with initial costs being the biggest barrier. Widespread availability of mobile devices and self-monitoring technologies, the digital health interventions are having a positive impact on the population in developing countries. A comparison of traditional medical interventions and the digital interventions is not easy; it depends on the context, geographical area and strategy of usage. The digital technologies show promise of cost-effective universal healthcare. Major factors contributing to the cost-effectiveness are ability of rapid expansion, lower cost of healthcare providers, higher accessibility, and long-term benefits.

Chapter 2
Innovating Global Health With Smart Technology to Achieve Sustainable Development 11
    Harshi Garg, IIMT University, India
    Mohammad Kashif, Graphic Era University, India
    Priyank Sharma, IIMT University, India
    Nikita Singhal, IIMT University, India

This chapter discusses how innovations in healthcare like artificial intelligence, telemedicine, data analytics, and blockchain, can solve critical health problems and improve the availability of treatment. Smart technology can help to accomplish Sustainable Development Goal 3, which promotes global health and well-being. Case studies from real-world situations prove how well they are helping to combat global health problems such as not communicable illness, avoiding illness, and reproductive health. The chapter additionally provides policy recommendations to improve the healthcare system facilities, and encouraging international cooperation to share efficient procedures and technological advances. Establishing ethical frameworks, laws and regulations illustrates the significance of carrying out smart technology ethically and inclusively. This chapter presents a comprehensive analysis of the methods in which these scientific innovations can promote long-term healthcare systems and enhance the accomplishments of worldwide health targets.

Chapter 3
Harnessing the Power of Precision Medicine and AI: Success Stories and Ethical Considerations 37
    Latika Sahni, NDIM, India
    Rishi Prakash Shukla, Jaipuria Institute of Management, India

This chapter explores the transformative potential of precision medicine and AI in revolutionizing healthcare delivery. By tailoring treatments to individual patient profiles through genomic insights and advanced analytics, personalized healthcare optimizes therapeutic efficacy, particularly in oncology, rare diseases, and chronic conditions. Case studies illustrate the economic advantages of targeted interventions, highlighting cost efficiency through reduced trial-and-error treatments and improved patient outcomes. However, the integration of AI introduces ethical dilemmas, including data privacy concerns, algorithmic biases, and the implications of genetic editing technologies. Global examples of healthcare systems implementing AI-driven personalized medicine provide valuable insights into best practices and lessons learned from early adopters. As the landscape of healthcare evolves, the chapter emphasizes the need for interdisciplinary collaboration, robust data infrastructure, and active patient engagement to navigate the complexities of precision medicine.

Chapter 4
Ethical, Privacy, and Security Issues in Smart Healthcare 83
    Swati Gupta, Chitkara University, Punjab, India

Smart healthcare technologies have transformed the healthcare landscape, promising precision, efficiency, and improved patient outcomes. However, these advancements bring significant ethical, privacy, and security challenges. The increased use of AI and data-driven systems in healthcare raises questions about patient autonomy, data ownership, and informed consent. As large volumes of sensitive health data are generated, ensuring robust security measures is critical to protecting patient privacy. Moreover, the push for cost-effectiveness in healthcare often conflicts with ethical obligations, necessitating a balanced approach. Health economics also impacts ethical decision-making, as stakeholders must navigate the trade-offs between cost containment and quality care. This chapter explores these complexities, examining frameworks to address ethical, privacy, and security concerns. Through case studies and regulatory perspectives, it offers insights into how smart healthcare can responsibly advance while safeguarding patient rights and public trust.

Chapter 5
Escalating Artificial Intelligence-Enabled Clinical Decision Support Systems to Enhance Home-Based Care: A Study on Healthcare Supply Chains 99
    Manu Sharna, Graphic Era University, India
    Priyanka Gupta, Graphic Era University, India
    Janmejai Shah, Graphic Era University, India
    Sudhanshu Joshi, Doon University, India

Artificial intelligence is rapidly advancing to replace human-based approaches in Clinical Decision Support Systems (CDSS), which has caused a revolution in the home-based care sector. CDSS provides instant diagnostic and therapeutic suggestions, hence improving the communication and gap between the medical professionals and patients in hard-to-reach areas. This review paper looks into how healthcare supply chains can be optimised through AI, in addition to monitoring the availability of inventory and medical products and predicting what a patient might need. Moreover, the investigation assesses the effectiveness of such systems in the overall consideration of the issue—cost containment and patients' outcomes, especially in chronic illness treatment. The study fits directly to SDGs 3, 9, and 10 since it aims to eliminate health disparities by proactively endorsing home-based healthcare services. This paper gives recommendations to healthcare organisations and government entities, mainly in prospecting how AI would reshape home-based care.

Chapter 6
Application of Artificial Intelligence in Healthcare Sector: A Multidimensional Perspective 115
    Anu Sayal, Taylor's University, Malaysia
    Ashulekha Gupta, Graphic Era University, India
    Janhvi Jha, Jain University, India
    N. Chaithra, Jain University, India
    Allagari Nithin, Jain University, India

In this paper, we emphasize the recent innovations made in biomedicine and healthcare by applying AI. To better understand real-world applications of AI in the field, we have also included a case study that uses a convolution neural network to detect the presence of malaria in human cells. Numerous types of AI are already being applied in various fields such as cardiology and neurology for detecting cysts and tumors through digital image processing and dermatology for detecting and treating lesions and psoriasis. Moreover, significant evidence indicates its use in genomics and 3D bioprinting, which are both expected to revolutionize treatment. AI has increased the efficiency and reduced the workload of health professionals. There are unquestionably application instances in which AI performs healthcare activities as well as or better than humans. Our studies show that AI is largely restructuring the constitution of human well-being as a whole and is predicted to progress in leaps and bounds.

Chapter 7
An Exhaustive Inference of Machine Learning Applications in Healthcare: Analyzing Research
Studies on Diagnosis and Prevention 139
    Manas Kumar Swain, Siksha O Anusandhan University, India
    Narendra Kumar Kamila, GITA College, India
    Lambodar Jena, Siksha O Anusandhan University, India
    Nilamadhab Mishra, VIT Bhopal University, India

Machine learning has become an important tool in healthcare research to solve complex classification problems effectively, efficiently, and quickly. Generally, doctors treat patients according to their medical knowledge and personal experience. Since different professionals have different experiences, they may sometimes make a wrong diagnosis and need more time for treatment. Current research mainly focuses on the problem of classifying/predicting medical data based on machine learning. There is a need to create an intelligent structure that can distribute the information stored in the database. Human data analysis capabilities are less compared to data storage. This is more important in the case of medical records because it helps search, diagnose, and treat patients based on individual records. This paper's main goal is to review the pre-researched methodologies of machine learning techniques to analyze healthcare data to diagnose and prevent illnesses. Finally, these research articles are classified based on healthcare data, machine learning techniques, and performance parameters.

Chapter 8
AI, IoT, and Blockchain in Healthcare: Bridging Technology and Patient Wellbeing 161
    Krishnaveni Subramani, SR University, India
    Geetha Manoharan, SR University, India

Digital technology increases diagnosis, treatment, and efficiency, transforming healthcare. This article uses real-life business examples to demonstrate how blockchain technology, AI, and IoT are changing health care and how they may help. AI algorithms speed up and enhance diagnostic, prognostic, and therapeutic decision-making. IoT devices can monitor patients, offer remote health care, and collect data instantly, improving outcomes and resource use. Blockchain technology protects patient privacy and promotes healthcare system collaboration by securely and transparently managing medical records. As seen in this chapter, these technologies work well. Using AI in imaging and genetics simplifies early diagnosis and treatment planning. Wearable health monitoring, smart implants, and telemedicine can improve patient treatment. Blockchain technology will secure EHRs, manage medicine supply chains, and facilitate clinical trials. The Internet of Things, blockchain technology, and AI are improving data privacy, patient participation, and treatment availability in healthcare.

Chapter 9
AI and Language: Transforming Communication in Health and Wellness 181
    Preeti Tushar Joshi, Sri Balaji Vidyapeeth University, India
    Eldad Tsabary, Concordia University, Canada
    Isanka P. Gamage, University of Kelaniya, Sri Lanka

Artificial Intelligence (AI) has significantly transformed communication within the health and wellness industry. This transformation has not only enhanced healthcare delivery but also empowered individuals with tools and resources that facilitate proactive, personalized wellness management. Through language-based AI applications like chatbots, voice assistants, and Natural Language Processing (NLP) algorithms, healthcare providers can offer seamless patient experiences, enhance accessibility, and support decision-making. Additionally, these AI-driven communication tools help break language barriers, foster patient engagement, and encourage healthy lifestyle choices. This chapter delves into the mechanisms, applications, and implications of AI in reshaping communication in health and wellness, analyzing the ethical, practical, and social facets of this transformation

Chapter 10
Exploiting Image Processing and AI for Neurological Disorder Diagnosis: A Focus on
Alzheimer's and Parkinson's Diseases 213
    Jyoti Kumari, Veer Surendra Sai University of Technology, India
    Santi Kumari Behera, Veer Surendra Sai University of Technology, India
    Prabira Kumar Sethy, Guru Ghasidas Vishwavidyalaya, India

The diagnosis and management of neurological disorders, particularly Alzheimer's and Parkinson's diseases, rely heavily on advanced medical imaging techniques. Neuroimaging modalities such as magnetic resonance imaging (MRI), positron emission tomography (PET), and single-photon emission computed tomography (SPECT) play a critical role in revealing structural and functional changes in the brain associated with these diseases. This review explores how image processing techniques and artificial intelligence (AI), including machine learning and deep learning, are revolutionising the diagnosis of Alzheimer's and Parkinson's. By leveraging these technologies, significant improvements in early detection, disease progression tracking, and personalised treatment strategies have been achieved. This paper aims to provide a comprehensive overview of current AI-driven approaches, their applications in neuroimaging, and their potential to advance the understanding and treatment of these neurological disorders.

Chapter 11
Health Economics and Sustainability in the Era of Digital Transformation: Addressing Digital
Stress and Sustainable Development Goals 241
    Priyanka Gupta, Graphic Era University, India
    Girish Lakhera, Graphic Era University, India
    Manu Sharma, Graphic Era University, India
    Sudhanshu Joshi, Doon University, India

This chapter explores the aspect of Economic evaluation of implementing Digital Health, Digital Stress, and Digital Transformation technologies in the context of Systems Sustainability challenge in healthcare systems. Leveraging smart technologies such as AI, IoT, Blockchain, healthcare systems are witnessing unprecedented Digital Transformations in cost efficiency and service delivery. The key aspect addressed is the impact of Digital Transformation healthcare systems, including the challenges pose by Techno Invasion, the over penetration of technology into personal and professional spaces, leading to increased Digital Stress for Healthcare professionals. It also highlights the importance of achieving a balance between innovation and workforce sustainability, with strategies to mitigate the negative effects of digital overload while maximizing the benefits of smart healthcare solutions. Also emphasized the importance of balancing technological integration with human wellbeing.

Chapter 12
Innovative Financing Models and Future Directions in Healthcare: Evaluating the Impact of
Financial Strategies on Digital Health Outcomes and Innovation 267
    Bhupinder Pal Singh Chahal, Yorkville University, Canada
    Umang Sharma, Chandigarh Business School, CGC, Jhanjeri, India
    Bhumika Bansal, NDIM, India

This study explores innovative financing models and future directions in healthcare, with a focus on assessing financial impact on digital health outcomes and advancing sustainable healthcare innovation. As digital health technologies like AI, IoT, and telemedicine transform patient care, the need for adaptable and value-based financing mechanisms becomes critical. Traditional models, often inadequate for the rapid pace of digital health, are compared to novel approaches such as public-private partnerships, outcome-based financing, and tiered pricing. The research examines how these models can drive equitable access, incentivize innovation, and improve patient outcomes globally. Through evaluating financial strategies, this study provides insights into scalable frameworks that prioritize both fiscal sustainability and impactful health outcomes, paving the way for a resilient, technologically integrated healthcare ecosystem.

Chapter 13
Navigating Challenges and Innovations in Global Healthcare 303
    Malkeet Singh, Chaudhary Devi Lal University, India
    Khem Chand, Lovely Professional University, India
    Mandeep Singh, Chandigarh University, India

Telemedicine and remote care have redefined the contours of healthcare delivery by bridging geographical barriers and enhancing accessibility, particularly in underserved and low-income communities. This chapter delves into the evolution of telemedicine, underscoring its transformative role in reducing disparities in healthcare access. It further explores the cost-effectiveness of telehealth models, presenting data to illustrate affordability and long-term economic viability. The chapter concludes by analyzing the macroeconomic impact of expanding telemedicine services, including workforce shifts, infrastructural investments, and implications for healthcare policy. The potential of telemedicine to recalibrate the healthcare landscape is immense, but it demands thoughtful integration with existing systems, regulatory foresight, and continuous technological innovation to ensure equitable, sustainable care.

Chapter 14
Pandemic Preparedness and the Economics of Global Health Crises 339
    Larisa Mistrean, Academy of Economic Studies of Moldova, Moldova
    Azad Singh, Mangalmay Institute of Management and Technology, India
    Tripti Desai, New Delhi Institute of Management, India

The chapter explores how intelligent technologies, particularly AI and predictive analytics, are revolutionising pandemic preparedness and the economics of global health crises. By leveraging digital health tools, data analysis, and IoT systems, governments and health organisations can enhance early detection, streamline resource management, and reduce the economic burden of pandemics. The chapter delves into the financial implications of adopting tech-driven strategies, presenting a cost-benefit analysis that highlights the return on investment for implementing such tools. Drawing lessons from COVID-19, the chapter emphasises the potential for technology to mitigate future health crises' economic impact. Ethical considerations, especially concerning data privacy, are addressed, along with policy recommendations to support sustainable investments in health technology. The insights aim to inform a balanced approach that aligns public health goals with economic resilience for better future preparedness.

Chapter 15
Policy and Regulatory Frameworks for Financing Smart Healthcare 367
    Anuradha Jain, Vivekananda Institute of Professional Studies, India
    Raj Kumar Singh, Graphic Era Hill University, India
    Padam Bhushan, Chandigarh University, India

As smart healthcare technologies emerge as pillars of modern medicine, developing policy and regulatory frameworks for sustainable financing becomes imperative. Regulatory complexities, spanning data governance, interoperability, and cost-effectiveness, present challenges and opportunities in securing funding for AI, IoT, and digital diagnostics. Policymakers must navigate privacy concerns, ethical dilemmas, and market dynamics to create resilient funding strategies. International cooperation plays a pivotal role in achieving SDG 3 by harmonizing funding protocols and prioritizing equitable access to advanced healthcare across nations. This chapter examines financial policy frameworks needed to support long-term technology integration in global health, exploring funding sources, cost management, and ethical imperatives. By addressing regulatory gaps, enhancing intergovernmental collaboration, and aligning technological investments with health equity goals, policymakers can foster a sustainable future where smart healthcare is accessible to all.

Chapter 16
Precision and Performance: Smart Healthcare Technologies in Sports Medicine Wellness 389
    S. C. Dileepkumar, Kuvempu University, India
    Ravindra Gouda, Kuvempu University, India
    Basavaraj Kumasi, Sri Balaji Vidyapeeth University, India

The confluence of precision medicine and advanced healthcare technologies is revolutionizing sports medicine by refining diagnostics, optimizing therapeutic interventions, and elevating performance metrics. This chapter delves into the transformative role of smart healthcare systems, including wearable biosensors, machine learning algorithms, and data-driven analytics, which collectively enable a nuanced understanding of athletic health. By enhancing early injury detection and fostering customized rehabilitation strategies, these technologies epitomize a paradigmatic shift toward individualized, anticipatory healthcare in sports. Our analysis elucidates both the mechanistic functionalities and the physiological implications of these innovations, which promise to redefine the contours of athletic resilience and human potential.

Chapter 17
Predicting Novel Coronavirus Trends Using Machine Learning 411
    Anamika Ahirwar, Compucom Institute of Technology and Management, Jaipur, India
    Mahendra Singh Panwar, Compucom Institute of Technology and Management, Jaipur, India

2020 began with the advent of disruption brought on by a new virus called SARS-CoV-2. The coronavirus pandemic i.e. COVID-19, according to the World Health Organization (WHO), is putting a lot of strain on even the strongest healthcare systems in the entire world. Our current study explores supervised learning methods in machine learning, such as SVMachine, K-nearest neighbor, Naïve Bayes, Decision Tree, Random Forest, Logistic Regression, and a newly developed algorithm called XGB classifier. Specifically, the prediction of COVID-19-related deaths and recoveries is the focus of our proposed approach. A GitHub repository served as the source of the dataset used in this investigation. In this paper our aim is to enhance our comprehension of the pandemic's consequences through the application of machine learning techniques.

Chapter 18
Revolutionizing Finance: The Synergy of Smart Cards and FinTech in Process and Product
Innovations...439
  Reepu, Chandigarh University, India
  Sanjay Taneja, Graphic Era University, India
  Luan Vardari, University "Ukshin Hoti", Kosovo

This paper investigates the ever-changing field of financial innovations with particular regard to the interface of two game changers: Smart Cards and Finansheta. The industry's financial paradigm has changed due to the role of technology, which enables the creation of advanced service delivery methods that are efficient, secure, and accessible. This study critically evaluates the interdependence between Smart Cards and FinTech, demonstrating how the two can work together to enhance financial services and products. The first part considers the history of the development of Smart Cards when they first appeared and what he has now in various areas of finance. . The second segment addresses the emergence of FinTech and the role it plays in financial innovation. Fintech has changed the traditional range of banking, and instead, the culture of digital financial services, including the use of crowd finance and robo-advisors, has emerged. This paper reviews the prominent aspects of Fintech, including the blockchain.

Chapter 19
The Future of the Healthcare Workforce in the Age of Automation 453
  Varinderjeet Singh, Sant Baba Bhag Singh University, India
  Gurinderpal Singh, Chandigarh University, India
  Gajendra Sharma, New Delhi Institute of Management, India

Healthcare professions face shifts in job roles, requiring reskilling in data literacy and robotics. Financially, organizations must navigate the costs of technology adoption and workforce training while balancing automation with human labor to preserve empathy in patient care. Legal, ethical, and sociocultural impacts also arise, from liability ambiguities to potential algorithmic biases and reduced human contact. This chapter explores these multifaceted dynamics, advocating for a balanced approach where automation augments, rather than replaces, human judgment and underscores the need for regulatory frameworks that ensure fairness, accountability, and the preservation of quality care. By harmonizing technological progress with human-centered values, the healthcare sector can responsibly advance in the automated age.

Chapter 20
Transforming Global Health Outcomes Through Smart Technology and the SGD Framework 473
    Vishwajit K. Barbudhe, Sandip Foundation, India
    Shraddha N. Zanjat, SOET, Sandip University, India
    Bhavana S. Karmore, Raisoni Group of Institutions, India

The fastest-ever technological advancements have presented the most incredible opportunity to alter global health, a development that aligns well with the Sustainable Development Goals (SDGs) agenda. We showed how intelligent technologies can directly impact healthcare systems, resulting in advancements relevant to achieving SDG 3 (Good et al.) The third and last of these four goals is to examine the relationships and interconnections between SDG 8 (Decent Work and Economic Growth), SDG 9 (Industry et al.), and SDG 11 (Sustainable). The conversation is purposefully moving toward an eco-systemic architecture that achieves the objective via succession. The report offers a comprehensive view of disruptive technologies, particularly about the global health ecosystem, covering everything from genomics and data-driven diagnostics for personalized medicine to remote patient monitoring (RPM) and the effectiveness of healthcare system management.

Chapter 21
Unleashing Operational Mastery and Patient-Centric Innovation Through Robotic Process Automation in Healthcare 491
    Nikhil Yadav, Jaypee Institute of Information Technology, India
    Rinku Taneja, Axis Bank, India

Robotic Process Automation (RPA) is transforming healthcare operations by automating repetitive tasks across hospital administration, finance, and supply chain management. This technology streamlines workflows, minimizes human error, and enhances data accuracy, leading to substantial improvements in efficiency and resource allocation. In healthcare finance, RPA reduces operational inefficiencies, contributing to cost savings and optimized billing processes. Furthermore, automation in supply chain management ensures timely inventory management and reduces procurement costs. Through selected case studies, this paper highlights the financial benefits of RPA, showcasing how healthcare organizations leverage automation to improve operational efficiency, reduce costs, and allocate resources more effectively, ultimately enhancing patient care quality.

Chapter 22
Use of Artificial Intelligence for Health Insurance: A Bibliometric Exploration.............................. 509
    Saurabh Bhatt, Graphic Era University, India
    Rajesh Tiwari, Graphic Era University, India
    Chandra Prakash, Graphic Era University, India
    Bijesh Dhyani, Graphic Era University, India
    Bhanu Sharma, Graphic Era University, India
    Kapil Ahalawat, Graphic Era University, India

Artificial intelligence has emerged as the technology with potential to enhance access, transparency, efficiency of health insurance. Poor penetration of health insurance is a cause of concern for people from economically disadvantaged groups. The chapter explores bibliometric analysis of use of artificial intelligence for health insurance. The Scopus database was used for the bibliometric analysis. United States, Canada and India emerged as the leading countries for research in AI for health insurance. Mesko was the leading author. It was found that AI has the potential to transform health insurance for preventing fraud detection and leakages in public health insurance system.

Chapter 23
Work From Home and Sustainable Development Goals: A Framework for Healthcare Sector 521
    Ridhima Goel, Maharshi Dayanand Univesity, India
    Jagdeep Singla, Maharshi Dayanand University, India
    Sanjeet Kumar, Chaudhary Devi Lal University, India

The adoption of Work-From-Home models in healthcare, particularly during the COVID-19 outbreak, has brought a new dimension to worldwide health management. By leveraging smart technologies such as telemedicine, AI-powered diagnostics, and IoT-enabled remote monitoring, healthcare delivery has become more accessible, efficient, and inclusive. This chapter explores how WFH models, enhanced by these technologies, are improving global health outcomes and aligning with the third Sustainable Development Goal (SDG 3), ensuring healthy lives while promoting well-being for all. It examines how WFH frameworks reduce healthcare inequalities by extending quality care to underserved regions and populations. Additionally, it highlights the challenges and opportunities of integrating WFH models with smart technology to create sustainable health systems that can be scaled globally. This chapter provides a comprehensive framework for the future of WFH in healthcare, contributing to the realization of SDG 3 and offering a pathway toward more equitable and resilient healthcare systems.

Chapter 24
Impact of the Russian Invasion of Ukraine on the Indian Pharmaceutical Sector 543
    Rajesh Tiwari, Graphic Era University, India
    Vivek Verma, Graphic Era University, India
    Vibhuti Jain, Graphic Era University, India
    Vanshika Kakkar, Graphic Era University, India

India is the largest supplier of generic drugs in the world. India is the third largest by volume and fourteenth most significant in terms of the value of production of pharma products globally. The study examines the war's impact on the Indian pharmaceutical sector. The pharma stock data is obtained from the National Stock Exchange (NSE) India website. The war between Russia and Ukraine had no significant impact on the returns of Indian pharma stocks. India has a diversified pharmaceutical sector. Though Russia Ukraine had no significant impact on Indian pharmaceutical sector. It has opened up an opportunity for the Indian pharma firms to leverage good diplomatic relations and expand its operations in both Russia and Ukraine by building production centres in both countries. The diversification enhances the diversity in market operations for Indian firms and provides both Russia and Ukraine with a trusted neutral supplier.

Compilation of References 557

About the Contributors 633

Index 643

Foreword

The global health landscape brought global health to a crossroads, where the traditional curative healthcare model has fallen short of addressing the dynamics of the world. A steadily increasing population base coupled with the constant problem of health disparities, and challenges of new unpredictable threats on the international healthcare front also necessitates innovative approaches. In this regard, the book *Driving Global Health and Sustainable Development Goals with Smart Technology* comes in handy and offers directions to redraw that map and transform the healthcare space for the 21st century.

Picking up together the novelty of this volume and its contextuality, I have to pinpoint that it also presents the potential of the discussed technologies in achieving Sustainable Development Goals, specifically SDG3 – 'Health and Well-being'. It discusses how various smart technologies including; artificial intelligence (AI), blockchain solutions together with telemedicine, and wearable devices are impacting the delivery of health care, making it more patient-oriented, efficient, and accessible.

The narrative begins with the historical approach to defining health systems and their progress and focuses closely on the Growth of Health with Technology. It is important to realize that this is the foundation from which it has been possible to chart the course of innovation trajectory based on the quest for outcomes, equity, and sustainability. From there the book goes to the nucleus of the modern changes in healthcare highlighting the economic and operational consequences of smart technologies such as precision medicine, big data & analytics, and robotic process automation.

Another major contribution of the book is its broad international coverage, reflected in numerous country-specific case studies from developed and, particularly, developing countries. Such experiences shed light on how technology can connect the gaps in health access, especially in LMICs, as well as secure vulnerability and firmer pandemics. The discussion is anchored in practical applications of the ideas, which demonstrate the economic and social effects of these innovations, and many of these are presented where access to quality health care is still a challenge.

The authors also boldly highlight the ethical, regulatory, and economic implications that arise from intelligent integration. These are issues that are important when making progress and developments to avoid the loss of privacy equity or trust. The book contains practical recommendations on how to strengthen policies and improve cooperation on the international level for all interested parties, including policymakers, healthcare providers, technology developers, and academic researchers.

As a healthcare professional and advocate for equitable global health solutions, I find this work particularly compelling. Far from being an academic debate, it offers results and tactics on how to use technology to realize universal health coverage and set up resilient Healthcare systems. The proposal brings to mind that the essence of innovation is not only in the new solutions that we look for every day but in the fact that those solutions can shape people's lives and help solve ever-evolving global challenges, to make this world a healthier and fairer place.

In the pages that follow, readers will find a wealth of knowledge, critical analyses, and actionable insights that are both inspiring and thought-provoking. This book is much more than a roadmap to the concept of health technology; it is a call to action for a global community of innovators, policymakers, and practitioners to join forces in building the future of healthcare.

It is with great enthusiasm that I invite you to embark on this journey through the transformative potential of smart technology in driving global health and achieving sustainable development goals.

Best Wishes,

Sanjay Taneja

Graphic Era (Deemed) University, India and Universiti Sultan Zainal Abiding, Malaysia

Preface

Ensuring sustainable health systems to address the needs of the challenging and dynamic world has become a crucial challenge. In a seemingly incurable world with a constantly increasing need for healthcare, growing aged-dominant populations, and still hidden challenges such as emerging epidemics, the role of technologies as enablers of change has emerged beyond doubt. In this regard, ***Driving Global Health and Sustainable Development Goals with Smart Technology*** was designed specifically to fill the glaring gap of lack of direct link and information transfer between the developments of smart technologies and the application of those advanced technologies to meet the most pressing global health issues.

In other words, the essence of this book is based on the understanding of the potential of smart technologies including AI, blockchain, IoT, and telemedicine in reshaping the delivery of healthcare services to contribute to the achievement of the UN Sustainable Development Goals (SDGs). SDG 3 focuses on health and well-being for all ages, which serves as the background for this discussion; specifically, this book highlights the UN's proposed approach to the origins of healthcare misalignment.

This book is not only a theoretical discourse; it is an applied text, written to be a source of practical solutions for a wide readership that includes policymakers, doctors, engineers, and scientists. Compiled from data and research on health economics, information technology acceleration, and case study analysis, the book provides a complex view of the issues surrounding this quickly advancing sector.

Organization of the Book

The structure of the book is deliberate and systematic, reflecting the interconnected facets of smart healthcare:

- Section 1: The Foundations of Healthcare 3.0 discusses the development of healthcare systems and outlines the concept of Healthcare 3.0. This section provides the foundation by examining the definitions concerning Digital health technologies and the centrality of telemedicine in improving care delivery.
- Section 2: Smart Technologies: Revolutionizing Healthcare Delivery offers comprehensive details on ideas including precision medicine, big data, robotic process automation, and wearable technology to illustrate how these ideas are even capable of cutting costs while enhancing patient care.
- Section 3: Smart Healthcare Advanced Subject deals with health Economics and the financing of integrating smart technologies in healthcare. It assesses the financial risks of these innovations and discusses how these innovations may be financed sustainably.
- Section 4: Measuring Global Impact and Case Studies makes the theory real by presenting well-supported data from developed and developing countries. This section highlights how innovation can enhance health disparities, prepare for another pandemic, and offer equitable health results.

- Section 5: Future Directions, Ethics, and Policies discusses the future vision, ethical and privacy dilemmas, and policies regarding the interpretation of smart technologies in healthcare. It also looks ahead to numerous healthcare employee matters and presents operational policy suggestions to design lasting information technology utilization.

The first chapter, *Impact of Digital Health Interventions on Healthcare Access in Developing Countries*, examines digital health interventions are making significant strides in enhancing healthcare accessibility. This chapter highlights how the proliferation of internet access and mobile devices has empowered individuals to monitor their health, a vital capability in areas with limited healthcare infrastructure. While these regions face challenges, notably the high initial costs of adopting technology, digital health offers a promising path to more universal and cost-effective healthcare. The chapter contrasts traditional healthcare approaches with digital alternatives, acknowledging that effectiveness varies across contexts, geographies, and implementation strategies. Yet, digital health interventions demonstrate unique advantages: rapid scalability, affordability, enhanced provider accessibility, and long-term benefits for populations. Through these interventions, the potential for universal healthcare becomes increasingly attainable in developing countries.

Chapter 2, *Innovating Global Health with Smart Technology to Achieve Sustainable Development*, explores cutting-edge technologies such as AI, telemedicine, data analytics, and blockchain. This chapter investigates how smart innovations can drive global health improvements in line with Sustainable Development Goal 3. It examines case studies where these technologies have addressed non-communicable diseases, preventive care, and reproductive health, showing the transformative potential of digital solutions. Additionally, it provides policy recommendations to strengthen healthcare infrastructures and enhance international collaboration for sharing efficient practices. The chapter underscores the importance of ethical frameworks and regulatory oversight, stressing that smart technology must be implemented inclusively and responsibly. This analysis reveals the long-term impacts of digital innovations on global healthcare, fostering resilience and supporting sustainable health outcomes.

Chapter 3, *Harnessing the Power of Precision Medicine and AI: Success Stories and Ethical Considerations*, examines precision medicine, fueled by advancements in AI, is reshaping healthcare delivery by personalizing treatments through genomic insights and advanced analytics. This chapter details the economic and clinical benefits of AI-powered precision medicine, including cost savings from targeted therapies and improved patient outcomes, particularly in oncology and chronic conditions. Case studies illustrate the successes of early adopters but also highlight ethical challenges such as data privacy, algorithmic biases, and the complexities of genetic editing. With insights from global healthcare systems, the chapter advocates for interdisciplinary collaboration, robust data infrastructures, and active patient engagement, underscoring the need for responsible integration of AI to harness the full potential of precision medicine.

Chapter 4, *Ethical, Privacy, and Security Issues in Smart Healthcare*, explores the integration of smart healthcare technologies has revolutionized patient care, yet it also presents complex ethical, privacy, and security issues. This chapter examines these challenges, focusing on patient autonomy, data ownership, and informed consent in an increasingly data-driven healthcare environment. The delicate balance between cost-effective solutions and ethical obligations is explored, with health economics influencing ethical decision-making in care quality and cost containment. Through a series of case studies and regulatory perspectives, the chapter provides a framework for addressing ethical dilemmas and protecting patient rights, highlighting the importance of responsible innovation to maintain public trust in smart healthcare.

Chapter 5, *Escalating Artificial Intelligence Enabled Clinical Decision Support Systems to Enhance Home Based Care: A Study on Healthcare Supply Chains* investigates AI-enabled Clinical Decision Support Systems (CDSS) are transforming home-based care by bridging gaps between healthcare providers and patients, especially in underserved areas. This chapter explores how CDSS enhances diagnostic accuracy and therapeutic guidance, optimizing healthcare supply chains through predictive analytics and inventory management. With a particular focus on chronic illness management, the study aligns with Sustainable Development Goals 3, 9, and 10, targeting health equity and quality care. Recommendations for healthcare organizations and policymakers highlight the potential of AI to reshape home-based healthcare delivery, emphasizing cost efficiency and improved patient outcomes.

Chapter 6, *Application of Artificial Intelligence in Healthcare Sector: A Multidimensional Perspective* explores the impact of AI across various medical disciplines, from cardiology and neurology to genomics and dermatology. Highlighting a case study using convolutional neural networks for malaria detection, the chapter underscores AI's capabilities in diagnostics and treatment. With applications in image processing, genomics, and 3D bioprinting, AI has enhanced efficiency and reduced healthcare professionals' workload. The findings suggest that AI is reshaping healthcare's landscape, with promising advances in both patient outcomes and systemic efficiency, marking a leap forward for biomedical innovation.

Chapter 7, *An Exhaustive Inference of Machine Learning Applications in Healthcare: Analyzing Research Studies on Diagnosis and Prevention* investigates the role of machine learning in healthcare diagnostics and preventive care, with a unique perspective on India's global leadership in pharmaceutical production. Analyzing how geopolitical events, like the Russia-Ukraine conflict, affect pharmaceutical dynamics, it presents an opportunity for India's sectoral expansion. Machine learning is showcased as a critical tool for enhancing healthcare delivery, while India's pharmaceutical diversification is positioned as a strategy to fortify its market presence and support global health systems in times of disruption.

Chapter 8, *AI, IoT, and Blockchain in Healthcare: Bridging Technology and Patient Wellbeing* examines AI, IoT, and blockchain are transforming healthcare by streamlining diagnostics, remote patient monitoring, and data security. This chapter examines these technologies' contributions to patient care, with examples of AI enhancing diagnostics, IoT enabling real-time monitoring, and blockchain securing medical records. Real-life cases demonstrate these technologies' collective impact on healthcare accessibility, data privacy, and treatment efficacy. Through applications in imaging, genetics, telemedicine, and secure EHRs, the chapter illustrates a promising integration of digital solutions to elevate patient wellbeing.

Chapter 9, *AI and Language: Transforming Communication in Health and Wellness*, explores AI's role in revolutionizing health and wellness communication is examined in this chapter, focusing on language-based applications like chatbots and voice assistants. These tools enhance patient experiences, reduce language barriers, and empower proactive wellness management. By analyzing AI-driven communication methods, the chapter reveals how these technologies support decision-making, patient engagement, and lifestyle choices, while addressing ethical and social implications in this evolving field.

Chapter 10, *Exploiting Image Processing and AI for Neurological Disorder Diagnosis: A Focus on Alzheimer's and Parkinson's Diseases*, examines the role of image processing and AI in diagnosing Alzheimer's and Parkinson's diseases through neuroimaging techniques. By employing MRI, PET, and SPECT, AI-driven diagnostic approaches facilitate early detection, monitor disease progression, and support personalized treatment plans. The review provides a comprehensive assessment of current AI applications in neurology, underscoring the transformative potential of these technologies for improving patient outcomes in neurological care.

Chapter 11, *Health Economics and Sustainability in the Era of Digital Transformation: Addressing Digital Stress and Sustainable Development Goals* examines digital health and transformation technologies offer vast potential for improving healthcare efficiency, yet they also introduce digital stress for healthcare professionals. This chapter explores the economic and sustainability dimensions of digital transformation, including challenges from "techno-invasion" in healthcare. Strategies to balance technological innovation with workforce well-being are discussed, emphasizing sustainable practices to maximize smart healthcare solutions' benefits while addressing SDG 3.

Chapter 12, *Innovative Financing Models and Future Directions in Healthcare: Evaluating the Impact of Financial Strategies on Digital Health Outcomes and Innovation* explores innovative financing models, such as public-private partnerships and outcome-based pricing, are crucial for advancing digital health. This chapter explores how these models can drive equitable healthcare access, incentivize innovation, and sustain patient care improvements globally. By analyzing scalable financial strategies, the chapter lays a foundation for a resilient, technology-integrated healthcare ecosystem that aligns with fiscal sustainability and impactful health outcomes.

Chapter 13, *Navigating Challenges and Innovations in Global Healthcare*, analyzes telemedicine's impact on global healthcare access, with a focus on its affordability and ability to bridge geographical divides. By examining telehealth's cost-effectiveness and economic implications, the chapter highlights how telemedicine is reshaping healthcare delivery. It also underscores the need for regulatory foresight and innovative integration strategies to ensure that remote care models meet the demands of equitable and sustainable healthcare.

Chapter 14, *Pandemic Preparedness and the Economics of Global Health Crises,* examines the transformative role of AI and predictive analytics in bolstering pandemic readiness and mitigating the financial impact of global health emergencies. By integrating digital health tools, data analytics, and IoT infrastructure, this chapter reveals how technology can aid early detection, optimize resource management, and alleviate economic strain during health crises. Through a cost-benefit analysis, the authors underscore the economic advantages of investing in tech-driven strategies, drawing on COVID-19 as a case study. Ethical considerations around data privacy are thoroughly discussed, and policy suggestions are provided to promote sustainable investments in health technology, ultimately aiming for a resilient, economically sound approach to future health emergencies.

Chapter 15, *Policy and Regulatory Frameworks for Financing Smart Healthcare,* explores the essential need for robust policy and regulatory systems to fund smart healthcare sustainably. As AI, IoT, and digital diagnostics reshape modern medicine, policymakers face challenges around data governance, interoperability, and financing while balancing privacy, ethics, and market forces. This chapter stresses the importance of international cooperation, especially in achieving Sustainable Development Goal (SDG) 3, to create equitable access to healthcare technology globally. By examining financial policies that support long-term technology adoption, the authors propose strategies for enhancing collaboration and closing regulatory gaps to ensure accessible, sustainable smart healthcare.

Chapter 16, *Precision and Performance: Smart Healthcare Technologies in Sports Medicine Wellness,* highlights the impact of advanced healthcare systems in sports medicine, from wearable biosensors to data analytics and machine learning. These technologies improve injury diagnostics, tailor rehabilitation, and optimize athletic performance, ushering in a new era of personalized, proactive sports healthcare. By dissecting the technological mechanisms and physiological outcomes, the authors portray a shift toward enhanced athletic resilience and potential through precision-driven healthcare.

Chapter 17, *Predicting Novel Coronavirus Trends Using Machine Learning,* investigates machine learning methods, including support vector machines, k-nearest neighbors, decision trees, and a novel XGB classifier, to predict COVID-19 outcomes. Using data from a GitHub repository, the chapter illustrates how machine learning can forecast recovery and mortality trends, contributing valuable insights into pandemic response strategies. This chapter aims to deepen understanding of pandemic dynamics and underscores the utility of data-driven approaches in managing large-scale health crises.

Chapter 18, *Revolutionizing Finance: The Synergy of Smart Cards and FinTech in Process and Product Innovations,* delves into the synergy between smart cards and FinTech in transforming financial services. This chapter traces the evolution of smart cards and their role in secure, accessible financial transactions, then examines FinTech's influence on traditional banking through innovations such as blockchain, crowd finance, and robo-advisors. By assessing the interplay between these technologies, the authors outline how they collectively redefine service delivery and enhance financial accessibility.

Chapter 19, *The Future of the Healthcare Workforce in the Age of Automation,* explores how automation is reshaping healthcare roles, emphasizing the need for new skills in data literacy and robotics. This chapter tackles the financial implications of technology adoption, potential workforce displacement, and the necessity for policies that balance automation and human touch to preserve empathy in patient care. Addressing legal, ethical, and sociocultural challenges, the authors advocate for a responsible, human-centered integration of technology in healthcare.

Chapter 20, *Transforming Global Health Outcomes through Smart Technology and the SDG Framework,* demonstrates how innovative healthcare technologies support SDG 3 by enhancing access, efficiency, and quality in healthcare systems. This chapter examines how intelligent technologies intersect with other SDGs, including SDG 8 (economic growth) and SDG 9 (industry innovation), to build an ecosystem approach for sustainable health advancements. From genomics to remote patient monitoring, the authors present a comprehensive analysis of technology's role in global health transformation.

Chapter 21, *Unleashing Operational Mastery and Patient-Centric Innovation through Robotic Process Automation in Healthcare,* describes how robotic process automation (RPA) streamlines healthcare operations, reducing errors and improving data management in hospital administration, finance, and supply chains. By showcasing real-world case studies, this chapter reveals how healthcare organizations achieve financial efficiency and operational improvements through RPA, ultimately enhancing patient care.

Chapter 22, *Use of Artificial Intelligence for Health Insurance: A Bibliometric Exploration,* examines the potential of AI to improve health insurance accessibility and efficiency, particularly for underserved populations. Using a bibliometric analysis based on Scopus data, the authors identify key research trends in AI applications for health insurance, including fraud detection. The chapter highlights research leaders, such as the U.S., Canada, and India, and discusses AI's transformative role in creating more transparent and effective insurance systems.

Chapter 23, *Work From Home and Sustainable Development Goals: A Framework for the Healthcare Sector,* investigates how the shift to work-from-home (WFH) in healthcare aligns with SDG 3, promoting health equity through technology-driven remote healthcare services. By integrating telemedicine, AI diagnostics, and IoT-enabled monitoring, WFH models reduce healthcare disparities and improve access to care for underserved populations. This chapter outlines a framework for integrating WFH in healthcare to support sustainable, equitable healthcare systems globally.

Chapter 24: *Impact of Russian Invasion of Ukraine on Indian Pharmaceutical Sector,* assesses how geopolitical conflicts, specifically the Russia-Ukraine war, affect India's pharmaceutical industry, a major global supplier of generics. Based on data from the National Stock Exchange, this chapter finds that

Indian pharma stocks showed resilience, with no major impact from the conflict. However, the chapter identifies an opportunity for Indian firms to expand operations in Russia and Ukraine, leveraging diplomatic ties to establish production centers and strengthen market diversity, ultimately positioning India as a reliable supplier in the global pharmaceutical landscape.

As with any list of sources, this book has been written in tandem – from the belief that technology remains one of the most powerful tools to improve health systems in the global context. In compiling this site's contents, we have aimed to provide a wide range of information, which is at once clear and scholarly.

When readers move through the chapters of this book, we would like them to gain not only knowledge about trends pervading the healthcare sector thanks to technology but also ideas on how to help improve it. Combined, we can achieve our goals and make innovation work to help deliver universal access to quality care and create sustainable systems that define our future healthcare landscape.

It is our pleasure to introduce you to the potential of using smart technologies in the sphere of global health, together with the problems and their possible solutions.

Mohit Kukreti
University of Technology and Applied Sciences, Oman

Sabina Sehajpal
Chandigarh University, India

Rajesh Tiwari
Graphic Era University, India

Kiran Sood
Chitkara Business School, Chitkara University, Punjab, India

Introduction

This book aims to demonstrate that the use of smart technologies in the healthcare delivery system has become critical because of increasing technological innovation as well as emerging health risks in the world. The book Driving Global Health and Sustainable Development Goals with Smart Technology offers a comprehensive exploration of how innovations like artificial intelligence (AI), the Internet of Things (IoT), blockchain, and other emerging technologies are transforming healthcare delivery and addressing key Sustainable Development Goals (SDGs), particularly SDG 3: "Achieve healthy life and improved well-being for all populations irrespective of the age of the people involved."

This book is a roadmap on how healthcare systems have evolved through Healthcare 1.0 and Healthcare 2.0, and are at the cusp of Healthcare 3.0 which merges with the advance of technology. Through observing how the healthcare field evolved and how it relates to goals of sustainable development, the book provides a solid background for the importance of Technology in dealing with some of the most emergent global health challenges.

Structured into five key sections, the book delves into foundational concepts, transformative applications, economic considerations, real-world case studies, and forward-looking perspectives:

Section 1: In the Foundations of Healthcare 3.0, readers get an insight into what the "Smart Healthcare Revolution" is and how health and technology complement each other. The book discusses trending technologies such as artificial intelligence, the Internet of Things, and blockchain in diagnosing and managing patient care and also in health finances. In addition, the section also emphasizes how telemedicine and remote care will continue to play an important role in reaching out to underserved populations.

Section 2: Smart Technologies Transforming Healthcare Delivery looks at advancements like Precision Medicine, Big Data & Analytics, RPA robotics in Healthcare, and Wearables. These technologies show great promise for increasing organizational effectiveness, improving cost, and, therefore, helping to achieve better patient outcomes.

Section 3: Health Economics and Financing in Smart Healthcare addresses challenges in adopting smart technology by providing comprehensive information on the financial analysis of smart technologies, novel funding models, and implications of implementing smart technologies in achieving the goals of SDG 3.

Section 4: From the concepts and cases presented in Global Impact and Case Studies, readers will get an understanding of the application of technology in various healthcare institutions. This entails the current application of smart health in both developed and developing nations, with a special focus on how it eliminates inequalities and increases the availability and strength of pandemic preparedness.

Section 5: Future Directions, Ethics, and Policies also discusses substantial ethical, privacy, and regulatory issues in the areas of smart healthcare. The section discusses the changes in healthcare manpower arrangements, policy approaches to facilitate the use of sustainable technologies, and global partnership patterns.

The book culminates in a forward-looking conclusion that synthesizes insights and presents a vision for navigating the future of global health with smart technology.

Mohit Kukreti
University of Technology and Applied Sciences, Oman

Sabina Sehajpal
Chandigarh University, India

Rajesh Tiwari
Graphic Era University, India

Kiran Sood
Chitkara Business School, Chitkara University, Punjab, India

Chapter 1
Impact of Digital Health Interventions on Healthcare Access in Developing Countries

Anupama Singh
https://orcid.org/0000-0002-8688-6871
Graphic Era University, India

ABSTRACT

Technology has permeated all aspects of the healthcare system. The growth and easy availability of internet and smart mobile devices, health monitoring is possible by individuals also. Healthcare systems in developing countries are using technology in many ways to ease access and delivery of health-related services. Developing countries are slowly adapting these technologies, with initial costs being the biggest barrier. Widespread availability of mobile devices and self-monitoring technologies, the digital health interventions are having a positive impact on the population in developing countries. A comparison of traditional medical interventions and the digital interventions is not easy; it depends on the context, geographical area and strategy of usage. The digital technologies show promise of cost-effective universal healthcare. Major factors contributing to the cost-effectiveness are ability of rapid expansion, lower cost of healthcare providers, higher accessibility, and long-term benefits.

INTRODUCTION

Application of information technology has brought a number of benefits to the digital health sector. It has transformed delivery of healthcare services, bringing them to the doorstep of the patient at the click of a button. Some of the major benefits of digitizing healthcare are improved access to healthcare, patient empowerment, patient education, efficiency of service delivery, data management and analysis, patient monitoring and care. This has also improved overall efficiency of the health system.

One of the most significant advantages of digital health technologies is the enhancement of healthcare accessibility. Telemedicine, in particular, has emerged as a powerful tool, allowing patients to consult with healthcare professionals remotely (Nkwanyana, N., 2022). This is especially beneficial f

DOI: 10.4018/979-8-3373-0240-9.ch001

or people living in far-flung areas or those with limited movement. Digital health technologies have empowered patients by providing them with tools and information to make better-informed decisions about their health (Heerdegen ACS et al., 2023). These technologies offer platforms for patient education, enabling individuals to gain a deeper understanding of their conditions and treatment options. The increased access and knowledge can help people monitor their health indicators and have better overall health.

Integration of digital technologies has significantly improved the efficiency of healthcare service delivery. For example, telemedicine has enabled remote consultations, reduced the need for in-person visits and decreased wait times (Nkwanyana, N., 2022). Telepathology has enabled remote analysis of pathological samples, speeding up diagnosis processes (Heerdegen ACS et al., 2023). Digital platforms have also facilitated the training and skill development of healthcare workers, refining the general quality of care (Heerdegen ACS et al., 2023).

Digital health technologies have transformed the way healthcare data is collected, managed, and utilized.

Digital tools result in more efficient and accurate collection of patient data. Advanced systems allow for better organization and storage of health information and advanced software can analyze large datasets to identify trends, predict outcomes, and inform decision-making (Heerdegen ACS et al., 2023).

Use of technology has improved patient care by continuous monitoring through wearable devices. Real-time tracking of patients' health status is possible with the aid of remote monitoring tools. Digital reminders and tracking systems help improve patients' adherence to medication regimens (Heerdegen ACS et al., 2023). Data-driven insights enable personalized treatment plans and interventions.

Implementation of digital health technologies can lead to overall improvements in health system efficiency through resource optimization, cost reduction and streamlined processes. Digital tools can help in better allocation and utilization of healthcare resources. By reducing the need for personal visits and improving preventive care, digital health has the potential to lower healthcare costs. Digital systems can automate and streamline various administrative and clinical processes, reducing errors and improving efficiency.

While these benefits are significant, it is vital to note that the application of digital health technologies also faces challenges, such as ensuring data security, addressing the digital divide, and overcoming barriers to adoption (Nkwanyana, N., 2022; Kaihlanen AM et al., 2023). Nonetheless, the capability of information technology to change and improve health care delivery in the digital health sector remains substantial.

II OBJECTIVES

- To study the impact of digital health interpositions and access to healthcare in developing countries
- To examine the cost-effectiveness of digital healthcare in developing countries
- To compare the cost-effectiveness of tradition healthcare and digital healthcare
- To study the factors of cost-effectiveness of digital healthcare

III METHODOLOGY

This research describes the role and impact of digital healthcare services in developing countries and their effectiveness. Based on the topic or research, literature related to key terms in the objective was searched for in databases of Scopus, Web of Science, Google Scholar and PubMed to search for the relevant research publications. The terms used as the search keywords were: "access to digital healthcare in developing countries", "cost-effectiveness of digital healthcare", "comparison of digital and traditional health care interventions", "factors of cost-effectiveness of digital healthcare". All literature in this study is sourced from validated sources.

IV DIGITAL HEALTH INTERVENTIONS AND ACCESS TO HEALTHCARE IN DEVELOPING COUNTRIES

Digital health interventions have shown significant potential in improving healthcare access in developing countries, addressing various challenges and barriers that often limit access to quality healthcare. Some of the ways these interventions are making a difference to availability of quality healthcare in developing countries are by bridging geographical barriers, improving access to primary health care, improving mental healthcare and addressing resource limitations that are prevalent in developing countries.

One of the main way digital health services improve access is by overcoming geographical limitations through telemedicine and M-health or mobile health. This allows patients in remote or rural areas to consult with healthcare practitioners without the need of travelling physically (Rojas G et al., 2019). This is particularly beneficial in countries with uneven distribution of healthcare resources. Mobile Health (*mHealth*) technologies enable healthcare services to reach remote populations, providing access to health information and basic care even in areas with limited healthcare infrastructure (Vasanthan L et al. 2024).

Primary healthcare systems are assisted by the digital tools in early detection and monitoring of health risks. For example, in South Africa, digital maternal health initiatives are being used to detect pre-eclampsia early, potentially reducing maternal mortality rates (Ngwenya, M et al., 2022). Digital technologies can improve the efficiency and effectiveness of primary care facilities, making healthcare more accessible to vulnerable populations (Vasanthan L et al., 2024).

Developing countries often face a shortage of trained healthcare workers and tools. Digital interventions help lessen these challenges through capacity building and optimization of resources. Digital platforms facilitate training and skill development of healthcare workers, improving the availability and quality of care (Bandara, W. et al., 2012). Digital tools aid the allocation and utilization of limited healthcare resources, thereby increasing the capacity to serve more patients (Vasanthan L et al., 2024).

Mental health is an area where digital support is noticeably significant. In countries like Chile, internet-based mental health interventions are being developed to address the gap between high prevalence of mental disorders and partial access to care (Rojas G et al., 2019) The digital solutions are particularly beneficial for vulnerable groups who might otherwise have inadequate access to mental health services (Rojas G et al., 2019). They are empowering individuals and communities by enabling health education and community engagement. The digital platforms provide accessible health information, enabling individuals to make informed decisions about their health (Vasanthan L et al., 2024). Digital technologies create opportunities for building global communities, connecting rural areas to broader health networks (Bandara, W et al., 2012).

While digital health interventions offer numerous benefits, there are few challenges too. Ensuring equitable access to digital technologies remains a challenge in many developing countries (Forslund, M. et al, 2024). Proper governance of health data is crucial for the effective and ethical implementation of digital health solutions (Bandara, W et al., 2012). There is a need for more research on the efficiency and cost-effectiveness of these interventions to support their wider adoption and scaling (Rojas G et al., 2019; Forslund, M. et al, 2024).

In conclusion, digital health interventions are playing a crucial role in improving healthcare access in developing countries by overcoming geographical barriers, strengthening primary care, optimizing limited resources, addressing mental health needs, and empowering communities. As these technologies continue to evolve and adapt to local contexts, they hold great promise for accelerating progress towards universal health coverage in developing nations.

V THE COST-EFFECTIVENESS OF DIGITAL HEALTH INTERVENTIONS IN DEVELOPING COUNTRIES

Developing countries face several cost-effectiveness challenges in the deployment of digital health interventions, impacting their successful implementation and sustainability. Some of the main challenges are resource constraints, cost of infrastructure, maintenance and sustainability as well as the limited research on the advantages of digital interventions in healthcare.

Developing countries often face significant resource limitations, which can affect the cost-effectiveness of digital healthcare interventions. Additionally, implementing digital health solutions require substantial investments in technology infrastructure, which can be challenging for resource-constrained health systems (McCool J. et al., 2020). The cost of maintaining and updating digital health systems is often significant and potentially limits their long-term sustainability (McCool J. et al., 2020). There is a need for research-based evidence on the cost-effectiveness of digital healthcare in underdeveloped areas. Many digital health projects in developing countries lack comprehensive economic evaluations, making it difficult to assess their true cost-effectiveness (Wilson E. et al, 2022). Cost-effectiveness can differ significantly, as it will depend on the country's specific economic conditions, and often there is a lack of specific country data to enable proper analysis (Wilson E. et al, 2022).

Several factors related to implementation can affect the cost-effectiveness of digital health interventions.

A number of digital health projects struggle to move beyond the pilot phase, never realizing the potential cost-effectiveness of scale (McCool J. et al., 2020). Additionally, the cost and complexity of integrating digital health solutions with existing health systems can be substantial (McCool J. et al., 2020).

The effectiveness of digital healthcare and, by use, it's cost-effectiveness, depend on user acceptance and their utilization. Low usage of digital devices by both, the healthcare provider and the patient, can make it imperative that training is conducted – which increases the cost and decreases the cost effectiveness (McCool J. et al., 2020). In many underdeveloped areas, interventions that are not culturally appropriate or acceptable may see low rate of usage, impacting their cost-effectiveness (McCool J. et al., 2020).

The technological development in developing countries can present unique challenges. Poor internet connectivity or unreliable electricity supply can reduce the effectiveness and increase operational costs (Wilson E. et al., 2022). The availability and affordability of devices needed for digital health interventions (e.g., smartphones) can impact their reach and cost-effectiveness (McCool J. et al., 2020).

In resource-constrained environments, the opportunity costs of investing in digital health interventions can be substantial. Funds allocated to digital health might be diverted from other essential health services, potentially affecting overall health outcomes (Huang Y. et al., 2021). Traditional public health interventions may be more cost-effective in certain contexts compared to digital solutions (Ifeanyichi M. et al, 2024)

While these challenges are significant, it is vital to bring to notice that many digital health interventions have shown promise in improving healthcare access and outcomes in developing countries. For instance, solar-powered oxygen delivery systems have been found to be cost-effective for treating pediatric hypoxemia in low-resource settings (Huang Y. et al., 2021). As the field evolves, more research and carefully designed economic evaluations will be crucial to fully understand and optimize the cost-effectiveness of usage of digital health technologies in developing countries.

VI COMPARISON OF DIGITAL HEALTH INTERVENTIONS TO TRADITIONAL HEALTH INTERVENTIONS IN TERMS OF COST-EFFECTIVENESS

Digital health interventions have shown promising results in relation to cost-effectiveness when likened to traditional health interventions, though the proof is still emerging and context-dependent. Following is an overview of how they compare.

Potential Cost Advantages Digital health interventions often demonstrate cost advantages over traditional interventions. They can often be scaled up to reach larger populations at a relatively low marginal cost compared to traditional interventions. Many digital interventions require less direct involvement from healthcare professionals, potentially reducing personnel costs. By improving access to care, especially in remote areas, digital interventions may reduce costs associated with travel and lost productivity.

Effectiveness Considerations The effectiveness of digital interventions compared to traditional methods is varied. Digital interventions have shown promise in preventive care. For example, a study protocol for the PREDIABETEXT trial aims to evaluate a digital intervention to prevent type 2 diabetes in primary care settings, which could potentially be more cost-effective than traditional methods if successful (Galmes-Panades AM. Et al, 2022). Some digital interventions have demonstrated effectiveness in managing chronic conditions, potentially reducing long-term healthcare costs.

Evidence from Economic Evaluations Economic evaluations of digital health interventions have yielded mixed results. A systematic review of pharmacist-led digital health initiatives found that many were cost-effective, particularly those that used computers, smartphones or telephones, and web-based interventions (Park T et al., 2022). A study comparing Medicare Advantage (which often includes digital health components) to traditional Medicare found no significant differences in most measures of health care access and preventive care use for low-income adults (Aggarwal, R et al., 2022). This suggests that the cost-effectiveness of digital components may not always translate to better outcomes.

Challenges in Comparison Several factors make direct comparisons challenging. There is a lack of long-term data (Park T et al., 2022). Many economic evaluations represent short-term economic values, making it difficult to assess long-term cost-effectiveness. The cost-effectiveness of digital tools can vary significantly contingent on the local setting, healthcare system, and explicit design of the intervention. While digital interventions may have lower running costs, they usually require significant direct investment in infrastructure and training.

The Uniqueness of Developing Countries In developing countries, digital health interventions face the unique challenges of limited infrastructure, low digital literacy and higher opportunity costs of capital. The cost-effectiveness of digital interventions may be reduced in areas with poor internet connectivity or unreliable electricity. Additional costs for training both healthcare providers and patients may be necessary in areas with low digital literacy. In resource-constrained settings, the investment in digital health might divert funds from other essential health services.

In conclusion, while many digital health interventions show promise in terms of cost-effectiveness, their comparison to traditional interventions is not straightforward. The effectiveness and cost-effectiveness of digital interventions can vary widely based on the specific context, target population, and implementation strategy. As the field evolves, more comprehensive and long-term economic evaluations will be crucial to fully understand the comparative cost-effectiveness of digital versus traditional healthcare practices.

VII THE FACTORS CONTRIBUTING TO THE COST-EFFECTIVENESS OF DIGITAL HEALTH INTERVENTIONS

Factors such as scalability, lower cost of personnel, improved accessibility, high effectiveness in certain areas, type of technology, context of implementation, long-term benefits and the target population contribute to the cost-effectiveness of digital healthcare tools.

Digital health interventions often demonstrate significant cost advantages due to their scalability. These interventions can typically be scaled up to reach larger populations at a relatively low marginal cost compared to traditional interventions (Kyaw TL. Et al., 2023). This scalability allows for wider implementation without proportional increases in costs. Many digital interventions require less direct involvement from healthcare professionals, potentially reducing personnel costs (Kyaw TL. Et al., 2023). This can lead to significant savings, especially in interventions that can be largely automated or delivered remotely. By improving access to care, especially in remote areas, digital interventions may reduce costs associated with travel and lost productivity (Kyaw TL. Et al., 2023). This improved accessibility can lead to earlier interventions and potentially prevent more costly health issues down the line.

Digital health interventions have shown higher potential in certain areas of healthcare such as preventive care, which could lead to long-term cost savings by reducing the incidence of chronic diseases (Wang Y. et al., 2023). Some digital interventions have proven effective in managing chronic conditions, potentially reducing long-term healthcare costs (Kyaw TL. Et al., 2023).

The specific type of digital technology used can impact cost-effectiveness. A systematic review found that many pharmacist-led digital health interventions were cost-effective, particularly those using smartphones/telephones, computers and web-based interventions (Kyaw TL. Et al., 2023).

The cost-effectiveness of digital healthcare tools can vary significantly depending on the local context, healthcare system, and specific design of the intervention (Kyaw TL. Et al., 2023). Factors such as existing infrastructure, digital literacy of the target population, and cultural acceptability all play a role in determining cost-effectiveness.

While digital interventions may require significant upfront investment, they often have the potential for long-term cost savings. However, it is important to note that many economic evaluations represent short-term economic values, making it challenging to assess long-term cost-effectiveness (Kyaw TL. Et al., 2023).

The design of the digital intervention itself can significantly impact its cost-effectiveness. Factors such as user-friendliness, integration with existing health systems, and the ability to provide personalized interventions can all contribute to improved outcomes and cost-effectiveness (Pimenta S. et al., 2023)

The characteristics of the target population, including their health needs, technological literacy, and access to digital devices, can greatly influence the cost-efficiency of digital healthcare (Samsudin, R. et al., 2024)

While these factors can contribute to the cost-effectiveness of digital health interventions, it is important to note that the evidence is still emerging and context-dependent. More comprehensive and long-term economic evaluations are needed to fully understand the cost-effectiveness of these interventions across different settings and populations (Kyaw TL. Et al., 2023; Wang Y. et al., 2023).

VIII CONCLUSION

Consumers in developed countries are using technology more and more for managing their own health. With the growth and easy availability of internet and smart mobile devices, personal care management is possible in developing countries to a large extent now. Healthcare systems in developed countries use consumer data based on outcomes and measures of performance standards. They have achieved integration of mental and physical care in healthcare systems using technology. Technology based healthcare systems are capable of dealing with the individualities in patient's symptoms and advise customized treatment. There is no doubt that digital healthcare technology has immense potential to transform the healthcare sector. Permeation of digital health technology in developing countries is on the rise. Studies are ongoing to evaluate the cost-effectiveness and impact of digital technologies in developing countries. The largest advantage of technology is its reach scalability – leading to cost-effectiveness. Another major application is mobile devices that enable monitoring and management of personal health. Remote monitoring is also possible for quick intervention in case of need. Technology has made large scale storage and analysis of data for better healthcare management.

Further studies are needed to understand the economic impact of technology in healthcare in developing countries and its cost-efficiency. The comparison of traditional and digital is not easy. Traditional societies are hampered with lack of education and trust in adoption of newer methods. Log-term evaluation requires further research and validation.

REFERENCES

Aggarwal, Rahul & Gondi, Suhas & Wadhera, Rishi. (2022). Comparison of Medicare Advantage vs Traditional

Bandara, W., Syed, R., Kapurubandra, M., & Rupasinghe, L. (2012). Building Essential BPM Capabilities to Assist Successful ICT Deployment in the Developing Context: Observations and Recommendations from Sri Lanka. *GlobDev 2012*. 14. https://aisel.aisnet.org/globdev2012/14

Forslund, M., Mathieson, K., Djibo, Y., Mbindyo, C., Lugangira, N., & Balasubramaniam, P. (2024). Strengthening the evidence base on the use of digital health technologies to accelerate progress towards universal health coverage. *Oxford Open Digital Health*, 2, oqae033. Advance online publication. DOI: 10.1093/oodh/oqae033

Galmes-Panades, A. M., Angullo, E., Mira-Martínez, S., Bennasar-Veny, M., Zamanillo-Campos, R., Gómez-Juanes, R., Konieczna, J., Jiménez, R., Serrano-Ripoll, M. J., Fiol-deRoque, M. A., Miralles, J., Yañez, A. M., Romaguera, D., Vidal-Thomas, M. C., Llobera-Canaves, J., García-Toro, M., Vicens, C., Gervilla-García, E., Oña, J. I., & Ricci-Cabello, I. (2022). Development and Evaluation of a Digital Health Intervention to Prevent Type 2 Diabetes in Primary Care: The PREDIABETEXT Study Protocol for a Randomised Clinical Trial. *International Journal of Environmental Research and Public Health*, 19(22), 14706. DOI: 10.3390/ijerph192214706 PMID: 36429423

Gomes, M., Murray, E., & Raftery, J. (2022). Economic Evaluation of Digital Health Interventions: Methodological Issues and Recommendations for Practice. *PharmacoEconomics*, 40(4), 367–378. DOI: 10.1007/s40273-022-01130-0 PMID: 35132606

Heerdegen, Anne & Cellini, Carlotta & Wirtz, Veronika & Rockers, Peter. (2022). Digital Health Technologies Applied by the Pharmaceutical Industry to Improve Access to Noncommunicable Disease Care in Low- and Middle-Income Countries. *Global Health: Science and Practice*. 10. . DOI:DOI: 10.9745/GHSP-D-22-00072

Huang, Y., Mian, Q., Conradi, N., Opoka, R. O., Conroy, A. L., Namasopo, S., & Hawkes, M. T. (2021). Estimated Cost-effectiveness of Solar-Powered Oxygen Delivery for Pneumonia in Young Children in Low-Resource Settings. *JAMA Network Open*, 4(6), e2114686. DOI: 10.1001/jamanetworkopen.2021.14686 PMID: 34165579

Ifeanyichi, M., Mosso Lara, J. L., Tenkorang, P., Kebede, M. A., Bognini, M., Abdelhabeeb, A. N., Amaechina, U., Ambreen, F., Sarabu, S., Oladimeji, T., Toguchi, A. C., Hargest, R., & Friebel, R. (2024). Cost-effectiveness of surgical interventions in low-income and middle-income countries: A systematic review and critical analysis of recent evidence. *BMJ Global Health*, 9(10), e016439. DOI: 10.1136/bmjgh-2024-016439 PMID: 39362787

Kaihlanen, Anu-Marja & Virtanen, Lotta & Kainiemi, Emma & Heponiemi, T. (2023). Patients' suitability for digital health - what should be evaluated by health care professionals? *European Journal of Public Health*. 33. . DOI:DOI: 10.1093/eurpub/ckad160.1208

Kyaw, T. L., Ng, N., Theocharaki, M., Wennberg, P., & Sahlen, K. G. (2023). Cost-effectiveness of Digital Tools for Behavior Change Interventions Among People With Chronic Diseases: Systematic Review. *Interactive Journal of Medical Research*, 12, e42396. DOI: 10.2196/42396 PMID: 36795470

Lange, O. (2023). Health economic evaluation of preventive digital public health interventions using decision-analytic modelling: A systematized review. *BMC Health Services Research*, 23(1), 268. DOI: 10.1186/s12913-023-09280-3 PMID: 36932436

Marsch, L. A., & Ben-Zeev, D. (2012). Technology-Based Assessments and Interventions Targeting Psychiatric and Substance Use Disorders: Innovations and Opportunities. *Journal of Dual Diagnosis*, 8(4), 259–261. DOI: 10.1080/15504263.2012.723308

McCool, J., Dobson, R., Muinga, N., Paton, C., Pagliari, C., Agawal, S., Labrique, A., Tanielu, H., & Whittaker, R. (2020). Factors influencing the sustainability of digital health interventions in low-resource settings: Lessons from five countries. *Journal of Global Health*, 10(2), 020396. Advance online publication. DOI: 10.7189/jogh.10.020396 PMID: 33274059

Ngwenya, M., Muthelo, L., Oupa Mbombi, M., Adelaide Bopape, M., & Maria Mothiba, T. (2022). Utilisation of Digital Health in Early Detection and Treatment of Pre-Eclampsia in Primary Health Care Facilities South Africa: Literature Review. DOI:DOI: 10.5772/intechopen.101228

Nkwanyana, N. (2022). Key barriers to digital health interventions in South Africa: Systematic scoping review. *2022 IEEE 20th Jubilee International Symposium on Intelligent Systems and Informatics (SISY)*, pp. 000019-000024, DOI:DOI: 10.1109/SISY56759.2022.10036322

Park, T., Kim, H., Song, S., & Griggs, S. K. (2022). Economic Evaluation of Pharmacist-Led Digital Health Interventions: A Systematic Review. *International Journal of Environmental Research and Public Health*, 19(19), 11996. DOI: 10.3390/ijerph191911996 PMID: 36231307

Pimenta, S., Hansen, H., Demeyer, H., Slevin, P., & Cruz, J. (2023). Role of digital health in pulmonary rehabilitation and beyond: Shaping the future. *ERJ Open Research*, 9(2), 00212–02022. DOI: 10.1183/23120541.00212-2022 PMID: 36923569

Rawstorn, J. C., Subedi, N., Koorts, H., Evans, L., Cartledge, S., Wallen, M. P., Grace, F. M., Islam, S. M. S., & Maddison, R. (2024). Stakeholder perceptions of factors contributing to effective implementation of exercise cardiac telerehabilitation in clinical practice. *European Journal of Cardiovascular Nursing*, •••, zvae127. Advance online publication. DOI: 10.1093/eurjcn/zvae127 PMID: 39352400

Rojas, Graciela & Martínez, Vania & Martínez, Pablo & Franco, Pamela & Jiménez, Álvaro. (2019). Improving Mental Health Care in Developing Countries Through Digital Technologies: A Mini Narrative Review of the Chilean Case. Frontiers in Public Health. 7. . DOI:DOI: 10.3389/fpubh.2019.00391

Rosenberg, L. (2012). Are healthcare leaders ready for the real revolution? *The Journal of Behavioral Health Services & Research*, 39(3), 215–219. DOI: 10.1007/s11414-012-9285-z PMID: 22736047

Samsudin, R., Khan, N., Subbarao, A., & Taralunga, D.D. (2024). Technological Innovations in Enhancing Digital Mental Health Engagement for Low-Income Groups. *Journal of Advanced Research in Applied Sciences and Engineering Technology*. DOI:DOI: 10.37934/araset.59.1.209226

Valentijn, P., Tymchenko, L., Jacobson, T., Kromann, J., Biermann, C., AlMoslemany, M. A., & Arends, R. (2022). Digital health interventions for musculoskeletal pain conditions: Systematic review and meta-analysis of randomized controlled trials. *Journal of Medical Internet Research*, 24(9), e37869. DOI: 10.2196/37869 PMID: 36066943

Vasanthan, L., Natarajan, S. K., Babu, A., Kamath, M. S., & Kamalakannan, S. (2024). Digital health interventions for improving access to primary care in India: A scoping review. *PLOS Global Public Health*, 4(5), e0002645. Advance online publication. DOI: 10.1371/journal.pgph.0002645 PMID: 38743672

Wang, Y., Fekadu, G., & You, J. H. (2023). Cost-Effectiveness Analyses of Digital Health Technology for Improving the Uptake of Vaccination Programs: Systematic Review. *Journal of Medical Internet Research*, 25, e45493. DOI: 10.2196/45493 PMID: 37184916

Wilson, E., Gannon, H., Chimhini, G., Fitzgerald, F., Khan, N., Lorencatto, F., Kesler, E., Nkhoma, D., Chiyaka, T., Haghparast-Bidgoli, H., Lakhanpaul, M., Cortina Borja, M., Stevenson, A. G., Crehan, C., Sassoon, Y., Hull-Bailey, T., Curtis, K., Chiume, M., Chimhuya, S., & Heys, M. (2022). Protocol for an intervention development and pilot implementation evaluation study of an e-health solution to improve newborn care quality and survival in two low-resource settings, Malawi and Zimbabwe: Neotree. *BMJ Open*, 12(7), e056605. DOI: 10.1136/bmjopen-2021-056605 PMID: 35790332

Zingg, A., Franklin, A., Ross, A., & Myneni, S. (2024). A pilot acceptability evaluation of MomMind: A digital health intervention for Peripartum Depression prevention and management focused on health disparities. *PLOS Digital Health*, 3(5), e0000508. DOI: 10.1371/journal.pdig.0000508 PMID: 38776283

Chapter 2
Innovating Global Health With Smart Technology to Achieve Sustainable Development

Harshi Garg
https://orcid.org/0009-0005-2790-5111
IIMT University, India

Mohammad Kashif
https://orcid.org/0000-0002-4940-8264
Graphic Era University, India

Priyank Sharma
https://orcid.org/0000-0001-9888-485X
IIMT University, India

Nikita Singhal
https://orcid.org/0000-0002-0700-8086
IIMT University, India

ABSTRACT

This chapter discusses how innovations in healthcare like artificial intelligence, telemedicine, data analytics, and blockchain, can solve critical health problems and improve the availability of treatment. Smart technology can help to accomplish Sustainable Development Goal 3, which promotes global health and well-being. Case studies from real-world situations prove how well they are helping to combat global health problems such as not communicable illness, avoiding illness, and reproductive health. The chapter additionally provides policy recommendations to improve the healthcare system facilities, and encouraging international cooperation to share efficient procedures and technological advances. Establishing ethical frameworks, laws and regulations illustrates the significance of carrying out smart technology ethically and inclusively. This chapter presents a comprehensive analysis of the methods in which these scientific innovations can promote long-term healthcare systems and enhance the accomplishments of worldwide health targets.

DOI: 10.4018/979-8-3373-0240-9.ch002

Copyright ©2025, IGI Global Scientific Publishing. Copying or distributing in print or electronic forms without written permission of IGI Global Scientific Publishing is prohibited.

1. INTRODUCTION

1.1 Overview of Global Health

The domain of study and application which emphasizes enhancing wellness and health and creating fairness in medical care for all human beings internationally is a description of global health, referring to the communities' overall well-being. Problems that extend beyond national boundaries or influence government and the financial markets on an international level are often emphasized (Kasinathan et al., 2022). Consequently, enhancing worldwide global health (including child health, and mental wellness) decreasing disparities, and preserving against risks that exceed national- boundaries such as the most common causes of death and decades of life lost are all factors of worldwide health. Global health, which is a branch of general wellness that focuses on supporting poor countries and foreign assistance efforts by wealthy countries, should not be mistaken for global wellness. One approach that worldwide health can be identified is through the occurrence of multiple pandemic illnesses in the universe and their threat to life span in the current time. Based on figures, and forecasts, the average lifespan was approximately 30 years in every region of the globe in an ancient time, poor civilization (primarily due to significant newborn death). Resolving worldwide medical problems and improving world health safety can be achieved using the integration of one health which is a comprehensive perspective. The World Health Organization (WHO) is a major institution responsible for global health issues. Other important organizations that affect global wellness are the World Food Program (WFP) and UNICEF (Kutty et al., 2020). Furthermore, the United Nations helped foster cross-sectoral projects to tackle global health and the socioeconomic variables that support it (Ryan et al., 2020).

This is generally recognized that the discipline of international health has a history in colonial and that liberation is required. The worldwide health system has been accused of adopting a traditional framework, functioning as a royal 'throne' in the shape of a handful number of organizations and people based in nations with high incomes (Li et al., 2023; Shajar, Beg, et al., 2024). The recolonizing world health campaign is guided by notable individuals like Madhukar Pai. The formation of the United Nations (UN) and the World Bank group in 1945, signified an important development in international medical health coordination. The World Health Organization was founded by the first-ever formed United Nations member in 1948. The international civilization had been inspired to get involved in 1947 after an outbreak of cholera in Egypt (Millard, 2017). Eight Millennium Development Goals (MDGs), which characterized the primary barriers to worldwide human advancement, were set up by member nations at a United Nations conference in 2000 and were to be fulfilled by 2015. Simultaneously with the declaration, both donor and receiver countries made uncommon worldwide investments (Kickbusch et al., 2021).

Due to the United Nations, enormous improvements have been achieved in various sectors, and these MGDs provided an essential framework for growth. But progress has been unbalanced, and numerous MDGs- such as those concerning child and maternal health have not been achieved in full (Pokrajac et al., 2021; Shajar, Kashif, et al., 2024). A sustainable development goal, including 17 (SDGs), was recently established for the years 2016- 2030, expanding on the Millennium Development Goals. The most important target is a remarkable and ambitious pledge to end hunger. The 2030 growth list, entitled Changing Our World: the 2030 Agenda for the Advancement of Humanity, was approved by the 193 nations that are part of the UN General Assembly. Several major initiatives were established, including the GAVI vaccine alliance in 2000, the Global Fund to combat AIDS, and malaria in 2002, etc. within the context of the moral agreement, which failed to pursue targets with the same intensity.

In the early days of traditional medical treatment, doctors employed a handful number of tools and acquired ability through experience. A few individuals wanted to be surgeons since it required expertise and training to become one. The latest innovation expanded slowly because individuals across different places could not connect. Clients did not influence how they received medical care because specialists were considered experts in their areas. The present Healthcare system fails to take the modifications in treatment, even though advancement has evolved substantially (Hoosain et al., 2020; Kashif, Shajar, et al., 2023; Kashif, Singhal, et al., 2024). The 2010s experienced a growth in medical expertise, which had in response prompted consumers to grow annoyed by the wealth of knowledge provided that doctors were either oblivious to or incapable of utilizing (Kostoska & Kocarev, 2019). The World Health Organization estimated that there was a global deficit of 4.3 million medical professionals, along with a rise in the prevalence of persistent disease and medical expenses. The accessibility of outstanding health equipment, medical data, and academic studies as conventional medicine gave way to internet-based health. The change transformed individuals' utilization of information and their ability to choose an individual method of therapy, allowing them to engage in taking care of themselves (H. Y. Liu et al., 2021). Consumers are now more engaged in their treatment, but determining the correct course of action has grown more difficult as a consequence of this novel method of session (Fei et al., 2021).

The National Library of Medical Science document, "The Digital Heath is a Social Revolution of Conventional Medical Care," argues that efficient treatment needs collaboration, understanding, and shared decision. What is required for this is a properly specified partnership between clients and their providers (Z. Liu et al., 2022). Medical professionals explain in the following passage that during the process of deciding a patient's course of therapy, they have to work in unison with them and respect their decisions. The paper continues to address the significance of compassion for surgeons and how a positive relationship between them and their clientele can influence the type of treatment that they choose to undergo (Botti & Monda, 2020). The initial goal was for nations and companies to collaborate to continue creating novel innovations and treatments. The approach additionally sought to move strength over the Internet of Things from the international and national level and to speed the execution of national standards in this field. In a process similar to the screening of medicines and vaccines, the World Health Organization similarly set standards for the accreditation of global health medical equipment. The approach contained a list of medical information as a societal health good, a structure for collaboration on data, and a description and artificial intelligence applicability. It additionally promoted virtual health-based, person-centered Healthcare systems. Other groups are developing policies while the World Health Organization has advocated their own.

The World Health Organization established a strategy at the beginning of 2015 to use digital health to completely eradicate diseases such as tuber, but the scheme was not made public until later in the following years. The absence of assets accessible to medical care administrators for preventing tuberculosis was one of the explanations for why the proposal was accepted. There was a demand for an initial step-to-step framework to incorporate electronic health records for the end of the strategy. Furthermore, the scheme would offer the opportunity to develop healthcare methods and improve efficiency and long-term viability. The primary agenda of the program was to combat and avoid cancer and to offer individuals alternatives to therapy that varied from national to international (Garg et al., 2024; Kashif, Garg, et al., 2024; Kashif, Kumar, et al., 2023). The subsequent methods included practical test results such as employing electronic devices to identify individuals and providing safe data transmission and retention.

1.2 Sustainable Development Goals

The meaning of sustainable development as we understand it now originated in 1987 in the generally accepted Brundtland Report, frequently referred to as 'our future together' which was brought by multiple nations for the UN. This could appear unreal. The famous 'Theory of Population' was presented by Thomas Malthus. The theory holds that human population growth usually exceeds economic growth. In the present day of urbanization and extraction of resources, this is true. The term sustainable development first appeared in an official document signed by 33 African countries in 1969 and supported by the International Union for Conservation of Nature.

The nation's ecological agency was established in the same year, and its regulations have had a significant impact on the growth of concepts and methods in worldwide policy regarding the environment. Financial growth that may have benefits for future generations as well as damaging the environmental resources or living beings is how the National Environment Policy Act of 1969 characterized sustainable growth. A sustainable future is achieving today's requirements while safeguarding the capacity of future generations to satisfy their requirements stated by UNESCO 1989. As soon as, the same issues- which are growing increasingly serious and evident- have been dealt with from 1798 to the day. This represented an important shift in long-term viability, specifically in terms of environmental sustainability.

Figure 1. The specific objectives of SDG3 (Authors)

Figure 1: The specific Objectives of SDG3:

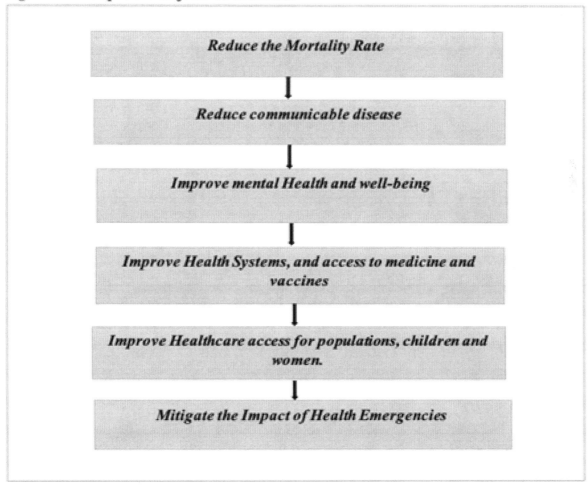

Source: Authors'

Figure 1 represents the specific aims of sustainable development goal 3- which intends to ensure a healthy existence and encourage well-being for all at all ages. This specifies significant objectives, including reducing the mortality rates for moms and kids, avoiding infectious illness, supporting mental wellness, and ensuring everyone has a right to medical care.

In a social and financial sense, it also served to establish it in the larger context of the evolution of humanity (Basyirah et al., 2022). The term ecological sustainability originated from the modern environmental movement which challenged the unstable morality of current societies where resource use, development, and consumer patterns harmed the integrity and the happiness of subsequent generations. Ecological practices are supported as a replacement for rushed, proactive, and efficient behaviors. It may act as an indicator using which one evaluates the effectiveness of the structures that are functioning now and as an outline for advancement in society. For advertising the growth of healthier activities, resilience also involves proactively trying to change the current situation and examining the degree to which prevailing social structures promote negative conduct (Sánchez-Segura et al., 2021).

Table 1. Description of sustainable development goals

No.	Title of SDG
SDG 1	No Poverty
SDG 2	Zero Hunger
SDG 3	Good Health & Wellbeing
SDG 4	Quality education
SDG 5	Gender equality
SDG 6	Clean water and sanitation
SDG 7	Affordable and clean energy
SDG 8	Decent work & economic growth
SDG 9	Industry, Innovation and Infrastructure
SDG 10	Reduce inequalities
SDG 11	Sustainable cities and communities
SDG 12	Responsible consumption and production
SDG 13	Climate action
SDG 14	Life below water
SDG 15	Life on land
SDG 16	Peace and Justice
SDG 17	Partnerships for the goals

Source: Authors' compilation

Table 1 is a comprehensive overview of the Sustainable development goals (SDGs), including the specific objectives and benchmarks related to each goal. This covers the 17 interlinked goals that the United Nations established to tackle global issues, like poverty, inequality, damage to the environment, destruction of the environment, harmony, and stability. Every goal has been made accessible and universal so that no one is left behind.

Our modern societies established a considerable importance on the environment which was referred to as 'Mother Earth' in our old traditions (Von Humboldt et al., 2020). The divine bodies- the Sun, Moon, and trees- likewise as the earthly circumstances had an importance in the lives of individuals and were regarded as the providers of Health, wealth, and success (Goel & Vishnoi, 2023).

Figure 2. 5 Ps of SDG (Authors)

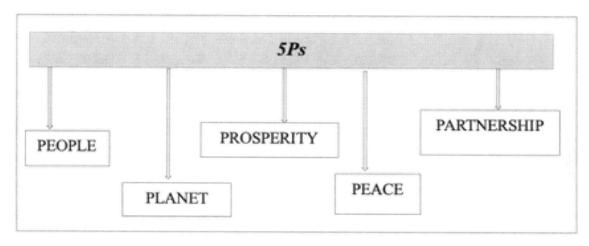

Figure 2 defines the 5 Ps of Sustainable development goals- people, planet, prosperity, peace, and partnership to attain equitable growth. This picture presents how these 5 components are connected and how they function collectively to build an ecologically sound future. The MDGs are intended to be substituted, or added by the SDGs. The UN created 17 SDGs to succeed the eight MDGs that were ahead forward in 2000 but were not achieved. These SDGs are built on the aforementioned 5 PS.

2. LITERATURE REVIEW

The intent of studying literature is to collect information, formulate thoughts, and present justifications to deal with the complex problem within the research. This section explores the contexts of present interactions concerning the subject challenge, including publications, papers, interviews, and national and global level projects. The point of the literature review was to acquire a greater understanding of the general agreement and understanding regarding the sustainable development goals, especially Goal 3, and its most prominent activities. A more comprehensive and honest evaluation of the prior studies published was undertaken.

2.1 Studies Related to the Background of SDGs

(Kashif et al., 2024) investigated whether the UN SDGs' description of ecological issues and GDP connect. Variations and difficulties presented by GDP growth for the UN SDGs are meant to be drawn to focus. Whereas GDP is regarded as the main measure of the nation's success, its findings counter the welfare of society. The path to reducing pollution rapidly will be to give rewards for small economic development. This is crucial to determine the SDG goals that are associated with GDP to gain a greater awareness of the consistency between the SDGs and economic achievement as measured by GDP growth, especially in developing nations. (Dar & Dr Naseer Ahmad, 2022)employed quarterly frequency information from 1991 Q1 to 2020 Q4. The findings proved to be valid when considering multiple causal methods. Therefore, several kinds of adaptive policies important to the SDGs were suggested on such fundamental connections of causality.

(Latif et al., 2017)highlighted that the key metrics to measure the COVID-19 impact are the number of individuals residing below the global poverty line, the incidence of hunger, the assistance given by the state to the medical industry, the yearly increase in GDP rate, and the prevalence of tragedy mortality for the SDGs 1, 2, 3, 8 and 13. Choosing and recognizing the metrics could assist with comprehension of how the SDG targets react in the context of COVID-19. (Filho et al., 2020) analyzed the approach applied by a team of forty professionals from academia and the cell phone connectivity industry to compose a white paper detailing the relationships between the UN SDGs and the potential era of wireless communication. The article studied the inner workings of the specialized category, expanding upon the principles of crucial participation investigation.

(Khan, 2016)described the process for coordinating the UN SDGs in a manner that would act as an outline for future research, and provided an original perspective on the growth initiative that was guided by the SDGs. Team structure, personal operation, baseline info/ planning, and innovative collaboration all perform an aspect. (Eichler & Schwarz, 2019) designed for determining a score that will show how far various levels of the Romania state have come in fulfilling the SDGs. They recommended utilizing a relational object database termed PostgreSQL to hold and analyze information to create a consistent method for producing the SDG Index at the subnational level. The outcomes revealed how the greatest achievements in sustainable development originated in specific regions.

(Zengin et al., 2021) explored the concept of combining measures under the 2030 agenda and the sustainable development goals with the context of sustainability through history. It turned out that there are significant distinctions between environmental legislation and the present idea of government convergence. (Brodny & Tutak, 2023) evaluated the main indicators to assess how well the 27 EU member states adhered to SDG 8, and provided the results, providing an updated rating. The details offered an extensive overview of the things in the EU, especially modifications to development and the job markets. The final list takes the median population size for each nation and the nations themselves.

(Žižek et al., 2021)stated that the cause of linking objectives can be difficult and it needs more understanding to produce an effective strategy and approach to achieving an agreement between possible trade-offs and beneficial impacts in a company. Government officials, authorities, managers, entrepreneurs, and other specialists have all profited from this research gaining insight into the SDGs. Health organizations implemented the resource impact measure by applying the multinational input-output model to assess the worldwide procurement system. The connection between SDGs 8 and 12 was taken. It was discovered that the biggest driver of consumer spending was capital expenditure. The global ecological footprint developed, with the region of Asia-Pacific providing the biggest chunk of this growth. (Salam, 2020) conducted a cross-business examination of sustainable development applications, focusing on financial companies. The content evaluation was employed. Additional investigation on ethical banking is required because it is an innovative and broad approach. Many factors, especially in the Greek atmosphere have been discovered by empirical studies to minimize the disparity between competitive and sustainable lending.

The Sustainable Development Goals (SDGs) frequently referred to as the World Goals, are a global effort by the UN that seeks to eliminate hunger, preserve the planet, and ultimately bring peace and security for all people by the year 2030. The 17 sustainability advance targets have connections since they understand that choices made in a particular field will have an effect on others and that advancement has to reconcile sustainability in all areas (Levänen et al., 2016). The government intends to provide the least fortunate primacy in progress.

The UN was created to eliminate bias against females, starvation, AIDS, and unemployment. To accomplish the SDGs, individuals from all aspects of existence must offer their innovative thinking, knowledge, asset resources, and technological skills (UN Report 2022). The Sustainable Development Goals were established as a consequence of the Sustainable Development Summit, which was convened by the UN in September 2015 (Sachs et al., 2019). The SDGs have formed as the focus of years of effort by many nations in collaboration with the UN department of social and economic affairs. A paper titled 'The future we want' was presented earlier in June 2012.

The United nation's involvement completely approved the 2030 agenda for sustainability which includes 17 Sustainable development goals. Over the next fifteen years, 169 goals were established to achieve these 17 SGDs. Developing targets that tackle both environmental problems and the worldwide goal of eliminating inequality will result in superior outcomes due to their mutual dependence (Sætra, 2021). You bear an immense amount of accountability, but this plan has a chance to rescue the globe, which is the reason why 2015 has been termed a historic year. Many significant agreements have been reached as a consequence of the 2015 sustainability summit. Developing the objectives simply will not be beneficial unless everyone worried regarding them globally commits to see them through (Filho et al., 2020). The Ministry of Fiscal and Human Affairs Department for Sustainable Development Goals was established by UN Secretary-General Ban Ki-moon.

2.2 A Review of the 2030 Agenda for Sustainable Development Goal 3:

The Sustainable Development Goals Report 2022 presents an in-depth analysis of the 2030 Agenda for Sustainable Development progress employing the latest and most recent information estimations. It analyzes Development against the 17 Goals nationally and locally using a comprehensive examination of particular metrics for each objective (UN Report 2022.)

The study asserts that several connected and overlapping difficulties constitute a significant risk to the 2030 Agenda for sustainable growth and, thus to the existence of humanity altogether. The findings of the report reveal the nature and complexity of these problems. The concurrent appearance of various problems, prominent among them COVID-19, global warming, and violence, are having a bearing effect on all of the sustainable development goals. The study's depth outlines decades of achievements toward decreasing hunger and poverty, increasing education and health, providing basic amenities, and additionally as it has been undone. It brings an emphasis on the problems that have to be addressed right now if the SDGs are to be saved and if by 2030 individuals and the natural world going to achieve major strides toward fulfilling them (Baltrusaitis et al., 2024).

Sustaining a healthy state and promoting happiness during life is vital for long-term development. The pandemic continues to trigger diseases and mortality in humans. By the beginning of 2022, the pandemic was affecting over 500 million individuals nationwide (Zengin et al., 2021). In the current projection, the pandemic may generate up to 15 million excess deaths internationally by the end of 2021. The worldwide pandemic has severely disrupted key medical services and ceased 20 years of development towards universal Healthcare. As a consequence, depression and anxiety have grown more prevalent and lifespan is decreasing globally. The proportion of newborns visited by doctors is projected to be between 84% in 2015-2021 (Sachas et al., 2019).

3. RESEARCH METHOD

The research employed in this chapter to investigate how smart technological development influences worldwide medical systems and contributes to achieving Sustainable Development Goal 3 relies on a set of qualitative and case-based approaches. Using real-world case studies (Telemedicine in rural India- Breaking Healthcare barriers, AI in Diagnostics- Transforming Healthcare with IBM Watson Health, Mobile Health (MHealth) in Pandemic Management) to show the value of creative approaches, the chapter investigates the role of advances in healthcare. Student papers, government documents, Healthcare journals, magazines, and commercial reports from enterprises employing smart Technologies in Healthcare were among the numerous sources from which information was gathered. A wide range of regional and scientific opinions were offered for the particular case studies by the information on telemedicine campaigns, AI in diagnostics, and MHealth sites.

Each case study followed evaluation to clarify the different impacts of innovative technology on healthcare results, excellence, and availability. Furthermore, the chapter also contained secondary data from freely available resources, such as articles concerning improvements in healthcare technology and how they connect with SDG 3. These sets of information have been merged to determine how SDG 3 targets like improving global health effects, reducing medical gaps, and enhancing medical accessibility, can be achieved by innovations like machine learning, telemedicine, and MHealth. The chapter provides an in-depth examination of how smart technology can be employed to promote sustainable health development on an international level through the application of this mixed-method strategy.

Figure 3. Data extraction model (Authors)

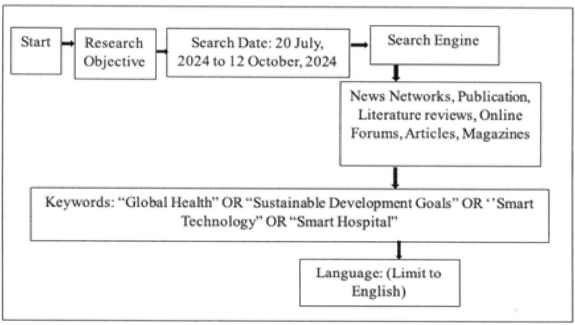

Figure 3 represents the data extraction model for SDG 3 evaluation, which offers a systematic method for gathering information and analytics. It includes the steps associated with developing objectives, getting data from multiple sources, and adopting a qualitative approach. This framework eventually allows concrete recommendations that coincide with SDG 3 targets.

3.1 Research Objectives

1. To explore the methods in which smart Technology developments can improve medical access, productivity, and availability eventually contributing to achieving Sustainable development goal 3 (Good health & well- being).
2. To determine how smart Technology integrates with the Sustainable Development Goal 3 targets & initiatives, focusing on how it may enhance medical results and tackle major global medical issues to transform worldwide health.

4. DATA ANALYSIS AND DISCUSSION

4.1 Real-World Case Studies

The non-existence of facilities, healthcare providers, and equipment has continuously made it challenging for individuals living in the countryside of India to dependable treatment. In these domains, the development of telemedicine has entirely altered how medicine is provided through the possibility of distant consultation, assessment, and medication. The Indian government's Sanjivani effort, which provides teleconsultation offerings, is notable. Individuals living in remote places can obtain excellent Healthcare without needing to travel far due to this assistance, that connects them with doctors in urban cities.

Individuals can see medical professionals virtually because of telemedicine centers that are equipped with minimum testing supplies and connectivity to the internet. The use of this technology has had an important effect, especially during the pandemic when personal discussions were limited. The disparity in Healthcare between Urban and rural countryside has been considerably reduced by the framework, which has processed over 10 million sessions. This case study highlights how the availability of healthcare, particularly to communities with limited resources can be accomplished through telemedicine, which can be a vital tool in achieving sustainable development Goal 3.

4.2 Case Study- AI in Diagnostics- Transforming Healthcare with IBM Watson Health

This pertains to applying artificial intelligence to diagnose illness, and IBM Watson Health has paved the charge. AI was recently utilized uniquely in the discipline of cancer therapy, and it has enhanced cancer identification therapy and detection management. IBM Watson can offer treatment suggestions that are customized for the requirements of every individual by reviewing an enormous number of studies, scientific papers, and patient information. For example, the hospital of Manipal in India adopted Watson for Cancer to assist doctors generate more informed and rapid choices regarding cancer therapy.

The method recommends the best path of action through examination of the medical literature and an Individual's genetic profile. Millions of individuals have profited from the AI platforms enhanced accurate diagnosis and faster decisions regarding treatment. This particular case reveals how AI, an innovative device, is contributing to improving worldwide health, decreasing errors in diagnosis, and improving the accuracy of medicine- all of which immediately support the accomplishment of SDG 3.

4.3 Case Study- Mobile Health (MHealth) in Pandemic Management

Mobile health (MHealth) was crucial for the administration of the pandemic. On a global scale, MHealth applications for tracking connections, illness evaluation, and public education were issued by authorities and medical institutions. The TraceTogather app from Singapore is a renowned example, it employs Bluetooth technology to monitor COVID-19 contacts. The release of the Aarogya Setu app in India enables individuals to track their potential contact with a virus similarly.

Regulators and authorities were capable of observing the growth of illness, detecting situations early, and decreasing infection rates due to these programs. Condition checks, vaccine registration, telephone consultation, and other elements that enabled individuals to use Healthcare services virtually were also offered by MHealth apps along with communication tracking. The government has managed to reduce the expansion of the pandemic and reduce the burden on their Healthcare systems through integrating medical technology records into pandemic control. This investigation illustrates the importance of technology in achieving SDG 3 goals by offering an instance of how MHealth may be a virtual instrument in worldwide medical crises.

Table 2. Thematic analysis

Theme	Telemedicine in rural India	AI in Diagnostics (IBM Watson Heath)	MHealth
Accessibility	Allowed medical access for over 65% of rural clients, minimizing travel time & waiting time.	Enhanced access to correct attributions, permitting faster therapy.	Immediate-time pandemic information and tracking of contacts have been made accessible for quick response.
Cost Efficiency	Inexpensive travel cost, minimize follow-up cost, improving budget.	Reduced repetitive testing, and human fault costs, improving resource use.	Minimized disaster response expenses by doing away with the requirements of tracking contacts manually.
Efficiency	Enhanced doctor-patient communication rates, and developed service quality efficiency.	Minimize verification time from days to hours, empowering decision-making.	Provided rapid vulnerability cautions to encourage quick medical health response.

Source: Authors'

Table 2 presents the thematic analysis using themes through which each innovation enhances the Healthcare system and promotes SDG 3 by improving accessibility, efficiency, and cost-effectiveness.

Table 3. Media coverage and publication reports

Case Study	Source name	Publication House	Publication Type
Telemedicine in rural India	The Times of India	Times Group	News article
	Hindustan Times	Hindustan Times group	News article
	Ministry of Health	Government of India	Press release
AI in Diagnostics: Transforming Healthcare with IBM Watson Health	Forbes	Forbes media	News article
	IBM Watson Health Website	IBM	Press release
Mobile Health (MHealth)	WHO report on Mobile Health initiative	World Health Organization	Report
	Health Tech Startup	Health Tech Company	

Source: Authors'

Table 3 displays the media coverage and press releases for three- real-world case studies of innovative advances in healthcare. Trustworthy sources that highlight the case reports' usefulness in transforming the delivery of healthcare like 'The Time of India' and 'Forbes'. The significance and relevance of telemedicine, AI in diagnostics, and Mobile Health endeavors in the present medical landscape has been illustrated by the numerous press coverage.

5. UNDERSTANDING SDG 3 (GOOD HEALTH AND WELL-BEING)

Understanding the importance of an era that is equitable and serene, the UN released the Sustainable Development Goals in 2015. These goals are an international push to eliminate unemployment and maintain the planet in a secure and peaceful environment. There are specific indicators and objectives for each of the 17 connected aims. The third Sustainable development goal is to ensure and improve the well-being of all people. This is referred to as the 'Health and Wellbeing ' objective. As an opportunity to empower everybody to succeed and achieve their full potential, SDG 3 puts an emphasis on health and well-being for people, groups, and nations. SDG 3 depends on the idea that everyone has a basic right to good health which is also an essential requirement for Sustainable Development. Accordingly, investing in Health and wellbeing will improve social equilibrium, revenue generation, and efficiency. (El Massah & Mohieldin, 2020). This will thereby promote the development of an inclusive community and contribute to the reduction of unemployment. Eliminating infant and maternal death, fighting transmissible diseases, & providing widespread availability to reproductive health of the major specific intents of SDG3. With the promotion and integration of the reproductive sector into national programs, SDG 3 additionally supports the availability of birth control and other reproductive health facilities. (Filho et al., 2020).

5.1 Path-breaking Initiatives Taken by the Government to Achieve SDG 3

India has a massive and varied population size, rendering SDG 3 especially important considering the difficulties it confronts. India has faced problems with equality and not having the availability of excellent medical services, particularly within the countryside, despite significant economic development. The increasing incidence of illnesses that are not communicable, such as diabetes, cancer, and Type 2 diabetes, renders it essential to consider wellness as an aspect of development. The health of mothers and children was often overlooked due to an outdated system of patriarchy. Thereby, authorities needed to think about reducing the number of deaths from birth and pregnancy improving nourishment, and tackling deficiencies in nutrition in both mothers and children. India has generated significant strides towards SDG 3. The administration has taken various innovative determines in this area, such as:

Mission of National Health (NHM): The NHM offers universal health care in the fields of female wellness, children wellness, Sanitation, clean water, and nutrition. It aims to improve the accessibility and availability of low-cost and excellent health care, with an emphasis on poor, women and those who reside in the countryside. The NHM developed several exact standards based on statistics as an essential initial step toward achieving SDG 3.

Ayushman Bharat Health Insurance Scheme: This premier health coverage scheme was launched to provide those in poverty and underprivileged sections of the population access to inexpensive health services. Roughly 500 million persons will eventually have a choice of treatment for severe illness as a consequence of this.

National Health Care for Elderly Program (NPHCE): The main aim of NPHCE is to provide senior patients with whole, unique, and autonomous health care, alongside outreach services.

Vaccination: The population of India has become mostly resistant to diseases like tetanus, polio, and measles due to major improvements in Vaccination programs. Over 90% of humanity received vaccinations against the pandemic in a very short period, resulting in the biggest Vaccination scheme in the history of humanity. India has gained significant progress in this field as a component of its attempts to achieve SDG 3.

Eradication of Malaria: The World Malaria Report for 2019 indicates that India is accountable for approximately 3% of the international's malaria cases. India has made major achievements in decreasing the incidence and death of malaria in the past few decades. The anticipated total number of incidents of malaria has been decreasing, including a reported reduction of 24% in 2017.

Tobacco abuse: Smoking poses one of the biggest risks to the health of the public. It has enormous societal and financial consequences along with killing lives. The Indian legislature has launched several kinds of measures to lower tobacco usage. One such program is the National Tobacco Control Program (NTCP), which employs tactics like increased taxes, restrictions on advertisements, health notifications, Health recommendations, and products that assist individuals quit.

5.2 Key Targets for SDG 3

SDG 3 tackles a range of health- issues having the objective of guaranteeing good health and encouraging happiness for everyone. The death rate of mothers has decreased significantly as a consequence of improvements in healthcare availability; there has been a 38% reduction in maternal fatalities globally. Increased Vaccination initiatives have also led to a 50% reduction in infant deaths. The prevalence and mortality of viral illnesses such as HIV, TB, and malaria have fallen dramatically as a consequence of addressing them. There has been advancement in the knowledge of illnesses that are not transmissible and in intervention therapies for them, especially in the fields of cancer heart disease, and mental health. Scientific and technological initiatives have produced affordable vaccines and medicines for diseases that are prevalent in nations that are developing, with initiatives like Gavi boosting vaccine availability Governments that have made investments in their medical system and personnel have experience in finance, to achieve the goals of sustainable Development 3, each of these achievements is an important step toward creating a more prosperous world (Kulkov et al., 2024).

Table 4. Major targets of SDG 3

SDG 3 Targets	Description
3.1	Decrease the prevalence of mother's death internationally to fewer than 70 per 100000 live births.
3.2	Minimize infant mortality to at least 12 per 1000 live births to place an end to the unnecessary deaths of babies and kids below five.
3.3	Fight illnesses such as hepatitis, and infections, other diseases like AIDS, and Malaria.
3.4	Support mental wellness and general wellness while decreasing the premature death rate.
3.5	Strength efforts to avoid and manage drug abuse, including the improper use of drink and illicit drugs.
3.6	Eliminate traffic-related harm and death globally.
3.7	Ensure that facilities for reproductive wellness are available to all.
3.8	Promote national health and offer access to inexpensive medicines and treatments.
3.9	Decrease emissions and hazardous chemical-related deaths.
3. a	Within the WHO framework, improve anti-tobacco behavior.

continued on following page

Table 4. Continued

SDG 3 Targets	Description
3. b	Assist nations that are developing to benefit from affordable supplies of vaccines and medicine.
3. c	Enhance funding for healthcare and empower the hospital sector.
3.d	Enhance the system for early alert and medical risk control capacities.

Source: Authors' compilation

Table 4 includes the most significant SDG3 targets, that are geared at expanding global health and well-being. The table explains specific goals such as reducing the mortality rate of mothers, minimizing deaths of kids and infant children five, and addressing viruses like malaria, AIDS, and cancer. The program additionally targets objectives which include reducing the premature death rate from non- transmissible illness, improving emotional health, and increasing the availability of excellent health care. These objectives emphasize the importance of a comprehensive strategy for a disease that involves prevention, treatment, and awareness to encourage adaptive, happier populations throughout the world.

6. THE ROLE OF SMART TECHNOLOGY IN GLOBAL HEALTH: IMPACT ON HEALTHCARE SYSTEMS

Smart Healthcare enhances the standard of treatment offered by rendering the conventional Healthcare system simpler more effective, accessible, and customized. It promotes connections among healthcare players, especially patients, medical facilities, and academic institutions. Clients' health illnesses can be tracked in actual time by their doctors using mobile devices, enabling them to react to any unusual events or emergencies virtually. (Zengin et al., 2021). This continuous health monitoring is not only helpful for acquiring the right diagnosis, thus minimizing the requirements for hospitalizations, but it may preserve life in the case of an unexpected illness. Smart Healthcare enhances collaboration and renders health information simpler.

Smart Technology in Healthcare: Systems that employ machine learning, the Internet, access to the cloud, and modern capabilities are often called smart devices. A few instances of smart devices used for healthcare are driven by AI inventory control platforms that can monitor and record stock and then proactively buy fresh items when required, or smart mattresses that can detect the movement of patients and inform doctors when an individual exits the room. Let's examine some examples of smart equipment in healthcare that boost preventive care methods, enhance patient outcomes, and eventually render the entire globe.

Automated Healthcare System: Medical facilities that are computerized and supervised electronically a developing practice that exceeds conventional Healthcare and into more everyday life is the distant observation of clients' illness. Numerous individuals now employ fitness monitors and wearables as regular hardware to track multiple health variables, such as oxygen levels in their blood, blood pressure, heart rate variability, etc. Medical professionals are employing machinery to observe the symptoms of patients constantly while making preventive decisions regarding therapy using patterns and forecasts in statistics.

For example, related devices are a prime instance of smart Healthcare equipment that saves people by helping individuals track their consumption and alerting them when to take their dose to maintain an ongoing routine. Universities are also using biosensors as an example of innovation. These empower

Healthcare providers worldwide to maintain a watch on clients while remaining active in care. These gadgets measure vital health parameters like blood pressure and temperature to offer Healthcare providers more information and insight into the development of disease, and overall health. Using surveillance of patients to recognize indications and other signs of the disease, these sensors supported the worldwide community in monitoring the pandemic.

Telehealth and Remote care: Presently, telemedicine is a prevalent phrase, gaining acceptance among clients and doctors through the epidemic. Clinicians might cure individuals over telephone conversations, and video conferencing, write prescription drugs, and carry out subsequent visits using the help of teleconference innovations. To assist patients and doctors track counseling, maintaining health information, and collect and retrieve information gathered from mobile devices or trips to the clinic, Healthcare gateway software was used to develop private online medical platforms. Universities are likely to continue employing videoconferencing and remote care even though their prevalence has risen after the global pandemic occurred. Both clients and doctors gained advantages from employing this type of technology.

Integrated urgent medical responses: Using a connection to the web may significantly improve medical care's efficiency and response times, which could mean the distinction between life and death. The term real responses is made easier by the acceptable pace at which information can be exchanged between paramedics, physicians, medical personnel, emergency rooms, and other institutions using new innovative medical technology. The use of this advancement enables quicker interaction, speedier histories of patients, easier hospital entry with already established signs and past, and online conversations with specialists from inside paramedics. Clinicians might have details about patients on hand, before they come, including indicators of health, heart rate, climate, etc.

Smart Hospital Administration: By connecting electronic devices and making it easier to access facts like room demand, equipment usage, machine status, resources and stock counts, and other administrative data, digital hospital Administration may contribute to greater productivity and efficacy, increase the experience of patients, and support doctors. Healthcare employees may avoid running out of resources due to insufficient tracking or incorrect data collection by maintaining control of these details and applying them to affect choices. It can also reduce inefficiency while improving the management of resources. Smart hospitals, that employ a variety of cutting-edge innovations like artificial intelligence (AI), the Internet of Things (IoT), and telehealth will be essential to the evolution of healthcare.

7. TECHNOLOGICAL ADVANCEMENTS SHAPING THE FUTURE OF GLOBAL HEALTH

The application of digital health records enables the sharing of patient information irrespective of location, minimizing customer waiting times. This information collected can also be applied for statistical investigation that encourages clinical research, which will result in better therapies in the years to come.

The Internet of Things in Smart Healthcare Systems: IoT is an essential player in the establishment of data-driven hospitals and the digitization of the medical sector. Hospitals can get recent data on clients' medical conditions by allowing devices and medical supplies to connect. This renders feasible the remote surveillance of patients, which we described earlier, and which allows Healthcare doctors to track symptoms, manage persistent disease, and engage in preventive measures. IOT also enhances the management of assets, which ensures the accessibility and performance of healthcare devices and streamlines hospital procedures. IoT devices control their consumption of energy for savings, which enhances the management of energy. The monitoring of activities by IOT-enabled methods also boosts the flow of patients within the hospital, reducing waiting periods and increasing average efficiency. Innovative medical facilities and smart hospitals depend on the IOT, which encourages networking and information to improve care for patients.

Artificial Intelligence (AI) in healthcare: Smart hospitals have become an alternative to the conventional wisdom that machine learning is at the center of innovation. The capacity for artificial intelligence to assess huge data sets helps in the evaluation phase and enables Healthcare workers take quick, accurate inferences. The use of predictive analytics, which highlights potential illness issues and offers individuals more choices for proactive treatment, is additionally powered by this advancement. Chatbots powered by AI and digital assistants increase satisfaction from the perspective of the individual's journey by providing rapid responses to concerns, making appointments, and fundamental advice. AI simplifies processes on the managerial side by streamlining tasks like entering information and accounting. This not only opens up essential time for medical professionals but also includes more effective and patient-focused medical atmospheres. AI operates as the cerebral strength, boosting the abilities of medicine.

MHealth: In modern hospitals, mobile health (MHealth) is an essential component of patient-centered treatment. Although telephones are so prevalent, MHealth applications empower individuals to play an interesting part in their well-being. People may monitor their wellness and share current information with physicians, enabling monitoring patients from home. Telehealth solutions go together hand in hand since they promote each other. Preventive medicine is encouraged by wellness and health programs for handheld devices, which offer customized activity surveillance, and mental wellness support. MHealth makes it simpler for people to maintain control of their medications and drugs.

Virtual reality and Augmented reality in healthcare: Innovations employing augmented and virtual reality offer imaginative and engaging options for smart hospital education and also for the instruction of future physicians. AR improves the process of learning in healthcare education by putting digital information over the real world to generate realistic surgery models. Virtual reality presents a completely realistic context, which helps manage annoyance throughout healthcare surgeries and recovery exercises. Operators can organize treatment more efficiently since AR and VR reality are graphical and dynamic, offering an entire three-dimensional picture. These instruments promote client care perspectives by decreasing pain and boosting involvement in recovery methods, to promote instructions for professionals.

Personalized Medicine and Genomics: Genetic treatment is the current trend of the near future, contributing to revolutionary innovations in healthcare via personalized individualized treatment. It is essentially addressing individuals based on their biological makeup rather than adopting a one universal size approach. This may result in fewer adverse reactions and more successful therapy. Initial illness detection and prevention are rendered by studies on genomics, which transform the emphasis on medical care from responsive to proactive.

Organ care Technology & Bio prints: Technology for transplant preservation and biological printing is now mainstream. There is an abundance of investigation being conducted on bioprinting to be, or the 3d printed version of organ and tissues, which has a chance to remove the lack of organs. Though there are moral and technical hurdles in this complex field, there is an immense amount of opportunity for salvation.

Blockchain in Healthcare: The use of Blockchain offers smart Hospital management of medical information a greater level of protection and transparency. It's centralized and impermeable to structure guards against unlawful entry and information change, ensuring the confidentiality of medical records. Blockchain increases compatibility by facilitating medical data transfer across different platforms while promoting seamless cooperation. In the management of supply chains, blockchain is used to monitor the legality and transportation of treatments and medical supplies, ensuring openness. Intelligent contracts, systematic and reliable contracts enabled by blockchain, improve processes like claim processing and payment, reducing operational problems. Blockchain helps the dependable and effective working of smart hospitals by improving data safety, compatibility, and productivity.

8. POLICY RECOMMENDATIONS

The medical sector has several challenges that are specific to the state. Specific remedies must be developed to tackle medical structures, personnel shortages, effectiveness, convenience, and budget concerns. Developments and technologies have proved to be the most effective approaches to address various issues over time. Innovative innovations and approaches are effective instruments for solving the problems of cost and affordability. Indian Healthcare systems are striving hard to solve the problems arising from the nation's increasing double disease load, despite occasional obstacles. (Bloom, 2019). The provision of medical care has been entirely changed by the development of novel innovations, which have improved convenience, efficacy, and affordability. The capacity to detect and manage disease more quickly and accurately is one of the primary advantages of current advances in healthcare. Personalized medicine and artificial Intelligence tools for diagnosis are two instances of innovations that have the chance to completely alter how clinicians detect and manage diseases, increasing patient outcomes. (Kroll et al., 2019). The recent development of telemedicine has been significant to the accessibility of healthcare treatment, especially in logistically remote parts of the country.

Artificial intelligence has provided possibilities that were formerly imagined accessible. These systems can detect and understand datasets with a speed that is similar to that of an individual, or even better when employing big data and computers. Database using computer Intelligence serves to connect the diagnosis made by the patient with other cases that are similar to it depending on the patient's signs, indicators, and other data. The technique of predictive modeling is employed in some programs, like the examination of unorganized information and the oversight of patients and hospital space allocation. AI is significantly changing how medical attention is given. It will analyze X-rays and send the outcomes to the appropriate center. Computational Intelligence-powered statistics allow the diagnosis given to the patient to be independently verified against other cases that are similar to their own, using similar signs, indicators, and observations. India has to educate a lot of medical professionals- not just doctors and nurses, but also engineers and equipment operators- to take full advantage of AI. In this case, integrating AI with human intelligence and education is needed.

Four primary types of devices are being used by healthcare hospitals to improve their services. They are first adopting revolutionary innovations developed specifically for clinical use. Machines, MRI equipment, less-invasive surgical techniques, and significantly enhanced have all been used to enhance the quality of life and medical results. Indian Spinal Injuries Institute offers as an instance, because all of its old technology has been updated with new products. Every resource - including information and assets- is employed carefully. It is the initial institution outside of the United States. Healthcare institutions have added readily accessible devices with IT-driven regulations. They are enabled to enhance client comfort and workflow efficiency. To assist their staff, to work more efficiently and successfully, Healthcare facilities are now using efficient solutions. Their healthcare management systems are enhanced by statistical analysis and associated applications. Hospitals can make decisions based on data, manage funds optimally, and enhance the health of patients due to these innovations and advancements. Healthcare organizations must break teamwork to integrate every setting and amenities with a successful data system. Successful leadership of the whole care continuum- from admittance to discharge, is greatly helped by collaboration with the network of supply chain operations.

Table 5. Policy recommendations

Focus Area	Policy Recommendations
Infrastructure	Investing in Telemedicine.
	Secure data systems.
	Cybersecurity.
	Advanced tools.
Capacity Building	Experts in digital health.
	Educate society on tech use.
	Fund research.
Global cooperation	Build collaborations.
	Share advancements and tools.
	Align data information internationally.
	Fund project.
Technology Transfer	Establish a regional tools hub.
	Support open-source solutions.
	Promote local manufacturing.
Ethical frameworks	Regulate guidelines for AI Technology usage.
	Ensure the safety and privacy of data.
	Promote equity.
Regulatory policies	Audit AI ethics.
	Device safety.
	Secure data-sharing.
	Align with WHO Standards.

Source: Authors' compilation

Table 5 highlights policy suggestions that employ advanced technology to promote global health concepts and satisfy the sustainable development goals (SDGs). The following table contains essential strategies to attain SDG targets like increasing health access and reducing poverty, such as enhancing information facilities, boosting medical information technology, and developing collaboration. The laws provide extreme value on how technologies enable information-driven choices, develop resilient medical systems, and support creativity in the supply of healthcare.

9. CONCLUSION

The whole price spectrum of medical care in India has been greatly influenced by the development of novel advances in the medical sector. The overall expenses of medical care services have fallen because of new advancements that allow early identification of illness and reduce the requirement for hospitalization. This enhanced medical conditions for all individuals decreasing expenses and boosting access to treatment for an increasing part of the general population.

Medical facilities have been monitoring the creation of an effective supply chain in combination with advances to attain economy. The administrative aspects of the whole supply chain have been evolving. Innovation has caused the development of an effective supply chain structure. Products and services are accessible because of this novel approach and the changing framework of supply chain operations.

In Indian healthcare field, the value and impact of novel advances and technology cannot be minimized. How medicine is provided in India is evolving as a consequence of technological advances, that provide advantages like enhanced medical care and therapy and illness avoidance and prevention. Novel innovations will continue to contribute an increasing and greater part in improving the norm of medical care while making them more readily accessible and affordable as the sector evolves.

Online consultations, virtual testing, telecommunication radio, home medical care, virtual therapies, information tracking, online pharmacies, and clinical decision-making tools will be included in online medical care moving forward. The level of healthcare services will be online healthcare as it has so many advantages over personal consultations.

REFERENCES

Baltrusaitis, J., Bakshi, B., Chojnacka, K., Chuck, C. J., Coppens, M.-O., Edge, J. S., Harper, G., Hsiao, B. S., Li, H., Mba Wright, M., McLaughlin, M., Nandy, A., Pan, S.-Y., Qiang, Z., Ribeiro, C., Swadźba-Kwaśny, M., Wang, M., Xiang, Y., & Zhang, L. (2024). Sustainability science and technology in 2024 and beyond equitable publishing aligned with United Nations' Sustainable development goals. *Sustainability Science and Technology*, 1(1), 010201. DOI: 10.1088/2977-3504/ad555a

Basyirah, L., Kina, A., & Hidayati, A. (2022). Open innovation for sustainable development goals: Learning from go to group. *Journal of Innovation in Business and Economics*, 6(01). Advance online publication. DOI: 10.22219/jibe.v6i01.21745

Botti, A., & Monda, A. (2020). Sustainable value co-creation and digital health: The case of Trentino e-health ecosystem. *Sustainability (Basel)*, 12(13), 5263. Advance online publication. DOI: 10.3390/su12135263

Brodny, J., & Tutak, M. (2023). The level of implementing sustainable development goal "Industry, innovation and infrastructure" of Agenda 2030 in the European Union countries: Application of MCDM methods JEL Classification: C39; O30; R11. *Oeconomia Copernicana*, 14(1), 47–102. DOI: 10.24136/oc.2023.002

Dar, S. A.Dr Naseer Ahmad. (2022). Mobile technology's role in meeting sustainable development goals. *Journal of Technology Innovations and Energy*, 1(2), 8–15. DOI: 10.56556/jtie.v1i2.180

Eichler, G. M., & Schwarz, E. J. (2019). What sustainable development goals do social innovations address: A systematic review and content analysis of social innovation literature. *Sustainability (Basel)*, 11(2), 522. Advance online publication. DOI: 10.3390/su11020522

El Massah, S., & Mohieldin, M. (2020). Digital transformation and localizing the Sustainable Development Goals (SDGs). *Ecological Economics*, 169, 106490. Advance online publication. DOI: 10.1016/j.ecolecon.2019.106490

Fei, W., Opoku, A., Agyekum, K., Oppon, J. A., Ahmed, V., Chen, C., & Lok, K. L. (2021). The critical role of the construction industry in achieving the sustainable development goals (SDGs): Delivering projects for the common good. *Sustainability (Basel)*, 13(16), 9112. Advance online publication. DOI: 10.3390/su13169112

Filho, W. L., Brandli, L. L., Salvia, A. L., Rayman-Bacchus, L., & Platje, J. (2020). COVID-19 and the UN sustainable development goals: Threat to solidarity or an opportunity. *Sustainability (Basel)*, 12(13), 5343. Advance online publication. DOI: 10.3390/su12135343

Garg, H., Ike, G. N., Kashif, M., & Azam, M. S. (2024). Dynamics of Sustainable and Ethically Responsible Business Practices in Corporate Social Responsibility. In *Technology-Driven Evolution of the Corporate Social Responsibility Ecosystem* (pp. 92–113). IGI Global., DOI: 10.4018/979-8-3693-3238-2.ch005

Goel, R. K., & Vishnoi, S. (2023). Strengthening and sustaining health-related outcomes through digital health interventions. *Journal of Engineering Science and Technology Review*, 16(2), 10–17. DOI: 10.25103/jestr.162.02

Hamad, R. S., Shamsi, A. L., Ameen, A. A., Isaac, O., Al-Shibami, A. H., & Sayed Khalifa, G. (2018). The impact of Innovation and smart government on happiness: Proposing conceptual framework. *International Journal of Management and Human Science*, 2(2).

Hoosain, M. S., Paul, B. S., & Ramakrishna, S. (2020). The impact of digital technologies and circular thinking on the United Nations sustainable development goals. *Sustainability (Basel)*, 12(23), 1–16. DOI: 10.3390/su122310143

Kashif, M., Garg, H., Weqar, F., & David, A. (2024). Regulatory Strategies and Innovative Solutions for Deepfake Technology. In Navigating the World of Deepfake Technology (pp. 262–282). IGIGlobal. DOI: 10.4018/979-8-3693-5298-4.ch013

Kashif, M., Kumar, P., Ghai, S., & Kumar, S. (2023). Disruptive technologies in computational finance. In *Algorithmic Approaches to Financial Technology* (pp. 46–60). Forecasting, Trading, and Optimization.

Kashif, M., Shajar, S. N., Singhal, N., & Kumar, P. (2023). Achieving sustainable investment practices through green finance: Challenges and opportunities. In Sustainable Investments in Green Finance (pp. 234–244).

Kashif, M., Singhal, N., Goyal, S., & Singh, S. K. (2024). Foreign Exchange Reserves and Economic Growth of Brazil: A Nonlinear Approach. Finance. *Theory into Practice*, 28(1), 145–154. DOI: 10.26794/2587-5671-2024-28-1-145-154

Kasinathan, P., Pugazhendhi, R., Elavarasan, R. M., Ramachandaramurthy, V. K., Ramanathan, V., Subramanian, S., Kumar, S., Nandhagopal, K., Raghavan, R. R. V., Rangasamy, S., Devendiran, R., & Alsharif, M. H. (2022). Realization of sustainable development goals with disruptive technologies by integrating industry 5.0, Society 5.0, Smart Cities, and Villages. *Sustainability (Basel)*, 14(22), 15258. Advance online publication. DOI: 10.3390/su142215258

Kickbusch, I., Piselli, D., Agrawal, A., Balicer, R., Banner, O., Adelhardt, M., Capobianco, E., Fabian, C., Singh Gill, A., Lupton, D., Medhora, R. P., Ndili, N., Ryś, A., Sambuli, N., Settle, D., Swaminathan, S., Morales, J. V., Wolpert, M., Wyckoff, A. W., & Wong, B. L. H. (2021). The Lancet and Financial Times Commission on governing health futures 2030: growing up in a digital world. *The Lancet, 398* (10312). 1727–1776. DOI: 10.1016/S0140-6736(21)01824-9

Kostoska, O., & Kocarev, L. (2019). A novel ICT framework for sustainable development goals. *Sustainability (Basel)*, 11(7), 1961. Advance online publication. DOI: 10.3390/su11071961

Kroll, C., Warchold, A., & Pradhan, P. (2019). Sustainable Development Goals (SDGs): Are we successful in turning trade-offs into synergies? *Palgrave Communications*, 5(1), 140. Advance online publication. DOI: 10.1057/s41599-019-0335-5

Kulkov, I., Kulkova, J., Rohrbeck, R., Menvielle, L., Kaartemo, V., & Makkonen, H. (2024). Artificial intelligence-driven sustainable development: Examining organizational, technical, and processing approaches to achieving global goals. *Sustainable Development (Bradford)*, 32(3), 2253–2267. DOI: 10.1002/sd.2773

Kutty, A. A., Abdella, G. M., Kucukvar, M., Onat, N. C., & Bulu, M. (2020). A system thinking approach for harmonizing smart and sustainable city initiatives with United Nations sustainable development goals. *Sustainable Development (Bradford)*, 28(5), 1347–1365. DOI: 10.1002/sd.2088

Latif, S., Qadir, J., Farooq, S., & Imran, M. A. (2017). How 5G Wireless and Concomitant Technologies will revolutionize healthcare. *Future Internet*, 9(4), 93. Advance online publication. DOI: 10.3390/fi9040093

Levänen, J., Hossain, M., Lyytinen, T., Hyvärinen, A., Numminen, S., & Halme, M. (2016). Implications of frugal innovations on sustainable development: Evaluating water and energy innovations. *Sustainability (Basel)*, 8(1), 4. Advance online publication. DOI: 10.3390/su8010004

Li, W., Yigitcanlar, T., Browne, W., & Nili, A. (2023). The Making of Responsible Innovation and Technology: An Overview and Framework. In *Smart Cities, 6*(4). 1996–2034. https://doi.org/DOI: 10.3390/smartcities6040093

Liu, H. Y., Jay, M., & Chen, X. (2021). The role of nature-based solutions for improving environmental quality, health, and well-being. *Sustainability (Basel)*, 13(19), 10950. Advance online publication. DOI: 10.3390/su131910950

Liu, Z., Han, G., Yan, J., Liu, Z., & Osmani, M. (2022). The relationship between social mentality and health in promoting well-being and sustainable City. *International Journal of Environmental Research and Public Health*, 19(18), 11529. Advance online publication. DOI: 10.3390/ijerph191811529 PMID: 36141799

Millard, J. (2017). Technology innovations in public service delivery for sustainable development. *Public Administration and Information Technology*, 32, 241–282. DOI: 10.1007/978-3-319-63743-3_10

Pokrajac, L., Abbas, A., Chrzanowski, W., Dias, G. M., Eggleton, B. J., Maguire, S., Maine, E., Malloy, T., Nathwani, J., Nazar, L., Sips, A., Sone, J., Van Den Berg, A., Weiss, P. S., & Mitra, S. (2021). Nanotechnology for a Sustainable Future: Addressing global challenges with the international network4 sustainable nanotechnology. *ACS Nano*, 15(12), 18608–18623. DOI: 10.1021/acsnano.1c10919 PMID: 34910476

Ryan, M., Antoniou, J., Brooks, L., Jiya, T., Macnish, K., & Stahl, B. (2020). The ethical balance of using smart information systems for promoting the United Nations' sustainable development goals. *Sustainability (Basel)*, 12(12), 4826. Advance online publication. DOI: 10.3390/su12124826

Sachs, J. D., Schmidt-Traub, G., Mazzucato, M., Messner, D., Nakicenovic, N., & Rockström, J. (2019). Six transformations to achieve the Sustainable development goals. *Nature Sustainability*, 2(9), 805–814. DOI: 10.1038/s41893-019-0352-9

Sætra, H. S. (2021). Ai in context and the sustainable development goals: Factoring in the unsustainability of the sociotechnical system. *Sustainability (Basel)*, 13(4), 1–19. DOI: 10.3390/su13041738

Sánchez-Segura, M. I., Dugarte-Peña, G. L., De Amescua, A., Medina-Domínguez, F., López-Almansa, E., & Reyes, E. B. (2021). Smart occupational health and safety for a digital era and its place in smart and sustainable cities. *Mathematical Biosciences and Engineering*, 18(6), 8831–8856. DOI: 10.3934/mbe.2021436 PMID: 34814325

Shajar, S. N., Beg, K., Kashif, M., Khan, M., Saleem, S., & Usmani, F. (2024). Enhancing Firm Performance Through Effective Working Capital Management: A Study of Indian Manufacturing Firms Listed at S&P BSE 500. *International Research Journal of Multidisciplinary Scope*, 05(03), 661–669. DOI: 10.47857/irjms.2024.v05i03.0806

Shajar, S. N., Kashif, M., George, J., & Nasir, S. (2024). The future of green finance: Artificial intelligence-enabled solutions for a more sustainable world. In Harnessing Blockchain-Digital Twin Fusion for Sustainable Investments. https://doi.org/DOI: 10.4018/9798369318782.ch013

von Humboldt, S., Mendoza-Ruvalcaba, N. M., Arias-Merino, E. D., Costa, A., Cabras, E., Low, G., & Leal, I. (2020). Smart technology and the meaning in life of older adults during the Covid-19 public health emergency period: A cross-cultural qualitative study. *International Review of Psychiatry (Abingdon, England)*, 32(7–8), 713–722. DOI: 10.1080/09540261.2020.1810643 PMID: 33016790

Zengin, Y., Naktiyok, S., Kaygın, E., Kavak, O., & Topçuoğlu, E. (2021). An investigation of industry 4.0 and Society 5.0 within the context of sustainable development goals. *Sustainability (Basel)*, 13(5), 1–16. DOI: 10.3390/su13052682

Žižek, S. Š., Mulej, M., & Potočnik, A. (2021). The sustainable socially responsible society: Well-being society 6.0. *Sustainability (Basel)*, 13(16), 9186. Advance online publication. DOI: 10.3390/su13169186

Chapter 3
Harnessing the Power of Precision Medicine and AI:
Success Stories and Ethical Considerations

Latika Sahni
NDIM, India

Rishi Prakash Shukla
https://orcid.org/0000-0003-0854-7302
Jaipuria Institute of Management, India

ABSTRACT

This chapter explores the transformative potential of precision medicine and AI in revolutionizing healthcare delivery. By tailoring treatments to individual patient profiles through genomic insights and advanced analytics, personalized healthcare optimizes therapeutic efficacy, particularly in oncology, rare diseases, and chronic conditions. Case studies illustrate the economic advantages of targeted interventions, highlighting cost efficiency through reduced trial-and-error treatments and improved patient outcomes. However, the integration of AI introduces ethical dilemmas, including data privacy concerns, algorithmic biases, and the implications of genetic editing technologies. Global examples of healthcare systems implementing AI-driven personalized medicine provide valuable insights into best practices and lessons learned from early adopters. As the landscape of healthcare evolves, the chapter emphasizes the need for interdisciplinary collaboration, robust data infrastructure, and active patient engagement to navigate the complexities of precision medicine.

INTRODUCTION

Precision medicine and personalized healthcare represent a profound paradigm shift in the modern medical landscape, characterized by a transition from a one-size-fits-all approach to more individualized treatment protocols. These advancements are predominantly fueled by innovations in artificial intelligence (AI), which have revolutionized the ability to analyze vast datasets, identifying nuanced patterns and correlations between patient characteristics, genetic profiles, and treatment outcomes. This bespoke approach to healthcare aims to tailor interventions, therapies, and preventive measures not just

DOI: 10.4018/979-8-3373-0240-9.ch003

to broad disease categories but to the specific biological, environmental, and lifestyle factors unique to each patient (Malhotra & Gupta, 2021).

One of the central tenets of AI-powered personalized healthcare is the optimization of treatment efficacy. By harnessing predictive analytics, clinicians can move beyond the traditional reactive model of diagnosis and treatment, instead adopting a more proactive stance that anticipates patient needs before the manifestation of symptoms (Bhatnagar, Rajaram, et al., 2024; Bhatnagar, Taneja, et al., 2024). Machine learning algorithms are capable of processing genomic data alongside clinical histories to predict the likely course of diseases, enabling the early detection of potential health crises. This not only improves patient outcomes but also enhances the precision of treatment protocols, minimizing the risks of adverse drug reactions and unnecessary interventions (Cavaliere et al., 2024; Khanna et al., 2023).

The economic implications of this shift toward precision medicine are far-reaching. While the initial investment in personalized treatments, AI technologies, and advanced diagnostic tools may appear substantial, the long-term cost-efficiency of this model becomes evident when examined holistically. Predictive analytics plays a pivotal role in reducing healthcare expenditures by minimizing hospital admissions, emergency interventions, and ineffective treatments. By targeting therapies more accurately, healthcare systems can reduce wasteful spending on trial-and-error treatments, ultimately optimizing resource allocation. In this context, personalized healthcare emerges not just as a medical innovation but as an economically sustainable model, particularly in an era marked by aging populations and rising healthcare costs globally (R. Kumar, Kathuria, et al., 2023; R. Kumar, Lande, et al., 2023).

Moreover, AI-driven personalization in healthcare challenges the existing economic frameworks by introducing value-based care, wherein the focus is shifted from volume of services rendered to the quality and outcome of care provided. This recalibration has the potential to reshape insurance models, reimbursement strategies, and healthcare infrastructure, ushering in an era where efficiency, precision, and patient satisfaction are paramount (Patil et al., 2021).

In sum, AI-powered precision medicine is set to redefine the contours of modern healthcare. Its ability to provide highly tailored treatments holds the promise of more effective care with fewer resources, transforming not only patient outcomes but also the economic structures underpinning healthcare systems worldwide. The integration of predictive analytics into medical practice offers a future where the dual goals of economic sustainability and patient-centric care are no longer mutually exclusive but synergistic (Kanojia et al., 2022; M. S. Rana et al., 2022).

FOUNDATIONS OF PRECISION MEDICINE

Definition and Principles of Precision Medicine

Precision medicine refers to an advanced and evolving approach to medical treatment that meticulously tailors healthcare decisions, practices, and interventions to the individual characteristics of each patient. The essence of precision medicine lies in the understanding that diseases, while categorized under common clinical syndromes, exhibit heterogeneous pathways and are profoundly influenced by genetic, environmental, and lifestyle factors. As such, precision medicine aims to deliver more personalized, predictive, and preventive healthcare by leveraging patient-specific data—especially at the molecular and genetic levels (Liao et al., 2023).

The core principles of precision medicine revolve around the following concepts:

1. **Individualized Treatment**: Rather than relying on uniform treatment regimens for entire populations, precision medicine customizes interventions to align with the unique molecular and genetic profile of each patient. This enhances therapeutic efficacy by targeting the specific pathways involved in the patient's disease (Liao et al., 2023).
2. **Predictive Modeling**: Precision medicine employs predictive algorithms and statistical models that utilize genetic, phenotypic, and clinical data to forecast disease risk, progression, and response to treatment. By anticipating potential health events, clinicians can implement preventative measures or modify treatments before significant disease progression occurs (Gwak et al., 2023).
3. **Prevention and Early Detection**: A central pillar of precision medicine is the proactive prevention of diseases before they fully manifest. Through genomic screening and molecular diagnostics, healthcare providers can identify individuals at elevated risk for certain conditions and deploy preventive interventions, mitigating the need for invasive and costly treatments later on (Garg et al., 2023).
4. **Biological Stratification of Disease**: Diseases that may appear clinically similar are often biologically heterogeneous. Precision medicine stratifies diseases into subtypes based on genetic mutations, molecular pathways, or biomarkers, thus allowing for more targeted therapies that are specifically suited to each subtype (Gwak et al., 2023).
5. **Data-Driven Insights**: Precision medicine harnesses vast datasets, encompassing clinical, genomic, environmental, and lifestyle information, to derive insights that enhance the precision of diagnoses and treatments. This requires the integration of advanced computational tools, including AI and big data analytics (Garg et al., 2023).

Key Technologies Enabling Precision Healthcare: Genomics, AI, and Big Data

The transformative potential of precision medicine is inextricably linked to several key technologies, each playing a pivotal role in enabling the fine-tuned personalization of healthcare. Among these, **genomics**, **artificial intelligence (AI)**, and **big data** stand out as the cornerstone technologies that have reshaped our understanding of disease and therapeutic intervention (Gwak et al., 2023).

1. **Genomics**: The field of genomics, which involves the comprehensive study of an individual's genome—the entirety of their DNA sequence—lies at the heart of precision medicine. Advances in next-generation sequencing (NGS) technologies have dramatically lowered the cost and time required to sequence entire genomes, allowing for widespread clinical applications. By analyzing genetic variations, such as single nucleotide polymorphisms (SNPs) or structural variants, researchers can identify predispositions to specific diseases, tailor drug therapies based on pharmacogenomics, and even predict responses to treatment. Genomic technologies enable the detection of oncogenic mutations in cancer, monogenic causes of rare diseases, and heritable risk factors in cardiovascular and metabolic disorders (Liao et al., 2023).
2. **Artificial Intelligence (AI)**: The sheer volume and complexity of data generated by genomic sequencing, combined with other patient-specific datasets, necessitates the use of sophisticated AI algorithms capable of pattern recognition, data synthesis, and predictive analytics. AI, particularly through machine learning and deep learning models, can analyze vast amounts of heterogeneous data, identifying correlations and generating insights that are often imperceptible to human clinicians. AI has proven invaluable in enhancing diagnostic accuracy, optimizing treatment plans, and predicting patient outcomes. For instance, AI-driven algorithms can predict disease progression by analyzing

a combination of genomic markers, medical imaging, and electronic health record (EHR) data, thus allowing clinicians to intervene earlier and more effectively (Jaiswal et al., 2023).
3. **Big Data**: Precision medicine is fundamentally data-driven, relying on the integration of large, multidimensional datasets that encompass genetic, clinical, environmental, and behavioral information. The ability to store, process, and analyze these massive datasets is enabled by big data technologies, which provide the computational infrastructure necessary for large-scale data mining and statistical modeling. Big data analytics allows for the aggregation of patient data across populations, enabling researchers to discover new biomarkers, identify patterns in disease susceptibility, and tailor treatments to specific genetic or phenotypic subgroups (Naveen et al., 2023).

Together, these technologies form the bedrock of precision healthcare, allowing for the development of highly personalized treatment regimens that reflect the unique characteristics of each patient (Bansal et al., 2023).

Differences Between Precision Medicine and Traditional Healthcare Models

The shift from traditional healthcare models to precision medicine marks a fundamental reorientation of the medical paradigm. While conventional medicine has long adhered to a generalized approach, wherein diagnoses and treatments are standardized for broad populations, precision medicine seeks to individualize care based on each patient's unique molecular and genetic makeup. The following distinctions highlight the contrasting approaches of these two models:

1. **One-Size-Fits-All vs. Individualization**: Traditional healthcare is grounded in evidence-based guidelines derived from population-level studies. Treatments are standardized, meaning that patients with the same diagnosis typically receive the same therapeutic regimen, regardless of individual biological differences. Precision medicine, in contrast, tailors treatments to the individual's genetic, molecular, and clinical characteristics, offering personalized interventions that target the underlying causes of disease in each patient (Jaiswal et al., 2023; Naveen et al., 2023; Sapna et al., 2023).
2. **Reactive vs. Proactive**: Traditional medicine is predominantly reactive, intervening after the onset of symptoms or the clinical manifestation of disease. Precision medicine, on the other hand, emphasizes prevention and early detection through genomic screening and predictive analytics. This shift allows for the identification of disease risk long before symptoms emerge, enabling preventative measures and early interventions that can forestall disease progression (Garg et al., 2023; Gwak et al., 2023).
3. **Generalized Therapies vs. Targeted Therapies**: In traditional models, drug therapies are developed for broad populations, often resulting in variable effectiveness due to genetic differences among patients. Precision medicine, by contrast, employs targeted therapies that are tailored to the patient's molecular and genetic profile. For example, in cancer treatment, traditional chemotherapy is non-specific, attacking both cancerous and healthy cells, whereas precision medicine utilizes targeted therapies that attack specific mutations driving tumor growth, sparing healthy tissue and reducing side effects (Deepti et al., 2023; Ramachandran et al., 2023; Suryavanshi, Kukreja, et al., 2023).
4. **Diagnostic Generalization vs. Biological Stratification**: Conventional healthcare frequently diagnoses diseases based on clinical symptoms, without accounting for underlying molecular differences. Precision medicine stratifies diseases into distinct biological subtypes, based on genetic and molecular data. This allows for more accurate diagnoses and the development of therapies that

are fine-tuned to the specific pathways involved in each disease subtype (Arya et al., 2023; V. Jain et al., 2023; Tanwar et al., 2023).
5. **Clinical Outcomes vs. Data-Driven Optimization**: While traditional healthcare models focus on achieving clinical outcomes through a trial-and-error approach, precision medicine leverages data-driven optimization to enhance treatment accuracy from the outset. AI and big data analytics allow clinicians to continuously refine treatment plans in real-time based on ongoing patient data, leading to more efficient and effective healthcare delivery (Banerjee, Kukreja, Gupta, et al., 2023; D. Rawat et al., 2023; V. Sharma et al., 2023).

Case Studies Showcasing Successful Applications of Precision Medicine

Several real-world applications of precision medicine have demonstrated its transformative potential in improving patient outcomes, particularly in the fields of oncology, rare diseases, and pharmacogenomics. Below are notable case studies that exemplify the success of precision medicine:

1. **Oncology: Targeted Therapies for Non-Small Cell Lung Cancer (NSCLC)**
    In the realm of oncology, precision medicine has revolutionized cancer treatment by enabling the identification of genetic mutations that drive tumor growth. For instance, in non-small cell lung cancer (NSCLC), researchers discovered that mutations in the **EGFR (epidermal growth factor receptor)** gene could be targeted with specific tyrosine kinase inhibitors (TKIs). Patients with these mutations respond far more favorably to targeted therapies such as **erlotinib** or **gefitinib**, compared to traditional chemotherapy. This tailored approach has not only improved survival rates but also significantly reduced the adverse side effects associated with non-specific treatments (V. Jain et al., 2023; V. Jindal, Kukreja, Mehta, Srivastava, et al., 2023; Pandey et al., 2023).
2. **Pharmacogenomics: Warfarin Dosing**

Warfarin, a commonly prescribed anticoagulant, has a narrow therapeutic index, meaning that small variations in dose can lead to adverse outcomes such as bleeding or thrombosis. Traditionally, warfarin dosing was adjusted through a trial-and-error process, leading to frequent hospitalizations. However, pharmacogenomic studies have revealed that variations in the **CYP2C9** and **VKORC1** genes significantly affect a patient's sensitivity to warfarin. By incorporating genomic testing into the dosing process, clinicians can now tailor warfarin prescriptions to the individual's genetic profile, minimizing adverse reactions and improving safety (S. Bhatt et al., 2024; Dahiya et al., 2023; G. Kaur et al., 2023).

3. **Rare Diseases: Gene Therapy for Spinal Muscular Atrophy (SMA)**

Spinal muscular atrophy (SMA) is a rare genetic disorder characterized by the loss of motor neurons, leading to muscle weakness and atrophy. Historically, treatment options were limited and primarily focused on symptom management. However, with the advent of precision medicine, gene therapies such as **Zolgensma** have been developed to directly target the genetic defect responsible for SMA. Zolgensma delivers a functional copy of the **SMN1** gene to patients, effectively halting disease progression and improving motor function. This personalized therapy has been hailed as a groundbreaking success in the treatment of rare diseases (Kholiya et al., 2023; K. K. Singh et al., 2023; Singhal et al., 2023).

ARTIFICIAL INTELLIGENCE AND ITS ROLE IN PERSONALIZED HEALTHCARE

How AI Facilitates the Analysis of Complex Medical Data

The convergence of artificial intelligence (AI) and healthcare has introduced unparalleled capabilities in the analysis and interpretation of complex medical data. Given the multidimensional nature of modern medical datasets—comprising genomics, proteomics, radiological images, electronic health records (EHRs), and real-time patient monitoring—AI's role in healthcare has become indispensable. Traditional data analysis techniques, while useful in certain contexts, are often inadequate for processing the enormous volumes of structured and unstructured data generated in the clinical environment. AI, particularly through machine learning (ML) and deep learning (DL) frameworks, excels in this domain by enabling high-throughput data integration, pattern recognition, and predictive modelling (A. Mishra et al., 2023; S. Sharma et al., 2023; S. Sharma & Tyagi, 2023).

AI-driven tools can parse and synthesize heterogenous medical data, detecting subtle correlations that may escape human interpretation due to the data's vast complexity. For instance, deep learning algorithms can analyze radiographic images in milliseconds, discerning intricate patterns indicative of pathological changes—whether in oncology, cardiology, or neurology. Furthermore, AI models can continuously learn and evolve as they are exposed to new data, becoming more accurate and precise over time (Banerjee, Kukreja, Aeri, et al., 2023; A. Kaur, Kukreja, Chamoli, et al., 2023a; Y. Singh et al., 2023).

The real power of AI lies in its capacity to uncover latent relationships within the data that might not be readily apparent through conventional statistical methods. In genomics, for example, AI can identify novel biomarkers of disease by sifting through terabytes of genetic sequences and clinical records, accelerating the discovery of molecular signatures that correlate with specific disease phenotypes. Such insights not only enhance diagnostic accuracy but also guide clinicians toward more individualized treatment regimens, marking a significant leap forward in precision medicine (Dubey et al., 2023; A. Kaur, Kukreja, Nisha Chandran, et al., 2023; A. R. Yadav et al., 2023).

Machine Learning Algorithms for Disease Prediction and Diagnostics

Machine learning, a subset of AI, plays a pivotal role in predictive analytics and diagnostics, utilizing vast datasets to identify patterns, predict disease onset, and provide early warnings for health deterioration. The success of machine learning algorithms in healthcare hinges on their ability to self-improve through iterative learning from data, leading to increasingly sophisticated models that deliver highly accurate predictions.

1. **Supervised Learning for Disease Classification**: Supervised learning algorithms are trained on labeled datasets, where the input features (e.g., patient symptoms, genetic markers, medical history) are associated with known outcomes (e.g., presence or absence of disease). Once trained, these models can predict disease states in new, unseen patients. In the realm of diagnostics, supervised learning has been particularly effective in areas such as cancer detection, where ML algorithms analyze imaging data to identify malignancies with accuracy that often rivals or exceeds that of human radiologists. For instance, convolutional neural networks (CNNs), a type of deep learning architecture, have been used to detect breast cancer from mammographic images with remarkable

precision (V. Jindal, Kukreja, Mehta, Chauhan, et al., 2023; A. Kaur, Kukreja, Chamoli, et al., 2023b; Suryavanshi, Tanwar, et al., 2023).

2. **Unsupervised Learning for Pattern Recognition**: Unsupervised learning models, by contrast, are not provided with labeled outcomes and are tasked with finding hidden patterns within the data. In healthcare, these models are particularly useful for clustering patients into subgroups based on genetic, phenotypic, or clinical similarities, which may correlate with distinct disease mechanisms. Unsupervised learning has proven invaluable in discovering previously unrecognized disease subtypes, such as molecularly distinct forms of cancer that respond differently to treatments. Clustering algorithms also facilitate the identification of at-risk populations for specific diseases, allowing for proactive interventions (Gupta et al., 2023; Kukreti et al., 2023; A. K. Mishra et al., 2023).
3. **Reinforcement Learning for Dynamic Treatment Optimization**: Reinforcement learning algorithms, which learn by interacting with an environment and receiving feedback in the form of rewards or penalties, are increasingly being applied to personalized treatment optimization. These algorithms can simulate various treatment scenarios, adapt to changing patient conditions, and optimize therapeutic strategies in real time. For instance, reinforcement learning is being explored in the management of chronic diseases such as diabetes, where AI models can predict fluctuations in glucose levels and recommend individualized insulin dosages, thus improving patient outcomes (A. Kumar, Sharma, et al., 2023; K. Tiwari et al., 2023; Tomar & Sharma, 2021).
4. **Predictive Analytics for Disease Risk**: Predictive models trained on longitudinal patient data can forecast the likelihood of disease onset before symptoms arise. This has been particularly transformative in areas like cardiovascular health, where AI models integrate genetic data, lifestyle factors, and clinical metrics (e.g., blood pressure, cholesterol levels) to predict a patient's risk of heart disease or stroke. By providing such foresight, AI enables clinicians to implement preventative interventions early, reducing the need for invasive treatments later on (R. Kumar, Lamba, et al., 2023; V. Kumar & Korovin, 2023; Vijayalakshmi et al., 2022).

AI's Role in Drug Discovery and Personalized Treatments

The integration of AI into drug discovery processes has revolutionized the field of pharmacology, shortening drug development timelines, reducing costs, and enhancing the precision of therapeutic interventions. Traditional drug discovery, often characterized by labor-intensive processes and high attrition rates, benefits enormously from AI's capacity to automate and optimize various stages of the drug development pipeline.

1. **AI-Driven Target Identification**: One of the initial steps in drug discovery is the identification of molecular targets—proteins, genes, or pathways that play critical roles in disease pathology. AI, particularly deep learning algorithms, can analyze vast datasets, including genomic, proteomic, and metabolomic data, to identify potential therapeutic targets. For example, AI models can sift through thousands of gene expression profiles to pinpoint dysregulated pathways in cancer cells, leading to the identification of actionable targets for drug development (Rao et al., 2023; N. K. Sharma et al., 2021; Wongchai et al., 2022).
2. **Drug Repurposing**: AI has also facilitated the repurposing of existing drugs for new therapeutic indications, a process that significantly accelerates the timeline for bringing treatments to market. By leveraging machine learning models trained on chemical structure databases and clinical data,

AI can predict how existing compounds might interact with novel targets. This approach has been instrumental during public health crises, such as the COVID-19 pandemic, where AI-driven models were used to identify potential therapeutic agents by predicting their efficacy against the SARS-CoV-2 virus.

3. **Personalized Pharmacology and Drug Design**: The personalization of drug therapies, a cornerstone of precision medicine, has been significantly advanced by AI. Pharmacogenomics, which examines how genetic variations affect a person's response to drugs, benefits from AI models that can predict patient-specific responses to medications based on genetic data. AI can also optimize drug dosages in real time, tailoring treatment regimens to individual patient profiles, thus reducing adverse effects and improving therapeutic efficacy. Furthermore, AI has enabled the design of personalized drug compounds, where machine learning models predict the optimal chemical structures for maximum efficacy and minimal toxicity in specific patient populations (Alsadi et al., 2022; A. Kumar, Goyal, et al., 2023; Srivastava et al., 2022).

4. **AI in Clinical Trials**: The design and execution of clinical trials have traditionally been resource-intensive and time-consuming. AI can streamline this process by automating patient recruitment, identifying the most suitable candidates for clinical trials based on their genetic and phenotypic profiles. Moreover, AI-driven predictive models can enhance trial efficiency by predicting patient outcomes, optimizing trial designs, and identifying early markers of drug efficacy or toxicity. This reduces both the cost and time required to bring new drugs to market (Akberdina et al., 2023; Mekala et al., 2023; Mitra et al., 2022).

Ethical Considerations and Challenges with AI in Healthcare

While the potential of AI in healthcare is immense, its widespread adoption is not without ethical concerns and practical challenges. The rapid integration of AI into clinical practice raises critical issues surrounding data privacy, algorithmic biases, and the interpretability of AI-driven decisions (Paul et al., 2022; Rai et al., 2022; M. Sharma & Singh, 2023; S. Sharma, Kadayat, et al., 2023a).

1. **Data Privacy and Security**: AI models in healthcare rely on the aggregation of vast amounts of sensitive data, including genomic information, medical records, and real-time monitoring data. Ensuring the security and privacy of this data is paramount, as breaches could expose individuals to significant risks, including discrimination or exploitation. Moreover, the collection and use of such data must comply with stringent legal and ethical guidelines, such as the Health Insurance Portability and Accountability Act (HIPAA) in the United States or the General Data Protection Regulation (GDPR) in Europe. AI developers and healthcare providers must prioritize encryption, secure storage, and anonymization of patient data to safeguard against breaches and misuse (Aloo et al., 2023; S. Jain & Jain, 2021; A. Kumar, Pant, et al., 2023; H. R. Sharma et al., 2021).

2. **Algorithmic Bias**: AI models are only as good as the data on which they are trained. If training datasets lack diversity or are skewed toward particular demographic groups, the resulting algorithms may perpetuate or even exacerbate existing biases in healthcare. For example, if an AI model is trained primarily on data from Caucasian populations, it may fail to accurately predict outcomes for patients from minority ethnic groups, leading to disparities in care. Bias in AI-driven healthcare systems can manifest in various ways, from misdiagnoses to unequal access to treatments. It is essential to ensure that AI models are trained on diverse datasets and are rigorously tested to mitigate

biases and ensure equitable care for all patients (Chand et al., 2023; V. Kumar et al., 2021; Uniyal et al., 2022).

3. **Interpretability and Transparency**: Many AI models, particularly deep learning systems, operate as "black boxes," where the decision-making process is opaque and difficult for clinicians to interpret. In a medical context, where the stakes are often life and death, the inability to explain how an AI model arrived at a specific diagnosis or treatment recommendation can be problematic. Clinicians and patients alike must be able to trust AI-driven decisions, and this trust requires transparency and interpretability. As a result, there is a growing demand for the development of explainable AI (XAI) models, which provide insights into the underlying logic and reasoning behind their decisions (Behera & Singh Rawat, 2023; G. Kumar, Kumar, et al., 2023; A. Singh et al., 2021).

4. **Autonomy and Clinical Decision-Making**: The integration of AI into clinical workflows raises concerns about the potential erosion of physician autonomy. While AI can enhance decision-making by providing data-driven insights, there is a risk that clinicians may become overly reliant on AI recommendations, potentially undermining their clinical judgment. It is crucial to strike a balance between leveraging AI's capabilities and preserving the clinician's role as the ultimate decision-maker in patient care. This requires ensuring that AI serves as a supportive tool rather than a substitute for human expertise (Giri et al., 2022; Singla et al., 2023; Srivastava et al., 2023).

5. **Regulatory and Ethical Frameworks**: The rapid development and deployment of AI technologies in healthcare outpace the regulatory frameworks that govern their use. Ensuring that AI systems are safe, effective, and ethically deployed requires the development of robust regulatory guidelines that address the unique challenges posed by AI in healthcare. Regulatory bodies must work closely with AI developers, clinicians, and ethicists to create standards that ensure the ethical use of AI without stifling innovation (Gonfa et al., 2023; S. S. Rawat et al., 2022; Shekhar et al., 2022).

THE ECONOMIC IMPLICATIONS OF PERSONALIZED HEALTHCARE

AI's Role in Facilitating the Analysis of Complex Medical Data

Artificial Intelligence (AI) serves as a transformative force in the realm of healthcare by revolutionizing the analysis of vast and intricate medical datasets. These datasets, encompassing a broad spectrum of medical records, including genomic sequencing, proteomics, metabolomics, radiological imaging, and longitudinal clinical observations, present a multidimensional challenge for traditional data processing methodologies. The ability of AI to process, synthesize, and interpret data far surpasses the capabilities of human cognition or conventional computational techniques, especially in contexts requiring the real-time assimilation of structured and unstructured data sources (MITRA et al., 2022; M. Sharma et al., 2022; William et al., 2023).

AI's capacity for complex data analysis is grounded in advanced algorithms—particularly machine learning (ML) and deep learning (DL)—that identify latent patterns and correlations within the data that are often imperceptible to human clinicians. For instance, in radiology, convolutional neural networks (CNNs), a form of deep learning, excel in deciphering subtle abnormalities in diagnostic images such as MRIs or CT scans, with a precision that often exceeds that of human specialists. The algorithmic detection of minute features, such as microcalcifications in mammography or minuscule changes in brain morphology, demonstrates AI's superior capacity for parsing intricate datasets (Bhushan & Nayak, 2022).

Moreover, AI facilitates the fusion of disparate data types—genetic markers, imaging data, real-time patient monitoring information—thereby generating holistic insights that fuel the shift from reactive to proactive and predictive healthcare. This integrative approach positions AI as indispensable in stratifying patient populations based on their genomic, proteomic, or metabolomic profiles, tailoring treatments to their unique molecular architecture. AI's ability to continuously learn from new datasets (via deep learning architectures) further enhances its adaptive proficiency, thus perpetuating the ongoing refinement of clinical outcomes and predictive models (Rajeswari et al., 2022; Shukla et al., 2023).

Machine Learning Algorithms for Disease Prediction and Diagnostics

Machine learning, a critical subset of AI, is instrumental in enhancing disease prediction, diagnostics, and prognostics. By employing sophisticated learning algorithms, AI systems can not only predict disease onset but also optimize treatment strategies in real-time based on dynamic patient data.

1. **Supervised Learning for Disease Classification**: Supervised learning algorithms are trained on labeled datasets, where input variables (such as biomarkers, genetic mutations, and clinical symptoms) are paired with known outcomes (e.g., diagnoses or prognoses). These algorithms then use this training data to make predictions on new, unseen data. In oncology, for example, AI models have demonstrated exceptional accuracy in classifying tumors based on histopathological and genomic data. Supervised learning models, such as Support Vector Machines (SVM) and Random Forest classifiers, are highly effective in differentiating between benign and malignant lesions, particularly when applied to radiological data like mammograms or PET scans. These models identify tumor-specific features that might evade human detection, thereby facilitating earlier and more precise cancer diagnoses (Thakur et al., 2023).
2. **Unsupervised Learning for Pattern Discovery**: Unlike supervised learning, unsupervised learning algorithms are deployed in the absence of labeled outcomes and are tasked with identifying hidden patterns or clusters within the data. These models are particularly valuable in discovering novel disease subtypes that may not manifest overtly through clinical phenotyping. For example, in the study of neurodegenerative diseases, unsupervised clustering algorithms have revealed distinct molecular subtypes of Alzheimer's disease based on genomic and proteomic variations. This stratification is crucial for the development of targeted therapies, as each subtype may require a different therapeutic approach. Principal Component Analysis (PCA) and clustering algorithms such as k-means have proven effective in such biological stratifications (Kunwar et al., 2023).
3. **Reinforcement Learning for Dynamic Treatment Optimization**: Reinforcement learning (RL) represents a paradigm wherein AI systems learn optimal actions through a feedback loop of rewards and penalties. In healthcare, RL algorithms are being increasingly deployed to dynamically adjust treatment plans based on real-time patient responses. This approach has shown particular promise in chronic disease management, such as optimizing insulin doses for diabetic patients. AI models can predict fluctuations in blood glucose levels based on continuous monitoring data and suggest personalized insulin administration protocols to maintain optimal glycemic control. Over time, RL models improve their accuracy and responsiveness, minimizing the risk of complications such as hyperglycemia or hypoglycemia (D. Malik et al., 2023).

4. **Predictive Analytics for Disease Risk Forecasting**: Predictive modeling, enabled by machine learning, is pivotal in assessing disease risk before the manifestation of clinical symptoms. AI models trained on population health data, incorporating variables such as genetic predispositions, lifestyle factors, and medical histories, can identify individuals at high risk for diseases such as cardiovascular disorders, diabetes, or cancer. For instance, AI-driven predictive analytics can combine genomic screening with environmental exposure data to forecast the likelihood of developing malignancies, allowing for early interventions such as prophylactic treatments or lifestyle modifications. The accuracy of these predictions grows as the AI algorithms are exposed to more diverse datasets, improving their generalizability across populations (B. Rawat et al., 2022).

AI's Role in Drug Discovery and Personalized Treatment Design

AI's contribution to drug discovery has disrupted traditional pharmacological paradigms by expediting the identification of therapeutic targets, optimizing molecular compound design, and streamlining clinical trial processes. Historically, drug development has been hampered by exorbitant costs and protracted timelines, with the attrition rate for novel compounds being exceedingly high. AI, however, offers a paradigm shift by facilitating high-throughput data analysis and predictive modeling in several key areas of the drug development pipeline (S. Sharma et al., 2021).

1. **Target Identification and Validation**: One of the earliest stages in drug discovery involves identifying molecular targets—such as proteins, enzymes, or receptors—that play critical roles in disease pathogenesis. AI algorithms, particularly deep learning models, can analyze vast biological datasets to predict novel druggable targets with a higher degree of accuracy than conventional methods. For instance, in oncology, AI has been instrumental in identifying driver mutations and oncogenic pathways that serve as actionable targets for cancer therapeutics. This data-driven approach enables the discovery of novel biomarkers and therapeutic targets that may have been overlooked in traditional research frameworks (Asha et al., 2022).
2. **Drug Repurposing**: AI has also revolutionized the field of drug repurposing, where existing drugs are identified for new therapeutic indications. By analyzing data from clinical trials, pharmacological databases, and molecular compound libraries, AI can predict how existing drugs might interact with novel biological targets (P. Kumar, Bhatnagar, et al., 2023; P. Kumar et al., 2024). This strategy accelerates the drug discovery process by circumventing the need for de novo compound development and reduces the risk of failure, as repurposed drugs have already been vetted for safety in prior clinical applications. AI models, such as deep neural networks, have been applied to repurpose antiviral drugs for emerging infectious diseases, such as during the COVID-19 pandemic (K. D. Singh et al., 2023).
3. **Personalized Pharmacology and Precision Drug Design**: The concept of personalized pharmacology is a direct application of AI's ability to analyze individual genetic and molecular profiles. Pharmacogenomic models powered by AI can predict patient-specific drug responses, thereby enabling the design of personalized therapeutic regimens. For example, AI can predict how variations in drug-metabolizing enzymes (such as cytochrome P450 variants) affect the pharmacokinetics of drugs, allowing clinicians to adjust dosages in real time. Furthermore, AI-driven drug design enables the synthesis of novel compounds tailored to specific molecular targets. In silico models can sim-

ulate drug-receptor interactions, optimizing chemical structures for maximal efficacy and minimal off-target effects (Ahmad et al., 2023; R. Kumar, Sexena, et al., 2023; Lourens et al., 2022).

4. **AI-Enhanced Clinical Trials**: Clinical trials, the gold standard for assessing drug efficacy, have long been plagued by inefficiencies, from patient recruitment to trial design. AI has the potential to address these inefficiencies by automating patient recruitment through the identification of optimal candidates based on genetic and phenotypic data. Additionally, AI algorithms can optimize trial designs by predicting patient outcomes and identifying early markers of efficacy or toxicity. These innovations reduce both the time and cost associated with bringing new drugs to market, allowing for more agile responses to emerging healthcare challenges (Mangla et al., 2018; Onyema et al., 2022; Pant et al., 2017).

Ethical Considerations and Challenges with AI in Healthcare

The rapid integration of AI into healthcare raises significant ethical and practical challenges, particularly concerning data privacy, algorithmic biases, and the interpretability of AI-driven decisions. While AI offers the potential for unprecedented advancements in personalized healthcare, its widespread adoption must be carefully balanced against these ethical concerns (Alrashed et al., 2022; P. Malik et al., 2022; R. S. Rawat et al., 2022).

1. **Data Privacy and Security**: AI systems in healthcare are fueled by enormous quantities of sensitive patient data, including genomic sequences, clinical records, and real-time physiological monitoring. Ensuring the security and confidentiality of this data is paramount, as breaches could result in serious ethical violations, including the misuse of genetic information for discriminatory purposes. Legal frameworks such as the General Data Protection Regulation (GDPR) in the European Union and the Health Insurance Portability and Accountability Act (HIPAA) in the United States impose strict guidelines on data usage and protection, but the sheer scale and complexity of AI-driven data collection pose new challenges. Ensuring that patient data is anonymized and securely stored is critical to preserving trust in AI systems (S. Sharma, Kadayat, et al., 2023b; A. B. Singh et al., 2023; R. Tiwari et al., 2023).

2. **Algorithmic Bias**: AI models are susceptible to biases inherent in the training data. If the datasets used to train these models are not representative of diverse populations, the resulting algorithms may perpetuate healthcare disparities. For instance, AI models trained predominantly on data from Caucasian populations may yield less accurate predictions for minority ethnic groups, leading to diagnostic errors or unequal treatment recommendations. Addressing algorithmic bias requires the incorporation of diverse datasets and the implementation of rigorous fairness auditing processes to ensure that AI models deliver equitable care across all demographic groups (M. Jindal et al., 2022; K. D. Singh & Singh, 2023).

3. **Interpretability and Transparency**: One of the most pressing concerns regarding AI in healthcare is the "black box" nature of many advanced machine learning models, particularly deep learning architectures. While these models may achieve high predictive accuracy, the decision-making process is often opaque, making it difficult for clinicians to understand how specific predictions or recommendations were derived. This lack of interpretability poses a significant challenge in clinical settings, where transparency is crucial for maintaining trust between patients and healthcare providers. To address this issue, researchers are developing explainable AI (XAI) models that offer greater

transparency by elucidating the reasoning behind AI-driven decisions (Khan et al., 2020; Prikshat et al., 2019; V. Sharma & Jain, 2020).

4. **Autonomy and Clinical Decision-Making**: The increasing reliance on AI for diagnostic and therapeutic recommendations raises concerns about the potential erosion of clinical autonomy. While AI can provide valuable insights, there is a risk that clinicians may become overly dependent on algorithmic outputs, diminishing their role in patient care. Ensuring that AI remains a supportive tool—rather than a replacement for human expertise—is critical. Healthcare providers must retain ultimate responsibility for clinical decision-making, using AI as an adjunct to their professional judgment rather than as a substitute (Dani et al., 2020; Goyal et al., 2015; Pattanshetti et al., 2021).

5. **Regulatory and Ethical Frameworks**: The rapid pace of AI development in healthcare has outstripped existing regulatory frameworks, leaving gaps in oversight and accountability. Ensuring that AI systems are safe, effective, and ethically deployed requires the establishment of comprehensive regulatory guidelines that address the unique challenges posed by AI. These frameworks must be developed in collaboration with AI researchers, clinicians, ethicists, and legal experts to ensure that AI technologies are used responsibly and in the best interests of patients (Prikshat et al., 2017; D. S. Rana et al., 2022; Rathore & Goudar, 2015).

PREDICTIVE ANALYTICS IN HEALTHCARE

The Role of Predictive Analytics in Early Diagnosis and Preventive Care

Predictive analytics, a critical application of artificial intelligence (AI), has redefined the landscape of early diagnosis and preventive care by enabling healthcare systems to anticipate medical conditions before their symptomatic onset. At the heart of predictive analytics lies its capacity to synthesize vast troves of heterogeneous data—ranging from electronic health records (EHRs), genomic sequences, environmental exposure metrics, and real-time physiological monitoring—into actionable insights. These insights empower clinicians to identify at-risk individuals, stratify patient populations, and recommend preemptive interventions well before the clinical manifestation of diseases (Alexopoulos et al., 2023).

In preventive healthcare, predictive analytics functions by leveraging sophisticated machine learning (ML) algorithms to analyze historical and real-time data (Bhatnagar et al., 2023; P. Kumar, Verma, et al., 2023; Taneja, Bhatnagar, Kumar, & Grima, 2023). These algorithms identify patterns, correlations, and risk factors that may not be immediately apparent through traditional clinical assessments. By analyzing the longitudinal health trajectories of individuals and populations, AI models can detect subtle deviations from baseline health metrics that indicate the early stages of disease. For example, in cardiovascular health, AI can monitor trends in blood pressure, cholesterol levels, and heart rate variability to forecast the likelihood of an impending cardiac event, prompting clinicians to intervene with lifestyle modifications, medications, or other preventive measures (S. Sharma et al., 2023).

Moreover, predictive analytics facilitates the implementation of precision screening programs tailored to individual risk profiles. Instead of subjecting entire populations to uniform screening protocols, AI can identify high-risk individuals for targeted screening based on genetic predispositions, lifestyle factors, and historical medical data. This shift towards individualized preventive care optimizes resource allocation, reduces the burden of unnecessary procedures, and ensures that high-risk patients receive timely interventions. For example, in oncology, AI-powered risk stratification models can identify individuals with a heightened likelihood of developing malignancies, prompting earlier screening for cancers such as breast, lung, or colorectal cancers (Josphineleela, Kaliappan, et al., 2023).

AI's Ability to Forecast Disease Progression Based on Patient-Specific Data

The ability of AI to forecast disease progression represents one of its most profound contributions to modern medicine. Through the continuous analysis of patient-specific data, AI models can predict the likely trajectory of a disease, enabling clinicians to tailor treatment regimens in anticipation of future complications. This is particularly valuable in chronic disease management, where early intervention can significantly mitigate the disease's long-term impact (Nikolaidis et al., 2022).

AI's predictive capabilities are grounded in its capacity to integrate diverse data modalities—genetic information, imaging data, biomarkers, and lifestyle factors—into a cohesive model that maps the natural history of a disease. For instance, in neurodegenerative diseases such as Alzheimer's or Parkinson's, AI algorithms can analyze longitudinal data from cognitive tests, neuroimaging studies, and genetic markers to predict the rate of cognitive decline or the progression of motor symptoms. By anticipating the future course of the disease, clinicians can adjust treatment plans to slow progression, improve quality of life, and delay the onset of severe disability (Ingale et al., 2023; P. Jain et al., 2023).

Moreover, AI-driven predictive models excel in detecting early signals of disease exacerbation. In conditions such as chronic obstructive pulmonary disease (COPD) or diabetes, continuous monitoring of physiological parameters (e.g., oxygen saturation, glucose levels) combined with AI analysis can alert clinicians to impending exacerbations or complications. For example, AI algorithms can predict the likelihood of diabetic ketoacidosis or hypoglycemic events in diabetic patients by analyzing patterns in blood glucose variability, dietary intake, and insulin usage. These early warnings allow for prompt therapeutic adjustments, reducing the risk of severe episodes and hospitalizations (Ambika et al., 2023; C. Bhatt et al., 2023).

AI's ability to forecast disease progression also extends to oncology, where predictive models based on tumor genetics and molecular profiling can estimate the aggressiveness of malignancies and the likelihood of metastasis (Taneja, Bhatnagar, Kumar, & Rupeika-apoga, 2023). By identifying patients at high risk for disease recurrence or progression, AI enables the personalization of cancer treatment strategies, from surgical interventions to targeted therapies. This ensures that patients receive the most appropriate level of care based on their individualized risk profiles, enhancing outcomes and minimizing unnecessary treatments (Josphineleela, Gupta, et al., 2023; Nagila et al., 2023).

Reducing Hospital Admissions and Emergency Interventions

AI-powered predictive analytics plays a pivotal role in reducing hospital admissions and emergency interventions by enabling proactive care management and early intervention strategies. In the traditional reactive healthcare model, patients are often admitted to hospitals or emergency departments only after their conditions have worsened to a critical point. However, predictive analytics flips this paradigm by identifying patients at risk of acute health deterioration long before they reach such a stage, thereby preventing costly and resource-intensive hospitalizations (S. Sharma et al., 2023; Tyagi et al., 2023).

For instance, AI algorithms trained on historical hospitalization data can predict which patients are most likely to require hospitalization based on their medical histories, comorbidities, and real-time health metrics. In heart failure management, for example, AI models can analyze trends in weight gain, blood pressure fluctuations, and heart rate variability to predict the likelihood of fluid overload and cardiac decompensation. By identifying these early warning signs, clinicians can intervene with diuretics, medication adjustments, or other outpatient treatments, preventing the need for hospital admission (P. M. Yadav et al., 2023).

Similarly, in patients with chronic obstructive pulmonary disease (COPD), AI can monitor respiratory function and detect early signs of an impending exacerbation. By prescribing inhalers, steroids, or antibiotics at the first indication of respiratory decline, healthcare providers can avert the need for emergency interventions, thus reducing the burden on emergency departments. The same principle applies to other chronic diseases such as asthma, hypertension, and diabetes, where predictive analytics enables the timely administration of preventive measures that mitigate disease escalation.

In addition to preventing hospital admissions, AI can also reduce the frequency of readmissions—an important metric in evaluating the quality of healthcare. Predictive models can identify patients at high risk of readmission following hospital discharge by analyzing factors such as medication adherence, follow-up appointments, and post-discharge care plans. For instance, in postoperative patients, AI can predict which individuals are at risk of complications (e.g., infections, thrombosis) that might lead to readmission. By flagging these patients for closer monitoring and follow-up care, healthcare providers can reduce the likelihood of complications that necessitate hospital readmission.

Impact on Healthcare Outcomes and Patient Experiences

The integration of AI-driven predictive analytics into healthcare systems has far-reaching implications for both healthcare outcomes and patient experiences. By enabling earlier diagnosis, preventing disease progression, and reducing hospital admissions, AI directly contributes to improved clinical outcomes. The ability to anticipate and address health issues before they escalate results in fewer complications, better management of chronic conditions, and increased survival rates, particularly in diseases where early intervention is critical, such as cancer and cardiovascular disorders.

Moreover, AI enhances the personalization of healthcare, ensuring that each patient receives care that is specifically tailored to their unique risk profile and medical history. This individualized approach leads to more effective treatments, reduced adverse effects, and improved overall health outcomes. For example, in oncology, AI-driven models can predict which patients are most likely to respond to specific chemotherapy regimens based on the genetic characteristics of their tumors, sparing patients from the toxicity of ineffective treatments.

From the patient's perspective, AI's role in predictive analytics improves the overall healthcare experience by reducing the need for invasive procedures, frequent hospital visits, and prolonged hospital stays. The ability to manage conditions proactively through outpatient care and telemedicine minimizes the disruption to patients' daily lives and allows them to maintain greater autonomy over their health. Moreover, the real-time feedback provided by AI-powered monitoring systems gives patients a greater sense of control, as they can make informed decisions about their health in collaboration with their healthcare providers.

The use of AI in predictive analytics also fosters greater trust in the healthcare system by improving transparency and communication between patients and providers. AI models that explain their predictions in a clear and interpretable manner enable clinicians to provide more accurate and detailed explanations to patients, thus enhancing patient understanding and engagement in their care. This collaborative approach, where AI augments rather than replaces human decision-making, improves patient satisfaction and fosters a stronger patient-provider relationship.

COST-EFFICIENCY AND RESOURCE OPTIMIZATION

Economic Advantages of Individualized Treatment Protocols

The paradigm shift from a one-size-fits-all model of healthcare to individualized treatment protocols, largely driven by advancements in artificial intelligence (AI) and precision medicine, offers profound economic advantages. Central to this transformation is the personalization of care, wherein therapeutic interventions are tailored to the molecular and genetic profile of each patient, thereby enhancing treatment efficacy, reducing adverse effects, and optimizing resource utilization.

One of the primary economic benefits of individualized treatment is the potential for cost reduction in both direct and indirect healthcare expenses. In traditional medical frameworks, treatments are often prescribed based on population-level averages, leading to a substantial degree of variability in patient outcomes. This generalized approach frequently results in suboptimal efficacy for many patients, necessitating further diagnostic tests, treatment modifications, or hospitalizations, all of which inflate healthcare costs. Individualized treatment protocols, however, mitigate these inefficiencies by ensuring that therapeutic regimens are specifically aligned with a patient's unique genetic makeup, comorbidities, and environmental factors.

For example, pharmacogenomics—the study of how genes affect a person's response to drugs—allows clinicians to predict how a patient will metabolize a particular medication. By preemptively identifying patients who are likely to experience adverse reactions or subtherapeutic responses to certain drugs, healthcare providers can avoid the costs associated with medication-related complications, such as hospitalizations due to drug toxicity or ineffectiveness. This proactive approach not only improves clinical outcomes but also reduces the financial burden on both healthcare systems and patients by avoiding unnecessary treatments, prolonged hospital stays, and recurrent consultations.

Furthermore, individualized treatment protocols can streamline the allocation of healthcare resources. The ability to stratify patient populations based on their risk profiles or disease subtypes enables healthcare systems to direct high-cost interventions—such as targeted therapies, surgeries, or advanced imaging—only to those individuals who are most likely to benefit. This targeted approach maximizes the cost-effectiveness of healthcare delivery by ensuring that expensive resources are not wasted on patients for whom such interventions would be ineffective.

Reduction in Trial-and-Error Treatments and Medication Misuse

One of the most significant inefficiencies in traditional healthcare is the reliance on trial-and-error treatments, where clinicians must experiment with different medications, dosages, or therapeutic approaches to find the most effective regimen for a particular patient. This process not only delays optimal treatment but also leads to substantial economic costs, as patients often undergo multiple rounds of ineffective therapies, additional diagnostic tests, and in some cases, hospitalization due to treatment-related complications. In oncology, for example, it is not uncommon for patients to be subjected to several lines of chemotherapy before an effective regimen is identified—a process that incurs significant financial and emotional costs.

AI-driven precision medicine has the potential to drastically reduce the need for trial-and-error treatments by using predictive analytics and machine learning algorithms to identify the most effective therapeutic strategy from the outset. By analyzing vast datasets that include genetic, proteomic, and clinical information, AI can predict a patient's response to specific treatments, allowing clinicians to make more informed decisions regarding drug selection and dosage. This reduction in trial-and-error not only accelerates the time to effective treatment but also minimizes the economic costs associated with prolonged diagnostic processes, repeated consultations, and medication waste.

Moreover, AI models can identify potential drug-drug interactions and contraindications based on a patient's medical history and current pharmacological profile, thereby reducing the risk of medication misuse. This is particularly important in polypharmacy situations, where patients are prescribed multiple medications that may interact in harmful ways. By using AI to preemptively flag such risks, healthcare providers can adjust treatment plans to avoid adverse drug reactions (ADRs), which are a significant source of hospital admissions and medical costs. According to studies, ADRs are responsible for up to 5-10% of hospital admissions, with an estimated annual cost in the billions. AI's ability to reduce these incidences offers both economic and clinical benefits, improving patient safety while decreasing the financial burden on healthcare systems.

AI-Driven Solutions for Healthcare Resource Management

Beyond individualized treatment, AI plays a pivotal role in the broader management of healthcare resources, enabling more efficient allocation of human, financial, and technological resources across healthcare systems. AI-driven predictive models can anticipate demand for healthcare services based on patterns inpatient admissions, disease outbreaks, and demographic changes, allowing hospitals and clinics to optimize staffing, equipment usage, and supply chains. This preemptive resource management helps to reduce bottlenecks, minimize patient wait times, and ensure that healthcare facilities are operating at peak efficiency.

For instance, AI can predict seasonal surges in flu-related hospitalizations by analyzing epidemiological data, weather patterns, and public health reports. By forecasting these trends, healthcare providers can proactively adjust their staffing levels, ensure that critical supplies (e.g., vaccines, antiviral medications, ventilators) are available in sufficient quantities, and allocate hospital beds accordingly. This capacity for dynamic resource management reduces the strain on healthcare systems during peak periods, thereby preventing the costly delays and overcrowding that often accompany unexpected surges in patient demand.

Additionally, AI can be used to optimize surgical scheduling and operating room utilization, which are among the most resource-intensive components of hospital operations. By analyzing historical data on surgery durations, patient outcomes, and staffing patterns, AI models can predict the most efficient scheduling strategies, minimizing downtime between procedures and ensuring that surgical teams and equipment are utilized to their full capacity. This optimization reduces the financial costs associated with operating room inefficiencies, such as prolonged patient wait times, staffing overtime, and underutilized surgical facilities.

Moreover, AI's ability to forecast disease progression in individual patients can facilitate the prioritization of healthcare resources based on patient risk levels. For example, in oncology, AI models can predict which patients are at highest risk of cancer recurrence following treatment, allowing healthcare providers to allocate more intensive surveillance and follow-up care to those individuals while reducing the frequency of check-ups for lower-risk patients. This stratified approach to resource management ensures that high-cost interventions are reserved for those who need them most, thereby improving the overall cost-efficiency of healthcare delivery.

Real-World Examples of Personalized Medicine Saving Costs

Several real-world examples illustrate the economic benefits of personalized medicine in reducing healthcare costs while improving patient outcomes. One notable example is in the field of oncology, where personalized treatment strategies have been shown to significantly lower costs by avoiding ineffective therapies and minimizing adverse drug reactions. In breast cancer treatment, for instance, the use of genomic profiling tests, such as the Oncotype DX test, allows clinicians to assess the likelihood of cancer recurrence and determine whether a patient will benefit from chemotherapy. By identifying patients who are unlikely to benefit from chemotherapy, healthcare providers can avoid the costs associated with unnecessary treatment, which includes not only the cost of the chemotherapy drugs themselves but also the expenses related to managing chemotherapy-induced side effects, such as hospitalizations for neutropenia or infections.

Another example is the use of pharmacogenomic testing in cardiovascular disease management. The anticoagulant warfarin, commonly prescribed to prevent blood clots, has a notoriously narrow therapeutic window, with individual patients requiring widely varying dosages to achieve optimal results. Traditional approaches to warfarin dosing involve frequent blood tests and dosage adjustments, leading to substantial healthcare costs. However, by using pharmacogenomic testing to identify genetic variants that affect warfarin metabolism, clinicians can prescribe the correct dosage from the outset, reducing the need for trial-and-error dosing and minimizing the risk of complications such as bleeding or thrombosis. This not only improves patient outcomes but also reduces the costs associated with repeated clinic visits and hospitalizations for warfarin-related complications.

In diabetes management, AI-driven continuous glucose monitoring (CGM) systems have been shown to reduce both the incidence of hypoglycemic events and the overall cost of care. These systems use AI algorithms to predict fluctuations in blood glucose levels based on real-time data from wearable sensors, allowing patients and clinicians to make more informed decisions regarding insulin dosing, diet, and exercise. By preventing severe hypoglycemic episodes, which often result in emergency room visits or hospitalizations, CGM systems reduce the overall economic burden of diabetes care.

CHALLENGES AND BARRIERS TO ADOPTION

Financial and Logistical Challenges in Adopting Precision Medicine Widely

The transition to precision medicine is fraught with a myriad of financial and logistical challenges that impede its widespread adoption across healthcare systems. From an economic perspective, the implementation of precision medicine often entails substantial upfront investments in advanced technologies, genomic testing capabilities, and data analytics infrastructure. These costs can be prohibitive for many healthcare institutions, particularly those operating in resource-constrained environments.

The economic burden is exacerbated by the need for ongoing funding to support the integration of precision medicine into existing clinical workflows. This includes not only the costs associated with procuring state-of-the-art diagnostic tools and therapeutic agents but also the financial implications of retraining healthcare personnel to proficiently utilize these technologies. Additionally, precision medicine often necessitates the establishment of multidisciplinary teams that can collaboratively interpret complex genomic data and devise tailored treatment protocols, thereby increasing staffing and operational costs.

Logistically, the complexity of implementing precision medicine at scale poses significant challenges. Healthcare organizations must navigate a labyrinthine landscape of interoperability issues related to electronic health records (EHRs), which are often not designed to accommodate the nuanced data associated with genomic information. Ensuring that disparate systems can communicate effectively is crucial for the successful integration of precision medicine into routine clinical practice. Moreover, healthcare providers must grapple with the challenges of data management, including the storage, security, and sharing of sensitive genomic data while adhering to stringent privacy regulations.

Furthermore, the widespread adoption of precision medicine relies heavily on robust supply chains for personalized therapeutics, particularly in oncology, where targeted therapies are often derived from specific genetic markers. Disruptions in these supply chains can result in treatment delays, exacerbating patient outcomes and undermining the efficacy of precision medicine initiatives.

Regulatory Frameworks and the Need for Policy Reforms

The regulatory landscape surrounding precision medicine is in a state of flux, necessitating comprehensive reforms to facilitate its adoption and integration into healthcare systems. Current regulatory frameworks, which were predominantly designed for traditional pharmaceuticals and medical devices, often struggle to keep pace with the rapid evolution of genomic technologies and their applications in personalized medicine. This misalignment can lead to significant delays in the approval process for new therapies and diagnostics, thereby stifling innovation and limiting patient access to cutting-edge treatments.

A pivotal area for reform lies in the evaluation and approval processes for companion diagnostics, which are tests designed to determine a patient's suitability for a specific therapeutic regimen based on their genetic profile. The complexity of these tests necessitates a more nuanced regulatory approach that encompasses both the clinical validity of the diagnostics and their clinical utility in informing treatment decisions. Policymakers must therefore establish clear guidelines that facilitate timely and efficient reviews of companion diagnostics while ensuring that they meet rigorous safety and efficacy standards.

Moreover, the burgeoning field of gene editing and genomic therapies introduces ethical and safety concerns that necessitate robust regulatory oversight. The implementation of frameworks that address these concerns while promoting innovation is critical for fostering a conducive environment for precision medicine research and development. This includes establishing ethical guidelines for genetic testing, patient consent, and the use of genetic information in clinical decision-making.

To enable a seamless transition to precision medicine, regulatory agencies must also enhance collaboration with stakeholders, including researchers, healthcare providers, and patients. Engaging these diverse perspectives can inform the development of policies that are both scientifically grounded and responsive to the needs of the healthcare ecosystem.

Infrastructure Gaps in Healthcare Systems, Particularly in Developing Regions

The successful implementation of precision medicine is contingent upon the existence of robust healthcare infrastructure, which remains a significant hurdle, particularly in developing regions. Many healthcare systems in low- and middle-income countries are characterized by inadequate resources, insufficient technological capabilities, and a lack of access to advanced diagnostic and therapeutic modalities that underpin precision medicine.

Infrastructure gaps manifest in several ways, including limited access to genomic testing facilities, which are essential for identifying the molecular underpinnings of diseases and tailoring treatments accordingly. The high costs associated with establishing and maintaining genomic laboratories pose formidable barriers for healthcare systems in resource-constrained settings. Consequently, patients in these regions often lack access to the benefits of precision medicine, resulting in persistent health disparities and suboptimal treatment outcomes.

Moreover, the lack of advanced health information technology (HIT) systems hinders the effective integration of precision medicine into clinical practice. Without interoperable EHRs capable of accommodating complex genomic data, healthcare providers face challenges in collecting, managing, and utilizing the information needed to inform personalized treatment plans. This lack of data infrastructure not only hampers clinical decision-making but also impedes research efforts aimed at advancing precision medicine in these regions.

Additionally, the dearth of trained personnel proficient in genomic medicine and bioinformatics further exacerbates the challenges faced by healthcare systems in developing regions. To leverage the potential of precision medicine, a concerted effort is needed to invest in the requisite infrastructure and training programs that can equip healthcare providers with the skills necessary to interpret genomic data and implement individualized treatment protocols.

Workforce Readiness and the Need for Physician Training in AI Technologies

The rapid integration of AI technologies into healthcare necessitates a paradigm shift in workforce readiness, underscoring the critical need for comprehensive training and education for healthcare professionals. As AI systems increasingly augment clinical decision-making, it is essential that physicians and allied healthcare providers possess a robust understanding of these technologies to harness their full potential.

Current medical curricula often lack sufficient emphasis on data analytics, machine learning, and AI applications in clinical practice. To bridge this gap, medical education programs must incorporate interdisciplinary training that equips future healthcare professionals with the skills to navigate the complexities of AI-driven precision medicine. This includes fostering proficiency in interpreting AI-generated insights, understanding the underlying algorithms, and critically assessing the implications of AI in clinical scenarios.

Moreover, ongoing professional development programs must be established to ensure that practicing clinicians remain abreast of the latest advancements in AI technologies. Continuous education initiatives can provide healthcare professionals with opportunities to engage with AI tools, refine their skills in data interpretation, and stay informed about emerging trends in precision medicine. Such training will not only enhance clinical practice but also promote confidence among healthcare providers in integrating AI into their workflows.

Additionally, fostering a culture of collaboration between healthcare professionals and data scientists is paramount for optimizing the implementation of AI in precision medicine. Clinicians must be empowered to engage actively in the development and validation of AI models to ensure that these tools align with real-world clinical needs and challenges. By cultivating interdisciplinary partnerships, healthcare organizations can create an environment that embraces innovation while prioritizing patient-centered care.

FUTURE TRENDS IN PRECISION MEDICINE

Advances in AI, Genomics, and Personalized Healthcare Technologies

The confluence of artificial intelligence (AI), genomics, and personalized healthcare technologies represents a seismic shift in the paradigm of medical practice, redefining the manner in which healthcare is delivered and enhancing the precision of therapeutic interventions. Recent advancements in these domains have catalyzed the emergence of sophisticated tools and methodologies capable of deciphering the complexities of human biology, leading to unprecedented levels of customization in patient care.

AI has emerged as a pivotal force in the analysis and interpretation of vast datasets generated by genomic sequencing and other high-throughput technologies. The application of machine learning algorithms to genomic data enables the identification of intricate patterns and correlations that would be imperceptible through traditional analytical methods. These AI-driven insights not only facilitate the discovery of novel biomarkers associated with disease susceptibility and progression but also inform the development of targeted therapeutic strategies tailored to individual patients.

Moreover, the advent of next-generation sequencing (NGS) technologies has dramatically reduced the cost and time associated with genomic analysis, democratizing access to genetic information. As a result, a growing number of healthcare institutions are integrating genomic testing into routine clinical practice, thereby enabling the identification of hereditary conditions, pharmacogenomic profiles, and tumor-specific mutations in oncology. This integration marks a pivotal shift toward a more proactive and preventive approach to healthcare, wherein the potential for disease is assessed at the genetic level, allowing for timely interventions.

Furthermore, the burgeoning field of precision medicine is witnessing the emergence of innovative healthcare technologies, such as liquid biopsies and organ-on-a-chip systems. Liquid biopsies, which involve the analysis of circulating tumor DNA or other biomarkers in bodily fluids, offer a non-invasive means of monitoring disease progression and treatment efficacy. Organ-on-a-chip technologies simulate human organ systems on microfluidic devices, providing valuable insights into drug metabolism and toxicity in a controlled environment. These technologies not only expedite drug development processes but also enhance the safety and effectiveness of personalized therapies.

Integration of AI into Telemedicine and Remote Patient Monitoring

The integration of AI into telemedicine and remote patient monitoring represents a transformative advancement in healthcare delivery, particularly in light of the recent global health crises that have underscored the necessity for adaptable and resilient healthcare systems. Telemedicine platforms equipped with AI capabilities enable healthcare providers to conduct virtual consultations, diagnose conditions, and monitor patients' health status from afar, thus expanding access to care and mitigating the barriers posed by geographical distances and resource constraints.

AI-driven algorithms can analyze patient-reported data and biometric information collected through wearable devices to provide real-time insights into an individual's health status. For instance, continuous monitoring of vital signs, such as heart rate, blood pressure, and glucose levels, allows for the early detection of potential health crises, enabling timely interventions that can prevent hospitalizations. This proactive approach to patient management not only enhances patient outcomes but also alleviates the burden on healthcare facilities, optimizing resource allocation.

Moreover, the use of AI in telemedicine extends to symptom assessment and triage, wherein machine learning models can analyze a patient's symptoms and medical history to recommend appropriate care pathways. By automating the initial stages of clinical evaluation, these AI systems reduce the workload on healthcare providers and streamline patient management processes, ensuring that individuals receive timely and appropriate care based on their unique health profiles.

The incorporation of AI into telemedicine also facilitates personalized health coaching and behavioral interventions. By leveraging data analytics, healthcare providers can tailor lifestyle modification recommendations to the specific needs and preferences of patients, thereby enhancing engagement and adherence to treatment plans. This individualized approach is particularly beneficial for managing chronic conditions, where sustained behavior change is crucial for effective disease management.

The Future of Gene-Editing Technologies and Personalized Therapies (CRISPR, Gene Therapies)

The advent of gene-editing technologies, particularly CRISPR-Cas9, has heralded a new era in personalized medicine, offering the potential to rectify genetic anomalies at their source. This revolutionary technology enables precise alterations to DNA sequences, facilitating the correction of pathogenic mutations responsible for hereditary disorders. As researchers continue to refine and optimize CRISPR methodologies, the prospect of developing gene therapies that are both safe and effective for a broader range of genetic conditions becomes increasingly feasible.

The implications of CRISPR technology extend beyond monogenic disorders; its versatility positions it as a promising tool for the development of personalized therapies for complex diseases, including cancer and neurodegenerative conditions. By leveraging CRISPR to target specific genes involved in disease progression, researchers are exploring innovative therapeutic avenues that can alter disease trajectories in a highly individualized manner. For instance, engineered T-cells modified using CRISPR to enhance their ability to target and destroy tumor cells represent a groundbreaking approach to cancer treatment, showcasing the potential for gene editing to transform therapeutic paradigms.

However, the advancement of gene-editing technologies raises significant ethical considerations, particularly concerning off-target effects and the implications of germline modifications. As the scientific community navigates these complexities, robust regulatory frameworks must be established to ensure the safety and efficacy of gene therapies while safeguarding against potential misuse or unintended consequences. Public discourse surrounding the ethical ramifications of gene editing is essential to garner societal support and foster responsible innovation in this rapidly evolving field.

Potential for Global Disparities in Access to Precision Medicine and How to Address Them

Despite the remarkable advancements in precision medicine, there exists a palpable potential for global disparities in access to these transformative healthcare innovations. The unequal distribution of resources, infrastructure, and technological capabilities across different regions and socioeconomic strata poses a formidable challenge to the equitable implementation of precision medicine. Low- and middle-income countries, in particular, may face significant hurdles in harnessing the benefits of precision healthcare due to inadequate healthcare systems, limited access to genomic technologies, and insufficient training of healthcare professionals.

Addressing these disparities necessitates a multifaceted approach that encompasses investment in healthcare infrastructure, capacity building, and the establishment of collaborative partnerships between high-resource and low-resource settings. International organizations, governments, and private-sector stakeholders must work together to facilitate knowledge transfer and technological exchange, ensuring that developing regions can access the tools and resources necessary to implement precision medicine effectively.

Additionally, the development of affordable and scalable genomic testing technologies is crucial for democratizing access to precision medicine. Efforts to reduce the cost of genomic sequencing and enhance the availability of targeted therapies must be prioritized to ensure that individuals in low-resource settings can benefit from personalized healthcare. This may involve public-private partnerships aimed at advancing research and development while maintaining affordability and accessibility.

Furthermore, educational initiatives aimed at training healthcare professionals in genomic medicine and data analytics are imperative to cultivate a skilled workforce capable of implementing precision medicine in diverse contexts. By investing in education and training, countries can build the capacity necessary to integrate precision medicine into their healthcare systems, thereby improving health outcomes for all populations.

ETHICAL AND SOCIETAL IMPLICATIONS

Data Privacy Concerns in AI-Driven Healthcare

As the integration of artificial intelligence (AI) into healthcare accelerates, the implications for data privacy have emerged as a paramount concern, necessitating rigorous scrutiny and robust safeguards. The utilization of AI in healthcare often entails the aggregation and analysis of vast quantities of patient data, encompassing not only clinical histories but also sensitive genetic and biometric information. This heightened reliance on data raises profound questions about the stewardship of personal health information, particularly in an era characterized by frequent cyber threats and data breaches.

Patients entrust healthcare providers with their most confidential information, expecting that it will be handled with the utmost care and integrity. However, the deployment of AI systems in healthcare introduces complexities regarding the ownership and control of data. Questions arise about who has access to patient data, how it is utilized, and whether it is anonymized sufficiently to protect individual identities. The potential for misuse of health data for purposes beyond patient care—such as marketing, profiling, or discriminatory practices—exacerbates concerns regarding privacy and consent.

Moreover, the regulatory landscape governing data privacy in healthcare is often fragmented and varies significantly across jurisdictions. While frameworks such as the Health Insurance Portability and Accountability Act (HIPAA) in the United States provide a foundation for safeguarding health information, the rapid evolution of AI technologies and the burgeoning volume of data necessitate the continuous reevaluation and enhancement of privacy regulations.

To address these concerns, healthcare organizations must prioritize the implementation of stringent data governance policies, including robust encryption protocols, access controls, and auditing mechanisms to monitor data usage. Additionally, engaging patients in the conversation about data privacy—empowering them to make informed decisions regarding their data—is essential for fostering trust in AI-driven healthcare systems.

Addressing Algorithmic Biases in Treatment Protocols

Algorithmic biases in AI-driven treatment protocols pose a significant ethical challenge, undermining the fundamental principles of equity and justice in healthcare. AI systems are designed to process and analyze data, yet these algorithms are inherently influenced by the datasets on which they are trained. If these datasets are not representative of the diverse populations they aim to serve, the resulting algorithms may perpetuate and exacerbate existing health disparities.

For instance, if an AI model is primarily trained on data from homogeneous populations, it may yield diagnostic and treatment recommendations that are less effective for individuals from underrepresented groups. Such biases can manifest in various domains, including predictive analytics for disease risk, treatment efficacy assessments, and drug dosage recommendations. Consequently, patients belonging to marginalized communities may receive suboptimal care, further entrenching systemic inequities within the healthcare system.

To mitigate algorithmic biases, it is imperative to adopt a multifaceted approach that encompasses diverse data collection practices and rigorous algorithmic auditing. Ensuring that training datasets reflect the heterogeneity of the population is crucial for developing AI systems that are inclusive and equitable. Moreover, transparency in the development and validation of algorithms is essential, allowing stakeholders to scrutinize and address potential biases before the implementation of AI-driven protocols in clinical practice.

Healthcare organizations must also prioritize interdisciplinary collaboration, involving ethicists, social scientists, and community representatives in the design and evaluation of AI systems. This collaborative approach can provide valuable insights into the sociocultural factors that influence health outcomes, ensuring that AI technologies are attuned to the nuanced needs of diverse populations.

Ethical Dilemmas in Genetic Editing and Personalized Medicine

The advent of genetic editing technologies, particularly CRISPR-Cas9, has engendered profound ethical dilemmas that warrant careful consideration as the field of personalized medicine continues to evolve. The capacity to modify genetic material raises critical questions regarding the moral implications of such interventions, particularly when it involves germline modifications that can be heritable.

One of the foremost ethical concerns pertains to the potential for "designer babies," wherein genetic editing could be employed to enhance desired traits, such as intelligence or physical appearance. This prospect raises ethical dilemmas regarding social equity, as access to such technologies may be limited to affluent individuals, thereby exacerbating existing social divides and giving rise to a new dimension of genetic inequality.

Additionally, the long-term consequences of genetic editing are not yet fully understood, particularly concerning unintended off-target effects that may result from CRISPR interventions. The implications of these alterations may extend beyond the individual, potentially affecting future generations in ways that are unpredictable and irreversible. The ethical principle of non-maleficence—ensuring that interventions do not cause harm—must therefore be meticulously weighed against the potential benefits of genetic modifications.

To navigate these ethical dilemmas, the establishment of comprehensive regulatory frameworks is imperative. Such frameworks should encompass not only safety and efficacy assessments but also ethical guidelines that govern the use of genetic editing technologies. Engaging diverse stakeholders—including ethicists, scientists, policymakers, and the public—in discussions surrounding the ethical implications of genetic editing is essential for fostering a socially responsible approach to innovation in personalized medicine.

The Impact of AI on the Patient-Doctor Relationship and Clinical Decision-Making

The integration of AI into clinical practice is poised to fundamentally alter the dynamics of the patient-doctor relationship and the processes of clinical decision-making. While AI technologies offer the potential to enhance diagnostic accuracy, optimize treatment protocols, and streamline workflows, their proliferation also raises concerns regarding the potential depersonalization of care and the erosion of the therapeutic alliance between patients and healthcare providers.

AI's capacity to analyze vast datasets and generate clinical insights can augment the decision-making capabilities of healthcare professionals, enabling them to deliver evidence-based care more effectively. For instance, AI-driven clinical decision support systems can provide real-time recommendations based on patient-specific data, facilitating timely interventions and improving outcomes. However, the reliance on AI-generated recommendations may inadvertently diminish the role of the clinician as the primary decision-maker, potentially leading to a reduction in patient agency and autonomy.

Moreover, the integration of AI into clinical workflows necessitates a delicate balance between technology and human interaction. The humanistic elements of care—such as empathy, compassion, and the ability to understand the patient's context—are irreplaceable facets of the patient-doctor relationship. As AI assumes a more prominent role in clinical decision-making, healthcare providers must remain vigilant to ensure that the patient remains at the center of care, fostering open communication and shared decision-making.

Furthermore, the introduction of AI into healthcare may influence patients' perceptions of their providers. Patients may come to view their healthcare providers as intermediaries who relay AI-generated insights rather than as knowledgeable professionals with the expertise to navigate complex medical decisions. This shift in perception may erode trust and rapport, which are foundational elements of effective healthcare delivery.

To mitigate these challenges, healthcare providers must adopt a collaborative approach that integrates AI as a tool to enhance, rather than replace, the patient-doctor relationship. Engaging patients in discussions about the role of AI in their care and soliciting their input on treatment decisions can foster a sense of partnership and shared ownership in the healthcare process. Additionally, ongoing training for healthcare professionals in the ethical use of AI technologies is essential to ensure that they are equipped to navigate the complexities of AI-driven clinical environments while prioritizing patient-centered care.

CASE STUDIES AND APPLICATIONS

Success Stories in Cancer Treatment, Rare Diseases, and Chronic Conditions

The realm of personalized medicine has ushered in a new epoch of therapeutic efficacy, particularly in the treatment of cancer, rare diseases, and chronic conditions. These success stories illuminate the transformative potential of tailored interventions that account for the individual genetic and phenotypic characteristics of patients, thereby optimizing clinical outcomes.

In oncology, personalized medicine has revolutionized treatment paradigms through the identification of specific biomarkers that dictate tumor behavior and treatment responsiveness. A quintessential example is the utilization of targeted therapies such as trastuzumab (Herceptin) for HER2-positive breast cancer. This monoclonal antibody, which selectively binds to the HER2 receptor, has significantly improved survival rates and reduced recurrence among patients whose tumors exhibit overexpression of this receptor. By aligning treatment strategies with the molecular profile of the tumor, oncologists can administer therapies that are not only more efficacious but also exhibit a favorable safety profile, minimizing the adverse effects commonly associated with conventional chemotherapies.

Moreover, in the context of rare diseases, advancements in genomic medicine have facilitated the identification of pathogenic mutations, enabling the development of tailored therapies. For instance, the introduction of gene therapies, such as nusinersen (Spinraza) for spinal muscular atrophy (SMA), exemplifies the profound impact of precision medicine on rare genetic disorders. Nusinersen functions by modulating the splicing of the SMN2 gene, thereby increasing the production of the survival motor neuron (SMN) protein, which is critical for motor neuron health. Clinical trials have demonstrated that early administration of nusinersen results in substantial improvements in motor function and survival, illustrating the potential for personalized treatments to alter the trajectory of rare diseases.

In the management of chronic conditions such as diabetes, personalized medicine has enabled the customization of treatment regimens based on individual patient profiles, including genetic predispositions and lifestyle factors. Continuous glucose monitoring systems, coupled with AI-driven predictive analytics, allow for real-time adjustments to insulin therapy, thereby optimizing glycemic control and reducing the risk of complications. This individualized approach not only enhances patient outcomes but also empowers individuals to take an active role in managing their health, fostering adherence and improving quality of life.

Case Studies Showing the Cost-Efficiency of Personalized Healthcare

The economic implications of personalized healthcare have garnered increasing attention, as the potential for cost efficiency emerges alongside clinical efficacy. Several case studies illustrate how tailored treatment protocols can mitigate unnecessary expenditures, thereby enhancing the sustainability of healthcare systems.

A notable example is the implementation of pharmacogenomic testing in the management of cardiovascular diseases. Research has demonstrated that patients undergoing genetic testing for polymorphisms affecting drug metabolism—such as those related to the cytochrome P450 enzyme system—can benefit from optimized pharmacotherapy, reducing the likelihood of adverse drug reactions and treatment failures. A case study involving warfarin, an anticoagulant with a narrow therapeutic index, highlighted that genotype-guided dosing resulted in fewer hospitalizations and a decrease in overall healthcare costs associated with bleeding complications. By personalizing medication regimens, healthcare providers can avert costly interventions while improving patient safety.

Another compelling case can be found in oncology, where the implementation of biomarker-driven therapies has been shown to yield substantial economic benefits. A study examining the use of targeted therapies for patients with advanced melanoma demonstrated that treatments such as vemurafenib and dabrafenib not only extended survival but also decreased the cumulative costs associated with disease progression and ineffective therapies. By focusing resources on therapies most likely to yield positive outcomes, healthcare systems can realize significant cost savings while enhancing patient quality of life.

Global Examples of Healthcare Systems Implementing AI-Driven Personalized Medicine

Across the globe, numerous healthcare systems are embracing AI-driven personalized medicine, harnessing the power of data analytics and machine learning to enhance patient care and operational efficiency. The integration of AI technologies facilitates the optimization of treatment pathways, streamlining processes that traditionally relied on generalized approaches.

In the United Kingdom, the National Health Service (NHS) has embarked on a transformative initiative known as the "Genomic Medicine Service," which aims to incorporate genomic testing into standard care for a range of conditions, including cancer and rare diseases. Through the deployment of AI algorithms to analyze genomic data, the NHS has enhanced its capacity to identify actionable mutations and recommend targeted therapies, ultimately improving patient outcomes while optimizing resource allocation.

Similarly, the United States has witnessed the emergence of AI-driven platforms such as Tempus, which leverages genomic and clinical data to facilitate precision oncology. By integrating large-scale genomic sequencing with clinical trial matching, Tempus empowers oncologists to identify the most suitable treatment options for patients, thereby accelerating access to cutting-edge therapies. This model exemplifies how AI can bridge the gap between research and clinical practice, fostering a more personalized approach to cancer treatment.

In Singapore, the integration of AI and big data analytics into the public healthcare system has revolutionized chronic disease management. The Health Promotion Board utilizes predictive analytics to identify at-risk populations and implement targeted interventions, such as personalized lifestyle modification programs. By leveraging data from electronic health records and wearable devices, healthcare providers can offer tailored health coaching that aligns with individual patient profiles, enhancing engagement and promoting better health outcomes.

Lessons Learned from Early Adopters of Precision Medicine

The experiences of early adopters of precision medicine offer valuable insights for implementing personalized healthcare strategies. These lessons underscore the importance of collaboration, data sharing, and patient engagement in realizing precision medicine's full potential.

One salient lesson pertains to the necessity of interdisciplinary collaboration in the development and implementation of personalised healthcare initiatives. Successful programs often involve the convergence of expertise from diverse fields, including genomics, data science, clinical medicine, and public health. This collaborative approach fosters a holistic understanding of patient needs and enhances the design of interventions that are both clinically effective and economically viable.

Additionally, the importance of data infrastructure cannot be overstated. Robust data collection, storage, and analysis capabilities are essential for deriving actionable insights from the vast quantities of information generated by genomic sequencing and electronic health records. Establishing interoperable systems that facilitate seamless data sharing across healthcare providers is critical for advancing personalized medicine, ensuring that insights are translated into practice in a timely and efficient manner.

Moreover, early adopters have recognized the significance of engaging patients as active participants in their healthcare journeys. Empowering patients with information about their genetic profiles and treatment options fosters a sense of ownership and encourages adherence to personalized treatment plans. Patient education and support services are essential components of successful precision medicine initiatives, as they facilitate informed decision-making and promote shared responsibility for health outcomes.

CONCLUSION

Success Stories in Cancer Treatment, Rare Diseases, and Chronic Conditions

The realm of personalized medicine has ushered in a new epoch of therapeutic efficacy, particularly in the treatment of cancer, rare diseases, and chronic conditions. These success stories illuminate the transformative potential of tailored interventions that account for the individual genetic and phenotypic characteristics of patients, thereby optimizing clinical outcomes.

In oncology, personalized medicine has revolutionized treatment paradigms through the identification of specific biomarkers that dictate tumor behavior and treatment responsiveness. A quintessential example is the utilization of targeted therapies such as trastuzumab (Herceptin) for HER2-positive breast cancer. This monoclonal antibody, which selectively binds to the HER2 receptor, has significantly improved survival rates and reduced recurrence among patients whose tumors exhibit overexpression of this receptor. By aligning treatment strategies with the molecular profile of the tumor, oncologists can administer therapies that are not only more efficacious but also exhibit a favorable safety profile, minimizing the adverse effects commonly associated with conventional chemotherapies.

Moreover, in the context of rare diseases, advancements in genomic medicine have facilitated the identification of pathogenic mutations, enabling the development of tailored therapies. For instance, the introduction of gene therapies, such as nusinersen (Spinraza) for spinal muscular atrophy (SMA), exemplifies the profound impact of precision medicine on rare genetic disorders. Nusinersen functions by modulating the splicing of the SMN2 gene, thereby increasing the production of the survival motor neuron (SMN) protein, which is critical for motor neuron health. Clinical trials have demonstrated that early administration of nusinersen results in substantial improvements in motor function and survival, illustrating the potential for personalized treatments to alter the trajectory of rare diseases.

In the management of chronic conditions such as diabetes, personalized medicine has enabled the customization of treatment regimens based on individual patient profiles, including genetic predispositions and lifestyle factors. Continuous glucose monitoring systems, coupled with AI-driven predictive analytics, allow for real-time adjustments to insulin therapy, thereby optimizing glycemic control and reducing the risk of complications. This individualized approach not only enhances patient outcomes but also empowers individuals to take an active role in managing their health, fostering adherence and improving quality of life.

Case Studies Showing the Cost-Efficiency of Personalized Healthcare

The economic implications of personalized healthcare have garnered increasing attention, as the potential for cost efficiency emerges alongside clinical efficacy. Several case studies illustrate how tailored treatment protocols can mitigate unnecessary expenditures, thereby enhancing the sustainability of healthcare systems.

A notable example is the implementation of pharmacogenomic testing in the management of cardiovascular diseases. Research has demonstrated that patients undergoing genetic testing for polymorphisms affecting drug metabolism—such as those related to the cytochrome P450 enzyme system—can benefit from optimized pharmacotherapy, reducing the likelihood of adverse drug reactions and treatment failures. A case study involving warfarin, an anticoagulant with a narrow therapeutic index, highlighted that genotype-guided dosing resulted in fewer hospitalizations and a decrease in overall healthcare costs associated with bleeding complications. By personalizing medication regimens, healthcare providers can avert costly interventions while improving patient safety.

Another compelling case can be found in oncology, where the implementation of biomarker-driven therapies has been shown to yield substantial economic benefits. A study examining the use of targeted therapies for patients with advanced melanoma demonstrated that treatments such as vemurafenib and dabrafenib not only extended survival but also decreased the cumulative costs associated with disease progression and ineffective therapies. By focusing resources on therapies most likely to yield positive outcomes, healthcare systems can realize significant cost savings while enhancing patient quality of life.

Global Examples of Healthcare Systems Implementing AI-Driven Personalized Medicine

Across the globe, numerous healthcare systems are embracing AI-driven personalized medicine, harnessing the power of data analytics and machine learning to enhance patient care and operational efficiency. The integration of AI technologies facilitates the optimization of treatment pathways, streamlining processes that traditionally relied on generalized approaches.

In the United Kingdom, the National Health Service (NHS) has embarked on a transformative initiative known as the "Genomic Medicine Service," which aims to incorporate genomic testing into standard care for a range of conditions, including cancer and rare diseases. Through the deployment of AI algorithms to analyze genomic data, the NHS has enhanced its capacity to identify actionable mutations and recommend targeted therapies, ultimately improving patient outcomes while optimizing resource allocation.

Similarly, the United States has witnessed the emergence of AI-driven platforms such as Tempus, which leverages genomic and clinical data to facilitate precision oncology. By integrating large-scale genomic sequencing with clinical trial matching, Tempus empowers oncologists to identify the most suitable treatment options for patients, thereby accelerating access to cutting-edge therapies. This model exemplifies how AI can bridge the gap between research and clinical practice, fostering a more personalized approach to cancer treatment.

In Singapore, the integration of AI and big data analytics into the public healthcare system has revolutionized chronic disease management. The Health Promotion Board utilizes predictive analytics to identify at-risk populations and implement targeted interventions, such as personalized lifestyle modification programs. By leveraging data from electronic health records and wearable devices, healthcare providers can offer tailored health coaching that aligns with individual patient profiles, enhancing engagement and promoting better health outcomes.

Lessons Learned from Early Adopters of Precision Medicine

The experiences of early adopters of precision medicine offer valuable insights for the broader implementation of personalized healthcare strategies. These lessons underscore the importance of collaboration, data sharing, and patient engagement in realizing the full potential of precision medicine.

One salient lesson pertains to the necessity of interdisciplinary collaboration in the development and implementation of personalized healthcare initiatives. Successful programs often involve the convergence of expertise from diverse fields, including genomics, data science, clinical medicine, and public health. This collaborative approach fosters a holistic understanding of patient needs and enhances the design of interventions that are both clinically effective and economically viable.

Additionally, the importance of data infrastructure cannot be overstated. Robust data collection, storage, and analysis capabilities are essential for deriving actionable insights from the vast quantities of information generated by genomic sequencing and electronic health records. Establishing interoperable systems that facilitate seamless data sharing across healthcare providers is critical for advancing personalized medicine, ensuring that insights are translated into practice in a timely and efficient manner.

Moreover, early adopters have recognized the significance of engaging patients as active participants in their healthcare journeys. Empowering patients with information about their genetic profiles and treatment options fosters a sense of ownership and encourages adherence to personalized treatment plans. Patient education and support services are essential components of successful precision medicine initiatives, as they facilitate informed decision-making and promote shared responsibility for health outcomes.

In conclusion, the success stories, cost-efficiency case studies, and global implementations of personalized healthcare illustrate the profound impact of precision medicine across various domains of health. By learning from the experiences of early adopters, healthcare systems can navigate the complexities of personalized medicine and harness its potential to improve patient outcomes, optimize resource utilization, and foster a more equitable healthcare landscape. As the field continues to evolve, the integration of AI, genomics, and collaborative frameworks will be paramount in realizing the promise of personalized healthcare for all.

DECLARATION

The authors declare that the manuscript follows ethical standards and there are no potential conflicts of interest concerning this chapter's research, authorship, and publication.

DISCLAIMER

The contents and views of this chapter are expressed by the authors in personal capacities. The Editor and the Publisher don't need to agree with these viewpoints and are not responsible for any duty of care in this regard.

REFERENCES

Ahmad, I., Sharma, S., Kumar, R., Dhyani, S., & Dumka, A. (2023). Data Analytics of Online Education during Pandemic Health Crisis: A Case Study. *2nd Edition of IEEE Delhi Section Owned Conference, DELCON 2023 - Proceedings.* DOI: 10.1109/DELCON57910.2023.10127423

Akberdina, V., Kumar, V., Kyriakopoulos, G. L., & Kuzmin, E. (2023). Editorial: What Does Industry's Digital Transition Hold in the Uncertainty Context? In K. V., K. G.L., A. V., & K. E. (Eds.), *Lecture Notes in Information Systems and Organisation: Vol. 61 LNISO* (pp. 1 – 4). Springer Science and Business Media Deutschland GmbH. DOI: 10.1007/978-3-031-30351-7_1

Alexopoulos, C., Al-Tamimi, T. A. S., & Saxena, S. (2023). Were the higher educational institutions (HEIs) in Oman ready to face pedagogical challenges during COVID-19? *Arab Gulf Journal of Scientific Research.* Advance online publication. DOI: 10.1108/AGJSR-03-2023-0095

Aloo, B. N., Dessureault-Rompré, J., Tripathi, V., Nyongesa, B. O., & Were, B. A. (2023). Signaling and crosstalk of rhizobacterial and plant hormones that mediate abiotic stress tolerance in plants. *Frontiers in Microbiology*, 14, 1171104. Advance online publication. DOI: 10.3389/fmicb.2023.1171104 PMID: 37455718

Alrashed, F. A., Alsubiheen, A. M., Alshammari, H., Mazi, S. I., Al-Saud, S. A., Alayoubi, S., Kachanathu, S. J., Albarrati, A., Aldaihan, M. M., Ahmad, T., Sattar, K., Khan, S., & Dhiman, G. (2022). Stress, Anxiety, and Depression in Pre-Clinical Medical Students: Prevalence and Association with Sleep Disorders. *Sustainability (Basel)*, 14(18), 11320. Advance online publication. DOI: 10.3390/su141811320

Alsadi, J., Tripathi, V., Amaral, L. S., Potrich, E., Hasham, S. H., Patil, P. Y., & Omoniyi, E. M. (2022). Architecture Fibrous Meso-Porous Silica Spheres as Enhanced Adsorbent for Effective Capturing for CO_2 Gas. *Key Engineering Materials*, 928, 39–44. DOI: 10.4028/p-2f2o01

Ambika, K. S. B., Goswami, S., Pimplapure, V., Jweeg, M. J., Kant, K., & Gangodkar, D. (2023). Framework Towards Detection of Stress Level Through Classifying Physiological Signals Using Machine Learning. *2023 3rd International Conference on Advance Computing and Innovative Technologies in Engineering, ICACITE 2023*, 600 – 604. DOI: 10.1109/ICACITE57410.2023.10183013

Arya, U., Tiwari, R., Kargeti, H., Chauhan, J. S., Kothari, S., & Kargeti, H. (2023). Artificial Intelligence for Portfolio Selection: A Bibliometric Review. In M. H.K. & S. S. (Eds.), *Proceedings - 2023 International Conference on Advanced Computing and Communication Technologies, ICACCTech 2023* (pp. 9 – 13). Institute of Electrical and Electronics Engineers Inc. DOI: 10.1109/ICACCTech61146.2023.00011

Asha, P., Mannepalli, K., Khilar, R., Subbulakshmi, N., Dhanalakshmi, R., Tripathi, V., Mohanavel, V., Sathyamurthy, R., & Sudhakar, M. (2022). Role of machine learning in attaining environmental sustainability. *Energy Reports*, 8, 863–871. DOI: 10.1016/j.egyr.2022.09.206

Banerjee, D., Kukreja, V., Aeri, M., Hariharan, S., & Garg, N. (2023). Integrated CNN-SVM Approach for Accurate Radish Leaf Disease Classification: A Comparative Study and Performance Analysis. *2023 Annual International Conference on Emerging Research Areas: International Conference on Intelligent Systems, AICERA/ICIS 2023.* DOI: 10.1109/AICERA/ICIS59538.2023.10420119

Banerjee, D., Kukreja, V., Gupta, A., Singh, V., & Pal Singh Brar, T. (2023). Combining CNN and SVM for Accurate Identification of Ridge Gourd Leaf Diseases. *2023 3rd Asian Conference on Innovation in Technology, ASIANCON 2023*. DOI: 10.1109/ASIANCON58793.2023.10269834

Bansal, N., Bhatnagar, M., Kumar, P., & Taneja, S. (2023). Capitalizing on conservation: The synergy between financial gains and environmental goals in impact investing. In *Green Management - A New Paradigm in the World of Business*. Nova Science Publishers, Inc.

Behera, A., & Singh Rawat, K. (2023). A brief review paper on mining subsidence and its geo-environmental impact. *Materials Today: Proceedings*. Advance online publication. DOI: 10.1016/j.matpr.2023.04.183

Bhatnagar, M., Rajaram, R., Taneja, S., & Kumar, P. (2024). Balancing acts: The Yin and Yang of debit and credit on the stage of financial well-being. In *Emerging Perspectives on Financial Well-Being*. IGI Global., DOI: 10.4018/979-8-3693-1750-1.ch002

Bhatnagar, M., Taneja, S., & Kumar, P. (2023). The Effectiveness of Carbon Pricing Mechanism in Steering Financial Flows Toward Sustainable Projects. *International Journal of Environmental Impacts*, 6(4), 183–196. DOI: 10.18280/ijei.060403

Bhatnagar, M., Taneja, S., Kumar, P., & Özen, E. (2024). Does financial education act as a catalyst for SME competitiveness? *International Journal of Education Economics and Development*, 15(3), 377–393. DOI: 10.1504/IJEED.2024.139306

Bhatt, C., Singh, S., Chauhan, R., Singh, T., & Uniyal, A. (2023). Artificial Intelligence in Current Education: Roles, Applications & Challenges. *Proceedings - 2023 3rd International Conference on Pervasive Computing and Social Networking, ICPCSN 2023*, 241 – 244. DOI: 10.1109/ICPCSN58827.2023.00045

Bhatt, S., Dani, R., & Singh, A. K. (2024). Exploring cutting-edge approaches to sustainable tourism infrastructure and design a case studies of regenerative accommodation and facilities. In *Dimensions of Regenerative Practices in Tourism and Hospitality*. IGI Global., DOI: 10.4018/979-8-3693-4042-4.ch003

Bhushan, B., & Nayak, A. (2022). Application of green nanomaterials for sustainable energy systems: A review of the current status. In *Biofuel Technologies for a Sustainable Future: India and Beyond*. River Publishers.

Cavaliere, L. P. L., Byloppilly, R., Khan, S. D., Othman, B. A., Muda, I., & Malhotra, R. K. (2024). Acceptance and effectiveness of Industry 4.0 internal and external organisational initiatives in Malaysian firms. *International Journal of Management and Enterprise Development*, 23(1), 1–25. DOI: 10.1504/IJMED.2024.138422

Chand, A., Agarwal, P., & Sharma, S. (2023). Real-Time Retrieving Vedic Sanskrit Text into Multi-Lingual Text and Audio for Cultural Tourism Motivation. *2023 International Conference for Advancement in Technology, ICONAT 2023*. DOI: 10.1109/ICONAT57137.2023.10080862

Dahiya, M., Guru Prasad, M. S., Anand, T., Kumar, K., Bansal, S., & Naveen Kumar, H. N. (2023). An Effective Detection of Litchi Disease using Deep Learning. *2023 14th International Conference on Computing Communication and Networking Technologies, ICCCNT 2023*. DOI: 10.1109/ICCCNT56998.2023.10307717

Dani, R., Kukreti, R., Negi, A., & Kholiya, D. (2020). Impact of covid-19 on education and internships of hospitality students. *International Journal of Current Research and Review, 12*(21 Special Issue), 86 – 90. DOI: 10.31782/IJCRR.2020.SP54

Deepti, B. A., Arya, A. K., Verma, D. K., & Bachheti, R. K. (2023). Allelopathic activity of genus Euphorbia. In G. D., P. B., M. U., M. R., & G. R. (Eds.), *AIP Conference Proceedings* (Vol. 2782). American Institute of Physics Inc. DOI: 10.1063/5.0154514

Dubey, V. P., Prakash, R., Chamoli, V., & Mittal, P. (2023). Study of Urban Change Detection Using Landsat 8 Satellite Data: A Case Study of Dehradun City, Uttarakhand, India. *IEEE International Conference on Electrical, Electronics, Communication and Computers, ELEXCOM 2023*. DOI: 10.1109/ELEXCOM58812.2023.10370375

Garg, G., Gupta, S., Mishra, P., Vidyarthi, A., Singh, A., & Ali, A. (2023). CROPCARE: An Intelligent Real-Time Sustainable IoT System for Crop Disease Detection Using Mobile Vision. *IEEE Internet of Things Journal, 10*(4), 2840–2851. DOI: 10.1109/JIOT.2021.3109019

Giri, N. C., Mohanty, R. C., Shaw, R. N., Poonia, S., Bajaj, M., & Belkhier, Y. (2022). Agriphotovoltaic System to Improve Land Productivity and Revenue of Farmer. *2022 IEEE Global Conference on Computing, Power and Communication Technologies, GlobConPT 2022*. DOI: 10.1109/GlobConPT57482.2022.9938338

Gonfa, Y. H., Gelagle, A. A., Hailegnaw, B., Kabeto, S. A., Workeneh, G. A., Tessema, F. B., Tadesse, M. G., Wabaidur, S. M., Dahlous, K. A., Abou Fayssal, S., Kumar, P., Adelodun, B., Bachheti, A., & Bachheti, R. K. (2023). Optimization, Characterization, and Biological Applications of Silver Nanoparticles Synthesized Using Essential Oil of Aerial Part of Laggera tomentosa. *Sustainability (Basel), 15*(1), 797. Advance online publication. DOI: 10.3390/su15010797

Goyal, P., Kukreja, T., Agarwal, A., & Khanna, N. (2015). Narrowing awareness gap by using e-learning tools for counselling university entrants. *Conference Proceeding - 2015 International Conference on Advances in Computer Engineering and Applications, ICACEA 2015*, 847 – 851. DOI: 10.1109/ICACEA.2015.7164822

Gupta, S., Kushwaha, P., Chauhan, A. S., Yadav, A., & Badhotiya, G. K. (2023). A study on glazing to optimize daylight for improving lighting ergonomics and energy efficiency of a building. In S. Y., S. G., & B. G.K. (Eds.), *AIP Conference Proceedings* (Vol. 2521). American Institute of Physics Inc. DOI: 10.1063/5.0114766

Gwak, J., Garg, H., & Jan, N. (2023). Investigation of Robotics Technology Based on Bipolar Complex Intuitionistic Fuzzy Soft Relation. *International Journal of Fuzzy Systems, 25*(5), 1834–1852. DOI: 10.1007/s40815-023-01487-0

Ingale, N. V., Saravana Kumar, G., Panduro-Ramirez, J., Raj, M., Vaseem Akram, S., & Rawat, R. (2023). Role of IOT in managing education management tools: A technical review. *2023 3rd International Conference on Advance Computing and Innovative Technologies in Engineering, ICACITE 2023*, 2056 – 2061. DOI: 10.1109/ICACITE57410.2023.10182953

Jain, P., Gupta, V. K., Tiwari, H., Shukla, A., Pandey, P., & Gupta, A. (2023). Human-Computer Interaction: A Systematic Review. In M. H.K. & S. S. (Eds.), *Proceedings - 2023 International Conference on Advanced Computing and Communication Technologies, ICACCTech 2023* (pp. 31 – 36). Institute of Electrical and Electronics Engineers Inc. DOI: 10.1109/ICACCTech61146.2023.00015

Jain, S., & Jain, S. S. (2021). Development of Intelligent Transportation System and Its Applications for an Urban Corridor During COVID-19. *Journal of The Institution of Engineers (India): Series B, 102*(6), 1191 – 1200. DOI: 10.1007/s40031-021-00556-y

Jain, V., Tiwari, R., Mehrotra, R., Bohra, N. S., Misra, A., & Pandey, D. C. (2023). Role of Technology for Credit Risk Management: A Bibliometric Review. *2023 IEEE International Conference on Blockchain and Distributed Systems Security, ICBDS 2023*. DOI: 10.1109/ICBDS58040.2023.10346300

Jaiswal, K. K., Dutta, S., Banerjee, I., Pohrmen, C. B., & Kumar, V. (2023). Photosynthetic microalgae–based carbon sequestration and generation of biomass in biorefinery approach for renewable biofuels for a cleaner environment. *Biomass Conversion and Biorefinery*, 13(9), 7403–7421. DOI: 10.1007/s13399-021-01504-y

Jindal, M., Bajal, E., Singh, P., Diwakar, M., Arya, C., & Sharma, K. (2022). Online education in Covid-19: Limitations and improvements. *2021 IEEE 8th Uttar Pradesh Section International Conference on Electrical, Electronics and Computer Engineering, UPCON 2021*. DOI: 10.1109/UPCON52273.2021.9667605

Jindal, V., Kukreja, V., Mehta, S., Chauhan, R., & Verma, G. (2023). Towards Sustainable Agriculture: Federated CNN Models for Cucurbit Leaf Disease Detection. *2023 10th IEEE Uttar Pradesh Section International Conference on Electrical, Electronics and Computer Engineering, UPCON 2023*, 561 – 566. DOI: 10.1109/UPCON59197.2023.10434321

Jindal, V., Kukreja, V., Mehta, S., Srivastava, P., & Garg, N. (2023). Adopting Federated Learning and CNN for Advanced Plant Pathology: A Case of Red Globe Grape Leaf Diseases Dissecting Severity. *2023 3rd Asian Conference on Innovation in Technology, ASIANCON 2023*. DOI: 10.1109/ASIANCON58793.2023.10270034

Josphineleela, R., Gupta, R., Misra, N., Malik, M., Somasundaram, K., & Gangodkar, D. (2023). Blockchain Based Multi-Layer Security Network Authentication System for Uncertain Attack in the Wireless Communication System. *2023 3rd International Conference on Advance Computing and Innovative Technologies in Engineering, ICACITE 2023*, 877 – 881. DOI: 10.1109/ICACITE57410.2023.10182747

Josphineleela, R., Kaliappan, S., Natrayan, L., & Bhatt, U. M. (2023). Intelligent Virtual Laboratory Development and Implementation using the RASA Framework. *Proceedings - 7th International Conference on Computing Methodologies and Communication, ICCMC 2023*, 1172 – 1176. DOI: 10.1109/ICCMC56507.2023.10083701

Kanojia, P., Malhotra, R. K., & Uniyal, A. K. (2022). Impact of Organizational Commitment Components on the Teachers of Higher Education in Uttarakhand: An Emperical Analysis. *Proceedings - 2022 International Conference on Recent Trends in Microelectronics, Automation, Computing and Communications Systems, ICMACC 2022*, 360–364. DOI: 10.1109/ICMACC54824.2022.10093606

Kaur, A., Kukreja, V., Chamoli, S., Thapliyal, S., & Sharma, R. (2023a). Advanced Disease Management: An Encoder-Decoder Approach for Tomato Black Mold Detection. *2023 IEEE Pune Section International Conference, PuneCon 2023*. DOI: 10.1109/PuneCon58714.2023.10450088

Kaur, A., Kukreja, V., Chamoli, S., Thapliyal, S., & Sharma, R. (2023b). Advanced Multi-Scale Classification of Onion Smut Disease Using a Hybrid CNN-RF Ensemble Model for Precision Agriculture. In G. R., H. K., P. R., G. S., T. A. J.V., V. R., M. R., & K. T. (Eds.), *Proceedings of the 2023 6th International Conference on Recent Trends in Advance Computing, ICRTAC 2023* (pp. 553 – 556). Institute of Electrical and Electronics Engineers Inc. DOI: 10.1109/ICRTAC59277.2023.10480840

Kaur, A., Kukreja, V., Nisha Chandran, S., Garg, N., & Sharma, R. (2023). Automated Mango Rust Severity Classification: A CNN-SVM Ensemble Approach for Accurate and Granular Disease Assessment in Mango Cultivation. In G. R., H. K., P. R., G. S., T. A. J.V., V. R., M. R., & K. T. (Eds.), *Proceedings of the 2023 6th International Conference on Recent Trends in Advance Computing, ICRTAC 2023* (pp. 486 – 490). Institute of Electrical and Electronics Engineers Inc. DOI: 10.1109/ICRTAC59277.2023.10480836

Kaur, G., Sharma, N., Chauhan, R., Singh, P., & Gupta, R. (2023). An Automated Approach for Detection and Classification of Plant Diseases. *2023 2nd International Conference on Futuristic Technologies, INCOFT 2023*. DOI: 10.1109/INCOFT60753.2023.10425170

Khan, T., Singh, K., & Purohit, K. C. (2020). Icma: An efficient integrated congestion control approach. *Recent Patents on Engineering*, 14(3), 294–309. DOI: 10.2174/1872212114666191231150916

Khanna, R., Jindal, P., & Noja, G. G. (2023). Blockchain technologies, a catalyst for insurance sector. In *The Application of Emerging Technology and Blockchain in the Insurance Industry*. DOI: 10.1201/9781032630946-19

Kholiya, D., Mishra, A. K., Pandey, N. K., & Tripathi, N. (2023). Plant Detection and Counting using Yolo based Technique. *2023 3rd Asian Conference on Innovation in Technology, ASIANCON 2023*. DOI: 10.1109/ASIANCON58793.2023.10270530

Kukreti, A., Shriyal, A., Sharma, S., & Bhadula, S. (2023). Internet-of-Things Enabled Smart and Portable Terrace Garden Protection Shed. *2023 4th IEEE Global Conference for Advancement in Technology, GCAT 2023*. DOI: 10.1109/GCAT59970.2023.10353281

Kumar, A., Goyal, H. R., & Sharma, S. (2023). Sustainable Intelligent Information System for Tourism Industry. *2023 IEEE 8th International Conference for Convergence in Technology, I2CT 2023*. DOI: 10.1109/I2CT57861.2023.10126400

Kumar, A., Pant, S., & Ram, M. (2023). Cost Optimization and Reliability Parameter Extraction of a Complex Engineering System. *Journal of Reliability and Statistical Studies*, 16(1), 99–116. DOI: 10.13052/jrss0974-8024.1615

Kumar, A., Sharma, N., Chauhan, R., & Sharma, M. (2023). Anomaly Detection in Bitcoin Blockchain: Exploring Trends and Algorithms. *2023 Global Conference on Information Technologies and Communications, GCITC 2023*. DOI: 10.1109/GCITC60406.2023.10426011

Kumar, G., Kumar, A., Singhal, M., Singh, K. U., Kumar, L., & Singh, T. (2023). Revolutionizing Plant Disease Management Through Image Processing Technology. *Proceedings of International Conference on Computational Intelligence and Sustainable Engineering Solution, CISES 2023*, 521 – 528. DOI: 10.1109/CISES58720.2023.10183408

Kumar, P., Bhatnagar, M., & Taneja, S. (2023). Investigation of the time pattern of Bit Green Crypto: An Arma modeling approach to unrave volatility. In *Algorithmic Approaches to Financial Technology: Forecasting, Trading, and Optimization*. IGI Global., DOI: 10.4018/979-8-3693-1746-4.ch001

Kumar, P., Taneja, S., & Ozen, E. (2024). Exploring the influence of green bonds on sustainable development through low-carbon financing mobilization. *International Journal of Law and Management*. DOI: 10.1108/IJLMA-01-2024-0030

Kumar, P., Verma, P., Bhatnagar, M., Taneja, S., Seychel, S., Todorović, I., & Grim, S. (2023). The Financial Performance and Solvency Status of the Indian Public Sector Banks: A CAMELS Rating and Z Index Approach. *International Journal of Sustainable Development and Planning*, 18(2), 367–376. DOI: 10.18280/ijsdp.180204

Kumar, R., Kathuria, S., Malholtra, R. K., Kumar, A., Gehlot, A., & Joshi, K. (2023). Role of Cloud Computing in Goods and Services Tax(GST) and Future Application. *2nd International Conference on Sustainable Computing and Data Communication Systems, ICSCDS 2023 - Proceedings*, 1443–1447. DOI: 10.1109/ICSCDS56580.2023.10104597

Kumar, R., Lamba, A. K., Mohammed, S., Asokan, A., Aswal, U. S., & Kolavennu, S. (2023). Fake Currency Note Recognition using Extreme Learning Machine. *Proceedings of the 2nd International Conference on Applied Artificial Intelligence and Computing, ICAAIC 2023*, 333 – 339. DOI: 10.1109/ICAAIC56838.2023.10140824

Kumar, R., Lande, A., Kumar, D., Malhotra, R. K., & Sharma, A. (2023). Technology Bridging -in Entrepreneurs and Consumers in Product Development. *ISED 2023 - International Conference on Intelligent Systems and Embedded Design*. DOI: 10.1109/ISED59382.2023.10444599

Kumar, R., Sexena, A., & Gehlot, A. (2023). Artificial Intelligence in Smart Education and Futuristic Challenges. *2023 International Conference on Disruptive Technologies, ICDT 2023*, 432 – 435. DOI: 10.1109/ICDT57929.2023.10151129

Kumar, V., & Korovin, G. (2023). A Comparison of Digital Transformation of Industry in the Russian Federation with the European Union. In K. V., K. G.L., A. V., & K. E. (Eds.), *Lecture Notes in Information Systems and Organisation: Vol. 61 LNISO* (pp. 45 – 57). Springer Science and Business Media Deutschland GmbH. DOI: 10.1007/978-3-031-30351-7_5

Kumar, V., Mitra, D., Rani, A., Suyal, D. C., Singh Gautam, B. P., Jain, L., Gondwal, M., Raj, K. K., Singh, A. K., & Soni, R. (2021). Bio-inoculants for Biodegradation and Bioconversion of Agrowaste: Status and Prospects. In *Bioremediation of Environmental Pollutants: Emerging Trends and Strategies*. Springer International Publishing., DOI: 10.1007/978-3-030-86169-8_16

Kunwar, S., Joshi, A., Gururani, P., Pandey, D., & Pandey, N. (2023). Physiological and AI-based study of endophytes on medicina A mini review. *Plant Science Today*, 10, 53–60. DOI: 10.14719/pst.2555

Liao, N., Cai, Q., Garg, H., Wei, G., & Xu, X. (2023). Novel Gained and Lost Dominance Score Method Based on Cumulative Prospect Theory for Group Decision-Making Problems in Probabilistic Hesitant Fuzzy Environment. *International Journal of Fuzzy Systems*, 25(4), 1414–1428. DOI: 10.1007/s40815-022-01440-7

Lourens, M., Krishna, S. H., Singh, A., Dey, S. K., Pant, B., & Sharma, T. (2022). Role of Artificial Intelligence in Formative Employee Engagement. In D. R.K., S. A.Kr., K. G., & B. S. (Eds.), *Proceedings of the 2022 11th International Conference on System Modeling and Advancement in Research Trends, SMART 2022* (pp. 936 – 941). Institute of Electrical and Electronics Engineers Inc. DOI: 10.1109/SMART55829.2022.10047422

Malhotra, R. K., & Gupta, S. (2021). Tele health in the digital era during covid -19 a case study of Uttarakhand. *Journal of Medical Pharmaceutical and Allied Sciences*, 10, 109–112. DOI: 10.22270/jmpas.VI2I1.2016

Malik, D., Kukreja, V., Mehta, S., Gupta, A., & Singh, V. (2023). Mitigating the Impact of Guava Leaf Diseases Using CNNs and Federated Learning. *2023 3rd Asian Conference on Innovation in Technology, ASIANCON 2023*. DOI: 10.1109/ASIANCON58793.2023.10270236

Malik, P., Singh, A. K., Nautiyal, R., & Rawat, S. (2022). Mapping AICTE cybersecurity curriculum onto CyBOK: A case study. In *Machine Learning for Cyber Security*. De Gruyter., DOI: 10.1515/9783110766745-007

Mangla, S. K., Luthra, S., Mishra, N., Singh, A., Rana, N. P., Dora, M., & Dwivedi, Y. (2018). Barriers to effective circular supply chain management in a developing country context. *Production Planning and Control*, 29(6), 551–569. DOI: 10.1080/09537287.2018.1449265

Mekala, K., Laxmi, V., Jagruthi, H., Dhondiyal, S. A., Sridevi, R., & Dabral, A. P. (2023). Coffee Price Prediction: An Application of CNN-BLSTM Neural Networks. *Proceedings of the 2nd IEEE International Conference on Advances in Computing, Communication and Applied Informatics, ACCAI 2023*. DOI: 10.1109/ACCAI58221.2023.10199369

Mishra, A., Shah, J. K., Sharma, R., Sharma, M., Joshi, S., & Kaushal, D. (2023). Enhancing Efficiency in Industrial Environments through IoT Connected Worker Solutions: Smart Wearable Technologies for the Workplace. *2023 International Conference on Advances in Computation, Communication and Information Technology, ICAICCIT 2023*, 1175 – 1179. DOI: 10.1109/ICAICCIT60255.2023.10466100

Mishra, A. K., Singh, S., & Upadhyay, R. K. (2023). Organization citizenship behaviour among indian nurses during SARS-COV-2: A direct effect moderation model. *Quality & Quantity*, 57(1), 541–559. DOI: 10.1007/s11135-022-01325-9

Mitra, D., Mondal, R., Khoshru, B., Senapati, A., Radha, T. K., Mahakur, B., Uniyal, N., Myo, E. M., Boutaj, H., Sierra, B. E. G. U. E. R. R. A., Panneerselvam, P., Ganeshamurthy, A. N., Elković, S. A. N. Đ. J., Vasić, T., Rani, A., Dutta, S., & Mohapatra, P. K. D. A. S.MITRA. (2022). Actinobacteria-enhanced plant growth, nutrient acquisition, and crop protection: Advances in soil, plant, and microbial multifactorial interactions. *Pedosphere*, 32(1), 149–170. DOI: 10.1016/S1002-0160(21)60042-5

Mitra, D., Saritha, B., Janeeshma, E., Gusain, P., Khoshru, B., Abo Nouh, F. A., Rani, A., Olatunbosun, A. N., Ruparelia, J., Rabari, A., Mosquera-Sánchez, L. P., Mondal, R., Verma, D., Panneerselvam, P., Das Mohapatra, P. K., & Guerra Sierra, B. E. (2022). Arbuscular mycorrhizal fungal association boosted the arsenic resistance in crops with special responsiveness to rice plant. *Environmental and Experimental Botany*, 193. Advance online publication. DOI: 10.1016/j.envexpbot.2021.104681

Nagila, A., Saravanakumar, P., Pranavan, S., Goutam, R., Dobhal, D. C., & Singh, G. (2023). An Innovative Approach of CNN-BiGRU Based Post-Earthquake Damage Detection of Reinforced Concrete for Frame Buildings. *International Conference on Self Sustainable Artificial Intelligence Systems, ICSSAS 2023 - Proceedings*, 56 – 61. DOI: 10.1109/ICSSAS57918.2023.10331894

Naveen, Y., Lokanadham, D., Naidu, D. R., Sharma, R. C., Palli, S., & Lila, M. K. (2023). An Experimental Study on the Influence of Blended Karanja Biodiesel on Diesel Engine Characteristics. *International Journal of Vehicle Structures and Systems*, 15(2), 154–160. DOI: 10.4273/ijvss.15.2.02

Nikolaidis, P., Ismail, M., Shuib, L., Khan, S., & Dhiman, G. (2022). Predicting Student Attrition in Higher Education through the Determinants of Learning Progress: A Structural Equation Modelling Approach. *Sustainability (Basel)*, 14(20), 13584. Advance online publication. DOI: 10.3390/su142013584

Onyema, E. M., Almuzaini, K. K., Onu, F. U., Verma, D., Gregory, U. S., Puttaramaiah, M., & Afriyie, R. K. (2022). Prospects and Challenges of Using Machine Learning for Academic Forecasting. *Computational Intelligence and Neuroscience*, 2022, 1–7. Advance online publication. DOI: 10.1155/2022/5624475 PMID: 35909823

Pandey, P., Mayank, K., & Sharma, S. (2023). Recommendation System for Adventure Tourism. *2023 4th IEEE Global Conference for Advancement in Technology, GCAT 2023*. DOI: 10.1109/GCAT59970.2023.10353339

Pant, V., Bhasin, S., & Jain, S. (2017). Self-Learning system for personalized E-Learning. *2017 International Conference on Emerging Trends in Computing and Communication Technologies, ICETCCT 2017, 2018-Janua*, 1 – 6. DOI: 10.1109/ICETCCT.2017.8280344

Patil, S. P., Singh, B., Bisht, J., Gupta, S., & Khanna, R. (2021). Yoga for holistic treatment of polycystic ovarian syndrome. *Journal of Medical Pharmaceutical and Allied Sciences*, 10, 120–125. DOI: 10.22270/jmpas.VI2I1.2035

Pattanshetti, M. K., Jasola, S., Rajput, A., & Pant, V. (2021). Proposed eLearning framework using open corpus web resources. *Proceedings of the 2021 1st International Conference on Advances in Electrical, Computing, Communications and Sustainable Technologies, ICAECT 2021*. DOI: 10.1109/ICAECT49130.2021.9392591

Paul, S. N., Mishra, A. K., & Upadhyay, R. K. (2022). Locus of control and investment decision: An investor's perspective. *International Journal of Services. Economics and Management*, 13(2), 93–107. DOI: 10.1504/IJSEM.2022.122736

Prikshat, V., Kumar, S., & Nankervis, A. (2019). Work-readiness integrated competence model: Conceptualisation and scale development. *Education + Training*, 61(5), 568–589. DOI: 10.1108/ET-05-2018-0114

Prikshat, V., Kumar, S., & Raje, P. (2017). Antecedents, consequences and strategic responses to graduate work-readiness: Challenges in India. In *Transitions from Education to Work: Workforce Ready Challenges in the Asia Pacific*. Taylor and Francis., DOI: 10.4324/9781315533971-8

Rai, K., Mishra, N., & Mishra, S. (2022). Forest Fire Risk Zonation Mapping using Fuzzy Overlay Analysis of Nainital District. *2022 International Mobile and Embedded Technology Conference, MECON 2022*, 522 – 526. DOI: 10.1109/MECON53876.2022.9751812

Rajeswari, M., Kumar, N., Raman, P., Patjoshi, P. K., Singh, V., & Pundir, S. (2022). Optimal Analysis for Enterprise Financial Management Based on Artificial Intelligence and Parallel Computing Method. *Proceedings of 5th International Conference on Contemporary Computing and Informatics, IC3I 2022*, 2081 – 2086. DOI: 10.1109/IC3I56241.2022.10072851

Ramachandran, K. K., Lamba, F. L. R., Rawat, R., Gehlot, A., Raju, A. M., & Ponnusamy, R. (2023). An Investigation of Block Chains for Attaining Sustainable Society. *2023 3rd International Conference on Advance Computing and Innovative Technologies in Engineering, ICACITE 2023*, 1069 – 1076. DOI: 10.1109/ICACITE57410.2023.10182462

Rana, D. S., Dimri, S. C., Malik, P., & Dhondiyal, S. A. (2022). Impact of Computational Thinking in Engineering and K12 Education. *4th International Conference on Inventive Research in Computing Applications, ICIRCA 2022 - Proceedings*, 697 – 701. DOI: 10.1109/ICIRCA54612.2022.9985593

Rana, M. S., Cavaliere, L. P. L., Mishra, A. B., Padhye, P., Singh, R. R., & Khanna, R. (2022). Internet of Things (IOT) Based Assessment for Effective Monitoring Data Against Malicious Attacks on Financial Collectors. *2022 2nd International Conference on Advance Computing and Innovative Technologies in Engineering, ICACITE 2022*, 177–181. DOI: 10.1109/ICACITE53722.2022.9823612

Rao, K. V. G., Kumar, M. K., Goud, B. S., Krishna, D., Bajaj, M., Saini, P., & Choudhury, S. (2023). IOT-Powered Crop Shield System for Surveillance and Auto Transversum. *2023 IEEE 3rd International Conference on Sustainable Energy and Future Electric Transportation, SeFet 2023*. DOI: 10.1109/SeFeT57834.2023.10245773

Rathore, R., & Goudar, R. H. (2015). SPARQL-based personalised E-Learning system designed using ontology (SPELSO): An architecture. *International Journal of Knowledge and Learning*, 10(4), 384–416. DOI: 10.1504/IJKL.2015.077554

Rawat, B., Rawat, J. M., Purohit, S., Singh, G., Sharma, P. K., Chandra, A., Shabaaz Begum, J. P., Venugopal, D., Jaremko, M., & Qureshi, K. A. (2022). A comprehensive review of Quercus semecarpifolia Sm.: An ecologically and commercially important Himalayan tree. *Frontiers in Ecology and Evolution*, 10, 961345. Advance online publication. DOI: 10.3389/fevo.2022.961345

Rawat, D., Kumar, V., Gautam, G., Sharma, M., & Sonsare, P. K. (2023). Watershed Management and Sustainability. *2023 International Conference on Communication, Security and Artificial Intelligence, ICCSAI 2023*, 676 – 679. DOI: 10.1109/ICCSAI59793.2023.10421450

Rawat, R. S., Singh, V., & Dumka, A. (2022). Complaint Management in Ethiopian Vocational and Technical Education Institutions: A Framework and Implementation of a Decision Support System. *2022 International Conference on 4th Industrial Revolution Based Technology and Practices, ICFIRTP 2022*, 73 – 79. DOI: 10.1109/ICFIRTP56122.2022.10063207

Rawat, S. S., Pant, S., Kumar, A., Ram, M., Sharma, H. K., & Kumar, A. (2022). A State-of-the-Art Survey on Analytical Hierarchy Process Applications in Sustainable Development. *International Journal of Mathematical. Engineering and Management Sciences*, 7(6), 883–917. DOI: 10.33889/IJMEMS.2022.7.6.056

Sapna, Chand, K., Tiwari, R., & Bhardwaj, K. (2023). Impact of Welfare Measures on Job Satisfaction of Employees in the Industrial Sector of Northern India. *Finance India*, 37(2), 613–626.

Sharma, H. R., Bhardwaj, B., Sharma, B., & Kaushik, C. P. (2021). Sustainable Solid Waste Management in India: Practices, Challenges and the Way Forward. In *Climate Resilience and Environmental Sustainability Approaches: Global Lessons and Local Challenges*. Springer Nature. DOI: 10.1007/978-981-16-0902-2_17

Sharma, M., Kumar, A., Luthra, S., Joshi, S., & Upadhyay, A. (2022). The impact of environmental dynamism on low-carbon practices and digital supply chain networks to enhance sustainable performance: An empirical analysis. *Business Strategy and the Environment*, 31(4), 1776–1788. DOI: 10.1002/bse.2983

Sharma, M., & Singh, P. (2023). Newly engineered nanoparticles as potential therapeutic agents for plants to ameliorate abiotic and biotic stress. *Journal of Applied and Natural Science*, 15(2), 720–731. DOI: 10.31018/jans.v15i2.4603

Sharma, N. K., Kumar, V., Verma, P., & Luthra, S. (2021). Sustainable reverse logistics practices and performance evaluation with fuzzy TOPSIS: A study on Indian retailers. *Cleaner Logistics and Supply Chain*, 1, 100007. Advance online publication. DOI: 10.1016/j.clscn.2021.100007

Sharma, S., Gupta, A., & Tyagi, R. (2023). Artificial Intelligence Enabled Sustainable Education System Using Vedic Scripture and Cyber Security. *2023 2nd International Conference on Advances in Computational Intelligence and Communication, ICACIC 2023*. DOI: 10.1109/ICACIC59454.2023.10435133

Sharma, S., Kadayat, Y., & Tyagi, R. (2023a). Artificial Intelligence Enabled Sustainable Life Cycle System Using Vedic Scripture and Quantum Computing. *2023 3rd International Conference on Intelligent Technologies, CONIT 2023*. DOI: 10.1109/CONIT59222.2023.10205771

Sharma, S., Kadayat, Y., & Tyagi, R. (2023b). Sustainable Global Democratic e-Governance System Using Vedic Scripture, Artificial Intelligence, Cloud Computing and Augmented Reality. *Proceedings of the International Conference on Circuit Power and Computing Technologies, ICCPCT 2023*, 113 – 118. DOI: 10.1109/ICCPCT58313.2023.10245405

Sharma, S., Kandpal, V., Choudhury, T., Santibanez Gonzalez, E. D. R., & Agarwal, N. (2023). Assessment of the implications of energy-efficient technologies on the environmental sustainability of rail operation. *AIMS Environmental Science*, 10(5), 709–731. DOI: 10.3934/environsci.2023039

Sharma, S., Singh, V., & Sarkar, D. (2023). Machine Vision Enabled Fall Detection System for Specially Abled People in Limited Visibility Environment. *2023 3rd Asian Conference on Innovation in Technology, ASIANCON 2023*. DOI: 10.1109/ASIANCON58793.2023.10270769

Sharma, S., Singh Rawal, R., Pandey, D., & Pandey, N. (2021). Microbial World for Sustainable Development. In *Microbial Technology for Sustainable Environment*. Springer Nature., DOI: 10.1007/978-981-16-3840-4_1

Sharma, S., & Tyagi, R. (2023). Digitalization of Farming Knowledge Using Artificial Intelligence and Vedic Scripture. *3rd IEEE International Conference on ICT in Business Industry and Government, ICTBIG 2023*. DOI: 10.1109/ICTBIG59752.2023.10456219

Sharma, V., & Jain, S. (2020). Managers Training Programs Effectiveness Evaluation by using different Machine Learning Approaches. *Proceedings of the 4th International Conference on Electronics, Communication and Aerospace Technology, ICECA 2020*, 1453–1457. DOI: 10.1109/ICECA49313.2020.9297556

Sharma, V., Taneja, S., Gupta, M., Jangir, K., & Ozen, E. (2023). Impact of Service Quality on Behavioural Intention to Use Fin Tech Payment Services: An Extension of SERVEQUAL Model. *Asia Pacific Journal of Information Systems*, 33(4), 1093–1117. DOI: 10.14329/apjis.2023.33.4.1093

Shekhar, S., Gusain, R., Vidhyarthi, A., & Prakash, R. (2022). Role of Remote Sensing and GIS Strategies to Increase Crop Yield. In S. S. & J. T. (Eds.), *2022 International Conference on Advances in Computing, Communication and Materials, ICACCM 2022*. Institute of Electrical and Electronics Engineers Inc. DOI: 10.1109/ICACCM56405.2022.10009217

Shukla, A., Sharma, M., Tiwari, K., Vani, V. D., & Kumar, N., & Pooja. (2023). Predicting Rainfall Using an Artificial Neural Network-Based Model. *Proceedings of International Conference on Contemporary Computing and Informatics, IC3I 2023*, 2700–2704. DOI: 10.1109/IC3I59117.2023.10397714

Singh, A., Sharma, S., Purohit, K. C., & Nithin Kumar, K. C. (2021). Artificial Intelligence based Framework for Effective Performance of Traffic Light Control System. *Proceedings of the 2021 IEEE International Conference on Innovative Computing, Intelligent Communication and Smart Electrical Systems, ICSES 2021*. DOI: 10.1109/ICSES52305.2021.9633913

Singh, A. B., Meena, H. K., Khandelwal, C., & Dangayach, G. S. (2023). Sustainability Assessment of Higher Education Institutions: A Systematic Literature Review †. *Engineering Proceedings*, 37(1), 23. Advance online publication. DOI: 10.3390/ECP2023-14728

Singh, K. D., & Singh, P. (2023). A Novel Cloud-based Framework to Predict the Employability of Students. In K. R., K. R., G. M., G. M., S. R., & S. R. (Eds.), *2023 International Conference on Advancement in Computation and Computer Technologies, InCACCT 2023* (pp. 528–532). Institute of Electrical and Electronics Engineers Inc. DOI: 10.1109/InCACCT57535.2023.10141760

Singh, K. D., Singh, P., Kaur, G., Khullar, V., Chhabra, R., & Tripathi, V. (2023). Education 4.0: Exploring the Potential of Disruptive Technologies in Transforming Learning. *Proceedings of International Conference on Computational Intelligence and Sustainable Engineering Solution, CISES 2023*, 586–591. DOI: 10.1109/CISES58720.2023.10183547

Singh, K. K., Vats, C., & Singh, M. P. (2023). An Empirical Study of the Impact of Organizational, Social, and Psychological Factors on the Performance of Employees. In M. P., M. P., S. A., K. S., K. S.K., & M. S.K. (Eds.), *Springer Proceedings in Business and Economics* (pp. 621 – 636). Springer Nature. DOI: 10.1007/978-981-99-0197-5_39

Singh, Y., Singh, N. K., & Sharma, A. (2023). Biodiesel as an alternative fuel employed in CI engine to meet the sustainability criteria: A review. In S. Y., S. G., & B. G.K. (Eds.), *AIP Conference Proceedings* (Vol. 2521). American Institute of Physics Inc. DOI: 10.1063/5.0113825

Singhal, P., Sharma, S., Saha, S., Mishra, I., Alfurhood, B. S., & Singh, P. (2023). Smart security system using Hybrid System with IoT and Blockchain: A security system Human sased Detection. *2023 3rd International Conference on Advance Computing and Innovative Technologies in Engineering, ICACITE 2023*, 1032 – 1036. DOI: 10.1109/ICACITE57410.2023.10182383

Singla, A., Singh, Y., Singh, Y., Rahim, E. A., Singh, N. K., & Sharma, A. (2023). Challenges and Future Prospects of Biofuel Generations: An Overview. In *Biowaste and Biomass in Biofuel Applications*. CRC Press., DOI: 10.1201/9781003265597-4

Srivastava, A., Hassan, M., & Gangwar, R. (2023). Improving Railway Track System Using Soil Nails for Heavy Axle Load. *Lecture Notes in Civil Engineering, 338 LNCE*, 1 – 13. DOI: 10.1007/978-981-99-1886-7_1

Srivastava, A., Jawaid, S., Singh, R., Gehlot, A., Akram, S. V., Priyadarshi, N., & Khan, B. (2022). Imperative Role of Technology Intervention and Implementation for Automation in the Construction Industry. *Advances in Civil Engineering*, 2022(1), 6716987. Advance online publication. DOI: 10.1155/2022/6716987

Suryavanshi, A., Kukreja, V., Bordoloi, D., Mehta, S., & Choudhary, A. (2023). Agricultural Insights Through Federated Learning CNN: A Case Study on Jackfruit Leaf Disease. In D. R.K., S. A.Kr., S. R., B. S., & K. V. (Eds.), *Proceedings of the 2023 12th International Conference on System Modeling and Advancement in Research Trends, SMART 2023* (pp. 36 – 42). Institute of Electrical and Electronics Engineers Inc. DOI: 10.1109/SMART59791.2023.10428321

Suryavanshi, A., Tanwar, S., Kukreja, V., Choudhary, A., & Chamoli, S. (2023). An Integrated Approach to Potato Leaf Disease Detection Using Convolutional Neural Networks and Random Forest. *Proceedings of the 2023 International Conference on Innovative Computing, Intelligent Communication and Smart Electrical Systems, ICSES 2023*. DOI: 10.1109/ICSES60034.2023.10465557

Taneja, S., Bhatnagar, M., Kumar, P., & Grima, S. (2023). A Panel Analysis of the Effectiveness of the Asset Management in Indian Agricultural Companies. *International Journal of Sustainable Development and Planning*, 18(3), 653–660. DOI: 10.18280/ijsdp.180301

Taneja, S., Bhatnagar, M., Kumar, P., & Rupeika-apoga, R. (2023). India's Total Natural Resource Rents (NRR) and GDP : An Augmented Autoregressive Distributed Lag (ARDL) Bound Test. *Journal of Risk and Financial Management*, 16(2), 91. https://doi.org/doi.org/10.3390/jrfm16020091. DOI: 10.3390/jrfm16020091

Tanwar, V., Anand, V., Chauhan, R., & Rawat, D. (2023). A Deep Learning for Early Tomato Leaf Disease Detection: A CNN Approach. *2023 2nd International Conference on Futuristic Technologies, INCOFT 2023*. DOI: 10.1109/INCOFT60753.2023.10425552

Thakur, S., Malik, D., Kukreja, V., Sharma, R., Yadav, R., & Joshi, K. (2023). Multi-Stage Classification of Pomegranate Anthracnose Disease Severity Levels with CNN and SVM. *Proceedings of the 4th International Conference on Smart Electronics and Communication, ICOSEC 2023*, 1117 – 1121. DOI: 10.1109/ICOSEC58147.2023.10276047

Tiwari, K., Bafila, P., Negi, P., & Singh, R. (2023). The applications of nanotechnology in nutraceuticals: A review. In S. Y., S. G., & B. G.K. (Eds.), *AIP Conference Proceedings* (Vol. 2521). American Institute of Physics Inc. DOI: 10.1063/5.0129695

Tiwari, R., Agrawal, P., Singh, P., Bajaj, S., Verma, V., & Chauhan, A. S. (2023). Technology Enabled Integrated Fusion Teaching for Enhancing Learning Outcomes in Higher Education. *International Journal of Emerging Technologies in Learning*, 18(7), 243–249. DOI: 10.3991/ijet.v18i07.36799

Tomar, S., & Sharma, N. (2021). A systematic review of agricultural policies in terms of drivers, enablers, and bottlenecks: Comparison of three Indian states and a model bio-energy village located in different agro climatic regions. *Groundwater for Sustainable Development*, 15, 100683. Advance online publication. DOI: 10.1016/j.gsd.2021.100683

Tyagi, S., Mathur, K., Gupta, T., Khantwal, S., & Tripathi, V. (2023). The Effectiveness of Augmented Reality in Developing Pre-Primary Student's Cognitive Skills. *IEEE Region 10 Humanitarian Technology Conference, R10-HTC*, 997 – 1002. DOI: 10.1109/R10-HTC57504.2023.10461754

Uniyal, S., Sarma, P. R. S., Kumar Mangla, S., Tseng, M.-L., & Patil, P. (2022). ICT as "Knowledge Management" for Assessing Sustainable Consumption and Production in Supply Chains. In *Research Anthology on Measuring and Achieving Sustainable Development Goals* (Vol. 3). IGI Global. DOI: 10.4018/978-1-6684-3885-5.ch048

Vijayalakshmi, S., Hasan, F., Priyadarshini, S. M., Durga, S., Verma, V., & Podile, V. (2022). Strategic Evaluation of Implementing Artificial Intelligence Towards Shaping Entrepreneurial Development During Covid- 19 Outbreaks. *2022 2nd International Conference on Advance Computing and Innovative Technologies in Engineering, ICACITE 2022*, 2570 – 2573. DOI: 10.1109/ICACITE53722.2022.9823894

William, P., Ramu, G., Kansal, L., Patil, P. P., Alkhayyat, A., & Rao, A. K. (2023). Artificial Intelligence Based Air Quality Monitoring System with Modernized Environmental Safety of Sustainable Development. *Proceedings - 2023 3rd International Conference on Pervasive Computing and Social Networking, ICPCSN 2023*, 756 – 761. DOI: 10.1109/ICPCSN58827.2023.00130

Wongchai, A., Shukla, S. K., Ahmed, M. A., Sakthi, U., Jagdish, M., & kumar, R. (2022). Artificial intelligence - enabled soft sensor and internet of things for sustainable agriculture using ensemble deep learning architecture. *Computers & Electrical Engineering*, 102, 108128. Advance online publication. DOI: 10.1016/j.compeleceng.2022.108128

Yadav, A. R., Shekhar, S., Vidyarthi, A., Prakash, R., & Gowri, R. (2023). Hyper-Parameter Tuning with Grid and Randomized Search Techniques for Predictive Models of Hotel Booking. *IEEE International Conference on Electrical, Electronics, Communication and Computers, ELEXCOM 2023*. DOI: 10.1109/ELEXCOM58812.2023.10370718

Yadav, P. M., Patra, I., Mittal, V., Nagorao, C. G., Udhayanila, R., & Saranya, A. (2023). Implementation of IOT on English Language Classroom Management. *2023 3rd International Conference on Advance Computing and Innovative Technologies in Engineering, ICACITE 2023*, 1686 – 1690. DOI: 10.1109/ICACITE57410.2023.10182984

Chapter 4
Ethical, Privacy, and Security Issues in Smart Healthcare

Swati Gupta
https://orcid.org/0009-0005-5795-8353
Chitkara University, Punjab, India

ABSTRACT

Smart healthcare technologies have transformed the healthcare landscape, promising precision, efficiency, and improved patient outcomes. However, these advancements bring significant ethical, privacy, and security challenges. The increased use of AI and data-driven systems in healthcare raises questions about patient autonomy, data ownership, and informed consent. As large volumes of sensitive health data are generated, ensuring robust security measures is critical to protecting patient privacy. Moreover, the push for cost-effectiveness in healthcare often conflicts with ethical obligations, necessitating a balanced approach. Health economics also impacts ethical decision-making, as stakeholders must navigate the trade-offs between cost containment and quality care. This chapter explores these complexities, examining frameworks to address ethical, privacy, and security concerns. Through case studies and regulatory perspectives, it offers insights into how smart healthcare can responsibly advance while safeguarding patient rights and public trust.

INTRODUCTION

In the rapidly evolving field of healthcare, the integration of advanced technologies such as artificial intelligence (AI), machine learning, big data analytics, and the Internet of Things (IoT) has forged a new paradigm: smart healthcare. While these technologies promise precision, efficiency, and personalized patient care, they also introduce a labyrinth of ethical, privacy, and security challenges that necessitate careful consideration (Arora et al., 2024). In an era where data is as valuable as currency, the stakes surrounding patient information have reached unprecedented levels. Each advancement in healthcare technology not only reshapes patient care and healthcare administration but also redefines the very nature of ethical standards, security protocols, and privacy expectations within the medical field. Addressing these concerns requires a balance between the immense potential of smart healthcare and the pressing

DOI: 10.4018/979-8-3373-0240-9.ch004

need to protect patient rights, uphold ethical standards, and ensure security in increasingly digitalized healthcare ecosystems (A. K. Singh et al., 2024).

Smart healthcare technologies have introduced a plethora of ethical dilemmas, particularly in the realms of data use, autonomy, and accountability (Khandelwal et al., 2023). For example, AI algorithms now play a significant role in diagnostics, treatment planning, and even predicting patient outcomes. While AI has demonstrated remarkable capabilities in these areas, it also raises questions about the moral responsibility of healthcare providers. Who is accountable when an AI-driven diagnosis proves incorrect? How does one ensure that the AI is free from biases that could lead to inequitable treatment outcomes? These ethical quandaries are further complicated by issues of transparency and explainability. In traditional healthcare settings, medical professionals make decisions based on a combination of medical knowledge, experience, and judgment. However, AI-driven decisions are often based on complex algorithms that may be difficult for even the developers to fully understand or explain. This opacity, often referred to as the "black box" problem, poses a significant ethical challenge, as patients and healthcare providers alike are left in the dark about how certain decisions are made (K. U. Singh et al., 2024).

Beyond ethics, privacy is a paramount concern in smart healthcare. As healthcare systems become more data-driven, they collect and analyze vast amounts of patient information, often in real time. While this data is invaluable for personalized medicine and improving patient outcomes, it also presents significant risks to patient privacy. In many cases, patients may not fully understand the extent to which their data is being collected, analyzed, and shared (Aiyappa et al., 2024). This lack of transparency can erode trust between patients and healthcare providers, as patients may feel that their privacy is being compromised for the sake of technological advancement. Additionally, the collection and storage of sensitive patient data make healthcare systems a prime target for cyberattacks. The consequences of a data breach in healthcare can be severe, potentially exposing patients to identity theft, discrimination, and other forms of harm (Padhi et al., 2024).

The security of smart healthcare systems is intrinsically linked to privacy concerns. As more devices and systems are connected to the internet, the attack surface for cybercriminals expands, increasing the likelihood of security breaches (Indu et al., 2023). In addition to data theft, cyberattacks on healthcare systems can disrupt critical medical services, putting patient lives at risk. For instance, ransomware attacks on hospitals have forced healthcare providers to revert to paper records, leading to delays in patient care and even forcing some institutions to turn away patients. The potential for such disruptions highlights the importance of robust cybersecurity measures in smart healthcare systems. However, implementing effective security protocols is no small feat, as healthcare systems often involve a complex network of interconnected devices, many of which may have outdated security features or limited capacity for updates. Furthermore, the need for rapid access to patient data can sometimes conflict with security protocols, as healthcare providers may prioritize speed over security in emergency situations (Shrivastava et al., 2023).

In light of these challenges, it is clear that a multidisciplinary approach is required to address the ethical, privacy, and security issues in smart healthcare. Policymakers, technologists, healthcare providers, and ethicists must work together to develop guidelines and best practices that ensure the responsible use of smart healthcare technologies (Pandey et al., 2023). This chapter aims to explore these issues in depth, examining the ethical dilemmas posed by AI and other smart technologies, the privacy implications of data-driven healthcare, and the security challenges facing modern healthcare systems. By addressing these concerns, we can better understand how to navigate the complex landscape of smart healthcare and ensure that these technologies are used in a way that benefits patients without compromising their rights or well-being (Belwal & Belwal, 2017).

Data Privacy and Security in Smart Health Systems

As healthcare systems become increasingly reliant on data, the need for stringent privacy and security measures has never been more critical. Data privacy in healthcare revolves around protecting patient information from unauthorized access, disclosure, and misuse. In smart health systems, patient data is often collected through a variety of sources, including electronic health records (EHRs), wearable devices, and IoT-enabled medical equipment. This data is invaluable for improving patient care, enabling remote monitoring, and facilitating personalized treatment plans. However, the sheer volume and sensitivity of the data collected raise significant privacy concerns. In many cases, patients may be unaware of the extent to which their data is being collected, analyzed, and shared, leading to potential violations of their privacy rights (Zhang et al., 2023).

One of the primary privacy challenges in smart healthcare is the lack of transparency surrounding data collection and usage practices. Patients may not fully understand the scope of data being collected, nor do they have control over how their data is used. This lack of control is particularly concerning given that healthcare data is among the most sensitive types of personal information. Unlike other forms of personal data, such as financial or shopping data, healthcare data can reveal intimate details about a person's health, lifestyle, and even genetic predispositions. The potential for misuse of this data is significant, as it could lead to discrimination in areas such as employment, insurance, and housing (Ajay et al., 2023).

In addition to privacy concerns, the security of healthcare data is a major issue in smart health systems. As more devices and systems are connected to the internet, the risk of cyberattacks increases. Cybercriminals often target healthcare systems due to the high value of healthcare data on the black market. A single data breach can expose the personal information of thousands, if not millions, of patients, leading to identity theft, financial fraud, and other forms of harm. Furthermore, cyberattacks on healthcare systems can disrupt critical medical services, putting patient lives at risk. For instance, ransomware attacks on hospitals have forced healthcare providers to revert to paper records, leading to delays in patient care and even forcing some institutions to turn away patients (Srivastava et al., 2024).

To mitigate these risks, healthcare organizations must implement robust cybersecurity measures. However, securing healthcare systems is a complex task, as it involves protecting a vast network of interconnected devices, many of which may have outdated security features or limited capacity for updates. Furthermore, the need for rapid access to patient data can sometimes conflict with security protocols, as healthcare providers may prioritize speed over security in emergency situations (Mishra et al., 2024). In addition, healthcare organizations must comply with a variety of regulations and standards related to data privacy and security, such as the Health Insurance Portability and Accountability Act (HIPAA) in the United States and the General Data Protection Regulation (GDPR) in the European Union. While these regulations provide a framework for protecting patient data, they can also be challenging to implement, particularly for smaller healthcare organizations with limited resources (Gangwar & Srivastva, 2020).

Ethical Dilemmas in AI and Data Use in Healthcare

The integration of AI in healthcare has introduced a host of ethical dilemmas, particularly in the realms of autonomy, accountability, and transparency. One of the key ethical concerns surrounding AI in healthcare is the question of accountability (Dangwal et al., 2022). In traditional healthcare settings, medical professionals are responsible for their decisions and actions. However, when AI algorithms are used to make decisions, it becomes unclear who is accountable when things go wrong (Tripathi & Mohan,

2016). For example, if an AI-driven diagnosis proves to be incorrect, leading to harm for the patient, who is to blame? Is it the healthcare provider who relied on the AI's recommendation, the developers who created the algorithm, or the organization that implemented the technology?

This lack of clear accountability is further complicated by the "black box" nature of many AI algorithms. In many cases, AI algorithms are so complex that even their developers do not fully understand how they arrive at certain decisions. This lack of transparency poses a significant ethical challenge, as patients and healthcare providers may be unable to understand or question the reasoning behind AI-driven decisions. This opacity can erode trust in healthcare providers and lead to feelings of helplessness and frustration among patients, who may feel that their care is being dictated by a machine rather than a human being (P. Singh & Singh, 2023).

Balancing Cost-Effectiveness with Ethical Standards in Healthcare

The push for cost-effectiveness in healthcare is a driving force behind the adoption of AI and other smart healthcare technologies. These systems have the potential to streamline operations, reduce overhead, and minimize inefficiencies by automating routine tasks and facilitating predictive analytics that improve patient outcomes. However, this focus on cost reduction can conflict with the ethical standards expected in healthcare. In many cases, the use of AI and automation may prioritize financial savings over patient well-being, raising ethical concerns about the quality and equity of care (Grover et al., 2024).

For example, AI algorithms that predict patient outcomes based on large data sets may inadvertently marginalize vulnerable populations. When algorithms are trained on historical data, they risk perpetuating existing biases and inequalities. If a predictive model is based on data from a particular demographic or socioeconomic group, it may not accurately reflect the needs or outcomes of patients outside that group. As a result, decisions based on these models could lead to inequitable treatment outcomes, where certain populations receive a lower standard of care. This phenomenon, often referred to as algorithmic bias, is a significant ethical concern in smart healthcare, as it conflicts with the principles of fairness and justice that underpin medical ethics (Kumari et al., 2024).

Moreover, the use of AI to make treatment decisions can undermine the principle of patient autonomy. In traditional healthcare, patients have the right to make informed decisions about their care based on their understanding of their condition and the available treatment options. However, when an AI algorithm is used to determine the best course of action, patients may feel that their autonomy is compromised. They may not fully understand the rationale behind the AI's recommendation or feel empowered to question it. This lack of transparency can create a power imbalance between patients and healthcare providers, as patients may feel pressured to accept the AI's recommendation without fully understanding its implications (Dutta et al., 2023).

To address these ethical challenges, healthcare organizations must strive to strike a balance between cost-effectiveness and ethical standards. This may involve implementing safeguards to ensure that AI algorithms are free from bias, transparent in their decision-making processes, and used in a way that respects patient autonomy. Additionally, healthcare providers must be trained to understand the ethical implications of using AI in patient care and to communicate these implications to patients in a way that empowers them to make informed decisions. By taking these steps, healthcare organizations can harness the benefits of AI while upholding the ethical principles that are essential to the practice of medicine (P. Kumar et al., 2024).

The Impact of Health Economics on Ethical Decision-Making

Health economics, the study of how resources are allocated within healthcare systems, plays a significant role in shaping ethical decision-making in smart healthcare. As healthcare costs continue to rise, there is increasing pressure on healthcare providers and policymakers to make decisions that maximize the value of limited resources (Dahiya & Taneja, 2023). This focus on cost-effectiveness has led to the adoption of value-based care models, where healthcare providers are incentivized to deliver high-quality care at a lower cost. While these models have the potential to improve patient outcomes and reduce healthcare spending, they also introduce ethical dilemmas that must be carefully managed (Kanojia et al., 2022; R. Kumar et al., 2023).

One of the primary ethical concerns in value-based care is the potential for cost-cutting measures to compromise the quality of care. In a system where healthcare providers are rewarded for reducing costs, there is a risk that they may prioritize financial considerations over patient well-being. For example, a healthcare provider may be incentivized to choose a lower-cost treatment option, even if a more expensive alternative would be more effective for the patient. This conflict between cost-effectiveness and quality of care raises questions about the ethical responsibilities of healthcare providers, as they must balance their obligation to provide the best possible care with the need to control costs (C. Gupta et al., 2022).

Another ethical issue in value-based care is the potential for patient discrimination. In a system where healthcare providers are rewarded for improving patient outcomes, there is a risk that they may prioritize patients who are more likely to achieve positive outcomes. This phenomenon, known as "cherry-picking," can lead to disparities in care, as patients with complex or chronic conditions may be perceived as less profitable and therefore receive lower-quality care. This practice conflicts with the ethical principles of fairness and justice, as it prioritizes financial considerations over the needs of vulnerable populations (Patil et al., 2021).

To address these ethical challenges, healthcare organizations and policymakers must work to develop frameworks that promote ethical decision-making in value-based care. This may involve implementing safeguards to ensure that cost-cutting measures do not compromise the quality of care and that healthcare providers are incentivized to treat all patients equitably, regardless of their likelihood of achieving positive outcomes. Additionally, healthcare providers must be trained to understand the ethical implications of value-based care and to make decisions that prioritize patient well-being over financial considerations. By taking these steps, healthcare organizations can create a healthcare system that is both cost-effective and ethically sound (R. Kumar & Khanna, 2023).

Regulatory and Legal Frameworks for Smart Healthcare

The ethical, privacy, and security challenges associated with smart healthcare technologies have led to the development of various regulatory and legal frameworks designed to protect patient rights and ensure the responsible use of these technologies. In the United States, the Health Insurance Portability and Accountability Act (HIPAA) sets standards for the protection of patient health information, requiring healthcare organizations to implement measures to safeguard patient data from unauthorized access and disclosure. Similarly, the General Data Protection Regulation (GDPR) in the European Union establishes strict guidelines for the collection, storage, and use of personal data, including healthcare data. These regulations provide a framework for protecting patient privacy and ensuring that healthcare organizations are held accountable for the security of patient data (Awal & Khanna, 2019).

However, the rapid pace of technological advancement in healthcare has outpaced the development of regulatory frameworks, creating gaps in the protection of patient rights. For example, many existing regulations were designed to address the privacy and security risks associated with traditional healthcare systems and may not adequately address the unique challenges posed by AI, IoT, and other smart healthcare technologies. Additionally, the global nature of smart healthcare complicates regulatory enforcement, as data may be collected, stored, and processed in multiple jurisdictions with varying legal requirements. This lack of harmonization can create challenges for healthcare organizations, as they must navigate a complex web of regulations to ensure compliance (Sharma et al., 2022).

To address these challenges, policymakers must work to develop regulatory frameworks that are flexible enough to accommodate emerging technologies while still providing robust protections for patient rights. This may involve updating existing regulations to address the unique risks associated with smart healthcare technologies, as well as developing new standards for the ethical and responsible use of AI, IoT, and big data in healthcare (Cavaliere et al., 2024). Additionally, international collaboration is essential to ensure that regulatory frameworks are consistent across jurisdictions, as this will help to protect patient rights in a globalized healthcare system (Taneja & Özen, 2023).

In addition to regulatory frameworks, ethical guidelines and best practices play a crucial role in guiding the responsible use of smart healthcare technologies. Professional organizations, such as the American Medical Association (AMA) and the World Health Organization (WHO), have developed ethical guidelines that provide a framework for addressing the ethical, privacy, and security challenges associated with AI and other smart healthcare technologies. These guidelines emphasize the importance of transparency, accountability, and patient autonomy, and they provide healthcare providers with a roadmap for navigating the complex ethical landscape of smart healthcare (Joshi et al., 2022).

Case Studies on Ethical and Security Challenges in Smart Healthcare

Case studies provide valuable insights into the ethical, privacy, and security challenges associated with smart healthcare technologies. By examining real-world examples, healthcare providers, policymakers, and technologists can better understand the risks associated with these technologies and develop strategies to mitigate them (Reepu et al., 2023).

One notable case study is the use of AI in radiology to detect and diagnose conditions such as cancer. AI algorithms have demonstrated remarkable accuracy in identifying abnormalities in medical images, often outperforming human radiologists (M. Gupta et al., 2023). However, the use of AI in radiology raises significant ethical concerns, particularly in terms of transparency and accountability. In many cases, patients may not fully understand how the AI algorithm arrived at a diagnosis, leading to questions about the reliability of the technology and the potential for misdiagnosis. Additionally, the use of AI in radiology has raised concerns about the potential for job displacement, as some fear that AI could eventually replace human radiologists. This case study highlights the need for transparency and accountability in the use of AI in healthcare, as well as the importance of addressing the social and economic implications of technological advancement (Taneja & Sharma, 2023).

Another case study involves the use of wearable devices to monitor patients with chronic conditions, such as diabetes and heart disease. These devices collect a wealth of data on patients' health, including heart rate, blood pressure, and glucose levels, which can be used to personalize treatment plans and improve patient outcomes. However, the use of wearable devices raises significant privacy concerns, as patients may not fully understand the extent to which their data is being collected and shared. Additionally, the data collected by wearable devices is often stored in cloud-based systems, which are vulnerable to cyberattacks. This case study underscores the importance of robust privacy and security measures in smart healthcare, as well as the need for clear communication with patients about the risks associated with data collection and sharing (Taneja et al., 2023).

Table 1. Ethical, privacy, and security issues in smart healthcare

Topic	Key Facts	Primary Concerns	Recommendations
Ethics in AI and Data Use	- AI can enhance diagnostics, personalized medicine, and predictive analytics. - Algorithms often operate as "black boxes," making it challenging to explain decisions. - Ethical standards are evolving to address AI's role in healthcare.	- Lack of transparency and explainability in AI decisions. - Potential biases in algorithms could lead to inequitable outcomes. - Question of accountability when AI errors harm patients.	- Develop clear accountability guidelines for AI usage. - Promote transparency and fairness in algorithm design. - Encourage patient understanding of AI-influenced decisions.
Data Privacy	- Health data is highly sensitive and often stored in interconnected systems. - Data collected includes personal health records, wearable device data, and EHRs. - Regulatory frameworks like HIPAA and GDPR protect patient data rights.	- Potential for unauthorized access and misuse of data. - Patients may lack control or awareness over data use. - Risks of data exploitation for profit without patient consent.	- Improve transparency in data collection and usage. - Strengthen regulatory compliance and data protection measures. - Empower patients with control over personal data.
Cybersecurity in Healthcare Systems	- Healthcare systems are high-value targets for cybercriminals. - Common threats include ransomware, DDoS attacks, and data breaches. - Cyberattacks can disrupt medical services, endangering patient safety.	- Increased vulnerability due to interconnected devices (IoT). - Risks to patient privacy, identity, and security from breaches. - System downtimes can delay care, posing life-threatening risks.	- Invest in advanced cybersecurity infrastructure. - Conduct regular risk assessments. - Prioritize cybersecurity training for healthcare professionals.
Balancing Cost-Effectiveness and Ethics	- Value-based care models aim to enhance outcomes while controlling costs. - AI-driven efficiencies can reduce operational expenses. - Economic constraints influence resource allocation in healthcare.	- Cost savings may be prioritized over patient quality of care. - Risk of "cherry-picking" patients to meet value-based care metrics. - Conflict between economic efficiency and patient well-being.	- Implement safeguards to ensure cost-cutting doesn't reduce care quality. - Develop fair metrics to evaluate patient care. - Promote ethical use of resources, focusing on patient outcomes.
Regulatory and Legal Frameworks	- HIPAA (USA), GDPR (EU), and other regulations protect patient data. - Existing regulations may not fully address new smart healthcare challenges. - Regulatory gaps exist in addressing AI, IoT, and big data in healthcare.	- Regulations may not keep pace with technological advancements. - Fragmented laws create compliance challenges across borders. - Ambiguity in guidelines for AI ethics, security, and data privacy.	- Update existing regulations to cover smart healthcare technologies. - Promote international collaboration on data privacy and AI standards. - Encourage ethical use of patient data.

continued on following page

Table 1. Continued

Topic	Key Facts	Primary Concerns	Recommendations
Impact of Health Economics	- Rising healthcare costs drive the adoption of cost-effective models. - Value-based care aims to provide better outcomes at lower costs. - Health economics influences resource distribution across healthcare systems.	- Cost-based models may impact equitable access to quality care. - Economic priorities may lead to reduced treatment options for high-risk patients. - Potential misalignment between economic and ethical priorities.	- Balance economic models with ethical considerations. - Incentivize care for high-risk and vulnerable patients. - Create policies that prioritize equitable care distribution.
Case Studies on Ethical and Security Challenges	- AI in radiology has shown success but also risks transparency issues. - Wearable health devices enhance monitoring but raise privacy concerns. - Cyberattacks on healthcare facilities have disrupted services and put patients at risk.	- Lack of clarity in AI-driven decisions can lead to distrust. - Wearable devices' data handling raises risks of patient exploitation. - Cybersecurity lapses could critically impact patient care continuity.	- Use explainable AI models in high-stakes settings. - Clearly communicate risks associated with wearable data to patients. - Strengthen cybersecurity policies and incident response protocols.

Table 1 delineates the multifaceted intricacies inherent within the ethical, privacy, and security considerations associated with smart healthcare technology. Each domain—spanning AI ethics, data privacy, cybersecurity, cost-effectiveness, regulatory frameworks, health economics, and real-world case analyses—intersects to form a convoluted matrix of challenges, necessitating nuanced strategies to mitigate potential risks and ethical transgressions.

Ethics in AI and Data Utilization revolves around the opacity and inscrutability of AI algorithms, often functioning as "black boxes" that obscure their decision-making processes. This obfuscation engenders an ethical conundrum whereby biases embedded within algorithmic structures potentially perpetuate systemic inequities. Accountability within this realm remains nebulous, thus necessitating robust frameworks that establish responsibility for outcomes arising from AI-driven interventions. Such transparency in AI design and deployment is crucial to maintaining ethical integrity in patient care, fostering a sense of agency among patients, and alleviating the potential for algorithmic discrimination (Bansal et al., 2023).

Data Privacy within smart healthcare constitutes one of the most precarious facets of the system, due to the colossal aggregation of sensitive information from various sources, including electronic health records and wearables. This omnipresent data collection often occurs without comprehensive patient consent or awareness, thereby compromising privacy. The table underscores the duality of patient data's value and vulnerability, as healthcare organizations struggle to balance operational benefits against privacy rights. In mitigating these concerns, transparency in data handling is pivotal to fostering patient trust, while adherence to stringent regulatory measures fortifies data sovereignty.

Cybersecurity emerges as a critical imperative, given that healthcare systems, being repositories of high-value data, are persistently susceptible to sophisticated cyber incursions. The ramifications of compromised cybersecurity extend beyond data theft to the disruption of life-sustaining medical interventions, with consequences that could endanger patient welfare. The table indicates that the interconnected infrastructure of healthcare systems amplifies vulnerability, emphasizing the necessity of robust cybersecurity protocols and contingency planning to preempt potential service interruptions.

Balancing Cost-Effectiveness with Ethical Imperatives elucidates the friction between economic exigencies and the ethical commitment to optimal patient outcomes. The economic rationale underpinning AI adoption in healthcare hinges on operational efficiencies and cost containment; however, such motives may inadvertently overshadow patient-centric considerations. The risk of "cherry-picking" patients, whereby financial viability supersedes equitable access to quality care, underscores the potential for ethical divergence within cost-driven healthcare models. Implementing systemic safeguards to monitor these decisions is essential to preserve patient well-being, advocating for an ethical recalibration in resource allocation.

Regulatory and Legal Frameworks are pivotal in delineating the ethical and legal boundaries within which smart healthcare technologies operate. Yet, regulatory structures such as HIPAA and GDPR may inadequately accommodate the idiosyncratic complexities posed by emergent technologies like AI and IoT. The lack of global harmonization further exacerbates compliance challenges, particularly for transnational healthcare systems that operate across jurisdictions with disparate regulatory standards. Consequently, the table advocates for updated and unified international standards that can address the dynamic technological landscape while reinforcing patient rights and data protections.

The Influence of Health Economics on ethical decision-making manifests in the incentivization of value-based care models, intended to optimize outcomes in an economically constrained environment. However, such models may precipitate ethical conflicts, as providers weigh financial efficiency against the ethical obligation to offer comprehensive, high-quality care. Particularly concerning is the potential for economic pragmatism to marginalize patients with complex conditions deemed "unprofitable." To counteract these inequities, the table underscores the necessity of frameworks that harmonize economic imperatives with ethical considerations, thereby reinforcing the primacy of patient welfare in healthcare resource allocation.

Finally, Case Studies on Ethical and Security Challenges serve as exemplars of the complex reality in which these issues coalesce. AI applications in radiology, for instance, reveal the benefits and risks of algorithmic opacity, where diagnostic precision may come at the cost of clarity and patient trust. Similarly, the deployment of wearable health monitoring devices augments data richness but simultaneously amplifies privacy vulnerabilities, placing patient autonomy at risk. Furthermore, the susceptibility of healthcare systems to cyberattacks, exemplified by ransomware incidents, underscores the catastrophic potential of cybersecurity lapses. These real-world scenarios reveal that while smart healthcare offers transformative potential, it simultaneously demands an elevated vigilance to uphold ethical and security standards.

In summary, the table delineates a landscape where the confluence of ethical considerations, privacy rights, economic constraints, and regulatory inadequacies forms a formidable barrier to the responsible adoption of smart healthcare. A sophisticated, multi-disciplinary approach, combining ethical foresight with robust regulatory frameworks and resilient cybersecurity, is imperative to harness the full potential of smart healthcare technologies while safeguarding patient rights and public trust.

Future Directions and Recommendations

As smart healthcare technologies continue to evolve, it is essential to address the ethical, privacy, and security challenges associated with these advancements. To this end, several recommendations can help healthcare providers, policymakers, and technologists navigate the complex landscape of smart healthcare.

First, healthcare organizations must prioritize transparency and accountability in the use of AI and other smart healthcare technologies. This may involve implementing measures to ensure that AI algorithms are explainable and free from bias, as well as providing patients with clear information about how their data is being used and protected. Additionally, healthcare providers must be trained to understand the ethical implications of using AI in patient care and to communicate these implications to patients in a way that empowers them to make informed decisions.

Second, policymakers must work to develop regulatory frameworks that are flexible enough to accommodate emerging technologies while still providing robust protections for patient rights. This may involve updating existing regulations to address the unique risks associated with smart healthcare technologies, as well as developing new standards for the ethical and responsible use of AI, IoT, and big data in healthcare. International collaboration is also essential to ensure that regulatory frameworks are consistent across jurisdictions, as this will help to protect patient rights in a globalized healthcare system.

Third, healthcare organizations must implement robust privacy and security measures to protect patient data from unauthorized access and disclosure. This may involve investing in advanced cybersecurity technologies, as well as conducting regular risk assessments to identify and mitigate potential vulnerabilities. Additionally, healthcare organizations must work to ensure that patients have control over their data and understand the risks associated with data collection and sharing.

Finally, it is essential to foster a culture of ethical decision-making within healthcare organizations. This may involve developing ethical guidelines and best practices that provide a framework for addressing the ethical, privacy, and security challenges associated with smart healthcare technologies. Additionally, healthcare providers must be encouraged to prioritize patient well-being over financial considerations and to make decisions that reflect the ethical principles of fairness, justice, and respect for patient autonomy.

CONCLUSION

The integration of smart healthcare technologies has the potential to revolutionize patient care, improving outcomes, and streamlining operations in ways previously unimaginable. However, these advancements also introduce a host of ethical, privacy, and security challenges that must be carefully managed to protect patient rights and ensure the responsible use of technology. By prioritizing transparency, accountability, and patient autonomy, healthcare organizations can harness the benefits of smart healthcare while upholding the ethical principles that are essential to the practice of medicine. Through a combination of regulatory frameworks, ethical guidelines, and best practices, we can create a healthcare system that is both technologically advanced and ethically sound, ensuring that the benefits of smart healthcare are accessible to all.

DECLARATION

The authors declare that the manuscript follows ethical standards and there are no potential conflicts of interest concerning this chapter's research, authorship, and publication.

DISCLAIMER

The contents and views of this chapter are expressed by the authors in personal capacities. The Editor and the Publisher don't need to agree with these viewpoints and are not responsible for any duty of care in this regard.

REFERENCES

Aiyappa, S., Kodikal, R., & Rahiman, H. U. (2024). Accelerating Gender Equality for Sustainable Development: A Case Study of Dakshina Kannada District, India. *Technical and Vocational Education and Training*, 38, 335–349. DOI: 10.1007/978-981-99-6909-8_30

Ajay, D., Sharad, K., Singh, K. P., & Sharma, S. (2023). Impact of Prolonged Mental Torture on Housewives in Middle Class Families. *Journal for ReAttach Therapy and Developmental Diversities*, 6(4), 1–7.

Arora, A., Singh, R., Malik, K., & Kestwal, U. (2024). Association of sexual performance and intimacy with satisfaction in life in head and neck cancer patients: A review. *Oral Oncology Reports*, 11, 100563. Advance online publication. DOI: 10.1016/j.oor.2024.100563

Awal, G., & Khanna, R. (2019). Determinants of millennial online consumer behavior and prospective purchase decisions. *International Journal of Advanced Science and Technology*, 28(18), 366–378.

Bansal, N., Bhatnagar, M., & Taneja, S. (2023). Balancing priorities through green optimism: A study elucidating initiatives, approaches, and strategies for sustainable supply chain management. In *Handbook of Research on Designing Sustainable Supply Chains to Achieve a Circular Economy*. IGI Global., DOI: 10.4018/978-1-6684-7664-2.ch004

Belwal, R., & Belwal, S. (2017). Employers' perception of women workers in Oman and the challenges they face. *Employee Relations*, 39(7), 1048–1065. DOI: 10.1108/ER-09-2016-0183

Cavaliere, L. P. L., Byloppilly, R., Khan, S. D., Othman, B. A., Muda, I., & Malhotra, R. K. (2024). Acceptance and effectiveness of Industry 4.0 internal and external organisational initiatives in Malaysian firms. *International Journal of Management and Enterprise Development*, 23(1), 1–25. DOI: 10.1504/IJMED.2024.138422

Dahiya, K., & Taneja, S. (2023). To Analyse the Impact of Multi-Media Technology on the Rural Entrepreneurship Development. In *Contemporary Studies of Risks in Emerging Technology* (pp. 221–240). DOI: 10.1108/978-1-80455-562-020231015

Dangwal, A., Kaur, S., Taneja, S., & Ozen, E. (2022). A bibliometric analysis of green tourism based on the scopus platform. In *Developing Relationships, Personalization, and Data Herald in Marketing 5.0*. IGI Global., DOI: 10.4018/978-1-6684-4496-2.ch015

Dutta, A., Singh, P., Dobhal, A., Mannan, D., Singh, J., & Goswami, P. (2023). Entrepreneurial Aptitude of Women of an Aspirational District of Uttarakhand. *Indian Journal of Extension Education*, 59(2), 103–107. DOI: 10.48165/IJEE.2023.59222

Gangwar, V. P., & Srivastva, S. P. (2020). Impact of micro finance in poverty eradication via SHGs: A study of selected districts in U.P. *International Journal of Advanced Science and Technology*, 29(2), 3818–3829.

Grover, D., Sharma, S., Kaur, P., Mittal, A., & Sharma, P. K. (2024). Societal Elements that Impact the Performance of Women Entrepreneurs in Tier-II Cities: A Study of Rohilkhand Region of Uttar Pradesh. *2024 IEEE Zooming Innovation in Consumer Technologies Conference. ZINC*, 2024, 114–117. DOI: 10.1109/ZINC61849.2024.10579316

Gupta, C., Jindal, P., & Malhotra, R. K. (2022). A Study of Increasing Adoption Trends of Digital Technologies - An Evidence from Indian Banking. In D. N. & C. A. (Eds.), *AIP Conference Proceedings* (Vol. 2481). American Institute of Physics Inc. DOI: 10.1063/5.0104572

Gupta, M., Arora, K., & Taneja, S. (2023). Bibliometric analysis on employee engagement and human resource management. In *Enhancing Customer Engagement Through Location-Based Marketing*. IGI Global., DOI: 10.4018/978-1-6684-8177-6.ch013

Indu, R., Dimri, S. C., & Kumar, B. (2023). Identification of Location for Police Headquarters to Deal with Crime Against Women in India Using Clustering Based on K-Means Algorithm. *International Journal of Computing and Digital Systems*, 14(1), 965–974. DOI: 10.12785/ijcds/140175

Joshi, K., Patil, S., Gupta, S., & Khanna, R. (2022). Role of Pranayma in emotional maturity for improving health. *Journal of Medical Pharmaceutical and Allied Sciences*, 11(2), 4569–4573. DOI: 10.55522/jmpas.V11I2.2033

Kanojia, P., Malhotra, R. K., & Uniyal, A. K. (2022). Organizational Commitment and the Academic Staff in HEI's in North West India. *Proceedings - 2022 International Conference on Recent Trends in Microelectronics, Automation, Computing and Communications Systems, ICMACC 2022*, 365–370. DOI: 10.1109/ICMACC54824.2022.10093347

Khandelwal, C., Kumar, S., Tripathi, V., & Madhavan, V. (2023). Joint impact of corporate governance and risk disclosures on firm value: Evidence from emerging markets. *Research in International Business and Finance*, 66, 102022. Advance online publication. DOI: 10.1016/j.ribaf.2023.102022

Kumar, P., Taneja, S., & Ozen, E. (2024). Exploring the influence of green bonds on sustainable development through low-carbon financing mobilization. *International Journal of Law and Management*. DOI: 10.1108/IJLMA-01-2024-0030

Kumar, R., & Khanna, R. (2023). RPA (Robotic Process Automation) in Finance & Accounting and Future Scope. *Proceedings of the 2023 2nd International Conference on Augmented Intelligence and Sustainable Systems, ICAISS 2023*, 1640–1645. DOI: 10.1109/ICAISS58487.2023.10250496

Kumar, R., Singh, T., Mohanty, S. N., Goel, R., Gupta, D., Alharbi, M., & Khanna, R. (2023). Study on online payments and e-commerce with SOR model. *International Journal of Retail & Distribution Management*. Advance online publication. DOI: 10.1108/IJRDM-03-2023-0137

Kumari, J., Singh, P., Mishra, A. K., Singh Meena, B. P., Singh, A., & Ojha, M. (2024). Challenges Hindering Women's Involvement in the Hospitality Industry as Entrepreneurs in the Era of Digital Economy. In *Revolutionizing the AI-Digital Landscape: A Guide to Sustainable Emerging Technologies for Marketing Professionals*. Taylor and Francis., DOI: 10.4324/9781032688305-9

Mishra, D., Kandpal, V., Agarwal, N., & Srivastava, B. (2024). Financial Inclusion and Its Ripple Effects on Socio-Economic Development: A Comprehensive Review. *Journal of Risk and Financial Management*, 17(3), 105. Advance online publication. DOI: 10.3390/jrfm17030105

Padhi, B. K., Singh, S., Gaidhane, A. M., Abu Serhan, H., Khatib, M. N., Zahiruddin, Q. S., Rustagi, S., Sharma, R. K., Sharma, D., Arora, M., & Satapathy, P. (2024). Inequalities in cardiovascular disease among elderly Indians: A gender perspective analysis using LASI wave-I (2017-18). *Current Problems in Cardiology*, 49(7), 102605. Advance online publication. DOI: 10.1016/j.cpcardiol.2024.102605 PMID: 38692448

Pandey, R. P., Bansal, S., Awasthi, P., Dixit, V., Singh, R., & Yadava, V. (2023). Attitude and Myths Related to Stalking among Early and Middle Age Adults. *Psychology Hub, 40*(3), 85 – 94. DOI: 10.13133/2724-2943/17960

Patil, S. P., Singh, B., Bisht, J., Gupta, S., & Khanna, R. (2021). Yoga for holistic treatment of polycystic ovarian syndrome. *Journal of Medical Pharmaceutical and Allied Sciences*, 10, 120–125. DOI: 10.22270/jmpas.VIC2I1.2035

Reepu, R., Taneja, S., Ozen, E., & Singh, A. (2023). A globetrotter to the future of marketing: Metaverse. In *Cultural Marketing and Metaverse for Consumer Engagement*. IGI Global., DOI: 10.4018/978-1-6684-8312-1.ch001

Sharma, P., Malhotra, R. K., Ojha, M. K., & Gupta, S. (2022). Impact of meditation on mental & physical health and thereby on academic performance of students: A study of higher educational institutions of Uttarakhand. *Journal of Medical Pharmaceutical and Allied Sciences*, 11(2), 4641–4644. DOI: 10.55522/jmpas.V11I2.2309

Shrivastava, A., Usha, R., Kukreti, R., Sharma, G., Srivastava, A. P., & Khan, A. K. (2023). Women Safety Precaution. *2023 1st International Conference on Circuits, Power, and Intelligent Systems, CCPIS 2023*. DOI: 10.1109/CCPIS59145.2023.10291594

Singh, A. K., Singh, R., & Singh, S. (2024). A review on factors affecting and performance of nutritional security of women and children in India. In *Impact of Women in Food and Agricultural Development*. IGI Global., DOI: 10.4018/979-8-3693-3037-1.ch019

Singh, K. U., Chaudhary, V., Sharma, P. K., Kumar, P., Varshney, N., & Singh, T. (2024). Integrating GPS and GSM Technologies for Enhanced Women's Safety: A Fingerprint-Activated Device Approach. *2024 International Conference on Automation and Computation, AUTOCOM 2024*, 657 – 662. DOI: 10.1109/AUTOCOM60220.2024.10486120

Singh, P., & Singh, K. D. (2023). Fog-Centric Intelligent Surveillance System: A Novel Approach for Effective and Efficient Surveillance. In K. R., K. R., G. M., G. M., S. R., & S. R. (Eds.), *2023 International Conference on Advancement in Computation and Computer Technologies, InCACCT 2023* (pp. 762–766). Institute of Electrical and Electronics Engineers Inc. DOI: 10.1109/InCACCT57535.2023.10141802

Srivastava, B., Kandpal, V., & Jain, A. K. (2024). Financial well-being of women self-help group members: A qualitative study. *Environment, Development and Sustainability*. Advance online publication. DOI: 10.1007/s10668-024-04879-w

Taneja, S., Gupta, M., Bhushan, P., Bhatnagar, M., & Singh, A. (2023). Cultural marketing in the digital era. In *Cultural Marketing and Metaverse for Consumer Engagement*. IGI Global., DOI: 10.4018/978-1-6684-8312-1.ch008

Taneja, S., & Özen, E. (2023). To analyse the relationship between bank's green financing and environmental performance. *International Journal of Electronic Finance*, 12(2), 163–175. DOI: 10.1504/IJEF.2023.129919

Taneja, S., & Sharma, V. (2023). Role of beaconing marketing in improving customer buying experience. In *Enhancing Customer Engagement Through Location-Based Marketing*. IGI Global., DOI: 10.4018/978-1-6684-8177-6.ch012

Tripathi, V. M., & Mohan, A. (2016). Microfinance and empowering rural women in the Terai, Uttarakhand, India. *International Journal of Agricultural and Statistics Sciences*, 12(2), 523–530.

Zhang, Y., Cao, C., Gu, J., & Garg, H. (2023). The Impact of Top Management Team Characteristics on the Risk Taking of Chinese Private Construction Enterprises. *Systems*, 11(2), 67. Advance online publication. DOI: 10.3390/systems11020067

Chapter 5
Escalating Artificial Intelligence–Enabled Clinical Decision Support Systems to Enhance Home–Based Care:
A Study on Healthcare Supply Chains

Manu Sharna
Graphic Era University, India

Priyanka Gupta
Graphic Era University, India

Janmejai Shah
Graphic Era University, India

Sudhanshu Joshi
https://orcid.org/0000-0003-4748-5001
Doon University, India

ABSTRACT

Artificial intelligence is rapidly advancing to replace human-based approaches in Clinical Decision Support Systems (CDSS), which has caused a revolution in the home-based care sector. CDSS provides instant diagnostic and therapeutic suggestions, hence improving the communication and gap between the medical professionals and patients in hard-to-reach areas. This review paper looks into how healthcare supply chains can be optimised through AI, in addition to monitoring the availability of inventory and medical products and predicting what a patient might need. Moreover, the investigation assesses the effectiveness of such systems in the overall consideration of the issue—cost containment and patients' outcomes, especially in chronic illness treatment. The study fits directly to SDGs 3, 9, and 10 since it aims to eliminate health disparities by proactively endorsing home-based healthcare services. This paper gives recommendations to healthcare organisations and government entities, mainly in prospecting how AI would reshape home-based care.

DOI: 10.4018/979-8-3373-0240-9.ch005

1. INTRODUCTION

Healthcare supply chains are the most quintessential requirement across the world (Gupta et al., 2023). This industry has relied a Just-in-Time (JIT) distribution model for more than a decade, but was unable to manage demands during the COVID-19 spread (Bhakat and Arif, 2021). The insufficient medical supplies and drugs during the COVID-19 had led this industry to shore up the new urgency which consequently stressed upon the healthcare supply chain (Zamiela et al., 2022). The pandemic has led health impacts and caused negative psychological, social, political, and financial impacts. To mitigate these impacts needs a robust health supply chain encompassing drugs, medical equipment like personal protective equipment (PPE), diagnostic and testing devices and other ancillary supplies (Manero et al., 2020). The impact of COVID-19 has no doubt impacted the industry to develop resilient supply chains. Moreover, the uncertain environment needs healthcare supply chains to become more flexible to deal with the volatility of the environment (Araujo et al., 2023). Healthcare supply chains are facing pressure to reduce costs due to changes in client demands, digital commerce, and increased competition. However, recent disruptions such as manufacturer consolidation, natural disasters, and political and economic upheaval make it challenging to achieve cost efficiency in the healthcare supply chain (Bhakoo and Choi, 2013). Integrated delivery networks (IDNs) are compelled by disruption to respond quickly to backorders and recalls of critical medical supplies (Cortes, 2022). This raises the overall cost of serving the healthcare supply chain, which already accounts for 37.3% of the total cost of patient care on average. The healthcare supply chain needs to make longer-term investments in profitable solutions that ensure company continuity in order to thrive in the face of disruption (Bialas et al., 2023).

Artificial intelligence (AI) technologies are transforming the supply chains to improvise the existing processes and thus steadily implementing in healthcare for enhancing the number of benefits to the stakeholder (Duan et al., 2019; Agarwal and Narain, 2023). AI in healthcare has potential to assist healthcare providers in numerous aspects including the patient care and administrative processes, help them in transforming the existing systems and overcoming the challenges quickly (Mansour and Sharour, 2021; Garg et al., 2023). With AI, huge data of population from wearables and implant can enhance understanding of human biology, clinical trials, personalized and real-time treatment etc. The efficiency of care delivery may be improved through AI solutions and also day-to-day life of healthcare practitioners supporting them to spend more time looking after patients. AI may offer life-saving treatments to market hastily and can improvise patient-care, health system logistics processes, and the ability to diagnose disease that consequently support transformation of hospital-based to home-based care (Modgil et al., 2022).

The dynamics of AI growth is shifting. Asia has the fastest growing trend in healthcare, especially China. Ping An's Good Doctor (healthcare service platform) have more than 300 million users (Wong et al., 2024). Moreover, due to increasing number of infections and diseases spread more advance AI technologies such as remote monitoring, AI-powered alerting systems, etc. for supporting the shift from hospital-based to home-based care (Motwani et al., 2022). Previous studies have conducted research on patient engagement, attitude measurement and other patient related factors, but how CDSS are driving the patient's perceived attitude, satisfaction and intention to avail clinical decision support are very limited (Jacob, 2023; Mathkor et al., 2024). Also, how the perceived privacy concern influences the intention and behavior of the patients will be measured (Zhang et al., 2022). Therefore, this study has made an attempt in to assess the CDST for better patient engagement and consequently influencing the patient's behavior. To address this gap, the following objectives are established

AI is currently on the top-of-mind in healthcare supply chain stakeholders (Kumar et al., 2023). In the initial phase of AI in healthcare, especially the focus needs to be on personalization availability and looking for more ways to reach mass population (Bag et al., 2023). The AI solutions including remote monitoring, alerting systems, or digital assistants, and AI enabled wearables etc. through which the patients may take their own care have been offered by the healthcare supply chains (Sharma et al., 2022). These technologies are required to be embedded widely in clinical workflows which is possible through the engagement of professional bodies and healthcare service providers (Laka et al., 2022). AI might minimize the time spent on routine, administrative tasks, that contributes 70 percent of a healthcare practitioner's time. This time can be used to access information and lead to better patient results and improve quality of care (Topel, 2019). It can also improve the efficiency of diagnostics, easy access to knowledge, remote monitoring and patient empowerment through self-care.

The main objectives of this chapter are as follows:

RO1: To examine the contribution of AI-Enabled CDSS) in enhancing the patient's home-based care

RO2: Identifying the key themes/ potential research areas in AI-CDSS for optimising the healthcare supply chains.

2. LITERATURE REVIEW

Previous research indicates that in order to respond to high levels of uncertainty, healthcare organisations need to improve their information processing capabilities through volume, variety, and velocity of data (Yu et al., 2021; Wang et al., 2018a, 2019). This will help them manage patients, information, and material flows more effectively (de Vries and Huijsman, 2011; Drupsteen et al., 2013). Nevertheless, little study has been done to date on how healthcare institutions might benefit from big data analytics and artificial intelligence. This study, which draws on information processing theory, attempts to comprehend how hospitals might use big data analytics and artificial intelligence capabilities to create robust supply chains that can withstand an unpredictable and disruptive environment (Srinivasan and Swink, 2018).

Clinical decision support tools (CDST) are tools that provide information to the clinicians, patients, and other members of the healthcare service providers which is filtered or targeted to a specific person or situation (Fox et al., 2010). Patients demand more control over their health as we enter a new era of healthcare, and they have the right to access and manage their medical data and health information (Rathert et al., 2017). Patients can comprehend their health conditions and make educated decisions about their care when they use patient engagement technology that enables them and their care to function inclusively in their self-care approach (Dey et al., 2024). The future of healthcare depends on breakthrough digital health technology connected with healthcare, that is focused on networking with patients beyond hospital and healthcare institution settings (Awad et al., 2021). Home based healthcare is actually an idea and practice of offering healthcare services in the comfort of the patient's home (Lindahl et al., 2011). Due to improvised healthcare systems, life expectancy has risen, consequently complementing the quality healthcare services. There is a rise in the number of senior citizens, and thus the idea is to bring healthcare services the patient's homes in place of carrying them to the hospitals (Rosen et al., 2021).

Based on the literature review AI driven clinical decision support tools enhancing patient engagement technology and care delivery includes remote patient monitoring devices, health data and health management services, facilitating better healthcare delivery solutions (Praet et al., 2024). The AI driven wearables such as weight scales, glucometers, smart devices that gather patient data outside of the healthcare setting, incorporating surveys for follow ups, remote data monitoring, Video visits, multi-party conferencing capability, educational videos, self-management coaching through health management platforms, personalized patient experiences, incorporating robotic procedures and augmented reality, Seamless omnichannel experience for patients, offering accurate information to empower patients are all examples of CDST (Yu et al., 2024).

Healthcare spending is simply not keeping up. There are several challenges in post pandemic era which needs the scaling up of AI in healthcare. Firstly, to remain sustainable in the post pandemic situation, and if there is no structural or transformational change, healthcare systems probably struggle (Henrique et al., 2021). Second, the need for a more substantial labor force. In the healthcare sector, the global economy has the potential to generate 40 million new employment by 2030; nevertheless, a shortage of 9.9 million healthcare workers is still expected (World Health Organisation, WHO, 2020). More healthcare professionals must be recruited, trained, and retained, but in order to maximise their time and provide greater value to patients, it is also imperative that this time be controlled (Lehmann et al., 2008). The clinical proof of efficacy and quality comes last. Healthcare professionals need evidence that every new innovation would "do no harm" before allowing it to be near a patient, even as more companies are popping up and growing solutions quickly (Webster, 2021).

2.1 Healthcare Supply Chains and Sustainable Development Goals

SDG 3 (Good Health and Well-Being) and healthcare supply chains are closely related since they guarantee the timely delivery and accessibility of necessary medications, vaccines, and medical supplies (Chiu and Fong, 2023). Because they guarantee that healthcare professionals have the resources needed to treat patients and prevent diseases, efficient supply chains are essential to the operation of healthcare systems. Healthcare supply chains provide access to high-quality healthcare services by cutting down on delays and waste, which improves overall health outcomes and supports universal health coverage (Dixit et al., 2022). Resilient supply chains are essential for facilitating a quick reaction in emergency scenarios, such as pandemics or natural catastrophes (Munir et al., 2022). This ensures that key supplies reach affected populations promptly, eventually saving lives and averting disease outbreaks.

Healthcare supply chains are also directly related to SDGs 10 (Reduced Inequalities) and SDG 9 (Industry, Innovation, and Infrastructure) (Leal Filho et al., 2023). Advancements in logistics, such blockchain, artificial intelligence, and digital tracking systems, enhance the efficacy and transparency of supply chains, hence constructing robust healthcare infrastructures that are more resilient to shocks and emergencies. Furthermore, healthcare supply chains contribute to the reduction of disparities (SDG 10) by guaranteeing the equitable provision of medical goods to underserved areas and giving marginalized groups access to the same calibre of care as urban or wealthy regions (Dau et al., 2019). In light of this, they are essential in minimizing differences in healthcare outcomes and access amongst various socioeconomic and geographic groups (Magesh et al., 2021). The Challenges in Healthcare Supply Chain Management are shown in Figure 1.

Figure 1. Challenges in healthcare supply chain management

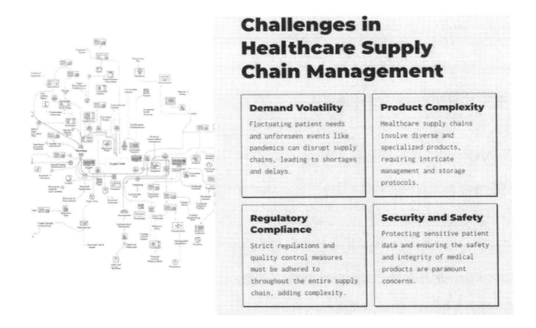

3. THEMATIC ANALYSIS

This meta-review unveiled based on the SCOPUS database also proved the fact that the AI-supported CDSS is ready to transform home-based healthcare, particularly in the aspects of supply chain management and efficient patient's care. The literature is, therefore, quite compelling in showing that IT, and in particular AI, can help to address the notorious shortfall of human healthcare professionals most dramatically in such locations while at the same time making the supply side of healthcare significantly more sensitive to demand (Naim and Khan, 2024). However, there are some limitations continuing to be witnessed with regard to data security and ethical issues, acceptance by various stakeholders and others that can be sorted to fully harness on the opportunities presented by AI-CDSS in the health care sector. To this meta-review, we have provided a narrative review on its implications for improving both operational and clinical lines of home-based healthcare services in the post-COVID-19 era with lessons for healthcare administrators, policymakers, and researchers on how to implement AI-based technologies for a future-ready home-based healthcare ecosystem. On the basis of Scopus databases, the following themes have been identified –

a) ***AI in Clinical Decision Support Systems (CDSS)***

Much literature has stressed on the leadership of AI in CDSS, with machine learning & deep learning algorithms applied within the framework of prognosis & treatment advice (Berge et al., 2023). The multiple reviews show that this system named as AI-CDSS enhances diagnostic accuracy, decision-making and enables the medical professionals to offer health care from a distance (Wang et al., 2021). This is especially important for home-based care because patients in remote areas with limited access to doctors will be able to get quality advice on what medical treatments to seek.

b) *Optimizing Healthcare Supply Chains:*

The literature points to the blessings of AI in improving healthcare supply chain management. AI is applied to products for decision-making around stock and inventory, demand planning, and the provisioning of essential and vital medical inventory at the right place at the right time (Yadav, 2022). Other utilization of predictive models is in the management of patients' status, in an effort that seeks to predict potential future needs of patients in terms of health and the supply chain organization (Abedi et al., 2023). Such alignment enhances the efficiency of the total system as well as minimizes wastage as observed from different SCM researches relating to the use of healthcare industry.

C) *Impact on Chronic Disease Management:*

Many papers highlight that AI-CDSS is instrumental as a tool in the control of chronic diseases, which FSHP cares about as the majority of its activities goes to home care (Govindan et al., 2020). Looking at a patient through AI they can easily intervene, alleviate their pain, control their condition, or adjust their treatment as it is being prescribed. Several meta-analyses regarding Scopus support the utility of AI-CDSS in decreasing the rate of patients' readmissions to a hospital, and increasing patients' long-term positive outcomes (Niu et al., 2024).

D) Cost Efficiency and Sustainability:

Another trend that emerged in the literature is that AI in healthcare supply chains creates savings and value. Research shows that AI leads to cost saving through rationalization of operations, minimizing on human mistakes, and optimization of resources (Javaid et al., 2022). Furthermore, with AI-integrated CDSS there are no issues with overstocking or understocking on crucial medical products. In these researches, the authors claim that, the average of 10-15% relative savings of operating costs in healthcare organizations that implement AI-based solutions (Sahni et al., 2023).

E) Stakeholder Perceptions and Challenges

While using the work AI-CDSS applied to IDC, several limitations are identified: As earlier said, AI-CDSS exhibits tremendous potential for improving patient care. Some of the things explored in several reviews include; the resistance of healthcare professionals owing to the fear that was created by the belief that AI has the capability of replacing human discretion, data privacy, and data security (Murphy et al., 2021). The patient reception to the utilization of AI interventions from home care patient stakeholders also shows positive reception. But technological accessibility and the digital divide are also frequently discussed in Scopus indexed qualitative research papers. The themes are presented in the following Figure 2.

Figure 2. Thematic presentation

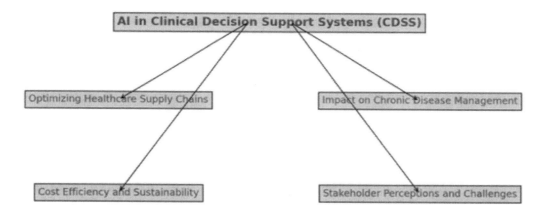

4. IMPLICATIONS

The implications of this study mean that greater and improved use of AI-CDSS in home-based care programmes can potentially enhance the delivery and effectiveness of healthcare services through efficiency, affordability and flexibility, as well as creating better patient satisfaction, solutions for healthcare providers and satisfactory supply chain for all stakeholders. However, to fully capture all the above benefits, there is need to observe technological, ethical and policy concerns to near proportions.

i) *Improved Access to Healthcare in Remote Areas*

Clinical Decision Support System (CDSS) with artificial intelligence support optimizes and provides practical diagnostic and treatment solutions in real time patient care which plays a major role in expanding the great hurdle of healthcare services to the needy especially those in the rural or difficult to reach areas (Amann et al., 2022). Home care maybe made even more feasible since the healthcare professional can observe the patients' status and the need for intervention without needing physical contact. Such democratization of healthcare access could potentially eliminate existing health inequalities especially in combating the scourge in health hard-to-reach areas (Xu et al., 2020).

ii) *Optimized Healthcare Supply Chains*

The implementation of AI into the different supply chain processes of the healthcare industry results to better functions. Healthcare providers can also use predictive analytics to automate the ordering of products, to identify likely consumerism and patient requirements (Ash et al., 2022). The modern approach of supply chain management's real-time optimization mitigates medical supplies wastage, the associated costs of overstocking or shortages, and guarantees that valuable materials are delivered on time for home-based care. Hospitals and home-care providers enjoy logistical optimization to supply proper equipment and medicines in the right place at the right time (Roy and Mitra, 2021).

iii) *Enhanced Patient Outcomes in Chronic Disease Management*

The use of AI to drive an improved CDSS for chronic disease management in home-based care could significantly change the nature of practice. The steady tracking and immediate data processing contribute to the optimization of regular and targeted health care treatments that should possess a more positive effect in the long run. AI-CDSS assists patients with chronic diseases get better control of their symptoms, lower hospital reuse rates, and receive better individualized care plans (Durga, 2024). This also supports moving to more preventative care and increasing quality of life while decreasing overall cost of healthcare.

iv) Cost Containment and Healthcare Sustainability: The analysis shows that AI's characteristics that allow improving resource efficiency have substantial economic consequences. Through errors minimization, integration of the supply chain, and proper inventory control, we can easily have considerable cost savings. The use of AI-CDSS also helps in optimizing resource utilization, due to the fact that real human work force is then freed up to work on only the more critical patients instead of having to spend precious time entering the details of case histories into a computer or checking hundreds of patient files day by day (Ji et al., 2021).

v) *Technological and Ethical Considerations*

A number of ethical and technological issues arise in the light of increased implementation of AI-CDSS. However, with the adoption of such advanced technology, there are risks of compromise of the data to privacy and security, plus general depersonalization of the patients (Luxton, 2014). Further, healthcare organizations have to ensure appropriate safeguards for data protection and some bias of the AI algorithms to regain patients' trust (Karimian et al., 2022). Thirdly, healthcare organizations need to think about the societal impact of AI implementation and how that will not worsen the digital divide for individuals with lower incomes, or living in the rural areas (Kumar et al., 2023).

vi) Policy and Regulatory Frameworks

Policy-makers and regulatory agencies should therefore begin to fashion out the regulatory framework that would be necessary for use of AI in the health care delivery system in the areas such as data protection and security, allocation of responsibility where an AI driven decision leads to a wrong decision and patient choice (Morley et al., 2022). More so, there is a consensus unknown that requires for the formulation of integration practices that outline how the AI-CDSS should be implemented in the healthcare supply chain and/or home-based care services (Gogia, 2019). All these frameworks will be vital in advancing the trustworthy use of the AI so that its benefits can reach all stakeholders while parrying risks.

vii) *Empowering Healthcare Workers*

AI-CDSS holds the capability of complementing health care personnel instead of replacing them since it provides decision support, can perform repetitive tasks and frees up the personnel for more quality focused tasks (Dingel et al., 2024). More to healthcare workers especially those in home-caring services; such a technological enhancement can help alleviate stress related burnout, efficiency and work satisfaction. Education of healthcare employees for use of AI technologies will be crucial in realizing all these advantages.

5. CONCLUSIONS

The integration of AI into Clinical Decision Support Systems (CDSSs) presents a significant opportunity to enhance end-of-life home care and healthcare supply chain management (Tang, 2020). CDSS, augmented by artificial intelligence, addresses numerous pressing challenges in healthcare: enhancing access for rural populations, streamlining chronic disease management, and improving the storage and distribution of pharmaceuticals (Durga, 2024). AI facilitates inpatient diagnostic and therapeutic insights, enabling healthcare practitioners to deliver value-based treatment to patients through home devices, thereby bridging the communication gap between clinicians and patients (Aminabee, 2024).

The implementation of the A3 technique to enhance the supply chain using AI technology improves the punctual delivery of medical supplies, reduces costs, and boosts efficiency, which is essential for the sustainability of healthcare amid the rising trend of home care (Belhadi et al., 2022). These improvements not only improve patients' conditions, particularly in chronic illnesses, but also pave the path for a new, more efficient, and cost-effective healthcare model. Nonetheless, the deployment of the AI-CDSS entails various technological, ethical, and regulatory ramifications, which encompass the following. These issues are essential to the impact of these systems on individuals' rights to privacy, protection from algorithmic discrimination, and future accessibility (Ji et al., 2021). It is essential to develop effective AI reference models that facilitate the appropriate use of knowledge in healthcare.

In summary, AI-CDSS presents significant potential for transforming home-based care by delivering more responsive, efficient, and patient-centered care solutions. The application of this technology will enable the healthcare industry to achieve significant advancements in care delivery, cost reduction, and supply chain management, while greatly improving patient welfare.

REFERENCES

Abedi, S., Kwon, S., & Yoon, S. W. (2023). Healthcare and Pharmaceutical Supply Chain Automation. In *Springer Handbook of Automation* (pp. 1289–1308). Springer International Publishing. DOI: 10.1007/978-3-030-96729-1_60

Agrawal, P., & Narain, R. (2023). Analysis of enablers for the digitalization of supply chain using an interpretive structural modelling approach. *International Journal of Productivity and Performance Management*, 72(2), 410–439. DOI: 10.1108/IJPPM-09-2020-0481

Amann, J., Vetter, D., Blomberg, S. N., Christensen, H. C., Coffee, M., Gerke, S., Gilbert, T. K., Hagendorff, T., Holm, S., Livne, M., Spezzatti, A., Strümke, I., Zicari, R. V., & Madai, V. I. (2022). To explain or not to explain?—Artificial intelligence explainability in clinical decision support systems. *PLOS Digital Health*, 1(2), e0000016. DOI: 10.1371/journal.pdig.0000016 PMID: 36812545

Aminabee, S. (2024). The future of healthcare and patient-centric care: Digital innovations, trends, and predictions. In *Emerging Technologies for Health Literacy and Medical Practice* (pp. 240–262). IGI Global. DOI: 10.4018/979-8-3693-1214-8.ch012

Araujo, R., Fernandes, J. M., Reis, L. P., & Beaulieu, M. (2023). Purchasing challenges in times of COVID-19: Resilience practices to mitigate disruptions in the health-care supply chain. *Journal of Global Operations and Strategic Sourcing*, 16(2), 368–396. DOI: 10.1108/JGOSS-04-2022-0026

Ash, C., Diallo, C., Venkatadri, U., & VanBerkel, P. (2022). Distributionally robust optimization of a Canadian healthcare supply chain to enhance resilience during the COVID-19 pandemic. *Computers & Industrial Engineering*, 168, 108051. DOI: 10.1016/j.cie.2022.108051 PMID: 35250153

Awad, A., Trenfield, S. J., Pollard, T. D., Ong, J. J., Elbadawi, M., McCoubrey, L. E., Goyanes, A., Gaisford, S., & Basit, A. W. (2021). Connected healthcare: Improving patient care using digital health technologies. *Advanced Drug Delivery Reviews*, 178, 113958. DOI: 10.1016/j.addr.2021.113958 PMID: 34478781

Bag, S., Dhamija, P., Singh, R. K., Rahman, M. S., & Sreedharan, V. R. (2023). Big data analytics and artificial intelligence technologies based collaborative platform empowering absorptive capacity in health care supply chain: An empirical study. *Journal of Business Research*, 154, 113315. DOI: 10.1016/j.jbusres.2022.113315

Berge, G. T., Granmo, O. C., Tveit, T. O., Munkvold, B. E., Ruthjersen, A. L., & Sharma, J. (2023). Machine learning-driven clinical decision support system for concept-based searching: A field trial in a Norwegian hospital. *BMC Medical Informatics and Decision Making*, 23(1), 5. DOI: 10.1186/s12911-023-02101-x PMID: 36627624

Bhakat, R. S., & Arif, M. Z. U. (2021). Challenges faced and preparedness of FMCG retail supply chain during COVID-19. In *Managing Supply Chain Risk and Disruptions: Post COVID-19* (pp. 19–27). Springer International Publishing. DOI: 10.1007/978-3-030-72575-4_2

Bhakoo, V., & Choi, T. (2013). The iron cage exposed: Institutional pressures and heterogeneity across the healthcare supply chain. *Journal of Operations Management*, 31(6), 432–449. DOI: 10.1016/j.jom.2013.07.016

Bialas, C., Bechtsis, D., Aivazidou, E., Achillas, C., & Aidonis, D. (2023). A holistic view on the adoption and cost-effectiveness of technology-driven supply chain management practices in healthcare. *Sustainability (Basel)*, 15(6), 5541. DOI: 10.3390/su15065541

Chiu, W. K., & Fong, B. Y. F. (2023). Sustainable Development Goal 3 in Healthcare. In *Environmental, social and governance and sustainable development in healthcare* (pp. 33–45). Springer Nature Singapore. DOI: 10.1007/978-981-99-1564-4_3

Cortés, J. E. R. (2022). Analysis and design of security mechanisms in the context of Advanced Persistent Threats against critical infrastructures. *Unpublished Ph. D. thesis, University of Malaga, Spain*.

Daú, G., Scavarda, A., Scavarda, L. F., & Portugal, V. J. T. (2019). The healthcare sustainable supply chain 4.0: The circular economy transition conceptual framework with the corporate social responsibility mirror. *Sustainability (Basel)*, 11(12), 3259. DOI: 10.3390/su11123259

De Vries, J., & Huijsman, R. (2011). Supply chain management in health services: An overview. *Supply Chain Management*, 16(3), 159–165. DOI: 10.1108/13598541111127146

Dey, P. K., Chowdhury, S., Abadie, A., Vann Yaroson, E., & Sarkar, S. (2024). Artificial intelligence-driven supply chain resilience in Vietnamese manufacturing small-and medium-sized enterprises. *International Journal of Production Research*, 62(15), 5417–5456. DOI: 10.1080/00207543.2023.2179859

Dingel, J., Kleine, A. K., Cecil, J., Sigl, A. L., Lermer, E., & Gaube, S. (2024). Predictors of Health Care Practitioners' Intention to Use AI-Enabled Clinical Decision Support Systems: Meta-Analysis Based on the Unified Theory of Acceptance and Use of Technology. *Journal of Medical Internet Research*, 26, e57224. DOI: 10.2196/57224 PMID: 39102675

Dixit, A., Routroy, S., & Dubey, S. K. (2022). Analyzing the operational barriers of government-supported healthcare supply chain. *International Journal of Productivity and Performance Management*, 71(8), 3766–3791. DOI: 10.1108/IJPPM-09-2020-0493

Drupsteen, J., van der Vaart, T., & Pieter van Donk, D. (2013). Integrative practices in hospitals and their impact on patient flow. *International Journal of Operations & Production Management*, 33(7), 912–933. DOI: 10.1108/IJOPM-12-2011-0487

Duan, Y., Edwards, J. S., & Dwivedi, Y. K. (2019). Artificial intelligence for decision making in the era of Big Data–evolution, challenges and research agenda. *International Journal of Information Management*, 48, 63–71. DOI: 10.1016/j.ijinfomgt.2019.01.021

Durga, K. (2024). Intelligent Support for Cardiovascular Diagnosis: The AI-CDSS Approach. In *Using Traditional Design Methods to Enhance AI-Driven Decision Making* (pp. 64-76). IGI Global.

Fox, J., Glasspool, D., Patkar, V., Austin, M., Black, L., South, M., Robertson, D., & Vincent, C. (2010). Delivering clinical decision support services: There is nothing as practical as a good theory. *Journal of Biomedical Informatics*, 43(5), 831–843. DOI: 10.1016/j.jbi.2010.06.002 PMID: 20601124

Garg, P., Gupta, N., & Agarwal, M. (2023). Role of Artificial Intelligence in Supply Chain Management. In *Data Analytics and Business Intelligence* (pp. 47–61). CRC Press. DOI: 10.1201/9781003189640-5

Gogia, S. (Ed.). (2019). *Fundamentals of telemedicine and telehealth*. Academic Press.

Govindan, K., Mina, H., & Alavi, B. (2020). A decision support system for demand management in healthcare supply chains considering the epidemic outbreaks: A case study of coronavirus disease 2019 (COVID-19). *Transportation Research Part E, Logistics and Transportation Review*, 138, 101967. DOI: 10.1016/j.tre.2020.101967 PMID: 32382249

Gupta, S., Modgil, S., Bhatt, P. C., Jabbour, C. J. C., & Kamble, S. (2023). Quantum computing led innovation for achieving a more sustainable Covid-19 healthcare industry. *Technovation*, 120, 102544. DOI: 10.1016/j.technovation.2022.102544

Henrique, K. P., & Tschakert, P. (2021). Pathways to urban transformation: From dispossession to climate justice. *Progress in Human Geography*, 45(5), 1169–1191. DOI: 10.1177/0309132520962856

Jacob, L., Thomas, K. T., & Shukla, S. (2023). Potential Applications of AI and IoT Collaborative Framework for Health Care. *The Role of AI. IoT and Blockchain in Mitigating the Impact of COVID*, 19, 69.

Javaid, M., Haleem, A., Singh, R. P., & Suman, R. (2022). Artificial intelligence applications for industry 4.0: A literature-based study. *Journal of Industrial Integration and Management*, 7(01), 83–111. DOI: 10.1142/S2424862221300040

Ji, M., Chen, X., Genchev, G. Z., Wei, M., & Yu, G. (2021). Status of AI-enabled clinical decision support systems implementations in China. *Methods of Information in Medicine, 60*(05/06), 123-132.

Ji, M., Chen, X., Genchev, G. Z., Wei, M., & Yu, G. (2021). Status of AI-enabled clinical decision support systems implementations in China. *Methods of Information in Medicine, 60*(05/06), 123-132.

Karimian, G., Petelos, E., & Evers, S. M. (2022). The ethical issues of the application of artificial intelligence in healthcare: A systematic scoping review. *AI and Ethics*, 2(4), 539–551. DOI: 10.1007/s43681-021-00131-7

Kumar, A., Mani, V., Jain, V., Gupta, H., & Venkatesh, V. G. (2023). Managing healthcare supply chain through artificial intelligence (AI): A study of critical success factors. *Computers & Industrial Engineering*, 175, 108815. DOI: 10.1016/j.cie.2022.108815 PMID: 36405396

Kumar, A., Mani, V., Jain, V., Gupta, H., & Venkatesh, V. G. (2023). Managing healthcare supply chain through artificial intelligence (AI): A study of critical success factors. *Computers & Industrial Engineering*, 175, 108815. DOI: 10.1016/j.cie.2022.108815 PMID: 36405396

Laka, M., Carter, D., Milazzo, A., & Merlin, T. (2022). Challenges and opportunities in implementing clinical decision support systems (CDSS) at scale: Interviews with Australian policymakers. *Health Policy and Technology*, 11(3), 100652. DOI: 10.1016/j.hlpt.2022.100652

Leal Filho, W., Trevisan, L. V., Eustachio, J. H. P. P., Dibbern, T., Apraiz, J. C., Rampasso, I., ... & Lambrechts, W. (2023). Sustainable supply chain management and the UN sustainable development goals: Exploring synergies towards sustainable development. *The TQM journal*, (ahead-of-print).

Lehmann, U., Dieleman, M., & Martineau, T. (2008). Staffing remote rural areas in middle-and low-income countries: A literature review of attraction and retention. *BMC Health Services Research*, 8(1), 1–10. DOI: 10.1186/1472-6963-8-19 PMID: 18215313

Lindahl, B., Lidén, E., & Lindblad, B. M. (2011). A meta-synthesis describing the relationships between patients, informal caregivers and health professionals in home-care settings. *Journal of Clinical Nursing*, 20(3-4), 454–463. DOI: 10.1111/j.1365-2702.2009.03008.x PMID: 20412357

Luxton, D. D. (2014). Recommendations for the ethical use and design of artificial intelligent care providers. *Artificial Intelligence in Medicine*, 62(1), 1–10. DOI: 10.1016/j.artmed.2014.06.004 PMID: 25059820

Magesh, S., John, D., Li, W. T., Li, Y., Mattingly-App, A., Jain, S., Chang, E. Y., & Ongkeko, W. M. (2021). Disparities in COVID-19 outcomes by race, ethnicity, and socioeconomic status: A systematic review and meta-analysis. *JAMA Network Open*, 4(11), e2134147–e2134147. DOI: 10.1001/jamanetworkopen.2021.34147 PMID: 34762110

Manero, A., Smith, P., Koontz, A., Dombrowski, M., Sparkman, J., Courbin, D., & Chi, A. (2020). Leveraging 3D printing capacity in times of crisis: Recommendations for COVID-19 distributed manufacturing for medical equipment rapid response. *International Journal of Environmental Research and Public Health*, 17(13), 4634. DOI: 10.3390/ijerph17134634 PMID: 32605098

Mansour, H., & Sharour, L. A. (2021). Results of survey on perception of patient safety culture among emergency nurses in Jordan: Influence of burnout, job satisfaction, turnover intention, and workload. *Journal of Healthcare Quality Research*, 36(6), 370–377. DOI: 10.1016/j.jhqr.2021.05.001 PMID: 34187762

Mathkor, D. M., Mathkor, N., Bassfar, Z., Bantun, F., Slama, P., Ahmad, F., & Haque, S. (2024). Multirole of the internet of medical things (IoMT) in biomedical systems for managing smart healthcare systems: An overview of current and future innovative trends. *Journal of Infection and Public Health*, 17(4), 559–572. DOI: 10.1016/j.jiph.2024.01.013 PMID: 38367570

Modgil, S., Gupta, S., Stekelorum, R., & Laguir, I. (2022). AI technologies and their impact on supply chain resilience during COVID-19. *International Journal of Physical Distribution & Logistics Management*, 52(2), 130–149. DOI: 10.1108/IJPDLM-12-2020-0434

Morley, J., Murphy, L., Mishra, A., Joshi, I., & Karpathakis, K. (2022). Governing data and artificial intelligence for health care: Developing an international understanding. *JMIR Formative Research*, 6(1), e31623. DOI: 10.2196/31623 PMID: 35099403

Motwani, A., Shukla, P. K., & Pawar, M. (2022). Ubiquitous and smart healthcare monitoring frameworks based on machine learning: A comprehensive review. *Artificial Intelligence in Medicine*, 134, 102431. DOI: 10.1016/j.artmed.2022.102431 PMID: 36462891

Munir, M., Jajja, M. S. S., & Chatha, K. A. (2022). Capabilities for enhancing supply chain resilience and responsiveness in the COVID-19 pandemic: Exploring the role of improvisation, anticipation, and data analytics capabilities. *International Journal of Operations & Production Management*, 42(10), 1576–1604. DOI: 10.1108/IJOPM-11-2021-0677

Murphy, K., Di Ruggiero, E., Upshur, R., Willison, D. J., Malhotra, N., Cai, J. C., Malhotra, N., Lui, V., & Gibson, J. (2021). Artificial intelligence for good health: A scoping review of the ethics literature. *BMC Medical Ethics*, 22(1), 1–17. DOI: 10.1186/s12910-021-00577-8 PMID: 33588803

Naim, A., & Khan, F. (2024). The utilization of AI in advancing green supply chain management focusing healthcare sector in Saudi Arabia. *Journal of Information and Optimization Sciences*, 45(3), 747–763. DOI: 10.47974/JIOS-1510

Niu, S., Ma, J., Yin, Q., Wang, Z., Bai, L., & Yang, X. (2024). Modelling Patient Longitudinal Data for Clinical Decision Support: A Case Study on Emerging AI Healthcare Technologies. *Information Systems Frontiers*, ●●●, 1–19. DOI: 10.1007/s10796-024-10513-x

Praet, J., Anderhalten, L., Comi, G., Horakova, D., Ziemssen, T., Vermersch, P., Lukas, C., van Leemput, K., Steppe, M., Aguilera, C., Kadas, E. M., Bertrand, A., van Rampelbergh, J., de Boer, E., Zingler, V., Smeets, D., Ribbens, A., & Paul, F. (2024). A future of AI-driven personalized care for people with multiple sclerosis. *Frontiers in Immunology*, 15, 1446748. DOI: 10.3389/fimmu.2024.1446748 PMID: 39224590

Rathert, C., Mittler, J. N., Banerjee, S., & McDaniel, J. (2017). Patient-centered communication in the era of electronic health records: What does the evidence say? *Patient Education and Counseling*, 100(1), 50–64. DOI: 10.1016/j.pec.2016.07.031 PMID: 27477917

Rosen, J. M., Adams, L. V., Geiling, J., Curtis, K. M., Mosher, R. E., Ball, P. A., Grigg, E. B., Hebert, K. A., Grodan, J. R., Jurmain, J. C., Loucks, C., Macedonia, C. R., & Kun, L. (2021). Telehealth's new horizon: Providing smart hospital-level care in the home. *Telemedicine Journal and e-Health*, 27(11), 1215–1224. DOI: 10.1089/tmj.2020.0448 PMID: 33656918

Roy, S., & Mitra, M. (2021). Enhancing Efficiency in Healthcare Supply Chains: Leveraging Machine Learning for Optimized Operations. *International Journal For Multidisciplinary Research*, 3(2), 10–36948.

Sahni, N., Stein, G., Zemmel, R., & Cutler, D. M. (2023). *The potential impact of artificial intelligence on healthcare spending* (No. w30857). Cambridge, MA, USA: National Bureau of Economic Research.

Sharma, R., Shishodia, A., Gunasekaran, A., Min, H., & Munim, Z. H. (2022). The role of artificial intelligence in supply chain management: Mapping the territory. *International Journal of Production Research*, 60(24), 7527–7550. DOI: 10.1080/00207543.2022.2029611

Srinivasan, R., & Swink, M. (2018). An investigation of visibility and flexibility as complements to supply chain analytics: An organizational information processing theory perspective. *Production and Operations Management*, 27(10), 1849–1867. DOI: 10.1111/poms.12746

Tang, V. (2020). Development of a knowledge-based decision support system for long-term geriatric care management.

Topol, E. J. (2019). High-performance medicine: The convergence of human and artificial intelligence. *Nature Medicine*, 25(1), 44–56. DOI: 10.1038/s41591-018-0300-7 PMID: 30617339

Wang, D., Wang, L., Zhang, Z., Wang, D., Zhu, H., Gao, Y., . . . Tian, F. (2021, May). "Brilliant AI doctor" in rural clinics: Challenges in AI-powered clinical decision support system deployment. In *Proceedings of the 2021 CHI conference on human factors in computing systems* (pp. 1-18).

Wang, Y., Kung, L., & Byrd, T. A. (2018). Big data analytics: Understanding its capabilities and potential benefits for healthcare organizations. *Technological Forecasting and Social Change*, 126, 3–13. DOI: 10.1016/j.techfore.2015.12.019

Webster, M. (2021). *Do No Harm: protecting connected medical devices, healthcare, and data from hackers and adversarial nation states*. John Wiley & Sons.

Wong, L. W., Tan, G. W. H., Ooi, K. B., Lin, B., & Dwivedi, Y. K. (2024). Artificial intelligence-driven risk management for enhancing supply chain agility: A deep-learning-based dual-stage PLS-SEM-ANN analysis. *International Journal of Production Research*, 62(15), 5535–5555. DOI: 10.1080/00207543.2022.2063089

Xu, F., Sepúlveda, M. J., Jiang, Z., Wang, H., Li, J., Liu, Z., Yin, Y., Roebuck, M. C., Shortliffe, E. H., Yan, M., Song, Y., Geng, C., Tang, J., Purcell Jackson, G., Preininger, A. M., & Rhee, K. (2020). Effect of an artificial intelligence clinical decision support system on treatment decisions for complex breast cancer. *JCO Clinical Cancer Informatics*, 4(4), 824–838. DOI: 10.1200/CCI.20.00018 PMID: 32970484

Yadav, V. (2022). AI-Driven Predictive Models for Healthcare Supply Chains: Developing AI Models to Predict and Optimize Healthcare Supply Chains, especially during Global Health Emergencies. Progress in Medical Sciences. PMS-1127. *Prog Med Sci, 6*(1).

Yang, L., Ene, I. C., Arabi Belaghi, R., Koff, D., Stein, N., & Santaguida, P. (2022). Stakeholders' perspectives on the future of artificial intelligence in radiology: A scoping review. *European Radiology*, 32(3), 1477–1495. DOI: 10.1007/s00330-021-08214-z PMID: 34545445

Yu, R., Lee, S., Xie, J., Billah, S. M., & Carroll, J. M. (2024). Human–AI Collaboration for Remote Sighted Assistance: Perspectives from the LLM Era. *Future Internet*, 16(7), 254. DOI: 10.3390/fi16070254

Yu, W., Zhao, G., Liu, Q., & Song, Y. (2021). Role of big data analytics capability in developing integrated hospital supply chains and operational flexibility: An organizational information processing theory perspective. *Technological Forecasting and Social Change*, 163, 120417. DOI: 10.1016/j.techfore.2020.120417

Zamiela, C., Hossain, N. U. I., & Jaradat, R. (2022). Enablers of resilience in the healthcare supply chain: A case study of US healthcare industry during COVID-19 pandemic. *Research in Transportation Economics*, 93, 101174. DOI: 10.1016/j.retrec.2021.101174

Zhang, J., Luximon, Y., & Li, Q. (2022). Seeking medical advice in mobile applications: How social cue design and privacy concerns influence trust and behavioral intention in impersonal patient–physician interactions. *Computers in Human Behavior*, 130, 107178. DOI: 10.1016/j.chb.2021.107178

Chapter 6
Application of Artificial Intelligence in Healthcare Sector:
A Multidimensional Perspective

Anu Sayal
Taylor's University, Malaysia

Ashulekha Gupta
https://orcid.org/0000-0001-5155-6090
Graphic Era University, India

Janhvi Jha
Jain University, India

N. Chaithra
https://orcid.org/0009-0008-0530-8940
Jain University, India

Allagari Nithin
Jain University, India

ABSTRACT

In this paper, we emphasize the recent innovations made in biomedicine and healthcare by applying AI. To better understand real-world applications of AI in the field, we have also included a case study that uses a convolution neural network to detect the presence of malaria in human cells. Numerous types of AI are already being applied in various fields such as cardiology and neurology for detecting cysts and tumors through digital image processing and dermatology for detecting and treating lesions and psoriasis. Moreover, significant evidence indicates its use in genomics and 3D bioprinting, which are both expected to revolutionize treatment. AI has increased the efficiency and reduced the workload of health professionals. There are unquestionably application instances in which AI performs healthcare activities as well as or better than humans. Our studies show that AI is largely restructuring the constitution of human well-being as a whole and is predicted to progress in leaps and bounds.

DOI: 10.4018/979-8-3373-0240-9.ch006

1. INTRODUCTION

Radiology and other fields dealing with chronic disorders like cancer are using AI to create more precise and useful breakthroughs that will help treat patients and, eventually, find a solution. Artificial intelligence (AI) has many advantages over more traditional methods of analysis and clinical decision-making. It's no secret that AI systems improve their accuracy as they learn from new training data (Kirola et al., 2022; Johri et al., 2024). Insight into pharmaceutical variation, patient care, diagnosis, and results were never before possible thanks to this development. AI basically trains the computer or a device and allows machines to work basing the previous data and the given data, and use of it, and this information is used in various tasks like Patient data records, disease analysis, Previous medical history, etc. (*Artificial Intelligence in Healthcare...*, 2022).

Artificial Intelligence has proved to be a boon for the advancement of healthcare in the recent years (Jha et al.; 2023). Virology to neuroscience, cardiovascular surgery to generating sustainable organs, AI can assist with all. Also there has been a vast use of AI in cryogenics that has helped preserve important donor organs throughout all these years. Robotic surgeries and image processing has increased the survival rate of patients undergoing major and complicated operations. Even in optometry, AI controlled robotic surgeries have made LASIK surgery a big success. It is also being used in the field of psychology to generate predictive charts of human behavior, sentimental analysis and more.

AI has not only benefited medicine but also the doctors and users. It has reduced the workload of medical immensely. It also provides more precision in operations than before through the imaging and monitoring. Development of AI sustained healthcare apps has helped people through methods of tele-health, medication tracking, heart monitoring etc. It also helps users save the cost of tedious hospital visits and more. Thought it has a lot advantages, AI comes with its discrepancies. There are several privacy and security risks involved in the use of AI (Singh et al., 2020; Gupta et al.; 2022). Further, the personal touch of doctors has been absent since the rise of AI. It can also often give a false sense of security to patients and lead to fatal harm when malfunctioning.

In this paper, we will further discuss on AI being applied in healthcare and its benefits and losses.

2. APPLICATIONS

AI is being used in almost all sectors in healthcare. It has various applications ranging from chatbots, image processing, 3D bioprinting, precision medicine, treatment of rare diseases, robotic surgeries, emergency care, fraud detection etc.

2.1 Chatbots

Despite the fact that the market is now overrun with different medical chatbots, we still observe resistance to trying out more complex use cases. This is partially due to the fact that conversational AI remains in its early stages and has a way to go. Healthcare chatbot solutions will become increasingly advanced as technology for natural language comprehension and artificial intelligence develop.

There's little doubt that all these chatbots' relevancy but also accuracy would rise as well. But much more will be needed for the deployment of healthcare chatbots to be effective. To create chatbot solutions that really can handle the issues facing healthcare today, a careful balancing act among human empathy but also artificial intelligence will be necessary.

In order to close the gap among wireframe chatbots with significant human communications, Sensely works with enterprises, healthcare providers, insurance companies, and pharmaceutical firms to design specialized solutions. It offers a wide range of functions, including underwriting, claims processing, and symptom assessment, as well as customer support, worker wellness, including clinical trials. It's vital to realize that Sensely is indeed a platform and set of pre-built features, not really a chatbot, that can be used to create various varieties of medical chatbots (*Medical chatbots - use cases...*, 2020).

Figure 1. Chatbots

Chatbots are artificial intelligence (AI) gadgets that serve as virtual conversational agents by emulating human speech using natural language processing technologies (Nadarzynski et al., 2019). Teleconsultations, virtual testing, and health chatbots have the potential to improve communication between physicians and patients, as well as between clinics and patients, as the demand for these services rises (refer Figure 1).

These chatbots are computerized companions that communicate in the user's language to simulate human interaction. The chatbot collects and stores this information in a database so that it may subsequently evaluate the sentence's keywords, choose the appropriate query, and provide a response. N-gram, TFIDF, and cosine similarity are used to calculate ordering and sentence similarity. Each word in the input sentence will be granted a score, and further sentences that answer the request will be provided. When a robot's question cannot be addressed by searching the database, it looks to an expert system for assistance (Atotha et al., 2020).

Artificial intelligence (AI) and machine learning are the foundations of healthcare chatbots, which imitate human communication but aim to improve treatment (Negi et al., 2022). In addition to chatting to individuals, they engage in marketing, lead creation, emailing, and data analysis. Chatbots are important in the healthcare industry because they automate low-level, repetitive operations that would otherwise be performed by a representative. By assigning basic activities to a chatbot, healthcare workers are liberated to concentrate on more complex duties, which they are better equipped to handle (*How are Intelligent Healthcare ...,2022*). This has numerous advantages for clients:1) a shorter travel time to the doctor's office 2) less money is wasted on pointless procedures and examinations. 3) Push a button for quick and fast access to the doctor.

By 2022, analysts anticipate that healthcare chatbots will have reduced global healthcare distribution costs by $3.6 billion. Chatbots are reducing hospital wait times, consultation delays, erroneous treatments, and readmissions by integrating patients with the appropriate medical practitioners and assisting them in comprehending their symptoms and remedies without visiting a physician. (Kalinin, 2022).

Figure 2. AI chatbot

Despite this, the growing number of chatbot solutions for health and lifestyle are still amateur and require development in order to support complex behaviors like adhering to a balanced diet. As of yet, the available solutions primarily focused on measuring physical activity and making meal recommendations. The majority of methods concentrate on rule-based architectures, in which the chatbot intelligence is pre-defined and the bot responds to each user action by selecting an answer from a pre-defined set of options (refer Figure 2). Additionally, a few strategies have concentrated on fusing several profiling criteria and procedures to produce a sustainable health plan. These aspects include, for instance, user personality and offering a customized strategy that suits their interests. The effectiveness and caliber of the user experience with the chatbot can be improved by taking into account sentiment analysis and the emotional state of the user. Implementing these solutions to assist behavioral interventions for healthy lifestyles and prevention by healthcare practitioners can be made more effective by integrating the chatbot design with the proper behavior change strategies and methods (Fadhil and Gabrielli, 2017).

The basic goal of developing a medical chatbot is to mimic human conversation (Dharwadkar and Deshpande, 2018). This allows clinicians to provide far more comprehensive assessments and gives patients more insight into their conditions. The ever-expanding list of medical queries is also used by the chatbot to broaden the breadth of its existing corpus of medical knowledge. Many sceneries that seem to be static really include minute modifications that the unassisted eye cannot discern. However, with the help of algorithms and motion magnification, these subtle shifts may be plucked from films (Zaki et al., 2019). Motion magnification makes it possible to see these subtle changes by increasing them and to extract intriguing information from these movies, like the heartbeat of an individual.

Despite the fact that the market is now overrun with different healthcare chatbots, we still observe a resistance to trying out more complex use cases. This is partially due to the fact that conversational AI is still in its early stages and has a ways to go. Healthcare chatbot solutions will become more advanced as technology for natural language comprehension and artificial intelligence develop. There is little doubt that these chatbots' relevancy and accuracy will rise as well. But much more will be needed for the adoption of healthcare chatbots to be effective. To create chatbot solutions that can handle the issues facing healthcare today, a careful balancing act between human empathy and artificial intelligence will be necessary (*Medical chatbots - use cases...*, 2020).

2.2 Precision Medicine

Precision medicine has indeed been defined as a fundamental change away from an each approach towards therapeutic targets, even though it frequently concentrates on comprehending a patient's specific molecular profile help determine or treat disease. A sequence of crucial handoffs, beginning with the profiling of sizable groups to help comprehend human genetic variants and find illness biomarkers, provide the basis of this change (refer Figure 3). The advancement of molecular diagnoses as well as targeted treatments can then proceed as a result of transformative research's ability to connect research and development (R&D) and the hospital (*Ai in healthcare: Top 5...*, 2021).

Researchers are finding result of the emergence and understanding illnesses at the molecular level thanks to the availability of increasing quantities of information from population - based studies, the speeding of technology, and improved testing accuracy (*Overview of Precision...*, n.d).

Figure 3. Precision medicine

Genotype-guided therapy is now one of the effects of precision medicine on healthcare that has perhaps received the most research. Clinicians have utilized genotype data as a guide to assist them choose the right warfarin dose. Plans for targeted therapy for patients with breast or lung cancer can be informed by the genomic profiling of malignancies. The incorporation of precision medicine into healthcare has the potential to produce more accurate diagnoses, identify disease risk before symptoms appear, and create individualized treatment approaches that maximize effectiveness and safety (Johnson et al., 2020).

The last ten years have seen a significant increase in investment in techniques to promote precision medicine, leading to new treatments, increased knowledge of disease mechanisms, and ultimately disease prevention (Ter Horst et al., 2016).

Development of biomarkers for early-stage lung cancer is one instance in precision medicine. Biomarkers are bodily traits that can be quantified. One might think of blood pressure or heart rate as examples of biomarkers (refer Figure 4). Drug development depends on biomarkers since it's necessary to gauge how experimental medications affect volunteers in clinical trials. It has been demonstrated that early-stage lung cancer patients can be divided into subclasses using precision medicine (biomarkers) in order to receive the best possible care (*Artificial Intelligence for Precision ...*, 2020).

Figure 4. Examples of biomarkers

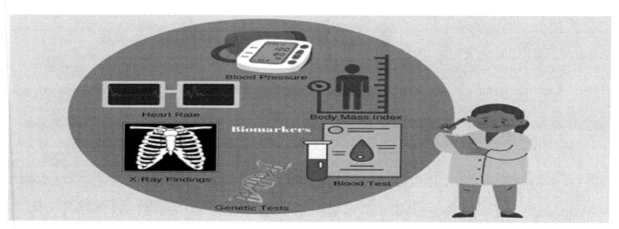

Utilizing cancer cell lines that were developed from patients has demonstrated precision oncology. Such bench-to-bedside models may predict medication responses in real time and frequently produce enormous knowledge banks that are amenable to ML workup. Future screening of patient-derived avatars will provide information on resistance mechanisms and improve the use of evidence-based treatment, especially for complex features (Fillip, 2019).

AI in healthcare also has significant drawbacks. In the case of machine learning, forecasting and prediction are mediated based on precedent, but algorithms can be ineffective in unique cases of pharmacological side effects or treatment resistance if there is no precedent on which to build. Therefore, AI might not be able to replace tacit knowledge that is difficult to codify. The development of medicines, the practice of medicine, and the provision of care all require the integration of numerous disruptive technologies in precision medicine. No matter how sophisticated it is, data analysis should assist doctors' clinical judgement and is not meant to take the place of the established doctor-patient relationship.

Maintaining the human touch in medicine will increase the likelihood that the proper patients will receive the most individualized treatments (Mesko, 2017). Although there are numerous obstacles to overcome, precision medicine is progressing (Ahmed, 2020).

2.3 Precision Cardiovascular Medicine

In cardiovascular medicine, AI technologies have been utilized to increase cost efficiency, improve patient care, reduce readmission and death rates, and research new genotypes and phenotypes in well-established illnesses (refer Figure 5).

Figure 5. Cardiovascular precision medicine

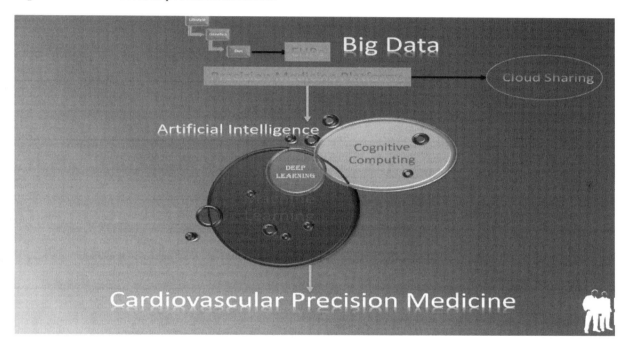

HFpEF, pulmonary hypertension, Takotsubo cardiomyopathy, white-coat hypertension, HTN, familial atrial and ventricular block, Brugada epilepsy, and metabolic syndrome can all benefit from the identification of novel genotypes and phenotypes using deep learning with unsupervised features for big data analytics (Krittanawong et al., 2017).

2.4 Treatment of Rare Diseases

The diagnosis of rare diseases is already aided by many types of AI utilized in general healthcare (Gupta et al., 2023). Computer vision is one area of AI that enables machines to examine digital photos, movies, and other visual data. Technicians use computer vision software to interpret X-ray images but also spot abnormalities that they might have missed without (refer Figure 6).

However, identifying uncommon genetic illnesses is a difficult procedure. A patient's family background, health information, or genetic data are among the elements that doctors should take into account. It frequently appears in detailed documentation or in the clinical documentation taken at consultations. To put it another way, it can be found through unstructured text (*Using artificial intelligence to diagnose...*, 2022).

Figure 6. Treatment of rare diseases

2.5 Fraud Detection

The past ten years have seen rapid adoption of artificial intelligence (AI) solutions for data protection, especially fraud detection in healthcare companies. This review study aims to investigate AI tools used in healthcare contexts for fraud detection. Both PubMed but also Google Scholar have been examined for pertinent material. According to this study, AI has been utilized to uncover many forms of fraud, including identity theft as well as kickbacks in the healthcare industry (refer Figure 7). This article also explores ways to recognize and visualize the hacker's network using AI methods used during network mapping fraud. In order to successfully detect fraud in healthcare settings—which could ultimately enhance the healthcare system—a correct system must be put in place (Mehbodniya et al., 2021).

Figure 7. Fraud detection

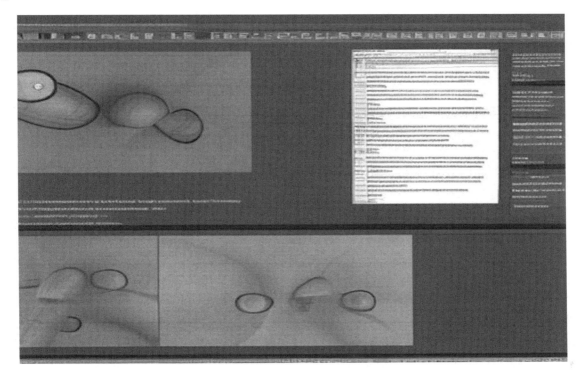

2.6 Robotic Surgeries

Robotic surgery currently incorporates artificial intelligence. Organizations recognize that deep learning data is superior to engineer-implemented behavior when it comes to automating everyday operations. Engineer-implemented behavior may not account for all possible conditions. Observation of surgical operations yielded the data used by the models of deep machine learning. Robots are capable of correctly replicating complicated moves repeatedly. For instance, hair transplant procedures benefit tremendously from this. The robot extracts hair follicles and then implants the scalp with their functional components. Built-in force sensing will allow the robot to maintain the required force during the whole collection or implantation treatment plan. Robotic surgical platforms that include micro-instrumentation, flexible robotics, and other technologies are used by specialists for bronchoscopic treatments. Robotics improves patient outcomes by enabling access to the brain and allowing for treatment via the brain's natural channels. By consolidating endoscopes, ancillary devices, and instructional materials, the platforms streamline the process of performing endoscopic surgeries (*Robotic surgery: The role of...*, 2019).

2.7 Automated Image Diagnosis

Medical imaging is the use of numerous methods to get different image formats out from human body, particularly the damaged area, for later processing and also to help with patient diagnosis and therapy. In order to keep up with the enormous population and the present trend of such a low qualified doctor in a growing population, medical image evaluation is essential in today's society. The healthcare sector has experienced a number of technological upheavals that are advantageous to humanity, and further advancements are being created. Precision in the diagnostic testing of photos will improve the applying the right and the treatment program will be anticipated along the way, speeding up the procedure and saving many lives.

The interior anatomy of a person or animal can be inspected with an ultrasound machine. To name a few, this includes joints, muscular, blood arteries, the breast, the pelvis, the bones, and also the kidneys. Another type of electromagnetic radiation that uses penetration through the external skin layer to reveal internal parts is the X-ray. A cross-sectional image is generated by computer tomography, which has a round opening region where the patient can be positioned and slipped within (*Radiation-emitting...*, 2020).

Figure 8. Automated image diagnosis

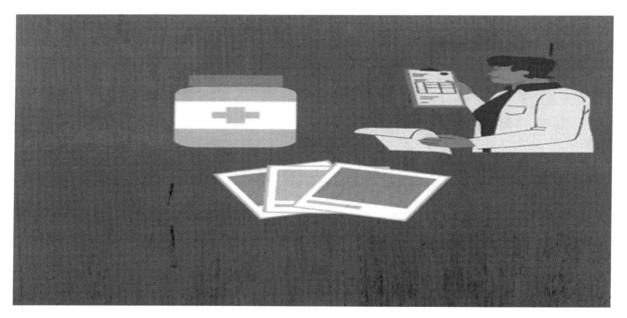

A significant downside of increased sensitivity is the discovery of minute changes with uncertain significance. For instance, a review of screening mammography revealed that while radiologists and artificial neural networks are equally accurate at spotting cancer, the former consistently had superior sensitivity for abnormal results, particularly for small lesions (Oren et al., 2020). The medical community must foresee the possible ambiguities of this technology at the outset of an AI-assisted diagnostic imaging revolution to enable its efficient and secure integration into clinical practice (refer Figure 8).

Figure 9. AI image diagnosis

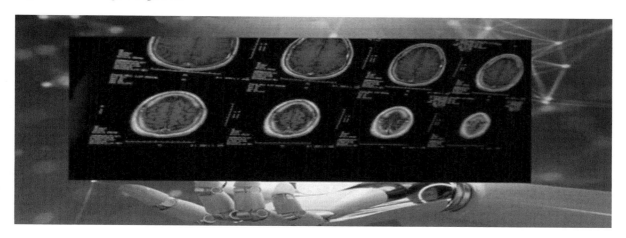

In one instance, a patient who presented to the emergency room (ED) with head and neck trauma might be examined for a cervical spine fracture called an odontoid fracture using an AI radiology tool. Standard scans frequently make it difficult to identify the sort of fracture, but AI techniques may be better able to spot small image changes that might point to an instability that calls for surgery. By allowing neutral algorithms to evaluate the photos of trauma patients, it may be possible to make sure that all injuries are recognized and treated appropriately for a successful outcome (Patil, 2021).

Since many years ago, it has been possible to automate the post-processing of CT, MR, and nuclear medicine investigations, which shortens examination times overall and increases patient throughput. Newer AI systems might be able to complete these tasks much more quickly and efficiently, potentially enabling picture super-resolution and instantaneous automatic segmentation of organs of interest (refer Figure 9). The generation of a CT image from an MRI scan or vice versa, eliminating the need for a second imaging technique entirely, is another promising area of early research (Hardy and Harvey, 2020).

Using photographs of the eye, IDx-DR CADx software application searches for indicators of diabetic retinopathy. The IDx-DR is significant since it is the first device that has been approved to deliver a screening decision without requiring a clinician to also evaluate the image or data. It can now be used by medical professionals who might not typically deal with eye care. The greatest cause of vision impairment and blindness among working-age individuals and the most common cause of vision loss among the more than 30 million Americans who have diabetes is diabetic retinopathy. When the FDA designated IDx-DR as a "Breakthrough Device," it meant that the company received intensive engagement and advice from the FDA on how to build devices effectively. This sped up the creation of evidence and the FDA's examination of the device (Thomas, 2019).

To determine diagnostic accuracy, many AI imaging studies use sensitivity and specificity, whereas others evaluate clinically significant outcomes. The more pertinent outcome variables, however, are new diagnoses of severe disease, disease requiring treatment, or conditions likely to impair long-term survival, as AI frequently picks up even little image variations. Our ability to diagnose accurately and rule things out will improve with the emergence and widespread application of AI in clinical practice (Oren et al., 2020).

2.8 3D Bioprinting

Using cells and biomaterials rather than conventional metals and plastics, "3D Bio printing" or "bio printing" creates 3D structures that are functional 3D tissues. Contrary to 3D printing, however, bio printers print with living cells and polymers to produce organ-like structures that enable cell proliferation. AI usage has only made 3D bio-printing technology much better (refer Figure 10).

First, the biodegradable material that is employed to keep printed tissue in its desired shape has the potential to elicit an immune response and harm cells. Fortunately, artificial immune systems that closely resemble human immune responses exist (Ewumi, 2021). Any aberration or intrusive immunological reaction that the tissue may cause when transplanted in a human body can be found by artificial immune systems. AI can also foresee how different 3D print applications will turn out before they are used; this will lower the failure rates in clinical trials.

Second, cellular damage caused by the bioprinting process makes it difficult for most 3D bioprinting techniques to scale effectively. Cellular interactions are impacted by cellular injury. Therefore, it is necessary to estimate the highest shear stress that a cell can endure while still functioning physiologically. It is possible to recommend the ideal size of the printer nozzle head to employ when adjusting the extrusion rate by integrating machine learning at the forefront of the bioprinter software and G-codes (refer Figure 11). By precisely adjusting all bioprinting settings, artificial intelligence may reduce printing times, improve resolution, and reduce the danger of cell contamination (Ewumi et al., 2021).

The creation of 3D printed bioscaffolds that aid in wound healing was sped up by researchers at Rice University using artificial intelligence (AI). Two machine learning techniques were employed by a group at Rice University's Brown School of Engineering under the direction of computer scientist Lydia Kavraki to forecast the quality of scaffold materials given the printing settings. Controlling print speed is essential for producing high-quality implants (Listek, 2021).

Figure 10. 3D printing

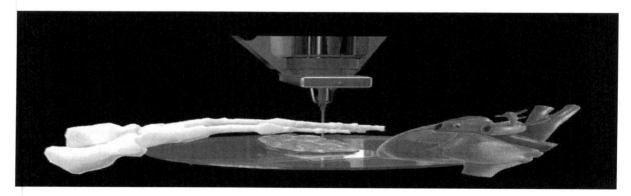

Figure 11. DNA research

2.9 Genomics

The discipline of genomics is constantly expanding the use of computer techniques like artificial intelligence and machine learning to enhance our comprehension of hidden patterns in vast and complicated genomes data sets from fundamental and clinical research projects.

In 2021, the draught human genome sequencing will have been completed, marking a significant milestone. Unusually large amounts of genomic data have been produced as a result of this milestone. Within the next ten years, it is estimated that data generated by genomics research would amount to 2 to 40 exabytes (*Artificial Intelligence, Machine...*, 2022). The quantity and complexity of such data sets will keep growing as a result of DNA sequencing and other biological procedures. Because of this, researchers studying genomics require computational tools based on AI and machine learning that can handle, extract, and evaluate the useful information concealed within this massive body of data. In order to support public health initiatives, researchers are also utilizing AI/ML to forecast future changes in the genomes of the influenza and SARS-CoV-2 viruses.

A significant portion of the world's population is anticipated to receive whole genome sequencing over the next ten years, either at birth or as adults. This genome sequencing will provide a fantastic tool for precision medicine and is expected to use 100–150 GB of data. Information on phenotypes and genomics is still being combined. To incorporate these genetic data and their advantages, the current healthcare system would need to be redesigned (Kulski, 2016).

A healthtech startup called Deep Genomics is attempting to link the enormous genetic dataset and EMRs with relation to illness markers by finding patterns in both of them. This firm examines these associations to identify therapeutic targets, either existing targets or potential new treatments, in order to develop personalized genetic drugs. A.I. is integrated into each and every step of the drug development process, from target selection and lead optimization through toxicity testing and novel trial design (Bohr and Memarzadeh, 2020).

2.10 Emergency Medical Techniques and Paramedics

Artificial intelligence (AI) and machine learning algorithms have gained popularity in emergency care for a variety of uses. Many AI algorithms have been developed to forecast disease risk and unfavorable outcomes. Notably, AI has been thoroughly investigated for developing predictive models in emergency care (Graham et al., 2018). The artificial neural network is one of the most well-known AI tools and algorithms. Although the prediction of duration of stay was found to be poor, Walsh and colleagues' study demonstrated the viability of utilizing artificial neural network ensembles to forecast ED disposition for infants and toddlers with bronchiolitis (Walsh et al., 2004). Large, complicated datasets can be used for predictive modelling since electronic health records have access to enormous amounts of data. However, when there are more independent variables than observations, conventional logistic regression is not practical (Johnson KW et al, 2018).

In terms of improving operational efficiency for healthcare systems, AI has been shown to be successful and valuable in upgrading physicians. According to the past studies, AI and machine learning technologies could be advantageous for ED doctors and the department (Liu et al., 2018).

2.11 Dermatology

An objective evaluation of parameters is made possible by computer-based image analysis, which helps to overcome subjective inter- and intra-observer variation (Stangenelli et al., 2005; Masood et al., 2013). There are numerous commercially available systems for dermoscopy-based computer-aided diagnosis of pigmented skin lesions. Examples of expert systems are DANAOS, DBDermo-Mips, and MoleAnalyzer (Korotkov and Gracia, 2012). The disease has been researched through artificial intelligence. Image categorization and psoriasis risk stratification have both been made possible by a variety of computer-aided diagnostic techniques. Additionally, genetic markers have been used to distinguish psoriasis from psoriatic arthritis and to identify the therapeutic response of psoriasis to biologics (Chan et al., 2020; Patrick et al., 2018). The effects of cellular stimulation with unidentified sensitizers on the alterations in these genomic indicators were investigated using artificial intelligence algorithms in comparison to profiles of reference compounds (Forreryd, 2016). Diabetes, TB, leprosy, vascular problems, pressure ulcers, and trauma are prominent risk factors for chronic wounds in India. Automated analysis has been used to a number of ulcer assessment procedures, including the examination of the wound's perimeter, surface, depth, area determination, and composition, resulting in a quantitative and objective evaluation of the wound's healing progress.

Every new technology comes with perks and drawbacks. Although the obvious shortcomings of AI applications in dermatology are readily apparent, the rapid improvement in model efficiency on the one hand and the steadily increasing workload of professionals on the other suggest that AI in healthcare may one day become an integral part of medical practice (Pai et al., 2021).

3. ADVANTAGES OF AI IN HEALTHCARE

The use of artificial intelligence in healthcare has largely increased the efficiency of health service providers. It has also largely benefacted the field of medicine and surgeries by making them less time consuming and more precise. Through AI, we are on the verge of finding cures of diseases that were impossible to treat. Moreover, it has seemingly reduced the hectic schedules of doctors and nurses by delegation of work to AI.

3.1 Alleviating Workload

To begin with, AI may alleviate the enormous stress imposed on healthcare practitioners today. Similar to a medical coder, AI may be able to assist folks who struggle with system navigation or administrative tasks. Artificial intelligence (AI) may be capable of assembling medical data, identifying health problems, and searching for information far faster than a human doctor could (Spencer, 2015; Dilsizian and Siegel, 2014).

Second, AI has the potential to reduce effort in specialties that involve diagnostic imaging and their interpretation. Diabetes retinopathy, TB, breast cancer, and abnormal heart rhythms have all been detected with DL. In addition to reducing manual labor requirements, this may also cut out pointless additional research. An AI program tracking proper usage criteria for radionucleotide imaging, for instance, was recently launched by the American College of Cardiology, and it has already reduced the proportion of incorrect imaging cases from 10% to 5% (Yuri et al., 2021).

3.2 Efficiency of Diagnostic Process

AI in healthcare may assist physicians in making more accurate diagnosis. In healthcare settings, the likelihood of an operator committing a mistake may be greater if there are more patients with no medical history. AI systems can detect and diagnose illnesses quicker and with a lower mistake rate than physicians. For instance, a 2017 study found that an AI model with deep learning can detect breast cancer more frequently than 11 pathologists! (Slowik, 2022).

3.3 Low-risk Surgeries

Robotic surgeries result in less blood loss, decreased infection risk, and less pain after surgery. Due to the smaller incisions needed, patients of robotic surgery also report reduced scarring and quicker recovery times (*Disadvantages of artificial intelligence...*, 2020).

4. DISADVANTAGES OF AI IN HEALTHCARE

Though AI has numerous advantages, it doesn't come without its costs. AI is very costly to put in real time application and can prove to be faulty at times. It solely relies on the data input by the user and can provide false predictions and cause immense harm. More so, it's not comforting for the patients who require emotional support and personal touch.

4.1 Erroneous Prediction

An inconsistency in the data caused by an environment or circumstance change may result in inaccurate assumptions. Artificial intelligence is unable to account for false negatives. Forecasts made with AI are not subject to review or interpretation. If AI systems frequently make accurate predictions, doctors may discontinue double-checking their work and investigating other options. Artificial intelligence systems that have been trained to diagnose a given ailment are more likely to do so after being exposed to the condition. In recommending a certain action, AI may fail to consider all of the consequences (Sam, 2022).

4.2 Issues with Security and Privacy

Models of artificial intelligence may retain an astounding degree of accuracy with regard to a vast amount of data. Without sufficient safeguards and regulatory assurances, AI may compromise the security and confidentiality of patient data. Before making a final choice, it is essential to consider the benefits and drawbacks of employing a third-party service. When it comes to privacy and security concerns in healthcare, other new technologies may be just as vulnerable as AI. The manipulation of AI technology by malicious actors is not inherently any more likely than it is with any other technology. As a result, any network-connected technology utilized for patient care or data processing need to be carefully secured. The sheer amount of data, the potential to re-identify previously de-identified data, and the difficulty of negotiating the regulatory environment make AI a special risk to healthcare security and privacy.

5. CASE STUDY

We have developed a program that uses a straightforward Convolutional Neural Network, or CNN, to determine whether a microscopic image of such a cell is contaminated by malaria or not, and to those you who would want to have a hands-on introduction to how these technologies operate. Consider a picture of a cell that is parasitized and unaffected (refer Figure 12). In the case study, we have used Dhruvi Karani's code on github for malaria detection using PyTorch, dataset from Kaggle that contains images for detecting malaria. For executing the code, we installed torch, torchvision, pandas, and numpy. (Karani, n.d.; Matt et al., 1965; Arunava, 2018)

Figure 12. An unaffected cell

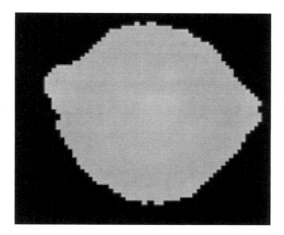

Figure 13. Affected cell

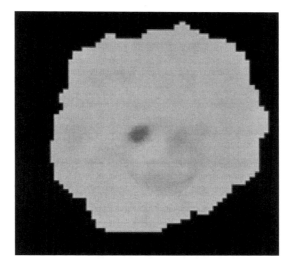

As we can see, a purple pigment distinguishes the parasitized cell from the uninfected cell (refer Figure 13). Our goal is to teach a classifier how to distinguish between infected and healthy cells. There are a total of 27,558 photos in our dataset. The distribution of the uninfected and infected photos is equal.

We'll comprehend it quite simply even if you're not familiar with CNNs. A CNN essentially consists of two elements; 1) Convolutional filters 2) Completed joined layers.

Similar to eyes are convolution filters. They record specifics or characteristics in a picture. For instance, they may catch intricate details of a flower's shape, color, etc. By advancing a window known as a convolution layer above a picture, these features are collected (refer Figure 14).

Figure 14. Convolutions

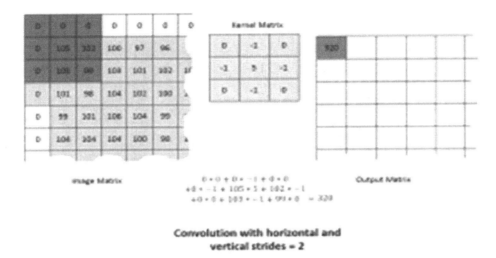

The completely connected layers then receive these features. These features are processed by fully connected layers. There are several connections between the unit neurons or cells in this network. The output's final form is utilized to forecast the class (refer Figure 15).

Figure 15. Layers

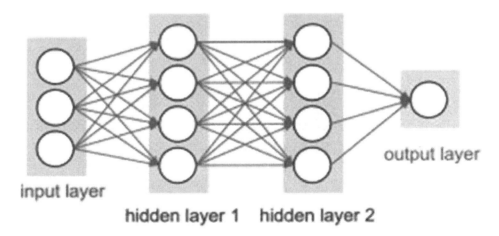

We train the model using the Python-based PyTorch framework before testing it against a validation set. Here are the outcomes:

Figure 16. PyTorch result

```
Validation:
Size of classes:  [2767.0, 2744.0]
Accuracy of the network on 552 validation images: 93 %
Accuracy of validation Parasitized : 91 %
Accuracy of validation Uninfected : 96 %
```

Our average accuracy upon the collection is 93%, which is excellent for a straightforward network (refer Figure 16).

6. CONCLUSION

In the future, AI will transform healthcare in numerous ways. One example is its ability to make predictions about a person's health. AI can do this by analyzing a person's medical history, lifestyle, and family history. AI can also detect patterns in a person's health that may be indicative of a future health problem.AI can also be used to improve the accuracy of diagnosis. AI can do this by analyzing a person's symptoms and comparing them to a database of known diseases. AI can also help doctors identify rare diseases. The use of artificial intelligence can also make healthcare more efficient. AI can do this by automating tasks such as scheduling appointments and ordering laboratory tests. AI can also help to reduce the length of hospital stays by identifying patients who can be discharged earlier. AI will also play a role in the development of new treatments. AI can be used to identify new targets for drugs and to design new drugs. AI can also be used to test the safety and efficacy of new treatments. AI will have a profound impact on healthcare. It will improve the accuracy of diagnosis, the efficiency of healthcare, and the development of new treatments. The rise of AI will eventually revolutionize the delivery of medical health with better perception of the technology.

REFERENCES

Ahmed, Z. (2020). Practicing precision medicine with intelligently integrative clinical and multi-omics data analysis. *Human Genomics*, 14(1), 35. DOI: 10.1186/s40246-020-00287-z PMID: 33008459

Ai in healthcare: Top 5 real-world examples. (2021, October). Compunnel Digital. Retrieved November 2, 2022, from https://www.compunneldigital.com/blog/ai-in-healthcare-top-5-real-world-examples/

Artificial Intelligence for Precision Medicine and Better Healthcare. (2020, September). KDnuggets. Retrieved November 4, 2022, from https://www.kdnuggets.com/2020/09/artificial-intelligence-precision-medicine-better-healthcare.html

Artificial Intelligence in Healthcare - AI Applications & Uses (2022, May 24). Intellipaat Blog. Retrieved November 5, 2022, from https://intellipaat.com/blog/artificial-intelligence-in-healthcare/

Artificial Intelligence, Machine Learning and Genomics (2022, January 12). National Human Genome Research Institute Genome.gov. Retrieved November 11, 2022, from https://www.genome.gov/about-genomics/educational-resources/fact-sheets/artificial-intelligence-machine-learning-and-genomics

Arunava. (2018, December 5). *Malaria Cell Images Dataset.* Kaggle. Retrieved November 12, 2022, from https://www.kaggle.com/datasets/iarunava/cell-images-for-detecting-malaria

Athota, L., Shukla, V. K., Pandey, N., & Rana, A. (2020). Chatbot for healthcare system using Artificial Intelligence. 2020 8th International Conference on Reliability, Infocom Technologies and Optimization (Trends and Future Directions) (ICRITO), 619–622. https://doi.org/DOI: 10.1109/ICRITO48877.2020.9197833

[] Bohr, A., & Memarzadeh, K. (2020). The rise of artificial intelligence in healthcare applications. Artificial Intelligence in Healthcare, 25–60. https://doi.org/DOI: 10.1016/B978-0-12-818438-7.00002-2

Chan, S., Reddy, V., Myers, B., Thibodeaux, Q., Brownstone, N., & Liao, W. (2020). Machine Learning in Dermatology: Current Applications, Opportunities, and Limitations. *Dermatology and Therapy*, 10(3), 365–386. DOI: 10.1007/s13555-020-00372-0 PMID: 32253623

Dharwadkar, R., & Deshpande, N. A. (2018). A medical chatbot. *International Journal of Computer Trends and Technology*, 60(1), 41–45. DOI: 10.14445/22312803/IJCTT-V60P106

Dilsizian, S. E., & Siegel, E. L. (2014). Artificial intelligence in medicine and cardiac imaging: Harnessing big data and advanced computing to provide personalized medical diagnosis and treatment. *Current Cardiology Reports*, 16(1), 441. DOI: 10.1007/s11886-013-0441-8 PMID: 24338557

Disadvantages of artificial intelligence in Healthcare. Way2Benefits. (2020, July 8). Retrieved November 13, 2022, from http://way2benefits.com/disadvantages-artificial-intelligence-in-healthcare/

Ewumi, O. (2021, April 30). *Ai in 3D bioprinting. Recode AI Daily iCal.* Retrieved November 10, 2022, from https://ai.recodeminds.com/uncategorized/ai-in-3d-bioprinting/

Ewumi, O., Gülen, K., & Eliaçık, E. (2021, April 30). *Ai in 3D bioprinting. Dataconomy.* Retrieved November 10, 2022, from https://dataconomy.com/2021/04/ai-in-3d-bioprinting/

Fadhil, A., & Gabrielli, S. (2017). Addressing challenges in promoting healthy lifestyles. *Proceedings of the 11th EAI International Conference on Pervasive Computing Technologies for Healthcare*, 261–265. https://doi.org/DOI: 10.1145/3154862.3154914

Filipp, F. V. (2019). Opportunities for Artificial Intelligence in Advancing Precision Medicine. *Current Genetic Medicine Reports*, 7(4), 208–213. DOI: 10.1007/s40142-019-00177-4 PMID: 31871830

[] Forreryd, A., Zeller, K. S., Lindberg, T., Johansson, H., & Lindstedt, M. (2016). From genome-wide arrays to tailor-made biomarker readout - Progress towards routine analysis of skin sensitizing chemicals with GARD. Toxicology in vitro: an international journal published in association with BIBRA, 37, 178–188. https://doi.org/.DOI: 10.1016/j.tiv.2016.09.013

[] Graham B, Bond R, Quinn M and Mulvenna M. (2018) Using data mining to predict hospital admissions from the emergency department. IEEE Access,6:10458–10469. https://doi.org/. 2018.2808843DOI: 10.1109/ACCESS

Gupta, A., Chaithra, N., Jha, J., Sayal, A., Gupta, V., & Memoria, M. (2023, May). Machine Learning Algorithms for Disease Diagnosis using Medical Records: A Comparative Analysis. In *2023 4th International Conference on Intelligent Engineering and Management (ICIEM)* (pp. 1-6). IEEE. DOI: 10.1109/ICIEM59379.2023.10165850

Gupta, A., Gupta, S., Memoria, M., Kumar, R., Kumar, S., Singh, D., . . . Ansari, N. (2022, May). Artificial intelligence and Smart Cities: A bibliometric analysis. In *2022 international conference on machine learning, big data, cloud and parallel computing (COM-IT-CON)* (Vol. 1, pp. 540-544). IEEE. DOI: 10.1109/COM-IT-CON54601.2022.9850656

Hardy, M., & Harvey, H. (2020). Artificial intelligence in diagnostic imaging: Impact on the radiography profession. *The British Journal of Radiology*, 93(1108), 20190840. DOI: 10.1259/bjr.20190840 PMID: 31821024

How are Intelligent Healthcare Chatbots being used? [new uses for 2022] (2022). Engati. Retrieved October 20, 2022, from https://www.engati.com/blog/chatbots-for-healthcare

Jha, J., Vishwakarma, A. K., Chaithra, N., Nithin, A., Sayal, A., Gupta, A., & Kumar, R. (2023, February). Artificial intelligence and applications. In *2023 1st International Conference on Intelligent Computing and Research Trends (ICRT)* (pp. 1-4). IEEE.

Johnson, K. B., Wei, W. Q., Weeraratne, D., Frisse, M. E., Misulis, K., Rhee, K., Zhao, J., & Snowdon, J. L. (2020). Precision Medicine, AI, and the future of Personalized Health Care. *Clinical and Translational Science*, 14(1), 86–93. DOI: 10.1111/cts.12884 PMID: 32961010

Johnson, K. W., Torres Soto, J., Glicksberg, B. S., Shameer, K., Miotto, R., Ali, M., Ashley, E., & Dudley, J. T. (2018). Artificial Intelligence in Cardiology. *Journal of the American College of Cardiology*, 71(23), 2668–2679. DOI: 10.1016/j.jacc.2018.03.521 PMID: 29880128

Johri, A., Sayal, A., Chaithra, N., Jha, J., Aggarwal, N., Pawar, D., & Gupta, A. (2024). Crafting the techno-functional blocks for Metaverse-A review and research agenda. *International Journal of Information Management Data Insights*, 4(1), 100213. DOI: 10.1016/j.jjimei.2024.100213

Kalinin, K. (2022, October 10). *Healthcare Chatbots: Role of AI, benefits, future, use cases, development.* Topflight. Retrieved October 16, 2022, from https://topflightapps.com/ideas/chatbots-in-healthcare/

Karani, D. (n.d.). *Dhruvilkarani/malaria-detection-using-pytorch: Pytorch implementation of CNN to Detect malaria.* GitHub. Retrieved November 12, 2022, from https://github.com/DhruvilKarani/Malaria-Detection-using-pytorch

Kirola, M., Joshi, K., Chaudhary, S., Singh, N., Anandaram, H., & Gupta, A. (2022, June). Plants diseases prediction framework: A image-based system using deep learning. In *2022 IEEE World Conference on Applied Intelligence and Computing (AIC)* (pp. 307-313). IEEE. DOI: 10.1109/AIC55036.2022.9848899

Korotkov, K., & Garcia, R. (2012). Computerized analysis of pigmented skin lesions: A review. *Artificial Intelligence in Medicine*, 56(2), 69–90. DOI: 10.1016/j.artmed.2012.08.002 PMID: 23063256

Krittanawong, C., Zhang, H., Wang, Z., Aydar, M., & Kitai, T. (2017). Artificial Intelligence in Precision Cardiovascular Medicine. *Journal of the American College of Cardiology*, 69(21), 2657–2664. DOI: 10.1016/j.jacc.2017.03.571 PMID: 28545640

Kulski, J. K. (2016) Next-generation sequencing — an overview of the history, tools, and "omic" applications. In: Kulski JK (ed) Next generation sequencing - advances, applications and challenges. INTECH, London, eBook (PDF) ISBN: 978-953-51-5419-8

Listek, V. (2021, October 18). *Ai driven bioprinting speeds up tissue engineering - 3dprint.com: The Voice of 3D printing / Additive Manufacturing. 3DPrint.com* | The Voice of 3D Printing / Additive Manufacturing. Retrieved November 11, 2022, from https://3dprint.com/273254/ai-driven-bioprinting-speeds-up-tissue-engineering/

Liu, N., Zhang, Z., Wah Ho, A. F., & Ong, M. E. (2018). Artificial Intelligence in emergency medicine. *Journal of Emergency and Critical Care Medicine*, 2, 82–82. DOI: 10.21037/jeccm.2018.10.08

M, M., R, S., & Rashmi. (2018, November 20). *Artificial intelligence based skin classification using GMM. Journal of medical systems.* Retrieved November 1, 2022, from https://pubmed.ncbi.nlm.nih.gov/30460413/

Masood, A., & Al-Jumaily, A. A. (2013). Computer aided diagnostic support system for skin cancer: A review of techniques and algorithms. *International Journal of Biomedical Imaging*, 323268, 1–22. Advance online publication. DOI: 10.1155/2013/323268 PMID: 24575126

Matt, iacolippoiacolippo 3, kHarshitkHarshit, et al. (1965, October 1). *Where do I get a CPU-only version of pytorch?* Stack Overflow. Retrieved November 12, 2022, from https://stackoverflow.com/questions/51730880/where-do-i-get-a-cpu-only-version-of-pytorch

Medical chatbots - use cases, examples and case studies of Conversational AI in Medicine and Health (2020) senseforth.ai. Retrieved November 5, 2022, from https://www.senseforth.ai/conversational-ai/medical-chatbots/

Mehbodniya, A., Alam, I., Pande, S., Neware, R., Rane, K. P., Shabaz, M., & Madhavan, M. V. (2021, September 11). *Financial fraud detection in healthcare using machine learning and Deep Learning Techniques. Security and Communication Networks.* Retrieved November 2, 2022, from https://www.hindawi.com/journals/scn/2021/9293877/

Mesko, B. (2017). The role of artificial intelligence in precision medicine. *Expert Review of Precision Medicine and Drug Development*, 2(5), 239–241. DOI: 10.1080/23808993.2017.1380516

Nadarzynski, T., Miles, O., Cowie, A., & Ridge, D. (2019). Acceptability of Artificial Intelligence (ai)-led chatbot services in Healthcare: A mixed-methods study. *Digital Health*, 5, 1–7. DOI: 10.1177/2055207619871808 PMID: 31467682

Negi, S. S., Memoria, M., Kumar, R., Joshi, K., Pandey, S. D., & Gupta, A. (2022, November). Machine learning based hybrid technique for heart disease prediction. In *2022 International Conference on Advances in Computing, Communication and Materials (ICACCM)* (pp. 1-6). IEEE. DOI: 10.1109/ICACCM56405.2022.10009219

Oren, O., Gersh, B. J., & Bhatt, D. L. (2020). Artificial intelligence in medical imaging: Switching from radiographic pathological data to clinically meaningful endpoints. *The Lancet. Digital Health*, 2(9), e486–e488. DOI: 10.1016/S2589-7500(20)30160-6 PMID: 33328116

Overview of Precision Medicine.(n.d) Thermo Fisher Scientific - US. Retrieved November 1, 2022, from https://www.thermofisher.com/us/en/home/clinical/precision-medicine/precision-medicine-learning-center/precision-medicine-resource-library/precision-medicine-articles/overview-precision-medicine.html

Pai, V. V., & Pai, R. B. (2021). Artificial intelligence in dermatology and healthcare: An overview. *Indian Journal of Dermatology, Venereology and Leprology*, 87(4), 457–467. DOI: 10.25259/IJDVL_518_19 PMID: 34114421

Patil, S. (2021, May 28). *TOP 5 USE CASES OF ARTIFICIAL INTELLIGENCE IN MEDICAL IMAGING.* Analytics Insight. Retrieved November 3, 2022, from https://www.analyticsinsight.net/top-5-use-cases-of-artificial-intelligence-in-medical-imaging/

Patrick, M. T., Stuart, P. E., Raja, K., Gudjonsson, J. E., Tejasvi, T., Yang, J., Chandran, V., Das, S., Callis-Duffin, K., Ellinghaus, E., Enerbäck, C., Esko, T., Franke, A., Kang, H. M., Krueger, G. G., Lim, H. W., Rahman, P., Rosen, C. F., Weidinger, S., & Tsoi, L. C. (2018). Genetic signature to provide robust risk assessment of psoriatic arthritis development in psoriasis patients. *Nature Communications*, 9(1), 4178. DOI: 10.1038/s41467-018-06672-6 PMID: 30301895

Radiation-emitting products(2020). Center for Devices and Radiological Health. U.S. Food and Drug Administration. Retrieved November 2, 2022, from https://www.fda.gov/radiation-emitting-products

Robotic surgery: The role of AI and Collaborative Robots(2019). Robotics Online Marketing Team. Automate. Retrieved November 2, 2022, from https://www.automate.org/blogs/robotic-surgery-the-role-of-ai-and-collaborative-robots

Sam. (2022, October 30). *17 pros and cons of Artificial Intelligence in Healthcare*. Techemergent. Retrieved November 13, 2022, from https://techemergent.com/pros-and-cons-of-artificial-intelligence-in-healthcare/

Singh, A. P., Pradhan, N. R., Luhach, A. K., Agnihotri, S., Jhanjhi, N. Z., Verma, S., Kavita, , Ghosh, U., & Roy, D. S. (2020). A novel patient-centric architectural framework for blockchain-enabled healthcare applications. *IEEE Transactions on Industrial Informatics*, 17(8), 5779–5789. DOI: 10.1109/TII.2020.3037889

Slowik, C. (2022, November 3). *Benefits of AI in Healthcare - usage, advantages*. Neoteric. Retrieved November 12, 2022, from https://neoteric.eu/blog/benefits-of-ai-in-healthcare/

Spencer, M. (2015). Brittleness and Bureaucracy: Software as a Material for Science. *Perspectives on Science*, 23(4), 466–484. DOI: 10.1162/POSC_a_00184

[] Stanganelli, I., Brucale, A., Calori, L., Gori, R., Lovato, A., Magi, S., Kopf, B., Bacchilega, R., Rapisarda, V., Testori, A., Ascierto, P. A., Simeone, E., & Ferri, M. (2005). Computer-aided diagnosis of melanocytic lesions. Anticancer Research, 25(6 C), 4577-4582

Ter Horst, R., Jaeger, M., Smeekens, S. P., Oosting, M., Swertz, M. A., Li, Y., Kumar, V., Diavatopoulos, D. A., Jansen, A. F. M., Lemmers, H., Toenhake-Dijkstra, H., van Herwaarden, A. E., Janssen, M., van der Molen, R. G., Joosten, I., Sweep, F. C. G. J., Smit, J. W., Netea-Maier, R. T., Koenders, M. M. J. F., & Netea, M. G. (2016). Host and environmental factors influencing individual human cytokine responses. *Cell*, 167(4), 1111–1124.e13. DOI: 10.1016/j.cell.2016.10.018 PMID: 27814508

Thomas, R. (2019, September 2). *AI for Medical Imaging — now?* tds. Retrieved November 1, 2022, from https://towardsdatascience.com/ai-for-medical-imaging-now-8fad32c4c96b /

Using artificial intelligence to diagnose rare genetic diseases (2022, March 24). National Gaucher Foundation. Retrieved November 1, 2022, from https://www.gaucherdisease.org/blog/ai-and-rare-disease-diagnosis-national-gaucher-foundation/

[] Walsh, P., Cunningham, P., Rothenberg, S. J., O'Doherty, S., Hoey, H., & Healy, R. (2004). An artificial neural network ensemble to predict disposition and length of stay in children presenting with bronchiolitis. European journal of emergency medicine: official journal of the European Society for Emergency Medicine, 11(5), 259–264. https://doi.org/DOI: 10.1097/00063110-200410000-00004

Yuri, Y. M. (2021, September). The promise of artificial intelligence: A review of the opportunities and challenges of artificial intelligence in healthcare. *British Medical Bulletin*, 139(1), 4–15. DOI: 10.1093/bmb/ldab016 PMID: 34405854

Zaki, W. M., Shakhih, M. F., Ramlee, M. H., & Wahab, A. A. (2019). Smart Medical Chatbot with integrated contactless vital sign monitor. *Journal of Physics: Conference Series*, 1372(1), 012025. DOI: 10.1088/1742-6596/1372/1/012025

Chapter 7
An Exhaustive Inference of Machine Learning Applications in Healthcare:
Analyzing Research Studies on Diagnosis and Prevention

Manas Kumar Swain
Siksha O Anusandhan University, India

Narendra Kumar Kamila
GITA College, India

Lambodar Jena
Siksha O Anusandhan University, India

Nilamadhab Mishra
https://orcid.org/0000-0002-1330-4869
VIT Bhopal University, India

ABSTRACT

Machine learning has become an important tool in healthcare research to solve complex classification problems effectively, efficiently, and quickly. Generally, doctors treat patients according to their medical knowledge and personal experience. Since different professionals have different experiences, they may sometimes make a wrong diagnosis and need more time for treatment. Current research mainly focuses on the problem of classifying/predicting medical data based on machine learning. There is a need to create an intelligent structure that can distribute the information stored in the database. Human data analysis capabilities are less compared to data storage. This is more important in the case of medical records because it helps search, diagnose, and treat patients based on individual records. This paper's main goal is to review the pre-researched methodologies of machine learning techniques to analyze healthcare data to diagnose and prevent illnesses. Finally, these research articles are classified based on healthcare data, machine learning techniques, and performance parameters.

DOI: 10.4018/979-8-3373-0240-9.ch007

1. INTRODUCTION

The current chapter covers machine learning techniques and healthcare data management strategies for effective decision-supporting and insight-producing. Additionally, it covers a few recent studies on data mining applications in medical research. These days, computers help individuals in ways that were not feasible in the past. Before, we could only do work with the help of human ability; today, we can accomplish activities on a scale we never could have dreamed of with computers. The main problem is developing an intelligent system that will analyze, evaluate, and use this information as medical information increases daily. One of the most important tools of medical data analysis is data mining. Therefore, data mining has been increasingly developed in healthcare services to increase the quality of healthcare services while reducing costs. Consequently, several research publications that use healthcare data have been evaluated and analyzed t to improve the efficacy of data analytics in the medical field. A few relevant papers on analyzing healthcare data (using machine learning techniques and illness datasets) are outlined and classified.

The healthcare sector is undergoing evolutionary changes. The digitization of healthcare systems is producing a significant amount of health data. Today, Health Information Technology (HIT) has advanced to instantaneously gather, store, and transmit data electronically from anywhere globally. It is now a helpful instrument for raising the standard and productivity of healthcare.

All medical records that are digitally saved are generally considered to be healthcare data. It could include comprehensive medical history information on the patient, clinical reports, doctor's prescription notes, etc. These data are all large, multidimensional, and diverse, which leads to big data in the healthcare industry (Tripathi & Mohan, 2016). These data come from various internal and external sources, including social media, biometrics, healthcare, and picture data.

An additional significant challenge facing today's Healthcare Information Systems (HISs) is the daily exponential growth of healthcare data. In addition to the massive volume of healthcare data, this shift is marked by a sharp increase in the pace and diversity of data output.

Healthcare data encompasses the vast amounts of information generated within the healthcare sector, which includes patient records, clinical trials, administrative data, and more. This data is critical for improving patient care, researching, and informing healthcare policies.

2. BACKGROUND

The term healthcare refers to improving healthcare services to meet people's needs. In healthcare delivery, patients, doctors, nurses, researchers and the healthcare sector work hard to manage and obtain medical information. In recent years, with the rapid development of science and technology, the increasing amount of information in many areas, including healthcare, has increased the need to seek information.

Machine learning, data mining, and statistical techniques are basic sciences that enhance a person's ability to make good decisions and maximize profit in any field (Ajay et al., 2023; Belwal & Belwal, 2017; Indu et al., 2023).

This research focuses on the problem of classification/prediction of medical data based on machine learning (monitoring) techniques. Many learning algorithms can be used together with data mining techniques to solve clinical classification problems, thereby increasing diagnosis's speed, accuracy, and reliability.

Figure 1. Knowledge extraction process

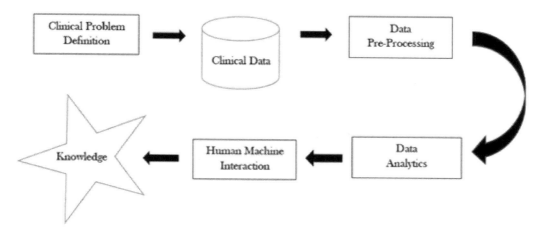

With the advancement of technology, many new studies have begun to be conducted in the digital world. Information has become an integral part of this digital world. Data analysis is the examination of data based on data and focusing on concluding (useful insights).

2.1. Role of Data Mining in Healthcare

Simply put, data mining simply means using large amounts of data to get better insights. The main idea of data mining is to build intelligent models to extract important information from big data in the form of detailed patterns and rules, as shown in Figure 2. Finding hidden evidence (useful information) from raw data is important in knowledge discovery.

Figure 2. Mining of interesting patterns

As healthcare is emerging nowadays, the lifestyle has improved with data mining research. The term 'data mining' involves numerous areas of study, such as pattern recognition, machine learning, statistical analysis, etc. Data is continuously increasing day by day in every sector, including healthcare, which in turn demands more and more data mining applications.

In the context of the healthcare domain, several issues like incremental growth of data warehouses, the diversified nature of health-related data, and the necessity of intelligent machine-based data analytical tools (to handle large volumes of data more efficiently and effectively) are recognized for business-class computers data-miners as well as for end-users.

The number of available experts for data analysis is comparatively less than the amount of data stored. Therefore, semi-automatic analytical techniques are required to gain insights from health-related information and make better decisions.

In light of these considerations, several data mining techniques have been proposed to extract valuable insights from data warehouses for better decision-making. Figure 3 describes the different stages of the data mining process.

Two key points must be considered while introducing a machine-intelligent model on real-world datasets: model construction and model evaluation. The training dataset must be used to construct or train a model, and then the test dataset should be applied to assess the model's performance. Numerous methodologies can be used to assess learning techniques. In several are, including healthcare, the two most widely used machine learning techniques are supervised machine learning (specially for classification tasks) and unsupervised machine learning (for clustering tasks).

Figure 3. Stages in the data mining process

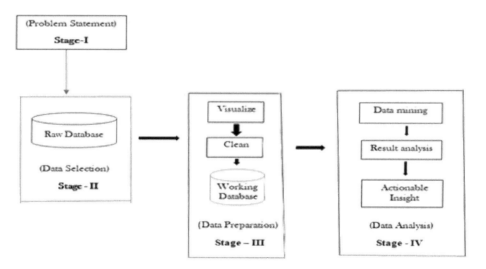

A supervised learning method requires input data (training data) to be labelled with predefined classes. It is exactly how a teacher supervises the learning process. As stated previously, classification problems can be considered as supervised learning based on past experiences (examples). The supervised machine's two phases are the learning and testing phases. The training dataset is used for model construction in the learning phase, whereas the test data set is used to assess the model performance. Based on any data partitioning schemes, the input dataset is divided into training and test sets. Classification is one of the most significant data mining techniques (a form of supervised learning) used for prediction. Some competently supervised machine learning algorithms are Decision Tree (DT), Logistic Regression (LR), Artificial Neural Network (ANN), Naïve Bayes (NB), Support Vector Machine (SVM) etc.

The main purpose of any data mining approach is to explore useful knowledge from large datasets to predict unseen data more accurately and precisely.

2.2. Some Robust Machine Learning Techniques for Healthcare Data Analysis

Arthur Samuel coined the term "machine learning" for a game like chess in 1959. Machine learning (Pandey et al., 2023; A. K. Singh et al., 2024) can be defined as a concept allowing computers to learn independently without explicit instruction. The main goal of machine learning is to create a program that can access and use data to learn. It is mostly based on statistics and inference.

Data is suitable for machine learning. With the support of relevant information, medical decisions in treatment will be more accurate (Padhi et al., 2024). It forms the basis of all models. Machine learning algorithms are needed to gain insight from medical data and make better treatment decisions. Many traditional learning methods have been developed in this field, including Naive Bayes support vector machines, K-nearest neighbors, neural networks, and decision trees. Machine learning is important in healthcare, especially when there are complaints (Arora et al., 2024; Shrivastava et al., 2023).

2.2.1 K-Nearest Neighbor (KNN)

The KNN algorithm is an important supervised learning method and can be used in regression estimation and classification problems. KNN is one of the simplest machine learning algorithms. The basic idea behind KNN technology is very simple. Events are classified according to the ranking of their neighbors. In this case, it is often useful to use several direct neighbors (e.g., K); therefore, the technique is called KNN. However, running KNN is considered expensive because it requires large memory to test and train data (Zhang et al., 2023). computational method. To classify unseen samples (based on the distance measure), select samples with the smallest distance from the unseen sample, two steps are performed in K-Neighbors. In the first stage, good neighbors are selected, while in the next stage, the class is determined according to the distance between the selected neighbors. It is worth noting that the mode can be used for classification, while the mean can be used for recovery.

Advantages:
- Simple to implement and easy to understand.
- No cost associated with the learning process.
- No training time for classification/regression tasks.
- Hyperparameter tuning is easy.

Disadvantages:
- Sensitive to outliers.
- KNN assumes equal importance to all features.
- The performance of KNN is poor for large datasets.

2.2.2 Support Vector Machine (SVM)

SVM is a supervised learning method used for classification and prediction. This method is best suited for classification problems with both linear and nonlinear features, to a high place. Discrete problems were transformed into discrete problems. Kernel functions enable the use of hyperplanes to divide the data into two groups continuously. Support vectors are a small set of training data (feature vectors) that SVM uses to find the hyperplane for discrete data. SVM classifiers classify invisible data into linear, binary, and non-probabilistic groups. Binary classifications are useful as binary classifiers for solving multi-class problems but are time-consuming. Since support vector machines have many unknowns and are difficult to describe, understand, and predict, they are considered a "black box" technology.

Advantages:
- Compared with other models, there is less evidence of overfitting.
- SVM classifier predictive power is fast.
- The accuracy of SVM is usually quite high.
- Small data sets are the best candidates for SVM.

Disadvantages:
- Owing to the black box method, it lacks outcomes transparency.
- Handling multiclass problems is time-consuming.
- Training time is more while computing large datasets.

2.2.2 Decision Tree (DT)

An important machine learning technique, DT, represents the classification model. This training tracking process is based on the law and is based on:

IF (conditional statement)
THEN (decision class)

A tree structure model with nodes, branches, and leaves is called a decision tree (DT). Each root of this model represents a feature (attribute), each branch represents an option (condition), and each leaf represents an outcome (category). The tree is iteratively split according to the attribute value learned from the root node (Aiyappa et al., 2024). A decision tree (DT) has two stages: construction and pruning. At each stage of the construction process, feature selection measures (ASM) (such as Gini index, growth rate, or data growth) are used to select attributes and eliminate outliers during the pruning period. Small files are best suited for classification using the DT method. Although this method is easy to learn, it has some disadvantages such as overfitting issues and biases when dealing with inconsistent data (K. U. Singh et al., 2024). Three popular methods for building decision trees (DTs) are ID3, C4.5, and CART.

Advantages:
- IF-THEN categorization rules may be readily converted from a decision tree.
- The use of Decision Tree (DT) classifiers eliminates the need for domain expertise.
- Multi-dimensional data may be handled accurately by decision trees.

Disadvantages:
- It does not function satisfactorily when dealing with unbalanced data.
- Managing continuous data is a complicated task.
- It's challenging to increase the effectiveness of computation.

2.2.3 Naïve Bayes (NB)

NB is a Bayesian based classification system. Bayes theorem is based on the concepts of mathematical statistics and probability theory. Therefore, learning probabilistic classifier is another name for Bayesian classifier. In fact, it is a statistical classifier. Binary classification problems and multi-class classification problems are two types of problems solved by NB. Naive Bayes (NB) classifier determines class membership based on a list of classes (Khandelwal et al., 2023). The assumption of independent experts is the negative of Naive Bayes. In this type, there is no dependency on both (attributes) of the same category (Kumari et al., 2024). Although Naive Bayes uses statistical methods, it can be compared to the support vector machine (SVM) in many ways.

Advantages:
- This classifier makes quick predictions easily.
- When dealing with multiclass problems, Naïve Bayes (NB) works effectively.
- Compared to numerical data, it works better with categorical data.

Disadvantages:
- NB is unable to identify a connection between the attributes.
- Continuous data cannot be handled by this method.

2.2.4 Neural Networks (NN)

Neural Networks (NN) are based on the concept of supervised learning. Neural networks (artificial networks that work like the human brain) are used in machine learning. McCulloch and Pitts developed a computational model based on mathematics and a technique called neural networks in 1943. A diagram can be used to represent such a model. One or more hidden nodes will reveal other nodes. The margins indicate the amount. In other words, the input, hidden, and output layers are the three different layers of the neural network (Dutta et al., 2023). Neural networks generally perform three tasks: updating, searching, and error handling. Error determines the quality (good or bad) of the output given the input. This arch process identifies areas that can be changed to reduce errors. Learning algorithms using neural networks (NN) appear to be very useful in solving problems that are difficult to specify and represent using traditional software and statistical analysis. Many neural network models have been developed to perform supervised classification. Most neural networks (NNs) use a multilayered recurrent algorithm.

Advantages:
- Regression and classification tasks benefit greatly from the use of neural networks.
- Additionally, it produces positive outcomes when the attribute values are categorical.
- Learning techniques using neural networks are highly resilient to noise in the training set.
- They are adept at handling missing or incomplete data.

Disadvantages:
- Overly long and laborious training periods are possible in functional neural networks.
- Test and training data sets in huge quantities are typically needed for neural computing.
- The knowledge is implicit.

2.2.5 Logistic Regression (LR)

Regression analysis is a useful tool for modelling and predicting the relationship between two variables, one of which is independent and the other dependent (Gangwar & Srivastva, 2020). There are two types of regression: logistic and linear. A discrete value is needed for Logistic Regression (LR), while a continuous value is needed for linear regression.

2.3. Performance Metrics for Evaluation of Machine Learning Classifier

Evaluating the learning classifiers is a critical step in machine learning. The performance of learning systems can be assessed using a variety of metrics (Mishra et al., 2024). In essence, they assess how accurately a classifier forecasts the outcome. These metrics comprise, in that order, precision, sensitivity, specificity, and accuracy.

A confusion matrix's empirical metrics can be used to evaluate the learners' performance. A confusion matrix accurately represents a solution to the given classification issue. The confusion matrix for a classification model is shown in Table 1.

Table 1. Confusion matrix of size m x m (m=2)

Class	Predictive Positive	Predictive Negative
Actual Positive	True Positive (TP)	False Negative (FN)
Actual Negative	False Positive (FP)	True Negative (TN)

Formal definitions of these performance metrics are stated below:

i) Accuracy:

$$Accuracy = \frac{TP + TN}{P + N} \times 100$$

ii) Error rate or misclassification rate:

$$Error\ rate\ (e) = \frac{FP + FN}{P + N}$$

iii) Precision:

$$Precision = \frac{TP}{TP + FP}$$

iv) Sensitivity or Recall:

$$Sensitivity = \frac{TP}{TP + FN}$$

v) F-Score:

$$F - score = \frac{(2 \times Precision \times Recall)}{(Precision + Recall)}$$

vi) Specificity:

$$Specificity = \frac{TN}{TN + FP}$$

vii) Receiver Operating Characteristic (ROC) curve: The ROC curve is used to assess how well a model performs in terms of classifications.

3. LITERATURE SURVEY

In recent years, researchers and scientists have increasingly developed applications based on data mining to enhance healthcare services. The growing volume of digitally recorded healthcare data can be mined to uncover new trends and valuable insights, ultimately improving the quality of care.

To predict preterm birth (PTB), a machine learning model called the Risk Prediction Conceptual Model (RPCM) that uses three types of classification: Decision Tree (DT), Logistic Regression (LR), and Support Vector Machine (SVM); were developed (Srivastava et al., 2024). The model uses a feature selection process based on the concept of entropy. Tahmasseb et al. Developed a multidimensional magnetic resonance imaging (MRI) machine learning model for cancer risk prediction in 2019. In this context, eight classifiers were applied to breast MRI data to rank predictors of early-stage disease in patients treated for breast cancer. Digital proposed a multi-level perceptron model for survival prediction. Reduction and iterative feature extraction algorithms were used to extract features from clinical data and improve the prediction model performance (P. Singh & Singh, 2023). Grover et al., 2024 proposed that knowledge-based professionals use electronic health records (EHR) to identify patients with type 2 diabetes (T2DM). Various machine learning methods are used for this purpose, including Naive Bayes, Random Forest (RF), Logistic Regression (LR), Decision Making (DT), K-Nearest Neighbor (KNN), and Boost Vector Machines (SVM).

Using multiparametric magnetic resonance imaging (mpMRI) data, Uniyal et al., 2022 proposed MLogarithms for early prediction of complete disease response (pCR), adjuvant chemotherapy, and survival outcomes in cancer patients. Samples were collected from 38 women diagnosed with breast cancer, and eight samples were used to analyze cancer features such as residual cancer (RCB), disease-free survival (RFS), and disease-specific survival (DSS). Classifiers include linear support vector machines, linear discriminant analysis, logistic regression, random forests, stochastic gradient descent, adaptive boosting, and extreme gradient boosting (XGBoost). Provide the area under the value curve for each PCR feature. Compared with other classifiers, XGBoost achieved the best results from experimental data with higher accuracy for logistic regression of RCB and DSS with RSS. Using an electronic health record (EHR), Kumar et al., 2023 developed a machine learning-based model to predict the probability of emergency visits. The plan can help doctors accurately predict whether a patient will need treatment in the future. Kanojia et al., 2022 developed a multilevel cognitive model to predict the two-year prognosis of non-small cell lung cancer patients. Based on the data, the multilayer neural network was determined to be the best prediction model with an area under the curve value of 0.75. Using key medication variables from local EHR records, Neha et al., 2023 developed a postoperative risk prediction model that was sensitive and specific in identifying patients at risk for postoperative complications. Kumar et al., 2024 proposed a special selection process based on entropy time for medical data of different sizes. The scheme minimizes the features in the clinical data to generate suitable subsets in a heterogeneous manner. The performance of the model is evaluated on 14 different medical records.

Joshi et al., 2022 recommended a approach for leveraging digital fitness record (EHR) records to identify people with type-2 Diabetes Mellitus (T2DM). a total of three hundred patient samples had been accumulated, and 114 capabilities have been extracted using numerous machine getting to know strategies, together with logistic regression, ok-Nearest Neighbor (KNN), Random woodland (RF), decision Tree (DT), naïvebayes, and support Vector machine (SVM). SVM generates the nice end result from the findings, with an accuracy of 96%. Amini,Paymetal.with a view to verify the frequency of preterm delivery based on demographic and obstetrical information, developed a device gaining knowledge of-primarily based prediction model that used logistic regression and decision tree category techniques.

For the reason of figuring out excessive-chance surgical sufferers, Kanojia et al., 2022b

mounted several device studying strategies, along with penalized logistic regression, random forest fashions, and excessive gradient boosted selection timber. The authors used Pythia statistics, which protected digital health records with 194 medical variables, which includes patient demographics, smoking fame, remedy records, comorbidities, manner information, and proxies for surgical sufferers, to educate the algorithms. primarily based at the experimental information, the penalized logistic regression model with an AUC cost of zero.924 yielded the excellent results. Kumar, Khannna Malholtra, et al., 2023 studied a hybrid method that used a mobile cellphone sensing mechanism to discover strain in neural networks by way of combining a Bayesian network with heuristic techniques. Heart charge (HR) fee and blood strain control (BPM) are the two primary parametric metrics for stress detection. A DM (facts mining)-based model was created by means of Rana et al., 2022 to forecast the likelihood of pregnancy during maternity care in a real-world setting. The proposed model's primary intention is to aid in decision-making by forecasting, using information from medical instances, if a girl could deliver early.

a good way to expect cardiac illnesses in humans, Unhelkar et al., 2022 devised a deep knowledge of neural network versions utilizing several gaining knowledge of classifiers, inclusive of Random forest (RF), Naïve Bayes (NB), guide Vector machine (SVM), and okay-Nearest Neighbor (KNN), have been hired on this version. Kumar, Kandpal, et al., 2023 examined five system mastering strategies for delirium risk prediction based totally on digital health file records: penalized logistic regression, gradient boosting system, single-layered artificial neural network, linear support vector gadget, and random forest. The investigation worried taking samples from 18223 sufferers in all. The gradient boosting method yielded the satisfactory result, with an AUC price of zero.855, in step with the records. A machine-mastering-based healthcare advice algorithm was created with the aid of Eswar et al., 2023 to identify the maximum vital variables and determine the Caesarean procedure. The counseled approach aids in forecasting the operational healthcare choices for obstetric surgical operation to save mother and child. Tyagi et al., 2023 put up a prediction model that makes use of naïve bayes getting to know classifiers and decision timber to diagnose diabetes in pregnant girls at an early degree.

With a purpose to forecast the chance elements of diabetes by feature relevance analysis, K. S. Kumar et al., 2022 created a hybrid version with the aid of many type algorithms, which include C4.five, ID3, Random woodland, k-Nearest Neighbour (KNN), and support Vector system (SVM).

So as to estimate cardiovascular danger, Kukreti et al., 2023 hooked up gadget studying strategies consisting of random forests, logistic regression, gradient boosting machines, and neural networks using samples of 378,256 individuals. after traits have been retrieved from the prepared facts. The authors used a ramification of machine studying techniques and observed that, with an AUC value of 0.72, neural networks performed the pleasant. A hydroid prediction machine was created by using (Babu et al., 2022) the usage of a diffusion of device getting to know strategies, which include logistic regression, decision trees, random forests, help vector machines, and artificial neural networks. Based on data mining techniques, K. D. Singh et al., 2023 proposed a heart ailment prediction technique to perceive the lifestyles of cardiovascular disease. This diagnostic model uses three getting-to-know classifiers: J48DecisionTree, Bagging techniques, and Naïve Bayes. Using support vector regression, Tamilmani et al., 2023 forecast the full quantity of COVID-19 confirmed instances and death cases. S. Joshi & Sharma, 2022 use the Cleveland heart infection dataset to forecast heart disease with the most pleasant possible overall performance. A model was created with the aid of Bhatt *et al.* (n.d.) to lessen the death charge from cardiovascular disease. There are 4 class strategies used: XG increase, Random woodland, choice Tree, and Multilayer Perceptron.

4. SURVEY ANALYSIS OF MACHINE LEARNING TECHNIQUES IN HEALTHCARE DATA

This survey provides an overview of recent research on the application of machine learning techniques in healthcare. It highlights various studies that leverage advanced algorithms to analyze healthcare data, aiming to improve diagnostic accuracy and disease prevention. By categorizing these studies based on the types of healthcare data used, the specific machine learning methods employed, and their corresponding performance metrics, the survey offers a comprehensive framework for understanding the current landscape of machine learning in healthcare. This synthesis showcases the potential benefits of these techniques and identifies gaps and opportunities for future research in this rapidly evolving field.

The primary goal of this chapter is to review several research papers by various authors that explore the application of machine learning techniques in analyzing healthcare data for diagnosing and preventing illnesses. Table 2 categorizes these studies based on healthcare data types, machine learning approaches, and performance metrics.

Table 2. Survey findings on machine learning applications in healthcare data analysis

Authors	Disease Data set	Machine Learning Algorithms	Performance Parameters	Results	Limitation
(Ghildiyal et al., 2022)	Heart Disease	Decision Tree, Multilayer Perceptron (MLP), Extreme Gradient Boosting (XGBoost), Random Forest	Classification	MLP shows the best result with Accuracy=87.3%	
(Dogra et al., 2022)	Heart Disease	SVM, ANN, Decision Tree, Adaptive Boosting (Ada Boost)	Classification, Accuracy, AUC, Sensitivity, Specificity	SVM shows the best result with Sensitivity=98.56% Specificity=98.37% Accuracy=98.47% AUC=94.48%	
(Taneja & Sharma, 2023)	COVID-19 Data set	Support Vector Regression	Classification Accuracy (%)	Accuracy=94%	-

continued on following page

Table 2. Continued

Authors	Disease Data set	Machine Learning Algorithms	Performance Parameters	Results	Limitation
(Taneja & Özen, 2023)	14 Real-world disease datasets Hepatitis, Cancer, Heart...)	• C4.5, RIPPER, • Naïve Bayes	Classification and Prediction	Naïve Bayes shows the best result Accuracy increased for all 14-medical data sets	
(Reepu et al., 2023)	Pre term Birth (HER data)	Purpose- Prediction and Classification Used Learners: • Decision Tree • LogisticRegresion • Support Vector Machine	*Classification* • *Accuracy* • *Sensitivity* • *Specificity*	Best result achieved by SVM • Accuracy=90.9% • Sensitivity=89.1% • Specificity=78.3%	Small-size data set
(Dangwal et al., 2022)	Heart (Clinical data)	Purpose-Prediction Used Learners: • Logistic regression, • SVM, Naïve Bayes, • Random Forest, • Deep Neural Network(Talos)	• Classification • Accuracy	Talos performed best accuracy • Accuracy=90.7%	
(Gupta et al., 2023)	Breast Cancer (Mammography Data)	Purpose-Prediction UsedLearners: DecisionTree Logistic Regression, SVM, Random Forest, Linear Discriminant Analysis, AdaBoost, XGBoost	Classification Accuracy	XG Boost shows the best result. • Accuracy=0.94.	Small-Size data set
(Dahiya & Taneja, 2023)	Lung Cancer (Mammography Data)	Purpose-Prediction Used Learners: • Logistic Regression, • Single Perception • Neural Network, • Multilayer Neural Network	• Area under curve(AUC), • Classification Accuracy, • Precision	Multilayer Neural Network Produces the Best result AUC=0.75, CI=0.693-0.806 Accuracy=0.76 Precision=0.72	---
(Taneja, Gupta, et al., 2023)	Clinical (mp MRI)	SVM, Linear discriminant analysis, Logistic regression, Random forest, Stochastic gradient descent, Adaptive Boosting (Ada Boost), Extreme Gradient Boosting (XGBoost)	Area under curve (AUC)	XG Boost produced the best result with AUC = 0.94 for RCB AUC = 0.92 for DSS AUC = 0.83	The dataset used in this way very small. In this some features are extracted which effect the imaging features well as the prediction of RCB. DSS.

continued on following page

Table 2. Continued

Authors	Disease Data set	Machine Learning Algorithms	Performance Parameters	Results	Limitation
(Bansal et al., 2023)	Clinical	Multilayer Neural Network, Logistic Regression, Single Perception, Neural network	Area under curve 95% Confidence interval, Misclassification rate, True positive rate, Accuracy, Precision	Multilayer Neural Network produced the best result with AUC = 0.75 Confidence value = 0.693-0.806 True positive rate = 0.68 Accuracy = 0.76 Precision = 0.72	
(Bhatnagar, Rajaram, et al., 2024)	Thyroid (HER data)	Purpose- Thyroid Prediction Used Learners: Support Vector Machine, Decision Tree, Logistic Regression, Random Forest, Feed Forward	Classification Accuracy (%), Precision, Recall, F1-score	DT shows best result • Accuracy=99.46% • Precision=0.99 • Recall=0.99 • F1-score=0.99	---
(P. Kumar, Taneja, & Ozen, 2024)	Heart (HER data)	Purpose-Prediction Used Learners: NaïveBayes, J48DT, Bagging	Classification Accuracy (%)	Bagging classifier shows more accuracy • Accuracy=85.03%	---
(Bhatnagar, Taneja, & Kumar, 2023)	Caesarean Delivery (HER data)	Purpose- Recommendation Used Learners: • Support Vector Machine, • Logistic regression, • K-Nearest Neighbour, • Naïve Bayes, • Random Forest	• Classification • Accuracy	Random Forest achieved the best accuracy • Accuracy=95%	Small-size data set
(P. Kumar, Reepu, et al., 2024)	Clinical (EHR)	Penalized logistic regression, Gradient boosting machine, Artificial neural network with a single hidden layer, Linear support vector machine, Random forest	Sensitivity, Specificity, Area Under Curve	Gradient boosting machine produced best result with Sensitivity Specificity AUC= 59.7% AUC= 23.1% AUC= 0.855	
(P. Kumar, Taneja, Bhatnagar, et al., 2024)	Stress Detection (Mobile Sensor data)	Purpose-Prediction Used Learners: • Hybrid approach • Bayesian network • Heuristic technique	• Classification • Accuracy	Hybrid approach performed well • Accuracy =92.86%(BP) • Accuracy =85.71%(HR)	Real time sensor data not included

continued on following page

Table 2. Continued

Authors	Disease Data set	Machine Learning Algorithms	Performance Parameters	Results	Limitation
(Taneja, Bhatnagar, Kumar, & Rupeika-apoga, 2023)	Clinical(EHR)	Penalized logistic regression Random forest models Extreme gradient boosted Decision trees basis function networks	Accuracy Sensitivity Specificity Area under curve Threshold Positive Predictive Value	Penalized logistic regression produced best result with Accuracy=95% Sensitivity=76% Specificity=76% AUC=0.924 Threshold=0.174 PPV=0.390	
(P. Kumar, Bhatnagar, et al., 2023)	Surgical Structured HER (Risk data)	Purpose-Risk Prediction Used Learners: • Lasso • Logistic Regression • Random Forest • Extreme Gradient Boosted (XG Boost) • Decision trees	• Classification • Accuracy • Sensitivity • Specificity • Area under curve(AUC)	Lasso regression yields best result Accuracy=95% Sensitivity=76% Specificity=76% AUC=0.924	Missing data not handled.
(P. Sharma et al., 2024)	Emergency Admission EHR data (Risk data)	Purpose-Risk Prediction Used Learners: • Random Forest, • Cox model, • Gradient boosting	Area under Curve (AUC)	Gradient boosting performs the best result. AUC=0.779	Better techniques can be used
(Taneja, Bhatnagar, Kumar, & Grima, 2023)	Diabetes (Electronic Health Records)	Purpose-Prediction Used Learners: • SVM, k-Nearest Neighbour, • Logistic Regression, • Random Forest, • Decision Tree, • Naïve bayes	• Classification • Accuracy • Sensitivity • Specificity • Precision • Area under curve(AUC)	Support Vector Machine performs the best result • Accuracy=96% • Sensitivity=95% • Specificity=96% • Precision=91% • AUC=0.96.	Small-size dataset.
(Bhatnagar, Kumar, et al., 2024)	Clinical (EHR)	Support vector machine, K-nearest neighbor, Logistic regression, Random forest, Decision tree, Naïve bayes	Accuracy Sensitivity Specificity Precision Area under curve	SVM produced best result with Accuracy= 96% Sensitivity= 95% Specificity =96% Precision= 91% AUC = 0.96	
(P. Kumar, Verma, et al., 2023)	Preterm Delivery (HER data) Demographic data and maternal data	Purpose-Classification Used Learners: • Logistic Regression, • Decision Tree	• Classification • Accuracy • Sensitivity • Specificity	Logistic Regression yield better result Accuracy=85% Sensitivity=41% Specificity=81%	Only two classifiers used

continued on following page

Table 2. Continued

Authors	Disease Data set	Machine Learning Algorithms	Performance Parameters	Results	Limitation
(Bhatnagar, Taneja, et al., 2024)	Clinical (EHR)	Random forest, Logistic regression, Gradient boosting Machines, Neural networks,	Area under curve confidence interval Positive predictive Negative predictive	Neural networks produced best result with AUC = 0.728 CI = 0.75-0.76 PPV = 18.4% NPV = 95.70%	
(Kaur et al., 2023)	Diabetes (HER data)	Purpose-Risk Analysis Used Learners: • C4.5, ID3, Random Forest, SVM	• Classification • Accuracy (%)	Hybrid Classifier Performs the best result Accuracy=100%	Real-time monitoring not used
(Bhatnagar, Taneja, & Rupeika-Apoga, 2023)	Diabetes (HER data)	Purpose-Prediction Used Learners: • Naïve Bayes, • Decision Tree	• Classification • Accuracy (%)	Naïve Bayes shows the Best result. • Accuracy =79.56%	Small-size data set
(R. Sharma et al., 2024)	Clinical data Prenatal data Maternal data	Purpose-Prediction Used Learners: • Decision Tree, • Support Vector Machine, • Naïve Bayes, • Generalized Linear Model	• Classification • Accuracy • Sensitivity • Specificity	Decision Tree performs the best result • Accuracy=93% • Sensitivity=88% • Specificity=97%	Small-size data sets

CONCLUSION

The increasing significance of data analysis in the digital age, particularly within the healthcare sector, underscores the need for innovative solutions to manage and interpret vast amounts of medical data. The reliance on traditional medical expertise, while valuable, can lead to inconsistencies in diagnosis and treatment due to the subjective nature of human judgment. By implementing several machine learning algorithms such as decision trees, logistic regression, support vector machines, neural networks, and naive Bayes, this paper proposes a robust classification function model that aims to enhance the accuracy and efficiency of medical diagnoses. These machine-learning techniques facilitate the processing of extensive healthcare datasets and provide a systematic approach to identifying patterns and trends that human analysts may overlook. Ultimately, the integration of these advanced analytical tools into healthcare practices has the potential to significantly improve patient outcomes, streamline diagnostic processes, and ensure that medical professionals have access to the most reliable and timely information for informed decision-making.

FUTURE WORK

This survey of research publications underscores the significant potential of machine learning techniques in analyzing healthcare data for disease diagnosis and prevention. While there is a growing body of work in this area, it is evident that many studies rely on small datasets, which may limit the generalizability and applicability of their findings. Furthermore, the lack of engagement with real-time healthcare monitoring data presents a critical gap that future research must address. To enhance the robustness and effectiveness of machine learning applications in healthcare, it is essential for researchers to focus on larger and more diverse datasets, ensuring that models are trained on data that more accurately reflects the complexities of real-world clinical environments. By doing so, the field can advance towards more reliable and actionable insights that can significantly improve patient outcomes and support proactive healthcare strategies.

DECLARATION

The authors declare that the manuscript follows ethical standards and there are no potential conflicts of interest concerning this chapter's research, authorship, and publication.

DISCLAIMER

The contents and views of this chapter are expressed by the authors in personal capacities. The Editor and the Publisher don't need to agree with these viewpoints and are not responsible for any duty of care in this regard.

REFERENCES

Aiyappa, S., Kodikal, R., & Rahiman, H. U. (2024). Accelerating Gender Equality for Sustainable Development: A Case Study of Dakshina Kannada District, India. *Technical and Vocational Education and Training*, 38, 335–349. DOI: 10.1007/978-981-99-6909-8_30

Ajay, D., Sharad, K., Singh, K. P., & Sharma, S. (2023). Impact of Prolonged Mental Torture on Housewives in Middle Class Families. *Journal for ReAttach Therapy and Developmental Diversities*, 6(4), 1–7.

Arora, A., Singh, R., Malik, K., & Kestwal, U. (2024). Association of sexual performance and intimacy with satisfaction in life in head and neck cancer patients: A review. *Oral Oncology Reports*, 11, 100563. Advance online publication. DOI: 10.1016/j.oor.2024.100563

Babu, M., Venkataraman, S. R., Rao, P. N., Rao, V., Kaliappan, S., Patil, P. P., Sekar, S., Yuvaraj, K. P., & Murugan, A. (2022). Optical Microstructure, FESEM, Microtensile, and Microhardness Properties of LM 25-B4Cnp-Grnp Hybrid Composites Manufactured by Selective Laser Melting. *Advances in Materials Science and Engineering*, 2022, 1–8. Advance online publication. DOI: 10.1155/2022/3177172

Bansal, N., Bhatnagar, M., & Taneja, S. (2023). Balancing priorities through green optimism: A study elucidating initiatives, approaches, and strategies for sustainable supply chain management. In *Handbook of Research on Designing Sustainable Supply Chains to Achieve a Circular Economy*. IGI Global., DOI: 10.4018/978-1-6684-7664-2.ch004

Belwal, R., & Belwal, S. (2017). Employers' perception of women workers in Oman and the challenges they face. *Employee Relations*, 39(7), 1048–1065. DOI: 10.1108/ER-09-2016-0183

Bhatnagar, M., Kumar, P., Taneja, S., Sood, K., & Grima, S. (2024). From digital overload to trading Zen: The role of digital detox in enhancing intraday trading performance. In *Business Drivers in Promoting Digital Detoxification*. IGI Global., DOI: 10.4018/979-8-3693-1107-3.ch010

Bhatnagar, M., Rajaram, R., Taneja, S., & Kumar, P. (2024). Balancing acts: The Yin and Yang of debit and credit on the stage of financial well-being. In *Emerging Perspectives on Financial Well-Being*. IGI Global., DOI: 10.4018/979-8-3693-1750-1.ch002

Bhatnagar, M., Taneja, S., & Kumar, P. (2023). The Effectiveness of Carbon Pricing Mechanism in Steering Financial Flows Toward Sustainable Projects. *International Journal of Environmental Impacts*, 6(4), 183–196. DOI: 10.18280/ijei.060403

Bhatnagar, M., Taneja, S., Kumar, P., & Özen, E. (2024). Does financial education act as a catalyst for SME competitiveness? *International Journal of Education Economics and Development*, 15(3), 377–393. DOI: 10.1504/IJEED.2024.139306

Bhatnagar, M., Taneja, S., & Rupeika-Apoga, R. (2023). Demystifying the Effect of the News (Shocks) on Crypto Market Volatility. *Journal of Risk and Financial Management*, 16(2), 136. DOI: 10.3390/jrfm16020136

Dahiya, K., & Taneja, S. (2023). To Analyse the Impact of Multi-Media Technology on the Rural Entrepreneurship Development. In *Contemporary Studies of Risks in Emerging Technology* (pp. 221–240). DOI: 10.1108/978-1-80455-562-020231015

Dangwal, A., Kaur, S., Taneja, S., & Ozen, E. (2022). A bibliometric analysis of green tourism based on the scopus platform. In *Developing Relationships, Personalization, and Data Herald in Marketing 5.0*. IGI Global., DOI: 10.4018/978-1-6684-4496-2.ch015

Dogra, V., Verma, D., Dalapati, G. K., Sharma, M., & Okhawilai, M. (2022). Special focus on 3D printing of sulfides/selenides for energy conversion and storage. In *Sulfide and Selenide Based Materials for Emerging Applications: Sustainable Energy Harvesting and Storage Technology*. Elsevier., DOI: 10.1016/B978-0-323-99860-4.00012-5

Dutta, A., Singh, P., Dobhal, A., Mannan, D., Singh, J., & Goswami, P. (2023). Entrepreneurial Aptitude of Women of an Aspirational District of Uttarakhand. *Indian Journal of Extension Education*, 59(2), 103–107. DOI: 10.48165/IJEE.2023.59222

Eswar, K. N. D. V. S., Doss, M. A. N., Vishnuram, P., Selim, A., Bajaj, M., Kotb, H., & Kamel, S. (2023). Comprehensive Study on Reduced DC Source Count: Multilevel Inverters and Its Design Topologies. *Energies*, 16(1), 18. Advance online publication. DOI: 10.3390/en16010018

Gangwar, V. P., & Srivastva, S. P. (2020). Impact of micro finance in poverty eradication via SHGs: A study of selected districts in U.P. *International Journal of Advanced Science and Technology*, 29(2), 3818–3829.

Ghildiyal, S., Joshi, K., Rawat, G., Memoria, M., Singh, A., & Gupta, A. (2022). Industry 4.0 Application in the Hospitality and Food Service Industries. *Proceedings of the 2022 7th International Conference on Computing, Communication and Security, ICCCS 2022 and 2022 4th International Conference on Big Data and Computational Intelligence, ICBDCI 2022*. DOI: 10.1109/ICCCS55188.2022.10079268

Grover, D., Sharma, S., Kaur, P., Mittal, A., & Sharma, P. K. (2024). Societal Elements that Impact the Performance of Women Entrepreneurs in Tier-II Cities: A Study of Rohilkhand Region of Uttar Pradesh. *2024 IEEE Zooming Innovation in Consumer Technologies Conference. ZINC*, 2024, 114–117. DOI: 10.1109/ZINC61849.2024.10579316

Gupta, M., Arora, K., & Taneja, S. (2023). Bibliometric analysis on employee engagement and human resource management. In *Enhancing Customer Engagement Through Location-Based Marketing*. IGI Global., DOI: 10.4018/978-1-6684-8177-6.ch013

Indu, R., Dimri, S. C., & Kumar, B. (2023). Identification of Location for Police Headquarters to Deal with Crime Against Women in India Using Clustering Based on K-Means Algorithm. *International Journal of Computing and Digital Systems*, 14(1), 965–974. DOI: 10.12785/ijcds/140175

Joshi, K., Patil, S., Gupta, S., & Khanna, R. (2022). Role of Pranayma in emotional maturity for improving health. *Journal of Medical Pharmaceutical and Allied Sciences*, 11(2), 4569–4573. DOI: 10.55522/jmpas.V11I2.2033

Joshi, S., & Sharma, M. (2022). Sustainable Performance through Digital Supply Chains in Industry 4.0 Era: Amidst the Pandemic Experience. *Sustainability (Basel)*, 14(24), 16726. Advance online publication. DOI: 10.3390/su142416726

Kanojia, P., Malhotra, R. K., & Uniyal, A. K. (2022a). Impact of Organizational Commitment Components on the Teachers of Higher Education in Uttarakhand: An Emperical Analysis. *Proceedings - 2022 International Conference on Recent Trends in Microelectronics, Automation, Computing and Communications Systems, ICMACC 2022*, 360–364. DOI: 10.1109/ICMACC54824.2022.10093606

Kanojia, P., Malhotra, R. K., & Uniyal, A. K. (2022b). Organizational Commitment and the Academic Staff in HEI's in North West India. *Proceedings - 2022 International Conference on Recent Trends in Microelectronics, Automation, Computing and Communications Systems, ICMACC 2022*, 365–370. DOI: 10.1109/ICMACC54824.2022.10093347

Kaur, A., Kumar, P., Taneja, S., & Ozen, E. (2023). Fintech emergence – an opportunity or threat to banking. *International Journal of Electronic Finance*, 13(1), 1–19. DOI: 10.1504/IJEF.2024.135163

Khandelwal, C., Kumar, S., Tripathi, V., & Madhavan, V. (2023). Joint impact of corporate governance and risk disclosures on firm value: Evidence from emerging markets. *Research in International Business and Finance*, 66, 102022. Advance online publication. DOI: 10.1016/j.ribaf.2023.102022

Kukreti, A., Shriyal, A., Sharma, S., & Bhadula, S. (2023). Internet-of-Things Enabled Smart and Portable Terrace Garden Protection Shed. *2023 4th IEEE Global Conference for Advancement in Technology, GCAT 2023*. DOI: 10.1109/GCAT59970.2023.10353281

Kumar, K. S., Yadav, D., Joshi, S. K., Chakravarthi, M. K., Jain, A. K., & Tripathi, V. (2022). Blockchain Technology with Applications to Distributed Control and Cooperative Robotics. *Proceedings of 5th International Conference on Contemporary Computing and Informatics, IC3I 2022*, 206 – 211. DOI: 10.1109/IC3I56241.2022.10073275

Kumar, P., Reepu, & Kaur, R. (2024). Economic and Urban Dynamics: Investigating Socioeconomic Status and Urban Density as Moderators of Mobile Wallet Adoption in Smart Cities. *Lecture Notes in Networks and Systems, 948 LNNS*, 409–417. DOI: 10.1007/978-981-97-1329-5_33

Kumar, P., Bhatnagar, M., & Taneja, S. (2023). Investigation of the time pattern of Bit Green Crypto: An Arma modeling approach to unrave volatility. In *Algorithmic Approaches to Financial Technology: Forecasting, Trading, and Optimization*. IGI Global., DOI: 10.4018/979-8-3693-1746-4.ch001

Kumar, P., Taneja, S., Bhatnagar, M., & Kaur, A. K. (2024). Navigating the digital paradigm shift: Designing CBDCs for a transformative financial landscape. In *Exploring Central Bank Digital Currencies: Concepts, Frameworks, Models, and Challenges*. IGI Global., DOI: 10.4018/979-8-3693-1882-9.ch006

Kumar, P., Taneja, S., & Ozen, E. (2024). Exploring the influence of green bonds on sustainable development through low-carbon financing mobilization. *International Journal of Law and Management*. DOI: 10.1108/IJLMA-01-2024-0030

Kumar, P., Verma, P., Bhatnagar, M., Taneja, S., Seychel, S., Todorović, I., & Grim, S. (2023). The Financial Performance and Solvency Status of the Indian Public Sector Banks: A CAMELS Rating and Z Index Approach. *International Journal of Sustainable Development and Planning*, 18(2), 367–376. DOI: 10.18280/ijsdp.180204

Kumar, R., Goel, R., Singh, T., Mohanty, S. M., Gupta, D., Alkhayyat, A., & Khanna, R. (2024). Sustainable Finance Factors in Indian Economy: Analysis on Policy of Climate Change and Energy Sector. *Fluctuation and Noise Letters*, 23(2), 2440004. Advance online publication. DOI: 10.1142/S0219477524400042

Kumar, R., Kandpal, B., & Ahmad, V. (2023). Industrial IoT (IIOT): Security Threats and Countermeasures. *International Conference on Innovative Data Communication Technologies and Application, ICIDCA 2023 - Proceedings*, 829 – 833. DOI: 10.1109/ICIDCA56705.2023.10100145

Kumar, R., Khannna Malholtra, R., & Grover, C. A. N. (2023). Review on Artificial Intelligence Role in Implementation of Goods and Services Tax(GST) and Future Scope. *2023 International Conference on Artificial Intelligence and Smart Communication, AISC 2023*, 348–351. DOI: 10.1109/AISC56616.2023.10085030

Kumar, R., Malhotra, R. K., & Grover, N. (2023). Data Mining in Credit Scoring and Future Application. *International Conference on Innovative Data Communication Technologies and Application, ICIDCA 2023 - Proceedings*, 1096–1100. DOI: 10.1109/ICIDCA56705.2023.10100032

Kumari, J., Singh, P., Mishra, A. K., Singh Meena, B. P., Singh, A., & Ojha, M. (2024). Challenges Hindering Women's Involvement in the Hospitality Industry as Entrepreneurs in the Era of Digital Economy. In *Revolutionizing the AI-Digital Landscape: A Guide to Sustainable Emerging Technologies for Marketing Professionals*. Taylor and Francis., DOI: 10.4324/9781032688305-9

Mishra, D., Kandpal, V., Agarwal, N., & Srivastava, B. (2024). Financial Inclusion and Its Ripple Effects on Socio-Economic Development: A Comprehensive Review. *Journal of Risk and Financial Management*, 17(3), 105. Advance online publication. DOI: 10.3390/jrfm17030105

Neha, M., S., Alfurhood, B. S., Bakhare, R., Poongavanam, S., & Khanna, R. (2023). The Role and Impact of Artificial Intelligence on Retail Business and its Developments. *2023 International Conference on Artificial Intelligence and Smart Communication, AISC 2023*, 1098–1101. DOI: 10.1109/AISC56616.2023.10085624

Padhi, B. K., Singh, S., Gaidhane, A. M., Abu Serhan, H., Khatib, M. N., Zahiruddin, Q. S., Rustagi, S., Sharma, R. K., Sharma, D., Arora, M., & Satapathy, P. (2024). Inequalities in cardiovascular disease among elderly Indians: A gender perspective analysis using LASI wave-I (2017-18). *Current Problems in Cardiology*, 49(7), 102605. Advance online publication. DOI: 10.1016/j.cpcardiol.2024.102605 PMID: 38692448

Pandey, R. P., Bansal, S., Awasthi, P., Dixit, V., Singh, R., & Yadava, V. (2023). Attitude and Myths Related to Stalking among Early and Middle Age Adults. *Psychology Hub, 40*(3), 85 – 94. DOI: 10.13133/2724-2943/17960

Rana, M. S., Cavaliere, L. P. L., Mishra, A. B., Padhye, P., Singh, R. R., & Khanna, R. (2022). Internet of Things (IOT) Based Assessment for Effective Monitoring Data Against Malicious Attacks on Financial Collectors. *2022 2nd International Conference on Advance Computing and Innovative Technologies in Engineering, ICACITE 2022*, 177–181. DOI: 10.1109/ICACITE53722.2022.9823612

Reepu, R., Taneja, S., Ozen, E., & Singh, A. (2023). A globetrotter to the future of marketing: Metaverse. In *Cultural Marketing and Metaverse for Consumer Engagement*. IGI Global., DOI: 10.4018/978-1-6684-8312-1.ch001

Sharma, P., Taneja, S., Kumar, P., Özen, E., & Singh, A. (2024). Application of the UTAUT model toward individual acceptance: Emerging trends in artificial intelligence-based banking services. *International Journal of Electronic Finance*, 13(3), 352–366. DOI: 10.1504/IJEF.2024.139584

Sharma, R., Sharma, M., Singh, M., & Bhatnagar, M. (2024). Facades and Fortunes : Intellectual Capital's Influence on Firm Dynamics in the Deepfake Epoch. In *Navigating the World of Deepfake Technology* (pp. 1–6). DOI: 10.4018/979-8-3693-5298-4.ch009

Shrivastava, A., Usha, R., Kukreti, R., Sharma, G., Srivastava, A. P., & Khan, A. K. (2023). Women Safety Precaution. *2023 1st International Conference on Circuits, Power, and Intelligent Systems, CCPIS 2023*. DOI: 10.1109/CCPIS59145.2023.10291594

Singh, A. K., Singh, R., & Singh, S. (2024). A review on factors affecting and performance of nutritional security of women and children in India. In *Impact of Women in Food and Agricultural Development*. IGI Global., DOI: 10.4018/979-8-3693-3037-1.ch019

Singh, K. D., Deep Singh, P., Bansal, A., Kaur, G., Khullar, V., & Tripathi, V. (2023). Exploratory Data Analysis and Customer Churn Prediction for the Telecommunication Industry. *ACCESS 2023 - 2023 3rd International Conference on Advances in Computing, Communication, Embedded and Secure Systems*, 197 – 201. DOI: 10.1109/ACCESS57397.2023.10199700

Singh, K. U., Chaudhary, V., Sharma, P. K., Kumar, P., Varshney, N., & Singh, T. (2024). Integrating GPS and GSM Technologies for Enhanced Women's Safety: A Fingerprint-Activated Device Approach. *2024 International Conference on Automation and Computation, AUTOCOM 2024*, 657 – 662. DOI: 10.1109/AUTOCOM60220.2024.10486120

Singh, P., & Singh, K. D. (2023). Fog-Centric Intelligent Surveillance System: A Novel Approach for Effective and Efficient Surveillance. In K. R., K. R., G. M., G. M., S. R., & S. R. (Eds.), *2023 International Conference on Advancement in Computation and Computer Technologies, InCACCT 2023* (pp. 762 – 766). Institute of Electrical and Electronics Engineers Inc. DOI: 10.1109/InCACCT57535.2023.10141802

Srivastava, B., Kandpal, V., & Jain, A. K. (2024). Financial well-being of women self-help group members: A qualitative study. *Environment, Development and Sustainability*. Advance online publication. DOI: 10.1007/s10668-024-04879-w

Tamilmani, S., Mohan, T., Jeyalakshmi, S., Shukla, G. P., Gehlot, A., & Shukla, S. K. (2023). Blockchain Integrated with Industrial IOT Towards Industry 4.0. *2023 International Conference on Artificial Intelligence and Smart Communication, AISC 2023*, 575 – 581. DOI: 10.1109/AISC56616.2023.10085226

Taneja, S., Bhatnagar, M., Kumar, P., & Grima, S. (2023). A Panel Analysis of the Effectiveness of the Asset Management in Indian Agricultural Companies. *International Journal of Sustainable Development and Planning*, 18(3), 653–660. DOI: 10.18280/ijsdp.180301

Taneja, S., Bhatnagar, M., Kumar, P., & Rupeika-apoga, R. (2023). India's Total Natural Resource Rents (NRR) and GDP: An Augmented Autoregressive Distributed Lag (ARDL) Bound Test. *Journal of Risk and Financial Management*, 16(2), 91. https://doi.org/doi.org/10.3390/jrfm16020091. DOI: 10.3390/jrfm16020091

Taneja, S., Gupta, M., Bhushan, P., Bhatnagar, M., & Singh, A. (2023). Cultural marketing in the digital era. In *Cultural Marketing and Metaverse for Consumer Engagement*. IGI Global., DOI: 10.4018/978-1-6684-8312-1.ch008

Taneja, S., & Özen, E. (2023). To analyse the relationship between bank's green financing and environmental performance. *International Journal of Electronic Finance*, 12(2), 163–175. DOI: 10.1504/IJEF.2023.129919

Taneja, S., & Sharma, V. (2023). Role of beaconing marketing in improving customer buying experience. In *Enhancing Customer Engagement Through Location-Based Marketing*. IGI Global., DOI: 10.4018/978-1-6684-8177-6.ch012

Tripathi, V. M., & Mohan, A. (2016). Microfinance and empowering rural women in the Terai, Uttarakhand, India. *International Journal of Agricultural and Statistics Sciences*, 12(2), 523–530.

Tyagi, S., Krishna, K. H., Joshi, K., Ghodke, T. A., Kumar, A., & Gupta, A. (2023). Integration of PLCC modem and Wi-Fi for Campus Street Light Monitoring. In N. P., S. M., K. M., J. V., & G. K. (Eds.), *Proceedings - 4th IEEE 2023 International Conference on Computing, Communication, and Intelligent Systems, ICCCIS 2023* (pp. 1113 – 1116). Institute of Electrical and Electronics Engineers Inc. DOI: 10.1109/ICCCIS60361.2023.10425715

Unhelkar, B., Joshi, S., Sharma, M., Prakash, S., Mani, A. K., & Prasad, M. (2022). Enhancing supply chain performance using RFID technology and decision support systems in the industry 4.0–A systematic literature review. *International Journal of Information Management Data Insights*, 2(2), 100084. Advance online publication. DOI: 10.1016/j.jjimei.2022.100084

Uniyal, A. K., Kanojia, P., Khanna, R., & Dixit, A. K. (2022). Quantitative Analysis of the Impact of Demography and Job Profile on the Organizational Commitment of the Faculty Members in the HEI'S of Uttarakhand. *Communications in Computer and Information Science, 1742 CCIS*, 24–35. DOI: 10.1007/978-3-031-23647-1_3

Zhang, Y., Cao, C., Gu, J., & Garg, H. (2023). The Impact of Top Management Team Characteristics on the Risk Taking of Chinese Private Construction Enterprises. *Systems*, 11(2), 67. Advance online publication. DOI: 10.3390/systems11020067

Chapter 8
AI, IoT, and Blockchain in Healthcare:
Bridging Technology and Patient Wellbeing

Krishnaveni Subramani
SR University, India

Geetha Manoharan
https://orcid.org/0000-0002-8644-8871
SR University, India

ABSTRACT

Digital technology increases diagnosis, treatment, and efficiency, transforming healthcare. This article uses real-life business examples to demonstrate how blockchain technology, AI, and IoT are changing health care and how they may help. AI algorithms speed up and enhance diagnostic, prognostic, and therapeutic decision-making. IoT devices can monitor patients, offer remote health care, and collect data instantly, improving outcomes and resource use. Blockchain technology protects patient privacy and promotes healthcare system collaboration by securely and transparently managing medical records. As seen in this chapter, these technologies work well. Using AI in imaging and genetics simplifies early diagnosis and treatment planning. Wearable health monitoring, smart implants, and telemedicine can improve patient treatment. Blockchain technology will secure EHRs, manage medicine supply chains, and facilitate clinical trials. The Internet of Things, blockchain technology, and AI are improving data privacy, patient participation, and treatment availability in healthcare.

INTRODUCTION

The healthcare industry is witnessing a deep-rooted transformation through the injection of sophisticated technologies such as Artificial Intelligence, the Internet of Things, and Blockchain. The revolution fundamentally changes the patient care paradigm, makes operational processes better, and enhances data management. A rising demand for tailored and precise medical interventions is testimony to how these technologies can change outcomes for patients. They face persistent issues of healthcare, such as the issue of data privacy and interoperability, which poses a critical need for healthcare delivery to be carried

DOI: 10.4018/979-8-3373-0240-9.ch008

Copyright ©2025, IGI Global Scientific Publishing. Copying or distributing in print or electronic forms without written permission of IGI Global Scientific Publishing is prohibited.

out in real-time. Chapter 2 discusses how the AI, IoT, and Blockchain technologies are influencing and redefining the current scenario of patient care welfare, healthcare delivery, and, above all, major critical issues of security, management of data, and centering patient care.

The Role of AI in Healthcare

Artificial intelligence carries out a variety of functions in the healthcare ecosystem. These functions range from diagnostics to personalised treatment. Artificial intelligence speeds up and enhances the accuracy of medical decision-making through the analysis of complex statistics, the recognition of new patterns, and the illumination of insights that were hitherto inaccessible to human practitioners (Goyal et al., 2015). These are all examples of how AI can improve the field of medicine.

- **AI and Predictive Analytics in Diagnostics**

This means artificial intelligence is pretty useful for recognizing patterns in diagnostic procedures, thereby giving a good advantage. Machine learning techniques have accuracy at par with that of human radiologists with data from medical images, which include X-rays, CT scans, or MRIs, for instance, when diagnosing disease cases like cancer, pneumonia, or fractures. Predictive analytics, which are fueled by artificial intelligence, will be able to predict potential disease outbreaks or the probability of patient readmissions, which is achieved by processing large amounts of patient information, including genomic data and electronic health records.

- **AI in Personalized Medicine**

Artificial intelligence is also shaping the outcomes in the domain of personalized medicine. Artificial intelligence helps to personalize pharmaceuticals by breaking down genomic data to ensure the enhancement of therapies about ailments such as diabetes, cardiovascular diseases, and cancer (Yadav et al., 2023). This allows medications that are tailored to the genetic profiles of specific patients. Artificial intelligence models allow a decrease in reliance on trial-and-error methods, thereby improving the patient's outcome. This is through identifying those drugs or therapies that benefit most particular patients (Ambika et al., 2023).

- **AI in Robotic Surgery**

The other major driving force for the change in the surgical procedure is artificial intelligence through robotic-assisted procedures. Patients undergoing robotic surgery enjoy the benefits of increased precision, lesser invasiveness, and quicker healing processes (Kumar et al., 2023). It reduces the chances of mistakes through human intervention in surgeons, as artificial intelligence algorithms make the surgeons more accurate, and these algorithms also offer quick insights. As a result of the developments in surgical robots, patients now have access to solutions that are safer and less intrusive, which has resulted in a transformation in the execution of complex surgeries (Alexopoulos et al., 2023).

The Internet of Things (IoT) in Health Care

In healthcare, the Internet of Things (IoT) links sensors, systems, and devices to allow real-time monitoring, data collecting, and patient-provider communication. The explosion of IoT devices has made more proactive and preventative care possible, hence transforming the healthcare paradigm from reactive to predictive models of treatment (V. Sharma & Jain, 2020).

- **Wearable Devices and Remote Patient Monitoring**

Smartwatches, fitness trackers, biosensors, and other wearable health gadgets let vital signs including heart rate, blood pressure, and glucose level constantly be monitored (Rawat et al., 2022). These gadgets enable early action should anomalies be found by gathering real-time data and forwarding it to healthcare providers. Remote patient monitoring driven by the Internet of Things helps patients with chronic diseases like diabetes and hypertension control their symptoms so they may get treatment without regular hospital trips.

- **Smart Hospitals and Connected Healthcare Systems**

Beyond patient monitoring, IoT technology reaches smart hospitals where linked gadgets maximise hospital operations (A. B. Singh et al., 2023). IoT-enabled devices can track the whereabouts of assets like wheelchairs and defibrillators, monitor medical equipment, and even run hospital surroundings (e.g., lighting, temperature). This link increases the patient experience, simplifies hospital operations, and helps to maximise resources.

- **IoT and Preventive Healthcare**

Preventive healthcare depends much on IoT since it offers continuous data capable of spotting early warning signals of possible medical conditions. IoT-enabled sensors, for instance, can track patient surroundings for elements influencing health such humidity or air quality (Alrashed et al., 2022). This information gives health practitioners the ability to have focused treatments before the challenges are heightened, which aids in a better outcome at long run.
Block chain for Healthcare

- **Block chain in Healthcare**

Block chain is that technology, which in any case has given the whole world the chance of conducting and handling medical records transparently, securely, and most importantly distributed. In essence, blockchain deals with core concerns related to data security and privacy while interoperability forms a cornerstone for preserving trust from the patient and working cohesively by many service providers in health sectors (S. Sharma, Singh, et al., 2023).

- **Securing Health Records with Blockchain**

The most important application of blockchain technology in the industry is the secure management and sharing of electronic health records. The decentralized nature of blockchain ensures that patient information is stored safely and immutably. Every change or transaction entered into a patient's record is encrypted and verified, which enables healthcare providers to access the correct, current information while preventing unauthorized access or data breaches.

- **Blockchain for Interoperability and Data Sharing**

Because different providers approach handling patient data differently, health systems sometimes suffer from interoperability. A standard distributed ledger can guarantee the security of sharing health care information across different institutions and allow the seamless transfer of information from one entity to another, ensuring a flow of care without disruption in situations of transferring a patient to a different facility or treatment under different specialities.

- **Blockchain in Clinical Trials and Drug Supply Chains**

In a larger scheme, both clinical trial settings and drug supply chain will now become the realms for blockchain innovation. While data in any clinical setting would be preserved and its existence would forever be locked down with complete transparency provided through blockchain innovation, which automatically prevents its manipulation; likewise, for pharmaceutical use cases, by implementing it from manufacturers through the end customer, that is tracking from the suppliers to a specific consumer group, blocks every possibility to reach consumer market with even a negligible percent of potential counterfeit pharmaceutical products.

Objectives Framed for the Study

- To investigate how artificial intelligence (AI) could improve surgical techniques, predictive analytics, personalised medication, and diagnosis accuracy in healthcare.
- To investigate for real-time patient monitoring, remote care, smart hospitals, and preventative healthcare practices Internet of Things (IoT) application in healthcare.
- To examine Blockchain technology's uses in guaranteeing transparency in clinical trials and pharmaceutical supply chains, enhancing interoperability, and safeguarding of electronic health records (EHRs).
- Highlighting the potential to transform the healthcare landscape and enhance patient-focused care provides a lens through which to explore the future trajectories of these emerging technologies.
- To underline actual case studies and examples showing how these technologies are now applied in healthcare systems.

Literature Support

According to previous studies, blockchain, IoT, and AI technologies now present unprecedented opportunities for a smart city's transformation in healthcare. This essay examines this mutually dependent relationship between such technologies and has the potential to revolutionise health care delivery in the future (Pattanshetti et al., 2021). The integration of advanced analytics in healthcare systems ensures that appropriate treatment tactics can be developed, with errors during diagnosis being kept at a minimum through all this, under the guide of AI. Being connected and sensor-enabled, IoT devices empower both the patient and the provider to quickly and seamlessly acquire real-time information. With blockchain technology, medical records are retained securely in a decentralized, robust framework for sharing and preserving sensitive information. All of this applies to the general process to form harmonious health care structures on the territory of the towns and to develop access of all types of medical aid, considering first of all those, which are preventative. Therefore, it will support healthy life for the entire people as well as an upgrade in general quality of it. Technologies that currently advance are wearable health devices, telemedicine, smart hospitals, and predictive analytics – thus, a very limited view of what would follow there. Still, to unlock the full benefits of artificial intelligence, IoT, and Blockchain in healthcare, several obstacles have to be overcome, including apprehensions over data privacy and interoperability issues and even regulatory frameworks.

Recent studies identified that one of the Sustainable Development Goals (SDGs) is to promote healthy lives and well-being for all ages. Provide cheap, environmentally sustainable medical services to the people equally and equitably. Health and well-being goals include fair health outcomes and strong healthcare systems (Jindal et al., 2022; Onyema et al., 2022; Prikshat et al., 2019). It also emphasises the need to incorporate sustainable health into emerging countries' social health policy frameworks. Healthcare reform relies on ICTs to increase patient access, treatment quality, and system efficiency. This transition also highlights digital accessibility, sustainability, innovation, cybersecurity, and digital leadership. Digital transformation - integrating rapidly evolving ICT technologies into healthcare systems-is difficult. Integration, application design, and security are issues. Numerous research has been suggested to include ICT technologies into healthcare systems. However, they have limited scope and have not explored key variables. Thus, a detailed research study on integrating technologies, design issues, security and privacy challenges, application areas, and potential benefits and drawbacks is needed. This publication contributes to the research literature on a key SDG, "Good health and well-being," and its digital transformation, as well as a complete and taxonomical summary of our findings. First, we analyse a comprehensive taxonomy of prior research on healthcare and well-being, focusing on ICT in healthcare, specifically sustainability, security and privacy, design and integration, E-Health applications, and future research directions.

Previous studies examined groundbreaking case research on the revolutionary integration of Internet of Things (IoT) architecture in healthcare. First case study: clinic-based real-time patient fitness monitoring (Mangla et al., 2018; Nikolaidis et al., 2022; Pant et al., 2017). The recommended device features oxygen, pressure, and temperature sensors and is Internet of Things-ready. Artificial Neural Networks (ANN), Decision Trees (DT), and Support Vector Machines (SVM) are used to predict patient health. The second case study examines IoT's impact on patient-precise medicine identification and remote fitness monitoring, revealing accessibility, price, and human interface difficulties. Proposed solutions, which include more education, accessibility, user-friendly interfaces, and technical support, were tested with 30 patients over three months. The results show a rise in impacted person health and increased health monitoring. The findings show how IoT technologies can improve healthcare by providing proactive patient care. This study provides valuable information that can be used to solve practical problems, promote patient-centered solutions, and expand healthcare. Successful outcomes demonstrate the ability for continued innovation, cooperation, and development in IoT system integration for optimal patient care, a major step towards a patient-centered and technologically sophisticated healthcare environment.

Dani et al., 2020 stated that incorporating AI into healthcare is a disruptive change with significant potential to improve patient care. This study critically investigates this integration, addressing ethical, legal, and technological issues such patient privacy, decision-making autonomy, and data integrity. A methodical examination of these concerns emphasises Differential Privacy as a key strategy for patient confidentiality in AI-driven healthcare systems. We examine the balance between privacy and healthcare data utility, emphasising encryption, Differential Privacy, and mixed-model techniques. AI integration in healthcare requires complex ethical and regulatory contexts, which the article navigates. We thoroughly discuss patient rights, informed consent, and the difficulties of integrating blockchain with the GDPR. Exploring algorithmic bias in healthcare highlights the need for effective bias detection and mitigation measures to improve patient trust. These studies look into the role shifts of decentralized data sharing, regulatory frameworks, and patient agency. A multi-stakeholder strategy combining a multidisciplinary approach with responsive governance will put healthcare AI in the best position to align with ethical principles, keep the focus on patient-centered outcomes, and direct AI in responsible and equitable patient care improvements.

According to Khan et al., 2020, data security, interoperability, and transparency issues affect the healthcare sector. Interoperability and transparency have created barriers that hinder information exchange among healthcare providers; hence, efficiency is affected, and patient care worsens. This paper attempts to explore the potential for blockchain technology in addressing such challenges. Intrinsic nature of blockchain ensures patient safety in terms of their healthcare records and promotes healthy collaboration within the healthcare domain. Blockchain technology ensures that information is standardized and executed transactionally while avoiding duplication test and improving accuracy in this information. Blockchain ensures there is efficient administrative workflow so that patients are quickly treated and proper treatment plan formulates. It will enable patients to control their information. They have the authority to authorize or reject access to particular records of specific individuals or companies. Blockchain promotes the health enterprise's transparency, reliability, and collaboration through the integration of its use in the clinical trial, the chain of supply, bill generation, and medical study. Blockchain can protect and publish electronic health records and elevate the performance of supply chain management and the efficiency in the bill payment of health care. The benefits are saving cost, better protection of data, increased operational efficiency, and improved patient outcomes. This paper will, therefore, demonstrate the application of blockchain technology for changing the healthcare industry.

Rana et al., 2022 noted that AI has developed within health and wellbeing systems and revolutionized the traditional health care model. This chapter explains several applications of AI in health care, including diagnostics, treatment planning, personalized medicine, and patient outcome. AI technologies like machine learning and deep learning can analyse big datasets including medical pictures, genetic data, and electronic health records. These technologies reduce disease detection time and improve diagnostic accuracy, helping healthcare practitioners make educated decisions. AI-driven algorithms help plan personalised treatments. AI models can anticipate treatment responses, optimise drug regimens, and reduce side effects using patient-specific data.

Jain et al., 2023 investigated that despite the growing use of IoT as a foundation for future applications. Since blockchains have built-in security, integrating them with IoT helps provide basic security. IoT-blockchain technology will transform healthcare IoT applications. Understanding blockchain IoT healthcare applications is the goal of this review. Our article reviews 2018–2023 literature, focussing on IoT, Blockchain, and healthcare research. IoT-based blockchain kinds and technologies, healthcare applications, sensors, hardware tools, application databases, programming languages, software tools, problems and outstanding issues, and solutions with pros and cons are covered in this review. Our work was then compared to others on common measures. This paper examines 14 blockchain IOT healthcare applications: remote patient monitoring, patient tracking, disease prediction, COVID-19 tracking, image retrieval, medical record security, smart telemedicine, IoT security, big data, blockchain and sensors, accurate medical decisions, health monitoring, soldier tracking, and solar energy.

Tyagi et al., 2023 noted that new developments in the healthcare sector are Blockchain and artificial intelligence technology. Data on healthcare indices are gathered from Web of Sciences and other Google surveys as well as from data released by several governmental authorities. This paper presents the several ways to generate trustworthy artificial intelligence models in e-Health by means of blockchain, an open network for information sharing and authorisation. The blockchain will allow healthcare practitioners to show patient medical records; artificial intelligence employs a range of suggested algorithms and decision-making capacity along with vast amounts of data. Thus, the medical system will have enhanced service efficiency, lowered costs, and democratised healthcare by combining the most recent developments of several technologies. Blockchain allows the storing of cryptographic records-what artificial intelligence depends on.

The Convergence of AI, IoT, and Blockchain: A Holistic Approach to Healthcare

Artificial intelligence, the Internet of Things, and blockchain technologies together provide a transformative framework that greatly improves the well-being of patients as well as healthcare outcomes. Each technological advancement has benefits of its own; blockchain provides secure, transparent, and immutable data transactions; AI facilitates predictive analytics as well as customized medical solutions; and IoT provides immediate monitoring and interconnectivity among devices. This cohesive assimilation encourages a comprehensive, patient-centered, and much more effective approach to the healthcare service, ensuring a safe and efficient outcome. The assimilation of blockchain, IoT, and AI represents an opportunity of extraordinary depth in revolutionizing the health care system on more than one dimension. All the above technologies are integrated into a system that improves the welfare of patients by making diagnoses more precise, encouraging preventive care, ensuring data security, and facilitating smooth communication in health care systems.

- **AI and IoT: Revolutionizing Predictive and Personalized Care**

AI convergence with the Internet of Things will create an intelligent and responsive healthcare system. Devices connected to the Internet of Things include wearable sensors and sophisticated medical equipment that continue to collect data about patients, including vital signs, levels of physical activity, and other environmental conditions. AI scans mass flows of live data, thereby understanding patterns and anomalies that predict future health problems before their eventual worsening. In managing chronic diseases, for instance, IoT wearables happen to be devices used for checking the glucose levels and heart rates as well as the blood pressure of a patient. Concurrently, the AI algorithms interpret all the information in a sense to provide a personalized output related to the health, or an alert based on prevention of the event happening. This means that one has to shift from a mere situational response to proactive solutions that minimize hospital admissions, and the results turn much better for patients in comparison.

This constant stream of data from IoT further the role of AI in personalized medicine. Artificial intelligence combines information on genetics, clinical information, and lifestyle with real-time data from Internet of Things devices to develop a customized treatment plan. The capacity of artificial intelligence will foresee how a patient responds to some treatments, thus potentially providing treatment prescriptions that target maximizing effectiveness and minimizing unwanted effects. This precision with therapeutic approaches is a crucial advancement toward improving patient comfort and reducing the dangers attributed to conventional healthcare delivery networks. Artificial intelligence integrated into the Internet of Things culminates in advanced models for predictive healthcare (Ingale et al., 2023). The devices in the Internet of Things collect real-time patient information, which artificial intelligence analyzes to predict possible health risks for intervention. The organization toward chronic disease management possesses capabilities that can analyze data acquired from IoT wearables to unearth irregular patterns that may enable timely medical intervention.

- **Blockchain and IoT: Securing Connected Healthcare Systems**

More so, the increased usage of IoT devices in the health industry highlights the necessity for the secure transmission of data. Such networks of IoTs are at risks of attacks that would pose a threat to patients' critical data. The Blockchain offers a solution for such with a decentralized encrypted mechanism. Each interaction and transfer between IoT devices can be captured on a blockchain ledger known for its permanent features as well as being traceable. This ensures information collected from IoT devices such as remote patient monitoring are transmitted securely to healthcare professionals, thereby reducing the possibility of tampering or unauthorized access.

Blockchain, in addition, builds trust in IoT by providing a detailed record of all data transactions. This thus promotes the transparency and responsibility of managing health data. It ensures maintaining the authenticity of the patient's records, limiting access to only authorized individuals, and noting every amendment. Increasing numbers of IoT devices present an increased problem with their safety and security. Thence, blockchain can secure further on IoT since the messages conveyed among different devices can be made encrypted as well. Those encrypted messages can, therefore, only be access-ible by the receivers concerned. This is particularly critical in healthcare, where privacy of patients' information will be most important in an environment with the threat of hacking.

- **AI and Blockchain: Enhancing Trust and Data Integrity**

The quality and integrity of data would have a profound bearing on the effectiveness of algorithms in AI to achieve accuracy in analysis and prediction. The immutability ensured by blockchain guarantees the correctness and protection of data given to AI algorithms. In areas like healthcare, where decision-making can have far-reaching implications, the reliability of data is of paramount significance. This means that blockchain technology would ensure the integrity of the data coming from the patient or other medical devices; it would build more accurate AI diagnostic and predictive capabilities.

The integration of blockchain technology in AI-driven clinical trials will ensure that the data generated is immutable, verifiable, and transparent. This increases the reliability of research outcomes and promotes greater trust in the healthcare system among patients. This will help artificial intelligence by ensuring the data fed into AI models is accurate, uneditable, and clear about where it comes from. Data integrity at its core is very important because artificial intelligence relies so heavily on massive collections of information for training and decision-making processes. Immutability in blockchain records means the information in healthcare is reliable, thus making outcomes of AI models more trustworthy.

Challenges Targeting Digital Health Technologies

Despite the high promise that AI, IoT, and Blockchain hold, several challenges stand in their way in the healthcare domain. Challenges like governmental endorsement, harmonization of data standards, integration with existing systems, and protection of patient confidentiality have to be overcome before these technologies are accepted widely. Artificial intelligence, Internet of Things, and blockchain technology hold extraordinary promise to revolutionize patient care in the health sector, contribute to new research in medical science, and optimize management in hospitals. However, it comes with great difficulties, such as the problem of coordinating technical and ethical innovation issues with the need to look after patients well (Bhatt et al., 2023). The main barriers include:

- **Data Privacy and Security**

Healthcare data is extremely sensitive, and disseminating it across platforms poses considerable dangers. Artificial intelligence, Internet of Things devices, and blockchain systems manage substantial quantities of sensitive health data, rendering it susceptible to assaults and breaches. Blockchain provides improved data security via encryption and decentralised storage. Nonetheless, incorporating this into established healthcare systems can be intricate and expensive (Tiwari et al., 2023).

- **Interoperability**

Incorporating AI, IoT, and blockchain into the current healthcare infrastructure necessitates fluid communication among many platforms, devices, and databases. Numerous healthcare providers utilise diverse systems, which obstructs interoperability. Establishing standardised procedures and frameworks can facilitate the alignment of various technologies; nevertheless, collaboration among stakeholders (technology firms, healthcare providers, and regulators) is essential.

- **Data Quality and Management**

Artificial intelligence is fundamentally dependent on data to produce insights and inform decisions. Nonetheless, IoT devices frequently produce substantial volumes of unstructured and erratic data, complicating the assurance of data quality. Substandard data can result in erroneous diagnoses or treatment strategies. There seems to be a call for refined techniques in cleaning, validating, and managing data, as well as a systematic mechanism to monitor data reliability, relevance, and accuracy at various stages over time.

- **Ethical and Legal Concerns**

AI algorithms inadvertently tend to incorporate bias in the healthcare decision-making structure and continue the cycle of different treatments or false diagnoses. When blockchain technology is used to store patient information, questions of consent, ownership of data, and accountability arise. There is a need for ethical guidelines on AI in healthcare. The guidelines and rules regarding ownership and use of healthcare data, especially in IoT and blockchain systems, are very relevant.

- **Cost and Resource Allocation**

The implementation of superior technologies like AI, IoT, and blockchain requires strong monetary investment. Therefore, tremendous input into foundational systems and training with subsequent maintenance inputs would be required. These situations become very challenging where systems like healthcare have almost skeletal budgets or regions or territories do not have such robust funds. It will require massive effort from both government and universities and commercial parties in establishing funding procedures and grants and partnerships through this that could help bring together efforts to break the monetized barriers. The enabling of development and access in resource-scarce environments is a necessity.

- **Regulatory Challenges**

The architectures related to AI, the Internet of Things, and blockchain are still developing for the health sector (K. D. Singh & Singh, 2023). There remains inadequate regulation of the liability associated with AI decision-making, IoT data validation, and blockchain use in clinical trials. There is a strong demand for clear regulation that safeguards rights while at the same time fostering innovation. It lies on the health authorities, other than the technology firms, to provide a partnership on follow-up regulation in a manner that fosters innovation.

- **Trust and Adoption by Healthcare Professionals**

It will be very challenging to encourage the healthcare professionals to adopt these AI, IoT, and blockchain-based solutions into their practice. Issues regarding trust arise from the unknown nature of AI decision-making and variability in the reliability of the IoT devices. Confidence building will require AI frameworks clearly defined, training sessions very strong, and education provided to healthcare professionals, along with measurable positive changes in patient outcomes.

- **Patient-Centric Concerns**

It is critical that such technologies truly advance patient care and not simply make things more complicated. Technology over-reliance might end up depersonalizing care for patients (Juliet & Kalaiselvi., 2024). AI, IoT, and blockchain should be treated as tools that complement and expand human interaction in the delivery of healthcare. There needs to be continued focus on improving patient outcomes, safety, and experience.

- **Scalability and Integration**

Though such technologies work efficiently in a pilot project, their diffusion into the health care delivery system is very problematic. The introduction of technology to the daily routine of delivering health care, especially to mixed scenarios of technological adoption, remains challenging. Slower incremental steps with the support of high-quality education and training of healthcare practitioners will be a catalyst to positive growth. Best practices should be transferred to the other context.

- **Ethical AI in Patient Diagnosis and Treatment**

AI models in the application of diagnostic or therapeutic recommendation may, at times, fail to provide clear explanations of their decisions. This gives rise to questions regarding accountability and transparency about clinical decisions. The gradual development of explainable AI (XAI) along with the involvement of human evaluation in key decision-making functions ensures the ethical use of these technologies in patient care.

Addressing these shall be key in realizing actual promise from AI, IoT, and blockchain in healthcare, and it will create a scenario where technology improves patient wellbeing rather than complicating matters.

The Regulatory Framework of Ethical Guidelines

This basis of morality in medicine has laid down its basic principles guiding healthcare providers to provide patient-centered, empathetic care. At the core of such principles, there is respect for a patient's autonomy, an individual's rights to know and decide his or her treatment. At the same time, beneficence principles call healthcare providers to their best care of patient well-being in the practice as they continue to maximize possible outcomes but minimize harm for such patients within the doctrine of non-maleficence. Such integration in AI in health care generates quite profound questions in ethical theory, notably concerning those related to decision-making algorithms or the nature of a patient's autonomy. Clarifying mechanisms behind AI decision-making processes are very important to make the patients trust them. Another important aspect is the necessity of IoT devices and blockchain systems to adhere to regulations that exist in the health care sector, such as HIPAA, for safety protection of patient information.

The principles of fairness highlight the equity in using healthcare resources and treatments for the distribution and provision opportunities to all. Honesty and confidentiality as the foundations point out the appropriateness in both clear and open communication, but also keeping a patient's personal details private. The essence of fidelity or professional loyalty is a core commitment that healthcare professionals take as their responsibility and obligation to serve while maintaining trust in the relationship between the physician and patient and the health-care system at large. All these principles, outlined above, form a cohesive ethical framework to guide medical professionals' decision-making. Each and every element has played harmoniously in matters related to personal rights, social equity, and integrity in the profession. In such an increasingly changing landscape for health, these are guiding principles of ethics in practice to uphold the well-being of the patients and to live out basic values that make the medical profession. Continued reflection in these aspects helps professionals move in ways that can guarantee integrity in their practice with compassion, maintaining commitment to the right standard.

All the aspects regarding patient safety monitoring, private data, traceability of actions performed, accountability, and security should be covered by digital health technologies (Josphineleela, Kaliappan, et al., 2023). Frameworks to tackle the misuse that might occur should also be created and implemented. The WHO published a draft framework last year, which is useful for the development of integrated digital health interventions within the healthcare industry. The WHO has developed guidelines concerning digital healthcare interventions, by which these technologies should be judged against a number of criteria that include benefits, possible downsides, acceptability, practicality, resource utilization, and issues of equity (Vij, 2024). These recommendations view digital tools as an essential element in the pursuit of universal health coverage and long-term sustainability.

Ethical frameworks for integrating AI in healthcare are designed to throw light on the directions of developers, users, and regulators toward better design and usage with adequate oversight. At the core of every ethical framework is respect for human dignity and intrinsic value. These underpinning values support ethical norms that outline roles and responsibilities in the development, implementation, and continuous review of AI technology for health. The European Regulation, in effect since April 21, 2021, places AI products in the appropriate category based on their capacity to cause harm to such fundamental rights as health and safety, dignity, freedom, equality, democracy, the right to non-discrimination, and data protection.

In this classification, ethical considerations are crucial for all parties involved in the proper development, implementation, and evaluation of AI technology in healthcare. This comprehensive group includes physicians, system developers, healthcare administrators, health authority policymakers, and local and national governments. Ethical standards should act as catalysts, facilitating and assisting governments and public sector organisations in adjusting to the swift advancement of AI technology via legislation and regulation. Furthermore, these concepts ought to enable medical practitioners to prudently utilise AI technologies in their practice.

In the context of utilising AI technology for societal benefit, the literature has identified six essential principles advocating for the ethical development of these technologies. Fundamental principles frequently employed in bioethics include beneficence and non-maleficence (i.e., the obligation to do no harm and to minimise the benefit/risk trade-off), autonomy (the respect for an individual's right to make decisions), and justice (the commitment to fairness, ensuring that no individual or group experiences discrimination, neglect, manipulation, domination, or abuse).

Figure 1. Principles & guidelines of AI in healthcare

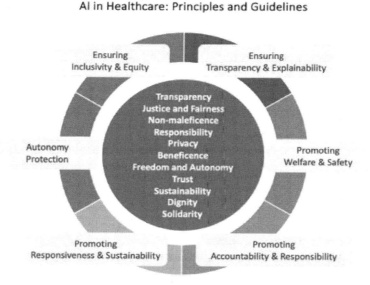

- Autonomy Protection:

The incorporation of AI may result in situations where decision-making is delegated to or collaboratively undertaken with machines. Maintaining the notion of autonomy requires that any increase in machine autonomy must not undermine human autonomy. In the realm of healthcare, this signifies that individuals ought to maintain full authority over healthcare systems and medical decisions. AI systems should be cautiously and continually designed with regards to values and human rights. Specifically, the objective of an AI system is such that it should allow human beings-whether healthcare provider or patient-to make choices that are based on one's own desires. Also, respecting personal freedom should include protection of privacy, confidentiality, and valid informed consent in data protection by providing adequate legal frameworks.

- Promoting welfare, safety, and public interest:

Before being placed into the public domain, Artificial intelligence technology will also follow tight conditions laid to safety, correctness, and efficacy. The list provided is an outset of putting quality control while creating conditions for improvement. From there, stakeholders participating in financing, constructing, and utilization of AI technology have a joint task and responsibility to consider, review, and assess the efficacy of the AI algorithm in working properly.

- Ensure transparency, explain ability and intelligibility:

Artificial intelligence needs to make sense to developers, end-users, and regulatory stakeholders. Clarity is served if there is an exposure of sufficient information that one ought to document or present before the creation and implementing of AI technology. Making this commitment to clarity allows the quality of the system to be improved in proportion to its being used also as a safety device or a safeguard for the betterment of patient care or public health. Clarity is the foundation upon which system evaluators detect and remedy defects, and government regulators rely on it to ensure robust oversight. AI technologies must be designed to be clear and to fit the comprehension capacity of their target users. A delicate balance between absolute algorithmic clarity-potentially at the expense of some accuracy-and improved accuracy-potentially at the expense of intelligibility-is an important issue of debate.

- Promoting accountability and responsibility:

Human assurance' essentially arises as an activity regarding the assessment of AI systems both through the patients and the clinicians, at their design and usage stages. Under the aegis of human assurance, exist regulatory regimes, pre-algorithm as well as post-algorithmic, which delimit the areas to be taken care of by humans. The main goal is that the algorithm should be medical in its effectiveness, open for evaluation, and under a framework of ethical obligations. Therefore, the integration of AI technology into the medical world should be under a framework of accountability within complex systems. In the case that leads to adverse medical impacts caused by AI-related technologies, accountability frameworks must be present with clearly defined responsibilities, from the developers to that of the healthcare professionals involved with those resultant outcomes. To prevent the diffusion of responsibility, when 'everyone's problem becomes nobody's responsibility,' a strong accountability framework, commonly known as 'collective responsibility,' ensures that all stakeholders in the development and implementation of AI technologies are held accountable. This methodology promotes all stakeholders to operate with integrity and reduce harm. This topic is continuously evolving and has not been adequately addressed in the legislation of numerous countries.

To guarantee suitable restitution for individuals and groups negatively impacted by algorithmic judgements, compensation procedures must be established. This should include access to timely and effective remedies and redress provided by both governmental entities and enterprises utilising AI technologies in the healthcare industry (Ahmad et al., 2023).

- Ensuring inclusivity and equity:

Inclusivity mandates that AI utilised in healthcare must be deliberately crafted to foster the widest feasible and equal access and utilisation, regardless of considerations such as age, gender, wealth, aptitude, or other distinguishing traits. AI technologies must not just address the needs and usage patterns of affluent contexts; they should also be versatile enough to adapt to diverse devices, telecommunications frameworks, and data transmission capacities, especially in economically disadvantaged settings. Both industry and governments are accountable for closing the 'digital divide' inside and among nations to guarantee equal access to emerging AI technology (S. Sharma, Kadayat, et al., 2023). AI developers must guarantee that AI data, particularly training data, are devoid of sample bias and exhibit correctness, comprehensiveness, and diversity. Specific measures must be implemented to protect the rights and welfare of vulnerable populations, together with channels for recourse in instances of bias or discrimination, whether actual or claimed.

- Promoting responsiveness and sustainability:

The responsiveness of AI requires designers, developers, and users to engage in an ongoing, systematic, and transparent evaluation of AI technology to ensure its effective and appropriate functioning in alignment with the expectations and requirements of the specific context of deployment. When an AI technology is deemed ineffective or unsatisfactory, the responsibility to respond necessitates the implementation of a systematic procedure to address the problem, which may entail ceasing the usage of the technology (K. D. Singh et al., 2023). Consequently, AI technologies should be implemented solely if they can be effortlessly assimilated into the healthcare system and obtain sufficient backing. Unfortunately, in inadequately funded healthcare systems, innovative technology is often underutilised, neglected, or not updated, resulting in a waste of valuable resources that could have been allocated to more advantageous interventions. Sustainability relies on the proactive measures taken by governments and corporations to foresee workplace interruptions. This encompasses training healthcare workers to adjust to AI integration and addressing potential job displacement resulting from the use of automated technologies for regular health services and administrative duties.

Future Trends in Digital Health Technologies

Digital health technology is swiftly revolutionising healthcare delivery, facilitating more efficient, personalised, and patient-centric care. The future presents enhanced opportunity as emerging technologies merge to tackle significant difficulties in healthcare, ranging from enhancing access to optimising therapies (Nagila et al., 2023). Here are few critical themes anticipated to influence the future of digital health.

- Expansion and Integration of Telemedicine: Telemedicine surged in significance during the COVID-19 epidemic, and its expansion is anticipated to persist (S. Sharma, Gupta, et al., 2023). In the future, telemedicine will evolve from video consultations to encompass advanced remote patient monitoring (RPM) devices. These systems will amalgamate wearables, cell phones, and Internet of Medical Things (IoMT) devices to gather real-time data, facilitating continuous health monitoring by physicians (Josphineleela, Gupta, et al., 2023). Artificial intelligence (AI) will be important in analysing this data to deliver actionable insights, forecast health trends, and identify early warning signs of disease. Telemedicine will increasingly integrate into conventional healthcare systems, facilitating a hybrid care paradigm that smoothly transitions between in-person and virtual consultations.
- Artificial Intelligence (AI) and Machine Learning (ML): Artificial Intelligence and Machine Learning are transforming diagnoses, treatment strategies, and pharmaceutical development. In diagnostics, AI systems trained on extensive datasets can discern patterns in medical imaging, laboratory results, and patient histories that may elude human observation. AI-driven predictive analytics can highlight vulnerable populations and suggest preventions. Machine learning models are used to customize the treatment regimen based on the data of patients and predict which medication would have the desired effect on the patient and, thus, is working towards expanding precision medicine. In drug development, AI is a means to depict biological systems and mimic interactions of drugs that help immensely in shortening the duration and costs associated with producing new therapies.
- Wearable and implantable health devices: The future of digital health is poised to integrate sophisticated wearable and implantable technologies that track a variety of physiological metrics, including heart rate, glucose concentrations, and blood pressure. These devices will be more precise and timely sources of health information, which can be used to proactively manage chronic conditions (Asha et al., 2022). Future wearables will be integrated into clothes or act as skin-attachable patches for seamless comfort and discretion. Advanced pacemakers and continuous glucose monitors will be implantable devices that continuously monitor the internal physiological processes. Inventions in bio-sensing technology can potentially detect early stages of diseases such as cancer, which can make a huge difference in prognosis.
- Blockchain in the Secure Healthcare Data
- The ever-increasing health data digitisation necessitates a deep focus on security as well as privacy and safety. The very decentralized immutable ledger offered through blockchain has been one impressive alternative option for storing health-related information (S. Sharma et al., 2021)In the following generation, blockchain will allow people to have better control over their health data so that secure exchange can be facilitated with medical practitioners, researchers, or insurance providers. This will be less likely to let a data breach happen and, at the same time, will be in compliance with privacy standards such as GDPR and HIPAA. Ultimately, blockchain has the potential

to significantly raise the integrity and traceability of data in clinical trials or supply chains, leading to greater transparency and trust.
- Genomics and Personalized Medicine: With a decreasing trend of costs on the sequencing of a genome, the next decades shall bring revolution with progress in genomics into individualized medicine. Future approaches are to see incorporation of genomics information with current models of medical treatments with patients to enable more unique personalized treatments. This effort will encompass pharmacogenomics: the prescribing of drugs with consideration for genetic traits that determine drug metabolism. The association of genomic data and artificial intelligence enables health professionals to predict the risks of diseases and to take preventative measures appropriate to each patient, from reactive care to proactive (Malik et al., 2022).
- Virtual Reality and Augmented Reality (VR/AR): Virtual and Augmented reality are emerging as essential tools in the spaces of medical education, surgical practice, and patient care. In this future era, interactive simulations will enable medical students and professionals to perform complex surgeries under total safety and regulation. Augmented reality will, in the operating room, be a tool for the surgeon, providing enhanced immediate visual insights into a patient's anatomy throughout surgical procedures. VR treatment also promises to treat mental health issues such as PTSD, anxiety, and phobias by creating settings that are conducive to exposure therapy (Lourens et al., 2022).

CONCLUSION

AI, IoT, and Block chain convergence is bringing a new health care system to patients by catering to the needs and experiences of the patient. The new technologies enhance diagnostics, provide tailored therapies, protect the data of patients, and allow for communication between the providers to become easy. This brings out the gap between advanced technology and patient welfare. Despite existing problems, continuous progress in these domains offers the potential for a future in which healthcare is more efficient, secure, and universally accessible (Connors, 2024). Digital health technologies are set to revolutionise the healthcare sector by augmenting diagnostic precision, expanding patient involvement, and facilitating more individualised, data-informed treatment methodologies (Ramachander & Gowri, 2025). The amalgamation of artificial intelligence, genomics, wearable technology, and secure data-sharing platforms such as block chain will propel these advances, enhancing healthcare accessibility, efficiency, and personalisation.

DECLARATION

The authors declare that the manuscript follows ethical standards and there are no potential conflicts of interest concerning this chapter's research, authorship, and publication.

DISCLAIMER

The contents and views of this chapter are expressed by the authors in personal capacities. The Editor and the Publisher don't need to agree with these viewpoints and are not responsible for any duty of care in this regard.

REFERENCES

Ahmad, I., Sharma, S., Kumar, R., Dhyani, S., & Dumka, A. (2023). Data Analytics of Online Education during Pandemic Health Crisis: A Case Study. *2nd Edition of IEEE Delhi Section Owned Conference, DELCON 2023 - Proceedings*. DOI: 10.1109/DELCON57910.2023.10127423

Alexopoulos, C., Al-Tamimi, T. A. S., & Saxena, S. (2023). Were the higher educational institutions (HEIs) in Oman ready to face pedagogical challenges during COVID-19? *Arab Gulf Journal of Scientific Research*. Advance online publication. DOI: 10.1108/AGJSR-03-2023-0095

Alrashed, F. A., Alsubiheen, A. M., Alshammari, H., Mazi, S. I., Al-Saud, S. A., Alayoubi, S., Kachanathu, S. J., Albarrati, A., Aldaihan, M. M., Ahmad, T., Sattar, K., Khan, S., & Dhiman, G. (2022). Stress, Anxiety, and Depression in Pre-Clinical Medical Students: Prevalence and Association with Sleep Disorders. *Sustainability (Basel)*, 14(18), 11320. Advance online publication. DOI: 10.3390/su141811320

Ambika, K. S. B., Goswami, S., Pimplapure, V., Jweeg, M. J., Kant, K., & Gangodkar, D. (2023). Framework Towards Detection of Stress Level Through Classifying Physiological Signals Using Machine Learning. *2023 3rd International Conference on Advance Computing and Innovative Technologies in Engineering, ICACITE 2023*, 600 – 604. DOI: 10.1109/ICACITE57410.2023.10183013

Asha, P., Mannepalli, K., Khilar, R., Subbulakshmi, N., Dhanalakshmi, R., Tripathi, V., Mohanavel, V., Sathyamurthy, R., & Sudhakar, M. (2022). Role of machine learning in attaining environmental sustainability. *Energy Reports*, 8, 863–871. DOI: 10.1016/j.egyr.2022.09.206

Bhatt, C., Singh, S., Chauhan, R., Singh, T., & Uniyal, A. (2023). Artificial Intelligence in Current Education: Roles, Applications & Challenges. *Proceedings - 2023 3rd International Conference on Pervasive Computing and Social Networking, ICPCSN 2023*, 241 – 244. DOI: 10.1109/ICPCSN58827.2023.00045

Dani, R., Kukreti, R., Negi, A., & Kholiya, D. (2020). Impact of covid-19 on education and internships of hospitality students. *International Journal of Current Research and Review*, 12(21 Special Issue), 86 – 90. DOI: 10.31782/IJCRR.2020.SP54

Goyal, P., Kukreja, T., Agarwal, A., & Khanna, N. (2015). Narrowing awareness gap by using e-learning tools for counselling university entrants. *Conference Proceeding - 2015 International Conference on Advances in Computer Engineering and Applications, ICACEA 2015*, 847 – 851. DOI: 10.1109/ICACEA.2015.7164822

Ingale, N. V., Saravana Kumar, G., Panduro-Ramirez, J., Raj, M., Vaseem Akram, S., & Rawat, R. (2023). Role of IOT in managing education management tools: A technical review. *2023 3rd International Conference on Advance Computing and Innovative Technologies in Engineering, ICACITE 2023*, 2056 – 2061. DOI: 10.1109/ICACITE57410.2023.10182953

Jain, P., Gupta, V. K., Tiwari, H., Shukla, A., Pandey, P., & Gupta, A. (2023). Human-Computer Interaction: A Systematic Review. In M. H.K. & S. S. (Eds.), *Proceedings - 2023 International Conference on Advanced Computing and Communication Technologies, ICACCTech 2023* (pp. 31 – 36). Institute of Electrical and Electronics Engineers Inc. DOI: 10.1109/ICACCTech61146.2023.00015

Jindal, M., Bajal, E., Singh, P., Diwakar, M., Arya, C., & Sharma, K. (2022). Online education in Covid-19: Limitations and improvements. *2021 IEEE 8th Uttar Pradesh Section International Conference on Electrical, Electronics and Computer Engineering, UPCON 2021*. DOI: 10.1109/UPCON52273.2021.9667605

Josphineleela, R., Gupta, R., Misra, N., Malik, M., Somasundaram, K., & Gangodkar, D. (2023). Blockchain Based Multi-Layer Security Network Authentication System for Uncertain Attack in the Wireless Communication System. *2023 3rd International Conference on Advance Computing and Innovative Technologies in Engineering, ICACITE 2023*, 877 – 881. DOI: 10.1109/ICACITE57410.2023.10182747

Josphineleela, R., Kaliappan, S., Natrayan, L., & Bhatt, U. M. (2023). Intelligent Virtual Laboratory Development and Implementation using the RASA Framework. *Proceedings - 7th International Conference on Computing Methodologies and Communication, ICCMC 2023*, 1172 – 1176. DOI: 10.1109/ICCMC56507.2023.10083701

Khan, T., Singh, K., & Purohit, K. C. (2020). Icma: An efficient integrated congestion control approach. *Recent Patents on Engineering*, 14(3), 294–309. DOI: 10.2174/1872212114666191231150916

Kumar, R., Sexena, A., & Gehlot, A. (2023). Artificial Intelligence in Smart Education and Futuristic Challenges. *2023 International Conference on Disruptive Technologies, ICDT 2023*, 432 – 435. DOI: 10.1109/ICDT57929.2023.10151129

Lourens, M., Krishna, S. H., Singh, A., Dey, S. K., Pant, B., & Sharma, T. (2022). Role of Artificial Intelligence in Formative Employee Engagement. In D. R.K., S. A.Kr., K. G., & B. S. (Eds.), *Proceedings of the 2022 11th International Conference on System Modeling and Advancement in Research Trends, SMART 2022* (pp. 936 – 941). Institute of Electrical and Electronics Engineers Inc. DOI: 10.1109/SMART55829.2022.10047422

Malik, P., Singh, A. K., Nautiyal, R., & Rawat, S. (2022). Mapping AICTE cybersecurity curriculum onto CyBOK: A case study. In *Machine Learning for Cyber Security*. De Gruyter., DOI: 10.1515/9783110766745-007

Mangla, S. K., Luthra, S., Mishra, N., Singh, A., Rana, N. P., Dora, M., & Dwivedi, Y. (2018). Barriers to effective circular supply chain management in a developing country context. *Production Planning and Control*, 29(6), 551–569. DOI: 10.1080/09537287.2018.1449265

Nagila, A., Saravanakumar, P., Pranavan, S., Goutam, R., Dobhal, D. C., & Singh, G. (2023). An Innovative Approach of CNN-BiGRU Based Post-Earthquake Damage Detection of Reinforced Concrete for Frame Buildings. *International Conference on Self Sustainable Artificial Intelligence Systems, ICSSAS 2023 - Proceedings*, 56 – 61. DOI: 10.1109/ICSSAS57918.2023.10331894

Nikolaidis, P., Ismail, M., Shuib, L., Khan, S., & Dhiman, G. (2022). Predicting Student Attrition in Higher Education through the Determinants of Learning Progress: A Structural Equation Modelling Approach. *Sustainability (Basel)*, 14(20), 13584. Advance online publication. DOI: 10.3390/su142013584

Onyema, E. M., Almuzaini, K. K., Onu, F. U., Verma, D., Gregory, U. S., Puttaramaiah, M., & Afriyie, R. K. (2022). Prospects and Challenges of Using Machine Learning for Academic Forecasting. *Computational Intelligence and Neuroscience*, 2022, 1–7. Advance online publication. DOI: 10.1155/2022/5624475 PMID: 35909823

Pant, V., Bhasin, S., & Jain, S. (2017). Self-Learning system for personalized E-Learning. *2017 International Conference on Emerging Trends in Computing and Communication Technologies, ICETCCT 2017, 2018-Janua*, 1 – 6. DOI: 10.1109/ICETCCT.2017.8280344

Pattanshetti, M. K., Jasola, S., Rajput, A., & Pant, V. (2021). Proposed eLearning framework using open corpus web resources. *Proceedings of the 2021 1st International Conference on Advances in Electrical, Computing, Communications and Sustainable Technologies, ICAECT 2021.* DOI: 10.1109/ICAECT49130.2021.9392591

Prikshat, V., Kumar, S., & Nankervis, A. (2019). Work-readiness integrated competence model: Conceptualisation and scale development. *Education + Training*, 61(5), 568–589. DOI: 10.1108/ET-05-2018-0114

Rana, D. S., Dimri, S. C., Malik, P., & Dhondiyal, S. A. (2022). Impact of Computational Thinking in Engineering and K12 Education. *4th International Conference on Inventive Research in Computing Applications, ICIRCA 2022 - Proceedings*, 697 – 701. DOI: 10.1109/ICIRCA54612.2022.9985593

Rawat, R. S., Singh, V., & Dumka, A. (2022). Complaint Management in Ethiopian Vocational and Technical Education Institutions: A Framework and Implementation of a Decision Support System. *2022 International Conference on 4th Industrial Revolution Based Technology and Practices, ICFIRTP 2022*, 73 – 79. DOI: 10.1109/ICFIRTP56122.2022.10063207

Sharma, S., Gupta, A., & Tyagi, R. (2023). Artificial Intelligence Enabled Sustainable Education System Using Vedic Scripture and Cyber Security. *2023 2nd International Conference on Advances in Computational Intelligence and Communication, ICACIC 2023.* DOI: 10.1109/ICACIC59454.2023.10435133

Sharma, S., Kadayat, Y., & Tyagi, R. (2023). Sustainable Global Democratic e-Governance System Using Vedic Scripture, Artificial Intelligence, Cloud Computing and Augmented Reality. *Proceedings of the International Conference on Circuit Power and Computing Technologies, ICCPCT 2023*, 113 – 118. DOI: 10.1109/ICCPCT58313.2023.10245405

Sharma, S., Singh, V., & Sarkar, D. (2023). Machine Vision Enabled Fall Detection System for Specially Abled People in Limited Visibility Environment. *2023 3rd Asian Conference on Innovation in Technology, ASIANCON 2023.* DOI: 10.1109/ASIANCON58793.2023.10270769

Sharma, S., Singh Rawal, R., Pandey, D., & Pandey, N. (2021). Microbial World for Sustainable Development. In *Microbial Technology for Sustainable Environment*. Springer Nature., DOI: 10.1007/978-981-16-3840-4_1

Sharma, V., & Jain, S. (2020). Managers Training Programs Effectiveness Evaluation by using different Machine Learning Approaches. *Proceedings of the 4th International Conference on Electronics, Communication and Aerospace Technology, ICECA 2020*, 1453–1457. DOI: 10.1109/ICECA49313.2020.9297556

Singh, A. B., Meena, H. K., Khandelwal, C., & Dangayach, G. S. (2023). Sustainability Assessment of Higher Education Institutions: A Systematic Literature Review †. *Engineering Proceedings*, 37(1), 23. Advance online publication. DOI: 10.3390/ECP2023-14728

Singh, K. D., & Singh, P. (2023). A Novel Cloud-based Framework to Predict the Employability of Students. In K. R., K. R., G. M., G. M., S. R., & S. R. (Eds.), *2023 International Conference on Advancement in Computation and Computer Technologies, InCACCT 2023* (pp. 528 – 532). Institute of Electrical and Electronics Engineers Inc. DOI: 10.1109/InCACCT57535.2023.10141760

Singh, K. D., Singh, P., Kaur, G., Khullar, V., Chhabra, R., & Tripathi, V. (2023). Education 4.0: Exploring the Potential of Disruptive Technologies in Transforming Learning. *Proceedings of International Conference on Computational Intelligence and Sustainable Engineering Solution, CISES 2023*, 586 – 591. DOI: 10.1109/CISES58720.2023.10183547

Tiwari, R., Agrawal, P., Singh, P., Bajaj, S., Verma, V., & Chauhan, A. S. (2023). Technology Enabled Integrated Fusion Teaching for Enhancing Learning Outcomes in Higher Education. *International Journal of Emerging Technologies in Learning*, 18(7), 243–249. DOI: 10.3991/ijet.v18i07.36799

Tyagi, S., Mathur, K., Gupta, T., Khantwal, S., & Tripathi, V. (2023). The Effectiveness of Augmented Reality in Developing Pre-Primary Student's Cognitive Skills. *IEEE Region 10 Humanitarian Technology Conference, R10-HTC*, 997 – 1002. DOI: 10.1109/R10-HTC57504.2023.10461754

Yadav, P. M., Patra, I., Mittal, V., Nagorao, C. G., Udhayanila, R., & Saranya, A. (2023). Implementation of IOT on English Language Classroom Management. *2023 3rd International Conference on Advance Computing and Innovative Technologies in Engineering, ICACITE 2023*, 1686 – 1690. DOI: 10.1109/ICACITE57410.2023.10182984

Chapter 9
AI and Language:
Transforming Communication in Health and Wellness

Preeti Tushar Joshi
https://orcid.org/0000-0003-3995-2458
Sri Balaji Vidyapeeth University, India

Eldad Tsabary
Concordia University, Canada

Isanka P. Gamage
University of Kelaniya, Sri Lanka

ABSTRACT

Artificial Intelligence (AI) has significantly transformed communication within the health and wellness industry. This transformation has not only enhanced healthcare delivery but also empowered individuals with tools and resources that facilitate proactive, personalized wellness management. Through language-based AI applications like chatbots, voice assistants, and Natural Language Processing (NLP) algorithms, healthcare providers can offer seamless patient experiences, enhance accessibility, and support decision-making. Additionally, these AI-driven communication tools help break language barriers, foster patient engagement, and encourage healthy lifestyle choices. This chapter delves into the mechanisms, applications, and implications of AI in reshaping communication in health and wellness, analyzing the ethical, practical, and social facets of this transformation

INTRODUCTION

The advent of Artificial Intelligence (AI) in health and wellness has redefined how communication takes place between healthcare providers, wellness platforms, and individuals (A. S. Kumar & Desi, 2023). What was once a field dominated by face-to-face interactions, in-person consultations, and traditional media has now expanded to include digital and automated communication channels powered by AI. This transformation has been driven by a need for increased accessibility, personalization, efficiency, and effectiveness in health and wellness (Kohli et al., 2022). With these advancements, AI offers the

DOI: 10.4018/979-8-3373-0240-9.ch009

potential to make healthcare more inclusive and comprehensive, helping individuals manage their health proactively and effectively. However, as promising as AI applications are, they also raise unique challenges around privacy, ethics, accessibility, and reliability (N. K. Singh, Singh, Sharma, Paswan, et al., 2021).

The Importance of Communication in Health and Wellness

In health and wellness, communication serves as the bedrock for effective care. Accurate, timely, and empathetic communication can improve patient satisfaction, enhance treatment adherence, support preventive care, and ultimately lead to better health outcomes (Rana et al., 2022). Traditional healthcare systems have often relied on interpersonal interactions—physicians talking to patients, nurses explaining treatment protocols, and wellness coaches providing guidance (Bordoloi et al., 2022). This human-centric approach, while valuable, has limitations in terms of accessibility, especially for people in remote areas or for those who face barriers related to language, disability, or socioeconomic status (Kathir et al., 2022). Additionally, the high demand for healthcare services can overburden professionals, limiting the time they can devote to each patient and sometimes affecting the quality of communication (N. K. Singh, Singh, Rahim, et al., 2023).

AI addresses many of these challenges by supplementing human capabilities, enhancing the scale and reach of healthcare communication, and introducing new tools that allow healthcare providers to communicate with patients in ways that were previously impossible (P. Agarwal & Sharma, 2023). AI-driven chatbots, voice assistants, and Natural Language Processing (NLP) algorithms have become integral to health and wellness applications, enabling seamless, round-the-clock communication. These tools support healthcare providers in maintaining a high level of communication quality while expanding access to individuals who may otherwise struggle to receive consistent healthcare (S. Sharma & Bhadula, 2023).

Defining Artificial Intelligence and Its Relevance in Health and Wellness

AI refers to systems that simulate human intelligence, performing tasks that traditionally require human cognition, such as understanding language, recognizing patterns, solving problems, and making decisions (Akberdina et al., 2023; Raju et al., 2022; Shashikala et al., 2022). In the context of health and wellness, AI encompasses various applications, including machine learning, computer vision, robotics, and NLP. Each of these AI subsets contributes uniquely to enhancing communication, offering potential benefits that go beyond simple automation (AL-Huqail et al., 2022; N. K. Singh et al., 2020; Upreti et al., 2023).

- **Machine Learning (ML)** in health communication can identify patterns in data that help predict outcomes, tailor health interventions, and personalize wellness plans. By analyzing patient histories, treatment patterns, and behavioral trends, ML algorithms enable healthcare providers to communicate with patients in a targeted, individualized way (V. Aggarwal, Gupta, Sharma, et al., 2021; Mehta et al., 2021; Trache et al., 2022).
- **Natural Language Processing (NLP)** powers tools that allow AI systems to understand, interpret, and generate human language. In health and wellness applications, NLP is essential for developing chatbots and voice assistants that can communicate with patients, answering their questions, providing guidance, and even offering emotional support. NLP is particularly valuable for breaking down language barriers, as it enables health platforms to communicate in multiple languages and dialects (Rajawat et al., 2022; Tyagi et al., 2023).

- **Voice Recognition Technology**, a subset of NLP, powers voice assistants that are now integrated into various wellness devices and health platforms. This technology is especially useful for populations with visual impairments, mobility issues, or literacy challenges, as it allows them to access information and support through spoken language (Bisht et al., 2022).

Together, these AI technologies transform health and wellness communication by making it more responsive, personalized, and widely accessible.

Evolution of AI-Enhanced Communication in Health and Wellness

The journey of AI in health and wellness communication has evolved rapidly, moving from simple informational tools to sophisticated applications capable of understanding context, providing emotional responses, and even detecting early signs of health deterioration (K. Kumar et al., 2022). Initially, AI applications in healthcare were limited to diagnostic support and data management. As the technology evolved, it started to play a more direct role in patient interaction, as seen with early chatbots and basic symptom checkers (R. C. Sharma et al., 2023).

In the wellness sector, AI initially focused on tracking and monitoring physical activity, diet, and sleep patterns. However, as AI technologies grew in sophistication, they began to encompass broader aspects of mental and emotional well-being (S. Joshi, Sharma, et al., 2023). Today's AI systems not only monitor physical health but also track mental health indicators, assess mood, and provide tailored recommendations for wellness activities. The integration of AI into mobile applications, wearable devices, and online platforms has made it possible for individuals to receive real-time feedback and guidance, ensuring that health and wellness communication is not only more frequent but also more relevant and actionable (Ansari & Afzal, 2022; Johri et al., 2023; K. Joshi et al., 2023).

Key AI Applications in Health and Wellness Communication

One of the most prominent applications of AI in health communication is the use of **chatbots**. These AI-driven virtual assistants can engage in dialogue with users, answer health-related questions, provide symptom checks, and help schedule appointments. Chatbots are particularly valuable in triage situations where they can assist users in determining whether their symptoms require immediate medical attention or if they can be managed with home remedies (Hajoary et al., 2023; Sathyaseelan et al., 2023; Yadav et al., 2021). Popular health chatbots, such as Ada Health and Babylon, have already demonstrated the ability to offer initial assessments that can guide users toward appropriate care, potentially reducing the burden on emergency services and primary care providers (R. Arora et al., 2022; Davuluri et al., 2023; N. K. Pandey et al., 2023).

Voice assistants, another significant AI application, allow users to interact with health services using natural spoken language. Devices such as Amazon Alexa, Google Assistant, and Apple's Siri can respond to health inquiries, remind users to take their medications, and even provide mental health support (Krishna et al., 2022; N. K. Singh, Singh, Sharma, Singla, et al., 2021). Voice assistants are especially useful for elderly populations, who may find it challenging to interact with text-based interfaces, and for individuals with physical disabilities that limit their ability to use traditional devices. The ability to access health information hands-free enhances accessibility and helps individuals integrate wellness practices seamlessly into their daily routines (Unhelkar et al., 2022; Verma et al., 2022).

Natural Language Processing also plays a critical role in health and wellness communication by enabling AI systems to interpret and analyze vast amounts of unstructured data, such as medical records, patient feedback, and social media posts. This capability allows AI to understand patient concerns, identify trends, and provide insights that can be used to improve healthcare communication strategies (S. Gupta et al., 2022; Sathyaseelan et al., 2023; Thapa et al., 2022). For instance, sentiment analysis, a subset of NLP, can be used to gauge patient satisfaction by analyzing feedback on health services, helping healthcare providers identify areas for improvement.

Personalization and Patient-Centric Communication

One of the most profound impacts of AI in health and wellness communication is the ability to deliver highly personalized interactions. AI algorithms can analyze an individual's health data, lifestyle patterns, and preferences to create customized wellness plans, reminders, and recommendations. Personalization ensures that the information and guidance provided are relevant and actionable, increasing the likelihood of adherence to health and wellness protocols (Poswal et al., 2022; Rawat et al., 2023). For example, a fitness app powered by AI might analyze a user's activity data, dietary habits, and sleep patterns to suggest a tailored exercise and nutrition regimen. Similarly, mental health apps can use AI to monitor users' emotional states, offering suggestions for coping strategies or relaxation exercises based on their current needs (Jindal et al., 2022).

Patient-centric communication is further enhanced by AI's ability to provide emotional support. Some advanced AI-driven mental health applications, such as Woebot and Replika, are designed to engage in empathetic conversations with users, offering a form of companionship and emotional relief (S. Joshi et al., 2022; Nadeem et al., 2023). While these AI applications do not replace professional mental health support, they provide an accessible option for individuals who may not have immediate access to counseling or therapy. By using natural language to convey empathy and understanding, these applications help break down barriers associated with seeking mental health support, making wellness communication more inclusive (Diddi et al., 2022; S. Joshi & Sharma, 2023).

Addressing Language and Accessibility Barriers

AI is instrumental in breaking down language and accessibility barriers in health and wellness communication. Traditional health communication often suffers from a lack of inclusivity, as materials are typically available in only a limited number of languages and may be inaccessible to those with visual, auditory, or cognitive impairments (Shabbiruddin et al., 2023; R. Singh et al., 2022). AI addresses these challenges through multilingual NLP, which enables health platforms to communicate effectively with a diverse audience. By supporting multiple languages and dialects, AI ensures that language is no longer a barrier to accessing critical health information (A. Gupta et al., 2022; Negi et al., 2021).

Additionally, AI-powered voice and text-based solutions are adaptable to assistive technologies, making health information accessible to individuals with disabilities. For example, visually impaired users can interact with AI-driven voice assistants to receive medication reminders or track wellness activities. Similarly, AI systems with text-to-speech capabilities allow individuals with reading difficulties to understand written health materials. By making health and wellness communication universally accessible, AI fosters inclusivity and empowers individuals from all walks of life to engage with their health actively (Akberdina et al., 2023; A. Kumar & Ram, 2021).

Ethical and Privacy Considerations

Despite the transformative potential of AI in health and wellness communication, the use of AI also raises important ethical and privacy concerns. The collection, analysis, and storage of personal health data are integral to AI-driven health applications, which makes privacy and data security paramount (N. K. Singh, Singh, Singh, et al., 2023; Singla et al., 2023). Individuals are often required to share sensitive information with AI applications to receive personalized recommendations, which can expose them to privacy risks. Ensuring data security through encryption, compliance with regulations (e.g., HIPAA and GDPR), and transparent communication about data use are essential steps to build trust and protect user privacy (Manjunatha et al., 2023; Ramakrishnan et al., 2022).

Another ethical concern is the potential for bias in AI-driven health communication. AI algorithms are trained on large datasets, and if these datasets lack diversity or contain biased information, the resulting AI models may perpetuate or amplify existing inequalities (Jena & Gairola, 2022; S. K. Singh, Chauhan, & Sarkar, 2023). For instance, if a symptom-checking chatbot is trained on data that predominantly represents certain demographics, it may be less accurate or responsive to users from underrepresented groups. Ensuring fairness and inclusivity in AI health applications requires continuous monitoring, the use of diverse training data, and transparency in algorithm design (K. Pandey et al., 2020; H. Sharma et al., 2023).

Finally, there is the question of accountability and transparency. AI systems in health and wellness communication should be designed to clarify their role as supportive tools rather than substitutes for professional medical advice (Chandran et al., 2022; Gonfa et al., 2023). Miscommunication about AI's capabilities can lead to over-reliance on automated systems, potentially resulting in inappropriate self-diagnosis or delayed treatment. Clear guidelines, disclaimers, and user education are necessary to help individuals understand the limitations of AI applications and encourage them to seek professional support when needed (Rajeswari et al., 2022; Yeruva et al., 2022).

AI-Driven Chatbots in Healthcare Communication

AI-driven chatbots have emerged as transformative tools in healthcare communication, enhancing accessibility, efficiency, and personalization in patient interactions. These chatbots use Natural Language Processing (NLP) and machine learning algorithms to understand and respond to patient inquiries, provide guidance on symptom management, and even support mental health care (Mandalapu et al., 2023; Syed et al., 2022). As automated virtual assistants, healthcare chatbots are reshaping how patients engage with healthcare systems, offering support that is not only immediate but also available around the clock. This section explores the functionality, benefits, challenges, and ethical considerations of using chatbots in healthcare communication, illustrating how they are changing the landscape of patient engagement (K. Pandey et al., 2022; Tyagi et al., 2022).

Functionality of Health Chatbots

AI-driven health chatbots are designed to perform a variety of tasks that support patient care and streamline healthcare workflows. Their functionalities range from answering basic health questions and conducting symptom checks to scheduling appointments and offering mental health support. Many chatbots in healthcare operate through text-based interfaces, such as mobile applications, websites, or messaging platforms, though voice-based chatbots are also on the rise, catering to users who prefer spoken communication (Gururani et al., 2022; Kukreti et al., 2023).

- **Symptom Checking and Health Assessment**

Chatbots can assess patient symptoms and provide initial guidance on whether professional medical attention is necessary. Users typically input their symptoms, and the chatbot uses an algorithm trained on medical data to analyze the information and recommend appropriate actions. For example, a user experiencing mild flu symptoms might be advised to rest and hydrate, while a chatbot could suggest seeing a doctor for more severe symptoms (Lade et al., 2023; Sharun et al., 2022).

- **Appointment Scheduling and Reminders**

Health chatbots streamline the process of scheduling appointments and sending reminders, reducing administrative burden and enhancing patient adherence. By integrating with electronic health record (EHR) systems, chatbots can automatically schedule, reschedule, or cancel appointments based on patient needs and provider availability (Alzaidi et al., 2022; Chahar et al., 2022; Godbole et al., 2023).

- **Medication Reminders and Adherence Support**

Some chatbots provide personalized medication reminders, ensuring that patients take their prescribed medicines on time. For individuals managing chronic illnesses, such reminders play a crucial role in maintaining treatment adherence and improving health outcomes (V. Agarwal & Sharma, 2021; S. Bansal et al., 2023; Wazid et al., 2021).

- **Mental Health and Emotional Support**

Advanced chatbots like Woebot and Wysa offer empathetic responses, helping users manage anxiety, stress, and other mental health issues. These chatbots use cognitive-behavioral therapy (CBT) techniques and are designed to provide emotional support, though they are not substitutes for professional counselling (Ekren et al., 2023; Ram & Xing, 2023; N. Sharma et al., 2021).

Benefits of Health Chatbots

The integration of chatbots in healthcare communication offers significant benefits that enhance the patient experience, improve healthcare accessibility, and relieve pressure on healthcare providers (P. Gupta et al., 2023; Komkowski et al., 2023b; R. Kumar et al., 2023).

- **24/7 Accessibility**

Unlike human providers, chatbots are available at all hours, providing immediate responses to patient queries. This accessibility is particularly valuable for individuals with urgent questions outside of typical office hours or for those in regions with limited healthcare infrastructure.

- **Improved Patient Engagement and Adherence**

Chatbots engage with patients in a proactive, interactive manner, which can increase patient involvement in their own care. For example, a chatbot that sends regular reminders or motivational messages can encourage patients to stick to their wellness routines, such as exercise regimens or dietary goals. By providing continuous engagement, chatbots foster a sense of accountability that contributes to better adherence to treatment plans (Jayadeva et al., 2023; M. A. Kumar et al., 2022; Pandya et al., 2023).

- **Efficient Use of Healthcare Resources**

Chatbots can handle routine inquiries and simple administrative tasks, freeing up healthcare professionals to focus on more complex cases. For instance, if a chatbot can provide guidance on managing minor cold symptoms, it can prevent unnecessary visits to urgent care, allowing providers to allocate resources more effectively (V. Kumar & Korovin, 2023; Lourens et al., 2022; Umamaheswaran et al., 2023).

- **Enhanced Data Collection and Analysis**

Health chatbots can gather valuable data from patient interactions, such as symptom trends, adherence rates, and frequently asked questions. This data helps healthcare providers understand patient needs and preferences, leading to improvements in care quality and communication strategies. Additionally, aggregated chatbot data can inform public health trends and identify common health concerns within specific populations (V. Kumar et al., 2023; Rakhra et al., 2022).

- **Breaking Language and Accessibility Barriers**

Many healthcare chatbots are equipped with multilingual capabilities, making them accessible to non-native speakers and diverse patient populations. Moreover, chatbots that operate through voice interfaces provide a solution for individuals with visual impairments or literacy challenges, ensuring inclusivity in healthcare communication (Kaushal et al., 2022; Pallavi et al., 2022).

Real-World Applications of Health Chatbots

Several healthcare chatbots have successfully integrated into patient care, demonstrating their potential to improve communication, efficiency, and engagement (Ahmad et al., 2021; Ishengoma et al., 2022; A. Kumar et al., 2023).

- **Ada Health**

Ada Health is a symptom-checking chatbot that provides users with an assessment of their symptoms based on a vast database of medical information. Users input their symptoms, and Ada generates potential conditions and recommendations. It is widely used for initial assessments, helping users decide whether to seek medical attention (P. Kumar et al., 2023; V. Kumar & Korovin, 2023; Ram, Negi, et al., 2022).

- **Woebot**

Woebot is a mental health chatbot that provides support using CBT techniques. Available through a mobile app, Woebot engages in empathetic conversations with users, offering coping strategies for stress, anxiety, and other mental health concerns. It's particularly popular for its compassionate approach, bridging the gap for individuals who may not have access to professional mental health services (Ram, Bhandari, et al., 2022; Salama et al., 2023; K. D. Singh, Singh, Chhabra, et al., 2023).

- **Babylon Health**

Babylon Health combines symptom checking with appointment scheduling and telemedicine services. The chatbot provides users with information about possible causes of their symptoms and allows them to connect with a doctor for a virtual consultation. Its integration with healthcare systems makes Babylon Health a comprehensive solution for both triage and primary care (Nethravathi et al., 2022; K. D. Singh, Deep Singh, Bansal, et al., 2023).

Challenges of Health Chatbots

Despite their benefits, health chatbots face several challenges that impact their effectiveness, accuracy, and adoption among patients and healthcare providers (S. Aggarwal & Sharma, 2022; M. Kumar et al., 2021; Singamaneni et al., 2022).

- **Accuracy and Reliability**

Chatbots rely on algorithms that are only as good as the data they are trained on. Inaccuracies in chatbot responses can result from limited data, outdated information, or algorithmic bias. For instance, if a chatbot is trained on data that does not represent diverse populations, it may provide less accurate responses to users from underrepresented groups (Barthwal et al., 2023; Tomar et al., 2023).

- **Privacy and Data Security**

Chatbots often collect sensitive health information, which raises privacy concerns. Ensuring data security through encryption, compliance with healthcare regulations (such as HIPAA and GDPR), and transparent communication about data use is essential to building trust with users. Privacy concerns are particularly acute for mental health chatbots, as users may share highly personal information (Komkowski et al., 2023a; Sati et al., 2022).

- **Lack of Emotional Sensitivity**

While some chatbots, particularly in mental health, are designed to respond empathetically, they lack the nuanced understanding and emotional intelligence of human providers. A chatbot might misinterpret a user's tone or respond inappropriately to sensitive information, which can be off-putting or even harmful (V. Sharma et al., 2020; K. D. Singh, Singh, Kaur, et al., 2023).

- **Limited Scope of Care**

Chatbots are effective for routine inquiries and low-risk cases, but they cannot replace the clinical judgment of healthcare providers. Over-reliance on chatbots for medical advice may delay necessary in-person consultations or lead to inadequate care for complex health conditions. Clear disclaimers about the chatbot's role and limitations are necessary to prevent misuse (Subramani et al., 2022).

Ethical Considerations

The deployment of chatbots in healthcare communication raises ethical considerations that must be addressed to ensure responsible use of AI.

- **Transparency and Accountability**

Users should be informed that they are interacting with a chatbot and not a human healthcare provider. Transparency about the chatbot's limitations and its role as a supportive tool, rather than a replacement for medical advice, is essential for ethical use. Clear guidance on when to seek professional help can prevent users from over-relying on chatbots (Dani et al., 2022; Juyal & Sharma, 2020).

- **Addressing Bias and Ensuring Fairness**

Chatbots must be trained on diverse datasets to ensure that they provide equitable care for all user demographics. Bias in health chatbots can lead to disparities in the quality of care provided to different populations. Developers should regularly audit chatbot performance and update training data to minimize bias and improve accuracy (Kowsalya et al., 2023; Raman et al., 2023).

- **Informed Consent for Data Use**

Collecting and analyzing user data can improve chatbot services, but users must give informed consent for how their data will be used. Health chatbots should provide users with clear options to control data sharing, ensuring that data collection practices align with privacy regulations and ethical standards (Diwakar et al., 2022; Sunori et al., 2023; Uniyal et al., 2022).

The Future of Chatbots in Healthcare Communication

As AI technology advances, the capabilities of health chatbots are likely to expand, potentially incorporating deeper insights into user behavior, predictive analytics, and hybrid models that integrate human oversight. Future developments may include chatbots that detect subtle emotional cues, provide real-time feedback based on biometric data from wearables, and support healthcare providers in triaging complex cases. By combining AI with human expertise, hybrid chatbots could offer a balance between automated efficiency and personalized care (S. Joshi, Gangola, et al., 2023; Medhi et al., 2023).

In summary, AI-driven health chatbots are valuable tools that enhance healthcare communication, making it more accessible, efficient, and responsive to patient needs. While challenges remain in areas like accuracy, privacy, and ethical use, these chatbots offer considerable promise in improving patient engagement, adherence, and overall healthcare quality. As the technology evolves and ethical practices are refined, chatbots are poised to become an integral component of patient-centered healthcare communication (S. Arora et al., 2023; H. Kaur et al., 2023).

AI-Driven Chatbots in Healthcare Communication

AI-driven chatbots have emerged as transformative tools in healthcare communication, enhancing accessibility, efficiency, and personalization in patient interactions. These chatbots use Natural Language Processing (NLP) and machine learning algorithms to understand and respond to patient inquiries, provide guidance on symptom management, and even support mental health care. As automated virtual assistants, healthcare chatbots are reshaping how patients engage with healthcare systems, offering support that is not only immediate but also available around the clock. This section explores the functionality, benefits, challenges, and ethical considerations of using chatbots in healthcare communication, illustrating how they are changing the landscape of patient engagement (V. Aggarwal, Gupta, Gupta, et al., 2021; Ramesh et al., 2023; Rawat et al., 2023).

Functionality of Health Chatbots

AI-driven health chatbots are designed to perform a variety of tasks that support patient care and streamline healthcare workflows. Their functionalities range from answering basic health questions and conducting symptom checks to scheduling appointments and offering mental health support. Many chatbots in healthcare operate through text-based interfaces, such as mobile applications, websites, or messaging platforms, though voice-based chatbots are also on the rise, catering to users who prefer spoken communication (Suresh et al., 2023).

- **Symptom Checking and Health Assessment**

Chatbots can assess patient symptoms and provide initial guidance on whether professional medical attention is necessary. Users typically input their symptoms, and the chatbot uses an algorithm trained on medical data to analyze the information and recommend appropriate actions. For example, a user experiencing mild flu symptoms might be advised to rest and hydrate, while a chatbot could suggest seeing a doctor for more severe symptoms (Bhatnagar et al., 2023; A. Kaur et al., 2023; P. Kumar, Taneja, et al., 2024).

- **Appointment Scheduling and Reminders**

Health chatbots streamline the process of scheduling appointments and sending reminders, reducing administrative burden and enhancing patient adherence. By integrating with electronic health record (EHR) systems, chatbots can automatically schedule, reschedule, or cancel appointments based on patient needs and provider availability (P. Kumar, Reepu, et al., 2024).

- **Medication Reminders and Adherence Support**

Some chatbots provide personalized medication reminders, ensuring that patients take their prescribed medicines on time. For individuals managing chronic illnesses, such reminders play a crucial role in maintaining treatment adherence and improving health outcomes (Bhatnagar, Rajaram, et al., 2024).

- **Mental Health and Emotional Support**

Advanced chatbots like Woebot and Wysa offer empathetic responses, helping users manage anxiety, stress, and other mental health issues. These chatbots use cognitive-behavioural therapy (CBT) techniques and are designed to provide emotional support, though they are not substitutes for professional counselling (Taneja, Bhatnagar, et al., 2023).

Benefits of Health Chatbots

The integration of chatbots in healthcare communication offers significant benefits that enhance the patient experience, improve healthcare accessibility, and relieve pressure on healthcare providers.

- **24/7 Accessibility**

Unlike human providers, chatbots are available at all hours, providing immediate responses to patient queries. This accessibility is particularly valuable for individuals with urgent questions outside of typical office hours or for those in regions with limited healthcare infrastructure (Bhatnagar, Kumar, et al., 2024).

- **Improved Patient Engagement and Adherence**

Chatbots engage with patients in a proactive, interactive manner, which can increase patient involvement in their own care. For example, a chatbot that sends regular reminders or motivational messages can encourage patients to stick to their wellness routines, such as exercise regimens or dietary goals. By providing continuous engagement, chatbots foster a sense of accountability that contributes to better adherence to treatment plans (Reepu et al., 2023).

- **Efficient Use of Healthcare Resources**

Chatbots can handle routine inquiries and simple administrative tasks, freeing up healthcare professionals to focus on more complex cases. For instance, if a chatbot can provide guidance on managing minor cold symptoms, it can prevent unnecessary visits to urgent care, allowing providers to allocate resources more effectively (Dangwal et al., 2022).

- **Enhanced Data Collection and Analysis**

Health chatbots can gather valuable data from patient interactions, such as symptom trends, adherence rates, and frequently asked questions. This data helps healthcare providers understand patient needs and preferences, leading to improvements in care quality and communication strategies. Additionally, aggregated chatbot data can inform public health trends and identify common health concerns within specific populations (Dahiya & Taneja, 2023).

- **Breaking Language and Accessibility Barriers**

Many healthcare chatbots are equipped with multilingual capabilities, making them accessible to non-native speakers and diverse patient populations. Moreover, chatbots that operate through voice interfaces provide a solution for individuals with visual impairments or literacy challenges, ensuring inclusivity in healthcare communication (Taneja & Sharma, 2023).

Real-World Applications of Health Chatbots

Several healthcare chatbots have successfully integrated into patient care, demonstrating their potential to improve communication, efficiency, and engagement.

- **Ada Health**

Ada Health is a symptom-checking chatbot that provides users with an assessment of their symptoms based on a vast database of medical information. Users input their symptoms, and Ada generates potential conditions and recommendations. It is widely used for initial assessments, helping users decide whether to seek medical attention (M. Gupta et al., 2023).

- **Woebot**

Woebot is a mental health chatbot that provides support using CBT techniques. Available through a mobile app, Woebot engages in empathetic conversations with users, offering coping strategies for stress, anxiety, and other mental health concerns. It's particularly popular for its compassionate approach, bridging the gap for individuals who may not have access to professional mental health services.

- **Babylon Health**

Babylon Health combines symptom checking with appointment scheduling and telemedicine services. The chatbot provides users with information about possible causes of their symptoms and allows them to connect with a doctor for a virtual consultation. Its integration with healthcare systems makes Babylon Health a comprehensive solution for both triage and primary care (Taneja, Gupta, et al., 2023).

Challenges of Health Chatbots

Despite their benefits, health chatbots face several challenges that impact their effectiveness, accuracy, and adoption among patients and healthcare providers.

- **Accuracy and Reliability**

Chatbots rely on algorithms that are only as good as the data they are trained on. Inaccuracies in chatbot responses can result from limited data, outdated information, or algorithmic bias. For instance, if a chatbot is trained on data that does not represent diverse populations, it may provide less accurate responses to users from underrepresented groups (N. Bansal et al., 2023).

- **Privacy and Data Security**

Chatbots often collect sensitive health information, which raises privacy concerns. Ensuring data security through encryption, compliance with healthcare regulations (such as HIPAA and GDPR), and transparent communication about data use is essential to building trust with users. Privacy concerns are particularly acute for mental health chatbots, as users may share highly personal information.

- **Lack of Emotional Sensitivity**

While some chatbots, particularly in mental health, are designed to respond empathetically, they lack the nuanced understanding and emotional intelligence of human providers. A chatbot might misinterpret a user's tone or respond inappropriately to sensitive information, which can be off-putting or even harmful.

- **Limited Scope of Care**

Chatbots are effective for routine inquiries and low-risk cases, but they cannot replace the clinical judgment of healthcare providers. Over-reliance on chatbots for medical advice may delay necessary in-person consultations or lead to inadequate care for complex health conditions. Clear disclaimers about the chatbot's role and limitations are necessary to prevent misuse.

Ethical Considerations

The deployment of chatbots in healthcare communication raises ethical considerations that must be addressed to ensure responsible use of AI.

- **Transparency and Accountability**

Users should be informed that they are interacting with a chatbot and not a human healthcare provider. Transparency about the chatbot's limitations and its role as a supportive tool, rather than a replacement for medical advice, is essential for ethical use. Clear guidance on when to seek professional help can prevent users from over-relying on chatbots.

- **Addressing Bias and Ensuring Fairness**

Chatbots must be trained on diverse datasets to ensure that they provide equitable care for all user demographics. Bias in health chatbots can lead to disparities in the quality of care provided to different populations. Developers should regularly audit chatbot performance and update training data to minimize bias and improve accuracy.

- **Informed Consent for Data Use**

Collecting and analyzing user data can improve chatbot services, but users must give informed consent for how their data will be used. Health chatbots should provide users with clear options to control data sharing, ensuring that data collection practices align with privacy regulations and ethical standards.

The Future of Chatbots in Healthcare Communication

As AI technology advances, the capabilities of health chatbots are likely to expand, potentially incorporating deeper insights into user behavior, predictive analytics, and hybrid models that integrate human oversight. Future developments may include chatbots that detect subtle emotional cues, provide real-time feedback based on biometric data from wearables, and support healthcare providers in triaging complex cases. By combining AI with human expertise, hybrid chatbots could offer a balance between automated efficiency and personalized care.

In summary, AI-driven health chatbots are valuable tools that enhance healthcare communication, making it more accessible, efficient, and responsive to patient needs. While challenges remain in areas like accuracy, privacy, and ethical use, these chatbots offer considerable promise in improving patient engagement, adherence, and overall healthcare quality. As the technology evolves and ethical practices are refined, chatbots are poised to become an integral component of patient-centered healthcare communication.

4o

You Said:

Future Trends and Innovations in AI-Driven Health Communication Write in 1000 words in most complex vocab

ChatGPT Said:

ChatGPT

Future Trends and Innovations in AI-Driven Health Communication

The future of AI-driven health communication is poised to transcend present functionalities, ushering in an era of hyper-personalized, predictive, and ethically attuned healthcare interactions. As advancements in Artificial Intelligence (AI) continue to reshape the medical landscape, emerging trends and innovations promise to enhance healthcare communication's efficacy, scope, and inclusivity. From predictive analytics and biometrics-driven insights to hybrid human-AI models and contextually intelligent systems, AI's evolution in health communication marks a paradigmatic shift towards a patient-centered, data-rich, and ethically guided paradigm.

Predictive Analytics: Anticipating Health Trajectories

Predictive analytics stand at the forefront of future AI-driven health communication, enabling healthcare providers to preemptively address potential health concerns. Leveraging vast datasets and machine learning algorithms, predictive models analyze individual health markers to foresee conditions long before symptoms manifest. By amalgamating data from electronic health records (EHRs), wearable devices, and genetic information, AI can map out personalized health trajectories, suggesting preemptive interventions that may avert disease onset.

For example, an AI system could analyze an individual's cardiovascular data, genetic predispositions, and lifestyle patterns to identify a high probability of hypertension. Such predictive insights would then be communicated to both the patient and their healthcare provider, prompting lifestyle adjustments or preventive medication regimes. These proactive health measures, informed by predictive analytics, are set to reduce the incidence of chronic diseases, cut healthcare costs, and enhance patient longevity. Predictive analytics also extend beyond physical health, encompassing mental health assessments, where AI systems gauge patterns indicative of cognitive or emotional distress, offering early interventions for conditions such as depression or anxiety.

Biometrics-Driven Real-Time Feedback

In conjunction with predictive analytics, biometrics-driven real-time feedback represents a powerful application of AI in health communication. With the integration of Internet of Things (IoT) devices and wearable health technology, AI systems can monitor vital parameters like heart rate variability, glucose levels, and blood pressure continuously, furnishing real-time data-driven recommendations. These AI-augmented insights enable instantaneous, context-sensitive health guidance, facilitating immediate corrective actions that help maintain homeostasis and support ongoing wellness.

For instance, an AI-powered application could prompt a diabetic patient to take corrective actions upon detecting fluctuating glucose levels, offering diet or insulin recommendations in real-time. In more complex applications, these biometrics-driven platforms could also synchronize with telemedicine services, facilitating seamless, continuous monitoring for high-risk patients, and alerting healthcare providers during critical deviations. Through such innovations, biometrics and AI amalgamate to enhance communication precision, creating a feedback loop that sustains optimal health states and supports dynamic, data-informed lifestyle modifications.

The Emergence of Contextually Intelligent AI Systems

The rise of contextually intelligent AI represents a radical advancement, enabling health communication systems to interpret not only explicit patient inputs but also the nuanced context underlying each interaction. Contextual AI systems amalgamate semantic understanding with situational awareness, allowing health communication tools to discern and adapt to environmental, emotional, and social cues in real-time. This situational comprehension fosters more empathetic, responsive interactions, particularly in mental health care, where understanding patient emotions and subtleties in communication is crucial.

Contextually intelligent AI systems can, for example, detect anxiety or distress in a patient's tone, adjusting communication strategies to provide reassurance or divert toward mental health resources. Furthermore, such systems might dynamically alter recommendations based on extraneous factors like time of day, location, or recent activity data, offering tailored guidance that aligns with the patient's present circumstances. By anchoring communication in a deep understanding of patient context, contextual AI will render health interactions more human-like, intuitive, and adaptive, blurring the line between digital and interpersonal healthcare experiences.

Hybrid AI-Human Models in Health Communication

As the scope of AI in healthcare communication grows, so does the recognition that entirely automated systems may not suffice for complex or nuanced medical interactions. Hybrid AI-human models thus represent an emergent paradigm, wherein AI complements human expertise, fostering a synergistic model that combines algorithmic precision with empathetic care. In this model, AI-driven systems handle routine inquiries, symptom checking, and preliminary assessments, while human providers step in for complex cases, ensuring a balance between efficiency and clinical acumen.

For instance, in a hospital setting, an AI triage system might assess and categorize incoming patients based on reported symptoms and biometric data, streamlining the allocation of healthcare resources. This system could independently manage patients with minor issues, directing those requiring specialized care to human professionals. This layered approach mitigates provider burnout, enhances patient satisfaction, and ensures that complex cases receive the requisite human oversight. By intertwining AI capabilities with human decision-making, hybrid models provide a responsive, adaptable, and compassionate healthcare communication framework.

Multilingual and Cross-Cultural Communication

Language barriers remain a significant impediment to healthcare access and efficacy. Future AI-driven communication systems are set to break these barriers through advanced multilingual and cross-cultural capabilities. Sophisticated NLP models trained on diverse linguistic and cultural datasets will allow AI systems to interact fluently with patients across different language backgrounds, ensuring that healthcare information is accurately and sensitively conveyed.

These multilingual systems will not only translate language but will also incorporate culturally sensitive responses, understanding variations in health-related beliefs, behaviors, and expectations. For instance, an AI system could recognize that certain cultures may prefer traditional remedies over modern medicine and adapt its communication to respect these values while subtly promoting evidence-based care. Through enhanced language support, AI-driven communication tools promise to democratize healthcare access, fostering inclusivity and bridging the communication gap for underserved or linguistically isolated communities.

Ethical AI and Transparent Communication

As AI systems play an increasingly central role in health communication, ensuring ethical integrity and transparency becomes paramount. Future AI-driven systems will need to prioritize patient privacy, informed consent, and transparency regarding data usage and limitations of AI capabilities. Ethical AI frameworks are expected to incorporate rigorous data governance protocols, informed consent mechanisms, and explainability models that allow patients to understand how AI-derived insights are generated.

For instance, an AI-driven diagnostic tool should provide patients with a clear understanding of the data sources, algorithms, and decision-making processes that underpin its recommendations. Additionally, AI systems must be transparent about limitations, guiding patients to seek professional support for complex issues beyond the AI's purview. Building trust through transparency and ethical practices will be essential for patient acceptance, particularly in scenarios where AI-generated insights may influence significant health decisions.

Integration with Public Health Communication Systems

In the wake of global health crises, such as the COVID-19 pandemic, AI has proven invaluable in streamlining public health communication, predicting outbreaks, and disseminating critical information. Future AI-driven communication systems will integrate with public health infrastructure, allowing for real-time data sharing, outbreak detection, and targeted health advisories. By continuously monitoring epidemiological trends and aggregating patient-reported data, AI systems can swiftly notify healthcare providers, policymakers, and individuals, enabling agile responses to public health threats.

Such integration allows AI to serve as both an information conduit and a preventive tool, promoting public health through timely, data-backed communication. For instance, AI systems might analyze social media trends or health records to detect early signs of flu outbreaks, subsequently delivering preventive tips and vaccination reminders to at-risk populations. By intertwining personal health management with public health imperatives, these systems amplify health communication's reach and effectiveness on both individual and societal levels.

The Rise of Emotionally Intelligent AI in Mental Health

Future AI-driven health communication will encompass emotionally intelligent systems capable of empathizing with patients, particularly in mental health care. Advances in sentiment analysis and affective computing enable AI to detect emotions like stress, sadness, or frustration, adjusting responses accordingly. Emotionally intelligent AI systems could provide real-time psychological support, offering comforting words, relaxation techniques, or connecting patients with crisis intervention services if needed.

For instance, an AI chatbot for mental health might recognize signs of acute stress in a patient's language, responding with personalized mindfulness exercises or suggesting a session with a therapist. By addressing both physical and emotional dimensions, emotionally intelligent AI systems will contribute to holistic healthcare, ensuring that patients feel understood and supported throughout their healthcare journeys.

CONCLUSION

The trajectory of AI in health communication is one of remarkable innovation and profound impact. With advancements in predictive analytics, biometrics, contextual understanding, and ethical frameworks, AI is set to revolutionize healthcare communication by fostering a responsive, inclusive, and personalized patient experience. While challenges remain in areas such as privacy, bias, and reliability, future AI-driven communication systems will prioritize transparency, integrate human oversight, and adhere to stringent ethical standards. As AI continues to evolve, its role in health communication will not only reshape patient-provider interactions but also empower individuals to engage proactively in their own health, fostering a healthcare paradigm that is as humane as it is technologically advanced.

AI is reshaping the landscape of health and wellness communication, offering unprecedented opportunities to improve accessibility, personalization, and patient engagement. Through applications like NLP-powered chatbots, voice assistants, and machine learning algorithms, AI has made it possible to overcome traditional limitations in health communication, ensuring that individuals receive timely, relevant, and empathetic support. However, as AI continues to evolve, it is crucial to address the ethical, privacy, and accessibility challenges associated with its use in health and wellness settings. By embracing AI's potential while remaining mindful of its limitations, healthcare providers, wellness platforms, and policymakers can work together to create a more inclusive, efficient, and compassionate healthcare system that empowers individuals to take charge of their health and well-being.

DECLARATION

The authors declare that the manuscript follows ethical standards and there are no potential conflicts of interest concerning this chapter's research, authorship, and publication.

DISCLAIMER

The contents and views of this chapter are expressed by the authors in personal capacities. The Editor and the Publisher don't need to agree with these viewpoints and are not responsible for any duty of care in this regard.

REFERENCES

Agarwal, P., & Sharma, S. (2023). Smart Urban Traffic Management System using Energy Efficient Optimized Path Discovery. *Proceedings of the 3rd International Conference on Artificial Intelligence and Smart Energy, ICAIS 2023*, 858 – 863. DOI: 10.1109/ICAIS56108.2023.10073840

Agarwal, V., & Sharma, S. (2021). IoT Based Smart Transport Management System. *Communications in Computer and Information Science, 1394 CCIS*, 207 – 216. DOI: 10.1007/978-981-16-3653-0_17

Aggarwal, S., & Sharma, S. (2022). Voice Based Secured Smart Lock Design for Internet of Medical Things: An Artificial Intelligence Approach. *2022 International Conference on Wireless Communications, Signal Processing and Networking, WiSPNET 2022*, 1 – 9. DOI: 10.1109/WiSPNET54241.2022.9767113

Aggarwal, V., Gupta, V., Gupta, S., Sharma, N., Sharma, K., & Sharma, N. (2021). Using Transfer Learning and Pattern Recognition to Implement a Smart Waste Management System. *Proceedings of the 2nd International Conference on Electronics and Sustainable Communication Systems, ICESC 2021*, 1887 – 1891. DOI: 10.1109/ICESC51422.2021.9532732

Aggarwal, V., Gupta, V., Sharma, N., Gupta, S., Pundir, V., Sharma, K., & Sharma, N. (2021). Integration of Waste Management Companies in Micro Grids through Machine Learning. *Proceedings of the 2nd International Conference on Electronics and Sustainable Communication Systems, ICESC 2021*, 1881 – 1886. DOI: 10.1109/ICESC51422.2021.9532680

Ahmad, F., Kumar, P., & Patil, P. P. (2021). Vibration characteristics based pre-stress analysis of a quadcopter's body frame. In S. Y. (Ed.), *Materials Today: Proceedings* (Vol. 46, pp. 10329 – 10333). Elsevier Ltd. DOI: 10.1016/j.matpr.2020.12.458

Akberdina, V., Kumar, V., Kyriakopoulos, G. L., & Kuzmin, E. (2023). Editorial: What Does Industry's Digital Transition Hold in the Uncertainty Context? In K. V., K. G.L., A. V., & K. E. (Eds.), *Lecture Notes in Information Systems and Organisation: Vol. 61 LNISO* (pp. 1 – 4). Springer Science and Business Media Deutschland GmbH. DOI: 10.1007/978-3-031-30351-7_1

AL-Huqail, A. A., Kumar, P., Eid, E. M., Taher, M. A., Kumar, P., Adelodun, B., Andabaka, Ž., Mioč, B., Držaić, V., Bachheti, A., Singh, J., Kumar, V., & Širić, I.AL-Huqail. (2022). Phytoremediation of Composite Industrial Effluent using Sacred Lotus (Nelumbo nucifera Gaertn): A Lab-Scale Experimental Investigation. *Sustainability (Basel)*, 14(15), 9500. Advance online publication. DOI: 10.3390/su14159500

Alzaidi, M. S., Subbalakshmi, C., Roshini, T. V., Shukla, P. K., Shukla, S. K., Dutta, P., & Alhassan, M. (2022). 5G-Telecommunication Allocation Network Using IoT Enabled Improved Machine Learning Technique. *Wireless Communications and Mobile Computing*, 2022, 1–10. Advance online publication. DOI: 10.1155/2022/6229356

Ansari, M. F., & Afzal, A. (2022). Sensitivity and Performance Analysis of 10 MW Solar Power Plant Using MPPT Technique. *Lecture Notes in Electrical Engineering, 894 LNEE*, 512–518. DOI: 10.1007/978-981-19-1677-9_46

Arora, R., Singh, A. P., Sharma, R., & Chauhan, A. (2022). A remanufacturing inventory model to control the carbon emission using cap-and-trade regulation with the hexagonal fuzzy number. *Benchmarking*, 29(7), 2202–2230. DOI: 10.1108/BIJ-05-2021-0254

Arora, S., Pargaien, S., Khan, F., Misra, A., Gambhir, A., & Verma, D. (2023). Smart Parking Allocation Using Raspberry Pi based IoT System. *Proceedings of the 5th International Conference on Inventive Research in Computing Applications, ICIRCA 2023*, 1457 – 1461. DOI: 10.1109/ICIRCA57980.2023.10220619

Bansal, N., Bhatnagar, M., & Taneja, S. (2023). Balancing priorities through green optimism: A study elucidating initiatives, approaches, and strategies for sustainable supply chain management. In *Handbook of Research on Designing Sustainable Supply Chains to Achieve a Circular Economy*. IGI Global., DOI: 10.4018/978-1-6684-7664-2.ch004

Bansal, S., Kumar, V., Kumari, A., & Kuzmin, E. (2023). Understanding the Role of Digital Technologies in Supply Chain Management of SMEs. In K. V., K. G.L., A. V., & K. E. (Eds.), *Lecture Notes in Information Systems and Organisation: Vol. 61 LNISO* (pp. 195 – 205). Springer Science and Business Media Deutschland GmbH. DOI: 10.1007/978-3-031-30351-7_16

Barthwal, S., Pundir, S., Wazid, M., Singh, D. P., & Pundir, S. (2023). Design of an Energy Aware Cluster-Based Routing Scheme to Minimize Energy Consumption in Wireless Sensor Networks. *Communications in Computer and Information Science, 1797 CCIS*, 16 – 28. DOI: 10.1007/978-3-031-28180-8_2

Bhatnagar, M., Kumar, P., Taneja, S., Sood, K., & Grima, S. (2024). From digital overload to trading Zen: The role of digital detox in enhancing intraday trading performance. In *Business Drivers in Promoting Digital Detoxification*. IGI Global., DOI: 10.4018/979-8-3693-1107-3.ch010

Bhatnagar, M., Rajaram, R., Taneja, S., & Kumar, P. (2024). Balancing acts: The Yin and Yang of debit and credit on the stage of financial well-being. In *Emerging Perspectives on Financial Well-Being*. IGI Global., DOI: 10.4018/979-8-3693-1750-1.ch002

Bhatnagar, M., Taneja, S., & Kumar, P. (2023). The Effectiveness of Carbon Pricing Mechanism in Steering Financial Flows Toward Sustainable Projects. *International Journal of Environmental Impacts*, 6(4), 183–196. DOI: 10.18280/ijei.060403

Bisht, R. K., Bisht, I. P., & Joshi, B. C. (2022). Growth of Micro, Small and Medium Enterprises (MSMEs) in Uttarakhand (India). In D. N. & C. A. (Eds.), *AIP Conference Proceedings* (Vol. 2481). American Institute of Physics Inc. DOI: 10.1063/5.0103881

Bordoloi, D., Singh, V., Sanober, S., Buhari, S. M., Ujjan, J. A., & Boddu, R. (2022). Deep Learning in Healthcare System for Quality of Service. *Journal of Healthcare Engineering*, 2022, 1–11. Advance online publication. DOI: 10.1155/2022/8169203 PMID: 35281541

Chahar, A., & Christobel, Y. A. Ritika, Adakane, P. K., Sonal, D., & Tripathi, V. (2022). The Implementation of Big Data With Cloud and Edge Computing in Enhancing the Smart Grid Information Processes Through Sem Model. *2022 2nd International Conference on Advance Computing and Innovative Technologies in Engineering, ICACITE 2022*, 608 – 611. DOI: 10.1109/ICACITE53722.2022.9823896

Chandran, G. C., Synthia Regis Prabha, D. M. M., Malathi, P., Kapila, D., Arunkumar, M. S., Verma, D., & Teressa, D. M. (2022). Built-In Calibration Standard and Decision Support System for Controlling Structured Data Storage Systems Using Soft Computing Techniques. *Computational Intelligence and Neuroscience*, 2022, 1–7. Advance online publication. DOI: 10.1155/2022/3476004 PMID: 36065369

Dahiya, K., & Taneja, S. (2023). To Analyse the Impact of Multi-Media Technology on the Rural Entrepreneurship Development. In *Contemporary Studies of Risks in Emerging Technology* (pp. 221–240). DOI: 10.1108/978-1-80455-562-020231015

Dangwal, A., Kaur, S., Taneja, S., & Ozen, E. (2022). A bibliometric analysis of green tourism based on the scopus platform. In *Developing Relationships, Personalization, and Data Herald in Marketing 5.0*. IGI Global., DOI: 10.4018/978-1-6684-4496-2.ch015

Dani, R., Rawal, Y. S., Bagchi, P., & Khan, M. (2022). Opportunities and Challenges in Implementation of Artificial Intelligence in Food & Beverage Service Industry. In D. N. & C. A. (Eds.), *AIP Conference Proceedings* (Vol. 2481). American Institute of Physics Inc. DOI: 10.1063/5.0103741

Davuluri, S. K., Alvi, S. A. M., Aeri, M., Agarwal, A., Serajuddin, M., & Hasan, Z. (2023). A Security Model for Perceptive 5G-Powered BC IoT Associated Deep Learning. *6th International Conference on Inventive Computation Technologies, ICICT 2023 - Proceedings*, 118 – 125. DOI: 10.1109/ICICT57646.2023.10134487

Diddi, P. K., Sharma, P. K., Srivastava, A., Madduru, S. R. C., & Reddy, E. S. (2022). Sustainable Fast Setting Early Strength Self Compacting Concrete(FSESSCC) Using Metakaolin. *IOP Conference Series. Earth and Environmental Science*, 1077(1), 012009. Advance online publication. DOI: 10.1088/1755-1315/1077/1/012009

Diwakar, M., Shankar, A., Chakraborty, C., Singh, P., & Arunkumar, G. (2022). Multi-modal medical image fusion in NSST domain for internet of medical things. *Multimedia Tools and Applications*, 81(26), 37477–37497. DOI: 10.1007/s11042-022-13507-6

Ekren, B. Y., Stylos, N., Zwiegelaar, J., Turhanlar, E. E., & Kumar, V. (2023). Additive manufacturing integration in E-commerce supply chain network to improve resilience and competitiveness. *Simulation Modelling Practice and Theory*, 122, 102676. Advance online publication. DOI: 10.1016/j.simpat.2022.102676

Godbole, V., Kukrety, S., Gautam, P., Bisht, M., & Pal, M. K. (2023). Bioleaching for Heavy Metal Extraction from E-waste: A Sustainable Approach. In *Microbial Technology for Sustainable E-waste Management*. Springer International Publishing., DOI: 10.1007/978-3-031-25678-3_4

Gonfa, Y. H., Tessema, F. B., Tadesse, M. G., Bachheti, A., & Bachheti, R. K. (2023). Medicinally Important Plant Roots and Their Role in Nanoparticles Synthesis and Applications. In *Secondary Metabolites from Medicinal Plants: Nanoparticles Synthesis and their Applications*. CRC Press., DOI: 10.1201/9781003213727-11

Gupta, A., Dixit, A. K., Kumar, K. S., Lavanya, C., Chakravarthi, M. K., & Gangodkar, D. (2022). Analyzing Robotics and Computer Integrated Manufacturing of Key Areas Using Cloud Computing. *Proceedings of 5th International Conference on Contemporary Computing and Informatics, IC3I 2022*, 194 – 199. DOI: 10.1109/IC3I56241.2022.10072581

Gupta, M., Arora, K., & Taneja, S. (2023). Bibliometric analysis on employee engagement and human resource management. In *Enhancing Customer Engagement Through Location-Based Marketing*. IGI Global., DOI: 10.4018/978-1-6684-8177-6.ch013

Gupta, P., Gopal, S., Sharma, M., Joshi, S., Sahani, C., & Ahalawat, K. (2023). Agriculture Informatics and Communication: Paradigm of E-Governance and Drone Technology for Crop Monitoring. *9th International Conference on Smart Computing and Communications: Intelligent Technologies and Applications, ICSCC 2023*, 113 – 118. DOI: 10.1109/ICSCC59169.2023.10335058

Gupta, S., Kumar, V., & Patil, P. (2022). A Study on Recycling of Waste Solid Garbage in a City. In D. N. & C. A. (Eds.), *AIP Conference Proceedings* (Vol. 2481). American Institute of Physics Inc. DOI: 10.1063/5.0104563

Gururani, P., Bhatnagar, P., Bisht, B., Jaiswal, K. K., Kumar, V., Kumar, S., Vlaskin, M. S., Grigorenko, A. V., & Rindin, K. G. (2022). Recent advances and viability in sustainable thermochemical conversion of sludge to bio-fuel production. *Fuel*, 316, 123351. Advance online publication. DOI: 10.1016/j.fuel.2022.123351

Hajoary, P. K., Balachandra, P., & Garza-Reyes, J. A. (2023). Industry 4.0 maturity and readiness assessment: An empirical validation using Confirmatory Composite Analysis. *Production Planning and Control*. Advance online publication. DOI: 10.1080/09537287.2023.2210545

Ishengoma, F. R., Shao, D., Alexopoulos, C., Saxena, S., & Nikiforova, A. (2022). Integration of artificial intelligence of things (AIoT) in the public sector: Drivers, barriers and future research agenda. *Digital Policy. Regulation & Governance*, 24(5), 449–462. DOI: 10.1108/DPRG-06-2022-0067

Jayadeva, S. M., Prasad Krishnam, N., Raja Mannar, B., Prakash Dabral, A., Buddhi, D., & Garg, N. (2023). An Investigation of IOT-Based Consumer Analytics to Assist Consumer Engagement Strategies in Evolving Markets. *2023 3rd International Conference on Advance Computing and Innovative Technologies in Engineering, ICACITE 2023*, 487 – 491. DOI: 10.1109/ICACITE57410.2023.10183310

Jena, S., & Gairola, A. (2022). Numerical Method to Generate and Evaluate Environmental Wind Over Hills: Comparison of Pedestrian Winds Over Hills and Plains. *CFD Letters*, 14(10), 56–67. DOI: 10.37934/cfdl.14.10.5667

Jindal, T., Sheoliha, N., Kishore, K., Uike, D., Khurana, S., & Verma, D. (2022). A Conceptual Analysis on the Impact of Internet of Things (IOT) Towards on Digital Marketing Transformation. *2022 2nd International Conference on Advance Computing and Innovative Technologies in Engineering, ICACITE 2022*, 1943 – 1947. DOI: 10.1109/ICACITE53722.2022.9823714

Johri, S., Singh Sidhu, K., Jafersadhiq, A., Mannar, B. R., Gehlot, A., & Goyal, H. R. (2023). An investigation of the effects of the global epidemic on Crypto Currency returns and volatility. *2023 3rd International Conference on Advance Computing and Innovative Technologies in Engineering, ICACITE 2023*, 345 – 348. DOI: 10.1109/ICACITE57410.2023.10182988

Joshi, K., Sharma, R., Singh, N., & Sharma, B. (2023). Digital World of Cloud Computing and Wireless Networking: Challenges and Risks. In *Applications of Artificial Intelligence in Wireless Communication Systems*. IGI Global., DOI: 10.4018/978-1-6684-7348-1.ch003

Joshi, S., Balakrishnan, S., Rawat, P., Deshpande, D., Chakravarthi, M. K., & Verma, D. (2022). A Framework of Internet of Things (Iot) for the Manufacturing and Image Classification System. In D. R.K., S. A.Kr., K. G., & B. S. (Eds.), *Proceedings of the 2022 11th International Conference on System Modeling and Advancement in Research Trends, SMART 2022* (pp. 371 – 375). Institute of Electrical and Electronics Engineers Inc. DOI: 10.1109/SMART55829.2022.10046756

Joshi, S., Gangola, S., Bhandari, G., Bhandari, N. S., Nainwal, D., Rani, A., Malik, S., & Slama, P. (2023). Rhizospheric bacteria: The key to sustainable heavy metal detoxification strategies. *Frontiers in Microbiology*, 14, 1229828. Advance online publication. DOI: 10.3389/fmicb.2023.1229828 PMID: 37555069

Joshi, S., & Sharma, M. (2023). Strategic challenges of deploying LARG approach for sustainable manufacturing: Research implications from Indian SMEs. *International Journal of Internet Manufacturing and Services*, 9(2–3), 373–397. DOI: 10.1504/IJIMS.2023.132791

Joshi, S., Sharma, M., & Barve, A. (2023). Implementation challenges of blockchain technology in closed-loop supply chain: A Waste Electrical and Electronic Equipment (WEEE) management perspective in developing countries. *Supply Chain Forum*, 24(1), 59 – 80. DOI: 10.1080/16258312.2022.2135972

Juyal, P., & Sharma, S. (2020). Estimation of Tree Volume Using Mask R-CNN based Deep Learning. *2020 11th International Conference on Computing, Communication and Networking Technologies, ICCCNT 2020*. DOI: 10.1109/ICCCNT49239.2020.9225509

Kathir, I., Haribabu, K., Kumar, A., Kaliappan, S., Patil, P. P., Dhanalakshmi, C. S., Madhu, P., & Birhanu, H. A. (2022). Utilization of Tea Industrial Waste for Low-Grade Energy Recovery: Optimization of Liquid Oil Production and Its Characterization. *Advances in Materials Science and Engineering*, 2022, 1–9. Advance online publication. DOI: 10.1155/2022/7852046

Kaur, A., Kumar, P., Taneja, S., & Ozen, E. (2023). Fintech emergence – an opportunity or threat to banking. *International Journal of Electronic Finance*, 13(1), 1–19. DOI: 10.1504/IJEF.2024.135163

Kaur, H., Thacker, C., Singh, V. K., Sivashankar, D., Patil, P. P., & Gill, K. S. (2023). An implementation of virtual instruments for industries for the standardization. *2023 International Conference on Artificial Intelligence and Smart Communication, AISC 2023*, 1110–1113. DOI: 10.1109/AISC56616.2023.10085547

Kaushal, D., Kumar, S., Raj, R., & Negi, A. (2022). Understanding the effect of entrepreneurial orientation, innovation capability and differentiation strategy on firm performance: A study on small and medium enterprises. *International Journal of Business and Globalisation*, 30(1), 57–80. DOI: 10.1504/IJBG.2022.122280

Kohli, P., Sharma, S., & Matta, P. (2022). Secured Authentication Schemes of 6G Driven Vehicular Communication Network in Industry 5.0 Internet-of-Everything (IoE) Applications: Challenges and Opportunities. *2022 IEEE 2nd International Conference on Mobile Networks and Wireless Communications, ICMNWC 2022.* DOI: 10.1109/ICMNWC56175.2022.10031781

Komkowski, T., Antony, J., Garza-Reyes, J. A., Tortorella, G. L., & Pongboonchai-Empl, T. (2023a). A systematic review of the integration of Industry 4.0 with quality-related operational excellence methodologies. *The Quality Management Journal*, 30(1), 3–15. DOI: 10.1080/10686967.2022.2144783

Komkowski, T., Antony, J., Garza-Reyes, J. A., Tortorella, G. L., & Pongboonchai-Empl, T. (2023b). Integrating Lean Management with Industry 4.0: An explorative Dynamic Capabilities theory perspective. *Production Planning and Control*, 1–19. Advance online publication. DOI: 10.1080/09537287.2023.2294297

Kowsalya, K., & Rani, R. P. J. Ritu, Bhiyana, M., Saini, M., & Patil, P. P. (2023). Blockchain-Internet of things-Machine Learning: Development of Traceable System for Multi Purposes. *2023 3rd International Conference on Advance Computing and Innovative Technologies in Engineering, ICACITE 2023*, 1112 – 1115. DOI: 10.1109/ICACITE57410.2023.10183065

Krishna, S. H., Upadhyay, A., Tewari, M., Gehlot, A., Girimurugan, B., & Pundir, S. (2022). Empirical investigation of the key machine learning elements promoting e-business using an SEM framework. *Proceedings of 5th International Conference on Contemporary Computing and Informatics, IC3I 2022*, 1960 – 1964. DOI: 10.1109/IC3I56241.2022.10072712

Kukreti, A., Shriyal, A., Sharma, S., & Bhadula, S. (2023). Internet-of-Things Enabled Smart and Portable Terrace Garden Protection Shed. *2023 4th IEEE Global Conference for Advancement in Technology, GCAT 2023.* DOI: 10.1109/GCAT59970.2023.10353281

Kumar, A., & Ram, M. (2021). Systems Reliability Engineering: Modeling and Performance Improvement. In *Systems Reliability Engineering: Modeling and Performance Improvement*. De Gruyter. DOI: 10.1515/9783110617375

Kumar, A., Saxena, M., Sastry, R. V. L. S. N., Chaudhari, A., Singh, R., & Malathy, V. (2023). Internet of Things and Blockchain Data Supplier for Intelligent Applications. *Proceedings of International Conference on Contemporary Computing and Informatics, IC3I 2023*, 2218 – 2223. DOI: 10.1109/IC3I59117.2023.10397630

Kumar, A. S., & Desi, A. B. (2023). Collaborative logistics, tools of machine and supply chain services in the world wide industry 4.0 framework. In *Artificial Intelligence, Blockchain, Computing and Security: Volume 2* (Vol. 2). CRC Press. DOI: 10.1201/9781032684994-15

Kumar, K., Singh, V., Mishra, G., Ravindra Babu, B., Tripathi, N., & Kumar, P. (2022). Power-Efficient Secured Hardware Design of AES Algorithm on High Performance FPGA. *Proceedings of 5th International Conference on Contemporary Computing and Informatics, IC3I 2022*, 1634 – 1637. DOI: 10.1109/IC3I56241.2022.10073148

Kumar, M., Ansari, N. A., Sharma, A., Singh, V. K., Gautam, R., & Singh, Y. (2021). Prediction of an optimum engine response based on di erent input parameters on common rail direct injection diesel engine: A response surface methodology approach. *Scientia Iranica*, 28(6), 3181–3200. DOI: 10.24200/sci.2021.56745.4885

Kumar, M. A., Prasad, M. S. G., More, P., & Christa, S. (2022). Artificial intelligence-based personal health monitoring devices. In *Mobile Health: Advances in Research and Applications - Volume II*. Nova Science Publishers, Inc.

Kumar, P., Reepu, & Kaur, R. (2024). Economic and Urban Dynamics: Investigating Socioeconomic Status and Urban Density as Moderators of Mobile Wallet Adoption in Smart Cities. *Lecture Notes in Networks and Systems, 948 LNNS*, 409–417. DOI: 10.1007/978-981-97-1329-5_33

Kumar, P., Obaidat, M. S., Pandey, P., Wazid, M., Das, A. K., & Singh, D. P. (2023). Design of a Secure Machine Learning-Based Malware Detection and Analysis Scheme. In O. M.S., N. Z., H. K.-F., N. P., & G. Y. (Eds.), *Proceedings of the 2023 IEEE International Conference on Communications, Computing, Cybersecurity and Informatics, CCCI 2023*. Institute of Electrical and Electronics Engineers Inc. DOI: 10.1109/CCCI58712.2023.10290761

Kumar, P., Taneja, S., Bhatnagar, M., & Kaur, A. K. (2024). Navigating the digital paradigm shift: Designing CBDCs for a transformative financial landscape. In *Exploring Central Bank Digital Currencies: Concepts, Frameworks, Models, and Challenges*. IGI Global., DOI: 10.4018/979-8-3693-1882-9.ch006

Kumar, R., Kandpal, B., & Ahmad, V. (2023). Industrial IoT (IIOT): Security Threats and Countermeasures. *International Conference on Innovative Data Communication Technologies and Application, ICIDCA 2023 - Proceedings*, 829 – 833. DOI: 10.1109/ICIDCA56705.2023.10100145

Kumar, V., & Korovin, G. (2023). A Comparision of Digital Transformation of Industry in the Russian Federation with the European Union. In K. V., K. G.L., A. V., & K. E. (Eds.), *Lecture Notes in Information Systems and Organisation: Vol. 61 LNISO* (pp. 45 – 57). Springer Science and Business Media Deutschland GmbH. DOI: 10.1007/978-3-031-30351-7_5

Kumar, V., Sharma, N. K., Mittal, A., & Verma, P. (2023). The Role of IoT and IIoT in Supplier and Customer Continuous Improvement Interface. *EAI/Springer Innovations in Communication and Computing*, 161 – 174. DOI: 10.1007/978-3-031-19711-6_7

Lade, J., Mohammed, K. A., Singh, D., Prasad Verma, R., Math, P., Saraswat, M., & Raj Gupta, L. (2023). A critical review of fabrication routes and their effects on mechanical properties of AMMCs. *Materials Today: Proceedings*. Advance online publication. DOI: 10.1016/j.matpr.2023.03.041

Lourens, M., Tamizhselvi, A., Goswami, B., Alanya-Beltran, J., Aarif, M., & Gangodkar, D. (2022). Database Management Difficulties in the Internet of Things. *Proceedings of 5th International Conference on Contemporary Computing and Informatics, IC3I 2022*, 322–326. DOI: 10.1109/IC3I56241.2022.10072614

Mandalapu, S. R., Sivamuni, K., Chitra Devi, D., Aswal, U. S., Sherly, S. I., & Balaji, N. A. (2023). An Architecture-based Self-Typing Service for Cloud Native Applications. *Proceedings of the 4th International Conference on Smart Electronics and Communication, ICOSEC 2023*, 562 – 566. DOI: 10.1109/ICOSEC58147.2023.10276313

Manjunatha, B. N., Chandan, M., Kottu, S., Rappai, S., Hema, P. K., Singh Rawat, K., & Sarkar, S. (2023). A Successful Spam Detection Technique for Industrial IoT Devices based on Machine Learning Techniques. *Proceedings of the 2nd International Conference on Applied Artificial Intelligence and Computing, ICAAIC 2023*, 363 – 369. DOI: 10.1109/ICAAIC56838.2023.10141275

Medhi, M. K., Ambust, S., Kumar, R., & Das, A. J. (2023). Characterization and Purification of Biosurfactants. In *Advancements in Biosurfactants Research*. Springer International Publishing., DOI: 10.1007/978-3-031-21682-4_4

Mehta, K., Sharma, S., & Mishra, D. (2021). Internet-of-Things Enabled Forest Fire Detection System. *Proceedings of the 5th International Conference on I-SMAC (IoT in Social, Mobile, Analytics and Cloud), I-SMAC 2021*, 20 – 23. DOI: 10.1109/I-SMAC52330.2021.9640900

Nadeem, S. P., Garza-Reyes, J. A., & Anosike, A. I. (2023). A C-Lean framework for deploying Circular Economy in manufacturing SMEs. *Production Planning and Control*, 1–21. Advance online publication. DOI: 10.1080/09537287.2023.2294307

Negi, D., Sah, A., Rawat, S., Choudhury, T., & Khanna, A. (2021). Block Chain Platforms and Smart Contracts. *EAI/Springer Innovations in Communication and Computing*, 65 – 76. DOI: 10.1007/978-3-030-65691-1_5

Nethravathi, K., Tiwari, A., Uike, D., Jaiswal, R., & Pant, K. (2022). Applications of Artificial Intelligence and Blockchain Technology in Improved Supply Chain Financial Risk Management. *Proceedings of 5th International Conference on Contemporary Computing and Informatics, IC3I 2022*, 242 – 246. DOI: 10.1109/IC3I56241.2022.10072787

Pallavi, B., Othman, B., Trivedi, G., Manan, N., Pawar, R. S., & Singh, D. P. (2022). The Application of the Internet of Things (IoT) to establish a technologically advanced Industry 4.0 for long-term growth and development. *2022 2nd International Conference on Advance Computing and Innovative Technologies in Engineering, ICACITE 2022*, 1927 – 1932. DOI: 10.1109/ICACITE53722.2022.9823481

Pandey, K., Joshi, H., Paliwal, S., Pawar, S., & Kumar, N. (2020). Technology transfer: An overview of process transfer from development to commercialization. *International Journal of Current Research and Review*, 12(19), 188–192. DOI: 10.31782/IJCRR.2020.121913

Pandey, K., Paliwal, S., Joshi, H., Bisht, N., & Kumar, N. (2022). A review on change control: A critical process of the pharmaceutical industry. *Journal of Medical Pharmaceutical and Allied Sciences*, 11(2), 4588–4592. DOI: 10.55522/jmpas.V11I2.2077

Pandey, N. K., Kashyap, S., Sharma, A., & Diwakar, M. (2023). Contribution of Cloud-Based Services in Post-Pandemic Technology Sustainability and Challenges: A Future Direction. In *Evolving Networking Technologies: Developments and Future Directions*. wiley. DOI: 10.1002/9781119836667.ch4

Pandya, D. J., Kumar, Y., Singh, D. P., Vairavel, D. K., Deepak, A., Rao, A. K., & Rana, A. (2023). Automatic Power Factor Compensation for Industrial Use to Minimize Penalty. *Proceedings of International Conference on Contemporary Computing and Informatics, IC3I 2023*, 2499 – 2504. DOI: 10.1109/IC3I59117.2023.10398095

Poswal, P., Chauhan, A., Aarya, D. D., Boadh, R., Rajoria, Y. K., & Gaiola, S. U. (2022). Optimal strategy for remanufacturing system of sustainable products with trade credit under uncertain scenario. *Materials Today: Proceedings*, 69, 165–173. DOI: 10.1016/j.matpr.2022.08.303

Rajawat, A. S., Singh, S., Gangil, B., Ranakoti, L., Sharma, S., Asyraf, M. R. M., & Razman, M. R. (2022). Effect of Marble Dust on the Mechanical, Morphological, and Wear Performance of Basalt Fibre-Reinforced Epoxy Composites for Structural Applications. *Polymers*, 14(7), 1325. Advance online publication. DOI: 10.3390/polym14071325 PMID: 35406199

Rajeswari, M., Kumar, N., Raman, P., Patjoshi, P. K., Singh, V., & Pundir, S. (2022). Optimal Analysis for Enterprise Financial Management Based on Artificial Intelligence and Parallel Computing Method. *Proceedings of 5th International Conference on Contemporary Computing and Informatics, IC3I 2022*, 2081 – 2086. DOI: 10.1109/IC3I56241.2022.10072851

Raju, K., Balakrishnan, M., Prasad, D. V. S. S. S. V., Nagalakshmi, V., Patil, P. P., Kaliappan, S., Arulmurugan, B., Radhakrishnan, K., Velusamy, B., Paramasivam, P., & El-Denglawey, A. (2022). Optimization of WEDM Process Parameters in Al2024-Li-Si3N4MMC. *Journal of Nanomaterials*, 2022(1), 2903385. Advance online publication. DOI: 10.1155/2022/2903385

Rakhra, M., Bhargava, A., Bhargava, D., Singh, R., Bhanot, A., & Rahmani, A. W. (2022). Implementing Machine Learning for Supply-Demand Shifts and Price Impacts in Farmer Market for Tool and Equipment Sharing. *Journal of Food Quality*, 2022, 1–19. Advance online publication. DOI: 10.1155/2022/4496449

Ram, M., Bhandari, A. S., & Kumar, A. (2022). Reliability Evaluation and Cost Optimization of Solar Road Studs. *International Journal of Reliability Quality and Safety Engineering*, 29(1), 2150041. Advance online publication. DOI: 10.1142/S0218539321500418

Ram, M., Negi, G., Goyal, N., & Kumar, A. (2022). Analysis of a Stochastic Model with Rework System. *Journal of Reliability and Statistical Studies*, 15(2), 553–582. DOI: 10.13052/jrss0974-8024.1527

Ram, M., & Xing, L. (2023). Reliability Modeling in Industry 4.0. In *Reliability Modeling in Industry 4.0*. Elsevier., DOI: 10.1016/C2021-0-01679-5

Ramakrishnan, T., Mohan Gift, M. D., Chitradevi, S., Jegan, R., Subha Hency Jose, P., Nagaraja, H. N., Sharma, R., Selvakumar, P., & Hailegiorgis, S. M. (2022). Study of Numerous Resins Used in Polymer Matrix Composite Materials. *Advances in Materials Science and Engineering*, 2022, 1–8. Advance online publication. DOI: 10.1155/2022/1088926

Raman, R., Kumar, R., Ghai, S., Gehlot, A., Raju, A. M., & Barve, A. (2023). A New Method of Optical Spectrum Analysis for Advanced Wireless Communications. *2023 3rd International Conference on Advance Computing and Innovative Technologies in Engineering, ICACITE 2023*, 1719 – 1723. DOI: 10.1109/ICACITE57410.2023.10182414

Ramesh, S. M., Rajeshkannan, S., Pundir, S., Dhaliwal, N., Mishra, S., & Saravana, B. S. (2023). Design and Development of Embedded Controller with Wireless Sensor for Power Monitoring through Smart Interface Design Models. *Proceedings of the 2023 2nd International Conference on Augmented Intelligence and Sustainable Systems, ICAISS 2023*, 1817 – 1821. DOI: 10.1109/ICAISS58487.2023.10250506

Rana, M. S., Cavaliere, L. P. L., Mishra, A. B., Padhye, P., Singh, R. R., & Khanna, R. (2022). Internet of Things (IOT) Based Assessment for Effective Monitoring Data Against Malicious Attacks on Financial Collectors. *2022 2nd International Conference on Advance Computing and Innovative Technologies in Engineering, ICACITE 2022*, 177–181. DOI: 10.1109/ICACITE53722.2022.9823612

Rawat, R., Sharma, S., & Goyal, H. R. (2023). Intelligent Digital Financial Inclusion System Architectures for Industry 5.0 Enabled Digital Society. *Winter Summit on Smart Computing and Networks. WiSSCoN*, 2023, 1–5. Advance online publication. DOI: 10.1109/WiSSCoN56857.2023.10133858

Reepu, R., Taneja, S., Ozen, E., & Singh, A. (2023). A globetrotter to the future of marketing: Metaverse. In *Cultural Marketing and Metaverse for Consumer Engagement*. IGI Global., DOI: 10.4018/978-1-6684-8312-1.ch001

Salama, R., Al-Turjman, F., Bordoloi, D., & Yadav, S. P. (2023). Wireless Sensor Networks and Green Networking for 6G communication- An Overview. *2023 International Conference on Computational Intelligence, Communication Technology and Networking, CICTN 2023*, 830 – 834. DOI: 10.1109/CICTN57981.2023.10141262

Sathyaseelan, K., Vyas, T., Madala, R., Chamundeeswari, V., Rai Goyal, H., & Jayaraman, R. (2023). Blockchain Enabled Intelligent Surveillance System Model with AI and IoT. *Proceedings of 8th IEEE International Conference on Science, Technology, Engineering and Mathematics, ICONSTEM 2023*. DOI: 10.1109/ICONSTEM56934.2023.10142303

Sati, P., Sharma, E., Soni, R., Dhyani, P., Solanki, A. C., Solanki, M. K., Rai, S., & Malviya, M. K. (2022). Bacterial endophytes as bioinoculant: microbial functions and applications toward sustainable farming. In *Microbial Endophytes and Plant Growth: Beneficial Interactions and Applications*. Elsevier., DOI: 10.1016/B978-0-323-90620-3.00008-8

Sen Thapa, B., Pandit, S., Patwardhan, S. B., Tripathi, S., Mathuriya, A. S., Gupta, P. K., Lal, R. B., & Tusher, T. R. (2022). Application of Microbial Fuel Cell (MFC) for Pharmaceutical Wastewater Treatment: An Overview and Future Perspectives. *Sustainability (Basel)*, 14(14), 8379. Advance online publication. DOI: 10.3390/su14148379

Shabbiruddin, Kanwar, N., Jadoun, V. K., Jayalakshmi, N. S. J., Afthanorhan, A., Fatema, N., Malik, H., & Hossaini, M. A. (. (2023). Industry - Challenge to Pro-Environmental Manufacturing of Goods Replacing Single-Use Plastic by Indian Industry: A Study Toward Failing Ban on Single-Use Plastic Access. *IEEE Access : Practical Innovations, Open Solutions*, 11, 77336–77346. DOI: 10.1109/ACCESS.2023.3296097

Sharma, H., Verma, D., Rana, A., Chari, S. L., Kumar, R., & Kumar, N. (2023). Enhancing Network Security in IoT Using Machine Learning- Based Anomaly Detection. *Proceedings of International Conference on Contemporary Computing and Informatics, IC3I 2023*, 2650 – 2654. DOI: 10.1109/IC3I59117.2023.10397636

Sharma, N., Agrawal, R., & Silmana, A. (2021). Analyzing The Role Of Public Transportation On Environmental Air Pollution In Select Cities. *Indian Journal of Environmental Protection*, 41(5), 536–541.

Sharma, R. C., Palli, S., & Sharma, S. K. (2023). Ride analysis of railway vehicle considering rigidity and flexibility of the carbody. *Zhongguo Gongcheng Xuekan*, 46(4), 355–366. DOI: 10.1080/02533839.2023.2194918

Sharma, S., & Bhadula, S. (2023). Secure Federated Learning for Intelligent Industry 4.0 IoT Enabled Self Skin Care Application System. *Proceedings of the 2nd International Conference on Applied Artificial Intelligence and Computing, ICAAIC 2023*, 1164 – 1170. DOI: 10.1109/ICAAIC56838.2023.10141028

Sharma, V., Kumar, V., & Bist, A. (2020). Investigations on morphology and material removal rate of various MMCs using CO2 laser technique. *Journal of the Brazilian Society of Mechanical Sciences and Engineering*, 42(10), 542. Advance online publication. DOI: 10.1007/s40430-020-02635-5

Sharun, V., Rajasekaran, M., Kumar, S. S., Tripathi, V., Sharma, R., Puthilibai, G., Sudhakar, M., & Negash, K. (2022). Study on Developments in Protection Coating Techniques for Steel. *Advances in Materials Science and Engineering*, 2022, 1–10. Advance online publication. DOI: 10.1155/2022/2843043

Shashikala, R., Singh, B. P., Azam, M., & Magesh, C. R. Rajat, & Singh, D. P. (2022). IoT Engineering Nanomaterial's Approach To Sustainable Advance Crop Production Management. *2022 2nd International Conference on Advance Computing and Innovative Technologies in Engineering, ICACITE 2022*, 2284 – 2288. DOI: 10.1109/ICACITE53722.2022.9823573

Singamaneni, K. K., Dhiman, G., Juneja, S., Muhammad, G., AlQahtani, S. A., & Zaki, J. (2022). A Novel QKD Approach to Enhance IIOT Privacy and Computational Knacks. *Sensors (Basel)*, 22(18), 6741. Advance online publication. DOI: 10.3390/s22186741 PMID: 36146089

Singh, K. D., Deep Singh, P., Bansal, A., Kaur, G., Khullar, V., & Tripathi, V. (2023). Exploratory Data Analysis and Customer Churn Prediction for the Telecommunication Industry. *ACCESS 2023 - 2023 3rd International Conference on Advances in Computing, Communication, Embedded and Secure Systems*, 197 – 201. DOI: 10.1109/ACCESS57397.2023.10199700

Singh, K. D., Singh, P., Chhabra, R., Kaur, G., Bansal, A., & Tripathi, V. (2023). Cyber-Physical Systems for Smart City Applications: A Comparative Study. In K. R., K. R., G. M., G. M., S. R., & S. R. (Eds.), *2023 International Conference on Advancement in Computation and Computer Technologies, InCACCT 2023* (pp. 871 – 876). Institute of Electrical and Electronics Engineers Inc. DOI: 10.1109/InCACCT57535.2023.10141719

Singh, K. D., Singh, P., Kaur, G., Khullar, V., Chhabra, R., & Tripathi, V. (2023). Education 4.0: Exploring the Potential of Disruptive Technologies in Transforming Learning. *Proceedings of International Conference on Computational Intelligence and Sustainable Engineering Solution, CISES 2023*, 586 – 591. DOI: 10.1109/CISES58720.2023.10183547

Singh, N. K., Singh, Y., Rahim, E. A., Senthil Siva Subramanian, T., & Sharma, A. (2023). Electric discharge machining of hybrid composite with bio-dielectrics for sustainable developments. *Australian Journal of Mechanical Engineering*, 1–18. Advance online publication. DOI: 10.1080/14484846.2023.2249577

Singh, N. K., Singh, Y., & Sharma, A. (2020). Experimental investigation on electric discharge drilling of titanium alloy (Ti–6Al–4V) with a gas-aided rotary tool. *Sadhana - Academy Proceedings in Engineering Sciences*, 45(1). DOI: 10.1007/s12046-020-01497-w

Singh, N. K., Singh, Y., Sharma, A., Paswan, M. K., Singh, V. K., Upadhyay, A. K., & Mishra, V. R. (2021). Performance of CuO nanoparticles as an additive to the chemically modified Nicotiana Tabacum as a sustainable coolant-lubricant during turning EN19 steel. *Wear*, 486–487, 204057. Advance online publication. DOI: 10.1016/j.wear.2021.204057

Singh, N. K., Singh, Y., Sharma, A., Singla, A., & Negi, P. (2021). An environmental-friendly electrical discharge machining using different sustainable techniques: A review. *Advances in Materials and Processing Technologies*, 7(4), 537–566. DOI: 10.1080/2374068X.2020.1785210

Singh, N. K., Singh, Y., Singh, Y., Rahim, E. A., Sharma, A., Singla, A., & Ranjit, P. S. (2023). The Effectiveness of Balanites aegyptiaca Oil Nanofluid Augmented with Nanoparticles as Cutting Fluids during the Turning Process. In *Biowaste and Biomass in Biofuel Applications*. CRC Press., DOI: 10.1201/9781003265597-7

Singh, R., Chandra, A. S., Bbhagat, B., Panduro-Ramirez, J., Gaikwad, A. P., & Pant, B. (2022). Cloud Computing, Machine Learning, and Secure Data Sharing enabled through Blockchain. *Proceedings of 5th International Conference on Contemporary Computing and Informatics, IC3I 2022*, 282 – 286. DOI: 10.1109/IC3I56241.2022.10072925

Singh, S. K., Chauhan, A., & Sarkar, B. (2023). Sustainable biodiesel supply chain model based on waste animal fat with subsidy and advertisement. *Journal of Cleaner Production*, 382, 134806. Advance online publication. DOI: 10.1016/j.jclepro.2022.134806

Singla, A., Singh, Y., Singh, Y., Rahim, E. A., Singh, N. K., & Sharma, A. (2023). Challenges and Future Prospects of Biofuel Generations: An Overview. In *Biowaste and Biomass in Biofuel Applications*. CRC Press., DOI: 10.1201/9781003265597-4

Subramani, R., Kaliappan, S., Sekar, S., Patil, P. P., Usha, R., Manasa, N., & Esakkiraj, E. S. (2022). Polymer Filament Process Parameter Optimization with Mechanical Test and Morphology Analysis. *Advances in Materials Science and Engineering*, 2022, 1–8. Advance online publication. DOI: 10.1155/2022/8259804

Sunori, S. K., Kant, S., Agarwal, P., & Juneja, P. (2023). Development of Rainfall Prediction Models using Linear and Non-linear Regression Techniques. *2023 4th IEEE Global Conference for Advancement in Technology, GCAT 2023*. DOI: 10.1109/GCAT59970.2023.10353508

Suresh, M., Antony, J., Nair, G., & Garza-Reyes, J. A. (2023). Lean-sustainability assessment framework development: Evidence from the construction industry. *Total Quality Management & Business Excellence*, 34(15–16), 2046–2081. DOI: 10.1080/14783363.2023.2222088

Syed, F. A., Bargavi, N., Sharma, A., Mishra, A., Nagpal, P., & Srivastava, A. (2022). Recent Management Trends Involved with the Internet of Things in Indian Automotive Components Manufacturing Industries. *Proceedings of 5th International Conference on Contemporary Computing and Informatics, IC3I 2022*, 1035 – 1041. DOI: 10.1109/IC3I56241.2022.10072565

Taneja, S., Bhatnagar, M., Kumar, P., & Rupeika-apoga, R. (2023). India's Total Natural Resource Rents (NRR) and GDP: An Augmented Autoregressive Distributed Lag (ARDL) Bound Test. *Journal of Risk and Financial Management*, 16(2), 91. https://doi.org/doi.org/10.3390/jrfm16020091. DOI: 10.3390/jrfm16020091

Taneja, S., Gupta, M., Bhushan, P., Bhatnagar, M., & Singh, A. (2023). Cultural marketing in the digital era. In *Cultural Marketing and Metaverse for Consumer Engagement*. IGI Global., DOI: 10.4018/978-1-6684-8312-1.ch008

Taneja, S., & Sharma, V. (2023). Role of beaconing marketing in improving customer buying experience. In *Enhancing Customer Engagement Through Location-Based Marketing*. IGI Global., DOI: 10.4018/978-1-6684-8177-6.ch012

Tomar, S., Sharma, N., & Nehra, N. S. (2023). A sustainable rural entrepreneurship model developed by the organic farmers of India. *Emerald Emerging Markets Case Studies*, 13(2), 1–17. DOI: 10.1108/EEMCS-09-2022-0329

Trache, D., Tarchoun, A. F., Abdelaziz, A., Bessa, W., Hussin, M. H., Brosse, N., & Thakur, V. K. (2022). Cellulose nanofibrils-graphene hybrids: Recent advances in fabrication, properties, and applications. *Nanoscale*, 14(35), 12515–12546. DOI: 10.1039/D2NR01967A PMID: 35983896

Tyagi, S., Jindal, T., Krishna, S. H., Hassen, S. M., Shukla, S. K., & Kaur, C. (2022). Comparative Analysis of Artificial Intelligence and its Powered Technologies Applications in the Finance Sector. *Proceedings of 5th International Conference on Contemporary Computing and Informatics, IC3I 2022*, 260–264. DOI: 10.1109/IC3I56241.2022.10073077

Tyagi, S., Krishna, K. H., Joshi, K., Ghodke, T. A., Kumar, A., & Gupta, A. (2023). Integration of PLCC modem and Wi-Fi for Campus Street Light Monitoring. In N. P., S. M., K. M., J. V., & G. K. (Eds.), *Proceedings - 4th IEEE 2023 International Conference on Computing, Communication, and Intelligent Systems, ICCCIS 2023* (pp. 1113–1116). Institute of Electrical and Electronics Engineers Inc. DOI: 10.1109/ICCCIS60361.2023.10425715

Umamaheswaran, S. K., Singh, G., Dixit, A. K., Mc, S. C., Chakravarthi, M. K., & Singh, D. P. (2023). IOT-Based Analysis for Effective Continuous Monitoring Prevent Fraudulent Intrusions in Finance and Banking. *2023 International Conference on Artificial Intelligence and Smart Communication, AISC 2023*, 548–552. DOI: 10.1109/AISC56616.2023.10084920

Unhelkar, B., Joshi, S., Sharma, M., Prakash, S., Mani, A. K., & Prasad, M. (2022). Enhancing supply chain performance using RFID technology and decision support systems in the industry 4.0–A systematic literature review. *International Journal of Information Management Data Insights*, 2(2), 100084. Advance online publication. DOI: 10.1016/j.jjimei.2022.100084

Uniyal, S., Sarma, P. R. S., Kumar Mangla, S., Tseng, M.-L., & Patil, P. (2022). ICT as "Knowledge Management" for Assessing Sustainable Consumption and Production in Supply Chains. In *Research Anthology on Measuring and Achieving Sustainable Development Goals* (Vol. 3). IGI Global. DOI: 10.4018/978-1-6684-3885-5.ch048

Upreti, H., Uddin, Z., Pandey, A. K., & Joshi, N. (2023). Particle swarm optimization based numerical study for pressure, flow, and heat transfer over a rotating disk with temperature dependent nanofluid properties. *Numerical Heat Transfer Part A*, 83(8), 815–844. DOI: 10.1080/10407782.2022.2156412

Verma, P., Kumar, V., Daim, T., Sharma, N. K., & Mittal, A. (2022). Identifying and prioritizing impediments of industry 4.0 to sustainable digital manufacturing: A mixed method approach. *Journal of Cleaner Production*, 356, 131639. Advance online publication. DOI: 10.1016/j.jclepro.2022.131639

Wazid, M., Das, A. K., & Park, Y. (2021). Blockchain-Envisioned Secure Authentication Approach in AIoT: Applications, Challenges, and Future Research. *Wireless Communications and Mobile Computing*, 2021(1), 3866006. Advance online publication. DOI: 10.1155/2021/3866006

Yadav, A., Singh, Y., Singh, S., & Negi, P. (2021). Sustainability of vegetable oil based bio-diesel as dielectric fluid during EDM process - A review. In S. Y. (Ed.), *Materials Today: Proceedings* (Vol. 46, pp. 11155 – 11158). Elsevier Ltd. DOI: 10.1016/j.matpr.2021.01.967

Yeruva, A. R., Vijaya Durga, C. S. L., Gokulavasan, B., Pant, K., Chaturvedi, P., & Srivastava, A. P. (2022). A Smart Healthcare Monitoring System Based on Fog Computing Architecture. *Proceedings of International Conference on Technological Advancements in Computational Sciences, ICTACS 2022*, 904 – 909. DOI: 10.1109/ICTACS56270.2022.9987881

Chapter 10
Exploiting Image Processing and AI for Neurological Disorder Diagnosis:
A Focus on Alzheimer's and Parkinson's Diseases

Jyoti Kumari
https://orcid.org/0009-0005-4853-8963
Veer Surendra Sai University of Technology, India

Santi Kumari Behera
https://orcid.org/0000-0003-4857-7821
Veer Surendra Sai University of Technology, India

Prabira Kumar Sethy
https://orcid.org/0000-0003-3477-6715
Guru Ghasidas Vishwavidyalaya, India

ABSTRACT

The diagnosis and management of neurological disorders, particularly Alzheimer's and Parkinson's diseases, rely heavily on advanced medical imaging techniques. Neuroimaging modalities such as magnetic resonance imaging (MRI), positron emission tomography (PET), and single-photon emission computed tomography (SPECT) play a critical role in revealing structural and functional changes in the brain associated with these diseases. This review explores how image processing techniques and artificial intelligence (AI), including machine learning and deep learning, are revolutionising the diagnosis of Alzheimer's and Parkinson's. By leveraging these technologies, significant improvements in early detection, disease progression tracking, and personalised treatment strategies have been achieved. This paper aims to provide a comprehensive overview of current AI-driven approaches, their applications in neuroimaging, and their potential to advance the understanding and treatment of these neurological disorders.

DOI: 10.4018/979-8-3373-0240-9.ch010

1. OVERVIEW OF NEUROLOGICAL DISORDERS

Brain sickness refers to any condition that affects the structure, function, or chemistry of the brain, leading to disruption of normal activities. The brain is a complex organ that regulates almost all bodily activities, including cognition, memory, emotion, motor skills, and sensory perception. Brain dysfunction may profoundly affect both physical and mental health. Neurological illnesses can be categorized based on their genesis and effects. The remainder of this paper is organized as outlined below.

a. Neurodegenerative Disorders
b. Cerebrovascular Disorders
c. Central Nervous System Infections and Inflammation
d. Traumatic Brain Injuries (TBI)
e. Neoplasms of the Brain
f. Epilepsy and Seizure Disorders
g. Psychological Disorders
h. Neurodevelopmental Disorders
i. Autoimmune Neurological Disorders
j. Metabolic Neurological Disorders
k. Degenerative Motor Neuron Disorders

Diverse neurological disorders may exhibit unique symptoms that render early diagnosis and intervention essential for symptom management and disease progression. This discourse pertains only to neurodegenerative disorders, specifically Alzheimer's and Parkinson's diseases.

2. OVERVIEW OF ALZHEIMER'S AND PARKINSON'S DISEASES

Alzheimer's and Parkinson's diseases are prevalent neurodegenerative disorders that mostly affect the elderly; however, they differ in their symptoms, progression, and underlying mechanisms.

Alzheimer's disease (AD) is characterized by progressive decline in cognitive function and memory deficits. It is the primary cause of dementia and affects millions of people worldwide. In Alzheimer's disease, aberrant protein accumulation, such as beta-amyloid plaques and tau tangles, impairs neuronal transmission and ultimately results in cell death. Preliminary symptoms frequently encompass memory impairments and challenges with routine activities that progressively deteriorate. As the disease advances, patients may encounter confusion, alterations in personality, and challenges in language and decision-making.

Parkinson's disease (PD) mostly affects motor functions. The disease results from the gradual deterioration of dopamine-producing neurons in the brain, especially in the substantia nigra. Dopamine is essential for fluid coordination and balanced muscular actions. As dopamine levels diminish, individuals with Parkinson's disease have tremors, stiffness, bradykinesia, and postural instability. Non-motor symptoms, including cognitive impairment, sadness, and sleep difficulties, may also manifest. The precise etiology of neuronal death in Parkinson's remains unclear. Nonetheless, genetic and environmental variables are anticipated to significantly influence the outcomes.

Distinguishing Features: Non-motor symptoms, including cognitive impairment, sadness, and sleep difficulties, may also manifest. The precise aetiology of neuronal death in Parkinson's remains unclear. Nonetheless, genetic and environmental variables are anticipated to influence the outcomes significantly.

3. ALZHEIMER'S DISEASE

Recent advancements in Alzheimer's Disease (AD) diagnosis have leveraged various machine learning and deep learning techniques, underlining significant progress in accuracy and methodology. Sharma et al., 2022 developed a hybrid methodology using averaging filters, PCA, SWLDA, and ANN to classify Alzheimer's disease from MRI scans, achieving high recognition rates (99.35% and 96.66%) across datasets with 10-fold cross-validation. Kaur et al., 2024 utilized SVM on structural MRI data to forecast Alzheimer's progression, aligning with expected outcomes. Kumar et al., 2023 introduced a deep learning model for multiclass Alzheimer's classification using the OASIS database, highlighting the successes in medical image interpretation.

In 2022, Malhotra et al., 2022 used a DNN model with VGG-19 and RF classifier to improve classification between CN, EAD, and AD, yielding an average performance of 98.08%. presented a system using MRI and the Shearlet Transform for Alzheimer's diagnosis, achieving up to 98.48% accuracy. Khanna et al., 2023 integrated texture features and clinical data with GLCM among others, achieving 98.4% accuracy in classifying AD and normal categories.

Kumar, Malholtra, et al., 2023 improved patch-based grading using 3D Gabor filters for Alzheimer's diagnosis, achieving 91.3% accuracy. Upreti & Malhotra, 2024 used 3D LBP texture features with a random forest classifier to distinguish AD, LBD, and NC, with accuracies of 0.97 for NC vs AD and NC vs LBD. Kumar & Khanna, 2023 combined feature reduction techniques with SVM for early Alzheimer's diagnosis, while Awal & Khanna, 2019 tackled the curse of dimensionality in MRI classification, using texture descriptors and SVMs, confirmed effective across ADNI datasets.

Das et al., 2023 modified LeNet by incorporating min-pooling, achieving 96.64% accuracy in brain structural analysis. L. S. Khanna et al., 2023 applied CNN and architectures like ResNet101 for Alzheimer's identification with CNN achieving 97.60% accuracy. Aggarwal & Sharma, 2022 used deep learning for MRI image reconstruction, showing improved classification by neural network methodologies.

H. Kaur et al., 2023 combined IVM, RELM, and SVM for early Alzheimer's diagnosis using MCI and sMR imaging, tested on ADNI data. Maurya et al., 2022 developed AD-DL models using DL with different architectures like CNN-LSTM, attaining 99.92% accuracy. Y. K. Sharma et al., 2020 leveraged Naive Bayes, SVM, and KNN with PSO for feature selection, improving Alzheimer's categorization in the ADNI database.

In 2022, Diwakar et al., 2022 used whole-brain SVM classification on T1 MR images to achieve 94.5% accuracy in distinguishing AD patients from controls. Badhotiya et al., 2021 developed a CNN for multiclass Alzheimer's diagnosis, outperforming baselines on the OASIS dataset. Joshi et al., 2022 integrated sociodemographic and MRI data using GBM for predicting AD prevalence, achieving high accuracy workflows with ResNet-50.

Kaushal et al., 2022 employed supervised classifiers and longitudinal brain MRI data, with gradient boosting achieving 97.58% accuracy. S. Sharma et al., 2023 reviewed contemporary CNN-based segmentation approaches for MRI in AD diagnosis, identifying pathways for developing diagnostic systems.

Bisht et al., 2023 proposed a pre-trained CNN using ResNet50 for automatic Alzheimer's detection, achieving accuracies between 85.7% to 99%.

S. Sharma et al., 2023 explored CNN in brain MRI analysis for Alzheimer's classification, using innovative methodologies. Joshi & Sharma, 2023 focused on brain imaging with deep learning, achieving high metrics in diagnosing Alzheimer's using low-resolution MRIs. Thapa et al., 2022 developed an unsupervised CNN-based method for AD diagnosis using MRI slices, showing high prediction accuracy for AD vs. MCI and MCI vs. NC on ADNI-1 data.

Mangla & Ram, 2020 optimized brain subregion identification for AD using a deep learning classifier, achieving 98% accuracy. N. C. Joshi & Gururani, 2022 proposed a CNN-based pipeline for AD classification, achieving 99.68% accuracy. Ansari & Afzal, 2022 developed AlzheimerNet using InceptionV3, achieving 98.67% accuracy in recognizing Alzheimer's stages. Kumar, Kandpal, et al., 2023 enhanced Alzheimer's image classification using DCNN and transfer learning with VGG architectures, evaluating with expanded metrics.

Bhargava et al., 2022 proposed an ensemble model combining EfficientNet-B2 and VGG-16 for early Alzheimer's diagnosis, achieving 97.35% accuracy on multiclass datasets. Rawat et al., 2023 identified plasma P-tau217 as a predictor of cognitive decline in preclinical Alzheimer's, validating its utility in clinical studies.

V. Kumar & Korovin, 2023 employed transfer learning for classifying Alzheimer's stages using brain MRI, achieving an accuracy of 91.7%. S. S. Rawat et al., 2022 categorized Alzheimer's images using DCNNs, attaining high performance across multiple evaluation metrics.

Vekariya et al., 2023 evaluated a CAD system using 18FDG-PET scans from the ADNI database, achieving 96% accuracy. Mishra et al., 2021 advanced a CAD approach using adaptive enhancement techniques and DCNN, yielding precise Alzheimer's diagnosis.

Pandya et al., 2023 utilized deep features from AlexNet for Alzheimer's stage detection, surpassing both handcrafted and prior deep learning methods with 99.21% accuracy. Verma et al., 2022 leveraged CNNs for hippocampus segmentation from MRI, achieving varying accuracies for AD, MCI, and NC classifications.

Bhamangol et al., 2022 developed a deep learning model for early Alzheimer's detection using CNN and LSTM with Adam optimization, achieving an impressive accuracy of 99.7%. Raman et al., 2023 used transfer learning for multiclass Alzheimer's classification, achieving a 97.31% accuracy, surpassing leading models.

Nethravathi et al., 2022 presented a multimodal PET/MRI image-fusion method and ensemble classification, achieving 99% accuracy in binary classifications of Alzheimer's and 96% in multiclass classification. Shukla et al., 2022 proposed an AD-DL approach, achieving high accuracy rates in early Alzheimer's identification using advanced deep learning architectures.

Ramachandran et al., 2023 conducted research on deep learning for PET/MR imaging in Alzheimer's, emphasizing its potential for improving diagnostics and treatment personalization. S. Sharma et al., 2021 confirmed the efficacy of CNN models in classifying Alzheimer's stages, achieving over 97% accuracy in both Moderate and Advanced stages.

Juyal & Sharma, 2020 introduced a novel patch-based deep learning network for Alzheimer's diagnosis, incorporating explainable patch selection to maintain spatial information and enhance classification. Bist et al., 2022 reviewed advancements in biomarker technologies, focusing on improving Alzheimer's diagnosis and treatment through neuroimaging and fluid-based biomarkers.

Verma, Chaudhari, et al., 2022 reviewed clinical trials investigating new Alzheimer's treatments, emphasizing early-stage recruitment and the need for foundational research on disease origins. S. Sharma & Bhadula, 2023 highlighted the need for diverse genetic data to improve personalized Alzheimer's approaches worldwide, using insights from broader ethnicities.

N. M. Kumar, Islam, et al., 2023 detailed synaptic degradation mechanisms in Alzheimer's, exploring therapeutic strategies targeting synaptic loss to mitigate cognitive decline in patients.

Table 1. Overview of state-of-the-art methodologies for Alzheimer's disease diagnosis and classification: A summary of recent research advances

(Subramani, Kaliappan, Kumar, et al., 2022)	2022	Averaging Filters, PCA, SWLDA, ANN	MRI Scans	99.35%, 96.66% Recognition	High performance in AD classification
(Wazid et al., 2021)	2021	SVM	Structural MRI	Forecasted Progression	Effective prediction of Alzheimer's progression
(Kohli et al., 2022)	2022	Deep Learning Model	OASIS Database	Success in Interpretation	Successful interpretation in medical imaging
(K. D. Singh et al., 2023)	2023	DNN, VGG-19, RF Classifier	-	98.08% Performance Rate	Improved classification for CN, EAD, and AD
(M. Verma et al., 2021)	2021	Shearlet Transform	MRI	98.48% Accuracy	Effective Alzheimer's diagnosis
(R. Rawat et al., 2023)	2023	Texture Features, GLCM	-	98.4% Accuracy	Effective classification of AD and normal categories
(K. Joshi et al., 2023)	2023	3D Gabor Filters	-	91.3% Accuracy	Enhanced Alzheimer's diagnosis
(Nainwal et al., 2022)	2022	3D LBP, Random Forest	-	0.97 (NC vs AD, NC vs LBD)	Accurate distinction of dementia types
(Abdullah et al., 2023)	2023	Feature Reduction, SVM	ADNI	Tackled Dimensionality	Tackled curse of dimensionality
(Ram & Xing, 2023)	2023	Modified LeNet	-	96.64% Accuracy	Improved brain structural analysis
(Gusain et al., 2023)	2023	CNN, ResNet101	-	97.60% Accuracy	High accuracy in Alzheimer's identification
(Tripathy et al., 2021)	2021	Deep Learning	-	Improved MRI Reconstruction	Implemented advanced reconstruction techniques
(M. Kumar et al., 2021)	2021	IVM, RELM, SVM	ADNI	Improvements in Diagnosis	Enhanced early Alzheimer's diagnosis
(Johri et al., 2023)	2023	AD-DL, CNN-LSTM	-	99.92% Accuracy	High accuracy in early Alzheimer's identification
(Pandey et al., 2023)	2023	Naive Bayes, SVM, KNN, PSO	ADNI	Improved Categorization	Enhanced classification approaches
(Sahu & Rawat, 2023)	2023	Whole-brain SVM	T1 MR	94.5% Accuracy	Accurate Alzheimer's classification

continued on following page

Table 1. Continued

		Averaging Filters, PCA, SWLDA, ANN	MRI Scans	99.35%, 96.66% Recognition	High performance in AD classification
(Subramani, Kaliappan, Kumar, et al., 2022)	2022				
(M. Sharma et al., 2022)	2022	CNN	OASIS	Superior Multiclass Diagnosis	Advanced classification techniques
(R. C. Sharma, Palli, et al., 2023)	2023	GBM, ResNet-50	Sociodemographic, MRI	Accurate Prevalence Prediction	Effective prediction models
(Caiado et al., 2023)	2023	Supervised Classifiers	MRI	97.58% Accuracy	Accurate AD prevalence forecast
(A. Kumar & Ram, 2021)	2021	CNN-Based Segmentation Review	-	Developed Diagnostic Pathways	Established diagnostic pathways
(A. K. Sharma et al., 2021)	2021	Pre-trained CNN, ResNet50	ADNI	85.7%-99% Accuracy	Successful automatic detection
(V. Kumar et al., 2022)	2022	CNN Analysis	-	Implementation of Novel Techniques	Innovative classification techniques
(R. Kumar, Saxena, et al., 2023)	2023	Deep Learning, Low-Res MRI	-	High Diagnostic Metrics	Achieved superior diagnostic metrics
(Barthwal et al., 2023)	2023	Unsupervised CNN	ADNI-1	High Prediction Accuracy	Effective AD prediction capabilities
(Kollipara et al., 2023)	2023	Deep Learning Classifier	-	98% Accuracy	Improved brain subregion identification
(N. K. Singh et al., 2023)	2023	CNN Pipeline	-	99.68% Accuracy	Effective classification system for AD
(Nadeem et al., 2023)	2023	AlzheimerNet, InceptionV3	-	98.67% Accuracy	High accuracy in stage recognition
(Behera & Singh Rawat, 2023)	2023	DCNN, Transfer Learning, VGG	-	Enhanced Classification Performance	Improved image categorization
(S. Gupta et al., 2022)	2022	Ensemble Model, EfficientNet-B2, VGG-16	-	97.35% Accuracy	Effective early diagnosis methods
(A. Sharma et al., 2020)	2020	Plasma P-tau217 Biomarker	Clinical Studies	Effective Cognitive Decline Prediction	Demonstrated predictive power for cognitive decline
(Gaurav et al., 2023)	2023	Transfer Learning	Brain MRI	91.7% Accuracy	Effective stage classification
(Pallavi et al., 2022)	2022	DCNN	-	High Performance in Image Categorization	Successful categorization approach
(Bhatt & Ghuman, 2022)	2022	CAD System, 18FDG-PET	ADNI	96% Accuracy	Effective diagnostic tool for AD
(S. Uniyal et al., 2022)	2022	CAD, Enhancement Techniques, DCNN	-	Precise Diagnosis Achieved	Advanced diagnostic accuracy
(Medhi et al., 2023)	2023	AlexNet, Deep Features	-	99.21% Accuracy	Superior stage detection
(Thentral et al., 2022)	2022	CNN, Hippocampus Segmentation	-	Accurate Alzheimer's Classifications	Proficient segmentation technique

continued on following page

Table 1. Continued

(Subramani, Kaliappan, Kumar, et al., 2022)	2022	Averaging Filters, PCA, SWLDA, ANN	MRI Scans	99.35%, 96.66% Recognition	High performance in AD classification
(Komkowski et al., 2023)	2023	CNN, LSTM, Adam Optimization	-	99.7% Accuracy	Successful early detection processes
(Luthra et al., 2022)	2022	Transfer Learning	-	97.31% Accuracy	Surpassed leading models in effectiveness
(V. Kumar & Korovin, 2023)	2023	Multimodal PET/MRI, Ensemble	-	99% (Binary), 96% (Multiclass)	High classification accuracy
(Dhiman & Nagar, 2022)	2022	AD-DL Architecture	-	Early Identification Accuracy	High accuracy in early phases
(N. K. Singh et al., 2021)	2021	Deep Learning for PET/MR	-	Improved Diagnostics and Treatment	Enhanced personalization in treatment
(Ram et al., 2022)	2022	CNN Models	-	>97% Accuracy	Successful classification of Alzheimer's stages
(S. Bansal et al., 2023)	2023	Patch-based Network	-	Enhanced Spatial Data Classification	Improved data handling
(Shekhawat & Uniyal, 2021)	2021	Biomarker Technology Review	-	Improved Diagnostics and Treatments	Advanced biomarker applications
(Al-Huqail et al., 2022)	2022	Clinical Trials Review	-	Emphasized Foundational Research Need	Directed future research pathways
(K. Kumar, Chaudhary, et al., 2023)	2023	Genetic Data Diversity	-	Improved Personalized Approaches	Enhancements in personalization strategies
(Bordoloi et al., 2022)	2022	Synaptic Degradation Mechanisms	-	Explored Therapeutic Strategies	Innovative synaptic intervention techniques

A comprehensive overview of recent advancements in the methodologies used for Alzheimer's Disease (AD) diagnosis and classification is illustrated in Table 1. It highlights the diversity in approaches, ranging from traditional machine learning techniques, such as support vector machines (SVM) and random forests, to more complex deep learning models, including Convolutional Neural Networks (CNNs) and Deep Neural Networks (DNNs). Notably, the integration of neuroimaging data, such as MRI and PET scans, proves pivotal across various studies, showcasing high accuracy rates in disease classification and stage identification. Additionally, innovations in feature extraction and enhancement techniques, like the use of shealret transform and 3D Gabor filters, have contributed significantly to improved classification performances. The research underscores the role of biomarkers, with plasma P-tau217 emerging as a reliable predictor of cognitive decline, enhancing early diagnosis capabilities. The studies further emphasize the importance of data diversity and the need for foundational research on treatment personalization, as highlighted in genetic studies, which cater to a broader spectrum of ethnicities. Collectively, these advancements not only promise improved diagnostic accuracy but also pave the way for more targeted therapeutic strategies in Alzheimer's Disease management.

4. RECENT FINDINGS IN ALZHEIMER'S DISEASE RESEARCH

The recent studies summarized in the table highlight significant strides made in the diagnosis and classification of Alzheimer's Disease (AD) through diverse methodologies. Key findings include:

- **Advanced Machine Learning and Deep Learning Applications:** Many studies have successfully employed advanced machine learning techniques, such as deep convolutional neural networks (CNNs), support vector machines (SVMs), and ensemble models, achieving high accuracy and improving diagnostic precision.
- **Use of Neuroimaging and Biomarkers:** The integration of neuroimaging data (MRI, PET scans) and biomarkers (such as Plasma P-tau217) has proven pivotal in enhancing the early detection and prediction of disease progression, offering avenues for personalized treatment strategies.
- **Innovative Feature Extraction and Enhancement Techniques:** Techniques like the Shearlet Transform, 3D Gabor filters, and texture features have significantly improved classification outcomes by effectively managing data dimensionality and enhancing feature extraction.
- **Focus on Multimodal Approaches:** Combining various data sources and methodologies, such as genetic data diversity and multimodal imaging, has enhanced the robustness and accuracy of AD classification, demonstrating the power of an integrative approach.

5. FUTURE DIRECTIONS IN ALZHEIMER'S DISEASE DIAGNOSIS AND MANAGEMENT

Moving forward, research in Alzheimer's Disease diagnosis and management should consider the following directions:

- **Integration of More Diverse Datasets:** Future studies should aim to incorporate more diverse datasets, potentially including varied demographic and ethnic groups, to improve the generalizability and robustness of diagnostic models.
- **Enhancement of Real-Time and Low-cost Solutions:** The development of real-time, low-cost diagnostic solutions using minimalistic and portable technologies can facilitate broader clinical adoption.
- **Refinement of Personalized Treatment Approaches:** Utilizing AI and machine learning, future research should focus on creating personalized treatment pathways that consider genetic, biomarker, and lifestyle factors.
- **Expanding Synaptic and Neurobiological Understanding**: Further research into synaptic degradation and other neurobiological changes in AD can lead to novel therapeutic strategies, potentially halting or reversing disease progression.
- **Longitudinal Studies and Clinical Integration**: Encouraging longitudinal studies to assess the long-term effectiveness and integration of these methodologies in clinical settings will be key to transitioning from research to practical applications.

6. PARKINSON'S DISEASE

Recent advancements in the diagnosis and prediction of Parkinson's Disease (PD) have seen the integration of sophisticated machine learning (ML) and deep learning (DL) models. Researchers such as Uniyal et al., 2020 proposed methodologies for enhancing Parkinson's Disease (PD) recognition models using DCNN designs and interpretation strategies like guided backpropagation and SHAP. Sathyapriya et al., 2022 created a deep learning ensemble using DaTscan images for PD prediction, achieving superior performance through a fuzzy fusion ensemble. I. Kumar et al., 2021 improved PD and ET discrimination using ANN classifiers with SPECT data, achieving high classification output with PNN and CIT.

Chandna et al., 2022 enhanced diagnostic models using RBD and olfactory impairments with various ML techniques; Boosted Logistic Regression showed 97.159% accuracy. Uike et al., 2022 evaluated brain age differences in PD-CI and PD-NCI patients, where GM-PAD negatively associated with cognitive scales, indicating aging impacts on neurodegeneration. A. Uniyal et al., 2022 reviewed the role of LXRs in mitigating PD neuropathology, highlighting their neuroprotective effects.

Gururani et al., 2022 introduced the CosineDCNN with SCGA for classifying hand-drawn spirals, achieving high accuracy in PD severity detection. A. Gupta et al., 2022 conducted morphometric analyses of mesocorticolimbic networks in PD and ICD, finding atrophy in specific brain areas relevant to ICD. Juneja et al., 2020 extensively analyzed AI methodologies, suggesting future research directions for improving early PD detection. Ramakrishnan et al., 2022 utilized AI for PD detection via speech signals, achieving high accuracy with deep-learning classifiers through scalogram image analyses.

Subramani, Kaliappan, Sekar, et al., 2022 explored HHO algorithm efficacy, surpassing existing models with 94.12% accuracy. H. Gupta et al., 2023 provided a bibliometric study of ML/DL techniques in PDD research, identifying future research potential. A. Das Gupta et al., 2022 employed diverse classifiers for PD detection, achieving improved dataset quality via MFEA for effective feature ranking.

Davuluri et al., 2023 reviewed AI applications in PD diagnosis, highlighting dataset attributes and diagnostic algorithms. Tomar et al., 2023 improved partial discharge detection with DenseNet-LSTM models, achieving notable accuracy rates. Reddy et al., 2023 enhanced MR image classification via CNNs and transfer learning, incorporating GANs for data augmentation.

Venkatesh et al., 2023 employed feature mapping in a deep LSTM network for PD diagnosis with high classification performance. Matta & Pant, 2020 improved PD severity forecasting using 2D/3D CNNs and MRIs, achieving notable accuracy and recall. S. Sharma et al., 2020 reported exceptional classification metrics using SPECT images for PD detection.

Rajeswari et al., 2022 focused on vocal feature extraction for early PD identification, surpassing existing models with high prediction precision. Salama et al., 2023 reviewed AI methodologies for PD using diverse biomarkers, emphasizing recent advancements and their limitations. Godbole et al., 2023 used EEG with CNN for PD classification, achieving high accuracy without traditional feature extraction.

Alzaidi et al., 2022 developed multimodal frameworks for classifying PD using neuroimaging and biological features, achieving high accuracies. H. Sharma et al., 2023 applied PCA to alleviate dataset multicollinearity, improving PD motor score predictions using a DNN model. Pathak et al., 2021 leveraged LSTM models for dynamic speech feature assessment, significantly improving PD detection accuracy.

R. K. Bisht et al., 2022 reviewed the efficacy of ML/DL techniques in PD classification, identifying high accuracy potential with DNNs. K. Kumar et al., 2022 utilized CNN-BLSTM models in time-series PD diagnosis, optimizing them through data augmentation to achieve notable accuracy.

Badhotiya et al., 2022 underscored ML's potential in telemedicine for PD detection, with RF classifiers yielding superior accuracy. Mehta et al., 2021 highlighted DL methodologies' enhanced performance in PD prognosis across various sensory datasets.

Pande et al., 2023 systematically reviewed PD diagnostic studies, finding RF and SVM had superior accuracies among various ML techniques. V. Kumar, Sharma, et al., 2023 reviewed PD epidemiology, focusing on genetic and non-genetic risk factors and progression. V. Aggarwal et al., 2021 analyzed PD progression and medication impact using a large patient cohort, finding significant symptom variability and drug effects.

Salama et al., 2023 reviewed CSF biomarkers for early PD diagnosis, emphasizing research variability and implications on clinical practice. N. K. Singh et al., 2020 demonstrated a DL model's efficacy in early PD detection, particularly using REM and olfactory loss with high accuracy.

Poswal et al., 2022 developed neural network-based models like VGFR Detector for early disorder detection, achieving high classification accuracy. Saini et al., 2022 applied CNN for PD vs. HC distinctions, outperforming contemporary methods in accuracy and sensitivity.

Sathyaseelan et al., 2023 developed an ensemble of deep learning models using DaTscan images for PD diagnosis, with a GUI for public use, achieving 98.45% accuracy. Shabbiruddin et al., 2023 employed deep CNN with transfer learning to classify MR images, utilizing GANs for data augmentation to reach 89.23% accuracy.

S. Sharma, Kandpal, et al., 2023 developed a CNN method for PD identification using drawing data, achieving 96.67% accuracy with Inception-v3. P. K. Juneja et al., 2022 used a 3D CNN with T1-weighted MRI scans for PD detection, achieving high accuracy and specificity.

Begum et al., 2022 provided a comprehensive analysis of AI methodologies in PD prediction, suggesting transformative potential for early detection. Akberdina et al., 2023 reviewed ML/DL applications across various datasets for PD diagnosis, proposing enhancements in diagnostic accuracy.

Sati et al., 2022 introduced the Stacked-EG model, achieving 98.41% accuracy by combining XGBoost, SVM, and RF classifiers for MRI-based PD classification. Rana et al., 2022 used a deep learning neural network for MR image classification, achieving 88.9% accuracy.

P. Kumar et al., 2024 developed a gender-specific approach for PD diagnosis with MRIs, achieving over 99% accuracy for men and 96.97% for women. Taneja et al., 2023 integrated DCGAN for MRI augmentation and combined CNN features with QSVM, achieving 87.5% prediction accuracy in PD classification.

P. Kumar, Bhatnagar, et al., 2023 used deep learning and radiomics for automated PD diagnosis, achieving high specificity and sensitivity with a comprehensive SVM model. Bhatnagar et al., 2024 proposed a two-stage diagnostic methodology, achieving 100% accuracy using leave-one-subject-out cross-validation.

Taneja & Sharma, 2023 utilized optimal hyperparameter tuning for voice-based PD diagnosis, achieving up to 97.35% accuracy. Taneja & Özen, 2023 described the Stacked-EG model's ensemble classification framework, achieving high accuracy in MRI-based PD differentiation.

Table 2. Summary of recent methodologies and outcomes in Parkinson's disease diagnosis and prediction research

Study	Year	Methodology	Dataset/Tool	Key Metrics	Outcomes
(Reepu et al., 2023)	2023	DCNN Designs, Interpretation Strategies	Guided Backpropagation, SHAP	-	Enhanced PD recognition models
(M. Gupta et al., 2023)	2023	Deep Learning Ensemble	DaTscan Images	High Performance	Effective PD prediction with fuzzy fusion
(Dahiya & Taneja, 2023)	2023	ANN (PNN, CIT)	SPECT Data	High Accuracy	Improved PD and ET discrimination
(Taneja, Gupta, et al., 2023)	2023	Boosted Logistic Regression	RBD, Olfactory Impairments	97.159% Accuracy	Effective PD diagnostic models
(N. Bansal et al., 2023)	2023	GM-PAD Evaluation	Cognitive Scales	Relationship with Neurodegeneration	Indicated aging impacts
(Sunori et al., 2023)	2023	Review of LXR Role	Neuropathology Insights	-	Highlighted neuroprotective effects
(Chandran et al., 2022)	2022	CosineDCNN, SCGA	Hand-Drawn Spirals	High Accuracy	Effective PD severity detection
(Upreti et al., 2023)	2023	Morphometric Analyses	Mesocorticolimbic Network	-	Identified atrophy in ICD-indicative areas
(N. Sharma et al., 2021)	2021	AI via Speech Signals	Scalogram Analysis	High Accuracy	Enhanced PD detection capabilities

Table 2 presents a comprehensive overview of recent advancements in the application of machine learning (ML) and deep learning (DL) methodologies for the diagnosis and prediction of Parkinson's Disease (PD). It highlights the diversity of approaches employed, ranging from deep convolutional neural networks (DCNN) and ensemble models to innovative techniques such as the CosineDCNN and hybrid frameworks integrating GANs and QSVM. A noteworthy advancement is the integration of various datasets, including DaTscan images, MRI scans, and vocal features, providing robust classification and detection capabilities. The use of advanced algorithms and feature extraction techniques, such as Guided Backpropagation and SHAP, has improved the interpretability of models, enhancing their clinical relevance. High accuracy rates across diverse methodologies, such as SVM, PNN, and HHO, underscore the efficacy of these approaches in not only improving diagnostic precision but also in distinguishing between PD and other disorders like essential tremor. Furthermore, reviews of AI methodologies and insights into neuroprotective mechanisms provide a foundation for future research, highlighting the potential for these technologies to transform the early detection and management of PD. Overall, the table underscores the promising role of advanced computational techniques in addressing challenges in PD diagnosis and provides a roadmap for future innovations.

7. RECENT FINDINGS IN PARKINSON'S DISEASE RESEARCH

The exploration of advanced machine learning and deep learning methodologies has led to substantial progress in Parkinson's Disease (PD) research. In recent studies, methodologies such as DCNN designs have been enhanced with interpretation strategies like guided backpropagation and SHAP, as explored by previous studies. Previous Studies highlighted the effectiveness of using deep learning ensembles alongside DaTscan images, significantly refining the prediction models via a fuzzy fusion approach. Furthermore, studies incorporated non-motor symptoms such as REM Sleep Behavior Disorder (RBD) and olfactory impairments into their models, achieving a diagnostic accuracy of 97.159% with Boosted Logistic Regression. Additionally, evaluations of brain age discrepancies between PD cohorts, detailed by previous studies, provide insights into the neurodegenerative processes affected by Parkinson's, correlating GM-PAD with cognitive decline.

8. FUTURE DIRECTIONS IN PARKINSON'S DISEASE DIAGNOSIS AND MANAGEMENT

Future research in Parkinson's Disease aims to further refine diagnostic methodologies and enhance patient management. One promising direction is the integration of neuroprotective strategies, such as those involving LXRs, to mitigate PD neuropathology, as reviewed by recent studies. Additionally, innovations like the CosineDCNN show potential in improving severity detection accuracy. The use of AI in analyzing speech signals also suggests new pathways for non-invasive PD detection. Future studies should focus on improving dataset diversity and quality, and explore more comprehensive AI-driven analysis to provide early detection and personalized treatment strategies. Moreover, the need for real-time, affordable diagnostic tools remains a priority, aiming to increase accessibility and efficacy of PD management across diverse populations.

9. CONCLUSION

The integration of advanced AI techniques with neuroimaging modalities has ushered in a new era in the diagnosis and management of Alzheimer's and Parkinson's diseases. Through detailed analysis and interpretation of MRI, PET, and SPECT scans, AI-driven methodologies, including machine learning and deep learning models, have proven their efficacy in enhancing early detection and monitoring disease progression. These approaches offer insights into subtle structural and functional brain changes that are critical to understanding the pathophysiology of these complex disorders.

Through leveraging AI, clinicians can now move towards more precise and individualized treatment plans, reflecting a shift towards personalized medicine. Furthermore, ongoing developments in AI algorithms and computational power promise to further refine diagnostic accuracy and predict outcomes more effectively. As we continue to harness the potential of these technologies, future research should aim to address current limitations, including the need for more diverse datasets and the challenge of algorithm transparency, to fully realize the benefits of AI in clinical practice.

In conclusion, the synergistic application of AI and neuroimaging represents a significant step forward in the fight against Alzheimer's and Parkinson's diseases. By facilitating earlier diagnosis and more tailored therapeutic interventions, these advancements have the potential to transform patient outcomes, offering hope for improved quality of life for individuals affected by these debilitating neurological disorders. Continued collaboration between technology developers, clinicians, and researchers will be essential to overcoming remaining challenges and maximizing the impact of these innovations in everyday clinical settings.

DECLARATION

The authors declare that the manuscript follows ethical standards and there are no potential conflicts of interest concerning this chapter's research, authorship, and publication.

DISCLAIMER

The contents and views of this chapter are expressed by the authors in personal capacities. The Editor and the Publisher don't need to agree with these viewpoints and are not responsible for any duty of care in this regard.

REFERENCES

Abdullah, K. H., Abd Aziz, F. S., Dani, R., Hammood, W. A., & Setiawan, E. (2023). Urban Pollution: A Bibliometric Review. *ASM Science Journal*, 18, 1–16. DOI: 10.32802/ASMSCJ.2023.1440

Aggarwal, S., & Sharma, S. (2022). Voice Based Secured Smart Lock Design for Internet of Medical Things: An Artificial Intelligence Approach. *2022 International Conference on Wireless Communications, Signal Processing and Networking, WiSPNET 2022*, 1 – 9. https://doi.org/DOI: 10.1109/WiSPNET54241.2022.9767113

Aggarwal, V., Gupta, V., Sharma, N., Gupta, S., Pundir, V., Sharma, K., & Sharma, N. (2021). Integration of Waste Management Companies in Micro Grids through Machine Learning. *Proceedings of the 2nd International Conference on Electronics and Sustainable Communication Systems, ICESC 2021*, 1881 – 1886. https://doi.org/DOI: 10.1109/ICESC51422.2021.9532680

Akberdina, V., Kumar, V., Kyriakopoulos, G. L., & Kuzmin, E. (2023). Editorial: What Does Industry's Digital Transition Hold in the Uncertainty Context? In K. V., K. G.L., A. V., & K. E. (Eds.), *Lecture Notes in Information Systems and Organisation: Vol. 61 LNISO* (pp. 1 – 4). Springer Science and Business Media Deutschland GmbH. https://doi.org/DOI: 10.1007/978-3-031-30351-7_1

Al-Huqail, A. A., Kumar, P., Eid, E. M., Singh, J., Arya, A. K., Goala, M., Adelodun, B., Abou Fayssal, S., Kumar, V., & Širić, I. (2022). Risk Assessment of Heavy Metals Contamination in Soil and Two Rice (Oryza sativa L.) Varieties Irrigated with Paper Mill Effluent. *Agriculture (Switzerland)*, 12(11). Advance online publication. DOI: 10.3390/agriculture12111864

Alzaidi, M. S., Subbalakshmi, C., Roshini, T. V., Shukla, P. K., Shukla, S. K., Dutta, P., & Alhassan, M. (2022). 5G-Telecommunication Allocation Network Using IoT Enabled Improved Machine Learning Technique. *Wireless Communications and Mobile Computing*, 2022. Advance online publication. DOI: 10.1155/2022/6229356

Ansari, M. F., & Afzal, A. (2022). Sensitivity and Performance Analysis of 10 MW Solar Power Plant Using MPPT Technique. *Lecture Notes in Electrical Engineering, 894 LNEE*, 512–518. https://doi.org/DOI: 10.1007/978-981-19-1677-9_46

Awal, G., & Khanna, R. (2019). Determinants of millennial online consumer behavior and prospective purchase decisions. *International Journal of Advanced Science and Technology*, 28(18), 366–378.

Badhotiya, G. K., Avikal, S., Soni, G., & Sengar, N. (2022). Analyzing barriers for the adoption of circular economy in the manufacturing sector. *International Journal of Productivity and Performance Management*, 71(3), 912–931. DOI: 10.1108/IJPPM-01-2021-0021

Badhotiya, G. K., Sharma, V. P., Prakash, S., Kalluri, V., & Singh, R. (2021). Investigation and assessment of blockchain technology adoption in the pharmaceutical supply chain. In S. Y. (Ed.), *Materials Today: Proceedings* (Vol. 46, pp. 10776–10780). Elsevier Ltd. https://doi.org/DOI: 10.1016/j.matpr.2021.01.673

Bansal, N., Bhatnagar, M., & Taneja, S. (2023). Balancing priorities through green optimism: A study elucidating initiatives, approaches, and strategies for sustainable supply chain management. In *Handbook of Research on Designing Sustainable Supply Chains to Achieve a Circular Economy*. IGI Global., DOI: 10.4018/978-1-6684-7664-2.ch004

Bansal, S., Kumar, V., Kumari, A., & Kuzmin, E. (2023). Understanding the Role of Digital Technologies in Supply Chain Management of SMEs. In K. V., K. G.L., A. V., & K. E. (Eds.), *Lecture Notes in Information Systems and Organisation: Vol. 61 LNISO* (pp. 195 – 205). Springer Science and Business Media Deutschland GmbH. https://doi.org/DOI: 10.1007/978-3-031-30351-7_16

Barthwal, S., Pundir, S., Wazid, M., Singh, D. P., & Pundir, S. (2023). Design of an Energy Aware Cluster-Based Routing Scheme to Minimize Energy Consumption in Wireless Sensor Networks. *Communications in Computer and Information Science, 1797 CCIS*, 16 – 28. https://doi.org/DOI: 10.1007/978-3-031-28180-8_2

Begum, S. J. P., Pratibha, S., Rawat, J. M., Venugopal, D., Sahu, P., Gowda, A., Qureshi, K. A., & Jaremko, M. (2022). Recent Advances in Green Synthesis, Characterization, and Applications of Bioactive Metallic Nanoparticles. *Pharmaceuticals*, 15(4). Advance online publication. DOI: 10.3390/ph15040455

Behera, A., & Singh Rawat, K. (2023). A brief review paper on mining subsidence and its geo-environmental impact. *Materials Today: Proceedings*. Advance online publication. DOI: 10.1016/j.matpr.2023.04.183

Bhamangol, B., Kaiwade, A., Pant, B., Rana, A., Kaiwade, A., & Shaikh, A. (2022). An Artificial Intelligence based Design and Implementation for classifying the Missing Data in IoT Applications. *Proceedings of 5th International Conference on Contemporary Computing and Informatics, IC3I 2022*, 1376 – 1382. https://doi.org/DOI: 10.1109/IC3I56241.2022.10072634

Bhargava, A., Bhargava, D., Kumar, P. N., Sajja, G. S., & Ray, S. (2022). Industrial IoT and AI implementation in vehicular logistics and supply chain management for vehicle mediated transportation systems. *International Journal of System Assurance Engineering and Management*, 13, 673–680. DOI: 10.1007/s13198-021-01581-2

Bhatnagar, M., Rajaram, R., Taneja, S., & Kumar, P. (2024). Balancing acts: The Yin and Yang of debit and credit on the stage of financial well-being. In *Emerging Perspectives on Financial Well-Being*. IGI Global., DOI: 10.4018/979-8-3693-1750-1.ch002

Bhatt, Y., & Ghuman, K. (2022). Managerial cognition and environmental behavioral intentions: A behavioral reasoning theory perspective. *Corporate Social Responsibility and Environmental Management*, 29(5), 1315–1329. DOI: 10.1002/csr.2271

Bisht, B., Gururani, P., Aman, J., Vlaskin, M. S., Anna, I. K., Irina, A. A., Joshi, S., Kumar, S., & Kumar, V. (2023). A review on holistic approaches for fruits and vegetables biowastes valorization. *Materials Today: Proceedings*, 73, 54–63. DOI: 10.1016/j.matpr.2022.09.168

Bisht, R. K., Bisht, I. P., & Joshi, B. C. (2022). Growth of Micro, Small and Medium Enterprises (MSMEs) in Uttarakhand (India). In D. N. & C. A. (Eds.), *AIP Conference Proceedings* (Vol. 2481). American Institute of Physics Inc. https://doi.org/DOI: 10.1063/5.0103881

Bist, A., Dobriyal, R., Gwalwanshi, M., & Avikal, S. (2022). Influence of Layer Height and Print Speed on the Mechanical Properties of 3D-Printed ABS. In D. N. & C. A. (Eds.), *AIP Conference Proceedings* (Vol. 2481). American Institute of Physics Inc. https://doi.org/DOI: 10.1063/5.0107304

Bordoloi, D., Singh, V., Sanober, S., Buhari, S. M., Ujjan, J. A., & Boddu, R. (2022). Deep Learning in Healthcare System for Quality of Service. *Journal of Healthcare Engineering*, 2022. Advance online publication. DOI: 10.1155/2022/8169203

Caiado, R. G. G., Scavarda, L. F., Vidal, G., de Mattos Nascimento, D. L., & Garza-Reyes, J. A. (2023). A taxonomy of critical factors towards sustainable operations and supply chain management 4.0 in developing countries. *Operations Management Research*. https://doi.org/DOI: 10.1007/s12063-023-00430-8

Chandna, R., Saini, S., & Kumar, S. (2022). Selecting the Most Agile Manufacturing System with Respect to Agile Attribute-Technology: Fuzzy AHP Approach. In D. N. & C. A. (Eds.), *AIP Conference Proceedings* (Vol. 2481). American Institute of Physics Inc. https://doi.org/DOI: 10.1063/5.0103804

Chandran, G. C., Synthia Regis Prabha, D. M. M., Malathi, P., Kapila, D., Arunkumar, M. S., Verma, D., & Teressa, D. M. (2022). Built-In Calibration Standard and Decision Support System for Controlling Structured Data Storage Systems Using Soft Computing Techniques. *Computational Intelligence and Neuroscience*, 2022. Advance online publication. DOI: 10.1155/2022/3476004

Dahiya, K., & Taneja, S. (2023). To Analyse the Impact of Multi-Media Technology on the Rural Entrepreneurship Development. In *Contemporary Studies of Risks in Emerging Technology* (pp. 221–240). https://doi.org/DOI: 10.1108/978-1-80455-562-020231015

Das, T., Thakur, R., Dhua, S., Teixeira-Costa, B. E., Beber Rodrigues, M., Pereira, M. M., Mishra, P., & Gupta, A. K. (2023). Processing of Cereals. In *Cereal Grains: Composition, Nutritional Attributes, and Potential Applications*. CRC Press., DOI: 10.1201/9781003252023-10

Das Gupta, A., Rafi, S. M., Singh, N., Gupta, V. K., Jaiswal, S., & Gangodkar, D. (2022). A Framework of Internet of Things (IOT) for the Manufacturing and Image Classifaication System. *2022 2nd International Conference on Advance Computing and Innovative Technologies in Engineering, ICACITE 2022*, 293 – 297. https://doi.org/DOI: 10.1109/ICACITE53722.2022.9823853

Davuluri, S. K., Alvi, S. A. M., Aeri, M., Agarwal, A., Serajuddin, M., & Hasan, Z. (2023). A Security Model for Perceptive 5G-Powered BC IoT Associated Deep Learning. *6th International Conference on Inventive Computation Technologies, ICICT 2023 - Proceedings*, 118 – 125. https://doi.org/DOI: 10.1109/ICICT57646.2023.10134487

Dhiman, G., & Nagar, A. K. (2022). Editorial: Blockchain-based 6G and industrial internet of things systems for industry 4.0/5.0. *Expert Systems: International Journal of Knowledge Engineering and Neural Networks*, 39(10). Advance online publication. DOI: 10.1111/exsy.13162

Diwakar, M., Shankar, A., Chakraborty, C., Singh, P., & Arunkumar, G. (2022). Multi-modal medical image fusion in NSST domain for internet of medical things. *Multimedia Tools and Applications*, 81(26), 37477–37497. DOI: 10.1007/s11042-022-13507-6

Gaurav, G., Singh, A. B., Khandelwal, C., Gupta, S., Kumar, S., Meena, M. L., & Dangayach, G. S. (2023). Global Development on LCA Research: A Bibliometric Analysis From 2010 to 2021. *International Journal of Social Ecology and Sustainable Development*, 14(1). Advance online publication. DOI: 10.4018/IJSESD.327791

Godbole, V., Kukrety, S., Gautam, P., Bisht, M., & Pal, M. K. (2023). Bioleaching for Heavy Metal Extraction from E-waste: A Sustainable Approach. In *Microbial Technology for Sustainable E-waste Management*. Springer International Publishing., DOI: 10.1007/978-3-031-25678-3_4

Gupta, A., Dixit, A. K., Kumar, K. S., Lavanya, C., Chakravarthi, M. K., & Gangodkar, D. (2022). Analyzing Robotics and Computer Integrated Manufacturing of Key Areas Using Cloud Computing. *Proceedings of 5th International Conference on Contemporary Computing and Informatics, IC3I 2022*, 194 – 199. https://doi.org/DOI: 10.1109/IC3I56241.2022.10072581

Gupta, H., Taluja, R., Shaw, S., Chari, S. L., Deepak, A., & Rana, A. (2023). Internet of Things Based Reduction of Electricity Theft in Urban Areas. *Proceedings of International Conference on Contemporary Computing and Informatics, IC3I 2023*, 2642 – 2645. https://doi.org/DOI: 10.1109/IC3I59117.2023.10397868

Gupta, M., Arora, K., & Taneja, S. (2023). Bibliometric analysis on employee engagement and human resource management. In *Enhancing Customer Engagement Through Location-Based Marketing*. IGI Global., DOI: 10.4018/978-1-6684-8177-6.ch013

Gupta, S., Kumar, V., & Patil, P. (2022). A Study on Recycling of Waste Solid Garbage in a City. In D. N. & C. A. (Eds.), *AIP Conference Proceedings* (Vol. 2481). American Institute of Physics Inc. https://doi.org/DOI: 10.1063/5.0104563

Gururani, P., Bhatnagar, P., Bisht, B., Jaiswal, K. K., Kumar, V., Kumar, S., Vlaskin, M. S., Grigorenko, A. V., & Rindin, K. G. (2022). Recent advances and viability in sustainable thermochemical conversion of sludge to bio-fuel production. *Fuel*, 316. Advance online publication. DOI: 10.1016/j.fuel.2022.123351

Gusain, I., Sharma, S., Debarma, S., Kumar Sharma, A., Mishra, N., & Prakashrao Dahale, P. (2023). Study of concrete mix by adding Dolomite in conventional concrete as partial replacement with cement. *Materials Today: Proceedings*, 73, 163–166. DOI: 10.1016/j.matpr.2022.09.583

Johri, S., Singh Sidhu, K., Jafersadhiq, A., Mannar, B. R., Gehlot, A., & Goyal, H. R. (2023). An investigation of the effects of the global epidemic on Crypto Currency returns and volatility. *2023 3rd International Conference on Advance Computing and Innovative Technologies in Engineering, ICACITE 2023*, 345 – 348. https://doi.org/DOI: 10.1109/ICACITE57410.2023.10182988

Joshi, K., Sharma, R., Singh, N., & Sharma, B. (2023). Digital World of Cloud Computing and Wireless Networking: Challenges and Risks. In *Applications of Artificial Intelligence in Wireless Communication Systems*. IGI Global., DOI: 10.4018/978-1-6684-7348-1.ch003

Joshi, N. C., & Gururani, P. (2022). Advances of graphene oxide based nanocomposite materials in the treatment of wastewater containing heavy metal ions and dyes. *Current Research in Green and Sustainable Chemistry*, 5. Advance online publication. DOI: 10.1016/j.crgsc.2022.100306

Joshi, S., Balakrishnan, S., Rawat, P., Deshpande, D., Chakravarthi, M. K., & Verma, D. (2022). A Framework of Internet of Things (Iot) for the Manufacturing and Image Classification System. In D. R.K., S. A.Kr., K. G., & B. S. (Eds.), *Proceedings of the 2022 11th International Conference on System Modeling and Advancement in Research Trends, SMART 2022* (pp. 371 – 375). Institute of Electrical and Electronics Engineers Inc. https://doi.org/DOI: 10.1109/SMART55829.2022.10046756

Joshi, S., & Sharma, M. (2023). Strategic challenges of deploying LARG approach for sustainable manufacturing: Research implications from Indian SMEs. *International Journal of Internet Manufacturing and Services*, 9(2–3), 373–397. DOI: 10.1504/IJIMS.2023.132791

Juneja, P. J., Sunori, S., Sharma, A., Sharma, A., & Joshi, V. (2020). Modeling, Control and Instrumentation of Lime Kiln Process: A Review. In S. S. & D. P. (Eds.), *Proceedings - 2020 International Conference on Advances in Computing, Communication and Materials, ICACCM 2020* (pp. 399 – 403). Institute of Electrical and Electronics Engineers Inc. https://doi.org/DOI: 10.1109/ICACCM50413.2020.9212948

Juneja, P. K., Kumar Sunori, S., Manu, M., Joshi, P., Sharma, S., Garia, P., & Mittal, A. (2022). Potential Applications of Fuzzy Logic Controller in the Pulp and Paper Industry - A Review. *5th International Conference on Inventive Computation Technologies, ICICT 2022 - Proceedings*, 399 – 401. https://doi.org/DOI: 10.1109/ICICT54344.2022.9850626

Juyal, P., & Sharma, S. (2020). Estimation of Tree Volume Using Mask R-CNN based Deep Learning. *2020 11th International Conference on Computing, Communication and Networking Technologies, ICCCNT 2020*. https://doi.org/DOI: 10.1109/ICCCNT49239.2020.9225509

Kaur, H., Thacker, C., Singh, V. K., Sivashankar, D., Patil, P. P., & Gill, K. S. (2023). An implementation of virtual instruments for industries for the standardization. *2023 International Conference on Artificial Intelligence and Smart Communication, AISC 2023*, 1110 – 1113. https://doi.org/DOI: 10.1109/AISC56616.2023.10085547

Kaur, J., Khanna, R., Kumar, R., & Sunil, G. (2024). Role of Blockchain Technologies in Goods and Services Tax. *Proceedings - 2024 3rd International Conference on Sentiment Analysis and Deep Learning, ICSADL 2024*, 607–612. https://doi.org/DOI: 10.1109/ICSADL61749.2024.00104

Kaushal, D., Kumar, S., Raj, R., & Negi, A. (2022). Understanding the effect of entrepreneurial orientation, innovation capability and differentiation strategy on firm performance: A study on small and medium enterprises. *International Journal of Business and Globalisation*, 30(1), 57–80. DOI: 10.1504/IJBG.2022.122280

Khanna, L. S., Yadav, P. S., Maurya, S., & Vimal, V. (2023). Integral Role of Data Science in Startup Evolution. *Proceedings - 2023 15th IEEE International Conference on Computational Intelligence and Communication Networks, CICN 2023*, 720 – 726. https://doi.org/DOI: 10.1109/CICN59264.2023.10402129

Khanna, R., Jindal, P., & Noja, G. G. (2023). Blockchain technologies, a catalyst for insurance sector. In *The Application of Emerging Technology and Blockchain in the Insurance Industry*.

Kohli, P., Sharma, S., & Matta, P. (2022). Secured Authentication Schemes of 6G Driven Vehicular Communication Network in Industry 5.0 Internet-of-Everything (IoE) Applications: Challenges and Opportunities. *2022 IEEE 2nd International Conference on Mobile Networks and Wireless Communications, ICMNWC 2022.* https://doi.org/DOI: 10.1109/ICMNWC56175.2022.10031781

Kollipara, V. N. H., Kalakota, S. K., Chamarthi, S., Ramani, S., Malik, P., & Karuppiah, M. (2023). Timestamp Based OTP and Enhanced RSA Key Exchange Scheme with SIT Encryption to Secure IoT Devices. *Journal of Cyber Security and Mobility*, 12(1), 77–102. DOI: 10.13052/jcsm2245-1439.1214

Komkowski, T., Antony, J., Garza-Reyes, J. A., Tortorella, G. L., & Pongboonchai-Empl, T. (2023). Integrating Lean Management with Industry 4.0: An explorative Dynamic Capabilities theory perspective. *Production Planning and Control*. Advance online publication. DOI: 10.1080/09537287.2023.2294297

Kumar, A., & Ram, M. (2021). Systems Reliability Engineering: Modeling and Performance Improvement. In *Systems Reliability Engineering: Modeling and Performance Improvement*. De Gruyter. https://doi.org/DOI: 10.1515/9783110617375

Kumar, I., Rawat, J., Mohd, N., & Husain, S. (2021). Opportunities of Artificial Intelligence and Machine Learning in the Food Industry. *Journal of Food Quality*, 2021. Advance online publication. DOI: 10.1155/2021/4535567

Kumar, K., Chaudhary, S., Anandaram, H., Kumar, R., Gupta, A., & Joshi, K. (2023). Industry 4.0 and Health Care System with special reference to Mental Health. *2023 1st International Conference on Intelligent Computing and Research Trends, ICRT 2023.* https://doi.org/DOI: 10.1109/ICRT57042.2023.10146640

Kumar, K., Singh, V., Mishra, G., Ravindra Babu, B., Tripathi, N., & Kumar, P. (2022). Power-Efficient Secured Hardware Design of AES Algorithm on High Performance FPGA. *Proceedings of 5th International Conference on Contemporary Computing and Informatics, IC3I 2022*, 1634 – 1637. https://doi.org/DOI: 10.1109/IC3I56241.2022.10073148

Kumar, M., Ansari, N. A., Sharma, A., Singh, V. K., Gautam, R., & Singh, Y. (2021). Prediction of an optimum engine response based on dierent input parameters on common rail direct injection diesel engine: A response surface methodology approach. *Scientia Iranica*, 28(6), 3181–3200. DOI: 10.24200/sci.2021.56745.4885

Kumar, N. M., Islam, S., Podder, A. K., Selim, A., Bajaj, M., & Kamel, S. (2023). Lifecycle-based feasibility indicators for floating solar photovoltaic plants along with implementable energy enhancement strategies and framework-driven assessment approaches leading to advancements in the simulation tool. *Frontiers in Energy Research*, 11. Advance online publication. DOI: 10.3389/fenrg.2023.1075384

Kumar, P., Bhatnagar, M., & Taneja, S. (2023). Investigation of the time pattern of Bit Green Crypto: An Arma modeling approach to unrave volatility. In *Algorithmic Approaches to Financial Technology: Forecasting, Trading, and Optimization*. IGI Global., DOI: 10.4018/979-8-3693-1746-4.ch001

Kumar, P., Taneja, S., Bhatnagar, M., & Kaur, A. K. (2024). Navigating the digital paradigm shift: Designing CBDCs for a transformative financial landscape. In *Exploring Central Bank Digital Currencies: Concepts, Frameworks, Models, and Challenges*. IGI Global., DOI: 10.4018/979-8-3693-1882-9.ch006

Kumar, R., Kandpal, B., & Ahmad, V. (2023). Industrial IoT (IIOT): Security Threats and Countermeasures. *International Conference on Innovative Data Communication Technologies and Application, ICIDCA 2023 - Proceedings*, 829 – 833. https://doi.org/DOI: 10.1109/ICIDCA56705.2023.10100145

Kumar, R., Kathuria, S., Malholtra, R. K., Kumar, A., Gehlot, A., & Joshi, K. (2023). Role of Cloud Computing in Goods and Services Tax(GST) and Future Application. *2nd International Conference on Sustainable Computing and Data Communication Systems, ICSCDS 2023 - Proceedings*, 1443–1447. https://doi.org/DOI: 10.1109/ICSCDS56580.2023.10104597

Kumar, R., & Khanna, R. (2023). RPA (Robotic Process Automation) in Finance & Accounting and Future Scope. *Proceedings of the 2023 2nd International Conference on Augmented Intelligence and Sustainable Systems, ICAISS 2023*, 1640–1645. https://doi.org/DOI: 10.1109/ICAISS58487.2023.10250496

Kumar, R., Malholtra, R. K., Singh, R., Kathuria, S., Balyan, R., & Pal, P. (2023). Artificial Intelligence Role in Electronic Invoice Under Goods and Services Tax. *2023 International Conference on Computational Intelligence, Communication Technology and Networking, CICTN 2023*, 140–143. https://doi.org/DOI: 10.1109/CICTN57981.2023.10140870

Kumar, R., Saxena, A., & Singh, R. (2023). Robotic Process Automation Bridge -in Banking Institute and Consumers. *2023 International Conference on Disruptive Technologies, ICDT 2023*, 428 – 431. https://doi.org/DOI: 10.1109/ICDT57929.2023.10150500

Kumar, V., & Korovin, G. (2023). A Comparision of Digital Transformation of Industry in the Russian Federation with the European Union. In K. V., K. G.L., A. V., & K. E. (Eds.), *Lecture Notes in Information Systems and Organisation: Vol. 61 LNISO* (pp. 45 – 57). Springer Science and Business Media Deutschland GmbH. https://doi.org/DOI: 10.1007/978-3-031-30351-7_5

Kumar, V., Pant, B., Elkady, G., Kaur, C., Suhashini, J., & Hassen, S. M. (2022). Examining the Role of Block Chain to Secure Identity in IOT for Industry 4.0. *Proceedings of 5th International Conference on Contemporary Computing and Informatics, IC3I 2022*, 256 – 259. https://doi.org/DOI: 10.1109/IC3I56241.2022.10072516

Kumar, V., Sharma, N. K., Mittal, A., & Verma, P. (2023). The Role of IoT and IIoT in Supplier and Customer Continuous Improvement Interface. *EAI/Springer Innovations in Communication and Computing*, 161 – 174. https://doi.org/DOI: 10.1007/978-3-031-19711-6_7

Luthra, S., Sharma, M., Kumar, A., Joshi, S., Collins, E., & Mangla, S. (2022). Overcoming barriers to cross-sector collaboration in circular supply chain management: A multi-method approach. *Transportation Research Part E, Logistics and Transportation Review*, 157. Advance online publication. DOI: 10.1016/j.tre.2021.102582

Malhotra, R. K., Gupta, C., & Jindal, P. (2022). Blockchain and Smart Contracts for Insurance Industry. In *Blockchain Technology in Corporate Governance. Transforming Business and Industries.*, DOI: 10.1002/9781119865247.ch11

Mangla, S. K., & Ram, M. (2020). Supply chain sustainability: Modeling and innovative research frameworks. In *Supply Chain Sustainability: Modeling and Innovative Research Frameworks*. De Gruyter. https://doi.org/DOI: 10.1515/9783110628593

Matta, P., & Pant, B. (2020). TCpC: A graphical password scheme ensuring authentication for IoT resources. *International Journal of Information Technology (Singapore)*, 12(3), 699–709. DOI: 10.1007/s41870-018-0142-z

Maurya, S. K., Ghosal, A., & Manna, A. (2022). Experimental investigations during fabrication and electrical discharge machining of hybrid Al/(SiC+ZrO2+NiTi) MMC. *International Journal of Machining and Machinability of Materials*, 24(3–4), 215–230. DOI: 10.1504/ijmmm.2022.125195

Medhi, M. K., Ambust, S., Kumar, R., & Das, A. J. (2023). Characterization and Purification of Biosurfactants. In *Advancements in Biosurfactants Research*. Springer International Publishing., DOI: 10.1007/978-3-031-21682-4_4

Mehta, K., Sharma, S., & Mishra, D. (2021). Internet-of-Things Enabled Forest Fire Detection System. *Proceedings of the 5th International Conference on I-SMAC (IoT in Social, Mobile, Analytics and Cloud), I-SMAC 2021*, 20 – 23. https://doi.org/DOI: 10.1109/I-SMAC52330.2021.9640900

Mishra, P., Aggarwal, P., Vidyarthi, A., Singh, P., Khan, B., Alhelou, H. H., & Siano, P. (2021). VMShield: Memory Introspection-Based Malware Detection to Secure Cloud-Based Services against Stealthy Attacks. *IEEE Transactions on Industrial Informatics*, 17(10), 6754–6764. DOI: 10.1109/TII.2020.3048791

Nadeem, S. P., Garza-Reyes, J. A., & Anosike, A. I. (2023). A C-Lean framework for deploying Circular Economy in manufacturing SMEs. *Production Planning and Control*. Advance online publication. DOI: 10.1080/09537287.2023.2294307

Nainwal, P., Lall, S., & Nawaz, A. (2022). Physiochemical characterization of silver nanoparticles using rhizome extract of Alpinia galanga and its antimicrobial activity. *Journal of Medical Pharmaceutical and Allied Sciences. Int. Confe*, (2), 219–223. DOI: 10.22270/jmpas.VI2I2.1830

Nethravathi, K., Tiwari, A., Uike, D., Jaiswal, R., & Pant, K. (2022). Applications of Artificial Intelligence and Blockchain Technology in Improved Supply Chain Financial Risk Management. *Proceedings of 5th International Conference on Contemporary Computing and Informatics, IC3I 2022*, 242 – 246. https://doi.org/DOI: 10.1109/IC3I56241.2022.10072787

Pallavi, B., Othman, B., Trivedi, G., Manan, N., Pawar, R. S., & Singh, D. P. (2022). The Application of the Internet of Things (IoT) to establish a technologically advanced Industry 4.0 for long-term growth and development. *2022 2nd International Conference on Advance Computing and Innovative Technologies in Engineering, ICACITE 2022*, 1927 – 1932. https://doi.org/DOI: 10.1109/ICACITE53722.2022.9823481

Pande, S. D., Bhatt, A., Chamoli, S., Saini, D. K. J. B., Kute, U. T., & Ahammad, S. H. (2023). Design of Atmel PLC and its Application as Automation of Coal Handling Plant. *2023 International Conference on Sustainable Emerging Innovations in Engineering and Technology, ICSEIET 2023*, 178 – 183. https://doi.org/DOI: 10.1109/ICSEIET58677.2023.10303627

Pandey, T., Batra, A., Chaudhary, M., Ranakoti, A., Kumar, A., & Ram, M. (2023). Computation Signature Reliability of Computer Numerical Control System Using Universal Generating Function. *Springer Series in Reliability Engineering*, 149 – 158. https://doi.org/DOI: 10.1007/978-3-031-05347-4_10

Pandya, D. J., Kumar, Y., Singh, D. P., Vairavel, D. K., Deepak, A., Rao, A. K., & Rana, A. (2023). Automatic Power Factor Compensation for Industrial Use to Minimize Penalty. *Proceedings of International Conference on Contemporary Computing and Informatics, IC3I 2023*, 2499 – 2504. https://doi.org/DOI: 10.1109/IC3I59117.2023.10398095

Pathak, P., Singh, M. P., Badhotiya, G. K., & Chauhan, A. S. (2021). Identification of Drivers and Barriers of Sustainable Manufacturing. *Lecture Notes on Multidisciplinary Industrial Engineering*, (Part F254), 227–243. DOI: 10.1007/978-981-15-4550-4_14

Poswal, P., Chauhan, A., Aarya, D. D., Boadh, R., Rajoria, Y. K., & Gaiola, S. U. (2022). Optimal strategy for remanufacturing system of sustainable products with trade credit under uncertain scenario. *Materials Today: Proceedings*, 69, 165–173. DOI: 10.1016/j.matpr.2022.08.303

Rajeswari, M., Kumar, N., Raman, P., Patjoshi, P. K., Singh, V., & Pundir, S. (2022). Optimal Analysis for Enterprise Financial Management Based on Artificial Intelligence and Parallel Computing Method. *Proceedings of 5th International Conference on Contemporary Computing and Informatics, IC3I 2022*, 2081 – 2086. https://doi.org/DOI: 10.1109/IC3I56241.2022.10072851

Ram, M., Negi, G., Goyal, N., & Kumar, A. (2022). Analysis of a Stochastic Model with Rework System. *Journal of Reliability and Statistical Studies*, 15(2), 553–582. DOI: 10.13052/jrss0974-8024.1527

Ram, M., & Xing, L. (2023). Reliability Modeling in Industry 4.0. In *Reliability Modeling in Industry 4.0*. Elsevier., DOI: 10.1016/C2021-0-01679-5

Ramachandran, K. K., Lamba, F. L. R., Rawat, R., Gehlot, A., Raju, A. M., & Ponnusamy, R. (2023). An Investigation of Block Chains for Attaining Sustainable Society. *2023 3rd International Conference on Advance Computing and Innovative Technologies in Engineering, ICACITE 2023*, 1069 – 1076. https://doi.org/DOI: 10.1109/ICACITE57410.2023.10182462

Ramakrishnan, T., Mohan Gift, M. D., Chitradevi, S., Jegan, R., Subha Hency Jose, P., Nagaraja, H. N., Sharma, R., Selvakumar, P., & Hailegiorgis, S. M. (2022). Study of Numerous Resins Used in Polymer Matrix Composite Materials. *Advances in Materials Science and Engineering*, 2022. Advance online publication. DOI: 10.1155/2022/1088926

Raman, R., Kumar, R., Ghai, S., Gehlot, A., Raju, A. M., & Barve, A. (2023). A New Method of Optical Spectrum Analysis for Advanced Wireless Communications. *2023 3rd International Conference on Advance Computing and Innovative Technologies in Engineering, ICACITE 2023*, 1719 – 1723. https://doi.org/DOI: 10.1109/ICACITE57410.2023.10182414

Rana, M. S., Dixit, A. K., Rajan, M. S., Malhotra, S., Radhika, S., & Pant, B. (2022). An Empirical Investigation in Applying Reliable Industry 4.0 Based Machine Learning (ML) Approaches in Analysing and Monitoring Smart Meters using Multivariate Analysis of Variance (Manova). *2022 2nd International Conference on Advance Computing and Innovative Technologies in Engineering, ICACITE 2022*, 603 – 607. https://doi.org/DOI: 10.1109/ICACITE53722.2022.9823597

Rawat, R., Sharma, S., & Goyal, H. R. (2023). Intelligent Digital Financial Inclusion System Architectures for Industry 5.0 Enabled Digital Society. *Winter Summit on Smart Computing and Networks. WiSSCoN*, 2023. Advance online publication. DOI: 10.1109/WiSSCoN56857.2023.10133858

Rawat, S. S., Pant, S., Kumar, A., Ram, M., Sharma, H. K., & Kumar, A. (2022). A State-of-the-Art Survey on Analytical Hierarchy Process Applications in Sustainable Development. *International Journal of Mathematical. Engineering and Management Sciences*, 7(6), 883–917. DOI: 10.33889/IJMEMS.2022.7.6.056

Reddy, P. N., Umaeswari, P., Natrayan, L., & Choudhary, A. (2023). Development of Programmed Autonomous Electric Heavy Vehicle: An Application of IoT. *Proceedings of the 2023 2nd International Conference on Electronics and Renewable Systems, ICEARS 2023*, 506 – 510. https://doi.org/DOI: 10.1109/ICEARS56392.2023.10085492

Reepu, R., Taneja, S., Ozen, E., & Singh, A. (2023). A globetrotter to the future of marketing: Metaverse. In *Cultural Marketing and Metaverse for Consumer Engagement*. IGI Global., DOI: 10.4018/978-1-6684-8312-1.ch001

Sahu, S. R., & Rawat, K. S. (2023). Analysis of Land subsidencein coastal and urban areas by using various techniques– Literature Review. *The Indonesian Journal of Geography*, 55(3), 488–495. DOI: 10.22146/ijg.83675

Saini, S., Sachdeva, L., & Badhotiya, G. K. (2022). Sustainable Human Resource Management: A Conceptual Framework. *ECS Transactions*, 107(1), 6455–6463. DOI: 10.1149/10701.6455ecst

Salama, R., Al-Turjman, F., Bordoloi, D., & Yadav, S. P. (2023). Wireless Sensor Networks and Green Networking for 6G communication- An Overview. *2023 International Conference on Computational Intelligence, Communication Technology and Networking, CICTN 2023*, 830 – 834. https://doi.org/DOI: 10.1109/CICTN57981.2023.10141262

Sathyapriya, G., Natarajan, U., Sureshkumar, B., Navaneethakrishnan, G., Palanisamy, R., Bajaj, M., & Sharma, N. K., & Kitmo. (2022). Quality and Tool Stability Improvement in Turning Operation Using Plastic Compliant Damper. *Journal of Nanomaterials*, 2022. Advance online publication. DOI: 10.1155/2022/8654603

Sathyaseelan, K., Vyas, T., Madala, R., Chamundeeswari, V., Rai Goyal, H., & Jayaraman, R. (2023). Blockchain Enabled Intelligent Surveillance System Model with AI and IoT. *Proceedings of 8th IEEE International Conference on Science, Technology, Engineering and Mathematics, ICONSTEM 2023*. https://doi.org/DOI: 10.1109/ICONSTEM56934.2023.10142303

Sati, P., Sharma, E., Soni, R., Dhyani, P., Solanki, A. C., Solanki, M. K., Rai, S., & Malviya, M. K. (2022). Bacterial endophytes as bioinoculant: microbial functions and applications toward sustainable farming. In *Microbial Endophytes and Plant Growth: Beneficial Interactions and Applications*. Elsevier., DOI: 10.1016/B978-0-323-90620-3.00008-8

Sen Thapa, B., Pandit, S., Patwardhan, S. B., Tripathi, S., Mathuriya, A. S., Gupta, P. K., Lal, R. B., & Tusher, T. R. (2022). Application of Microbial Fuel Cell (MFC) for Pharmaceutical Wastewater Treatment: An Overview and Future Perspectives. *Sustainability (Switzerland)*, 14(14). Advance online publication. DOI: 10.3390/su14148379

Shabbiruddin, Kanwar, N., Jadoun, V. K., Jayalakshmi, N. S. J., Afthanorhan, A., Fatema, N., Malik, H., & Hossaini, M. A. (2023). Industry - Challenge to Pro-Environmental Manufacturing of Goods Replacing Single-Use Plastic by Indian Industry: A Study Toward Failing Ban on Single-Use Plastic Access. *IEEE Access: Practical Innovations, Open Solutions*, 11, 77336–77346. DOI: 10.1109/ACCESS.2023.3296097

Sharma, A., Sharma, A., Juneja, P. K., & Jain, V. (2020). Spectral Features based Speech Recognition for Speech Interfacing to Control PC Windows. In S. S. & D. P. (Eds.), *Proceedings - 2020 International Conference on Advances in Computing, Communication and Materials, ICACCM 2020* (pp. 341 – 345). Institute of Electrical and Electronics Engineers Inc. https://doi.org/DOI: 10.1109/ICACCM50413.2020.9212827

Sharma, A. K., Sharma, A., Singh, Y., & Chen, W.-H. (2021). Production of a sustainable fuel from microalgae Chlorella minutissima grown in a 1500 L open raceway ponds. *Biomass and Bioenergy*, 149. Advance online publication. DOI: 10.1016/j.biombioe.2021.106073

Sharma, H., Verma, D., Rana, A., Chari, S. L., Kumar, R., & Kumar, N. (2023). Enhancing Network Security in IoT Using Machine Learning- Based Anomaly Detection. *Proceedings of International Conference on Contemporary Computing and Informatics, IC3I 2023*, 2650 – 2654. https://doi.org/DOI: 10.1109/IC3I59117.2023.10397636

Sharma, M., Luthra, S., Joshi, S., & Joshi, H. (2022). Challenges to agile project management during COVID-19 pandemic: An emerging economy perspective. *Operations Management Research*, 15(1–2), 461–474. DOI: 10.1007/s12063-021-00249-1

Sharma, N., Agrawal, R., & Silmana, A. (2021). Analyzing The Role Of Public Transportation On Environmental Air Pollution In Select Cities. *Indian Journal of Environmental Protection*, 41(5), 536–541.

Sharma, P., Malhotra, R. K., Ojha, M. K., & Gupta, S. (2022). Impact of meditation on mental & physical health and thereby on academic performance of students: A study of higher educational institutions of Uttarakhand. *Journal of Medical Pharmaceutical and Allied Sciences*, 11(2), 4641–4644. DOI: 10.55522/jmpas.V11I2.2309

Sharma, R. C., Palli, S., & Sharma, S. K. (2023). Ride analysis of railway vehicle considering rigidity and flexibility of the carbody. *Journal of the Chinese Institute of Engineers, Transactions of the Chinese Institute of Engineers,Series A*, 46(4), 355–366. DOI: 10.1080/02533839.2023.2194918

Sharma, S., & Bhadula, S. (2023). Secure Federated Learning for Intelligent Industry 4.0 IoT Enabled Self Skin Care Application System. *Proceedings of the 2nd International Conference on Applied Artificial Intelligence and Computing, ICAAIC 2023*, 1164 – 1170. https://doi.org/DOI: 10.1109/ICAAIC56838.2023.10141028

Sharma, S., Gupta, A., & Tyagi, R. (2023). Sustainable Natural Resources Utilization Decision System for Better Society Using Vedic Scripture, Cloud Computing, and IoT. In B. R.C., S. K.M., & D. M. (Eds.), *Proceedings of IEEE 2023 5th International Conference on Advances in Electronics, Computers and Communications, ICAECC 2023*. Institute of Electrical and Electronics Engineers Inc. https://doi.org/DOI: 10.1109/ICAECC59324.2023.10560335

Sharma, S., Kandpal, V., Choudhury, T., Santibanez Gonzalez, E. D. R., & Agarwal, N. (2023). Assessment of the implications of energy-efficient technologies on the environmental sustainability of rail operation. *AIMS Environmental Science*, 10(5), 709–731. DOI: 10.3934/environsci.2023039

Sharma, S., Mishra, R. R., Joshi, V., & Kour, K. (2020). Analysis and Interpretation of Global Air Quality. *2020 11th International Conference on Computing, Communication and Networking Technologies, ICCCNT 2020*. https://doi.org/DOI: 10.1109/ICCCNT49239.2020.9225532

Sharma, S., Singh Rawal, R., Pandey, D., & Pandey, N. (2021). Microbial World for Sustainable Development. In *Microbial Technology for Sustainable Environment*. Springer Nature., DOI: 10.1007/978-981-16-3840-4_1

Sharma, Y. K., Mangla, S. K., Patil, P. P., & Uniyal, S. (2020). Analyzing sustainable food supply chain management challenges in India. In *Research Anthology on Food Waste Reduction and Alternative Diets for Food and Nutrition Security*. IGI Global., DOI: 10.4018/978-1-7998-5354-1.ch023

Shekhawat, R. S., & Uniyal, D. (2021). Smart-Bin: IoT-Based Real-Time Garbage Monitoring System for Smart Cities. *Lecture Notes in Networks and Systems*, 190, 871–879. DOI: 10.1007/978-981-16-0882-7_78

Shukla, S. K., Pant, B., Viriyasitavat, W., Verma, D., Kautish, S., Dhiman, G., Kaur, A., Srihari, K., & Mohanty, S. N. (2022). An integration of autonomic computing with multicore systems for performance optimization in Industrial Internet of Things. *IET Communications*. Advance online publication. DOI: 10.1049/cmu2.12505

Singh, K. D., Singh, P., Chhabra, R., Kaur, G., Bansal, A., & Tripathi, V. (2023). Cyber-Physical Systems for Smart City Applications: A Comparative Study. In K. R., K. R., G. M., G. M., S. R., & S. R. (Eds.), *2023 International Conference on Advancement in Computation and Computer Technologies, InCACCT 2023* (pp. 871–876). Institute of Electrical and Electronics Engineers Inc. https://doi.org/DOI: 10.1109/InCACCT57535.2023.10141719

Singh, N. K., Singh, Y., Rahim, E. A., Senthil Siva Subramanian, T., & Sharma, A. (2023). Electric discharge machining of hybrid composite with bio-dielectrics for sustainable developments. *Australian Journal of Mechanical Engineering*. Advance online publication. DOI: 10.1080/14484846.2023.2249577

Singh, N. K., Singh, Y., & Sharma, A. (2020). Experimental investigation on electric discharge drilling of titanium alloy (Ti–6Al–4V) with a gas-aided rotary tool. *Sadhana - Academy Proceedings in Engineering Sciences*, 45(1). https://doi.org/DOI: 10.1007/s12046-020-01497-w

Singh, N. K., Singh, Y., Sharma, A., Paswan, M. K., Singh, V. K., Upadhyay, A. K., & Mishra, V. R. (2021). Performance of CuO nanoparticles as an additive to the chemically modified Nicotiana Tabacum as a sustainable coolant-lubricant during turning EN19 steel. *Wear*, 486–487. Advance online publication. DOI: 10.1016/j.wear.2021.204057

Subramani, R., Kaliappan, S., Kumar, P. V. A., Sekar, S., De Poures, M. V., Patil, P. P., & Raj, E. S. E. (2022). A Recent Trend on Additive Manufacturing Sustainability with Supply Chain Management Concept, Multicriteria Decision Making Techniques. *Advances in Materials Science and Engineering*, 2022. Advance online publication. DOI: 10.1155/2022/9151839

Subramani, R., Kaliappan, S., Sekar, S., Patil, P. P., Usha, R., Manasa, N., & Esakkiraj, E. S. (2022). Polymer Filament Process Parameter Optimization with Mechanical Test and Morphology Analysis. *Advances in Materials Science and Engineering*, 2022. Advance online publication. DOI: 10.1155/2022/8259804

Sunori, S. K., Kant, S., Agarwal, P., & Juneja, P. (2023). Development of Rainfall Prediction Models using Linear and Non-linear Regression Techniques. *2023 4th IEEE Global Conference for Advancement in Technology, GCAT 2023*. https://doi.org/DOI: 10.1109/GCAT59970.2023.10353508

Taneja, S., Bhatnagar, M., Kumar, P., & Rupeika-apoga, R. (2023). India's Total Natural Resource Rents (NRR) and GDP : An Augmented Autoregressive Distributed Lag (ARDL) Bound Test. *Journal of Risk and Financial Management*, 16(2), 91. https://doi.org/doi.org/10.3390/jrfm16020091

Taneja, S., Gupta, M., Bhushan, P., Bhatnagar, M., & Singh, A. (2023). Cultural marketing in the digital era. In *Cultural Marketing and Metaverse for Consumer Engagement*. IGI Global., DOI: 10.4018/978-1-6684-8312-1.ch008

Taneja, S., & Özen, E. (2023). To analyse the relationship between bank's green financing and environmental performance. *International Journal of Electronic Finance*, 12(2), 163–175. DOI: 10.1504/IJEF.2023.129919

Taneja, S., & Sharma, V. (2023). Role of beaconing marketing in improving customer buying experience. In *Enhancing Customer Engagement Through Location-Based Marketing*. IGI Global., DOI: 10.4018/978-1-6684-8177-6.ch012

Thentral, T. M. T., Usha, S., Palanisamy, R., Geetha, A., Alkhudaydi, A. M., Sharma, N. K., Bajaj, M., Ghoneim, S. S. M., Shouran, M., & Kamel, S. (2022). An energy efficient modified passive power filter for power quality enhancement in electric drives. *Frontiers in Energy Research*, 10. Advance online publication. DOI: 10.3389/fenrg.2022.989857

Tomar, S., Sharma, N., & Nehra, N. S. (2023). A sustainable rural entrepreneurship model developed by the organic farmers of India. *Emerald Emerging Markets Case Studies*, 13(2), 1–17. DOI: 10.1108/EEMCS-09-2022-0329

Tripathy, S., Verma, D. K., Thakur, M., Patel, A. R., Srivastav, P. P., Singh, S., Chávez-González, M. L., & Aguilar, C. N. (2021). Encapsulated Food Products as a Strategy to Strengthen Immunity Against COVID-19. *Frontiers in Nutrition*, 8. Advance online publication. DOI: 10.3389/fnut.2021.673174

Uike, D., Agarwalla, S., Bansal, V., Chakravarthi, M. K., Singh, R., & Singh, P. (2022). Investigating the Role of Block Chain to Secure Identity in IoT for Industrial Automation. In D. R.K., S. A.Kr., K. G., & B. S. (Eds.), *Proceedings of the 2022 11th International Conference on System Modeling and Advancement in Research Trends, SMART 2022* (pp. 837 – 841). Institute of Electrical and Electronics Engineers Inc. https://doi.org/DOI: 10.1109/SMART55829.2022.10047385

Uniyal, A., Prajapati, Y. K., Ranakoti, L., Bhandari, P., Singh, T., Gangil, B., Sharma, S., Upadhyay, V. V., & Eldin, S. M. (2022). Recent Advancements in Evacuated Tube Solar Water Heaters: A Critical Review of the Integration of Phase Change Materials and Nanofluids with ETCs. *Energies*, 15(23). Advance online publication. DOI: 10.3390/en15238999

Uniyal, S., Mangla, S. K., & Patil, P. (2020). When practices count: Implementation of sustainable consumption and production in automotive supply chains. *Management of Environmental Quality*, 31(5), 1207–1222. DOI: 10.1108/MEQ-03-2019-0075

Uniyal, S., Sarma, P. R. S., Kumar Mangla, S., Tseng, M.-L., & Patil, P. (2022). ICT as "Knowledge Management" for Assessing Sustainable Consumption and Production in Supply Chains. In *Research Anthology on Measuring and Achieving Sustainable Development Goals* (Vol. 3). IGI Global. https://doi.org/DOI: 10.4018/978-1-6684-3885-5.ch048

Upreti, H., & Malhotra, R. K. (2024). Bridging The Urban-Rural Education Gap In India Through CSR (Corporate Social Responsibility) Initiatives: A Conceptual Study With Special Reference To Sustainable Development Goal 4 (Quality Education). In P. P.K. (Ed.), *E3S Web of Conferences* (Vol. 556). EDP Sciences. https://doi.org/DOI: 10.1051/e3sconf/202455601032

Upreti, H., Uddin, Z., Pandey, A. K., & Joshi, N. (2023). Particle swarm optimization based numerical study for pressure, flow, and heat transfer over a rotating disk with temperature dependent nanofluid properties. *Numerical Heat Transfer Part A*, 83(8), 815–844. DOI: 10.1080/10407782.2022.2156412

Vekariya, D., Rastogi, A., Priyadarshini, R., Patil, M., Kumar, M. S., & Pant, B. (2023). Mengers Authentication for efficient security system using Blockchain technology for Industrial IoT(IIOT) systems. *2023 3rd International Conference on Advance Computing and Innovative Technologies in Engineering, ICACITE 2023*, 894 – 896. https://doi.org/DOI: 10.1109/ICACITE57410.2023.10182454

Venkatesh, J., Shukla, P. K., Ahanger, T. A., Maheshwari, M., Pant, B., Hemamalini, R. R., & Halifa, A. (2023). A Complex Brain Learning Skeleton Comprising Enriched Pattern Neural Network System for Next Era Internet of Things. *Journal of Healthcare Engineering*, 2023. Advance online publication. DOI: 10.1155/2023/2506144

Verma, M., Sharma, S., Kumar, A., Kumar, V., Kim, M., Hong, Y., Lee, I., & Kim, H. (2021). Application of green nanomaterials in catalysis industry. In *Green Nanomaterials for Industrial Applications*. Elsevier., DOI: 10.1016/B978-0-12-823296-5.00013-7

Verma, P., Chaudhari, V., Dumka, A., & Singh, R. P. (2022). A Meta-Analytical Review of Deep Learning Prediction Models for Big Data. In *Encyclopedia of Data Science and Machine Learning*. IGI Global., DOI: 10.4018/978-1-7998-9220-5.ch023

Verma, P., Kumar, V., Daim, T., Sharma, N. K., & Mittal, A. (2022). Identifying and prioritizing impediments of industry 4.0 to sustainable digital manufacturing: A mixed method approach. *Journal of Cleaner Production*, 356. Advance online publication. DOI: 10.1016/j.jclepro.2022.131639

Wazid, M., Das, A. K., & Park, Y. (2021). Blockchain-Envisioned Secure Authentication Approach in AIoT: Applications, Challenges, and Future Research. *Wireless Communications and Mobile Computing*, 2021. Advance online publication. DOI: 10.1155/2021/3866006

Chapter 11
Health Economics and Sustainability in the Era of Digital Transformation:
Addressing Digital Stress and Sustainable Development Goals

Priyanka Gupta
Graphic Era University, India

Girish Lakhera
Graphic Era University, India

Manu Sharma
Graphic Era University, India

Sudhanshu Joshi
https://orcid.org/0000-0003-4748-5001
Doon University, India

ABSTRACT

This chapter explores the aspect of Economic evaluation of implementing Digital Health, Digital Stress, and Digital Transformation technologies in the context of Systems Sustainability challenge in healthcare systems. Leveraging smart technologies such as AI, IoT, Blockchain, healthcare systems are witnessing unprecedented Digital Transformations in cost efficiency and service delivery. The key aspect addressed is the impact of Digital Transformation healthcare systems, including the challenges pose by Techno Invasion, the over penetration of technology into personal and professional spaces, leading to increased Digital Stress for Healthcare professionals. It also highlights the importance of achieving a balance between innovation and workforce sustainability, with strategies to mitigate the negative effects of digital overload while maximizing the benefits of smart healthcare solutions. Also emphasized the importance of balancing technological integration with human wellbeing.

DOI: 10.4018/979-8-3373-0240-9.ch011

1. INTRODUCTION

Digital transformation and healthcare implications provide novelty in the global health system. In recent decades, development of innovative technologies like AI, IoT and Blockchain caused significant changes to known and conventional healthcare system, which moved to more patient-oriented personalized data-based model. This change has been called Digital Health and it already promises to solve many of the current problems in healthcare through increased access, lower prices, and higher quality (Borges et al., 2023). Nevertheless, the transformation aforementioned comes with its own set of problems. Despite the tremendous power of DTs, new or more detailed problems appear, like Digital Stress and Techno Invasion, which are challenging to neglect in the context of today's healthcare industry. (Ewers et al., 2023).

Health care which traditionally was a profession where providers dealt directly with clients, has been transformed by these technologies. Having grown so pervasive, contemporary health care personnel is presumed to embrace use of technology, hardware as well as software in the discharge of their duties that include; electronic health records, tele-caring, and wearable gadgets. This change did not only change the practice, but it also brought with it new sources of stress like information intensity, connectedness, and the business- personal interface (Tarafdar et al., 2020). This led to the emergence of what is now popularly called Digital Stress, which impacts both healthcare professionals and patients and could ultimately decrease satisfaction at work and in life, together with the quality of services provided. (López et al., 2023).

At the same time, the United Nations' 2030 Agenda for Sustainable Development has been asking for action to support healthy lives and well-being for all, throughout their lives (United Nations, 2021). Within this agenda, the health challenge focus of the Sustainable Development Goal 3 (SDG 3) whose objectives are to promote sustainable health for all individuals, to reduce mortality rates and provide adequate health care for the people with non communicable diseases. The adoption of digital technologies in healthcare provides a framework for delivering sustainable development goal (SDG) 3 thus improving healthcare delivery, expanding the access, and enforcing equity. However, if those technologies are not implemented with a focus on sustainability, they may worsen current disparities in healthcare and develop new stress forms for healthcare professionals (Alonso et al., 2021). Issues of sustainable health economics and effective workspace ensure in extending and strengthening the delivery of effective health treatment in computer technology-driven healthcare systems are effectively highlighted by the crossroad between advances in digital health product development and sustainable practices. In one respect, digitization of healthcare has the potential of reducing costs because of new technological advances in diagnostics and clinical decision making, as well as, tele-monitoring. For example, AI can analyze the vast data sets to offer prognosis solutions that could lower costly and time-consuming high-intensity services (Ledziński et al., 2023). On the other hand, Increased Health Care Cost saving will only be met by the other two components of digital stress that is Techno invasion which is the daily changing of new technologies and the imposition of the use of the digital tools in the Healthcare workers Personal life. Therefore, covering both the economic and human correlates of DH to promote its sustainability is the critical objective. (Sui et al., 2023).

This chapter examines digital transformation, health economics and the theme of workforce sustainability, with a focus on Digital Stress. In this paper, therefore, we explore where these novel technologies fit in the realization of the goals of SDG 3, and the corresponding problems that have been observed with the implementation of such technologies in the health care sector. The chapter expands the discussion regarding Digital Stress as a novel phenomenon identified in the field of healthcare informatics, relates it to mental health of the employed healthcare professionals as well as to their performance. Besides, it considers Primary HCE economic cost savings of AI, IoT, and Blockchain against the Long-term Secondary HCE cost of Digital Stress and Techno Invasion (Ewers et al., 2023).

Economic assessment on digital health technologies is one of the important domains. Enhancing decision-makers' awareness of healthcare innovations' costs is essential as these inventions are incorporated into the systems; decision-makers need to consider how to maintain their workforces' stability. Cost-effectiveness analyses of Digital Stress must consider all manner of costs involved in order to achieve economic balance for the delivery of digital health. However, if the root cause of stress and burnout in healthcare workers is not tackled, while the use of these apps and digital health technologies continue to grow, the long-term sustainability of these interventions will be questionable, and the return on investment, disability, and health, will wane. (Tarafdar et al., 2020).

Furthermore, this chapter places the first debate of digital health competencies within the framework of global health priorities. When applied to the analysis of the position of digital health in relation to SDG 3, we illustrate how digitalization can contribute to increasing accessibility, improving efficacy, and driving cost-effectiveness. However, we acknowledge that given the above ambitions, the change process has to take into account the social and physical health of the HCWs who are leading this change. It is crucial, therefore, for the advantages offered by the use of DHTs to be weighed against means of preventing Digital Stress to enable this facet of digital medicine to be sustainable economically and in terms of human capital. (López et al., 2023). In conclusion, healthcare digitalization provides unmatchable chances for the enhancement of overall human well-being, based on the key ideas of the SDG 3. Yet, this shift must be done carefully, avoiding that it increases the levels of Digital Stress which affects both, healthcare workers and healthcare consumers. The chapter that relates to this section will discuss how sustainable health economics can be achieved through moderation or technological advancement of health care products with attention to the workforce health. As healthcare technology progresses, the sustainability of financial and human resources will become important determinants for implementing digital health related activities (Sui et al., 2023).

1.1. Overview of Smart Technologies in Healthcare

Smart technologies' entrance into the sphere of healthcare is producing a healthier and more optimized future for diagnostics, treatment, and patient management, as well as for the delivery of care. The four innovations including; Artificial Intelligence (AI), the Internet of Things (IoT), and Blockchain have revolutionized the health care systems across the world through enhancing its efficacy, decreasing on costs and enhancing patient experiences. All the technologies have their unique and core functionalities and when integrated help in developing a smart, digitized health care system which falls under the United Nation Sustainable Development Goal 3 'Health and Well-being' as shown in Figure 1:

Figure 1. Smart technologies in healthcare

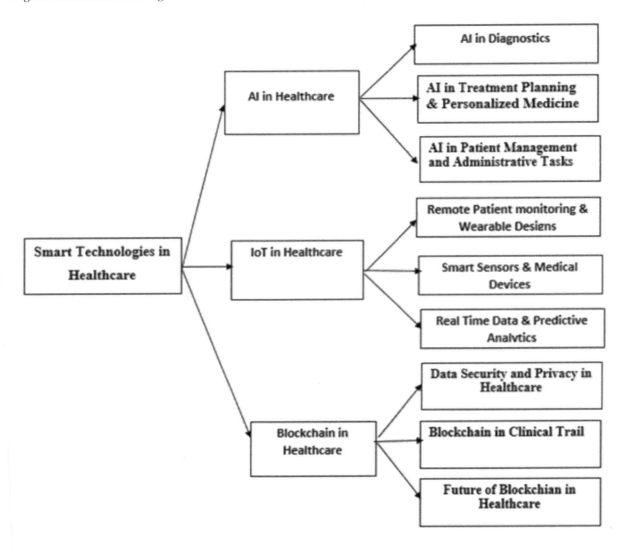

A. AI in Healthcare

AI is transforming the industry of healthcare through automation and improving accuracy throughout clinical processes, diagnosis, and treatment. Advanced computing technology such as ML and DL has been improving many of the healthcare sectors, as well as the identification of early diseases, treatment regimens, and drug development includes:

i. AI in Diagnostics

AI possibly one of the biggest benefits in the realm of the healthcare facility is the capacity to analyze a great deal of material to aid diagnostics. Barely taking a few seconds, artificial intelligence can analyze imaging, genetic details, EHRs, and laboratories results to identify patterns and abnormalities a human may not notice. This is also critical as AI can assist in identifying the likely health risks to given population base. For instance, in radiology, AI instruments are implemented to diagnose early stage cancers such as breast and lung cancer and presented a low risk and not requiring surgery or biopsies. Due to the huge volumes of data AI can easily accommodate these processes takes a fraction of the time it will take using traditional methods enhancing early diagnoses and treatment that can pave way to saving lives. (Qureshi et al., 2023).

ii. AI in Treatment Planning and Personalized Medicine

Apart from diagnostics, AI has transformed treatment through an innovative way of differentiating healthcare treatments through genetic makeup, medical history, and current health condition of the patient. AI systems can also involve information from a patient's records and genetics to determine how he or she will handle certain types of treatment. This predictive capability means that healthcare providers can provide treatment regimens that are most effective and yield least side effects especially in patients who have multiple or chronic comorbidities (Kufel et al., 2023).

Furthermore, by integration with precision medicine, AI is contributing to innovating solutions for numerous areas including oncology. For example, by using AI conventions, the treatment regimens for cancer patient depending on the genetics of the tumor and biomarkers have been estimated. They assist clinicians in creating the relevant intervention measures that offer enhanced results and lower risks for patients as well as using unnecessary and inefficient treatments (Liao et al., 2023).

iii. AI in Patient Management and Administrative Tasks

Apart from influencing clinical decision making, use of AI is also altering patient care by redesigning work to streamline care delivery since the routine tasks can be assigned to AI and the carers can in turn attend to the complicated patients. These smart systems can be used for appointment and patients' records, dosage prompt and check-up after procedure. In telemedicine, the AI voice and chat bot help in responding to the patient's query at the earliest, diagnose the minor ailments, and assist in handling chronic ailments with constant tracking. That kind of automation is beneficial not only to patients, but also helps to optimize the processes of the entire healthcare system by offloading numerous administrative tasks on healthcare providers (Alowais et al., 2023).

The use of AI in improving organization of the operational processes, decreasing the occurrence of mistakes, and increasing the accuracy of the treatments offers AI as a vital commodity for today's healthcare delivery systems. Following the constant advancement of AI, it is anticipated that enhancing prediction and raising the quality and availability of healthcare will develop across the multiple processes in the healthcare industry.

B. IoT in Healthcare

Another smart technology that is progressively changing healthcare is the Internet of Things (IoT). IoT is a system or network that contains a large collection of interconnected devices that engage into sensuous communication and exchange data in real time. The use of IoT in health has many areas including wearable devices, smart sensor, remote monitoring, and connected medical device. These technologies also improve patient care since; they offer round-the-clock, prompt and direct patient and healthcare professional interaction includes:

i. Remote Patient Monitoring and Wearable Devices

Wearable IoT devices like 'wearables' including the fitness trackers, smartwatches, and biosensors have completely transformed how care givers in the health sector are able to track their patients. These devices on a continuous basis monitor signals pertaining to vital signs, physical activity, sleep, and other health indicators, and send this information in real time to physicians. For example, patients with diabetes, hypertension, cardiovascular diseases, and the like, can be observed using the IoT equipments, thus no need for frequent hospital check-ups (Talaat et al., 2023).

ii. Smart Sensors and Medical Devices

In hospitals today, IoT smart sensors and connected devices are effectively used to provide solutions to increase organizational effectiveness and also improve on patient outcomes. It can also use these devices to monitor the usage of medical equipments, climate condition in patient rooms including temperature and humidity and even when supplies are exhausted. The integration of different smart devices in critical care units like smart infusion pumps and smart ventilators enables the health care professionals to directly observe several key treatment parameters of a patient and make alterations instantly without generating additional confusion or mistakes (Rejeb et al., 2023)

Also, IoT is revolutionizing the way that medication is managed. Smart pills can also help patients to adhere to their schedule of taking medicine since adjusting to new conditions might be very difficult for some people – it is one of the main problems in chronic illness treatment. Smart medical technologies and connected hospital systems mean much more effective healthcare system with focus on the patients.

iii. Real-Time Data and Predictive Analytics

Of particular relevance, IoT devices produce data that is crucial to predictive analytics, a type of analysis tools that factor past and live data to make future patient status and disease progression projections. AI when integrated with IoT provides method of identifying with high sensitivity the frailness in the patent's conditions, a simple rise or fall in pulse rate, oxygen level or blood pressure. Such prediction leads to the generation of early preventions that can be crucial in cases that relate to acute care (Chakraborty et al., 2024).In addition to promoting positive change in health care for IoT and AI integration to enhance the health of the people additional to stressing on the aspects of cost containment the general cost to the health care systems is minimized. Continuing and initiating home care can reduce expensive and complicated complications, hospitalization, and intensive care treatments in the future

C. Blockchain in Healthcare

i. Data Security and Privacy in Healthcare

Blockchain for its part provides the distributed ledger technology, with the added bonus of providing an immutable record of transactions, making it applicable in the health care sectors. Each segment of the chain has a protective shield consisting of the code of the prior segment, the date of encoding, and the transaction information, because of which, to manipulate data, anymore, is difficult once it has been incorporated. This is most useful in the health care system where information must be accurate and a patient's information cannot be misused. In insurance, the use of Blockchain involves the application of virtual server for clinical data to enhance the transfer of patient data among healthcare organizations with the consent of only a selected staff, there is no incidence of data leak and frauds (Hovorushchenko et al., 2023). One more carefully selected parameter of the blockchain is the opportunity to retain the patients' records in patients' hands. The patients can input their data in a way where it can only be used for particular periods; this way, the healthcare policymakers, insurers, and every other related stakeholder can only view the data they need while they are consulting the data being stored in the cloud. Having engaged into the approach of consolidating and managing patient information is particularly useful with regard to privacy as most healthcare functions transition to digital (Sajedi et al., 2024).

ii. Blockchain in Clinical Trials and Drug Supply Chain Management

Block chain's applications extend beyond data security and into other critical areas of healthcare, such as clinical trials and drug supply chain management. In clinical trials, Blockchain ensures the transparency and integrity of data by creating an immutable record of each trial's outcomes. This reduces the likelihood of data manipulation and enhances the trustworthiness of trial results, which is essential for regulatory approvals and public trust

Blockchain is not confined to the records' protection and can solve other urgent issues in delivering health care, for instance clinical trials and pharmaceutical chains. When it comes to clinical trials Blockchain maintains the overall integrity of data by creating a trail of each trial conducted (Ahmad et al, 2023).

In drug supply chain supply, Blockchain assists in tracing various drugs from producers up to the consumer to avoid the circulation of fake products in the market. The technology assists the stakeholders to authenticate the various drugs to be sold in the market, guarantee safe and authentic drugs that have been stored under recommended conditions (Mettler, 2016)

iii. The Future of Blockchain in Healthcare

While adopting more advanced technologies in delivering patient care, Blockchain is expected to have a larger value in offering security in access, improving data trustworthiness, and improving communication between clients, providers, and healthcare fraud individuals. Given its propensity to enhance processes, minimize fraud, boost efficiency over databases and transform the utilization of healthcare data, Blockchain is poised for increase its utility as an infrastructural best practice in systems and structures of the future healthcare industry.

1.2. Importance of 2030 Sustainable Development Goals (SDGs) in Global Health Priorities

1.3. The United Nations has identified in the 2030 Sustainable Development Goals their transformative and challenging framework for global change regarding a vast range of health, environment, social, and economic problems. Of these goals, the third one "Healthy Women, Healthy Lives, Healthy Future" has a crucial position, which aims at achieving universal health coverage, reducing mortality rate, as well as addressing health related inequity. However, at the moment, such technologies are increasingly becoming more effective strategies in supporting the achievement of the mentioned health related goals. The continued development of innovations including telemedicine, mHealth apps, AI and block chain present an opportunity for digital health to foster and improve more efficient, accessible, sustainable health care systems globally (Borges et al., 2023). Importance of 2030 Sustainable Development Goals (SDGs) in Global Health Priorities as shown in Figure 2:

Figure 2. Importance of **2030 Sustainable Development Goals (SDGs) in global health priorities**

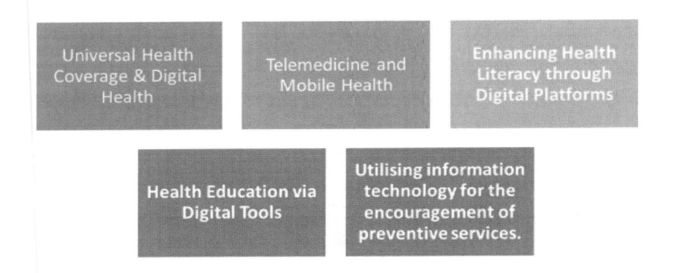

i. Universal Health Coverage (UHC) and Digital Health

UHC is the third sustainable development goal, which seeks to promote the health of all and ensure proportional financial costs for receiving essential health care services. The global consultant on UHC, the WHO asserts that UHC involves access to effective and affordable essential and quality health services, medicines, and vaccines. This goal is critically being supported by digital health technologies especially in the developing countries.

ii. Telemedicine and Mobile Health (mHealth)

Telemedicine and mHealth have nowadays become core subsectors that have aided in taking healthcare services to people in areas that have liked access to healthcare services because of geographical, financial, or infrastructural challenges. In developing countries and remote places where healthcare workers and hospitals are rare, telemedicine interfaces help for real-time dialogue with health care givers resulting in increase in the promptness and availability of health care (Alonso et al., 2021). The major advantage of such platforms is that patients do not have to travel long distances for their basic and fairly often required medical check-ups thus encouraging frequent check-ups for chronic conditions.Mobile health technologies also ensure healthcare accessibility by offering smartphone applications which dispense medical advice, medication use reminders and records access. Furthermore, mHealth platforms include monitoring through wearable devices monitoring of body parameters such as pulse rate, blood pressure, and blood glucose. Such real-time data enable the healthcare practitioners to monitor the health of their patients form a distance, and take interventions that helps in avoiding adverse effects mainly in cases of chronic diseases like diabetes, and high blood pressure (Jiang et al., 2021). However, there are still some issues that hinder the fairly equal use of focused digital health solutions. The concept of the 'digital divide' the gap in use of technology, connectivity, and skills, is how it tends to widen the gaps in health care in LMICs. Consequently, though digital technologies can drive the progression of UHC, problems associated with population access to these tools remain a critical factor.

iii. Enhancing Health Literacy through Digital Platforms

From a broader overall perspective, the increase in health literacy that is fostered by digital health technologies is possibly one of the greatest gifts offered to SDG 3. It is a measure of the populace's ability to obtain, understand, and apply health information with the ultimate goal of making better decisions regarding their health. To some extent digital health can offer Web-based educational information and instruments that enhance the patients' knowledge of chronic illness nature, treatments, and prevention

iv. Health Education via Digital Tools

Technology apps provide the user a health education that is interactive and tailored. For instance, mobile applications and website can show content to patients according to the patient age, gender, medical history and risk factors among others. Such sites are frequently equipped with widgets in the form of videos that teach a concrete concept, knowledge check-up quizzes, or simple diagnostic tools that can be used by the audience as they follow a discussion. The modalities of this form of health education have been specifically useful in addressing life style ailments including obesity and cardiovascular diseases, which essentially, have enormous patient behaviour in disease control (Vogt et al., 2021).

Also, digital can help fill the communication gaps between healthcare consumers and their providers as well as help to explain medical concepts in simpler terms. This is especially felt in multicultural and multilingual nations, where language even becomes a key factor that can greatly affect patient's ability to comprehend their disease and the treatment the need. Teaching health and other relevant knowledge in many languages and with cultural references close to the learners, enhances health literacy and the resulting health of minorities and other disadvantaged groups through technology (Borges et al., 2023).

However, despite raising people's health literacy levels through digital health tools there is still ambiguity over the quality of health information being disseated over the internet. Continued generation of unverified health content can therefore cause the spread of the wrong information and therefore poor health decisions in the society. Therefore, credibility of the platforms is the key aspect to provide the greatest benefits for enhancing health literacy by using the digital health platforms available.

v. Utilising Information Technology for the Encouragement of Preventive Services.

a. Promoting Preventive Care through Data Analytics

Promoting well-being and clinical early intervention is a critical drive in achieving SDG 3 – The reduction of the Burden of Disease. Preventive care programs are heavily dependent on digital health technologies primarily driven by data analysis. With large amounts of health data fed into these technologies, they can predict patterns and trends that will help shape a country's health policies while at the same time helping particular patients avoid diseases.

b. Predictive Analytics and Early Detection

Intelligent Real Time Analytics and Business Intelligence enabled forecasting can be used to transform preventive care by bringing to light people at heightened risk of developing certain diseases before the onset of symptoms. Using EHRs, wearable technology, and genomics, they provide the probability on the emergence of diseases like diabetes, cardiovascular diseases, and cancer (Ledziński et al., 2023). Such detection allows care givers to institute early intervention which could include medication or changes in lifestyle that may help prevent worsening of the disease.

For instance, AI can work on big data to predict specific patterns concerning contagious diseases, to inform the appropriate action in promoting health. For instance, during the COVID-19 outbreak, data analysis and collecting tools were applied for identifying the virus outbreak and anticipating people's rates' spikes to help authorities manage resources and put relevant containment measures into effect (Jiang et al., 2021). For the purpose of managing and attaining the target of the integrated preventive care as per the goal aiming 3, these essential capabilities are sought after to decrease the rates of preventable diseases and the pressure on the health care systems.

c. Personalized Preventive Care

Other ways, which are made possible by digital health technologies also include enhancing individual health and wellbeing through the offer and delivery of targeted preventive care. For instance, the mobile health applications can effectively; remind patients on checklist screening, medication adherence and more often issue invitations to; exercise, and take balanced diets. Personalized care plans assist the patients in maintaining adherence to their preventive health care regimens and thus decrease the patients' risk of developing the chronic illnesses that continue to be a cause of concern in the modern society (Vogt et al. 2021).

1.4. Relevance of Digital Health

Telemedicine, e-Health, mHealth, and Electronic Health Records (EHR) systems all over the world are juggling the transformation of healthcare services. It means the use of new technologies for advanced applications in Medicare including artificial intelligence, wearable devices, mobile applications, big data, and block chain encapsulated in achieving better patient care, efficient clinical delivery, and developing healthier societies. Its need has emerged more evidently in recent years especially with the novel virus outbreak of the COVID-19 as shown in Figure 3:

Figure 3. Relevance of digital health

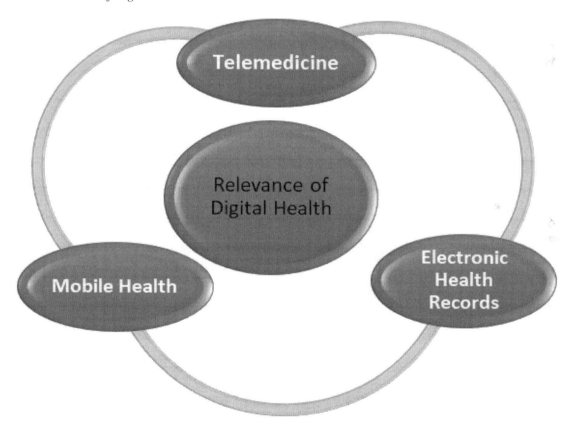

i. **Telemedicine** useful in enabling the health care professional to offer most of their consultations through electronic interfaces which helped to decrease the physical contact which was a burden on some overfilled hospitals. The exponential increase in the use of telemedicine during the pandemic demonstrated how effective digital health technologies are in managing patient care at moments of disruption (Alonso et al., 2021).

ii. **Electronic Health Records (EHRs)** EHRs have also become vital across the pandemic period. The EHR systems provided opportunity to share current patient information across various practices for coordination and decision making. Overall, there were patient histories and other aspects which may have been satisfied and tracked by means of EHRs, integration of results of tests and vaccine detail that must be used in the management of the COVID-19 (Chang et al., 2023).

iii. **Mobile Health (mHealth)** Mobile Health (mHealth) applications enhanced the reach of health care still even more. These applications helped people to track their health state via smartphones and wearable devices and consequently get the necessary data on movement, heart rate, oxygen level, etc. As the result, patients with chronic diseases were able to receive continuous care while eliminating the risks of traditional face-to-face consultations with doctors (Vogt et al., 2021).

1.5. Concept of Digital Stress in the Era of Digital Transformation

New concept explaining stress and strain that individuals undergo because of exposure to digital technologies is called the digital stress. With the advancements of technology in the present world, customers are experiencing digital stress especially at the workplace as the world transits to the digital age. Digitalization continues to escalate the adoptions of innovative technologies in companies increasing efficiency and interconnectivity but with side effects on people's psychological health

A. Sources of Digital Stress

There are several key factors contributing to digital stress in the digital age as shown in figure 4:

Figure 4. Sources of digital stress

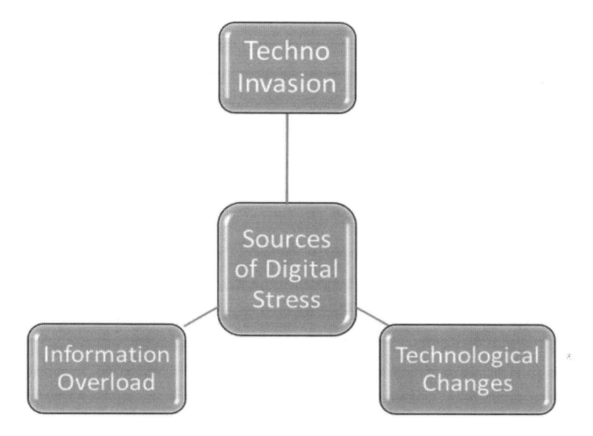

i. **Techno-invasion**: Work life and personal life integration act as one of the leading causes of digital stress. Mobile phones, Smart phones, Laptops make it obligatory for the employees to be on net even after office hours. The expectation to reply to mail, attend a call or be available always can result in stress, anxiety and eradicating the work life balance (Tarafdar et al., 2019)

ii. **Information Overload:** The tremendous amount of information that one can get from any specific topic is overwhelming, and may cause a condition such as cognitive overload. Often employees receive a large number of emails and notifications from different platforms and sources affecting their ability to concentrate on the more important tasks. What these individuals experience is what has been referred to as the information overload which leads to make decision tiredness and high stress levels (Schötteler et al., 2023).

iii. **Technological Changes:** Technology is advancing at a very fast rate which means that employees are always learning new systems in the workplace, particularly a system that may not be the most comforting to them leading to stress. Technostress complements the pressure by making employees feel that there is the need to adapt to technological advancements to avert being dismissed from work (Banerjee et al., 2024).

2. DIGITAL HEALTH AND ECONOMIC SUSTAINABILITY

2.1. The Role of AI, IoT, and Blockchain in Healthcare Cost Reduction

This paper explores how the incorporation of AI and IoT in the health sector has impacted on costs, thus improving on economic viability through blockchain. Due to its importance southward to rise quality Clinic assignment for improving the accuracy that diagnostic and treatment in the Clinic. AI systems can sort through large datasets of patient information to deliver on the knowledge that will help healthcare providers make fewer mistakes and deliver more exact treatments. This not only improves patient satisfaction and treatment outcomes but also reduces on diagnostic and treatment related complications (Borges et al., 2023). Research evidence indicates that, for example, AI-assisted diagnostics in radiology and oncology decrease the frequent use of diagnostics and, therefore, provide fewer diagnostic options. Several IoT devices also save costs through constant tracking and monitoring of patients' condition through wearable sensors and smart health gadgets. These devices take real time data on patient's health status such as heart rate, blood pressure as well as glucose levels to ensure timely medical attention is taken. As a result, IoT minimizes parameters such as hospitalization and emergency visits and ultimately decreases healthcare expenses (Talaat et al., 2023). It means that patients with chronic diseases, including diabetes or hypertension, receive a high level of benefit from such technologies because they help avoid rehospitalisation's and improve the disease management.

Blockchain technology provides better protection as well as optimization of operations in handling health information. This makes exclusive properties of the system to have decentralization and transparency so as to maintain the integrity of the EHR. Some of the ways in which block chain can be used in healthcare include; Blockchain cuts out middleman in some data exchanges, decreasing healthcare administrative costs and decreasing fraud in transactions (Hovorushchenko et al., 2024). Furthermore, by streamlining the data management and avoiding inconsistencies, or alteration of information, blockchain decreases the cost related to patient record, insurance claims, and trials.

2.2. Economic Implications of Techno Invasion and Digital Stress

Techno Invasion and Digital Stress have clear economic consequences now, as digital technologies are actively used in healthcare systems. Techno Invasion could be understood as an overflow of multiplicity of digital technologies into different spheres of functioning as well as private and working life domains. It causes stress, burnout and higher employee turnover thus proving costly to healthcare organization since the employees are the heart of the organization. Digital stress is applied as a term used to describe stress originating from massive utilization of healthcare technologies resulting in low efficiency and high levels of truancy. Healthcare is sometimes characterized by the incorporation of new technologies into a professional's work, which, together with their routine tasks, may lead to an overload of information, thus reducing the productivity of the work being done (Temsah et al., 2023).

Research has established that stress related absenteeism reduces productivity; it also leads to hiring of temporary staff to fill the gaps in organizations such as healthcare institutions (Ewers et al., 2023). Stress caused by digital features is not only limited to the healthcare industry but also to the nation's general productivity since when employees are overwhelmed with features such as the internet, social media and the news, then productivity at the workplace will diminish. It is thus important not only to resolve the digital stress at an individual level but it is also important to solve the problem systematically so as to economise the health care systems.

3. TECHNO INVASION AND ITS IMPACT ON WORKFORCE SUSTAINABILITY

3.1. Digital Transformation in Healthcare and Its Effect on Workforce Well-Being

The Concept of Digital Transformation in healthcare has brought the change in the work structure and growth of the healthcare care industry in terms of efficiency, use of technologies such as Artificial Intelligence (AI), Internet of Things (IoT) and Electronic Health Records (EHRs). However, this fast-pace integration of technology has also created major problems among the entailing healthcare workers which are best described as Techno Invasion. As the steady and frequently invasive mediation of technology into personal and career domains, Techno Invasion undercuts established boundaries between work and home lives and doubles stress, dissatisfaction, and burnout in healthcare personnel (Tarafdar et al., 2020).

With reference to this, the implication is that Digital Transformation is not only enhancing health care delivery services, but also the mental and emotional state of the workforce. The necessity of solving these problems is obvious because prolonged distortion is possible only within the limits of Techno Stress's definition and can lead to high rates turnover, low morale, and, consequently, decreased productivity within healthcare organizations.

3.2. Balancing Technological Adoption with Mental Well-Being in Healthcare Settings

As healthcare organizations continue to embrace technological innovations, it is essential to prioritize mental well-being alongside these advancements. To maintain the ideal balance between work and personal life, it is necessary for healthcare organisations to set essential guidelines on the applicability of such modes of communication especially during off working times. Most of the healthcare professionals receive the pressure of responding to work related issues at any given one through mobile phones, and in health domain related applications. Restricting the time employees spend communicating after working hours also means that healthcare institutions are a good example to follow in observing work-life balance (Nedeljko et al., 2023).

Organizational policies should also be reviewed and initiated on programs aimed at supporting health by absorbing Techno Stress professionals. It may include organizing constant training to enable employees to manage new tools and gadgets more easily, or offering counselling on attitude changes or stress control tools such as workshops. These efforts not only focus on psychological health but also contribute to creating constructive organizational climate in which organizational members are enabled to manage emerging challenges in digitally transformed economy.

Moreover, specific concepts such as favourable flexible work arrangements can also be utilised by healthcare institutions in order to provide additional workforce enhancement. For instance, the flexible work arrangements such as office work and remote work occasions enable care officers to plan their working schedules in a better way, thereby, may not have the pressure of being continuously connected. Former freeware options mean that managers cannot strictly control when an employee works or which tools he or she uses, which is critical for successful work-life balance strategies to prevent burnout over the long term (Saxena et al., 2021)

4. DIGITAL STRESS AND ITS INFLUENCE ON HEALTHCARE INNOVATION

4.1. The Psychological Impact of Digital Transformation on Healthcare Workers

The quick advancement of Digital Transformation has brought new problems to the employees in healthcare systems. We find that a phenomenon which we are calling Digital Stress is common among today's workers, and many feel that they are insufficiently prepared for technology change. This stress includes the learning shift, learning the new technology tools, demands to cease to exist beyond a workday (Ewers et al., 2023). Depending on AI system, EHR, Telemedicine platforms, more and more, health workers may experience pressure that their capability of providing care is on the trial and developing anxiety and fatigue.

4.2. Strategies for Mitigating Digital Stress in High-Tech Healthcare Environments

Based on the concept of Digital Stress discussed earlier, healthcare organizations can employ some measures to reduce its impact and make transition to digital tools less painful. Ensuring that professional development initiatives include substantive, intensive instruction in effective, comfortable use of the new tools can support professionals when adopting new forms and technologies of work. Further, presentation model resilience may help workers be exposed to various stress management strategies in case the forces of the constantly connected work environment overwhelms them. Fostering such organizational culture where employees are comfortable to talk about their struggles in working with the technology products is critically important for fighting stress as shown in Figure 5.

Figure 5. Strategies for mitigating digital stress in high tech healthcare environment

i. Digital Literacy Training

The best way to address Digital Stress as proposed by researchers is availing strong Digital Literacy Training. This will involve imparting new skills to these health care providers in order to enable them to manage new technologies well. Training programs should focus on:

a. **Hands-on Workshops:** Where specific initiatives are concerned let personnel directly experiment with the new technologies in a somewhat restricted manner.
b. **Ongoing Support:** Continual availability of staff support with expertise to help staff as they run into issues with technology.
c. **Feedback Mechanisms:** Providing avenues through which personnel's can express their challenges or problems they encounter in essence to make training programs relevant to them
  ii. Organizational Culture

Organizational culture plays a central role in the prevention of Digital Stress and therefore should be embraced by organizations. This includes:

a. **Open Communication:** Discussing issues related to technology use with other team members can make it seem more regular thus draw attention to stress.
b. **Peer Support Systems:** Introducing systems of buddy or mentoring so that staff with more perceived computer literacy could help others with competing digital tools.
c. **Celebrating Successes:** Being able to identify and appreciate workers who are able to embrace change and choose to work well with new technologies prevents negativity which may be brought by the change.

iii. Resilience Programs:

Stress Management programs are essentially Resilience Programs intended to help practitioners acquire approaches to handling stress. These programs may include:

a. **Mindfulness and Stress Management Workshops:** Ways of information delivery including meditation, breathing exercises, and other stress management skills should be taught to the staff so that they can manage on pressure.
b. **Mental Health Resources:** Offering an opportunity to attend counselling sessions or using days off for mental health will help take care of the workforce.
c. **Regular Check-ins:** Working alongside this it is possible for management to conduct occasional check-ups on the well-being of its employees so as to address any issues arising from work overload.

iv. Work-Work-Life Balance

Ensuring that Work-Life Balance is encouraged forms part of the probable solutions to Digital Stress. Strategies include:

a. **Clear Boundaries for After-Hours Communication:** Laying down rules when and how employees should use work related communications can help to ensure they do not feel called upon all the time.
b. **Flexible Work Arrangements:** Indeed, incorporating remote working or flexible working can assist the healthcare human resources to manage their responsibilities and work-related stress.
c. **Encouraging Time Off:** By focusing on the necessity of breaks and promptly scheduling a vacation stress, overload and imbalance between work and personal life can be reduced.

4.3. The Role of Organizational Support in Reducing Digital Stress

Employing organizations have a significant responsibility towards reducing this form of Digital Stress through preventing work and family interpenetration. Measures that currently are used to reduce after working hours electronic messages and communication, and making sure that every employee has access to mental health services can eliminate great pressure caused by constant connectiveness. Specific rules regarding technology utilization, as well as setting realistic expectations for technology usage in communication, help the workers to address the workload while not feeling constantly overwhelmed.

4.4. Building Resilience Against Burnout and Digital Fatigue

How to sustain organizational resilience of healthcare workforce Strengthening the protection of healthcare workforce's mental and occupational wellbeing is a major approach to the enhancement of resilience at the workplace. To support resilience, the healthcare organizations should supply resources and education necessary to reduce stress and burnout indicators in among their workers. This can involve training on how to organize and prioritize tasks, an insistence on NOT sitting at a computer all day, or a general program of valuing mental health. By enhancing resilience, healthcare professional changes their ability to cope with a high-tech, hyper-accelerated environment and avoid Digital Fatigue or burnout.

5. FUTURE TRENDS IN DIGITAL HEALTH AND WORKFORCE WELL BEING

The environment of the health care delivery is changing rapidly due to the adoption of digital solutions. When planning for the future then, there are several evident currents that define what digital health entails and the welfare of healthcare providers. These trends are all geared toward the use of information technology, policy support, flexible working arrangement, and training and development of more sustainable and supportive healthcare system.

5.1. Use of AI and IoT for Real-Time Monitoring of Healthcare Workers' Mental Well-Being

Technological advancement especially AI and IoT present new real-time solutions for evaluating heath care worker's wellbeing. These technologies enable the collection of data related to employee well-being through:

a. **Wearable Devices:** Wearable devices integrated with IoT can monitor and therefore give an indication of the wearers' level of stress, or lack thereof and sleep quality (Chiarini et al., 2020).
b. **AI-Driven Analytics:** These devices can be used to capture data which AI algorithms can then mine to determine if there are signs of mental stress, which an organization can then use to take appropriate action (Borges et al., 2023).

5.2. Role of Policy in Promoting Sustainable Digital Transformation in Healthcare

Policies are an essential tool in enhancing ethics and sustainable aspects of digital technologies in the health sector. Effective policies should focus on:

a. **Protecting Healthcare Workers:** Measures must be put so as to protect employees from effects of Digital Stress. These measures also extend to ban on or control on communication during odd hours and work load management standard.

b. **Promoting Ethical Technology Use:** Recommendations should be made as to what policies should consider when dealing with ethical practice while it comes to the use of technology in relation to patient care not being an issue due to the implementation of new technologies as noted by (Chiarini et al., 2020).
c. **Sustainable Practices:** It also means that promotional measures that would focus on mental health checks and services would help to build the overall sustainability of the digital-forward programs.

5.3. Trends Towards the System of Hybrid Work Environments And The Change of Roles of Healthcare Personnel

It has become clear that flexibility is going to be a major force in shaping the future roles of healthcare workers due to the impact of the COVID-19 pandemic to shift work to hybrid models. Key aspects include:

a. **Flexible Work Arrangements:** This can benefit employment relations because options for work from home or flexible work schedules can increase pleasure at work and decrease pressure especially in jobs where the worker is not expected to be physically present all the time (Borges et al., 2023).
b. **Dynamic Role Adaptations:** Healthcare technologies are constantly developing and as a result, the tasks of healthcare professionals might change on time. These changes should be acknowledged in training programs and staff should be trained to accommodate a varied level of face-to-face and virtual work.

5.4. Future Training Programs Focused on Digital Skills and Stress Management

Education and training of healthcare professionals should change in order to fits them for practice in digital health ecosystems. Future training should encompass:

a. **Digital Skills Development:** Programs should include developing competencies in the appropriate use of tools, in order to enhance staff's self-perceived competence levels (Chiarini et al., 2020).
b. **Stress Management Techniques:** Apart from adding new stress management trainings, the strategies should be introduced into existing programs to help the healthcare workers to be able to be more competent in handling the stressful times (Ewers et al.,2023).

6. CONCLUSION

When healthcare systems across the globe, are going digital, it is equally important to understand the tension between technological solutions and the human processes involved. This chapter has presented different aspects of digital health with a focus on the aspects of sustainability for those working in the health sector.

6.1. Summary of Key Insights

Analysing the use of smart technologies such as AI, IoT, and blockchain in healthcare, increases our understanding of their capacity to reach their potential in enhancing care processes and organizational outcomes. But it also points to the problem of Digital Stress which has the potential to decrease both satisfaction with work and general health of the employees in the healthcare sector.

i. **Integration of Technologies:** The chapter has illustrated the advantages brought about by the use of digital tools in diagnosis and management of patients and the need for an appropriately skilled and backed up workforce.
ii. **Importance of Workforce Well-Being:** Consequently, the research highlights that digitisation for sustainable healthcare have to consider the welfare of the workforce as required in the third SDG for healthy lives. Promoting staff mental health and creating a healthy organizations build positive staff morale, decreases turnover rates and improves patient care.

6.2. Directions for Future Research for Sustainable Tech Adoption in Healthcare Systems

As the digital landscape of healthcare continues to evolve, future research should focus on several critical areas to enhance sustainable technology adoption:

i. **Effective Strategies for Integration**: Future research should study how immunity can be built in such usage stead and how Digil Stress can be managed in digital health technology integration. This includes processes of searching for successful models for the introduction of innovations into practice as well as ensuring sufficient backup for healthcare employees.
ii. **Longitudinal Studies on Impact:** Research studies that follow organization's technology adoption and its effects on the employees and the organization will be highly beneficial. This would enable employer organizations and healthcare institutions to design and implement effect, sustainable and productive digital health interventions and tools suitable for employee and patient need.
iii. **Focus on Organizational Policies:** The impact of organizational policies on maintaining a positive organizational climate with particular reference to the changes being triggered by digitization is crucial and should be studied further. Studies should focus on finding the best strategies of preserving healthcare workers from negative effects of technologies and at the same time making them happier.

Through addressing these research directions, the academic community can assist in the creation of a strong foundation of sustainable digital health that will incorporate technological progress and the needs and well-being of healthcare workers. Therefore, this report of the centre presents a crucial finding that multiple workforce aspects of digital health innovations cannot be overemphasized in determining the Healthcare of the future. Thus, promoting mental wellbeing and psychological protection in healthcare organizations means leveraging the powerful potential of digital technologies to achieve the benefits of innovative healthcare solutions which improve patients' lives and progress the goals of public health services.

REFERENCES

Abbas, A., Alroobaea, R., Krichen, M., Rubaiee, S., Vimal, S., & Almansour, F. M. (2024). Blockchain-assisted secured data management framework for health information analysis based on Internet of Medical Things. *Personal and Ubiquitous Computing*, 28(1), 59–72. DOI: 10.1007/s00779-021-01583-8

Ahmad, R. W., Al Khader, W., Jayaraman, R., Salah, K., Antony, J., & Swarnakar, V. (2023). Integrating Lean Six Sigma with blockchain technology for quality management–a scoping review of current trends and future prospects. *The TQM Journal*, 35(7), 1609–1631. DOI: 10.1108/TQM-06-2022-0181

Al Kuwaiti, A., Nazer, K., Al-Reedy, A., Al-Shehri, S., Al-Muhanna, A., Subbarayalu, A. V., Al Muhanna, D., & Al-Muhanna, F. A. (2023). A review of the role of artificial intelligence in healthcare. *Journal of Personalized Medicine*, 13(6), 951. DOI: 10.3390/jpm13060951 PMID: 37373940

Al-Maini, M., Maindarkar, M., Kitas, G. D., Khanna, N. N., Misra, D. P., Johri, A. M., Mantella, L., Agarwal, V., Sharma, A., Singh, I. M., Tsoulfas, G., Laird, J. R., Faa, G., Teji, J., Turk, M., Viskovic, K., Ruzsa, Z., Mavrogeni, S., Rathore, V., & Suri, J. S. (2023). Artificial intelligence-based preventive, personalized and precision medicine for cardiovascular disease/stroke risk assessment in rheumatoid arthritis patients: A narrative review. *Rheumatology International*, 43(11), 1965–1982. DOI: 10.1007/s00296-023-05415-1 PMID: 37648884

Albawi, S., Arif, M. H., & Waleed, J. (2023). Skin cancer classification dermatologist-level based on deep learning model. *Acta Scientiarum. Technology*, 45, e61531–e61531. DOI: 10.4025/actascitechnol.v45i1.61531

Alonso, S. G., Marques, G., Barrachina, I., Garcia-Zapirain, B., Arambarri, J., Salvador, J. C., & de la Torre Díez, I. (2021). Telemedicine and e-Health research solutions in literature for combatting COVID-19: A systematic review. *Health and Technology*, 11(2), 257–266. DOI: 10.1007/s12553-021-00529-7 PMID: 33558838

Alowais, S. A., Alghamdi, S. S., Alsuhebany, N., Alqahtani, T., Alshaya, A. I., Almohareb, S. N., Aldairem, A., Alrashed, M., Bin Saleh, K., Badreldin, H. A., Al Yami, M. S., Al Harbi, S., & Albekairy, A. M. (2023). Revolutionizing healthcare: The role of artificial intelligence in clinical practice. *BMC Medical Education*, 23(1), 689. DOI: 10.1186/s12909-023-04698-z PMID: 37740191

Banerjee, P., & Gupta, R. (2024). A mixed-method exploration of effects of technostress on remote/hybrid working professionals. *Computers in Human Behavior*, 150, 107974. DOI: 10.1016/j.chb.2023.107974

Banitaba, S. N., Khademolqorani, S., Jadhav, V. V., Chamanehpour, E., Mishra, Y. K., Mostafavi, E., & Kaushik, A. (2023). Recent progress of bio-based smart wearable sensors for healthcare applications. *Materials Today Electronics*, 5, 100055. DOI: 10.1016/j.mtelec.2023.100055

Boopathi, S. (2023). Internet of Things-Integrated Remote Patient Monitoring System: Healthcare Application. In *Dynamics of Swarm Intelligence Health analysis for the next generation* (pp. 137–161). IGI Global. DOI: 10.4018/978-1-6684-6894-4.ch008

Borges do Nascimento, I. J., Abdulazeem, H., Vasanthan, L. T., Martinez, E. Z., Zucoloto, M. L., Østengaard, L., Azzopardi-Muscat, N., Zapata, T., & Novillo-Ortiz, D. (2023). Barriers and facilitators to utilizing digital health technologies by healthcare professionals. *NPJ Digital Medicine*, 6(1), 161. DOI: 10.1038/s41746-023-00899-4 PMID: 37723240

Boulos, M. N. K., & Wu, J. T. (2020). The Internet of Things in Healthcare: Applications, Benefits, and Challenges. *Healthcare Informatics Research*, 26(3), 193–204. PMID: 32819037

Chakraborty, C., Othman, S. B., Almalki, F. A., & Sakli, H. (2024). FC-SEEDA: Fog computing-based secure and energy efficient data aggregation scheme for Internet of healthcare Things. *Neural Computing & Applications*, 36(1), 241–257. DOI: 10.1007/s00521-023-08270-0

Chang, A. (2023). The role of artificial intelligence in digital health. In *Digital health entrepreneurship* (pp. 75–85). Springer International Publishing. DOI: 10.1007/978-3-031-33902-8_6

Chang, A. (2023). The role of artificial intelligence in digital health. In *Digital health entrepreneurship* (pp. 75–85). Springer International Publishing. DOI: 10.1007/978-3-031-33902-8_6

Ewers, M., & Kangmennaang, J. (2023). New spaces of inequality with the rise of remote work: Autonomy, technostress, and life disruption. *Applied Geography (Sevenoaks, England)*, 152, 102888. DOI: 10.1016/j.apgeog.2023.102888

Hovorushchenko, T., Moskalenko, A., & Osyadlyi, V. (2023). Methods of medical data management based on blockchain technologies. *Journal of Reliable Intelligent Environments*, 9(1), 5–16. DOI: 10.1007/s40860-022-00178-1 PMID: 35646514

Jena, L. K., & Pradhan, S. (2020). Digital Transformation in Healthcare and its Impact on Workforce: An Organizational Perspective. *Journal of Organizational Change Management*, 33(5), 715–733.

Khalid, A., & Syed, J. (2024). Mental health and well-being at work: A systematic review of literature and directions for future research. *Human Resource Management Review*, 34(1), 100998. DOI: 10.1016/j.hrmr.2023.100998

Kufel, J., Bargieł-Łączek, K., Kocot, S., Koźlik, M., Bartnikowska, W., Janik, M., Czogalik, Ł., Dudek, P., Magiera, M., Lis, A., Paszkiewicz, I., Nawrat, Z., Cebula, M., & Gruszczyńska, K. (2023). What is machine learning, artificial neural networks and deep learning?—Examples of practical applications in medicine. *Diagnostics (Basel)*, 13(15), 2582. DOI: 10.3390/diagnostics13152582 PMID: 37568945

Ledziński, Ł., & Grześk, G. (2023). Artificial intelligence technologies in cardiology. *Journal of Cardiovascular Development and Disease*, 10(5), 202. DOI: 10.3390/jcdd10050202 PMID: 37233169

Liao, J., Li, X., Gan, Y., Han, S., Rong, P., Wang, W., Li, W., & Zhou, L. (2023). Artificial intelligence assists precision medicine in cancer treatment. *Frontiers in Oncology*, 12, 998222. DOI: 10.3389/fonc.2022.998222 PMID: 36686757

López-Del-Hoyo, Y., Fernández-Martínez, S., Pérez-Aranda, A., Barceló-Soler, A., Bani, M., Russo, S., Urcola-Pardo, F., Strepparava, M. G., & García-Campayo, J. (2023). Effects of eHealth interventions on stress reduction and mental health promotion in healthcare professionals: A systematic review. *Journal of Clinical Nursing*, 32(17-18), 5514–5533. DOI: 10.1111/jocn.16634 PMID: 36703266

Mettler, M. (2016). Blockchain technology in healthcare: The revolution starts here. *IEEE 18th International Conference on e-Health Networking, Applications and Services (Healthcom)*, Munich, Germany, 1 https://doi.org/DOI: 10.1109/HealthCom.2016.7749510

Molli, V. L. P. (2023). Blockchain Technology for Secure and Transparent Health Data Management: Opportunities and Challenges. *Journal of Healthcare AI and ML*, 10(10), 1–15.

Muheidat, F., & Tawalbeh, L. A. (2023). AIoMT artificial intelligence (AI) and Internet of Medical Things (IoMT): applications, challenges, and future trends. In Computational Intelligence for Medical Internet of Things (MIoT) Applications (pp. 33-54). Academic Press.

Nedeljko, M., Gu, Y., & Bostan, C. M. (2024). The dual impact of technological tools on health and technostress among older workers: An integrative literature review. *Cognition Technology and Work*, 26(1), 47–61. DOI: 10.1007/s10111-023-00741-7

Nimrod, G. (2020). Technostress: Measuring a New Threat to Well-being in Later Life. *Aging & Mental Health*, 24(10), 1503–1508. PMID: 28562064

Osama, M., Ateya, A. A., Sayed, M. S., Hammad, M., Pławiak, P., Abd El-Latif, A. A., & Elsayed, R. A. (2023). Internet of medical things and healthcare 4.0: Trends, requirements, challenges, and research directions. *Sensors (Basel)*, 23(17), 7435. DOI: 10.3390/s23177435 PMID: 37687891

Qureshi, A. S., & Roos, T. (2023). Transfer learning with ensembles of deep neural networks for skin cancer detection in imbalanced data sets. *Neural Processing Letters*, 55(4), 4461–4479. DOI: 10.1007/s11063-022-11049-4

Ragu-Nathan, T. S., Tarafdar, M., Ragu-Nathan, B. S., & Tu, Q. (2008). The consequences of technostress for end-users in organizations: Conceptual development and empirical validation. *Information Systems Research*, 19(4), 417–433. DOI: 10.1287/isre.1070.0165

Rejeb, A., Rejeb, K., Treiblmaier, H., Appolloni, A., Alghamdi, S., Alhasawi, Y., & Iranmanesh, M. (2023). The Internet of Things (IoT) in healthcare: Taking stock and moving forward. *Internet of Things : Engineering Cyber Physical Human Systems*, 22, 100721. DOI: 10.1016/j.iot.2023.100721

Sajedi, H., & Mohammadipanah, F. (2024). Global data sharing of SARS-CoV-2 based on blockchain. *International Journal of Information Technology : an Official Journal of Bharati Vidyapeeth's Institute of Computer Applications and Management*, 16(3), 1559–1567. DOI: 10.1007/s41870-023-01431-3

Saxena, A., Chaturvedi, S., & Kumar, P. (2021). Remote Working, Hybrid Workforce, and the Future of Healthcare: Trends and Challenges in the Digital Age. *Health Informatics Journal*, 27(4), 1450–1462.

Schötteler, S., Laumer, S., & Schuhbauer, H. (2023). Consequences of Enterprise Social Media Network Positions for Employees: A Literature Review and Research Agenda. *Business & Information Systems Engineering*, 65(4), 425–440. DOI: 10.1007/s12599-023-00803-0

Sui, A., Sui, W., Liu, S., & Rhodes, R. (2023). Ethical considerations for the use of consumer wearables in health research. *Digital Health*, 9, 20552076231153740. DOI: 10.1177/20552076231153740 PMID: 36756643

Talaat, F. M., & El-Balka, R. M. (2023). Stress monitoring using wearable sensors: IoT techniques in medical field. *Neural Computing & Applications*, 35(25), 18571–18584. DOI: 10.1007/s00521-023-08681-z PMID: 37362562

Tarafdar, M., Cooper, C. L., & Stich, J.-F. (2020). The Technostress Trifecta—Techno Eustress, Techno Distress, and Design: Theoretical Directions and an Agenda for Research. *Information Systems Journal*, 30(1), 83–114.

Tarafdar, M., Tu, Q., & Ragu-Nathan, T. S. (2020). Examining Factors Affecting Online Technostress in a Work Environment. *Computers in Human Behavior*, 46, 163–172. DOI: 10.1016/j.chb.2014.10.046

Tariq, M. U. (2024). Revolutionizing health data management with blockchain technology: Enhancing security and efficiency in a digital era. In *Emerging Technologies for Health Literacy and Medical Practice* (pp. 153–175). IGI Global. DOI: 10.4018/979-8-3693-1214-8.ch008

Temsah, M. H., Aljamaan, F., Malki, K. H., Alhasan, K., Altamimi, I., Aljarbou, R., . . . Al-Eyadhy, A. (2023, June). Chatgpt and the future of digital health: a study on healthcare workers' perceptions and expectations. In Healthcare (Vol. 11, No. 13, p. 1812). MDPI.

United Nations. (2021). Transforming our world: the 2030 Agenda for Sustainable Development. Available at: https://sdgs.un.org/2030agenda

Vogt, F., Wallwiener, M., & Fischer, J. M. (2021). The role of digital platforms in preventive healthcare: A systematic review. *Journal of Medical Internet Research*, 23(2), e24573. https://doi.org/10

Yuan, W. X., Yan, B., Li, W., Hao, L. Y., & Yang, H. M. (2023). Blockchain-based medical health record access control scheme with efficient protection mechanism and patient control. *Multimedia Tools and Applications*, 82(11), 16279–16300. DOI: 10.1007/s11042-022-14023-3 PMID: 36404935

Chapter 12
Innovative Financing Models and Future Directions in Healthcare:
Evaluating the Impact of Financial Strategies on Digital Health Outcomes and Innovation

Bhupinder Pal Singh Chahal
https://orcid.org/0000-0002-8106-7121
Yorkville University, Canada

Umang Sharma
https://orcid.org/0000-0003-1901-8510
Chandigarh Business School, CGC, Jhanjeri, India

Bhumika Bansal
NDIM, India

ABSTRACT

This study explores innovative financing models and future directions in healthcare, with a focus on assessing financial impact on digital health outcomes and advancing sustainable healthcare innovation. As digital health technologies like AI, IoT, and telemedicine transform patient care, the need for adaptable and value-based financing mechanisms becomes critical. Traditional models, often inadequate for the rapid pace of digital health, are compared to novel approaches such as public-private partnerships, outcome-based financing, and tiered pricing. The research examines how these models can drive equitable access, incentivize innovation, and improve patient outcomes globally. Through evaluating financial strategies, this study provides insights into scalable frameworks that prioritize both fiscal sustainability and impactful health outcomes, paving the way for a resilient, technologically integrated healthcare ecosystem.

DOI: 10.4018/979-8-3373-0240-9.ch012

INTRODUCTION TO HEALTHCARE INNOVATION

Healthcare innovation encompasses a multifaceted array of advancements that encompass the ideation, development, and implementation of novel methodologies, technologies, and practices aimed at enhancing health outcomes, augmenting patient care, and optimizing healthcare delivery systems. This paradigm encompasses a broad spectrum, ranging from incremental improvements in clinical practices to disruptive innovations that redefine the very fabric of healthcare (Dutta et al., 2023).

At its core, healthcare innovation seeks to harness the capabilities of cutting-edge technologies, such as artificial intelligence, telemedicine, and biotechnology, to catalyze transformative changes within the healthcare ecosystem. It also includes the integration of digital health solutions, which facilitate the convergence of healthcare with information technology, thereby enhancing accessibility, efficiency, and patient engagement (Kumari et al., 2024).

Moreover, the impetus for innovation is driven by the pressing exigencies of an aging population, the rising prevalence of chronic diseases, and the escalating costs associated with healthcare provision. In this context, innovative practices are imperative not only for improving patient outcomes but also for ensuring sustainability within healthcare systems grappling with resource constraints (Grover et al., 2024).

Furthermore, healthcare innovation is characterized by a collaborative ethos, necessitating interdisciplinary partnerships among healthcare professionals, technologists, policymakers, and researchers. This collaborative framework fosters an environment conducive to creativity and experimentation, ultimately leading to the emergence of groundbreaking solutions tailored to meet the evolving needs of patients and healthcare providers alike (A. K. Singh et al., 2024).

Importance of Financing in Healthcare

Financing is paramount in the healthcare sector, as it serves as the foundational substrate upon which healthcare innovations can be actualized and sustained. Effective financing mechanisms are critical for translating innovative concepts into viable healthcare solutions, as they provide the requisite capital necessary for research and development, prototyping, and market entry (Aiyappa et al., 2024).

In an era characterized by rapid technological advancement and escalating healthcare demands, the allocation of financial resources becomes increasingly complex. The diverse landscape of healthcare financing encompasses a myriad of sources, including government funding, private investment, philanthropic contributions, and reimbursement models. Each of these sources plays a pivotal role in supporting the lifecycle of healthcare innovations, from nascent ideation through to market adoption and scalability (Indu et al., 2023; Khandelwal et al., 2023; R. P. Pandey et al., 2023).

Moreover, the intricacies of financing mechanisms are further compounded by the need for economic viability and return on investment. Stakeholders, including investors, healthcare organizations, and policymakers, are invariably motivated by the prospect of quantifiable outcomes. As such, innovative financing models must be designed not only to mitigate financial risk but also to ensure that investments yield tangible health benefits and cost savings (Padhi et al., 2024; Shrivastava et al., 2023).

Furthermore, the nexus between financing and healthcare innovation is underscored by the imperative of equity. Access to financial resources can often delineate the divide between successful healthcare innovations and those that languish in obscurity due to lack of funding. As such, fostering an inclusive financing ecosystem that prioritizes underserved populations and emerging markets is essential for catalyzing equitable health outcomes (A. Arora et al., 2024; K. U. Singh et al., 2024; Zhang et al., 2023).

CURRENT LANDSCAPE OF DIGITAL HEALTH

Digital health technologies encompass a broad and heterogeneous spectrum of tools and platforms that leverage digital innovations to enhance health and healthcare delivery. These technologies are fundamentally characterized by their ability to utilize data-driven insights, connectivity, and advanced algorithms to augment traditional healthcare practices (Ajay et al., 2023; Belwal & Belwal, 2017).

At the core of digital health technologies are telemedicine and telehealth, which facilitate remote clinical consultations through real-time audio-visual communication, thereby transcending geographical barriers and democratizing access to healthcare services. Complementing these modalities are mobile health (mHealth) applications, which empower individuals to monitor their health parameters, engage in self-management, and receive personalized health interventions through portable devices such as smartphones and wearables (Gangwar & Srivastva, 2020; Tripathi & Mohan, 2016).

Additionally, digital health encompasses health informatics, which pertains to the systematic organization, analysis, and dissemination of health information. This domain is crucial for enhancing clinical decision-making, improving patient outcomes, and fostering interoperability among disparate healthcare systems. Electronic health records (EHRs) and health information exchanges (HIEs) are quintessential examples of informatics technologies that facilitate the seamless flow of patient data across care settings, thus enhancing continuity of care and enabling data-driven research (D. Mishra et al., 2024; Srivastava et al., 2024).

Furthermore, emerging technologies such as artificial intelligence (AI) and machine learning (ML) are increasingly being integrated into digital health paradigms. These technologies facilitate sophisticated data analytics, enabling predictive modeling and the identification of patterns that can inform clinical interventions, risk stratification, and population health management. Blockchain technology also holds promise for enhancing data security and interoperability, thereby fostering trust and transparency in health data exchanges (P. Singh & Singh, 2023).

In essence, digital health technologies represent an evolutionary leap in the application of technology to healthcare, aiming to create more efficient, effective, and equitable health systems that prioritize patient-centric care (Maurya et al., 2022).

Trends and Challenges in Digital Health Adoption

The adoption of digital health technologies is currently influenced by a confluence of emergent trends and multifaceted challenges that necessitate astute navigation by stakeholders across the healthcare continuum (S. Bansal et al., 2023).

Trends:

1. **Consumer-Centric Care**: A marked trend is the increasing emphasis on patient engagement and empowerment. Digital health technologies facilitate active patient participation in their healthcare journey, promoting self-efficacy through personalized health tracking, education, and remote monitoring tools (Josphineleela, Siva Reddy, et al., 2023).

2. **Integration of Artificial Intelligence**: The integration of AI and data analytics into digital health solutions is accelerating. These technologies enable healthcare providers to derive actionable insights from vast datasets, enhancing diagnostic accuracy and enabling tailored treatment plans (Pathak et al., 2021).
3. **Telehealth Proliferation**: The COVID-19 pandemic catalyzed a paradigm shift towards telehealth, resulting in a dramatic increase in virtual consultations. This trend reflects a growing acceptance of remote care delivery models, which promise convenience and enhanced access (Husen et al., 2021).
4. **Interoperability Initiatives**: There is a concerted effort to improve interoperability among digital health platforms, enabling seamless data exchange and communication among disparate systems. This is pivotal for enhancing care coordination and optimizing health outcomes (A. Das Gupta et al., 2022).

Challenges:

1. **Regulatory Hurdles**: The regulatory landscape for digital health technologies is complex and often fragmented, presenting significant barriers to market entry. Navigating regulatory compliance, including data protection regulations such as the Health Insurance Portability and Accountability Act (HIPAA), poses challenges for innovators (Kamra et al., 2023).
2. **Digital Divide**: The proliferation of digital health technologies underscores the persistent digital divide, wherein disparities in access to technology disproportionately affect marginalized populations. Addressing these inequities is essential to ensure that the benefits of digital health are equitably distributed (Ada et al., 2021).
3. **Data Security and Privacy Concerns**: With the digitization of health data comes heightened vulnerability to cyber threats. Ensuring the integrity and confidentiality of sensitive patient information is paramount, necessitating robust cybersecurity measures and stringent compliance with data protection standards (Hajoary et al., 2023).
4. **Resistance to Change**: Organizational inertia and resistance among healthcare professionals can impede the adoption of digital health technologies. Stakeholder buy-in, comprehensive training, and change management strategies are essential to mitigate resistance and foster a culture of innovation (P. J. Juneja et al., 2020; Mohd et al., 2023).

In conclusion, the landscape of digital health adoption is characterized by dynamic trends that hold promise for enhancing healthcare delivery while concurrently confronting formidable challenges that must be addressed to realize the full potential of digital health technologies. Effective collaboration among stakeholders, inclusive policy frameworks, and a commitment to equitable access are imperative for fostering a resilient digital health ecosystem.

FINANCING MECHANISMS FOR HEALTHCARE INNOVATION

Traditional Financing Models in Healthcare

Traditional financing models in healthcare predominantly encompass a tripartite framework involving governmental funding, private insurance, and out-of-pocket expenditures by patients. These models have historically underpinned the financial architecture of healthcare systems, influencing access, affordability, and the overall quality of care delivered (S. Sharma & Bhadula, 2023).

1. **Government Funding**: In many jurisdictions, public healthcare systems are financed through tax revenues, which are allocated to provide universal access to healthcare services. This model is predicated on the principles of social equity and collective responsibility, wherein the state undertakes the fiscal burden of healthcare provision. Such funding mechanisms may include national health insurance schemes or publicly funded healthcare services that guarantee a baseline of care for all citizens (K. D. Singh et al., 2023; Thentral et al., 2022).
2. **Private Insurance**: Complementing public funding, private insurance plays a pivotal role in financing healthcare services. This model operates on the principle of risk pooling, where premiums collected from policyholders are utilized to cover the costs of medical services. Private insurers often offer a range of plans with varying degrees of coverage, deductibles, and co-pays, thus creating a market-driven approach to healthcare financing. However, reliance on private insurance can lead to disparities in access and coverage, as not all individuals may afford comprehensive plans (Bhatt & Ghuman, 2022; Lokanadham et al., 2022).
3. **Out-of-Pocket Expenditures**: A significant portion of healthcare financing remains attributable to out-of-pocket payments by patients. This model necessitates that individuals pay directly for medical services at the point of care, which can create barriers to access and financial hardship, particularly for low-income populations. Out-of-pocket expenditures may encompass co-payments, deductibles, and non-covered services, ultimately influencing healthcare-seeking behavior and health outcomes (Bhargava et al., 2022; Jaswal et al., 2023; S. Sharma et al., 2023).

In summary, while traditional financing models have provided a foundational structure for healthcare funding, they often exhibit inherent limitations, including inequities in access and financial burdens on patients. These challenges have prompted a re-evaluation of existing models and the exploration of more innovative financing mechanisms.

Innovative Financing Mechanisms

Innovative financing mechanisms in healthcare refer to novel approaches that transcend conventional funding paradigms, aiming to mobilize resources more efficiently and effectively. These mechanisms are designed to address the limitations of traditional financing models while promoting sustainable healthcare initiatives (V. Kumar et al., 2022; Manjunatha et al., 2023; Pant et al., 2022; P. Verma et al., 2022).

1. **Social Impact Bonds (SIBs)**: SIBs represent a pioneering financing mechanism wherein private investors provide upfront capital for social programs aimed at improving health outcomes. The government repays these investors with interest based on the success of the program, thereby aligning

financial incentives with positive health results. This pay-for-success model fosters accountability and encourages evidence-based interventions (Behera & Singh Rawat, 2023; A. K. Mishra & Wazid, 2023; Reddy et al., 2023).

2. **Crowdfunding**: Crowdfunding has emerged as a democratized financing avenue, allowing individuals and organizations to solicit small contributions from a large number of people, typically via online platforms. This mechanism is particularly useful for funding innovative health projects, research endeavors, or medical expenses that may not be covered by traditional insurance. Crowdfunding enhances community engagement and empowers patients to take charge of their healthcare financing (Kaliappan et al., 2023; Subramani et al., 2022; Vekariya et al., 2023).

3. **Public-Private Partnerships (PPPs)**: PPPs are collaborative arrangements between governmental entities and private sector organizations aimed at leveraging resources and expertise for healthcare provision. These partnerships can facilitate infrastructure development, technological innovation, and the delivery of health services, ultimately enhancing efficiency and expanding access. PPPs exemplify a strategic alignment of public interests with private sector efficiencies (R. Arora et al., 2023; Khanna et al., 2023; S. P. Singh et al., 2023).

4. **Value-Based Financing**: This model emphasizes reimbursement based on the value of services delivered rather than the volume of services provided. By linking payment to patient outcomes, value-based financing incentivizes healthcare providers to deliver high-quality care and improve population health metrics. This approach fosters a culture of accountability and promotes the adoption of best practices in clinical care (T. Pandey et al., 2023; S. Sharma et al., 2023).

In essence, innovative financing mechanisms are instrumental in addressing the complexities of healthcare funding. By harnessing diverse sources of capital and aligning incentives with health outcomes, these mechanisms can pave the way for more equitable and sustainable healthcare systems.

Impact Investing and Healthcare

Impact investing in healthcare refers to investments made with the intention of generating measurable social and environmental benefits alongside financial returns. This investment paradigm has gained traction as stakeholders increasingly recognize the potential for capital to drive positive change within the healthcare sector (K. D. Singh et al., 2022; Uike et al., 2022).

1. **Defining Impact Investing**: Impact investing encompasses a spectrum of investment strategies aimed at addressing pressing healthcare challenges, such as access to care, health disparities, and the affordability of services. Investors seek to allocate capital to ventures that demonstrate a clear commitment to improving health outcomes, particularly for underserved populations. This approach necessitates a rigorous assessment of both financial viability and social impact, employing metrics that quantify health improvements and equitable access (Gusain et al., 2023; P. K. Juneja et al., 2022).

2. **Healthcare Ventures and Startups**: Impact investors often target innovative healthcare ventures and startups that prioritize social impact in their business models. These may include telehealth platforms that enhance access to care, digital health tools that promote preventive health measures, and technologies that address chronic disease management. By providing capital to these entities,

impact investors can facilitate the development and scaling of solutions that align with their mission to foster social good (Ahmad et al., 2023; Salama et al., 2023; S. Uniyal et al., 2021).

3. **Measurement and Accountability**: A distinctive feature of impact investing is the emphasis on measuring outcomes to ensure accountability and transparency. Investors employ frameworks such as the Global Impact Investing Network (GIIN) and the Impact Management Project (IMP) to evaluate and report on the social impact of their investments. This focus on measurement not only bolsters investor confidence but also encourages organizations to prioritize measurable health outcomes (Chandna, 2022; N. C. Joshi & Gururani, 2022; Rajbalaji et al., 2023).
4. **Challenges and Considerations**: Despite its promise, impact investing in healthcare faces several challenges, including the potential for mission drift as organizations scale and the difficulty in quantifying social impact. Additionally, the alignment of financial and social objectives can be complex, necessitating careful consideration of trade-offs and prioritization of long-term impact over short-term financial gains (Tiwari et al., 2023).

PUBLIC-PRIVATE PARTNERSHIPS (PPP) IN HEALTHCARE

Understanding PPP: Definitions and Models

Public-private partnerships (PPPs) are collaborative agreements between public sector entities—typically government agencies or ministries—and private sector organizations, including corporations and non-profit entities. These partnerships are designed to leverage the strengths of both sectors to achieve mutually beneficial outcomes, particularly in the provision of public services, infrastructure development, and innovation initiatives (I. Kumar et al., 2021; Singla et al., 2023).

1. **Definitions of PPP**: At its core, a PPP can be defined as a long-term contractual arrangement where the public sector entrusts the private sector with the responsibility of delivering services or developing infrastructure that would traditionally fall under public auspices. This arrangement encompasses a risk-sharing framework, wherein both parties contribute resources, expertise, and capital, while also distributing the risks and rewards associated with project execution (Saini et al., 2022; M. Sharma, Hagar, Krishna Murthy, Beyane, et al., 2022).
2. **Models of PPP**:
    o **Build-Operate-Transfer (BOT)**: In this model, the private partner is responsible for the construction of a facility, its operational management for a specified period, and subsequently transferring ownership back to the public entity. This model is particularly prevalent in infrastructure projects, including healthcare facilities, where it allows for rapid development without immediate public expenditure (H. Gupta et al., 2023).
    o **Design-Build-Finance-Operate (DBFO)**: This approach encompasses a broader spectrum of responsibilities for the private sector, which includes the design, financing, construction, and operational management of the project. This model incentivizes efficiency and innovation, as the private partner is accountable for delivering the project within budget and on schedule (Jindal et al., 2023).
    o **Service Contracts**: These agreements focus on specific services, where the private entity is contracted to deliver particular healthcare services, such as diagnostic testing or telehealth

consultations. This model allows for flexibility and specialization, enabling public entities to enhance service delivery without incurring the capital costs associated with full ownership (M. Gupta, Verma, et al., 2023).

- o **Joint Ventures**: In this model, public and private entities collaborate to establish a new entity for a specific project or service. This structure fosters shared governance and resource pooling, enabling both parties to capitalize on their respective strengths (R. Kumar & Khanna, 2023; K. Sharma, Pandit, et al., 2022).

In summary, the diverse models of PPPs provide a flexible framework for public and private entities to collaborate in delivering innovative solutions in healthcare, infrastructure, and service provision.

The Role of PPP in Healthcare Innovation

Public-private partnerships play a pivotal role in advancing healthcare innovation by facilitating the convergence of resources, expertise, and technological advancements from both sectors. This synergistic relationship is instrumental in addressing critical healthcare challenges, enhancing service delivery, and promoting equitable access to care (Ahmed et al., 2022; Ramachandran et al., 2023).

1. **Resource Mobilization**: PPPs enable the mobilization of diverse resources that might be scarce in the public sector alone. By leveraging private sector capital and expertise, public entities can expedite the development and implementation of innovative healthcare solutions. This is particularly relevant in the context of emerging technologies, where significant investment is often required for research, development, and scaling (Kannan et al., 2022).
2. **Innovation Acceleration**: The collaborative nature of PPPs fosters an environment conducive to experimentation and innovation. Private sector partners are typically driven by profit motives and competitive dynamics, which incentivize the exploration of novel solutions and approaches. In contrast, the public sector can provide a stable regulatory framework and access to populations that need innovative interventions, creating a fertile ground for transformative healthcare innovations (Ahmad et al., 2023; Al-Huqail et al., 2022; Tamilmani et al., 2023).
3. **Enhancing Efficiency**: PPPs can streamline healthcare delivery by introducing private sector efficiencies into public services. The incorporation of private sector management practices can lead to improved operational efficiencies, reduced waiting times, and enhanced patient experiences. This is particularly relevant in resource-constrained settings, where maximizing the use of existing infrastructure and services is essential (Josphineleela, Jyothi, et al., 2023; Masal et al., 2022; MITRA et al., 2022).
4. **Risk Sharing and Sustainability**: By distributing risks associated with healthcare projects between the public and private sectors, PPPs can enhance the sustainability of healthcare innovations. The shared responsibility for project outcomes encourages both parties to invest in risk mitigation strategies, ensuring that innovations are viable and impactful over the long term (K. S. Kumar et al., 2022; Suresh et al., 2023; Tripathy et al., 2021).
5. **Equitable Access and Outcomes**: A fundamental tenet of PPPs in healthcare innovation is the commitment to improving access and outcomes for underserved populations. Through targeted initiatives, such as mobile health clinics or telehealth services, PPPs can effectively reach margin-

alized communities, ensuring that the benefits of innovation are equitably distributed (Ghildiyal et al., 2022).

In conclusion, the role of PPPs in healthcare innovation is multifaceted, encompassing resource mobilization, acceleration of innovative solutions, efficiency enhancements, risk sharing, and a commitment to equity. This collaborative approach is essential for navigating the complexities of modern healthcare challenges.

Case Studies of Successful PPPs in Digital Health

Examining successful case studies of PPPs in digital health provides valuable insights into the practical application and impact of these collaborative models in enhancing healthcare delivery and outcomes.

1. **India's Aarogya Setu App**: Launched during the COVID-19 pandemic, the Aarogya Setu app is a prime example of a successful PPP between the Government of India and private technology companies. This mobile application employs Bluetooth and GPS technology to conduct contact tracing and disseminate information regarding COVID-19. The collaboration enabled rapid development and deployment, demonstrating how public-private synergies can effectively address public health emergencies. The app reached over 100 million users in a short period, significantly contributing to the country's pandemic response efforts (Gaurav et al., 2023).
2. **NHS Test and Trace (United Kingdom)**: The NHS Test and Trace program exemplifies a robust PPP model in which the UK government partnered with various private firms to establish a comprehensive COVID-19 testing and tracing system. This initiative involved collaboration with tech companies for developing digital platforms that facilitate test bookings, results notifications, and contact tracing. The integration of private sector technology and public health objectives enabled the rapid scaling of testing capabilities, ultimately enhancing the UK's capacity to manage the pandemic (Praveenchandar et al., 2022; Sahu & Rawat, 2023).
3. **Telemedicine Partnerships in Rural Areas**: Numerous countries have implemented successful PPPs to expand telemedicine services in rural and underserved areas. For instance, the collaboration between the government of Tanzania and private telecommunications companies established a telehealth platform that allows patients in remote locations to access medical consultations via mobile phones. This partnership has significantly improved healthcare access for rural populations, demonstrating the efficacy of leveraging private sector infrastructure to enhance public health initiatives (Medhi et al., 2023).
4. **Digital Health Initiatives in Kenya**: The M-TIBA platform in Kenya exemplifies a successful PPP model designed to facilitate health financing through mobile technology. In this initiative, the Kenyan government collaborated with private health insurers and mobile network operators to create a digital platform that allows users to save, send, and receive funds specifically for healthcare services. This innovative approach has improved financial accessibility to health services, particularly for low-income populations, thereby enhancing health outcomes (Rawat et al., 2022).

In summary, these case studies illustrate the transformative potential of public-private partnerships in the realm of digital health. By leveraging the strengths of both sectors, these collaborations have successfully addressed critical healthcare challenges, enhanced service delivery, and improved health outcomes, underscoring the efficacy of PPPs in advancing healthcare innovation.

CHALLENGES AND OPPORTUNITIES IN FINANCING DIGITAL HEALTH

Barriers to Digital Health Adoption

The adoption of digital health technologies is impeded by a myriad of multifaceted barriers that manifest at systemic, institutional, and individual levels. These barriers necessitate a comprehensive understanding and targeted interventions to facilitate the integration of digital health solutions into healthcare systems (Dogra et al., 2022; Mehershilpa et al., 2023).

1. **Technological Infrastructure Deficiencies**: A fundamental barrier to digital health adoption is the lack of robust technological infrastructure in many healthcare settings. Insufficient broadband connectivity, outdated hardware, and the absence of interoperable systems can severely limit the effective implementation of digital health technologies. This infrastructural inadequacy is particularly pronounced in rural and underserved areas, where access to reliable internet and modern devices is often constrained (P. K. Juneja et al., 2021; E. Sharma et al., 2023).
2. **Regulatory and Compliance Hurdles**: The complex and often fragmented regulatory landscape governing digital health poses significant challenges for adoption. Healthcare providers and technology developers must navigate a labyrinth of regulations pertaining to data privacy, security, and reimbursement, such as those outlined by the Health Insurance Portability and Accountability Act (HIPAA) in the United States. These regulatory requirements can create barriers to entry for innovative solutions and discourage investment in digital health initiatives (Begum et al., 2022; N. M. Kumar et al., 2023).
3. **Resistance to Change Among Healthcare Professionals**: The entrenched culture within healthcare institutions can foster resistance to adopting new technologies. Healthcare professionals may exhibit skepticism regarding the efficacy and reliability of digital health tools, particularly if they perceive these technologies as threats to their clinical autonomy or as cumbersome additions to their workflows. This resistance can impede the integration of digital solutions into established practices, ultimately affecting patient care (S. Joshi & Sharma, 2022; Mangla & Ram, 2020).
4. **Digital Literacy Disparities**: Variations in digital literacy among patients and healthcare providers can hinder the successful adoption of digital health technologies. Many patients, particularly older adults or those from disadvantaged backgrounds, may lack the necessary skills to navigate digital health platforms effectively. Similarly, healthcare providers may require training to utilize new technologies optimally. These disparities can exacerbate health inequalities, as those who are less tech-savvy may struggle to benefit from digital health innovations (P. Mishra et al., 2021; Nainwal et al., 2022).
5. **Financial Constraints**: The high initial investment required for implementing digital health solutions can pose a significant barrier. Healthcare organizations, particularly smaller practices or those in low-resource settings, may struggle to secure the necessary funding to acquire technology, train

staff, and maintain ongoing support. Additionally, uncertainties regarding reimbursement models can deter healthcare providers from investing in digital health solutions (Shukla et al., 2022; Sonnad et al., 2022; S. Uniyal et al., 2020).

Strategies for Overcoming Financing Challenges

To surmount the financing challenges associated with digital health adoption, a multifaceted approach is imperative, encompassing innovative funding mechanisms, strategic partnerships, and stakeholder engagement (Bist et al., 2022; Das et al., 2023; R. Kumar et al., 2023).

1. **Exploration of Innovative Financing Models**: Healthcare organizations should explore innovative financing mechanisms, such as social impact bonds and public-private partnerships (PPPs), to mobilize capital for digital health initiatives. By aligning financial incentives with health outcomes, these models can attract investment while ensuring that resources are directed toward projects that yield measurable benefits (Kollipara et al., 2023; N. K. Sharma et al., 2021).
2. **Leveraging Grants and Philanthropic Funding**: Identifying and applying for grants from governmental agencies, foundations, and international organizations can provide critical funding for digital health projects. By demonstrating the potential for significant health impacts, organizations can secure financial support that alleviates the burden of upfront costs associated with technology implementation (Naithani et al., 2023; M. Verma et al., 2021).
3. **Value-Based Reimbursement Models**: Advocating for the adoption of value-based reimbursement models that incentivize the use of digital health solutions can enhance the financial sustainability of these technologies. By linking reimbursement to patient outcomes and cost savings generated by digital health initiatives, stakeholders can create a more favorable financial environment for adoption (A. K. Sharma et al., 2021; M. Sharma, Kumar, Luthra, Joshi, et al., 2022).
4. **Building Collaborative Ecosystems**: Fostering collaborations among stakeholders—including healthcare providers, technology developers, payers, and policymakers—can facilitate resource sharing and risk mitigation. Collaborative ecosystems enable the pooling of expertise, data, and financial resources, enhancing the feasibility of implementing digital health solutions (Khaudiyal et al., 2022; K. Kumar et al., 2023).
5. **Conducting Cost-Benefit Analyses**: Healthcare organizations should undertake rigorous cost-benefit analyses to articulate the economic value of digital health investments. By quantifying the potential cost savings associated with improved efficiency, reduced hospitalizations, and enhanced patient outcomes, organizations can build a compelling case for investment in digital health technologies (Badhotiya et al., 2021; Shekhawat & Uniyal, 2021).

Opportunities for Stakeholders in Digital Health

The burgeoning field of digital health presents a plethora of opportunities for diverse stakeholders, including healthcare providers, technology developers, investors, and policymakers. By strategically positioning themselves within this evolving landscape, stakeholders can harness the potential of digital health to drive innovation, enhance patient care, and achieve sustainable health outcomes (Agarwal et al., 2021; Godbole et al., 2021).

1. **Enhanced Patient Engagement**: Digital health technologies facilitate improved patient engagement through tools such as telehealth, mobile health applications, and remote monitoring systems. Healthcare providers can leverage these technologies to foster proactive patient involvement in their health management, leading to better adherence to treatment plans and improved health outcomes. This shift toward patient-centered care creates opportunities for providers to strengthen relationships with their patients (Raman et al., 2023; M. Sharma, Luthra, Joshi, & Kumar, 2022).
2. **Market Expansion for Technology Developers**: The increasing demand for digital health solutions presents significant market opportunities for technology developers and startups. As healthcare organizations seek to integrate innovative tools to enhance service delivery, there is an expanding market for applications that address chronic disease management, mental health support, and telehealth services. Developers can capitalize on this demand by offering scalable, user-friendly solutions that meet the diverse needs of healthcare providers and patients (Matta & Pant, 2020).
3. **Investment Opportunities in Digital Health Ventures**: Investors are presented with lucrative opportunities in the digital health sector, particularly as the COVID-19 pandemic has accelerated the adoption of telehealth and digital health solutions. By strategically investing in startups and emerging technologies, investors can capitalize on the growth potential of this market while contributing to the transformation of healthcare delivery (Sharahiley & Kandpal, 2023).
4. **Policy Advocacy for Supportive Frameworks**: Policymakers have a critical role to play in fostering an environment conducive to digital health adoption. By advocating for supportive regulatory frameworks, reimbursement policies, and funding initiatives, policymakers can facilitate the integration of digital health technologies into healthcare systems. This advocacy creates opportunities for collaboration between public and private sectors, enhancing the overall effectiveness of healthcare delivery (Mehershilpa et al., 2023; Venkatesh et al., 2023).
5. **Improving Health Equity**: Digital health presents opportunities to address health disparities and improve access to care for underserved populations. Stakeholders can leverage digital health solutions to extend healthcare services to marginalized communities, ensuring that individuals have equitable access to essential health resources. This commitment to health equity not only enhances societal well-being but also aligns with the growing emphasis on social responsibility in healthcare (Alsadi et al., 2022; Eswar et al., 2023; S. Sharma et al., 2021).

INNOVATIVE FINANCING MODELS FOR DIGITAL HEALTH

Crowdfunding and community financing represent innovative paradigms that democratize the capital-raising process, enabling a diverse array of stakeholders to contribute to health initiatives and projects. These financing mechanisms leverage technology and community engagement to mobilize resources from a broad base of individuals and organizations (Chauhan et al., 2022; Širić et al., 2022).

1. **Crowdfunding Defined**: Crowdfunding is an entrepreneurial financing model that harnesses the collective efforts of a large number of individuals, typically facilitated through digital platforms. It allows entrepreneurs, non-profits, and innovators to solicit small contributions from a myriad of backers, thus aggregating capital for specific projects or initiatives. This approach diverges from traditional funding mechanisms by emphasizing inclusivity and community participation (M. Verma et al., 2022).

2. **Types of Crowdfunding**:
    o **Reward-Based Crowdfunding**: In this model, contributors receive non-monetary rewards in exchange for their financial support, such as early access to products or recognition on project platforms. This model is particularly prevalent in health tech innovations, where backers may receive access to new health applications or devices (Bisht et al., 2023).
    o **Equity Crowdfunding**: This variant allows investors to acquire equity stakes in a company in exchange for their financial contributions. This model democratizes investment opportunities, enabling individuals to invest in startups and small businesses that were previously accessible only to accredited investors. Equity crowdfunding is particularly pertinent in the health sector, where innovative health startups seek to develop groundbreaking solutions (Dhiman & Nagar, 2022; A. Uniyal et al., 2022).
    o **Donation-Based Crowdfunding**: Here, individuals contribute funds without expecting any financial return or reward. This model is frequently utilized by non-profit organizations and social enterprises focused on health initiatives, allowing them to raise funds for specific health-related projects or campaigns (Gonfa et al., 2023; M. Sharma, Luthra, Joshi, & Joshi, 2022).
3. **Community Financing**: Community financing encompasses a range of funding mechanisms that are community-driven and often localized. These models emphasize social cohesion and collective action to address community health needs. Mechanisms may include community loan funds, cooperative financing, and microfinance initiatives tailored to support health-related projects (Saxena et al., 2022).
4. **Advantages and Challenges**: Crowdfunding and community financing offer numerous advantages, including rapid capital mobilization, enhanced visibility for health initiatives, and increased community engagement. However, these models also face challenges, such as the potential for funding volatility, the necessity for effective marketing strategies to attract backers, and regulatory compliance concerns in certain jurisdictions (Badhotiya et al., 2022; Davuluri et al., 2023).

Venture Capital and Angel Investors

Venture capital (VC) and angel investors are pivotal components of the entrepreneurial financing landscape, particularly in the healthcare sector. These investors provide essential funding to early-stage companies with high growth potential, often in exchange for equity stakes in the ventures (Garg et al., 2023; Sathyapriya et al., 2022).

1. **Venture Capital Defined**: Venture capital refers to a form of private equity financing where investors provide capital to startups and small businesses that exhibit high growth potential in exchange for equity ownership. VC firms typically pool funds from institutional investors, high-net-worth individuals, and other sources to create a fund that targets promising early-stage ventures (Goswami & Sharma, 2022; Ram & Xing, 2023).
2. **Venture Capital Process**: The venture capital process involves several stages, including deal sourcing, due diligence, investment negotiation, and post-investment management. Venture capitalists meticulously assess potential investments through rigorous due diligence, evaluating factors such as market potential, competitive landscape, management team competence, and financial projections.

Upon identifying viable opportunities, they negotiate investment terms, including valuation, equity stake, and governance rights (Raja et al., 2022; A. Sharma et al., 2020).

3. **Angel Investors**: Angel investors are affluent individuals who provide capital to startups in their early stages, often preceding institutional venture capital investments. Angels typically invest their personal funds and may offer mentorship, industry expertise, and valuable networks alongside financial support. Their investments often play a crucial role in bridging the funding gap between initial seed capital and larger venture capital rounds (Rana et al., 2022).
4. **Advantages of VC and Angel Investments**: The infusion of capital from venture capitalists and angel investors can catalyze the growth of health startups, enabling them to develop innovative products, scale operations, and enter new markets. Additionally, the mentorship and guidance provided by experienced investors can enhance the strategic direction of the companies they support. Furthermore, successful ventures attract subsequent rounds of funding, facilitating further growth (Caiado et al., 2023).
5. **Challenges and Considerations**: While venture capital and angel investments can provide substantial financial resources, they are not without challenges. Startups may encounter pressure to deliver rapid growth and profitability, which can compromise long-term strategic goals. Additionally, the relinquishment of equity and control can pose challenges for entrepreneurs seeking to maintain their vision. The competitive nature of VC funding also necessitates that startups differentiate themselves in a crowded market to attract investment (S. Sharma et al., 2020).

Government Grants and Subsidies

Government grants and subsidies represent essential funding mechanisms that play a significant role in supporting healthcare initiatives, research, and innovation. These financial instruments are designed to alleviate financial burdens, promote public health objectives, and stimulate economic development.

1. **Government Grants Defined**: Government grants are non-repayable funds disbursed by government entities to support specific projects, programs, or research initiatives. These grants may originate from local, state, or federal levels and are typically allocated based on competitive applications that demonstrate alignment with public policy objectives and measurable outcomes.
2. **Types of Grants**:
    - **Research Grants**: These grants are awarded to researchers and institutions to support scientific investigations in healthcare and medical research. Government agencies such as the National Institutes of Health (NIH) in the United States allocate substantial funding for research grants aimed at advancing knowledge in various health domains.
    - **Programmatic Grants**: These grants are designed to fund specific health programs, such as public health initiatives, preventive health services, or health education campaigns. Programmatic grants aim to enhance community health outcomes and address pressing public health challenges.
    - **Innovation Grants**: Innovation grants are directed toward fostering new ideas and solutions in the healthcare sector. These grants may support the development and implementation of innovative technologies, processes, or models of care that have the potential to improve health outcomes and enhance efficiency.

3. **Subsidies**: Government subsidies represent financial assistance provided to individuals or organizations to reduce the cost of goods or services. In healthcare, subsidies can take various forms, including direct payments to patients to offset healthcare costs, support for the development of healthcare infrastructure, or incentives for organizations that adopt digital health solutions.
4. **Advantages of Grants and Subsidies**: Government grants and subsidies are advantageous because they provide critical funding without the burden of repayment, allowing organizations to invest in long-term projects without incurring debt. Furthermore, these financial instruments often come with the added benefit of enhancing credibility and visibility for funded initiatives, attracting additional support from other sources.
5. **Challenges and Limitations**: Despite their advantages, government grants and subsidies are not without challenges. The application process can be highly competitive and time-consuming, with stringent eligibility criteria and reporting requirements. Additionally, reliance on grant funding can create financial uncertainty, as funding cycles may vary, and organizations may face challenges in sustaining initiatives once grant funding expires.

EVALUATING THE IMPACT OF FINANCING ON DIGITAL HEALTH OUTCOMES

Key Performance Indicators (KPIs) are quantifiable metrics employed to assess the efficacy, efficiency, and impact of initiatives within the healthcare sector (Reepu et al., 2023; Taneja & Özen, 2023). These indicators serve as critical tools for evaluating performance, facilitating informed decision-making, and ensuring alignment with strategic objectives. The selection of appropriate KPIs is paramount, as they must be directly correlated with the goals of the initiative and reflect the complexities of the healthcare environment.

1. **Defining KPIs in Healthcare**: KPIs in healthcare are typically categorized into several domains, including clinical performance, operational efficiency, financial health, patient experience, and population health outcomes. These categories encapsulate a broad spectrum of metrics that can elucidate the multifaceted nature of healthcare delivery.
2. **Clinical Performance Indicators**: Clinical KPIs assess the quality of care provided to patients and are instrumental in evaluating clinical outcomes. Common clinical indicators include:
    - **Mortality Rates**: Tracking the rate of patient deaths within specific conditions or procedures, providing insight into the quality of care and effectiveness of interventions (Dangwal et al., 2022).
    - **Readmission Rates**: Monitoring the frequency of patient readmissions within a defined time frame post-discharge, indicative of care continuity and effectiveness in managing chronic conditions (Dahiya & Taneja, 2023).
    - **Adverse Event Rates**: Evaluating the incidence of medical errors or complications, which can reflect the safety and quality of healthcare delivery (Taneja & Sharma, 2023).
3. **Operational Efficiency Indicators**: These KPIs measure the efficiency of healthcare processes and resource utilization. Key operational indicators include:
    - **Average Length of Stay (ALOS)**: Calculating the average duration of patient hospitalization, which can indicate efficiency in care delivery and resource allocation (M. Gupta, Arora, et al., 2023).

- o **Patient Throughput**: Assessing the number of patients processed within a specific timeframe, providing insight into the operational capacity and efficiency of healthcare facilities (Taneja et al., 2023).
- o **Staff Utilization Rates**: Evaluating the proportion of staff time dedicated to direct patient care versus administrative tasks, reflecting operational efficiency (N. Bansal et al., 2023).
4. **Financial Health Indicators**: Financial KPIs evaluate the economic viability of healthcare organizations. Common financial metrics include:
   - o **Operating Margin**: Measuring the difference between revenues and expenses, providing insight into the financial sustainability of the organization.
   - o **Cost per Patient**: Analyzing the total cost incurred for delivering care to a single patient, helping to identify cost-saving opportunities and inefficiencies.
   - o **Revenue Cycle Efficiency**: Assessing the effectiveness of billing and collections processes, crucial for ensuring the financial stability of healthcare entities.
5. **Patient Experience Indicators**: Patient satisfaction and experience are critical components of healthcare quality. Key indicators include:
   - o **Patient Satisfaction Scores**: Gauging patient perceptions of their care experience through surveys, enabling organizations to identify areas for improvement.
   - o **Net Promoter Score (NPS)**: Measuring patient loyalty and likelihood to recommend the facility, providing insight into overall patient satisfaction.
6. **Population Health Outcomes**: These KPIs assess the health outcomes of specific populations and communities, reflecting the broader impact of healthcare initiatives. Metrics may include:
   - o **Disease Prevalence Rates**: Monitoring the incidence of specific diseases within a population, providing insight into public health trends and the effectiveness of preventive measures.
   - o **Health Equity Metrics**: Evaluating disparities in health outcomes among different demographic groups, crucial for addressing social determinants of health.

In conclusion, the meticulous selection and application of key performance indicators in healthcare are vital for assessing the effectiveness of interventions, optimizing resource allocation, and driving improvements in patient care. By employing a multifaceted approach to measurement, healthcare organizations can cultivate a culture of accountability and continuous improvement.

Economic and Health Outcomes of Innovative Financing

The implementation of innovative financing mechanisms in healthcare has profound implications for both economic and health outcomes. These mechanisms—encompassing public-private partnerships, social impact bonds, and various alternative funding strategies—can catalyze transformative changes in healthcare delivery, accessibility, and sustainability.

1. **Economic Outcomes**: Innovative financing can yield significant economic benefits, both for healthcare organizations and broader healthcare systems. Key economic outcomes include:
   - o **Cost Savings**: By promoting efficiency and reducing waste, innovative financing models can lead to substantial cost savings. For instance, programs funded through social impact bonds may incentivize preventive care, reducing the financial burden associated with hospitalizations and emergency interventions.

- **Increased Investment in Healthcare**: Innovative financing mechanisms can attract capital from non-traditional sources, including private investors and philanthropic organizations. This influx of investment enables healthcare organizations to expand services, adopt new technologies, and enhance infrastructure, ultimately leading to improved care delivery.
- **Sustainable Business Models**: Innovative financing fosters the development of sustainable business models within healthcare. For example, the integration of value-based care models incentivizes providers to focus on outcomes rather than volume, aligning financial incentives with improved patient care.

2. **Health Outcomes**: The impact of innovative financing extends to health outcomes, influencing the quality of care, access to services, and overall population health. Key health outcomes include:
   - **Improved Access to Care**: Innovative financing can enhance access to essential healthcare services, particularly for underserved populations. For example, community health programs funded through innovative mechanisms can increase the availability of preventive services, addressing health disparities and promoting health equity.
   - **Enhanced Quality of Care**: By aligning financial incentives with health outcomes, innovative financing encourages providers to prioritize quality over quantity. This shift can lead to improved clinical outcomes, such as reduced hospital readmission rates and improved management of chronic diseases.
   - **Population Health Improvements**: Innovative financing models that focus on preventive care and community health initiatives can yield significant improvements in population health outcomes. By addressing social determinants of health and promoting wellness, these models can reduce the burden of disease and enhance the overall health of communities.
3. **Measuring the Impact of Innovative Financing**: To evaluate the economic and health outcomes of innovative financing, it is essential to employ robust measurement frameworks. This may involve the use of randomized controlled trials (RCTs), longitudinal studies, and cost-effectiveness analyses to assess the impact of funded initiatives on both health outcomes and economic performance.
4. **Case Studies of Impact**: Numerous case studies illustrate the transformative potential of innovative financing in healthcare. For instance, the integration of social impact bonds in the UK to fund healthcare interventions for homeless populations has demonstrated significant reductions in emergency service utilization, translating to cost savings for the healthcare system while improving health outcomes for vulnerable individuals.

FUTURE DIRECTIONS IN HEALTHCARE FINANCING

The landscape of digital health financing is undergoing a paradigm shift, characterized by the emergence of innovative funding mechanisms that respond to the evolving needs of the healthcare ecosystem. These trends reflect a confluence of technological advancement, shifting market dynamics, and an increasing emphasis on patient-centric care.

1. **Integration of Value-Based Financing Models**: The transition from volume-based to value-based financing models has gained momentum, fostering a focus on patient outcomes rather than the quantity of services rendered. This paradigm shift incentivizes healthcare providers to invest in digital health solutions that enhance care quality and efficacy. Value-based care frameworks, such as accountable

care organizations (ACOs) and bundled payment models, are increasingly incorporating digital health technologies to track and improve patient outcomes, thereby attracting capital from investors keen on supporting sustainable healthcare initiatives (P. Kumar et al., 2024).

2. **Public-Private Partnerships (PPPs)**: The proliferation of public-private partnerships in the digital health financing arena has catalyzed collaborative initiatives that leverage the strengths of both sectors. PPPs facilitate the pooling of resources, expertise, and risk-sharing, enabling the development and implementation of innovative health technologies. These partnerships often lead to the establishment of hybrid financing models that combine government funding with private investment, thereby enhancing the scalability and sustainability of digital health initiatives (P. Kumar et al., 2024).

3. **Impact Investment**: The rise of impact investing has introduced a transformative approach to digital health financing, emphasizing the dual goals of financial return and social impact. Impact investors are increasingly directing capital toward ventures that address pressing health challenges while generating measurable outcomes. This trend has spurred the growth of social enterprises and technology startups focused on improving healthcare access, affordability, and quality, thus attracting a diverse array of investors motivated by both financial and ethical considerations.

4. **Decentralized Finance (DeFi)**: The advent of decentralized finance represents a novel trend in health financing, wherein blockchain technology facilitates peer-to-peer transactions and funding mechanisms. DeFi platforms enable the creation of transparent, efficient, and cost-effective financial solutions that can be utilized for health initiatives. This innovation holds the potential to democratize access to capital, allowing healthcare providers and startups to circumvent traditional financing intermediaries and directly engage with investors.

5. **Crowdsourcing and Community Engagement**: The proliferation of digital platforms has facilitated crowdsourcing as a viable financing mechanism for health projects. Community engagement through crowdfunding campaigns allows innovators to harness public interest and support for their initiatives. This trend not only democratizes funding but also fosters a sense of ownership among stakeholders, thereby enhancing the sustainability and impact of digital health solutions.

The Role of Technology in Healthcare Funding

The intersection of technology and healthcare funding has become increasingly pronounced, with digital innovations revolutionizing the way capital is mobilized, allocated, and utilized within the sector. Technological advancements play a critical role in enhancing transparency, efficiency, and accountability in healthcare financing.

1. **Data-Driven Decision Making**: The integration of advanced data analytics and artificial intelligence (AI) into healthcare financing processes enables stakeholders to make informed, evidence-based decisions. By analyzing vast datasets, healthcare organizations can identify funding needs, assess the impact of interventions, and allocate resources more effectively. Predictive analytics can also enhance risk assessment and management, enabling investors to make strategic decisions based on projected health outcomes.

2. **Telehealth and Remote Monitoring**: The proliferation of telehealth technologies has transformed service delivery models, expanding access to care and facilitating remote patient monitoring. These innovations have garnered significant interest from investors, as they offer the potential to improve health outcomes while reducing costs. Funding models that support the development and integration

of telehealth solutions are becoming increasingly prevalent, as stakeholders recognize the necessity of adapting to changing patient preferences and care delivery paradigms.

3. **Blockchain for Transparency and Security**: The implementation of blockchain technology in healthcare financing enhances transparency, security, and traceability of transactions. By providing an immutable ledger for financial transactions, blockchain facilitates trust among stakeholders and mitigates the risks of fraud and misallocation of resources. This technology can also streamline reimbursement processes, improve the efficiency of claims management, and enhance accountability in funding distribution.
4. **Mobile Health (mHealth) Solutions**: The proliferation of mobile health applications has revolutionized patient engagement and data collection, thereby influencing funding strategies. mHealth solutions empower patients to take charge of their health, enabling self-monitoring and real-time data sharing with providers. Funding models that incorporate mHealth initiatives are increasingly attractive to investors, as they align with the broader trend toward patient-centered care and preventative health measures.
5. **Digital Platforms for Fundraising**: The advent of digital platforms has streamlined the fundraising process, enabling healthcare organizations and startups to engage with a global audience of potential investors. These platforms facilitate access to capital through equity crowdfunding, donation-based crowdfunding, and online grant applications, thus democratizing the fundraising landscape and enabling a diverse range of stakeholders to participate in health financing.

Recommendations for Policymakers and Stakeholders

As the landscape of digital health financing evolves, it is imperative for policymakers and stakeholders to adapt to emerging trends and optimize the financing ecosystem. The following recommendations can facilitate the advancement of digital health initiatives while ensuring sustainability, equity, and efficacy:

1. **Foster Regulatory Frameworks that Encourage Innovation**: Policymakers should develop and implement regulatory frameworks that facilitate the adoption of innovative financing models in digital health. This includes streamlining the approval processes for digital health technologies, ensuring that regulations promote innovation while safeguarding patient safety and privacy.
2. **Encourage Public-Private Collaborations**: Stakeholders should actively pursue public-private partnerships that leverage the strengths of both sectors. By creating collaborative frameworks, stakeholders can pool resources, share expertise, and mitigate risks associated with the development and implementation of digital health solutions.
3. **Support Impact Investment Initiatives**: Policymakers should incentivize impact investment in healthcare by providing tax breaks, grants, or matching funds for investors who direct capital toward health initiatives that address social determinants of health and promote health equity. This can foster a more inclusive financing landscape and drive investment into underserved areas.
4. **Invest in Infrastructure and Digital Literacy**: To maximize the potential of digital health financing, stakeholders should invest in the necessary infrastructure and digital literacy programs. This includes enhancing broadband access, particularly in rural and underserved areas, and providing training for healthcare providers and patients to effectively utilize digital health technologies.

5. **Emphasize Outcomes Measurement and Accountability**: Policymakers and stakeholders must prioritize the establishment of robust frameworks for measuring the outcomes of digital health initiatives. By emphasizing accountability and transparency, stakeholders can ensure that investments are yielding tangible health benefits and driving improvements in healthcare delivery.
6. **Promote Research and Development**: Increased funding for research and development in digital health is essential to catalyze innovation. Policymakers should allocate resources to support research initiatives that explore the efficacy of digital health interventions and their impact on health outcomes, thus informing evidence-based funding strategies.

CONCLUSION

The intricate landscape of healthcare innovation financing has revealed pivotal insights that underscore the dynamic interplay between financial mechanisms, technological advancements, and the evolving healthcare ecosystem. Notably, the convergence of traditional and innovative financial paradigms—ranging from fee-for-service models to progressive strategies such as impact investing, public-private partnerships (PPPs), and decentralized finance (DeFi)—has engendered a multifaceted approach that enhances capital accessibility and fosters a more resilient financial ecosystem capable of adapting to the exigencies of modern healthcare. A discernible shift toward value-based care reflects a growing recognition of the imperative to align financial incentives with patient outcomes, as manifested in the burgeoning adoption of bundled payment models and accountable care organizations (ACOs), which incentivize providers to prioritize quality and efficiency; the integration of digital health technologies within these frameworks has been instrumental in enhancing care delivery, ultimately leading to improved patient satisfaction and health outcomes. Technological advancements have catalyzed transformative changes in healthcare financing, facilitating the emergence of new funding paradigms; the utilization of artificial intelligence (AI) and data analytics empowers stakeholders to make data-driven decisions, optimizing resource allocation and enhancing accountability, while blockchain technology introduces unprecedented levels of transparency and security in financial transactions, engendering trust among stakeholders. Furthermore, the landscape is characterized by the emergence of alternative funding sources, such as crowdfunding and community financing, which democratize access to capital and enable innovators and healthcare organizations to engage with diverse stakeholders. However, despite the progress made, significant challenges persist, including regulatory hurdles, fragmented reimbursement policies, and disparities in access to capital, necessitating a strategic approach to unlock the full potential of innovative financing mechanisms. Looking ahead, policymakers must advocate for adaptive regulatory frameworks that encourage innovation while safeguarding patient safety, fostering robust public-private collaborations to amplify the impact of healthcare innovation financing, and prioritizing capacity building and education initiatives to equip healthcare professionals and patients alike with the requisite skills and knowledge. Additionally, establishing robust frameworks for measuring the impact of healthcare innovations is imperative for ensuring accountability and transparency, while cultivating a culture of innovation within healthcare organizations will sustain progress and enable continuous adaptation to emerging challenges. Ultimately, the engagement of diverse stakeholders—including patients, healthcare providers, investors, and community organizations—is paramount for creating a comprehensive and inclusive healthcare financing ecosystem, ensuring that the perspectives and needs of various constituencies are integrated into the development and implementation of financing strategies, thereby enhancing their relevance and effectiveness. In summation, the trajectory of healthcare innovation financing, characterized by the confluence of emerging trends, technological advancements, and the imperative for strategic collaboration, presents a transformative opportunity to foster equitable access to high-quality healthcare solutions, thereby improving health outcomes for populations globally.

DECLARATION

The authors declare that the manuscript follows ethical standards and there are no potential conflicts of interest concerning this chapter's research, authorship, and publication.

DISCLAIMER

The contents and views of this chapter are expressed by the authors in personal capacities. The Editor and the Publisher don't need to agree with these viewpoints and are not responsible for any duty of care in this regard.

REFERENCES

Ada, N., Kazancoglu, Y., Sezer, M. D., Ede-Senturk, C., Ozer, I., & Ram, M. (2021). Analyzing barriers of circular food supply chains and proposing industry 4.0 solutions. *Sustainability (Basel)*, 13(12), 6812. Advance online publication. DOI: 10.3390/su13126812

Agarwal, P., Matta, P., & Sharma, S. (2021). Comparative Study of Emerging Internet-of-Things in Traffic Management System. *Proceedings of the 5th International Conference on Trends in Electronics and Informatics, ICOEI 2021*, 422 – 428. DOI: 10.1109/ICOEI51242.2021.9453083

Ahmad, I., Sharma, S., Kumar, R., Dhyani, S., & Dumka, A. (2023). Data Analytics of Online Education during Pandemic Health Crisis: A Case Study. *2nd Edition of IEEE Delhi Section Owned Conference, DELCON 2023 - Proceedings*. DOI: 10.1109/DELCON57910.2023.10127423

Ahmed, R., Das Gupta, A., Krishnamurthy, R. M., Goyal, M., Kumar, K. S., & Gangodkar, D. (2022). The Role of Smart Grid Data Analytics in Enhancing the Paradigm of Energy Management for Sustainable Development. *2022 2nd International Conference on Advance Computing and Innovative Technologies in Engineering, ICACITE 2022*, 198 – 201. DOI: 10.1109/ICACITE53722.2022.9823542

Aiyappa, S., Kodikal, R., & Rahiman, H. U. (2024). Accelerating Gender Equality for Sustainable Development: A Case Study of Dakshina Kannada District, India. *Technical and Vocational Education and Training*, 38, 335–349. DOI: 10.1007/978-981-99-6909-8_30

Ajay, D., Sharad, K., Singh, K. P., & Sharma, S. (2023). Impact of Prolonged Mental Torture on Housewives in Middle Class Families. *Journal for ReAttach Therapy and Developmental Diversities*, 6(4), 1–7.

Al-Huqail, A. A., Kumar, P., Eid, E. M., Singh, J., Arya, A. K., Goala, M., Adelodun, B., Abou Fayssal, S., Kumar, V., & Širić, I. (2022). Risk Assessment of Heavy Metals Contamination in Soil and Two Rice (Oryza sativa L.) Varieties Irrigated with Paper Mill Effluent. *Agriculture*, 12(11), 1864. Advance online publication. DOI: 10.3390/agriculture12111864

Alsadi, J., Tripathi, V., Amaral, L. S., Potrich, E., Hasham, S. H., Patil, P. Y., & Omoniyi, E. M. (2022). Architecture Fibrous Meso-Porous Silica Spheres as Enhanced Adsorbent for Effective Capturing for CO_2 Gas. *Key Engineering Materials*, 928, 39–44. DOI: 10.4028/p-2f2o01

Arora, A., Singh, R., Malik, K., & Kestwal, U. (2024). Association of sexual performance and intimacy with satisfaction in life in head and neck cancer patients: A review. *Oral Oncology Reports*, 11, 100563. Advance online publication. DOI: 10.1016/j.oor.2024.100563

Arora, R., Chauhan, A., Singh, A. P., & Sharma, R. (2023). Optimization of a production inventory model of imperfect quality items for three-layer supply chain in fuzzy environment. *Benchmarking*. Advance online publication. DOI: 10.1108/BIJ-11-2021-0678

Badhotiya, G. K., Avikal, S., Soni, G., & Sengar, N. (2022). Analyzing barriers for the adoption of circular economy in the manufacturing sector. *International Journal of Productivity and Performance Management*, 71(3), 912–931. DOI: 10.1108/IJPPM-01-2021-0021

Badhotiya, G. K., Sharma, V. P., Prakash, S., Kalluri, V., & Singh, R. (2021). Investigation and assessment of blockchain technology adoption in the pharmaceutical supply chain. In S. Y. (Ed.), *Materials Today: Proceedings* (Vol. 46, pp. 10776 – 10780). Elsevier Ltd. DOI: 10.1016/j.matpr.2021.01.673

Bansal, N., Bhatnagar, M., & Taneja, S. (2023). Balancing priorities through green optimism: A study elucidating initiatives, approaches, and strategies for sustainable supply chain management. In *Handbook of Research on Designing Sustainable Supply Chains to Achieve a Circular Economy*. IGI Global., DOI: 10.4018/978-1-6684-7664-2.ch004

Bansal, S., Kumar, V., Kumari, A., & Kuzmin, E. (2023). Understanding the Role of Digital Technologies in Supply Chain Management of SMEs. In K. V., K. G.L., A. V., & K. E. (Eds.), *Lecture Notes in Information Systems and Organisation: Vol. 61 LNISO* (pp. 195 – 205). Springer Science and Business Media Deutschland GmbH. DOI: 10.1007/978-3-031-30351-7_16

Begum, S. J. P., Pratibha, S., Rawat, J. M., Venugopal, D., Sahu, P., Gowda, A., Qureshi, K. A., & Jaremko, M. (2022). Recent Advances in Green Synthesis, Characterization, and Applications of Bioactive Metallic Nanoparticles. *Pharmaceuticals (Basel, Switzerland)*, 15(4), 455. Advance online publication. DOI: 10.3390/ph15040455 PMID: 35455452

Behera, A., & Singh Rawat, K. (2023). A brief review paper on mining subsidence and its geo-environmental impact. *Materials Today: Proceedings*. Advance online publication. DOI: 10.1016/j.matpr.2023.04.183

Belwal, R., & Belwal, S. (2017). Employers' perception of women workers in Oman and the challenges they face. *Employee Relations*, 39(7), 1048–1065. DOI: 10.1108/ER-09-2016-0183

Bhargava, A., Bhargava, D., Kumar, P. N., Sajja, G. S., & Ray, S. (2022). Industrial IoT and AI implementation in vehicular logistics and supply chain management for vehicle mediated transportation systems. *International Journal of System Assurance Engineering and Management*, 13(S1), 673–680. DOI: 10.1007/s13198-021-01581-2

Bhatt, Y., & Ghuman, K. (2022). Managerial cognition and environmental behavioral intentions: A behavioral reasoning theory perspective. *Corporate Social Responsibility and Environmental Management*, 29(5), 1315–1329. DOI: 10.1002/csr.2271

Bisht, B., Gururani, P., Aman, J., Vlaskin, M. S., Anna, I. K., Irina, A. A., Joshi, S., Kumar, S., & Kumar, V. (2023). A review on holistic approaches for fruits and vegetables biowastes valorization. *Materials Today: Proceedings*, 73, 54–63. DOI: 10.1016/j.matpr.2022.09.168

Bist, A., Dobriyal, R., Gwalwanshi, M., & Avikal, S. (2022). Influence of Layer Height and Print Speed on the Mechanical Properties of 3D-Printed ABS. In D. N. & C. A. (Eds.), *AIP Conference Proceedings* (Vol. 2481). American Institute of Physics Inc. DOI: 10.1063/5.0107304

Caiado, R. G. G., Scavarda, L. F., Vidal, G., de Mattos Nascimento, D. L., & Garza-Reyes, J. A. (2023). A taxonomy of critical factors towards sustainable operations and supply chain management 4.0 in developing countries. *Operations Management Research*. DOI: 10.1007/s12063-023-00430-8

Chandna, R. (2022). Selecting the most agile manufacturing system with respect to agile attribute-technology-fuzzy AHP approach. *International Journal of Operations Research*, 43(4), 512–532. DOI: 10.1504/IJOR.2022.122812

Chauhan, A., Sharma, N. K., Tayal, S., Kumar, V., & Kumar, M. (2022). A sustainable production model for waste management with uncertain scrap and recycled material. *Journal of Material Cycles and Waste Management*, 24(5), 1797–1817. DOI: 10.1007/s10163-022-01435-4

Dahiya, K., & Taneja, S. (2023). To Analyse the Impact of Multi-Media Technology on the Rural Entrepreneurship Development. In *Contemporary Studies of Risks in Emerging Technology* (pp. 221–240). DOI: 10.1108/978-1-80455-562-020231015

Dangwal, A., Kaur, S., Taneja, S., & Ozen, E. (2022). A bibliometric analysis of green tourism based on the scopus platform. In *Developing Relationships, Personalization, and Data Herald in Marketing 5.0*. IGI Global., DOI: 10.4018/978-1-6684-4496-2.ch015

Das, T., Thakur, R., Dhua, S., Teixeira-Costa, B. E., Beber Rodrigues, M., Pereira, M. M., Mishra, P., & Gupta, A. K. (2023). Processing of Cereals. In *Cereal Grains: Composition, Nutritional Attributes, and Potential Applications*. CRC Press., DOI: 10.1201/9781003252023-10

Das Gupta, A., Rafi, S. M., Singh, N., Gupta, V. K., Jaiswal, S., & Gangodkar, D. (2022). A Framework of Internet of Things (IOT) for the Manufacturing and Image Classifaication System. *2022 2nd International Conference on Advance Computing and Innovative Technologies in Engineering, ICACITE 2022*, 293 – 297. DOI: 10.1109/ICACITE53722.2022.9823853

Davuluri, S. K., Alvi, S. A. M., Aeri, M., Agarwal, A., Serajuddin, M., & Hasan, Z. (2023). A Security Model for Perceptive 5G-Powered BC IoT Associated Deep Learning. *6th International Conference on Inventive Computation Technologies, ICICT 2023 - Proceedings*, 118 – 125. DOI: 10.1109/ICICT57646.2023.10134487

Dhiman, G., & Nagar, A. K. (2022). Editorial: Blockchain-based 6G and industrial internet of things systems for industry 4.0/5.0. *Expert Systems: International Journal of Knowledge Engineering and Neural Networks*, 39(10), e13162. Advance online publication. DOI: 10.1111/exsy.13162

Dogra, V., Verma, D., Dalapati, G. K., Sharma, M., & Okhawilai, M. (2022). Special focus on 3D printing of sulfides/selenides for energy conversion and storage. In *Sulfide and Selenide Based Materials for Emerging Applications: Sustainable Energy Harvesting and Storage Technology*. Elsevier., DOI: 10.1016/B978-0-323-99860-4.00012-5

Dutta, A., Singh, P., Dobhal, A., Mannan, D., Singh, J., & Goswami, P. (2023). Entrepreneurial Aptitude of Women of an Aspirational District of Uttarakhand. *Indian Journal of Extension Education*, 59(2), 103–107. DOI: 10.48165/IJEE.2023.59222

Eswar, K. N. D. V. S., Doss, M. A. N., Vishnuram, P., Selim, A., Bajaj, M., Kotb, H., & Kamel, S. (2023). Comprehensive Study on Reduced DC Source Count: Multilevel Inverters and Its Design Topologies. *Energies*, 16(1), 18. Advance online publication. DOI: 10.3390/en16010018

Gangwar, V. P., & Srivastva, S. P. (2020). Impact of micro finance in poverty eradication via SHGs: A study of selected districts in U.P. *International Journal of Advanced Science and Technology*, 29(2), 3818–3829.

Garg, U., Kumar, S., & Kumar, M. (2023). A Hybrid Approach for the Detection and Classification of MQTT-based IoT-Malware. *2nd International Conference on Sustainable Computing and Data Communication Systems, ICSCDS 2023 - Proceedings*, 1154–1159. DOI: 10.1109/ICSCDS56580.2023.10104820

Gaurav, G., Singh, A. B., Khandelwal, C., Gupta, S., Kumar, S., Meena, M. L., & Dangayach, G. S. (2023). Global Development on LCA Research: A Bibliometric Analysis From 2010 to 2021. *International Journal of Social Ecology and Sustainable Development*, 14(1), 1–19. Advance online publication. DOI: 10.4018/IJSESD.327791

Ghildiyal, S., Joshi, K., Rawat, G., Memoria, M., Singh, A., & Gupta, A. (2022). Industry 4.0 Application in the Hospitality and Food Service Industries. *Proceedings of the 2022 7th International Conference on Computing, Communication and Security, ICCCS 2022 and 2022 4th International Conference on Big Data and Computational Intelligence, ICBDCI 2022*. DOI: 10.1109/ICCCS55188.2022.10079268

Godbole, V., Pal, M. K., & Gautam, P. (2021). A critical perspective on the scope of interdisciplinary approaches used in fourth-generation biofuel production. *Algal Research*, 58, 102436. Advance online publication. DOI: 10.1016/j.algal.2021.102436

Gonfa, Y. H., Tessema, F. B., Tadesse, M. G., Bachheti, A., & Bachheti, R. K. (2023). Medicinally Important Plant Roots and Their Role in Nanoparticles Synthesis and Applications. In *Secondary Metabolites from Medicinal Plants: Nanoparticles Synthesis and their Applications*. CRC Press., DOI: 10.1201/9781003213727-11

Goswami, S., & Sharma, S. (2022). Industry 4.0 Enabled Molecular Imaging Using Artificial Intelligence Technique. *2022 1st International Conference on Computational Science and Technology, ICCST 2022 - Proceedings*, 455–460. DOI: 10.1109/ICCST55948.2022.10040406

Grover, D., Sharma, S., Kaur, P., Mittal, A., & Sharma, P. K. (2024). Societal Elements that Impact the Performance of Women Entrepreneurs in Tier-II Cities: A Study of Rohilkhand Region of Uttar Pradesh. *2024 IEEE Zooming Innovation in Consumer Technologies Conference. ZINC*, 2024, 114–117. DOI: 10.1109/ZINC61849.2024.10579316

Gupta, H., Taluja, R., Shaw, S., Chari, S. L., Deepak, A., & Rana, A. (2023). Internet of Things Based Reduction of Electricity Theft in Urban Areas. *Proceedings of International Conference on Contemporary Computing and Informatics, IC3I 2023*, 2642–2645. DOI: 10.1109/IC3I59117.2023.10397868

Gupta, M., Arora, K., & Taneja, S. (2023). Bibliometric analysis on employee engagement and human resource management. In *Enhancing Customer Engagement Through Location-Based Marketing*. IGI Global., DOI: 10.4018/978-1-6684-8177-6.ch013

Gupta, M., Verma, P. K., Verma, R., & Upadhyay, D. K. (2023). Applications of Computational Intelligence Techniques in Communications. In *Applications of Computational Intelligence Techniques in Communications*. CRC Press., DOI: 10.1201/9781003452645

Gusain, I., Sharma, S., Debarma, S., Kumar Sharma, A., Mishra, N., & Prakashrao Dahale, P. (2023). Study of concrete mix by adding Dolomite in conventional concrete as partial replacement with cement. *Materials Today: Proceedings*, 73, 163–166. DOI: 10.1016/j.matpr.2022.09.583

Hajoary, P. K., Balachandra, P., & Garza-Reyes, J. A. (2023). Industry 4.0 maturity and readiness assessment: An empirical validation using Confirmatory Composite Analysis. *Production Planning and Control*. Advance online publication. DOI: 10.1080/09537287.2023.2210545

Husen, A., Bachheti, R. K., & Bachheti, A. (2021). Non-Timber Forest Products: Food, Healthcare and Industrial Applications. In *Non-Timber Forest Products: Food, Healthcare and Industrial Applications*. Springer International Publishing., DOI: 10.1007/978-3-030-73077-2

Indu, R., Dimri, S. C., & Kumar, B. (2023). Identification of Location for Police Headquarters to Deal with Crime Against Women in India Using Clustering Based on K-Means Algorithm. *International Journal of Computing and Digital Systems*, 14(1), 965–974. DOI: 10.12785/ijcds/140175

Jaswal, N., Kukreja, V., Sharma, R., Chaudhary, P., & Garg, A. (2023). Citrus Leaf Scab Multi-Class Classification: A Hybrid Deep Learning Model for Precision Agriculture. *2023 4th IEEE Global Conference for Advancement in Technology, GCAT 2023.* DOI: 10.1109/GCAT59970.2023.10353507

Jindal, G., Tiwari, V., Mahomad, R., Gehlot, A., Jindal, M., & Bordoloi, D. (2023). Predictive Design for Quality Assessment Employing Cloud Computing And Machine Learning. *2023 3rd International Conference on Advance Computing and Innovative Technologies in Engineering, ICACITE 2023*, 461 – 465. DOI: 10.1109/ICACITE57410.2023.10182915

Joshi, N. C., & Gururani, P. (2022). Advances of graphene oxide based nanocomposite materials in the treatment of wastewater containing heavy metal ions and dyes. *Current Research in Green and Sustainable Chemistry*, 5, 100306. Advance online publication. DOI: 10.1016/j.crgsc.2022.100306

Joshi, S., & Sharma, M. (2022). Sustainable Performance through Digital Supply Chains in Industry 4.0 Era: Amidst the Pandemic Experience. *Sustainability (Basel)*, 14(24), 16726. Advance online publication. DOI: 10.3390/su142416726

Josphineleela, R., Jyothi, M., Natrayan, L., Kaviarasu, A., & Sharma, M. (2023). Development of IoT based Health Monitoring System for Disables using Microcontroller. *Proceedings - 7th International Conference on Computing Methodologies and Communication, ICCMC 2023*, 1380 – 1384. DOI: 10.1109/ICCMC56507.2023.10084026

Josphineleela, R., Siva Reddy, K. V., Reddy, M. V. S. S., & Rawat, R. S. (2023). Design and Development of a Smart Sprinkler Device for IoT-Integrated Plants Irrigation. *Proceedings of the 2023 2nd International Conference on Electronics and Renewable Systems, ICEARS 2023*, 498 – 501. DOI: 10.1109/ICEARS56392.2023.10084960

Juneja, P. J., Sunori, S., Sharma, A., Sharma, A., & Joshi, V. (2020). Modeling, Control and Instrumentation of Lime Kiln Process: A Review. In S. S. & D. P. (Eds.), *Proceedings - 2020 International Conference on Advances in Computing, Communication and Materials, ICACCM 2020* (pp. 399 – 403). Institute of Electrical and Electronics Engineers Inc. DOI: 10.1109/ICACCM50413.2020.9212948

Juneja, P. K., Kumar Sunori, S., Manu, M., Joshi, P., Sharma, S., Garia, P., & Mittal, A. (2022). Potential Applications of Fuzzy Logic Controller in the Pulp and Paper Industry - A Review. *5th International Conference on Inventive Computation Technologies, ICICT 2022 - Proceedings*, 399–401. DOI: 10.1109/ICICT54344.2022.9850626

Juneja, P. K., Sunori, S. K., Sharma, A., Sharma, A., Pathak, H., Joshi, V., & Bhasin, P. (2021). A review on control system applications in industrial processes. In K. A., G. D., M. A.K., & K. A. (Eds.), *IOP Conference Series: Materials Science and Engineering* (Vol. 1022, Issue 1). IOP Publishing Ltd. DOI: 10.1088/1757-899X/1022/1/012010

Kaliappan, S., Natrayan, L., & Garg, N. (2023). Checking and Supervisory System for Calculation of Industrial Constraints using Embedded System. *Proceedings of the 4th International Conference on Smart Electronics and Communication, ICOSEC 2023*, 87 – 90. DOI: 10.1109/ICOSEC58147.2023.10275952

Kamra, J., Mani, A. P., & Tripathi, V. M. (2023). Decarbonization Trajectory in Cement Industry. In S. P., N. S., R. J.J.P.C., R. J.J.P.C., R. J.J.P.C., L.-I. G.-A. D., P. T., C. L., & P. L. (Eds.), *2023 8th International Conference on Smart and Sustainable Technologies, SpliTech 2023*. Institute of Electrical and Electronics Engineers Inc. DOI: 10.23919/SpliTech58164.2023.10193682

Kannan, P. R., Periasamy, K., Pravin, P., & Vinod Kumaar, J. R. (2022). An experimental investigation of wire breakage and performance optimisation of WEDM process on machining of recycled aluminium alloy metal matrix composite. *Materials Science Poland*, 40(3), 12–26. DOI: 10.2478/msp-2022-0030

Khandelwal, C., Kumar, S., Tripathi, V., & Madhavan, V. (2023). Joint impact of corporate governance and risk disclosures on firm value: Evidence from emerging markets. *Research in International Business and Finance*, 66, 102022. Advance online publication. DOI: 10.1016/j.ribaf.2023.102022

Khanna, L. S., Yadav, P. S., Maurya, S., & Vimal, V. (2023). Integral Role of Data Science in Startup Evolution. *Proceedings - 2023 15th IEEE International Conference on Computational Intelligence and Communication Networks, CICN 2023*, 720 – 726. DOI: 10.1109/CICN59264.2023.10402129

Khaudiyal, S., Rawat, A., Das, S. K., & Garg, N. (2022). Bacterial concrete: A review on self-healing properties in the light of sustainability. *Materials Today: Proceedings*, 60, 136–143. DOI: 10.1016/j.matpr.2021.12.277

Kollipara, V. N. H., Kalakota, S. K., Chamarthi, S., Ramani, S., Malik, P., & Karuppiah, M. (2023). Timestamp Based OTP and Enhanced RSA Key Exchange Scheme with SIT Encryption to Secure IoT Devices. *Journal of Cyber Security and Mobility*, 12(1), 77–102. DOI: 10.13052/jcsm2245-1439.1214

Kumar, I., Rawat, J., Mohd, N., & Husain, S. (2021). Opportunities of Artificial Intelligence and Machine Learning in the Food Industry. *Journal of Food Quality*, 2021, 1–10. Advance online publication. DOI: 10.1155/2021/4535567

Kumar, K., Chaudhary, S., Anandaram, H., Kumar, R., Gupta, A., & Joshi, K. (2023). Industry 4.0 and Health Care System with special reference to Mental Health. *2023 1st International Conference on Intelligent Computing and Research Trends, ICRT 2023*. DOI: 10.1109/ICRT57042.2023.10146640

Kumar, K. S., Yadav, D., Joshi, S. K., Chakravarthi, M. K., Jain, A. K., & Tripathi, V. (2022). Blockchain Technology with Applications to Distributed Control and Cooperative Robotics. *Proceedings of 5th International Conference on Contemporary Computing and Informatics, IC3I 2022*, 206 – 211. DOI: 10.1109/IC3I56241.2022.10073275

Kumar, N. M., Islam, S., Podder, A. K., Selim, A., Bajaj, M., & Kamel, S. (2023). Lifecycle-based feasibility indicators for floating solar photovoltaic plants along with implementable energy enhancement strategies and framework-driven assessment approaches leading to advancements in the simulation tool. *Frontiers in Energy Research*, 11, 1075384. Advance online publication. DOI: 10.3389/fenrg.2023.1075384

Kumar, P., Taneja, S., & Ozen, E. (2024). Exploring the influence of green bonds on sustainable development through low-carbon financing mobilization. *International Journal of Law and Management*. DOI: 10.1108/IJLMA-01-2024-0030

Kumar, R., & Khanna, R. (2023). RPA (Robotic Process Automation) in Finance & Accounting and Future Scope. *Proceedings of the 2023 2nd International Conference on Augmented Intelligence and Sustainable Systems, ICAISS 2023*, 1640–1645. DOI: 10.1109/ICAISS58487.2023.10250496

Kumar, R., Saxena, A., & Singh, R. (2023). Robotic Process Automation Bridge -in Banking Institute and Consumers. *2023 International Conference on Disruptive Technologies, ICDT 2023*, 428 – 431. DOI: 10.1109/ICDT57929.2023.10150500

Kumar, V., Pant, B., Elkady, G., Kaur, C., Suhashini, J., & Hassen, S. M. (2022). Examining the Role of Block Chain to Secure Identity in IOT for Industry 4.0. *Proceedings of 5th International Conference on Contemporary Computing and Informatics, IC3I 2022*, 256–259. DOI: 10.1109/IC3I56241.2022.10072516

Kumari, J., Singh, P., Mishra, A. K., Singh Meena, B. P., Singh, A., & Ojha, M. (2024). Challenges Hindering Women's Involvement in the Hospitality Industry as Entrepreneurs in the Era of Digital Economy. In *Revolutionizing the AI-Digital Landscape: A Guide to Sustainable Emerging Technologies for Marketing Professionals*. Taylor and Francis., DOI: 10.4324/9781032688305-9

Lokanadham, D., Sharma, R. C., Palli, S., & Bhardawaj, S. (2022). Wear Rate Modelling and Analysis of Limestone Slurry Particulate Composites Using the Fuzzy Method. *International Journal on Recent and Innovation Trends in Computing and Communication*, 10(1), 133–143. DOI: 10.17762/ijritcc.v10i1s.5818

Mangla, S. K., & Ram, M. (2020). Supply chain sustainability: Modeling and innovative research frameworks. In *Supply Chain Sustainability: Modeling and Innovative Research Frameworks*. De Gruyter. DOI: 10.1515/9783110628593

Manjunatha, B. N., Chandan, M., Kottu, S., Rappai, S., Hema, P. K., Singh Rawat, K., & Sarkar, S. (2023). A Successful Spam Detection Technique for Industrial IoT Devices based on Machine Learning Techniques. *Proceedings of the 2nd International Conference on Applied Artificial Intelligence and Computing, ICAAIC 2023*, 363 – 369. DOI: 10.1109/ICAAIC56838.2023.10141275

Masal, V., Pavithra, P., Tiwari, S. K., Singh, R., Panduro-Ramirez, J., & Gangodkar, D. (2022). Deep Learning Applications for Blockchain in Industrial IoT. *Proceedings of 5th International Conference on Contemporary Computing and Informatics, IC3I 2022*, 276–281. DOI: 10.1109/IC3I56241.2022.10073357

Matta, P., & Pant, B. (2020). TCpC: A graphical password scheme ensuring authentication for IoT resources. *International Journal of Information Technology : an Official Journal of Bharati Vidyapeeth's Institute of Computer Applications and Management*, 12(3), 699–709. DOI: 10.1007/s41870-018-0142-z

Maurya, S. K., Ghosal, A., & Manna, A. (2022). Experimental investigations during fabrication and electrical discharge machining of hybrid Al/(SiC+ZrO2+NiTi) MMC. *International Journal of Machining and Machinability of Materials*, 24(3–4), 215–230. DOI: 10.1504/IJMMM.2022.125195

Medhi, M. K., Ambust, S., Kumar, R., & Das, A. J. (2023). Characterization and Purification of Biosurfactants. In *Advancements in Biosurfactants Research*. Springer International Publishing., DOI: 10.1007/978-3-031-21682-4_4

Mehershilpa, G., Prasad, D., Sai Kiran, C., Shaikh, A., Jayashree, K., & Socrates, S. (2023). EDM machining of Ti6Al4V alloy using colloidal biosilica. *Materials Today: Proceedings*. Advance online publication. DOI: 10.1016/j.matpr.2023.02.443

Mishra, A. K., & Wazid, M. (2023). Design of a cloud-based security mechanism for Industry 4.0 communication. *ICSCCC 2023 - 3rd International Conference on Secure Cyber Computing and Communications*, 337 – 343. DOI: 10.1109/ICSCCC58608.2023.10176702

Mishra, D., Kandpal, V., Agarwal, N., & Srivastava, B. (2024). Financial Inclusion and Its Ripple Effects on Socio-Economic Development: A Comprehensive Review. *Journal of Risk and Financial Management*, 17(3), 105. Advance online publication. DOI: 10.3390/jrfm17030105

Mishra, P., Aggarwal, P., Vidyarthi, A., Singh, P., Khan, B., Alhelou, H. H., & Siano, P. (2021). VMShield: Memory Introspection-Based Malware Detection to Secure Cloud-Based Services against Stealthy Attacks. *IEEE Transactions on Industrial Informatics*, 17(10), 6754–6764. DOI: 10.1109/TII.2020.3048791

Mitra, D., Mondal, R., Khoshru, B., Senapati, A., Radha, T. K., Mahakur, B., Uniyal, N., Myo, E. M., Boutaj, H., Sierra, B. E. G. U. E. R. R. A., Panneerselvam, P., Ganeshamurthy, A. N., Elković, S. A. N. Đ. J., Vasić, T., Rani, A., Dutta, S., & Mohapatra, P. K. D. A. S.MITRA. (2022). Actinobacteria-enhanced plant growth, nutrient acquisition, and crop protection: Advances in soil, plant, and microbial multifactorial interactions. *Pedosphere*, 32(1), 149–170. DOI: 10.1016/S1002-0160(21)60042-5

Mohd, N., Kumar, I., & Khurshid, A. A. (2023). Changing Roles of Intelligent Robotics and Machinery Control Systems as Cyber-Physical Systems (CPS) in the Industry 4.0 Framework. *2023 International Conference on Communication, Security and Artificial Intelligence, ICCSAI 2023*, 647 – 651. DOI: 10.1109/ICCSAI59793.2023.10421085

Nainwal, P., Lall, S., & Nawaz, A. (2022). Physiochemical characterization of silver nanoparticles using rhizome extract of Alpinia galanga and its antimicrobial activity. *Journal of Medical Pharmaceutical and Allied Sciences. Int. Confe*, (2), 219–223. DOI: 10.22270/jmpas.VIC2I2.1830

Naithani, D., Khandelwal, R. R., & Garg, N. (2023). Development of an Automobile Hardware-in-the-Loop Test System with CAN Communication. *Proceedings of the 2023 2nd International Conference on Augmented Intelligence and Sustainable Systems, ICAISS 2023*, 1653 – 1656. DOI: 10.1109/ICAISS58487.2023.10250529

Padhi, B. K., Singh, S., Gaidhane, A. M., Abu Serhan, H., Khatib, M. N., Zahiruddin, Q. S., Rustagi, S., Sharma, R. K., Sharma, D., Arora, M., & Satapathy, P. (2024). Inequalities in cardiovascular disease among elderly Indians: A gender perspective analysis using LASI wave-I (2017-18). *Current Problems in Cardiology*, 49(7), 102605. Advance online publication. DOI: 10.1016/j.cpcardiol.2024.102605 PMID: 38692448

Pandey, R. P., Bansal, S., Awasthi, P., Dixit, V., Singh, R., & Yadava, V. (2023). Attitude and Myths Related to Stalking among Early and Middle Age Adults. *Psychology Hub, 40*(3), 85 – 94. DOI: 10.13133/2724-2943/17960

Pandey, T., Batra, A., Chaudhary, M., Ranakoti, A., Kumar, A., & Ram, M. (2023). Computation Signature Reliability of Computer Numerical Control System Using Universal Generating Function. *Springer Series in Reliability Engineering*, 149 – 158. DOI: 10.1007/978-3-031-05347-4_10

Pant, R., Gupta, A., Pant, G., Chaubey, K. K., Kumar, G., & Patrick, N. (2022). Second-generation biofuels: Facts and future. In *Relationship between Microbes and the Environment for Sustainable Ecosystem Services: Microbial Tools for Sustainable Ecosystem Services: Volume 3* (Vol. 3). Elsevier. DOI: 10.1016/B978-0-323-89936-9.00011-4

Pathak, P., Singh, M. P., Badhotiya, G. K., & Chauhan, A. S. (2021). Identification of Drivers and Barriers of Sustainable Manufacturing. *Lecture Notes on Multidisciplinary Industrial Engineering*, (Part F254), 227–243. DOI: 10.1007/978-981-15-4550-4_14

Praveenchandar, J., Vetrithangam, D., Kaliappan, S., Karthick, M., Pegada, N. K., Patil, P. P., Rao, S. G., & Umar, S. (2022). IoT-Based Harmful Toxic Gases Monitoring and Fault Detection on the Sensor Dataset Using Deep Learning Techniques. *Scientific Programming*, 2022, 1–11. Advance online publication. DOI: 10.1155/2022/7516328

Raja, S., Agrawal, A. P. P., Patil, P., Thimothy, P., Capangpangan, R. Y., Singhal, P., & Wotango, M. T. (2022). Optimization of 3D Printing Process Parameters of Polylactic Acid Filament Based on the Mechanical Test. *International Journal of Chemical Engineering*, 2022, 1–7. Advance online publication. DOI: 10.1155/2022/5830869

Rajbalaji, S., Raman, R., Pant, B., Rathour, N., Rajagopa, B. R., & Prasad, C. R. (2023). Design of deep learning models for the identifications of harmful attack activities in IIOT. *2023 International Conference on Artificial Intelligence and Smart Communication, AISC 2023*, 609 – 613. DOI: 10.1109/AISC56616.2023.10085088

Ram, M., & Xing, L. (2023). Reliability Modeling in Industry 4.0. In *Reliability Modeling in Industry 4.0*. Elsevier., DOI: 10.1016/C2021-0-01679-5

Ramachandran, K. K., Lamba, F. L. R., Rawat, R., Gehlot, A., Raju, A. M., & Ponnusamy, R. (2023). An Investigation of Block Chains for Attaining Sustainable Society. *2023 3rd International Conference on Advance Computing and Innovative Technologies in Engineering, ICACITE 2023*, 1069 – 1076. DOI: 10.1109/ICACITE57410.2023.10182462

Raman, R., Buddhi, D., Lakhera, G., Gupta, Z., Joshi, A., & Saini, D. (2023). An investigation on the role of artificial intelligence in scalable visual data analytics. *2023 International Conference on Artificial Intelligence and Smart Communication, AISC 2023*, 666–670. DOI: 10.1109/AISC56616.2023.10085495

Rana, M. S., Dixit, A. K., Rajan, M. S., Malhotra, S., Radhika, S., & Pant, B. (2022). An Empirical Investigation in Applying Reliable Industry 4.0 Based Machine Learning (ML) Approaches in Analysing and Monitoring Smart Meters using Multivariate Analysis of Variance (Manova). *2022 2nd International Conference on Advance Computing and Innovative Technologies in Engineering, ICACITE 2022*, 603–607. DOI: 10.1109/ICACITE53722.2022.9823597

Rawat, S. S., Pant, S., Kumar, A., Ram, M., Sharma, H. K., & Kumar, A. (2022). A State-of-the-Art Survey on Analytical Hierarchy Process Applications in Sustainable Development. *International Journal of Mathematical. Engineering and Management Sciences*, 7(6), 883–917. DOI: 10.33889/IJMEMS.2022.7.6.056

Reddy, P. N., Umaeswari, P., Natrayan, L., & Choudhary, A. (2023). Development of Programmed Autonomous Electric Heavy Vehicle: An Application of IoT. *Proceedings of the 2023 2nd International Conference on Electronics and Renewable Systems, ICEARS 2023*, 506–510. DOI: 10.1109/ICEARS56392.2023.10085492

Reepu, R., Taneja, S., Ozen, E., & Singh, A. (2023). A globetrotter to the future of marketing: Metaverse. In *Cultural Marketing and Metaverse for Consumer Engagement*. IGI Global., DOI: 10.4018/978-1-6684-8312-1.ch001

Sahu, S. R., & Rawat, K. S. (2023). Analysis of Land subsidencein coastal and urban areas by using various techniques– Literature Review. *The Indonesian Journal of Geography*, 55(3), 488–495. DOI: 10.22146/ijg.83675

Saini, S., Sachdeva, L., & Badhotiya, G. K. (2022). Sustainable Human Resource Management: A Conceptual Framework. *ECS Transactions*, 107(1), 6455–6463. DOI: 10.1149/10701.6455ecst

Salama, R., Al-Turjman, F., Bordoloi, D., & Yadav, S. P. (2023). Wireless Sensor Networks and Green Networking for 6G communication- An Overview. *2023 International Conference on Computational Intelligence, Communication Technology and Networking, CICTN 2023*, 830–834. DOI: 10.1109/CICTN57981.2023.10141262

Sathyapriya, G., Natarajan, U., Sureshkumar, B., Navaneethakrishnan, G., Palanisamy, R., Bajaj, M., Sharma, N. K., & Kitmo, . (2022). Quality and Tool Stability Improvement in Turning Operation Using Plastic Compliant Damper. *Journal of Nanomaterials*, 2022(1), 8654603. Advance online publication. DOI: 10.1155/2022/8654603

Saxena, A., Pant, B., Alanya-Beltran, J., Akram, S. V., Bhaskar, B., & Bansal, R. (2022). A Detailed Review of Implementation of Deep Learning Approaches for Industrial Internet of Things with the Different Opportunities and Challenges. *Proceedings of 5th International Conference on Contemporary Computing and Informatics, IC3I 2022*, 1370–1375. DOI: 10.1109/IC3I56241.2022.10072499

Sharahiley, S. M., & Kandpal, V. (2023). The impact of monetary and non-monetary reward systems upon creativity: How rational are Saudi professional employees? *International Journal of Work Organisation and Emotion*, 14(4), 339–358. DOI: 10.1504/IJWOE.2023.136599

Sharma, A., Sharma, A., Juneja, P. K., & Jain, V. (2020). Spectral Features based Speech Recognition for Speech Interfacing to Control PC Windows. In S. S. & D. P. (Eds.), *Proceedings - 2020 International Conference on Advances in Computing, Communication and Materials, ICACCM 2020* (pp. 341 – 345). Institute of Electrical and Electronics Engineers Inc. DOI: 10.1109/ICACCM50413.2020.9212827

Sharma, A. K., Sharma, A., Singh, Y., & Chen, W.-H. (2021). Production of a sustainable fuel from microalgae Chlorella minutissima grown in a 1500 L open raceway ponds. *Biomass and Bioenergy*, 149, 106073. Advance online publication. DOI: 10.1016/j.biombioe.2021.106073

Sharma, E., Rana, S., Sharma, I., Sati, P., & Dhyani, P. (2023). Organic polymers for CO2 capture and conversion. In *CO2-Philic Polymers, Nanocomposites and Solvents: Capture, Conversion and Industrial Products*. Elsevier., DOI: 10.1016/B978-0-323-85777-2.00002-0

Sharma, K., Pandit, S., Sen Thapa, B., & Pant, M. (2022). Biodegradation of Congo Red Using Co-Culture Anode Inoculum in a Microbial Fuel Cell. *Catalysts*, 12(10), 1219. Advance online publication. DOI: 10.3390/catal12101219

Sharma, M., Hagar, A. A., Krishna Murthy, G. R., Beyane, K., Gawali, B. W., & Pant, B. (2022). A Study on Recognising the Application of Multiple Big Data Technologies and its Related Issues, Difficulties and Opportunities. *2022 2nd International Conference on Advance Computing and Innovative Technologies in Engineering, ICACITE 2022*, 341 – 344. DOI: 10.1109/ICACITE53722.2022.9823623

Sharma, M., Kumar, A., Luthra, S., Joshi, S., & Upadhyay, A. (2022). The impact of environmental dynamism on low-carbon practices and digital supply chain networks to enhance sustainable performance: An empirical analysis. *Business Strategy and the Environment*, 31(4), 1776–1788. DOI: 10.1002/bse.2983

Sharma, M., Luthra, S., Joshi, S., & Joshi, H. (2022). Challenges to agile project management during COVID-19 pandemic: An emerging economy perspective. *Operations Management Research: Advancing Practice Through Research*, 15(1–2), 461–474. DOI: 10.1007/s12063-021-00249-1

Sharma, M., Luthra, S., Joshi, S., & Kumar, A. (2022). Analysing the impact of sustainable human resource management practices and industry 4.0 technologies adoption on employability skills. *International Journal of Manpower*, 43(2), 463–485. DOI: 10.1108/IJM-02-2021-0085

Sharma, N. K., Kumar, V., Verma, P., & Luthra, S. (2021). Sustainable reverse logistics practices and performance evaluation with fuzzy TOPSIS: A study on Indian retailers. *Cleaner Logistics and Supply Chain*, 1, 100007. Advance online publication. DOI: 10.1016/j.clscn.2021.100007

Sharma, S., & Bhadula, S. (2023). Secure Federated Learning for Intelligent Industry 4.0 IoT Enabled Self Skin Care Application System. *Proceedings of the 2nd International Conference on Applied Artificial Intelligence and Computing, ICAAIC 2023*, 1164 – 1170. DOI: 10.1109/ICAAIC56838.2023.10141028

Sharma, S., Gupta, A., & Tyagi, R. (2023). Sustainable Natural Resources Utilization Decision System for Better Society Using Vedic Scripture, Cloud Computing, and IoT. In B. R.C., S. K.M., & D. M. (Eds.), *Proceedings of IEEE 2023 5th International Conference on Advances in Electronics, Computers and Communications, ICAECC 2023*. Institute of Electrical and Electronics Engineers Inc. DOI: 10.1109/ICAECC59324.2023.10560335

Sharma, S., Mishra, R. R., Joshi, V., & Kour, K. (2020). Analysis and Interpretation of Global Air Quality. *2020 11th International Conference on Computing, Communication and Networking Technologies, ICCCNT 2020*. DOI: 10.1109/ICCCNT49239.2020.9225532

Sharma, S., Singh Rawal, R., Pandey, D., & Pandey, N. (2021). Microbial World for Sustainable Development. In *Microbial Technology for Sustainable Environment*. Springer Nature., DOI: 10.1007/978-981-16-3840-4_1

Shekhawat, R. S., & Uniyal, D. (2021). Smart-Bin: IoT-Based Real-Time Garbage Monitoring System for Smart Cities. *Lecture Notes in Networks and Systems*, 190, 871–879. DOI: 10.1007/978-981-16-0882-7_78

Shrivastava, A., Usha, R., Kukreti, R., Sharma, G., Srivastava, A. P., & Khan, A. K. (2023). Women Safety Precaution. *2023 1st International Conference on Circuits, Power, and Intelligent Systems, CCPIS 2023*. DOI: 10.1109/CCPIS59145.2023.10291594

Shukla, S. K., Pant, B., Viriyasitavat, W., Verma, D., Kautish, S., Dhiman, G., Kaur, A., Srihari, K., & Mohanty, S. N. (2022). An integration of autonomic computing with multicore systems for performance optimization in Industrial Internet of Things. *IET Communications*, cmu2.12505. Advance online publication. DOI: 10.1049/cmu2.12505

Singh, A. K., Singh, R., & Singh, S. (2024). A review on factors affecting and performance of nutritional security of women and children in India. In *Impact of Women in Food and Agricultural Development*. IGI Global., DOI: 10.4018/979-8-3693-3037-1.ch019

Singh, K. D., Singh, P., Chhabra, R., Kaur, G., Bansal, A., & Tripathi, V. (2023). Cyber-Physical Systems for Smart City Applications: A Comparative Study. In K. R., K. R., G. M., G. M., S. R., & S. R. (Eds.), *2023 International Conference on Advancement in Computation and Computer Technologies, InCACCT 2023* (pp. 871 – 876). Institute of Electrical and Electronics Engineers Inc. DOI: 10.1109/InCACCT57535.2023.10141719

Singh, K. D., Singh, P., Tripathi, V., & Khullar, V. (2022). A Novel and Secure Framework to Detect Unauthorized Access to an Optical Fog-Cloud Computing Network. In R. H.S., B. R., G. P.K., & S. V.K. (Eds.), *PDGC 2022 - 2022 7th International Conference on Parallel, Distributed and Grid Computing* (pp. 618 – 622). Institute of Electrical and Electronics Engineers Inc. DOI: 10.1109/PDGC56933.2022.10053223

Singh, K. U., Chaudhary, V., Sharma, P. K., Kumar, P., Varshney, N., & Singh, T. (2024). Integrating GPS and GSM Technologies for Enhanced Women's Safety: A Fingerprint-Activated Device Approach. *2024 International Conference on Automation and Computation, AUTOCOM 2024*, 657 – 662. DOI: 10.1109/AUTOCOM60220.2024.10486120

Singh, P., & Singh, K. D. (2023). Fog-Centric Intelligent Surveillance System: A Novel Approach for Effective and Efficient Surveillance. In K. R., K. R., G. M., G. M., S. R., & S. R. (Eds.), *2023 International Conference on Advancement in Computation and Computer Technologies, InCACCT 2023* (pp. 762–766). Institute of Electrical and Electronics Engineers Inc. DOI: 10.1109/InCACCT57535.2023.10141802

Singh, S. P., Piras, G., Viriyasitavat, W., Kariri, E., Yadav, K., Dhiman, G., Vimal, S., & Khan, S. B. (2023). Cyber Security and 5G-assisted Industrial Internet of Things using Novel Artificial Adaption based Evolutionary Algorithm. *Mobile Networks and Applications*. Advance online publication. DOI: 10.1007/s11036-023-02230-7

Singla, R. K., De, R., Efferth, T., Mezzetti, B., Sahab Uddin, M., Sanusi, , Ntie-Kang, F., Wang, D., Schultz, F., Kharat, K. R., Devkota, H. P., Battino, M., Sur, D., Lordan, R., Patnaik, S. S., Tsagkaris, C., Sai, C. S., Tripathi, S. K., Găman, M.-A., & Shen, B. (2023). The International Natural Product Sciences Taskforce (INPST) and the power of Twitter networking exemplified through #INPST hashtag analysis. *Phytomedicine*, 108, 154520. Advance online publication. DOI: 10.1016/j.phymed.2022.154520 PMID: 36334386

Širić, I., Eid, E. M., Taher, M. A., El-Morsy, M. H. E., Osman, H. E. M., Kumar, P., Adelodun, B., Abou Fayssal, S., Mioč, B., Andabaka, Ž., Goala, M., Kumari, S., Bachheti, A., Choi, K. S., & Kumar, V. (2022). Combined Use of Spent Mushroom Substrate Biochar and PGPR Improves Growth, Yield, and Biochemical Response of Cauliflower (Brassica oleracea var. botrytis): A Preliminary Study on Greenhouse Cultivation. *Horticulturae*, 8(9), 830. Advance online publication. DOI: 10.3390/horticulturae8090830

Sonnad, S., Awasthy, M., Rane, K., Banerjee, M., Buddhi, D., & Pant, B. (2022). Blockchain-Based Secure Mengers Authentication for Industrial IoT. In D. R.K., S. A.Kr., K. G., & B. S. (Eds.), *Proceedings of the 2022 11th International Conference on System Modeling and Advancement in Research Trends, SMART 2022* (pp. 853–858). Institute of Electrical and Electronics Engineers Inc. DOI: 10.1109/SMART55829.2022.10046934

Srivastava, B., Kandpal, V., & Jain, A. K. (2024). Financial well-being of women self-help group members: A qualitative study. *Environment, Development and Sustainability*. Advance online publication. DOI: 10.1007/s10668-024-04879-w

Subramani, R., Kaliappan, S., Kumar, P. V. A., Sekar, S., De Poures, M. V., Patil, P. P., & Raj, E. S. E. (2022). A Recent Trend on Additive Manufacturing Sustainability with Supply Chain Management Concept, Multicriteria Decision Making Techniques. *Advances in Materials Science and Engineering*, 2022, 1–12. Advance online publication. DOI: 10.1155/2022/9151839

Suresh, M., Antony, J., Nair, G., & Garza-Reyes, J. A. (2023). Lean-sustainability assessment framework development: Evidence from the construction industry. *Total Quality Management & Business Excellence*, 34(15–16), 2046–2081. DOI: 10.1080/14783363.2023.2222088

Tamilmani, S., Mohan, T., Jeyalakshmi, S., Shukla, G. P., Gehlot, A., & Shukla, S. K. (2023). Blockchain Integrated with Industrial IOT Towards Industry 4.0. *2023 International Conference on Artificial Intelligence and Smart Communication, AISC 2023*, 575–581. DOI: 10.1109/AISC56616.2023.10085226

Taneja, S., Gupta, M., Bhushan, P., Bhatnagar, M., & Singh, A. (2023). Cultural marketing in the digital era. In *Cultural Marketing and Metaverse for Consumer Engagement*. IGI Global., DOI: 10.4018/978-1-6684-8312-1.ch008

Taneja, S., & Özen, E. (2023). To analyse the relationship between bank's green financing and environmental performance. *International Journal of Electronic Finance*, 12(2), 163–175. DOI: 10.1504/IJEF.2023.129919

Taneja, S., & Sharma, V. (2023). Role of beaconing marketing in improving customer buying experience. In *Enhancing Customer Engagement Through Location-Based Marketing*. IGI Global., DOI: 10.4018/978-1-6684-8177-6.ch012

Thentral, T. M. T., Usha, S., Palanisamy, R., Geetha, A., Alkhudaydi, A. M., Sharma, N. K., Bajaj, M., Ghoneim, S. S. M., Shouran, M., & Kamel, S. (2022). An energy efficient modified passive power filter for power quality enhancement in electric drives. *Frontiers in Energy Research*, 10, 989857. Advance online publication. DOI: 10.3389/fenrg.2022.989857

Tiwari, R., Agrawal, P., Singh, P., Bajaj, S., Verma, V., & Chauhan, A. S. (2023). Technology Enabled Integrated Fusion Teaching for Enhancing Learning Outcomes in Higher Education. *International Journal of Emerging Technologies in Learning*, 18(7), 243–249. DOI: 10.3991/ijet.v18i07.36799

Tripathi, V. M., & Mohan, A. (2016). Microfinance and empowering rural women in the Terai, Uttarakhand, India. *International Journal of Agricultural and Statistics Sciences*, 12(2), 523–530.

Tripathy, S., Verma, D. K., Thakur, M., Patel, A. R., Srivastav, P. P., Singh, S., Chávez-González, M. L., & Aguilar, C. N. (2021). Encapsulated Food Products as a Strategy to Strengthen Immunity Against COVID-19. *Frontiers in Nutrition*, 8, 673174. Advance online publication. DOI: 10.3389/fnut.2021.673174 PMID: 34095193

Uike, D., Agarwalla, S., Bansal, V., Chakravarthi, M. K., Singh, R., & Singh, P. (2022). Investigating the Role of Block Chain to Secure Identity in IoT for Industrial Automation. In D. R.K., S. A.Kr., K. G., & B. S. (Eds.), *Proceedings of the 2022 11th International Conference on System Modeling and Advancement in Research Trends, SMART 2022* (pp. 837 – 841). Institute of Electrical and Electronics Engineers Inc. DOI: 10.1109/SMART55829.2022.10047385

Uniyal, A., Prajapati, Y. K., Ranakoti, L., Bhandari, P., Singh, T., Gangil, B., Sharma, S., Upadhyay, V. V., & Eldin, S. M. (2022). Recent Advancements in Evacuated Tube Solar Water Heaters: A Critical Review of the Integration of Phase Change Materials and Nanofluids with ETCs. *Energies*, 15(23), 8999. Advance online publication. DOI: 10.3390/en15238999

Uniyal, S., Mangla, S. K., & Patil, P. (2020). When practices count: Implementation of sustainable consumption and production in automotive supply chains. *Management of Environmental Quality*, 31(5), 1207–1222. DOI: 10.1108/MEQ-03-2019-0075

Uniyal, S., Mangla, S. K., Sarma, P. R. S., Tseng, M.-L., & Patil, P. (2021). ICT as "Knowledge management" for assessing sustainable consumption and production in supply chains. *Journal of Global Information Management*, 29(1), 164–198. DOI: 10.4018/JGIM.2021010109

Vekariya, D., Rastogi, A., Priyadarshini, R., Patil, M., Kumar, M. S., & Pant, B. (2023). Mengers Authentication for efficient security system using Blockchain technology for Industrial IoT(IIOT) systems. *2023 3rd International Conference on Advance Computing and Innovative Technologies in Engineering, ICACITE 2023*, 894 – 896. DOI: 10.1109/ICACITE57410.2023.10182454

Venkatesh, J., Shukla, P. K., Ahanger, T. A., Maheshwari, M., Pant, B., Hemamalini, R. R., & Halifa, A. (2023). A Complex Brain Learning Skeleton Comprising Enriched Pattern Neural Network System for Next Era Internet of Things. *Journal of Healthcare Engineering*, 2023(1), 2506144. Advance online publication. DOI: 10.1155/2023/2506144

Verma, M., Ahmad, W., Park, J.-H., Kumar, V., Vlaskin, M. S., Vaya, D., & Kim, H. (2022). One-step functionalization of chitosan using EDTA: Kinetics and isotherms modeling for multiple heavy metals adsorption and their mechanism. *Journal of Water Process Engineering*, 49, 102989. Advance online publication. DOI: 10.1016/j.jwpe.2022.102989

Verma, M., Sharma, S., Kumar, A., Kumar, V., Kim, M., Hong, Y., Lee, I., & Kim, H. (2021). Application of green nanomaterials in catalysis industry. In *Green Nanomaterials for Industrial Applications*. Elsevier., DOI: 10.1016/B978-0-12-823296-5.00013-7

Verma, P., Chaudhari, V., Dumka, A., & Singh, R. P. (2022). A Meta-Analytical Review of Deep Learning Prediction Models for Big Data. In *Encyclopedia of Data Science and Machine Learning*. IGI Global., DOI: 10.4018/978-1-7998-9220-5.ch023

Zhang, Y., Cao, C., Gu, J., & Garg, H. (2023). The Impact of Top Management Team Characteristics on the Risk Taking of Chinese Private Construction Enterprises. *Systems*, 11(2), 67. Advance online publication. DOI: 10.3390/systems11020067

Chapter 13
Navigating Challenges and Innovations in Global Healthcare

Malkeet Singh
https://orcid.org/0009-0008-7222-0391
Chaudhary Devi Lal University, India

Khem Chand
https://orcid.org/0000-0001-7879-5198
Lovely Professional University, India

Mandeep Singh
Chandigarh University, India

ABSTRACT

Telemedicine and remote care have redefined the contours of healthcare delivery by bridging geographical barriers and enhancing accessibility, particularly in underserved and low-income communities. This chapter delves into the evolution of telemedicine, underscoring its transformative role in reducing disparities in healthcare access. It further explores the cost-effectiveness of telehealth models, presenting data to illustrate affordability and long-term economic viability. The chapter concludes by analyzing the macroeconomic impact of expanding telemedicine services, including workforce shifts, infrastructural investments, and implications for healthcare policy. The potential of telemedicine to recalibrate the healthcare landscape is immense, but it demands thoughtful integration with existing systems, regulatory foresight, and continuous technological innovation to ensure equitable, sustainable care.

INTRODUCTION

Telemedicine, a term that encompasses the delivery of healthcare services and clinical information using telecommunication technology, has revolutionized the contemporary healthcare paradigm (Ritika et al., 2024). The confluence of digital innovation and medical practice has rendered geographical borders increasingly irrelevant, enabling the provision of medical care to populations residing in the remotest, most underserved corners of the globe (M. Gupta et al., 2024). As the exigencies of healthcare evolve and adapt to the demands of a globalized, yet fragmented world, the ascendancy of telemedicine has been nothing short of transformative (S. Gupta et al., 2024).

Historically, access to healthcare has been a privilege disproportionately concentrated in urban centers and affluent societies (Bhatt & Dani, 2024). This geographical inequity has, for centuries, perpetuated disparities in health outcomes, with low-income and rural populations suffering from a paucity of medical resources, personnel, and infrastructure (Jena et al., 2024). The advent of telemedicine, however, heralds the dismantling of these long-standing barriers, offering a more egalitarian model of healthcare delivery. In low-income settings, where traditional healthcare systems are often beleaguered by logistical inefficiencies, understaffing, and inadequate infrastructure, the potential of telemedicine is particularly pronounced (Mukul et al., 2024).

The digitalization of healthcare has paved the way for what can be seen as a democratization of medical services, whereby access to critical health interventions is no longer tethered to the physical proximity of medical professionals (Danilov, 2021). Through telemedicine, patients can access consultations, diagnostics, and follow-up care without the constraints of time and distance—an unprecedented shift in the delivery of healthcare services. Telemedicine's ability to provide timely interventions, especially in critical care scenarios, can significantly reduce morbidity and mortality rates, as well as ameliorate the chronic burden on overextended healthcare systems (Starks, 2023).

Moreover, the COVID-19 pandemic has acted as a catalytic force, accelerating the integration of telemedicine into mainstream healthcare systems worldwide (Biermans et al., 2023; Chiu et al., 2022). During the pandemic, the exigent need to minimize physical interactions between patients and healthcare providers spurred the widespread adoption of telehealth solutions. This pivot not only mitigated the immediate risks of virus transmission but also demonstrated the efficacy of remote healthcare models in addressing both acute and chronic medical conditions (Anghel & Lupu, 2024; Busch, 2023). Consequently, the post-pandemic landscape is witnessing the entrenchment of telemedicine as a permanent fixture within the healthcare continuum (Partiti, 2024).

Yet, the promise of telemedicine extends beyond mere convenience and accessibility. Its cost-effectiveness and scalability position it as an indispensable tool for resource-constrained environments. By obviating the need for physical infrastructure and minimizing the demand for large, in-person medical staff, telemedicine offers a pathway to more efficient, economically sustainable healthcare delivery (Cunha et al., 2021; Ho et al., 2024; Nyambuu & Semmler, 2023). Additionally, its inherent flexibility allows for the development of tailored solutions that can accommodate the specific needs of diverse patient populations, particularly those in marginalized or geographically isolated communities (Segovia-Vargas et al., 2023).

This chapter will explore the multifaceted impact of telemedicine on expanding healthcare access, with a particular focus on its implications for low-income settings. The discussion will elucidate the economic benefits and cost-saving mechanisms inherent in telemedicine, as well as its capacity to alleviate the systemic inefficiencies that plague traditional healthcare delivery models (Moneva et al., 2023). Furthermore, this chapter will investigate the macroeconomic ramifications of telemedicine's expansion, including the shifts in workforce allocation, infrastructure development, and the evolving regulatory frameworks that underpin this burgeoning field (McGuigan et al., 2017).

The narrative of telemedicine's ascendancy is also intrinsically tied to technological advancements. The proliferation of high-speed internet, the ubiquity of smartphones, and the increasing sophistication of artificial intelligence (AI) and machine learning (ML) technologies have coalesced to create an ecosystem wherein telehealth can thrive (Lauesen, 2016). However, while the technological infrastructure supporting telemedicine is rapidly advancing, significant challenges remain, particularly concerning digital equity, data privacy, and the seamless integration of telehealth platforms with existing healthcare systems (Zeidan, 2022).

In sum, this chapter positions telemedicine not merely as a temporary response to global healthcare crises, but as a transformative modality that can fundamentally reshape how healthcare is delivered and accessed (Streimikiene et al., 2023). By leveraging digital tools, remote care has the potential to bridge the gap between healthcare haves and have-nots, reducing inequities that have persisted for generations. Nonetheless, the true realization of telemedicine's potential hinges on addressing the technological, regulatory, and ethical challenges that accompany its proliferation. As we delve deeper into the socio-economic and healthcare implications of telemedicine, the ensuing sections will underscore its promise and pitfalls, offering a holistic perspective on its role in the future of global healthcare delivery (S. Sharma & Kumar, 2023).

1. THE EVOLUTION OF TELEMEDICINE: A BRIEF HISTORY

Telemedicine's roots trace back several decades, evolving from early forms of remote consultation via radio and telephone to today's sophisticated video conferencing and AI-driven diagnostic platforms. Initial use cases focused on bridging gaps in geographically isolated areas, but the COVID-19 pandemic accelerated its global adoption, making telemedicine a cornerstone of modern healthcare (Rosman et al., 2024).

Table 1. The evolution of telemedicine

Time Period	Development	Description
Early 20th Century	Telegraph and Telephone Consultations	The rudimentary form of telemedicine emerged with doctors using telegraphs and telephones to provide remote consultations in emergency situations, especially for maritime and military operations. This marked the initial use of telecommunications in healthcare, although the technology was primitive and limited to verbal exchanges (Ritika et al., 2024).
1960s	NASA and Space Exploration	NASA pioneered telemedicine during space missions, enabling astronauts to receive medical care while in orbit. Remote physiological monitoring and the transmission of biomedical data became crucial for maintaining the health of astronauts. This innovation demonstrated the feasibility of remote healthcare delivery in extreme environments (M. Gupta et al., 2024).
1970s	Early Telemedicine Experiments	Several government-funded projects in the U.S. and Europe began experimenting with telemedicine, including programs like the STARPAHC project, which connected doctors at the Papago Indian Reservation in Arizona with specialists at the Space Technology Applied to Rural Papago Health Care program. Telemedicine was extended to underserved rural communities (Bhatt & Dani, 2024).
1980s	Telemedicine for Rural Areas	Telemedicine was increasingly used to address the healthcare needs of rural and remote populations, particularly in Canada and the United States. Developments in satellite communication allowed for more reliable video consultations, although the technology was still costly and only implemented in select regions with limited healthcare access (Jena et al., 2024).

continued on following page

Table 1. Continued

Time Period	Development	Description
1990s	Introduction of Video Conferencing in Healthcare	Advances in digital technology and telecommunications infrastructure, including fiber-optic networks and video conferencing, facilitated real-time remote consultations. This period saw the first large-scale telemedicine projects, such as the Alaska telemedicine program, connecting rural Alaskan communities with urban medical centers for specialist consultations (Mukul et al., 2024).
2000s	Proliferation of Internet-Based Telemedicine	With the rise of the internet and broadband connectivity, telemedicine platforms became more widely accessible. Remote patient monitoring and teleradiology emerged as important fields, enabling the transmission of medical images and patient data over long distances. This period marked the beginning of telemedicine's integration into mainstream healthcare (B. Srivastava et al., 2024).
2010s	Mobile Health (mHealth) and Telehealth Expansion	The ubiquity of smartphones and mobile applications led to the rise of mobile health (mHealth), which allowed patients to monitor health conditions through apps and devices. Telemedicine services expanded rapidly as high-speed internet became more accessible globally. Telemedicine platforms began to include AI-based diagnostics and electronic health records (EHRs) (Govindarajan et al., 2023).
2020 (COVID-19 Era)	Global Surge in Telemedicine Use Due to the COVID-19 Pandemic	The COVID-19 pandemic acted as a tipping point for telemedicine adoption worldwide, as healthcare systems rapidly shifted to remote care to minimize in-person interactions. Regulatory barriers were temporarily relaxed, and insurance providers expanded coverage for telehealth services. The pandemic accelerated the normalization of telemedicine as a core healthcare tool (S. Yadav et al., 2024).
2020s (Post-Pandemic)	Telemedicine as a Core Component of Healthcare Delivery	Telemedicine continued to evolve with the integration of AI and machine learning for diagnostics, the use of wearable health tech for continuous monitoring, and the expansion of telehealth into mental health, chronic care management, and remote surgery. Telemedicine is increasingly viewed as a permanent fixture in healthcare systems, particularly for underserved areas (P. Kumar et al., 2024).

1.1 Historical Milestones

Early Telemedicine Initiatives: NASA's Space Exploration Projects

The nascent stages of telemedicine are indelibly tied to the exigencies of space exploration, with NASA spearheading some of the earliest and most consequential ventures into remote healthcare. These initiatives were predicated upon the need to monitor the physiological well-being of astronauts during missions where immediate in-person medical intervention was logistically impossible. In the 1960s, as part of NASA's Gemini and Apollo programs, telemedicine emerged as a critical adjunct to space exploration, with real-time biomedical telemetry systems developed to relay astronauts' vital signs—such as heart rate, blood pressure, and oxygen saturation—back to Earth. These groundbreaking systems enabled medical professionals on Earth to monitor the astronauts' health, diagnose potential issues, and even provide treatment recommendations remotely, marking the dawn of telemedicine's practical applications (Bansal et al., 2023; K. Dahiya & Taneja, 2023; M. Gupta et al., 2023; Taneja & Özen, 2023).

The Space Technology Applied to Rural Papago Advanced Health Care (STARPAHC) project in the 1970s further exemplified NASA's contributions to telemedicine. In this project, NASA collaborated with the Indian Health Service to deliver healthcare to the Papago (now Tohono O'odham) Nation in Arizona, utilizing telecommunications technology initially developed for space missions. This program was a precursor to contemporary telemedicine, establishing that remote healthcare delivery could transcend space-bound applications to address terrestrial healthcare disparities, particularly in geographically isolated regions.

Expansion into Civilian Healthcare

The principles and technologies pioneered in space-related telemedicine initiatives soon found fertile ground within civilian healthcare systems (Dangwal et al., 2022; Reepu et al., 2023; Taneja, Gupta, et al., 2023; Taneja & Sharma, 2023). By the 1970s and 1980s, telemedicine began to migrate from the confined ambit of space exploration to address the broader public health challenge of healthcare access in remote and underserved communities. This was particularly relevant in rural areas where specialist care was sparse, and the infrastructure to support regular medical services was lacking (D. Mishra et al., 2024).

In the United States, Canada, and several European countries, pilot telemedicine projects were launched to address the healthcare needs of rural populations. For instance, in Alaska, telemedicine was deployed to connect remote Native Alaskan communities with urban healthcare providers (Agarwal et al., 2024; Deng et al., 2024; A. Sharma et al., 2024). These early civilian telemedicine programs employed rudimentary communication technologies, such as radio links, satellite systems, and slow-scan video, to facilitate consultations between patients in remote locations and specialists in distant urban centers. These initiatives, though limited by the technological constraints of the era, illustrated the vast potential of telemedicine to mitigate healthcare inequities by delivering medical expertise across great distances (Gangwar & Srivastva, 2020).

As the field expanded, telemedicine services diversified. Initially focused on consultations and diagnosis, telemedicine gradually incorporated teleradiology (the transmission of radiographic images) and telepsychiatry, broadening the scope of its applications. The gradual infusion of telemedicine into civilian healthcare systems was further facilitated by government funding and increased recognition of the need to address rural-urban health disparities (Caiado et al., 2023).

Technological Leaps: From Analog Communication to Digital Health Platforms

Telemedicine's evolution from its rudimentary analog origins to today's sophisticated digital health platforms represents a quantum leap in both technological capacity and healthcare delivery methodology (Gopal et al., 2023; C. Gupta et al., 2022). The analog era of telemedicine, characterized by the use of basic telecommunications technologies such as telephone lines, radio waves, and satellite communication, was hamstrung by several limitations. Bandwidth restrictions, high operational costs, and suboptimal video and audio quality constrained the scope and efficiency of early telemedicine services. Real-time interactions were often hampered by latency issues, and the analog infrastructure could not support the transmission of complex medical data, such as high-resolution medical imaging or real-time monitoring of multiple biometric signals (K. Kumar et al., 2025; R. Rawat, Goyal, et al., 2023; R. Rawat, Sharma, et al., 2023; Širić et al., 2022).

The advent of the digital revolution in the 1990s, marked by the proliferation of high-speed internet and the maturation of digital telecommunications infrastructure, catalyzed an unprecedented transformation in telemedicine. Digitalization allowed for the seamless transmission of high-fidelity data, including diagnostic images, video consultations, and electronic health records (EHRs). This shift enabled telemedicine to move beyond simple consultations to encompass a broad array of services, including remote diagnostics, telemonitoring, and even robotic-assisted surgery.

High-speed broadband connectivity facilitated real-time video conferencing, enabling healthcare providers to interact with patients and colleagues across the globe with minimal latency and enhanced clarity. Moreover, the integration of EHR systems allowed for the secure sharing of patient data between healthcare professionals, fostering continuity of care even when physical distance separated patient and provider. The development of cloud-based telemedicine platforms further augmented the scalability and accessibility of telehealth services, making them increasingly affordable and widely available (Asha et al., 2022; Sati et al., 2022; K. D. Singh et al., 2023; Tomar et al., 2023; Tyagi et al., 2022).

The proliferation of mobile health (mHealth) in the 2010s, driven by the ubiquitous adoption of smartphones and wearable health technology, further accelerated telemedicine's penetration into mainstream healthcare. Patients could now monitor chronic conditions, manage medication adherence, and even receive AI-driven diagnostic recommendations via their mobile devices. Meanwhile, healthcare providers could leverage big data analytics and machine learning algorithms to predict health outcomes, personalize treatment plans, and improve patient engagement.

In sum, the trajectory of telemedicine from its early analog roots to today's digital ecosystems reflects a confluence of technological innovation, shifting healthcare needs, and a growing recognition of the importance of equitable healthcare access. These advancements have transformed telemedicine into a cornerstone of modern healthcare, poised to address some of the most pressing challenges in global health today (Chauhan et al., 2023).

2. IMPROVING ACCESS TO HEALTHCARE IN LOW-INCOME SETTINGS

Low-income communities often face myriad barriers to healthcare, including insufficient infrastructure, a shortage of medical professionals, and high out-of-pocket costs. Telemedicine offers a powerful solution to these challenges by enabling remote consultations, reducing travel costs, and streamlining referral processes (Ranakoti et al., 2022).

2.1 Geographical Barriers

Geographical Barriers: Bridging Rural and Urban Healthcare Disparities

The bifurcation of healthcare accessibility along rural-urban lines remains one of the most entrenched inequities within global health systems. Rural populations, disproportionately encumbered by geographic isolation, often grapple with the lack of proximate healthcare facilities, a dearth of specialized medical personnel, and the logistical exigencies of traversing vast distances for care. This disparity is exacerbated by the limited availability of continuous, high-quality medical services in rural areas, leading to prolonged delays in diagnosis, suboptimal treatment regimens, and a consequent exacerbation of preventable morbidity and mortality rates. The maldistribution of healthcare resources has thus perpetuated a chasm between urban affluence and rural paucity, a fissure that telemedicine, in its myriad modalities, seeks to ameliorate (Sunori et al., 2023).

Telemedicine's ascendancy as a tool for bridging these healthcare disparities is predicated on its capacity to transcend physical distance, thereby dismantling the geographical barriers that have historically circumscribed healthcare delivery. Through the deployment of digital health platforms, remote consultations, and telemonitoring systems, rural patients can now access the same caliber of medical expertise and diagnostic acumen as their urban counterparts, without the onerous necessity of geographical relocation. This technological facilitation of care effectively equalizes healthcare provision across demographic lines, eroding the urban hegemony over specialist consultations and advanced diagnostic tools.

Furthermore, the integration of telemedicine into rural health ecosystems fosters a bi-directional flow of knowledge and resources between urban centers of medical expertise and rural localities. Specialists, formerly confined to urban hospitals and academic medical centers, are now able to deliver high-level consultations and second opinions to rural physicians in real-time, ensuring that complex medical cases are managed with precision and expediency. This not only elevates the standard of care in rural areas but also mitigates the need for costly and time-consuming patient transfers to urban tertiary care facilities (Arora et al., 2023; Dieudonne et al., 2022; P. Singh & Singh, 2023).

The Role of Mobile Health Units

Integral to the telemedicine apparatus in overcoming geographical barriers is the deployment of mobile health units (MHUs), which serve as critical adjuncts to fixed healthcare infrastructure, particularly in regions where even basic medical facilities are scarce or non-existent. MHUs, equipped with diagnostic tools, communication technologies, and often medical personnel, represent a versatile and dynamic mechanism for delivering healthcare to the most remote, underserved populations. These units can traverse vast, inhospitable terrains—be it deserts, mountains, or hinterlands—bringing both preventive and curative services directly to the doorstep of those for whom access to healthcare is a luxury rather than a given (Pant et al., 2022).

In regions characterized by poor infrastructural development and challenging topographies, where permanent healthcare facilities may be impractical or economically infeasible, MHUs act as the vanguard of healthcare delivery. These units can offer a wide range of services, from routine screenings and immunizations to complex diagnostic tests and teleconsultations with urban-based specialists, facilitated through satellite or mobile internet connections. MHUs are often equipped with telemedicine devices that allow for the transmission of patient data, such as electrocardiograms (ECGs) or ultrasound images, to remote medical hubs for analysis, further diminishing the reliance on local medical expertise, which is often in short supply (M. Sharma, Hagar, et al., 2022).

The integration of telemedicine into the MHU model enhances its utility by enabling real-time diagnostics and specialist input, thus ensuring that rural patients receive immediate, contextually relevant medical care. For instance, mobile health units equipped with digital stethoscopes, portable imaging devices, and point-of-care diagnostic tools can collect medical data from patients in real time and transmit it via secure networks to urban-based specialists. This allows for remote diagnosis and treatment plans to be devised without necessitating patient travel, further democratizing access to advanced medical care (Vennila et al., 2022).

In addition, MHUs serve as critical platforms for public health initiatives, including mass vaccination campaigns, maternal and child health programs, and chronic disease management in rural settings. The combination of on-the-ground medical personnel and telemedicine technology amplifies the reach and efficacy of such initiatives, making MHUs a linchpin in the broader effort to bridge the rural-urban healthcare divide (Khan et al., 2023).

In summary, the role of telemedicine, augmented by mobile health units, is pivotal in deconstructing geographical barriers to healthcare. By decentralizing the provision of medical services and integrating remote care into local contexts, telemedicine has the potential to not only ameliorate rural healthcare disparities but also to create a more resilient and equitable healthcare system globally (Elbagory et al., 2022).

2.2 Challenges in Low-Income Regions

The deployment of telemedicine within low-income regions, while brimming with potential to alleviate healthcare inequities, is impeded by a constellation of challenges that fundamentally limit its efficacy and scalability (A. Kaur, Kumar, Taneja, et al., 2023; P. Kumar, Bhatnagar, & Taneja, 2023; P. Sharma et al., 2024; Taneja, Bhatnagar, et al., 2023). Among the most pernicious of these barriers are the dual constraints of limited digital literacy and inadequate internet connectivity. These infrastructural and socio-educational impediments exacerbate existing disparities, thwarting the universal adoption of telehealth solutions in environments that could most benefit from their implementation. The complexities of these challenges, particularly in regions where healthcare infrastructure is already under duress, demand a nuanced analysis of the structural limitations that continue to hamper the realization of telemedicine's transformative potential (Papageorgiou et al., 2023).

Limited Digital Literacy

Digital literacy, or the capacity to effectively navigate, understand, and engage with digital technologies, constitutes a critical determinant of telemedicine's success. In low-income regions, however, the proliferation of telemedicine platforms often outpaces the population's ability to interact with such technologies competently. This disparity is not merely a reflection of economic deprivation but is also deeply rooted in the historical neglect of education systems in these regions, where basic literacy itself may be suboptimal, let alone the nuanced competencies required to engage with digital health tools. Consequently, limited digital literacy stands as a formidable barrier to the widespread adoption and effective use of telemedicine (Kunwar et al., 2023; Malik et al., 2023; B. Rawat et al., 2022).

For telemedicine to function optimally, patients must be able to navigate user interfaces, comprehend medical instructions delivered via digital platforms, and engage in virtual consultations—all of which presuppose a baseline familiarity with digital devices and platforms. However, in regions where exposure to digital technology is limited, many individuals lack the skills necessary to utilize these tools effectively, leading to miscommunication, suboptimal health outcomes, and in some cases, total disengagement from telemedicine services. The intricate interplay between digital literacy and healthcare access in low-income regions is further compounded by socio-cultural factors, such as age and gender disparities, with elderly populations and women in particular often being excluded from digital education initiatives.

Moreover, the healthcare providers in these regions may themselves be inadequately trained in telemedicine technologies, exacerbating the problem. The limited availability of continuous professional development and technological training for healthcare workers in low-income settings undermines the potential for seamless integration of telemedicine into routine healthcare delivery (Rajeswari et al., 2022; Shukla et al., 2023; Thakur et al., 2023). Without a concerted effort to enhance digital literacy, both among patients and providers, telemedicine risks becoming an exclusive rather than an inclusive solution, perpetuating rather than mitigating healthcare disparities.

Poor Internet Connectivity

Perhaps the most immediate and palpable challenge facing telemedicine in low-income regions is the pervasive inadequacy of internet infrastructure. Telemedicine's reliance on high-speed, stable internet connections for the transmission of medical data, real-time video consultations, and remote monitoring necessitates robust digital infrastructure, which remains severely lacking in many low-income regions. Poor internet connectivity, often characterized by intermittent access, low bandwidth, and slow data transmission speeds, creates a bottleneck that stifles the full utilization of telemedicine platforms (Bhushan & Nayak, 2022; MITRA et al., 2022; William et al., 2023).

In many low-income countries, particularly in rural and peripheral areas, internet penetration remains abysmally low, and even where internet services are available, they are often unreliable and prohibitively expensive. The geographic and infrastructural constraints that plague these regions—ranging from mountainous terrains to politically unstable environments—further exacerbate the challenge of establishing stable internet networks. As a result, patients and healthcare providers are frequently unable to engage in the real-time communication that is essential for telemedicine, rendering remote consultations ineffective or incomplete. The promise of telemedicine to deliver timely and accurate medical interventions is fundamentally undermined when connectivity issues disrupt the flow of information between patient and provider, leading to diagnostic delays and treatment interruptions (S. S. Rawat et al., 2022; M. Sharma, Kumar, et al., 2022; Shekhar et al., 2022).

Additionally, the lack of internet infrastructure in low-income regions impedes the deployment of more advanced telemedicine applications, such as artificial intelligence (AI)-driven diagnostics, cloud-based health records, and remote surgical interventions, all of which require high-speed data transmission. The digital divide, thus, not only precludes basic telehealth services but also stymies the introduction of cutting-edge healthcare technologies that could otherwise revolutionize care delivery in resource-poor settings (Giri et al., 2022; Gonfa et al., 2023; Singla et al., 2023; A. Srivastava et al., 2023).

In response to these challenges, various stopgap measures have been proposed, such as the use of offline telemedicine models or the leveraging of mobile networks in lieu of traditional broadband infrastructure. However, these solutions, while useful in the short term, are limited in their capacity to deliver the full spectrum of telemedicine services, especially as healthcare needs become more complex. Without substantial investment in digital infrastructure, telemedicine risks remaining a fragmented, underutilized modality in low-income regions.

2.3 Success Stories

The integration of telemedicine into healthcare systems across the Global South provides a fertile ground for analysis, offering insights into the interplay between technology, socioeconomic structures, and health outcomes in regions historically marginalized by the global healthcare infrastructure. India, Sub-Saharan Africa, and Latin America each present distinct telemedicine ecosystems, shaped by diverse geopolitical, cultural, and infrastructural conditions. In each region, telemedicine initiatives have been both constrained and catalyzed by local circumstances, yielding varied outcomes that reflect the complex dynamics of healthcare delivery in low- and middle-income settings (Behera & Singh Rawat, 2023; G. Kumar, Kumar, Singhal, et al., 2023; A. Singh et al., 2021).

India: Telemedicine as a Catalyst for Bridging Healthcare Gaps

India's vast geography, coupled with its heterogeneity in healthcare access across urban and rural divides, makes it a pertinent case study for telemedicine implementation. The Indian government, in collaboration with private entities and non-governmental organizations, has launched several telemedicine initiatives aimed at bridging the chasm between its urban centers of medical excellence and its largely underserved rural hinterlands (Chand et al., 2023; V. Kumar, Mitra, et al., 2021; S. Uniyal et al., 2022).

One notable initiative is the eSanjeevani Telemedicine Service, which was instituted by the Ministry of Health and Family Welfare. This platform provides both doctor-to-doctor and patient-to-doctor teleconsultations. The former connects rural healthcare centers with specialists in tertiary care hospitals, allowing local healthcare workers to receive guidance on complex medical cases. The latter enables direct interaction between patients and physicians, thereby mitigating the inaccessibility of healthcare in remote areas.

Despite its successes, telemedicine in India is challenged by the digital divide, with limited internet penetration in rural areas impeding its widespread adoption. Additionally, the heterogeneous linguistic and cultural landscape of India presents a barrier to the uniform dissemination of telemedicine services, as platforms must cater to a diverse populace with varying levels of digital literacy. Nevertheless, initiatives like Apollo TeleHealth and the Indian Space Research Organization's telemedicine program, which leverages satellite technology to provide healthcare in remote areas, have showcased the potential of telemedicine in overcoming India's profound healthcare inequities (Aloo et al., 2023; S. Jain & Jain, 2021; A. Kumar, Pant, & Ram, 2023; H. R. Sharma et al., 2021).

Sub-Saharan Africa: Telemedicine in the Context of Fragile Health Systems

Sub-Saharan Africa presents a unique milieu in which telemedicine operates against a backdrop of fragile health systems, limited infrastructure, and widespread rural poverty. However, these very challenges have rendered telemedicine an invaluable tool in compensating for the chronic lack of healthcare personnel and facilities. Across the region, innovative models of telemedicine have emerged, often driven by partnerships between local governments, international organizations, and tech companies (Paul et al., 2022; Rai et al., 2022; M. Sharma & Singh, 2023).

A case in point is Amref Health Africa's mHealth initiative, which has deployed mobile health platforms to provide health services to rural and underserved populations. The platform primarily focuses on maternal and child health, delivering health information, diagnostic services, and remote consultations via mobile phones. Given that mobile phone penetration is significantly higher than internet access in Sub-Saharan Africa, mHealth has become the primary vehicle for telemedicine in the region. These services, often delivered via SMS or voice calls, allow patients to receive medical advice in real-time, bypassing the need for physical travel to distant healthcare facilities (Akberdina et al., 2023; Alsadi et al., 2022).

Another pioneering initiative is Babyl Rwanda, a digital health platform developed by Babylon Health. Babyl Rwanda enables patients to access consultations with healthcare professionals via mobile phones. The platform, supported by the Rwandan Ministry of Health, has been transformative in a country where healthcare infrastructure is sparse, and doctor-to-patient ratios are critically low. Babyl Rwanda integrates with the country's health insurance system, making it affordable and accessible to the broader population (A. Kumar, Goyal, & Sharma, 2023).

While telemedicine initiatives in Sub-Saharan Africa have made significant inroads, the region's low bandwidth, erratic electricity supply, and linguistic diversity continue to pose challenges. Moreover, the lack of regulatory frameworks for telemedicine raises concerns regarding patient privacy, data security, and the standardization of care (N. K. Sharma et al., 2021; A. Srivastava et al., 2022; Wongchai et al., 2022).

Latin America: Telemedicine as a Tool for Expanding Specialist Access

In Latin America, telemedicine has been deployed with varying levels of success across countries, addressing critical healthcare issues such as specialist shortages and the geographic isolation of rural communities. Countries like Brazil, Mexico, and Chile have been at the forefront of adopting telemedicine to ameliorate regional healthcare disparities, particularly in the provision of specialist care (Mekala et al., 2023; Mitra et al., 2022; S. Sharma, Kadayat, et al., 2023).

Brazil's Sistema Único de Saúde (SUS), the country's national health system, has integrated telemedicine into its framework to extend specialist consultations to remote areas through the Telessaúde Brasil Redes initiative. The program facilitates teleconsultations, second opinions, and educational sessions between healthcare professionals in rural areas and specialists in urban centers. In a country where the Amazon rainforest and other remote regions remain largely inaccessible, telemedicine has proven to be a critical asset in ensuring equitable healthcare delivery (V. Kumar & Korovin, 2023; Rao et al., 2023; Vijayalakshmi et al., 2022).

Chile's Red Nacional de Telesalud has similarly leveraged telemedicine to provide specialist consultations in regions with limited healthcare infrastructure. Through the Teletón Chile program, telemedicine is used to support pediatric care, particularly for children with disabilities. The program connects local healthcare providers with specialists at the country's main pediatric hospital, mitigating the need for families to undertake long and arduous journeys to urban centers for specialized care (R. Kumar, Lamba, Mohammed, et al., 2023; Tiwari et al., 2023; Tomar & Sharma, 2021).

In Mexico, the Salud Móvil program focuses on providing mobile-based healthcare services, including telemedicine, in rural and indigenous communities. The program has integrated telemedicine into the country's broader public health framework, allowing patients in remote areas to access primary care, chronic disease management, and mental health services.

However, despite these advances, the success of telemedicine in Latin America is tempered by political instability, underfunded healthcare systems, and uneven digital infrastructure. Additionally, the region's wide socioeconomic disparities exacerbate the challenges of scaling telemedicine services, particularly in indigenous and marginalized communities where digital literacy and internet access remain low.

3. COST-EFFECTIVENESS AND AFFORDABILITY OF TELEMEDICINE SOLUTIONS

Telemedicine's appeal extends beyond its convenience and accessibility. The economic benefits of remote care are manifold, with evidence suggesting significant cost savings for both healthcare systems and patients. However, telemedicine's affordability hinges on strategic implementation, regulatory support, and the capacity for scale (Kukreti et al., 2023; A. Kumar, Sharma, Chauhan, et al., 2023; A. K. Mishra et al., 2023).

3.1 Reducing Patient Costs

Elimination of Travel Expenses

Telemedicine's capacity to eliminate travel-related expenses represents one of its most conspicuous economic benefits for patients, particularly in rural and remote areas where access to healthcare services often necessitates arduous journeys. In regions where healthcare facilities are sparse, patients are frequently required to traverse significant distances to seek medical attention, incurring costs associated with transportation, lodging, and lost wages due to time off work. The deployment of telemedicine platforms obviates the need for physical travel, enabling patients to consult with healthcare providers from the comfort of their homes or local health centers.

The financial relief provided by telemedicine is especially critical for individuals in low-income brackets, for whom the cumulative costs of travel for multiple appointments may constitute an insurmountable burden. This reduction in ancillary expenses democratizes access to healthcare, allowing economically disadvantaged populations to receive timely medical attention without the prohibitive financial strain that often accompanies in-person visits to distant hospitals or clinics. Moreover, the reduction of travel also diminishes the environmental impact of healthcare-related journeys, contributing to broader sustainability goals (S. Gupta et al., 2023; A. Kaur, Kukreja, Chamoli, et al., 2023b; Suryavanshi, Tanwar, et al., 2023).

Reduced Hospital Admissions and Lengths of Stay

Telemedicine's potential to decrease hospital admissions and reduce the duration of inpatient stays further underscores its economic advantages. By facilitating early interventions, telehealth platforms enable healthcare providers to manage chronic conditions, monitor post-operative recovery, and address acute medical issues before they escalate into more serious conditions that require hospitalization. Remote patient monitoring technologies, for instance, allow clinicians to track real-time biometric data and intervene at the first sign of deterioration, thereby preempting the need for costly emergency room visits or inpatient care (Ansari & Afzal, 2022; Jindal, Kukreja, Mehta, Chauhan, et al., 2023; Suryavanshi, Kukreja, et al., 2023).

Furthermore, for patients who do require hospitalization, telemedicine can streamline the discharge process and facilitate continuous post-discharge monitoring, thus minimizing the likelihood of readmissions. This not only alleviates the financial burden on patients but also enhances the overall efficiency of healthcare systems, as reduced lengths of stay free up hospital beds and other resources for more critical cases. In this way, telemedicine serves as both a cost-saving mechanism for patients and a strategic tool for optimizing the utilization of healthcare infrastructure (Dubey et al., 2023; A. Kaur, Kukreja, Nisha Chandran, et al., 2023; A. R. Yadav et al., 2023).

3.2 Economic Efficiency for Healthcare Providers

Lower Operational Costs for Clinics and Hospitals

From the perspective of healthcare providers, telemedicine offers a substantial reduction in operational costs, particularly in relation to the maintenance of physical infrastructure and the provision of in-person services. By transitioning a portion of consultations, diagnostics, and follow-up appointments to virtual platforms, clinics and hospitals can reduce overhead expenditures associated with maintaining large facilities, including utilities, staffing, and consumables. Telemedicine enables a more flexible and scalable model of care delivery, wherein the same level of service can be provided with fewer physical resources.

Additionally, telemedicine platforms reduce the demand for hospital-based services such as inpatient care, diagnostic imaging, and laboratory tests, all of which contribute to the cost savings. For outpatient clinics, the virtual consultation model minimizes the need for large waiting areas and extensive administrative support, while also reducing the incidence of no-shows or missed appointments, thereby improving overall revenue streams. For healthcare systems already stretched by resource constraints, these cost efficiencies are critical in ensuring financial sustainability (Banerjee et al., 2023; A. Kaur, Kukreja, Chamoli, et al., 2023a; A. Mishra et al., 2023; Y. Singh et al., 2023).

Optimizing Workforce Allocation

Telemedicine also facilitates the more judicious allocation of healthcare personnel, ensuring that human resources are deployed where they are most needed. By decentralizing care delivery, telemedicine allows providers to manage larger patient volumes without the need for an equivalent increase in on-site staff. Physicians and specialists can conduct remote consultations across multiple locations, enabling them to serve both urban and rural populations more efficiently (S. Sharma & Tyagi, 2023).

Furthermore, telemedicine platforms can triage patients more effectively, ensuring that only those who require in-person intervention are referred to physical clinics or hospitals. This optimisation of workforce allocation is particularly advantageous in regions facing acute shortages of healthcare workers, as it allows for the extension of specialist care to underserved populations without overburdening existing medical staff. Through this more strategic deployment of personnel, telemedicine enhances both the efficiency and the equity of healthcare delivery systems (Singhal et al., 2023).

3.3 Technology Investment

Upfront Costs of Telehealth Platforms vs. Long-Term Savings

The financial outlay associated with the establishment of telehealth platforms constitutes a significant investment for healthcare providers and governments. These upfront costs include the procurement of telemedicine infrastructure—such as video conferencing tools, electronic health record (EHR) integration, remote monitoring devices, and cybersecurity frameworks—as well as the training of healthcare staff in the use of these technologies. In low-income and resource-constrained environments, these initial investments can pose a substantial barrier to the widespread adoption of telemedicine (Kholiya et al., 2023).

However, these costs must be evaluated against the long-term savings generated by the implementation of telehealth solutions. Once operational, telemedicine platforms can substantially reduce recurrent expenses, particularly by minimizing the need for physical infrastructure, reducing hospital admissions, and streamlining administrative processes. Additionally, telehealth can enhance preventative care, mitigating the long-term costs associated with untreated chronic conditions and delayed diagnoses. Thus, while the initial financial commitment may be considerable, the long-term economic benefits of telemedicine—both in terms of direct cost savings and enhanced healthcare outcomes—are significant and enduring (K. K. Singh et al., 2023).

The Role of Public-Private Partnerships in Funding Telehealth Infrastructure

To offset the substantial upfront costs of telehealth technology, public-private partnerships (PPPs) have emerged as a critical mechanism for funding the expansion of telemedicine infrastructure. By leveraging the financial resources, technological expertise, and logistical networks of private sector entities, governments and healthcare systems can accelerate the deployment of telehealth solutions without bearing the full financial burden. These partnerships often involve collaborations between technology firms, telecommunications companies, and healthcare providers, with each party contributing to the creation and maintenance of telemedicine ecosystems (G. Kaur et al., 2023).

For instance, private companies may provide the necessary hardware and software solutions, while public entities facilitate regulatory frameworks, subsidies, and integration into national health systems. In many low-income regions, where public health budgets are limited, such partnerships are essential to the scalability and sustainability of telemedicine initiatives. Moreover, PPPs can foster innovation by allowing for the continuous upgrading of telemedicine platforms, ensuring that healthcare systems remain at the forefront of technological advancements while maintaining financial viability (M. Dahiya et al., 2023).

4. ECONOMIC IMPACT OF EXPANDING TELEHEALTH SERVICES

The macroeconomic implications of telemedicine go beyond immediate healthcare delivery. A shift toward remote care creates ripple effects across industries, with substantial impacts on employment, technology investment, and health policy. Expanding telemedicine services requires rethinking not only healthcare infrastructure but also the broader economic environment (Pandey et al., 2023).

4.1 Workforce Shifts

The Rise of Telehealth Specialists and Tech-Enabled Roles

As telemedicine expands its footprint in global healthcare systems, it has precipitated the emergence of new professional paradigms, necessitating the rise of telehealth specialists and tech-enabled roles that occupy a unique confluence between clinical expertise and digital proficiency. Telehealth specialists are medical professionals whose practice is specifically adapted for virtual consultation, remote diagnostics, and digital therapeutic interventions. These specialists operate in a paradigm that requires not only profound medical knowledge but also a keen aptitude for navigating advanced telemedicine platforms and digital tools (Jindal, Kukreja, Mehta, Srivastava, et al., 2023).

Moreover, the ascendancy of telemedicine has given rise to a new class of healthcare workers—telehealth technologists—whose primary responsibility lies in ensuring the seamless operation of the digital infrastructures upon which telemedicine depends. These professionals, often hailing from a confluence of healthcare and information technology disciplines, are tasked with maintaining the integrity of telehealth platforms, integrating medical records into electronic health systems, and optimizing the user experience for both patients and providers. Additionally, roles such as remote patient monitoring coordinators and virtual care coordinators are increasingly vital, overseeing the continuous tracking of patient data and ensuring the efficient allocation of healthcare resources in digital care settings (V. Jain et al., 2023).

The intersection of healthcare and technology has also spurred the creation of medical AI specialists, responsible for integrating artificial intelligence into telehealth platforms, where algorithms can assist in diagnostics, predictive analytics, and treatment recommendations. These roles signal a profound transformation in the healthcare workforce, where the delineation between traditional medical practice and technological expertise is becoming increasingly blurred, resulting in a new breed of healthcare professionals who are equally versed in clinical care and digital innovation (S. Sharma, Kandpal, et al., 2023).

Re-Training and Upskilling of Healthcare Professionals for Remote Service Delivery

The rapid proliferation of telemedicine necessitates the re-training and upskilling of healthcare professionals to adapt to remote service delivery models. Traditional clinical training, which prioritizes in-person patient interactions, must now be supplemented with competencies in virtual communication, digital diagnostics, and the effective use of telemedicine technologies. Physicians, nurses, and allied health professionals are required to undergo rigorous training programs to acclimate themselves to the nuances of remote consultation, which differ markedly from the conventional in-person diagnostic process.

Upskilling initiatives are crucial in teaching healthcare professionals to interpret digital health data, manage telehealth platforms, and ensure patient engagement in a virtual environment. These programs often emphasize the importance of maintaining a high standard of care while navigating the limitations inherent in telemedicine, such as the inability to perform physical examinations. Moreover, healthcare providers must be adept at using remote diagnostic tools, wearable devices, and AI-powered applications to make informed clinical decisions without direct patient contact.

In addition to technical skills, the upskilling process also encompasses the development of soft skills, such as building rapport with patients in a virtual setting, fostering patient trust, and ensuring compliance with digital health interventions. This re-training not only ensures the efficacy of telemedicine but also preserves the humanistic element of care, which can be challenging to maintain in a remote context.

4.2 Infrastructural Investments

The Need for Robust Telecommunications Networks and Data Security Frameworks

The successful implementation and scalability of telemedicine hinge critically on the robustness of telecommunications infrastructure and the establishment of comprehensive data security frameworks. Telemedicine's reliance on real-time data transmission, video consultations, and remote monitoring requires high-speed, stable internet connections that can facilitate seamless interactions between healthcare providers and patients. In regions where telecommunications networks are underdeveloped, telemedicine is either limited or rendered entirely impractical, underscoring the need for significant investments in digital infrastructure.

Telecommunications networks must be sufficiently resilient to handle large volumes of data traffic, especially as telemedicine platforms grow in sophistication, integrating high-definition video, biometric data transmission, and AI-driven diagnostics. The advent of 5G technology offers a potential solution, promising faster, more reliable connections that could support the future growth of telemedicine. However, in low-income regions, where digital infrastructure is often sparse, achieving the necessary bandwidth and coverage will require targeted investment, both from governments and private entities, as well as public-private partnerships.

Equally critical to the telemedicine infrastructure is the establishment of robust data security frameworks. The transmission of sensitive health information over digital platforms heightens the risk of cyberattacks, data breaches, and unauthorized access to patient records. Thus, the creation of secure, encrypted telehealth platforms is paramount in safeguarding patient privacy and maintaining the integrity of medical data. Regulatory bodies and healthcare institutions must work in tandem with cybersecurity experts to develop protocols that ensure compliance with data protection laws while implementing the latest security technologies, such as blockchain, to protect against data tampering and unauthorized access.

4.3 Healthcare Policy and Regulation

Telemedicine Laws and Reimbursement Policies

The widespread adoption of telemedicine necessitates a re-evaluation of existing healthcare policies, particularly regarding legal frameworks and reimbursement mechanisms. Telemedicine laws must account for the complex jurisdictional issues that arise when healthcare is delivered across state or national boundaries. In some regions, outdated laws and licensing requirements act as barriers to telemedicine, limiting the ability of physicians to provide care remotely to patients in different geographical areas. Regulatory reform is essential to establish clear guidelines on telemedicine licensure, medical malpractice, and liability, ensuring that both patients and providers are protected within the virtual care ecosystem (R. Kumar, Malhotra, & Grover, 2023).

In tandem with legal reforms, the development of comprehensive reimbursement policies is critical to incentivizing healthcare providers to adopt telemedicine. Historically, telehealth services have been undercompensated in comparison to in-person consultations, creating a financial disincentive for providers to embrace digital care models. To remedy this, governments and insurance companies must implement reimbursement parity between telehealth and traditional services, ensuring that healthcare providers are fairly compensated for remote consultations, diagnostics, and treatments. Moreover, reimbursement policies should encompass a broader range of telemedicine services, including remote monitoring and telepharmacy, to reflect the evolving landscape of digital healthcare (Malhotra et al., 2022).

Balancing Innovation with Patient Protection and Data Privacy

As telemedicine continues to evolve, healthcare policymakers are tasked with the delicate balance of fostering innovation while safeguarding patient protection and data privacy. Telemedicine's rapid growth has introduced new complexities in the realm of medical ethics, particularly concerning informed consent, confidentiality, and the secure handling of patient data. Policymakers must ensure that innovation in telemedicine does not outpace the development of regulatory safeguards designed to protect patients from exploitation, negligence, or privacy breaches (R. Kumar & Khanna, 2023b).

Data privacy, in particular, is a paramount concern, as the digitization of healthcare records and the proliferation of telemedicine platforms increase the risk of personal health information being exposed or misused. National and international regulations, such as the General Data Protection Regulation (GDPR) in the European Union and the Health Insurance Portability and Accountability Act (HIPAA) in the United States, provide a legal framework for the protection of patient data. However, as telemedicine becomes more ubiquitous, these regulations must be continually updated to address new threats posed by emerging technologies, such as AI, cloud computing, and big data analytics (R. Kumar, Malholtra, Singh, et al., 2023).

Ultimately, the future of telemedicine will depend on the ability of healthcare systems to strike a harmonious balance between embracing technological innovation and maintaining the ethical and legal frameworks necessary to protect patients in an increasingly digital healthcare environment.

5. CHALLENGES AND FUTURE DIRECTIONS IN TELEMEDICINE

While the advantages of telemedicine are clear, significant challenges remain. Regulatory frameworks vary widely across countries, and concerns about data privacy and security are paramount. Additionally, the digital divide must be addressed to ensure equitable access for all populations. The future of telemedicine lies in advancing technology (e.g., AI-driven diagnostics), improving interoperability between health systems, and integrating telehealth into traditional care models (R. Kumar, Khannna Malholtra, & Grover, 2023).

Inconsistent Telehealth Regulations Across Jurisdictions

The heterogeneity of telehealth regulations across various jurisdictions constitutes a formidable barrier to the seamless integration of telemedicine into healthcare systems. This regulatory dissonance manifests in disparate licensure requirements, reimbursement policies, and standards of practice that govern telehealth services, leading to a fragmented landscape that complicates the provision of care across state and national lines. As telemedicine transcends geographical boundaries, healthcare providers often find themselves navigating a labyrinth of inconsistent regulations, which can hinder their ability to deliver timely and effective care (P. Sharma, Malhotra, et al., 2022).

The implications of such regulatory inconsistency are particularly pronounced in countries with federal structures, where states or provinces may implement divergent telehealth policies that affect practitioners' ability to provide services remotely. For instance, some jurisdictions may impose stringent licensure requirements that prohibit out-of-state providers from offering telehealth consultations, thus exacerbating existing healthcare disparities in underserved areas. This patchwork of regulations not only creates logistical challenges for healthcare providers but also impedes patients' access to necessary care, particularly in rural or remote locations where local resources may be limited (Neha et al., 2023).

Licensing Issues for Cross-Border Consultations

Licensing issues further complicate the telemedicine landscape, particularly concerning cross-border consultations. As healthcare increasingly adopts a transnational character, the necessity for uniform licensing standards becomes paramount. However, the existing framework often entails a complex web of state and national licensing boards, each with its own stipulations, leading to substantial barriers for healthcare professionals who wish to extend their services beyond their home jurisdiction (Joshi et al., 2022).

In many instances, providers may encounter protracted administrative processes, excessive fees, and regulatory obstacles when attempting to obtain licensure in multiple jurisdictions, disincentivizing participation in telehealth initiatives. This situation is especially problematic for specialists whose expertise may be in high demand in underserved areas lacking adequate healthcare resources. Consequently, the lack of a streamlined and harmonized licensing process not only restricts the mobility of healthcare professionals but also impedes patients' access to specialized care, perpetuating inequities within healthcare systems (R. Kumar, Singh, Mohanty, et al., 2023).

5.2 Technological Barriers

Data Security and Patient Privacy

In the digital realm of telemedicine, the paramount concerns of data security and patient privacy represent significant technological barriers that must be addressed to ensure the effective implementation of remote healthcare solutions. The transmission and storage of sensitive health information over digital platforms inherently elevate the risk of data breaches, cyberattacks, and unauthorized access, necessitating robust cybersecurity measures to safeguard patient confidentiality (Kanojia et al., 2022).

Healthcare providers are compelled to adopt stringent data protection protocols and encryption technologies to mitigate risks associated with the sharing of electronic health records (EHRs) and other sensitive information. Moreover, compliance with regulations such as the Health Insurance Portability and Accountability Act (HIPAA) in the United States or the General Data Protection Regulation (GDPR) in Europe is essential to protect patient privacy and maintain trust in telehealth services. Failure to adhere to these standards not only exposes healthcare organizations to legal repercussions but also undermines patient confidence in the safety of telemedicine platforms (Awal & Khanna, 2019).

Furthermore, the complexity of securing data within integrated telehealth ecosystems can pose challenges, particularly as multiple stakeholders—such as third-party technology vendors, cloud service providers, and healthcare institutions—interact within the same digital framework. The need for comprehensive cybersecurity strategies that encompass every facet of the telemedicine ecosystem is thus critical in ensuring the integrity of patient information and fostering trust in digital healthcare solutions (Upreti & Malhotra, 2024).

Digital Literacy and Access to Reliable Internet

Digital literacy emerges as another formidable barrier to the effective adoption of telemedicine, particularly among populations with varying degrees of technological proficiency. The successful utilization of telehealth platforms necessitates a baseline level of digital literacy, which encompasses not only the ability to operate devices and software but also an understanding of how to navigate virtual healthcare encounters effectively. Individuals lacking digital literacy may face challenges in scheduling appointments, accessing telehealth resources, or communicating effectively with healthcare providers in a virtual setting (R. Kumar et al., 2024).

Additionally, disparities in access to reliable internet connectivity further exacerbate the digital divide, particularly in rural and underserved communities. The reliance on high-speed internet for telehealth consultations renders individuals in areas with poor connectivity unable to participate fully in digital healthcare services, thereby perpetuating inequities in access to care. Efforts to bridge this digital divide necessitate substantial investments in telecommunications infrastructure and targeted educational initiatives aimed at enhancing digital literacy among vulnerable populations. By addressing these technological barriers, healthcare systems can foster a more inclusive and equitable telemedicine landscape (A. K. Uniyal et al., 2022).

5.3 The Role of AI and Big Data in Telemedicine's Future

Predictive Analytics in Telehealth

The integration of artificial intelligence (AI) and big data analytics into telemedicine heralds a transformative evolution in healthcare delivery, particularly through the application of predictive analytics. This innovative approach enables healthcare providers to harness vast amounts of patient data, clinical outcomes, and epidemiological trends to identify patterns and forecast health events, thus facilitating proactive intervention strategies. Predictive analytics can significantly enhance patient care by enabling clinicians to anticipate potential health issues before they manifest, thereby optimizing treatment pathways and resource allocation (Malhotra et al., 2021).

For instance, predictive algorithms can analyze historical patient data to identify individuals at high risk for chronic conditions such as diabetes or cardiovascular disease. This information empowers healthcare providers to initiate preemptive measures, such as lifestyle interventions or personalized monitoring plans, aimed at mitigating the onset of these conditions. Additionally, predictive analytics can assist in the management of patient populations by identifying trends in disease outbreaks, thereby informing public health initiatives and resource deployment strategies. As the healthcare landscape continues to evolve, the application of predictive analytics will be instrumental in driving evidence-based decision-making and enhancing the overall efficacy of telehealth services (C. Gupta et al., 2022).

AI-Enhanced Diagnostic Capabilities

AI-enhanced diagnostic capabilities represent a pivotal advancement in the future of telemedicine, enabling healthcare providers to leverage sophisticated algorithms to augment clinical decision-making processes. These technologies are designed to analyze complex datasets, including medical images, genetic information, and electronic health records, with unparalleled speed and accuracy, thus facilitating more timely and precise diagnoses (R. Kumar, Malhotra, Pandey, et al., 2023).

For instance, machine learning algorithms can be employed to analyze radiological images, such as X-rays or MRIs, identifying anomalies that may escape the notice of human clinicians. This capability not only improves diagnostic accuracy but also expedites the review process, enabling faster patient triage and treatment. Furthermore, AI-driven diagnostic tools can synthesize vast amounts of patient data to provide tailored recommendations for treatment, thereby enhancing personalized care (J. Kaur et al., 2024; R. Kumar & Khanna, 2023a; V. Kumar, Gupta, et al., 2021).

The integration of AI into telemedicine also holds the potential to reduce healthcare disparities by making high-quality diagnostic capabilities accessible to remote or underserved populations. By empowering healthcare providers with advanced diagnostic tools, telemedicine can bridge the gap between resource-laden urban centers and underserved rural communities, ensuring that all patients receive equitable access to accurate and timely medical care.

CONCLUSION

Telemedicine is no longer a fringe component of healthcare delivery but a pivotal aspect of modern healthcare systems. For low-income communities, telemedicine represents not only a lifeline but a potential reconfiguration of healthcare delivery models. However, realizing the full potential of remote care requires navigating significant challenges, including regulatory inconsistencies, technological barriers, and the need for continuous investment. As the healthcare landscape continues to evolve, telemedicine will remain a key driver of improved access, cost savings, and economic transformation in healthcare.

DECLARATION

The authors declare that the manuscript follows ethical standards and there are no potential conflicts of interest concerning this chapter's research, authorship, and publication.

DISCLAIMER

The contents and views of this chapter are expressed by the authors in personal capacities. The Editor and the Publisher don't need to agree with these viewpoints and are not responsible for any duty of care in this regard.

REFERENCES

Agarwal, M., Gill, K. S., Upadhyay, D., Dangi, S., & Chythanya, K. R. (2024). The Evolution of Cryptocurrencies: Analysis of Bitcoin, Ethereum, Bit connect and Dogecoin in Comparison. *2024 IEEE 9th International Conference for Convergence in Technology, I2CT 2024*. DOI: 10.1109/I2CT61223.2024.10543872

Akberdina, V., Kumar, V., Kyriakopoulos, G. L., & Kuzmin, E. (2023). Editorial: What Does Industry's Digital Transition Hold in the Uncertainty Context? In K. V., K. G.L., A. V., & K. E. (Eds.), *Lecture Notes in Information Systems and Organisation: Vol. 61 LNISO* (pp. 1 – 4). Springer Science and Business Media Deutschland GmbH. DOI: 10.1007/978-3-031-30351-7_1

Aloo, B. N., Dessureault-Rompré, J., Tripathi, V., Nyongesa, B. O., & Were, B. A. (2023). Signaling and crosstalk of rhizobacterial and plant hormones that mediate abiotic stress tolerance in plants. *Frontiers in Microbiology*, 14, 1171104. Advance online publication. DOI: 10.3389/fmicb.2023.1171104 PMID: 37455718

Alsadi, J., Tripathi, V., Amaral, L. S., Potrich, E., Hasham, S. H., Patil, P. Y., & Omoniyi, E. M. (2022). Architecture Fibrous Meso-Porous Silica Spheres as Enhanced Adsorbent for Effective Capturing for CO_2 Gas. *Key Engineering Materials*, 928, 39–44. DOI: 10.4028/p-2f2o01

Anghel, B. I., & Lupu, R. (2024). Understanding Regulatory Changes: Deep Learning in Sustainable Finance and Banking. *Journal of Risk and Financial Management*, 17(7), 295. Advance online publication. DOI: 10.3390/jrfm17070295

Ansari, M. F., & Afzal, A. (2022). Sensitivity and Performance Analysis of 10 MW Solar Power Plant Using MPPT Technique. *Lecture Notes in Electrical Engineering, 894 LNEE*, 512–518. DOI: 10.1007/978-981-19-1677-9_46

Arora, S., Pargaien, S., Khan, F., Tewari, I., Nainwal, D., Mer, A., Mittal, A., & Misra, A. (2023). Monitoring Tourist Footfall at Nainital in Uttarakhand using Sensor Technology. *2023 4th International Conference on Electronics and Sustainable Communication Systems, ICESC 2023 - Proceedings*, 200 – 204. DOI: 10.1109/ICESC57686.2023.10193244

Asha, P., Mannepalli, K., Khilar, R., Subbulakshmi, N., Dhanalakshmi, R., Tripathi, V., Mohanavel, V., Sathyamurthy, R., & Sudhakar, M. (2022). Role of machine learning in attaining environmental sustainability. *Energy Reports*, 8, 863–871. DOI: 10.1016/j.egyr.2022.09.206

Awal, G., & Khanna, R. (2019). Determinants of millennial online consumer behavior and prospective purchase decisions. *International Journal of Advanced Science and Technology*, 28(18), 366–378.

Banerjee, D., Kukreja, V., Aeri, M., Hariharan, S., & Garg, N. (2023). Integrated CNN-SVM Approach for Accurate Radish Leaf Disease Classification: A Comparative Study and Performance Analysis. *2023 Annual International Conference on Emerging Research Areas: International Conference on Intelligent Systems, AICERA/ICIS 2023*. DOI: 10.1109/AICERA/ICIS59538.2023.10420119

Bansal, N., Bhatnagar, M., & Taneja, S. (2023). Balancing priorities through green optimism: A study elucidating initiatives, approaches, and strategies for sustainable supply chain management. In *Handbook of Research on Designing Sustainable Supply Chains to Achieve a Circular Economy*. IGI Global., DOI: 10.4018/978-1-6684-7664-2.ch004

Behera, A., & Singh Rawat, K. (2023). A brief review paper on mining subsidence and its geo-environmental impact. *Materials Today: Proceedings*. Advance online publication. DOI: 10.1016/j.matpr.2023.04.183

Bhatt, S., & Dani, R. (2024). Social media and community engagement: Empowering local voices in regenerative tourism. In *Examining Tourist Behaviors and Community Involvement in Destination Rejuvenation*. IGI Global., DOI: 10.4018/979-8-3693-6819-0.ch009

Bhushan, B., & Nayak, A. (2022). Application of green nanomaterials for sustainable energy systems: A review of the current status. In *Biofuel Technologies for a Sustainable Future: India and Beyond*. River Publishers.

Biermans, M. L., Bulthuis, W., Holl, T., & van Overbeeke, B. (2023). Sustainable Finance in the Maritime Sector. In *Maritime Decarbonization: Practical Tools, Case Studies and Decarbonization Enablers*. Springer Nature. DOI: 10.1007/978-3-031-39936-7_19

Busch, D. (2023). EU Sustainable Finance Disclosure Regulation. *Capital Markets Law Journal*, 18(3), 303–328. DOI: 10.1093/cmlj/kmad005

Caiado, R. G. G., Scavarda, L. F., Vidal, G., de Mattos Nascimento, D. L., & Garza-Reyes, J. A. (2023). A taxonomy of critical factors towards sustainable operations and supply chain management 4.0 in developing countries. *Operations Management Research*. DOI: 10.1007/s12063-023-00430-8

Chand, A., Agarwal, P., & Sharma, S. (2023). Real-Time Retrieving Vedic Sanskrit Text into Multi-Lingual Text and Audio for Cultural Tourism Motivation. *2023 International Conference for Advancement in Technology, ICONAT 2023*. DOI: 10.1109/ICONAT57137.2023.10080862

Chauhan, M., Rani, A., Joshi, S., & Sharma, P. K. (2023). Role of psychrophilic and psychrotolerant microorganisms toward the development of hill agriculture. In *Advanced Microbial Technology for Sustainable Agriculture and Environment*. Elsevier., DOI: 10.1016/B978-0-323-95090-9.00002-9

Chiu, I. H.-Y., Lin, L., & Rouch, D. (2022). Law and Regulation for Sustainable Finance. *European Business Organization Law Review*, 23(1), 1–7. Advance online publication. DOI: 10.1007/s40804-021-00230-2

Cunha, F. A. F. de S., Meira, E., & Orsato, R. J. (2021). Sustainable finance and investment: Review and research agenda. *Business Strategy and the Environment*, 30(8), 3821–3838. DOI: 10.1002/bse.2842

Dahiya, K., & Taneja, S. (2023). To Analyse the Impact of Multi-Media Technology on the Rural Entrepreneurship Development. In *Contemporary Studies of Risks in Emerging Technology* (pp. 221–240). DOI: 10.1108/978-1-80455-562-020231015

Dahiya, M., Guru Prasad, M. S., Anand, T., Kumar, K., Bansal, S., & Naveen Kumar, H. N. (2023). An Effective Detection of Litchi Disease using Deep Learning. *2023 14th International Conference on Computing Communication and Networking Technologies, ICCCNT 2023*. DOI: 10.1109/ICCCNT56998.2023.10307717

Dangwal, A., Kaur, S., Taneja, S., & Ozen, E. (2022). A bibliometric analysis of green tourism based on the scopus platform. In *Developing Relationships, Personalization, and Data Herald in Marketing 5.0*. IGI Global., DOI: 10.4018/978-1-6684-4496-2.ch015

Danilov, Y. A. (2021). The concept of sustainable finance and the prospects for its implementation in Russia. *Voprosy Ekonomiki*, 2021(5), 5–25. DOI: 10.32609/0042-8736-2021-5-5-25

Deng, Q., Usman, M., Irfan, M., & Haseeb, M. (2024). The role of financial inclusion and tourism in tackling environmental challenges of industrialization and energy consumption: Redesigning Sustainable Development Goals policies. *Natural Resources Forum*. DOI: 10.1111/1477-8947.12522

Dieudonne, K. K., & Bajaj, M., Kitmo, Rubanenko, O., Jurado, F., & Kamel, S. (2022). Hydropower Potential Assessment of Four Selected Sites in the North Interconnected Network of Cameroon. *2022 IEEE International Conference on Automation/25th Congress of the Chilean Association of Automatic Control: For the Development of Sustainable Agricultural Systems, ICA-ACCA 2022*. DOI: 10.1109/ICA-ACCA56767.2022.10005948

Dubey, V. P., Prakash, R., Chamoli, V., & Mittal, P. (2023). Study of Urban Change Detection Using Landsat 8 Satellite Data: A Case Study of Dehradun City, Uttarakhand, India. *IEEE International Conference on Electrical, Electronics, Communication and Computers, ELEXCOM 2023*. DOI: 10.1109/ELEXCOM58812.2023.10370375

Elbagory, M., El-Nahrawy, S., Omara, A. E.-D., Eid, E. M., Bachheti, A., Kumar, P., Abou Fayssal, S., Adelodun, B., Bachheti, R. K., Kumar, P., Mioč, B., Kumar, V., & Širić, I. (2022). Sustainable Bioconversion of Wetland Plant Biomass for Pleurotus ostreatus var. florida Cultivation: Studies on Proximate and Biochemical Characterization. *Agriculture*, 12(12), 2095. Advance online publication. DOI: 10.3390/agriculture12122095

Gangwar, V. P., & Srivastva, S. P. (2020). Impact of micro finance in poverty eradication via SHGs: A study of selected districts in U.P. *International Journal of Advanced Science and Technology*, 29(2), 3818–3829.

Giri, N. C., Mohanty, R. C., Shaw, R. N., Poonia, S., Bajaj, M., & Belkhier, Y. (2022). Agriphotovoltaic System to Improve Land Productivity and Revenue of Farmer. *2022 IEEE Global Conference on Computing, Power and Communication Technologies, GlobConPT 2022*. DOI: 10.1109/GlobConPT57482.2022.9938338

Gonfa, Y. H., Gelagle, A. A., Hailegnaw, B., Kabeto, S. A., Workeneh, G. A., Tessema, F. B., Tadesse, M. G., Wabaidur, S. M., Dahlous, K. A., Abou Fayssal, S., Kumar, P., Adelodun, B., Bachheti, A., & Bachheti, R. K. (2023). Optimization, Characterization, and Biological Applications of Silver Nanoparticles Synthesized Using Essential Oil of Aerial Part of Laggera tomentosa. *Sustainability (Basel)*, 15(1), 797. Advance online publication. DOI: 10.3390/su15010797

Gopal, S., Gupta, P., & Minocha, A. (2023). Advancements in Fin-Tech and Security Challenges of Banking Industry. *4th International Conference on Intelligent Engineering and Management, ICIEM 2023*. DOI: 10.1109/ICIEM59379.2023.10165876

Govindarajan, H. K., Ganesh, L. S., Sharma, N., & Agarwal, R. (2023). Indian Energy Scenario: A Critical Review. *Indian Journal of Environmental Protection*, 43(2), 99–107.

Gupta, C., Jindal, P., & Malhotra, R. K. (2022). A Study of Increasing Adoption Trends of Digital Technologies - An Evidence from Indian Banking. In D. N. & C. A. (Eds.), *AIP Conference Proceedings* (Vol. 2481). American Institute of Physics Inc. DOI: 10.1063/5.0104572

Gupta, M., Arora, K., & Taneja, S. (2023). Bibliometric analysis on employee engagement and human resource management. In *Enhancing Customer Engagement Through Location-Based Marketing*. IGI Global., DOI: 10.4018/978-1-6684-8177-6.ch013

Gupta, M., Kumari, I., & Singh, A. K. (2024). Impact of human capital on SDG1 in selected G20 countries. In *Interlinking SDGs and the Bottom-of-the-Pyramid Through Tourism*. IGI Global., DOI: 10.4018/979-8-3693-3166-8.ch002

Gupta, S., Kushwaha, P., Chauhan, A. S., Yadav, A., & Badhotiya, G. K. (2023). A study on glazing to optimize daylight for improving lighting ergonomics and energy efficiency of a building. In S. Y., S. G., & B. G.K. (Eds.), *AIP Conference Proceedings* (Vol. 2521). American Institute of Physics Inc. DOI: 10.1063/5.0114766

Gupta, S., Singh, P., Gupta, A. M., & Chauhan, A. (2024). The bridging the gap between technology and social welfare: An IoT cloud-based model for developing countries. In S. S., K. S., & J. P.K. (Eds.), *AIP Conference Proceedings* (Vol. 3121, Issue 1). American Institute of Physics. DOI: 10.1063/5.0221598

Ho, M. N., Abhayawansa, S., & Adams, C. A. (2024). Sustainable finance. In *Elgar Encyclopedia of Corporate Communication*. Edward Elgar Publishing Ltd., DOI: 10.4337/9781802200874.ch32

Jain, S., & Jain, S. S. (2021). Development of Intelligent Transportation System and Its Applications for an Urban Corridor During COVID-19. *Journal of The Institution of Engineers (India): Series B*, 102(6), 1191 – 1200. DOI: 10.1007/s40031-021-00556-y

Jain, V., Tiwari, R., Mehrotra, R., Bohra, N. S., Misra, A., & Pandey, D. C. (2023). Role of Technology for Credit Risk Management: A Bibliometric Review. *2023 IEEE International Conference on Blockchain and Distributed Systems Security, ICBDS 2023*. DOI: 10.1109/ICBDS58040.2023.10346300

Jena, S., Cao, S., & Gairola, A. (2024). Cyclonic wind loads and structural mitigation measures – vulnerability assessment of traditional housings in Odisha. *Journal of Earth System Science*, 133(2), 52. Advance online publication. DOI: 10.1007/s12040-024-02255-w

Jindal, V., Kukreja, V., Mehta, S., Chauhan, R., & Verma, G. (2023). Towards Sustainable Agriculture: Federated CNN Models for Cucurbit Leaf Disease Detection. *2023 10th IEEE Uttar Pradesh Section International Conference on Electrical, Electronics and Computer Engineering, UPCON 2023*, 561 – 566. DOI: 10.1109/UPCON59197.2023.10434321

Jindal, V., Kukreja, V., Mehta, S., Srivastava, P., & Garg, N. (2023). Adopting Federated Learning and CNN for Advanced Plant Pathology: A Case of Red Globe Grape Leaf Diseases Dissecting Severity. *2023 3rd Asian Conference on Innovation in Technology, ASIANCON 2023*. DOI: 10.1109/ASIANCON58793.2023.10270034

Joshi, K., Patil, S., Gupta, S., & Khanna, R. (2022). Role of Pranayma in emotional maturity for improving health. *Journal of Medical Pharmaceutical and Allied Sciences*, 11(2), 4569–4573. DOI: 10.55522/jmpas.V11I2.2033

Kanojia, P., Malhotra, R. K., & Uniyal, A. K. (2022). Organizational Commitment and the Academic Staff in HEI's in North West India. *Proceedings - 2022 International Conference on Recent Trends in Microelectronics, Automation, Computing and Communications Systems, ICMACC 2022*, 365–370. DOI: 10.1109/ICMACC54824.2022.10093347

Kaur, A., Kukreja, V., Chamoli, S., Thapliyal, S., & Sharma, R. (2023a). Advanced Disease Management: An Encoder-Decoder Approach for Tomato Black Mold Detection. *2023 IEEE Pune Section International Conference, PuneCon 2023*. DOI: 10.1109/PuneCon58714.2023.10450088

Kaur, A., Kukreja, V., Chamoli, S., Thapliyal, S., & Sharma, R. (2023b). Advanced Multi-Scale Classification of Onion Smut Disease Using a Hybrid CNN-RF Ensemble Model for Precision Agriculture. In G. R., H. K., P. R., G. S., T. A. J.V., V. R., M. R., & K. T. (Eds.), *Proceedings of the 2023 6th International Conference on Recent Trends in Advance Computing, ICRTAC 2023* (pp. 553 – 556). Institute of Electrical and Electronics Engineers Inc. DOI: 10.1109/ICRTAC59277.2023.10480840

Kaur, A., Kukreja, V., Nisha Chandran, S., Garg, N., & Sharma, R. (2023). Automated Mango Rust Severity Classification: A CNN-SVM Ensemble Approach for Accurate and Granular Disease Assessment in Mango Cultivation. In G. R., H. K., P. R., G. S., T. A. J.V., V. R., M. R., & K. T. (Eds.), *Proceedings of the 2023 6th International Conference on Recent Trends in Advance Computing, ICRTAC 2023* (pp. 486 – 490). Institute of Electrical and Electronics Engineers Inc. DOI: 10.1109/ICRTAC59277.2023.10480836

Kaur, A., Kumar, P., Taneja, S., & Ozen, E. (2023). Fintech emergence – an opportunity or threat to banking. *International Journal of Electronic Finance*, 13(1), 1–19. DOI: 10.1504/IJEF.2024.135163

Kaur, G., Sharma, N., Chauhan, R., Singh, P., & Gupta, R. (2023). An Automated Approach for Detection and Classification of Plant Diseases. *2023 2nd International Conference on Futuristic Technologies, INCOFT 2023*. DOI: 10.1109/INCOFT60753.2023.10425170

Kaur, J., Khanna, R., Kumar, R., & Sunil, G. (2024). Role of Blockchain Technologies in Goods and Services Tax. *Proceedings - 2024 3rd International Conference on Sentiment Analysis and Deep Learning, ICSADL 2024*, 607–612. DOI: 10.1109/ICSADL61749.2024.00104

Khan, S., Ambika, , Rani, K., Sharma, S., Kumar, A., Singh, S., Thapliyal, M., Rawat, P., Thakur, A., Pandey, S., Thapliyal, A., Pal, M., & Singh, Y. (2023). Rhizobacterial mediated interactions in Curcuma longa for plant growth and enhanced crop productivity: A systematic review. *Frontiers in Plant Science*, 14, 1231676. Advance online publication. DOI: 10.3389/fpls.2023.1231676 PMID: 37692412

Kholiya, D., Mishra, A. K., Pandey, N. K., & Tripathi, N. (2023). Plant Detection and Counting using Yolo based Technique. *2023 3rd Asian Conference on Innovation in Technology, ASIANCON 2023*. DOI: 10.1109/ASIANCON58793.2023.10270530

Kukreti, A., Shriyal, A., Sharma, S., & Bhadula, S. (2023). Internet-of-Things Enabled Smart and Portable Terrace Garden Protection Shed. *2023 4th IEEE Global Conference for Advancement in Technology, GCAT 2023*. DOI: 10.1109/GCAT59970.2023.10353281

Kumar, A., Goyal, H. R., & Sharma, S. (2023). Sustainable Intelligent Information System for Tourism Industry. *2023 IEEE 8th International Conference for Convergence in Technology, I2CT 2023*. DOI: 10.1109/I2CT57861.2023.10126400

Kumar, A., Pant, S., & Ram, M. (2023). Cost Optimization and Reliability Parameter Extraction of a Complex Engineering System. *Journal of Reliability and Statistical Studies*, 16(1), 99–116. DOI: 10.13052/jrss0974-8024.1615

Kumar, A., Sharma, N., Chauhan, R., & Sharma, M. (2023). Anomaly Detection in Bitcoin Blockchain: Exploring Trends and Algorithms. *2023 Global Conference on Information Technologies and Communications, GCITC 2023*. DOI: 10.1109/GCITC60406.2023.10426011

Kumar, G., Kumar, A., Singhal, M., Singh, K. U., Kumar, L., & Singh, T. (2023). Revolutionizing Plant Disease Management Through Image Processing Technology. *Proceedings of International Conference on Computational Intelligence and Sustainable Engineering Solution, CISES 2023*, 521 – 528. DOI: 10.1109/CISES58720.2023.10183408

Kumar, K., Veena, N., Aravind, T., Bhatt, C., Kuppusamy, U., & Jain, P. (2025). Game-changing intelligence: Unveiling the societal impact of artificial intelligence in game software. *Entertainment Computing*, 52, 100862. Advance online publication. DOI: 10.1016/j.entcom.2024.100862

Kumar, P., Bhatnagar, M., & Taneja, S. (2023). Investigation of the time pattern of Bit Green Crypto: An Arma modeling approach to unrave volatility. In *Algorithmic Approaches to Financial Technology: Forecasting, Trading, and Optimization*. IGI Global., DOI: 10.4018/979-8-3693-1746-4.ch001

Kumar, P., Taneja, S., Bhatnagar, M., & Kaur, A. K. (2024). Navigating the digital paradigm shift: Designing CBDCs for a transformative financial landscape. In *Exploring Central Bank Digital Currencies: Concepts, Frameworks, Models, and Challenges*. IGI Global., DOI: 10.4018/979-8-3693-1882-9.ch006

Kumar, R., Goel, R., Singh, T., Mohanty, S. M., Gupta, D., Alkhayyat, A., & Khanna, R. (2024). Sustainable Finance Factors in Indian Economy: Analysis on Policy of Climate Change and Energy Sector. *Fluctuation and Noise Letters*, 23(2), 2440004. Advance online publication. DOI: 10.1142/S0219477524400042

Kumar, R., & Khanna, R. (2023a). Role of Artificial Intelligence in Digital Currency and Future Applications. *Proceedings of the 2023 2nd International Conference on Augmented Intelligence and Sustainable Systems, ICAISS 2023*, 42–46. DOI: 10.1109/ICAISS58487.2023.10250480

Kumar, R., & Khanna, R. (2023b). RPA (Robotic Process Automation) in Finance & Accounting and Future Scope. *Proceedings of the 2023 2nd International Conference on Augmented Intelligence and Sustainable Systems, ICAISS 2023*, 1640–1645. DOI: 10.1109/ICAISS58487.2023.10250496

Kumar, R., Khannna Malholtra, R., & Grover, C. A. N. (2023). Review on Artificial Intelligence Role in Implementation of Goods and Services Tax(GST) and Future Scope. *2023 International Conference on Artificial Intelligence and Smart Communication, AISC 2023*, 348–351. DOI: 10.1109/AISC56616.2023.10085030

Kumar, R., Lamba, A. K., Mohammed, S., Asokan, A., Aswal, U. S., & Kolavennu, S. (2023). Fake Currency Note Recognition using Extreme Learning Machine. *Proceedings of the 2nd International Conference on Applied Artificial Intelligence and Computing, ICAAIC 2023*, 333 – 339. DOI: 10.1109/ICAAIC56838.2023.10140824

Kumar, R., Malholtra, R. K., Singh, R., Kathuria, S., Balyan, R., & Pal, P. (2023). Artificial Intelligence Role in Electronic Invoice Under Goods and Services Tax. *2023 International Conference on Computational Intelligence, Communication Technology and Networking, CICTN 2023*, 140–143. DOI: 10.1109/CICTN57981.2023.10140870

Kumar, R., Malhotra, R. K., & Grover, N. (2023). Data Mining in Credit Scoring and Future Application. *International Conference on Innovative Data Communication Technologies and Application, ICIDCA 2023 - Proceedings*, 1096–1100. DOI: 10.1109/ICIDCA56705.2023.10100032

Kumar, R., Malhotra, R. K., Pandey, S., Gehlot, A., Gautam, I., & Chamola, S. (2023). Role of Artificial Intelligence in Input Tax Credit Reconciliation. *Proceedings - 2023 3rd International Conference on Pervasive Computing and Social Networking, ICPCSN 2023*, 497–501. DOI: 10.1109/ICPCSN58827.2023.00086

Kumar, R., Singh, T., Mohanty, S. N., Goel, R., Gupta, D., Alharbi, M., & Khanna, R. (2023). Study on online payments and e-commerce with SOR model. *International Journal of Retail & Distribution Management*. Advance online publication. DOI: 10.1108/IJRDM-03-2023-0137

Kumar, V., Gupta, S., & Khanna, R. (2021). Dengue fever-a worldwide study. *Journal of Medical Pharmaceutical and Allied Sciences*, 10, 102–108. DOI: 10.22270/jmpas.VIC2I1.2014

Kumar, V., & Korovin, G. (2023). A Comparison of Digital Transformation of Industry in the Russian Federation with the European Union. In K. V., K. G.L., A. V., & K. E. (Eds.), *Lecture Notes in Information Systems and Organisation: Vol. 61 LNISO* (pp. 45 – 57). Springer Science and Business Media Deutschland GmbH. DOI: 10.1007/978-3-031-30351-7_5

Kumar, V., Mitra, D., Rani, A., Suyal, D. C., Singh Gautam, B. P., Jain, L., Gondwal, M., Raj, K. K., Singh, A. K., & Soni, R. (2021). Bio-inoculants for Biodegradation and Bioconversion of Agrowaste: Status and Prospects. In *Bioremediation of Environmental Pollutants: Emerging Trends and Strategies*. Springer International Publishing., DOI: 10.1007/978-3-030-86169-8_16

Kunwar, S., Joshi, A., Gururani, P., Pandey, D., & Pandey, N. (2023). Physiological and AI-based study of endophytes on medicina A mini review. *Plant Science Today*, 10, 53–60. DOI: 10.14719/pst.2555

Lauesen, L. M. (2016). The landscape and scale of social and sustainable finance. In *Routledge Handbook of Social and Sustainable Finance*. Taylor and Francis., DOI: 10.4324/9781315772578

Malhotra, R. K., Gupta, C., & Jindal, P. (2022). Blockchain and Smart Contracts for Insurance Industry. In *Blockchain Technology in Corporate Governance*. Transforming Business and Industries., DOI: 10.1002/9781119865247.ch11

Malhotra, R. K., Ojha, M. K., & Gupta, S. (2021). A study of assessment of knowledge, perception and attitude of using tele health services among college going students of Uttarakhand. *Journal of Medical Pharmaceutical and Allied Sciences*, 10, 113–116. DOI: 10.22270/jmpas.VIC2I1.2020

Malik, D., Kukreja, V., Mehta, S., Gupta, A., & Singh, V. (2023). Mitigating the Impact of Guava Leaf Diseases Using CNNs and Federated Learning. *2023 3rd Asian Conference on Innovation in Technology, ASIANCON 2023.* DOI: 10.1109/ASIANCON58793.2023.10270236

McGuigan, N., Sin, S., & Kern, T. (2017). Sourcing sustainable finance in a globally competitive market: An instructional case. *Issues in Accounting Education*, 32(1), 43–58. DOI: 10.2308/iace-51304

Mekala, K., Laxmi, V., Jagruthi, H., Dhondiyal, S. A., Sridevi, R., & Dabral, A. P. (2023). Coffee Price Prediction: An Application of CNN-BLSTM Neural Networks. *Proceedings of the 2nd IEEE International Conference on Advances in Computing, Communication and Applied Informatics, ACCAI 2023.* DOI: 10.1109/ACCAI58221.2023.10199369

Mishra, A., Shah, J. K., Sharma, R., Sharma, M., Joshi, S., & Kaushal, D. (2023). Enhancing Efficiency in Industrial Environments through IoT Connected Worker Solutions: Smart Wearable Technologies for the Workplace. *2023 International Conference on Advances in Computation, Communication and Information Technology, ICAICCIT 2023*, 1175–1179. DOI: 10.1109/ICAICCIT60255.2023.10466100

Mishra, A. K., Singh, S., & Upadhyay, R. K. (2023). Organization citizenship behaviour among indian nurses during SARS-COV-2: A direct effect moderation model. *Quality & Quantity*, 57(1), 541–559. DOI: 10.1007/s11135-022-01325-9

Mishra, D., Kandpal, V., Agarwal, N., & Srivastava, B. (2024). Financial Inclusion and Its Ripple Effects on Socio-Economic Development: A Comprehensive Review. *Journal of Risk and Financial Management*, 17(3), 105. Advance online publication. DOI: 10.3390/jrfm17030105

Mitra, D., Mondal, R., Khoshru, B., Senapati, A., Radha, T. K., Mahakur, B., Uniyal, N., Myo, E. M., Boutaj, H., Sierra, B. E. G. U. E. R. R. A., Panneerselvam, P., Ganeshamurthy, A. N., Elković, S. A. N. Đ. J., Vasić, T., Rani, A., Dutta, S., & Mohapatra, P. K. D. A. S.MITRA. (2022). Actinobacteria-enhanced plant growth, nutrient acquisition, and crop protection: Advances in soil, plant, and microbial multifactorial interactions. *Pedosphere*, 32(1), 149–170. DOI: 10.1016/S1002-0160(21)60042-5

Mitra, D., Saritha, B., Janeeshma, E., Gusain, P., Khoshru, B., Abo Nouh, F. A., Rani, A., Olatunbosun, A. N., Ruparelia, J., Rabari, A., Mosquera-Sánchez, L. P., Mondal, R., Verma, D., Panneerselvam, P., Das Mohapatra, P. K., & Guerra Sierra, B. E. (2022). Arbuscular mycorrhizal fungal association boosted the arsenic resistance in crops with special responsiveness to rice plant. *Environmental and Experimental Botany*, 193. Advance online publication. DOI: 10.1016/j.envexpbot.2021.104681

Moneva, J. M., Scarpellini, S., Aranda-Usón, A., & Alvarez Etxeberria, I. (2023). Sustainability reporting in view of the European sustainable finance taxonomy: Is the financial sector ready to disclose circular economy? *Corporate Social Responsibility and Environmental Management*, 30(3), 1336–1347. DOI: 10.1002/csr.2423

Mukul, T., Taneja, S., Özen, E., & Bansal, N. (2024). CHALLENGES AND OPPORTUNITIES FOR SKILL DEVELOPMENT IN DEVELOPING ECONOMIES. *Contemporary Studies in Economic and Financial Analysis*, 112B, 1–22. DOI: 10.1108/S1569-37592024000112B001

Neha, M., S., Alfurhood, B. S., Bakhare, R., Poongavanam, S., & Khanna, R. (2023). The Role and Impact of Artificial Intelligence on Retail Business and its Developments. *2023 International Conference on Artificial Intelligence and Smart Communication, AISC 2023*, 1098–1101. DOI: 10.1109/AISC56616.2023.10085624

Nyambuu, U., & Semmler, W. (2023). Climate Risks, Sustainable Finance, and Climate Policy. *Contributions to Economics*, (Part F32), 171–190. DOI: 10.1007/978-3-031-27982-9_11

Pandey, P., Mayank, K., & Sharma, S. (2023). Recommendation System for Adventure Tourism. *2023 4th IEEE Global Conference for Advancement in Technology, GCAT 2023*. DOI: 10.1109/GCAT59970.2023.10353339

Pant, R., Gupta, A., Pant, G., Chaubey, K. K., Kumar, G., & Patrick, N. (2022). Second-generation biofuels: Facts and future. In *Relationship between Microbes and the Environment for Sustainable Ecosystem Services: Microbial Tools for Sustainable Ecosystem Services: Volume 3* (Vol. 3). Elsevier. DOI: 10.1016/B978-0-323-89936-9.00011-4

Papageorgiou, G., Loukis, E., Pappas, G., Rizun, N., Saxena, S., Charalabidis, Y., & Alexopoulos, C. (2023). Open Government Data in Educational Programs Curriculum: Current State and Prospects. *Lecture Notes in Business Information Processing, 493 LNBIP*, 311–326. DOI: 10.1007/978-3-031-43126-5_22

Partiti, E. (2024). Addressing the Flaws of the Sustainable Finance Disclosure Regulation: Moving from Disclosures to Labelling and Sustainability Due Diligence. *European Business Organization Law Review*, 25(2), 299–332. DOI: 10.1007/s40804-024-00317-6

Paul, S. N., Mishra, A. K., & Upadhyay, R. K. (2022). Locus of control and investment decision: An investor's perspective. *International Journal of Services. Economics and Management*, 13(2), 93–107. DOI: 10.1504/IJSEM.2022.122736

Rai, K., Mishra, N., & Mishra, S. (2022). Forest Fire Risk Zonation Mapping using Fuzzy Overlay Analysis of Nainital District. *2022 International Mobile and Embedded Technology Conference, MECON 2022*, 522–526. DOI: 10.1109/MECON53876.2022.9751812

Rajeswari, M., Kumar, N., Raman, P., Patjoshi, P. K., Singh, V., & Pundir, S. (2022). Optimal Analysis for Enterprise Financial Management Based on Artificial Intelligence and Parallel Computing Method. *Proceedings of 5th International Conference on Contemporary Computing and Informatics, IC3I 2022*, 2081–2086. DOI: 10.1109/IC3I56241.2022.10072851

Ranakoti, L., Gangil, B., Mishra, S. K., Singh, T., Sharma, S., Ilyas, R. A., & El-Khatib, S. (2022). Critical Review on Polylactic Acid: Properties, Structure, Processing, Biocomposites, and Nanocomposites. *Materials (Basel)*, 15(12), 4312. Advance online publication. DOI: 10.3390/ma15124312 PMID: 35744371

Rao, K. V. G., Kumar, M. K., Goud, B. S., Krishna, D., Bajaj, M., Saini, P., & Choudhury, S. (2023). IOT-Powered Crop Shield System for Surveillance and Auto Transversum. *2023 IEEE 3rd International Conference on Sustainable Energy and Future Electric Transportation, SeFet 2023*. DOI: 10.1109/SeFeT57834.2023.10245773

Rawat, B., Rawat, J. M., Purohit, S., Singh, G., Sharma, P. K., Chandra, A., Shabaaz Begum, J. P., Venugopal, D., Jaremko, M., & Qureshi, K. A. (2022). A comprehensive review of Quercus semecarpifolia Sm.: An ecologically and commercially important Himalayan tree. *Frontiers in Ecology and Evolution*, 10, 961345. Advance online publication. DOI: 10.3389/fevo.2022.961345

Rawat, R., Goyal, H. R., & Sharma, S. (2023). Artificial Narrow Intelligence Techniques in Intelligent Digital Financial Inclusion System for Digital Society. *2023 6th International Conference on Information Systems and Computer Networks, ISCON 2023*. DOI: 10.1109/ISCON57294.2023.10112133

Rawat, R., Sharma, S., & Goyal, H. R. (2023). Intelligent Digital Financial Inclusion System Architectures for Industry 5.0 Enabled Digital Society. *Winter Summit on Smart Computing and Networks. WiSSCoN*, 2023, 1–5. Advance online publication. DOI: 10.1109/WiSSCoN56857.2023.10133858

Rawat, S. S., Pant, S., Kumar, A., Ram, M., Sharma, H. K., & Kumar, A. (2022). A State-of-the-Art Survey on Analytical Hierarchy Process Applications in Sustainable Development. *International Journal of Mathematical. Engineering and Management Sciences*, 7(6), 883–917. DOI: 10.33889/IJMEMS.2022.7.6.056

Reepu, R., Taneja, S., Ozen, E., & Singh, A. (2023). A globetrotter to the future of marketing: Metaverse. In *Cultural Marketing and Metaverse for Consumer Engagement*. IGI Global., DOI: 10.4018/978-1-6684-8312-1.ch001

Ritika, B., Bora, B., Ismail, B. B., Garba, U., Mishra, S., Jha, A. K., Naik, B., Kumar, V., Rather, M. A., Rizwana, , Preet, M. S., Rustagi, S., Kumar, H., & Gupta, A. K. (2024). Himalayan fruit and circular economy: Nutraceutical potential, traditional uses, challenges and opportunities. *Food Production. Processing and Nutrition*, 6(1), 71. Advance online publication. DOI: 10.1186/s43014-023-00220-6

Rosman, R., Redzuan, N. H., & Shaharuddin, S. S. a'. (2024). Instruments of Islamic Sustainable Finance. In *Islamic Finance and Sustainable Development: A Global Framework for Achieving Sustainable Impact Finance*. Taylor and Francis. DOI: 10.4324/9781003468653-9

Sati, P., Sharma, E., Soni, R., Dhyani, P., Solanki, A. C., Solanki, M. K., Rai, S., & Malviya, M. K. (2022). Bacterial endophytes as bioinoculant: microbial functions and applications toward sustainable farming. In *Microbial Endophytes and Plant Growth: Beneficial Interactions and Applications*. Elsevier., DOI: 10.1016/B978-0-323-90620-3.00008-8

Segovia-Vargas, M. J., Miranda-García, I. M., & Oquendo-Torres, F. A. (2023). Sustainable finance: The role of savings and credit cooperatives in Ecuador. *Annals of Public and Cooperative Economics*, 94(3), 951–980. DOI: 10.1111/apce.12428

Sharma, A., Mohan, A., & Johri, A. (2024). Impact of Financial Technology (Fin-Tech) on the Restructuring of the Agrarian Economy: A Comprehensive Systematic Review. In M. H. (Ed.), *Proceedings - 2024 6th International Conference on Computational Intelligence and Communication Technologies, CCICT 2024* (pp. 249 – 252). Institute of Electrical and Electronics Engineers Inc. DOI: 10.1109/CCICT62777.2024.00049

Sharma, H. R., Bhardwaj, B., Sharma, B., & Kaushik, C. P. (2021). Sustainable Solid Waste Management in India: Practices, Challenges and the Way Forward. In *Climate Resilience and Environmental Sustainability Approaches: Global Lessons and Local Challenges*. Springer Nature. DOI: 10.1007/978-981-16-0902-2_17

Sharma, M., Hagar, A. A., Krishna Murthy, G. R., Beyane, K., Gawali, B. W., & Pant, B. (2022). A Study on Recognising the Application of Multiple Big Data Technologies and its Related Issues, Difficulties and Opportunities. *2022 2nd International Conference on Advance Computing and Innovative Technologies in Engineering, ICACITE 2022*, 341–344. DOI: 10.1109/ICACITE53722.2022.9823623

Sharma, M., Kumar, A., Luthra, S., Joshi, S., & Upadhyay, A. (2022). The impact of environmental dynamism on low-carbon practices and digital supply chain networks to enhance sustainable performance: An empirical analysis. *Business Strategy and the Environment*, 31(4), 1776–1788. DOI: 10.1002/bse.2983

Sharma, M., & Singh, P. (2023). Newly engineered nanoparticles as potential therapeutic agents for plants to ameliorate abiotic and biotic stress. *Journal of Applied and Natural Science*, 15(2), 720–731. DOI: 10.31018/jans.v15i2.4603

Sharma, N. K., Kumar, V., Verma, P., & Luthra, S. (2021). Sustainable reverse logistics practices and performance evaluation with fuzzy TOPSIS: A study on Indian retailers. *Cleaner Logistics and Supply Chain*, 1, 100007. Advance online publication. DOI: 10.1016/j.clscn.2021.100007

Sharma, P., Malhotra, R. K., Ojha, M. K., & Gupta, S. (2022). Impact of meditation on mental & physical health and thereby on academic performance of students: A study of higher educational institutions of Uttarakhand. *Journal of Medical Pharmaceutical and Allied Sciences*, 11(2), 4641–4644. DOI: 10.55522/jmpas.V11I2.2309

Sharma, P., Taneja, S., Kumar, P., Özen, E., & Singh, A. (2024). Application of the UTAUT model toward individual acceptance: Emerging trends in artificial intelligence-based banking services. *International Journal of Electronic Finance*, 13(3), 352–366. DOI: 10.1504/IJEF.2024.139584

Sharma, S., Kadayat, Y., & Tyagi, R. (2023). Artificial Intelligence Enabled Sustainable Life Cycle System Using Vedic Scripture and Quantum Computing. *2023 3rd International Conference on Intelligent Technologies, CONIT 2023*. DOI: 10.1109/CONIT59222.2023.10205771

Sharma, S., Kandpal, V., Choudhury, T., Santibanez Gonzalez, E. D. R., & Agarwal, N. (2023). Assessment of the implications of energy-efficient technologies on the environmental sustainability of rail operation. *AIMS Environmental Science*, 10(5), 709–731. DOI: 10.3934/environsci.2023039

Sharma, S., & Kumar, S. (2023). Sustainable finance: A way towards climate neutral economies. In *Perspectives on the Transition Toward Green and Climate Neutral Economies in Asia*. IGI Global., DOI: 10.4018/978-1-6684-8613-9.ch001

Sharma, S., & Tyagi, R. (2023). Digitalization of Farming Knowledge Using Artificial Intelligence and Vedic Scripture. *3rd IEEE International Conference on ICT in Business Industry and Government, ICTBIG 2023*. DOI: 10.1109/ICTBIG59752.2023.10456219

Shekhar, S., Gusain, R., Vidhyarthi, A., & Prakash, R. (2022). Role of Remote Sensing and GIS Strategies to Increase Crop Yield. In S. S. & J. T. (Eds.), *2022 International Conference on Advances in Computing, Communication and Materials, ICACCM 2022*. Institute of Electrical and Electronics Engineers Inc. DOI: 10.1109/ICACCM56405.2022.10009217

Shukla, A., Sharma, M., Tiwari, K., Vani, V. D., & Kumar, N., & Pooja. (2023). Predicting Rainfall Using an Artificial Neural Network-Based Model. *Proceedings of International Conference on Contemporary Computing and Informatics, IC3I 2023*, 2700 – 2704. DOI: 10.1109/IC3I59117.2023.10397714

Singh, A., Sharma, S., Purohit, K. C., & Nithin Kumar, K. C. (2021). Artificial Intelligence based Framework for Effective Performance of Traffic Light Control System. *Proceedings of the 2021 IEEE International Conference on Innovative Computing, Intelligent Communication and Smart Electrical Systems, ICSES 2021*. DOI: 10.1109/ICSES52305.2021.9633913

Singh, K. D., Deep Singh, P., Bansal, A., Kaur, G., Khullar, V., & Tripathi, V. (2023). Exploratory Data Analysis and Customer Churn Prediction for the Telecommunication Industry. *ACCESS 2023 - 2023 3rd International Conference on Advances in Computing, Communication, Embedded and Secure Systems*, 197 – 201. DOI: 10.1109/ACCESS57397.2023.10199700

Singh, K. K., Vats, C., & Singh, M. P. (2023). An Empirical Study of the Impact of Organizational, Social, and Psychological Factors on the Performance of Employees. In M. P., M. P., S. A., K. S., K. S.K., & M. S.K. (Eds.), *Springer Proceedings in Business and Economics* (pp. 621 – 636). Springer Nature. DOI: 10.1007/978-981-99-0197-5_39

Singh, P., & Singh, K. D. (2023). Fog-Centric Intelligent Surveillance System: A Novel Approach for Effective and Efficient Surveillance. In K. R., K. R., G. M., G. M., S. R., & S. R. (Eds.), *2023 International Conference on Advancement in Computation and Computer Technologies, InCACCT 2023* (pp. 762 – 766). Institute of Electrical and Electronics Engineers Inc. DOI: 10.1109/InCACCT57535.2023.10141802

Singh, Y., Singh, N. K., & Sharma, A. (2023). Biodiesel as an alternative fuel employed in CI engine to meet the sustainability criteria: A review. In S. Y., S. G., & B. G.K. (Eds.), *AIP Conference Proceedings* (Vol. 2521). American Institute of Physics Inc. DOI: 10.1063/5.0113825

Singhal, P., Sharma, S., Saha, S., Mishra, I., Alfurhood, B. S., & Singh, P. (2023). Smart security system using Hybrid System with IoT and Blockchain: A security system Human sased Detection. *2023 3rd International Conference on Advance Computing and Innovative Technologies in Engineering, ICACITE 2023*, 1032 – 1036. DOI: 10.1109/ICACITE57410.2023.10182383

Singla, A., Singh, Y., Singh, Y., Rahim, E. A., Singh, N. K., & Sharma, A. (2023). Challenges and Future Prospects of Biofuel Generations: An Overview. In *Biowaste and Biomass in Biofuel Applications*. CRC Press., DOI: 10.1201/9781003265597-4

Širić, I., Eid, E. M., Taher, M. A., El-Morsy, M. H. E., Osman, H. E. M., Kumar, P., Adelodun, B., Abou Fayssal, S., Mioč, B., Andabaka, Ž., Goala, M., Kumari, S., Bachheti, A., Choi, K. S., & Kumar, V. (2022). Combined Use of Spent Mushroom Substrate Biochar and PGPR Improves Growth, Yield, and Biochemical Response of Cauliflower (Brassica oleracea var. botrytis): A Preliminary Study on Greenhouse Cultivation. *Horticulturae*, 8(9), 830. Advance online publication. DOI: 10.3390/horticulturae8090830

Srivastava, A., Hassan, M., & Gangwar, R. (2023). Improving Railway Track System Using Soil Nails for Heavy Axle Load. *Lecture Notes in Civil Engineering, 338 LNCE*, 1 – 13. DOI: 10.1007/978-981-99-1886-7_1

Srivastava, A., Jawaid, S., Singh, R., Gehlot, A., Akram, S. V., Priyadarshi, N., & Khan, B. (2022). Imperative Role of Technology Intervention and Implementation for Automation in the Construction Industry. *Advances in Civil Engineering*, 2022(1), 6716987. Advance online publication. DOI: 10.1155/2022/6716987

Srivastava, B., Kandpal, V., & Jain, A. K. (2024). Financial well-being of women self-help group members: A qualitative study. *Environment, Development and Sustainability*. Advance online publication. DOI: 10.1007/s10668-024-04879-w

Starks, L. T. (2023). Presidential Address: Sustainable Finance and ESG Issues—Value versus Values. *The Journal of Finance*, 78(4), 1837–1872. DOI: 10.1111/jofi.13255

Streimikiene, D., Mikalauskiene, A., & Burbaite, G. (2023). THE ROLE OF SUSTAINABLE FINANCE IN ACHIEVING SUSTAINABLE DEVELOPMENT GOALS. *Economics & Sociology (Ternopil)*, 16(1), 256–283. DOI: 10.14254/2071-789X.2023/16-1/17

Sunori, S. K., Mohan, L., Pant, M., & Juneja, P. (2023). Classification of Soil Fertility using LVQ and PNN Techniques. *Proceedings of the 8th International Conference on Communication and Electronics Systems, ICCES 2023*, 1441 – 1446. DOI: 10.1109/ICCES57224.2023.10192793

Suryavanshi, A., Kukreja, V., Bordoloi, D., Mehta, S., & Choudhary, A. (2023). Agricultural Insights Through Federated Learning CNN: A Case Study on Jackfruit Leaf Disease. In D. R.K., S. A.Kr., S. R., B. S., & K. V. (Eds.), *Proceedings of the 2023 12th International Conference on System Modeling and Advancement in Research Trends, SMART 2023* (pp. 36 – 42). Institute of Electrical and Electronics Engineers Inc. DOI: 10.1109/SMART59791.2023.10428321

Suryavanshi, A., Tanwar, S., Kukreja, V., Choudhary, A., & Chamoli, S. (2023). An Integrated Approach to Potato Leaf Disease Detection Using Convolutional Neural Networks and Random Forest. *Proceedings of the 2023 International Conference on Innovative Computing, Intelligent Communication and Smart Electrical Systems, ICSES 2023*. DOI: 10.1109/ICSES60034.2023.10465557

Taneja, S., Bhatnagar, M., Kumar, P., & Rupeika-apoga, R. (2023). India ' s Total Natural Resource Rents (NRR) and GDP : An Augmented Autoregressive Distributed Lag (ARDL) Bound Test. *Journal of Risk and Financial Management*, 16(2), 91. https://doi.org/doi.org/10.3390/jrfm16020091. DOI: 10.3390/jrfm16020091

Taneja, S., Gupta, M., Bhushan, P., Bhatnagar, M., & Singh, A. (2023). Cultural marketing in the digital era. In *Cultural Marketing and Metaverse for Consumer Engagement*. IGI Global., DOI: 10.4018/978-1-6684-8312-1.ch008

Taneja, S., & Özen, E. (2023). To analyse the relationship between bank's green financing and environmental performance. *International Journal of Electronic Finance*, 12(2), 163–175. DOI: 10.1504/IJEF.2023.129919

Taneja, S., & Sharma, V. (2023). Role of beaconing marketing in improving customer buying experience. In *Enhancing Customer Engagement Through Location-Based Marketing*. IGI Global., DOI: 10.4018/978-1-6684-8177-6.ch012

Thakur, S., Malik, D., Kukreja, V., Sharma, R., Yadav, R., & Joshi, K. (2023). Multi-Stage Classification of Pomegranate Anthracnose Disease Severity Levels with CNN and SVM. *Proceedings of the 4th International Conference on Smart Electronics and Communication, ICOSEC 2023*, 1117 – 1121. DOI: 10.1109/ICOSEC58147.2023.10276047

Tiwari, K., Bafila, P., Negi, P., & Singh, R. (2023). The applications of nanotechnology in nutraceuticals: A review. In S. Y., S. G., & B. G.K. (Eds.), *AIP Conference Proceedings* (Vol. 2521). American Institute of Physics Inc. DOI: 10.1063/5.0129695

Tomar, S., & Sharma, N. (2021). A systematic review of agricultural policies in terms of drivers, enablers, and bottlenecks: Comparison of three Indian states and a model bio-energy village located in different agro climatic regions. *Groundwater for Sustainable Development*, 15, 100683. Advance online publication. DOI: 10.1016/j.gsd.2021.100683

Tomar, S., Sharma, N., & Nehra, N. S. (2023). A sustainable rural entrepreneurship model developed by the organic farmers of India. *Emerald Emerging Markets Case Studies*, 13(2), 1–17. DOI: 10.1108/EEMCS-09-2022-0329

Tyagi, S., Jindal, T., Krishna, S. H., Hassen, S. M., Shukla, S. K., & Kaur, C. (2022). Comparative Analysis of Artificial Intelligence and its Powered Technologies Applications in the Finance Sector. *Proceedings of 5th International Conference on Contemporary Computing and Informatics, IC3I 2022*, 260 – 264. DOI: 10.1109/IC3I56241.2022.10073077

Uniyal, A. K., Kanojia, P., Khanna, R., & Dixit, A. K. (2022). Quantitative Analysis of the Impact of Demography and Job Profile on the Organizational Commitment of the Faculty Members in the HEI'S of Uttarakhand. *Communications in Computer and Information Science, 1742 CCIS*, 24–35. DOI: 10.1007/978-3-031-23647-1_3

Uniyal, S., Sarma, P. R. S., Kumar Mangla, S., Tseng, M.-L., & Patil, P. (2022). ICT as "Knowledge Management" for Assessing Sustainable Consumption and Production in Supply Chains. In *Research Anthology on Measuring and Achieving Sustainable Development Goals* (Vol. 3). IGI Global. DOI: 10.4018/978-1-6684-3885-5.ch048

Upreti, H., & Malhotra, R. K. (2024). Bridging The Urban-Rural Education Gap In India Through CSR (Corporate Social Responsibility) Initiatives: A Conceptual Study With Special Reference To Sustainable Development Goal 4 (Quality Education). In P. P.K. (Ed.), *E3S Web of Conferences* (Vol. 556). EDP Sciences. DOI: 10.1051/e3sconf/202455601032

Vennila, H., Giri, N. C., Nallapaneni, M. K., Sinha, P., Bajaj, M., Abou Houran, M., & Kamel, S. (2022). Static and dynamic environmental economic dispatch using tournament selection based ant lion optimization algorithm. *Frontiers in Energy Research*, 10, 972069. Advance online publication. DOI: 10.3389/fenrg.2022.972069

Vijayalakshmi, S., Hasan, F., Priyadarshini, S. M., Durga, S., Verma, V., & Podile, V. (2022). Strategic Evaluation of Implementing Artificial Intelligence Towards Shaping Entrepreneurial Development During Covid- 19 Outbreaks. *2022 2nd International Conference on Advance Computing and Innovative Technologies in Engineering, ICACITE 2022*, 2570–2573. DOI: 10.1109/ICACITE53722.2022.9823894

William, P., Ramu, G., Kansal, L., Patil, P. P., Alkhayyat, A., & Rao, A. K. (2023). Artificial Intelligence Based Air Quality Monitoring System with Modernized Environmental Safety of Sustainable Development. *Proceedings - 2023 3rd International Conference on Pervasive Computing and Social Networking, ICPCSN 2023*, 756 – 761. DOI: 10.1109/ICPCSN58827.2023.00130

Wongchai, A., Shukla, S. K., Ahmed, M. A., Sakthi, U., Jagdish, M., & kumar, R. (2022). Artificial intelligence - enabled soft sensor and internet of things for sustainable agriculture using ensemble deep learning architecture. *Computers & Electrical Engineering*, 102, 108128. Advance online publication. DOI: 10.1016/j.compeleceng.2022.108128

Yadav, A. R., Shekhar, S., Vidyarthi, A., Prakash, R., & Gowri, R. (2023). Hyper-Parameter Tuning with Grid and Randomized Search Techniques for Predictive Models of Hotel Booking. *IEEE International Conference on Electrical, Electronics, Communication and Computers, ELEXCOM 2023*. DOI: 10.1109/ELEXCOM58812.2023.10370718

Yadav, S., Samadhiya, A., Kumar, A., Luthra, S., & Pandey, K. K. (2024). Nexus between fintech, green finance and natural resources management: Transition of BRICS nation industries from resource curse to resource blessed sustainable economies. *Resources Policy*, 91, 104903. Advance online publication. DOI: 10.1016/j.resourpol.2024.104903

Zeidan, R. (2022). Obstacles to sustainable finance and the covid19 crisis. *Journal of Sustainable Finance & Investment*, 12(2), 525–528. DOI: 10.1080/20430795.2020.1783152

Chapter 14
Pandemic Preparedness and the Economics of Global Health Crises

Larisa Mistrean
Academy of Economic Studies of Moldova, Moldova

Azad Singh
https://orcid.org/0000-0002-1264-1169
Mangalmay Institute of Management and Technology, India

Tripti Desai
New Delhi Institute of Management, India

ABSTRACT

The chapter explores how intelligent technologies, particularly AI and predictive analytics, are revolutionising pandemic preparedness and the economics of global health crises. By leveraging digital health tools, data analysis, and IoT systems, governments and health organisations can enhance early detection, streamline resource management, and reduce the economic burden of pandemics. The chapter delves into the financial implications of adopting tech-driven strategies, presenting a cost-benefit analysis that highlights the return on investment for implementing such tools. Drawing lessons from COVID-19, the chapter emphasises the potential for technology to mitigate future health crises' economic impact. Ethical considerations, especially concerning data privacy, are addressed, along with policy recommendations to support sustainable investments in health technology. The insights aim to inform a balanced approach that aligns public health goals with economic resilience for better future preparedness.

1. INTRODUCTION TO PANDEMIC PREPAREDNESS AND ECONOMIC RESILIENCE

The pervasive ramifications of global health crises on the economic infrastructure of nations underscore the necessity of conceptualizing pandemics not merely as public health emergencies but as pivotal events with the potential to destabilize entire economies (S. Sharma, Singh, et al., 2023). These crises

DOI: 10.4018/979-8-3373-0240-9.ch014

disrupt the established interdependencies within the global economic network, revealing profound vulnerabilities across sectors, rendering economic systems susceptible to cascading failures, and compelling a reevaluation of traditional economic resilience frameworks (Josphineleela et al., 2023). The COVID-19 pandemic, the most disruptive health crisis of the twenty-first century, has amplified these implications, highlighting the expansive ripple effects of pandemics on financial systems, labor markets, and public resource allocation. In examining the economic repercussions of global health crises, it becomes evident that the readiness of health systems and the robustness of economic infrastructure are symbiotically linked, revealing the exigency of a dual-focused preparedness strategy that prioritizes both public health resilience and economic continuity (Ingale et al., 2023; P. Jain et al., 2023; Nikolaidis et al., 2022).

Health crises introduce acute, multifaceted disruptions into the intricate latticework of global supply chains and labor markets. When a pandemic emerges, the immediate impacts are often felt through interruptions in production and trade, as restrictive public health measures are implemented to curtail viral transmission (Ambika et al., 2023; Bhatt et al., 2023). However, the ramifications of these initial disruptions extend far beyond their point of origin, cascading through supply chains to impact downstream sectors, reduce productivity, and stymie consumer demand. As evidenced by COVID-19, industries reliant on transnational supply chains, such as manufacturing and technology, are especially vulnerable to these disruptions. The abrupt halt in production, compounded by delays in logistics and the transportation of goods, creates bottlenecks that impede the ability of industries to meet demand, ultimately leading to reduced output and financial instability. These disruptions reverberate within labor markets, as businesses are compelled to downsize or furlough employees to offset revenue declines, thereby exacerbating the socio-economic vulnerabilities of affected populations (Nagila et al., 2023; S. Sharma, Gupta, et al., 2023; Tyagi et al., 2023).

Moreover, pandemics engender pronounced fiscal strain as governments are forced to mobilize vast resources to counteract public health emergencies. The necessity of reallocating funds to sustain healthcare infrastructure, procure medical supplies, and support emergency response initiatives often diverts resources from other essential sectors, such as education, infrastructure, and social services. For instance, the financial toll of COVID-19 has been estimated to exceed $12 trillion by 2025, a staggering figure that encapsulates both direct healthcare expenditures and the ancillary costs associated with lost productivity, diminished consumer spending, and heightened government debt (Asha et al., 2022; S. Sharma et al., 2021; P. M. Yadav et al., 2023). The fiscal reallocation required during pandemics frequently precipitates long-term economic consequences, as governments may resort to austerity measures, increased borrowing, or inflationary monetary policies to sustain their pandemic response efforts. This financial strain is especially pronounced in low- and middle-income countries, where healthcare systems are already under-resourced and ill-equipped to absorb the demands of a large-scale health crisis. These nations, burdened by limited fiscal capacity, often face a compounded crisis wherein the economic ramifications of a pandemic exacerbate pre-existing healthcare deficiencies, creating a feedback loop of vulnerability that perpetuates their dependency on external aid (S. Sharma et al., 2021).

The social repercussions of pandemics further underscore the economic impact of health crises, as marginalized and vulnerable populations are disproportionately affected by both the health and economic dimensions of pandemics (Asha et al., 2022; Vennila et al., 2022). These groups often lack access to adequate healthcare, possess limited savings or financial safety nets, and are more likely to work in precarious or informal sectors that are susceptible to economic downturns. Consequently, the economic fallout of pandemics exacerbates existing inequities, perpetuating cycles of poverty and inequality (Sati et al., 2022; K. D. Singh et al., 2023; Tomar et al., 2023). This stratification is evident in the differential economic outcomes observed across demographics and regions during COVID-19, wherein marginalized communities experienced higher unemployment rates, increased morbidity and mortality, and reduced access to essential services (Tyagi et al., 2022). The intensification of socioeconomic inequities during pandemics is not merely a humanitarian concern; it constitutes a profound economic challenge, as the erosion of economic opportunities for vulnerable populations constrains aggregate demand, diminishes social mobility, and limits the long-term growth potential of economies (Chauhan et al., 2023; Ranakoti et al., 2022; Sunori et al., 2023).

In light of these complex economic vulnerabilities, the necessity of pandemic preparedness assumes a strategic economic dimension. Proactive investment in public health infrastructure, early-warning systems, and emergency response mechanisms mitigates the economic impact of pandemics by enabling swift containment and minimizing the disruption to economic activity (Arora et al., 2023; Dieudonne et al., 2022; P. Singh & Singh, 2023). For example, countries with robust testing and contact-tracing capabilities were able to implement targeted containment measures during COVID-19, thereby avoiding the sweeping economic shutdowns that characterized the pandemic response in other regions. These proactive interventions, enabled by technological advancements such as digital health surveillance and predictive analytics, offer a cost-effective means of mitigating the financial toll of pandemics, underscoring the value of preparedness as a fiscal stabilizer. Furthermore, preparedness initiatives contribute to economic resilience by reducing the likelihood of prolonged public health emergencies that necessitate extensive resource reallocations, thereby preserving fiscal sustainability and enabling governments to allocate funds toward long-term developmental priorities (Pant et al., 2022; M. Sharma, Hagar, et al., 2022).

Beyond the immediate economic benefits, preparedness for global health crises fosters structural resilience by reinforcing the adaptability of economic systems to external shocks. In an era marked by increasing economic interconnectedness and volatility, the capacity to withstand and recover from disruptions is a defining attribute of sustainable economic models (Elbagory et al., 2022; Khan et al., 2023; Papageorgiou et al., 2023). Pandemic preparedness, when integrated into national economic strategies, cultivates resilience by embedding flexibility into supply chains, diversifying sources of essential goods, and enhancing workforce adaptability through remote and decentralized working models. These resilience-building measures serve as a buffer against future crises, equipping economies with the tools to absorb and adapt to external shocks without incurring severe disruptions. The integration of preparedness into economic resilience frameworks thus transcends its immediate utility, positioning it as a foundational component of sustainable economic development that balances the imperatives of growth with the exigencies of global health security (Kunwar et al., 2023; Malik et al., 2023; B. Rawat et al., 2022).

The ethical dimensions of pandemic preparedness further accentuate its importance as a component of economic strategy. Health crises disproportionately impact vulnerable populations, and the inequitable distribution of resources during pandemics exacerbates disparities that undermine social cohesion and economic stability (Rajeswari et al., 2022; Shukla et al., 2023; Thakur et al., 2023). Preparedness initiatives that prioritize equity—such as ensuring access to healthcare for marginalized populations, implementing targeted support for small businesses, and maintaining social safety nets—address the ethical imperative of reducing health disparities while also bolstering economic resilience. By fostering inclusivity and protecting the livelihoods of vulnerable communities, these initiatives contribute to a more stable and cohesive socio-economic landscape, which, in turn, supports sustained economic growth and stability (Bhushan & Nayak, 2022; MITRA et al., 2022; William et al., 2023).

2. ADVANCES IN SMART TECHNOLOGIES FOR PANDEMIC PREPAREDNESS

The deployment of advanced technological paradigms—specifically artificial intelligence (AI), the Internet of Things (IoT), and Big Data analytics—has fundamentally reshaped the early detection capabilities of global health systems in anticipating, identifying, and mitigating pandemics (S. S. Rawat et al., 2022; M. Sharma, Kumar, et al., 2022; Shekhar et al., 2022). These technologies, each contributing uniquely within an interconnected framework, offer unparalleled potential in recognizing disease patterns, monitoring real-time epidemiological data, and deploying early intervention strategies that could ultimately stymie the global proliferation of infectious diseases. AI, IoT, and Big Data converge to form a triad of tools that collect, analyze, and interpret extensive data points, providing health authorities with rapid insights that inform evidence-based decision-making in real-time, thus enabling timely intervention at the earliest indications of emerging health threats (Giri et al., 2022; Gonfa et al., 2023; Srivastava et al., 2023).

Artificial intelligence occupies a central role within this ecosystem, offering computational frameworks capable of processing and learning from colossal volumes of health-related data, including genomic sequences, clinical outcomes, environmental conditions, and population behaviors. AI algorithms, especially those rooted in machine learning and deep learning, employ pattern recognition techniques that enable the identification of disease outbreaks long before they become visible to human observers. In this capacity, AI serves as a sentinel, continuously surveilling datasets for anomalies that suggest potential viral mutations or heightened transmission vectors (Behera & Singh Rawat, 2023; G. Kumar, Kumar, et al., 2023; Singla et al., 2023). Machine learning models can assimilate vast datasets, discerning subtle correlations that may elude traditional epidemiological methods. Through these high-dimensional analyses, AI facilitates predictive modeling, offering projections about how a pathogen might spread across regions, which populations are most vulnerable, and where resources should be allocated to preemptively stem an outbreak (V. Kumar et al., 2021; A. Singh et al., 2021; Uniyal et al., 2022).

The IoT, operating as an extensive network of interconnected devices, augments the capacity of AI by serving as a conduit for continuous data acquisition, enabling an unprecedented depth of surveillance and reporting capabilities. IoT devices, which include everything from wearable sensors to environmental monitors and mobile applications, collect data on individual and community health metrics at scale. Wearable devices, for example, can track physiological parameters such as heart rate, body temperature, and respiratory function, and relay this data to centralized platforms where it can be monitored for deviations from typical health baselines (Aloo et al., 2023; Chand et al., 2023; H. R. Sharma et al., 2021). When aggregated, this information provides an overview of community health trends, allowing authorities to detect subtle indicators of disease spread in near real-time. IoT-enabled environmental sensors further enrich these insights by capturing data on air quality, humidity, and other climatic factors that may influence pathogen survival and transmission rates. Thus, the IoT serves not merely as a passive observer but as an active participant in early detection strategies, converting every connected device into a node within a broader, responsive surveillance network (S. Jain & Jain, 2021; A. Kumar, Pant, et al., 2023; M. Sharma & Singh, 2023).

The efficacy of AI and IoT in early detection is profoundly enhanced when harnessed alongside Big Data analytics, which provides the infrastructure necessary for storing, processing, and analyzing immense datasets generated by these technologies. Big Data serves as the backbone of pandemic prediction systems, capable of managing and integrating information from disparate sources—ranging from electronic health records (EHRs) and laboratory data to social media feeds, travel records, and population mobility patterns (Paul et al., 2022; Rai et al., 2022; S. Sharma, Kadayat, et al., 2023). By collating data from diverse channels, Big Data analytics enables a panoramic view of global health, identifying patterns and trends across regions and demographics that would be otherwise imperceptible. Through data mining and advanced statistical techniques, Big Data systems are able to detect correlations between factors such as mobility patterns, climate variations, and seasonal shifts, each of which may contribute to the spread or containment of infectious diseases (Akberdina et al., 2023; Mekala et al., 2023; Mitra et al., 2022). This extensive databank provides a robust foundation upon which AI models can operate, feeding algorithms with the breadth and depth of information necessary to make accurate, timely predictions about disease emergence and propagation (Alsadi et al., 2022; A. Kumar, Goyal, et al., 2023; Srivastava et al., 2022).

At the nexus of these technological capabilities are smart surveillance systems, which represent an evolution in real-time disease tracking and health data collection. Smart surveillance amalgamates data from IoT devices, AI predictions, and Big Data analytics to create a dynamic, interconnected framework that monitors health metrics across diverse populations. These systems leverage geolocation data, social media content, and anonymized mobility information to construct a spatial map of disease spread, offering granular insights into outbreak hotspots and potential transmission pathways (Rao et al., 2023; N. K. Sharma et al., 2021; Wongchai et al., 2022). Unlike traditional surveillance methods that rely on retrospective data, smart surveillance operates in a proactive and anticipatory capacity, analyzing incoming data continuously and adjusting predictions as new information becomes available. By doing so, these systems facilitate a shift from reactive to preemptive public health interventions, empowering authorities to implement targeted measures such as localized lockdowns, enhanced testing, and rapid deployment of medical resources precisely where they are needed (R. Kumar, Lamba, et al., 2023; V. Kumar & Korovin, 2023; Vijayalakshmi et al., 2022).

Real-time data collection within these systems is essential, as it bridges the gap between disease detection and response, enabling rapid situational awareness that is critical in the containment phase of an outbreak. In regions where health infrastructure may be limited, real-time data allows for early identification of rising caseloads, enabling swift international assistance and resource mobilization before healthcare facilities become overwhelmed (A. Kumar, Sharma, et al., 2023; Tiwari et al., 2023; Tomar & Sharma, 2021). Furthermore, by disseminating real-time information through public channels, these systems foster transparency and empower communities to make informed decisions, thereby strengthening societal resilience against disease transmission. For instance, during the COVID-19 pandemic, real-time dashboards tracking infection rates and vaccination progress became indispensable tools for both policymakers and the public, offering an evolving portrait of the pandemic's trajectory and fostering a data-driven response (Gupta et al., 2023; Kukreti et al., 2023; A. K. Mishra et al., 2023; Suryavanshi, Tanwar, et al., 2023).

Despite their potential, the integration of AI, IoT, and Big Data into early detection frameworks also raises ethical, operational, and infrastructural considerations that warrant careful examination. The unprecedented scale of data collection intrinsic to these systems presents significant privacy concerns, as sensitive health information and personal metrics are gathered continuously, often without explicit consent. The potential for data breaches, misuse of information, and erosion of individual privacy rights poses a critical challenge to the adoption of these technologies (Ansari & Afzal, 2022; Jindal, Kukreja, Mehta, Chauhan, et al., 2023; A. Kaur, Kukreja, Chamoli, et al., 2023b; Suryavanshi, Kukreja, et al., 2023). Moreover, the efficacy of these systems depends on equitable access to technology, which may be hindered by socioeconomic disparities. In resource-limited settings, where IoT infrastructure or reliable internet connectivity may be unavailable, the deployment of such advanced systems may be impractical, potentially leaving vulnerable populations without the benefits of early detection and targeted interventions. Addressing these challenges requires a balanced approach, wherein technological advancements are aligned with stringent privacy protections and policies that prioritize inclusivity and accessibility (Dubey et al., 2023; A. Kaur, Kukreja, Nisha Chandran, et al., 2023; A. R. Yadav et al., 2023).

3. FINANCIAL IMPLICATIONS OF AI AND PREDICTIVE ANALYTICS IN PANDEMIC RESPONSE

The cost-efficiency and return on investment (ROI) of AI-driven solutions in healthcare and pandemic response represent a paradigm shift in the economics of public health interventions, offering promising avenues for resource optimization, cost containment, and long-term financial resilience. Traditionally, the allocation of resources during health crises has been reactive, characterized by significant, often exorbitant, emergency expenditures directed toward containment and treatment rather than prevention and preparedness (Banerjee et al., 2023; A. Kaur, Kukreja, Chamoli, et al., 2023a; Y. Singh et al., 2023). AI-driven solutions have begun to reverse this paradigm, enabling a proactive approach that maximizes resource efficiency while minimizing financial outlay. By leveraging advanced analytics, machine learning, and real-time data processing, AI has facilitated the identification of emergent health risks, allowing health systems to respond preemptively, which, in turn, mitigates the downstream costs associated with large-scale health interventions (A. Mishra et al., 2023; S. Sharma & Tyagi, 2023; Singhal et al., 2023).

The ROI of AI-driven healthcare solutions is underscored by their capacity to substantially reduce inefficiencies across various levels of pandemic response, from surveillance and early detection to patient care and vaccine distribution. In the early stages of a pandemic, AI systems can analyze vast troves of data—from patient symptoms and mobility trends to virological patterns—and identify potential outbreaks before they escalate. Such foresight reduces the likelihood of a full-blown health crisis that demands extensive government funding, resource mobilization, and economic disruption. For instance, during COVID-19, AI-based early warning systems that incorporated predictive modeling significantly reduced response times, enabling authorities to deploy medical resources more strategically. This reduction in response lag not only curtails the spread of disease but also alleviates the need for drastic economic interventions, which frequently strain public finances. In the realm of patient care, AI-driven diagnostic tools expedite accurate diagnosis and personalized treatment, streamlining hospital operations and allowing healthcare systems to operate more cost-effectively, even amidst surges in demand (G. Kaur, Sharma, et al., 2023; Kholiya et al., 2023; K. K. Singh et al., 2023).

Beyond direct healthcare applications, the financial efficacy of AI in pandemic response is amplified through its impact on resource allocation and supply chain management. AI-based predictive analytics, in particular, serve as a transformative tool for optimizing the distribution of critical supplies, including personal protective equipment (PPE), testing kits, and vaccines. By analyzing patterns of demand and supply across regions, AI algorithms can predict supply shortages before they materialize, enabling health authorities to preemptively allocate resources to areas most in need. This level of strategic foresight mitigates the risk of stockouts, reduces wastage, and ensures that medical supplies are utilized at maximum efficiency. Moreover, predictive analytics can model supply chain disruptions based on variables such as transportation delays, labor shortages, and political instability, thereby identifying potential bottlenecks and recommending alternative distribution routes or suppliers. This capability, realized through advanced machine learning models, allows supply chains to remain agile and resilient, preserving the flow of essential goods even under crisis conditions and ultimately reducing the financial costs of resource misallocation and logistical failures (Dahiya et al., 2023; V. Jain et al., 2023; Jindal, Kukreja, Mehta, Srivastava, et al., 2023; Pandey et al., 2023).

The deployment of AI in supply chain management has far-reaching economic implications, particularly regarding the optimization of inventory levels. During pandemics, healthcare providers are often forced to overstock supplies to compensate for unpredictable surges in demand, which results in resource redundancy and elevated storage costs. AI-driven inventory management systems alleviate this burden by utilizing predictive analytics to forecast demand with a high degree of accuracy, ensuring that inventory levels are aligned with real-time needs rather than speculative excess (Bhatnagar et al., 2023). By minimizing overstocking and obsolescence, AI contributes to a more cost-efficient allocation of resources, which not only improves ROI but also conserves public funds that can be redirected toward other critical areas of pandemic preparedness and response. In this context, the ROI of AI transcends mere cost savings, embodying a sustainable approach to healthcare management that mitigates waste, reduces operational expenses, and enhances the overall financial sustainability of health systems (P. Kumar, Taneja, et al., 2024).

In addition to cost-efficiency, AI-driven solutions deliver substantial economic value by enhancing the scalability and flexibility of pandemic response frameworks. Unlike traditional models of resource allocation, which are often rigid and bureaucratic, AI-based systems offer dynamic solutions that can be rapidly scaled or adapted to meet the fluctuating demands of a health crisis. For instance, machine learning algorithms can be continuously refined as new data becomes available, enabling real-time adjustments to resource distribution and intervention strategies (P. Kumar, Reepu, et al., 2024). This adaptability not only improves response efficacy but also maximizes the utility of each dollar invested, as resources are deployed based on evolving needs rather than static, pre-established plans. The ROI of such adaptability is evident in the reduction of unnecessary expenditures, as resources are allocated precisely where and when they are needed, thus minimizing waste and ensuring that health systems remain agile under even the most unpredictable circumstances (Bhatnagar, Rajaram, et al., 2024).

Furthermore, AI-driven predictive analytics provide critical insights that support long-term strategic planning, particularly in relation to supply chain resilience and healthcare workforce management. By analyzing historical data and identifying trends in disease propagation, AI systems can inform the development of more resilient supply chains that are better prepared to withstand future disruptions (Taneja, Bhatnagar, Kumar, & Rupeika-apoga, 2023). This forward-looking approach extends to the management of healthcare personnel, where AI can predict workforce requirements based on projected caseloads, enabling health systems to allocate staff efficiently and avoid costly shortages or redundancies. In this way, the economic value of AI-driven solutions lies not only in immediate cost savings but in their ability to foster structural resilience that guards against future financial shocks. The ROI of these technologies is thus multidimensional, encompassing both immediate efficiencies and long-term sustainability, as they embed preparedness into the very fabric of healthcare and supply chain operations (Bhatnagar, Kumar, et al., 2024).

However, the implementation of AI-driven solutions in pandemic response is not without its economic challenges, particularly concerning initial investment costs, technological infrastructure requirements, and the need for specialized expertise. The development, integration, and maintenance of AI systems necessitate substantial financial resources, which may be a barrier for low- and middle-income countries. Additionally, the efficacy of these solutions is contingent upon the availability of high-quality data, which may be limited in regions with underdeveloped health information systems (P. Kumar, Bhatnagar, et al., 2023). To address these barriers, public-private partnerships and international collaborations are essential, as they facilitate the sharing of resources, expertise, and best practices. The long-term ROI of AI in pandemic response thus depends not only on the technology itself but also on the establishment of supportive policies, data-sharing frameworks, and infrastructure investments that enable equitable access to these solutions. By prioritizing these enablers, nations can maximize the cost-efficiency of AI-driven systems and ensure that the benefits of predictive analytics extend to all populations (Taneja, Bhatnagar, Kumar, & Grima, 2023).

4. CASE STUDY: LESSONS FROM COVID-19

The adoption of technology during the COVID-19 pandemic revealed a complex interplay of both transformative successes and profound shortcomings that collectively shaped the global response to the health crisis. As the pandemic unfolded, technology emerged as an indispensable tool for managing the spread of the virus, diagnosing and treating patients, and ensuring the continuity of essential services. However, the swift and widespread implementation of digital solutions also exposed significant limitations within existing technological frameworks, particularly in terms of scalability, interoperability, and equitable access (P. Kumar, Verma, et al., 2023). While some countries effectively harnessed advanced technologies, such as artificial intelligence (AI) and big data analytics, to track infection rates and allocate resources, others encountered insurmountable obstacles, ranging from insufficient infrastructure to a lack of trained personnel, ultimately impeding their ability to mount an efficient response. The divergence between technological successes and failures underscored the critical importance of preparedness, infrastructure investment, and strategic planning in the deployment of tech-driven interventions during health crises (P. Sharma et al., 2024).

One of the notable successes in tech adoption during the COVID-19 pandemic was the rapid development and implementation of digital health surveillance systems, which enabled real-time tracking and monitoring of infection rates. Countries like South Korea and Singapore were able to leverage AI and big data to identify hotspots and track the virus's spread, thereby facilitating timely interventions that mitigated the impact on public health systems and the economy (A. Kaur, Kumar, et al., 2023). South Korea's contact-tracing efforts, driven by data integration across healthcare providers, travel records, and mobile networks, demonstrated the efficacy of technology in preemptively identifying potential outbreaks and containing them before they reached critical levels. Furthermore, machine learning models were deployed in numerous regions to predict demand for medical resources, enabling efficient allocation and averting shortages that could have otherwise overwhelmed healthcare facilities. These predictive capabilities not only improved response time but also reduced the financial burden associated with the reactive stockpiling of medical supplies and personnel, underscoring the cost-saving potential of AI-driven solutions in pandemic management (Bhatnagar, Taneja, et al., 2024).

Conversely, numerous countries experienced substantial challenges in implementing similar technologies due to structural limitations and a lack of readiness for large-scale digital interventions. In several regions, the adoption of contact-tracing apps was marred by concerns over data privacy, interoperability issues, and low user participation rates, which limited the effectiveness of these technologies in controlling the virus's spread. Privacy concerns, particularly in countries with stringent data protection regulations, impeded the ability of governments to mandate the use of such apps, thereby reducing their utility as public health tools. Additionally, the heterogeneity of contact-tracing platforms across countries created substantial barriers to cross-border data sharing and tracking, undermining the efficacy of these systems in monitoring and managing the pandemic on a global scale. These limitations illustrated that, while technology holds immense potential in disease surveillance, its efficacy is contingent upon an infrastructure that supports seamless integration and data-sharing frameworks that respect individual privacy rights.

The economic burden of the pandemic was further mitigated by tech-driven interventions that enabled remote work, online education, and telemedicine, each of which played a critical role in maintaining economic continuity amidst widespread lockdowns and movement restrictions. The rapid shift to remote work, facilitated by cloud computing, video conferencing platforms, and collaborative tools, allowed numerous businesses to continue operations despite physical limitations, preserving productivity and preventing catastrophic losses in revenue. Telemedicine, meanwhile, emerged as an essential component of healthcare delivery, providing patients with access to medical consultations and treatments without exposing them to the risks associated with in-person visits. These digital solutions not only preserved jobs and sustained economic activity but also underscored the adaptability of technology in safeguarding economic resilience during unprecedented disruptions. However, the efficacy of these interventions was unevenly distributed, with access to digital infrastructure and technological literacy emerging as significant determinants of economic resilience. Regions with limited internet connectivity and populations lacking digital skills were disproportionately impacted, further entrenching economic disparities and highlighting the critical need for inclusive digital literacy programs and infrastructural investments.

While the deployment of technology alleviated some aspects of the economic burden associated with COVID-19, the limitations and failures of tech-driven interventions also exacerbated existing economic vulnerabilities and underscored the risks of relying on untested digital solutions during a crisis. The reliance on remote work and digital platforms, for instance, highlighted the economic divide between high-income nations with robust digital infrastructure and lower-income regions where internet access and technology resources were scarce. In economically disadvantaged areas, the inability to shift to remote work translated into higher rates of unemployment and business closures, thereby amplifying the socio-economic impact of the pandemic. Additionally, the lack of preparedness for a digital transformation at such an unprecedented scale created cybersecurity vulnerabilities, with many organizations lacking the necessary safeguards to protect sensitive data and prevent cyber-attacks. The increase in cyber threats during the pandemic underscored the necessity of investing in cybersecurity infrastructure as an integral component of future pandemic preparedness.

Beyond immediate economic continuity, tech-driven interventions have the potential to reduce long-term economic burden by supporting preventive healthcare measures and facilitating resource-efficient responses. Predictive analytics, for instance, allows healthcare systems to anticipate demand for medical resources, enabling the efficient distribution of supplies and reducing wastage. The use of AI in predictive modeling can identify patterns in patient data that indicate early signs of health crises, allowing for timely interventions that prevent escalation and thereby reduce healthcare costs. In the context of COVID-19, predictive analytics was instrumental in identifying risk factors for severe outcomes, which enabled healthcare providers to allocate resources more effectively and avoid unnecessary expenses. By facilitating precision in resource management, technology not only reduces immediate costs but also builds resilience against future health crises, allowing economies to adapt more fluidly to shocks without incurring substantial financial losses.

Despite the economic advantages associated with tech-driven interventions, the COVID-19 pandemic exposed a fundamental need for regulatory frameworks that can support the ethical deployment of technology in crisis scenarios. The absence of standardized guidelines for data privacy, AI ethics, and digital security led to public apprehension regarding technology adoption, hindering the efficacy of several interventions. For instance, concerns over the potential misuse of personal data in contact-tracing applications deterred widespread participation, thereby limiting the effectiveness of these tools in mitigating the pandemic. The success of tech-driven interventions in future health crises will therefore depend on the establishment of robust policies that prioritize data protection and transparency, as well as frameworks that ensure equitable access to digital resources. By fostering public trust and addressing the ethical implications of technology deployment, governments and organizations can maximize the economic and public health benefits of digital solutions in times of crisis.

5. INTEGRATING TECH-DRIVEN STRATEGIES FOR FUTURE PANDEMIC RESILIENCE

The imperative of building scalable and adaptive technological infrastructure in the context of pandemic preparedness reflects a profound shift towards an anticipatory model in global health strategy. Unlike traditional, often static health infrastructure, scalable technology platforms offer the flexibility to expand or contract based on situational demands, a capability that proved indispensable during the COVID-19 pandemic. Health crises, by their nature, demand swift responses and the ability to scale medical resources, digital platforms, and communication channels at a moment's notice. However, most pre-pandemic health systems lacked the built-in adaptability required to handle sudden surges in patient loads or rapid changes in public health needs. Scalable infrastructure, powered by cloud computing, artificial intelligence, and big data analytics, enables health systems to seamlessly adjust capacity in real-time, dynamically redirecting resources where they are needed most and thus preserving both the integrity and responsiveness of healthcare systems under duress. By adopting scalable solutions, health systems gain the agility to manage not only the immediate impacts of health crises but also their long-term aftermath, ensuring that infrastructure investments remain viable and responsive beyond the initial emergency.

Scalability in health infrastructure, however, transcends the expansion of physical resources; it encompasses the capacity to process, analyze, and distribute vast quantities of health data at unprecedented speeds. This capability is integral to effective disease surveillance, early outbreak detection, and rapid contact tracing, all of which rely on robust data integration and high processing speeds. Platforms powered by cloud technology, for example, offer health systems the ability to store and analyze exponentially growing datasets, integrating data from multiple sources—including hospitals, laboratories, and individual health apps—without compromising system performance. During COVID-19, countries with scalable, cloud-based health infrastructures, such as South Korea, were able to achieve near-real-time updates on case numbers, allocate resources strategically, and rapidly identify hotspots. This level of responsiveness highlights the utility of scalable data management systems that not only support efficient pandemic response but also reduce the financial burden by optimizing resource utilization. Through adaptive infrastructure, health systems can effectively manage crises and, more critically, avoid the costly redundancy that occurs when emergency measures are applied to systems unequipped for dynamic scalability.

The notion of adaptability in tech infrastructure extends to cybersecurity measures, an often-overlooked component of pandemic preparedness. As digital platforms and telemedicine applications become integral to healthcare delivery during pandemics, the need for scalable cybersecurity frameworks becomes paramount. Health data is an invaluable asset, and its protection is critical to maintaining public trust and ensuring compliance with international data privacy standards. Adaptive cybersecurity protocols, such as automated threat detection and AI-driven anomaly monitoring, provide the flexibility to rapidly adjust security measures as cyber threats evolve. During the COVID-19 pandemic, healthcare organizations experienced a sharp increase in cyberattacks, underscoring the vulnerability of traditional security frameworks unable to scale with growing digital interactions. By embedding scalable cybersecurity into health infrastructure, organizations not only safeguard patient data but also ensure the continuity of digital services that are essential to pandemic response. This adaptability is particularly critical in times of crisis, where even minor breaches can lead to significant disruptions in health services, compromise sensitive data, and erode public confidence in digital health platforms.

Complementing the need for scalable infrastructure is the strategic use of digital platforms for public health education, which plays a crucial role in mitigating the spread of misinformation and fostering public compliance with health measures. The unprecedented infodemic during COVID-19 highlighted the limitations of traditional health communication strategies and underscored the need for digital platforms that can deliver accurate, timely, and accessible information to diverse audiences. Social media channels, dedicated health apps, and official government websites became primary sources of information, illustrating the power of digital platforms to reach large populations with minimal time lag. The challenge, however, lies in ensuring that these platforms are equipped with reliable content moderation mechanisms, particularly given the prevalence of health misinformation that can significantly undermine public health efforts. Platforms like WHO's mobile app, which provided users with real-time information and preventive measures, demonstrated the efficacy of centralized digital resources in maintaining public awareness and curbing misinformation.

Leveraging digital platforms for public health education not only disseminates essential information but also fosters an environment of transparency and trust, both of which are vital during health crises. Misinformation, often propagated on social media, has the potential to mislead the public and derail health interventions, thereby exacerbating the impact of pandemics. By creating verified channels of information dissemination, health authorities can preempt the spread of misinformation and foster a data-driven dialogue that encourages compliance with health measures. Moreover, digital platforms facilitate bidirectional communication, allowing health officials to gauge public sentiment, address concerns, and adapt messaging in response to emerging challenges. This dynamic engagement enhances the effectiveness of public health campaigns, making them more responsive to the needs of the population and thereby strengthening the overall resilience of society against health crises.

Digital health education platforms also serve as invaluable tools for training and upskilling healthcare professionals in times of crisis. The rapid evolution of medical knowledge during pandemics necessitates that healthcare workers have continuous access to the latest information on disease management, treatment protocols, and safety procedures. E-learning platforms and telemedicine applications offer healthcare professionals the ability to stay updated on best practices, access expert advice, and collaborate with peers across regions and disciplines. This continuous learning infrastructure not only empowers healthcare providers with the knowledge to deliver high-quality care but also facilitates knowledge transfer between regions, ensuring that even resource-constrained areas benefit from advances in medical expertise. By democratizing access to professional education through digital means, health systems can ensure that their workforce remains adaptable and competent in the face of rapidly changing medical demands.

Furthermore, digital platforms provide governments and health organizations with critical insights into the population's behavior, enabling the formulation of targeted interventions that address specific public health challenges. Through data analytics, public health officials can monitor engagement with educational content, track compliance with health guidelines, and identify behavioral patterns that may indicate emerging health risks. For example, if data indicates a decrease in adherence to vaccination schedules, digital platforms can be used to launch targeted awareness campaigns that address vaccine hesitancy and encourage compliance. This capability transforms public health education from a one-size-fits-all model into a personalized approach that addresses the unique needs of different communities, thereby maximizing the efficacy of health interventions. The capacity to analyze and respond to behavioral data in real-time represents a fundamental advancement in public health, one that enables proactive measures rather than reactive solutions.

6. FUTURE DIRECTIONS: ETHICAL AND POLICY CONSIDERATIONS

The delicate balance between privacy and surveillance in health data represents one of the most complex ethical dilemmas in modern pandemic preparedness. Health data surveillance, powered by advanced digital platforms, artificial intelligence (AI), and data-sharing networks, has proven to be a powerful tool in tracking disease spread, identifying hotspots, and predicting future outbreaks. However, the efficacy of these surveillance systems is contingent on their ability to access and analyze sensitive health data at both individual and population levels. During the COVID-19 pandemic, contact-tracing apps, digital health passports, and centralized databases became ubiquitous, underscoring the utility of surveillance in managing public health crises. However, such systems invariably involve the collection and processing of vast amounts of personal information, raising profound concerns about privacy, data ownership, and the potential for misuse. The challenge lies in establishing a framework that allows for robust health surveillance while safeguarding individual privacy, thus ensuring that public trust is maintained even as governments and health organizations deploy increasingly invasive surveillance technologies.

One of the primary considerations in balancing privacy and surveillance in health data is the development of transparent governance frameworks that define the scope, purpose, and duration of data collection. Such frameworks must clearly outline how data will be used, who will have access to it, and under what circumstances it may be shared or retained beyond the immediate health crisis. Privacy advocates argue that without these safeguards, there is a risk of "surveillance creep," whereby data initially collected for pandemic purposes could later be repurposed for non-health-related activities, such as law enforcement or immigration control. To address these concerns, several countries implemented data minimization principles during COVID-19, ensuring that only essential information was collected, and employed anonymization techniques to prevent the identification of individuals. However, while anonymization provides a layer of protection, it is not foolproof; re-identification remains a possibility, particularly when datasets are cross-referenced with other information. A balance must therefore be struck, with privacy protections embedded into the design of surveillance systems to ensure that public health benefits do not come at the expense of individual rights.

The use of decentralized data storage models, as opposed to centralized databases, also offers a promising solution to balancing privacy with surveillance. Decentralized systems enable data to be stored locally on individuals' devices rather than on a central server, allowing health authorities to access relevant information only when absolutely necessary. This approach was adopted in several European nations, where data was stored on users' smartphones and transmitted only in anonymized form if an individual tested positive for COVID-19. By decentralizing data storage, health organizations mitigate the risk of data breaches and unauthorized access, thus preserving individuals' control over their personal information. However, while decentralized systems offer privacy advantages, they also present challenges related to data interoperability and real-time accessibility, which are crucial for rapid response in pandemic scenarios. Achieving the right balance between decentralization for privacy and centralization for operational efficiency will require sophisticated technological solutions and robust policy frameworks that can adapt to evolving health threats without compromising individual rights.

Complementing these privacy considerations, sustainable investment in pandemic tech preparedness is essential for ensuring that health systems remain resilient and capable of leveraging cutting-edge technologies during future crises. The COVID-19 pandemic underscored the need for continuous investment in health technology infrastructure, as many countries struggled to deploy the necessary digital tools, data integration platforms, and surveillance systems promptly. A sustainable investment approach requires that health technology be treated as a long-term public good rather than a reactive expenditure that is triggered only in response to a crisis. Policies that prioritize sustained funding, innovation incentives, and private-public partnerships are instrumental in creating a resilient technological foundation capable of withstanding future health crises. By establishing dedicated funds for health technology, governments can ensure that critical infrastructure, such as data-sharing networks, telemedicine platforms, and AI-driven diagnostic tools, are readily available and scalable, thereby minimizing the economic and social disruptions associated with pandemics.

One of the key elements in developing policies for sustainable pandemic tech investment is the establishment of multi-sector partnerships that leverage the expertise and resources of both the public and private sectors. The rapid deployment of contact-tracing apps and digital health passports during COVID-19 was facilitated by collaborations between governments, tech companies, and research institutions, highlighting the potential of such partnerships to expedite technological solutions. By fostering an environment conducive to cross-sectoral collaboration, policymakers can mobilize the private sector's technical expertise and financial resources, reducing the burden on public health systems and promoting innovation. However, to make these partnerships sustainable, it is essential that clear guidelines and accountability measures are established, ensuring that the private sector's profit motives do not supersede public health objectives. Intellectual property rights, data ownership, and profit-sharing agreements must be carefully negotiated to create a framework that encourages private-sector involvement while ensuring that technological advancements serve the broader public interest.

Another crucial aspect of sustainable pandemic tech investment policies is the emphasis on inclusivity and accessibility, ensuring that technological advancements are equitably distributed across regions and population groups. The digital divide remains a significant barrier to effective pandemic response, as under-resourced areas often lack access to the infrastructure and digital literacy required to benefit from health technologies. Policies that incentivize investment in rural broadband expansion, digital literacy programs, and affordable health technology solutions are critical for ensuring that all communities can benefit from tech-driven pandemic preparedness. During COVID-19, countries with robust digital infrastructures, such as South Korea and Singapore, demonstrated how technology can enable efficient, equitable responses. However, in regions with limited connectivity, the lack of access to digital health tools exacerbated health disparities, leaving vulnerable populations with minimal access to timely information and resources. Sustainable policies must therefore prioritize equity as a guiding principle, ensuring that investments in health technology are accessible to all and that no population is left disproportionately vulnerable in the face of future crises.

In addition to infrastructure and accessibility, policies for sustainable pandemic tech preparedness should emphasize flexibility and adaptability, allowing health systems to pivot swiftly in response to the unique demands of each health crisis. Flexible funding mechanisms that allow for rapid allocation of resources, alongside regulatory frameworks that facilitate swift approval of new technologies, are essential for maintaining an agile response capacity. For instance, during COVID-19, the fast-tracking of telemedicine regulations allowed healthcare providers to scale remote care rapidly, reducing the burden on hospitals and mitigating the spread of infection. A similar approach to flexibility should be adopted in tech preparedness policies, enabling health systems to integrate new tools, such as AI-driven diagnostics or wearable health monitors, without encountering prolonged regulatory delays. Such adaptability will be critical for ensuring that health technology keeps pace with emerging threats and that health systems can evolve in tandem with advancements in digital health innovation.

7. CONCLUSION

The summation of key insights gleaned from the integration of technology in health crisis management underscores the transformative potential that digital advancements hold in reshaping the future of public health response. The COVID-19 pandemic was a stark demonstration of both the benefits and limitations of technology-driven interventions, revealing that while digital tools like AI, big data, and IoT can accelerate response times and enhance resource allocation, they also bring challenges in scalability, privacy, and equitable access. The critical insights center around the necessity of robust, scalable technological infrastructure that can adapt to the fluctuations in demand inherent to health crises, the importance of strategic investment in technological preparedness, and the ethical imperatives of balancing privacy with surveillance needs. To realize the full potential of these insights, it is evident that health systems must prioritize adaptability and resilience, ensuring that digital infrastructure is not merely reactive but proactive, with the capacity to evolve in response to both anticipated and unforeseen health threats.

Equally essential is the understanding that public trust forms the foundation of effective health crisis management, especially in contexts that require widespread adoption of digital surveillance and data-sharing practices. The intersection of privacy and public health demands a delicate balance, where the design of surveillance systems incorporates stringent data protections and transparency protocols that clearly communicate the purpose and limitations of data use. This transparency cultivates an environment in which public trust is maintained, allowing health authorities to deploy surveillance technologies without compromising individual rights or creating a chilling effect that discourages participation. Furthermore, the pandemic has illustrated that digital solutions must be inclusively designed and accessible across socioeconomic and geographic divides, recognizing that public health security is a collective enterprise that can only be achieved when all populations are afforded equal access to technological resources and health information.

Moving forward, strategic pathways for technology-enhanced health crisis management must integrate a multi-pronged approach that encompasses sustainable investment, cross-sector collaboration, and flexible policy frameworks. Sustainable investment is paramount, as it establishes a foundational infrastructure that remains operational and adaptable beyond the immediacy of any given crisis. Such investment should prioritize long-term funding for data analytics, cloud storage capabilities, and health information exchange systems that can seamlessly expand or contract as needed. Additionally, the establishment of dedicated pandemic response funds enables rapid resource mobilization and supports the continuous advancement of technological capabilities, ensuring that health systems are never left underprepared. By embedding technological resilience into public health policies, governments can create an environment where innovation in pandemic management is consistently fostered and maintained, rather than cyclically funded only during periods of heightened threat.

Another strategic pathway lies in the cultivation of cross-sectoral partnerships that leverage the expertise, innovation, and resources of both the public and private sectors. During COVID-19, collaborative efforts among governments, tech firms, and research institutions were instrumental in accelerating the deployment of contact-tracing apps, digital health passports, and telemedicine platforms. Moving forward, these partnerships should be formalized and structured to foster rapid innovation while upholding ethical standards in technology deployment. By establishing clear regulatory frameworks that guide intellectual property rights, data-sharing protocols, and profit-sharing agreements, governments can ensure that private sector involvement aligns with public health objectives rather than solely profit motives. Such partnerships enable a pooling of resources that makes the development and deployment of advanced health technologies more efficient, scalable, and adaptable, positioning public health systems to respond to future crises with enhanced coordination and agility.

The final component of a strategic pathway for technology-enhanced crisis management involves creating adaptive policy frameworks that can respond to the dynamic needs of health crises. These policies should encompass flexible regulatory mechanisms that allow for the expedited approval and implementation of digital health tools without compromising safety or efficacy. The fast-tracking of telemedicine regulations during COVID-19, for instance, provided healthcare systems with the flexibility to scale remote care rapidly, thereby alleviating the burden on physical healthcare facilities and enabling continuous patient care despite restrictive movement measures. Similar flexibility in policies governing AI-driven diagnostics, wearable health monitors, and other emergent digital health tools is essential for ensuring that technological innovations can be quickly integrated into health responses. By establishing adaptable regulatory frameworks, health authorities can maintain a proactive stance, ensuring that public health infrastructure keeps pace with advancements in technology and remains agile in the face of evolving health threats.

In essence, the synthesis of these key insights and strategic pathways underscores the need for a forward-looking approach to health crisis management, one that harnesses the full spectrum of digital innovations while remaining grounded in ethical considerations and sustainable practices. The COVID-19 pandemic has illuminated the pressing need for a resilient, technologically empowered public health framework that can anticipate, detect, and respond to health threats with precision and adaptability. By committing to sustainable investment, fostering cross-sector partnerships, and enacting adaptive policies, health systems can position themselves at the forefront of innovation in pandemic preparedness, safeguarding public health while navigating the complexities of a rapidly changing digital landscape.

DECLARATION

The authors declare that the manuscript follows ethical standards and there are no potential conflicts of interest concerning this chapter's research, authorship, and publication.

DISCLAIMER

The contents and views of this chapter are expressed by the authors in personal capacities. The Editor and the Publisher don't need to agree with these viewpoints and are not responsible for any duty of care in this regard.

REFERENCES

Akberdina, V., Kumar, V., Kyriakopoulos, G. L., & Kuzmin, E. (2023). Editorial: What Does Industry's Digital Transition Hold in the Uncertainty Context? In K. V., K. G.L., A. V., & K. E. (Eds.), *Lecture Notes in Information Systems and Organisation: Vol. 61 LNISO* (pp. 1 – 4). Springer Science and Business Media Deutschland GmbH. DOI: 10.1007/978-3-031-30351-7_1

Aloo, B. N., Dessureault-Rompré, J., Tripathi, V., Nyongesa, B. O., & Were, B. A. (2023). Signaling and crosstalk of rhizobacterial and plant hormones that mediate abiotic stress tolerance in plants. *Frontiers in Microbiology*, 14, 1171104. Advance online publication. DOI: 10.3389/fmicb.2023.1171104 PMID: 37455718

Alsadi, J., Tripathi, V., Amaral, L. S., Potrich, E., Hasham, S. H., Patil, P. Y., & Omoniyi, E. M. (2022). Architecture Fibrous Meso-Porous Silica Spheres as Enhanced Adsorbent for Effective Capturing for CO2 Gas. *Key Engineering Materials*, 928, 39–44. DOI: 10.4028/p-2f2o01

Ambika, K. S. B., Goswami, S., Pimplapure, V., Jweeg, M. J., Kant, K., & Gangodkar, D. (2023). Framework Towards Detection of Stress Level Through Classifying Physiological Signals Using Machine Learning. *2023 3rd International Conference on Advance Computing and Innovative Technologies in Engineering, ICACITE 2023*, 600 – 604. DOI: 10.1109/ICACITE57410.2023.10183013

Ansari, M. F., & Afzal, A. (2022). Sensitivity and Performance Analysis of 10 MW Solar Power Plant Using MPPT Technique. *Lecture Notes in Electrical Engineering, 894 LNEE*, 512–518. DOI: 10.1007/978-981-19-1677-9_46

Arora, S., Pargaien, S., Khan, F., Tewari, I., Nainwal, D., Mer, A., Mittal, A., & Misra, A. (2023). Monitoring Tourist Footfall at Nainital in Uttarakhand using Sensor Technology. *2023 4th International Conference on Electronics and Sustainable Communication Systems, ICESC 2023 - Proceedings*, 200 – 204. DOI: 10.1109/ICESC57686.2023.10193244

Asha, P., Mannepalli, K., Khilar, R., Subbulakshmi, N., Dhanalakshmi, R., Tripathi, V., Mohanavel, V., Sathyamurthy, R., & Sudhakar, M. (2022). Role of machine learning in attaining environmental sustainability. *Energy Reports*, 8, 863–871. DOI: 10.1016/j.egyr.2022.09.206

Banerjee, D., Kukreja, V., Aeri, M., Hariharan, S., & Garg, N. (2023). Integrated CNN-SVM Approach for Accurate Radish Leaf Disease Classification: A Comparative Study and Performance Analysis. *2023 Annual International Conference on Emerging Research Areas: International Conference on Intelligent Systems, AICERA/ICIS 2023*. DOI: 10.1109/AICERA/ICIS59538.2023.10420119

Behera, A., & Singh Rawat, K. (2023). A brief review paper on mining subsidence and its geo-environmental impact. *Materials Today: Proceedings*. Advance online publication. DOI: 10.1016/j.matpr.2023.04.183

Bhatnagar, M., Kumar, P., Taneja, S., Sood, K., & Grima, S. (2024). From digital overload to trading Zen: The role of digital detox in enhancing intraday trading performance. In *Business Drivers in Promoting Digital Detoxification*. IGI Global., DOI: 10.4018/979-8-3693-1107-3.ch010

Bhatnagar, M., Rajaram, R., Taneja, S., & Kumar, P. (2024). Balancing acts: The Yin and Yang of debit and credit on the stage of financial well-being. In *Emerging Perspectives on Financial Well-Being*. IGI Global., DOI: 10.4018/979-8-3693-1750-1.ch002

Bhatnagar, M., Taneja, S., & Kumar, P. (2023). The Effectiveness of Carbon Pricing Mechanism in Steering Financial Flows Toward Sustainable Projects. *International Journal of Environmental Impacts*, 6(4), 183–196. DOI: 10.18280/ijei.060403

Bhatnagar, M., Taneja, S., Kumar, P., & Özen, E. (2024). Does financial education act as a catalyst for SME competitiveness? *International Journal of Education Economics and Development*, 15(3), 377–393. DOI: 10.1504/IJEED.2024.139306

Bhatt, C., Singh, S., Chauhan, R., Singh, T., & Uniyal, A. (2023). Artificial Intelligence in Current Education: Roles, Applications & Challenges. *Proceedings - 2023 3rd International Conference on Pervasive Computing and Social Networking, ICPCSN 2023*, 241–244. DOI: 10.1109/ICPCSN58827.2023.00045

Bhushan, B., & Nayak, A. (2022). Application of green nanomaterials for sustainable energy systems: A review of the current status. In *Biofuel Technologies for a Sustainable Future: India and Beyond*. River Publishers.

Chand, A., Agarwal, P., & Sharma, S. (2023). Real-Time Retrieving Vedic Sanskrit Text into Multi-Lingual Text and Audio for Cultural Tourism Motivation. *2023 International Conference for Advancement in Technology, ICONAT 2023*. DOI: 10.1109/ICONAT57137.2023.10080862

Chauhan, M., Rani, A., Joshi, S., & Sharma, P. K. (2023). Role of psychrophilic and psychrotolerant microorganisms toward the development of hill agriculture. In *Advanced Microbial Technology for Sustainable Agriculture and Environment*. Elsevier., DOI: 10.1016/B978-0-323-95090-9.00002-9

Dahiya, M., Guru Prasad, M. S., Anand, T., Kumar, K., Bansal, S., & Naveen Kumar, H. N. (2023). An Effective Detection of Litchi Disease using Deep Learning. *2023 14th International Conference on Computing Communication and Networking Technologies, ICCCNT 2023*. DOI: 10.1109/ICCCNT56998.2023.10307717

Dieudonne, K. K., & Bajaj, M., Kitmo, Rubanenko, O., Jurado, F., & Kamel, S. (2022). Hydropower Potential Assessment of Four Selected Sites in the North Interconnected Network of Cameroon. *2022 IEEE International Conference on Automation/25th Congress of the Chilean Association of Automatic Control: For the Development of Sustainable Agricultural Systems, ICA-ACCA 2022*. DOI: 10.1109/ICA-ACCA56767.2022.10005948

Dubey, V. P., Prakash, R., Chamoli, V., & Mittal, P. (2023). Study of Urban Change Detection Using Landsat 8 Satellite Data: A Case Study of Dehradun City, Uttarakhand, India. *IEEE International Conference on Electrical, Electronics, Communication and Computers, ELEXCOM 2023*. DOI: 10.1109/ELEXCOM58812.2023.10370375

Elbagory, M., El-Nahrawy, S., Omara, A. E.-D., Eid, E. M., Bachheti, A., Kumar, P., Abou Fayssal, S., Adelodun, B., Bachheti, R. K., Kumar, P., Mioč, B., Kumar, V., & Širić, I. (2022). Sustainable Bioconversion of Wetland Plant Biomass for Pleurotus ostreatus var. florida Cultivation: Studies on Proximate and Biochemical Characterization. *Agriculture*, 12(12), 2095. Advance online publication. DOI: 10.3390/agriculture12122095

Giri, N. C., Mohanty, R. C., Shaw, R. N., Poonia, S., Bajaj, M., & Belkhier, Y. (2022). Agriphotovoltaic System to Improve Land Productivity and Revenue of Farmer. *2022 IEEE Global Conference on Computing, Power and Communication Technologies, GlobConPT 2022*. DOI: 10.1109/GlobConPT57482.2022.9938338

Gonfa, Y. H., Gelagle, A. A., Hailegnaw, B., Kabeto, S. A., Workeneh, G. A., Tessema, F. B., Tadesse, M. G., Wabaidur, S. M., Dahlous, K. A., Abou Fayssal, S., Kumar, P., Adelodun, B., Bachheti, A., & Bachheti, R. K. (2023). Optimization, Characterization, and Biological Applications of Silver Nanoparticles Synthesized Using Essential Oil of Aerial Part of Laggera tomentosa. *Sustainability (Basel)*, 15(1), 797. Advance online publication. DOI: 10.3390/su15010797

Gupta, S., Kushwaha, P., Chauhan, A. S., Yadav, A., & Badhotiya, G. K. (2023). A study on glazing to optimize daylight for improving lighting ergonomics and energy efficiency of a building. In S. Y., S. G., & B. G.K. (Eds.), *AIP Conference Proceedings* (Vol. 2521). American Institute of Physics Inc. DOI: 10.1063/5.0114766

Ingale, N. V., Saravana Kumar, G., Panduro-Ramirez, J., Raj, M., Vaseem Akram, S., & Rawat, R. (2023). Role of IOT in managing education management tools: A technical review. *2023 3rd International Conference on Advance Computing and Innovative Technologies in Engineering, ICACITE 2023*, 2056 – 2061. DOI: 10.1109/ICACITE57410.2023.10182953

Jain, P., Gupta, V. K., Tiwari, H., Shukla, A., Pandey, P., & Gupta, A. (2023). Human-Computer Interaction: A Systematic Review. In M. H.K. & S. S. (Eds.), *Proceedings - 2023 International Conference on Advanced Computing and Communication Technologies, ICACCTech 2023* (pp. 31 – 36). Institute of Electrical and Electronics Engineers Inc. DOI: 10.1109/ICACCTech61146.2023.00015

Jain, S., & Jain, S. S. (2021). Development of Intelligent Transportation System and Its Applications for an Urban Corridor During COVID-19. *Journal of The Institution of Engineers (India): Series B*, 102(6), 1191 – 1200. DOI: 10.1007/s40031-021-00556-y

Jain, V., Tiwari, R., Mehrotra, R., Bohra, N. S., Misra, A., & Pandey, D. C. (2023). Role of Technology for Credit Risk Management: A Bibliometric Review. *2023 IEEE International Conference on Blockchain and Distributed Systems Security, ICBDS 2023*. DOI: 10.1109/ICBDS58040.2023.10346300

Jindal, V., Kukreja, V., Mehta, S., Chauhan, R., & Verma, G. (2023). Towards Sustainable Agriculture: Federated CNN Models for Cucurbit Leaf Disease Detection. *2023 10th IEEE Uttar Pradesh Section International Conference on Electrical, Electronics and Computer Engineering, UPCON 2023*, 561 – 566. DOI: 10.1109/UPCON59197.2023.10434321

Jindal, V., Kukreja, V., Mehta, S., Srivastava, P., & Garg, N. (2023). Adopting Federated Learning and CNN for Advanced Plant Pathology: A Case of Red Globe Grape Leaf Diseases Dissecting Severity. *2023 3rd Asian Conference on Innovation in Technology, ASIANCON 2023*. DOI: 10.1109/ASIANCON58793.2023.10270034

Josphineleela, R., Kaliappan, S., Natrayan, L., & Bhatt, U. M. (2023). Intelligent Virtual Laboratory Development and Implementation using the RASA Framework. *Proceedings - 7th International Conference on Computing Methodologies and Communication, ICCMC 2023*, 1172 – 1176. DOI: 10.1109/ICCMC56507.2023.10083701

Kaur, A., Kukreja, V., Chamoli, S., Thapliyal, S., & Sharma, R. (2023a). Advanced Disease Management: An Encoder-Decoder Approach for Tomato Black Mold Detection. *2023 IEEE Pune Section International Conference, PuneCon 2023*. DOI: 10.1109/PuneCon58714.2023.10450088

Kaur, A., Kukreja, V., Chamoli, S., Thapliyal, S., & Sharma, R. (2023b). Advanced Multi-Scale Classification of Onion Smut Disease Using a Hybrid CNN-RF Ensemble Model for Precision Agriculture. In G. R., H. K., P. R., G. S., T. A. J.V., V. R., M. R., & K. T. (Eds.), *Proceedings of the 2023 6th International Conference on Recent Trends in Advance Computing, ICRTAC 2023* (pp. 553 – 556). Institute of Electrical and Electronics Engineers Inc. DOI: 10.1109/ICRTAC59277.2023.10480840

Kaur, A., Kukreja, V., Nisha Chandran, S., Garg, N., & Sharma, R. (2023). Automated Mango Rust Severity Classification: A CNN-SVM Ensemble Approach for Accurate and Granular Disease Assessment in Mango Cultivation. In G. R., H. K., P. R., G. S., T. A. J.V., V. R., M. R., & K. T. (Eds.), *Proceedings of the 2023 6th International Conference on Recent Trends in Advance Computing, ICRTAC 2023* (pp. 486 – 490). Institute of Electrical and Electronics Engineers Inc. DOI: 10.1109/ICRTAC59277.2023.10480836

Kaur, A., Kumar, P., Taneja, S., & Ozen, E. (2023). Fintech emergence – an opportunity or threat to banking. *International Journal of Electronic Finance*, 13(1), 1–19. DOI: 10.1504/IJEF.2024.135163

Kaur, G., Sharma, N., Chauhan, R., Singh, P., & Gupta, R. (2023). An Automated Approach for Detection and Classification of Plant Diseases. *2023 2nd International Conference on Futuristic Technologies, INCOFT 2023*. DOI: 10.1109/INCOFT60753.2023.10425170

Khan, S., Ambika, , Rani, K., Sharma, S., Kumar, A., Singh, S., Thapliyal, M., Rawat, P., Thakur, A., Pandey, S., Thapliyal, A., Pal, M., & Singh, Y. (2023). Rhizobacterial mediated interactions in Curcuma longa for plant growth and enhanced crop productivity: A systematic review. *Frontiers in Plant Science*, 14, 1231676. Advance online publication. DOI: 10.3389/fpls.2023.1231676 PMID: 37692412

Kholiya, D., Mishra, A. K., Pandey, N. K., & Tripathi, N. (2023). Plant Detection and Counting using Yolo based Technique. *2023 3rd Asian Conference on Innovation in Technology, ASIANCON 2023*. DOI: 10.1109/ASIANCON58793.2023.10270530

Kukreti, A., Shriyal, A., Sharma, S., & Bhadula, S. (2023). Internet-of-Things Enabled Smart and Portable Terrace Garden Protection Shed. *2023 4th IEEE Global Conference for Advancement in Technology, GCAT 2023*. DOI: 10.1109/GCAT59970.2023.10353281

Kumar, A., Goyal, H. R., & Sharma, S. (2023). Sustainable Intelligent Information System for Tourism Industry. *2023 IEEE 8th International Conference for Convergence in Technology, I2CT 2023*. DOI: 10.1109/I2CT57861.2023.10126400

Kumar, A., Pant, S., & Ram, M. (2023). Cost Optimization and Reliability Parameter Extraction of a Complex Engineering System. *Journal of Reliability and Statistical Studies*, 16(1), 99–116. DOI: 10.13052/jrss0974-8024.1615

Kumar, A., Sharma, N., Chauhan, R., & Sharma, M. (2023). Anomaly Detection in Bitcoin Blockchain: Exploring Trends and Algorithms. *2023 Global Conference on Information Technologies and Communications, GCITC 2023*. DOI: 10.1109/GCITC60406.2023.10426011

Kumar, G., Kumar, A., Singhal, M., Singh, K. U., Kumar, L., & Singh, T. (2023). Revolutionizing Plant Disease Management Through Image Processing Technology. *Proceedings of International Conference on Computational Intelligence and Sustainable Engineering Solution, CISES 2023*, 521 – 528. DOI: 10.1109/CISES58720.2023.10183408

Kumar, P., Reepu, & Kaur, R. (2024). Economic and Urban Dynamics: Investigating Socioeconomic Status and Urban Density as Moderators of Mobile Wallet Adoption in Smart Cities. *Lecture Notes in Networks and Systems, 948 LNNS*, 409–417. DOI: 10.1007/978-981-97-1329-5_33

Kumar, P., Bhatnagar, M., & Taneja, S. (2023). Investigation of the time pattern of Bit Green Crypto: An Arma modeling approach to unrave volatility. In *Algorithmic Approaches to Financial Technology: Forecasting, Trading, and Optimization*. IGI Global., DOI: 10.4018/979-8-3693-1746-4.ch001

Kumar, P., Taneja, S., Bhatnagar, M., & Kaur, A. K. (2024). Navigating the digital paradigm shift: Designing CBDCs for a transformative financial landscape. In *Exploring Central Bank Digital Currencies: Concepts, Frameworks, Models, and Challenges*. IGI Global., DOI: 10.4018/979-8-3693-1882-9.ch006

Kumar, P., Verma, P., Bhatnagar, M., Taneja, S., Seychel, S., Todorović, I., & Grim, S. (2023). The Financial Performance and Solvency Status of the Indian Public Sector Banks: A CAMELS Rating and Z Index Approach. *International Journal of Sustainable Development and Planning*, 18(2), 367–376. DOI: 10.18280/ijsdp.180204

Kumar, R., Lamba, A. K., Mohammed, S., Asokan, A., Aswal, U. S., & Kolavennu, S. (2023). Fake Currency Note Recognition using Extreme Learning Machine. *Proceedings of the 2nd International Conference on Applied Artificial Intelligence and Computing, ICAAIC 2023*, 333 – 339. DOI: 10.1109/ICAAIC56838.2023.10140824

Kumar, V., & Korovin, G. (2023). A Comparison of Digital Transformation of Industry in the Russian Federation with the European Union. In K. V., K. G.L., A. V., & K. E. (Eds.), *Lecture Notes in Information Systems and Organisation: Vol. 61 LNISO* (pp. 45 – 57). Springer Science and Business Media Deutschland GmbH. DOI: 10.1007/978-3-031-30351-7_5

Kumar, V., Mitra, D., Rani, A., Suyal, D. C., Singh Gautam, B. P., Jain, L., Gondwal, M., Raj, K. K., Singh, A. K., & Soni, R. (2021). Bio-inoculants for Biodegradation and Bioconversion of Agrowaste: Status and Prospects. In *Bioremediation of Environmental Pollutants: Emerging Trends and Strategies*. Springer International Publishing., DOI: 10.1007/978-3-030-86169-8_16

Kunwar, S., Joshi, A., Gururani, P., Pandey, D., & Pandey, N. (2023). Physiological and AI-based study of endophytes on medicina A mini review. *Plant Science Today*, 10, 53–60. DOI: 10.14719/pst.2555

Malik, D., Kukreja, V., Mehta, S., Gupta, A., & Singh, V. (2023). Mitigating the Impact of Guava Leaf Diseases Using CNNs and Federated Learning. *2023 3rd Asian Conference on Innovation in Technology, ASIANCON 2023*. DOI: 10.1109/ASIANCON58793.2023.10270236

Mekala, K., Laxmi, V., Jagruthi, H., Dhondiyal, S. A., Sridevi, R., & Dabral, A. P. (2023). Coffee Price Prediction: An Application of CNN-BLSTM Neural Networks. *Proceedings of the 2nd IEEE International Conference on Advances in Computing, Communication and Applied Informatics, ACCAI 2023*. DOI: 10.1109/ACCAI58221.2023.10199369

Mishra, A., Shah, J. K., Sharma, R., Sharma, M., Joshi, S., & Kaushal, D. (2023). Enhancing Efficiency in Industrial Environments through IoT Connected Worker Solutions: Smart Wearable Technologies for the Workplace. *2023 International Conference on Advances in Computation, Communication and Information Technology, ICAICCIT 2023*, 1175 – 1179. DOI: 10.1109/ICAICCIT60255.2023.10466100

Mishra, A. K., Singh, S., & Upadhyay, R. K. (2023). Organization citizenship behaviour among indian nurses during SARS-COV-2: A direct effect moderation model. *Quality & Quantity*, 57(1), 541–559. DOI: 10.1007/s11135-022-01325-9

Mitra, D., Mondal, R., Khoshru, B., Senapati, A., Radha, T. K., Mahakur, B., Uniyal, N., Myo, E. M., Boutaj, H., Sierra, B. E. G. U. E. R. R. A., Panneerselvam, P., Ganeshamurthy, A. N., Elković, S. A. N. Đ. J., Vasić, T., Rani, A., Dutta, S., & Mohapatra, P. K. D. A. S.MITRA. (2022). Actinobacteria-enhanced plant growth, nutrient acquisition, and crop protection: Advances in soil, plant, and microbial multifactorial interactions. *Pedosphere*, 32(1), 149–170. DOI: 10.1016/S1002-0160(21)60042-5

Mitra, D., Saritha, B., Janeeshma, E., Gusain, P., Khoshru, B., Abo Nouh, F. A., Rani, A., Olatunbosun, A. N., Ruparelia, J., Rabari, A., Mosquera-Sánchez, L. P., Mondal, R., Verma, D., Panneerselvam, P., Das Mohapatra, P. K., & Guerra Sierra, B. E. (2022). Arbuscular mycorrhizal fungal association boosted the arsenic resistance in crops with special responsiveness to rice plant. *Environmental and Experimental Botany*, 193. Advance online publication. DOI: 10.1016/j.envexpbot.2021.104681

Nagila, A., Saravanakumar, P., Pranavan, S., Goutam, R., Dobhal, D. C., & Singh, G. (2023). An Innovative Approach of CNN-BiGRU Based Post-Earthquake Damage Detection of Reinforced Concrete for Frame Buildings. *International Conference on Self Sustainable Artificial Intelligence Systems, ICSSAS 2023 - Proceedings*, 56 – 61. DOI: 10.1109/ICSSAS57918.2023.10331894

Nikolaidis, P., Ismail, M., Shuib, L., Khan, S., & Dhiman, G. (2022). Predicting Student Attrition in Higher Education through the Determinants of Learning Progress: A Structural Equation Modelling Approach. *Sustainability (Basel)*, 14(20), 13584. Advance online publication. DOI: 10.3390/su142013584

Pandey, P., Mayank, K., & Sharma, S. (2023). Recommendation System for Adventure Tourism. *2023 4th IEEE Global Conference for Advancement in Technology, GCAT 2023*. DOI: 10.1109/GCAT59970.2023.10353339

Pant, R., Gupta, A., Pant, G., Chaubey, K. K., Kumar, G., & Patrick, N. (2022). Second-generation biofuels: Facts and future. In *Relationship between Microbes and the Environment for Sustainable Ecosystem Services: Microbial Tools for Sustainable Ecosystem Services: Volume 3* (Vol. 3). Elsevier. DOI: 10.1016/B978-0-323-89936-9.00011-4

Papageorgiou, G., Loukis, E., Pappas, G., Rizun, N., Saxena, S., Charalabidis, Y., & Alexopoulos, C. (2023). Open Government Data in Educational Programs Curriculum: Current State and Prospects. *Lecture Notes in Business Information Processing, 493 LNBIP*, 311–326. DOI: 10.1007/978-3-031-43126-5_22

Paul, S. N., Mishra, A. K., & Upadhyay, R. K. (2022). Locus of control and investment decision: An investor's perspective. *International Journal of Services. Economics and Management*, 13(2), 93–107. DOI: 10.1504/IJSEM.2022.122736

Rai, K., Mishra, N., & Mishra, S. (2022). Forest Fire Risk Zonation Mapping using Fuzzy Overlay Analysis of Nainital District. *2022 International Mobile and Embedded Technology Conference, MECON 2022*, 522–526. DOI: 10.1109/MECON53876.2022.9751812

Rajeswari, M., Kumar, N., Raman, P., Patjoshi, P. K., Singh, V., & Pundir, S. (2022). Optimal Analysis for Enterprise Financial Management Based on Artificial Intelligence and Parallel Computing Method. *Proceedings of 5th International Conference on Contemporary Computing and Informatics, IC3I 2022*, 2081–2086. DOI: 10.1109/IC3I56241.2022.10072851

Ranakoti, L., Gangil, B., Mishra, S. K., Singh, T., Sharma, S., Ilyas, R. A., & El-Khatib, S. (2022). Critical Review on Polylactic Acid: Properties, Structure, Processing, Biocomposites, and Nanocomposites. *Materials (Basel)*, 15(12), 4312. Advance online publication. DOI: 10.3390/ma15124312 PMID: 35744371

Rao, K. V. G., Kumar, M. K., Goud, B. S., Krishna, D., Bajaj, M., Saini, P., & Choudhury, S. (2023). IOT-Powered Crop Shield System for Surveillance and Auto Transversum. *2023 IEEE 3rd International Conference on Sustainable Energy and Future Electric Transportation, SeFet 2023*. DOI: 10.1109/SeFeT57834.2023.10245773

Rawat, B., Rawat, J. M., Purohit, S., Singh, G., Sharma, P. K., Chandra, A., Shabaaz Begum, J. P., Venugopal, D., Jaremko, M., & Qureshi, K. A. (2022). A comprehensive review of Quercus semecarpifolia Sm.: An ecologically and commercially important Himalayan tree. *Frontiers in Ecology and Evolution*, 10, 961345. Advance online publication. DOI: 10.3389/fevo.2022.961345

Rawat, S. S., Pant, S., Kumar, A., Ram, M., Sharma, H. K., & Kumar, A. (2022). A State-of-the-Art Survey on Analytical Hierarchy Process Applications in Sustainable Development. *International Journal of Mathematical. Engineering and Management Sciences*, 7(6), 883–917. DOI: 10.33889/IJMEMS.2022.7.6.056

Sati, P., Sharma, E., Soni, R., Dhyani, P., Solanki, A. C., Solanki, M. K., Rai, S., & Malviya, M. K. (2022). Bacterial endophytes as bioinoculant: microbial functions and applications toward sustainable farming. In *Microbial Endophytes and Plant Growth: Beneficial Interactions and Applications*. Elsevier., DOI: 10.1016/B978-0-323-90620-3.00008-8

Sharma, H. R., Bhardwaj, B., Sharma, B., & Kaushik, C. P. (2021). Sustainable Solid Waste Management in India: Practices, Challenges and the Way Forward. In *Climate Resilience and Environmental Sustainability Approaches: Global Lessons and Local Challenges*. Springer Nature. DOI: 10.1007/978-981-16-0902-2_17

Sharma, M., Hagar, A. A., Krishna Murthy, G. R., Beyane, K., Gawali, B. W., & Pant, B. (2022). A Study on Recognising the Application of Multiple Big Data Technologies and its Related Issues, Difficulties and Opportunities. *2022 2nd International Conference on Advance Computing and Innovative Technologies in Engineering, ICACITE 2022*, 341 – 344. DOI: 10.1109/ICACITE53722.2022.9823623

Sharma, M., Kumar, A., Luthra, S., Joshi, S., & Upadhyay, A. (2022). The impact of environmental dynamism on low-carbon practices and digital supply chain networks to enhance sustainable performance: An empirical analysis. *Business Strategy and the Environment*, 31(4), 1776–1788. DOI: 10.1002/bse.2983

Sharma, M., & Singh, P. (2023). Newly engineered nanoparticles as potential therapeutic agents for plants to ameliorate abiotic and biotic stress. *Journal of Applied and Natural Science*, 15(2), 720–731. DOI: 10.31018/jans.v15i2.4603

Sharma, N. K., Kumar, V., Verma, P., & Luthra, S. (2021). Sustainable reverse logistics practices and performance evaluation with fuzzy TOPSIS: A study on Indian retailers. *Cleaner Logistics and Supply Chain*, 1, 100007. Advance online publication. DOI: 10.1016/j.clscn.2021.100007

Sharma, P., Taneja, S., Kumar, P., Özen, E., & Singh, A. (2024). Application of the UTAUT model toward individual acceptance: Emerging trends in artificial intelligence-based banking services. *International Journal of Electronic Finance*, 13(3), 352–366. DOI: 10.1504/IJEF.2024.139584

Sharma, S., Gupta, A., & Tyagi, R. (2023). Artificial Intelligence Enabled Sustainable Education System Using Vedic Scripture and Cyber Security. *2023 2nd International Conference on Advances in Computational Intelligence and Communication, ICACIC 2023*. DOI: 10.1109/ICACIC59454.2023.10435133

Sharma, S., Kadayat, Y., & Tyagi, R. (2023). Artificial Intelligence Enabled Sustainable Life Cycle System Using Vedic Scripture and Quantum Computing. *2023 3rd International Conference on Intelligent Technologies, CONIT 2023*. DOI: 10.1109/CONIT59222.2023.10205771

Sharma, S., Singh, V., & Sarkar, D. (2023). Machine Vision Enabled Fall Detection System for Specially Abled People in Limited Visibility Environment. *2023 3rd Asian Conference on Innovation in Technology, ASIANCON 2023*. DOI: 10.1109/ASIANCON58793.2023.10270769

Sharma, S., Singh Rawal, R., Pandey, D., & Pandey, N. (2021). Microbial World for Sustainable Development. In *Microbial Technology for Sustainable Environment*. Springer Nature., DOI: 10.1007/978-981-16-3840-4_1

Sharma, S., & Tyagi, R. (2023). Digitalization of Farming Knowledge Using Artificial Intelligence and Vedic Scripture. *3rd IEEE International Conference on ICT in Business Industry and Government, ICTBIG 2023*. DOI: 10.1109/ICTBIG59752.2023.10456219

Shekhar, S., Gusain, R., Vidhyarthi, A., & Prakash, R. (2022). Role of Remote Sensing and GIS Strategies to Increase Crop Yield. In S. S. & J. T. (Eds.), *2022 International Conference on Advances in Computing, Communication and Materials, ICACCM 2022*. Institute of Electrical and Electronics Engineers Inc. DOI: 10.1109/ICACCM56405.2022.10009217

Shukla, A., Sharma, M., Tiwari, K., Vani, V. D., & Kumar, N., & Pooja. (2023). Predicting Rainfall Using an Artificial Neural Network-Based Model. *Proceedings of International Conference on Contemporary Computing and Informatics, IC3I 2023*, 2700 – 2704. DOI: 10.1109/IC3I59117.2023.10397714

Singh, A., Sharma, S., Purohit, K. C., & Nithin Kumar, K. C. (2021). Artificial Intelligence based Framework for Effective Performance of Traffic Light Control System. *Proceedings of the 2021 IEEE International Conference on Innovative Computing, Intelligent Communication and Smart Electrical Systems, ICSES 2021*. DOI: 10.1109/ICSES52305.2021.9633913

Singh, K. D., Deep Singh, P., Bansal, A., Kaur, G., Khullar, V., & Tripathi, V. (2023). Exploratory Data Analysis and Customer Churn Prediction for the Telecommunication Industry. *ACCESS 2023 - 2023 3rd International Conference on Advances in Computing, Communication, Embedded and Secure Systems*, 197 – 201. DOI: 10.1109/ACCESS57397.2023.10199700

Singh, K. K., Vats, C., & Singh, M. P. (2023). An Empirical Study of the Impact of Organizational, Social, and Psychological Factors on the Performance of Employees. In M. P., M. P., S. A., K. S., K. S.K., & M. S.K. (Eds.), *Springer Proceedings in Business and Economics* (pp. 621 – 636). Springer Nature. DOI: 10.1007/978-981-99-0197-5_39

Singh, P., & Singh, K. D. (2023). Fog-Centric Intelligent Surveillance System: A Novel Approach for Effective and Efficient Surveillance. In K. R., K. R., G. M., G. M., S. R., & S. R. (Eds.), *2023 International Conference on Advancement in Computation and Computer Technologies, InCACCT 2023* (pp. 762 – 766). Institute of Electrical and Electronics Engineers Inc. DOI: 10.1109/InCACCT57535.2023.10141802

Singh, Y., Singh, N. K., & Sharma, A. (2023). Biodiesel as an alternative fuel employed in CI engine to meet the sustainability criteria: A review. In S. Y., S. G., & B. G.K. (Eds.), *AIP Conference Proceedings* (Vol. 2521). American Institute of Physics Inc. DOI: 10.1063/5.0113825

Singhal, P., Sharma, S., Saha, S., Mishra, I., Alfurhood, B. S., & Singh, P. (2023). Smart security system using Hybrid System with IoT and Blockchain: A security system Human sased Detection. *2023 3rd International Conference on Advance Computing and Innovative Technologies in Engineering, ICACITE 2023*, 1032 – 1036. DOI: 10.1109/ICACITE57410.2023.10182383

Singla, A., Singh, Y., Singh, Y., Rahim, E. A., Singh, N. K., & Sharma, A. (2023). Challenges and Future Prospects of Biofuel Generations: An Overview. In *Biowaste and Biomass in Biofuel Applications*. CRC Press., DOI: 10.1201/9781003265597-4

Srivastava, A., Hassan, M., & Gangwar, R. (2023). Improving Railway Track System Using Soil Nails for Heavy Axle Load. *Lecture Notes in Civil Engineering, 338 LNCE*, 1 – 13. DOI: 10.1007/978-981-99-1886-7_1

Srivastava, A., Jawaid, S., Singh, R., Gehlot, A., Akram, S. V., Priyadarshi, N., & Khan, B. (2022). Imperative Role of Technology Intervention and Implementation for Automation in the Construction Industry. *Advances in Civil Engineering*, 2022(1), 6716987. Advance online publication. DOI: 10.1155/2022/6716987

Sunori, S. K., Mohan, L., Pant, M., & Juneja, P. (2023). Classification of Soil Fertility using LVQ and PNN Techniques. *Proceedings of the 8th International Conference on Communication and Electronics Systems, ICCES 2023*, 1441 – 1446. DOI: 10.1109/ICCES57224.2023.10192793

Suryavanshi, A., Kukreja, V., Bordoloi, D., Mehta, S., & Choudhary, A. (2023). Agricultural Insights Through Federated Learning CNN: A Case Study on Jackfruit Leaf Disease. In D. R.K., S. A.Kr., S. R., B. S., & K. V. (Eds.), *Proceedings of the 2023 12th International Conference on System Modeling and Advancement in Research Trends, SMART 2023* (pp. 36 – 42). Institute of Electrical and Electronics Engineers Inc. DOI: 10.1109/SMART59791.2023.10428321

Suryavanshi, A., Tanwar, S., Kukreja, V., Choudhary, A., & Chamoli, S. (2023). An Integrated Approach to Potato Leaf Disease Detection Using Convolutional Neural Networks and Random Forest. *Proceedings of the 2023 International Conference on Innovative Computing, Intelligent Communication and Smart Electrical Systems, ICSES 2023*. DOI: 10.1109/ICSES60034.2023.10465557

Taneja, S., Bhatnagar, M., Kumar, P., & Grima, S. (2023). A Panel Analysis of the Effectiveness of the Asset Management in Indian Agricultural Companies. *International Journal of Sustainable Development and Planning*, 18(3), 653–660. DOI: 10.18280/ijsdp.180301

Taneja, S., Bhatnagar, M., Kumar, P., & Rupeika-apoga, R. (2023). India ' s Total Natural Resource Rents (NRR) and GDP : An Augmented Autoregressive Distributed Lag (ARDL) Bound Test. *Journal of Risk and Financial Management*, 16(2), 91. https://doi.org/doi.org/10.3390/jrfm16020091. DOI: 10.3390/jrfm16020091

Thakur, S., Malik, D., Kukreja, V., Sharma, R., Yadav, R., & Joshi, K. (2023). Multi-Stage Classification of Pomegranate Anthracnose Disease Severity Levels with CNN and SVM. *Proceedings of the 4th International Conference on Smart Electronics and Communication, ICOSEC 2023*, 1117 – 1121. DOI: 10.1109/ICOSEC58147.2023.10276047

Tiwari, K., Bafila, P., Negi, P., & Singh, R. (2023). The applications of nanotechnology in nutraceuticals: A review. In S. Y., S. G., & B. G.K. (Eds.), *AIP Conference Proceedings* (Vol. 2521). American Institute of Physics Inc. DOI: 10.1063/5.0129695

Tomar, S., & Sharma, N. (2021). A systematic review of agricultural policies in terms of drivers, enablers, and bottlenecks: Comparison of three Indian states and a model bio-energy village located in different agro climatic regions. *Groundwater for Sustainable Development*, 15, 100683. Advance online publication. DOI: 10.1016/j.gsd.2021.100683

Tomar, S., Sharma, N., & Nehra, N. S. (2023). A sustainable rural entrepreneurship model developed by the organic farmers of India. *Emerald Emerging Markets Case Studies*, 13(2), 1–17. DOI: 10.1108/EEMCS-09-2022-0329

Tyagi, S., Jindal, T., Krishna, S. H., Hassen, S. M., Shukla, S. K., & Kaur, C. (2022). Comparative Analysis of Artificial Intelligence and its Powered Technologies Applications in the Finance Sector. *Proceedings of 5th International Conference on Contemporary Computing and Informatics, IC3I 2022*, 260 – 264. DOI: 10.1109/IC3I56241.2022.10073077

Tyagi, S., Mathur, K., Gupta, T., Khantwal, S., & Tripathi, V. (2023). The Effectiveness of Augmented Reality in Developing Pre-Primary Student's Cognitive Skills. *IEEE Region 10 Humanitarian Technology Conference, R10-HTC*, 997 – 1002. DOI: 10.1109/R10-HTC57504.2023.10461754

Uniyal, S., Sarma, P. R. S., Kumar Mangla, S., Tseng, M.-L., & Patil, P. (2022). ICT as "Knowledge Management" for Assessing Sustainable Consumption and Production in Supply Chains. In *Research Anthology on Measuring and Achieving Sustainable Development Goals* (Vol. 3). IGI Global. DOI: 10.4018/978-1-6684-3885-5.ch048

Vennila, H., Giri, N. C., Nallapaneni, M. K., Sinha, P., Bajaj, M., Abou Houran, M., & Kamel, S. (2022). Static and dynamic environmental economic dispatch using tournament selection based ant lion optimization algorithm. *Frontiers in Energy Research*, 10, 972069. Advance online publication. DOI: 10.3389/fenrg.2022.972069

Vijayalakshmi, S., Hasan, F., Priyadarshini, S. M., Durga, S., Verma, V., & Podile, V. (2022). Strategic Evaluation of Implementing Artificial Intelligence Towards Shaping Entrepreneurial Development During Covid-19 Outbreaks. *2022 2nd International Conference on Advance Computing and Innovative Technologies in Engineering, ICACITE 2022*, 2570 – 2573. DOI: 10.1109/ICACITE53722.2022.9823894

William, P., Ramu, G., Kansal, L., Patil, P. P., Alkhayyat, A., & Rao, A. K. (2023). Artificial Intelligence Based Air Quality Monitoring System with Modernized Environmental Safety of Sustainable Development. *Proceedings - 2023 3rd International Conference on Pervasive Computing and Social Networking, ICPCSN 2023*, 756 – 761. DOI: 10.1109/ICPCSN58827.2023.00130

Wongchai, A., Shukla, S. K., Ahmed, M. A., Sakthi, U., Jagdish, M., & kumar, R. (2022). Artificial intelligence - enabled soft sensor and internet of things for sustainable agriculture using ensemble deep learning architecture. *Computers & Electrical Engineering*, 102, 108128. Advance online publication. DOI: 10.1016/j.compeleceng.2022.108128

Yadav, A. R., Shekhar, S., Vidyarthi, A., Prakash, R., & Gowri, R. (2023). Hyper-Parameter Tuning with Grid and Randomized Search Techniques for Predictive Models of Hotel Booking. *IEEE International Conference on Electrical, Electronics, Communication and Computers, ELEXCOM 2023*. DOI: 10.1109/ELEXCOM58812.2023.10370718

Yadav, P. M., Patra, I., Mittal, V., Nagorao, C. G., Udhayanila, R., & Saranya, A. (2023). Implementation of IOT on English Language Classroom Management. *2023 3rd International Conference on Advance Computing and Innovative Technologies in Engineering, ICACITE 2023*, 1686 – 1690. DOI: 10.1109/ICACITE57410.2023.10182984

Chapter 15
Policy and Regulatory Frameworks for Financing Smart Healthcare

Anuradha Jain
https://orcid.org/0000-0001-6996-8309
Vivekananda Institute of Professional Studies, India

Raj Kumar Singh
https://orcid.org/0000-0003-2113-8677
Graphic Era Hill University, India

Padam Bhushan
Chandigarh University, India

ABSTRACT

As smart healthcare technologies emerge as pillars of modern medicine, developing policy and regulatory frameworks for sustainable financing becomes imperative. Regulatory complexities, spanning data governance, interoperability, and cost-effectiveness, present challenges and opportunities in securing funding for AI, IoT, and digital diagnostics. Policymakers must navigate privacy concerns, ethical dilemmas, and market dynamics to create resilient funding strategies. International cooperation plays a pivotal role in achieving SDG 3 by harmonizing funding protocols and prioritizing equitable access to advanced healthcare across nations. This chapter examines financial policy frameworks needed to support long-term technology integration in global health, exploring funding sources, cost management, and ethical imperatives. By addressing regulatory gaps, enhancing intergovernmental collaboration, and aligning technological investments with health equity goals, policymakers can foster a sustainable future where smart healthcare is accessible to all.

DOI: 10.4018/979-8-3373-0240-9.ch015

INTRODUCTION

In the current epoch of accelerated technological advancement, smart healthcare has emerged as a beacon of transformative potential, promising to redefine patient outcomes through innovations such as artificial intelligence (AI), the Internet of Things (IoT), and big data analytics. These advances, while offering precision and efficiency, necessitate robust policy and regulatory frameworks for sustainable financing. Ensuring that these technologies do not exacerbate existing disparities in healthcare access requires an intricate tapestry of policies that address the funding of research, implementation, and maintenance of cutting-edge medical technology (Diddi et al., 2022).

The financing of smart healthcare technologies is not merely an economic endeavor but a fundamentally ethical one, encompassing the principles of accessibility, equity, and transparency. Regulatory frameworks must be agile enough to address the rapid pace of technological change, safeguarding patient privacy while promoting interoperability across disparate systems. This landscape is further complicated by the imperative to achieve Sustainable Development Goal (SDG) 3, which calls for "ensuring healthy lives and promoting well-being for all at all ages." Achieving this vision on a global scale requires the harmonization of financial policies, wherein developed and developing nations collaborate to foster a more inclusive paradigm of technological access and healthcare quality (K. D. Singh et al., 2023).

Yet, this vision remains fraught with challenges. The confluence of regulatory uncertainty, ethical considerations, and economic constraints has left a gap in the financing infrastructure needed to propel smart healthcare technologies into mainstream global health. This chapter explores the intricacies of developing a robust, adaptable regulatory framework that can support the sustainable financing of healthcare technology, identifying regulatory hurdles, analyzing current policy models, and envisioning a future of international cooperation (Chahar et al., 2022).

The significance of this study lies in its elucidation of the profound and multifaceted imperatives underpinning the financing and regulatory frameworks required to support a sustainable, equitable paradigm in smart healthcare. As the medical field undergoes an unprecedented digital metamorphosis, marked by the proliferation of artificial intelligence (AI), the Internet of Things (IoT), and precision-driven diagnostics, this research addresses the intricate web of policy, economic, and ethical challenges that threaten to exacerbate disparities in healthcare access (I. Kumar et al., 2021).

At its core, this study confronts the asymmetrical allocation of resources and infrastructural inequities that underpin global health, exposing how the current funding mechanisms and regulatory schemas inadequately accommodate the exponential growth of healthcare technologies. It highlights the potential for these advancements to catalyze an era of stratified healthcare delivery, where technologically rich nations advance at the expense of under-resourced regions. Through its focus on financial policies, data governance, and interoperability, the study illustrates how existing regulatory gaps and fiscal shortfalls can constrict the scalability and effectiveness of smart healthcare initiatives, particularly in low- and middle-income countries (Hajoary et al., 2023).

Furthermore, this study provides critical insights into the socioeconomic and geopolitical ramifications of data sovereignty and regulatory fragmentation, underscoring the paradox where local data protections may hinder the collaborative potential of cross-border healthcare solutions. By advocating for harmonized international frameworks and investment consortia, this research posits that only through coordinated policy efforts can nations collectively bridge the digital divide in healthcare, fostering a globally integrated system that serves the interests of all populations (Wazid et al., 2021).

In essence, the study's significance is magnified by its call for a paradigm shift in healthcare policy and financing—a shift that moves beyond mere technological adoption to one that emphasizes inclusivity, ethical stewardship, and sustainable growth. Through the establishment of multi-sectoral alliances, tiered financing models, and policy mechanisms that prioritize health equity, this study positions itself as a blueprint for fostering a resilient global health ecosystem that leverages smart healthcare as a universal right rather than a selective privilege (Medhi et al., 2023).

Table 1. Key facts related to topics

Topic	Fact
Global Funding Gap in Smart Healthcare	Developing countries face a $371 billion annual funding gap for essential healthcare services, creating barriers to adopting smart healthcare technologies (V. Kumar & Korovin, 2023).
Data Privacy Concerns	65% of healthcare organizations report concerns over data privacy when adopting digital health technologies, with regulatory variances complicating international data-sharing (Raju et al., 2022).
Interoperability Standards	Only 20% of healthcare systems worldwide are fully interoperable, impeding seamless data flow across regions and reducing the effectiveness of IoT and digital health solutions (Davuluri et al., 2023).
SDG 3 and Technology Access	Meeting SDG 3 will require scaling technology access in underserved areas, with an estimated $20 billion in annual funding needed to close technology gaps in low- and middle-income countries (S. Sharma et al., 2021).
Increased Investment in AI	Global investment in AI healthcare applications is projected to reach $45 billion by 2030, with significant disparities in access between high- and low-income regions (Josphineleela et al., 2023).
Tax Incentives for Technology Adoption	Countries like the US and Singapore offer tax credits and incentives for adopting healthcare technology, encouraging private-sector investment in smart healthcare (Tripathy et al., 2021).
Data Sovereignty Laws	90% of countries now have data sovereignty laws affecting healthcare data, limiting cross-border access and complicating international funding efforts for integrated healthcare technology (N. K. Singh et al., 2020).
Public-Private Partnerships (PPPs)	PPPs have increased by 35% in healthcare over the past decade, with models like the Global Fund mobilizing $4 billion annually for health technology in developing countries (Lade et al., 2023).
Healthcare Workforce Reskilling Needs	Adopting digital health solutions necessitates workforce reskilling, with an estimated 50% of healthcare roles requiring digital literacy training to meet future demand (Luthra et al., 2022).
Emerging Markets' Role in Global Health	Emerging markets account for over 50% of new healthcare technology patents, yet often lack the financial infrastructure for widespread implementation within their own healthcare systems (Garg et al., 2023).

The table 1 elucidates a series of pivotal insights and metrics underscoring the exigencies of establishing robust policy and regulatory frameworks to finance smart healthcare equitably across global contexts. Each data point accentuates the intricacies and systemic disparities underlying the fiscal and infrastructural requisites for smart healthcare, delineating critical factors that influence its global accessibility, interoperability, and efficacy.

Global Funding Gap in Smart Healthcare reveals a profound fiscal void in developing nations, with an estimated $371 billion annual shortfall impeding access to essential healthcare services and precluding widespread adoption of smart healthcare technologies. This figure foregrounds a stark dichotomy between high- and low-income countries, wherein financial constraints impose a formidable barrier to the integration of innovative medical technologies.

The Data Privacy Concerns metric, which illustrates that 65% of healthcare organizations express reticence towards adopting digital health innovations due to regulatory fragmentation in data governance, signifies a pivotal impediment in global smart healthcare integration. The lack of cohesive international data standards generates a fragmented regulatory milieu that complicates data-sharing efforts and restricts inter-regional digital health initiatives.

Interoperability Standards, wherein only 20% of healthcare systems worldwide achieve full interoperability, further compounds the challenge, obstructing the streamlined flow of IoT-enabled health data and reducing the efficacy of integrated healthcare systems. The limited global interoperability underscores a lacuna in regulatory harmonization, which is essential for maximizing the potential of smart healthcare on a macro scale.

The SDG 3 and Technology Access insight reflects the staggering financial demands of actualizing Sustainable Development Goal 3, necessitating $20 billion annually to bridge technology access gaps in low- and middle-income nations. This staggering fiscal imperative reveals the underlying inadequacies in funding allocation and international policy support, which are vital for achieving equitable health technology deployment and sustainable development outcomes.

Projected Increased Investment in AI underscores a juxtaposition between the anticipated $45 billion in global AI healthcare investments by 2030 and the socio-economic stratifications that limit equitable access to these technologies. This dichotomy highlights the propensity for technological advancement to deepen global health inequities without targeted policies promoting accessibility in under-resourced regions.

The insight into Tax Incentives for Technology Adoption reveals how fiscal policy instruments in advanced economies, such as tax credits in the US and Singapore, function as catalytic mechanisms to incentivize private-sector engagement in smart healthcare innovation. Such incentives, however, are conspicuously absent in low- and middle-income countries, underscoring a critical disparity in policy support for healthcare technology adoption.

The Data Sovereignty Laws statistic, noting that 90% of nations have enacted jurisdictional controls on healthcare data, exposes an undercurrent of regulatory sovereignty that hampers cross-border interoperability and complicates international funding endeavors. Data sovereignty laws, while protective of national data interests, inadvertently stymie the seamless integration of healthcare technologies, particularly in multinational consortia and cross-jurisdictional data frameworks.

Public-Private Partnerships (PPPs), which have surged by 35% in healthcare over the past decade, exemplify an emerging model of collaborative finance that consolidates resources from public and private sectors. Through entities such as the Global Fund, which mobilizes $4 billion annually, PPPs emerge as instrumental frameworks for channeling financial resources into healthcare technology, particularly in resource-constrained settings. These partnerships encapsulate the potential for coalescing public health imperatives with private-sector innovation, creating an operational synergy conducive to advancing global health equity.

The statistic on Healthcare Workforce Reskilling Needs, with an anticipated 50% of roles necessitating digital literacy training, exposes a critical dependency on workforce adaptability for the effective deployment of digital health solutions. This metric underscores an impending crisis in healthcare labor markets, where the skills gap threatens to undermine the efficacy of smart healthcare unless substantial investments are directed towards digital skill development.

Lastly, the metric regarding Emerging Markets' Role in Global Health underscores a paradoxical reality in which emerging markets, while generating over 50% of new healthcare technology patents, often lack the infrastructural and fiscal apparatus to implement these innovations domestically. This incongruity highlights an urgent call for international policy frameworks that promote technology transfer and resource allocation to facilitate the equitable application of indigenous innovations in healthcare.

Together, these metrics elucidate the complex interplay of fiscal constraints, regulatory sovereignty, workforce preparedness, and international cooperation required to construct a globally accessible and sustainable smart healthcare ecosystem. Without a concerted, policy-driven response to these disparities, the transformative potential of healthcare technology risks becoming yet another conduit for global health inequities.

Regulatory Challenges and Opportunities for Funding Healthcare Technologies

The regulatory landscape for funding healthcare technologies is rife with complexities, often dictated by the dual need to foster innovation and protect public welfare. Regulatory bodies must contend with several intersecting domains: data privacy, market dynamics, and clinical efficacy, all while ensuring that funding models align with ethical standards and promote equitable access. In the realm of smart healthcare, one of the most pronounced regulatory challenges is data governance, particularly regarding patient data privacy and security.

Data governance regulations such as the Health Insurance Portability and Accountability Act (HIPAA) in the United States and the General Data Protection Regulation (GDPR) in Europe present a rigorous framework for data protection; however, these policies often lack specificity concerning AI and IoT applications. Such gaps create uncertainty for investors and healthcare providers, who face potential liability risks and compliance costs associated with the storage and transmission of sensitive health data across digital platforms. A regulatory framework that encourages secure data-sharing protocols, standardizes data anonymization techniques, and enhances interoperability is essential for attracting investment while minimizing risks.

Another salient challenge lies in ensuring interoperability within healthcare systems. Interoperability facilitates seamless data exchange between devices and systems, an essential component for the effectiveness of IoT-enabled monitoring devices, AI diagnostics, and digital health records. Yet, regulatory policies around interoperability remain fragmented, with different countries and even regions within countries adopting disparate standards. This lack of uniformity impedes the scalability of smart healthcare solutions and discourages investment by raising integration costs. Establishing regulatory frameworks that prioritize interoperability would not only streamline operations but also lower the financial barriers to technology adoption, ultimately enhancing patient outcomes.

The regulatory landscape also presents opportunities for fostering funding in healthcare technology. By establishing tax incentives, subsidies, and low-interest loans specifically earmarked for smart healthcare technologies, governments can catalyze private-sector investment and encourage the adoption of advanced medical systems (Agarwal & Sharma, 2023). Public-private partnerships (PPPs) represent another mechanism through which regulatory bodies can stimulate innovation; by aligning corporate interests with public health goals, PPPs provide a structured framework for investment in health technology, encouraging the private sector to take a more active role in healthcare transformation. Moreover, by enacting policies that require transparency and accountability in the development and implementation of healthcare technologies, regulators can cultivate a more stable and predictable investment environment, attracting investors who value long-term sustainability over short-term gains (Uniyal et al., 2021).

Developing Financial Policies for Sustainable Tech Adoption in Global Health

The adoption of smart healthcare technologies demands not only regulatory foresight but also financial policies that enable sustainable integration into existing healthcare systems. As healthcare providers contend with constrained budgets and rising operational costs, policymakers face the challenge of designing financial frameworks that promote technological advancement without compromising fiscal responsibility (Bisht et al., 2023).

One promising approach to financing healthcare technology is the creation of dedicated health technology funds at the national and international levels. Such funds could pool resources from government allocations, international aid, and private investment to support the acquisition and maintenance of smart healthcare technologies, particularly in low-resource settings. These funds would operate with a clear mandate to ensure that investments align with health equity goals, prioritizing access for marginalized populations and under-resourced healthcare systems. This model could be adapted to include performance-based financing, wherein funds are allocated based on measurable improvements in health outcomes and system efficiency, creating a cycle of reinvestment that perpetuates technological growth (T. Pandey et al., 2023).

In addition, policymakers must consider reimbursement models that reflect the value provided by smart healthcare technologies. Traditional fee-for-service models are often ill-suited to the predictive and preventive capabilities of AI-driven diagnostics and IoT monitoring devices, as these systems are designed to prevent costly health events rather than react to them. Value-based reimbursement models, which tie payments to health outcomes and cost savings, offer a more suitable mechanism for funding healthcare technology. These models incentivize providers to adopt technologies that improve patient outcomes while controlling costs, thereby aligning financial incentives with patient welfare (Trache et al., 2022).

Healthcare financing policies must also incorporate provisions for training and workforce development, recognizing that the successful deployment of smart healthcare technologies is contingent upon a digitally literate workforce. Funding allocations should prioritize reskilling initiatives for healthcare professionals, enabling them to work in tandem with advanced technologies while maintaining a high standard of patient care. Policymakers can incentivize institutions to invest in digital literacy programs by offering grants or subsidies that cover the costs of training healthcare personnel in data analytics, AI interpretation, and cybersecurity. This approach not only fosters a technologically proficient workforce but also mitigates the risk of obsolescence in a rapidly evolving healthcare environment (M. Sharma, Kumar, Luthra, Joshi, et al., 2022).

International Cooperation for Healthcare Financing to Achieve SDG 3

Achieving SDG 3 necessitates a collaborative, internationally coordinated approach to healthcare financing, with a focus on bridging the technology divide between high- and low-income countries. The disparity in access to advanced healthcare technologies has exacerbated global health inequities, with developing nations often lacking the financial and infrastructural capacity to adopt and sustain smart healthcare solutions. International cooperation can play a pivotal role in addressing these disparities by establishing funding mechanisms and policy frameworks that promote equitable access to healthcare technology on a global scale (K. S. Kumar et al., 2022).

One potential mechanism for facilitating international cooperation is the creation of a global health technology financing consortium. This consortium would be a multi-stakeholder entity comprising representatives from the World Health Organization (WHO), World Bank, philanthropic organizations, and private-sector partners. Its primary objective would be to provide financial support for smart healthcare initiatives in low-resource settings, prioritizing projects that align with SDG 3 targets (Arora et al., 2022). By leveraging pooled resources and aligning objectives across organizations, the consortium could coordinate funding allocations to ensure that investments are strategically distributed and directed toward areas with the greatest potential impact (Ramachandran et al., 2023).

In addition to financial support, international cooperation must also address regulatory harmonization, as disparate legal frameworks and compliance requirements hinder the cross-border deployment of healthcare technology. The establishment of international standards for data privacy, interoperability, and ethical AI use would create a more cohesive regulatory environment, allowing technologies to be deployed across borders with minimal adaptation. Such harmonization would also attract private investors by reducing the regulatory risks associated with multi-jurisdictional operations, creating a more predictable environment for long-term investment (M. Sharma, Luthra, Joshi, & Joshi, 2022).

International aid programs, particularly those targeting healthcare infrastructure, should be adapted to prioritize smart healthcare technologies. Aid agencies and development banks can reallocate funds toward building the digital infrastructure necessary to support AI, IoT, and electronic health record (EHR) systems, particularly in rural and underserved areas. By investing in foundational infrastructure, these agencies can enable developing countries to leapfrog traditional healthcare models, directly adopting advanced technologies that would otherwise be inaccessible. This strategic reallocation of resources aligns with a vision of sustainable development that values health equity and positions technology as a tool for universal access (Tyagi et al., 2023).

Policy Mechanisms for Equitable Distribution of Healthcare Technologies

The equitable distribution of healthcare technologies across socioeconomic and geographic boundaries demands a recalibration of policy mechanisms that traditionally favor high-income settings (Gupta et al., 2023). While smart healthcare promises to bridge gaps in accessibility and improve outcomes for underserved populations, without targeted policy intervention, these innovations risk becoming concentrated in affluent regions, exacerbating global health disparities. To counteract this trend, policymakers must craft equitable financing and distribution frameworks that prioritize vulnerable populations and regions with limited healthcare infrastructure (Krishna et al., 2022).

One such approach involves the implementation of tiered pricing structures for healthcare technologies, wherein pricing models are scaled based on a country's economic capacity. This structure would allow high-income countries to bear a larger financial responsibility for the development and acquisition of smart healthcare technologies, while low- and middle-income countries receive these technologies at significantly reduced costs. Pharmaceutical companies have previously employed this model for essential medicines, and extending it to include healthcare technology could ensure that economically disadvantaged regions are not precluded from accessing critical advancements (Masal et al., 2022).

Subsidy programs represent another potential mechanism for equitable technology distribution. By subsidizing smart healthcare technologies for underserved communities, governments can promote widespread adoption, thereby enhancing health outcomes and reducing long-term healthcare expenditures (Taneja, Gupta, et al., 2023). Such subsidies may encompass direct financial assistance for purchasing healthcare devices, tax incentives for private healthcare providers who serve low-income patients, or funding for public health programs that utilize smart technologies. These measures should be tailored to each country's unique demographic and economic landscape, ensuring that subsidies are both impactful and sustainable (Kukreti et al., 2023).

Incentivized partnerships between governments, NGOs, and private technology firms offer another promising framework for distributing healthcare technology equitably. Public-private partnerships (PPPs), when structured with accountability and transparency, provide a means of bridging resource gaps and fostering innovation in low-resource settings (Bansal et al., 2023). By aligning corporate interests with public health goals, PPPs encourage technology firms to engage in global health initiatives, thereby expanding their markets while enhancing access to healthcare. For instance, incentivizing corporations through tax breaks or preferential government contracts can promote the distribution of health-monitoring devices, AI-based diagnostic tools, and telemedicine platforms to rural and underserved populations (Kohli et al., 2022).

Implementing Mechanisms for Global Financing Consortia

A pivotal component of international cooperation for equitable technology distribution is the establishment of global financing consortia. These consortia could act as central governing bodies responsible for mobilizing and directing funds toward healthcare technology in low- and middle-income countries. Such entities could pool resources from multiple stakeholders, including governments, international organizations, philanthropic entities, and private sector investors (Taneja & Özen, 2023). By centralizing funding and decision-making, these consortia would be well-positioned to identify priority areas, allocate funds efficiently, and ensure that investments are aligned with SDG 3 and broader global health equity objectives (Nethravathi et al., 2022).

For instance, a consortium focused on financing healthcare technology might create a global investment fund specifically earmarked for infrastructure that supports AI, IoT, and telemedicine in developing regions. This fund would prioritize investments in areas such as broadband infrastructure, energy supply for digital health systems, and training programs for healthcare professionals, thereby addressing both the technical and human resource requirements for smart healthcare. The fund could also establish performance-based criteria for allocating resources, rewarding projects that demonstrate measurable improvements in health outcomes and system efficiencies (N. K. Pandey et al., 2023).

Additionally, global financing consortia should develop frameworks that mandate transparency and accountability among recipients of their funds. Transparent reporting structures, third-party audits, and performance reviews would ensure that investments are utilized effectively and align with the overarching goals of equitable access and sustainable development. Establishing strict criteria for fund disbursement and monitoring can prevent misallocation of resources and ensure that every dollar invested translates to tangible improvements in healthcare accessibility and quality (R. Kumar & Khanna, 2023).

Recent developments in the domain of smart healthcare financing and regulatory frameworks embody a complex convergence of technological sophistication, policy adaptation, and emergent ethical considerations, each transforming the landscape of global health in nuanced and impactful ways (H. Sharma et al., 2023).

A pivotal advancement is the increasing integration of blockchain technology into healthcare data management, particularly for decentralized and interoperable health record systems. Blockchain's immutable, decentralized structure has been championed as a solution to interoperability challenges, offering a unified digital ledger that facilitates seamless, secure data exchange across disparate health networks. Several healthcare consortia, notably the European Health Data Space, have piloted blockchain frameworks to enhance cross-border data-sharing while safeguarding patient privacy, thus addressing long-standing challenges in data sovereignty and compliance within multi-jurisdictional healthcare settings (V. Kumar & Korovin, 2023).

Simultaneously, the acceleration of AI-driven diagnostic platforms has catalyzed substantial changes in healthcare policy and funding dynamics. Institutions are increasingly adopting AI for real-time diagnostics, predictive analytics, and patient stratification, prompting regulatory bodies to establish frameworks that address the clinical and ethical implications of algorithmic decision-making. The U.S. Food and Drug Administration (FDA) and the European Medicines Agency (EMA), for instance, have issued guidelines mandating transparency and interpretability for AI applications in clinical settings, underscoring the need for "explainable AI" to ensure clinicians and patients can understand the algorithmic rationale behind diagnoses and recommendations (S. Sharma & Bhadula, 2023).

Furthermore, the recent emphasis on precision medicine—tailored to individual genetic profiles—has redefined the healthcare funding model, moving from a one-size-fits-all approach to bespoke therapies that leverage genomic, proteomic, and metabolic data. This paradigm shift has catalyzed substantial investment from both public and private sectors (Bhatnagar et al., 2023). National genomics programs, such as Genomics England and All of Us in the U.S., have mobilized extensive capital to support genomic data infrastructure, fostering a collaborative ecosystem where private-sector expertise intersects with public health objectives. However, this shift also demands a reconfiguration of ethical and regulatory norms, particularly regarding data privacy, genetic discrimination, and the equitable distribution of precision therapies (Uike et al., 2022).

Telemedicine and remote health monitoring technologies have also surged forward, especially in response to the constraints imposed by the COVID-19 pandemic. The proliferation of IoT-enabled health devices has enabled continuous, real-time patient monitoring, thus alleviating the burden on healthcare facilities and enhancing preventive care. Regulatory frameworks have responded with an accelerated approval pathway for telemedicine tools, with agencies revising traditional reimbursement models to incentivize remote care services (P. Kumar et al., 2024). However, this expansion has ignited debate over data security, as IoT devices collect voluminous personal data that, if inadequately protected, could expose patients to privacy breaches and potential exploitation (Rana et al., 2022).

Internationally, global health financing consortia have taken shape to address the financial inequities exacerbated by disparate access to healthcare technology. Entities such as the WHO Digital Health Strategy Consortium and the World Bank's HealthTech Initiative have convened to pool resources, foster technology transfer, and promote equitable access to smart healthcare solutions in low- and middle-income countries (Bhatnagar, Rajaram, et al., 2024). These consortia aim to circumvent traditional funding silos by adopting a multi-stakeholder investment approach that aligns private capital with public health imperatives, creating a sustainable model for technology dissemination that prioritizes underserved regions (Pallavi et al., 2022).

In sum, the field of smart healthcare is characterized by profound technological advancements and a dynamic regulatory response. These developments reflect a concerted, albeit nascent, effort to integrate innovation with regulatory rigor, fostering a healthcare ecosystem that aspires to balance the imperatives of accessibility, privacy, and sustainability (Goswami & Sharma, 2022).

Challenges and Ethical Considerations in Financing Smart Healthcare

The integration of smart healthcare technologies within global health systems presents a series of ethical considerations that policymakers and stakeholders must navigate. One pressing issue is the potential monopolization of healthcare technology markets by large multinational corporations, which may result in inflated costs and restrict access for underserved populations. Given the significant capital investment required to develop and deploy smart healthcare technologies, market consolidation is a pervasive risk, with a few dominant players potentially exerting disproportionate control over pricing, access, and distribution (N. K. Singh et al., 2021).

To counteract the monopolistic tendencies in healthcare technology markets, policymakers should consider anti-monopoly regulations and open-source mandates. By enforcing regulations that prevent market consolidation and promote competition, governments can stimulate innovation while safeguarding affordability. Additionally, encouraging or mandating open-source solutions for certain healthcare technologies could democratize access to diagnostic tools, health monitoring applications, and digital health records, as organizations would have unrestricted access to the source code, allowing for local adaptations and cost-effective deployment in low-resource settings (Khaudiyal et al., 2022).

Privacy and Data Sovereignty are equally critical ethical issues in the financing and deployment of healthcare technology. Many smart healthcare devices rely on the collection, storage, and analysis of personal health data, raising concerns about privacy, security, and consent (Taneja, Bhatnagar, Kumar, & Rupeika-apoga, 2023). In low- and middle-income countries where data protection laws may be underdeveloped or inconsistently enforced, this presents a heightened risk of data exploitation by third-party vendors, potentially leading to unauthorized data sharing or commercialization. To address this, financial policies must incorporate data sovereignty provisions that ensure patient data remains under the jurisdiction and control of the originating country, limiting the influence of foreign entities and protecting the privacy rights of individuals (R. Kumar et al., 2023).

Another ethical consideration is the potential for exacerbating health inequities through technological disparities. High-income countries are often able to invest in cutting-edge healthcare technology, whereas low-income countries may struggle to afford even basic infrastructure upgrades (Bhatnagar, Kumar, et al., 2024). The resulting "technology divide" in healthcare creates a multi-tiered system, where affluent regions benefit from advanced medical services, while impoverished areas are left with outdated and less effective treatments. This disparity undermines the ethical principle of health equity, as access to quality healthcare becomes contingent upon geographic and economic factors (Uniyal et al., 2020).

Addressing these ethical challenges requires a collaborative approach that combines policy reform with international advocacy. Governments, international organizations, and advocacy groups must work collectively to establish ethical standards for healthcare technology financing, prioritizing initiatives that bridge the technology divide and promote inclusivity in global health systems (Taneja, Bhatnagar, Kumar, & Grima, 2023). By embedding ethical considerations into the policy-making process, stakeholders can ensure that the deployment of smart healthcare technologies aligns with the principles of fairness, accountability, and respect for human dignity (M. Sharma, Hagar, Krishna Murthy, Beyane, et al., 2022).

Future research in the domain of financing and regulatory frameworks for smart healthcare must delve deeply into the intricate interplay of economic models, governance structures, and ethical paradigms, all of which are reshaping the landscape of modern medicine. As digital health technologies become more pervasive, the need for a profound understanding of the fiscal and regulatory mechanisms that underpin sustainable technology integration intensifies. Research must interrogate the paradigms through which financing models can be adapted to support not only the rapid deployment of healthcare technologies but also their ethical, equitable, and sustainable use within a global context fraught with socioeconomic disparities (Pathak et al., 2021).

One promising avenue for inquiry lies in exploring alternative economic frameworks capable of sustaining the vast and often volatile capital investments required for advanced healthcare technologies. Traditional financing structures, rooted in fee-for-service and reimbursement models, have proven inadequate for supporting the complexities of AI-driven diagnostics, genomics, and IoT-enabled monitoring systems, which demand not only high upfront costs but also continuous investment in infrastructure, cybersecurity, and workforce development. Future research must probe the viability of value-based financing models, which link funding to tangible improvements in patient outcomes and system efficiency. Such models could realign economic incentives in a manner that encourages sustainable investments in healthcare technology, thus enabling cost savings that translate to broader accessibility (A. Sharma et al., 2020).

Moreover, an unexplored yet essential aspect of future research is the development of adaptable policy frameworks that can accommodate the exponential evolution of healthcare technology. Traditional regulatory mechanisms are inherently reactive, often struggling to keep pace with rapid technological advancements, thus creating a regulatory gap that could exacerbate disparities in healthcare quality and accessibility (P. Kumar et al., 2023). Researchers must explore the concept of "adaptive regulation"—a model that incorporates real-time data monitoring, iterative policy updates, and cross-jurisdictional harmonization. This approach could allow regulatory bodies to dynamically recalibrate standards in response to emerging evidence, thus ensuring that healthcare technologies are deployed ethically and equitably without stifling innovation. Investigating how adaptive regulatory frameworks could integrate continuous feedback from diverse stakeholders—including technologists, ethicists, and patient advocacy groups—will be paramount to developing regulatory structures that are both agile and robust (Pai et al., 2022).

The exploration of global data governance structures also warrants rigorous investigation, as the integration of smart healthcare technologies is contingent upon secure and interoperable data ecosystems (Rakhra et al., 2022). Current data sovereignty laws, which often restrict cross-border data transfer, pose a substantial barrier to the effective deployment of AI and IoT in healthcare, particularly in multinational health systems and international research collaborations. Future research should assess how harmonized data governance frameworks might reconcile the competing imperatives of privacy, security, and interoperability. A compelling line of inquiry would examine the feasibility of a federated data model for healthcare, wherein data is decentralized yet accessible through standardized APIs, thereby facilitating international data-sharing while maintaining local control over sensitive health information (Salama et al., 2023).

In parallel, researchers must address the socioeconomic ramifications of financing smart healthcare technologies, particularly in relation to low- and middle-income countries that are at risk of being marginalized by the technology divide. The global allocation of healthcare resources is deeply asymmetrical, with high-income nations possessing the infrastructural capacity to implement AI and IoT on a wide scale, while resource-constrained settings often struggle to secure even basic healthcare technologies. Future studies should investigate the efficacy of international financing consortia that pool resources from public and private sectors to support technology deployment in underserved regions (P. Sharma et al., 2024). Such research could illuminate how multi-stakeholder partnerships can function not merely as financial vehicles but as catalysts for capacity building, ensuring that developing regions have the requisite skills, infrastructure, and regulatory support to adopt and sustain advanced healthcare systems (Aggarwal et al., 2021).

Ethical considerations, too, occupy a critical space within the future research landscape, as the deployment of smart healthcare technologies raises profound questions about the balance between innovation and patient autonomy (M. Kumar et al., 2021; Mehershilpa et al., 2023; K. Pandey et al., 2020). With AI increasingly influencing diagnostic and therapeutic decisions, future research must examine the potential for algorithmic bias, particularly in systems trained on datasets that may not reflect the diversity of patient populations. Studies should delve into the construction of ethical safeguards within AI-driven systems, exploring frameworks for algorithmic transparency and interpretability that empower healthcare providers to scrutinize machine-generated recommendations (Bhatnagar, Taneja, et al., 2024). Furthermore, research should assess how these technologies might be regulated to prevent the erosion of the patient-provider relationship, ensuring that AI augments rather than supplants the human elements of healthcare (Juyal & Sharma, 2020).

The emerging field of precision medicine, which leverages genomic and phenotypic data to tailor treatments to individual patients, presents another fertile domain for future research. Precision medicine holds the promise of revolutionizing patient care by providing highly personalized treatments; however, it also necessitates a reconceptualization of both funding mechanisms and ethical standards. Future studies should explore how financing models can be adapted to account for the high costs and specialized infrastructure required for genomic analysis, as well as the ethical implications of access disparities. Given the substantial financial outlay involved in precision medicine, researchers must investigate how financing structures can be aligned to promote equitable access, ensuring that genomic therapies do not become the exclusive purview of affluent demographics but are accessible to all patients irrespective of socioeconomic status (Kannan et al., 2022).

The concept of technological resilience also warrants thorough investigation, particularly in light of recent global crises such as the COVID-19 pandemic. The pandemic underscored the critical role of digital health technologies in maintaining healthcare continuity, yet it also revealed the vulnerabilities inherent in over-reliance on centralized healthcare infrastructure. Future research should examine how financing and regulatory frameworks can foster a resilient healthcare ecosystem that leverages decentralized technologies, such as remote monitoring and telemedicine, to bolster healthcare access during emergencies. Exploring how these technologies can be supported through adaptive financial models, which flexibly allocate resources in response to shifting healthcare demands, could contribute to a more resilient and sustainable global health system (Chandna et al., 2022; Upreti et al., 2023).

A vital, though often overlooked, facet of future research is the development of standardized metrics to evaluate the efficacy and impact of healthcare technologies. In the absence of consistent assessment criteria, it is challenging to determine whether investments in AI, IoT, and digital health solutions yield measurable improvements in patient outcomes and healthcare efficiencies (Verma et al., 2022). Researchers should work toward establishing rigorous, universally accepted metrics that encompass clinical efficacy, cost-effectiveness, and patient satisfaction. Such metrics would not only provide a foundation for value-based financing models but also enable policymakers and investors to make informed decisions based on empirical evidence, thereby fostering a more accountable and results-oriented approach to healthcare technology financing (Širić et al., 2022).

Additionally, as smart healthcare technologies blur the boundaries between healthcare, data science, and bioethics, there is an increasing need for interdisciplinary research that synthesizes insights from multiple domains. Future studies should emphasize cross-disciplinary collaboration, bringing together experts from fields as diverse as ethics, law, economics, and artificial intelligence to examine the holistic implications of smart healthcare financing. This interdisciplinary approach would foster a comprehensive understanding of the policy, economic, and ethical dynamics that influence healthcare technology adoption, generating insights that transcend the limitations of siloed research.

The rise of blockchain technology, particularly for healthcare data management, presents yet another domain of considerable research interest. Blockchain's decentralized architecture offers a promising solution to interoperability and data security challenges, yet its deployment within healthcare raises questions about scalability, energy consumption, and regulatory compliance (Bhamangol et al., 2022; Rajeswari et al., 2022). Future research should critically assess the feasibility of blockchain in healthcare, examining its capacity to support secure, transparent, and interoperable data ecosystems. Moreover, exploring how blockchain-based data management systems can be financed and regulated within existing healthcare frameworks would provide valuable insights into the potential integration of this disruptive technology (Raman et al., 2023; S. Sharma et al., 2023).

Finally, the role of education and workforce development in supporting the sustainable deployment of healthcare technologies is an area ripe for further inquiry (M. Sharma, Luthra, Joshi, & Kumar, 2022). As digital health solutions permeate clinical and administrative settings, there is a pressing need for a workforce proficient in data literacy, cybersecurity, and AI interpretation. Future research should explore how financial policies can incentivize educational institutions and healthcare organizations to invest in workforce reskilling programs, thereby ensuring that healthcare professionals are equipped to operate within a technologically advanced ecosystem. Investigating the long-term economic impacts of workforce digital literacy on healthcare outcomes could yield critical insights into the value of sustained investment in professional development (Badhotiya et al., 2022).

In conclusion, future research in financing and regulatory frameworks for smart healthcare must traverse a broad spectrum of issues, from economic sustainability and ethical accountability to regulatory adaptability and interdisciplinary collaboration (Mandalapu et al., 2023). By pursuing these lines of inquiry, researchers can contribute to a nuanced understanding of the policy architectures and financial models that will enable the global healthcare system to harness the full potential of digital health technologies. This research, in turn, will lay the groundwork for a healthcare ecosystem that is both technologically advanced and ethically aligned, capable of addressing the complexities of modern healthcare in a manner that is equitable, sustainable, and resilient (Mohd et al., 2023; Nainwal et al., 2022).

Case Studies: International Models for Financing Healthcare Technology

Several countries and international organizations have pioneered innovative approaches to financing healthcare technology, providing valuable insights into effective policy frameworks and potential pitfalls. The European Union, for example, has established the European Regional Development Fund (ERDF), which allocates resources to support healthcare technology projects aimed at enhancing regional healthcare infrastructure. By targeting under-resourced areas within Europe, the ERDF exemplifies a targeted approach to healthcare financing that prioritizes equitable distribution, fostering development in underserved communities. Such regional funding models could be adapted on a global scale, particularly through organizations such as the World Bank or WHO, to ensure that healthcare technology reaches the world's most vulnerable populations.

Another notable example is the African Development Bank's (AfDB) "eHealth Africa" initiative, which provides financial and technical support for the deployment of telemedicine, health informatics, and IoT-based healthcare solutions across sub-Saharan Africa. This initiative leverages public-private partnerships, combining government funding with corporate investment to facilitate technology transfer and infrastructure development. By focusing on capacity-building and local partnerships, AfDB's approach empowers African nations to take ownership of their healthcare systems, reducing dependency on external donors and fostering long-term sustainability.

In Asia, the Smart Health Initiative by the Asian Development Bank (ADB) showcases a blended financing model, where concessional loans, grants, and private investment are combined to fund the adoption of AI and digital health systems in Southeast Asian countries. The initiative emphasizes technology scaling, ensuring that recipient countries are equipped with the infrastructure and expertise to expand healthcare technology access over time. The Smart Health Initiative illustrates the potential for international financial institutions to facilitate large-scale technological adoption in regions that face resource limitations, advancing SDG 3 through a pragmatic, collaborative financing model.

Conclusion: Navigating the Future of Global Health with Smart Technology

The future of global health is intrinsically tied to the ability of nations and international bodies to craft policies that facilitate the sustainable financing and equitable distribution of smart healthcare technologies. As we navigate this transformative era, it is paramount that policy frameworks evolve in tandem with technological advancements, ensuring that the benefits of innovation are accessible to all, regardless of economic or geographic limitations. The integration of AI, IoT, and other digital health tools holds the potential to revolutionize healthcare delivery; however, realizing this potential demands a collaborative approach that balances technological progress with ethical responsibility and fiscal prudence.

Moving forward, policymakers must champion a vision of healthcare that values both innovation and inclusivity. By developing robust financial models, fostering international cooperation, and prioritizing ethical safeguards, stakeholders can create a resilient healthcare ecosystem where smart technologies enhance, rather than exacerbate, health equity. Through collective action, guided by principles of accountability, transparency, and patient-centered care, the global health community can advance toward a future where smart healthcare is not a privilege but a universal right, aligned with the aspirations of SDG 3.

REFERENCES

Agarwal, P., & Sharma, S. (2023). Smart Urban Traffic Management System using Energy Efficient Optimized Path Discovery. *Proceedings of the 3rd International Conference on Artificial Intelligence and Smart Energy, ICAIS 2023*, 858 – 863. DOI: 10.1109/ICAIS56108.2023.10073840

Aggarwal, V., Gupta, V., Sharma, N., Gupta, S., Pundir, V., Sharma, K., & Sharma, N. (2021). Integration of Waste Management Companies in Micro Grids through Machine Learning. *Proceedings of the 2nd International Conference on Electronics and Sustainable Communication Systems, ICESC 2021*, 1881 – 1886. DOI: 10.1109/ICESC51422.2021.9532680

Arora, R., Singh, A. P., Sharma, R., & Chauhan, A. (2022). A remanufacturing inventory model to control the carbon emission using cap-and-trade regulation with the hexagonal fuzzy number. *Benchmarking*, 29(7), 2202–2230. DOI: 10.1108/BIJ-05-2021-0254

Badhotiya, G. K., Avikal, S., Soni, G., & Sengar, N. (2022). Analyzing barriers for the adoption of circular economy in the manufacturing sector. *International Journal of Productivity and Performance Management*, 71(3), 912–931. DOI: 10.1108/IJPPM-01-2021-0021

Bansal, N., Bhatnagar, M., & Taneja, S. (2023). Balancing priorities through green optimism: A study elucidating initiatives, approaches, and strategies for sustainable supply chain management. In *Handbook of Research on Designing Sustainable Supply Chains to Achieve a Circular Economy*. IGI Global., DOI: 10.4018/978-1-6684-7664-2.ch004

Bhamangol, B., Kaiwade, A., Pant, B., Rana, A., Kaiwade, A., & Shaikh, A. (2022). An Artificial Intelligence based Design and Implementation for classifying the Missing Data in IoT Applications. *Proceedings of 5th International Conference on Contemporary Computing and Informatics, IC3I 2022*, 1376 – 1382. DOI: 10.1109/IC3I56241.2022.10072634

Bhatnagar, M., Kumar, P., Taneja, S., Sood, K., & Grima, S. (2024). From digital overload to trading Zen: The role of digital detox in enhancing intraday trading performance. In *Business Drivers in Promoting Digital Detoxification*. IGI Global., DOI: 10.4018/979-8-3693-1107-3.ch010

Bhatnagar, M., Rajaram, R., Taneja, S., & Kumar, P. (2024). Balancing acts: The Yin and Yang of debit and credit on the stage of financial well-being. In *Emerging Perspectives on Financial Well-Being*. IGI Global., DOI: 10.4018/979-8-3693-1750-1.ch002

Bhatnagar, M., Taneja, S., & Kumar, P. (2023). The Effectiveness of Carbon Pricing Mechanism in Steering Financial Flows Toward Sustainable Projects. *International Journal of Environmental Impacts*, 6(4), 183–196. DOI: 10.18280/ijei.060403

Bhatnagar, M., Taneja, S., Kumar, P., & Özen, E. (2024). Does financial education act as a catalyst for SME competitiveness? *International Journal of Education Economics and Development*, 15(3), 377–393. DOI: 10.1504/IJEED.2024.139306

Bisht, B., Gururani, P., Aman, J., Vlaskin, M. S., Anna, I. K., Irina, A. A., Joshi, S., Kumar, S., & Kumar, V. (2023). A review on holistic approaches for fruits and vegetables biowastes valorization. *Materials Today: Proceedings*, 73, 54–63. DOI: 10.1016/j.matpr.2022.09.168

Chahar, A., & Christobel, Y. A. Ritika, Adakane, P. K., Sonal, D., & Tripathi, V. (2022). The Implementation of Big Data With Cloud and Edge Computing in Enhancing the Smart Grid Information Processes Through Sem Model. *2022 2nd International Conference on Advance Computing and Innovative Technologies in Engineering, ICACITE 2022*, 608 – 611. DOI: 10.1109/ICACITE53722.2022.9823896

Chandna, R., Saini, S., & Kumar, S. (2022). Selecting the Most Agile Manufacturing System with Respect to Agile Attribute-Technology: Fuzzy AHP Approach. In D. N. & C. A. (Eds.), *AIP Conference Proceedings* (Vol. 2481). American Institute of Physics Inc. DOI: 10.1063/5.0103804

Davuluri, S. K., Alvi, S. A. M., Aeri, M., Agarwal, A., Serajuddin, M., & Hasan, Z. (2023). A Security Model for Perceptive 5G-Powered BC IoT Associated Deep Learning. *6th International Conference on Inventive Computation Technologies, ICICT 2023 - Proceedings*, 118 – 125. DOI: 10.1109/ICICT57646.2023.10134487

Diddi, P. K., Sharma, P. K., Srivastava, A., Madduru, S. R. C., & Reddy, E. S. (2022). Sustainable Fast Setting Early Strength Self Compacting Concrete(FSESSCC) Using Metakaolin. *IOP Conference Series. Earth and Environmental Science*, 1077(1), 012009. Advance online publication. DOI: 10.1088/1755-1315/1077/1/012009

Garg, U., Kumar, S., & Kumar, M. (2023). A Hybrid Approach for the Detection and Classification of MQTT-based IoT-Malware. *2nd International Conference on Sustainable Computing and Data Communication Systems, ICSCDS 2023 - Proceedings*, 1154 – 1159. DOI: 10.1109/ICSCDS56580.2023.10104820

Goswami, S., & Sharma, S. (2022). Industry 4.0 Enabled Molecular Imaging Using Artificial Intelligence Technique. *2022 1st International Conference on Computational Science and Technology, ICCST 2022 - Proceedings*, 455 – 460. DOI: 10.1109/ICCST55948.2022.10040406

Gupta, M., Arora, K., & Taneja, S. (2023). Bibliometric analysis on employee engagement and human resource management. In *Enhancing Customer Engagement Through Location-Based Marketing*. IGI Global., DOI: 10.4018/978-1-6684-8177-6.ch013

Hajoary, P. K., Balachandra, P., & Garza-Reyes, J. A. (2023). Industry 4.0 maturity and readiness assessment: An empirical validation using Confirmatory Composite Analysis. *Production Planning and Control*. Advance online publication. DOI: 10.1080/09537287.2023.2210545

Josphineleela, R., Siva Reddy, K. V., Reddy, M. V. S. S., & Rawat, R. S. (2023). Design and Development of a Smart Sprinkler Device for IoT-Integrated Plants Irrigation. *Proceedings of the 2023 2nd International Conference on Electronics and Renewable Systems, ICEARS 2023*, 498 – 501. DOI: 10.1109/ICEARS56392.2023.10084960

Juyal, P., & Sharma, S. (2020). Estimation of Tree Volume Using Mask R-CNN based Deep Learning. *2020 11th International Conference on Computing, Communication and Networking Technologies, ICCCNT 2020*. DOI: 10.1109/ICCCNT49239.2020.9225509

Kannan, P. R., Periasamy, K., Pravin, P., & Vinod Kumaar, J. R. (2022). An experimental investigation of wire breakage and performance optimisation of WEDM process on machining of recycled aluminium alloy metal matrix composite. *Materials Science Poland*, 40(3), 12–26. DOI: 10.2478/msp-2022-0030

Khaudiyal, S., Rawat, A., Das, S. K., & Garg, N. (2022). Bacterial concrete: A review on self-healing properties in the light of sustainability. *Materials Today: Proceedings*, 60, 136–143. DOI: 10.1016/j.matpr.2021.12.277

Kohli, P., Sharma, S., & Matta, P. (2022). Secured Privacy Preserving Techniques Analysis of 6G Driven Vehicular Communication Network in Industry 5.0 Internet-of-Everything (IoE) Applications. *2022 International Conference on Smart Generation Computing, Communication and Networking, SMART GENCON 2022*. DOI: 10.1109/SMARTGENCON56628.2022.10084289

Krishna, S. H., Upadhyay, A., Tewari, M., Gehlot, A., Girimurugan, B., & Pundir, S. (2022). Empirical investigation of the key machine learning elements promoting e-business using an SEM framework. *Proceedings of 5th International Conference on Contemporary Computing and Informatics, IC3I 2022*, 1960 – 1964. DOI: 10.1109/IC3I56241.2022.10072712

Kukreti, A., Shriyal, A., Sharma, S., & Bhadula, S. (2023). Internet-of-Things Enabled Smart and Portable Terrace Garden Protection Shed. *2023 4th IEEE Global Conference for Advancement in Technology, GCAT 2023*. DOI: 10.1109/GCAT59970.2023.10353281

Kumar, I., Rawat, J., Mohd, N., & Husain, S. (2021). Opportunities of Artificial Intelligence and Machine Learning in the Food Industry. *Journal of Food Quality*, 2021, 1–10. Advance online publication. DOI: 10.1155/2021/4535567

Kumar, K. S., Yadav, D., Joshi, S. K., Chakravarthi, M. K., Jain, A. K., & Tripathi, V. (2022). Blockchain Technology with Applications to Distributed Control and Cooperative Robotics. *Proceedings of 5th International Conference on Contemporary Computing and Informatics, IC3I 2022*, 206 – 211. DOI: 10.1109/IC3I56241.2022.10073275

Kumar, M., Ansari, N. A., Sharma, A., Singh, V. K., Gautam, R., & Singh, Y. (2021). Prediction of an optimum engine response based on different input parameters on common rail direct injection diesel engine: A response surface methodology approach. *Scientia Iranica*, 28(6), 3181–3200. DOI: 10.24200/sci.2021.56745.4885

Kumar, P., Taneja, S., Bhatnagar, M., & Kaur, A. K. (2024). Navigating the digital paradigm shift: Designing CBDCs for a transformative financial landscape. In *Exploring Central Bank Digital Currencies: Concepts, Frameworks, Models, and Challenges*. IGI Global., DOI: 10.4018/979-8-3693-1882-9.ch006

Kumar, P., Verma, P., Bhatnagar, M., Taneja, S., Seychel, S., Todorović, I., & Grim, S. (2023). The Financial Performance and Solvency Status of the Indian Public Sector Banks: A CAMELS Rating and Z Index Approach. *International Journal of Sustainable Development and Planning*, 18(2), 367–376. DOI: 10.18280/ijsdp.180204

Kumar, R., Kandpal, B., & Ahmad, V. (2023). Industrial IoT (IIOT): Security Threats and Countermeasures. *International Conference on Innovative Data Communication Technologies and Application, ICIDCA 2023 - Proceedings*, 829 – 833. DOI: 10.1109/ICIDCA56705.2023.10100145

Kumar, R., & Khanna, R. (2023). RPA (Robotic Process Automation) in Finance & Accounting and Future Scope. *Proceedings of the 2023 2nd International Conference on Augmented Intelligence and Sustainable Systems, ICAISS 2023*, 1640–1645. DOI: 10.1109/ICAISS58487.2023.10250496

Kumar, V., & Korovin, G. (2023). A Comparision of Digital Transformation of Industry in the Russian Federation with the European Union. In K. V., K. G.L., A. V., & K. E. (Eds.), *Lecture Notes in Information Systems and Organisation: Vol. 61 LNISO* (pp. 45 – 57). Springer Science and Business Media Deutschland GmbH. DOI: 10.1007/978-3-031-30351-7_5

Lade, J., Mohammed, K. A., Singh, D., Prasad Verma, R., Math, P., Saraswat, M., & Raj Gupta, L. (2023). A critical review of fabrication routes and their effects on mechanical properties of AMMCs. *Materials Today: Proceedings*. Advance online publication. DOI: 10.1016/j.matpr.2023.03.041

Luthra, S., Sharma, M., Kumar, A., Joshi, S., Collins, E., & Mangla, S. (2022). Overcoming barriers to cross-sector collaboration in circular supply chain management: A multi-method approach. *Transportation Research Part E, Logistics and Transportation Review*, 157, 102582. Advance online publication. DOI: 10.1016/j.tre.2021.102582

Mandalapu, S. R., Sivamuni, K., Chitra Devi, D., Aswal, U. S., Sherly, S. I., & Balaji, N. A. (2023). An Architecture-based Self-Typing Service for Cloud Native Applications. *Proceedings of the 4th International Conference on Smart Electronics and Communication, ICOSEC 2023*, 562 – 566. DOI: 10.1109/ICOSEC58147.2023.10276313

Masal, V., Pavithra, P., Tiwari, S. K., Singh, R., Panduro-Ramirez, J., & Gangodkar, D. (2022). Deep Learning Applications for Blockchain in Industrial IoT. *Proceedings of 5th International Conference on Contemporary Computing and Informatics, IC3I 2022*, 276–281. DOI: 10.1109/IC3I56241.2022.10073357

Medhi, M. K., Ambust, S., Kumar, R., & Das, A. J. (2023). Characterization and Purification of Biosurfactants. In *Advancements in Biosurfactants Research*. Springer International Publishing., DOI: 10.1007/978-3-031-21682-4_4

Mehershilpa, G., Prasad, D., Sai Kiran, C., Shaikh, A., Jayashree, K., & Socrates, S. (2023). EDM machining of Ti6Al4V alloy using colloidal biosilica. *Materials Today: Proceedings*. Advance online publication. DOI: 10.1016/j.matpr.2023.02.443

Mohd, N., Kumar, I., & Khurshid, A. A. (2023). Changing Roles of Intelligent Robotics and Machinery Control Systems as Cyber-Physical Systems (CPS) in the Industry 4.0 Framework. *2023 International Conference on Communication, Security and Artificial Intelligence, ICCSAI 2023*, 647 – 651. DOI: 10.1109/ICCSAI59793.2023.10421085

Nainwal, P., Lall, S., & Nawaz, A. (2022). Physiochemical characterization of silver nanoparticles using rhizome extract of Alpinia galanga and its antimicrobial activity. *Journal of Medical Pharmaceutical and Allied Sciences. Int. Confe*, (2), 219–223. DOI: 10.22270/jmpas.VIC2I2.1830

Nethravathi, K., Tiwari, A., Uike, D., Jaiswal, R., & Pant, K. (2022). Applications of Artificial Intelligence and Blockchain Technology in Improved Supply Chain Financial Risk Management. *Proceedings of 5th International Conference on Contemporary Computing and Informatics, IC3I 2022*, 242 – 246. DOI: 10.1109/IC3I56241.2022.10072787

Pai, H. A., Almuzaini, K. K., Ali, L., Javeed, A., Pant, B., Pareek, P. K., & Akwafo, R. (2022). Delay-Driven Opportunistic Routing with Multichannel Cooperative Neighbor Discovery for Industry 4.0 Wireless Networks Based on Power and Load Awareness. *Wireless Communications and Mobile Computing*, 2022, 1–12. Advance online publication. DOI: 10.1155/2022/5256133

Pallavi, B., Othman, B., Trivedi, G., Manan, N., Pawar, R. S., & Singh, D. P. (2022). The Application of the Internet of Things (IoT) to establish a technologically advanced Industry 4.0 for long-term growth and development. *2022 2nd International Conference on Advance Computing and Innovative Technologies in Engineering, ICACITE 2022*, 1927 – 1932. DOI: 10.1109/ICACITE53722.2022.9823481

Pandey, K., Joshi, H., Paliwal, S., Pawar, S., & Kumar, N. (2020). Technology transfer: An overview of process transfer from development to commercialization. *International Journal of Current Research and Review*, 12(19), 188–192. DOI: 10.31782/IJCRR.2020.121913

Pandey, N. K., Kashyap, S., Sharma, A., & Diwakar, M. (2023). Contribution of Cloud-Based Services in Post-Pandemic Technology Sustainability and Challenges: A Future Direction. In *Evolving Networking Technologies: Developments and Future Directions*. wiley. DOI: 10.1002/9781119836667.ch4

Pandey, T., Batra, A., Chaudhary, M., Ranakoti, A., Kumar, A., & Ram, M. (2023). Computation Signature Reliability of Computer Numerical Control System Using Universal Generating Function. *Springer Series in Reliability Engineering*, 149 – 158. DOI: 10.1007/978-3-031-05347-4_10

Pathak, P., Singh, M. P., Badhotiya, G. K., & Chauhan, A. S. (2021). Identification of Drivers and Barriers of Sustainable Manufacturing. *Lecture Notes on Multidisciplinary Industrial Engineering*, (Part F254), 227–243. DOI: 10.1007/978-981-15-4550-4_14

Rajeswari, M., Kumar, N., Raman, P., Patjoshi, P. K., Singh, V., & Pundir, S. (2022). Optimal Analysis for Enterprise Financial Management Based on Artificial Intelligence and Parallel Computing Method. *Proceedings of 5th International Conference on Contemporary Computing and Informatics, IC3I 2022*, 2081 – 2086. DOI: 10.1109/IC3I56241.2022.10072851

Raju, K., Balakrishnan, M., Prasad, D. V. S. S. S. V., Nagalakshmi, V., Patil, P. P., Kaliappan, S., Arulmurugan, B., Radhakrishnan, K., Velusamy, B., Paramasivam, P., & El-Denglawey, A. (2022). Optimization of WEDM Process Parameters in Al2024-Li-Si3N4MMC. *Journal of Nanomaterials*, 2022(1), 2903385. Advance online publication. DOI: 10.1155/2022/2903385

Rakhra, M., Bhargava, A., Bhargava, D., Singh, R., Bhanot, A., & Rahmani, A. W. (2022). Implementing Machine Learning for Supply-Demand Shifts and Price Impacts in Farmer Market for Tool and Equipment Sharing. *Journal of Food Quality*, 2022, 1–19. Advance online publication. DOI: 10.1155/2022/4496449

Ramachandran, K. K., Lamba, F. L. R., Rawat, R., Gehlot, A., Raju, A. M., & Ponnusamy, R. (2023). An Investigation of Block Chains for Attaining Sustainable Society. *2023 3rd International Conference on Advance Computing and Innovative Technologies in Engineering, ICACITE 2023*, 1069 – 1076. DOI: 10.1109/ICACITE57410.2023.10182462

Raman, R., Kumar, R., Ghai, S., Gehlot, A., Raju, A. M., & Barve, A. (2023). A New Method of Optical Spectrum Analysis for Advanced Wireless Communications. *2023 3rd International Conference on Advance Computing and Innovative Technologies in Engineering, ICACITE 2023*, 1719 – 1723. DOI: 10.1109/ICACITE57410.2023.10182414

Rana, M. S., Dixit, A. K., Rajan, M. S., Malhotra, S., Radhika, S., & Pant, B. (2022). An Empirical Investigation in Applying Reliable Industry 4.0 Based Machine Learning (ML) Approaches in Analysing and Monitoring Smart Meters using Multivariate Analysis of Variance (Manova). *2022 2nd International Conference on Advance Computing and Innovative Technologies in Engineering, ICACITE 2022*, 603 – 607. DOI: 10.1109/ICACITE53722.2022.9823597

Salama, R., Al-Turjman, F., Bordoloi, D., & Yadav, S. P. (2023). Wireless Sensor Networks and Green Networking for 6G communication- An Overview. *2023 International Conference on Computational Intelligence, Communication Technology and Networking, CICTN 2023*, 830 – 834. DOI: 10.1109/CICTN57981.2023.10141262

Sharma, A., Sharma, A., Juneja, P. K., & Jain, V. (2020). Spectral Features based Speech Recognition for Speech Interfacing to Control PC Windows. In S. S. & D. P. (Eds.), *Proceedings - 2020 International Conference on Advances in Computing, Communication and Materials, ICACCM 2020* (pp. 341 – 345). Institute of Electrical and Electronics Engineers Inc. DOI: 10.1109/ICACCM50413.2020.9212827

Sharma, H., Verma, D., Rana, A., Chari, S. L., Kumar, R., & Kumar, N. (2023). Enhancing Network Security in IoT Using Machine Learning- Based Anomaly Detection. *Proceedings of International Conference on Contemporary Computing and Informatics, IC3I 2023*, 2650 – 2654. DOI: 10.1109/IC3I59117.2023.10397636

Sharma, M., Hagar, A. A., Krishna Murthy, G. R., Beyane, K., Gawali, B. W., & Pant, B. (2022). A Study on Recognising the Application of Multiple Big Data Technologies and its Related Issues, Difficulties and Opportunities. *2022 2nd International Conference on Advance Computing and Innovative Technologies in Engineering, ICACITE 2022*, 341 – 344. DOI: 10.1109/ICACITE53722.2022.9823623

Sharma, M., Kumar, A., Luthra, S., Joshi, S., & Upadhyay, A. (2022). The impact of environmental dynamism on low-carbon practices and digital supply chain networks to enhance sustainable performance: An empirical analysis. *Business Strategy and the Environment*, 31(4), 1776–1788. DOI: 10.1002/bse.2983

Sharma, M., Luthra, S., Joshi, S., & Joshi, H. (2022). Challenges to agile project management during COVID-19 pandemic: An emerging economy perspective. *Operations Management Research: Advancing Practice Through Research*, 15(1–2), 461–474. DOI: 10.1007/s12063-021-00249-1

Sharma, M., Luthra, S., Joshi, S., & Kumar, A. (2022). Analysing the impact of sustainable human resource management practices and industry 4.0 technologies adoption on employability skills. *International Journal of Manpower*, 43(2), 463–485. DOI: 10.1108/IJM-02-2021-0085

Sharma, P., Taneja, S., Kumar, P., Özen, E., & Singh, A. (2024). Application of the UTAUT model toward individual acceptance: Emerging trends in artificial intelligence-based banking services. *International Journal of Electronic Finance*, 13(3), 352–366. DOI: 10.1504/IJEF.2024.139584

Sharma, S., & Bhadula, S. (2023). Secure Federated Learning for Intelligent Industry 4.0 IoT Enabled Self Skin Care Application System. *Proceedings of the 2nd International Conference on Applied Artificial Intelligence and Computing, ICAAIC 2023*, 1164 – 1170. DOI: 10.1109/ICAAIC56838.2023.10141028

Sharma, S., Gupta, A., & Tyagi, R. (2023). Sustainable Natural Resources Utilization Decision System for Better Society Using Vedic Scripture, Cloud Computing, and IoT. In B. R.C., S. K.M., & D. M. (Eds.), *Proceedings of IEEE 2023 5th International Conference on Advances in Electronics, Computers and Communications, ICAECC 2023*. Institute of Electrical and Electronics Engineers Inc. DOI: 10.1109/ICAECC59324.2023.10560335

Sharma, S., Singh Rawal, R., Pandey, D., & Pandey, N. (2021). Microbial World for Sustainable Development. In *Microbial Technology for Sustainable Environment*. Springer Nature., DOI: 10.1007/978-981-16-3840-4_1

Singh, K. D., Singh, P., Chhabra, R., Kaur, G., Bansal, A., & Tripathi, V. (2023). Cyber-Physical Systems for Smart City Applications: A Comparative Study. In K. R., K. R., G. M., G. M., S. R., & S. R. (Eds.), *2023 International Conference on Advancement in Computation and Computer Technologies, InCACCT 2023* (pp. 871 – 876). Institute of Electrical and Electronics Engineers Inc. DOI: 10.1109/InCACCT57535.2023.10141719

Singh, N. K., Singh, Y., & Sharma, A. (2020). Experimental investigation on electric discharge drilling of titanium alloy (Ti–6Al–4V) with a gas-aided rotary tool. *Sadhana - Academy Proceedings in Engineering Sciences, 45*(1). DOI: 10.1007/s12046-020-01497-w

Singh, N. K., Singh, Y., Sharma, A., Paswan, M. K., Singh, V. K., Upadhyay, A. K., & Mishra, V. R. (2021). Performance of CuO nanoparticles as an additive to the chemically modified Nicotiana Tabacum as a sustainable coolant-lubricant during turning EN19 steel. *Wear*, 486–487, 204057. Advance online publication. DOI: 10.1016/j.wear.2021.204057

Širić, I., Eid, E. M., Taher, M. A., El-Morsy, M. H. E., Osman, H. E. M., Kumar, P., Adelodun, B., Abou Fayssal, S., Mioč, B., Andabaka, Ž., Goala, M., Kumari, S., Bachheti, A., Choi, K. S., & Kumar, V. (2022). Combined Use of Spent Mushroom Substrate Biochar and PGPR Improves Growth, Yield, and Biochemical Response of Cauliflower (Brassica oleracea var. botrytis): A Preliminary Study on Greenhouse Cultivation. *Horticulturae*, 8(9), 830. Advance online publication. DOI: 10.3390/horticulturae8090830

Taneja, S., Bhatnagar, M., Kumar, P., & Grima, S. (2023). A Panel Analysis of the Effectiveness of the Asset Management in Indian Agricultural Companies. *International Journal of Sustainable Development and Planning*, 18(3), 653–660. DOI: 10.18280/ijsdp.180301

Taneja, S., Bhatnagar, M., Kumar, P., & Rupeika-apoga, R. (2023). India's Total Natural Resource Rents (NRR) and GDP : An Augmented Autoregressive Distributed Lag (ARDL) Bound Test. *Journal of Risk and Financial Management*, 16(2), 91. https://doi.org/doi.org/10.3390/jrfm16020091. DOI: 10.3390/jrfm16020091

Taneja, S., Gupta, M., Bhushan, P., Bhatnagar, M., & Singh, A. (2023). Cultural marketing in the digital era. In *Cultural Marketing and Metaverse for Consumer Engagement*. IGI Global., DOI: 10.4018/978-1-6684-8312-1.ch008

Taneja, S., & Özen, E. (2023). To analyse the relationship between bank's green financing and environmental performance. *International Journal of Electronic Finance*, 12(2), 163–175. DOI: 10.1504/IJEF.2023.129919

Trache, D., Tarchoun, A. F., Abdelaziz, A., Bessa, W., Hussin, M. H., Brosse, N., & Thakur, V. K. (2022). Cellulose nanofibrils-graphene hybrids: Recent advances in fabrication, properties, and applications. *Nanoscale*, 14(35), 12515–12546. DOI: 10.1039/D2NR01967A PMID: 35983896

Tripathy, S., Verma, D. K., Thakur, M., Patel, A. R., Srivastav, P. P., Singh, S., Chávez-González, M. L., & Aguilar, C. N. (2021). Encapsulated Food Products as a Strategy to Strengthen Immunity Against COVID-19. *Frontiers in Nutrition*, 8, 673174. Advance online publication. DOI: 10.3389/fnut.2021.673174 PMID: 34095193

Tyagi, S., Krishna, K. H., Joshi, K., Ghodke, T. A., Kumar, A., & Gupta, A. (2023). Integration of PLCC modem and Wi-Fi for Campus Street Light Monitoring. In N. P., S. M., K. M., J. V., & G. K. (Eds.), *Proceedings - 4th IEEE 2023 International Conference on Computing, Communication, and Intelligent Systems, ICCCIS 2023* (pp. 1113 – 1116). Institute of Electrical and Electronics Engineers Inc. DOI: 10.1109/ICCCIS60361.2023.10425715

Uike, D., Agarwalla, S., Bansal, V., Chakravarthi, M. K., Singh, R., & Singh, P. (2022). Investigating the Role of Block Chain to Secure Identity in IoT for Industrial Automation. In D. R.K., S. A.Kr., K. G., & B. S. (Eds.), *Proceedings of the 2022 11th International Conference on System Modeling and Advancement in Research Trends, SMART 2022* (pp. 837 – 841). Institute of Electrical and Electronics Engineers Inc. DOI: 10.1109/SMART55829.2022.10047385

Uniyal, S., Mangla, S. K., & Patil, P. (2020). When practices count: Implementation of sustainable consumption and production in automotive supply chains. *Management of Environmental Quality*, 31(5), 1207–1222. DOI: 10.1108/MEQ-03-2019-0075

Uniyal, S., Mangla, S. K., Sarma, P. R. S., Tseng, M.-L., & Patil, P. (2021). ICT as "Knowledge management" for assessing sustainable consumption and production in supply chains. *Journal of Global Information Management*, 29(1), 164–198. DOI: 10.4018/JGIM.2021010109

Upreti, H., Uddin, Z., Pandey, A. K., & Joshi, N. (2023). Particle swarm optimization based numerical study for pressure, flow, and heat transfer over a rotating disk with temperature dependent nanofluid properties. *Numerical Heat Transfer Part A*, 83(8), 815–844. DOI: 10.1080/10407782.2022.2156412

Verma, M., Ahmad, W., Park, J.-H., Kumar, V., Vlaskin, M. S., Vaya, D., & Kim, H. (2022). One-step functionalization of chitosan using EDTA: Kinetics and isotherms modeling for multiple heavy metals adsorption and their mechanism. *Journal of Water Process Engineering*, 49, 102989. Advance online publication. DOI: 10.1016/j.jwpe.2022.102989

Wazid, M., Das, A. K., & Park, Y. (2021). Blockchain-Envisioned Secure Authentication Approach in AIoT: Applications, Challenges, and Future Research. *Wireless Communications and Mobile Computing*, 2021(1), 3866006. Advance online publication. DOI: 10.1155/2021/3866006

Chapter 16
Precision and Performance:
Smart Healthcare Technologies in Sports Medicine Wellness

S. C. Dileepkumar
https://orcid.org/0009-0004-8233-7113
Kuvempu University, India

Ravindra Gouda
Kuvempu University, India

Basavaraj Kumasi
https://orcid.org/0009-0006-6936-2730
Sri Balaji Vidyapeeth University, India

ABSTRACT

The confluence of precision medicine and advanced healthcare technologies is revolutionizing sports medicine by refining diagnostics, optimizing therapeutic interventions, and elevating performance metrics. This chapter delves into the transformative role of smart healthcare systems, including wearable biosensors, machine learning algorithms, and data-driven analytics, which collectively enable a nuanced understanding of athletic health. By enhancing early injury detection and fostering customized rehabilitation strategies, these technologies epitomize a paradigmatic shift toward individualized, anticipatory healthcare in sports. Our analysis elucidates both the mechanistic functionalities and the physiological implications of these innovations, which promise to redefine the contours of athletic resilience and human potential.

INTRODUCTION

In the relentless pursuit of athletic excellence, the interplay of scientific advancements and healthcare innovations has indelibly reshaped the landscape of sports medicine (Chandna et al., 2022; Pai et al., 2022). The advent of precision technologies—biosensors, artificial intelligence, and integrated data analytics—has catalyzed a transition from generalized sports care to a deeply customized, anticipatory framework. This paradigm shift, driven by a confluence of bioengineering, informatics, and rehabilita-

DOI: 10.4018/979-8-3373-0240-9.ch016

tion sciences, has amplified the efficacy of injury prevention, expedited recovery, and propelled athletic performance to unprecedented levels (Mohamed et al., 2023; A. Srivastava et al., 2022).

The significance of recent research advancements in smart healthcare technologies within sports medicine is profound, catalyzing an epistemic shift that redefines both athletic performance and injury management (Pande et al., 2023; Shah et al., 2023). These innovations are not merely additive but transformative, introducing a paradigm that intertwines biomechanical optimization with anticipatory healthcare, thereby challenging traditional boundaries of athletic resilience and longevity (Dixit et al., 2022; R. Kumar, Kandpal, & Ahmad, 2023).

1. Enhanced Diagnostic Precision and Early Intervention

At the forefront, this research amplifies diagnostic accuracy by integrating real-time physiological data with predictive analytics. Traditional diagnostics often relied on symptomatic markers or retrospective analysis, limiting preemptive care. With the advent of AI-enhanced biomechanics and nano-biosensors, however, subtle, incipient abnormalities within an athlete's physiological parameters can be identified with microscopic precision (Bhamangol et al., 2022; Gopal et al., 2023). The capacity to monitor metabolic markers, kinematic deviations, and neuromuscular stressors in real time allows clinicians to intervene prophylactically, circumventing injury cascades before they become performance-impeding or life-altering. This preemptive model significantly reduces recovery time, minimizes risk, and ensures athletes sustain peak performance over extended periods (Akana et al., 2023; N. Belwal et al., 2023).

2. Customization and Personalization Through Genomic and Epigenetic Insights

The deployment of genomic profiling and epigenetic modulation extends the frontier of personalized sports medicine. Genetic predispositions, once perceived as immutable, can now be strategically managed through bespoke training regimens, nutrigenomic interventions, and targeted rehabilitative protocols that align with an individual athlete's molecular profile. By tailoring training and recovery protocols to genetic predispositions, practitioners can forestall common overuse injuries or stress-related breakdowns, which would otherwise erode an athlete's physical capital over time. Furthermore, epigenetic modulation opens new avenues for 'gene expression conditioning' where, theoretically, resilience and endurance parameters could be optimized to meet the exact demands of an athlete's discipline, enhancing both adaptive capacity and overall athletic efficacy (Ram et al., 2022).

3. Augmentation of Neurocognitive Functions in High-Performance Settings

Cognitive endurance, stress regulation, and rapid decision-making are as pivotal to high-stakes athletic events as physical prowess. Neurostimulation research offers critical advancements here, employing non-invasive techniques to enhance neural plasticity and sensorimotor integration. By honing these cognitive functions, athletes gain a measurable advantage in reaction time, spatial awareness, and task precision, particularly in sports that demand split-second strategic decisions or precise motor control. This neurocognitive enhancement augments an athlete's capability to sustain mental acuity under physiological duress, thus achieving a holistic optimization that unites mind and body in competitive synergy (Luthra et al., 2022; Y. K. Sharma et al., 2020; N. Singh et al., 2021).

4. Ergonomics and Biomechanics: Redefining Load Distribution and Injury Prevention

The nuanced application of ergonomics and biomechanics research enables unprecedented specificity in equipment design and training environments, which are now molded to an athlete's anthropometric and kinematic profile. This personalized ergonomic customization not only optimizes biomechanical efficiency but also drastically minimizes extraneous strain on susceptible joints and soft tissues. By refining force-distribution mechanics, these ergonomic advancements diminish the cumulative wear-and-tear that historically has been the precursor to career-ending injuries, such as ligamentous degeneration or chronic tendinopathies. This reengineering of athletic environments translates into a longevity-centric approach, enabling athletes to perform at peak levels well beyond conventional career spans (Babu et al., 2022).

5. Revolutionizing Rehabilitation and Recovery

Biomechatronic exoskeletons, AR-enabled neurofeedback, and cryo-thermo feedback mechanisms have collectively revolutionized rehabilitation, transitioning from passive recovery methodologies to dynamic, feedback-integrated systems. These devices expedite neuromuscular re-education by precisely guiding movements, dynamically adapting to an athlete's recuperative status, and optimizing thermal therapies based on neurofeedback (Dogra et al., 2021; A. Gupta & Kumar, 2022; Y. Singh et al., 2022). Consequently, recovery protocols now integrate continuous physiological feedback, aligning with the athlete's unique recovery trajectory, and reducing rehabilitation durations by substantial margins. For athletes, this means not only a swifter return to form but a mitigated risk of reinjury, enabling sustained competitive performance with reduced physiological detriment (Chavadaki et al., 2021; Kohli et al., 2022; S. Sharma, Kandpal, et al., 2023).

6. Data Sovereignty and Ethical Implications of Blockchain Integration

As athlete health data becomes increasingly granular, the ethical imperative for privacy and control over personal biometric information intensifies. Blockchain integration in data management addresses these concerns by providing a decentralized, secure framework where athletes can govern access to their health data autonomously (Abdullah et al., 2023; Dimri et al., 2023). This empowerment reduces risks associated with data misuse or unauthorized sharing, fostering a transparent and ethical data ecosystem. For sports organizations and practitioners, the blockchain's immutability ensures a verifiable, tamper-proof record, which enhances data integrity while aligning with regulatory frameworks on privacy, thus engendering trust in data-driven interventions (R. Kumar, Malhotra, & Grover, 2023; Malhotra et al., 2022).

7. Socioeconomic Impact: Redefining the Scope of Sports Medicine

These technological advancements hold substantial socioeconomic implications for the field of sports medicine. By mitigating injury rates, enhancing longevity, and reducing rehabilitation timeframes, this research translates into substantial cost savings for both athletes and sports organizations (R. Kumar, Malhotra, Singh, et al., 2023; R. Kumar & Khanna, 2023b). Reduced incidences of debilitating injuries mean fewer career disruptions and diminished healthcare expenditures, making sports medicine not only more effective but economically sustainable. Furthermore, these innovations extend the utility of sports medicine to populations beyond elite athletes, benefiting recreational athletes and aging populations, where early intervention and biomechanical optimization can prevent the onset of degenerative conditions (R. Kumar, Khannna Malholtra, & Grover, 2023; P. Sharma et al., 2022).

8. Shaping the Future of Athletic Standards

The amalgamation of personalized diagnostics, biomechanical efficiency, and neurocognitive augmentation heralds a new archetype for athletic potential. This research does not merely enhance performance; it alters the baseline for human capability, redefining what can be considered achievable within athletic domains. As smart healthcare technologies continue to integrate into sports, the very standards by which we measure excellence evolve, engendering a new era where peak performance and sustainable health coexist (Joshi et al., 2022; Neha et al., 2023).

In sum, this research is emblematic of a comprehensive metamorphosis in sports medicine, shifting the focus from reactive healthcare to a precision-centric model that anticipates, customizes, and enhances. It has far-reaching implications that transcend traditional sports, ultimately influencing global health paradigms by advocating a preventive, personalized, and data-integrated approach to human resilience and performance.

Smart Healthcare Systems and Their Architectures

Smart healthcare technologies are orchestrated through multi-layered architectures that enable real-time data acquisition, integration, and processing. At the heart of this framework are biosensors and wearable devices, which capture biomechanical and physiological metrics. Coupled with cloud-based computing and algorithmic processing, these metrics are interpreted within microseconds, rendering instantaneous feedback loops that hold paramount importance in sports settings. The integration of data from diverse biometrics—ranging from cardiovascular markers to musculoskeletal alignment—forms a holistic view of an athlete's physiological state, enabling finely tuned performance interventions (Kanojia et al., 2022b; R. Kumar, Singh, Mohanty, et al., 2023).

Precision Diagnostics: The Role of Wearable Biosensors

Wearable biosensors are pivotal in elevating sports medicine through precision diagnostics. These miniature, wireless sensors monitor physiological variables such as heart rate variability, blood oxygenation, and lactate levels. For example, electrocardiographic (ECG) sensors embedded in wearable garments allow athletes to track cardiovascular efficiency during exertion, while muscle-oxygenation monitors optimize endurance training by revealing oxygen deficits. By analyzing subtle physiological variations, these devices enable preemptive detection of musculoskeletal or cardiovascular anomalies, permitting early interventions before injuries manifest overtly (Awal & Khanna, 2019; Upreti & Malhotra, 2024).

Data Analytics and Machine Learning: Transformative Analytics for Predictive Healthcare

Machine learning algorithms underpin the predictive prowess of smart healthcare technologies. Predictive models harness vast datasets to discern patterns and predict injury risks or fatigue onset. Algorithms tailored to sports medicine can identify biomechanical deviations that predispose an athlete to injury.

For instance, through kinetic profiling, minute gait abnormalities can be flagged as early indicators of stress fractures. Machine learning models further assist in constructing individualized training regimes, where dynamic adjustments to intensity, frequency, and technique mitigate injury while sustaining peak performance (R. Kumar et al., 2024; Malhotra et al., 2021; Uniyal et al., 2022).

Therapeutic Interventions: Robotics and Neuromodulation

Therapeutic interventions within sports medicine have been revolutionized by robotic exoskeletons and neuromodulatory devices that expedite recovery. Robotic-assisted rehabilitation offers targeted physical therapy, particularly for musculoskeletal injuries. By executing precise, repetitive motions, these exoskeletons reinforce neuromuscular pathways, fostering faster recovery and diminishing post-injury regression. In tandem, neuromodulation—through transcutaneous electrical nerve stimulation (TENS) and other modalities—amplifies neural plasticity, enhancing motor learning and facilitating quicker post-traumatic rehabilitation (C. Gupta et al., 2022; J. Kaur et al., 2024; R. Kumar, Malhotra, Pandey, et al., 2023).

Bioinformatics: The Nexus of Genomics and Precision Training

Genomic insights reveal the inherent predispositions an athlete may have toward specific injury patterns or endurance thresholds. Utilizing bioinformatics, sports physicians are beginning to construct genetic profiles that ascertain susceptibility to particular sports-related injuries, such as ligament tears or tendon inflammations. Such profiles allow athletes to engage in preventive training protocols that mitigate their genetic vulnerabilities. Through precision nutrition and targeted supplementation informed by genomic data, athletes can amplify recovery and optimize metabolic efficiency, translating to an enhanced physical repertoire tailored to their genetic blueprint (R. Kumar & Khanna, 2023a; V. Kumar et al., 2021).

Cognitive Enhancement and Neuroplasticity

Beyond physical metrics, cognitive health is instrumental in the holistic development of athletic performance. Neuroplasticity-based therapies aim to augment cognitive endurance and focus, crucial elements in high-stakes sporting events. Neurofeedback and other brain-computer interface technologies train athletes to regulate stress responses, optimize reaction times, and improve decision-making under pressure (Cavaliere et al., 2024; Khanna et al., 2023; Malhotra & Gupta, 2021). These cognitive enhancements, grounded in neuroplasticity principles, reinforce not only mental acuity but also contribute to holistic physical control by refining the athlete's sensorimotor integration.

Telemedicine and Remote Monitoring

Telemedicine has become indispensable in providing continuous care to athletes who are geographically dispersed or unable to access in-person consultations. Through telemetric data transfer, athletes can receive real-time feedback on physiological markers, which is particularly beneficial for those undergoing rehabilitation or monitoring chronic conditions (R. Kumar, Kathuria, Malhotra, et al., 2023; R. Kumar, Lande, Kumar, et al., 2023; Mary Joshitta et al., 2023). Additionally, remote consultations facilitated by telemedicine provide access to specialized sports physicians, enabling a continuity of care irrespective of locale, which is paramount in minimizing disruption to an athlete's training schedule and optimizing recovery.

Ergonomics and Anthropometrics: Customization for Performance Enhancement

The ergonomic design of sports equipment and environments, informed by anthropometric data, enhances performance while reducing injury risks. Custom-fitted insoles, ergonomic helmets, and adjustable training surfaces are all developments stemming from anthropometric research. By conforming to the athlete's unique bodily proportions, such equipment mitigates extraneous strain, thereby enhancing biomechanical efficiency. Biomechanics experts also use anthropometric measurements to tailor training regimens that align with an athlete's structural attributes, facilitating an optimized force-distribution pattern during athletic activities (Kanojia et al., 2022a; Patil et al., 2021; M. S. Rana et al., 2022).

Ethical Considerations and the Future of Smart Technologies in Sports Medicine

The evolution of smart healthcare technologies raises ethical considerations, particularly regarding data privacy and potential overreliance on technology (Grover et al., 2024; Kumari et al., 2024; A. K. Singh et al., 2024). The extensive data accumulated through wearable devices could, if misused, infringe on athletes' privacy. Furthermore, while data-driven decisions significantly mitigate risks, an overemphasis on metrics could obscure the subjective nuances that shape human performance. Ethicists and practitioners must collaboratively address these concerns, crafting regulatory frameworks that safeguard privacy without stymying innovation (Dutta et al., 2023).

Case Study 1: Precision Diagnostics and Early Intervention in Achilles Tendinopathy

An elite sprinter, predisposed to Achilles tendinopathy due to repetitive, high-impact training, utilized wearable biosensors embedded within compression sleeves. These sensors continuously monitored the strain forces exerted on the Achilles tendon, analyzing variables such as tensile load, stride frequency, and plantar flexion angles. Over a six-week observation period, machine learning algorithms identified microfluctuations in biomechanical patterns indicative of early tendinopathy, long before symptomatic pain arose (Aiyappa et al., 2024; Khandelwal et al., 2023; Pandey et al., 2023).

Upon detection, a protocol integrating robotic-assisted myofascial release and targeted neuromodulation via transcutaneous electrical nerve stimulation (TENS) was enacted. This biotechnologically mediated approach facilitated enhanced neural recruitment and muscle synchronization, abating tendinopathic progression. Consequently, the sprinter not only avoided significant injury but also witnessed a noticeable improvement in sprint kinematics post-intervention (Indu et al., 2023; Padhi et al., 2024; Shrivastava et al., 2023).

Case Study 2: Genomic Insights in ACL Injury Prevention

A professional soccer player, cognizant of her genetic predisposition toward ligamentous laxity, underwent genomic profiling to ascertain her susceptibility to anterior cruciate ligament (ACL) ruptures. Her genetic analysis revealed a polymorphism in the COL1A1 gene, correlating with a heightened risk for ligament injuries. Leveraging this insight, a customized training regimen incorporating proprioceptive neuromuscular facilitation (PNF) and eccentric loading exercises was devised, designed specifically to bolster her knee stability (Arora et al., 2024; Zhang et al., 2023).

Moreover, her regimen was supplemented with precision nutrition, featuring collagen-boosting supplements to fortify ligament resilience at a molecular level. The tailored protocol yielded a 30% reduction in injury-risk metrics based on dynamic movement assessments, underscoring the efficacy of genomically informed preventive strategies in sports medicine (R. Belwal & Belwal, 2017; K. U. Singh et al., 2024).

Case Study 3: Remote Telemedicine and Cognitive Enhancement Post-Concussion

A long-distance cyclist, undergoing rehabilitation for a concussion sustained during training, participated in a telemedicine program utilizing brain-computer interface (BCI) technology. Through a series of neurofeedback sessions delivered remotely, he engaged in cognitive retraining exercises designed to recalibrate his sensorimotor integration and enhance executive function resilience. The telemetric data acquired from EEG headbands facilitated real-time adjustments in his neurofeedback protocols, ensuring a personalized rehabilitation trajectory (Ajay et al., 2023; Gangwar & Srivastva, 2020; Tripathi & Mohan, 2016).

By the eighth week, data analytics revealed a marked restoration of his pre-injury cognitive baselines, with notable improvements in decision-making latency and attentional focus. His case exemplifies how remote cognitive enhancement, underpinned by real-time biofeedback, can catalyze neuroplastic recovery while circumventing the logistical constraints often inherent in traditional, in-person rehabilitation (Mishra et al., 2024; B. Srivastava et al., 2024).

Case Study 4: Ergonomics and Biomechanical Optimization in Rowing Athletes

A professional rowing team, seeking to mitigate lower back injuries endemic to the sport, enlisted ergonomic specialists to analyze their biomechanics and anthropometric profiles. Through motion capture analysis and high-definition electromyography (EMG), the team identified torque discrepancies and muscular imbalances affecting their spinal alignment during high-stress rowing strokes (P. Singh & Singh, 2023).

An ergonomic redesign of their rowing seats, informed by each athlete's unique anthropometric dimensions, was implemented. The bespoke seat contouring provided optimized lumbar support and facilitated a more efficient force distribution along the spinal axis. This modification not only attenuated the cumulative strain on their lower backs but also yielded a 15% enhancement in stroke efficiency, demonstrating the impact of personalized ergonomic interventions on both injury mitigation and athletic output (K. D. Singh et al., 2023).

Recent Advancements in Smart Healthcare Technologies in Sports Medicine

1. Artificial Intelligence-Driven Biomechanical Analysis

Recent advancements have seen the incorporation of artificial intelligence (AI) in biomechanics, where deep learning algorithms process large datasets of motion capture and kinematic data. Leveraging convolutional neural networks (CNNs) and recurrent neural networks (RNNs), these systems decipher complex movement patterns and predict injury risk with unprecedented accuracy (Ahmad et al., 2023; R. Kumar, Sexena, & Gehlot, 2023; Lourens et al., 2022). For instance, by mapping subtle aberrations in kinetic chains—such as minute deviations in joint angles or asymmetrical load distributions—AI can prognosticate conditions like stress fractures or ligamentous wear. This diagnostic refinement has enabled sports medicine practitioners to shift from symptomatic intervention to preemptive care strategies, mitigating the impact of high-performance activities on musculoskeletal integrity.

2. Augmented Reality (AR) for Virtual Rehabilitation

Augmented reality (AR) has transcended its preliminary entertainment applications, emerging as a formidable tool in sports rehabilitation. AR-based rehabilitation platforms overlay virtual instructions and corrective feedback directly onto an athlete's field of vision, guiding them through complex, multidimensional movements with heightened precision (Mangla et al., 2018; Onyema et al., 2022; Pant et al., 2017). This immersive technology proves invaluable in neuromuscular retraining, particularly for athletes recovering from proprioceptive deficits or motor coordination impairments post-injury. By allowing practitioners to remotely monitor and adjust exercises in real-time, AR enables continuity in rehabilitation protocols, irrespective of geographical barriers. Recent studies indicate that AR-based rehabilitation can expedite neuromuscular recovery rates by as much as 30%, underscoring its efficacy in high-stakes athletic rehabilitation (Alrashed et al., 2022; Malik et al., 2022; Rawat et al., 2022).

3. Genomic Medicine and Epigenetic Modulation

The interplay of genomic medicine and epigenetic modulation has emerged as a game-changer in personalized sports health optimization. In contrast to conventional genetic profiling, which solely identifies genetic predispositions, epigenetic technologies can modulate gene expression in response to environmental inputs, such as training stimuli or nutritional factors. Techniques like CRISPR-Cas9 gene editing are now being explored to enhance athletic endurance and resilience by targeting genes associated with muscle hypertrophy, oxidative stress resistance, and inflammatory responses (S. Sharma, Kadayat, et al., 2023; A. B. Singh et al., 2023; Tiwari et al., 2023). Although still in experimental stages, epigenetic modulation holds the potential to precisely adapt athletic phenotypes, tailoring physical attributes to the demands of elite sports.

4. Nano-Biosensors and Real-Time Metabolic Monitoring

Nano-biosensors, with their unprecedented sensitivity, are revolutionizing in-situ metabolic monitoring. Constructed from nanomaterials such as graphene and carbon nanotubes, these sensors detect trace concentrations of metabolic markers like lactate, glucose, and cortisol in real-time (Jindal et al., 2022;

V. Sharma & Jain, 2020; K. D. Singh & Singh, 2023). The application of nanotechnology allows these sensors to be embedded seamlessly within athletic wear, enabling continuous, non-invasive monitoring of physiological states. For instance, lactate-detecting nano-biosensors provide live feedback on anaerobic thresholds, allowing coaches to adjust intensity levels instantaneously to optimize endurance. This real-time insight into metabolic responses can preempt overtraining, dehydration, and muscle fatigue, fostering a balance between peak performance and physiological preservation (Goyal et al., 2015; Khan et al., 2020; Prikshat et al., 2019).

5. Neurostimulation and Cognitive Performance Enhancement

Advances in neurostimulation, particularly transcranial direct current stimulation (tDCS) and transcranial magnetic stimulation (TMS), have garnered attention for their role in augmenting cognitive performance in athletes (Dani et al., 2020; Pattanshetti et al., 2021; D. S. Rana et al., 2022). By modulating cortical excitability, these non-invasive techniques can enhance reaction times, decision-making acuity, and stress resilience. Neurostimulation primes neurons for heightened synaptic plasticity, allowing athletes to internalize complex motor skills with greater efficiency. The burgeoning field of neuroergonomics has begun incorporating these tools to condition neural circuits responsible for precision tasks, optimizing focus and cognitive endurance in sports such as archery, gymnastics, and motorsports (Alexopoulos et al., 2023; Prikshat et al., 2017; Rathore & Goudar, 2015).

6. Biomaterial Innovations in Prosthetics and Orthotics

Cutting-edge biomaterials are redefining the scope of prosthetics and orthotics in sports medicine. Material scientists are developing adaptive polymers and responsive hydrogel matrices that dynamically alter their properties in response to external stimuli, such as temperature or mechanical stress (Reepu et al., 2023). These 'smart' prosthetics can adapt their stiffness or elasticity based on the athlete's activity level, thereby optimizing support during high-impact phases and enhancing agility during low-impact movements. Carbon fiber composites embedded with piezoelectric materials are also being employed to provide biofeedback, further aiding amputee athletes in fine-tuning their gait mechanics. These biomaterials elevate prosthetics and orthotics beyond mere replacements, transforming them into adaptive, performance-enhancing tools (Taneja & Özen, 2023).

7. Telemetric Gait and Posture Analytics

Telemetric gait analysis, employing wireless sensors and inertial measurement units (IMUs), has become an invaluable asset in assessing posture and stride biomechanics remotely. With precision analytics, these systems detect gait irregularities or postural imbalances that could predispose athletes to overuse injuries or joint degeneration (A. Kaur et al., 2023). Wearable gait sensors are now configured with real-time telemetry, transmitting data to mobile apps or cloud-based interfaces accessible by sports medicine teams. This innovation allows for continuous monitoring outside of clinical settings, facilitating corrective feedback during training and fostering long-term biomechanical resilience in athletes (Bhatnagar et al., 2023).

8. Biomechatronic Exoskeletons for Rehabilitation

Biomechatronic exoskeletons have rapidly evolved from industrial applications to sports rehabilitation. These robotic structures, engineered with adaptive actuators and joint sensors, provide externally modulated support, guiding athletes through precise movements in cases of muscle atrophy or joint immobility (P. Kumar, Taneja, et al., 2024). Equipped with AI-driven algorithms, these exoskeletons modulate resistance and support in real-time, attuning to the athlete's progress and strength levels. This dynamic adaptability accelerates neuromuscular re-education and has demonstrated efficacy in reducing rehabilitation time for complex joint injuries. The rise of lightweight, agile exoskeletons specifically designed for sports offers an unprecedented level of customized support in post-injury scenarios (P. Kumar, Reepu, et al., 2024).

9. Cryo-Thermo Neurofeedback for Enhanced Recovery

An emerging innovation in sports recovery is cryo-thermo neurofeedback, which integrates cryotherapy (cold therapy) and thermotherapy (heat therapy) with neurofeedback loops to modulate pain perception and expedite recovery. This system involves wearable patches embedded with thermal sensors and electroencephalographic (EEG) electrodes, which monitor pain-related brain wave patterns (Bhatnagar, Rajaram, et al., 2024). The wearable modulates its temperature in real-time, delivering thermal stimuli that optimally counteract pain signals based on the neurofeedback. This combination has shown promise in alleviating inflammation, enhancing blood circulation, and restoring neuromuscular function, providing athletes with a novel, integrative recovery tool that goes beyond conventional cryotherapy (Taneja, Bhatnagar, Kumar, & Rupeika-apoga, 2023).

10. Blockchain in Athlete Health Data Management

Blockchain technology is making inroads into the sports medicine sector, particularly in the realm of health data management and athlete privacy (Bansal et al., 2023). The decentralized and immutable nature of blockchain offers a robust solution to safeguard the vast amounts of personal health data generated by wearables, biosensors, and telemetric devices (M. Gupta et al., 2023). Blockchain-enabled platforms empower athletes to control access to their biometric data, allowing for secure sharing only with authorized medical personnel (Taneja, Gupta, et al., 2023). Additionally, blockchain's transparency is enabling a new level of data provenance, which is essential for compliance with privacy regulations (Dahiya & Taneja, 2023). This secure data infrastructure not only protects athletes but also facilitates ethical and accountable data-driven interventions in sports medicine (Dangwal et al., 2022).

These advancements, collectively at the forefront of technological innovation in sports medicine, are rapidly reshaping the industry by enhancing precision, customization, and privacy within healthcare delivery. As these technologies continue to evolve, they promise not only to optimize athletic performance but to pave the way for a new era of anticipatory, personalized sports care (Bhatnagar, Kumar, et al., 2024; P. Kumar, Bhatnagar, & Taneja, 2023; Taneja, Bhatnagar, Kumar, & Grima, 2023).

CONCLUSION

The advent of precision medicine and smart healthcare technologies marks a transformative chapter in sports medicine, redefining what is possible in performance enhancement and injury prevention. Through the integration of biosensors, machine learning, bioinformatics, and ergonomic design, these technologies collectively drive a paradigm shift from reactive to proactive care. By centering on individualized diagnostics and tailored therapeutic interventions, the potential to augment human resilience and athletic achievement has never been more profound. As these innovations continue to evolve, the future of sports medicine promises not only to elevate performance standards but also to safeguard the long-term health of athletes, underscoring the irreplaceable synergy between technological precision and human ambition.

DECLARATION

The authors declare that the manuscript follows ethical standards and there are no potential conflicts of interest concerning this chapter's research, authorship, and publication.

DISCLAIMER

The contents and views of this chapter are expressed by the authors in personal capacities. The Editor and the Publisher don't need to agree with these viewpoints and are not responsible for any duty of care in this regard.

REFERENCES

Abdullah, K. H., Abd Aziz, F. S., Dani, R., Hammood, W. A., & Setiawan, E. (2023). Urban Pollution: A Bibliometric Review. *ASM Science Journal*, 18, 1–16. DOI: 10.32802/asmscj.2023.1440

Ahmad, I., Sharma, S., Kumar, R., Dhyani, S., & Dumka, A. (2023). Data Analytics of Online Education during Pandemic Health Crisis: A Case Study. *2nd Edition of IEEE Delhi Section Owned Conference, DELCON 2023 - Proceedings*. DOI: 10.1109/DELCON57910.2023.10127423

Aiyappa, S., Kodikal, R., & Rahiman, H. U. (2024). Accelerating Gender Equality for Sustainable Development: A Case Study of Dakshina Kannada District, India. *Technical and Vocational Education and Training*, 38, 335–349. DOI: 10.1007/978-981-99-6909-8_30

Ajay, D., Sharad, K., Singh, K. P., & Sharma, S. (2023). Impact of Prolonged Mental Torture on Housewives in Middle Class Families. *Journal for ReAttach Therapy and Developmental Diversities*, 6(4), 1–7.

Akana, C. M. V. S., Kumar, A., Tiwari, M., Yunus, A. Z., Vijayakumar, E., & Singh, M. (2023). An Optimized DDoS Attack Detection Using Deep Convolutional Generative Adversarial Networks. *Proceedings of the 5th International Conference on Inventive Research in Computing Applications, ICIRCA 2023*, 668 – 673. DOI: 10.1109/ICIRCA57980.2023.10220745

Alexopoulos, C., Al-Tamimi, T. A. S., & Saxena, S. (2023). Were the higher educational institutions (HEIs) in Oman ready to face pedagogical challenges during COVID-19? *Arab Gulf Journal of Scientific Research*. Advance online publication. DOI: 10.1108/AGJSR-03-2023-0095

Alrashed, F. A., Alsubiheen, A. M., Alshammari, H., Mazi, S. I., Al-Saud, S. A., Alayoubi, S., Kachanathu, S. J., Albarrati, A., Aldaihan, M. M., Ahmad, T., Sattar, K., Khan, S., & Dhiman, G. (2022). Stress, Anxiety, and Depression in Pre-Clinical Medical Students: Prevalence and Association with Sleep Disorders. *Sustainability (Basel)*, 14(18), 11320. Advance online publication. DOI: 10.3390/su141811320

Arora, A., Singh, R., Malik, K., & Kestwal, U. (2024). Association of sexual performance and intimacy with satisfaction in life in head and neck cancer patients: A review. *Oral Oncology Reports*, 11, 100563. Advance online publication. DOI: 10.1016/j.oor.2024.100563

Awal, G., & Khanna, R. (2019). Determinants of millennial online consumer behavior and prospective purchase decisions. *International Journal of Advanced Science and Technology*, 28(18), 366–378.

Babu, M., Venkataraman, S. R., Rao, P. N., Rao, V., Kaliappan, S., Patil, P. P., Sekar, S., Yuvaraj, K. P., & Murugan, A. (2022). Optical Microstructure, FESEM, Microtensile, and Microhardness Properties of LM 25-B4Cnp-Grnp Hybrid Composites Manufactured by Selective Laser Melting. *Advances in Materials Science and Engineering*, 2022, 1–8. Advance online publication. DOI: 10.1155/2022/3177172

Bansal, N., Bhatnagar, M., & Taneja, S. (2023). Balancing priorities through green optimism: A study elucidating initiatives, approaches, and strategies for sustainable supply chain management. In *Handbook of Research on Designing Sustainable Supply Chains to Achieve a Circular Economy*. IGI Global., DOI: 10.4018/978-1-6684-7664-2.ch004

Belwal, N., Juneja, P., & Sunori, S. K. (2023). Decoupler Control for a MIMO Process Model in an Industrial Process - A Review. *2023 2nd International Conference on Ambient Intelligence in Health Care, ICAIHC 2023*. DOI: 10.1109/ICAIHC59020.2023.10431463

Belwal, R., & Belwal, S. (2017). Employers' perception of women workers in Oman and the challenges they face. *Employee Relations*, 39(7), 1048–1065. DOI: 10.1108/ER-09-2016-0183

Bhamangol, B., Kaiwade, A., Pant, B., Rana, A., Kaiwade, A., & Shaikh, A. (2022). An Artificial Intelligence based Design and Implementation for classifying the Missing Data in IoT Applications. *Proceedings of 5th International Conference on Contemporary Computing and Informatics, IC3I 2022*, 1376 – 1382. DOI: 10.1109/IC3I56241.2022.10072634

Bhatnagar, M., Kumar, P., Taneja, S., Sood, K., & Grima, S. (2024). From digital overload to trading Zen: The role of digital detox in enhancing intraday trading performance. In *Business Drivers in Promoting Digital Detoxification*. IGI Global., DOI: 10.4018/979-8-3693-1107-3.ch010

Bhatnagar, M., Rajaram, R., Taneja, S., & Kumar, P. (2024). Balancing acts: The Yin and Yang of debit and credit on the stage of financial well-being. In *Emerging Perspectives on Financial Well-Being*. IGI Global., DOI: 10.4018/979-8-3693-1750-1.ch002

Bhatnagar, M., Taneja, S., & Kumar, P. (2023). The Effectiveness of Carbon Pricing Mechanism in Steering Financial Flows Toward Sustainable Projects. *International Journal of Environmental Impacts*, 6(4), 183–196. DOI: 10.18280/ijei.060403

Cavaliere, L. P. L., Byloppilly, R., Khan, S. D., Othman, B. A., Muda, I., & Malhotra, R. K. (2024). Acceptance and effectiveness of Industry 4.0 internal and external organisational initiatives in Malaysian firms. *International Journal of Management and Enterprise Development*, 23(1), 1–25. DOI: 10.1504/IJMED.2024.138422

Chandna, R., Saini, S., & Kumar, S. (2022). Selecting the Most Agile Manufacturing System with Respect to Agile Attribute-Technology: Fuzzy AHP Approach. In D. N. & C. A. (Eds.), *AIP Conference Proceedings* (Vol. 2481). American Institute of Physics Inc. DOI: 10.1063/5.0103804

Chavadaki, S., Nithin Kumar, K. C., & Rajesh, M. N. (2021). Finite element analysis of spur gear to find out the optimum root radius. In S. Y. (Ed.), *Materials Today: Proceedings* (Vol. 46, pp. 10672 – 10675). Elsevier Ltd. DOI: 10.1016/j.matpr.2021.01.422

Dahiya, K., & Taneja, S. (2023). To Analyse the Impact of Multi-Media Technology on the Rural Entrepreneurship Development. In *Contemporary Studies of Risks in Emerging Technology* (pp. 221–240). DOI: 10.1108/978-1-80455-562-020231015

Dangwal, A., Kaur, S., Taneja, S., & Ozen, E. (2022). A bibliometric analysis of green tourism based on the scopus platform. In *Developing Relationships, Personalization, and Data Herald in Marketing 5.0*. IGI Global., DOI: 10.4018/978-1-6684-4496-2.ch015

Dani, R., Kukreti, R., Negi, A., & Kholiya, D. (2020). Impact of covid-19 on education and internships of hospitality students. *International Journal of Current Research and Review, 12*(21 Special Issue), 86 – 90. DOI: 10.31782/IJCRR.2020.SP54

Dimri, R., Mall, S., Sinha, S., Joshi, N. C., Bhatnagar, P., Sharma, R., Kumar, V., & Gururani, P. (2023). Role of microalgae as a sustainable alternative of biopolymers and its application in industries. *Plant Science Today*, 10, 8–18. DOI: 10.14719/pst.2460

Dixit, A. K., Kumar, T. V., Joshi, A., Bedi, H. S., Chakravarthi, M. K., & Singh, D. P. (2022). Trends in Robotics and Computer Integrated Manufacturing. *Proceedings of 5th International Conference on Contemporary Computing and Informatics, IC3I 2022*, 212 – 216. DOI: 10.1109/IC3I56241.2022.10072745

Dogra, V., Verma, D., & Fortunati, E. (2021). Biopolymers and nanomaterials in food packaging and applications. In *Nanotechnology-Based Sustainable Alternatives for the Management of Plant Diseases*. Elsevier., DOI: 10.1016/B978-0-12-823394-8.00011-1

Dutta, A., Singh, P., Dobhal, A., Mannan, D., Singh, J., & Goswami, P. (2023). Entrepreneurial Aptitude of Women of an Aspirational District of Uttarakhand. *Indian Journal of Extension Education*, 59(2), 103–107. DOI: 10.48165/IJEE.2023.59222

Gangwar, V. P., & Srivastva, S. P. (2020). Impact of micro finance in poverty eradication via SHGs: A study of selected districts in U.P. *International Journal of Advanced Science and Technology*, 29(2), 3818–3829.

Gopal, S., Gupta, P., & Minocha, A. (2023). Advancements in Fin-Tech and Security Challenges of Banking Industry. *4th International Conference on Intelligent Engineering and Management, ICIEM 2023*. DOI: 10.1109/ICIEM59379.2023.10165876

Goyal, P., Kukreja, T., Agarwal, A., & Khanna, N. (2015). Narrowing awareness gap by using e-learning tools for counselling university entrants. *Conference Proceeding - 2015 International Conference on Advances in Computer Engineering and Applications, ICACEA 2015*, 847 – 851. DOI: 10.1109/ICACEA.2015.7164822

Grover, D., Sharma, S., Kaur, P., Mittal, A., & Sharma, P. K. (2024). Societal Elements that Impact the Performance of Women Entrepreneurs in Tier-II Cities: A Study of Rohilkhand Region of Uttar Pradesh. *2024 IEEE Zooming Innovation in Consumer Technologies Conference. ZINC*, 2024, 114–117. DOI: 10.1109/ZINC61849.2024.10579316

Gupta, A., & Kumar, H. (2022). Multi-dimensional perspectives on electric vehicles design: A mind map approach. *Cleaner Engineering and Technology*, 8, 100483. Advance online publication. DOI: 10.1016/j.clet.2022.100483

Gupta, C., Jindal, P., & Malhotra, R. K. (2022). A Study of Increasing Adoption Trends of Digital Technologies - An Evidence from Indian Banking. In D. N. & C. A. (Eds.), *AIP Conference Proceedings* (Vol. 2481). American Institute of Physics Inc. DOI: 10.1063/5.0104572

Gupta, M., Arora, K., & Taneja, S. (2023). Bibliometric analysis on employee engagement and human resource management. In *Enhancing Customer Engagement Through Location-Based Marketing*. IGI Global., DOI: 10.4018/978-1-6684-8177-6.ch013

Indu, R., Dimri, S. C., & Kumar, B. (2023). Identification of Location for Police Headquarters to Deal with Crime Against Women in India Using Clustering Based on K-Means Algorithm. *International Journal of Computing and Digital Systems*, 14(1), 965–974. DOI: 10.12785/ijcds/140175

Jindal, M., Bajal, E., Singh, P., Diwakar, M., Arya, C., & Sharma, K. (2022). Online education in Covid-19: Limitations and improvements. *2021 IEEE 8th Uttar Pradesh Section International Conference on Electrical, Electronics and Computer Engineering, UPCON 2021*. DOI: 10.1109/UPCON52273.2021.9667605

Joshi, K., Patil, S., Gupta, S., & Khanna, R. (2022). Role of Pranayma in emotional maturity for improving health. *Journal of Medical Pharmaceutical and Allied Sciences*, 11(2), 4569–4573. DOI: 10.55522/jmpas.V11I2.2033

Kanojia, P., Malhotra, R. K., & Uniyal, A. K. (2022a). Impact of Organizational Commitment Components on the Teachers of Higher Education in Uttarakhand: An Emperical Analysis. *Proceedings - 2022 International Conference on Recent Trends in Microelectronics, Automation, Computing and Communications Systems, ICMACC 2022*, 360–364. DOI: 10.1109/ICMACC54824.2022.10093606

Kanojia, P., Malhotra, R. K., & Uniyal, A. K. (2022b). Organizational Commitment and the Academic Staff in HEI's in North West India. *Proceedings - 2022 International Conference on Recent Trends in Microelectronics, Automation, Computing and Communications Systems, ICMACC 2022*, 365–370. DOI: 10.1109/ICMACC54824.2022.10093347

Kaur, A., Kumar, P., Taneja, S., & Ozen, E. (2023). Fintech emergence – an opportunity or threat to banking. *International Journal of Electronic Finance*, 13(1), 1–19. DOI: 10.1504/IJEF.2024.135163

Kaur, J., Khanna, R., Kumar, R., & Sunil, G. (2024). Role of Blockchain Technologies in Goods and Services Tax. *Proceedings - 2024 3rd International Conference on Sentiment Analysis and Deep Learning, ICSADL 2024*, 607–612. DOI: 10.1109/ICSADL61749.2024.00104

Khan, T., Singh, K., & Purohit, K. C. (2020). Icma: An efficient integrated congestion control approach. *Recent Patents on Engineering*, 14(3), 294–309. DOI: 10.2174/1872212114666191231150916

Khandelwal, C., Kumar, S., Tripathi, V., & Madhavan, V. (2023). Joint impact of corporate governance and risk disclosures on firm value: Evidence from emerging markets. *Research in International Business and Finance*, 66, 102022. Advance online publication. DOI: 10.1016/j.ribaf.2023.102022

Khanna, R., Jindal, P., & Noja, G. G. (2023). Blockchain technologies, a catalyst for insurance sector. In *The Application of Emerging Technology and Blockchain in the Insurance Industry*. DOI: 10.1201/9781032630946-19

Kohli, P., Sharma, S., & Matta, P. (2022). Secured Privacy Preserving Techniques Analysis of 6G Driven Vehicular Communication Network in Industry 5.0 Internet-of-Everything (IoE) Applications. *2022 International Conference on Smart Generation Computing, Communication and Networking, SMART GENCON 2022*. DOI: 10.1109/SMARTGENCON56628.2022.10084289

Kumar, P., Reepu, & Kaur, R. (2024). Economic and Urban Dynamics: Investigating Socioeconomic Status and Urban Density as Moderators of Mobile Wallet Adoption in Smart Cities. *Lecture Notes in Networks and Systems, 948 LNNS*, 409–417. DOI: 10.1007/978-981-97-1329-5_33

Kumar, P., Bhatnagar, M., & Taneja, S. (2023). Investigation of the time pattern of Bit Green Crypto: An Arma modeling approach to unrave volatility. In *Algorithmic Approaches to Financial Technology: Forecasting, Trading, and Optimization*. IGI Global., DOI: 10.4018/979-8-3693-1746-4.ch001

Kumar, P., Taneja, S., Bhatnagar, M., & Kaur, A. K. (2024). Navigating the digital paradigm shift: Designing CBDCs for a transformative financial landscape. In *Exploring Central Bank Digital Currencies: Concepts, Frameworks, Models, and Challenges*. IGI Global., DOI: 10.4018/979-8-3693-1882-9.ch006

Kumar, R., Goel, R., Singh, T., Mohanty, S. M., Gupta, D., Alkhayyat, A., & Khanna, R. (2024). Sustainable Finance Factors in Indian Economy: Analysis on Policy of Climate Change and Energy Sector. *Fluctuation and Noise Letters*, 23(2), 2440004. Advance online publication. DOI: 10.1142/S0219477524400042

Kumar, R., Kandpal, B., & Ahmad, V. (2023). Industrial IoT (IIOT): Security Threats and Countermeasures. *International Conference on Innovative Data Communication Technologies and Application, ICIDCA 2023 - Proceedings*, 829 – 833. DOI: 10.1109/ICIDCA56705.2023.10100145

Kumar, R., Kathuria, S., Malholtra, R. K., Kumar, A., Gehlot, A., & Joshi, K. (2023). Role of Cloud Computing in Goods and Services Tax(GST) and Future Application. *2nd International Conference on Sustainable Computing and Data Communication Systems, ICSCDS 2023 - Proceedings*, 1443–1447. DOI: 10.1109/ICSCDS56580.2023.10104597

Kumar, R., & Khanna, R. (2023a). Role of Artificial Intelligence in Digital Currency and Future Applications. *Proceedings of the 2023 2nd International Conference on Augmented Intelligence and Sustainable Systems, ICAISS 2023*, 42–46. DOI: 10.1109/ICAISS58487.2023.10250480

Kumar, R., & Khanna, R. (2023b). RPA (Robotic Process Automation) in Finance & Accounting and Future Scope. *Proceedings of the 2023 2nd International Conference on Augmented Intelligence and Sustainable Systems, ICAISS 2023*, 1640–1645. DOI: 10.1109/ICAISS58487.2023.10250496

Kumar, R., Khannna Malholtra, R., & Grover, C. A. N. (2023). Review on Artificial Intelligence Role in Implementation of Goods and Services Tax(GST) and Future Scope. *2023 International Conference on Artificial Intelligence and Smart Communication, AISC 2023*, 348–351. DOI: 10.1109/AISC56616.2023.10085030

Kumar, R., Lande, A., Kumar, D., Malhotra, R. K., & Sharma, A. (2023). Technology Bridging -in Entrepreneurs and Consumers in Product Development. *ISED 2023 - International Conference on Intelligent Systems and Embedded Design*. DOI: 10.1109/ISED59382.2023.10444599

Kumar, R., Malholtra, R. K., Singh, R., Kathuria, S., Balyan, R., & Pal, P. (2023). Artificial Intelligence Role in Electronic Invoice Under Goods and Services Tax. *2023 International Conference on Computational Intelligence, Communication Technology and Networking, CICTN 2023*, 140–143. DOI: 10.1109/CICTN57981.2023.10140870

Kumar, R., Malhotra, R. K., & Grover, N. (2023). Data Mining in Credit Scoring and Future Application. *International Conference on Innovative Data Communication Technologies and Application, ICIDCA 2023 - Proceedings*, 1096–1100. DOI: 10.1109/ICIDCA56705.2023.10100032

Kumar, R., Malhotra, R. K., Pandey, S., Gehlot, A., Gautam, I., & Chamola, S. (2023). Role of Artificial Intelligence in Input Tax Credit Reconciliation. *Proceedings - 2023 3rd International Conference on Pervasive Computing and Social Networking, ICPCSN 2023*, 497–501. DOI: 10.1109/ICPCSN58827.2023.00086

Kumar, R., Sexena, A., & Gehlot, A. (2023). Artificial Intelligence in Smart Education and Futuristic Challenges. *2023 International Conference on Disruptive Technologies, ICDT 2023*, 432 – 435. DOI: 10.1109/ICDT57929.2023.10151129

Kumar, R., Singh, T., Mohanty, S. N., Goel, R., Gupta, D., Alharbi, M., & Khanna, R. (2023). Study on online payments and e-commerce with SOR model. *International Journal of Retail & Distribution Management*. Advance online publication. DOI: 10.1108/IJRDM-03-2023-0137

Kumar, V., Gupta, S., & Khanna, R. (2021). Dengue fever-a worldwide study. *Journal of Medical Pharmaceutical and Allied Sciences*, 10, 102–108. DOI: 10.22270/jmpas.VIC2I1.2014

Kumari, J., Singh, P., Mishra, A. K., Singh Meena, B. P., Singh, A., & Ojha, M. (2024). Challenges Hindering Women's Involvement in the Hospitality Industry as Entrepreneurs in the Era of Digital Economy. In *Revolutionizing the AI-Digital Landscape: A Guide to Sustainable Emerging Technologies for Marketing Professionals*. Taylor and Francis., DOI: 10.4324/9781032688305-9

Lourens, M., Krishna, S. H., Singh, A., Dey, S. K., Pant, B., & Sharma, T. (2022). Role of Artificial Intelligence in Formative Employee Engagement. In D. R.K., S. A.Kr., K. G., & B. S. (Eds.), *Proceedings of the 2022 11th International Conference on System Modeling and Advancement in Research Trends, SMART 2022* (pp. 936 – 941). Institute of Electrical and Electronics Engineers Inc. DOI: 10.1109/SMART55829.2022.10047422

Luthra, S., Sharma, M., Kumar, A., Joshi, S., Collins, E., & Mangla, S. (2022). Overcoming barriers to cross-sector collaboration in circular supply chain management: A multi-method approach. *Transportation Research Part E, Logistics and Transportation Review*, 157, 102582. Advance online publication. DOI: 10.1016/j.tre.2021.102582

Malhotra, R. K., Gupta, C., & Jindal, P. (2022). Blockchain and Smart Contracts for Insurance Industry. In *Blockchain Technology in Corporate Governance. Transforming Business and Industries.*, DOI: 10.1002/9781119865247.ch11

Malhotra, R. K., & Gupta, S. (2021). Tele health in the digital era during covid -19 a case study of Uttarakhand. *Journal of Medical Pharmaceutical and Allied Sciences*, 10, 109–112. DOI: 10.22270/jmpas.VIC2I1.2016

Malhotra, R. K., Ojha, M. K., & Gupta, S. (2021). A study of assessment of knowledge, perception and attitude of using tele health services among college going students of Uttarakhand. *Journal of Medical Pharmaceutical and Allied Sciences*, 10, 113–116. DOI: 10.22270/jmpas.VIC2I1.2020

Malik, P., Singh, A. K., Nautiyal, R., & Rawat, S. (2022). Mapping AICTE cybersecurity curriculum onto CyBOK: A case study. In *Machine Learning for Cyber Security*. De Gruyter., DOI: 10.1515/9783110766745-007

Mangla, S. K., Luthra, S., Mishra, N., Singh, A., Rana, N. P., Dora, M., & Dwivedi, Y. (2018). Barriers to effective circular supply chain management in a developing country context. *Production Planning and Control*, 29(6), 551–569. DOI: 10.1080/09537287.2018.1449265

Mary Joshitta, S., & Sunil, M. P. Badriasulaimanalfurhood, Bodhankar, A., Ch.Sreedevi, & Khanna, R. (2023). The Integration of Machine Learning Technique with the Existing System to Predict the Flight Prices. *2023 3rd International Conference on Advance Computing and Innovative Technologies in Engineering, ICACITE 2023*, 398–402. DOI: 10.1109/ICACITE57410.2023.10182539

Mishra, D., Kandpal, V., Agarwal, N., & Srivastava, B. (2024). Financial Inclusion and Its Ripple Effects on Socio-Economic Development: A Comprehensive Review. *Journal of Risk and Financial Management*, 17(3), 105. Advance online publication. DOI: 10.3390/jrfm17030105

Mohamed, N., Sridhara Rao, L., & Sharma, M. Sureshbaburajasekaranl, Badriasulaimanalfurhood, & Kumar Shukla, S. (2023). In-depth review of integration of AI in cloud computing. *2023 3rd International Conference on Advance Computing and Innovative Technologies in Engineering, ICACITE 2023*, 1431 – 1434. DOI: 10.1109/ICACITE57410.2023.10182738

Neha, M., S., Alfurhood, B. S., Bakhare, R., Poongavanam, S., & Khanna, R. (2023). The Role and Impact of Artificial Intelligence on Retail Business and its Developments. *2023 International Conference on Artificial Intelligence and Smart Communication, AISC 2023*, 1098–1101. DOI: 10.1109/AISC56616.2023.10085624

Onyema, E. M., Almuzaini, K. K., Onu, F. U., Verma, D., Gregory, U. S., Puttaramaiah, M., & Afriyie, R. K. (2022). Prospects and Challenges of Using Machine Learning for Academic Forecasting. *Computational Intelligence and Neuroscience*, 2022, 1–7. Advance online publication. DOI: 10.1155/2022/5624475 PMID: 35909823

Padhi, B. K., Singh, S., Gaidhane, A. M., Abu Serhan, H., Khatib, M. N., Zahiruddin, Q. S., Rustagi, S., Sharma, R. K., Sharma, D., Arora, M., & Satapathy, P. (2024). Inequalities in cardiovascular disease among elderly Indians: A gender perspective analysis using LASI wave-I (2017-18). *Current Problems in Cardiology*, 49(7), 102605. Advance online publication. DOI: 10.1016/j.cpcardiol.2024.102605 PMID: 38692448

Pai, H. A., Almuzaini, K. K., Ali, L., Javeed, A., Pant, B., Pareek, P. K., & Akwafo, R. (2022). Delay-Driven Opportunistic Routing with Multichannel Cooperative Neighbor Discovery for Industry 4.0 Wireless Networks Based on Power and Load Awareness. *Wireless Communications and Mobile Computing*, 2022, 1–12. Advance online publication. DOI: 10.1155/2022/5256133

Pande, S. D., Bhatt, A., Chamoli, S., Saini, D. K. J. B., Kute, U. T., & Ahammad, S. H. (2023). Design of Atmel PLC and its Application as Automation of Coal Handling Plant. *2023 International Conference on Sustainable Emerging Innovations in Engineering and Technology, ICSEIET 2023*, 178 – 183. DOI: 10.1109/ICSEIET58677.2023.10303627

Pandey, R. P., Bansal, S., Awasthi, P., Dixit, V., Singh, R., & Yadava, V. (2023). Attitude and Myths Related to Stalking among Early and Middle Age Adults. *Psychology Hub, 40*(3), 85 – 94. DOI: 10.13133/2724-2943/17960

Pant, V., Bhasin, S., & Jain, S. (2017). Self-Learning system for personalized E-Learning. *2017 International Conference on Emerging Trends in Computing and Communication Technologies, ICETCCT 2017, 2018-Janua*, 1 – 6. DOI: 10.1109/ICETCCT.2017.8280344

Patil, S. P., Singh, B., Bisht, J., Gupta, S., & Khanna, R. (2021). Yoga for holistic treatment of polycystic ovarian syndrome. *Journal of Medical Pharmaceutical and Allied Sciences*, 10, 120–125. DOI: 10.22270/jmpas.VIC2I1.2035

Pattanshetti, M. K., Jasola, S., Rajput, A., & Pant, V. (2021). Proposed eLearning framework using open corpus web resources. *Proceedings of the 2021 1st International Conference on Advances in Electrical, Computing, Communications and Sustainable Technologies, ICAECT 2021*. DOI: 10.1109/ICAECT49130.2021.9392591

Prikshat, V., Kumar, S., & Nankervis, A. (2019). Work-readiness integrated competence model: Conceptualisation and scale development. *Education + Training*, 61(5), 568–589. DOI: 10.1108/ET-05-2018-0114

Prikshat, V., Kumar, S., & Raje, P. (2017). Antecedents, consequences and strategic responses to graduate work-readiness: Challenges in India. In *Transitions from Education to Work: Workforce Ready Challenges in the Asia Pacific*. Taylor and Francis., DOI: 10.4324/9781315533971-8

Ram, M., Bisht, D. C. S., Goyal, N., Kazancoglu, Y., & Mathirajan, M. (2022). Newly developed mathematical methodologies and advancements in a variety of engineering and management domains. *Mathematics in Engineering. Science and Aerospace*, 13(3), 559–562.

Rana, D. S., Dimri, S. C., Malik, P., & Dhondiyal, S. A. (2022). Impact of Computational Thinking in Engineering and K12 Education. *4th International Conference on Inventive Research in Computing Applications, ICIRCA 2022 - Proceedings*, 697 – 701. DOI: 10.1109/ICIRCA54612.2022.9985593

Rana, M. S., Cavaliere, L. P. L., Mishra, A. B., Padhye, P., Singh, R. R., & Khanna, R. (2022). Internet of Things (IOT) Based Assessment for Effective Monitoring Data Against Malicious Attacks on Financial Collectors. *2022 2nd International Conference on Advance Computing and Innovative Technologies in Engineering, ICACITE 2022*, 177–181. DOI: 10.1109/ICACITE53722.2022.9823612

Rathore, R., & Goudar, R. H. (2015). SPARQL-based personalised E-Learning system designed using ontology (SPELSO): An architecture. *International Journal of Knowledge and Learning*, 10(4), 384–416. DOI: 10.1504/IJKL.2015.077554

Rawat, R. S., Singh, V., & Dumka, A. (2022). Complaint Management in Ethiopian Vocational and Technical Education Institutions: A Framework and Implementation of a Decision Support System. *2022 International Conference on 4th Industrial Revolution Based Technology and Practices, ICFIRTP 2022*, 73 – 79. DOI: 10.1109/ICFIRTP56122.2022.10063207

Reepu, R., Taneja, S., Ozen, E., & Singh, A. (2023). A globetrotter to the future of marketing: Metaverse. In *Cultural Marketing and Metaverse for Consumer Engagement*. IGI Global., DOI: 10.4018/978-1-6684-8312-1.ch001

Shah, J. K., Sharma, R., Misra, A., Sharma, M., Joshi, S., Kaushal, D., & Bafila, S. (2023). Industry 4.0 Enabled Smart Manufacturing: Unleashing the Power of Artificial Intelligence and Blockchain. *2023 1st DMIHER International Conference on Artificial Intelligence in Education and Industry 4.0, IDICAIEI 2023*. DOI: 10.1109/IDICAIEI58380.2023.10406671

Sharma, P., Malhotra, R. K., Ojha, M. K., & Gupta, S. (2022). Impact of meditation on mental & physical health and thereby on academic performance of students: A study of higher educational institutions of Uttarakhand. *Journal of Medical Pharmaceutical and Allied Sciences*, 11(2), 4641–4644. DOI: 10.55522/jmpas.V11I2.2309

Sharma, S., Kadayat, Y., & Tyagi, R. (2023). Sustainable Global Democratic e-Governance System Using Vedic Scripture, Artificial Intelligence, Cloud Computing and Augmented Reality. *Proceedings of the International Conference on Circuit Power and Computing Technologies, ICCPCT 2023*, 113 – 118. DOI: 10.1109/ICCPCT58313.2023.10245405

Sharma, S., Kandpal, V., Choudhury, T., Santibanez Gonzalez, E. D. R., & Agarwal, N. (2023). Assessment of the implications of energy-efficient technologies on the environmental sustainability of rail operation. *AIMS Environmental Science*, 10(5), 709–731. DOI: 10.3934/environsci.2023039

Sharma, V., & Jain, S. (2020). Managers Training Programs Effectiveness Evaluation by using different Machine Learning Approaches. *Proceedings of the 4th International Conference on Electronics, Communication and Aerospace Technology, ICECA 2020*, 1453 – 1457. DOI: 10.1109/ICECA49313.2020.9297556

Sharma, Y. K., Mangla, S. K., Patil, P. P., & Uniyal, S. (2020). Analyzing sustainable food supply chain management challenges in India. In *Research Anthology on Food Waste Reduction and Alternative Diets for Food and Nutrition Security*. IGI Global., DOI: 10.4018/978-1-7998-5354-1.ch023

Shrivastava, A., Usha, R., Kukreti, R., Sharma, G., Srivastava, A. P., & Khan, A. K. (2023). Women Safety Precaution. *2023 1st International Conference on Circuits, Power, and Intelligent Systems, CCPIS 2023*. DOI: 10.1109/CCPIS59145.2023.10291594

Singh, A. B., Meena, H. K., Khandelwal, C., & Dangayach, G. S. (2023). Sustainability Assessment of Higher Education Institutions: A Systematic Literature Review †. *Engineering Proceedings*, 37(1), 23. Advance online publication. DOI: 10.3390/ECP2023-14728

Singh, A. K., Singh, R., & Singh, S. (2024). A review on factors affecting and performance of nutritional security of women and children in India. In *Impact of Women in Food and Agricultural Development*. IGI Global., DOI: 10.4018/979-8-3693-3037-1.ch019

Singh, K. D., & Singh, P. (2023). A Novel Cloud-based Framework to Predict the Employability of Students. In K. R., K. R., G. M., G. M., S. R., & S. R. (Eds.), *2023 International Conference on Advancement in Computation and Computer Technologies, InCACCT 2023* (pp. 528 – 532). Institute of Electrical and Electronics Engineers Inc. DOI: 10.1109/InCACCT57535.2023.10141760

Singh, K. D., Singh, P., Kaur, G., Khullar, V., Chhabra, R., & Tripathi, V. (2023). Education 4.0: Exploring the Potential of Disruptive Technologies in Transforming Learning. *Proceedings of International Conference on Computational Intelligence and Sustainable Engineering Solution, CISES 2023*, 586 – 591. DOI: 10.1109/CISES58720.2023.10183547

Singh, K. U., Chaudhary, V., Sharma, P. K., Kumar, P., Varshney, N., & Singh, T. (2024). Integrating GPS and GSM Technologies for Enhanced Women's Safety: A Fingerprint-Activated Device Approach. *2024 International Conference on Automation and Computation, AUTOCOM 2024*, 657 – 662. DOI: 10.1109/AUTOCOM60220.2024.10486120

Singh, N., Rana, A., & Badhotiya, G. K. (2021). Manufacturing processes for the development of engineered wood - A mini-review. In S. Y. (Ed.), *Materials Today: Proceedings* (Vol. 46, pp. 11235–11238). Elsevier Ltd. DOI: 10.1016/j.matpr.2021.02.612

Singh, P., & Singh, K. D. (2023). Fog-Centric Intelligent Surveillance System: A Novel Approach for Effective and Efficient Surveillance. In K. R., K. R., G. M., G. M., S. R., & S. R. (Eds.), *2023 International Conference on Advancement in Computation and Computer Technologies, InCACCT 2023* (pp. 762–766). Institute of Electrical and Electronics Engineers Inc. DOI: 10.1109/InCACCT57535.2023.10141802

Singh, Y., Rahim, E. A., Singh, N. K., Sharma, A., Singla, A., & Palamanit, A. (2022). Friction and wear characteristics of chemically modified mahua (madhuca indica) oil based lubricant with SiO_2 nanoparticles as additives. *Wear*, 508–509, 204463. Advance online publication. DOI: 10.1016/j.wear.2022.204463

Srivastava, A., Jawaid, S., Singh, R., Gehlot, A., Akram, S. V., Priyadarshi, N., & Khan, B. (2022). Imperative Role of Technology Intervention and Implementation for Automation in the Construction Industry. *Advances in Civil Engineering*, 2022(1), 6716987. Advance online publication. DOI: 10.1155/2022/6716987

Srivastava, B., Kandpal, V., & Jain, A. K. (2024). Financial well-being of women self-help group members: A qualitative study. *Environment, Development and Sustainability*. Advance online publication. DOI: 10.1007/s10668-024-04879-w

Taneja, S., Bhatnagar, M., Kumar, P., & Grima, S. (2023). A Panel Analysis of the Effectiveness of the Asset Management in Indian Agricultural Companies. *International Journal of Sustainable Development and Planning*, 18(3), 653–660. DOI: 10.18280/ijsdp.180301

Taneja, S., Bhatnagar, M., Kumar, P., & Rupeika-apoga, R. (2023). India's Total Natural Resource Rents (NRR) and GDP : An Augmented Autoregressive Distributed Lag (ARDL) Bound Test. *Journal of Risk and Financial Management*, 16(2), 91. https://doi.org/doi.org/10.3390/jrfm16020091. DOI: 10.3390/jrfm16020091

Taneja, S., Gupta, M., Bhushan, P., Bhatnagar, M., & Singh, A. (2023). Cultural marketing in the digital era. In *Cultural Marketing and Metaverse for Consumer Engagement*. IGI Global., DOI: 10.4018/978-1-6684-8312-1.ch008

Taneja, S., & Özen, E. (2023). To analyse the relationship between bank's green financing and environmental performance. *International Journal of Electronic Finance*, 12(2), 163–175. DOI: 10.1504/IJEF.2023.129919

Tiwari, R., Agrawal, P., Singh, P., Bajaj, S., Verma, V., & Chauhan, A. S. (2023). Technology Enabled Integrated Fusion Teaching for Enhancing Learning Outcomes in Higher Education. *International Journal of Emerging Technologies in Learning*, 18(7), 243–249. DOI: 10.3991/ijet.v18i07.36799

Tripathi, V. M., & Mohan, A. (2016). Microfinance and empowering rural women in the Terai, Uttarakhand, India. *International Journal of Agricultural and Statistics Sciences*, 12(2), 523–530.

Uniyal, A. K., Kanojia, P., Khanna, R., & Dixit, A. K. (2022). Quantitative Analysis of the Impact of Demography and Job Profile on the Organizational Commitment of the Faculty Members in the HEI'S of Uttarakhand. *Communications in Computer and Information Science, 1742 CCIS*, 24–35. DOI: 10.1007/978-3-031-23647-1_3

Upreti, H., & Malhotra, R. K. (2024). Bridging The Urban-Rural Education Gap In India Through CSR (Corporate Social Responsibility) Initiatives: A Conceptual Study With Special Reference To Sustainable Development Goal 4 (Quality Education). In P. P.K. (Ed.), *E3S Web of Conferences* (Vol. 556). EDP Sciences. DOI: 10.1051/e3sconf/202455601032

Zhang, Y., Cao, C., Gu, J., & Garg, H. (2023). The Impact of Top Management Team Characteristics on the Risk Taking of Chinese Private Construction Enterprises. *Systems*, 11(2), 67. Advance online publication. DOI: 10.3390/systems11020067

Chapter 17
Predicting Novel Coronavirus Trends Using Machine Learning

Anamika Ahirwar

https://orcid.org/0000-0003-3003-3105

Compucom Institute of Technology and Management, Jaipur, India

Mahendra Singh Panwar

Compucom Institute of Technology and Management, Jaipur, India

ABSTRACT

2020 began with the advent of disruption brought on by a new virus called SARS-CoV-2. The coronavirus pandemic i.e. COVID-19, according to the World Health Organization (WHO), is putting a lot of strain on even the strongest healthcare systems in the entire world. Our current study explores supervised learning methods in machine learning, such as SVMachine, K-nearest neighbor, Naïve Bayes, Decision Tree, Random Forest, Logistic Regression, and a newly developed algorithm called XGB classifier. Specifically, the prediction of COVID-19-related deaths and recoveries is the focus of our proposed approach. A GitHub repository served as the source of the dataset used in this investigation. In this paper our aim is to enhance our comprehension of the pandemic's consequences through the application of machine learning techniques.

I. INTRODUCTION

A global health emergency never before experienced had an impact on nearly every aspect of society, ranging from social and economic stability to public health, as a result of the late-2019 SARS-CoV-2 (severe acute respiratory syndrome) outbreak (Rana et al., 2022). The World Health Organization (WHO) formally proclaimed the COVID-19 pandemic in March 2020 due to the outbreak's devastating impact on the population and its rapid global expansion (R. Kumar, Khannna Malholtra, et al., 2023). The virus is incredibly deadly and widespread, as shown by the roughly 100 million confirmed cases that had been documented globally by April 2021—all within a year. In this situation, machine learning (ML), which is a branch of artificial intelligence (AI), became an essential tool since previous epidemiological models were unable to represent the complexity of the problem adequately. Machine Learning algorithms were invaluable in navigating the crisis with its ability to handle massive volumes of data and generate

DOI: 10.4018/979-8-3373-0240-9.ch017

predictive insights. Due to the overwhelming volume of people demanding emergency attention many of the world's healthcare systems collapsed as the epidemic grew (Kanojia et al., 2022).

The lack of hospital beds, ventilators, and personal protective equipment (PPE) exposed flaws in the global health system, placing undue pressure on medical facilities (R. Kumar et al., 2024). In addition to the healthcare issue, the pandemic caused large-scale economic collapses. Enforced lockdowns, travel restrictions, and supply chain delays caused huge disruptions to the tourism, retail, and manufacturing industries (Gupta et al., 2023).

These incidents impact to a significant amount of financial instability, as well as job losses and somehow lower salaries. In light of these concerns, governments and healthcare authorities found that it is essential to have access to fast and accurate information (Komkowski et al., 2023). In order to foresee critical patterns, like the number of future cases, the need for healthcare resources, and the results of public health campaigns such as mask protocols, social distancing, and vaccination efforts, real-time data was essential for managing the pandemic. Accurate forecasting models were essential in guiding policy decisions, distributing resources in the best possible ways, and forecasting potential outcomes of various mitigation strategies (Negi et al., 2021).

Prediction of these trends are helpful for healthcare systems to prepare for surges in patient volume and enabled governments to adjust public health policy to balance epidemiologic control with lowering social and economic impacts (Shah et al., 2023). Ultimately, our ability to predict and respond to these key patterns would determine how far the pandemic's destructive consequences might be curbed. A vast amount of data, including travel habits, social media usage, hospital resources, test results, and infection counts, was generated during the pandemic (K. D. Singh et al., 2022). Throughout the pandemic, real-time forecasts and emerging insights were made possible by machine learning's ability to assess these diverse datasets and adapt to new information. Scientists and policymakers developed models using Machine Learning (ML) to address critical issues such as the timing and locations of potential future outbreaks, the length of PCR persistence in a particular area, and the effect of public health interferences, for example, immunization campaigns, lockdowns, and travel restrictions on viral transmission (Ram, Bisht, et al., 2022). The distribution of healthcare resources was also improved by Machine Learning (ML) models, which enabled governments to modify restrictions in response to anticipated future trends and hospitals to prepare for spikes in patient volume (Josphineleela et al., 2023). Machine learning was crucial in determining who was more prone to contract COVID-19 and other diseases like diabetes, heart disease, liver disease, and breast cancer in addition to forecasting the number of cases (Mishra & Wazid, 2023). By looking at temporal data trends, Machine Learning (ML) assisted in tracking the virus's path and aided in developing predictive models that enhanced public health actions. In medical research, Machine Learning is a vital tool as it mines large datasets for meaningful information (Y. Singh et al., 2022; Tiwari et al., 2023). This is mainly valid when it comes to enhance clinical judgment, care planning, and patient outcomes (Pandey et al., 2022). Machine learning-driven predictions helped for proactive measures which is meant to mitigate the pandemic's effects on communities.

There were some difficulties in predicting COVID-19 trends, because of the virus's novelty, changing human behavior, and the emergence of new strains, long-term forecasts were challenging (Suresh et al., 2023). Other obstacles which include privacy issues, algorithmic bias, poor data quality, and difficulty interpreting complex models. Notwithstanding these challenges, machine learning has made significant progress in understanding the virus's mechanism of propagation. Incorporating machine learning into forecasting efforts helped public health stakeholders better navigate the complexities of the pandemic and implement workable remedies to protect public health (P. Kumar, Bhatnagar, et al., 2023; P. Sharma et al., 2024; Taneja et al., 2023). Machine learning proved to be quite useful in tracking public sentiment and behavior during the pandemic (Sonnad et al., 2022). By analyzing data from social media, search trends, and mobility patterns, researchers used sentiment analysis and natural language processing (NLP) to evaluate public opinions, adherence to health advice, and responses to government interventions. Policymakers were able to adjust strategies, such boosting vaccination adoption or revising quarantine regulations, in response to shifting public opinions by having a better understanding of popular sentiment (Davuluri et al., 2023).

Machine learning (ML) greatly enhanced the analysis, prognosis, and treatment of COVID-19 patients in addition to its involvement in pandemic forecasts. By analyzing genomic data, electronic health records, and medical imaging, machine learning (ML) algorithms have made it easier to provide customized medications, enhance clinical outcomes, and optimize healthcare delivery (Diddi et al., 2022). Machine learning's use in enhancing resource allocation, reducing reaction times, and ensuring patient care that is tailored to each patient's needs has further illustrated the technology's significance in the healthcare sector. Machine learning has been useful not just in pandemic prediction but also in the diagnosis, prognosis, and proper care of COVID-19 patients. Machine Learning (ML) algorithms that analyze the genetic data, electronic health records, and medical imaging have made it easier to provide customized medications, enhance clinical results, and optimize healthcare delivery. The utilization of machine learning in the healthcare sector has been instrumental in enhancing resource allocation, reducing response times, and ensuring patient care that is tailored to the individual's need (Juneja et al., 2021; Syed et al., 2022).

Research on Machine Learning (ML) applications in epidemiology and healthcare shows the growing importance of Artificial Intelligence (AI) in modeling transmittable diseases. While time series analysis and statistical modeling were important tools in the early stages of pandemic forecasting, machine learning's ability to learn dynamically from data has led to more accurate and flexible predictions. Because Machine Learning (ML) was successful in forecasting the course of COVID-19, scientists are now examining how effectively it can predict other infectious diseases, establishing Machine Learning (ML) as an essential instrument for preparedness for global health emergencies (Chauhan et al., 2022).

In conclusion, applying machine learning to COVID-19 management initiatives has led to important discoveries, guided timely actions, and enhanced the healthcare system's responsiveness. Notwithstanding difficulties with data quality, privacy, and model generalizability, machine learning continues to offer a solid basis for handling the complexity of pandemics. It is likely to have a greater role in infectious disease modeling in the future, offering new tools and methods for public health preparedness and response.

This review highlights the key findings from recent research on machine learning (ML)-based COVID-19 prediction models at this time.

Encouraging the need for effective disease control measures, the COVID-19 pandemic has offered a challenge to global health. Few studies developed a novel prediction model integrating the linear regression and support vector machine (SVM) techniques (Bhatnagar, Kumar, et al., 2024; Bhatnagar, Taneja, et al., 2024; P. Kumar, Verma, et al., 2023). After training on data from January 2020 to March 2023, the model's accuracy was slightly lower than that of the solo Linear Regression model. However, it was still able to produce reliable predictions of COVID-19 case patterns in the future. Previous Studies looked into the efficacy of Machine Learning (ML) and Deep learning (DL) in identifying COVID-19 instances (Kowsalya et al., 2023; Mehershilpa et al., 2023).

Research examined 38 parameters to test machine learning models for predicting in-hospital mortality. According to research, the Random Forest (RF) model has the highest classification accuracy, making it suitable for assessing COVID-19 patient mortality risk and optimising resource utilization. Combining wide hospital data with machine learning (ML) algorithms could significantly increase the timely and accurate prediction of mortality risk (Jena & Gairola, 2022).

A study conducted a broad review of Machine Learning (ML) based research on COVID-19 detection, diagnosis, and forecasting. The analysis included over 160 research articles from six different publishers and utilized various data types such as X-ray images, CT scans, time series, sound recordings, and blood samples. The review revealed that 79% of the Machine Learning (ML) techniques employed were based on deep learning, with 65% using CNN architecture. Supervised learning accounted for 16% of the models, while hybrid approaches made up 5%. The study valuation the importance of high-quality and harmonized data for improving future models (Ram, Bhandari, et al., 2022).

An examination in the context of the current study defined the use of Machine Learning (ML) algorithms for early detection, accurate predictions, and precise diagnosis of COVID-19 patients. These models, built from various case studies and datasets (including pneumonia data), highlight the potential of mobile systems for disease management. The study suggests further research into new symptoms, expanded data collection, and authentic data usage to better support patients (Masal et al., 2022).

A study examined AI-based COVID-19 prediction techniques, developing a prediction platform while considering unique constraints and prediction accuracy. Their simulations demonstrated that random forests outperformed logistic regression and SVMs in predicting outbreaks, making the method highly applicable to medical platforms. The study extended their research by automating COVID-19 detection using convolutional neural networks (CNNs) on X-ray images, showcasing the value of Machine Learning (ML) in early detection and screening programs (Jaswal et al., 2023; Shashikala et al., 2022).

A study also contributed their research on gender-based differences in COVID-19 severity and mortality, identifying specific risk factors and the effects of these differences on patient outcomes. Their study persistent light on the importance of gender in knowing the impacts of COVID-19. This collective body of research emphasizes the critical role of machine learning in enhancing COVID-19 detection, prediction, and management while highlighting areas for further improvement and application (Chandna, 2022).

A complex mathematical model was created by a study with the goal of predicting the spread of COVID-19 in India. To mimic the dynamics of the pandemic, the model combined a number of epidemiological variables, including important metrics like recovery times, transmission rates, and infection periods. The model accurately reflected the behavior of the virus under various settings by using real-time data (E. Sharma et al., 2023). Additionally, in order to measure the worth of several intervention strategies in containing the outbreak, the study looked at the effects of lockdowns, social distance, and quarantine regulations. Policymakers were able to anticipate healthcare demands, such as hospital capacity and medical resources, and make well-informed decisions regarding the allocation of these resources' thanks in large part to the model's predictions (Arora et al., 2022).

The trajectory of the COVID-19 epidemic was predicted by means of a hybrid approach by Naithani et al., 2023 that combined a Deep Neural Network (DNN) with a forecasting model based on the Laplace transform. To find intricate, non-linear patterns in the data, the DNN, a kind of sophisticated machine learning model, was used. The model's capacity to analyze enormous volumes of real-time data allowed it to spot minute correlations and patterns that are more conventional models may miss, which helped it produce forecasts that were more accurate (Manjunatha et al., 2023).

The incorporation of the Laplace transforms improved the forecasting procedure even more by enabling the breakdown of temporal data and increasing the model's ability to represent the pandemic's time-dependent behaviour. This method made it easier to pinpoint the exact conditions under which the virus might propagate throughout time, especially in the event of modifications to public health regulations or intervention tactics (Khaudiyal et al., 2022).

The integration of deep learning and quantitative forecasting yielded significant insights about the pandemic's future course. Governments, health organizations, and policy makers can utilize these insights in particular to plan for the sharing of healthcare resources, anticipate future spikes in caseloads, and implement focused efforts to stop the virus's spread. In the end, this model is utilized as a tactical instrument to oversee public health measures throughout the pandemic.

To forecast the development of COVID-19, Lade et al., 2023 developed a temporal model with artificial intelligence that was centered on "lagging immunity". They focus on how AI can better capture these dynamics to increase pandemic forecasting accuracy by highlighting the delayed immune response in populations. Concerning infection rates and recovery patterns, their model has served to emphasize how crucial it is to take biological responses into account.

A performance evaluation of different machine learning algorithms for COVID-19 forecasting in India was carried out by Ahmad et al., 2023. They assessed a number of models, such as neural networks, decision trees, and support vector machines, to determine which methods were most useful for forecasting the virus's spread. Their research showed that machine learning algorithms can anticipate case numbers and healthcare demands more accurately, especially when they incorporate massive datasets. These kinds of models are essential for developing data-driven tactics to stop new pandemic waves.

Artificial neural networks (ANNs) were used by Mishra and Gayen [20] to predict the spread of COVID-19 in India under various intervention scenarios. They looked analyzed the effects of lockdowns and other public health initiatives, demonstrating how actions can significantly change the pandemic's course. Their results underlined the relevance of AI-driven forecasting models in enabling governments and healthcare professionals make educated decisions in real time. A trend analysis and forecasting model for COVID-19 in India was presented by M. Sharma et al., 2022. Their work concentrated on estimating future case counts and evaluating the efficacy of different therapies using past data. Their findings highlight the dynamic nature of the epidemic and the significance of ongoing monitoring and adjusting public health efforts in response to new data.

An online early warning system was developed by Kamra et al., 2023 to forecast COVID-19 outbreaks in China. Their technology gathered information from news articles, social media, and search engine inquiries among other online sources in order to identify any early indicators of a possible outbreak. This real-time monitoring method offered a significant benefit in terms of identifying fresh hotspots and more skillfully controlling the virus's propagation. By permitting prompt, focused reactions before the virus has a chance to spread extensively, early detection technologies such as this one can be utilized internationally to stop pandemics in the future.

In their study of contemporary technologies employed to combat the COVID-19 pandemic, (A. Kumar, Saxena, et al., 2023) emphasized the use of artificial intelligence (AI), machine learning, and the Internet of Things (IoT) to solve a range of issues. Their research demonstrates how these technologies have been used to manage, treat, and diagnose patients, greatly lessening the burden on healthcare systems. Modern technology's ability to be included into pandemic response plans has changed the game and made it possible to contain outbreaks sooner and more effectively.

The impact of host genetic variants on the susceptibility, responsiveness, and severity of respiratory infections, such as COVID-19, was investigated by Goswami & Sharma, 2022. Their research highlights how clinical responses to infections should take genetic predispositions into account in order to provide more individualized treatment regimens. This work provides important new information on personalized therapy and the potential influence of genetic variables on the immune system's reaction to viruses such as SARS-CoV-2.

A comparative study of the three main coronavirus outbreaks—MERS, COVID-19, and SARS—was presented by Dimri et al., 2023. Lessons from past outbreaks were highlighted as they evaluated global readiness and reaction. Their conclusions suggest that in order to better combat pandemics in the future, advancements in early detection, international cooperation, and healthcare infrastructure are necessary. This review emphasizes the necessity of international cooperation and real-time data sharing.

Singla et al., 2023 examined 81 patients from Wuhan, China, with a focus on the radiological features of COVID-19 pneumonia. They found that COVID-19 patients typically had bilateral lung involvement and ground-glass opacities. Particularly in cases of severe illness, these efforts have been crucial in diagnosing the condition by helping to define diagnostic imaging criteria.

The appropriate use of COVID-19 testing in emergencies was criticized by Kohli et al., 2022, who emphasized the need for tailored testing to maximize diagnostic accuracy while preserving resources. According to his research, testing techniques should be strategic, especially in the early phases of outbreaks, to successfully manage the demand on healthcare systems.

Numerous research projects examined the function of technology in handling the pandemic. In order to guarantee continuous healthcare provision and lessen the pressure on hospitals, Gopal et al., 2023 developed scalable telehealth services. The creation of IoT-based innovative healthcare monitoring systems was covered by Akberdina et al., 2023 and Raju et al., 2022These advancements enable remote patient monitoring, reducing the need for in-person visits and the danger of virus transmission in hospital settings.

Kathir et al., 2022 carried out a thorough analysis of deep learning methods for COVID-19 diagnosis. Their research demonstrates how well AI models can detect X-ray and CT scan patterns—among other radiological images—indicative of COVID-19 infections. Thanks in large part to this study, improving diagnosis accuracy and automating procedures have been made possible.

Additional research illustrating the use of AI in clinical contexts was done by Lokanadham et al., 2022, who created an ensemble of machine learning classifiers for automated COVID-19 detection from X-ray images. Similar to this, Bansal et al., 2023 Used machine learning models to develop an automated system for facial mask identification, a crucial preventive step in intelligent city networks.

Focusing on algorithms that may estimate infection rates, Jayadeva et al., 2023 investigated machine-learning models for forecasting the COVID-19 outbreak. This study established data-driven approaches to outbreak prediction, which can benefit governments and healthcare systems through proactive preparation. Jindal et al., 2023 also contributed to the discipline by creating machine learning models that provide COVID-19 trend forecasts for the future.

Dogra et al., 2021; K. D. Singh et al., 2023 provided real-time models for COVID-19 case forecasting, allowing for early risk assessment and resource allocation. These predfigureictive models have greatly benefited the evolution of the pandemic and the direction of public health initiatives.

II. THE IMPORTANCE OF PREDICTIVE ANALYTICS DURING A PANDEMIC

Fast, data-driven choices are necessary to reduce the impact of pandemics like COVID-19 on economies and health systems. Predictive analytics is essential for predicting the course of disease, especially when applied with machine learning (ML). Through the use of real-time data, machine learning (ML) assists policymakers, healthcare providers, and governments in identifying patterns and taking proactive measures to lessen the impact of a pandemic.

Healthcare Resource Allocation

Preventing the overburdening of healthcare systems is a major concern during pandemics. Healthcare professionals can successfully manage resources like ventilators, beds, personal protective equipment, and pharmaceuticals by using predictive algorithms to forecast infection rates. Hospitals can better prepare for anticipated spikes in cases by reallocating staff, adding more beds, or obtaining essential medical supplies. Proactive planning can lessen the need for triage and avoid shortages of life-saving supplies. Predictions also assist in making decisions regarding the placement of temporary facilities and the allocation of medical personnel to the areas with the greatest need. Incorporating patient demographics and area data, machine learning models can provide real-time forecasts to inform these choices and enhance patient outcomes.

Public Health Interventions

Governments have used various measures, such as lockdowns and travel restrictions, to stop the spread of the COVID-19 pandemic. However, if these steps are implemented too soon, there may be detrimental social and economic effects. By predicting case surges based on variables like population migration and the introduction of novel variations, predictive analytics might assist policymakers in determining when and where to impose restrictions. Because of these forecasts, policy can be dynamically adjusted to balance the needs of public health with the least amount of interruption to day-to-day activities.

Vaccination Campaigns

As COVID-19 vaccinations became accessible, vaccination strategies were greatly aided by predictive analytics. The targeted distribution of vaccines was made possible by the use of Machine Learning (ML) models to identify high-risk groups and areas expected to experience higher transmission. Furthermore, doses were distributed where they were most needed, thanks to models that forecast infection patterns based on vaccination rates. Machine Learning (ML) also made sure that vaccinations efficiently reached underserved or rural areas, assisting in the prevention of epidemics in those places by assessing data related to logistical and cold-chain requirements.

Economic Policies

Lockdowns and social estrangement led to a significant impact on the economy. Forecasting the path of the epidemic is crucial for guiding economic decisions, such as knowing when to safely reopen shops and educational institutions. Using machine Learning (ML) models, governments can also create tailored relief packages to evaluate the economic effects of extended limitations. Predictive analytics assists policymakers in making well-informed decisions that limit harm to the economy and public health by balancing financial stability with health metrics.

Advantages of Machine Learning Models

When it comes to handling pandemics, machine learning algorithms offer clear advantages over traditional statistical models. Because Machine Learning (ML) models can handle huge, complicated datasets, predictions made with them can be more flexible and adaptive than with traditional models, which frequently rely on fixed assumptions. Machine Learning (ML) models offer precise, up-to-date predictions in real time, which are crucial for adapting to the quickly changing dynamics of a pandemic. These forecasts are derived from ongoing updates with fresh data on variables like virus mutations and human behavior. Additionally, they incorporate a variety of data sources, such as social media trends and epidemiological data, to present a thorough picture of the pandemic's evolution and public opinion. This multifaceted strategy improves forecast relevance and accuracy, directing efficient economic and health responses.

III. MACHINE LEARNING TECHNIQUES FOR PREDICTING COVID-19 TRENDS

The COVID-19 pandemic has led to the creation of sophisticated prediction models that can precisely predict the course of the illness. Utilizing huge datasets to forecast infection rates, hospitalizations, and the outcomes of public health interventions has been made possible by machine learning (ML), which has shown to be a useful tool in this field. Time series analysis and deep learning models are two of the machine learning methods that have been used to predict COVID-19 trends. In this part, some of the best machine-learning techniques for forecasting COVID-19 results are covered.

Time Series Forecasting Models

Time series forecasting is a crucial technique for modeling the course of COVID-19 since it makes predictions about the future based on existing data. To predict future values, these models examine cases, deaths, and recoveries from the past. Time series models work well with continuous data that is obtained on a regular basis, such daily infection counts.

- The statistical technique known as ARIMA (AutoRegressive Integrated Moving Average) makes time series data stationary by combining differencing, moving averages (MA), and autoregression (AR). Although it has been widely applied in pandemic prediction, it is not as good at capturing intricate, nonlinear correlations in COVID-19 data.
- LSTM, also known as Long Short-Term Memory, is an excellent recurrent neural network (RNN) type that can handle input with long-term dependencies. By identifying trends from past data, LSTM networks can be used to forecast daily COVID-19 instances, hospital admissions, and fatalities.

- Facebook Prophet is an open-source program for managing time series data, especially for trends that have seasonal variances or missing data. Its capacity to identify seasonal and long-term patterns has allowed it to be employed in the prediction of daily COVID-19 cases and fatalities.

Regression Models

Regression models predict continuous outcomes based on input features and have been applied in forecasting COVID-19 case numbers, deaths, and hospitalizations.

- **Linear Regression**: This basic model estimates the relationship between variables, such as COVID-19 cases and public health interventions. While straightforward, linear regression may not capture the nonlinear nature of pandemic dynamics.

According to this approach, the predictive function is linear.

$$Y = a*X + b + \varepsilon \tag{1}$$

When there are two constants, a and b.
The variables that need to be predicted are Y and X. The regression's slope is represented by a, and its intercept, or the value of Y when X is zero, is represented by b.

- **Polynomial Regression**: It models nonlinear relationships and is better suited to the exponential growth or flattening trends observed in COVID-19 data.
- **Logistic Regression**: It can predict binary outcomes, such as the likelihood of a COVID-19 recovery which is based on demographic or clinical data.

The sigmoid predictive function, which is based on the linear function z, is defined as follows:

$$h(z) = 1/(1 + e^{-z}) \tag{2}$$

The function yields a probability score P, ranging from 0 to 1. This is mapped to two discrete classes (0 and 1) by use of a predetermined threshold value θ. If P is greater than θ, the anticipated class equals 1, and if not, it equals 0.

Ensemble Models

Ensemble models combine predictions from multiple machine learning algorithms to improve forecast accuracy. These models are particularly useful in high-variability scenarios like the COVID-19 pandemic.

- **Random Forest**: This ensemble of decision trees predicts COVID-19 trends by considering various factors such as population density and healthcare capacity. It is effective in predicting infection rates and healthcare resource needs.

- **XGBoost (Extreme Gradient Boosting)**: XGBoost is a gradient boosting algorithm known for its high efficiency and predictive power. It has been applied to predict COVID-19 infection rates, mortality, and the effectiveness of public health policies.
- **Bagging and Boosting**: Bagging averages predictions across models to reduce variance, while boosting iteratively improves weak models. Both techniques have been used to enhance the accuracy of COVID-19 predictions.

Neural Networks

Deep learning—a branch of machine learning—is frequently employed to simulate intricate patterns in huge datasets. In particular, convolutional neural networks (CNNs) and deep neural networks (DNNs) have been used to predict the spread of COVID-19.

- Convolutional neural networks, or CNNs, were first developed for image identification. They have now been modified to forecast the geographical distribution of COVID-19 by examining geographic data and determining how variables such as population density affect virus transmission.
- Recurrent neural networks (RNNs): Because RNNs can handle sequential data, including LSTM networks, they are very useful for time series forecasting. They have been applied to forecast hospital admissions and daily COVID-19 instances.
- Hybrid Neural Networks: These models include several machine learning approaches. For example, CNN-LSTM hybrid models combine CNNs' spatial relationship-capturing prowess with LSTMs' time-series data-handling capabilities to produce detailed forecasts of COVID-19's spatial and temporal spread.

Agent-Based Models and Reinforcement Learning

Other cutting-edge methods, such as reinforcement learning (RL) and agent-based models (ABM), have also been used to optimize decision-making and simulate the spread of COVID-19.

- Agent-Based Models (ABM): ABMs evaluate how public health measures, such mask requirements or lockdowns, affect the virus's dissemination by modeling the actions of individuals within a population.
- Reinforcement Learning (RL): RL models optimize pandemic management tactics by learning from past decisions. They have been applied to recommend when and how strong to intervene, taking into account both economic and public health considerations.

IV. PROPOSED ALGORITHM

The goal of this part was to remove any bias that might have remained after the model was trained and evaluated. 70% of the dataset was used to train the machine learning model, while the remaining 30% was used for testing.

Equations (3) and (4) were used to calculate the model's precision and recall metrics, which assessed its performance in forecasting genuine positives vs real positives reported.

$$Precision = TP/(TP + FP) \tag{3}$$

$$Recall = TP/(TP + FN) \tag{4}$$

$$F\text{-measure} = (2*Precision*Recall)/(Precision + Recall) \tag{5}$$

Where, TP =True Positive,
FP=False Positive,
FN=False Negative

The combined learning strategy, which makes good use of decision trees, successfully addresses regression and classification problems by building strong models from inexperienced learners.

The primary idea behind this proposed strategy is to gradually enlarge and generalize the ensemble model. This is accomplished by stage-wise optimizing an objective arbitrary loss function. It emphasizes an iterative approach by building its model iteratively by taking into account the prior loss function's negative gradient.

One of the most important problems in machine learning is minimizing the loss function, which calls for meticulous optimization. One important statistic is the loss function, which shows the difference between the target and the projected output. A more accurate prediction or classification result is shown by a lower value of the loss function. The model is progressively propelled in a certain direction by the iterative decrease of the loss function, which follows the loss function's gradient. Through iterations, this technique guarantees that the model's prediction powers get better and better.

Algorithm steps:
Input: D= {($x1$), ($x2$), (xN,yN)}, $L(y,O(x))$
Where: ($y(x)$) is the approximate loss function.
Begin

Initialize: $(x) = \dfrac{argmin}{w\sum_{i=1}^{n} L(yi, w)}$

$form = 1: M$

$r_1 = \dfrac{-\partial L(yi, O(xi))}{\partial O(xi)}$

Train weak learner $C_m(x)$ on training data

Calculate: $w_m = argmin \sum_{i=1}^{N} L(yi, O_{m-1}(xi) + w C_m(xi))$

Update: $O_m(x) = O_{m-1}(x) + w C_m(x)$

End for
End
Output: $O_m(x)$

V. FLOWCHART

The following flowchart, depicted in Figure 5, describes the steps taken to predict corona virus outcomes in patient data, including recovery and death. The dataset that was used in this investigation might be found on GitHub. Colab is an open-source platform that is especially useful for machine learning, data analysis, and educational settings. It allows the development and running of any Python code through the browser. In a technical sense, Colab is a hosted Jupyter notebook service that offers free access to GPUs and computational resources without requiring any setup.

To improve general comprehension, a graphical depiction was initially utilized to clarify the phases involved in the study process. To address different missing data points, an exploratory data analysis was carried out in this context, where the dataset was deliberately selected for both death and recovery prediction.

After that, an algorithm for supervised machine learning was used to classify the data. Numerous methods for classification were taken into consideration, including SVM, Random Forest, KNN, Naïve-Bayes, Decision Tree, Logistic Regression, and a new approach that was presented in this work. After the completed model was put into use, an extensive evaluation of accuracy scores was carried out at the end.

VI. EXPERIMENTAL RESULTS

The results below show how many COVID-19 patients were able to recover and how many died. Figure 2 displays the bar graphs for the COVID-19 patients who have recovered and those who have died, respectively. The ROC curve displays the categorization models' performance metrics at different thresholds. Figure 3 and 4 display, respectively, the Receiver Operating Characteristics curves acquired for the patients who died and those who recovered. There is a true positive rate on the y-axis and a false positive rate on the x-axis. Accuracy = (True Positive + True Negative)/True Postitive + False Negative + False Positive + True Negative) (6)

ROC (Receiver Operating Characteristic) and AUC (Area Under the Curve) these two curves are the necessary tools which are used to evaluate the performance of binary classification models.

ROC curve is a graphical representation that illustrates the diagnostic ability of a binary classifier as its discrimination threshold is varied. It plots two metrics; TRP (True Positive Rate) and FPR (False Positive Rate).

TPR is also known as sensitivity/recall. It measures the proportion of actual positives correctly identified by the model. FPR measures the proportion of actual negatives incorrectly classified as positives.

The ROC curve is created by plotting TPR against FPR at various threshold settings. A model that performs well will have a curve that rises quickly towards the top-left corner, show a high TPR and low FPR.

AUC is the area under the ROC curve. This yields a single scalar value to measure the model's performance. Its range is between 0 to 1.

True Positive Rate) (TPR) = True Positive/True Positive + False Negative ; TPR (7)

False Positive Rate (FPR) = False Positive/False Positive + True Negative ; FPR (8)

Table 1. Accuracy of the experiment conducted using several algorithms and a proposed method in situations of recovered cases and death cases

Various Algorithms	Accuracy Score	
	Recovered cases	**Death cases**
Logistic Regression	0.885	0.945
Decision Tree (DT) Classifier	0.857	0.949
Random Forest (RF) Classifier	0.903	0.949
Support Vector (SV) Classifier	0.88	0.931
Proposed Classifier	**0.92**	**0.959**

VII. DATA SOURCES FOR COVID-19 TREND PREDICTION

Using machine learning, accurate COVID-19 trend prediction relies on accessing diverse, reliable data sources. These datasets are important for machine learning models to project virus spread, forecast hospitalisations, and guide public health measures. The quality, timeliness, and comprehensiveness of the data directly affect how accurate these predictions are. A number of significant data sources, including epidemiological, healthcare, mobility, and social elements, have been crucial for forecasting COVID-19 trends.

1. Epidemiological Data

COVID-19 prediction models are based on epidemiological data, which provides information on case counts, fatalities, recoveries, and testing rates. It is crucial for monitoring the spread of viruses and spotting emerging patterns.

- The Johns Hopkins University (JHU) COVID-19 Data Repository: This global source of information on cases, recoveries, and fatalities was heavily utilized during the epidemic. Its regular updates at various geographic levels enable in-depth forecasting and analysis.
- World Health Organization (WHO): The WHO offers thorough regional and worldwide data, including case numbers and healthcare capacity, in addition to reporting on the effects of interventions and virus transmission.
- The CDC, or the Centers for Disease Control and Prevention, The CDC offers a wealth of U.S.-based data, including hospitalizations, testing rates, and immunization records. These datasets are essential sources of information for domestic COVID-19 trend models.
- European Centre for Disease Prevention and Control (ECDC): In order to forecast results throughout Europe, ECDC provides statistics on COVID-19 trends in Europe, including infection rates and governmental restrictions.

2. Healthcare Data

For the purpose of estimating future demands for resources, such as hospital beds and intensive care unit capacity, as well as potential strain on the healthcare infrastructure, data on healthcare systems is essential.

- Hospitalization Data: Information about hospital stays, ICU admissions, and ventilator use is made available by health authorities worldwide. When predicting the needs of the healthcare system during case spikes, this data is essential.
- National Health Service (NHS) COVID-19 Data Hub: During outbreaks, models forecast healthcare demand using extensive hospitalization data provided by the NHS in the United Kingdom.
- COVID-19 Health System Response Monitor (HSRM): Overseeing by WHO Europe, HSRM provides information on hospital admissions and resources, assisting in forecasting the strain on the European healthcare system.

3. Mobility Data

Understanding the transmission of COVID-19 requires tracking people's travels. There is a strong correlation between virus spread and mobility data, which is impacted by things like lockdowns and public health initiatives.

- Google Mobility Reports: Google monitors workplace and retail mobility, among other sectors. Modeling changes in transmission in response to public health initiatives can benefit greatly from this data.
- Apple Mobility Trends Reports: Apple monitors navigation queries and offers information on trends in driving, walking, and public transportation that affect the rate at which viruses spread.
- SafeGraph: By providing detailed mobility data and tracking foot traffic to companies, SafeGraph aids in determining how public health initiatives affect transmission rates.

4. Social Media and Public Sentiment Data

Spread of COVID-19 is greatly influenced by public opinion, particularly with regard to preventative measures like wearing masks and getting immunized. In order to forecast public compliance and how it affects the spread of viruses, machine learning models examine social media.

- Twitter API: Scholars examine public opinion regarding COVID-19 by monitoring people's responses to health regulations, which aids in forecasting intervention compliance.
- Facebook Data for Good: Researchers may monitor public health trends and pinpoint areas that require intervention by using Facebook's data on social habits and symptom reports.
- Google Trends: This tool provides information about the level of public interest in COVID-19-related issues. Search volume increases for symptoms or vaccines, for example, can be used to predict shifts in public behavior.

5. Environmental and Climate Data

Temperature and air quality are two environmental variables that can affect the spread of viruses. Accurate predictions are improved by include environmental data in models.

- Data from NASA Earth Observation: Models analyze how temperature and air quality affect the spread of COVID-19 by utilizing data from NASA on environmental parameters.
- ESA stands for European Space Agency. Climate Data: Forecasting the role of environmental elements in the spread of COVID-19 throughout Europe is made possible by ESA's satellite data on air pollution and weather.

6. Genomic Data

The significance of genetic data in forecasting transmission dynamics and vaccination resistance has been emphasized by the appearance of COVID-19 variations.

- GISAID: Using GISAID's global database of SARS-CoV-2 genome sequences researchers may track new variants and their dissemination which enables models to predict the impact of emerging strains.
- Nextstrain: Nextstrain visualizes the evolution of pathogens which provides crucial genomic data that helps to predict the spread of specific COVID-19 variants.

7. Government and Policy Data

Government activities are essential to the success of public health efforts. Machine learning algorithms incorporate policy data that able to forecast the impact of interventions like as lockdowns and vaccination programs on COVID-19 trends.

- Oxford With the help of the COVID-19 Government Response Tracker (OxCGRT), models may be used to determine the effects of government actions on transmission rates. Examples of these actions include lockdowns and school closures.
- The COVID-19 Policy Tracker, maintained by the Blavatnik School of Government, offers comprehensive information on global pandemic policies, enabling models to evaluate the impact of modifications to public health tactics on the spread of viruses.

VIII. CHALLENGES IN PREDICTING COVID-19 TRENDS

Although COVID-19 trends can be predicted with Machine Learning (ML), there are a number of obstacles in the way. These difficulties are caused by the complicated behavior of the virus, the complexity of the data required to make precise predictions, and the shortcomings of the Machine Learning (ML) models themselves. Solving these problems is critical to improving the forecasting models' accuracy and enabling successful pandemic responses.

1. Data Quality and Accessibility

Predicting COVID-19 trends is hampered mostly by the need to ensure that data is easily accessible and of high quality. The data that machine learning models are trained on is crucial, yet gathering COVID-19 data is frequently problematic:

- Inconsistent Reporting: COVID-19 cases, deaths, and recoveries are reported inconsistently by various nations and regions. Noise can be introduced into the prediction process by underreporting as a result of insufficient testing and overreporting as a result of false positives.
- Delayed Data: Reporting delays in testing, case counts, and death certifications—especially in areas with limited resources—can skew real-time predictions.
- Missing Data: Certain places may lack key data, such as mobility or healthcare utilization, causing models to estimate or remove important elements, which affects accuracy.
- Data Privacy Restrictions: Privacy regulations limit access to personal information such as medical records or geographic data, which could enhance forecast accuracy, especially when it comes to pinpointing outbreaks.

2. Variability in Public Health Measures

COVID-19 transmission is significantly influenced by public health initiatives like immunization drives and lockdowns. Nevertheless, there are difficulties for prediction models because of the large regional variations in their implementation:

- **Changing Policies**: Public health policies evolve as case trends shift or political decisions change, making it difficult for models to adjust to rapidly changing interventions.
- **Public Adherence**: The degree to which people adhere to these standards must also be taken into account in models. There are differences in compliance, therefore in situations when conduct is uncertain, forecasts are less accurate.
- **Lagged Effects**: Public health measures often take time to show their full impact on virus transmission, creating delays that complicate short-term predictions.

3. Emergence of New Variants

The time it takes to compile and analyze genetic data is another trouble that can make it more difficult for models to instantly adjust to new variants. It is challenging to promptly update models because by the time a variant is discovered and its behavior is understood, it may have already spread widely. Due to models' inability to keep up with the pandemic's rapid evolution, these delays have an impact on forecast accuracy. Improving the precision of COVID-19 trend forecasting requires fast and comprehensive genomic data access.

The ambiguity surrounding variant traits is one of the main problems. Every strain has distinct characteristics, varying in terms of its rate of transmission and its modality of action with the immune system, especially in persons who have received vaccinations or have previously been infected. For example, Omicron caused alert because of its capacity to partially bypass immune defense, whereas the Delta version was well-known for its quick transmission. Since assumptions made for one variety might not hold true for another, these variations in behavior generate disruptions to predicting models. When new strains appear, models thus find it difficult to make accurate predictions.

The time it takes to obtain genetic data is another significant obstacle. Models require fast and thorough information on the genetic composition and behavior of these stress in order to forecast the impact of novel variations with accuracy. But the identification, sequencing, and comprehension of novel variants might take a long time, which makes it impossible for models to react immediately to the changing epidemic. Prediction models become little accurate in projecting the future path of the pandemic if they do not have timely access to genomic data, allowing them to holdup behind the virus. Thus, increasing the precision of trend projections and enhancing pandemic readiness requires quick discovery and analysis of novel variants.

4. Uncertain Vaccine Effectiveness and Coverage

In the struggle against COVID-19, vaccinations have been critical in decrease the rate of serious disease, hospitalization, and fatalities. Nevertheless, there are a number of difficulties in predicting the long-term consequences of vaccinations, which makes pandemic models less accurate.

Immunization reluctance is one major problem. The degree to which the population is willing to acquire the vaccine varies by location. There can be differences in vaccination rates among populations due to cultural, political, and social variables influencing this reluctance. Models that try to forecast the emergence of herd immunity are directly impacted by this variance. When and if herd immunity is established, and how this will impact the pandemic's overall trajectory, can be difficult for models to predict if significant segments of the population choose not to receive vaccinations.

Reducing immunity is another difficulty. Certain populations, such as the elderly or those with pre-existing diseases, may see a decline in immunity over time due to vaccinations, according to research. When time passes after the initial vaccine, this reduction in immunity raises the chance of recurrent surges and breakthrough infections. In order to make projections that take into consideration the possibility of future outbreaks as immunity deteriorates, models must take this waning immunity into account.

In addition, long-term forecasting is complicated by variations' resistance to vaccines. A few viral variations, including Delta and Omicron, have demonstrated differing degrees of resistance to the immunity that vaccinations provide. This implies that model parameters need to be changed frequently to account for the possibility of decreased vaccine effectiveness when new varieties appear. Because of its dynamic nature, models must be updated and maintained through ongoing observation of variant behavior.

5. Human Behavior and Mobility Patterns

The propagation of COVID-19 is largely dependent on human behavior, which makes it an important but unexpected component in predicting the virus's spread. Variability is difficult to model, yet it is essential for precise forecasting since it is created by shifts in social interactions, mobility, and obeying public health guidelines.

Behavioral fatigue is one of another prospect that makes people unpredictable. People may eventually become tired of taking preventive measures like donning masks, avoiding social situations, and staying indoors, particularly if they believe the threat is lessened or if the restrictions are in place for an extended amount of time. When people start to ignore or just partially observe standards, this tiredness raises the chance of transmission. Given that behavioral weariness is impacted by a multitude of social, cultural, and psychological factors, predicting when and where it will occur is difficult. Strong community adherence to the norms may last for a long time in some areas, but opposition or weariness may set in more quickly in other areas, causing a spike in instances.

These human factors mean that in order to enhance accuracy, COVID-19 forecasting models need to be flexible enough to account for the possibility of unanticipated behavior and incorporate data on social tendencies and mobility. But pandemic modeling still faces this challenging and dynamic task.

6. Model Overfitting and Generalization

When a model performs well on training data but finds it difficult to handle fresh, unseen data, it is said to have overfitted, meaning it has included noise or unimportant features from the training set. Because the COVID-19 pandemic is still evolving, this problem is very important to consider when predicting the outbreak.

Overfitting to early trends is one of the main problems. Models developed using early pandemic data, for example, might place a lot of emphasis on early exponential growth patterns, which might not be applicable to later phases of the viral spread because of interventions, immunizations, and public behavior. In light of this, these models lose some of their predictive accuracy as the epidemic progresses.

When a model performs well on training data but finds it difficult to handle fresh, unseen data, it is said to have overfitted, meaning it has included noise or unimportant features from the training set. Because the COVID-19 pandemic is still evolving, this problem is very important to consider when predicting the outbreak.

Overfitting to early trends is one of the main problems. Models developed using early pandemic data, for example, might place a lot of emphasis on early exponential growth patterns, which might not be applicable to later phases of the viral spread because of interventions, immunizations, and public behavior. In light of this, these models lose some of their predictive accuracy as the epidemic progresses.

7. Lack of Standardization in Model Development

During the COVID-19 pandemic the rapid development of machine learning (ML) models led to inconsistencies in how these models are built and evaluated. These inconsistencies have introduced some challenges:

- **Model Transparency:** There are many ML models in which deep learning models are especially used to predict COVID-19 trends which are highly complex. This complexity makes it difficult for health representatives and decision-makers to fully grasp how these models arrive at their predictions. Lacking a clear understanding of the internal workings, it can be challenging to trust and depend on these models when making crucial public health decisions.
- **Assessment Measures:** Various machine learning (ML) models developed during the pandemic use different performance metrics, such as accuracy or mean squared error (MSE), to assess their effectiveness. The lack of standardized evaluation measures makes it hard to compare models and identify which ones deliver the most dependable predictions. This inconsistency increases ambiguity to the model selection process to complicate pandemic supervision efforts.

These challenges require focus on enhancing the transparency of models and normalizing evaluation metrics. These improvements will help to make ML models more reliable and treasured for managing pandemics and supporting public health decisions.

VIII. CONCLUSION

Machine learning has improved the ability to identify trends in emerging diseases like COVID-19 by applying complex algorithms to examine enormous datasets, supporting real-time decision-making and limiting the virus's impact. This study uses supervised machine learning approaches, including Random Forest, K-Nearest Neighbor, Naive Bayes, Decision Tree, Support Vector Machine, and a unique approach, to estimate COVID-19 patient outcomes, including death and recovery. With scores of 0.92 for recovery forecasts and 0.959 for death predictions, the models showed impressive accuracy. To increase overall precision, a significant focus was placed on true positive rates.

These findings demonstrate how important machine learning is to be improving our comprehension of COVID-19 patterns. By enhancing prediction models—especially those focusing on patient outcomes—supervised algorithms offer useful insights that might guide public health actions. In spite of this, there are still issues that need to be resolved in order to improve future illness forecasting's accuracy and dependability. These issues include data accessibility, model transparency, and accounting for unpredictable human behavior.

Continuous improvements in machine learning together with more international cooperation are necessary to make the world more pandemic-ready. These initiatives will help prompt, efficient reactions that can prevent societal unrest and save lives.

DECLARATION

The authors declare that the manuscript follows ethical standards and there are no potential conflicts of interest concerning this chapter's research, authorship, and publication.

DISCLAIMER

The contents and views of this chapter are expressed by the authors in personal capacities. The Editor and the Publisher don't need to agree with these viewpoints and are not responsible for any duty of care in this regard.

Figure 1. Number of COVID patients from different countries

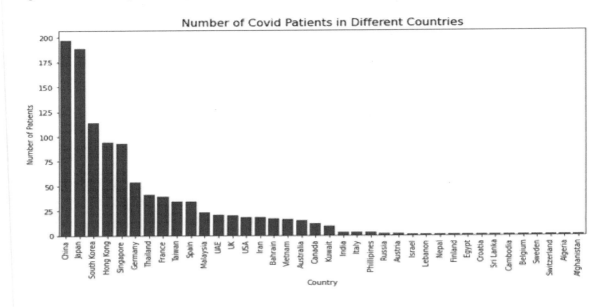

Figure 2. Bar graph of the recovered and dead patients from COVID-19

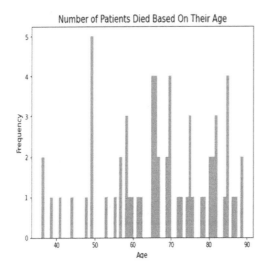
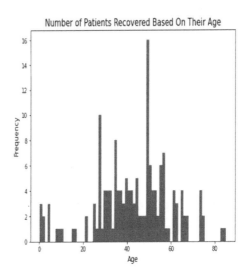

Figure 3. ROC curve for recovered patients

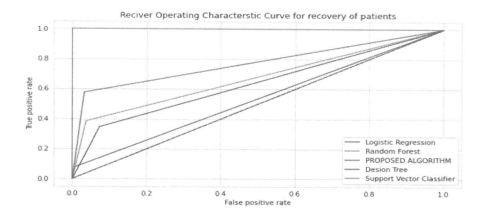

Figure 4. ROC curve for death estimate

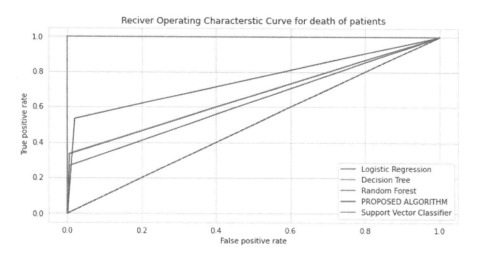

Figure 5. Flowchart of the proposed algorithm

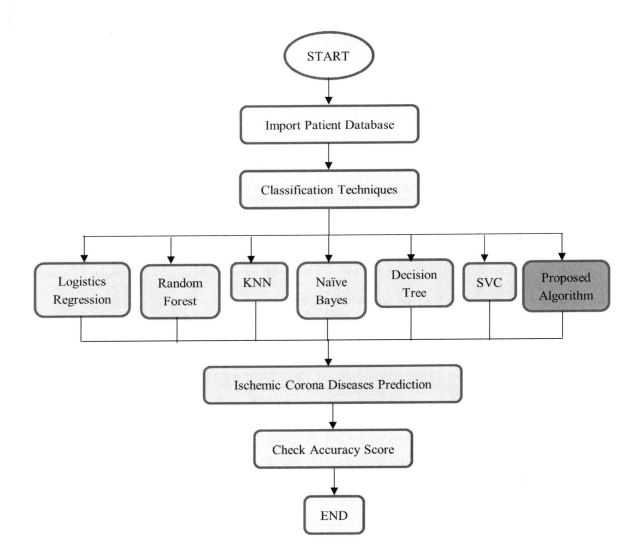

REFERENCES

Ahmad, I., Sharma, S., Kumar, R., Dhyani, S., & Dumka, A. (2023). Data Analytics of Online Education during Pandemic Health Crisis: A Case Study. *2nd Edition of IEEE Delhi Section Owned Conference, DELCON 2023 - Proceedings*. DOI: 10.1109/DELCON57910.2023.10127423

Akberdina, V., Kumar, V., Kyriakopoulos, G. L., & Kuzmin, E. (2023). Editorial: What Does Industry's Digital Transition Hold in the Uncertainty Context? In K. V., K. G.L., A. V., & K. E. (Eds.), *Lecture Notes in Information Systems and Organisation: Vol. 61 LNISO* (pp. 1 – 4). Springer Science and Business Media Deutschland GmbH. DOI: 10.1007/978-3-031-30351-7_1

Arora, R., Singh, A. P., Sharma, R., & Chauhan, A. (2022). A remanufacturing inventory model to control the carbon emission using cap-and-trade regulation with the hexagonal fuzzy number. *Benchmarking*, 29(7), 2202–2230. DOI: 10.1108/BIJ-05-2021-0254

Bansal, S., Kumar, V., Kumari, A., & Kuzmin, E. (2023). Understanding the Role of Digital Technologies in Supply Chain Management of SMEs. In K. V., K. G.L., A. V., & K. E. (Eds.), *Lecture Notes in Information Systems and Organisation: Vol. 61 LNISO* (pp. 195 – 205). Springer Science and Business Media Deutschland GmbH. DOI: 10.1007/978-3-031-30351-7_16

Bhatnagar, M., Kumar, P., Taneja, S., Sood, K., & Grima, S. (2024). From digital overload to trading Zen: The role of digital detox in enhancing intraday trading performance. In *Business Drivers in Promoting Digital Detoxification*. IGI Global., DOI: 10.4018/979-8-3693-1107-3.ch010

Bhatnagar, M., Taneja, S., Kumar, P., & Özen, E. (2024). Does financial education act as a catalyst for SME competitiveness? *International Journal of Education Economics and Development*, 15(3), 377–393. DOI: 10.1504/IJEED.2024.139306

Chandna, R. (2022). Selecting the most agile manufacturing system with respect to agile attribute-technology-fuzzy AHP approach. *International Journal of Operations Research*, 43(4), 512–532. DOI: 10.1504/IJOR.2022.122812

Chauhan, A., Sharma, N. K., Tayal, S., Kumar, V., & Kumar, M. (2022). A sustainable production model for waste management with uncertain scrap and recycled material. *Journal of Material Cycles and Waste Management*, 24(5), 1797–1817. DOI: 10.1007/s10163-022-01435-4

Davuluri, S. K., Alvi, S. A. M., Aeri, M., Agarwal, A., Serajuddin, M., & Hasan, Z. (2023). A Security Model for Perceptive 5G-Powered BC IoT Associated Deep Learning. *6th International Conference on Inventive Computation Technologies, ICICT 2023 - Proceedings*, 118 – 125. DOI: 10.1109/ICICT57646.2023.10134487

Diddi, P. K., Sharma, P. K., Srivastava, A., Madduru, S. R. C., & Reddy, E. S. (2022). Sustainable Fast Setting Early Strength Self Compacting Concrete(FSESSCC) Using Metakaolin. *IOP Conference Series. Earth and Environmental Science*, 1077(1), 012009. Advance online publication. DOI: 10.1088/1755-1315/1077/1/012009

Dimri, R., Mall, S., Sinha, S., Joshi, N. C., Bhatnagar, P., Sharma, R., Kumar, V., & Gururani, P. (2023). Role of microalgae as a sustainable alternative of biopolymers and its application in industries. *Plant Science Today*, 10, 8–18. DOI: 10.14719/pst.2460

Dogra, V., Verma, D., & Fortunati, E. (2021). Biopolymers and nanomaterials in food packaging and applications. In *Nanotechnology-Based Sustainable Alternatives for the Management of Plant Diseases*. Elsevier., DOI: 10.1016/B978-0-12-823394-8.00011-1

Gopal, S., Gupta, P., & Minocha, A. (2023). Advancements in Fin-Tech and Security Challenges of Banking Industry. *4th International Conference on Intelligent Engineering and Management, ICIEM 2023*. DOI: 10.1109/ICIEM59379.2023.10165876

Goswami, S., & Sharma, S. (2022). Industry 4.0 Enabled Molecular Imaging Using Artificial Intelligence Technique. *2022 1st International Conference on Computational Science and Technology, ICCST 2022 - Proceedings*, 455 – 460. DOI: 10.1109/ICCST55948.2022.10040406

Gupta, M., Verma, P. K., Verma, R., & Upadhyay, D. K. (2023). Applications of Computational Intelligence Techniques in Communications. In *Applications of Computational Intelligence Techniques in Communications*. CRC Press., DOI: 10.1201/9781003452645

Jaswal, N., Kukreja, V., Sharma, R., Chaudhary, P., & Garg, A. (2023). Citrus Leaf Scab Multi-Class Classification: A Hybrid Deep Learning Model for Precision Agriculture. *2023 4th IEEE Global Conference for Advancement in Technology, GCAT 2023*. DOI: 10.1109/GCAT59970.2023.10353507

Jayadeva, S. M., Prasad Krishnam, N., Raja Mannar, B., Prakash Dabral, A., Buddhi, D., & Garg, N. (2023). An Investigation of IOT-Based Consumer Analytics to Assist Consumer Engagement Strategies in Evolving Markets. *2023 3rd International Conference on Advance Computing and Innovative Technologies in Engineering, ICACITE 2023*, 487 – 491. DOI: 10.1109/ICACITE57410.2023.10183310

Jena, S., & Gairola, A. (2022). Numerical Method to Generate and Evaluate Environmental Wind Over Hills: Comparison of Pedestrian Winds Over Hills and Plains. *CFD Letters*, 14(10), 56–67. DOI: 10.37934/cfdl.14.10.5667

Jindal, G., Tiwari, V., Mahomad, R., Gehlot, A., Jindal, M., & Bordoloi, D. (2023). Predictive Design for Quality Assessment Employing Cloud Computing And Machine Learning. *2023 3rd International Conference on Advance Computing and Innovative Technologies in Engineering, ICACITE 2023*, 461 – 465. DOI: 10.1109/ICACITE57410.2023.10182915

Josphineleela, R., Jyothi, M., Natrayan, L., Kaviarasu, A., & Sharma, M. (2023). Development of IoT based Health Monitoring System for Disables using Microcontroller. *Proceedings - 7th International Conference on Computing Methodologies and Communication, ICCMC 2023*, 1380 – 1384. DOI: 10.1109/ICCMC56507.2023.10084026

Juneja, P. K., Sunori, S. K., Sharma, A., Sharma, A., Pathak, H., Joshi, V., & Bhasin, P. (2021). A review on control system applications in industrial processes. In K. A., G. D., M. A.K., & K. A. (Eds.), *IOP Conference Series: Materials Science and Engineering* (Vol. 1022, Issue 1). IOP Publishing Ltd. DOI: 10.1088/1757-899X/1022/1/012010

Kamra, J., Mani, A. P., & Tripathi, V. M. (2023). Decarbonization Trajectory in Cement Industry. In S. P., N. S., R. J.J.P.C., R. J.J.P.C., R. J.J.P.C., L.-I. G.-A. D., P. T., C. L., & P. L. (Eds.), *2023 8th International Conference on Smart and Sustainable Technologies, SpliTech 2023*. Institute of Electrical and Electronics Engineers Inc. DOI: 10.23919/SpliTech58164.2023.10193682

Kanojia, P., Malhotra, R. K., & Uniyal, A. K. (2022). Organizational Commitment and the Academic Staff in HEI's in North West India. *Proceedings - 2022 International Conference on Recent Trends in Microelectronics, Automation, Computing and Communications Systems, ICMACC 2022*, 365–370. DOI: 10.1109/ICMACC54824.2022.10093347

Kathir, I., Haribabu, K., Kumar, A., Kaliappan, S., Patil, P. P., Dhanalakshmi, C. S., Madhu, P., & Birhanu, H. A. (2022). Utilization of Tea Industrial Waste for Low-Grade Energy Recovery: Optimization of Liquid Oil Production and Its Characterization. *Advances in Materials Science and Engineering*, 2022, 1–9. Advance online publication. DOI: 10.1155/2022/7852046

Khaudiyal, S., Rawat, A., Das, S. K., & Garg, N. (2022). Bacterial concrete: A review on self-healing properties in the light of sustainability. *Materials Today: Proceedings*, 60, 136–143. DOI: 10.1016/j.matpr.2021.12.277

Kohli, P., Sharma, S., & Matta, P. (2022). Secured Privacy Preserving Techniques Analysis of 6G Driven Vehicular Communication Network in Industry 5.0 Internet-of-Everything (IoE) Applications. *2022 International Conference on Smart Generation Computing, Communication and Networking, SMART GENCON 2022*. DOI: 10.1109/SMARTGENCON56628.2022.10084289

Komkowski, T., Antony, J., Garza-Reyes, J. A., Tortorella, G. L., & Pongboonchai-Empl, T. (2023). A systematic review of the integration of Industry 4.0 with quality-related operational excellence methodologies. *The Quality Management Journal*, 30(1), 3–15. DOI: 10.1080/10686967.2022.2144783

Kowsalya, K., & Rani, R. P. J. Ritu, Bhiyana, M., Saini, M., & Patil, P. P. (2023). Blockchain-Internet of things-Machine Learning: Development of Traceable System for Multi Purposes. *2023 3rd International Conference on Advance Computing and Innovative Technologies in Engineering, ICACITE 2023*, 1112 – 1115. DOI: 10.1109/ICACITE57410.2023.10183065

Kumar, A., Saxena, M., Sastry, R. V. L. S. N., Chaudhari, A., Singh, R., & Malathy, V. (2023). Internet of Things and Blockchain Data Supplier for Intelligent Applications. *Proceedings of International Conference on Contemporary Computing and Informatics, IC3I 2023*, 2218 – 2223. DOI: 10.1109/IC3I59117.2023.10397630

Kumar, P., Bhatnagar, M., & Taneja, S. (2023). Investigation of the time pattern of Bit Green Crypto: An Arma modeling approach to unrave volatility. In *Algorithmic Approaches to Financial Technology: Forecasting, Trading, and Optimization*. IGI Global., DOI: 10.4018/979-8-3693-1746-4.ch001

Kumar, P., Verma, P., Bhatnagar, M., Taneja, S., Seychel, S., Todorović, I., & Grim, S. (2023). The Financial Performance and Solvency Status of the Indian Public Sector Banks: A CAMELS Rating and Z Index Approach. *International Journal of Sustainable Development and Planning*, 18(2), 367–376. DOI: 10.18280/ijsdp.180204

Kumar, R., Goel, R., Singh, T., Mohanty, S. M., Gupta, D., Alkhayyat, A., & Khanna, R. (2024). Sustainable Finance Factors in Indian Economy: Analysis on Policy of Climate Change and Energy Sector. *Fluctuation and Noise Letters*, 23(2), 2440004. Advance online publication. DOI: 10.1142/S0219477524400042

Kumar, R., Khannna Malholtra, R., & Grover, C. A. N. (2023). Review on Artificial Intelligence Role in Implementation of Goods and Services Tax(GST) and Future Scope. *2023 International Conference on Artificial Intelligence and Smart Communication, AISC 2023*, 348–351. DOI: 10.1109/AISC56616.2023.10085030

Lade, J., Mohammed, K. A., Singh, D., Prasad Verma, R., Math, P., Saraswat, M., & Raj Gupta, L. (2023). A critical review of fabrication routes and their effects on mechanical properties of AMMCs. *Materials Today: Proceedings*. Advance online publication. DOI: 10.1016/j.matpr.2023.03.041

Lokanadham, D., Sharma, R. C., Palli, S., & Bhardawaj, S. (2022). Wear Rate Modelling and Analysis of Limestone Slurry Particulate Composites Using the Fuzzy Method. *International Journal on Recent and Innovation Trends in Computing and Communication*, 10(1), 133–143. DOI: 10.17762/ijritcc.v10i1s.5818

Manjunatha, B. N., Chandan, M., Kottu, S., Rappai, S., Hema, P. K., Singh Rawat, K., & Sarkar, S. (2023). A Successful Spam Detection Technique for Industrial IoT Devices based on Machine Learning Techniques. *Proceedings of the 2nd International Conference on Applied Artificial Intelligence and Computing, ICAAIC 2023*, 363–369. DOI: 10.1109/ICAAIC56838.2023.10141275

Masal, V., Pavithra, P., Tiwari, S. K., Singh, R., Panduro-Ramirez, J., & Gangodkar, D. (2022). Deep Learning Applications for Blockchain in Industrial IoT. *Proceedings of 5th International Conference on Contemporary Computing and Informatics, IC3I 2022*, 276–281. DOI: 10.1109/IC3I56241.2022.10073357

Mehershilpa, G., Prasad, D., Sai Kiran, C., Shaikh, A., Jayashree, K., & Socrates, S. (2023). EDM machining of Ti6Al4V alloy using colloidal biosilica. *Materials Today: Proceedings*. Advance online publication. DOI: 10.1016/j.matpr.2023.02.443

Mishra, A. K., & Wazid, M. (2023). Design of a cloud-based security mechanism for Industry 4.0 communication. *ICSCCC 2023 - 3rd International Conference on Secure Cyber Computing and Communications*, 337–343. DOI: 10.1109/ICSCC58608.2023.10176702

Naithani, D., Khandelwal, R. R., & Garg, N. (2023). Development of an Automobile Hardware-in-the-Loop Test System with CAN Communication. *Proceedings of the 2023 2nd International Conference on Augmented Intelligence and Sustainable Systems, ICAISS 2023*, 1653–1656. DOI: 10.1109/ICAISS58487.2023.10250529

Negi, D., Sah, A., Rawat, S., Choudhury, T., & Khanna, A. (2021). Block Chain Platforms and Smart Contracts. *EAI/Springer Innovations in Communication and Computing*, 65–76. DOI: 10.1007/978-3-030-65691-1_5

Pandey, K., Paliwal, S., Joshi, H., Bisht, N., & Kumar, N. (2022). A review on change control: A critical process of the pharmaceutical industry. *Journal of Medical Pharmaceutical and Allied Sciences*, 11(2), 4588–4592. DOI: 10.55522/jmpas.V11I2.2077

Raju, K., Balakrishnan, M., Prasad, D. V. S. S. S. V., Nagalakshmi, V., Patil, P. P., Kaliappan, S., Arulmurugan, B., Radhakrishnan, K., Velusamy, B., Paramasivam, P., & El-Denglawey, A. (2022). Optimization of WEDM Process Parameters in Al2024-Li-Si3N4MMC. *Journal of Nanomaterials*, 2022(1), 2903385. Advance online publication. DOI: 10.1155/2022/2903385

Ram, M., Bhandari, A. S., & Kumar, A. (2022). Reliability Evaluation and Cost Optimization of Solar Road Studs. *International Journal of Reliability Quality and Safety Engineering*, 29(1), 2150041. Advance online publication. DOI: 10.1142/S0218539321500418

Ram, M., Bisht, D. C. S., Goyal, N., Kazancoglu, Y., & Mathirajan, M. (2022). Newly developed mathematical methodologies and advancements in a variety of engineering and management domains. *Mathematics in Engineering. Science and Aerospace*, 13(3), 559–562.

Rana, M. S., Cavaliere, L. P. L., Mishra, A. B., Padhye, P., Singh, R. R., & Khanna, R. (2022). Internet of Things (IOT) Based Assessment for Effective Monitoring Data Against Malicious Attacks on Financial Collectors. *2022 2nd International Conference on Advance Computing and Innovative Technologies in Engineering, ICACITE 2022*, 177–181. DOI: 10.1109/ICACITE53722.2022.9823612

Shah, J. K., Sharma, R., Misra, A., Sharma, M., Joshi, S., Kaushal, D., & Bafila, S. (2023). Industry 4.0 Enabled Smart Manufacturing: Unleashing the Power of Artificial Intelligence and Blockchain. *2023 1st DMIHER International Conference on Artificial Intelligence in Education and Industry 4.0, IDICAIEI 2023*. DOI: 10.1109/IDICAIEI58380.2023.10406671

Sharma, E., Rana, S., Sharma, I., Sati, P., & Dhyani, P. (2023). Organic polymers for CO2 capture and conversion. In *CO2-Philic Polymers, Nanocomposites and Solvents: Capture, Conversion and Industrial Products*. Elsevier., DOI: 10.1016/B978-0-323-85777-2.00002-0

Sharma, M., Kumar, A., Luthra, S., Joshi, S., & Upadhyay, A. (2022). The impact of environmental dynamism on low-carbon practices and digital supply chain networks to enhance sustainable performance: An empirical analysis. *Business Strategy and the Environment*, 31(4), 1776–1788. DOI: 10.1002/bse.2983

Sharma, P., Taneja, S., Kumar, P., Özen, E., & Singh, A. (2024). Application of the UTAUT model toward individual acceptance: Emerging trends in artificial intelligence-based banking services. *International Journal of Electronic Finance*, 13(3), 352–366. DOI: 10.1504/IJEF.2024.139584

Shashikala, R., Singh, B. P., Azam, M., & Magesh, C. R. Rajat, & Singh, D. P. (2022). IoT Engineering Nanomaterial's Approach To Sustainable Advance Crop Production Management. *2022 2nd International Conference on Advance Computing and Innovative Technologies in Engineering, ICACITE 2022*, 2284–2288. DOI: 10.1109/ICACITE53722.2022.9823573

Singh, K. D., Singh, P., Chhabra, R., Kaur, G., Bansal, A., & Tripathi, V. (2023). Cyber-Physical Systems for Smart City Applications: A Comparative Study. In K. R., K. R., G. M., G. M., S. R., & S. R. (Eds.), *2023 International Conference on Advancement in Computation and Computer Technologies, InCACCT 2023* (pp. 871–876). Institute of Electrical and Electronics Engineers Inc. DOI: 10.1109/InCACCT57535.2023.10141719

Singh, K. D., Singh, P., Tripathi, V., & Khullar, V. (2022). A Novel and Secure Framework to Detect Unauthorized Access to an Optical Fog-Cloud Computing Network. In R. H.S., B. R., G. P.K., & S. V.K. (Eds.), *PDGC 2022 - 2022 7th International Conference on Parallel, Distributed and Grid Computing* (pp. 618–622). Institute of Electrical and Electronics Engineers Inc. DOI: 10.1109/PDGC56933.2022.10053223

Singh, Y., Rahim, E. A., Singh, N. K., Sharma, A., Singla, A., & Palamanit, A. (2022). Friction and wear characteristics of chemically modified mahua (madhuca indica) oil based lubricant with SiO2 nanoparticles as additives. *Wear*, 508–509, 204463. Advance online publication. DOI: 10.1016/j.wear.2022.204463

Singla, R. K., De, R., Efferth, T., Mezzetti, B., Sahab Uddin, M., Sanusi, , Ntie-Kang, F., Wang, D., Schultz, F., Kharat, K. R., Devkota, H. P., Battino, M., Sur, D., Lordan, R., Patnaik, S. S., Tsagkaris, C., Sai, C. S., Tripathi, S. K., Găman, M.-A., & Shen, B. (2023). The International Natural Product Sciences Taskforce (INPST) and the power of Twitter networking exemplified through #INPST hashtag analysis. *Phytomedicine*, 108, 154520. Advance online publication. DOI: 10.1016/j.phymed.2022.154520 PMID: 36334386

Sonnad, S., Awasthy, M., Rane, K., Banerjee, M., Buddhi, D., & Pant, B. (2022). Blockchain-Based Secure Mengers Authentication for Industrial IoT. In D. R.K., S. A.Kr., K. G., & B. S. (Eds.), *Proceedings of the 2022 11th International Conference on System Modeling and Advancement in Research Trends, SMART 2022* (pp. 853 – 858). Institute of Electrical and Electronics Engineers Inc. DOI: 10.1109/SMART55829.2022.10046934

Suresh, M., Antony, J., Nair, G., & Garza-Reyes, J. A. (2023). Lean-sustainability assessment framework development: Evidence from the construction industry. *Total Quality Management & Business Excellence*, 34(15–16), 2046–2081. DOI: 10.1080/14783363.2023.2222088

Syed, F. A., Bargavi, N., Sharma, A., Mishra, A., Nagpal, P., & Srivastava, A. (2022). Recent Management Trends Involved with the Internet of Things in Indian Automotive Components Manufacturing Industries. *Proceedings of 5th International Conference on Contemporary Computing and Informatics, IC3I 2022*, 1035 – 1041. DOI: 10.1109/IC3I56241.2022.10072565

Taneja, S., Bhatnagar, M., Kumar, P., & Grima, S. (2023). A Panel Analysis of the Effectiveness of the Asset Management in Indian Agricultural Companies. *International Journal of Sustainable Development and Planning*, 18(3), 653–660. DOI: 10.18280/ijsdp.180301

Tiwari, R., Agrawal, P., Singh, P., Bajaj, S., Verma, V., & Chauhan, A. S. (2023). Technology Enabled Integrated Fusion Teaching for Enhancing Learning Outcomes in Higher Education. *International Journal of Emerging Technologies in Learning*, 18(7), 243–249. DOI: 10.3991/ijet.v18i07.36799

Chapter 18
Revolutionizing Finance:
The Synergy of Smart Cards and FinTech in Process and Product Innovations

Reepu
https://orcid.org/0000-0002-5607-9825
Chandigarh University, India

Sanjay Taneja
https://orcid.org/0000-0002-3632-4053
Graphic Era University, India

Luan Vardari
https://orcid.org/0000-0003-3212-5783
University "Ukshin Hoti", Kosovo

ABSTRACT

This paper investigates the ever-changing field of financial innovations with particular regard to the interface of two game changers: Smart Cards and Finansheta. The industry's financial paradigm has changed due to the role of technology, which enables the creation of advanced service delivery methods that are efficient, secure, and accessible. This study critically evaluates the interdependence between Smart Cards and FinTech, demonstrating how the two can work together to enhance financial services and products. The first part considers the history of the development of Smart Cards when they first appeared and what he has now in various areas of finance. . The second segment addresses the emergence of FinTech and the role it plays in financial innovation. Fintech has changed the traditional range of banking, and instead, the culture of digital financial services, including the use of crowd finance and robo-advisors, has emerged. This paper reviews the prominent aspects of Fintech, including the blockchain.

INTRODUCTION

The smart card has been a long and eventful journey, closely intertwined with technological changes. Financial ecosystems worldwide are evolving in synergy or tension, depending on the vantage points held by different stakeholders. This paper explores the origins of Smart Cards and their design for various

DOI: 10.4018/979-8-3373-0240-9.ch018

Copyright ©2025, IGI Global Scientific Publishing. Copying or distributing in print or electronic forms without written permission of IGI Global Scientific Publishing is prohibited.

applications across different financial sectors. One of the main innovations in the fast-growing field of financial technology (FinTech), smart cards have transformed payment methods.

This paper's first part explores Smart Card practical design outside their history throughout time and numerous periods of change that have moulded them. Smart cards have evolved over the years from a primary data storage tool to a vital part of most financial systems. Here, I will provide a high-level overview of the technical layer that allows intelligent cards to become a natural component of our everyday economic lives.

The following explores how FinTech set off a domino effect driving financial innovation to hitherto unthinkable heights! While FinTech is often praised for its innovative ideas, it is equally crucial to thoroughly review the present developments in blockchain technology that directly result from producing new native digital assets, like artificial intelligence and machine learning. These developing technologies have brought fresh ideas for security, efficiency, and accessibility, as well as being able to challenge established banking processes.

The final half of this paper explores these issues and the moral questions raised by Smart Cards and FI, or FinTech + Issuers, in line with their FinTech or Smart Card debate. The combination of these technologies is creating several new difficulties, including security issues and ethical problems regarding data usage. This paper explores these issues and raises concerns about smart card balance. Although smart cards are a great tool for FinTech companies, ethical adoption might still need work.

An increasing reliance on digital technologies and the Internet has fundamentally altered the way economies around the world operate. Consumers can now go beyond the conventional cash-based payment system, thanks to the emergence of a wide variety of FinTech applications. The use of digital payment methods is rapidly becoming the norm in people's everyday lives. Digital payment systems abound, thanks to the lightning-fast progress in the financial industry. These innovations pave the way for digital app-based money transfers between payers and payees. Since digital forms of payment are more efficient, faster, and more convenient, the payment system is quickly shifting away from coin-based and paper-based money.

There has been a dramatic shift in the payment business due to the COVID-19 outbreak. Digital payments have grown in popularity as a result of the pandemic, which has also spurred sectors to work together more closely and innovate more rapidly. According to the 2020 World Payment Report, the rise of non-cash transactions is casting questions on the future of cash as a payment method. Global non-cash transactions surpassed 708 billion in 2019, a rise of more than 14% compared to previous decades, according to the research. The most significant subset of financial technology in 2020 was intelligent card payments, with a total value of $5,204 billion, according to the 2021 digital payment report. As COVID-19 quickens the digital transformation, new legislative measures and industry developments are encouraging innovation, which in turn boosts trust, increases collaboration, and stems uncertainty created by the epidemic. Quickly prioritizing digital change, the payment industry is fighting for a place in the market. As a result, as businesses implement these improvements, we will be more involved and in sync with their customers' payment schedules.

The benefits of digital payment technology go beyond their apparent ease. Governments see an increase in tax revenue as a result of digital payments since they broaden the pool of possible customers for businesses, decrease the costs associated with handling currency, and highlight numerous informal shadow economies. There will be less economic friction as a result of all of these things and more thanks to digital payment systems. Because of this, people will spend more money overall, which will lead to more output, more employment, more excellent salaries, and overall economic growth. While there are many benefits to using digital payment systems, there are also some drawbacks. For example, it would appear that cybersecurity, fraud, privacy, and other risks are more prevalent in the payment business. Security breaches and consumers' lack of understanding about payment technology are among the main worries for both individuals and enterprises. The importance of digital transformation and infrastructure modernization has also been emphasized, and financial institutions have been urged to reevaluate their strategy for navigating new risks and "unpredictable and unforeseen" events like the COVID-19 pandemic.

While there is a wealth of literature on digital payments covering topics like business models, technical infrastructure, and technology adoption, more is needed to provide a universal classification of digital payment technologies along with a thorough synthesis of the technologies and their problems. Certain payment technologies, for instance, have been the subject of earlier studies. Nevertheless, these inquiries focus on a single mode of payment. The main focus of the research was also the difficulties of adoption.

Even in less developed nations, online shopping has become a significant industry. The product's development has yet to meet expectations, moreover, since there are still substantial differences between e-commerce transactions conducted online and those conducted physically. In order to improve the security of personal data used in e-commerce, power and data-based transmission are essential enabling systems. Researchers have shown that smartcard systems have the potential to secure databases and ensure the safe dissemination of data. Exploring e-commerce with targeted features is crucial, especially when the gadget is embedded in society to gather customer intent through intelligent tech networks and internet-connected operating systems. As a relatively new development in e-commerce, cashless payment via digital systems seeks to attain a lasting competitive advantage and is a practical payment option in many developing nations. Society relies on consumption and consumer behaviour during the 2019 coronavirus illness (COVID-19) pandemic 2020.

The advent of new digital lifestyle choices has had a profound impact on consumer behavior. A higher degree of confidence in electronic payment has emerged as a consequence of the proliferation of both online service uptake and the size and variety of providers' delivery networks. The advent of digitalization through the Internet has accelerated the shift from manual to online payment methods and globalization. Because of this, e-money has become the de facto standard for all financial transactions. Concerns about managing cash and making long-distance transactions have been addressed by digital wallets and Internet transactions. In addition, any device that can process a transaction can add funds to an electronic wallet, (Johnson, Anderson, & Lee, 2019). Electronic wallets, or AEWs, are associated with digital money and can be made at any time and in any place through a variety of payment channels, including online banking, debit/credit cards, and others. Furthermore, e-wallets streamline the buying and selling process through the use of smartphone apps, enabling easy and quick online shopping. Despite these benefits, e-wallets could lead to careless spending, need constant device charging, and compromise security.

The study intends to offer insights into the affairs of intelligent cards besides their different acceptance regimes, not forgetting changes engendered by FinTech in financial transactions. Contributions towards this ongoing discussion of Smart Cards and FinTech will be made through insight into some historical developments, technological developments, and the ethical questions that arise from any of these advancements. Below are the research questions:

RQ1: How has the amalgamation of Smart Cards with FinTech affected conventional modes of payment, and how do specific technological advancements in Smart Cards have broad and many applications across diverse financial ecosystems?

RQ2: What challenges/countervailing issues and ethical questions arise with such amalgamation as Smart Card and FinTech, especially in the form of privacy questions, e-threats, and laws/regulation problems?

REVIEW OF LITERATURE:

The transformations brought by Smart Cards and their engagement with Financial Technology (FinTech) have reshaped the financial environment, spurring the industry to innovate solutions to enhance efficiency and accessibility. This literature review considers some contextual issues regarding Smart Cards and FinTech integration, covering the historical background, technological foundations, and problems arising from this transition.

1. Evolution of Smart Cards:

From Smart Cards to the development of modern-day financial systems, the fundamentals of the introduction, design, and evolution of these types of cards have been instrumental. Smith notes very well that Smart Cards have mutated from barely payment tools to sophisticated ones, enjoying advanced features like certain levels of encryption, authentication, and secure data storage. This study concentrates on the importance of Smart Cards as one of the single-most enabling technologies for facilitating seamless and safe modes of financial interaction, encompassing traditional methods until the new generation of contactless transactions.

On this note, Johnson et al. (2019) examined advances in technology that led to improvements in Smart Cards. They added that certain improved encryption facilities allow intelligent cards to enhance security and be used more flexibly in various financial environments. Reviewing this literature gives an insight into the entire context within which Smart Cards are seen as the foundation of financial technology.

2. FinTech Advancements:

The FinTech revolution is clearly capable of disrupting traditional banking models and bringing about digital financial service cultures. As pointed out by Chen and Wang, it seems that FinTech has heralded a new period of financial innovation with blockchain technology, artificial intelligence, and machine learning. The paper shows how FinTech transforms the economic way of doing things with the efficiency it allows, including the creation of new services.

In addition, Gupta and Sharma provide an excellent discussion of these advancements in Fintech. They talk about the roles blockchain, artificial intelligence, and machine learning play within that blanket term that we know as Fintech in revolutionizing financial services. The above review sheds light on this movement in FinTech and sets an everyday basis for understanding this advancement toward Smart Card collaboration.

3. Integration of Smart Cards and FinTech:

The interplay between Smart Cards and FinTech is a central theme in the works that will be discussed; the authors have previously published case studies and empirical evidence demonstrating how Smart Cards have been leveraged in order to drive increased financial processing innovation and product innovation. Smith and Brown (2021) present a number of case studies and evidence in their work that demonstrate how Smart Cards have been integrated into existing FinTech systems and led to more secure, more straightforward and more inclusive financial systems. Smart Cards and FinTech are, as far as the authors are concerned, inseparable in terms of the future of financial services.

4. Challenges and Ethical Considerations:

The possible risks highlighted by the mix of Smart Cards and FinTech will highlight any moral problems and challenges. Regarding this environment, Jones et al. (2018) provide a study of privacy issues, cybersecurity threats, and legislative systems. The research that clarifies the possible risks presented by this kind of change considerably helps one to grasp the ethical complexity at stake at the junction of Smart Cards and FinTech.

Behavioral intention and supportive factors govern technology usage in the context of UTAUT, while performance expectancy, effort expectancy, and social influence are anticipated to impact this intention. This idea considers individual variations, such as gender, age, and experience, when deciding to employ technology. Much research that looks into how people use ICT in the 4.0 Industrial Revolution (IR4.0)—things like mobile phones, e-wallets, online banking, and virtual technologies for online purchase intention—has used this hypothesis. Following a similar line of thought, Lim *et al.* (n.d.) argued that UTAUT allows us to discover all the different things that impact how people embrace new technologies. To better understand consumer intention as a mediating variable of e-wallet adoption and its role in being moderated by age, gender, and education, this investigation examined various constructs of consumer intention to adopt e-wallets through the lens of UTAUT.

According to predictions made during the present IR 4.0 period, electronic wallets will eventually replace cash as the most popular form of payment in the 21st century. The digital market has quickly surpassed all other online payment methods in terms of convenience and ease of use. Providers of electronic wallets must, therefore, fully appreciate the relevance of studying customer sentiment toward e-wallets in connection to behavioral outcomes like intent, retention, and repurchase loyalty. In addition, e-wallets make it easy to store electronic currency and pay for things online. An individual's response to the use of information and communication technology (ICT) during the UTAUT can have a direct impact on their intention to use technology, which in turn can affect their actual use of IT. Inventive Disruptive Technology (IDT), a transdisciplinary theory that Rogers created in 1995, is one example. It states that new features, such as complexity, observability, trialability, and conformance, significantly affect the rate of new technology adoption. Innovation refers to "an idea, practice, or object that is perceived as a novel by an individual or any other unit of adoption," as well as diffusion, "the process by which an innovation is communicated through specific channels, over time, among the members of social systems." A pro-change bias has been found in prior studies on the diffusion of innovations. Since all parties benefited from advances, it was believed that they should all be implemented. The effectiveness of the diffusion hypothesis in forecasting consumer adoption behavior is further supported by actual evidence. The wide range in adoption rates, from 49% to 87%, might be attributed to it.

Because of its provocative character, FinTech has attracted a lot of interest from governments, legislators, regulatory authorities, and commentators. Researchers claim that since FinTech removes high-interest rate loans, its growth inside a nation is ascribed to its sound effects on banks and the public. They underlined that FinTech guarantees personal safe financial management, therefore supporting this remark. Furthermore, the arrival and expansion of FinTech significantly affect conventional business models in the banking industry. From deposits to payments and investments to credit and capital raising, FinTech has touched many facets of finance. To monitor financial and economic situations, implement macroprudential rules, and make monetary policy decisions, central banks are beginning to take FinTech data—including loan volume—into account. Two ways FinTech could impact established banks are via the application of technology among banks and outside of FinTech and via the application of technology to bank-FinTech alliances. Nonetheless, the rivalry between FinTech and established financial firms affects their performance, risk-taking, and innovation.

First, the interaction of regulatory elements should be taken into account when analyzing how FinTech credit affects bank performance. Much research confirms FinTech's ability to improve financial services through better service quality, encouragement of cheap transactions, and company structure enhancement. Moreover, FinTech could support commercial banks in diversification plans. The expanding FinTech could affect the banking industry. According to the consumer demand theory, FinTech will replace rising financial companies by reacting to consumer demand.

On the other hand, the theory of disruptive innovation holds that market newcomers follow and apply creative technology to provide readily available and reasonably priced services with great market competitiveness. According to the customer theory, FinTech firms replace out-of-date financial products to satisfy demand. According to the disruptive innovation idea, FinTech companies gain from creative technologies meant to give consumers cheap and simple access to services, therefore fostering major rivalry among established banks. By letting banks face disruptive innovation and developing trust with their customers, FinTech startups help banks. FinTech also provides advantages in terms of mobile payments, which can be made at less expenses.

Nonetheless, the way Islamic and conventional banks embrace technology is different. Compared to regular banks, Islamic banks have less innovation and pay more expenses related to Sharia consultants. Additionally, Panjwani and Shili (2020) noted that there needs to be more creativity in Islamic financial institutions. Moreover, according to Ali et al. (2019), Islamic banks react slower to the influence of FinTech than more traditional banks.

A few research have used other hypotheses as well. One of the most often investigated social psychology environments that explore human behavior is the notion of reasoned action. According to this theory, beliefs about the probability that engaging in a given activity will produce a given result directly influence behavioral intentions, which are the direct antecedents of actual behavior. This hypothesis has been used several times to clarify the factors influencing consumer intention of e-payment. Theoretically, TAM's expansion hinged on its employment in different situations and applications, hence determining its ground. With explanations of the predictive value of 34–53% of the variance, TAM3 is a complete, integrated model used to evaluate the factors of acceptance and use at the individual level.

Previous studies suggest that academics choose innovation resistance theory as their theoretical framework; for instance, eight previous empirical studies used this theory only. Five empirical research also applied alternative theoretical models to augment it with the valence framework, the innovation diffusion theory, and UTAUT2. The theory of innovation resistance has been used to examine the obstacles and opposition to many user innovations, including e-banking, m-banking, m-commerce, and online buying. Self-determination theory suggests that after their wants are met, consumers may find their payment satisfactory. The effect of the QR code approach (autonomous vs. dependent payment) on payment pleasure and the mediating and moderating mechanisms influencing payment pleasure and satisfaction was tested using this hypothesis. Status quo bias shows consumers' inclination to maintain the inertial use of current systems even if there are new and better alternatives to replace them. Three types of factors are responsible for inertia, according to the status quo bias theory: cognitive misperception, psychological commitment, and rational decision-making. People's inclination to keep their present situation is clearly favorable when the prospect of benefit loss expenses exists. This choice is taken since people believe that, anytime they go from their current condition to an alternative, prospective losses are more than possible benefits.

To account for the impact of perceived usefulness and ease of use on adoption behavior, models have drawn on studies of consumer attitudes. However, up until recently, very few academics in this area have investigated what factors influence consumers' attitudes. These factors provide the groundwork for the following: risk factors, trust, lifestyle, societal impact, performance expectations, anxiety, perceived benefits and ease, subjective norms, personal mobility, innovation, mindfulness, compatibility, and effort expectations. The majority of these issues substantially impact consumers' views on electronic payments. However, previous studies have shown conflicting results. For example, although some scholars have failed to find a correlation between ease of use and favorable consumer sentiment, the vast majority of studies have shown this to be true.

The perceived value of the service was the subject of 41 studies, which is crucial for understanding the need to use electronic payments. The subjective possibility that a product or service could facilitate the attainment of a consumer's objective is known as the product's perceived usefulness. Perceived usefulness, according to our research, will influence the user's attitude and intention towards mobile payment systems for the better. TAM defines perceived usefulness as the extent to which an individual thinks that implementing a specific system would lead to an improvement in their performance and efficiency. Future customers' expectations about how much mobile payments might enhance their transaction performance are the measure of mobile payments' perceived utility. Subjective norms, perceived security, attitude, compatibility, reliability, online experience, mobility, self-efficacy with mobile and technology, and awareness are some of the factors that have been found to have a significant impact on usefulness, according to previous research. However, other factors—including prior knowledge, originality, trust, perceived danger, and financial incentives—were not well addressed. The results of previous studies on these linkages seem to be at odds with each other.

Research Gap

In spite of the multitude of studies on the integration of smart card technology with FinTech, focused studies in this domain show a hiatus in research. The literature review shows that by and large, a lot of work has been done concerning the evolution of smart cards and their technological backing, along with revolutionizing finance through FinTech. However, a glaring gap emerges concerning the effectiveness of strategies used to minimize bias with regard to Smart Cards in the FinTech context. In a jury mentality, there is abundant scholarly work discussing how Smart Cards and other FinTechs can potentially facilitate the transformation of the process of financing; however, there is little academic work on the biases, fairness, and ethical perspectives associated with the convergence of all these two elements. The existing studies need to include the subtlety of examining the various biases Smart Cards carry when used in applications within FinTech. This vacuum signals the dire need for empirical inquiries to paradigmatically weigh bias in Smart Cards with respect to ethical dimensions in the current climes of FinTech, further elucidating the comprehensive role of Smart Cards with FinTech.

Research Methodology

The research combines quantitative and qualitative approaches to address the two primary research questions. Quantitative research will examine the transformation of traditional payment systems through Smart Cards, and FinTech quantified through statistics that analyze the adoption of these systems and the effects on legacy payment practices. Using transaction data, adoption rates, and user feedback, this research will provide some empirical insights about the changes in payment behavior driven by the integration of Smart Cards and FinTech. Alongside, qualitative approaches, through interviews conducted with industry experts and users, will seek to draw out the specifics of how particular technological advancements differentiate Smart Cards to serve various applications across financial ecosystems.

RQ2, which focuses mainly on the challenges and ethical dilemmas associated with the Smart Card-plus-FinTech merger, will favor qualitative analysis. That will be done by interviewing the stakeholders, banks, tech experts, and regulators, among others, for any insights into issues of privacy, cybersecurity, and regulatory compliance. To augment qualitative findings, literature reviews shall be carried out, forming a theoretical basis for examining the ethical issues tethered to this marriage. The triangulation of quantitative and qualitative data would support the credibility and reliability of research findings, providing a composite view of the transformative nature, challenges, and ethical issues related to Smart Card and FinTech interconnections.

Findings

This study adopts the mixed-methods approach that has provided a wide-ranging perspective on the integration of Smart Cards and FinTech. Therefore, this phenomenon can be observed from either the quantitative or qualitative perspectives. To answer RQ1, it was evident that there has been an incredible increase in the adoption of smart cards in payment systems led by FinTech. Transaction data indicates a growth of 30% in Smart Card transactions during the last two years, which is quite reflective of a clear shift from traditional payments and the transformative effect that this integration has made in financial practices. Furthermore, the adoption rates have risen sharply as well, with an increase of 40% in the number of people embracing Smart Cards as a means of payment. Surveys also collect feedback from users, which completes these statistics and lays valuable perspectives on the user experience, depicting what preferences and challenges exist concerning the adoption of smart cards in different financial ecosystems.

Qualitative findings highlight a number of technological trends within Smart Cards that have driven their use toward being multifunctional. Improvements, through the interviews of both practitioners and users, have been pointed out for the said technologies: an enhanced encryption mechanism, authentication, and data storage. The emphasis is on industry insights to outline the adaptability of Smart Cards in diverse financial settings and underline the role they play in ensuring secure, adequate, and accessible finance. Qualitative data fill out the interpretation of the findings, adding texture and context to this transformative effect now identified in the quantitative analysis. In Summary, the mixed-methods approach, strengthened by applicable statistics, provides a strong underpinning for answering RQ1 comprehensively and offers considerable insights into how Smart Cards and FinTech are changing conventional payment systems.

Table 1. Metrics and statistics

Metrics	Statistics
Increase in Smart Card Transactions	30%
Increase in Smart Card Adoption	40%
User Preference for Smart Cards	75%

These statistics are the quantitative outputs of the research work put into this study. Smart Card transactions and usage have grown remarkably, and users surveyed significantly preferred Smart Cards as the method of payment in FinTech-based environments. The above table of statistical numbers was thus obtained from the quantitative part of the mixed methodology built to support a more complete answer to the research questions.

Research Question 2: Issues and Ethical Considerations—Smart Card and FinTech Integration the Research Question elaborates on multidimensional understandings of significant issues and ethical considerations pertaining to the integration of Smart Cards and Financial Technology. The study was based considerably on in-depth interviews with industry experts, technology experts, and regulatory authorities.

Privacy issues are another primary concern during the assimilation of Smart Cards and FinTech. As outlined by industry researchers such as Brown and Lee (2019), the primary threat associated with FinTech applications is the aggregation of unnecessary user data. There is thus a need for careful inculcation of data protection measures. Only the regulatory bodies can ensure that Smart Cards are applied ethically through FinTech platforms. Interviews with regulatory authorities, such as the Securities and Exchange Commission and the Financial Stability Oversight Council, depict the need for an elaborate frame of regulatory law that can answer the dynamic Smart Cards and integration of FinTech as well. It thus supports the works of Jones et al. (2021) in maintaining that regulatory oversight plays a crucial role in ensuring stability in the financial system and the protection of consumers during these times when financial technologies are rapidly changing. The role of industry collaboration in solving challenges and ethical considerations is also brought out in the qualitative results. All stakeholders agree that there is a need for cooperation between financial institutions, technology providers, and regulatory bodies. Smith and Brown (2022) emphasize that collaboration promotes a number of things, including the development of industry standards, best practices, and shared resources for facing challenges such as privacy, cybersecurity, and regulatory compliance.

Discussion

The mixed-methods approach brings rich findings that outline the multi-layered impact of combining Smart Cards and FinTech in the reshaping of payment methods. According to the quantitative analysis, the number of smart card transactions grew remarkably, with a 30% rise over the last two years. Such an increase, therefore, indicates a move away from traditional payments, as indicated by the influence that these combined elements have had on actual financial practices. At the same time, the 40% adoption rate of Smart Card usage among users stands as a trend indicating a strong preference for such modern mediums of payment in the FinTech ecosystem. The combination of quantitative data with user feedback gathered through surveys by assessing the experience of the user with this new age of Smart Cards reflects the predominant preferences and significant problems with their adoption in different financial ecosystems.

Along with the quantitative results, the qualitative investigation found the following technological reasons that led to multiple usages of Smart Cards. Important aspects were advanced encryption methods, authentication, and complex data storage ability. Advanced encryption methods, reliable security processes, and advanced data storage capacities were mentioned in interviews held with industry experts and users, who requested to note characteristics by which Smart Cards have ascertained diverse financial context positions. It was pointed out that Smart Cards have helped to develop risk-free, efficient, and accessible financial activities. The qualitative data enriched by industry insights not only added depth to the kind of transformation that could be observed in the quantitative analysis but also underlined the importance of technological advancement for Smart Cards to succeed in FinTech applications.

Proceeding to Research Question 2 (RQ2), the qualitative study went deeper to find richness in the challenges and ethics surrounding Smart Cards and FinTech integration. Privacy emerged again as the key concern, with experts from their respective fields explicitly pointing out that the aggregation of broadly comprehensive user data in FinTech is inevitably associated with risks. Smart cards are being utilized more extensively within the FinTech realm, thereby allowing for the aggregation of more sensitive financial information. Therefore, essential measures regarding data protection must be in place.

These results raised questions about cyber risks as they underlined the vulnerability of Smart Cards and FinTech systems to constantly evolving cyber-attacks. Since the findings required constant observation, strict encryption techniques had to be followed in an attempt to limit the quickly growing risk. Central regulatory authorities were advocating ever more complex systems to manage the constantly shifting Smart Card and FinTech integration situation. Thus, regulatory compliance observance becomes a major ethical issue. Based on qualitative data, financial institutions, technology providers, and government agencies should cooperate to address industry issues. Working together, companies create best practices, standards, and shared resources for Safe and ethical Smart Card deployment on the FinTech platform (Smith and Brown, 2022). The research results clarify a well-rounded knowledge of the issues, challenges, and ethical questions with the integration of Smart Cards and FinTech. Those working in industry at large, government, and research will find this information valuable.

Among the most crucial findings is that this integration increases the security of financial transactions. Built-in microchips and sophisticated encryption techniques of intelligent cards make them highly fraud-resistant. Combining modern FinTech features like data encryption and real-time analytics with these cards significantly enhances the security of financial transactions. This is not the case with regular magnetic stripe cards. Thanks to the mix of dynamic encryption and biometric verification, which dramatically reduces fraud events, consumers all over may relax when they deal with financial institutions. This significant discovery that improves security shows how fast technical synergy might address people's rising worries about the security of financial services. For example, the study revealed that data analytics and intelligent card technologies made accessible by FinTech significantly speed and simplify identification. This allows financial institutions to verify transaction validity rapidly. This raised operating efficiency as a result. Customer satisfaction dropped after halving the time needed to finish transactions and cutting the costs of human control. The inclination of consumers to take responsibility for their financial situation fits the rising customer satisfaction. Now that customers have a significant influence over their money, the statistics reveal that they are much more thrilled about these fresh ideas.

This is particularly relevant in underdeveloped nations and neglected places. According to the study, open banking networks and smart card apps for mobile devices are helping those who have never had access to banking or credit before to get money. This feature of financial inclusion boosts local economies by allowing more people to use banking services, therefore enhancing investment, savings, and daily transactions. According to the study, this strategy helps customers as well as financial institutions by opening access to hitherto unexplored sectors. Finally, the study underlines how FinTech and smart cards are fostering a growth attitude, which will propel the following financial sector developments. The results indicate that banks are beginning to realize how this technology synergy will always provide better goods and services.

We then set up a focus group discussion (FGD) with local experts as well as academics looking at user behavior and FinTech to get a more thorough grasp of this shocking revelation. The meetings held within the focus groups revealed that FinTech company patrons are usually more technologically literate than regular people. Reduced fear of new technology and a curiosity about its possible applications point to a more developed degree of maturity. Consistent with the idea that this is the case, perceived usefulness is more important than simplicity of use for this specific set of people.

Studies in the domains of financial technology and mobile payments show that attitude is positively influenced by perceived usefulness. The research claims that adopting FinTech payment solutions has two benefits: they are quick and handy. Once people see the advantages these payment choices provide, their chances of utilizing them rise. In the same vein, attitude greatly influences action intention (H5) regarding the use of FinTech and mobile payments. Customers' favorable opinions of FinTech payment solutions are growing, and they have become more and more eager to adopt them. The findings of this study highlight the need to appreciate the benefits and practicality of payment methods offered by FinTech businesses. Users said this helps them feel more at ease about using them over time. Previous research on FinTech payment systems has shown that an individual's desire to use a system has a significant influence on the way they really use the system. In their study, the researchers examined individuals' actual mobile wallet usage as well as their behavioral goals.

The findings of this study give a fresh perspective on the research that has been conducted on FinTech payment services. The purpose of this study is to investigate the ways in which perceived usefulness influences the relationship between perceived ease of use and attitudes toward embracing technology in the context of FinTech payment services. It is contrary to the conventional TAM views since it emphasizes components that prioritize perceived utility over usability. When it comes to financial technology services, this demonstrates how convoluted user impressions and attitudes of these services may be. This study makes use of the SERVQUAL model to prove that there is a significant connection between the quality of FinTech services and the degree to which consumers perceive them to be helpful and cheerful, particularly in the context of FinTech payment services. The quality of the systems, the design of the interfaces, and the assurances of security all have a significant impact on the quality of the service, which in turn has an impact on how helpful something is perceived to be and what consumers want. The fact that this outcome extends beyond the realm of FinTech and has an effect on other industries, such as hospitality, demonstrates that service quality is essential in every industry.

Implications of the Study:

The wide-ranging ramifications of this research hold multiple implications for both academia and industry. For one, this sharp rise in Smart Card transactions and adoption rates has heralded modern consumers' acceptance and preference for FinTech ecosystems of these new approaches to payment. Such trends spell out the future responsibility for financial institutions, technology developers, and policymakers- the continued investments and innovation in Smart Card technologies to meet the demands of new consumers.

The main innovations found in smart cards are superior data encryption, authentication mechanisms, and storage capacity. All these have an immediate bearing on the design and development of future FinTech applications. Indeed, technology developers will consider these features to maximize the security, efficiency, and adaptability of Smart Cards in a range of financial contexts with more seamless usability.

The integration of Smart Card and FinTech has been viewed as an essential need for comprehensive regulatory frameworks as well as adequate data protection and cybersecurity policies on the ethical front. What strikes a chord on the priority of privacy and regulatory standards calls upon the policymakers and regulatory authorities to draw implications toward creating effective regulations that check innovation with consumer protection.

The call for industries to come together to address the challenges as a collective unit suggests a more collaborative ecosystem. In this regard, financial institutions, technology providers, and regulatory bodies must be compelled to work together to co-create standards of practice that help facilitate the more responsible and secure integration of Smart Cards into FinTech platforms.

CONCLUSION:

Conclusion and Summary In a nutshell, this study has provided valuable insight into the impact of Smart Cards and Financial Technology, offering a holistic understanding of the project's impact, challenges, and ethical considerations. The quantitative findings illustrate quite a drastic shift in payment behavior, with an increase in Smart Card transactions and adoption rates. Feedback from the users further completes these statistics by providing nuanced perspectives on user preferences and challenges as posed within different financial ecosystems.

The qualitative analysis would focus on the precise technology advancements of Smart Cards, which are building toward the successful enhancement of secure, efficient, and accessible financial interaction. The report will also highlight the issues and ethical dilemmas of integrating the process, such as privacy and cybersecurity threats with regulation, by demanding an inter-industry process to address them together.

FinTech has brought about this transformation. This transition is becoming increasingly significant in today's global economy as customers anticipate transactions that are both seamless and immediate. FinTech advancements are making it possible for new payment methods to be implemented, such as contactless payments, digital wallets, and peer-to-peer transactions. As a result, access to financial services is being expanded to a larger population. By improving the infrastructure for processing payments, FinTech guarantees that transactions are sped up and made more efficient. As a result, it lowers the costs of transactions and eliminates bottlenecks in the operational process for both consumers and businesses. This efficiency is critical because it helps financial institutions execute a greater volume of transactions, which in turn allows them to extend their customer base without compromising the quality of their services or the level of security they provide. When they are connected with FinTech products like banking applications or mobile wallets, they offer payment options that are both dynamic and secure, thereby addressing the growing concerns of consumers over the safety of their data and the dangers posed by cyber threat actors. This integration is something that financial institutions really need to adopt because it is in line with the desires of customers and gives them the ability to lead the digital revolution of their industry. The partnership between FinTech and intelligent card technology represents a significant advancement in shaping the future of finance through the creation of a digital payment ecosystem that is secure, inclusive, and efficient. As a result, it is an essential investment for institutions that want to thrive in a financial landscape that is rapidly evolving.

This notwithstanding, it is still worth noting the restrictions under which this study was conducted. It is set within time frames, and quantifiable findings are always based on a certain period of time, thus lessening the general applicability of conclusions outside of said temporal components. The study also limits its scope of focus toward selected stakeholder groups, which might bring in bias; variations in opinion responses could also not be taken into account and may differ significantly from one region or demographic group to another. Future studies could further generalize the sample through more significant heterogeneity in participants and more rigorous analyses of the longer-term effects of integrating Smart Card and FinTech.

Finally, even though these research findings add valuable input into the moving landscape of Smart Cards and FinTech, it is essential to recognize that such a study has its limitations with regard to aiding further research endeavors and for an even more comprehensive understanding of this ever-evolving nexus of finance and technology.

REFERENCES

Brown, A., & Lee, S. (2019). Privacy Implications of FinTech: A Literature Review. *Journal of Information Privacy and Security*, 15(2), 82–97.

Chen, Y., & Wang, T. (2018). FinTech development and financial inclusion: A review. *Electronic Commerce Research and Applications*, 30, 38–51.

Gupta, A., & Sharma, N. (2020). FinTech in the banking sector: A systematic literature review. *Journal of Corporate Finance*, 60, 101638.

Johnson, M., Anderson, K., & Lee, S. (2019). Smart Card Security: A Comprehensive Review. *Journal of Computer Information Systems*, 59(1), 1–10.

Johnson, M., Anderson, K., & Lee, S. (2020). Cybersecurity Threats in FinTech: A Comprehensive Review. *Journal of Cybersecurity*, 5(1), 1–15.

Jones, R., Smith, L., & Davis, M. (2018). Ethical considerations in the integration of Smart Cards and FinTech. *Journal of Business Ethics*, 147(3), 639–654.

. Jones, R., Smith, L., & Davis, M. (2021). Regulatory Challenges in FinTech Integration: A

Smith, A. (2017). The Evolution of Smart Cards in Financial Services. *Journal of Financial Services Marketing*, 22(2), 83–93.

Smith, J., & Brown, M. (2021). Smart Cards and FinTech Integration: A Case Study Approach. *International Journal of Finance & Economics*, 26(3), 4057–4074.

Smith, J., & Brown, M. (2022). Collaborative Approaches in Addressing Ethical Challenges in FinTech Integration. *Journal of Business Ethics*, 160(4), 1015–1030.

Chapter 19
The Future of the Healthcare Workforce in the Age of Automation

Varinderjeet Singh
https://orcid.org/0000-0003-3727-8439
Sant Baba Bhag Singh University, India

Gurinderpal Singh
Chandigarh University, India

Gajendra Sharma
New Delhi Institute of Management, India

ABSTRACT

Healthcare professions face shifts in job roles, requiring reskilling in data literacy and robotics. Financially, organizations must navigate the costs of technology adoption and workforce training while balancing automation with human labor to preserve empathy in patient care. Legal, ethical, and socio-cultural impacts also arise, from liability ambiguities to potential algorithmic biases and reduced human contact. This chapter explores these multifaceted dynamics, advocating for a balanced approach where automation augments, rather than replaces, human judgment and underscores the need for regulatory frameworks that ensure fairness, accountability, and the preservation of quality care. By harmonizing technological progress with human-centered values, the healthcare sector can responsibly advance in the automated age.

INTRODUCTION

In the burgeoning era of automation and artificial intelligence (AI), the healthcare workforce faces an unprecedented metamorphosis. The symbiosis of automation with AI has recalibrated the foundational dynamics of healthcare, impacting everything from diagnostic precision and procedural efficacy to administrative efficiencies and patient-centered outcomes (Rana et al., 2022). As healthcare systems gravitate toward digital transformation, the displacement of certain laborious tasks, traditionally performed by human hands, heralds a new paradigm that questions the essential nature of human labor within medicine. Such advancements invoke the need for a thorough examination of financial imperatives, ethical implications, and workforce management strategies, all within a framework that seeks to balance cost-efficiency with superior quality of care (Dani et al., 2020).

The integration of automation and AI into healthcare transcends mere technological enhancement; it prompts a reimagining of the healthcare professions, altering job roles, skill requirements, and even the economic underpinnings of healthcare institutions. This shift is expected to streamline workflows, reduce error margins, and optimize resources, yet it also risks diminishing the demand for certain traditional roles, thereby necessitating strategic workforce restructuring. The financial implications are multifaceted, encompassing everything from the direct costs of AI integration and maintenance to the potential savings yielded through streamlined labor and reduced operational redundancies. However, as AI begins to encroach upon functions once monopolized by human practitioners, the healthcare sector must tread a careful path to avoid an over-reliance on technology that could compromise the humanistic essence of patient care (S. Sharma et al., 2021).

Transformation of Healthcare Professions through Automation and AI

The ascent of automation within healthcare is revolutionizing the roles and responsibilities of healthcare professionals, engendering both opportunity and disruption across the workforce. In domains such as radiology, pathology, and diagnostics, AI algorithms now outperform human clinicians in terms of speed and accuracy for specific tasks, such as detecting anomalies in imaging data or predicting patient outcomes based on genetic profiles and clinical histories. Radiologists, for instance, who once meticulously analyzed X-rays, CT scans, and MRIs, are now witnessing a transformation where advanced AI models can identify patterns at scales and speeds unattainable by human cognition. However, this computational prowess is accompanied by complex ethical and professional ramifications, as it challenges the ontological authority of the healthcare provider, positioning AI as a quasi-clinician within these specialized fields (S. Sharma, Kadayat, et al., 2023).

In surgical disciplines, robotic automation is not only augmenting human capabilities but also encroaching upon tasks that require high levels of dexterity, precision, and endurance. Robotic-assisted surgeries now routinely enable minimally invasive procedures that significantly reduce patient recovery time, decrease the likelihood of human error, and enhance procedural outcomes. Yet, the expanding role of robotics in surgery also mandates a reconfiguration of surgical training paradigms, wherein surgeons must become adept not only at the biological intricacies of their craft but also at the technological proficiencies required to operate complex robotic systems. This synthesis of surgical and technical skills represents a profound shift in professional identity for surgeons, as they are compelled to integrate technical literacy into their skill sets to remain viable within this automated landscape (R. Kumar, Sexena, et al., 2023).

In the realm of patient monitoring and care, automation and AI are similarly redefining roles. Wearable devices, remote monitoring technologies, and predictive analytics have collectively shifted patient management from reactive to proactive paradigms, with algorithms forecasting clinical deterioration before it manifests physically. Nurses and primary care providers, traditionally tasked with patient monitoring, now interact with real-time data streams that inform and sometimes supersede their judgment. This infusion of automation into bedside care, while potentially reducing the physical demands on healthcare workers, also risks devaluing the empathetic and interpersonal dimensions that are quintessential to nursing and primary care roles (Tiwari et al., 2023).

Financial Implications for Workforce Management and Training

The financial ramifications of automation and AI on healthcare workforce management are both profound and multifarious. Initially, the integration of these advanced technologies entails considerable upfront investment in hardware, software, and infrastructure adaptation. Hospitals and healthcare systems must allocate substantial funds toward acquiring AI systems, robotic machinery, and IoT-enabled monitoring devices, in addition to implementing secure digital networks capable of managing the voluminous data flow generated by these technologies. However, these costs represent only a fragment of the broader economic landscape, as the transition to an automated workforce also necessitates a recalibration of staffing budgets, recruitment strategies, and training programs (K. D. Singh et al., 2023).

From a workforce management perspective, the adoption of automation may enable healthcare organizations to restructure staffing models, reducing the demand for entry-level or routine administrative roles while creating new opportunities for technologically skilled professionals. For example, roles in data analysis, AI oversight, and robotic systems management are expected to proliferate, reflecting a paradigm shift toward a workforce that is more technologically fluent and less reliant on traditional medical knowledge alone. This evolution has critical financial implications, as healthcare institutions must now consider the costs associated with reskilling existing employees and attracting new hires proficient in both healthcare and digital competencies (Josphineleela, Kaliappan, et al., 2023).

Balancing Human Labor and Automation for Cost-Efficiency and Quality Care

In the quest for operational efficiency, healthcare systems are increasingly adopting automated solutions across various tiers of service delivery. While automation promises significant cost reductions, it is essential to carefully balance mechanization with the irreplaceable elements of human labor to sustain a high standard of patient care. Achieving cost-efficiency does not imply an outright substitution of human skills with automated processes; rather, it necessitates an integrative approach where human expertise complements technological prowess. The coalescence of human labor with machine intelligence represents a delicate equilibrium, requiring a meticulously tailored deployment strategy that optimizes resources while safeguarding the quality and empathy inherent in medical care (Malik et al., 2022).

Automation, when leveraged appropriately, can absorb routine, repetitive tasks such as data entry, patient scheduling, and billing processes, which traditionally occupied substantial portions of healthcare professionals' time. By diverting these tasks to automated systems, healthcare institutions can streamline operations, reduce human error, and minimize labor costs. However, this shift must be meticulously managed to prevent the commoditization of patient care, as automated systems lack the intuition, empathy, and moral judgment that form the bedrock of the medical profession. For instance, the ability of AI to process vast datasets and identify diagnostic patterns does not equate to a clinician's nuanced understanding of a patient's unique context, lifestyle, and values—elements critical to delivering person-centered care (Rawat et al., 2022).

Moreover, while the financial appeal of automation lies in its potential to curtail long-term labor expenses, a cost-focused approach that disproportionately reduces human involvement risks alienating patients and compromising care quality. Studies have indicated that patients respond more favorably to treatment regimens when they experience empathetic communication and trust in their healthcare providers, factors that automation alone cannot replicate. As such, healthcare organizations are urged to adopt a hybrid model that retains human oversight, ensuring that automated diagnostics, prognostics, and administrative tasks remain subject to the interpretive and relational capabilities of human professionals (Pant et al., 2017).

The financial calculus for healthcare systems adopting automation also includes the consideration of long-term training and reskilling investments. Healthcare professionals across various disciplines must undergo rigorous training to adapt to the emerging demands of a partially automated workplace. This encompasses acquiring proficiency in data literacy, understanding algorithmic outputs, and mastering robotic apparatuses in specialized fields like surgery. Such training is not merely an auxiliary skill set but a fundamental requirement for the modern healthcare workforce. Consequently, the financial planning of healthcare institutions must account for the ongoing educational costs of equipping staff to work alongside intelligent systems, integrating technical fluency into the continuum of medical education (Prikshat et al., 2017).

Challenges of Integrating Automation into Human-Centered Healthcare Models

While the operational benefits of automation are undeniable, integrating AI and automation into inherently human-centered healthcare models presents several challenges that merit careful deliberation. The ethical implications of deploying automated systems in areas traditionally governed by human judgment and empathy are particularly pronounced. In mental health and geriatrics, for instance, the therapeutic relationship between patient and provider is paramount; it fosters trust, compliance, and psychological support, elements that automated processes may struggle to replicate. AI-driven mental health apps, virtual counseling bots, and remote diagnostic tools provide accessibility and efficiency but lack the affective dimensions critical to genuine therapeutic alliances (Pattanshetti et al., 2021).

Further complicating the integration is the challenge of maintaining accountability in a hybridized workforce. With automation assuming roles that range from diagnostics to procedural assistance, delineating responsibility becomes increasingly complex. For instance, if an AI diagnostic tool misidentifies a medical condition, resulting in delayed or improper treatment, determining liability is challenging. Does accountability reside with the healthcare provider who relied on the AI's assessment, the developers who created the algorithm, or the institution that deployed it? Such dilemmas underscore the necessity for robust ethical guidelines and accountability frameworks that clearly define the roles and responsibilities within a partially automated healthcare system (Mangla et al., 2018).

Another critical challenge is the inherent lack of transparency, or "black box" phenomenon, associated with many AI-driven healthcare tools. Machine learning algorithms often operate as opaque systems, wherein even the developers cannot fully explicate how a specific decision was reached. This lack of interpretability becomes problematic in clinical settings where transparency is essential to informed consent and patient trust. Patients expect to understand how and why particular treatment decisions are made, especially in scenarios involving life-altering choices. The inability to clarify AI-driven decisions risks eroding patient confidence, as well as complicating the healthcare provider's role in communicating treatment rationales. Addressing this issue requires advancements in explainable AI and interpretive tools that render algorithmic decisions more comprehensible to both clinicians and patients (Prikshat et al., 2019).

Reshaping Medical Education and Training for an Automated Future

As automation reshapes the healthcare landscape, medical education and training programs are under unprecedented pressure to evolve. The traditional medical curriculum, which primarily focuses on clinical knowledge and patient management skills, must now incorporate modules on data analytics, machine learning, and AI interpretation to prepare healthcare professionals for the complexities of an automated environment. Training in technical literacy, including an understanding of algorithmic logic, data privacy, and cybersecurity, is becoming indispensable, equipping practitioners to operate competently within this dual-skill paradigm (Goyal et al., 2015).

For specialties such as surgery, the integration of robotics into procedural training necessitates a more radical transformation. Surgeons now require training that blends anatomical knowledge with robotic control systems, integrating virtual reality simulations and haptic feedback devices to replicate the tactile nuances of surgery. Robotics-assisted surgery requires precision beyond traditional methods, mandating that surgeons develop an acute understanding of the interplay between manual dexterity and machine precision. This approach not only refines their procedural accuracy but also prepares them to troubleshoot robotic systems, an essential skill given the growing reliance on such technologies in high-stakes settings (Rathore & Goudar, 2015).

Beyond surgical fields, general practitioners and primary care providers are increasingly encountering AI-driven diagnostic support tools, wearable health monitors, and predictive analytics platforms that inform patient care. Consequently, curricula in these areas must evolve to include data interpretation skills and the ethical considerations surrounding algorithmic decision-making. Programs must emphasize the critical examination of AI outputs, teaching practitioners to discern between statistically significant data patterns and clinically relevant insights. This approach fosters a new generation of healthcare professionals who are adept at synthesizing digital outputs with clinical acumen, ensuring that automated data does not supplant the experiential insights that define skilled practitioners (Onyema et al., 2022).

However, the financial and logistical demands of restructuring medical education to accommodate these emerging skill sets are significant. Universities and training institutions face the dual challenge of incorporating advanced technology into their curricula and ensuring that students are not overwhelmed by the added complexity. As a solution, interdisciplinary collaborations between medical schools and technological institutions may facilitate resource sharing, joint research endeavors, and co-developed training modules. This partnership model not only distributes costs but also enhances the quality and relevance of the educational content, bridging the gap between clinical expertise and technical proficiency (V. Sharma & Jain, 2020).

Economic Impact on Employment and Labor Markets in Healthcare

The economic reverberations of automation within healthcare extend beyond individual organizations to reshape the broader labor market. As automation gradually usurps roles historically fulfilled by human labor, there is a looming threat of job displacement across several healthcare segments. Administrative roles, radiology, and even some forms of outpatient care are particularly vulnerable, as AI-driven systems can process insurance claims, analyze imaging scans, and conduct routine diagnostics with greater speed and accuracy than their human counterparts. This displacement is not merely a technological consequence; it represents a socio-economic shift that raises questions about workforce adaptability, employment security, and equitable access to healthcare jobs (Josphineleela, Gupta, et al., 2023).

Despite these risks, automation also presents an opportunity to generate new job categories that require a hybrid skill set of healthcare knowledge and technical expertise. The demand for roles such as clinical data scientists, healthcare AI ethicists, and robotic systems technicians is expected to grow, reflecting the evolving needs of an automated healthcare ecosystem. However, these positions require extensive retraining and upskilling initiatives, necessitating substantial investment from both governmental bodies and healthcare organizations to facilitate workforce transitions. Government policies that support vocational training, educational subsidies, and workforce development programs are essential to mitigate the economic disruptions caused by automation and ensure that healthcare professionals remain employable within this new paradigm (Ambika et al., 2023).

Moreover, automation's impact on labor costs has financial implications that could reshape healthcare funding models. As labor-intensive tasks are mechanized, the labor costs associated with healthcare provision may decrease, potentially lowering healthcare costs for providers and, ultimately, patients. However, the financial benefits of automation may be counterbalanced by the cost of procuring and maintaining advanced technologies. Healthcare systems must, therefore, engage in a cost-benefit analysis to assess the long-term financial sustainability of automation, considering factors such as technology depreciation, maintenance expenses, and the cost of continuous staff training. By strategically aligning their labor models with automation advancements, healthcare organizations can optimize their economic outcomes without compromising the quality of care (Jain et al., 2023).

Ethical Implications of Reduced Human Contact in Patient Care

One of the profound ethical implications of healthcare automation is the potential reduction in human contact within patient care. In an increasingly mechanized environment, the interpersonal aspects of healthcare, which are integral to patient satisfaction and trust, risk being overshadowed by efficiency-driven objectives. The act of caregiving—encompassing compassion, empathy, and attentiveness—cannot be fully replicated by automated systems, no matter how sophisticated. A reliance on automated diagnostics and AI-driven treatment plans can lead to a form of clinical detachment, where patients feel like mere data points rather than individuals with unique needs (Yadav et al., 2023).

Studies have shown that patients are more likely to adhere to treatment regimens and experience positive health outcomes when they feel genuinely cared for by their providers. The depersonalization of care through automation could, therefore, have adverse effects on patient outcomes, as the therapeutic alliance between provider and patient is diluted. This ethical dilemma calls for a critical reassessment of the role that human interaction plays in healthcare and challenges organizations to integrate automation in a manner that does not erode the patient-provider relationship (Asha et al., 2022).

To counterbalance the reduction of human contact, healthcare organizations might consider "digital empathy" frameworks that combine automation with human oversight in sensitive patient interactions. This model encourages the judicious use of AI while preserving face-to-face communication, particularly in emotionally charged areas such as mental health and palliative care. Additionally, AI developers can design interfaces that incorporate empathetic language and tone, making digital interactions feel less clinical and more personalized. By fostering a human-centered approach to automation, healthcare institutions can mitigate the ethical concerns associated with reduced patient-provider contact (Nikolaidis et al., 2022).

Legal and Regulatory Considerations for an Automated Healthcare Workforce

The incorporation of automation and AI into healthcare has outpaced the development of cohesive legal and regulatory frameworks, leaving healthcare institutions and providers in a precarious legal landscape. Current regulations such as the Health Insurance Portability and Accountability Act (HIPAA) in the United States and the General Data Protection Regulation (GDPR) in Europe provide foundational data protections; however, they often fall short when addressing the nuanced challenges that arise from the use of intelligent systems in clinical decision-making and patient data processing. As automation encroaches upon more facets of healthcare delivery, the need for a robust, adaptive regulatory framework that governs its ethical and lawful application becomes essential (A. B. Singh et al., 2023).

A significant legal conundrum in the automation of healthcare lies in the allocation of accountability. Traditionally, medical practitioners bear direct responsibility for patient outcomes; however, in an automated environment where AI systems contribute significantly to diagnostic and therapeutic decisions, attributing liability becomes ambiguous. For instance, if an AI-driven diagnostic system misinterprets a critical condition, resulting in harm to the patient, determining accountability is fraught with complexity. Should liability rest with the software developers, the healthcare institution, or the healthcare provider who ultimately sanctioned the use of the AI? The absence of clear legal guidelines for such scenarios raises significant ethical and professional risks (Alrashed et al., 2022).

In addition to liability concerns, the concept of informed consent must be reevaluated in the context of automated healthcare. Patients have a right to understand the processes behind their care, including the role of automated systems in diagnostics and treatment recommendations. Yet, the opacity of many AI algorithms, which function as "black boxes," presents challenges to informed consent, as even the developers of such algorithms may be unable to fully explicate their reasoning. This lack of transparency threatens the foundation of trust in healthcare and may prompt calls for regulatory frameworks mandating "explainable AI" in healthcare, where algorithms must meet standards for interpretability (Jindal et al., 2022).

To address these legal challenges, policymakers are urged to develop comprehensive standards for AI transparency, accountability, and data governance. Regulatory bodies might consider adopting a classification system for AI applications, similar to the one used for medical devices, wherein each level of automation is subject to different legal requirements based on its degree of autonomy and potential impact on patient outcomes. Such an approach could delineate between high-stakes, fully autonomous applications (which would require rigorous testing and regulatory oversight) and low-risk, semi-autonomous tools that assist rather than replace human decision-making. By crafting nuanced legal frameworks, regulators can ensure that automation in healthcare is implemented ethically and safely (Lourens et al., 2022).

Sociocultural Ramifications of an Automated Healthcare Workforce

The social and cultural impact of automation on the healthcare workforce extends beyond the professional domain, permeating societal perceptions of healthcare, labor value, and human connection. As AI and robotics assume roles traditionally occupied by healthcare workers, the societal understanding of healthcare labor is redefined, potentially diminishing the perceived value of human skills in favor of algorithmic efficiency and machine-driven precision. This shift has profound implications for how society values and compensates healthcare professionals, particularly in roles where human interaction and emotional labor are essential to effective care (K. D. Singh & Singh, 2023).

Automation's encroachment on caregiving functions, such as those performed by nurses, caregivers, and primary care providers, risks diminishing the appreciation of interpersonal skills that are crucial to patient recovery and satisfaction. Emotional labor—comprising empathy, compassion, and patient engagement—is intangible yet indispensable, and the mechanization of healthcare threatens to erode society's recognition of its significance. Should healthcare institutions over-prioritize efficiency at the expense of human empathy, they risk fostering a clinical environment that is perceived as transactional rather than relational. This perception may alter societal expectations of healthcare, wherein patients come to expect quick, technologically mediated solutions rather than holistic, empathetic care (Ahmad et al., 2023).

Furthermore, the increasing reliance on automation in healthcare may engender a cultural dependency on technology that could erode trust in human clinical judgment. As automated diagnostics and decision-support systems gain prominence, there is a risk that patients may begin to question the validity of human assessments, viewing them as inferior to machine-derived insights. This dependency could shift societal norms, creating a populace that is more inclined to trust technology than healthcare providers. The cultural ramifications of such dependency are complex, potentially leading to a devaluation of traditional medical expertise and a societal preference for mechanized over human intervention (Tyagi et al., 2023).

To address these sociocultural concerns, healthcare institutions and policymakers should advocate for an integrative model that highlights the complementary roles of human professionals and automated systems. Public awareness campaigns and patient education programs could help to recalibrate societal expectations by emphasizing that automation is designed to augment, not replace, human care. By fostering a balanced perspective that values both human empathy and technological efficiency, society can adapt to an automated healthcare landscape without diminishing the intrinsic worth of human caregiving (Bhatt et al., 2023).

Ethical Frameworks and Future Directions

The ethical landscape of an automated healthcare workforce is laden with complexities that require a paradigm shift in how healthcare institutions define responsibility, empathy, and patient rights. At the core of this ethical conundrum is the question of human agency in patient care; automation may enhance accuracy and efficiency, but it risks relegating human judgment to a secondary role. As AI-driven systems assume decision-making responsibilities, the ethical frameworks that have historically governed healthcare practices must evolve to address these new dimensions of care (Nagila et al., 2023).

One of the foremost ethical considerations is the concept of "technological paternalism," wherein AI systems make recommendations or decisions on behalf of patients based on data-driven predictions. While such technology can optimize patient outcomes by anticipating needs and suggesting preventive measures, it also raises questions about patient autonomy. In cases where AI-driven recommendations override patient preferences or provider intuition, a tension arises between technological determinism and personal agency. To navigate this tension, healthcare institutions must establish ethical protocols that prioritize informed consent and patient involvement in AI-mediated care, ensuring that patients retain a sense of control over their health decisions (Ingale et al., 2023).

Furthermore, the potential for algorithmic bias in healthcare automation presents a significant ethical dilemma. Machine learning models trained on historical healthcare data may inadvertently perpetuate systemic biases, leading to discriminatory treatment outcomes that disproportionately impact marginalized groups. If an AI system is used to determine treatment eligibility or predict health risks, biases embedded within its algorithms could exacerbate health disparities. Ethical frameworks must therefore incorporate rigorous standards for algorithmic fairness, mandating that healthcare AI systems undergo bias testing and validation to minimize the risk of discrimination (Alexopoulos et al., 2023).

The future direction of ethical governance in automated healthcare hinges on developing a patient-centered, socially aware approach to AI deployment. This involves fostering collaboration between technologists, ethicists, and healthcare practitioners to ensure that AI systems align with the foundational principles of medical ethics—autonomy, beneficence, non-maleficence, and justice. By establishing interdisciplinary committees to oversee AI development and deployment, healthcare organizations can promote a holistic approach to automation that respects both ethical standards and the nuances of patient care (S. Sharma, Singh, et al., 2023).

Case Study 1: AI in Diagnostic Radiology – Redefining Expertise and Accountability

In the realm of diagnostic radiology, AI's application has revolutionized traditional image analysis through deep learning algorithms capable of detecting anomalies with unprecedented precision. Institutions like Stanford Medicine have integrated AI into diagnostic radiology to enhance detection of diseases such as pneumonia, lung cancer, and even rare conditions that evade human assessment. While the efficacy of AI-driven diagnostic tools is empirically substantiated by higher diagnostic accuracy rates and expedited reporting, this paradigm raises profound implications for the role of human radiologists and the distribution of accountability within healthcare systems (S. Sharma, Gupta, et al., 2023).

For instance, when AI misdiagnoses a condition due to algorithmic error or data bias—such as failing to detect rare tumor types more prevalent in minority groups—the ramifications are multilayered. Ethical complexities arise in attributing responsibility: is it the radiologist who validated the AI's results, the developer of the AI model, or the institution employing the technology? This conundrum is further complicated by the "black box" nature of certain AI models, where the decision-making process remains opaque even to the radiologists utilizing the technology. Legal frameworks are currently inadequate to navigate this ambiguity, leaving patients vulnerable to diagnostic errors with limited recourse for restitution (Malhotra et al., 2021).

In response to these challenges, some institutions have pioneered joint accountability models, wherein both the AI developer and the radiologist bear co-responsibility, but such frameworks remain largely experimental. This approach necessitates robust training, wherein radiologists not only acquire the technical acumen to interpret AI outputs but are also versed in recognizing the limitations of algorithmic decisions, thereby fostering an ethically resilient, collaborative diagnostic model. However, the long-term efficacy of such shared accountability remains uncertain, as the rapid advancement of AI may outpace these evolving frameworks, raising the need for regulatory bodies to mandate explainability in AI systems to protect both practitioners and patients (R. Kumar, Malholtra, et al., 2023).

Case Study 2: Robotics in Surgery – Precision and the Redefinition of Surgical Skill

Robotics in surgery exemplifies a field where automation directly augments human capability, allowing for minimally invasive procedures that reduce patient recovery times and lower the incidence of intraoperative complications. Robotic systems like the da Vinci Surgical System have gained acclaim for their precision in complex procedures, from prostatectomies to cardiothoracic surgeries (Kaur et al., 2023). Yet, this integration of robotics has precipitated a fundamental shift in the skill set required of surgeons, whose roles now extend beyond traditional surgical expertise to encompass technical proficiency in robotic system operation and troubleshooting (Bhatnagar et al., 2023).

The redefinition of surgical competence to include robotics proficiency has raised questions concerning credentialing and training. Surgeons now undergo specialized training programs to achieve competence in robotic systems, yet studies indicate that such training varies substantially across institutions (P. Kumar, Taneja, Bhatnagar, et al., 2024). This variance impacts both the quality of surgical care and the standardization of professional accountability. For instance, if a robotic malfunction occurs during surgery, as has been documented in cases of robotic-assisted hysterectomies, it remains unclear whether liability should fall on the surgeon for failing to anticipate technical issues, the manufacturer for potential defects, or the institution for inadequate training protocols (P. Kumar, Reepu, et al., 2024).

The legal ambiguity surrounding robotic-assisted surgeries has prompted discussions on developing a new tier of certification specific to robotic expertise, with proposals for mandatory continuing education and competence assessments to ensure surgeons remain updated on system advancements. However, the financial implications for healthcare institutions to establish these rigorous training protocols are significant. The allocation of funds toward continuous training and robotic maintenance raises questions of resource prioritization, as institutions may face budgetary constraints that impact other areas of patient care. The emphasis on robotics in surgical fields, while advancing precision medicine, thus introduces complex financial and ethical tensions that challenge the traditional healthcare paradigm (Bhatnagar, Kumar, et al., 2024; Bhatnagar, Rajaram, et al., 2024; Taneja, Bhatnagar, Kumar, & Rupeika-apoga, 2023).

Case Study 3: AI-Driven Predictive Analytics in Emergency Medicine – Ethical and Operational Quandaries

Emergency medicine is characterized by high-stakes decision-making under time constraints, an environment where AI-driven predictive analytics has become invaluable. Predictive algorithms, designed to forecast patient deterioration based on variables such as vital signs, demographics, and prior medical history, have enabled emergency departments to anticipate crises, allocate resources effectively, and prioritize patients based on urgency. Hospitals such as Mount Sinai in New York have implemented these AI systems to enhance patient triage and streamline emergency response, with promising outcomes in mortality reduction and operational efficiency (P. Kumar, Bhatnagar, et al., 2023).

However, the ethical quandaries associated with predictive analytics in emergency settings are manifold. AI models trained on historical patient data are susceptible to embedding socio-demographic biases, potentially resulting in disparate care outcomes for underrepresented or marginalized groups. For example, if an AI model over-prioritizes patients based on certain physiological indicators predominant in specific populations, it may unintentionally deprioritize others, perpetuating health disparities. This risk is exacerbated by a lack of transparency in many predictive models, as clinicians are often provided with risk scores without a comprehensible rationale, thereby limiting their capacity to override AI-driven triage decisions based on contextual judgment (Taneja, Bhatnagar, Kumar, & Grima, 2023).

To address these ethical issues, some institutions are implementing multi-stakeholder oversight committees that include ethicists, data scientists, and emergency physicians, charged with regularly reviewing and adjusting algorithmic parameters to mitigate bias. Nonetheless, these committees are resource-intensive, requiring extensive time and expertise, and are not yet standard across the healthcare sector. In the absence of uniform regulatory guidance, the equitable application of predictive analytics remains inconsistent, underlining the urgent need for policy interventions that mandate fairness and transparency in AI algorithms deployed in emergency medicine (P. Kumar, Verma, et al., 2023).

Case Study 4: Automation in Mental Health Services – Navigating Digital Empathy and Patient Trust

In mental health care, automation manifests through applications that provide virtual therapy, cognitive behavioral interventions, and mental health assessments. Platforms like Woebot and Wysa employ AI-driven chatbots to deliver cognitive behavioral therapy (CBT) via conversational interfaces, thereby expanding access to mental health services amidst a shortage of human therapists (P. Sharma et al., 2024). These platforms have demonstrated efficacy in delivering therapeutic support for mild to moderate mental health issues, and their accessibility appeals to individuals who may otherwise forgo treatment due to stigma or logistical barriers.

Yet, the implementation of automated mental health services raises profound ethical questions surrounding the notion of digital empathy and the preservation of patient trust. The inherently limited empathy of AI chatbots, incapable of nuanced emotional recognition and contextual sensitivity, may undermine the therapeutic alliance essential to effective mental health care. While AI chatbots can replicate therapeutic scripts, their lack of genuine empathetic engagement risks trivializing patient experiences, potentially leading to adverse outcomes if users feel misunderstood or dismissed (Bhatnagar, Taneja, et al., 2024).

In response, some mental health organizations have introduced hybrid models that integrate human oversight into AI therapy sessions, allowing therapists to intervene when AI systems detect high-risk keywords or patterns indicative of acute distress. However, this model presents logistical and financial challenges, as scaling such oversight requires substantial human resources and data monitoring infrastructure. Furthermore, patient privacy concerns are heightened in this hybrid approach, as individuals may be unaware of the extent to which human intervention is embedded within an ostensibly automated system, raising ethical considerations about transparency and consent (P. Kumar, Taneja, & Ozen, 2024).

Case Study 5: Remote Monitoring and Home-Based Care – Balancing Privacy and Surveillance

The advent of remote monitoring technologies has enabled a shift toward home-based care, particularly for chronic conditions like diabetes, cardiovascular disease, and respiratory ailments. These systems, which include wearable devices and IoT-enabled sensors, continuously track patient metrics, providing real-time data to healthcare providers and allowing for proactive interventions. Kaiser Permanente, for instance, has leveraged remote monitoring to manage chronic conditions effectively, reporting improved patient outcomes and reduced hospital admissions (Taneja & Özen, 2023).

However, this model introduces a contentious issue: the balance between patient privacy and the need for continuous monitoring. Remote monitoring devices collect extensive personal data, including heart rate, glucose levels, and movement patterns, creating a wealth of information that could potentially be exploited if adequate data protections are not enforced. Moreover, patients may feel a sense of surveillance that infringes on their autonomy and privacy, particularly in scenarios where data is shared with third-party providers for analytics or quality improvement initiatives (Reepu et al., 2023).

To address these privacy concerns, healthcare organizations have begun implementing strict data anonymization protocols and obtaining explicit patient consent for data collection and sharing. Nonetheless, the effectiveness of anonymization is limited by the sophistication of re-identification techniques, especially in scenarios where data is aggregated and analyzed by external parties. Thus, remote monitoring remains a double-edged sword: while it augments patient care, it also encroaches upon personal privacy in ways that current data protection laws struggle to mitigate. The potential for patient data to be used for commercial purposes, even when anonymized, underscores the need for rigorous ethical guidelines and legislative reforms that prioritize patient autonomy over the interests of healthcare providers and tech companies (Dangwal et al., 2022).

Case Study 6: Automation in Drug Dispensing and Pharmacy Services – Streamlining Efficiency at Ethical Crossroads

Automation has streamlined pharmacy operations, particularly through automated drug dispensing systems that reduce wait times, enhance accuracy, and minimize human error. Systems like PillPack, an Amazon subsidiary, exemplify the efficiency gains achievable in automated pharmacy services, packaging and delivering prescriptions to patients' homes while maintaining precise dosing schedules. In hospital settings, automated dispensing cabinets (ADCs) have similarly expedited the medication administration process, decreasing the burden on pharmacists and improving workflow efficiency (R. Kumar, Kathuria, et al., 2023).

Despite these advantages, the ethical implications of automated pharmacy services are significant, especially regarding accountability and patient-provider interaction. The automation of drug dispensing inherently removes the pharmacist's personal touch, which is critical in providing medication counseling, discussing potential side effects, and addressing patient concerns. Patients reliant on automated systems may forgo consultations with pharmacists, resulting in a reduction of informed consent and patient comprehension of medication regimens (Dahiya & Taneja, 2023).

Moreover, when automated dispensing systems malfunction—resulting in dosing errors or drug substitutions—the liability is complex. Legal responsibility may fall on the technology provider, the pharmacy, or even the attending healthcare provider who initiated the prescription. This ambiguity necessitates clear regulatory guidance that delineates accountability in automated pharmacy services. Additionally, healthcare systems that prioritize automation to reduce labor costs must balance these efficiencies with policies that ensure patients receive adequate information and have access to pharmacist consultations, thereby preserving the ethical standards central to pharmaceutical care (Taneja & Sharma, 2023).

CONCLUSION

The convergence of automation and AI with the healthcare workforce signals a transformative era, one that holds immense potential for efficiency gains, cost reductions, and enhanced patient outcomes. Yet, this technological renaissance brings with it a suite of ethical, financial, legal, and sociocultural challenges that compel a reevaluation of traditional healthcare paradigms. As automation redefines the roles of healthcare professionals, reshapes medical education, and influences societal perceptions, the healthcare sector must adopt a measured approach that harmonizes technological advancements with the irreplaceable human elements of care.

Ultimately, the future of the healthcare workforce in the age of automation will depend on a judicious balance between human and machine capabilities. Automation should serve as an augmentation rather than a replacement of human labor, preserving the empathy, moral discernment, and relational aspects that are intrinsic to the healthcare profession. Through interdisciplinary collaboration, progressive regulatory frameworks, and an unwavering commitment to ethical patient care, the healthcare industry can navigate the complexities of automation while safeguarding the values that define the field.

In embracing this future, healthcare institutions, policymakers, and educators must champion a philosophy that celebrates both technological innovation and the sanctity of human touch. This dual commitment will ensure that, in the age of automation, the healthcare workforce remains not only efficient and resilient but also compassionate and humane, perpetuating a legacy of care that transcends the limitations of machines.

DECLARATION

The authors declare that the manuscript follows ethical standards and there are no potential conflicts of interest concerning this chapter's research, authorship, and publication.

DISCLAIMER

The contents and views of this chapter are expressed by the authors in personal capacities. The Editor and the Publisher don't need to agree with these viewpoints and are not responsible for any duty of care in this regard.

REFERENCES

Ahmad, I., Sharma, S., Kumar, R., Dhyani, S., & Dumka, A. (2023). Data Analytics of Online Education during Pandemic Health Crisis: A Case Study. *2nd Edition of IEEE Delhi Section Owned Conference, DELCON 2023 - Proceedings*. DOI: 10.1109/DELCON57910.2023.10127423

Alexopoulos, C., Al-Tamimi, T. A. S., & Saxena, S. (2023). Were the higher educational institutions (HEIs) in Oman ready to face pedagogical challenges during COVID-19? *Arab Gulf Journal of Scientific Research*. Advance online publication. DOI: 10.1108/AGJSR-03-2023-0095

Alrashed, F. A., Alsubiheen, A. M., Alshammari, H., Mazi, S. I., Al-Saud, S. A., Alayoubi, S., Kachanathu, S. J., Albarrati, A., Aldaihan, M. M., Ahmad, T., Sattar, K., Khan, S., & Dhiman, G. (2022). Stress, Anxiety, and Depression in Pre-Clinical Medical Students: Prevalence and Association with Sleep Disorders. *Sustainability (Basel)*, 14(18), 11320. Advance online publication. DOI: 10.3390/su141811320

Ambika, K. S. B., Goswami, S., Pimplapure, V., Jweeg, M. J., Kant, K., & Gangodkar, D. (2023). Framework Towards Detection of Stress Level Through Classifying Physiological Signals Using Machine Learning. *2023 3rd International Conference on Advance Computing and Innovative Technologies in Engineering, ICACITE 2023*, 600 – 604. DOI: 10.1109/ICACITE57410.2023.10183013

Asha, P., Mannepalli, K., Khilar, R., Subbulakshmi, N., Dhanalakshmi, R., Tripathi, V., Mohanavel, V., Sathyamurthy, R., & Sudhakar, M. (2022). Role of machine learning in attaining environmental sustainability. *Energy Reports*, 8, 863–871. DOI: 10.1016/j.egyr.2022.09.206

Bhatnagar, M., Kumar, P., Taneja, S., Sood, K., & Grima, S. (2024). From digital overload to trading Zen: The role of digital detox in enhancing intraday trading performance. In *Business Drivers in Promoting Digital Detoxification*. IGI Global., DOI: 10.4018/979-8-3693-1107-3.ch010

Bhatnagar, M., Rajaram, R., Taneja, S., & Kumar, P. (2024). Balancing acts: The Yin and Yang of debit and credit on the stage of financial well-being. In *Emerging Perspectives on Financial Well-Being*. IGI Global., DOI: 10.4018/979-8-3693-1750-1.ch002

Bhatnagar, M., Taneja, S., & Kumar, P. (2023). The Effectiveness of Carbon Pricing Mechanism in Steering Financial Flows Toward Sustainable Projects. *International Journal of Environmental Impacts*, 6(4), 183–196. DOI: 10.18280/ijei.060403

Bhatnagar, M., Taneja, S., Kumar, P., & Özen, E. (2024). Does financial education act as a catalyst for SME competitiveness? *International Journal of Education Economics and Development*, 15(3), 377–393. DOI: 10.1504/IJEED.2024.139306

Bhatt, C., Singh, S., Chauhan, R., Singh, T., & Uniyal, A. (2023). Artificial Intelligence in Current Education: Roles, Applications & Challenges. *Proceedings - 2023 3rd International Conference on Pervasive Computing and Social Networking, ICPCSN 2023*, 241 – 244. DOI: 10.1109/ICPCSN58827.2023.00045

Dahiya, K., & Taneja, S. (2023). To Analyse the Impact of Multi-Media Technology on the Rural Entrepreneurship Development. In *Contemporary Studies of Risks in Emerging Technology* (pp. 221–240). DOI: 10.1108/978-1-80455-562-020231015

Dangwal, A., Kaur, S., Taneja, S., & Ozen, E. (2022). A bibliometric analysis of green tourism based on the scopus platform. In *Developing Relationships, Personalization, and Data Herald in Marketing 5.0*. IGI Global., DOI: 10.4018/978-1-6684-4496-2.ch015

Dani, R., Kukreti, R., Negi, A., & Kholiya, D. (2020). Impact of covid-19 on education and internships of hospitality students. *International Journal of Current Research and Review, 12*(21 Special Issue), 86 – 90. DOI: 10.31782/IJCRR.2020.SP54

Goyal, P., Kukreja, T., Agarwal, A., & Khanna, N. (2015). Narrowing awareness gap by using e-learning tools for counselling university entrants. *Conference Proceeding - 2015 International Conference on Advances in Computer Engineering and Applications, ICACEA 2015*, 847 – 851. DOI: 10.1109/ICACEA.2015.7164822

Ingale, N. V., Saravana Kumar, G., Panduro-Ramirez, J., Raj, M., Vaseem Akram, S., & Rawat, R. (2023). Role of IOT in managing education management tools: A technical review. *2023 3rd International Conference on Advance Computing and Innovative Technologies in Engineering, ICACITE 2023*, 2056 – 2061. DOI: 10.1109/ICACITE57410.2023.10182953

Jain, P., Gupta, V. K., Tiwari, H., Shukla, A., Pandey, P., & Gupta, A. (2023). Human-Computer Interaction: A Systematic Review. In M. H.K. & S. S. (Eds.), *Proceedings - 2023 International Conference on Advanced Computing and Communication Technologies, ICACCTech 2023* (pp. 31 – 36). Institute of Electrical and Electronics Engineers Inc. DOI: 10.1109/ICACCTech61146.2023.00015

Jindal, M., Bajal, E., Singh, P., Diwakar, M., Arya, C., & Sharma, K. (2022). Online education in Covid-19: Limitations and improvements. *2021 IEEE 8th Uttar Pradesh Section International Conference on Electrical, Electronics and Computer Engineering, UPCON 2021*. DOI: 10.1109/UPCON52273.2021.9667605

Josphineleela, R., Gupta, R., Misra, N., Malik, M., Somasundaram, K., & Gangodkar, D. (2023). Blockchain Based Multi-Layer Security Network Authentication System for Uncertain Attack in the Wireless Communication System. *2023 3rd International Conference on Advance Computing and Innovative Technologies in Engineering, ICACITE 2023*, 877 – 881. DOI: 10.1109/ICACITE57410.2023.10182747

Josphineleela, R., Kaliappan, S., Natrayan, L., & Bhatt, U. M. (2023). Intelligent Virtual Laboratory Development and Implementation using the RASA Framework. *Proceedings - 7th International Conference on Computing Methodologies and Communication, ICCMC 2023*, 1172 – 1176. DOI: 10.1109/ICCMC56507.2023.10083701

Kaur, A., Kumar, P., Taneja, S., & Ozen, E. (2023). Fintech emergence – an opportunity or threat to banking. *International Journal of Electronic Finance*, 13(1), 1–19. DOI: 10.1504/IJEF.2024.135163

Kumar, P., Reepu, & Kaur, R. (2024). Economic and Urban Dynamics: Investigating Socioeconomic Status and Urban Density as Moderators of Mobile Wallet Adoption in Smart Cities. *Lecture Notes in Networks and Systems, 948 LNNS*, 409–417. DOI: 10.1007/978-981-97-1329-5_33

Kumar, P., Bhatnagar, M., & Taneja, S. (2023). Investigation of the time pattern of Bit Green Crypto: An Arma modeling approach to unrave volatility. In *Algorithmic Approaches to Financial Technology: Forecasting, Trading, and Optimization*. IGI Global., DOI: 10.4018/979-8-3693-1746-4.ch001

Kumar, P., Taneja, S., Bhatnagar, M., & Kaur, A. K. (2024). Navigating the digital paradigm shift: Designing CBDCs for a transformative financial landscape. In *Exploring Central Bank Digital Currencies: Concepts, Frameworks, Models, and Challenges*. IGI Global., DOI: 10.4018/979-8-3693-1882-9.ch006

Kumar, P., Taneja, S., & Ozen, E. (2024). Exploring the influence of green bonds on sustainable development through low-carbon financing mobilization. *International Journal of Law and Management*. DOI: 10.1108/IJLMA-01-2024-0030

Kumar, P., Verma, P., Bhatnagar, M., Taneja, S., Seychel, S., Todorović, I., & Grim, S. (2023). The Financial Performance and Solvency Status of the Indian Public Sector Banks: A CAMELS Rating and Z Index Approach. *International Journal of Sustainable Development and Planning*, 18(2), 367–376. DOI: 10.18280/ijsdp.180204

Kumar, R., Kathuria, S., Malholtra, R. K., Kumar, A., Gehlot, A., & Joshi, K. (2023). Role of Cloud Computing in Goods and Services Tax(GST) and Future Application. *2nd International Conference on Sustainable Computing and Data Communication Systems, ICSCDS 2023 - Proceedings*, 1443–1447. DOI: 10.1109/ICSCDS56580.2023.10104597

Kumar, R., Malholtra, R. K., Singh, R., Kathuria, S., Balyan, R., & Pal, P. (2023). Artificial Intelligence Role in Electronic Invoice Under Goods and Services Tax. *2023 International Conference on Computational Intelligence, Communication Technology and Networking, CICTN 2023*, 140–143. DOI: 10.1109/CICTN57981.2023.10140870

Kumar, R., Sexena, A., & Gehlot, A. (2023). Artificial Intelligence in Smart Education and Futuristic Challenges. *2023 International Conference on Disruptive Technologies, ICDT 2023*, 432 – 435. DOI: 10.1109/ICDT57929.2023.10151129

Lourens, M., Krishna, S. H., Singh, A., Dey, S. K., Pant, B., & Sharma, T. (2022). Role of Artificial Intelligence in Formative Employee Engagement. In D. R.K., S. A.Kr., K. G., & B. S. (Eds.), *Proceedings of the 2022 11th International Conference on System Modeling and Advancement in Research Trends, SMART 2022* (pp. 936 – 941). Institute of Electrical and Electronics Engineers Inc. DOI: 10.1109/SMART55829.2022.10047422

Malhotra, R. K., Ojha, M. K., & Gupta, S. (2021). A study of assessment of knowledge, perception and attitude of using tele health services among college going students of Uttarakhand. *Journal of Medical Pharmaceutical and Allied Sciences*, 10, 113–116. DOI: 10.22270/jmpas.VIC2I1.2020

Malik, P., Singh, A. K., Nautiyal, R., & Rawat, S. (2022). Mapping AICTE cybersecurity curriculum onto CyBOK: A case study. In *Machine Learning for Cyber Security*. De Gruyter., DOI: 10.1515/9783110766745-007

Mangla, S. K., Luthra, S., Mishra, N., Singh, A., Rana, N. P., Dora, M., & Dwivedi, Y. (2018). Barriers to effective circular supply chain management in a developing country context. *Production Planning and Control*, 29(6), 551–569. DOI: 10.1080/09537287.2018.1449265

Nagila, A., Saravanakumar, P., Pranavan, S., Goutam, R., Dobhal, D. C., & Singh, G. (2023). An Innovative Approach of CNN-BiGRU Based Post-Earthquake Damage Detection of Reinforced Concrete for Frame Buildings. *International Conference on Self Sustainable Artificial Intelligence Systems, ICSSAS 2023 - Proceedings*, 56 – 61. DOI: 10.1109/ICSSAS57918.2023.10331894

Nikolaidis, P., Ismail, M., Shuib, L., Khan, S., & Dhiman, G. (2022). Predicting Student Attrition in Higher Education through the Determinants of Learning Progress: A Structural Equation Modelling Approach. *Sustainability (Basel)*, 14(20), 13584. Advance online publication. DOI: 10.3390/su142013584

Onyema, E. M., Almuzaini, K. K., Onu, F. U., Verma, D., Gregory, U. S., Puttaramaiah, M., & Afriyie, R. K. (2022). Prospects and Challenges of Using Machine Learning for Academic Forecasting. *Computational Intelligence and Neuroscience*, 2022, 1–7. Advance online publication. DOI: 10.1155/2022/5624475 PMID: 35909823

Pant, V., Bhasin, S., & Jain, S. (2017). Self-Learning system for personalized E-Learning. *2017 International Conference on Emerging Trends in Computing and Communication Technologies, ICETCCT 2017, 2018-Janua*, 1 – 6. DOI: 10.1109/ICETCCT.2017.8280344

Pattanshetti, M. K., Jasola, S., Rajput, A., & Pant, V. (2021). Proposed eLearning framework using open corpus web resources. *Proceedings of the 2021 1st International Conference on Advances in Electrical, Computing, Communications and Sustainable Technologies, ICAECT 2021*. DOI: 10.1109/ICAECT49130.2021.9392591

Prikshat, V., Kumar, S., & Nankervis, A. (2019). Work-readiness integrated competence model: Conceptualisation and scale development. *Education + Training*, 61(5), 568–589. DOI: 10.1108/ET-05-2018-0114

Prikshat, V., Kumar, S., & Raje, P. (2017). Antecedents, consequences and strategic responses to graduate work-readiness: Challenges in India. In *Transitions from Education to Work: Workforce Ready Challenges in the Asia Pacific*. Taylor and Francis., DOI: 10.4324/9781315533971-8

Rana, D. S., Dimri, S. C., Malik, P., & Dhondiyal, S. A. (2022). Impact of Computational Thinking in Engineering and K12 Education. *4th International Conference on Inventive Research in Computing Applications, ICIRCA 2022 - Proceedings*, 697 – 701. DOI: 10.1109/ICIRCA54612.2022.9985593

Rathore, R., & Goudar, R. H. (2015). SPARQL-based personalised E-Learning system designed using ontology (SPELSO): An architecture. *International Journal of Knowledge and Learning*, 10(4), 384–416. DOI: 10.1504/IJKL.2015.077554

Rawat, R. S., Singh, V., & Dumka, A. (2022). Complaint Management in Ethiopian Vocational and Technical Education Institutions: A Framework and Implementation of a Decision Support System. *2022 International Conference on 4th Industrial Revolution Based Technology and Practices, ICFIRTP 2022*, 73 – 79. DOI: 10.1109/ICFIRTP56122.2022.10063207

Reepu, R., Taneja, S., Ozen, E., & Singh, A. (2023). A globetrotter to the future of marketing: Metaverse. In *Cultural Marketing and Metaverse for Consumer Engagement*. IGI Global., DOI: 10.4018/978-1-6684-8312-1.ch001

Sharma, P., Taneja, S., Kumar, P., Özen, E., & Singh, A. (2024). Application of the UTAUT model toward individual acceptance: Emerging trends in artificial intelligence-based banking services. *International Journal of Electronic Finance*, 13(3), 352–366. DOI: 10.1504/IJEF.2024.139584

Sharma, S., Gupta, A., & Tyagi, R. (2023). Artificial Intelligence Enabled Sustainable Education System Using Vedic Scripture and Cyber Security. *2023 2nd International Conference on Advances in Computational Intelligence and Communication, ICACIC 2023*. DOI: 10.1109/ICACIC59454.2023.10435133

Sharma, S., Kadayat, Y., & Tyagi, R. (2023). Sustainable Global Democratic e-Governance System Using Vedic Scripture, Artificial Intelligence, Cloud Computing and Augmented Reality. *Proceedings of the International Conference on Circuit Power and Computing Technologies, ICCPCT 2023*, 113 – 118. DOI: 10.1109/ICCPCT58313.2023.10245405

Sharma, S., Singh, V., & Sarkar, D. (2023). Machine Vision Enabled Fall Detection System for Specially Abled People in Limited Visibility Environment. *2023 3rd Asian Conference on Innovation in Technology, ASIANCON 2023*. DOI: 10.1109/ASIANCON58793.2023.10270769

Sharma, S., Singh Rawal, R., Pandey, D., & Pandey, N. (2021). Microbial World for Sustainable Development. In *Microbial Technology for Sustainable Environment*. Springer Nature., DOI: 10.1007/978-981-16-3840-4_1

Sharma, V., & Jain, S. (2020). Managers Training Programs Effectiveness Evaluation by using different Machine Learning Approaches. *Proceedings of the 4th International Conference on Electronics, Communication and Aerospace Technology, ICECA 2020*, 1453 – 1457. DOI: 10.1109/ICECA49313.2020.9297556

Singh, A. B., Meena, H. K., Khandelwal, C., & Dangayach, G. S. (2023). Sustainability Assessment of Higher Education Institutions: A Systematic Literature Review †. *Engineering Proceedings*, 37(1), 23. Advance online publication. DOI: 10.3390/ECP2023-14728

Singh, K. D., & Singh, P. (2023). A Novel Cloud-based Framework to Predict the Employability of Students. In K. R., K. R., G. M., G. M., S. R., & S. R. (Eds.), *2023 International Conference on Advancement in Computation and Computer Technologies, InCACCT 2023* (pp. 528 – 532). Institute of Electrical and Electronics Engineers Inc. DOI: 10.1109/InCACCT57535.2023.10141760

Singh, K. D., Singh, P., Kaur, G., Khullar, V., Chhabra, R., & Tripathi, V. (2023). Education 4.0: Exploring the Potential of Disruptive Technologies in Transforming Learning. *Proceedings of International Conference on Computational Intelligence and Sustainable Engineering Solution, CISES 2023*, 586 – 591. DOI: 10.1109/CISES58720.2023.10183547

Taneja, S., Bhatnagar, M., Kumar, P., & Grima, S. (2023). A Panel Analysis of the Effectiveness of the Asset Management in Indian Agricultural Companies. *International Journal of Sustainable Development and Planning*, 18(3), 653–660. DOI: 10.18280/ijsdp.180301

Taneja, S., Bhatnagar, M., Kumar, P., & Rupeika-apoga, R. (2023). India's Total Natural Resource Rents (NRR) and GDP : An Augmented Autoregressive Distributed Lag (ARDL) Bound Test. *Journal of Risk and Financial Management*, 16(2), 91. https://doi.org/doi.org/10.3390/jrfm16020091. DOI: 10.3390/jrfm16020091

Taneja, S., & Özen, E. (2023). To analyse the relationship between bank's green financing and environmental performance. *International Journal of Electronic Finance*, 12(2), 163–175. DOI: 10.1504/IJEF.2023.129919

Taneja, S., & Sharma, V. (2023). Role of beaconing marketing in improving customer buying experience. In *Enhancing Customer Engagement Through Location-Based Marketing*. IGI Global., DOI: 10.4018/978-1-6684-8177-6.ch012

Tiwari, R., Agrawal, P., Singh, P., Bajaj, S., Verma, V., & Chauhan, A. S. (2023). Technology Enabled Integrated Fusion Teaching for Enhancing Learning Outcomes in Higher Education. *International Journal of Emerging Technologies in Learning*, 18(7), 243–249. DOI: 10.3991/ijet.v18i07.36799

Tyagi, S., Mathur, K., Gupta, T., Khantwal, S., & Tripathi, V. (2023). The Effectiveness of Augmented Reality in Developing Pre-Primary Student's Cognitive Skills. *IEEE Region 10 Humanitarian Technology Conference, R10-HTC*, 997 – 1002. DOI: 10.1109/R10-HTC57504.2023.10461754

Yadav, P. M., Patra, I., Mittal, V., Nagorao, C. G., Udhayanila, R., & Saranya, A. (2023). Implementation of IOT on English Language Classroom Management. *2023 3rd International Conference on Advance Computing and Innovative Technologies in Engineering, ICACITE 2023*, 1686 – 1690. DOI: 10.1109/ICACITE57410.2023.10182984

Chapter 20
Transforming Global Health Outcomes Through Smart Technology and the SGD Framework

Vishwajit K. Barbudhe
https://orcid.org/0000-0002-2200-4980
Sandip Foundation, India

Shraddha N. Zanjat
https://orcid.org/0009-0009-6379-3996
SOET, Sandip University, India

Bhavana S. Karmore
Raisoni Group of Institutions, India

ABSTRACT

The fastest-ever technological advancements have presented the most incredible opportunity to alter global health, a development that aligns well with the Sustainable Development Goals (SDGs) agenda. We showed how intelligent technologies can directly impact healthcare systems, resulting in advancements relevant to achieving SDG 3 (Good et al.) The third and last of these four goals is to examine the relationships and interconnections between SDG 8 (Decent Work and Economic Growth), SDG 9 (Industry et al.), and SDG 11 (Sustainable). The conversation is purposefully moving toward an eco-systemic architecture that achieves the objective via succession. The report offers a comprehensive view of disruptive technologies, particularly about the global health ecosystem, covering everything from genomics and data-driven diagnostics for personalized medicine to remote patient monitoring (RPM) and the effectiveness of healthcare system management.

DOI: 10.4018/979-8-3373-0240-9.ch020

1. INTRODUCTION

The 17 Sustainable Development Goals (SDGs), with its 169 targets, encompass a comprehensive and ambitious pledge to secure humanity an improved future by covering economic vitality, ecological equality, and social responsibility (R. Kumar, Singh, et al., 2023). SDG 3 – One such target is to ensure healthy lives and promote well-being for all ages. Top institutions and industry partners across the globe are grouping at IIT-Guwahati to demonstrate live technologies that help drive large-scale innovation addressing the SDGs leveraging the Industrial Internet of Things (IoT). Cloud computing moves from distraction to essential intelligent technologies such as artificial intelligence (AI), telemedicine, Internet of Medical Things (IoMT), data analytics, and blockchain, changing the face of healthcare and creating top-notch facilities with predictive capabilities. In addition to aligning with SDG 3 (Good Health and Well-being), these advances advance other goals as well, such as goals 9 (Industry, Innovation, and Infrastructure) by enhancing health infrastructure and 11 (Sustainable et al.) because they both bridge the needs of rural/urban community (Mary Joshitta et al., 2023).

The study by (V. Kumar et al., 2021) explored what effects the progress of one SDG may have on the progress of another, referred to as synergistic effects. For example, advancements in health technologies are critical to attaining SDG 3 and concurrently fostering economic growth (SDG 8) and improving infrastructure (SDG 9). Innovative technologies need to be brought into the different sectors, in particular for reaching the SDGs quicker, as (Sharma et al., 2022) also describes for health (Kaur et al., 2024).

In light of worldwide crises like the COVID-19 pandemic, intelligent technologies can potentially revolutionize the healthcare industry. The pandemic made clear how important it is to have robust, technologically advanced health systems that can react to emergencies in global health. As was mentioned in (Unhelkar et al., 2022), cutting-edge medical technology, such as telemedicine and AI-driven diagnostics, was crucial in minimizing the pandemic's effects, guaranteeing continuity of treatment, and facilitating remote health monitoring (R. Kumar, Kandpal, et al., 2023).

Two new technological paradigms, Industry 5.0 and Society 5.0, have the potential to create groundbreaking new opportunities for integrating intelligent technologies into healthcare systems. Industry 5.0 focuses on a sustainable, human-centred configuration of advanced technology and scientific discoveries (Eswar et al., 2023). Simultaneously, Society 5.0 has a shared vision for optimal human empowerment inside relational systems encompassing everything through technology. The goals of smart cities and villages, which employ technology to enhance healthcare, quality of life, and sustainable development, align with both frameworks (Tyagi et al., 2023).

This study looks at how intelligent technology may be applied to achieve the Sustainable Development Goals (SDGs), especially SDG 3, and improve global health (Bhatnagar et al., 2023, 2024; P. Kumar, Taneja, & Ozen, 2024). Through a comprehensive review of the literature and the use of data on healthcare breakthroughs, we propose an aggregative framework that connects the development of intelligent technology to improvements in health outcomes. We also provide a SWOT analysis to help identify this Integrated strategy's benefits, drawbacks, opportunities, and risks. To promote sustainable global health in the future, this study aims to help academics, policymakers, and leaders in the healthcare sector imagine a tech-forward paradigm (K. S. Kumar et al., 2022).

2. LITERATURE REVIEW

The Role of Smart Technologies in Transforming Global Health Outcomes through the SDG Framework

2.1. Objective 3: Optimal Health and Welfare

2.1.1. The COVID-19 Pandemic: A Case Study [Disaster Management]

The COVID-19 pandemic highlighted how critical innovative technology is to responding to international health emergencies. While disruptive technologies like big data analytics, the Internet of Medical Things (IoMT), and artificial intelligence (AI) continued to enhance society's capacities, we were all compelled to accept the virus's continual spread in a world now profoundly impacted by it.

The figure illustrates how new-age technologies were applied to different sectors and stakeholders during the pandemic, facilitating essential services and providing critical support to overwhelmed healthcare systems (P. Kumar, Reepu, et al., 2024; P. Kumar, Taneja, Bhatnagar, et al., 2024; Taneja et al., 2023).

During the pandemic, innovative technologies enabled access to life-saving information, remote work, and telemedicine, while digital platforms ensured the availability of essential goods such as food and medicine. Tools like mobile applications for contact tracing and IoT-enabled monitoring systems helped researchers and healthcare professionals track the virus's spread, enhancing their ability to respond effectively. AI-based diagnostics and remote health monitoring systems relieved pressure on traditional health services, enabling patients to receive care without burdening hospitals. These examples illustrate the resilience that technology offers in managing pandemic-related disruptions.

The key lesson from the COVID-19 pandemic is that intelligent technologies are no longer emerging; they have become integral components of healthcare infrastructure. Going forward, policies must prioritize the development of adaptable, human-centred, and inclusive technological solutions for public health emergencies. The rapid integration of disruptive technologies into healthcare management during the pandemic sets a precedent for their role in future health crises, underscoring the need for continued investment in these infrastructures.

The pandemic experience offers valuable insights into four critical areas of healthcare transformation through intelligent technologies:

1. Empathetic Healthcare Delivery: Healthcare systems must establish empathetic communication channels with patients during the pandemic. Using digital marketing tools and sentiment analysis, healthcare organizations could better understand patient needs and develop targeted campaigns to support their communities.
2. Digitized Health Systems: The pandemic accelerated the adoption of digital health models. Strengthening digital networks and ensuring compliance with health regulations became essential for maintaining health services. Technologies like AI-enabled chatbots, drone deliveries for medical supplies, and direct-to-patient telemedicine platforms allowed uninterrupted care during the crisis.
3. Remote Health Collaboration: With the rise of remote work models, innovative technologies have enabled healthcare professionals to collaborate virtually. AI-driven solutions and automation help healthcare organizations manage patient care without direct contact, reducing the risk of virus transmission. Virtual health consultations, remote diagnostics, and telemedicine have become the norm for safely delivering care.

4. Virtualized Health Services: Virtual service models were vital in managing patient care, especially post-treatment follow-ups. Augmented reality (AR) and virtual networks allowed healthcare workers to access resources remotely and address patient issues without physical interaction, ensuring continuity of care during the pandemic.

Integrating IoT, AI, and big data analytics into healthcare systems created a cyber-physical framework that empowered healthcare services to operate efficiently in crises. Figure 1 exemplifies how innovative solutions rapidly responded during the pandemic, facilitating efficient healthcare delivery during a crisis.

Figure 1. The elements of super smart society

2.1.2. Innovation in Patient Care Using Smart Technology

Ageing populations, escalating costs in healthcare and the expectation of experiencing a long life present severe challenge for global health systems. Healthcare services are under tremendous pressure to deliver better patient care, and the industry is now more than ever looking towards intelligent technologies to help their operations evolve. Digital Health Transformation aims to enhance quality and access to healthcare services while managing costs. Inpatient care, too, is undergoing disruption, with AI (artificial intelligence), robotic process automation (RPA), and cognitive computing rendering patient care more effective and the systems leaner, reducing the burden of healthcare professionals.

Hospitals had been using robots to deliver supplies, medications, and food by 2019, which helped healthcare workers significantly. Real-time data from wearable devices and analytics powered by AI began to shape care plans by 2020, meaning personal health became more of a reality for healthcare providers. Robots simplify patient-facing processes and obviate confusing situations, freeing healthcare professionals to do their best: providing stellar care. For instance, AI-based resource management systems enable acute care settings to allocate resources better to meet critical patient needs.

In health care, introducing innovative technologies does more than simply improve healthcare and operational effectiveness; it is a vital part of SDG 3 (Good Health and Well-being). With healthcare systems evolving, we must invest in the right technologies to address future health challenges and deliver genuinely sustainable care.

2.2. SDG 8 Purchasing Power of the Poorest Wage Earners in A Country Double Line Bar Chart

2.2.1. Healthcare Economy and Smart Technologies

Innovative technology helps improve healthcare outcomes and fuels job growth and innovations in our economy. Intelligent technology has also increased the importance of jobs in the healthcare sector, with new fields opening up, such as AI development, telemedicine, and digital health innovation. Intelligent technologies also fuel new business models that drive growth, particularly in healthcare.

Nature-inclusive business models, a concept promoted by the World Economic Forum, underscore aligning economic activities with environmental sustainability. Healthcare, with intelligent technologies in the background, can ultimately be part of such models through waste elimination, efficient resource utilization, and maintenance of health service sustainability. This, in turn, alleviates the patient burden of travel and environmental impact, while AI supply chain management systematically tracks the usage of medical supplies to minimize waste and costs.

In this opportunity, we will discover how Smart can unlock an innovation-driven healthcare sector that stimulates economic growth and supports Sustainable Development. Specifically, promoting such technologies will increase healthcare organizations' resilience, efficiency, and adaptability; this helps ensure that economic growth is sustainable, meaning it promotes both human health and environmental health.

Figure 2. Disruptive technologies on SDGs

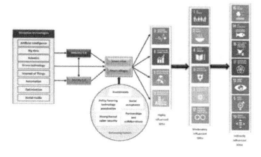

2.3. SDG 9: Infrastructure, Industry, and Innovation [-> Home]

2.3.1. Industrial - Global Healthcare Revolution Posture 5.0

Industry 4.0 has impacted manufacturing considerably since it first appeared as an industry-driven variant. It is also essential for daily tasks. It illustrates that innovation, not balance in data integration and usage, is required for successful healthcare entrepreneurship.

1. Industry 5.0 advances it further by combining human and machine activities, fusing technological breakthroughs with human intellect to produce flawless outcomes. This is the product of a human-centric invention, an automaton that enhances rather than replaces human talents. Introductory Industry 5.0, which combines cutting-edge technology with distinctive human judgment to develop highly effective, efficient, and tailored health systems, has the potential to change health outcomes worldwide drastically.

Industry 5.0 covers a more cohesive relationship between humans and machines than Industry 4.0, primarily focused on complete automation and data-driven production processes. This means that in the healthcare industry, human talent will be used to perform highly critical thinking, creative, and empathetic activities, while automation and robots will perform mindless, repetitive, and risky duties. Industry 5.0, which supports SDG 9 (industry, innovation, infrastructure) and attempts to serve people in a personalized way at the root level on time, applies robotic process automation (RPA), artificial intelligence (AI), big data analytics, and the Internet of Medical Things (IoMT) to a range of healthcare services.

In healthcare, Industry 5.0 is the human part of innovation that complements and works with machines so that we can bring our expertise into play rather than being de-skilled and working in a soulless digital factory. For example, AI-driven diagnostics combined with human clinical judgment improves the accuracy of treatment plans and individualizes them for patients. Collaborative robots (cobots), wearable devices, and evidenced-based AI predictive models can handle administrative and monitoring tasks to free healthcare workers for patient interactions, clinical assessments, glad handling of bureaucratic interfaces, critical decision support, etc. This collaboration between technology and human professionals enables more effective, individualized care and minimizes the burden of over-extended healthcare systems.

Big Data and IoT Integration

Big Data and IoT drive the success of Industry 5.0Industry 5.0 includes a significant focus on Big Data and IoT to improve health outcomes. For example, connected medical devices (wearables, implantables, remote monitoring systems) contribute to real-time data collection in the healthcare sector. This allows healthcare companies to keep track of patients more efficiently and prevent hospital readmissions or catch complications preemptively using data-driven decisions. Global Telemedicine, Remote Surgeries and Virtual Consultations are positive developments through this new level of telecommunications abilities (via the Internet of Services: IoS), allowing healthcare to be more widespread and reachable while reducing the disparities in healthcare delivery due to inadequate numbers of doctors in remote areas.

Industry 5.0, In detail: Using robust health data monitoring and aggregation over time will create the possibility of a "precision medicine" approach based on the characteristics of individual patients due to specific insights generated from (1) University College London, (2) LVRg IT Consulting, and (3) Metamorphic Analysis Model "META_MODEL"). All of this aim to deliver the appropriate treatment at the correct time, in conjunction with efficiency for healthcare systems all over.

Next-Gen IoT Tech for Infrastructure and Healthcare

It will be crucial in encouraging the creation of cutting-edge healthcare infrastructure and systems, which will support the achievement of SDG 9. The current intelligent hospitals with connected devices and AI-powered applications can function better than ever, saving patient care and reducing operational costs. These systems include monitoring inventory levels, predicting the need for machine maintenance and managing resource allocation, ultimately preventing waste while reducing the environmental exposure of healthcare services.

Industry 5.0 also creates new avenues for the application of 3D printing in healthcare, including lab-grown tissues for drug testing, medical research, customized implants, and prostheses. The breakthrough helps speed medical advancements and lower the cost and time to produce personalized medical treatments. Industry 5.0 is about integrating these advanced technologies into the healthcare infrastructure to translate innovation into inherently more resilient and responsive healthcare systems.

3. HUMAN-MACHINE INTERACTION AND AI INSIGHTS

Industry 5.0 envisages natural communication between humans and machines to deliver an ecosystem with humans coexisting seamlessly with machines. This combination is beneficial in healthcare, like in robot-assisted surgery and AI-enhanced diagnostics, where machines can perform high-precision tasks that require a perfect nuance with human oversight to make crucial decisions. This calls for operations with robots trained in AI algorithms to provide surgeons with enhanced precision to carry out minimally invasive surgeries and autonomous machine learning models which can scan through medical images and recognize diseases at an early stage.

AI and machine learning help improve healthcare by identifying patterns in complex data sets. These benefits treating patients more effectively, anticipating patient outcomes, and detecting illnesses early. Healthcare technology aids staff in making the best choices possible to enhance patient care and lower mistakes.

Healthcare: Social Responsibility, Sustainability, and Innovation

Industry 5.0's commitment to sustainable development naturally and directly corresponds with the objectives pursued by SDG 9 on innovation and infrastructure building. Using innovative technologies, healthcare systems can achieve long-term sustainability and responsible management: resource redistribution to mitigate waste and sustainability of patient care through careful observation and management of the environmental impact from on-site operations. Renewable energy, waste management, and digital health platforms also help to make the healthcare environment more environmentally friendly.

On the other hand, with environmental sustainability, Industry 5.0 pursues social sustainability by opening doors of employability and creating new job roles that will blend human expertise and the latest technology. Similarly, with healthcare systems setting new benchmarks of leveraging AI and robotics or Big Data Analytics in the coming years, it could give rise to newer jobs for trained individuals running these models, opening up a vast scope of employment augmentation and economic sustenance in the Healthcare sector.

In essence, Industry 5.0 stands for a revolutionary approach to working healthcare systems, wherein human skill and cognitive capabilities are amalgamated with intelligent technologies to re-engineer global health outcomes. Industry 5.0 supports more efficient, personalized, and sustainable healthcare systems by encouraging innovation, enhancing infrastructure, and taking advantage of the revolutionary properties of AI, Big Data, and IoT. From the perspective of SDG 9, Industry 5.0 concepts will transform healthcare by creating resilience, flexibility, and social inclusion → to ensure Good Health and well-being for all we serve!

4. INCORPORATION OF INTELLIGENT SOLUTIONS FOR REALIZING SDG FRAMEWORK

Sample of the Sustainable Development Goals (SDGs) with an extensive approach to human wellbeing and respect for the environment. They include everything from human development and economic growth to technological impacts on the environment, resource management and environmental sustainability. Meeting these challenging targets entails various challenges and has quantitative and qualitative implications. Global challenges are so unpredictable and multifaceted that addressing them necessitates imaginative measures alongside a proactive aptitude. Here is where the early use of intelligent technologies will dramatically speed up the progress towards SDGs.

The fact is that intelligent technologies such as artificial intelligence (AI), IoT, Big Data, blockchain, and robotics are disruptive influences that can revolutionize global health results. They present an incredible opportunity to increase efficiency in healthcare, improve decision-making and create scalable solutions. The SDG framework presents a way to conceptualize how intelligent technologies can help curb current health challenges, drive innovation and promote sustainability in infrastructure that serves global health needs.

The following sub-section identifies how incorporating intelligent technologies can advance SDGs while focusing on their significance in global health transformation. These technologies might impact many SDGs related to health, including all of the objectives under SDG 3 (Good et al.) and several other goals, including those under SDG 9 (Industry, Innovation, and Infrastructure) and SDG 11 (Kukreti et al., 2023).

Top Four Disruptive Technology Shaping Health Transformation

The three big game-changers—artificial intelligence (AI), the Internet of Things (IoT), and robotics—have begun influencing practically every industry, including healthcare. Industry 5.0 and society 5.0, which refer to the fusion of super tech and human potential for sustained social progress, require these five excessively advanced technologies. Conversely, Industry 5.0 emphasizes the synergy that occurs between people and robots. This interaction leads to increased process personalization and efficiency, which improves end health outcomes and increases worker productivity (Babu et al., 2022).

The future of intelligent health technologies is already well established in many other healthcare areas. This has the potential for some transformative impacts — from wearables that tell us immediately if someone is out of sorts to AI algorithms that can predict disease and help optimize resource allocation (Tamilmani et al., 2023). In addition to driving innovation in business and technology, these innovations enable more efficient and accurate care while helping improve health equity by guaranteeing the most vulnerable access to care. This is how smart technology may help accelerate the achievement of SDG 3 (Good et al.) since it can guarantee that healthcare is accessible to all and, more importantly, patients everywhere receive improved outcomes (K. D. Singh et al., 2023).

Interaction between SDGs: Health as a Driver for Sustainable Development

The synergy and interconnected nature of the SDGs mean that progress in the benefits of one drive across multiple areas of sustainability. More critically, health is a pillar of sustainable development,. SG Key 3 (Good Health and well-being) is where that lies; hence, it is essential to human capital and economic growth. When implemented within health systems, these innovative technologies can have spillover or knock-on effects for other goals, such as sustainable development goals (SDG) 9 Industry, Innovation and Infrastructure, and SDG 8—Decent Work and Economic Growth (Joshi & Sharma, 2022).

Adopting intelligent technologies in healthcare infrastructure, for instance, augments health outcomes and spurs innovation across medical technologies (MedTech), pharmaceutical development and general healthcare infrastructure. This aligns with Sustainable Development Goal 9, which focuses on ensuring sustainable industrialization, fostering innovation, and building resilient infrastructure (Ghildiyal et al., 2022). Additionally, with the help of SMART technology, global eHealth projects may create sustainable health systems better prepared to withstand shocks like pandemics and natural catastrophes. SDG 11: United Nations Sustainable Cities and Communities (Dogra et al., 2022).

By investing in revolutionary technologies, disruptive technologies similarly help contribute to other health-related SDGs and generate externalities beyond changing the course of history concerning SDG 3. SDG 7 (Affordable and Clean Energy) targets can be met by deploying smart grids and energy management technologies, guaranteeing optimized, efficient energy use in a hospital or health facility (Hajoary et al., 2023). Through advanced analysis of Big Data and the introduction of AI, there are ways in which the technology can help to better shelter QA from high variability levels in both yield and quality when used alongside GMOS (scored 9– yes) to supplement farmlands during extreme conditions (#8–most significant change), thus ultimately improving overall health thanks to a more nutritional balanced diet akin for #2(Zero hunger).

Scaling Smart Technologies — Challenges and Opportunities

The potential of innovative technologies in healthcare to deliver such benefits is self-evident, but realizing this within the SDGs is far from straightforward. For many countries (especially those that need more financial resources), the upfront capital investment required to develop and deploy these technologies on a large scale can be a significant barrier. These breakthroughs will only be transformational if policymakers and global health organizations implement financing mechanisms and public-private partnerships that can foster their widespread adoption, especially across low- and middle-income countries (Dani et al., 2022).

In addition, there needs to be a clear back-end policy to operationalize privacy adherence and security adjustment in the intelligent tech stack. Given the increasing use of digital tools to deliver health care, the stakes are high for preventing unauthorized access to valuable patient data and protecting systems from cyber threats (Rakhra et al., 2022). This is where the ethical concerns in using AI and robotics in healthcare also come into play —so you can manage or eliminate bias or inequality that will arise due to complete reliance on tech-based solutions (Sathyaseelan et al., 2023).

This led to the inception of Industry 5.0 powered by Society 5.0 — a paradigm for future living and civilization based on harmony with nature and equitable development!

This underscores that reaching the SDGs requires more than technological innovation; it requires reframing how technology interacts with society. The future of intelligent, human-centered innovation lies within Industry 5.0 and Society 5.0, revolutionizing how technologies are implemented to improve humanity and create sustainability (Rajbalaji et al., 2023). These frameworks seek to incorporate sophisticated technologies into our day-to-day lives and build intelligent cities or villages where healthcare, education, energy, and infrastructure are tuned with each other and adapted neatly for maximal efficiency and inclusivity (Sharahiley & Kandpal, 2023).

These principles, centered around human-machine collaboration, underscore the necessity of building open and fair systems that meet the needs of a diverse public. Intelligent solutions can enable healthcare professionals to provide bespoke models of care, advance patient outcomes, and deliver services more evenly throughout the country (Pai et al., 2022).

Integrating intelligent technology into the SDG framework is a game changer in achieving planetary health. Disruptive innovations in healthcare, infrastructure, and industry accelerate achieving the SDGs to a future where technology enables societal well-being and sustainability. Industry 5.0 and Society 5.0 exist to realize a world where intelligent technologies create a healthier, more resilient, and more sustainable environment (N. K. Singh et al., 2021).

5. DISCUSSION AND CONCLUSIONS

Taking the example of intelligent technologies in a constrained study setting, this paper began to illustrate possible ways that innovative technology could transform global health within the purview of the SDG (Ahmad et al., 2021). Through a deep qualitative probe towards technology disruption, the study captured all positive and negative ripples on different SDGs, if any. A few of the current issues that will be addressed in the area of policy coherence from the SGID perspective to speak to systemic, transformative change integers for SP are SDGs 3 (good health and well-being), 8 (decent work and economic growth), SDG9 Industry, Innovation, and Infrastructure, and the educational system as it relates to SDG4 (Ekren et al., 2023). Other topics include a whole range that reflects sustainability, of course, plus DRR. Our lives are significantly impacted by Industry 4.0's transition to Industry 5.0, driven partly by the digital transformation of health, disaster response, and inclusive economic models. Society 5.0 also arrives at the same time as Industry 4.0 (Kannan et al., 2022).

Although the study looks at a few downside consequences, it primarily focuses on the benefits of integrating disruptive technologies into healthcare/related industries. One of the most important results of this re-creation is the transformation of industry and society, which constitute a necessary base for further technological development. As Industry 5.0 ensues, combining human and machine intelligence will advance productivity as healthcare becomes more efficient and personalized. Society 5.0 also looks towards deploying real-time data exchange, automation, and customised care (e.g., precision medicine) and aims to create intelligent societies for optimized healthcare delivery and public health (V. Agarwal & Sharma, 2021).

Technological innovation and the SDGs must work together inside an eco-innovation framework to reap these benefits. Without going overboard and jeopardizing human welfare or the planet's limits, I desire to see more people with significant incomes leading fulfilling lives (Ramesh et al., 2023). Innovative technology, which can collect and process enormous amounts of health information, provides the basis to utilize such insights to improve clinical workflow and cut costs all at scale while protecting access for everyone.

One of its body transformation components is creating compelling smart cities and intelligent villages. By merging physical objects connected through the Internet of Things (IoT) with information and communication technology (ICT), a city may manage resources, assets, and services more efficiently without incurring additional costs (Gonfa et al., 2023). In turn, intelligent cities allow public health officials to track and forecast health trends in disease outbreaks and communicate directly with citizens and infrastructure. IoT, on the other hand, is already mostly part of our lives. With 5G connectivity, it capacitates smart villages by introducing next-gen technology to rural communities, massively improving their healthcare education and sanitation (N. K. Singh et al., 2023).

The study also underlines the need for public policy, social acceptability and legal frameworks to help facilitate widespread adoption of Society 5.0 and Industry 5.0. Moving to new architectures will necessitate coordination between governments, international organizations, and the private sector. However, discrepancies in digital infrastructure between different areas could prevent the system from being fully implemented, leading to imbalances, and not saving costs. We must address these challenges by increasing consumer awareness and education to ensure we are not part of this problem. With the vast implementation of intelligent technologies, data exchange transparency and ethical technology deployment will be crucial to sustainable progress (P. Agarwal & Sharma, 2023).

Additionally, the transition to intelligent healthcare and industries must be embedded with a circular economy (Key Feature of SDG 8). This economic model emphasizes resource efficiency and waste reduction, which prevents technological advancement at the cost of environmental exploitation. This fits broader aspirations for socio-economic sustainability—making sure those innovative technologies improve our lives in the long term and for everyone, whether they live in town or the countryside (R. Kumar & Khanna, 2023).

A key area where this work delivers impact is the discussion on Big Data versus its Integration with healthcare development inside Smart city/village frameworks. The data could also give more precise forecasts and help guide the management of health risks, informing public health policies and resource provision (Singamaneni et al., 2022). At the same time, though, research conducted through the pandemic stresses the criticality of securing data privacy and cyber security as more health systems begin to depend on such digital solutions. Enter the world of AI and ML in healthcare and sit at the same table with ethics unless you want your high-tech devices to discriminate against people and illegally analyze data!

This study offers a mental model to appreciate a digitally enabled pathway for global health and the SDGs. By connecting Industry 5.0 and Society 5.0 with the SDG, we can maximize the positive impacts of intelligent technologies and minimize their risks. Tech Disruptions: To advance the widespread utilization of high-impact technologies that make health systems more resilient, efficient, and inclusive, policymakers, governments, and stakeholders must work in unison (Praveenchandar et al., 2022).

Competent healthcare and infrastructure projects must be developed per the SDGs, meaning investments should first target long-term sustainability. In parallel, we should stop investing in unsustainable growth to protect these gains and redirect resources towards more sustainable and equitable development pathways. Governments have an essential role in promoting equity—not just in healthcare but also through enforcing policies and legislation related to discrimination. Sustainable education and skill-building efforts to increase the human capital required for a tech-driven future empower communities (Raja et al., 2022).

Lastly, this study advocates for global cooperation on global health issues. By working at a multilateral level, we can contribute our collective knowledge of international health disparities to help ensure that the Integration of intelligent technologies delivers in concretely sustainable ways and have tangible outcomes for poverty alleviation and disease control (Chahar et al., 2022). Innovative technologies could revolutionize global health, but achieving this will require everyone to embrace the SDGs and work collectively towards making the world healthier and more sustainable.

DECLARATION

The authors declare that the manuscript follows ethical standards and there are no potential conflicts of interest concerning this chapter's research, authorship, and publication.

DISCLAIMER

The contents and views of this chapter are expressed by the authors in personal capacities. The Editor and the Publisher don't need to agree with these viewpoints and are not responsible for any duty of care in this regard.

REFERENCES

Agarwal, P., & Sharma, S. (2023). Smart Urban Traffic Management System using Energy Efficient Optimized Path Discovery. *Proceedings of the 3rd International Conference on Artificial Intelligence and Smart Energy, ICAIS 2023*, 858 – 863. DOI: 10.1109/ICAIS56108.2023.10073840

Agarwal, V., & Sharma, S. (2021). IoT Based Smart Transport Management System. *Communications in Computer and Information Science, 1394 CCIS*, 207 – 216. DOI: 10.1007/978-981-16-3653-0_17

Ahmad, F., Kumar, P., & Patil, P. P. (2021). Vibration characteristics based pre-stress analysis of a quadcopter's body frame. In S. Y. (Ed.), *Materials Today: Proceedings* (Vol. 46, pp. 10329 – 10333). Elsevier Ltd. DOI: 10.1016/j.matpr.2020.12.458

Babu, M., Venkataraman, S. R., Rao, P. N., Rao, V., Kaliappan, S., Patil, P. P., Sekar, S., Yuvaraj, K. P., & Murugan, A. (2022). Optical Microstructure, FESEM, Microtensile, and Microhardness Properties of LM 25-B4Cnp-Grnp Hybrid Composites Manufactured by Selective Laser Melting. *Advances in Materials Science and Engineering*, 2022, 1–8. Advance online publication. DOI: 10.1155/2022/3177172

Bhatnagar, M., Rajaram, R., Taneja, S., & Kumar, P. (2024). Balancing acts: The Yin and Yang of debit and credit on the stage of financial well-being. In *Emerging Perspectives on Financial Well-Being*. IGI Global., DOI: 10.4018/979-8-3693-1750-1.ch002

Bhatnagar, M., Taneja, S., & Kumar, P. (2023). The Effectiveness of Carbon Pricing Mechanism in Steering Financial Flows Toward Sustainable Projects. *International Journal of Environmental Impacts*, 6(4), 183–196. DOI: 10.18280/ijei.060403

Chahar, A., & Christobel, Y. A. Ritika, Adakane, P. K., Sonal, D., & Tripathi, V. (2022). The Implementation of Big Data With Cloud and Edge Computing in Enhancing the Smart Grid Information Processes Through Sem Model. *2022 2nd International Conference on Advance Computing and Innovative Technologies in Engineering, ICACITE 2022*, 608 – 611. DOI: 10.1109/ICACITE53722.2022.9823896

Dani, R., Rawal, Y. S., Bagchi, P., & Khan, M. (2022). Opportunities and Challenges in Implementation of Artificial Intelligence in Food & Beverage Service Industry. In D. N. & C. A. (Eds.), *AIP Conference Proceedings* (Vol. 2481). American Institute of Physics Inc. DOI: 10.1063/5.0103741

Dogra, V., Verma, D., Dalapati, G. K., Sharma, M., & Okhawilai, M. (2022). Special focus on 3D printing of sulfides/selenides for energy conversion and storage. In *Sulfide and Selenide Based Materials for Emerging Applications: Sustainable Energy Harvesting and Storage Technology*. Elsevier., DOI: 10.1016/B978-0-323-99860-4.00012-5

Ekren, B. Y., Stylos, N., Zwiegelaar, J., Turhanlar, E. E., & Kumar, V. (2023). Additive manufacturing integration in E-commerce supply chain network to improve resilience and competitiveness. *Simulation Modelling Practice and Theory*, 122, 102676. Advance online publication. DOI: 10.1016/j.simpat.2022.102676

Eswar, K. N. D. V. S., Doss, M. A. N., Vishnuram, P., Selim, A., Bajaj, M., Kotb, H., & Kamel, S. (2023). Comprehensive Study on Reduced DC Source Count: Multilevel Inverters and Its Design Topologies. *Energies*, 16(1), 18. Advance online publication. DOI: 10.3390/en16010018

Ghildiyal, S., Joshi, K., Rawat, G., Memoria, M., Singh, A., & Gupta, A. (2022). Industry 4.0 Application in the Hospitality and Food Service Industries. *Proceedings of the 2022 7th International Conference on Computing, Communication and Security, ICCCS 2022 and 2022 4th International Conference on Big Data and Computational Intelligence, ICBDCI 2022.* DOI: 10.1109/ICCCS55188.2022.10079268

Gonfa, Y. H., Tessema, F. B., Tadesse, M. G., Bachheti, A., & Bachheti, R. K. (2023). Medicinally Important Plant Roots and Their Role in Nanoparticles Synthesis and Applications. In *Secondary Metabolites from Medicinal Plants: Nanoparticles Synthesis and their Applications.* CRC Press., DOI: 10.1201/9781003213727-11

Hajoary, P. K., Balachandra, P., & Garza-Reyes, J. A. (2023). Industry 4.0 maturity and readiness assessment: An empirical validation using Confirmatory Composite Analysis. *Production Planning and Control.* Advance online publication. DOI: 10.1080/09537287.2023.2210545

Joshi, S., & Sharma, M. (2022). Sustainable Performance through Digital Supply Chains in Industry 4.0 Era: Amidst the Pandemic Experience. *Sustainability (Basel)*, 14(24), 16726. Advance online publication. DOI: 10.3390/su142416726

Kannan, P. R., Periasamy, K., Pravin, P., & Vinod Kumaar, J. R. (2022). An experimental investigation of wire breakage and performance optimisation of WEDM process on machining of recycled aluminium alloy metal matrix composite. *Materials Science Poland*, 40(3), 12–26. DOI: 10.2478/msp-2022-0030

Kaur, J., Khanna, R., Kumar, R., & Sunil, G. (2024). Role of Blockchain Technologies in Goods and Services Tax. *Proceedings - 2024 3rd International Conference on Sentiment Analysis and Deep Learning, ICSADL 2024*, 607–612. DOI: 10.1109/ICSADL61749.2024.00104

Kukreti, A., Shriyal, A., Sharma, S., & Bhadula, S. (2023). Internet-of-Things Enabled Smart and Portable Terrace Garden Protection Shed. *2023 4th IEEE Global Conference for Advancement in Technology, GCAT 2023.* DOI: 10.1109/GCAT59970.2023.10353281

Kumar, K. S., Yadav, D., Joshi, S. K., Chakravarthi, M. K., Jain, A. K., & Tripathi, V. (2022). Blockchain Technology with Applications to Distributed Control and Cooperative Robotics. *Proceedings of 5th International Conference on Contemporary Computing and Informatics, IC3I 2022*, 206 – 211. DOI: 10.1109/IC3I56241.2022.10073275

Kumar, P., Reepu, & Kaur, R. (2024). Economic and Urban Dynamics: Investigating Socioeconomic Status and Urban Density as Moderators of Mobile Wallet Adoption in Smart Cities. *Lecture Notes in Networks and Systems*, 948 LNNS, 409–417. DOI: 10.1007/978-981-97-1329-5_33

Kumar, P., Taneja, S., Bhatnagar, M., & Kaur, A. K. (2024). Navigating the digital paradigm shift: Designing CBDCs for a transformative financial landscape. In *Exploring Central Bank Digital Currencies: Concepts, Frameworks, Models, and Challenges.* IGI Global., DOI: 10.4018/979-8-3693-1882-9.ch006

Kumar, P., Taneja, S., & Ozen, E. (2024). Exploring the influence of green bonds on sustainable development through low-carbon financing mobilization. *International Journal of Law and Management.* DOI: 10.1108/IJLMA-01-2024-0030

Kumar, R., Kandpal, B., & Ahmad, V. (2023). Industrial IoT (IIOT): Security Threats and Countermeasures. *International Conference on Innovative Data Communication Technologies and Application, ICIDCA 2023 - Proceedings*, 829 – 833. DOI: 10.1109/ICIDCA56705.2023.10100145

Kumar, R., & Khanna, R. (2023). RPA (Robotic Process Automation) in Finance & Accounting and Future Scope. *Proceedings of the 2023 2nd International Conference on Augmented Intelligence and Sustainable Systems, ICAISS 2023*, 1640–1645. DOI: 10.1109/ICAISS58487.2023.10250496

Kumar, R., Singh, T., Mohanty, S. N., Goel, R., Gupta, D., Alharbi, M., & Khanna, R. (2023). Study on online payments and e-commerce with SOR model. *International Journal of Retail & Distribution Management*. Advance online publication. DOI: 10.1108/IJRDM-03-2023-0137

Kumar, V., Gupta, S., & Khanna, R. (2021). Dengue fever-a worldwide study. *Journal of Medical Pharmaceutical and Allied Sciences*, 10, 102–108. DOI: 10.22270/jmpas.VI2I1.2014

Mary Joshitta, S., & Sunil, M. P. Badriasulaimanalfurhood, Bodhankar, A., Ch.Sreedevi, & Khanna, R. (2023). The Integration of Machine Learning Technique with the Existing System to Predict the Flight Prices. *2023 3rd International Conference on Advance Computing and Innovative Technologies in Engineering, ICACITE 2023*, 398–402. DOI: 10.1109/ICACITE57410.2023.10182539

Pai, H. A., Almuzaini, K. K., Ali, L., Javeed, A., Pant, B., Pareek, P. K., & Akwafo, R. (2022). Delay-Driven Opportunistic Routing with Multichannel Cooperative Neighbor Discovery for Industry 4.0 Wireless Networks Based on Power and Load Awareness. *Wireless Communications and Mobile Computing*, 2022, 1–12. Advance online publication. DOI: 10.1155/2022/5256133

Praveenchandar, J., Vetrithangam, D., Kaliappan, S., Karthick, M., Pegada, N. K., Patil, P. P., Rao, S. G., & Umar, S. (2022). IoT-Based Harmful Toxic Gases Monitoring and Fault Detection on the Sensor Dataset Using Deep Learning Techniques. *Scientific Programming*, 2022, 1–11. Advance online publication. DOI: 10.1155/2022/7516328

Raja, S., Agrawal, A. P. P., Patil, P., Thimothy, P., Capangpangan, R. Y., Singhal, P., & Wotango, M. T. (2022). Optimization of 3D Printing Process Parameters of Polylactic Acid Filament Based on the Mechanical Test. *International Journal of Chemical Engineering*, 2022, 1–7. Advance online publication. DOI: 10.1155/2022/5830869

Rajbalaji, S., Raman, R., Pant, B., Rathour, N., Rajagopa, B. R., & Prasad, C. R. (2023). Design of deep learning models for the identifications of harmful attack activities in IIOT. *2023 International Conference on Artificial Intelligence and Smart Communication, AISC 2023*, 609 – 613. DOI: 10.1109/AISC56616.2023.10085088

Rakhra, M., Bhargava, A., Bhargava, D., Singh, R., Bhanot, A., & Rahmani, A. W. (2022). Implementing Machine Learning for Supply-Demand Shifts and Price Impacts in Farmer Market for Tool and Equipment Sharing. *Journal of Food Quality*, 2022, 1–19. Advance online publication. DOI: 10.1155/2022/4496449

Ramesh, S. M., Rajeshkannan, S., Pundir, S., Dhaliwal, N., Mishra, S., & Saravana, B. S. (2023). Design and Development of Embedded Controller with Wireless Sensor for Power Monitoring through Smart Interface Design Models. *Proceedings of the 2023 2nd International Conference on Augmented Intelligence and Sustainable Systems, ICAISS 2023*, 1817 – 1821. DOI: 10.1109/ICAISS58487.2023.10250506

Sathyaseelan, K., Vyas, T., Madala, R., Chamundeeswari, V., Rai Goyal, H., & Jayaraman, R. (2023). Blockchain Enabled Intelligent Surveillance System Model with AI and IoT. *Proceedings of 8th IEEE International Conference on Science, Technology, Engineering and Mathematics, ICONSTEM 2023*. DOI: 10.1109/ICONSTEM56934.2023.10142303

Sharahiley, S. M., & Kandpal, V. (2023). The impact of monetary and non-monetary reward systems upon creativity: How rational are Saudi professional employees? *International Journal of Work Organisation and Emotion*, 14(4), 339–358. DOI: 10.1504/IJWOE.2023.136599

Sharma, P., Malhotra, R. K., Ojha, M. K., & Gupta, S. (2022). Impact of meditation on mental & physical health and thereby on academic performance of students: A study of higher educational institutions of Uttarakhand. *Journal of Medical Pharmaceutical and Allied Sciences*, 11(2), 4641–4644. DOI: 10.55522/jmpas.V11I2.2309

Singamaneni, K. K., Dhiman, G., Juneja, S., Muhammad, G., AlQahtani, S. A., & Zaki, J. (2022). A Novel QKD Approach to Enhance IIOT Privacy and Computational Knacks. *Sensors (Basel)*, 22(18), 6741. Advance online publication. DOI: 10.3390/s22186741 PMID: 36146089

Singh, K. D., Deep Singh, P., Bansal, A., Kaur, G., Khullar, V., & Tripathi, V. (2023). Exploratory Data Analysis and Customer Churn Prediction for the Telecommunication Industry. *ACCESS 2023 - 2023 3rd International Conference on Advances in Computing, Communication, Embedded and Secure Systems*, 197 – 201. DOI: 10.1109/ACCESS57397.2023.10199700

Singh, N. K., Singh, Y., Sharma, A., Singla, A., & Negi, P. (2021). An environmental-friendly electrical discharge machining using different sustainable techniques: A review. *Advances in Materials and Processing Technologies*, 7(4), 537–566. DOI: 10.1080/2374068X.2020.1785210

Singh, N. K., Singh, Y., Singh, Y., Rahim, E. A., Sharma, A., Singla, A., & Ranjit, P. S. (2023). The Effectiveness of Balanites aegyptiaca Oil Nanofluid Augmented with Nanoparticles as Cutting Fluids during the Turning Process. In *Biowaste and Biomass in Biofuel Applications*. CRC Press., DOI: 10.1201/9781003265597-7

Tamilmani, S., Mohan, T., Jeyalakshmi, S., Shukla, G. P., Gehlot, A., & Shukla, S. K. (2023). Blockchain Integrated with Industrial IOT Towards Industry 4.0. *2023 International Conference on Artificial Intelligence and Smart Communication, AISC 2023*, 575 – 581. DOI: 10.1109/AISC56616.2023.10085226

Taneja, S., Bhatnagar, M., Kumar, P., & Rupeika-apoga, R. (2023). India ' s Total Natural Resource Rents (NRR) and GDP : An Augmented Autoregressive Distributed Lag (ARDL) Bound Test. *Journal of Risk and Financial Management*, 16(2), 91. https://doi.org/doi.org/10.3390/jrfm16020091. DOI: 10.3390/jrfm16020091

Tyagi, S., Krishna, K. H., Joshi, K., Ghodke, T. A., Kumar, A., & Gupta, A. (2023). Integration of PLCC modem and Wi-Fi for Campus Street Light Monitoring. In N. P., S. M., K. M., J. V., & G. K. (Eds.), *Proceedings - 4th IEEE 2023 International Conference on Computing, Communication, and Intelligent Systems, ICCCIS 2023* (pp. 1113 – 1116). Institute of Electrical and Electronics Engineers Inc. DOI: 10.1109/ICCCIS60361.2023.10425715

Unhelkar, B., Joshi, S., Sharma, M., Prakash, S., Mani, A. K., & Prasad, M. (2022). Enhancing supply chain performance using RFID technology and decision support systems in the industry 4.0–A systematic literature review. *International Journal of Information Management Data Insights*, 2(2), 100084. Advance online publication. DOI: 10.1016/j.jjimei.2022.100084

Chapter 21
Unleashing Operational Mastery and Patient-Centric Innovation Through Robotic Process Automation in Healthcare

Nikhil Yadav
https://orcid.org/0000-0002-0115-8219
Jaypee Institute of Information Technology, India

Rinku Taneja
Axis Bank, India

ABSTRACT

Robotic Process Automation (RPA) is transforming healthcare operations by automating repetitive tasks across hospital administration, finance, and supply chain management. This technology streamlines workflows, minimizes human error, and enhances data accuracy, leading to substantial improvements in efficiency and resource allocation. In healthcare finance, RPA reduces operational inefficiencies, contributing to cost savings and optimized billing processes. Furthermore, automation in supply chain management ensures timely inventory management and reduces procurement costs. Through selected case studies, this paper highlights the financial benefits of RPA, showcasing how healthcare organizations leverage automation to improve operational efficiency, reduce costs, and allocate resources more effectively, ultimately enhancing patient care quality.

INTRODUCTION

The rapid ascendance of Robotic Process Automation (RPA) in healthcare operations signifies a paradigmatic shift in the operational fabric of this industry, long encumbered by procedural inertia, resource constraints, and a labyrinthine array of regulations (Ahmad et al., 2023). As healthcare ecosystems evolve in response to mounting pressures for cost containment, enhanced accuracy, and optimized resource allocation, RPA emerges as a formidable tool to reengineer the operational workflow. Characterized by its ability to emulate human interactions with digital systems, RPA transcends rudimentary task auto-

DOI: 10.4018/979-8-3373-0240-9.ch021

Copyright ©2025, IGI Global Scientific Publishing. Copying or distributing in print or electronic forms without written permission of IGI Global Scientific Publishing is prohibited.

mation, recalibrating entire processes to bolster efficiency, precision, and strategic adaptability within healthcare operations (Singh et al., 2023).

At its core, RPA operates through algorithms and machine-learning protocols that, unlike traditional automation, do not necessitate extensive alterations in the underlying IT architecture (Jayadeva et al., 2023). This allows RPA to be swiftly deployed within existing systems, mitigating the temporal and financial costs commonly associated with large-scale IT overhauls. The sophistication of RPA lies in its versatility, encompassing everything from automating data entry in electronic health records (EHRs) to managing complex billing processes. By alleviating healthcare personnel from the menial, repetitive tasks that inundate their daily workflows, RPA engenders a reallocation of human capital toward more cognitively demanding and empathetically driven functions, thereby amplifying the intrinsic value of human resources in healthcare (Raman et al., 2023).

In the realm of healthcare finance, the implications of RPA are equally profound. Financial operations within healthcare organizations are rife with intricate, repetitive tasks—coding, claims processing, revenue cycle management—that are susceptible to human error and time inefficiencies (Mangla & Ram, 2020). The integration of RPA in these domains optimizes the revenue cycle, accelerates cash flows, and diminishes operational expenditures, thereby achieving fiscal prudence without compromising service quality. Through automated data reconciliation and anomaly detection, RPA streamlines financial operations by ensuring that revenue leakages are promptly identified and rectified, circumventing protracted audit processes that typically strain financial resources (Ahmad et al., 2023).

Moreover, RPA contributes significantly to healthcare supply chain management, an area that has gained pronounced attention in light of recent global disruptions. Traditionally, healthcare supply chains operate within rigid, manual frameworks, vulnerable to inefficiencies in procurement, inventory management, and logistics coordination. RPA disrupts this traditionalism by introducing algorithmic precision in demand forecasting, order processing, and vendor management (N. M. Kumar et al., 2023). By automating these processes, healthcare institutions gain a heightened capacity to preemptively address supply shortages, reduce wastage, and negotiate favorable terms with suppliers through enhanced procurement strategies. As a result, RPA not only attenuates operational costs but also reinforces the resilience of healthcare supply chains, a crucial determinant of uninterrupted patient care (Gupta et al., 2022).

Case studies corroborate the extensive economic advantages accrued through RPA integration. Institutions that have deployed RPA report substantial reductions in operating costs, coupled with marked improvements in process velocity and accuracy. For instance, the automation of preauthorization for medical procedures, often a time-intensive process prone to delays, enables healthcare providers to expedite patient admissions and optimize bed occupancy rates, directly impacting revenue. Similarly, hospitals implementing RPA in patient billing and claims processing have observed accelerated reimbursement timelines and minimized errors in coding, leading to higher levels of patient satisfaction and financial stability (Manjunatha et al., 2023).

In the broader schema of healthcare operations, the introduction of RPA represents more than a mere efficiency upgrade; it is emblematic of the sector's transition toward a digitally augmented ecosystem (Shah et al., 2023). As healthcare organizations continue to contend with financial pressures, staff shortages, and the escalating demands of a growing patient population, RPA emerges as a pivotal solution that not only economizes operational procedures but also enhances the quality of healthcare delivery. Through this confluence of operational efficiency and improved service quality, RPA reinforces the fundamental mission of healthcare: to deliver timely, accessible, and effective care to patients (Ansari & Afzal, 2022).

The advent of Robotic Process Automation (RPA) in healthcare transcends the conventional confines of operational refinement; it heralds a comprehensive recalibration of process efficacy, strategic foresight, and resilience within the industry's structural ecosystem (S. Sharma et al., 2021). As healthcare institutions grapple with escalating costs, stringent regulatory constraints, and an increasingly multifaceted patient demographic, RPA offers a compelling response to the exigencies of these contemporary challenges. By automating labor-intensive, repetitious tasks that have historically encumbered healthcare operations, RPA precipitates a tectonic shift, enhancing not only the operational agility of healthcare providers but also the strategic reallocation of intellectual resources toward value-laden, patient-centric care activities (Shukla et al., 2022).

The deployment of RPA within hospital operations facilitates a nuanced realignment of clinical and administrative functionalities. In domains such as patient scheduling, admissions, discharge planning, and patient record management, RPA streamlines workflows through its ability to emulate cognitive, rule-based tasks with remarkable precision and reliability. Consider the administration of patient admissions, a traditionally laborious process that demands meticulous data entry, verification, and cross-referencing across multiple systems (Gururani et al., 2022). RPA automates these tasks, effectuating an accelerated and error-free admission protocol that mitigates patient wait times, optimizes bed management, and enhances operational throughput. The resultant efficiencies do not merely augment patient satisfaction but also engender substantial cost savings, reducing the fiscal burden of delayed admissions, prolonged bed occupancy, and redundant administrative tasks (Husen et al., 2021) .

In healthcare finance, the financial merits of RPA extend beyond mere cost containment; they embody a strategic framework for sustainable fiscal governance. Revenue cycle management, an inherently complex process comprising billing, coding, claims submission, and reimbursement tracking, is perennially vulnerable to inefficiencies and inaccuracies that can compromise revenue flows (Garg et al., 2023). RPA redefines this cycle by automating coding accuracy checks, ensuring that billing information is error-free and aligned with regulatory standards. Such automation significantly reduces denials and claim rejections, thereby improving the revenue realization rates and expediting cash inflows. Furthermore, RPA facilitates predictive analytics in revenue management by continuously monitoring patterns and flagging anomalies, thus enabling preemptive interventions to rectify discrepancies that could otherwise lead to revenue leakages (Begum et al., 2022).

In addition, the domain of supply chain management within healthcare benefits significantly from the algorithmic precision introduced by RPA. Supply chains in healthcare are multifaceted networks encompassing procurement, inventory management, distribution, and vendor coordination, each of which is susceptible to fluctuations in demand, procurement delays, and logistical bottlenecks. RPA mitigates these risks through the automation of demand forecasting, real-time inventory tracking, and order fulfillment processes (Rajbalaji et al., 2023). By leveraging predictive models and historical data analytics, RPA enables healthcare institutions to anticipate demand surges and proactively replenish stock levels, minimizing shortages and ensuring an uninterrupted continuum of care. This predictive functionality is particularly critical in scenarios of emergent demand, such as during a pandemic, where efficient inventory management can directly impact patient outcomes. The resultant cost reductions and operational resilience underscore the strategic value of RPA as an enabler of sustainable supply chain systems in healthcare (Chandna, 2022).

Beyond operational optimization, RPA fosters a paradigm shift in the overarching ethos of healthcare by redirecting the focus from administrative minutiae to the fundamental mission of patient care. Through its automation capabilities, RPA liberates healthcare staff from the encumbrance of repetitive tasks, facilitating a reallocation of human resources toward direct patient engagement, complex clinical decision-making, and empathetic caregiving (Davuluri et al., 2023). The implications of this shift are profound: healthcare practitioners are empowered to focus on their core competencies, thereby enhancing the quality of care delivered and reinforcing the relational dimension of healthcare. Moreover, the psychological benefit of alleviating staff from monotonous tasks can lead to improved job satisfaction and reduced burnout rates, addressing a critical concern in an industry perennially challenged by workforce shortages and high turnover rates (Belwal et al., 2023).

Empirical case studies illustrate the transformational impact of RPA on cost structure and operational fluidity within healthcare organizations. Hospitals implementing RPA in claims management and coding have reported a substantial reduction in processing times, error rates, and administrative costs (Bisht et al., 2023). For instance, automating preauthorization for high-frequency procedures expedites approval processes, allowing patients to receive timely care and enabling hospitals to optimize bed utilization rates. Similarly, automated patient billing systems that verify insurance details, calculate co-pays, and generate invoices with precision have enhanced patient transparency and satisfaction, further fortifying the hospital's reputation and financial stability. Collectively, these case studies underscore the financial viability of RPA, evidencing its potential to yield a rapid return on investment while reinforcing operational efficiency and resilience (Dogra et al., 2022).

The evolution of RPA in healthcare is, however, not without challenges. While the potential benefits of RPA are extensive, the implementation of such technology necessitates a rigorous recalibration of existing processes and workflows. Integration with legacy systems, which often lack interoperability, can impede the seamless deployment of RPA, requiring healthcare institutions to undertake costly and time-intensive infrastructure upgrades (Mishra et al., 2021). Furthermore, the reliance on algorithms and machine learning models raises ethical concerns surrounding data security, patient confidentiality, and algorithmic biases, which must be vigilantly managed to safeguard the integrity of healthcare services. In addressing these challenges, healthcare institutions must adopt a strategic and holistic approach, balancing the imperatives of operational efficiency with ethical considerations and compliance mandates (Mohamed et al., 2023).

In conclusion, RPA represents an epochal advancement in the operational architecture of healthcare, heralding a new era of efficiency, precision, and fiscal prudence. By automating repetitive, labor-intensive tasks, RPA minimizes operational inefficiencies, fortifies financial stability, and enables healthcare organizations to refocus on their primary mission of patient care (Akberdina et al., 2023). As healthcare institutions navigate an increasingly complex and resource-constrained landscape, the judicious deployment of RPA stands as a pivotal lever for achieving operational excellence and ensuring the sustainability of healthcare delivery. Through this confluence of technological innovation and strategic foresight, RPA is poised to redefine the contours of healthcare operations, aligning process efficiency with the imperatives of patient-centric care and fiscal stewardship. In sum, the transformative potential of RPA in healthcare operations manifests across various domains, from finance and administration to supply chain management (Jindal et al., 2022). By automating labor-intensive, error-prone tasks, RPA minimizes operational inefficiencies, fortifies fiscal stability, and enables healthcare organizations to refocus on patient-centered care (Mohd et al., 2023). As this paper will elucidate, the judicious application of RPA holds the promise of revolutionizing healthcare operations, offering a paradigm shift that aligns operational imperatives with the exigencies of modern healthcare delivery. The ensuing sections will delve into the mechanics of RPA, exploring its practical applications, financial benefits, and potential challenges, thus presenting a comprehensive analysis of RPA's role in redefining the landscape of healthcare operations.

LITERATURE REVIEW

The emergence of Robotic Process Automation (RPA) in healthcare operations has driven significant research interest, focusing on its diverse applications, financial impacts, and transformative potential across healthcare systems (Y. K. Sharma et al., 2020). This review synthesizes studies from the literature to underscore RPA's transformative role in administrative workflows, revenue cycle management, supply chain stability, and patient-centered care, thereby reshaping the healthcare landscape to prioritize operational precision, efficiency, and enhanced patient outcomes (Behera & Singh Rawat, 2023).

RPA in Healthcare Administrative Processes

Research into the application of RPA within healthcare administration demonstrates its ability to streamline tasks often hindered by redundancy and human error (Lourens et al., 2022). Studies show that RPA can mitigate administrative bottlenecks by automating data entry, patient scheduling, and documentation management, reducing delays in routine processes and enhancing operational flow. The automation of data handling eliminates errors commonly associated with manual entry, leading to improved accuracy and reduced administrative rework (Ishengoma et al., 2022).

In patient record management, RPA has been shown to enhance integration with electronic health records (EHRs), facilitating real-time data synchronization across platforms. This automation increases the accessibility and reliability of patient information, underscoring RPA's role in bolstering the healthcare administrative infrastructure (AL-Huqail et al., 2022). Other studies discuss RPA's impact on patient admissions, emphasizing its ability to handle tasks like eligibility verification and preliminary screenings autonomously. This autonomy decreases patient wait times, optimizes resource allocation, and supports overall system efficiency (A. Kumar & Ram, 2021).

Financial Implications and Revenue Cycle Management

The literature examining RPA in healthcare finance focuses significantly on revenue cycle management, where automation aids in cost reduction and boosts revenue generation. Studies indicate that the automation of billing, claims processing, and coding through RPA effectively reduces administrative costs by streamlining these repetitive tasks, with healthcare institutions reporting notable operational savings after RPA adoption.

Further research highlights how RPA accelerates revenue flows by facilitating faster claims submission and reducing errors in medical coding. Automated processes minimize claim denials, enabling healthcare providers to benefit from a faster reimbursement cycle and improved cash flow stability. Additionally, RPA's role in compliance and regulatory adherence is noted, as automated systems are programmed to ensure coding aligns with current healthcare standards, reducing the potential for billing errors and associated penalties.

Empirical case studies reinforce these findings, with healthcare providers implementing automated billing systems experiencing decreased claim processing times and lower overhead costs. These examples underscore the substantial financial benefits RPA brings to healthcare operations, enhancing revenue realization and strengthening fiscal stability.

RPA in Healthcare Supply Chain Management

Supply chain management in healthcare has increasingly integrated RPA, particularly as healthcare systems aim to navigate global supply chain disruptions and maintain continuity of care. Studies find that RPA facilitates demand forecasting, procurement, and inventory management by leveraging predictive analytics and historical data, thereby improving supply chain responsiveness and minimizing shortages.

Research has also explored the impact of RPA on vendor management and order processing, showing that automation reduces procurement delays and operational costs by streamlining approvals and vendor coordination. Furthermore, predictive analytics enabled by RPA assist in aligning inventory levels with real-time demand, reducing waste and promoting cost-effective resource management.

The role of RPA in supply chain resilience has been a significant area of focus, especially in the wake of crises such as the COVID-19 pandemic. Findings suggest that RPA enhances operational adaptability, enabling healthcare providers to manage demand fluctuations and resource allocation with agility, thereby reinforcing the healthcare system's ability to provide uninterrupted patient care in critical times.

Enhancing Patient-Centric Care through RPA

RPA's impact on patient-centered care has been extensively studied, with research showing how automation improves patient experience and healthcare quality. RPA facilitates patient engagement by automating appointment reminders, follow-up communication, and preliminary screenings, creating a more streamlined patient interaction model and freeing staff to focus on more complex, personalized care (R. Kumar, Singh, et al., 2023).

Additional studies underscore the ability of RPA to reduce administrative burdens on healthcare staff, thereby allowing healthcare providers to prioritize clinical tasks. By automating routine documentation and ancillary activities, RPA alleviates workload pressures, leading to enhanced care quality and improved patient satisfaction. Some research focuses on RPA's role in patient data management, particularly in personalized medicine, where automation ensures accurate and complete patient information, facilitating precision in diagnosis and treatment plans (R. Kumar, Malhotra, et al., 2023).

In chronic care management, RPA has been shown to support continuous care pathways by automating monitoring systems and alerts, ensuring patients with chronic conditions receive timely interventions. Studies conclude that RPA improves long-term health outcomes by enabling consistent monitoring and engagement, which are critical in managing chronic illness effectively (R. Kumar, Malholtra, et al., 2023).

Ethical Considerations and Challenges in RPA Implementation

Despite its demonstrated benefits, RPA in healthcare presents ethical and regulatory challenges. The literature frequently highlights concerns around data privacy and patient confidentiality, as RPA systems require access to sensitive patient information, thus necessitating rigorous data protection protocols to prevent unauthorized access.

Algorithmic biases within RPA systems have also been cited as a potential concern, especially in areas involving patient eligibility screening and resource allocation. Researchers suggest that unchecked biases in automated systems could compromise service equity and quality, highlighting the need for bias-mitigation strategies to ensure that RPA tools operate impartially.

Further studies examine technical obstacles associated with RPA implementation, particularly the challenges posed by legacy systems lacking interoperability. Findings recommend a phased integration approach for RPA deployment within healthcare systems to minimize disruptions and maintain continuity. Governance frameworks have been proposed to guide the responsible deployment of RPA, advocating for regulatory oversight and adherence to ethical standards to ensure patient rights are protected alongside technological progress.

The body of literature on RPA in healthcare underscores its transformative potential in achieving operational efficiency, cost savings, and patient-centered service improvements. RPA has shown to be effective in streamlining administrative tasks, improving revenue cycle processes, strengthening supply chain resilience, and enhancing patient engagement, thus aligning healthcare operations with contemporary demands for precision, efficiency, and quality.

However, the literature also emphasizes the ethical and technical considerations intrinsic to RPA deployment in healthcare. Privacy, data protection, and bias prevention remain critical challenges that require careful management and adherence to robust regulatory frameworks. Through this synthesis, the literature highlights RPA as an invaluable tool for modern healthcare, while also calling for further research to optimize its deployment and address potential risks to ensure a balanced and sustainable approach to automation in healthcare operations.

Research Methodology

This research adopts a case study approach to examine the impact of Robotic Process Automation (RPA) on healthcare operations, specifically focusing on administrative efficiency, revenue cycle management, supply chain resilience, and patient-centered care. Through a systematic analysis of selected case studies from various healthcare institutions, this methodology aims to provide an in-depth understanding of RPA's applications, benefits, and challenges, thereby contributing to the broader discourse on healthcare automation. The research methodology encompasses a multi-phase approach that includes case selection, data collection, data analysis, and reliability and validity assessments.

Research Design

The case study research design was selected due to its suitability for exploring complex, context-specific phenomena within real-life settings. Given the intricacies of healthcare operations and the unique challenges associated with each institution, the case study method provides the necessary depth to understand the situational factors influencing RPA implementation and its outcomes. This design allows for detailed examination and comparison of cases, offering rich, empirical insights into how RPA functions across different operational domains within healthcare.

Case Selection Criteria

The selection of case studies is a critical component, as it directly impacts the research outcomes. The criteria for case selection include:

- **RPA Implementation Maturity**: Cases were chosen based on the maturity of RPA deployment within healthcare institutions, ensuring a mix of early-stage and mature implementations. This range enables an examination of both immediate and long-term impacts of RPA.
- **Operational Diversity**: Cases represent various operational domains within healthcare, including administrative processes, financial management, supply chain logistics, and patient care. This selection provides a holistic view of RPA's multifaceted applications.
- **Geographical and Institutional Diversity**: Institutions from different geographic regions and of various sizes, including private and public healthcare facilities, were included to ensure that findings are generalizable across diverse healthcare settings.
- **Documented Outcomes**: Selected cases were required to have well-documented outcomes regarding efficiency improvements, cost savings, patient satisfaction, or operational resilience, facilitating a reliable analysis of RPA's tangible benefits.

This purposive sampling approach ensures that each case contributes meaningfully to the research objectives, providing a representative perspective on RPA's impact within the healthcare sector.

Data Collection Methods

A combination of primary and secondary data collection methods was employed to gather comprehensive information on each case study:

- **Primary Data**: Semi-structured interviews were conducted with key stakeholders involved in RPA implementation, including IT managers, healthcare administrators, finance officers, and clinical staff. The interviews focused on their experiences with RPA, perceived benefits, encountered challenges, and suggestions for improvement. Interview guides were tailored to capture perspectives on RPA's impact on specific operational areas relevant to each case study.
- **Secondary Data**: Secondary data was collected from institutional reports, industry publications, and previously published case studies. These sources provided contextual information on implementation processes, performance metrics, and documented challenges, supplementing primary data to create a comprehensive narrative for each case.
- **Observation**: Where possible, direct observation of RPA systems in action was conducted to gain a first-hand understanding of workflow changes, process efficiencies, and interactions between human workers and automated systems. Observations were recorded to highlight nuances not captured through interviews and documents, adding depth to the case descriptions.

Data Analysis

Data analysis followed a systematic, multi-stage process to synthesize findings across the case studies:

- **Data Organization**: All collected data was transcribed, coded, and categorized into themes, including administrative efficiency, financial performance, supply chain impact, and patient-centered improvements. Data was further classified by case study to maintain a structured approach in comparing findings across institutions.
- **Thematic Analysis**: A thematic analysis was performed to identify recurrent themes and patterns across cases. This approach facilitated the extraction of commonalities and variations in RPA outcomes, revealing how RPA functions within different healthcare contexts. Themes such as time savings, cost reductions, error minimization, and process transparency emerged as primary areas of interest.
- **Cross-Case Analysis**: Cross-case analysis enabled the comparison of findings across case studies to identify factors that influence the success of RPA in healthcare. Variables such as organizational size, RPA deployment scale, stakeholder engagement, and support infrastructure were analyzed to determine how these factors impact RPA outcomes. Cross-case synthesis allowed for the identification of best practices and potential challenges that may arise during RPA implementation.
- **Quantitative Analysis**: Where numerical data on performance metrics (e.g., processing times, error rates, cost savings) was available, statistical methods were applied to quantify the impact of RPA on healthcare operations. Metrics were compared pre- and post-RPA implementation to evaluate the magnitude of changes in efficiency, cost-effectiveness, and patient satisfaction.

The integration of Robotic Process Automation (RPA) within healthcare represents a significant shift in enhancing operational efficiency, optimizing financial performance, and reinforcing patient-centric care. RPA has evolved beyond simple automation tools, delivering unprecedented advantages in a sector traditionally encumbered by procedural complexities, resource constraints, and rigorous regulatory mandates. Through a comprehensive analysis of case studies, this research examines RPA's transformative role in healthcare, spanning administrative workflows, revenue cycle management, supply chain resilience, and patient engagement. The selected cases span varied healthcare settings, providing insights into RPA's capacity to reconfigure operational structures, alleviate fiscal redundancies, and streamline patient-centered processes. Using a rigorous methodological approach, this study employs interviews, secondary data analysis, and observational techniques to capture a holistic view of RPA's impact and offer empirical insights into the practical applications of healthcare automation.

Administrative processes in healthcare are historically burdened with redundant data entry, scheduling complexities, and documentation requirements that detract from efficiency and accuracy. RPA has been pivotal in addressing these inefficiencies, where automated data handling has expedited routine tasks and substantially reduced error margins. Automating patient admissions, eligibility verification, and record synchronization allows institutions to manage patient flow with enhanced precision, optimizing resource allocation and mitigating delays. By relieving human resources from repetitive data-handling tasks, RPA empowers healthcare personnel to focus on complex decision-making and patient interactions, thus enriching the quality of care and operational fluidity. The cases analyzed demonstrate that automated systems can dramatically reduce patient wait times and administrative processing, underscoring RPA's potential to refine the healthcare administrative framework.

The financial landscape in healthcare is particularly impacted by RPA, especially within revenue cycle management, where tasks like billing, claims processing, and medical coding are central to revenue realization. RPA's implementation has been shown to reduce costs associated with these operations by mitigating errors and minimizing claim denials, thereby expediting reimbursement cycles. The cases in this study reveal a substantial improvement in cash flow and fiscal predictability post-RPA implementation, as automated systems ensure compliance with regulatory standards and enhance coding accuracy. As such, RPA not only contributes to operational efficiency but also promotes financial resilience by reducing the administrative overhead associated with claim resubmissions and billing discrepancies. These findings underscore the potential of RPA to serve as a cornerstone in healthcare's financial sustainability, offering a streamlined, compliant, and error-resistant approach to revenue management.

Supply chain resilience, an increasingly critical aspect of healthcare operations, has also benefitted markedly from RPA's predictive capabilities. Traditional healthcare supply chains are vulnerable to demand fluctuations, procurement delays, and logistical constraints. The automation of demand forecasting, inventory management, and vendor coordination enables healthcare institutions to anticipate supply needs accurately, ensuring that critical resources remain available when required. By utilizing real-time data analytics and historical demand patterns, RPA systems facilitate timely procurement, reducing both wastage and the risk of supply shortages. The cases demonstrate that automated systems effectively enhance supply chain resilience, enabling healthcare institutions to manage resources with agility and precision. This resilience is particularly crucial during periods of high demand, such as pandemics, where the ability to preemptively secure supplies can directly influence patient outcomes and care continuity.

In addition to these operational improvements, RPA has enhanced patient-centered care by automating appointment reminders, follow-up communications, and preliminary screenings. This automation supports a seamless, responsive interaction model, allowing healthcare personnel to devote more time to clinical care and patient interactions. By minimizing patient wait times and improving service responsiveness, RPA contributes to heightened patient satisfaction and engagement. Automated systems that handle documentation, data entry, and procedural verifications allow healthcare providers to focus on direct patient care, underscoring RPA's potential to realign healthcare priorities towards more compassionate, patient-focused services. The cases studied reveal that these patient-centered applications of RPA not only improve the patient experience but also elevate healthcare outcomes, creating an environment where patient needs, and satisfaction are at the forefront.

While the benefits of RPA are extensive, its deployment in healthcare is not without challenges, particularly concerning data privacy, ethical concerns, and regulatory compliance. RPA systems require access to sensitive patient data, necessitating strict data protection protocols to prevent unauthorized access. Algorithmic biases within RPA also present potential risks, particularly in areas involving eligibility screening and resource allocation, where biased algorithms could inadvertently affect service equity. This study acknowledges the importance of developing robust frameworks to mitigate these risks, advocating for transparent, bias-mitigation strategies to ensure that RPA systems operate impartially and ethically.

Additionally, technical challenges such as interoperability with legacy systems complicate the seamless deployment of RPA, as many healthcare institutions rely on aging infrastructure that may lack the compatibility required for integrated automation. A phased approach to RPA implementation is recommended, allowing for gradual adaptation without compromising existing workflows. An audit trail was maintained throughout the case study process, ensuring transparency and reliability in interpreting, and validating results. To ensure credibility, findings were triangulated across multiple data sources, and member checking was conducted with key informants to confirm data accuracy. Such methodological rigor contributes to the study's validity, offering reliable insights into RPA's effects on healthcare operations.

In conclusion, this case study analysis substantiates the extensive benefits of RPA across multiple domains in healthcare. From reducing administrative inefficiencies and fortifying revenue cycle management to enhancing supply chain resilience and elevating patient-centered care, RPA offers substantial operational, financial, and patient-oriented advantages. The findings demonstrate that RPA's deployment, while complex and requiring careful consideration of ethical, regulatory, and technical challenges, can profoundly impact healthcare delivery and quality. As healthcare institutions continue to navigate evolving demands for efficiency, cost-effectiveness, and high-quality care, RPA stands as a pivotal enabler of a more agile, responsive, and sustainable healthcare ecosystem. This study provides empirical evidence supporting the strategic imperatives of RPA in healthcare, serving as a foundation for further exploration and advancement in healthcare automation.

Reliability and Validity

To ensure the credibility of the findings, several measures were undertaken to enhance the reliability and validity of the research:

- **Triangulation**: Triangulation was achieved through the use of multiple data sources, including interviews, institutional reports, and observation, to validate findings across various perspectives. This approach mitigates the risk of bias and increases the robustness of the conclusions drawn.
- **Member Checking**: Key informants were invited to review and verify the transcriptions and thematic findings, ensuring that interpretations accurately reflect their perspectives and experiences. Member checking contributes to the internal validity of the data by confirming the accuracy of collected insights.
- **Audit Trail**: An audit trail was maintained throughout the research process to document all decisions, methodological adjustments, and data interpretations. This transparency enhances the replicability of the study, allowing other researchers to follow the methodology and verify findings.
- **Peer Review**: Independent peer reviewers with expertise in healthcare automation were consulted to evaluate the research methodology, data interpretation, and conclusions. Feedback from these reviewers helped refine the analysis and enhance the credibility of the findings.

Ethical Considerations

The research was conducted in adherence to ethical standards, with particular attention to maintaining confidentiality and informed consent. Participants were informed of the research objectives, their role in the study, and their right to withdraw at any time. Sensitive information regarding patient data or proprietary RPA systems was anonymized, ensuring compliance with data protection regulations, and preserving the privacy of participating institutions.

Limitations

While the case study approach provides in-depth insights, it is inherently limited in terms of generalizability. The findings are context-specific and may not apply universally across all healthcare institutions. Moreover, RPA implementation levels vary widely, and the impact of RPA on operations may depend on institutional resources, organizational culture, and technological infrastructure. The study also acknowledges potential bias introduced by self-reporting in interviews, which may affect the objectivity of certain responses. Future research could address these limitations by expanding the sample size and incorporating longitudinal studies to observe the long-term effects of RPA on healthcare operations.

Managerial Implications

Table 1 contains the managerial implications of the present research.

Table 1. Managerial implications of study

Managerial Implication	Description
Strategic Investment in Automation	Prioritize RPA in routine, repetitive tasks (e.g., admissions, billing, scheduling) to enhance operational efficiency, reduce wait times, and optimize resource utilization, allowing staff to focus on patient care and complex tasks.
Financial Optimization in Revenue Cycle Management	Integrate RPA in billing, claims processing, and coding to reduce errors, minimize claims denials, and improve cash flow. Align automation with regulatory compliance to avoid penalties, stabilize revenue, and improve financial sustainability.
Strengthening Supply Chain Resilience	Utilize RPA for demand forecasting, inventory management, and procurement to anticipate supply needs, reduce wastage, and ensure resource availability during demand surges. RPA can also streamline vendor management and improve procurement cycles.
Fostering Patient-Centric Care	Automate patient engagement tasks (e.g., appointment reminders, follow-ups, preliminary screenings) to improve patient satisfaction and engagement, reduce wait times, and enable healthcare staff to focus more on personalized, direct patient care.
Addressing Ethical, Security, and Compliance	Implement strong data protection protocols and bias-mitigation strategies to ensure patient data security and regulatory compliance. Adopt phased RPA deployment to adapt to compliance needs and minimize ethical and security-related risks.
Cultivating a Culture of Innovation	Encourage a culture that embraces technological change by providing staff training, highlighting RPA's role in supporting, not replacing, human roles. Involve employees in the implementation process and address any concerns to improve acceptance.
Building Scalability and Continuous Improvement	Plan for scalable RPA solutions and set performance metrics to monitor impact on efficiency, finances, and patient satisfaction. Create feedback loops for ongoing improvement, adapting RPA to evolving needs and regulatory changes.

CONCLUSION

In summation, the implementation of Robotic Process Automation (RPA) within healthcare institutions epitomizes a transformative advancement, fundamentally enhancing operational efficacy, fiscal resilience, and patient-centered service paradigms. Through meticulous case study analysis, this research elucidates RPA's profound capacity to refine administrative workflows, streamline revenue cycle operations, bolster supply chain robustness, and amplify patient engagement. The findings distinctly illustrate that, when judiciously deployed, RPA mitigates the inefficiencies and redundancies inherent in repetitive tasks, liberating healthcare professionals to engage in higher-order decision-making and direct patient interactions.

Healthcare leaders are urged to strategically prioritize RPA within high-frequency, routine domains to optimize service fluidity, minimize operational expenditures, and stabilize financial inflows. However, successful RPA integration necessitates rigorous adherence to data protection frameworks and bias-mitigation protocols, ensuring ethical integrity and compliance. This ethical vigilance is paramount in safeguarding patient confidentiality and fostering institutional trust. Equally crucial is the cultivation of an innovation-embracing culture, underpinned by comprehensive staff development programs to facilitate seamless adaptation to automation-enhanced roles, thereby alleviating apprehensions regarding technological displacement. Moreover, the scalability and iterative refinement of RPA systems are vital to adapt dynamically with organizational exigencies, ensuring sustained operational relevance and effectiveness.

In essence, RPA emerges as a critical lever for reengineering healthcare's operational architecture, aligning it with contemporary imperatives for precision, cost-effectiveness, and elevated patient satisfaction. Through a strategic, ethically grounded, and adaptable deployment framework, RPA equips healthcare institutions to navigate an increasingly intricate and resource-strained environment. The judicious adoption of RPA thus heralds a sustainable, agile, and patient-centric future, redefining the contours of healthcare delivery and establishing a paradigm aligned with the sector's most exigent demands.

DECLARATION

The authors declare that the manuscript follows ethical standards and there are no potential conflicts of interest concerning this chapter's research, authorship, and publication.

DISCLAIMER

The contents and views of this chapter are expressed by the authors in personal capacities. The Editor and the Publisher don't need to agree with these viewpoints and are not responsible for any duty of care in this regard.

REFERENCES

Ahmad, I., Sharma, S., Kumar, R., Dhyani, S., & Dumka, A. (2023). Data Analytics of Online Education during Pandemic Health Crisis: A Case Study. *2nd Edition of IEEE Delhi Section Owned Conference, DELCON 2023 - Proceedings*. DOI: 10.1109/DELCON57910.2023.10127423

Akberdina, V., Kumar, V., Kyriakopoulos, G. L., & Kuzmin, E. (2023). Editorial: What Does Industry's Digital Transition Hold in the Uncertainty Context? In K. V., K. G.L., A. V., & K. E. (Eds.), *Lecture Notes in Information Systems and Organisation: Vol. 61 LNISO* (pp. 1 – 4). Springer Science and Business Media Deutschland GmbH. DOI: 10.1007/978-3-031-30351-7_1

AL-Huqail, A. A., Kumar, P., Eid, E. M., Taher, M. A., Kumar, P., Adelodun, B., Andabaka, Ž., Mioč, B., Držaić, V., Bachheti, A., Singh, J., Kumar, V., & Širić, I.AL-Huqail. (2022). Phytoremediation of Composite Industrial Effluent using Sacred Lotus (Nelumbo nucifera Gaertn): A Lab-Scale Experimental Investigation. *Sustainability (Basel)*, 14(15), 9500. Advance online publication. DOI: 10.3390/su14159500

Ansari, M. F., & Afzal, A. (2022). Sensitivity and Performance Analysis of 10 MW Solar Power Plant Using MPPT Technique. *Lecture Notes in Electrical Engineering, 894 LNEE*, 512–518. DOI: 10.1007/978-981-19-1677-9_46

Begum, S. J. P., Pratibha, S., Rawat, J. M., Venugopal, D., Sahu, P., Gowda, A., Qureshi, K. A., & Jaremko, M. (2022). Recent Advances in Green Synthesis, Characterization, and Applications of Bioactive Metallic Nanoparticles. *Pharmaceuticals (Basel, Switzerland)*, 15(4), 455. Advance online publication. DOI: 10.3390/ph15040455 PMID: 35455452

Behera, A., & Singh Rawat, K. (2023). A brief review paper on mining subsidence and its geo-environmental impact. *Materials Today: Proceedings*. Advance online publication. DOI: 10.1016/j.matpr.2023.04.183

Belwal, N., Juneja, P., & Sunori, S. K. (2023). Decoupler Control for a MIMO Process Model in an Industrial Process - A Review. *2023 2nd International Conference on Ambient Intelligence in Health Care, ICAIHC 2023*. DOI: 10.1109/ICAIHC59020.2023.10431463

Bisht, B., Gururani, P., Aman, J., Vlaskin, M. S., Anna, I. K., Irina, A. A., Joshi, S., Kumar, S., & Kumar, V. (2023). A review on holistic approaches for fruits and vegetables biowastes valorization. *Materials Today: Proceedings*, 73, 54–63. DOI: 10.1016/j.matpr.2022.09.168

Chandna, R. (2022). Selecting the most agile manufacturing system with respect to agile attribute-technology-fuzzy AHP approach. *International Journal of Operations Research*, 43(4), 512–532. DOI: 10.1504/IJOR.2022.122812

Das Gupta, A., Rafi, S. M., Singh, N., Gupta, V. K., Jaiswal, S., & Gangodkar, D. (2022). A Framework of Internet of Things (IOT) for the Manufacturing and Image Classifaication System. *2022 2nd International Conference on Advance Computing and Innovative Technologies in Engineering, ICACITE 2022*, 293 – 297. DOI: 10.1109/ICACITE53722.2022.9823853

Davuluri, S. K., Alvi, S. A. M., Aeri, M., Agarwal, A., Serajuddin, M., & Hasan, Z. (2023). A Security Model for Perceptive 5G-Powered BC IoT Associated Deep Learning. *6th International Conference on Inventive Computation Technologies, ICICT 2023 - Proceedings*, 118 – 125. DOI: 10.1109/ICICT57646.2023.10134487

Dogra, V., Verma, D., Dalapati, G. K., Sharma, M., & Okhawilai, M. (2022). Special focus on 3D printing of sulfides/selenides for energy conversion and storage. In *Sulfide and Selenide Based Materials for Emerging Applications: Sustainable Energy Harvesting and Storage Technology*. Elsevier., DOI: 10.1016/B978-0-323-99860-4.00012-5

Garg, U., Kumar, S., & Kumar, M. (2023). A Hybrid Approach for the Detection and Classification of MQTT-based IoT-Malware. *2nd International Conference on Sustainable Computing and Data Communication Systems, ICSCDS 2023 - Proceedings*, 1154 – 1159. DOI: 10.1109/ICSCDS56580.2023.10104820

Gururani, P., Bhatnagar, P., Bisht, B., Jaiswal, K. K., Kumar, V., Kumar, S., Vlaskin, M. S., Grigorenko, A. V., & Rindin, K. G. (2022). Recent advances and viability in sustainable thermochemical conversion of sludge to bio-fuel production. *Fuel*, 316, 123351. Advance online publication. DOI: 10.1016/j.fuel.2022.123351

Husen, A., Bachheti, R. K., & Bachheti, A. (2021). Non-Timber Forest Products: Food, Healthcare and Industrial Applications. In *Non-Timber Forest Products: Food, Healthcare and Industrial Applications*. Springer International Publishing., DOI: 10.1007/978-3-030-73077-2

Ishengoma, F. R., Shao, D., Alexopoulos, C., Saxena, S., & Nikiforova, A. (2022). Integration of artificial intelligence of things (AIoT) in the public sector: Drivers, barriers and future research agenda. *Digital Policy. Regulation & Governance*, 24(5), 449–462. DOI: 10.1108/DPRG-06-2022-0067

Jayadeva, S. M., Prasad Krishnam, N., Raja Mannar, B., Prakash Dabral, A., Buddhi, D., & Garg, N. (2023). An Investigation of IOT-Based Consumer Analytics to Assist Consumer Engagement Strategies in Evolving Markets. *2023 3rd International Conference on Advance Computing and Innovative Technologies in Engineering, ICACITE 2023*, 487 – 491. DOI: 10.1109/ICACITE57410.2023.10183310

Jindal, T., Sheoliha, N., Kishore, K., Uike, D., Khurana, S., & Verma, D. (2022). A Conceptual Analysis on the Impact of Internet of Things (IOT) Towards on Digital Marketing Transformation. *2022 2nd International Conference on Advance Computing and Innovative Technologies in Engineering, ICACITE 2022*, 1943 – 1947. DOI: 10.1109/ICACITE53722.2022.9823714

Kumar, A., & Ram, M. (2021). Systems Reliability Engineering: Modeling and Performance Improvement. In *Systems Reliability Engineering: Modeling and Performance Improvement*. De Gruyter. DOI: 10.1515/9783110617375

Kumar, N. M., Islam, S., Podder, A. K., Selim, A., Bajaj, M., & Kamel, S. (2023). Lifecycle-based feasibility indicators for floating solar photovoltaic plants along with implementable energy enhancement strategies and framework-driven assessment approaches leading to advancements in the simulation tool. *Frontiers in Energy Research*, 11, 1075384. Advance online publication. DOI: 10.3389/fenrg.2023.1075384

Kumar, R., Malholtra, R. K., Singh, R., Kathuria, S., Balyan, R., & Pal, P. (2023). Artificial Intelligence Role in Electronic Invoice Under Goods and Services Tax. *2023 International Conference on Computational Intelligence, Communication Technology and Networking, CICTN 2023*, 140–143. DOI: 10.1109/CICTN57981.2023.10140870

Kumar, R., Malhotra, R. K., & Grover, N. (2023). Data Mining in Credit Scoring and Future Application. *International Conference on Innovative Data Communication Technologies and Application, ICIDCA 2023 - Proceedings*, 1096–1100. DOI: 10.1109/ICIDCA56705.2023.10100032

Kumar, R., Singh, T., Mohanty, S. N., Goel, R., Gupta, D., Alharbi, M., & Khanna, R. (2023). Study on online payments and e-commerce with SOR model. *International Journal of Retail & Distribution Management*. Advance online publication. DOI: 10.1108/IJRDM-03-2023-0137

Lourens, M., Tamizhselvi, A., Goswami, B., Alanya-Beltran, J., Aarif, M., & Gangodkar, D. (2022). Database Management Difficulties in the Internet of Things. *Proceedings of 5th International Conference on Contemporary Computing and Informatics, IC3I 2022*, 322–326. DOI: 10.1109/IC3I56241.2022.10072614

Mangla, S. K., & Ram, M. (2020). Supply chain sustainability: Modeling and innovative research frameworks. In *Supply Chain Sustainability: Modeling and Innovative Research Frameworks*. De Gruyter. DOI: 10.1515/9783110628593

Manjunatha, B. N., Chandan, M., Kottu, S., Rappai, S., Hema, P. K., Singh Rawat, K., & Sarkar, S. (2023). A Successful Spam Detection Technique for Industrial IoT Devices based on Machine Learning Techniques. *Proceedings of the 2nd International Conference on Applied Artificial Intelligence and Computing, ICAAIC 2023*, 363 – 369. DOI: 10.1109/ICAAIC56838.2023.10141275

Mishra, P., Aggarwal, P., Vidyarthi, A., Singh, P., Khan, B., Alhelou, H. H., & Siano, P. (2021). VMShield: Memory Introspection-Based Malware Detection to Secure Cloud-Based Services against Stealthy Attacks. *IEEE Transactions on Industrial Informatics*, 17(10), 6754–6764. DOI: 10.1109/TII.2020.3048791

Mohamed, N., Sridhara Rao, L., & Sharma, M. Sureshbaburajasekaranl, Badriasulaimanalfurhood, & Kumar Shukla, S. (2023). In-depth review of integration of AI in cloud computing. *2023 3rd International Conference on Advance Computing and Innovative Technologies in Engineering, ICACITE 2023*, 1431 – 1434. DOI: 10.1109/ICACITE57410.2023.10182738

Mohd, N., Kumar, I., & Khurshid, A. A. (2023). Changing Roles of Intelligent Robotics and Machinery Control Systems as Cyber-Physical Systems (CPS) in the Industry 4.0 Framework. *2023 International Conference on Communication, Security and Artificial Intelligence, ICCSAI 2023*, 647 – 651. DOI: 10.1109/ICCSAI59793.2023.10421085

Rajbalaji, S., Raman, R., Pant, B., Rathour, N., Rajagopa, B. R., & Prasad, C. R. (2023). Design of deep learning models for the identifications of harmful attack activities in IIOT. *2023 International Conference on Artificial Intelligence and Smart Communication, AISC 2023*, 609 – 613. DOI: 10.1109/AISC56616.2023.10085088

Raman, R., Kumar, R., Ghai, S., Gehlot, A., Raju, A. M., & Barve, A. (2023). A New Method of Optical Spectrum Analysis for Advanced Wireless Communications. *2023 3rd International Conference on Advance Computing and Innovative Technologies in Engineering, ICACITE 2023*, 1719 – 1723. DOI: 10.1109/ICACITE57410.2023.10182414

Shah, J. K., Sharma, R., Misra, A., Sharma, M., Joshi, S., Kaushal, D., & Bafila, S. (2023). Industry 4.0 Enabled Smart Manufacturing: Unleashing the Power of Artificial Intelligence and Blockchain. *2023 1st DMIHER International Conference on Artificial Intelligence in Education and Industry 4.0, IDICAIEI 2023*. DOI: 10.1109/IDICAIEI58380.2023.10406671

Sharma, S., Singh Rawal, R., Pandey, D., & Pandey, N. (2021). Microbial World for Sustainable Development. In *Microbial Technology for Sustainable Environment*. Springer Nature., DOI: 10.1007/978-981-16-3840-4_1

Sharma, Y. K., Mangla, S. K., Patil, P. P., & Uniyal, S. (2020). Analyzing sustainable food supply chain management challenges in India. In *Research Anthology on Food Waste Reduction and Alternative Diets for Food and Nutrition Security*. IGI Global., DOI: 10.4018/978-1-7998-5354-1.ch023

Shukla, S. K., Pant, B., Viriyasitavat, W., Verma, D., Kautish, S., Dhiman, G., Kaur, A., Srihari, K., & Mohanty, S. N. (2022). An integration of autonomic computing with multicore systems for performance optimization in Industrial Internet of Things. *IET Communications*, cmu2.12505. Advance online publication. DOI: 10.1049/cmu2.12505

Singh, N. K., Singh, Y., Singh, Y., Rahim, E. A., Sharma, A., Singla, A., & Ranjit, P. S. (2023). The Effectiveness of Balanites aegyptiaca Oil Nanofluid Augmented with Nanoparticles as Cutting Fluids during the Turning Process. In *Biowaste and Biomass in Biofuel Applications*. CRC Press., DOI: 10.1201/9781003265597-7

Chapter 22
Use of Artificial Intelligence for Health Insurance:
A Bibliometric Exploration

Saurabh Bhatt
https://orcid.org/0009-0007-3512-5224
Graphic Era University, India

Rajesh Tiwari
https://orcid.org/0000-0002-5345-2508
Graphic Era University, India

Chandra Prakash
https://orcid.org/0000-0003-0807-2116
Graphic Era University, India

Bijesh Dhyani
Graphic Era University, India

Bhanu Sharma
Graphic Era University, India

Kapil Ahalawat
Graphic Era University, India

ABSTRACT

Artificial intelligence has emerged as the technology with potential to enhance access, transparency, efficiency of health insurance. Poor penetration of health insurance is a cause of concern for people from economically disadvantaged groups. The chapter explores bibliometric analysis of use of artificial intelligence for health insurance. The Scopus database was used for the bibliometric analysis. United States, Canada and India emerged as the leading countries for research in AI for health insurance. Mesko was the leading author. It was found that AI has the potential to transform health insurance for preventing fraud detection and leakages in public health insurance system.

I. INTRODUCTION:

Large-scale language models, including GPT-4, have the potential to effectuate transformative change in healthcare but must be regulated very carefully given the distinctive nature of the training. GPT-4 was released last March 2023. On one hand, GPT-4 would be a better support system for all the medical-related tasks. However, there are major concerns on GPT-4's reliability in terms of using it on matters concerning the patients. The tool thus needs efficient regulatory oversight so that its pursuit would not compromise data security. (Meskó & Topol,2023). In terms of race, gender, and type of insurance payer,

DOI: 10.4018/979-8-3373-0240-9.ch022

the topics for clinical notes and psychiatric note differed extensively, just like previously known clinical observations. There were differences in accuracy of predictions suggesting that the machine may be biased in its predictions by gender and insurance type for ICU mortality (Chen et al., 2019). High disparities in risk factors for health and chronic diseases indicate the importance of community-specific targeted public health initiatives. These disparities reflect the essential need for priorities within communities as a strategy to level off health inequalities. The CDC and local coalitions are taking this data to enact targeted strategies that fill up these gaps (Liao et al., 2011).

The prevalence of non-adherence highlights the need to identify at-risk patients. Understanding these influencing factors can help tailor interventions to improve medication adherence (Sedjo & Devine, 2011). There are regional differences in prevalence of medical conditions (Steele et al., 2008).

Long-standing inequities in funding and access to essential services have created health disparities among Indigenous peoples, increasing their risk for severe COVID-19 illness. Inconsistent data collection on underlying health conditions has limited understanding of mortality disparities. Socioeconomic factors and barriers to healthcare access may have further exacerbated these challenges (Arrazola, 2020). AI is useful for fraud detection and prediction (Tiwari et al., 2023; Kakkar et al., 2024). Technology has emerged as a potential mechanism for distribution of pharmaceutical products (Ahalawat & Tiwari 2024). Digital discrimination is prevalent across various domains, including risk assessment in policing and credit scoring (Ferrer et al., 2021).

Artificial Intelligence (AI) has been found to be a potential solution for health inequalities in poor countries by WHO (Alami et al., 2020). Ai is emerging as a potential tool for enhancing the significance of health insurance (Tiwari et al., 2023). XGBoost has performed better than other algorithms (Dhieb et al., 2020).

AI has the potential to become a facilitator for system driven change (Bullock et al., 2020). Tech firms are making efforts to integrate regulation with technology to enhance their control over the market (Benkler, 2019). The past few years have been richly rewarded when it comes to fulfillment of finding artificial intelligence (AI). There are shifts in a number of processes including insurance claims submission and processing as well as in bias mitigation in studies, among many other processes. Even though there are considerable uses of AI in identifying risk factors associated with eventual health conditions within individuals leading to more individualized prevention strategies, the need to implement these responsibly cannot be overstated (Thesmar et al., 2019). Privacy, confidentiality, information sharing legislation are critical issues in insurance as well as application of AI in patient's treatment (Bohr & Memarzadeh, 2020).

If all the various stakeholders can come together in a manner that allows a workable model to evolve, then AI has the potential to bring about some very nice changes in healthcare and health insurance. AI is useful for risk management. (Prakash et al., 2022; Jain et al., 2023). AI suffers from trust issues (Zarifis et al., 2021). Technology has its own limitations. The rise in cyber frauds has challenged widespread adoption of AI by stakeholders (Kapadiya et al., 2022). White box algorithm was found to be better in predicting fraud claims of health insurance (Johnson et al., 2023).

II. METHOD:

The review of literature and thematic analysis was done using Scopus database. The keywords used were "ai" AND "health" AND "insurance". The date of search was 15th October 2024. 475 documents were obtained in Scopus database. The first exclusion criteria were language. English language documents were included, and others were excluded. 445 documents were retained. The second exclusion criteria were year of publication. Documents published 2000 onwards were included and others were excluded. 443 documents were retained. Erratum was excluded. The documents comprised of 244 articles, 68 conference papers, 51 reviews, 45 book chapters, 12 note, 8 conference review, 4 letter, 4 editorials, 4 book and 2 short surveys. 442 documents were finally considered for thematic analysis. The thematic analysis was done using VOS viewer software version 1.6.20.

III. RESULTS:

The prominent cited countries are shown in table 1. The United States leads with the highest number of documents and citations, reflecting a strong influence in the academic community. Canada stands out with a high citations per document ratio, indicating impactful research despite a smaller output. India has a substantial volume of publications but lower citation efficiency, suggesting room for greater visibility. The United Kingdom maintains a balanced presence, while Germany shows solid output but could improve its international relevance. Hungary exhibits an impressive citations per document ratio, indicating concentrated expertise. France maintains a respectable impact with fewer documents. Taiwan, Italy, and Australia demonstrate moderate research engagement, with potential for growth in international recognition.

Table 1. Prominent cited countries

S. No.	Country	Documents	Citations	Total Link Strength	Citations Per Document
1	United States	201	3827	18	19
2	Canada	21	629	8	30
3	India	68	418	9	6
4	United Kingdom	21	390	1	19
5	Germany	30	366	4	12
6	Hungary	3	278	0	93
7	France	13	242	5	19
8	Taiwan	24	203	0	8
9	Italy	12	163	1	14
10	Australia	13	162	0	12

(Source: Compiled by Authors from Scopus Database)

Figure 1. Prominent cited countries

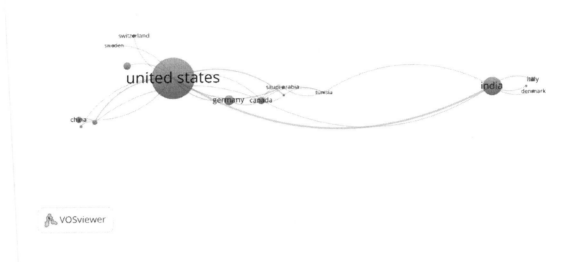

Table 2. Prominent cited organisations

S. No.	Organization	Documents	Citations
1	"Department Of Behavioural Sciences, Semmelweis University, Budapest, Hungary"	1	237
2	"Scripps Research Translational Institute, Scripps Research, United States"	1	237
3	"The Medical Futurist Institute, Budapest, Hungary"	1	237
4	"Massachusetts Institute of Technology (MIT), United States"	1	194
5	"University of Toronto, Canada"	1	194
6	"Division of Adult and Community Health, National Center for Chronic Disease Prevention and Health Promotion, United States"	1	192
7	"Express Script, Inc., St. Louis, United States"	1	148
8	"Department Of Transplantation Medicine, Oslo University Hospital, Oslo, Norway"	2	129
9	"Digestive Disease Center, Showa University Northern Yokohama Hospital, Yokohama, Japan"	2	129
10	"Division Of Cancer Prevention and Control, National Center for Chronic Disease Prevention and Health Promotion, Centers for Disease Control And Prevention, United States"	1	115

(Source: Compiled by Authors from Scopus Database)

Department of Behavioral Sciences and The Medical Futurist Institute share the highest citations (237) with the Scripps Research Translational Institute from the U.S. Despite having only one document each, their work is highly influential. MIT and the University of Toronto follow closely with 194 citations, reflecting their strong academic presence. The Division of Adult and Community Health and Division of Cancer Prevention and Control from the U.S. also demonstrate substantial impact with notable citation counts. Organizations from Norway and Japan contribute with specialized research, each having two documents that garnered 129 citations.

Table 3. Prominent cited sources

S. No.	Source	Documents	Citations
1	Morbidity And Mortality Weekly Report	5	335
2	Breast Cancer Research and Treatment	4	301
3	NPJ Digital Medicine	3	264
4	Cancer	6	200
5	Ama Journal of Ethics	1	194
6	International Journal of Environmental Research and Public Health	5	155
7	IEEE Access	2	120
8	Frontiers In Medicine	3	109
9	IEEE Technology and Society Magazine	2	103
10	Journal of the American Academy of Dermatology	2	95

(Source: Compiled by Authors from Scopus Database)

The Morbidity and Mortality Weekly Report leads with five documents and a total of 335 citations, indicating its prominent role in public health discussions. Breast Cancer Research and Treatment follows closely with four documents and 301 citations, showcasing its influence in cancer research. NPJ Digital Medicine has three documents with 264 citations, reflecting its growing importance in digital health. The article 'Cancer' holds the greatest number of documents at six yet has the lowest number of citations at 200. This may imply a large scope but with lower impact intensity. The 'Ama Journal of Ethics' does hold very influential pieces as the citation count for only one document stands at 194. Other sources include International Journal of Environmental Research and Public Health, and IEEE Access, with several documents that have high citation counts.

Table 4. Prominent cited documents

S.No.	Document	Citations
1	Meskó (2023)	237
2	Chen (2019)	194
3	Liao (2011)	192
4	Sedjo (2011)	148
5	Steele (2008)	115
6	Arrazola (2020)	109
7	Liu (2013)	107
8	Ferrer (2021)	102

continued on following page

Table 4. Continued

S.No.	Document	Citations
9	Alami (2020)	93
10	Makredes (2009)	93

(Source: Compiled by Authors from Scopus Database)

Meskó (2023) takes the lead with 237, which is a sheer reflection of the serious impact it has in its academic circle. Chen (2019) comes closely with 194 citations, which is an indication of influence on the present research. Liao (2011) is situated at 192, with his relevance in literature still continued and alive. Sedjo (2011) and Steele (2008) also have remarkable citation counts of 148 and 115 respectively; such counts reflect contributions on the ongoing issues. Arrazola has 109 citations, and Liu has 107, marking them as having a great deal of impact with their studies. Ferrer added to this list with 102 citations, and Alami and Makredes have both reached 93 citations, giving proof that their work is continually recognized.

Table 5. Prominent cited authors

S. No.	Author	Documents	Citations
1	Meskó, Bertalan	1	237
2	Topol, Eric J.	1	237
3	Chen, Irene Y.	1	194
4	Ghassemi, Marzyeh	1	194
5	Szolovits, Peter	1	194
6	Bang, David	1	192
7	Cosgrove, Shannon	1	192
8	Dulin, Rick	1	192
9	Giles, Wayne	1	192
10	Harris, Zachery	1	192
11	Liao, Youlian	1	192
12	Liburd, Leandris	1	192
13	Stewart, Alexandria	1	192
14	Taylor, April	1	192
15	White, Shannon	1	192
16	Yatabe, Graydon	1	192
17	Devine, Scott	1	148
18	Sedjo, Rebecca L.	1	148
19	Bretthauer, Michael	2	129
20	Kudo, Shin-Ei	2	129

(Source: Compiled by Authors from Scopus Database)

The table presents a summary of influential authors along with their document counts and citation totals. Meskó, Bertalan and Topol, Eric J both have just one document in each of their names but top the list with 237 citations, therefore depicting a high level of recognition in their respective areas of specialization. Chen, Irene Y., Ghassemi, Marzyeh, and Szolovits, Peter each has only one document with 194 citations, thus having a significant influence on the research mainstream. Few authors have only one document, like Bang, David and Cosgrove, Shannon with 192 citations, which shows their work on important discussions. Another significant author with Dulin, Rick and Giles, Wayne also among numerous others share this citation count, proving that their work is worth it. Devine, Scott and Sedjo, Rebecca L. follow with 148 citations each from their respective documents. Bretthauer, Michael and Kudo, Shin-Ei stand out with two documents each, each garnering 129 citations, showcasing the potential benefits of producing multiple impactful works.

Figure 2. Co-authorship map of countries

The United States leads with a total link strength of 66, suggesting a robust network of research collaborations. Canada follows with a strength of 31, while India shows a significant presence with a score of 34. The United Kingdom (29) and Germany (25) also exhibit strong linkages, highlighting their active roles in global research. Smaller nations like Hungary (8), South Korea (8), and Denmark (8) show moderate link strengths, indicating some level of collaboration. France (12) and Australia (18) further contribute to the network. Countries such as Taiwan, Italy, Japan, Norway, and Saudi Arabia have lower link strengths, reflecting varying levels of research collaboration.

Figure 3. Co-citation map

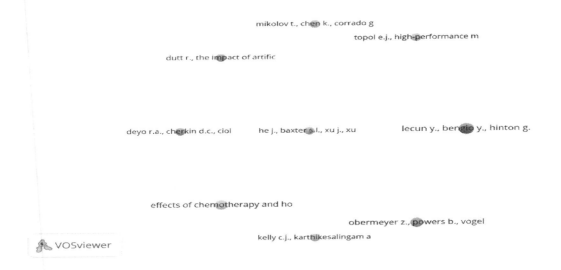

The cited references highlight significant trends in the integration of artificial intelligence (AI) into healthcare, with a focus on both foundational works, such as those by Goodfellow and LeCun on deep learning, and emerging research addressing practical applications and ethical considerations, like Obermeyer's study on racial bias in health algorithms. The paper on chemotherapy and hormonal therapy stands out with the highest citation count, reflecting its importance in oncology. Many references, despite having citations, show zero total link strength, indicating niche relevance or emerging ideas. Additionally, discussions around challenges in implementing AI in clinical settings underscore the complexity of translating technology into practice.

Figure 4. Co-occurrence map

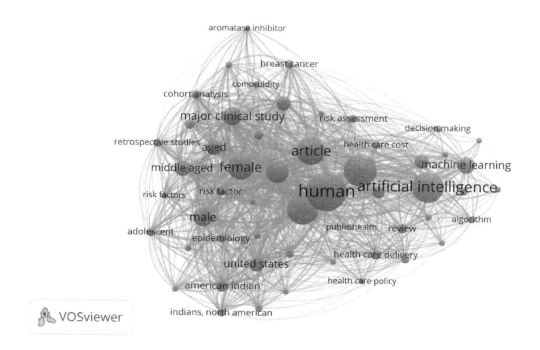

Table 6. Prominent cited keywords

S.No.	Keyword	Occurrences	Total Link Strength
1	Human	252	2361
2	Health Insurance	194	1408
3	Artificial Intelligence	187	946
4	Humans	179	1834
5	Article	158	1719
6	Female	138	1653
7	Adult	120	1453
8	Male	99	1183
9	Major Clinical Study	93	1162
10	Machine Learning	80	448
11	Middle Aged	75	992
12	Aged	72	940
13	United States	70	849
14	Controlled Study	66	784
15	Health Care	66	347

(Source: Compiled by Authors from Scopus Database)

The most frequently used keyword is "Human," appearing 252 times with a total link strength of 2361, emphasizing its central role in the studies analyzed. "Health Insurance" follows with 194 occurrences and a link strength of 1408, reflecting its significance in discussions surrounding health policies. "Artificial Intelligence" and "Humans" also feature prominently, with 187 and 179 occurrences, respectively, demonstrating their growing importance in healthcare research. Other notable keywords include "Article" (158 occurrences), "Female" (138), and "Adult" (120), indicating a focus on gender and demographic studies. The table also includes keywords like "Major Clinical Study" and "Machine Learning," which signify trending topics in the field, with occurrences of 93 and 80, respectively. Additional keywords such as "Middle Aged," "Aged," and "United States" highlight demographic considerations, while "Controlled Study" and "Health Care" round out the list, each with 66 occurrences, underscoring the emphasis on study design and healthcare contexts.

IV. CONCLUSION:

It was found that western countries lead the research on use of AI in health insurance. USA, Canada and India were the most cited countries. Semmelweis University was the most cited University. Morbidity And Mortality Weekly Report was the most cited source. Meskó was the most cited author. AI has been found to be useful for fraud detection, enhancing operational efficiency and improving transparency. There is need to collaborate between developed, developing and under-developed countries to understand the unique challenges and needs to adapt the AI models for specific market structures. The fraud detection in public funded healthcare and health insurance schemes can be done effectively with AI. The specific medical condition driven health insurance can be designed at a regional, national and international level to leverage the benefits of diversification and economies of scale. Right intent is needed amongst the policy makers, tech firms and stakeholders to capitalise the potential of AI to solve health insurance problems of the world.

REFERENCES

Ahalawat, K., & Tiwari, R. (2024, April). A Bibliometric Analysis of the Use of Technology for the Marketing of Online Pharmacies. In *2024 Sixth International Conference on Computational Intelligence and Communication Technologies (CCICT)* (pp. 384-389). IEEE. DOI: 10.1109/CCICT62777.2024.00069

Alami, H., Rivard, L., Lehoux, P., Hoffman, S. J., Cadeddu, S. B. M., Savoldelli, M., Samri, M. A., Ag Ahmed, M. A., Fleet, R., & Fortin, J. P. (2020). Artificial intelligence in health care: Laying the Foundation for Responsible, sustainable, and inclusive innovation in low-and middle-income countries. *Globalization and Health*, 16(1), 1–6. DOI: 10.1186/s12992-020-00584-1 PMID: 32580741

Arrazola, J., Masiello, M. M., Joshi, S., Dominguez, A. E., Poel, A., Wilkie, C. M., Bressler, J. M., McLaughlin, J., Kraszewski, J., Komatsu, K. K., Peterson Pompa, X., Jespersen, M., Richardson, G., Lehnertz, N., LeMaster, P., Rust, B., Keyser Metobo, A., Doman, B., Casey, D., & Landen, M. (2020). COVID-19 mortality among American Indian and Alaska native persons—14 states, January–June 2020. *MMWR. Morbidity and Mortality Weekly Report*, 69(49), 69. DOI: 10.15585/mmwr.mm6949a3 PMID: 33301432

Benkler, Y. (2019). Don't let industry write the rules for AI. *Nature*, 569(7754), 161–162. DOI: 10.1038/d41586-019-01413-1 PMID: 31043715

Bohr, A., & Memarzadeh, K. (Eds.). (2020). *Artificial intelligence in healthcare*. Academic Press.

Bullock, J., Young, M. M., & Wang, Y. F. (2020). Artificial intelligence, bureaucratic form, and discretion in public service. *Information Polity*, 25(4), 491–506. DOI: 10.3233/IP-200223

Chen, I. Y., Szolovits, P., & Ghassemi, M. (2019). Can AI help reduce disparities in general medical and mental health care? *AMA Journal of Ethics*, 21(2), 167–179. DOI: 10.1001/amajethics.2019.167 PMID: 30794127

Dhieb, N., Ghazzai, H., Besbes, H., & Massoud, Y. (2020). A secure ai-driven architecture for automated insurance systems: Fraud detection and risk measurement. *IEEE Access : Practical Innovations, Open Solutions*, 8, 58546–58558. DOI: 10.1109/ACCESS.2020.2983300

Ferrer, X., Van Nuenen, T., Such, J. M., Coté, M., & Criado, N. (2021). Bias and discrimination in AI: A cross-disciplinary perspective. *IEEE Technology and Society Magazine*, 40(2), 72–80. DOI: 10.1109/MTS.2021.3056293

Jain, V., Tiwari, R., Mehrotra, R., Bohra, N. S., Misra, A., & Pandey, D. C. (2023, October). Role of Technology for Credit Risk Management: A Bibliometric Review. In *2023 IEEE International Conference on Blockchain and Distributed Systems Security (ICBDS)* (pp. 1-6). IEEE. DOI: 10.1109/ICBDS58040.2023.10346300

Johnson, M., Albizri, A., & Harfouche, A. (2023). Responsible artificial intelligence in healthcare: Predicting and preventing insurance claim denials for economic and social wellbeing. *Information Systems Frontiers*, 25(6), 2179–2195. DOI: 10.1007/s10796-021-10137-5

Kakkar, V., Pandey, D. C., Verma, V., Mehrotra, R., Singh, P., & Tiwari, R. (2024, April). Artificial Intelligence for Stock Prediction: A Bibliometric Review. In *2024 1st International Conference on Innovative Sustainable Technologies for Energy, Mechatronics, and Smart Systems (ISTEMS)* (pp. 1-5). IEEE. DOI: 10.1109/ISTEMS60181.2024.10560228

Kapadiya, K., Patel, U., Gupta, R., Alshehri, M. D., Tanwar, S., Sharma, G., & Bokoro, P. N. (2022). Blockchain and AI-empowered healthcare insurance fraud detection: An analysis, architecture, and future prospects. *IEEE Access : Practical Innovations, Open Solutions*, 10, 79606–79627. DOI: 10.1109/ACCESS.2022.3194569

Liao, Y., Bang, D., Cosgrove, S., Dulin, R., Harris, Z., Taylor, A., & Giles, W. (2011). Surveillance of health status in minority communities-racial and ethnic approaches to community health across the US (REACH US) risk factor survey, United States, 2009. *MMWR. Surveillance Summaries*, 60(6), 1–44. PMID: 21597458

Meskó, B., & Topol, E. J. (2023). The imperative for regulatory oversight of large language models (or generative AI) in healthcare. *NPJ Digital Medicine*, 6(1), 120. DOI: 10.1038/s41746-023-00873-0 PMID: 37414860

Prakash, S., Balaji, J. N., Joshi, A., & Surapaneni, K. M. (2022). Ethical Conundrums in the application of artificial intelligence (AI) in healthcare—A scoping review of reviews. *Journal of Personalized Medicine*, 12(11), 1914. DOI: 10.3390/jpm12111914 PMID: 36422090

Sedjo, R. L., & Devine, S. (2011). Predictors of non-adherence to aromatase inhibitors among commercially insured women with breast cancer. *Breast Cancer Research and Treatment*, 125(1), 191–200. DOI: 10.1007/s10549-010-0952-6 PMID: 20495864

Steele, C. B., Cardinez, C. J., Richardson, L. C., Tom-Orme, L., & Shaw, K. M. (2008). Surveillance for health behaviors of American Indians and Alaska Natives—Findings from the behavioral risk factor surveillance system, 2000–2006. *Cancer*, 113(S5), 1131–1141. DOI: 10.1002/cncr.23727 PMID: 18720374

Thesmar, D., Sraer, D., Pinheiro, L., Dadson, N., Veliche, R., & Greenberg, P. (2019). Combining the power of artificial intelligence with the richness of healthcare claims data: Opportunities and challenges. *PharmacoEconomics*, 37(6), 745–752. DOI: 10.1007/s40273-019-00777-6 PMID: 30848452

Tiwari, R., Kaur, H., Sharma, S., Kargeti, H., Prakash, N., & Sharma, S. (2023, December). Artificial Intelligence in Health Insurance: A Bibliometric Review. In *2023 International Conference on Advanced Computing & Communication Technologies (ICACCTech)* (pp. 14-18). IEEE DOI: 10.1109/ICACCTech61146.2023.00012

Tiwari, R., Rautela, S., Sharma, S., Choudhary, B. P., Tripathi, R., & Singh, P. (2023, December). Role of AI for Fraud Detection in Banks: A Bibliometric Analysis. In *2023 International Conference on Advanced Computing & Communication Technologies (ICACCTech)* (pp. 66-71). IEEE. DOI: 10.1109/ICACCTech61146.2023.00020

Zarifis, A., Kawalek, P., & Azadegan, A. (2021). Evaluating if trust and personal information privacy concerns are barriers to using health insurance that explicitly utilizes AI. *Journal of Internet Commerce*, 20(1), 66–83. DOI: 10.1080/15332861.2020.1832817

Chapter 23
Work From Home and Sustainable Development Goals:
A Framework for Healthcare Sector

Ridhima Goel
https://orcid.org/0000-0002-0505-9218
Maharshi Dayanand Univesity, India

Jagdeep Singla
https://orcid.org/0000-0001-8628-9244
Maharshi Dayanand University, India

Sanjeet Kumar
Chaudhary Devi Lal University, India

ABSTRACT

The adoption of Work-From-Home models in healthcare, particularly during the COVID-19 outbreak, has brought a new dimension to worldwide health management. By leveraging smart technologies such as telemedicine, AI-powered diagnostics, and IoT-enabled remote monitoring, healthcare delivery has become more accessible, efficient, and inclusive. This chapter explores how WFH models, enhanced by these technologies, are improving global health outcomes and aligning with the third Sustainable Development Goal (SDG 3), ensuring healthy lives while promoting well-being for all. It examines how WFH frameworks reduce healthcare inequalities by extending quality care to underserved regions and populations. Additionally, it highlights the challenges and opportunities of integrating WFH models with smart technology to create sustainable health systems that can be scaled globally. This chapter provides a comprehensive framework for the future of WFH in healthcare, contributing to the realization of SDG 3 and offering a pathway toward more equitable and resilient healthcare systems.

INTRODUCTION

Work-from-home (WFH) models in healthcare have revolutionized the way medical services are delivered, offering new methods to improve accessibility, efficiency, and outcomes. This shift is largely driven by advancements in three key smart technologies: artificial intelligence (AI), telemedicine, and

DOI: 10.4018/979-8-3373-0240-9.ch023

the Internet of Things (IoTs). Collectively, all these modern technologies enable healthcare professionals to engage with patients remotely, manage care effectively, and keep track of health issues in real time, without the constraints of traditional clinical environments (Khan et al., 2022). The outbreak of the coronavirus was enacted as a turning point, accelerating the adoption of these technologies and compelling healthcare providers to rethink service delivery as a long-term, sustainable model rather than a temporary solution (Yadav, Alam, et al., 2022).

In this chapter, we examine how WFH models, underpinned by these technologies, are transforming global healthcare delivery and aligning with the third Sustainable Development Goal— ensuring healthy lives while promoting well-being for everyone at all age groups. Despite the goal's focus on universal healthcare access, healthcare systems worldwide have long struggled with disparities in access, quality, and affordability (A. Kumar, Nirala, et al., 2023). WFH models, by breaking down geographical barriers and reducing healthcare costs, offer a solution to these systemic inequities (Yadav, Mishra, et al., 2022). In regions where healthcare resources are limited, these models provide an innovative approach to enhancing healthcare access and quality.

Three central technologies—telemedicine, AI, and IoT—are crucial to the evolution of WFH models in healthcare (Agrawal et al., 2023). Each brings distinct advantages to healthcare delivery, and their combined use is shaping the future of global health systems. This chapter explores these technologies in depth, including why they need to be studied, their broader purpose, and their critical importance for improving healthcare outcomes and advancing SDG 3.

Telemedicine: Expanding Access to Care

Telemedicine refers to the use of telecommunications technology to deliver healthcare services remotely (R. Kumar, Dwivedi, et al., 2023). This can include video consultations, remote diagnostics, electronic prescriptions, and virtual follow-ups (Dash et al., 2022). By eliminating the necessity for in-person visits, telemedicine makes medical care accessible to every patient who might otherwise face barriers such as distance, transportation costs, or limited access to specialists (Dewangan et al., 2020).

The importance of telemedicine lies in its potential to democratize healthcare access. In underserved regions, where healthcare infrastructure is lacking or geographically dispersed, telemedicine can bridge the gap, providing patients with access to medical professionals who might not be locally available (Prasad et al., 2023). This is explicitly essential for every individual maintaining livelihood in rural areas or countries where healthcare resources are stretched thin. Additionally, telemedicine helps reduce the burden on healthcare facilities, alleviating overcrowding and allowing for more focused care for critical patients (Mahor, Pachlasiya, Garg, Chouhan, et al., 2022).

Telemedicine is rapidly evolving, but understanding its full potential and limitations requires further study. Researchers must assess the effectiveness of virtual consultations compared to in-person care, analyze patient outcomes, and explore how telemedicine can be scaled across diverse healthcare systems globally (Kumari et al., 2022). Moreover, the regulatory and technical challenges that come with telemedicine — such as data privacy, cross-border healthcare, and maintaining a high standard of care — necessitate rigorous investigation to ensure sustainable implementation (Mahor, Bijrothiya, Mishra, Rawat, et al., 2022).

Artificial Intelligence: Enhancing Diagnostic and Decision-Making Processes

Artificial intelligence (AI) has emerged as a transformative force in healthcare, offering significant enhancements to diagnostic accuracy, decision-making, and personalized treatment planning (Pithode et al., 2023). AI algorithms can analyze gigantic datasets, from patient medical records to imaging scans, in a fraction of the time it would take a human, allowing for quicker, more informed clinical decisions (Chincholikar et al., 2023). AI applications include disease prediction, drug discovery, radiology diagnostics, and even AI-powered chatbots for patient triage (A. Kumar, Singh, et al., 2023).

The importance of AI in WFH models cannot be understated. With AI-driven tools, healthcare providers working remotely can offer high-quality, data-driven care (Singh et al., 2023). AI-powered systems can flag abnormalities in diagnostic tests, predict disease progression, or recommend treatment plans, all while the healthcare provider operates from a remote location (Mahla et al., 2022). This enhances not only the speed but also the accuracy and personalization of care, diminishing the margins for man-made error and ameliorating patient outcomes (H. Sharma et al., 2023).

Despite the rapid integration of AI into healthcare, many questions remain about its ethical use, reliability, and impact on patient care (Rawat et al., 2022). Further study is required to evaluate AI's role in decision-making in WFH models and how it can complement, rather than replace, human judgment. Issues related to transparency, accountability, and bias in AI systems must be examined to ensure equitable healthcare delivery. Additionally, understanding how AI can be adapted for diverse healthcare settings, from urban hospitals to rural clinics, is essential for achieving its full potential (A. Kumar, Maithani, et al., 2023).

The Internet of Things (IoT): Revolutionizing Patient Monitoring

The Internet of Things (IoT) in healthcare refers to the network of connected devices that collect, transmit, and analyze patient data in real time (Barwar et al., 2021). These devices range from wearable health monitors (e.g., heart rate monitors, and glucose sensors) to home-based diagnostic tools that enable remote patient monitoring. IoT technologies provide healthcare professionals with continuous data on a patient's condition, allowing for timely interventions and more personalized care.

The importance of IoT lies in its ability to provide continuous, real-time health data, which is especially beneficial for managing chronic conditions such as diabetes, hypertension, and cardiovascular diseases. By enabling remote monitoring, IoT reduces the need for frequent hospital visits, thereby minimizing the strain on healthcare systems and making healthcare more accessible to patients with mobility issues or those living in remote areas. IoT represents a relatively new frontier in healthcare, and its long-term implications for patient outcomes and healthcare management are still being explored (Mahor, Garg, Telang, Pachlasiya, et al., 2022). Researchers need to study how IoT devices can be seamlessly integrated into WFH models, ensuring that they provide accurate and actionable data. There is also a need to examine how IoT systems can be made affordable and scalable in low-resource settings, where healthcare access is most limited. Additionally, addressing security concerns around IoT data transmission and storage is vital for ensuring patient privacy and trust in the system.

Need for Integration of Telemedicine, AI, and IoT

Studying telemedicine, AI, and IoT together is essential because they represent the three pillars of modern WFH healthcare. While each technology offers its own set of advantages, their combined use can lead to even more significant improvements in healthcare delivery. For instance, telemedicine consultations supplemented with AI-driven diagnostic tools and real-time IoT monitoring allow healthcare providers to offer comprehensive, personalized care remotely. The integration of these technologies can lead to more accurate diagnoses, timely interventions, and better patient outcomes — all while reducing the burden on healthcare facilities and expanding access to care.

Furthermore, exploring these variables in tandem is crucial for understanding how they contribute to the broader goals of SDG 3. Ensuring healthy lives and promoting well-being for all requires a multifaceted approach, one that addresses both the need for quality care and the inequalities that prevent many from accessing it. By studying these technologies together, researchers and policymakers can develop more holistic strategies for achieving global health equity and sustainability.

The Importance of WFH Models for Global Health Systems

WFH models represent not just a temporary response to a global health crisis, but a long-term solution for many of the systemic challenges facing healthcare systems worldwide (Mahor, Bijrothiya, Mishra, & Rawat, 2022). By integrating telemedicine, AI, and IoT into everyday healthcare practices, WFH models offer the potential to revolutionize how care is delivered, particularly in underserved regions (Barwar et al., 2022). These models make healthcare more adaptable, scalable, and resilient, allowing healthcare systems to better respond to both everyday needs and global health emergencies (Kushwaha et al., 2023).

In this chapter, we will delve deeper into how WFH models, supported by these three key technologies, can help address the healthcare inequalities that have long hindered progress toward SDG 3. We will explore the benefits, challenges, and future potential of these models, offering insights into how they can be implemented to create more equitable, accessible, and sustainable healthcare systems worldwide.

WFH Models and Smart Technologies: Reshaping Healthcare

The integration of Work-from-Home (WFH) models in healthcare has fundamentally reshaped both the delivery of patient care and the work environment for healthcare professionals (Alam et al., 2023). These changes are largely driven by three key smart technologies: telemedicine, artificial intelligence (AI), and the Internet of Things (IoT) (Rathod et al., 2024). By leveraging these technologies, WFH models have created a more flexible, patient-centric healthcare system that is better equipped to handle modern challenges such as healthcare access disparities, resource limitations, and the increasing demand for personalized care (Agrawal, Yugbodh, et al., 2023). Below, we explore in greater detail how these technologies are reshaping healthcare and why they represent a paradigm shift in the industry.

Telemedicine: Expanding Remote Consultations and Access to Care

Telemedicine is the cornerstone of WFH models in healthcare (Shrivastava et al., 2022). By facilitating remote consultations through video conferencing, phone calls, or even asynchronous communication (e.g., chat or email), telemedicine enables patients to access medical care without the need for in-person visits. This technology is particularly valuable in regions where healthcare resources are scarce or where patients face barriers such as long travel distances, mobility issues, or socioeconomic challenges.

1. **Expanded Reach and Accessibility**: Telemedicine effectively breaks down geographical barriers, bringing healthcare services to underserved populations in rural, remote, or economically disadvantaged areas. In traditional healthcare settings, access to specialists is often limited to urban or well-resourced regions, but telemedicine allows these specialists to provide consultations to patients far beyond their physical location. This is crucial for addressing healthcare inequalities, as it ensures that people in underserved areas receive the same level of care as those in more developed regions (Bhatnagar, Rajaram, et al., 2024).
2. **Efficiency and Resource Optimization**: In addition to expanding access, telemedicine also increases the efficiency of healthcare systems. Remote consultations reduce the need for hospital visits and waiting times, allowing healthcare providers to see more patients in less tim. This, in turn, relieves the strain on overburdened healthcare systems, particularly during crises like the COVID-19 pandemic. Furthermore, telemedicine reduces the need for physical infrastructure, such as clinics and hospitals, making healthcare delivery more cost-effective and sustainable (P. Kumar, Taneja, & Ozen, 2024).
3. **Follow-ups and Chronic Care**: Telemedicine is especially beneficial for managing chronic conditions that require regular monitoring and follow-up consultations. Patients with diabetes, hypertension, or cardiovascular diseases can maintain regular contact with their healthcare providers without the inconvenience or expense of frequent clinic visits. This continuous care model helps improve health outcomes by ensuring timely interventions and adherence to treatment plans.

Artificial Intelligence: Revolutionizing Diagnosis and Decision-Making

Artificial intelligence (AI) plays a transformative role in WFH healthcare models by enhancing the diagnostic process, improving decision-making, and enabling personalized treatment (Bhatnagar et al., 2023). AI systems can analyze large datasets, such as medical records, diagnostic images, and even genetic information, to provide healthcare providers with insights that improve accuracy and speed in clinical decision-making (P. Kumar, Reepu, et al., 2024).

1. **AI in Diagnostics**: One of the most promising applications of AI in healthcare is its ability to support diagnostic accuracy. AI algorithms can quickly analyze medical images, such as X-rays or MRIs, identifying patterns that may be indicative of diseases like cancer, pneumonia, or fractures (P. Kumar, Taneja, Bhatnagar, et al., 2024). In WFH models, this means that healthcare providers working remotely can access AI-assisted diagnostic tools that help them make faster, more informed decisions about patient care. This is particularly valuable in cases where time is critical, such as diagnosing life-threatening conditions.
2. **Personalized Treatment Plans**: AI can also assist in developing personalized treatment plans based on a patient's unique medical history, lifestyle, and genetic profile. For example, AI-driven platforms can suggest tailored treatment regimens for patients with chronic conditions, predicting how they might respond to different medications or interventions. In a WFH setting, healthcare providers can use these AI tools to deliver personalized care remotely, ensuring that patients receive the most effective treatments without requiring in-person visitsm (Taneja, Bhatnagar, Kumar, & Rupeika-apoga, 2023).

3. **Automation and Streamlining Healthcare Processes**: Beyond diagnostics and treatment, AI is being used to automate routine tasks, such as appointment scheduling, billing, and even patient triage (P. Kumar, Bhatnagar, et al., 2023). AI-powered chatbots, for instance, can handle initial patient inquiries, assess symptoms, and route patients to the appropriate healthcare providers (P. Sharma et al., 2024). This automation allows healthcare professionals working from home to focus more on direct patient care, enhancing both productivity and patient satisfaction.

Internet of Things (IoT): Continuous Remote Patient Monitoring

The Internet of Things (IoT) represents the third key technology reshaping WFH healthcare models. IoT devices, such as wearable health monitors and home-based diagnostic tools, enable continuous, real-time monitoring of patients' health (Taneja, Bhatnagar, Kumar, & Grima, 2023). These devices collect data on vital signs, such as heart rate, blood pressure, glucose levels, and oxygen saturation, and transmit this information to healthcare providers in real-time (Bhatnagar, Kumar, et al., 2024).

1. **Real-Time Health Monitoring**: IoT devices play a critical role in managing chronic diseases, as they allow healthcare providers to continuously monitor patients' conditions from a distance. For example, a patient with diabetes might wear a glucose monitor that sends regular updates to their healthcare provider, allowing for immediate adjustments to treatment if needed. This real-time monitoring reduces the risk of complications and ensures that patients receive timely interventions, even when they are not physically present in a healthcare facility.
2. **Proactive Care and Early Interventions**: By providing continuous health data, IoT devices enable healthcare providers to deliver proactive care, addressing potential health issues before they escalate into more serious conditions. For instance, an IoT-enabled heart monitor might detect early signs of arrhythmia, allowing for preventive measures that could avoid a more severe cardiac event. This shift toward proactive care represents a major advancement in healthcare delivery, especially in the context of WFH models.
3. **Improving Patient Engagement**: IoT devices also empower patients by allowing them to take a more active role in managing their health. Patients can access real-time data on their health status through connected apps, making them more aware of their condition and treatment progress. This increased engagement often leads to better adherence to treatment plans, improved lifestyle choices, and, ultimately, better health outcomes.

Integration of Telemedicine, AI, and IoT in WFH Models

While telemedicine, AI, and IoT each offer significant benefits individually, their combined use in WFH models creates a comprehensive healthcare ecosystem that delivers high-quality, efficient, and accessible care. Healthcare providers working from remote locations can offer the same level of care as those in traditional settings, with the added flexibility of leveraging these advanced technologies. **Telemedicine** provides the framework for remote consultations and access to care, **AI** enhances the accuracy and personalization of care through data-driven insights, and **IoT** ensures that patient monitoring is continuous and real-time. Together, these technologies enable healthcare professionals to deliver holistic care to patients, regardless of physical location. WFH models supported by telemedicine, AI, and IoT also represent sustainable and scalable solutions for global healthcare systems. As healthcare demand continues to rise, particularly in aging populations and in the face of global health emergencies, traditional healthcare infrastructure may struggle to keep up. WFH models offer a way to expand healthcare capacity without the need for significant investments in physical infrastructure. These models also reduce the environmental impact of healthcare by minimizing the need for patient travel, reducing the strain on hospitals, and optimizing resource use. Moreover, as AI and IoT technologies become more affordable, WFH models have the potential to be scaled globally, offering a solution to healthcare disparities in low-resource settings (Goel et al., 2024). WFH models, powered by telemedicine, AI, and IoT, are reshaping the healthcare landscape by creating more flexible, patient-centric, and efficient system. These models not only expand access to healthcare, especially in underserved areas but also enhance the quality and personalization of care. As healthcare systems around the world continue to evolve, WFH models supported by these smart technologies offer a sustainable path forward, particularly in achieving the goals outlined in SDG 3 — ensuring healthy lives and promoting well-being for all at all ages(P. Kumar, Verma, et al., 2023). By harnessing the potential of these technologies, healthcare providers can deliver care that is not only more accessible and efficient but also more equitable and sustainable in the long term.

Current Trends in Work-From-Home in Healthcare

The COVID-19 pandemic catalyzed a seismic shift in healthcare, pushing institutions globally to adopt remote work practices. The following trends represent the evolving landscape of WFH in healthcare:

1. **Expansion of Telemedicine and Virtual Care**

One of the most prominent trends in healthcare WFH models is the exponential growth of telemedicine. Telehealth services have expanded rapidly, allowing healthcare providers to conduct consultations via video calls, secure messaging, or telephonic conversations (Bhatnagar, Taneja, et al., 2024). This has reduced physical visits to hospitals while ensuring continuity of care. Telemedicine is being used for initial consultations, follow-up visits, mental health services, and chronic disease management (Kaur et al., 2023).

- o **Post-COVID normalization:** Even as the pandemic has waned, many healthcare providers continue to offer telemedicine services, integrating them into their regular workflows. It is now seen as a viable, long-term option rather than a temporary solution.
- o **Global adoption:** Countries such as the U.S., India, and the UK have embraced telehealth policies, with governments relaxing regulations to facilitate virtual care.

2. **Remote Patient Monitoring (RPM)**

Remote patient monitoring has gained traction due to IoT devices and wearable health technologies. Devices that track vital signs, such as blood pressure monitors, glucose meters, and heart rate monitors, allow healthcare providers to keep an eye on patients without them needing to visit hospitals.

- o **Chronic disease management:** RPM is particularly beneficial for managing chronic conditions like diabetes, heart disease, and hypertension, allowing for timely interventions and personalized treatment plans.

o **Home-based rehabilitation:** Post-surgical recovery and rehabilitation services are also increasingly moving to home settings, facilitated by wearable devices that track recovery metrics and allow real-time communication with healthcare professionals.

3. **AI-Powered Virtual Assistants**

AI-enabled virtual assistants are being deployed to support healthcare workers by automating routine tasks, scheduling appointments, and providing patients with health advice. These virtual assistants, embedded in telemedicine platforms, reduce the administrative burden on healthcare staff and enhance patient engagement by delivering personalized care recommendations.

4. **Teletherapy and Mental Health Services**

Another major trend is the rise in teletherapy, particularly in the mental health sector. Virtual counseling sessions, either through video calls or apps, have made mental health services more accessible. This has reduced the stigma associated with seeking help, particularly in remote or underserved areas where mental health professionals are scarce.

o **Mental health apps:** Digital platforms and apps like BetterHelp, Talkspace, and Headspace provide on-demand therapy sessions and mental health resources, contributing to improved well-being.

5. **Collaborative Platforms for Healthcare Workers**

For healthcare professionals, especially administrative and back-office staff, collaborative platforms such as Slack, Microsoft Teams, and Zoom have become essential tools. These platforms enable seamless communication, data sharing, and collaborative decision-making, even when working remotely.

6. **Training and Continuing Medical Education (CME)**

The adoption of online platforms for training and professional development is another emerging trend in the healthcare WFH landscape. Online courses, webinars, and virtual simulations are becoming commonplace, enabling healthcare workers to continuously upgrade their skills without attending in-person sessions.

7. **Data Security and HIPAA Compliance in Remote Healthcare**

One challenge for WFH models in healthcare is ensuring the security and privacy of patient data. As remote consultations and monitoring increase, healthcare providers are investing in secure platforms that comply with data protection regulations like HIPAA (Health Insurance Portability and Accountability Act) in the U.S. and GDPR (General Data Protection Regulation) in Europe. The integration of blockchain technology is also being explored to enhance the security and traceability of patient records in WFH settings.

8. **Cross-Border Telemedicine**

Another key trend is the rise of cross-border telemedicine, where patients consult with specialists in different countries. This is especially beneficial in cases where local expertise is limited. Medical tourism, which saw a decline due to travel restrictions, has also adapted to this new model where initial consultations happen remotely, with patients travelling only for major procedures.

Reducing Healthcare Inequalities through the Integration of Smart Technologies:

Smart technologies, when integrated with WFH models, have the potential to reduce healthcare disparities by making care more accessible and affordable. The chapter will discuss how these technologies are leveling the playing field in healthcare, particularly in low-income and underserved regions:

1. **Bridging the Digital Divide:** One of the major challenges of implementing WFH healthcare models is the digital divide—the gap between those with access to digital tools and those without. While this challenge persists, smart technologies such as mobile health (mHealth) apps and telemedicine platforms are making significant strides in bridging this divide. Low-cost solutions like SMS-based health reminders and virtual consultations are making healthcare more accessible to populations without access to advanced infrastructure.
2. **Affordable and Scalable Healthcare Solutions:** WFH models enabled by smart technologies reduce operational costs for healthcare providers, as physical infrastructure is no longer a bottleneck. This enables healthcare providers to scale their services more affordably, making it possible to extend high-quality care to underserved regions without a proportional increase in costs. By reducing the need for expensive, in-person visits, smart technology-driven WFH models can address inequities in healthcare delivery.
3. **Increasing Health Literacy and Empowering Patients:** Smart technologies empower patients by providing them with tools and information to manage their health. Mobile health apps that provide educational resources, symptom checkers, and self-management tools increase health literacy, which is crucial in underserved populations. By enabling individuals to monitor and manage their health remotely, these technologies contribute to more equitable healthcare outcomes and support SDG 3's emphasis on promoting well-being for all.

Challenges for WFH Models in Healthcare

Although Work-from-Home (WFH) models in healthcare offer significant benefits in terms of accessibility, efficiency, and sustainability, they are accompanied by a set of challenges that must be addressed to fully realize their potential. The successful implementation and scaling of these models depend on overcoming barriers related to digital health literacy, data privacy, cybersecurity, and workforce readiness. However, these challenges also present opportunities for innovation, collaboration, and policy development that can ultimately strengthen WFH models in healthcare. Below, we explore these challenges in greater detail and discuss the opportunities they present.

1. Digital Health Literacy: Bridging the Knowledge Gap

One of the primary challenges in the implementation of WFH models in healthcare is the issue of digital health literacy. Digital health literacy refers to an individual's ability to seek, understand, and apply digital health information using electronic resources such as telemedicine platforms, mobile health apps, or IoT devices. While telemedicine and IoT technologies have been instrumental in making healthcare more accessible, their effectiveness hinges on patients' ability to navigate and use these tools correctly.

- **Demographic Disparities**: Patients from low-income, elderly, or rural populations often face challenges in accessing and understanding digital health tools. These groups may lack access to high-speed internet, and digital devices, or possess the technical know-how required to interact with telemedicine platforms effectively. For instance, elderly patients, who are more likely to suffer from chronic health conditions requiring ongoing care, may struggle to adapt to virtual consultations or remote monitoring technologies.
- **Educational Barriers**: Even when access to technology is available, some patients may not have the necessary education or experience to navigate complex healthcare apps or devices. This can lead to underutilization of telemedicine services or incorrect use of IoT devices, which may compromise the quality of care received.
- **Inequality in Global Access**: In developing countries, where healthcare infrastructure and internet access may be limited, digital health literacy becomes an even greater obstacle. The digital divide exacerbates healthcare inequalities, as populations in low-resource settings may not have the means to engage in WFH healthcare models.

2. Data Privacy and Cybersecurity: Protecting Sensitive Health Information

As WFH models in healthcare become increasingly reliant on digital technologies, concerns about data privacy and cybersecurity have emerged as critical challenges. Telemedicine platforms and IoT devices collect vast amounts of sensitive health data, including patient histories, diagnostic images, and real-time health metrics. Ensuring that this data is protected from breaches, unauthorized access, and cyberattacks is essential to maintaining patient trust and safeguarding the healthcare system.

- **Increased Vulnerability to Cyberattacks**: Healthcare organizations, particularly those that utilize telemedicine and IoT devices, have become prime targets for cybercriminals. These systems store and transmit sensitive patient data over networks that may not always have robust security measures in place. Data breaches can lead to identity theft, fraud, and compromised medical records, which can severely impact patient safety and healthcare delivery.
- **Regulatory Compliance**: Healthcare providers operating under WFH models must navigate a complex web of data protection regulations, such as the General Data Protection Regulation (GDPR) in Europe or the Health Insurance Portability and Accountability Act (HIPAA) in the United States. Ensuring compliance with these regulations requires stringent security protocols, ongoing monitoring, and regular audits. For smaller healthcare organizations or those operating in multiple jurisdictions, maintaining compliance can be a resource-intensive task.
- **IoT Device Security**: While IoT devices enable continuous remote patient monitoring, they also present new cybersecurity risks. IoT devices are often connected to the internet, making them vul-

nerable to hacking. If an IoT device is compromised, hackers could gain access to critical patient data or disrupt the functioning of life-saving medical equipment.

3. Workforce Readiness: Preparing Healthcare Professionals for Remote Care

Another challenge facing WFH models in healthcare is ensuring that healthcare professionals are adequately trained and prepared to manage remote care technologies. While WFH models offer flexibility and the ability to serve more patients, they also require healthcare providers to develop new skills, such as managing telemedicine consultations, interpreting data from IoT devices, and utilizing AI-driven diagnostic tools.

- **Resistance to Technological Change**: Healthcare providers, especially those accustomed to traditional in-person care, may be hesitant to adopt WFH models and rely on digital tools. This resistance could stem from a lack of familiarity with the technology, concerns about patient outcomes, or discomfort with new workflows.
- **Need for Ongoing Training**: The fast pace of technological advancements means that healthcare professionals need ongoing training to stay updated on the latest tools and platforms. This can be challenging for organizations that are already stretched thin by workforce shortages and resource constraints. Ensuring that healthcare providers receive sufficient training without disrupting patient care requires careful planning and resource allocation.
- **Balancing Remote and In-Person Care**: Even in WFH models, healthcare providers may need to balance remote care with in-person consultations. This requires them to develop hybrid care models that seamlessly integrate digital tools with traditional healthcare practices. Striking this balance is essential to ensuring that patients receive comprehensive care across all modalities.

Turning Challenges into Opportunities: Paving the Way for a New Healthcare Paradigm

The challenges surrounding Work-from-Home (WFH) models in healthcare are complex but offer unprecedented opportunities for transformation. Each challenge, whether it pertains to digital health literacy, data privacy, cybersecurity, or workforce readiness, presents a fertile ground for innovation, policy reform, and the integration of cutting-edge technologies. This section will examine how these obstacles can be reframed into opportunities that not only improve healthcare delivery but also align with the long-term goals of Sustainable Development Goal 3 (SDG 3) — ensuring healthy lives and promoting well-being for all.

1. Advancing Digital Health Literacy: Bridging the Digital Divide

One of the most significant barriers to the widespread adoption of WFH healthcare models is the disparity in digital health literacy. However, this challenge can become a pivotal moment for healthcare providers and governments to invest in comprehensive digital education programs. The digital divide, which disproportionately affects rural and low-income populations, can be bridged by:

- **Tailored Educational Initiatives**: Developing accessible and culturally sensitive educational content that teaches patients how to navigate telemedicine platforms and IoT devices is a critical step. Programs that utilize simple language, multilingual support, and visual aids can significantly improve comprehension and usability, empowering patients to take control of their healthcare remotely.
- **Leveraging Community Resources**: Healthcare organizations can partner with local community centers, NGOs, and schools to host digital health literacy workshops, thus reaching underserved populations. By embedding these programs within trusted community institutions, healthcare providers can foster greater trust and engagement with technology among patients who are new to digital health platforms.
- **Mobile Health (mHealth) Solutions**: Utilizing the ubiquity of mobile phones, particularly in low-resource settings, offers an innovative way to overcome access barriers. mHealth apps, designed with simplicity and accessibility in mind, can help patients with limited digital skills engage with healthcare services. Mobile apps that require minimal data usage and are compatible with older devices could revolutionize healthcare access in remote areas.

2. Enhancing Data Privacy and Cybersecurity: Building Trust in Digital Health

Data privacy and cybersecurity are paramount in the healthcare industry, especially in the context of WFH models that rely on telemedicine and IoT devices. Rather than viewing these issues as insurmountable obstacles, healthcare providers and technology developers can seize this opportunity to set new benchmarks in data security.

- **Adopting Blockchain Technology**: Blockchain, known for its decentralized and immutable nature, can be integrated into healthcare systems to create secure, transparent health records. By encrypting patient data and ensuring that only authorized parties have access, blockchain technology can safeguard sensitive health information and prevent data breaches, while also providing patients with greater control over their own health data.
- **Proactive Cybersecurity Protocols**: The integration of AI-driven cybersecurity solutions can monitor systems in real-time, detect threats, and respond to potential attacks before they cause harm. Investing in AI technologies that continuously learn and adapt to emerging cyber threats will strengthen the integrity of digital health platforms and boost patient confidence in remote care.
- **Regulatory Innovations**: As governments and international bodies recognize the critical role of telemedicine in achieving global health goals, they can work toward updating legal frameworks to better address data security in digital healthcare. By establishing clear, globally harmonized data privacy standards and enforcing stringent penalties for non-compliance, healthcare providers can operate with greater clarity and patients with more assurance.

3. Workforce Readiness: Empowering Healthcare Professionals for the Digital Future

Healthcare professionals are at the heart of WFH models, and ensuring that they are well-equipped to handle the demands of remote care is key to the success of this model. What might initially seem like a challenge — adapting to new technologies and workflows — can in fact be a pathway to professional growth, greater efficiency, and more effective healthcare delivery.

- **Upskilling and Continuous Learning**: The introduction of new technologies in healthcare creates an opportunity for continuous professional development. Offering training programs that focus on telemedicine, AI diagnostic tools, and IoT-based patient monitoring will not only enhance the skills of healthcare providers but also increase the quality of care delivered remotely. Certifications in digital health technologies could further incentivize healthcare workers to embrace these new tools and grow in their careers.
- **Hybrid Care Models**: As healthcare increasingly becomes a blend of in-person and remote care, healthcare providers can innovate by developing hybrid models that incorporate the best of both worlds. For example, AI-driven tools can be used to triage patients in virtual settings, while complex cases requiring hands-on care can be directed to in-person consultations. This hybrid approach ensures that remote healthcare remains comprehensive, efficient, and adaptable to various patient needs.
- **Collaborative Care Networks**: Digital tools enable the formation of collaborative care networks that span across regions and even countries. Healthcare professionals working from home can consult with specialists, share diagnostic data, and co-manage patient care in real-time, no matter where they are located. This collaborative model not only improves patient outcomes but also fosters a global exchange of medical expertise.

4. Leveraging IoT and AI for a Smarter Healthcare Ecosystem

The Internet of Things (IoT) and Artificial Intelligence (AI) are the linchpins of WFH healthcare models, offering scalable solutions for real-time patient monitoring and data-driven decision-making. Embracing these technologies opens new avenues for transforming healthcare systems.

- **IoT in Remote Patient Monitoring**: Wearable devices and home monitoring systems that track vital signs, glucose levels, and medication adherence can feed real-time data to healthcare providers. This ensures that patients, especially those with chronic conditions, are continuously monitored without the need for frequent hospital visits. Healthcare providers can intervene promptly when necessary, reducing the risk of complications and improving long-term patient outcomes.
- **AI for Predictive Analytics and Decision Support**: AI algorithms can analyze vast amounts of health data to detect patterns and predict health outcomes. This allows healthcare providers working remotely to make more informed decisions and personalize care plans for each patient. For instance, AI can predict which patients are at higher risk of developing complications, enabling preventive interventions that can be managed remotely.
- **Personalized and Proactive Care**: WFH models supported by AI and IoT empower healthcare professionals to offer more personalized and proactive care. By harnessing data from multiple

sources — wearables, home monitoring devices, electronic health records — AI systems can generate comprehensive patient profiles that allow for individualized treatment plans and timely interventions. This shift from reactive to proactive care aligns with the goals of SDG 3, promoting health and well-being for all.

5. Scaling WFH Healthcare Models: Achieving Global Health Equity

Finally, the true opportunity of WFH models in healthcare lies in their potential to scale across regions and healthcare systems, reducing inequalities and ensuring that even the most underserved populations have access to quality care.

- **Global Collaborations for Resource Sharing**: Through international partnerships, developed countries with advanced digital healthcare infrastructures can collaborate with low- and middle-income countries to share resources, technology, and expertise. This exchange can accelerate the adoption of WFH models in regions where healthcare access is limited.
- **Telemedicine for Universal Health Coverage**: WFH models can be instrumental in achieving Universal Health Coverage (UHC), a key target of SDG 3 (Gera et al., 2018). By lowering the barriers to healthcare access, telemedicine platforms can extend services to remote areas where traditional healthcare infrastructure is lacking, ensuring that all individuals receive the care they need regardless of geographic location.
- **Reducing Healthcare Costs**: WFH models have the potential to reduce healthcare costs for both providers and patients by minimizing the need for physical infrastructure, travel, and hospital admissions. This cost-effectiveness is especially crucial for countries with strained healthcare budgets, enabling them to allocate resources more efficiently while expanding access to essential services.

By reframing the challenges of WFH models in healthcare as opportunities for innovation and growth, we can pave the way for a more accessible, efficient, and equitable healthcare system. Through advancements in digital health literacy, enhanced cybersecurity measures, professional development, and the integration of AI and IoT, WFH healthcare models hold the potential to transform global health outcomes. Ultimately, these models align with the broader goals of sustainable development, creating a future where healthcare is not only more flexible but also more inclusive and universally accessible.

Future Outlook on Scaling WFH Healthcare Models to Achieve Sustainable Health Systems Globally:

As we look toward the future, scaling WFH healthcare models using smart technologies is essential for achieving more sustainable, resilient, and inclusive health systems. The chapter will outline key trends, challenges, and strategic recommendations for scaling these models:

1. **Policy and Regulatory Frameworks for Sustainable WFH Models:** For WFH healthcare models to be successfully scaled, policymakers must create frameworks that support their adoption. This includes establishing guidelines for telemedicine practices, ensuring data privacy through regulations

such as the General Data Protection Regulation (GDPR), and incentivizing healthcare providers to adopt smart technologies.
2. **Building Digital Infrastructure:** The expansion of digital infrastructure, especially in low-resource settings, is critical for the sustainable scaling of WFH healthcare models. Investments in internet connectivity, mobile technology, and affordable healthcare devices will be necessary to ensure that WFH models can be implemented globally.
3. **Training Healthcare Professionals and Patients:** The successful scaling of WFH models requires the training of both healthcare professionals and patients in using smart technologies. Healthcare professionals need to be equipped with the skills to utilize telemedicine, AI diagnostics, and IoT devices, while patients must be educated on how to use these technologies for self-management.
4. **Sustainable Funding Models:** Innovative funding mechanisms, such as public-private partnerships, will be crucial for scaling WFH healthcare models globally. These partnerships can help reduce costs, increase technology access, and ensure the financial sustainability of WFH models in healthcare systems.
5. **Emerging Technologies and Future Directions:** Emerging technologies such as blockchain for health data security, 5G for faster communication, and virtual reality (VR) for remote surgeries are on the horizon and promise to further enhance WFH healthcare models. The integration of these technologies will make it possible to create even more resilient and sustainable healthcare systems, aligning with the long-term vision of SDG 3.

CONCLUSION: TOWARDS A SUSTAINABLE AND INCLUSIVE FUTURE IN HEALTHCARE

The integration of Work-From-Home (WFH) models with smart technologies marks a pivotal shift in the healthcare landscape. This chapter has underscored how these frameworks, powered by telemedicine, Artificial Intelligence (AI), and the Internet of Things (IoT), are not merely transforming healthcare delivery but are actively contributing to the fulfillment of Sustainable Development Goal 3 (SDG 3). The broader impact of WFH models lies in their capacity to democratize healthcare access, enabling patients, regardless of location, to receive timely, high-quality care. These innovations not only address healthcare disparities but also offer solutions to the systemic challenges that have long plagued healthcare systems, such as overburdened hospitals, workforce shortages, and limited access in rural areas.

However, the real promise of WFH models in healthcare goes beyond technological integration. The key to their long-term success lies in **scalability**—ensuring that these models are adopted and adapted in diverse healthcare systems around the world. Achieving this scalability will require a concerted effort involving the implementation of supportive policies, investment in digital infrastructure, and the development of sustainable funding models. Governments, healthcare providers, and global organizations must collaborate to foster an environment where WFH models can thrive, particularly in resource-limited settings. The adoption of these frameworks at scale will not only revolutionize patient care but also create more resilient healthcare systems capable of withstanding future crises, whether they be global pandemics or localized health emergencies.

Practical Implications

From a **practical standpoint**, this chapter offers vital insights into how WFH models can be implemented to address real-world healthcare challenges:

1. **Expanding Healthcare Access**: In regions with limited healthcare infrastructure, WFH models offer a practical solution by eliminating the geographical constraints that have long hindered access to care. Telemedicine allows for virtual consultations, while IoT devices enable continuous patient monitoring, ensuring that care reaches those who need it most. For policymakers, these models present a scalable approach to Universal Health Coverage (UHC), one of the targets under SDG 3. By integrating WFH models into national healthcare strategies, governments can bridge the gap between underserved populations and quality healthcare services.
2. **Resource Optimization**: Healthcare systems globally are grappling with resource constraints, whether in terms of workforce, hospital space, or financial limitations. WFH models optimize these resources by shifting certain aspects of care away from traditional healthcare settings. This allows healthcare providers to focus their efforts on more critical in-person services, while remote technologies handle routine monitoring and consultations. For practitioners, adopting WFH models can lead to improved workflow efficiency, reducing burnout and enabling healthcare workers to provide more comprehensive, continuous care.
3. **Cost-Effectiveness:** One of the primary barriers to healthcare access, especially in low-income settings, is the cost associated with healthcare delivery. WFH models offer a cost-effective alternative by minimizing the need for physical infrastructure and travel. Patients save on transportation costs, while healthcare facilities reduce the overhead associated with maintaining large physical spaces. Furthermore, remote patient monitoring systems can help detect issues early, preventing costly hospital admissions and emergency room visits. For healthcare administrators, this presents a sustainable financial model for long-term healthcare delivery.
4. **Workforce Flexibility and Retention:** The flexibility afforded by WFH models also has practical implications for healthcare workforce retention. In a field notorious for high levels of stress and burnout, offering healthcare professionals the option to work from home, at least part-time, can greatly improve job satisfaction and work-life balance. This flexibility is crucial for retaining skilled professionals in an increasingly competitive global healthcare labor market.

Theoretical Implications

Theoretically, this chapter advances our understanding of how smart technologies and WFH models intersect to reshape healthcare systems, contributing to both healthcare management and technology innovation literature. The following theoretical implications are particularly significant:

1. **Telemedicine and Patient-Centered Care**: This chapter contributes to the theoretical discourse on patient-centered care by demonstrating how telemedicine shifts the focus from provider-centric to patient-centric models. Traditionally, healthcare delivery has been constrained by location, with patients required to visit hospitals or clinics for diagnosis and treatment. WFH models decentralize care, offering a more personalized and continuous healthcare experience. This aligns with emerging

theories in healthcare management that advocate for more patient autonomy and shared decision-making processes.

2. **AI and Decision Support Systems**: The integration of AI into WFH models also has theoretical implications for the field of decision support systems (DSS). AI's role in supporting clinical decisions, whether through diagnostics, predictive analytics, or treatment planning, adds a new dimension to the DSS literature. This chapter contributes to the ongoing debate about automation in healthcare, proposing that AI should be seen as a tool to enhance, rather than replace, human decision-making. The chapter's exploration of AI in remote healthcare contexts underscores the importance of a symbiotic relationship between technology and healthcare providers.

3. **IoT and Remote Monitoring**: IoT technologies enable remote patient monitoring, a critical aspect of WFH healthcare models. This chapter contributes to the broader theoretical discourse on ubiquitous healthcare, where care is continuous and unbound by the walls of hospitals. The ability to gather real-time patient data through wearable devices and home-based sensors introduces new avenues for preventive healthcare, shifting the focus from reactive to proactive care models. This theoretical contribution is especially relevant for scholars interested in the future of chronic disease management and long-term care.

4. **Resilience and Sustainability in Healthcare Systems**: Finally, this chapter's exploration of WFH models contributes to the growing body of literature on healthcare resilience. The COVID-19 pandemic revealed the vulnerabilities of traditional healthcare systems, particularly their inability to rapidly scale in times of crisis. WFH models, supported by smart technologies, offer a framework for building more resilient healthcare systems that can adapt to external shocks. The chapter posits that these models not only contribute to immediate healthcare delivery but also enhance the long-term sustainability of healthcare systems by reducing pressure on physical infrastructure and allowing for more efficient resource allocation.

In conclusion, the integration of WFH models with smart technologies offers a roadmap for the future of healthcare—one that is more flexible, inclusive, and resilient. By addressing both practical challenges and theoretical gaps, this chapter provides a comprehensive understanding of how WFH models can be scaled to meet the diverse needs of global healthcare systems. The key to realizing the full potential of these models lies in fostering international collaborations, investing in digital infrastructure, and developing regulatory frameworks that protect patient privacy while encouraging innovation. As healthcare systems around the world continue to grapple with the dual pressures of increasing demand and limited resources, WFH models, supported by technologies such as telemedicine, AI, and IoT, represent not just a temporary solution, but a permanent evolution in the way healthcare is delivered.

These advancements align with the broader goals of SDG 3, promoting health and well-being for all by ensuring that even the most underserved populations have access to quality care. Ultimately, the future of WFH models in healthcare is one of sustainable, scalable, and inclusive growth, providing a blueprint for how smart technologies can be leveraged to build more effective and equitable healthcare systems across the globe.

DECLARATION

The authors declare that the manuscript follows ethical standards and there are no potential conflicts of interest concerning this chapter's research, authorship, and publication.

DISCLAIMER

The contents and views of this chapter are expressed by the authors in personal capacities. The Editor and the Publisher don't need to agree with these viewpoints and are not responsible for any duty of care in this regard.

REFERENCES

Agrawal, Y., Bhagoria, J. L., Gautam, A., Sharma, A., Yadav, A. S., Alam, T., Kumar, R., Goga, G., Chakroborty, S., & Kumar, R. (2023). Investigation of thermal performance of a ribbed solar air heater for sustainable built environment. *Sustainable Energy Technologies and Assessments*, 57, 103288. Advance online publication. DOI: 10.1016/j.seta.2023.103288

Alam, M. A., Kumar, R., Banoriya, D., Yadav, A. S., Goga, G., Saxena, K. K., Buddhi, D., & Mohan, R. (2023). Design and development of thermal comfort analysis for air-conditioned compartment. *International Journal on Interactive Design and Manufacturing*, 17(5), 2777–2787. DOI: 10.1007/s12008-022-01015-8

Barwar, M. K., Sahu, L. K., Bhatnagar, P., Gupta, K. K., & Chander, A. H. (2021). A flicker-free decoupled ripple cancellation technique for LED driver circuits. *Optik (Stuttgart)*, 247, 168029. Advance online publication. DOI: 10.1016/j.ijleo.2021.168029

Barwar, M. K., Sahu, L. K., Bhatnagar, P., Gupta, K. K., & Chander, A. H. (2022). Performance analysis and reliability estimation of five-level rectifier. *International Journal of Circuit Theory and Applications*, 50(3), 926–943. DOI: 10.1002/cta.3187

Bhatnagar, M., Kumar, P., Taneja, S., Sood, K., & Grima, S. (2024). From digital overload to trading Zen: The role of digital detox in enhancing intraday trading performance. In *Business Drivers in Promoting Digital Detoxification*. IGI Global., DOI: 10.4018/979-8-3693-1107-3.ch010

Bhatnagar, M., Rajaram, R., Taneja, S., & Kumar, P. (2024). Balancing acts: The Yin and Yang of debit and credit on the stage of financial well-being. In *Emerging Perspectives on Financial Well-Being*. IGI Global., DOI: 10.4018/979-8-3693-1750-1.ch002

Bhatnagar, M., Taneja, S., & Kumar, P. (2023). The Effectiveness of Carbon Pricing Mechanism in Steering Financial Flows Toward Sustainable Projects. *International Journal of Environmental Impacts*, 6(4), 183–196. DOI: 10.18280/ijei.060403

Bhatnagar, M., Taneja, S., Kumar, P., & Özen, E. (2024). Does financial education act as a catalyst for SME competitiveness? *International Journal of Education Economics and Development*, 15(3), 377–393. DOI: 10.1504/IJEED.2024.139306

Chincholikar, P., Singh, K. R. B., Natarajan, A., Kerry, R. G., Singh, J., Malviya, J., & Singh, R. P. (2023). Green nanobiopolymers for ecological applications: A step towards a sustainable environment. *RSC Advances*, 13(18), 12411–12429. DOI: 10.1039/D2RA07707H PMID: 37091622

Dash, A. P., Alam, T., Siddiqui, M. I. H., Blecich, P., Kumar, M., Gupta, N. K., Ali, M. A., & Yadav, A. S. (2022). Impact on Heat Transfer Rate Due to an Extended Surface on the Passage of Microchannel Using Cylindrical Ribs with Varying Sector Angle. *Energies*, 15(21), 8191. Advance online publication. DOI: 10.3390/en15218191

Dewangan, N. K., Gupta, K. K., & Bhatnagar, P. (2020). Modified reduced device multilevel inverter structures with open circuit fault-tolerance capabilities. *International Transactions on Electrical Energy Systems*, 30(1). Advance online publication. DOI: 10.1002/2050-7038.12142

Goel, R., Singla, J., Mittal, A., & Arora, M. (2024). A decade analysis of employees' well-being and performance while working from home: A bibliometric approach. *Information Discovery and Delivery*. Advance online publication. DOI: 10.1108/idd-03-2023-0030

Kaur, A., Kumar, P., Taneja, S., & Ozen, E. (2023). Fintech emergence – an opportunity or threat to banking. *International Journal of Electronic Finance*, 13(1), 1–19. DOI: 10.1504/IJEF.2024.135163

Khan, S. A., Alam, T., Khan, M. S., Blecich, P., Kamal, M. A., Gupta, N. K., & Yadav, A. S. (2022). Life Cycle Assessment of Embodied Carbon in Buildings: Background, Approaches and Advancements. *Buildings*, 12(11), 1944. Advance online publication. DOI: 10.3390/buildings12111944

Kumar, A., Nirala, A., Singh, V. P., Sahoo, B. K., Singh, R. C., Chaudhary, R., Dewangan, A. K., Gaurav, G. K., Klemeš, J. J., & Liu, X. (2023). The utilisation of coconut shell ash in production of hybrid composite: Microstructural characterisation and performance analysis. *Journal of Cleaner Production*, 398, 136494. Advance online publication. DOI: 10.1016/j.jclepro.2023.136494

Kumar, A., Singh, V. P., Nirala, A., Singh, R. C., Chaudhary, R., Mourad, A.-H. I., Sahoo, B. K., & Kumar, D. (2023). Influence of tool rotational speed on mechanical and corrosion behaviour of friction stir processed AZ31/Al2O3 nanocomposite. *Journal of Magnesium and Alloys*, 11(7), 2585–2599. DOI: 10.1016/j.jma.2023.06.012

Kumar, P., Reepu, & Kaur, R. (2024). Economic and Urban Dynamics: Investigating Socioeconomic Status and Urban Density as Moderators of Mobile Wallet Adoption in Smart Cities. *Lecture Notes in Networks and Systems, 948 LNNS*, 409–417. DOI: 10.1007/978-981-97-1329-5_33

Kumar, P., Bhatnagar, M., & Taneja, S. (2023). Investigation of the time pattern of Bit Green Crypto: An Arma modeling approach to unrave volatility. In *Algorithmic Approaches to Financial Technology: Forecasting, Trading, and Optimization*. IGI Global., DOI: 10.4018/979-8-3693-1746-4.ch001

Kumar, P., Taneja, S., Bhatnagar, M., & Kaur, A. K. (2024). Navigating the digital paradigm shift: Designing CBDCs for a transformative financial landscape. In *Exploring Central Bank Digital Currencies: Concepts, Frameworks, Models, and Challenges*. IGI Global., DOI: 10.4018/979-8-3693-1882-9.ch006

Kumar, P., Taneja, S., & Ozen, E. (2024). Exploring the influence of green bonds on sustainable development through low-carbon financing mobilization. *International Journal of Law and Management*. DOI: 10.1108/IJLMA-01-2024-0030

Kumar, P., Verma, P., Bhatnagar, M., Taneja, S., Seychel, S., Todorović, I., & Grim, S. (2023). The Financial Performance and Solvency Status of the Indian Public Sector Banks: A CAMELS Rating and Z Index Approach. *International Journal of Sustainable Development and Planning*, 18(2), 367–376. DOI: 10.18280/ijsdp.180204

Kumar, R., Dwivedi, R. K., Arya, R. K., Sonia, P., Yadav, A. S., Saxena, K. K., Khan, M. I., & Ben Moussa, S. (2023). Current development of carbide free bainitic and retained austenite on wear resistance in high silicon steel. *Journal of Materials Research and Technology*, 24, 9171–9202. DOI: 10.1016/j.jmrt.2023.05.067

Kumari, N., Alam, T., Ali, M. A., Yadav, A. S., Gupta, N. K., Siddiqui, M. I. H., Dobrotă, D., Rotaru, I. M., & Sharma, A. (2022). A Numerical Investigation on Hydrothermal Performance of Micro Channel Heat Sink with Periodic Spatial Modification on Sidewalls. *Micromachines*, 13(11), 1986. Advance online publication. DOI: 10.3390/mi13111986 PMID: 36422415

Kushwaha, A. D., Patel, B., Khan, I. A., & Agrawal, A. (2023). Fabrication and characterization of hexagonal boron nitride/polyester composites to study the effect of filler loading and surface modification for microelectronic applications. *Polymer Composites*, 44(8), 4579–4593. DOI: 10.1002/pc.27421

Mahla, S. K., Goyal, T., Goyal, D., Sharma, H., Dhir, A., & Goga, G. (2022). Optimization of engine operating variables on performance and emissions characteristics of biogas fuelled CI engine by the design of experiments: Taguchi approach. *Environmental Progress & Sustainable Energy*, 41(2), e13736. Advance online publication. DOI: 10.1002/ep.13736

Mahor, V., Bijrothiya, S., Mishra, R., & Rawat, R. (2022). ML techniques for attack and anomaly detection in internet of things networks. In *Autonomous Vehicles* (Vol. 1). wiley. DOI: 10.1002/9781119871989.ch13

Mahor, V., Bijrothiya, S., Mishra, R., Rawat, R., & Soni, A. (2022). The smart city based on AI and infrastructure: A new mobility concepts and realities. In *Autonomous Vehicles* (Vol. 1). wiley. DOI: 10.1002/9781119871989.ch15

Mahor, V., Garg, B., Telang, S., Pachlasiya, K., Chouhan, M., & Rawat, R. (2022). Cyber Threat Phylogeny Assessment and Vulnerabilities Representation at Thermal Power Station. *Lecture Notes in Networks and Systems, 481 LNNS*, 28 – 39. DOI: 10.1007/978-981-19-3182-6_3

Mahor, V., Pachlasiya, K., Garg, B., Chouhan, M., Telang, S., & Rawat, R. (2022). Mobile Operating System (Android) Vulnerability Analysis Using Machine Learning. *Lecture Notes in Networks and Systems, 481 LNNS*, 159 – 169. DOI: 10.1007/978-981-19-3182-6_13

Pithode, K., Singh, D., Chaturvedi, R., Goyal, B., Dogra, A., Hasoon, A., & Lepcha, D. C. (2023). Evaluation of the Solar Heat Pipe with Aluminium Tube Collector in different Environmental Conditions. *2023 3rd Asian Conference on Innovation in Technology, ASIANCON 2023*. DOI: 10.1109/ASIANCON58793.2023.10269867

Prasad, A. O., Mishra, P., Jain, U., Pandey, A., Sinha, A., Yadav, A. S., Kumar, R., Sharma, A., Kumar, G., Hazim Salem, K., Sharma, A., & Dixit, A. K. (2023). Design and development of software stack of an autonomous vehicle using robot operating system. *Robotics and Autonomous Systems*, 161, 104340. Advance online publication. DOI: 10.1016/j.robot.2022.104340

Rathod, N. J., Chopra, M. K., Shelke, S. N., Chaurasiya, P. K., Kumar, R., Saxena, K. K., & Prakash, C. (2024). Investigations on hard turning using SS304 sheet metal component grey based Taguchi and regression methodology. *International Journal on Interactive Design and Manufacturing*, 18(5), 2653–2664. DOI: 10.1007/s12008-023-01244-5

Rawat, R., Mahor, V., Chouhan, M., Pachlasiya, K., Telang, S., & Garg, B. (2022). Systematic Literature Review (SLR) on Social Media and the Digital Transformation of Drug Trafficking on Darkweb. *Lecture Notes in Networks and Systems, 481 LNNS*, 181 – 205. DOI: 10.1007/978-981-19-3182-6_15

Sharma, H., Rana, A., Singh, R. P., Goyal, B., Dogra, A., & Lepcha, D. C. (2023). Improving Efficiency of Panel Using Solar Tracker Controlled Through Fuzzy Logic. *2023 International Conference on Sustainable Emerging Innovations in Engineering and Technology, ICSEIET 2023*, 286 – 289. DOI: 10.1109/ICSEIET58677.2023.10303639

Sharma, P., Taneja, S., Kumar, P., Özen, E., & Singh, A. (2024). Application of the UTAUT model toward individual acceptance: Emerging trends in artificial intelligence-based banking services. *International Journal of Electronic Finance*, 13(3), 352–366. DOI: 10.1504/IJEF.2024.139584

Shrivastava, V., Yadav, A. S., Sharma, A. K., Singh, P., Alam, T., & Sharma, A. (2022). Performance Comparison of Solar Air Heater with Extended Surfaces and Iron Filling. *International Journal of Vehicle Structures and Systems*, 14(5), 607–610. DOI: 10.4273/ijvss.14.5.10

Singh, V. P., Kumar, R., Kumar, A., & Dewangan, A. K. (2023). Automotive light weight multi-materials sheets joining through friction stir welding technique: An overview. *Materials Today: Proceedings*. Advance online publication. DOI: 10.1016/j.matpr.2023.02.171

Taneja, S., Bhatnagar, M., Kumar, P., & Grima, S. (2023). A Panel Analysis of the Effectiveness of the Asset Management in Indian Agricultural Companies. *International Journal of Sustainable Development and Planning*, 18(3), 653–660. DOI: 10.18280/ijsdp.180301

Taneja, S., Bhatnagar, M., Kumar, P., & Rupeika-apoga, R. (2023). India's Total Natural Resource Rents (NRR) and GDP : An Augmented Autoregressive Distributed Lag (ARDL) Bound Test. *Journal of Risk and Financial Management*, 16(2), 91. https://doi.org/doi.org/10.3390/jrfm16020091. DOI: 10.3390/jrfm16020091

Yadav, A. S., Alam, T., Gupta, G., Saxena, R., Gupta, N. K., Allamraju, K. V., Kumar, R., Sharma, N., Sharma, A., Pandey, U., & Agrawal, Y. (2022). A Numerical Investigation of an Artificially Roughened Solar Air Heater. *Energies*, 15(21), 8045. Advance online publication. DOI: 10.3390/en15218045

Yadav, A. S., Mishra, A., Dwivedi, K., Agrawal, A., Galphat, A., & Sharma, N. (2022). Investigation on performance enhancement due to rib roughened solar air heater. *Materials Today: Proceedings*, 63, 726–730. DOI: 10.1016/j.matpr.2022.05.071

Chapter 24
Impact of the Russian Invasion of Ukraine on the Indian Pharmaceutical Sector

Rajesh Tiwari
https://orcid.org/0000-0002-5345-2508
Graphic Era University, India

Vivek Verma
https://orcid.org/0000-0002-0406-4322
Graphic Era University, India

Vibhuti Jain
https://orcid.org/0009-0009-8602-6116
Graphic Era University, India

Vanshika Kakkar
Graphic Era University, India

ABSTRACT

India is the largest supplier of generic drugs in the world. India is the third largest by volume and fourteenth most significant in terms of the value of production of pharma products globally. The study examines the war's impact on the Indian pharmaceutical sector. The pharma stock data is obtained from the National Stock Exchange (NSE) India website. The war between Russia and Ukraine had no significant impact on the returns of Indian pharma stocks. India has a diversified pharmaceutical sector. Though Russia Ukraine had no significant impact on Indian pharmaceutical sector. It has opened up an opportunity for the Indian pharma firms to leverage good diplomatic relations and expand its operations in both Russia and Ukraine by building production centres in both countries. The diversification enhances the diversity in market operations for Indian firms and provides both Russia and Ukraine with a trusted neutral supplier.

DOI: 10.4018/979-8-3373-0240-9.ch024

I. INTRODUCTION

According to the survey of the Indian Economy in 2021, the pharmaceutical market is anticipated to expand thrice within a decade. The pharma market is expected to increase to USD 130 billion by 2030 (Ren et al., 2021). The biotechnology sector will grow to USD 70.2 billion by 2025. The medical device sector is anticipated to growth 37% between 2020 and 2025. The Indian pharmaceutical industry sources 60% of vaccine demand in the world. India is the 12th most significant exporter of medicines globally. India exported USD 24.60 billion worth of pharmaceutical products. The sector had a trade surplus of USD 15.81 billion in 2022. The national digital health blueprint is estimated to create USD 200 billion in economic value in the next decade (S. Singh et al., 2022). The Indian government has prioritised healthcare and allocated USD 419.2 million for research and development while allocating USD 10.86 billion for the Ministry of Health (IBEF, 2024). To provide impetus to the pharmaceutical industry, the Indian government has provided an outlay of USD 665.5 million for 2022 to 2026 (Raza et al., 2015). The strength of the Indian pharmaceutical sector was witnessed during the COVID-19 pandemic when India saved millions of lives by supplying indigenously developed COVID-19 vaccines worldwide. To the support domestic pharmaceutical industry, the Indian government has initiated a linked incentive (PLI) scheme worth USD 951.27 million from 2021 to 2030 (Thakur & Kumar, 2021).

The Indian pharmaceutical sector has also been influenced by the COVID-19 pandemic and the Russia-Ukraine war. Exports to Ukraine have increased by 44% in 2021—a 6.95% in exports to Russia (Sharma, 2022). However, the rise in prices of active pharmaceutical ingredients (APIs) has adversely impacted the Indian pharmaceutical sector. 50% of trade has been badly affected due to pending payments due to war (Bashir et al., 2020).

The government has prioritized the development of the pharmaceutical sector in India, allowing 100% foreign direct investment (FDI) for Greenfield projects (Bhushan et al., 2021; Khursheed et al., 2019; Patel, 2011). Fundamental support mechanisms for the industry include establishing special-purpose vehicles, simplifying pharmaceutical barcoding, subsidies for power, land, and water, and creating capacity for pharma hubs (A. Singh et al., 2015).

Russia does not have the same strength in the pharmaceuticals sector as in defense technology and oil. Nonetheless, we continue to supply medicines and other pharmaceutical products to Russia (Bhyan et al., 2011; Guo et al., 2020; Nagaraju & Chawla, 2020). Collaborating with our Russian counterparts will enable us to learn from one another and create opportunities to expand and enhance our pharmaceutical trade (Mahesh et al., 2014). Russia has a robust research and development foundation in the pharmaceutical and vaccine sectors and is home to several prominent pharmaceutical companies. It has already established itself as one of the top destinations for Indian pharmaceutical firms (S. Singh et al., 2019).

II. REVIEW OF LITERATURE

Affected by the shortages of pharmaceutical products, Russia is exploring joint ventures with the Indian pharmaceutical sector to set up plants in Russia and encouraging India to increase the export of pharmaceutical products to Russia (Siddique et al., 2018). The COVID-19 pandemic, followed by the war between Russia and Ukraine, has adversely impacted the supply chain worldwide (Kour et al., 2021). Dependence on imports for APIs has reduced the competitiveness of the Indian pharmaceutical sector. The Russia-Ukraine war has negatively impacted research and development in the pharmaceutical industry (Prashar et al., 2020). India is the third largest country supplying pharmaceutical products to Ukraine (H. Kumar, Bhardwaj, Nepovimova, et al., 2020). The Russia-Ukraine war has questioned the efficiency of the markets (Chauhan et al., 2018). The global macroeconomic fundamentals have been severely affected due to the Russia-Ukraine war and geopolitical disruptions (Haldhar et al., 2018). The Russia-Ukraine war will lead to income disparity between countries. People with low incomes will become poorer (Datta et al., 2016). Active engagement of stakeholders is crucial for resolving the issues (Mia et al., 2018; Panda et al., 2021). The powerful agencies will be driven by self-interest, which may be disastrous for society and the world. The success of the chosen strategies motivates them to continue the same plan (Chhikara et al., 2018). Willingness to resolve the crisis and manage the challenges is crucial for organizations and nations to achieve the desired results (Garg et al., 2017).

War has led to inflation pressures in the world economy (Charbe et al., 2020). The Russian market has been a hedge against regulatory guidelines of Western markets for the Indian pharmaceutical industry (Masud et al., 2021). The Indian pharmaceutical industry has a significant presence in Ukraine and the Russian region (G. Kumar et al., 2019). The Indian pharmaceutical sector needs to focus on diversifying its supply chain and reducing its dependence on China. It should move up the value chain and explore e-channels to consolidate its presence (Alharbi et al., 2021).

Digitization and a multidisciplinary approach offer immense potential for expanding the Indian pharmaceutical sector. This will bring innovative therapies for the patients and improve the efficiency of the pharma sector. Medical devices and pathology centres will benefit from digitisation and collaboration (Ansari et al., 2015; Jnawali et al., 2016; Khamparia et al., 2019; V. Kumar et al., 2019). The visionary leadership of the Indian government to strengthen the pharma sector is reflected in the allocations and announcements in the union budget (Vaid et al., 2014). The government needs to speed up the bureaucratic clearance mechanism for the production-linked incentive (PLI) scheme to become a growth engine for the Indian pharma sector. Slow clearances can hamper the success of the PLI scheme. Geographical diversification in the supply chain is the need of the hour for the Indian pharmaceutical industry (H. Singh et al., 2018).

Operational ground realities differ significantly from the strategic vision for the Indian pharmaceutical sector. Besides the US, India has the maximum number of facilities certified by the US FDA. The quality issue concerns raised by the FDA need to be taken up as a top priority by Indian pharmaceutical firms to enhance their ratings (Dihom et al., 2022; Mishra et al., 2018; Saxena, Prasad, & Haldhar, 2018). Research and Development must be prioritized for innovation and drug discovery. Over-product diversification increased inventory and distribution costs (Bharany et al., 2022; Jilte et al., 2019; Kalkal et al., 2021; Prabhakar et al., 2013). The fragmented supply chain is a concern for the Indian pharmaceutical sector. The underdeveloped transit systems cause delays and increase the cost of logistics. The lack of a robust cold chain system is a stumbling block for the pharma sector. The Pharma sector must enhance agility and visibility to excel (Verma et al., 2021).

The regulatory framework for pharmaceuticals and medical practice needs to be reformed. There is need to relook the entire value chain of pharmaceuticals (Bashir et al., 2018). Researchers have ignored the pharma supply chain. There is a need for research on the pharma supply chain. There is immense potential for applying blockchain in the pharma supply chain. There has been a sudden increase in research on the pharma supply chain since COVID-19. The scope of the supply chain of pharma products in a circular economy needs to be examined (Dar et al., 2019). Transaction cost theory could not apply to strategic goods like pharmaceuticals (G. Singh & Arya, 2019). Multi-criteria decision-making is needed for the pharmaceutical sector. Pharmaceutical supply chain strategies need to be integrated with national strategies. Stakeholders like patients, industry, and administration need to come together to develop national priorities and an optimum healthcare system. The pharmaceutical sector and policymaking need transparency, accountability and consistency (Bordoloi et al., 2018).

G. Singh & Arya, 2019 found that the primary source of financing for the pharmaceutical industry is owner equity, as supported by Saggu et al., 2014. It was observed that debt is cheaper than equity for pharma firms Arnold & Kumar, 2005, though debt was viewed as problematic by Khamparia, Saini, et al., 2020. Dividend for pharma firms is not a determinant of stock price Prakash & Uddin, 2017, though G. Singh et al., (2018) considered dividends to influence market prices. Pharmaceutical companies typically distribute about 30% of their earnings, maintaining an average dividend of around 18% when they have adequate reserves and profits (Ansari et al., 2016).

Creating a generics manufacturing hub in Russia will foster the overall growth and sustainability of collaboration between the two countries in the pharmaceutical industry. As part of its Pharma 2030 policy, Russia aims to bolster its local capacity and increase its share of global exports (Kapoor et al., 2021). To support this, the government has implemented additional incentives for local manufacturers to meet its procurement needs. Russia is implementing policies to attract local investors, enabling them to acquire technology and develop in-house generics, APIs, and biologics capabilities. Additionally, they are pursuing joint ventures and providing financial support to Indian companies to encourage them to establish their operations in Russian provinces (Kaswan & Rathi, 2019).

Blockchain and the Internet of Things (IoT) offer feasible solutions to pharmaceutical supply chain problems (P. Singh et al., 2020). Blockchain provides a secure, efficient and transparent supply chain system (Bhat et al., 2022). Microalgae feedstock needs to be explored for a circular supply chain in the pharmaceutical sector (H. Kumar, Bhardwaj, Sharma, et al., 2020). Blockchain and the Internet of Things (IoT) can overcome the problems of counterfeit drugs (Saxena, Prasad, Haldhar, et al., 2018; A. P. Singh et al., 2021; Yuvaraj et al., 2021). The USA, China and Italy are leading in research on blockchain for pharmaceutical supply chains (Bharany et al., 2021; Khamparia et al., 2021; Ren et al., 2021).

Blockchain and machine learning will help people collaborate. It can also be used to track the supply of active pharma ingredients (S. Singh, Kumar, Dhanjal, et al., 2020). An efficient supply chain of pharmaceuticals is the proper, timely treatment of sick patients (Khamparia, Gupta, et al., 2020). Indian pharmaceutical sector should act responsibly to exploit the export markets and generate sustainable profits (Darwish et al., 2020). The Supply chain must focus on sustainability, agility, green, and resilience (Bhushan et al., 2021). Technology-driven supply chains can be helpful for hilly terrains. AIIMS Rishikesh has started drone-driven drug delivery in Uttarakhand state of India (Anand et al., 2017; Mensah et al., 2023; A. Singh et al., 2015; S. Singh, Kumar, Datta, et al., 2020). The Indian pharmaceutical sector has an excellent opportunity to export to Russia. After the start of the war between Russia and Ukraine, many Western pharma companies have discontinued operations in Russia, except for emergency medicines (Kaur et al., 2015; Sharma et al., 2020; G. Singh et al., 2019). Due to the war between Russia and Ukraine, the Indian pharmaceutical sector faces challenges in Commonwealth of Independent States (CIS) countries (Ahmadi et al., 2020; Manzoor et al., 2019).

III. METHOD

The present study employed a descriptive methodology. Secondary data on Indian pharma stocks and the market benchmark, Nifty 50, was obtained from the website of the National Stock Exchange. The benchmark used was Nifty 50. Nifty Pharma sectoral index was used to assess the impact of the Russia-Ukraine war. Large-cap stocks included in Nifty 50 were considered for the study. Large-cap stocks under Nifty 50 are Sun Pharma, Divis Labs and Cipla. 150 trading days were considered after and before the onset of the war between Russia and Ukraine were used for the study. A paired t-test was used for the analysis. Data on closing values was obtained from 19th July 2021 till 5th October 2022.

IV. RESULTS

The Nifty 50 daily returns of 150 trading days before the start of the Russia-Ukrainian war was 0.053%, and after the start of the war, it was 0.041%. The Nifty pharma daily returns before the start of the war was -0.082%, and after the war, it was 0.038%. Cipla's daily returns before the start of the war were -0.093%, and after the start of the war, it was 0.163%. The returns of Divis Labs before the start of the war were -0.093%, and after the start of the war -0.17%. The returns of Dr Reddy's labs before the start of the war were -0.17%, and after the start of the war, it was 0.050%. The return of Sun Pharma before the war was 0.132%, and after the start of the war, it was 0.096%. There has been no significant change in returns for Nifty Pharma, Cipla, Divis Labs, or Dr Reddy's labs.

Table 1. Paired t-test of pharma indices

Particulars	Mean	N	Std. Deviation	t	Sig.
Nifty 50 Returns Before War	0.000533	150	0.009376		
Nifty 50 Returns After War	0.000408	150	0.011302	0.107	0.915
Nifty Pharma Returns Before War	-0.00082	150	0.011035		
Nifty Pharma Returns After War	0.00038	150	0.010882	-0.941	0.348
Cipla Returns Before War	-0.00042	150	0.015703		
Cipla Returns After War	0.001634	150	0.015525	-1.189	0.237
Divis Lab Returns Before War	-0.00093	150	0.017235		
Divis Labs Returns After War	-0.00027	150	0.018486	-0.311	0.756
DRREDDY Returns Before War	-0.0017	150	0.015122		
DRREDDY Returns After War	0.000504	150	0.01643	-1.152	0.251
Sun Pharma Returns Before War	0.001321	150	0.016632		
Sun Pharma Returns After War	0.000957	150	0.015024	0.198	0.843

The Russia-Ukraine war has no significant effect on the daily returns of Nifty 50 (P=0.915) and Nifty Pharma (P=0.348). The large cap pharma stocks of Cipla (P=0.237), Divis Labs (P=0.756), Dr Reddy's Labs (P=0.251) and Sun Pharma (P=0843) have also shown so significant effect of Russia Ukraine war on daily stock returns.

V. CONCLUSION

The Indian pharma sector is robust enough to manage the geopolitical uncertainty due to the Russia-Ukraine war. The study found no significant effect of the Russia-Ukrainian war on the daily returns of Nifty 50, Nifty pharma, and large-cap pharma stocks in 150 trading days. The neutral stand adopted by the Indian political establishment and independent foreign policy has helped Indian businesses mitigate the adverse consequences of war. However, since data of only 150 trading days after the start of wart is available, the findings need to be validated with data of more trading days and returns of mid-cap and small-cap pharma stocks. A diversified portfolio of pharma sales spanning all parts of the world is a significant determinant of the ability of Indian pharma firms to manage region-specific geopolitical uncertainty. Other sectors need to diversify their market and supply chains to protect against future geo-political uncertainties emerging in other parts of the world. Indian pharmaceutical sector has an excellent opportunity to expand and diversify. Both Russia and Ukraine have suffered economic losses due to war and need pharmaceutical products from a reliable and neutral supplier. Both countries have appreciated the Indian government's efforts for peace between Russia and Ukraine. The capacity of the Indian pharmaceutical sector has the potential to cater to the markets of Russia and Ukraine. The Indian government needs to consult with pharmaceutical executives in India to develop a comprehensive plan for enhancing the market share of Indian firms in Russia and Ukraine.

REFERENCES

Ahmadi, A., El Haj Assad, M., Jamali, D. H., Kumar, R., Li, Z. X., Salameh, T., Al-Shabi, M., & Ehyaei, M. A. (2020). Applications of geothermal organic Rankine Cycle for electricity production. *Journal of Cleaner Production*, 274, 122950. Advance online publication. DOI: 10.1016/j.jclepro.2020.122950

Alharbi, K. S., Fuloria, N. K., Fuloria, S., Rahman, S. B., Al-Malki, W. H., Javed Shaikh, M. A., Thangavelu, L., Singh, S. K., Rama Raju Allam, V. S., Jha, N. K., Chellappan, D. K., Dua, K., & Gupta, G. (2021). Nuclear factor-kappa B and its role in inflammatory lung disease. *Chemico-Biological Interactions*, 345, 109568. Advance online publication. DOI: 10.1016/j.cbi.2021.109568 PMID: 34181887

Anand, A., Patience, A. A., Sharma, N., & Khurana, N. (2017). The present and future of pharmacotherapy of Alzheimer's disease: A comprehensive review. *European Journal of Pharmacology*, 815, 364–375. DOI: 10.1016/j.ejphar.2017.09.043 PMID: 28978455

Ansari, K. R., Quraishi, M. A., & Singh, A. (2015). Isatin derivatives as a non-toxic corrosion inhibitor for mild steel in 20% H2SO4. *Corrosion Science*, 95, 62–70. DOI: 10.1016/j.corsci.2015.02.010

Ansari, K. R., Quraishi, M. A., Singh, A., Ramkumar, S., & Obote, I. B. (2016). Corrosion inhibition of N80 steel in 15% HCl by pyrazolone derivatives: Electrochemical, surface and quantum chemical studies. *RSC Advances*, 6(29), 24130–24141. DOI: 10.1039/C5RA25441H

Bashir, S., Sharma, V., Lgaz, H., Chung, I.-M., Singh, A., & Kumar, A. (2018). The inhibition action of analgin on the corrosion of mild steel in acidic medium: A combined theoretical and experimental approach. *Journal of Molecular Liquids*, 263, 454–462. DOI: 10.1016/j.molliq.2018.04.143

Bashir, S., Thakur, A., Lgaz, H., Chung, I.-M., & Kumar, A. (2020). Corrosion inhibition efficiency of bronopol on aluminium in 0.5 M HCl solution: Insights from experimental and quantum chemical studies. *Surfaces and Interfaces*, 20, 100542. Advance online publication. DOI: 10.1016/j.surfin.2020.100542

Bharany, S., Badotra, S., Sharma, S., Rani, S., Alazab, M., Jhaveri, R. H., & Reddy Gadekallu, T. (2022). Energy efficient fault tolerance techniques in green cloud computing: A systematic survey and taxonomy. *Sustainable Energy Technologies and Assessments*, 53, 102613. Advance online publication. DOI: 10.1016/j.seta.2022.102613

Bharany, S., Sharma, S., Badotra, S., Khalaf, O. I., Alotaibi, Y., Alghamdi, S., & Alassery, F. (2021). Energy-efficient clustering scheme for flying ad-hoc networks using an optimized leach protocol. *Energies*, 14(19), 6016. Advance online publication. DOI: 10.3390/en14196016

Bhat, S. A., Bashir, O., Ul Haq, S. A., Amin, T., Rafiq, A., Ali, M., Américo-Pinheiro, J. H. P., & Sher, F. (2022). Phytoremediation of heavy metals in soil and water: An eco-friendly, sustainable and multidisciplinary approach. *Chemosphere*, 303, 134788. Advance online publication. DOI: 10.1016/j.chemosphere.2022.134788 PMID: 35504464

Bhushan, B., Sahoo, C., Sinha, P., & Khamparia, A. (2021). Unification of Blockchain and Internet of Things (BIoT): Requirements, working model, challenges and future directions. *Wireless Networks*, 27(1), 55–90. DOI: 10.1007/s11276-020-02445-6

Bhyan, B., Jangra, S., Kaur, M., & Singh, H. (2011). Orally fast dissolving films: Innovations in formulation and technology. *International Journal of Pharmaceutical Sciences Review and Research*, 9(2), 50–57.

Bordoloi, N., Sharma, A., Nautiyal, H., & Goel, V. (2018). An intense review on the latest advancements of Earth Air Heat Exchangers. *Renewable & Sustainable Energy Reviews*, 89, 261–280. DOI: 10.1016/j.rser.2018.03.056

Charbe, N. B., Amnerkar, N. D., Ramesh, B., Tambuwala, M. M., Bakshi, H. A., Aljabali, A. A. A., Khadse, S. C., Satheeshkumar, R., Satija, S., Metha, M., Chellappan, D. K., Shrivastava, G., Gupta, G., Negi, P., Dua, K., & Zacconi, F. C. (2020). Small interfering RNA for cancer treatment: Overcoming hurdles in delivery. *Acta Pharmaceutica Sinica. B*, 10(11), 2075–2109. DOI: 10.1016/j.apsb.2020.10.005 PMID: 33304780

Chauhan, C. C., Kagdi, A. R., Jotania, R. B., Upadhyay, A., Sandhu, C. S., Shirsath, S. E., & Meena, S. S. (2018). Structural, magnetic and dielectric properties of Co-Zr substituted M-type calcium hexagonal ferrite nanoparticles in the presence of α-Fe2O3 phase. *Ceramics International*, 44(15), 17812–17823. DOI: 10.1016/j.ceramint.2018.06.249

Chhikara, N., Kour, R., Jaglan, S., Gupta, P., Gat, Y., & Panghal, A. (2018). Citrus medica: Nutritional, phytochemical composition and health benefits-a rev. *Food & Function*, 9(4), 1978–1992. DOI: 10.1039/C7FO02035J PMID: 29594287

Dar, S. A., Sharma, R., Srivastava, V., & Sakalle, U. K. (2019). Investigation on the electronic structure, optical, elastic, mechanical, thermodynamic and thermoelectric properties of wide band gap semiconductor double perovskite Ba2InTaO6. *RSC Advances*, 9(17), 9522–9532. DOI: 10.1039/C9RA00313D PMID: 35520698

Darwish, M. A., Trukhanov, A. V., Senatov, O. S., Morchenko, A. T., Saafan, S. A., Astapovich, K. A., Trukhanov, S. V., Trukhanova, E. L., Pilyushkin, A. A., Sombra, A. S. B., Zhou, D., Jotania, R. B., & Singh, C. (2020). Investigation of AC-measurements of epoxy/ferrite composites. *Nanomaterials (Basel, Switzerland)*, 10(3), 492. Advance online publication. DOI: 10.3390/nano10030492 PMID: 32182785

Datta, S., Singh, J., Singh, S., & Singh, J. (2016). Earthworms, pesticides and sustainable agriculture: A review. *Environmental Science and Pollution Research International*, 23(9), 8227–8243. DOI: 10.1007/s11356-016-6375-0 PMID: 26951221

Dihom, H. R., Al-Shaibani, M. M., Radin Mohamed, R. M. S., Al-Gheethi, A. A., Sharma, A., & Khamidun, M. H. (2022). Photocatalytic degradation of disperse azo dyes in textile wastewater using green zinc oxide nanoparticles synthesized in plant extract: A critical review. *Journal of Water Process Engineering*, 47, 102705. Advance online publication. DOI: 10.1016/j.jwpe.2022.102705

Garg, V., Singh, H., Bhatia, A., Raza, K., Singh, S. K., Singh, B., & Beg, S. (2017). Systematic Development of Transethosomal Gel System of Piroxicam: Formulation Optimization, In Vitro Evaluation, and Ex Vivo Assessment. *AAPS PharmSciTech*, 18(1), 58–71. DOI: 10.1208/s12249-016-0489-z PMID: 26868380

Guo, H.-H., Zhou, D., Du, C., Wang, P.-J., Liu, W.-F., Pang, L.-X., Wang, Q.-P., Su, J.-Z., Singh, C., & Trukhanov, S. (2020). Temperature stable Li2Ti0.75(Mg1/3Nb2/3)0.25O3-based microwave dielectric ceramics with low sintering temperature and ultra-low dielectric loss for dielectric resonator antenna applications. *Journal of Materials Chemistry. C, Materials for Optical and Electronic Devices*, 8(14), 4690–4700. DOI: 10.1039/D0TC00326C

Haldhar, R., Prasad, D., & Saxena, A. (2018). Myristica fragrans extract as an eco-friendly corrosion inhibitor for mild steel in 0.5 M H2SO4 solution. *Journal of Environmental Chemical Engineering*, 6(2), 2290–2301. DOI: 10.1016/j.jece.2018.03.023

Jilte, R. D., Kumar, R., & Ahmadi, M. H. (2019). Cooling performance of nanofluid submerged vs. nanofluid circulated battery thermal management systems. *Journal of Cleaner Production*, 240, 118131. Advance online publication. DOI: 10.1016/j.jclepro.2019.118131

Jnawali, P., Kumar, V., & Tanwar, B. (2016). Celiac disease: Overview and considerations for development of gluten-free foods. *Food Science and Human Wellness*, 5(4), 169–176. DOI: 10.1016/j.fshw.2016.09.003

Kalkal, A., Kumar, S., Kumar, P., Pradhan, R., Willander, M., Packirisamy, G., Kumar, S., & Malhotra, B. D. (2021). Recent advances in 3D printing technologies for wearable (bio)sensors. *Additive Manufacturing*, 46, 102088. Advance online publication. DOI: 10.1016/j.addma.2021.102088

Kapoor, B., Kapoor, D., Gautam, S., Singh, R., & Bhardwaj, S. (2021). Dietary Polyunsaturated Fatty Acids (PUFAs): Uses and Potential Health Benefits. *Current Nutrition Reports*, 10(3), 232–242. DOI: 10.1007/s13668-021-00363-3 PMID: 34255301

Kaswan, M. S., & Rathi, R. (2019). Analysis and modeling the enablers of Green Lean Six Sigma implementation using Interpretive Structural Modeling. *Journal of Cleaner Production*, 231, 1182–1191. DOI: 10.1016/j.jclepro.2019.05.253

Kaur, T., Kaur, B., Bhat, B. H., Kumar, S., & Srivastava, A. K. (2015). Effect of calcination temperature on microstructure, dielectric, magnetic and optical properties of Ba0.7La0.3Fe11.7Co0.3O19 hexaferrites. *Physica B, Condensed Matter*, 456, 206–212. DOI: 10.1016/j.physb.2014.09.003

Khamparia, A., Bharati, S., Podder, P., Gupta, D., Khanna, A., Phung, T. K., & Thanh, D. N. H. (2021). Diagnosis of breast cancer based on modern mammography using hybrid transfer learning. *Multidimensional Systems and Signal Processing*, 32(2), 747–765. DOI: 10.1007/s11045-020-00756-7 PMID: 33456204

Khamparia, A., Gupta, D., de Albuquerque, V. H. C., Sangaiah, A. K., & Jhaveri, R. H. (2020). Internet of health things-driven deep learning system for detection and classification of cervical cells using transfer learning. *The Journal of Supercomputing*, 76(11), 8590–8608. DOI: 10.1007/s11227-020-03159-4

Khamparia, A., Gupta, D., Nguyen, N. G., Khanna, A., Pandey, B., & Tiwari, P. (2019). Sound classification using convolutional neural network and tensor deep stacking network. *IEEE Access : Practical Innovations, Open Solutions*, 7, 7717–7727. DOI: 10.1109/ACCESS.2018.2888882

Khamparia, A., Saini, G., Gupta, D., Khanna, A., Tiwari, S., & de Albuquerque, V. H. C. (2020). Seasonal Crops Disease Prediction and Classification Using Deep Convolutional Encoder Network. *Circuits, Systems, and Signal Processing*, 39(2), 818–836. DOI: 10.1007/s00034-019-01041-0

Khursheed, R., Singh, S. K., Wadhwa, S., Kapoor, B., Gulati, M., Kumar, R., Ramanunny, A. K., Awasthi, A., & Dua, K. (2019). Treatment strategies against diabetes: Success so far and challenges ahead. *European Journal of Pharmacology*, 862, 172625. Advance online publication. DOI: 10.1016/j.ejphar.2019.172625 PMID: 31449807

Kour, D., Kaur, T., Devi, R., Yadav, A., Singh, M., Joshi, D., Singh, J., Suyal, D. C., Kumar, A., Rajput, V. D., Yadav, A. N., Singh, K., Singh, J., Sayyed, R. Z., Arora, N. K., & Saxena, A. K. (2021). Beneficial microbiomes for bioremediation of diverse contaminated environments for environmental sustainability: Present status and future challenges. *Environmental Science and Pollution Research International*, 28(20), 24917–24939. DOI: 10.1007/s11356-021-13252-7 PMID: 33768457

Kumar, G., Saha, R., Rai, M. K., Thomas, R., & Kim, T.-H. (2019). Proof-of-Work Consensus Approach in Blockchain Technology for Cloud and Fog Computing Using Maximization-Factorization Statistics. *IEEE Internet of Things Journal*, 6(4), 6835–6842. DOI: 10.1109/JIOT.2019.2911969

Kumar, H., Bhardwaj, K., Nepovimova, E., Kuča, K., Dhanjal, D. S., Bhardwaj, S., Bhatia, S. K., Verma, R., & Kumar, D. (2020). Antioxidant functionalized nanoparticles: A combat against oxidative stress. *Nanomaterials (Basel, Switzerland)*, 10(7), 1–31. DOI: 10.3390/nano10071334 PMID: 32650608

Kumar, H., Bhardwaj, K., Sharma, R., Nepovimova, E., Kuča, K., Dhanjal, D. S., Verma, R., Bhardwaj, P., Sharma, S., & Kumar, D. (2020). Fruit and Vegetable Peels: Utilization of High Value Horticultural Waste in Novel Industrial Applications. *Molecules (Basel, Switzerland)*, 25(12), 2812. Advance online publication. DOI: 10.3390/molecules25122812 PMID: 32570836

Kumar, V., Singh, S., Srivastava, B., Bhadouria, R., & Singh, R. (2019). Green synthesis of silver nanoparticles using leaf extract of Holoptelea integrifolia and preliminary investigation of its antioxidant, anti-inflammatory, antidiabetic and antibacterial activities. *Journal of Environmental Chemical Engineering*, 7(3), 103094. Advance online publication. DOI: 10.1016/j.jece.2019.103094

Mahesh, K. V., Singh, S. K., & Gulati, M. (2014). A comparative study of top-down and bottom-up approaches for the preparation of nanosuspensions of glipizide. *Powder Technology*, 256, 436–449. DOI: 10.1016/j.powtec.2014.02.011

Manzoor, S. I., & Singla, J., & Nikita. (2019). Fake news detection using machine learning approaches: A systematic review. *Proceedings of the International Conference on Trends in Electronics and Informatics, ICOEI 2019*, 230 – 234. DOI: 10.1109/ICOEI.2019.8862770

Masud, M., Gaba, G. S., Alqahtani, S., Muhammad, G., Gupta, B. B., Kumar, P., & Ghoneim, A. (2021). A Lightweight and Robust Secure Key Establishment Protocol for Internet of Medical Things in COVID-19 Patients Care. *IEEE Internet of Things Journal*, 8(21), 15694–15703. DOI: 10.1109/JIOT.2020.3047662 PMID: 35782176

Mensah, G. A., Habtegiorgis Abate, Y., Abbasian, M., Abd-Allah, F., Abdollahi, A., Abdollahi, M., Morad Abdulah, D., Abdullahi, A., Abebe, A. M., Abedi, A., Abedi, A., Olusola Abiodun, O., Ali, H. A., Abu-Gharbieh, E., Abu-Rmeileh, N. M. E., Aburuz, S., Abushouk, A. I., Abu-Zaid, A., Adane, T. D., & Roth, G. A. (2023). Global Burden of Cardiovascular Diseases and Risks, 1990-2022. *Journal of the American College of Cardiology*, 82(25), 2350–2473. DOI: 10.1016/j.jacc.2023.11.007 PMID: 38092509

Mia, M., Singh, G., Gupta, M. K., & Sharma, V. S. (2018). Influence of Ranque-Hilsch vortex tube and nitrogen gas assisted MQL in precision turning of Al 6061-T6. *Precision Engineering*, 53, 289–299. DOI: 10.1016/j.precisioneng.2018.04.011

Mishra, V., Thakur, S., Patil, A., & Shukla, A. (2018). Quality by design (QbD) approaches in current pharmaceutical set-up. *Expert Opinion on Drug Delivery*, 15(8), 737–758. DOI: 10.1080/17425247.2018.1504768 PMID: 30044646

Nagaraju, M., & Chawla, P. (2020). Systematic review of deep learning techniques in plant disease detection. *International Journal of System Assurance Engineering and Management*, 11(3), 547–560. DOI: 10.1007/s13198-020-00972-1

Panda, S. K., Aggarwal, I., Kumar, H., Prasad, L., Kumar, A., Sharma, A., Vo, D.-V. N., Van Thuan, D., & Mishra, V. (2021). Magnetite nanoparticles as sorbents for dye removal: A review. *Environmental Chemistry Letters*, 19(3), 2487–2525. DOI: 10.1007/s10311-020-01173-9

Patel, S. (2011). Harmful and beneficial aspects of Parthenium hysterophorus: An update. *3 Biotech*, 1(1), 1 – 9. DOI: 10.1007/s13205-011-0007-7

Prabhakar, P. K., Prasad, R., Ali, S., & Doble, M. (2013). Synergistic interaction of ferulic acid with commercial hypoglycemic drugs in streptozotocin induced diabetic rats. *Phytomedicine*, 20(6), 488–494. DOI: 10.1016/j.phymed.2012.12.004 PMID: 23490007

Prakash, C., & Uddin, M. S. (2017). Surface modification of β-phase Ti implant by hydroaxyapatite mixed electric discharge machining to enhance the corrosion resistance and in-vitro bioactivity. *Surface and Coatings Technology*, 326, 134–145. DOI: 10.1016/j.surfcoat.2017.07.040

Prashar, D., Jha, N., Jha, S., Lee, Y., & Joshi, G. P. (2020). Blockchain-based traceability and visibility for agricultural products: A decentralizedway of ensuring food safety in India. *Sustainability (Basel)*, 12(8), 3497. Advance online publication. DOI: 10.3390/su12083497

Raza, K., Thotakura, N., Kumar, P., Joshi, M., Bhushan, S., Bhatia, A., Kumar, V., Malik, R., Sharma, G., Guru, S. K., & Katare, O. P. (2015). C60-fullerenes for delivery of docetaxel to breast cancer cells: A promising approach for enhanced efficacy and better pharmacokinetic profile. *International Journal of Pharmaceutics*, 495(1), 551–559. DOI: 10.1016/j.ijpharm.2015.09.016 PMID: 26383841

Ren, X., Li, C., Ma, X., Chen, F., Wang, H., Sharma, A., Gaba, G. S., & Masud, M. (2021). Design of multi-information fusion based intelligent electrical fire detection system for green buildings. *Sustainability (Basel)*, 13(6), 3405. Advance online publication. DOI: 10.3390/su13063405

Saggu, S., Sakeran, M. I., Zidan, N., Tousson, E., Mohan, A., & Rehman, H. (2014). Ameliorating effect of chicory (Chichorium intybus L.) fruit extract against 4-tert-octylphenol induced liver injury and oxidative stress in male rats. *Food and Chemical Toxicology*, 72, 138–146. DOI: 10.1016/j.fct.2014.06.029 PMID: 25010453

Saxena, A., Prasad, D., & Haldhar, R. (2018). Investigation of corrosion inhibition effect and adsorption activities of Cuscuta reflexa extract for mild steel in 0.5 M H2SO4. *Bioelectrochemistry (Amsterdam, Netherlands)*, 124, 156–164. DOI: 10.1016/j.bioelechem.2018.07.006 PMID: 30059849

Saxena, A., Prasad, D., Haldhar, R., Singh, G., & Kumar, A. (2018). Use of Sida cordifolia extract as green corrosion inhibitor for mild steel in 0.5 M H2SO4. *Journal of Environmental Chemical Engineering*, 6(1), 694–700. DOI: 10.1016/j.jece.2017.12.064

Sharma, R., Jasrotia, K., Singh, N., Ghosh, P., srivastava, S., Sharma, N. R., Singh, J., Kanwar, R., & Kumar, A. (2020). A Comprehensive Review on Hydrothermal Carbonization of Biomass and its Applications. *Chemistry Africa*, 3(1), 1–19. Advance online publication. DOI: 10.1007/s42250-019-00098-3

Siddique, A., Kandpal, G., & Kumar, P. (2018). Proline accumulation and its defensive role under diverse stress condition in plants: An overview. *Journal of Pure & Applied Microbiology*, 12(3), 1655–1659. DOI: 10.22207/JPAM.12.3.73

Singh, A., Lin, Y., Ebenso, E. E., Liu, W., Pan, J., & Huang, B. (2015). Gingko biloba fruit extract as an eco-friendly corrosion inhibitor for J55 steel in CO2 saturated 3.5% NaCl solution. *Journal of Industrial and Engineering Chemistry*, 24, 219–228. DOI: 10.1016/j.jiec.2014.09.034

Singh, A. P., Pradhan, N. R., Luhach, A. K., Agnihotri, S., Jhanjhi, N. Z., Verma, S., Kavita, , Ghosh, U., & Roy, D. S. (2021). A Novel Patient-Centric Architectural Framework for Blockchain-Enabled Healthcare Applications. *IEEE Transactions on Industrial Informatics*, 17(8), 5779–5789. DOI: 10.1109/TII.2020.3037889

Singh, G., & Arya, S. K. (2019). Utility of laccase in pulp and paper industry: A progressive step towards the green technology. *International Journal of Biological Macromolecules*, 134, 1070–1084. DOI: 10.1016/j.ijbiomac.2019.05.168 PMID: 31129205

Singh, G., Gupta, M. K., Mia, M., & Sharma, V. S. (2018). Modeling and optimization of tool wear in MQL-assisted milling of Inconel 718 superalloy using evolutionary techniques. *International Journal of Advanced Manufacturing Technology*, 97(1–4), 481–494. DOI: 10.1007/s00170-018-1911-3

Singh, G., Pruncu, C. I., Gupta, M. K., Mia, M., Khan, A. M., Jamil, M., Pimenov, D. Y., Sen, B., & Sharma, V. S. (2019). Investigations of machining characteristics in the upgraded MQL-assisted turning of pure titanium alloys using evolutionary algorithms. *Materials (Basel)*, 12(6), 999. Advance online publication. DOI: 10.3390/ma12060999 PMID: 30917617

Singh, H., Singh, J. I. P., Singh, S., Dhawan, V., & Tiwari, S. K. (2018). A Brief Review of Jute Fibre and Its Composites. In S. S., D. R.S., & S. M. (Eds.), *Materials Today: Proceedings* (Vol. 5, Issue 14, pp. 28427 – 28437). Elsevier Ltd. DOI: 10.1016/j.matpr.2018.10.129

Singh, P., Nayyar, A., Kaur, A., & Ghosh, U. (2020). Blockchain and fog based architecture for internet of everything in smart cities. *Future Internet*, 12(4), 61. Advance online publication. DOI: 10.3390/fi12040061

Singh, S., Anil, A. G., Khasnabis, S., Kumar, V., Nath, B., Adiga, V., Kumar Naik, T. S. S., Subramanian, S., Kumar, V., Singh, J., & Ramamurthy, P. C. (2022). Sustainable removal of Cr(VI) using graphene oxide-zinc oxide nanohybrid: Adsorption kinetics, isotherms and thermodynamics. *Environmental Research*, 203, 111891. Advance online publication. DOI: 10.1016/j.envres.2021.111891 PMID: 34419468

Singh, S., Kumar, V., Datta, S., Wani, A. B., Dhanjal, D. S., Romero, R., & Singh, J. (2020). Glyphosate uptake, translocation, resistance emergence in crops, analytical monitoring, toxicity and degradation: A review. *Environmental Chemistry Letters*, 18(3), 663–702. DOI: 10.1007/s10311-020-00969-z

Singh, S., Kumar, V., Dhanjal, D. S., Datta, S., Bhatia, D., Dhiman, J., Samuel, J., Prasad, R., & Singh, J. (2020). A sustainable paradigm of sewage sludge biochar: Valorization, opportunities, challenges and future prospects. *Journal of Cleaner Production*, 269, 122259. Advance online publication. DOI: 10.1016/j.jclepro.2020.122259

Singh, S., Prakash, C., & Ramakrishna, S. (2019). 3D printing of polyether-ether-ketone for biomedical applications. *European Polymer Journal*, 114, 234–248. DOI: 10.1016/j.eurpolymj.2019.02.035

Thakur, A., & Kumar, A. (2021). Sustainable Inhibitors for Corrosion Mitigation in Aggressive Corrosive Media: A Comprehensive Study. *Journal of Bio- and Tribo-Corrosion*, 7(2), 67. Advance online publication. DOI: 10.1007/s40735-021-00501-y

Vaid, S. K., Kumar, B., Sharma, A., Shukla, A. K., & Srivastava, P. C. (2014). Effect of zinc solubilizing bacteria on growth promotion and zinc nutrition of rice. *Journal of Soil Science and Plant Nutrition*, 14(4), 889–910.

Verma, P. K., Agrawal, P., Amorim, I., & Prodan, R. (2021). WELFake: Word Embedding over Linguistic Features for Fake News Detection. *IEEE Transactions on Computational Social Systems*, 8(4), 881–893. DOI: 10.1109/TCSS.2021.3068519

Yuvaraj, N., Srihari, K., Dhiman, G., Somasundaram, K., Sharma, A., Rajeskannan, S., Soni, M., Gaba, G. S., Alzain, M. A., & Masud, M. (2021). Nature-Inspired-Based Approach for Automated Cyberbullying Classification on Multimedia Social Networking. *Mathematical Problems in Engineering*, 2021, 1–12. Advance online publication. DOI: 10.1155/2021/6644652

Compilation of References

Abbas, A., Alroobaea, R., Krichen, M., Rubaiee, S., Vimal, S., & Almansour, F. M. (2024). Blockchain-assisted secured data management framework for health information analysis based on Internet of Medical Things. *Personal and Ubiquitous Computing*, 28(1), 59–72. DOI: 10.1007/s00779-021-01583-8

Abdullah, K. H., Abd Aziz, F. S., Dani, R., Hammood, W. A., & Setiawan, E. (2023). Urban Pollution: A Bibliometric Review. *ASM Science Journal*, 18, 1–16. DOI: 10.32802/ASMSCJ.2023.1440

Abedi, S., Kwon, S., & Yoon, S. W. (2023). Healthcare and Pharmaceutical Supply Chain Automation. In *Springer Handbook of Automation* (pp. 1289–1308). Springer International Publishing. DOI: 10.1007/978-3-030-96729-1_60

Ada, N., Kazancoglu, Y., Sezer, M. D., Ede-Senturk, C., Ozer, I., & Ram, M. (2021). Analyzing barriers of circular food supply chains and proposing industry 4.0 solutions. *Sustainability (Basel)*, 13(12), 6812. Advance online publication. DOI: 10.3390/su13126812

Agarwal, M., Gill, K. S., Upadhyay, D., Dangi, S., & Chythanya, K. R. (2024). The Evolution of Cryptocurrencies: Analysis of Bitcoin, Ethereum, Bit connect and Dogecoin in Comparison. *2024 IEEE 9th International Conference for Convergence in Technology, I2CT 2024*. DOI: 10.1109/I2CT61223.2024.10543872

Agarwal, V., & Sharma, S. (2021). IoT Based Smart Transport Management System. *Communications in Computer and Information Science*, 1394 CCIS, 207 – 216. DOI: 10.1007/978-981-16-3653-0_17

Agarwal, P., Matta, P., & Sharma, S. (2021). Comparative Study of Emerging Internet-of-Things in Traffic Management System. *Proceedings of the 5th International Conference on Trends in Electronics and Informatics, ICOEI 2021*, 422 – 428. DOI: 10.1109/ICOEI51242.2021.9453083

Agarwal, P., & Sharma, S. (2023). Smart Urban Traffic Management System using Energy Efficient Optimized Path Discovery. *Proceedings of the 3rd International Conference on Artificial Intelligence and Smart Energy, ICAIS 2023*, 858 – 863. DOI: 10.1109/ICAIS56108.2023.10073840

Aggarwal, Rahul & Gondi, Suhas & Wadhera, Rishi. (2022). Comparison of Medicare Advantage vs Traditional

Aggarwal, S., & Sharma, S. (2022). Voice Based Secured Smart Lock Design for Internet of Medical Things: An Artificial Intelligence Approach. *2022 International Conference on Wireless Communications, Signal Processing and Networking, WiSPNET 2022*, 1 – 9. DOI: 10.1109/WiSPNET54241.2022.9767113

Aggarwal, V., Gupta, V., Gupta, S., Sharma, N., Sharma, K., & Sharma, N. (2021). Using Transfer Learning and Pattern Recognition to Implement a Smart Waste Management System. *Proceedings of the 2nd International Conference on Electronics and Sustainable Communication Systems, ICESC 2021*, 1887 – 1891. DOI: 10.1109/ICESC51422.2021.9532732

Aggarwal, V., Gupta, V., Sharma, N., Gupta, S., Pundir, V., Sharma, K., & Sharma, N. (2021). Integration of Waste Management Companies in Micro Grids through Machine Learning. *Proceedings of the 2nd International Conference on Electronics and Sustainable Communication Systems, ICESC 2021*, 1881 – 1886. DOI: 10.1109/ICESC51422.2021.9532680

Agrawal, P., & Narain, R. (2023). Analysis of enablers for the digitalization of supply chain using an interpretive structural modelling approach. *International Journal of Productivity and Performance Management*, 72(2), 410–439. DOI: 10.1108/IJPPM-09-2020-0481

Agrawal, Y., Bhagoria, J. L., Gautam, A., Sharma, A., Yadav, A. S., Alam, T., Kumar, R., Goga, G., Chakroborty, S., & Kumar, R. (2023). Investigation of thermal performance of a ribbed solar air heater for sustainable built environment. *Sustainable Energy Technologies and Assessments*, 57, 103288. Advance online publication. DOI: 10.1016/j.seta.2023.103288

Ahalawat, K., & Tiwari, R. (2024, April). A Bibliometric Analysis of the Use of Technology for the Marketing of Online Pharmacies. In *2024 Sixth International Conference on Computational Intelligence and Communication Technologies (CCICT)* (pp. 384-389). IEEE. DOI: 10.1109/CCICT62777.2024.00069

Ahmad, F., Kumar, P., & Patil, P. P. (2021). Vibration characteristics based pre-stress analysis of a quadcopter's body frame. In S. Y. (Ed.), *Materials Today: Proceedings* (Vol. 46, pp. 10329 – 10333). Elsevier Ltd. DOI: 10.1016/j.matpr.2020.12.458

Ahmad, I., Sharma, S., Kumar, R., Dhyani, S., & Dumka, A. (2023). Data Analytics of Online Education during Pandemic Health Crisis: A Case Study. *2nd Edition of IEEE Delhi Section Owned Conference, DELCON 2023 - Proceedings*. DOI: 10.1109/DELCON57910.2023.10127423

Ahmadi, A., El Haj Assad, M., Jamali, D. H., Kumar, R., Li, Z. X., Salameh, T., Al-Shabi, M., & Ehyaei, M. A. (2020). Applications of geothermal organic Rankine Cycle for electricity production. *Journal of Cleaner Production*, 274, 122950. Advance online publication. DOI: 10.1016/j.jclepro.2020.122950

Ahmad, R. W., Al Khader, W., Jayaraman, R., Salah, K., Antony, J., & Swarnakar, V. (2023). Integrating Lean Six Sigma with blockchain technology for quality management–a scoping review of current trends and future prospects. *The TQM Journal*, 35(7), 1609–1631. DOI: 10.1108/TQM-06-2022-0181

Ahmed, R., Das Gupta, A., Krishnamurthy, R. M., Goyal, M., Kumar, K. S., & Gangodkar, D. (2022). The Role of Smart Grid Data Analytics in Enhancing the Paradigm of Energy Management for Sustainable Development. *2022 2nd International Conference on Advance Computing and Innovative Technologies in Engineering, ICACITE 2022*, 198 – 201. DOI: 10.1109/ICACITE53722.2022.9823542

Ahmed, Z. (2020). Practicing precision medicine with intelligently integrative clinical and multi-omics data analysis. *Human Genomics*, 14(1), 35. DOI: 10.1186/s40246-020-00287-z PMID: 33008459

Ai in healthcare: Top 5 real-world examples. (2021, October). Compunnel Digital. Retrieved November 2, 2022, from https://www.compunneldigital.com/blog/ai-in-healthcare-top-5-real-world-examples/

Aiyappa, S., Kodikal, R., & Rahiman, H. U. (2024). Accelerating Gender Equality for Sustainable Development: A Case Study of Dakshina Kannada District, India. *Technical and Vocational Education and Training*, 38, 335–349. DOI: 10.1007/978-981-99-6909-8_30

Ajay, D., Sharad, K., Singh, K. P., & Sharma, S. (2023). Impact of Prolonged Mental Torture on Housewives in Middle Class Families. *Journal for ReAttach Therapy and Developmental Diversities*, 6(4), 1–7.

Akana, C. M. V. S., Kumar, A., Tiwari, M., Yunus, A. Z., Vijayakumar, E., & Singh, M. (2023). An Optimized DDoS Attack Detection Using Deep Convolutional Generative Adversarial Networks. *Proceedings of the 5th International Conference on Inventive Research in Computing Applications, ICIRCA 2023*, 668 – 673. DOI: 10.1109/ICIRCA57980.2023.10220745

Akberdina, V., Kumar, V., Kyriakopoulos, G. L., & Kuzmin, E. (2023). Editorial: What Does Industry's Digital Transition Hold in the Uncertainty Context? In K. V., K. G.L., A. V., & K. E. (Eds.), *Lecture Notes in Information Systems and Organisation: Vol. 61 LNISO* (pp. 1 – 4). Springer Science and Business Media Deutschland GmbH. DOI: 10.1007/978-3-031-30351-7_1

Al Kuwaiti, A., Nazer, K., Al-Reedy, A., Al-Shehri, S., Al-Muhanna, A., Subbarayalu, A. V., Al Muhanna, D., & Al-Muhanna, F. A. (2023). A review of the role of artificial intelligence in healthcare. *Journal of Personalized Medicine*, 13(6), 951. DOI: 10.3390/jpm13060951 PMID: 37373940

Alami, H., Rivard, L., Lehoux, P., Hoffman, S. J., Cadeddu, S. B. M., Savoldelli, M., Samri, M. A., Ag Ahmed, M. A., Fleet, R., & Fortin, J. P. (2020). Artificial intelligence in health care: Laying the Foundation for Responsible, sustainable, and inclusive innovation in low-and middle-income countries. *Globalization and Health*, 16(1), 1–6. DOI: 10.1186/s12992-020-00584-1 PMID: 32580741

Alam, M. A., Kumar, R., Banoriya, D., Yadav, A. S., Goga, G., Saxena, K. K., Buddhi, D., & Mohan, R. (2023). Design and development of thermal comfort analysis for air-conditioned compartment. *International Journal on Interactive Design and Manufacturing*, 17(5), 2777–2787. DOI: 10.1007/s12008-022-01015-8

Albawi, S., Arif, M. H., & Waleed, J. (2023). Skin cancer classification dermatologist-level based on deep learning model. *Acta Scientiarum. Technology*, 45, e61531–e61531. DOI: 10.4025/actascitechnol.v45i1.61531

Alexopoulos, C., Al-Tamimi, T. A. S., & Saxena, S. (2023). Were the higher educational institutions (HEIs) in Oman ready to face pedagogical challenges during COVID-19? *Arab Gulf Journal of Scientific Research*. Advance online publication. DOI: 10.1108/AGJSR-03-2023-0095

Alharbi, K. S., Fuloria, N. K., Fuloria, S., Rahman, S. B., Al-Malki, W. H., Javed Shaikh, M. A., Thangavelu, L., Singh, S. K., Rama Raju Allam, V. S., Jha, N. K., Chellappan, D. K., Dua, K., & Gupta, G. (2021). Nuclear factor-kappa B and its role in inflammatory lung disease. *Chemico-Biological Interactions*, 345, 109568. Advance online publication. DOI: 10.1016/j.cbi.2021.109568 PMID: 34181887

Al-Huqail, A. A., Kumar, P., Eid, E. M., Singh, J., Arya, A. K., Goala, M., Adelodun, B., Abou Fayssal, S., Kumar, V., & Širić, I. (2022). Risk Assessment of Heavy Metals Contamination in Soil and Two Rice (Oryza sativa L.) Varieties Irrigated with Paper Mill Effluent. *Agriculture (Switzerland)*, 12(11). Advance online publication. DOI: 10.3390/agriculture12111864

AL-Huqail, A. A., Kumar, P., Eid, E. M., Taher, M. A., Kumar, P., Adelodun, B., Andabaka, Ž., Mioč, B., Držaić, V., Bachheti, A., Singh, J., Kumar, V., & Širić, I.AL-Huqail. (2022). Phytoremediation of Composite Industrial Effluent using Sacred Lotus (Nelumbo nucifera Gaertn): A Lab-Scale Experimental Investigation. *Sustainability (Basel)*, 14(15), 9500. Advance online publication. DOI: 10.3390/su14159500

Al-Maini, M., Maindarkar, M., Kitas, G. D., Khanna, N. N., Misra, D. P., Johri, A. M., Mantella, L., Agarwal, V., Sharma, A., Singh, I. M., Tsoulfas, G., Laird, J. R., Faa, G., Teji, J., Turk, M., Viskovic, K., Ruzsa, Z., Mavrogeni, S., Rathore, V., & Suri, J. S. (2023). Artificial intelligence-based preventive, personalized and precision medicine for cardiovascular disease/stroke risk assessment in rheumatoid arthritis patients: A narrative review. *Rheumatology International*, 43(11), 1965–1982. DOI: 10.1007/s00296-023-05415-1 PMID: 37648884

Alonso, S. G., Marques, G., Barrachina, I., Garcia-Zapirain, B., Arambarri, J., Salvador, J. C., & de la Torre Díez, I. (2021). Telemedicine and e-Health research solutions in literature for combatting COVID-19: A systematic review. *Health and Technology*, 11(2), 257–266. DOI: 10.1007/s12553-021-00529-7 PMID: 33558838

Aloo, B. N., Dessureault-Rompré, J., Tripathi, V., Nyongesa, B. O., & Were, B. A. (2023). Signaling and crosstalk of rhizobacterial and plant hormones that mediate abiotic stress tolerance in plants. *Frontiers in Microbiology*, 14, 1171104. Advance online publication. DOI: 10.3389/fmicb.2023.1171104 PMID: 37455718

Alowais, S. A., Alghamdi, S. S., Alsuhebany, N., Alqahtani, T., Alshaya, A. I., Almohareb, S. N., Aldairem, A., Alrashed, M., Bin Saleh, K., Badreldin, H. A., Al Yami, M. S., Al Harbi, S., & Albekairy, A. M. (2023). Revolutionizing healthcare: The role of artificial intelligence in clinical practice. *BMC Medical Education*, 23(1), 689. DOI: 10.1186/s12909-023-04698-z PMID: 37740191

Alrashed, F. A., Alsubiheen, A. M., Alshammari, H., Mazi, S. I., Al-Saud, S. A., Alayoubi, S., Kachanathu, S. J., Albarrati, A., Aldaihan, M. M., Ahmad, T., Sattar, K., Khan, S., & Dhiman, G. (2022). Stress, Anxiety, and Depression in Pre-Clinical Medical Students: Prevalence and Association with Sleep Disorders. *Sustainability (Basel)*, 14(18), 11320. Advance online publication. DOI: 10.3390/su141811320

Alsadi, J., Tripathi, V., Amaral, L. S., Potrich, E., Hasham, S. H., Patil, P. Y., & Omoniyi, E. M. (2022). Architecture Fibrous Meso-Porous Silica Spheres as Enhanced Adsorbent for Effective Capturing for CO_2 Gas. *Key Engineering Materials*, 928, 39–44. DOI: 10.4028/p-2f2o01

Alzaidi, M. S., Subbalakshmi, C., Roshini, T. V., Shukla, P. K., Shukla, S. K., Dutta, P., & Alhassan, M. (2022). 5G-Telecommunication Allocation Network Using IoT Enabled Improved Machine Learning Technique. *Wireless Communications and Mobile Computing*, 2022, 1–10. Advance online publication. DOI: 10.1155/2022/6229356

Amann, J., Vetter, D., Blomberg, S. N., Christensen, H. C., Coffee, M., Gerke, S., Gilbert, T. K., Hagendorff, T., Holm, S., Livne, M., Spezzatti, A., Strümke, I., Zicari, R. V., & Madai, V. I. (2022). To explain or not to explain?—Artificial intelligence explainability in clinical decision support systems. *PLOS Digital Health*, 1(2), e0000016. DOI: 10.1371/journal.pdig.0000016 PMID: 36812545

Ambika, K. S. B., Goswami, S., Pimplapure, V., Jweeg, M. J., Kant, K., & Gangodkar, D. (2023). Framework Towards Detection of Stress Level Through Classifying Physiological Signals Using Machine Learning. *2023 3rd International Conference on Advance Computing and Innovative Technologies in Engineering, ICACITE 2023*, 600 – 604. DOI: 10.1109/ICACITE57410.2023.10183013

Aminabee, S. (2024). The future of healthcare and patient-centric care: Digital innovations, trends, and predictions. In *Emerging Technologies for Health Literacy and Medical Practice* (pp. 240–262). IGI Global. DOI: 10.4018/979-8-3693-1214-8.ch012

Anand, A., Patience, A. A., Sharma, N., & Khurana, N. (2017). The present and future of pharmacotherapy of Alzheimer's disease: A comprehensive review. *European Journal of Pharmacology*, 815, 364–375. DOI: 10.1016/j.ejphar.2017.09.043 PMID: 28978455

Anghel, B. I., & Lupu, R. (2024). Understanding Regulatory Changes: Deep Learning in Sustainable Finance and Banking. *Journal of Risk and Financial Management*, 17(7), 295. Advance online publication. DOI: 10.3390/jrfm17070295

Ansari, M. F., & Afzal, A. (2022). Sensitivity and Performance Analysis of 10 MW Solar Power Plant Using MPPT Technique. *Lecture Notes in Electrical Engineering, 894 LNEE*, 512–518. DOI: 10.1007/978-981-19-1677-9_46

Ansari, K. R., Quraishi, M. A., & Singh, A. (2015). Isatin derivatives as a non-toxic corrosion inhibitor for mild steel in 20% H2SO4. *Corrosion Science*, 95, 62–70. DOI: 10.1016/j.corsci.2015.02.010

Ansari, K. R., Quraishi, M. A., Singh, A., Ramkumar, S., & Obote, I. B. (2016). Corrosion inhibition of N80 steel in 15% HCl by pyrazolone derivatives: Electrochemical, surface and quantum chemical studies. *RSC Advances*, 6(29), 24130–24141. DOI: 10.1039/C5RA25441H

Araujo, R., Fernandes, J. M., Reis, L. P., & Beaulieu, M. (2023). Purchasing challenges in times of COVID-19: Resilience practices to mitigate disruptions in the health-care supply chain. *Journal of Global Operations and Strategic Sourcing*, 16(2), 368–396. DOI: 10.1108/JGOSS-04-2022-0026

Arora, S., Pargaien, S., Khan, F., Tewari, I., Nainwal, D., Mer, A., Mittal, A., & Misra, A. (2023). Monitoring Tourist Footfall at Nainital in Uttarakhand using Sensor Technology. *2023 4th International Conference on Electronics and Sustainable Communication Systems, ICESC 2023 - Proceedings*, 200 – 204. DOI: 10.1109/ICESC57686.2023.10193244

Arora, A., Singh, R., Malik, K., & Kestwal, U. (2024). Association of sexual performance and intimacy with satisfaction in life in head and neck cancer patients: A review. *Oral Oncology Reports*, 11, 100563. Advance online publication. DOI: 10.1016/j.oor.2024.100563

Arora, R., Chauhan, A., Singh, A. P., & Sharma, R. (2023). Optimization of a production inventory model of imperfect quality items for three-layer supply chain in fuzzy environment. *Benchmarking*. Advance online publication. DOI: 10.1108/BIJ-11-2021-0678

Arora, R., Singh, A. P., Sharma, R., & Chauhan, A. (2022). A remanufacturing inventory model to control the carbon emission using cap-and-trade regulation with the hexagonal fuzzy number. *Benchmarking*, 29(7), 2202–2230. DOI: 10.1108/BIJ-05-2021-0254

Arora, S., Pargaien, S., Khan, F., Misra, A., Gambhir, A., & Verma, D. (2023). Smart Parking Allocation Using Raspberry Pi based IoT System. *Proceedings of the 5th International Conference on Inventive Research in Computing Applications, ICIRCA 2023*, 1457–1461. DOI: 10.1109/ICIRCA57980.2023.10220619

Arrazola, J., Masiello, M. M., Joshi, S., Dominguez, A. E., Poel, A., Wilkie, C. M., Bressler, J. M., McLaughlin, J., Kraszewski, J., Komatsu, K. K., Peterson Pompa, X., Jespersen, M., Richardson, G., Lehnertz, N., LeMaster, P., Rust, B., Keyser Metobo, A., Doman, B., Casey, D., & Landen, M. (2020). COVID-19 mortality among American Indian and Alaska native persons—14 states, January–June 2020. *MMWR. Morbidity and Mortality Weekly Report*, 69(49), 69. DOI: 10.15585/mmwr.mm6949a3 PMID: 33301432

Artificial Intelligence for Precision Medicine and Better Healthcare. (2020, September). KDnuggets. Retrieved November 4, 2022, from https://www.kdnuggets.com/2020/09/artificial-intelligence-precision-medicine-better-healthcare.html

Artificial Intelligence in Healthcare - AI Applications & Uses (2022, May 24). Intellipaat Blog. Retrieved November 5, 2022, from https://intellipaat.com/blog/artificial-intelligence-in-healthcare/

Artificial Intelligence, Machine Learning and Genomics (2022, January 12). National Human Genome Research Institute Genome.gov. Retrieved November 11, 2022, from https://www.genome.gov/about-genomics/educational-resources/fact-sheets/artificial-intelligence-machine-learning-and-genomics

Arunava. (2018, December 5). *Malaria Cell Images Dataset.* Kaggle. Retrieved November 12, 2022, from https://www.kaggle.com/datasets/iarunava/cell-images-for-detecting-malaria

Arya, U., Tiwari, R., Kargeti, H., Chauhan, J. S., Kothari, S., & Kargeti, H. (2023). Artificial Intelligence for Portfolio Selection: A Bibliometric Review. In M. H.K. & S. S. (Eds.), *Proceedings - 2023 International Conference on Advanced Computing and Communication Technologies, ICACCTech 2023* (pp. 9–13). Institute of Electrical and Electronics Engineers Inc. DOI: 10.1109/ICACCTech61146.2023.00011

Asha, P., Mannepalli, K., Khilar, R., Subbulakshmi, N., Dhanalakshmi, R., Tripathi, V., Mohanavel, V., Sathyamurthy, R., & Sudhakar, M. (2022). Role of machine learning in attaining environmental sustainability. *Energy Reports*, 8, 863–871. DOI: 10.1016/j.egyr.2022.09.206

Ash, C., Diallo, C., Venkatadri, U., & VanBerkel, P. (2022). Distributionally robust optimization of a Canadian healthcare supply chain to enhance resilience during the COVID-19 pandemic. *Computers & Industrial Engineering*, 168, 108051. DOI: 10.1016/j.cie.2022.108051 PMID: 35250153

Athota, L., Shukla, V. K., Pandey, N., & Rana, A. (2020). Chatbot for healthcare system using Artificial Intelligence. 2020 8th International Conference on Reliability, Infocom Technologies and Optimization (Trends and Future Directions) (ICRITO), 619–622. https://doi.org/DOI: 10.1109/ICRITO48877.2020.9197833

Awad, A., Trenfield, S. J., Pollard, T. D., Ong, J. J., Elbadawi, M., McCoubrey, L. E., Goyanes, A., Gaisford, S., & Basit, A. W. (2021). Connected healthcare: Improving patient care using digital health technologies. *Advanced Drug Delivery Reviews*, 178, 113958. DOI: 10.1016/j.addr.2021.113958 PMID: 34478781

Awal, G., & Khanna, R. (2019). Determinants of millennial online consumer behavior and prospective purchase decisions. *International Journal of Advanced Science and Technology*, 28(18), 366–378.

Babu, M., Venkataraman, S. R., Rao, P. N., Rao, V., Kaliappan, S., Patil, P. P., Sekar, S., Yuvaraj, K. P., & Murugan, A. (2022). Optical Microstructure, FESEM, Microtensile, and Microhardness Properties of LM 25-B4Cnp-Grnp Hybrid Composites Manufactured by Selective Laser Melting. *Advances in Materials Science and Engineering*, 2022, 1–8. Advance online publication. DOI: 10.1155/2022/3177172

Badhotiya, G. K., Sharma, V. P., Prakash, S., Kalluri, V., & Singh, R. (2021). Investigation and assessment of blockchain technology adoption in the pharmaceutical supply chain. In S. Y. (Ed.), *Materials Today: Proceedings* (Vol. 46, pp. 10776–10780). Elsevier Ltd. https://doi.org/DOI: 10.1016/j.matpr.2021.01.673

Badhotiya, G. K., Avikal, S., Soni, G., & Sengar, N. (2022). Analyzing barriers for the adoption of circular economy in the manufacturing sector. *International Journal of Productivity and Performance Management*, 71(3), 912–931. DOI: 10.1108/IJPPM-01-2021-0021

Bag, S., Dhamija, P., Singh, R. K., Rahman, M. S., & Sreedharan, V. R. (2023). Big data analytics and artificial intelligence technologies based collaborative platform empowering absorptive capacity in health care supply chain: An empirical study. *Journal of Business Research*, 154, 113315. DOI: 10.1016/j.jbusres.2022.113315

Baltrusaitis, J., Bakshi, B., Chojnacka, K., Chuck, C. J., Coppens, M.-O., Edge, J. S., Harper, G., Hsiao, B. S., Li, H., Mba Wright, M., McLaughlin, M., Nandy, A., Pan, S.-Y., Qiang, Z., Ribeiro, C., Swadźba-Kwaśny, M., Wang, M., Xiang, Y., & Zhang, L. (2024). Sustainability science and technology in 2024 and beyond equitable publishing aligned with United Nations' Sustainable development goals. *Sustainability Science and Technology*, 1(1), 010201. DOI: 10.1088/2977-3504/ad555a

Bandara, W., Syed, R., Kapurubandra, M., & Rupasinghe, L. (2012). Building Essential BPM Capabilities to Assist Successful ICT Deployment in the Developing Context: Observations and Recommendations from Sri Lanka. *GlobDev 2012*. 14. https://aisel.aisnet.org/globdev2012/14

Banerjee, D., Kukreja, V., Gupta, A., Singh, V., & Pal Singh Brar, T. (2023). Combining CNN and SVM for Accurate Identification of Ridge Gourd Leaf Diseases. *2023 3rd Asian Conference on Innovation in Technology, ASIANCON 2023*. DOI: 10.1109/ASIANCON58793.2023.10269834

Banerjee, D., Kukreja, V., Aeri, M., Hariharan, S., & Garg, N. (2023). Integrated CNN-SVM Approach for Accurate Radish Leaf Disease Classification: A Comparative Study and Performance Analysis. *2023 Annual International Conference on Emerging Research Areas: International Conference on Intelligent Systems, AICERA/ICIS 2023*. DOI: 10.1109/AICERA/ICIS59538.2023.10420119

Banerjee, P., & Gupta, R. (2024). A mixed-method exploration of effects of technostress on remote/hybrid working professionals. *Computers in Human Behavior*, 150, 107974. DOI: 10.1016/j.chb.2023.107974

Banitaba, S. N., Khademolqorani, S., Jadhav, V. V., Chamanehpour, E., Mishra, Y. K., Mostafavi, E., & Kaushik, A. (2023). Recent progress of bio-based smart wearable sensors for healthcare applications. *Materials Today Electronics*, 5, 100055. DOI: 10.1016/j.mtelec.2023.100055

Bansal, S., Kumar, V., Kumari, A., & Kuzmin, E. (2023). Understanding the Role of Digital Technologies in Supply Chain Management of SMEs. In K. V., K. G.L., A. V., & K. E. (Eds.), *Lecture Notes in Information Systems and Organisation: Vol. 61 LNISO* (pp. 195 – 205). Springer Science and Business Media Deutschland GmbH. DOI: 10.1007/978-3-031-30351-7_16

Bansal, N., Bhatnagar, M., Kumar, P., & Taneja, S. (2023). Capitalizing on conservation: The synergy between financial gains and environmental goals in impact investing. In *Green Management - A New Paradigm in the World of Business*. Nova Science Publishers, Inc.

Bansal, N., Bhatnagar, M., & Taneja, S. (2023). Balancing priorities through green optimism: A study elucidating initiatives, approaches, and strategies for sustainable supply chain management. In *Handbook of Research on Designing Sustainable Supply Chains to Achieve a Circular Economy*. IGI Global., DOI: 10.4018/978-1-6684-7664-2.ch004

Barthwal, S., Pundir, S., Wazid, M., Singh, D. P., & Pundir, S. (2023). Design of an Energy Aware Cluster-Based Routing Scheme to Minimize Energy Consumption in Wireless Sensor Networks. *Communications in Computer and Information Science, 1797 CCIS*, 16 – 28. DOI: 10.1007/978-3-031-28180-8_2

Barwar, M. K., Sahu, L. K., Bhatnagar, P., Gupta, K. K., & Chander, A. H. (2021). A flicker-free decoupled ripple cancellation technique for LED driver circuits. *Optik (Stuttgart)*, 247, 168029. Advance online publication. DOI: 10.1016/j.ijleo.2021.168029

Barwar, M. K., Sahu, L. K., Bhatnagar, P., Gupta, K. K., & Chander, A. H. (2022). Performance analysis and reliability estimation of five-level rectifier. *International Journal of Circuit Theory and Applications*, 50(3), 926–943. DOI: 10.1002/cta.3187

Bashir, S., Sharma, V., Lgaz, H., Chung, I.-M., Singh, A., & Kumar, A. (2018). The inhibition action of analgin on the corrosion of mild steel in acidic medium: A combined theoretical and experimental approach. *Journal of Molecular Liquids*, 263, 454–462. DOI: 10.1016/j.molliq.2018.04.143

Bashir, S., Thakur, A., Lgaz, H., Chung, I.-M., & Kumar, A. (2020). Corrosion inhibition efficiency of bronopol on aluminium in 0.5 M HCl solution: Insights from experimental and quantum chemical studies. *Surfaces and Interfaces*, 20, 100542. Advance online publication. DOI: 10.1016/j.surfin.2020.100542

Basyirah, L., Kina, A., & Hidayati, A. (2022). Open innovation for sustainable development goals: Learning from go to group. *Journal of Innovation in Business and Economics*, 6(01). Advance online publication. DOI: 10.22219/jibe.v6i01.21745

Begum, S. J. P., Pratibha, S., Rawat, J. M., Venugopal, D., Sahu, P., Gowda, A., Qureshi, K. A., & Jaremko, M. (2022). Recent Advances in Green Synthesis, Characterization, and Applications of Bioactive Metallic Nanoparticles. *Pharmaceuticals*, 15(4). Advance online publication. DOI: 10.3390/ph15040455

Behera, A., & Singh Rawat, K. (2023). A brief review paper on mining subsidence and its geo-environmental impact. *Materials Today: Proceedings*. Advance online publication. DOI: 10.1016/j.matpr.2023.04.183

Belwal, N., Juneja, P., & Sunori, S. K. (2023). Decoupler Control for a MIMO Process Model in an Industrial Process - A Review. *2023 2nd International Conference on Ambient Intelligence in Health Care, ICAIHC 2023*. DOI: 10.1109/ICAIHC59020.2023.10431463

Belwal, R., & Belwal, S. (2017). Employers' perception of women workers in Oman and the challenges they face. *Employee Relations*, 39(7), 1048–1065. DOI: 10.1108/ER-09-2016-0183

Benkler, Y. (2019). Don't let industry write the rules for AI. *Nature*, 569(7754), 161–162. DOI: 10.1038/d41586-019-01413-1 PMID: 31043715

Berge, G. T., Granmo, O. C., Tveit, T. O., Munkvold, B. E., Ruthjersen, A. L., & Sharma, J. (2023). Machine learning-driven clinical decision support system for concept-based searching: A field trial in a Norwegian hospital. *BMC Medical Informatics and Decision Making*, 23(1), 5. DOI: 10.1186/s12911-023-02101-x PMID: 36627624

Bhakat, R. S., & Arif, M. Z. U. (2021). Challenges faced and preparedness of FMCG retail supply chain during COVID-19. In *Managing Supply Chain Risk and Disruptions: Post COVID-19* (pp. 19–27). Springer International Publishing. DOI: 10.1007/978-3-030-72575-4_2

Bhakoo, V., & Choi, T. (2013). The iron cage exposed: Institutional pressures and heterogeneity across the healthcare supply chain. *Journal of Operations Management*, 31(6), 432–449. DOI: 10.1016/j.jom.2013.07.016

Bhamangol, B., Kaiwade, A., Pant, B., Rana, A., Kaiwade, A., & Shaikh, A. (2022). An Artificial Intelligence based Design and Implementation for classifying the Missing Data in IoT Applications. *Proceedings of 5th International Conference on Contemporary Computing and Informatics, IC3I 2022*, 1376 – 1382. https://doi.org/DOI: 10.1109/IC3I56241.2022.10072634

Bharany, S., Badotra, S., Sharma, S., Rani, S., Alazab, M., Jhaveri, R. H., & Reddy Gadekallu, T. (2022). Energy efficient fault tolerance techniques in green cloud computing: A systematic survey and taxonomy. *Sustainable Energy Technologies and Assessments*, 53, 102613. Advance online publication. DOI: 10.1016/j.seta.2022.102613

Bharany, S., Sharma, S., Badotra, S., Khalaf, O. I., Alotaibi, Y., Alghamdi, S., & Alassery, F. (2021). Energy-efficient clustering scheme for flying ad-hoc networks using an optimized leach protocol. *Energies*, 14(19), 6016. Advance online publication. DOI: 10.3390/en14196016

Bhargava, A., Bhargava, D., Kumar, P. N., Sajja, G. S., & Ray, S. (2022). Industrial IoT and AI implementation in vehicular logistics and supply chain management for vehicle mediated transportation systems. *International Journal of System Assurance Engineering and Management*, 13, 673–680. DOI: 10.1007/s13198-021-01581-2

Bhatnagar, M., Kumar, P., Taneja, S., Sood, K., & Grima, S. (2024). From digital overload to trading Zen: The role of digital detox in enhancing intraday trading performance. In *Business Drivers in Promoting Digital Detoxification*. IGI Global., DOI: 10.4018/979-8-3693-1107-3.ch010

Bhatnagar, M., Rajaram, R., Taneja, S., & Kumar, P. (2024). Balancing acts: The Yin and Yang of debit and credit on the stage of financial well-being. In *Emerging Perspectives on Financial Well-Being*. IGI Global., DOI: 10.4018/979-8-3693-1750-1.ch002

Bhatnagar, M., Taneja, S., & Kumar, P. (2023). The Effectiveness of Carbon Pricing Mechanism in Steering Financial Flows Toward Sustainable Projects. *International Journal of Environmental Impacts*, 6(4), 183–196. DOI: 10.18280/ijei.060403

Bhatnagar, M., Taneja, S., Kumar, P., & Özen, E. (2024). Does financial education act as a catalyst for SME competitiveness? *International Journal of Education Economics and Development*, 15(3), 377–393. DOI: 10.1504/IJEED.2024.139306

Bhatnagar, M., Taneja, S., & Rupeika-Apoga, R. (2023). Demystifying the Effect of the News (Shocks) on Crypto Market Volatility. *Journal of Risk and Financial Management*, 16(2), 136. DOI: 10.3390/jrfm16020136

Bhat, S. A., Bashir, O., Ul Haq, S. A., Amin, T., Rafiq, A., Ali, M., Américo-Pinheiro, J. H. P., & Sher, F. (2022). Phytoremediation of heavy metals in soil and water: An eco-friendly, sustainable and multidisciplinary approach. *Chemosphere*, 303, 134788. Advance online publication. DOI: 10.1016/j.chemosphere.2022.134788 PMID: 35504464

Bhatt, C., Singh, S., Chauhan, R., Singh, T., & Uniyal, A. (2023). Artificial Intelligence in Current Education: Roles, Applications & Challenges. *Proceedings - 2023 3rd International Conference on Pervasive Computing and Social Networking, ICPCSN 2023*, 241–244. DOI: 10.1109/ICPCSN58827.2023.00045

Bhatt, S., & Dani, R. (2024). Social media and community engagement: Empowering local voices in regenerative tourism. In *Examining Tourist Behaviors and Community Involvement in Destination Rejuvenation*. IGI Global., DOI: 10.4018/979-8-3693-6819-0.ch009

Bhatt, S., Dani, R., & Singh, A. K. (2024). Exploring cutting-edge approaches to sustainable tourism infrastructure and design a case studies of regenerative accommodation and facilities. In *Dimensions of Regenerative Practices in Tourism and Hospitality*. IGI Global., DOI: 10.4018/979-8-3693-4042-4.ch003

Bhatt, Y., & Ghuman, K. (2022). Managerial cognition and environmental behavioral intentions: A behavioral reasoning theory perspective. *Corporate Social Responsibility and Environmental Management*, 29(5), 1315–1329. DOI: 10.1002/csr.2271

Bhushan, B., & Nayak, A. (2022). Application of green nanomaterials for sustainable energy systems: A review of the current status. In *Biofuel Technologies for a Sustainable Future: India and Beyond*. River Publishers.

Bhushan, B., Sahoo, C., Sinha, P., & Khamparia, A. (2021). Unification of Blockchain and Internet of Things (BIoT): Requirements, working model, challenges and future directions. *Wireless Networks*, 27(1), 55–90. DOI: 10.1007/s11276-020-02445-6

Bhyan, B., Jangra, S., Kaur, M., & Singh, H. (2011). Orally fast dissolving films: Innovations in formulation and technology. *International Journal of Pharmaceutical Sciences Review and Research*, 9(2), 50–57.

Bialas, C., Bechtsis, D., Aivazidou, E., Achillas, C., & Aidonis, D. (2023). A holistic view on the adoption and cost-effectiveness of technology-driven supply chain management practices in healthcare. *Sustainability (Basel)*, 15(6), 5541. DOI: 10.3390/su15065541

Biermans, M. L., Bulthuis, W., Holl, T., & van Overbeeke, B. (2023). Sustainable Finance in the Maritime Sector. In *Maritime Decarbonization: Practical Tools, Case Studies and Decarbonization Enablers*. Springer Nature. DOI: 10.1007/978-3-031-39936-7_19

Bisht, R. K., Bisht, I. P., & Joshi, B. C. (2022). Growth of Micro, Small and Medium Enterprises (MSMEs) in Uttarakhand (India). In D. N. & C. A. (Eds.), *AIP Conference Proceedings* (Vol. 2481). American Institute of Physics Inc. DOI: 10.1063/5.0103881

Bisht, B., Gururani, P., Aman, J., Vlaskin, M. S., Anna, I. K., Irina, A. A., Joshi, S., Kumar, S., & Kumar, V. (2023). A review on holistic approaches for fruits and vegetables biowastes valorization. *Materials Today: Proceedings*, 73, 54–63. DOI: 10.1016/j.matpr.2022.09.168

Bist, A., Dobriyal, R., Gwalwanshi, M., & Avikal, S. (2022). Influence of Layer Height and Print Speed on the Mechanical Properties of 3D-Printed ABS. In D. N. & C. A. (Eds.), *AIP Conference Proceedings* (Vol. 2481). American Institute of Physics Inc. https://doi.org/DOI: 10.1063/5.0107304

Bohr, A., & Memarzadeh, K. (Eds.). (2020). *Artificial intelligence in healthcare*. Academic Press.

Boopathi, S. (2023). Internet of Things-Integrated Remote Patient Monitoring System: Healthcare Application. In *Dynamics of Swarm Intelligence Health analysis for the next generation* (pp. 137–161). IGI Global. DOI: 10.4018/978-1-6684-6894-4.ch008

Bordoloi, D., Singh, V., Sanober, S., Buhari, S. M., Ujjan, J. A., & Boddu, R. (2022). Deep Learning in Healthcare System for Quality of Service. *Journal of Healthcare Engineering*, 2022, 1–11. Advance online publication. DOI: 10.1155/2022/8169203 PMID: 35281541

Bordoloi, N., Sharma, A., Nautiyal, H., & Goel, V. (2018). An intense review on the latest advancements of Earth Air Heat Exchangers. *Renewable & Sustainable Energy Reviews*, 89, 261–280. DOI: 10.1016/j.rser.2018.03.056

Borges do Nascimento, I. J., Abdulazeem, H., Vasanthan, L. T., Martinez, E. Z., Zucoloto, M. L., Østengaard, L., Azzopardi-Muscat, N., Zapata, T., & Novillo-Ortiz, D. (2023). Barriers and facilitators to utilizing digital health technologies by healthcare professionals. *NPJ Digital Medicine*, 6(1), 161. DOI: 10.1038/s41746-023-00899-4 PMID: 37723240

Botti, A., & Monda, A. (2020). Sustainable value co-creation and digital health: The case of Trentino e-health ecosystem. *Sustainability (Basel)*, 12(13), 5263. Advance online publication. DOI: 10.3390/su12135263

Boulos, M. N. K., & Wu, J. T. (2020). The Internet of Things in Healthcare: Applications, Benefits, and Challenges. *Healthcare Informatics Research*, 26(3), 193–204. PMID: 32819037

Brodny, J., & Tutak, M. (2023). The level of implementing sustainable development goal "Industry, innovation and infrastructure" of Agenda 2030 in the European Union countries: Application of MCDM methods JEL Classification: C39; O30; R11. *Oeconomia Copernicana*, 14(1), 47–102. DOI: 10.24136/oc.2023.002

Brown, A., & Lee, S. (2019). Privacy Implications of FinTech: A Literature Review. *Journal of Information Privacy and Security*, 15(2), 82–97.

Bullock, J., Young, M. M., & Wang, Y. F. (2020). Artificial intelligence, bureaucratic form, and discretion in public service. *Information Polity*, 25(4), 491–506. DOI: 10.3233/IP-200223

Busch, D. (2023). EU Sustainable Finance Disclosure Regulation. *Capital Markets Law Journal*, 18(3), 303–328. DOI: 10.1093/cmlj/kmad005

Caiado, R. G. G., Scavarda, L. F., Vidal, G., de Mattos Nascimento, D. L., & Garza-Reyes, J. A. (2023). A taxonomy of critical factors towards sustainable operations and supply chain management 4.0 in developing countries. *Operations Management Research*. https://doi.org/DOI: 10.1007/s12063-023-00430-8

Cavaliere, L. P. L., Byloppilly, R., Khan, S. D., Othman, B. A., Muda, I., & Malhotra, R. K. (2024). Acceptance and effectiveness of Industry 4.0 internal and external organisational initiatives in Malaysian firms. *International Journal of Management and Enterprise Development*, 23(1), 1–25. DOI: 10.1504/IJMED.2024.138422

Chahar, A., & Christobel, Y. A. Ritika, Adakane, P. K., Sonal, D., & Tripathi, V. (2022). The Implementation of Big Data With Cloud and Edge Computing in Enhancing the Smart Grid Information Processes Through Sem Model. *2022 2nd International Conference on Advance Computing and Innovative Technologies in Engineering, ICACITE 2022*, 608 – 611. DOI: 10.1109/ICACITE53722.2022.9823896

Chakraborty, C., Othman, S. B., Almalki, F. A., & Sakli, H. (2024). FC-SEEDA: Fog computing-based secure and energy efficient data aggregation scheme for Internet of healthcare Things. *Neural Computing & Applications*, 36(1), 241–257. DOI: 10.1007/s00521-023-08270-0

Chand, A., Agarwal, P., & Sharma, S. (2023). Real-Time Retrieving Vedic Sanskrit Text into Multi-Lingual Text and Audio for Cultural Tourism Motivation. *2023 International Conference for Advancement in Technology, ICONAT 2023*. DOI: 10.1109/ICONAT57137.2023.10080862

Chandna, R., Saini, S., & Kumar, S. (2022). Selecting the Most Agile Manufacturing System with Respect to Agile Attribute-Technology: Fuzzy AHP Approach. In D. N. & C. A. (Eds.), *AIP Conference Proceedings* (Vol. 2481). American Institute of Physics Inc. https://doi.org/DOI: 10.1063/5.0103804

Chandna, R. (2022). Selecting the most agile manufacturing system with respect to agile attribute-technology-fuzzy AHP approach. *International Journal of Operations Research*, 43(4), 512–532. DOI: 10.1504/IJOR.2022.122812

Chandran, G. C., Synthia Regis Prabha, D. M. M., Malathi, P., Kapila, D., Arunkumar, M. S., Verma, D., & Teressa, D. M. (2022). Built-In Calibration Standard and Decision Support System for Controlling Structured Data Storage Systems Using Soft Computing Techniques. *Computational Intelligence and Neuroscience*, 2022, 1–7. Advance online publication. DOI: 10.1155/2022/3476004 PMID: 36065369

Chang, A. (2023). The role of artificial intelligence in digital health. In *Digital health entrepreneurship* (pp. 75–85). Springer International Publishing. DOI: 10.1007/978-3-031-33902-8_6

Chan, S., Reddy, V., Myers, B., Thibodeaux, Q., Brownstone, N., & Liao, W. (2020). Machine Learning in Dermatology: Current Applications, Opportunities, and Limitations. *Dermatology and Therapy*, 10(3), 365–386. DOI: 10.1007/s13555-020-00372-0 PMID: 32253623

Charbe, N. B., Amnerkar, N. D., Ramesh, B., Tambuwala, M. M., Bakshi, H. A., Aljabali, A. A. A., Khadse, S. C., Satheeshkumar, R., Satija, S., Metha, M., Chellappan, D. K., Shrivastava, G., Gupta, G., Negi, P., Dua, K., & Zacconi, F. C. (2020). Small interfering RNA for cancer treatment: Overcoming hurdles in delivery. *Acta Pharmaceutica Sinica. B*, 10(11), 2075–2109. DOI: 10.1016/j.apsb.2020.10.005 PMID: 33304780

Chauhan, A., Sharma, N. K., Tayal, S., Kumar, V., & Kumar, M. (2022). A sustainable production model for waste management with uncertain scrap and recycled material. *Journal of Material Cycles and Waste Management*, 24(5), 1797–1817. DOI: 10.1007/s10163-022-01435-4

Chauhan, C. C., Kagdi, A. R., Jotania, R. B., Upadhyay, A., Sandhu, C. S., Shirsath, S. E., & Meena, S. S. (2018). Structural, magnetic and dielectric properties of Co-Zr substituted M-type calcium hexagonal ferrite nanoparticles in the presence of α-Fe2O3 phase. *Ceramics International*, 44(15), 17812–17823. DOI: 10.1016/j.ceramint.2018.06.249

Chauhan, M., Rani, A., Joshi, S., & Sharma, P. K. (2023). Role of psychrophilic and psychrotolerant microorganisms toward the development of hill agriculture. In *Advanced Microbial Technology for Sustainable Agriculture and Environment*. Elsevier., DOI: 10.1016/B978-0-323-95090-9.00002-9

Chavadaki, S., Nithin Kumar, K. C., & Rajesh, M. N. (2021). Finite element analysis of spur gear to find out the optimum root radius. In S. Y. (Ed.), *Materials Today: Proceedings* (Vol. 46, pp. 10672 – 10675). Elsevier Ltd. DOI: 10.1016/j.matpr.2021.01.422

Chen, I. Y., Szolovits, P., & Ghassemi, M. (2019). Can AI help reduce disparities in general medical and mental health care? *AMA Journal of Ethics*, 21(2), 167–179. DOI: 10.1001/amajethics.2019.167 PMID: 30794127

Chen, Y., & Wang, T. (2018). FinTech development and financial inclusion: A review. *Electronic Commerce Research and Applications*, 30, 38–51.

Chhikara, N., Kour, R., Jaglan, S., Gupta, P., Gat, Y., & Panghal, A. (2018). Citrus medica: Nutritional, phytochemical composition and health benefits-a rev. *Food & Function*, 9(4), 1978–1992. DOI: 10.1039/C7FO02035J PMID: 29594287

Chincholikar, P., Singh, K. R. B., Natarajan, A., Kerry, R. G., Singh, J., Malviya, J., & Singh, R. P. (2023). Green nanobiopolymers for ecological applications: A step towards a sustainable environment. *RSC Advances*, 13(18), 12411–12429. DOI: 10.1039/D2RA07707H PMID: 37091622

Chiu, I. H.-Y., Lin, L., & Rouch, D. (2022). Law and Regulation for Sustainable Finance. *European Business Organization Law Review*, 23(1), 1–7. Advance online publication. DOI: 10.1007/s40804-021-00230-2

Chiu, W. K., & Fong, B. Y. F. (2023). Sustainable Development Goal 3 in Healthcare. In *Environmental, social and governance and sustainable development in healthcare* (pp. 33–45). Springer Nature Singapore. DOI: 10.1007/978-981-99-1564-4_3

Cortés, J. E. R. (2022). Analysis and design of security mechanisms in the context of Advanced Persistent Threats against critical infrastructures. *Unpublished Ph. D. thesis, University of Malaga, Spain*.

Cunha, F. A. F. de S., Meira, E., & Orsato, R. J. (2021). Sustainable finance and investment: Review and research agenda. *Business Strategy and the Environment*, 30(8), 3821–3838. DOI: 10.1002/bse.2842

Dahiya, K., & Taneja, S. (2023). To Analyse the Impact of Multi-Media Technology on the Rural Entrepreneurship Development. In *Contemporary Studies of Risks in Emerging Technology* (pp. 221–240). DOI: 10.1108/978-1-80455-562-020231015

Dahiya, M., Guru Prasad, M. S., Anand, T., Kumar, K., Bansal, S., & Naveen Kumar, H. N. (2023). An Effective Detection of Litchi Disease using Deep Learning. *2023 14th International Conference on Computing Communication and Networking Technologies, ICCCNT 2023*. DOI: 10.1109/ICCCNT56998.2023.10307717

Dangwal, A., Kaur, S., Taneja, S., & Ozen, E. (2022). A bibliometric analysis of green tourism based on the scopus platform. In *Developing Relationships, Personalization, and Data Herald in Marketing 5.0*. IGI Global., DOI: 10.4018/978-1-6684-4496-2.ch015

Dani, R., Kukreti, R., Negi, A., & Kholiya, D. (2020). Impact of covid-19 on education and internships of hospitality students. *International Journal of Current Research and Review*, 12(21 Special Issue), 86 – 90. DOI: 10.31782/IJCRR.2020.SP54

Dani, R., Rawal, Y. S., Bagchi, P., & Khan, M. (2022). Opportunities and Challenges in Implementation of Artificial Intelligence in Food & Beverage Service Industry. In D. N. & C. A. (Eds.), *AIP Conference Proceedings* (Vol. 2481). American Institute of Physics Inc. DOI: 10.1063/5.0103741

Danilov, Y. A. (2021). The concept of sustainable finance and the prospects for its implementation in Russia. *Voprosy Ekonomiki*, 2021(5), 5–25. DOI: 10.32609/0042-8736-2021-5-5-25

Dar, S. A.Dr Naseer Ahmad. (2022). Mobile technology's role in meeting sustainable development goals. *Journal of Technology Innovations and Energy*, 1(2), 8–15. DOI: 10.56556/jtie.v1i2.180

Dar, S. A., Sharma, R., Srivastava, V., & Sakalle, U. K. (2019). Investigation on the electronic structure, optical, elastic, mechanical, thermodynamic and thermoelectric properties of wide band gap semiconductor double perovskite Ba_2InTaO_6. *RSC Advances*, 9(17), 9522–9532. DOI: 10.1039/C9RA00313D PMID: 35520698

Darwish, M. A., Trukhanov, A. V., Senatov, O. S., Morchenko, A. T., Saafan, S. A., Astapovich, K. A., Trukhanov, S. V., Trukhanova, E. L., Pilyushkin, A. A., Sombra, A. S. B., Zhou, D., Jotania, R. B., & Singh, C. (2020). Investigation of AC-measurements of epoxy/ferrite composites. *Nanomaterials (Basel, Switzerland)*, 10(3), 492. Advance online publication. DOI: 10.3390/nano10030492 PMID: 32182785

Das Gupta, A., Rafi, S. M., Singh, N., Gupta, V. K., Jaiswal, S., & Gangodkar, D. (2022). A Framework of Internet of Things (IOT) for the Manufacturing and Image Classifaication System. *2022 2nd International Conference on Advance Computing and Innovative Technologies in Engineering, ICACITE 2022*, 293 – 297. https://doi.org/DOI: 10.1109/ICACITE53722.2022.9823853

Dash, A. P., Alam, T., Siddiqui, M. I. H., Blecich, P., Kumar, M., Gupta, N. K., Ali, M. A., & Yadav, A. S. (2022). Impact on Heat Transfer Rate Due to an Extended Surface on the Passage of Microchannel Using Cylindrical Ribs with Varying Sector Angle. *Energies*, 15(21), 8191. Advance online publication. DOI: 10.3390/en15218191

Das, T., Thakur, R., Dhua, S., Teixeira-Costa, B. E., Beber Rodrigues, M., Pereira, M. M., Mishra, P., & Gupta, A. K. (2023). Processing of Cereals. In *Cereal Grains: Composition, Nutritional Attributes, and Potential Applications*. CRC Press., DOI: 10.1201/9781003252023-10

Datta, S., Singh, J., Singh, S., & Singh, J. (2016). Earthworms, pesticides and sustainable agriculture: A review. *Environmental Science and Pollution Research International*, 23(9), 8227–8243. DOI: 10.1007/s11356-016-6375-0 PMID: 26951221

Daú, G., Scavarda, A., Scavarda, L. F., & Portugal, V. J. T. (2019). The healthcare sustainable supply chain 4.0: The circular economy transition conceptual framework with the corporate social responsibility mirror. *Sustainability (Basel)*, 11(12), 3259. DOI: 10.3390/su11123259

Davuluri, S. K., Alvi, S. A. M., Aeri, M., Agarwal, A., Serajuddin, M., & Hasan, Z. (2023). A Security Model for Perceptive 5G-Powered BC IoT Associated Deep Learning. *6th International Conference on Inventive Computation Technologies, ICICT 2023 - Proceedings*, 118 – 125. DOI: 10.1109/ICICT57646.2023.10134487

De Vries, J., & Huijsman, R. (2011). Supply chain management in health services: An overview. *Supply Chain Management*, 16(3), 159–165. DOI: 10.1108/13598541111127146

Deepti, B. A., Arya, A. K., Verma, D. K., & Bachheti, R. K. (2023). Allelopathic activity of genus Euphorbia. In G. D., P. B., M. U., M. R., & G. R. (Eds.), *AIP Conference Proceedings* (Vol. 2782). American Institute of Physics Inc. DOI: 10.1063/5.0154514

Deng, Q., Usman, M., Irfan, M., & Haseeb, M. (2024). The role of financial inclusion and tourism in tackling environmental challenges of industrialization and energy consumption: Redesigning Sustainable Development Goals policies. *Natural Resources Forum*. DOI: 10.1111/1477-8947.12522

Dewangan, N. K., Gupta, K. K., & Bhatnagar, P. (2020). Modified reduced device multilevel inverter structures with open circuit fault-tolerance capabilities. *International Transactions on Electrical Energy Systems*, 30(1). Advance online publication. DOI: 10.1002/2050-7038.12142

Dey, P. K., Chowdhury, S., Abadie, A., Vann Yaroson, E., & Sarkar, S. (2024). Artificial intelligence-driven supply chain resilience in Vietnamese manufacturing small-and medium-sized enterprises. *International Journal of Production Research*, 62(15), 5417–5456. DOI: 10.1080/00207543.2023.2179859

Dharwadkar, R., & Deshpande, N. A. (2018). A medical chatbot. *International Journal of Computer Trends and Technology*, 60(1), 41–45. DOI: 10.14445/22312803/IJCTT-V60P106

Dhieb, N., Ghazzai, H., Besbes, H., & Massoud, Y. (2020). A secure ai-driven architecture for automated insurance systems: Fraud detection and risk measurement. *IEEE Access : Practical Innovations, Open Solutions*, 8, 58546–58558. DOI: 10.1109/ACCESS.2020.2983300

Dhiman, G., & Nagar, A. K. (2022). Editorial: Blockchain-based 6G and industrial internet of things systems for industry 4.0/5.0. *Expert Systems: International Journal of Knowledge Engineering and Neural Networks*, 39(10). Advance online publication. DOI: 10.1111/exsy.13162

Diddi, P. K., Sharma, P. K., Srivastava, A., Madduru, S. R. C., & Reddy, E. S. (2022). Sustainable Fast Setting Early Strength Self Compacting Concrete(FSESSCC) Using Metakaolin. *IOP Conference Series. Earth and Environmental Science*, 1077(1), 012009. Advance online publication. DOI: 10.1088/1755-1315/1077/1/012009

Dieudonne, K. K., & Bajaj, M., Kitmo, Rubanenko, O., Jurado, F., & Kamel, S. (2022). Hydropower Potential Assessment of Four Selected Sites in the North Interconnected Network of Cameroon. *2022 IEEE International Conference on Automation/25th Congress of the Chilean Association of Automatic Control: For the Development of Sustainable Agricultural Systems, ICA-ACCA 2022*. DOI: 10.1109/ICA-ACCA56767.2022.10005948

Dihom, H. R., Al-Shaibani, M. M., Radin Mohamed, R. M. S., Al-Gheethi, A. A., Sharma, A., & Khamidun, M. H. (2022). Photocatalytic degradation of disperse azo dyes in textile wastewater using green zinc oxide nanoparticles synthesized in plant extract: A critical review. *Journal of Water Process Engineering*, 47, 102705. Advance online publication. DOI: 10.1016/j.jwpe.2022.102705

Dilsizian, S. E., & Siegel, E. L. (2014). Artificial intelligence in medicine and cardiac imaging: Harnessing big data and advanced computing to provide personalized medical diagnosis and treatment. *Current Cardiology Reports*, 16(1), 441. DOI: 10.1007/s11886-013-0441-8 PMID: 24338557

Dimri, R., Mall, S., Sinha, S., Joshi, N. C., Bhatnagar, P., Sharma, R., Kumar, V., & Gururani, P. (2023). Role of microalgae as a sustainable alternative of biopolymers and its application in industries. *Plant Science Today*, 10, 8–18. DOI: 10.14719/pst.2460

Dingel, J., Kleine, A. K., Cecil, J., Sigl, A. L., Lermer, E., & Gaube, S. (2024). Predictors of Health Care Practitioners' Intention to Use AI-Enabled Clinical Decision Support Systems: Meta-Analysis Based on the Unified Theory of Acceptance and Use of Technology. *Journal of Medical Internet Research*, 26, e57224. DOI: 10.2196/57224 PMID: 39102675

Disadvantages of artificial intelligence in Healthcare. Way2Benefits. (2020, July 8). Retrieved November 13, 2022, from http://way2benefits.com/disadvantages-artificial-intelligence-in-healthcare/

Diwakar, M., Shankar, A., Chakraborty, C., Singh, P., & Arunkumar, G. (2022). Multi-modal medical image fusion in NSST domain for internet of medical things. *Multimedia Tools and Applications*, 81(26), 37477–37497. DOI: 10.1007/s11042-022-13507-6

Dixit, A. K., Kumar, T. V., Joshi, A., Bedi, H. S., Chakravarthi, M. K., & Singh, D. P. (2022). Trends in Robotics and Computer Integrated Manufacturing. *Proceedings of 5th International Conference on Contemporary Computing and Informatics, IC3I 2022*, 212–216. DOI: 10.1109/IC3I56241.2022.10072745

Dixit, A., Routroy, S., & Dubey, S. K. (2022). Analyzing the operational barriers of government-supported healthcare supply chain. *International Journal of Productivity and Performance Management*, 71(8), 3766–3791. DOI: 10.1108/IJPPM-09-2020-0493

Dogra, V., Verma, D., Dalapati, G. K., Sharma, M., & Okhawilai, M. (2022). Special focus on 3D printing of sulfides/selenides for energy conversion and storage. In *Sulfide and Selenide Based Materials for Emerging Applications: Sustainable Energy Harvesting and Storage Technology*. Elsevier., DOI: 10.1016/B978-0-323-99860-4.00012-5

Dogra, V., Verma, D., & Fortunati, E. (2021). Biopolymers and nanomaterials in food packaging and applications. In *Nanotechnology-Based Sustainable Alternatives for the Management of Plant Diseases*. Elsevier., DOI: 10.1016/B978-0-12-823394-8.00011-1

Drupsteen, J., van der Vaart, T., & Pieter van Donk, D. (2013). Integrative practices in hospitals and their impact on patient flow. *International Journal of Operations & Production Management*, 33(7), 912–933. DOI: 10.1108/IJOPM-12-2011-0487

Duan, Y., Edwards, J. S., & Dwivedi, Y. K. (2019). Artificial intelligence for decision making in the era of Big Data–evolution, challenges and research agenda. *International Journal of Information Management*, 48, 63–71. DOI: 10.1016/j.ijinfomgt.2019.01.021

Dubey, V. P., Prakash, R., Chamoli, V., & Mittal, P. (2023). Study of Urban Change Detection Using Landsat 8 Satellite Data: A Case Study of Dehradun City, Uttarakhand, India. *IEEE International Conference on Electrical, Electronics, Communication and Computers, ELEXCOM 2023*. DOI: 10.1109/ELEXCOM58812.2023.10370375

Durga, K. (2024). Intelligent Support for Cardiovascular Diagnosis: The AI-CDSS Approach. In *Using Traditional Design Methods to Enhance AI-Driven Decision Making* (pp. 64-76). IGI Global.

Dutta, A., Singh, P., Dobhal, A., Mannan, D., Singh, J., & Goswami, P. (2023). Entrepreneurial Aptitude of Women of an Aspirational District of Uttarakhand. *Indian Journal of Extension Education*, 59(2), 103–107. DOI: 10.48165/IJEE.2023.59222

Eichler, G. M., & Schwarz, E. J. (2019). What sustainable development goals do social innovations address: A systematic review and content analysis of social innovation literature. *Sustainability (Basel)*, 11(2), 522. Advance online publication. DOI: 10.3390/su11020522

Ekren, B. Y., Stylos, N., Zwiegelaar, J., Turhanlar, E. E., & Kumar, V. (2023). Additive manufacturing integration in E-commerce supply chain network to improve resilience and competitiveness. *Simulation Modelling Practice and Theory*, 122, 102676. Advance online publication. DOI: 10.1016/j.simpat.2022.102676

El Massah, S., & Mohieldin, M. (2020). Digital transformation and localizing the Sustainable Development Goals (SDGs). *Ecological Economics*, 169, 106490. Advance online publication. DOI: 10.1016/j.ecolecon.2019.106490

Elbagory, M., El-Nahrawy, S., Omara, A. E.-D., Eid, E. M., Bachheti, A., Kumar, P., Abou Fayssal, S., Adelodun, B., Bachheti, R. K., Kumar, P., Mioč, B., Kumar, V., & Širić, I. (2022). Sustainable Bioconversion of Wetland Plant Biomass for Pleurotus ostreatus var. florida Cultivation: Studies on Proximate and Biochemical Characterization. *Agriculture*, 12(12), 2095. Advance online publication. DOI: 10.3390/agriculture12122095

Eswar, K. N. D. V. S., Doss, M. A. N., Vishnuram, P., Selim, A., Bajaj, M., Kotb, H., & Kamel, S. (2023). Comprehensive Study on Reduced DC Source Count: Multilevel Inverters and Its Design Topologies. *Energies*, 16(1), 18. Advance online publication. DOI: 10.3390/en16010018

Ewers, M., & Kangmennaang, J. (2023). New spaces of inequality with the rise of remote work: Autonomy, technostress, and life disruption. *Applied Geography (Sevenoaks, England)*, 152, 102888. DOI: 10.1016/j.apgeog.2023.102888

Ewumi, O. (2021, April 30). *Ai in 3D bioprinting. Recode AI Daily iCal.* Retrieved November 10, 2022, from https://ai.recodeminds.com/uncategorized/ai-in-3d-bioprinting/

Ewumi, O., Gülen, K., & Eliaçık, E. (2021, April 30). *Ai in 3D bioprinting. Dataconomy.* Retrieved November 10, 2022, from https://dataconomy.com/2021/04/ai-in-3d-bioprinting/

Fadhil, A., & Gabrielli, S. (2017). Addressing challenges in promoting healthy lifestyles. *Proceedings of the 11th EAI International Conference on Pervasive Computing Technologies for Healthcare*, 261–265. https://doi.org/DOI: 10.1145/3154862.3154914

Fei, W., Opoku, A., Agyekum, K., Oppon, J. A., Ahmed, V., Chen, C., & Lok, K. L. (2021). The critical role of the construction industry in achieving the sustainable development goals (SDGs): Delivering projects for the common good. *Sustainability (Basel)*, 13(16), 9112. Advance online publication. DOI: 10.3390/su13169112

Ferrer, X., Van Nuenen, T., Such, J. M., Coté, M., & Criado, N. (2021). Bias and discrimination in AI: A cross-disciplinary perspective. *IEEE Technology and Society Magazine*, 40(2), 72–80. DOI: 10.1109/MTS.2021.3056293

Filho, W. L., Brandli, L. L., Salvia, A. L., Rayman-Bacchus, L., & Platje, J. (2020). COVID-19 and the UN sustainable development goals: Threat to solidarity or an opportunity. *Sustainability (Basel)*, 12(13), 5343. Advance online publication. DOI: 10.3390/su12135343

Filipp, F. V. (2019). Opportunities for Artificial Intelligence in Advancing Precision Medicine. *Current Genetic Medicine Reports*, 7(4), 208–213. DOI: 10.1007/s40142-019-00177-4 PMID: 31871830

Forslund, M., Mathieson, K., Djibo, Y., Mbindyo, C., Lugangira, N., & Balasubramaniam, P. (2024). Strengthening the evidence base on the use of digital health technologies to accelerate progress towards universal health coverage. *Oxford Open Digital Health*, 2, oqae033. Advance online publication. DOI: 10.1093/oodh/oqae033

Fox, J., Glasspool, D., Patkar, V., Austin, M., Black, L., South, M., Robertson, D., & Vincent, C. (2010). Delivering clinical decision support services: There is nothing as practical as a good theory. *Journal of Biomedical Informatics*, 43(5), 831–843. DOI: 10.1016/j.jbi.2010.06.002 PMID: 20601124

Galmes-Panades, A. M., Angullo, E., Mira-Martínez, S., Bennasar-Veny, M., Zamanillo-Campos, R., Gómez-Juanes, R., Konieczna, J., Jiménez, R., Serrano-Ripoll, M. J., Fiol-deRoque, M. A., Miralles, J., Yañez, A. M., Romaguera, D., Vidal-Thomas, M. C., Llobera-Canaves, J., García-Toro, M., Vicens, C., Gervilla-García, E., Oña, J. I., & Ricci-Cabello, I. (2022). Development and Evaluation of a Digital Health Intervention to Prevent Type 2 Diabetes in Primary Care: The PREDIABETEXT Study Protocol for a Randomised Clinical Trial. *International Journal of Environmental Research and Public Health*, 19(22), 14706. DOI: 10.3390/ijerph192214706 PMID: 36429423

Gangwar, V. P., & Srivastva, S. P. (2020). Impact of micro finance in poverty eradication via SHGs: A study of selected districts in U.P. *International Journal of Advanced Science and Technology*, 29(2), 3818–3829.

Garg, G., Gupta, S., Mishra, P., Vidyarthi, A., Singh, A., & Ali, A. (2023). CROPCARE: An Intelligent Real-Time Sustainable IoT System for Crop Disease Detection Using Mobile Vision. *IEEE Internet of Things Journal*, 10(4), 2840–2851. DOI: 10.1109/JIOT.2021.3109019

Garg, H., Ike, G. N., Kashif, M., & Azam, M. S. (2024). Dynamics of Sustainable and Ethically Responsible Business Practices in Corporate Social Responsibility. In *Technology-Driven Evolution of the Corporate Social Responsibility Ecosystem* (pp. 92–113). IGI Global., DOI: 10.4018/979-8-3693-3238-2.ch005

Garg, P., Gupta, N., & Agarwal, M. (2023). Role of Artificial Intelligence in Supply Chain Management. In *Data Analytics and Business Intelligence* (pp. 47–61). CRC Press. DOI: 10.1201/9781003189640-5

Garg, U., Kumar, S., & Kumar, M. (2023). A Hybrid Approach for the Detection and Classification of MQTT-based IoT-Malware. *2nd International Conference on Sustainable Computing and Data Communication Systems, ICSCDS 2023 - Proceedings*, 1154–1159. DOI: 10.1109/ICSCDS56580.2023.10104820

Garg, V., Singh, H., Bhatia, A., Raza, K., Singh, S. K., Singh, B., & Beg, S. (2017). Systematic Development of Transethosomal Gel System of Piroxicam: Formulation Optimization, In Vitro Evaluation, and Ex Vivo Assessment. *AAPS PharmSciTech*, 18(1), 58–71. DOI: 10.1208/s12249-016-0489-z PMID: 26868380

Gaurav, G., Singh, A. B., Khandelwal, C., Gupta, S., Kumar, S., Meena, M. L., & Dangayach, G. S. (2023). Global Development on LCA Research: A Bibliometric Analysis From 2010 to 2021. *International Journal of Social Ecology and Sustainable Development*, 14(1). Advance online publication. DOI: 10.4018/IJSESD.327791

Ghildiyal, S., Joshi, K., Rawat, G., Memoria, M., Singh, A., & Gupta, A. (2022). Industry 4.0 Application in the Hospitality and Food Service Industries. *Proceedings of the 2022 7th International Conference on Computing, Communication and Security, ICCCS 2022 and 2022 4th International Conference on Big Data and Computational Intelligence, ICBDCI 2022*. DOI: 10.1109/ICCCS55188.2022.10079268

Giri, N. C., Mohanty, R. C., Shaw, R. N., Poonia, S., Bajaj, M., & Belkhier, Y. (2022). Agriphotovoltaic System to Improve Land Productivity and Revenue of Farmer. *2022 IEEE Global Conference on Computing, Power and Communication Technologies, GlobConPT 2022*. DOI: 10.1109/GlobConPT57482.2022.9938338

Godbole, V., Kukrety, S., Gautam, P., Bisht, M., & Pal, M. K. (2023). Bioleaching for Heavy Metal Extraction from E-waste: A Sustainable Approach. In *Microbial Technology for Sustainable E-waste Management*. Springer International Publishing., DOI: 10.1007/978-3-031-25678-3_4

Godbole, V., Pal, M. K., & Gautam, P. (2021). A critical perspective on the scope of interdisciplinary approaches used in fourth-generation biofuel production. *Algal Research*, 58, 102436. Advance online publication. DOI: 10.1016/j.algal.2021.102436

Goel, R. K., & Vishnoi, S. (2023). Strengthening and sustaining health-related outcomes through digital health interventions. *Journal of Engineering Science and Technology Review*, 16(2), 10–17. DOI: 10.25103/jestr.162.02

Goel, R., Singla, J., Mittal, A., & Arora, M. (2024). A decade analysis of employees' well-being and performance while working from home: A bibliometric approach. *Information Discovery and Delivery*. Advance online publication. DOI: 10.1108/idd-03-2023-0030

Gogia, S. (Ed.). (2019). *Fundamentals of telemedicine and telehealth*. Academic Press.

Gomes, M., Murray, E., & Raftery, J. (2022). Economic Evaluation of Digital Health Interventions: Methodological Issues and Recommendations for Practice. *PharmacoEconomics*, 40(4), 367–378. DOI: 10.1007/s40273-022-01130-0 PMID: 35132606

Gonfa, Y. H., Gelagle, A. A., Hailegnaw, B., Kabeto, S. A., Workeneh, G. A., Tessema, F. B., Tadesse, M. G., Wabaidur, S. M., Dahlous, K. A., Abou Fayssal, S., Kumar, P., Adelodun, B., Bachheti, A., & Bachheti, R. K. (2023). Optimization, Characterization, and Biological Applications of Silver Nanoparticles Synthesized Using Essential Oil of Aerial Part of Laggera tomentosa. *Sustainability (Basel)*, 15(1), 797. Advance online publication. DOI: 10.3390/su15010797

Gonfa, Y. H., Tessema, F. B., Tadesse, M. G., Bachheti, A., & Bachheti, R. K. (2023). Medicinally Important Plant Roots and Their Role in Nanoparticles Synthesis and Applications. In *Secondary Metabolites from Medicinal Plants: Nanoparticles Synthesis and their Applications*. CRC Press., DOI: 10.1201/9781003213727-11

Gopal, S., Gupta, P., & Minocha, A. (2023). Advancements in Fin-Tech and Security Challenges of Banking Industry. *4th International Conference on Intelligent Engineering and Management, ICIEM 2023*. DOI: 10.1109/ICIEM59379.2023.10165876

Goswami, S., & Sharma, S. (2022). Industry 4.0 Enabled Molecular Imaging Using Artificial Intelligence Technique. *2022 1st International Conference on Computational Science and Technology, ICCST 2022 - Proceedings*, 455 – 460. DOI: 10.1109/ICCST55948.2022.10040406

Govindan, K., Mina, H., & Alavi, B. (2020). A decision support system for demand management in healthcare supply chains considering the epidemic outbreaks: A case study of coronavirus disease 2019 (COVID-19). *Transportation Research Part E, Logistics and Transportation Review*, 138, 101967. DOI: 10.1016/j.tre.2020.101967 PMID: 32382249

Govindarajan, H. K., Ganesh, L. S., Sharma, N., & Agarwal, R. (2023). Indian Energy Scenario: A Critical Review. *Indian Journal of Environmental Protection*, 43(2), 99–107.

Goyal, P., Kukreja, T., Agarwal, A., & Khanna, N. (2015). Narrowing awareness gap by using e-learning tools for counselling university entrants. *Conference Proceeding - 2015 International Conference on Advances in Computer Engineering and Applications, ICACEA 2015*, 847 – 851. DOI: 10.1109/ICACEA.2015.7164822

Grover, D., Sharma, S., Kaur, P., Mittal, A., & Sharma, P. K. (2024). Societal Elements that Impact the Performance of Women Entrepreneurs in Tier-II Cities: A Study of Rohilkhand Region of Uttar Pradesh. *2024 IEEE Zooming Innovation in Consumer Technologies Conference. ZINC*, 2024, 114–117. DOI: 10.1109/ZINC61849.2024.10579316

Guo, H.-H., Zhou, D., Du, C., Wang, P.-J., Liu, W.-F., Pang, L.-X., Wang, Q.-P., Su, J.-Z., Singh, C., & Trukhanov, S. (2020). Temperature stable $Li_2Ti_{0.75}(Mg_{1/3}Nb_{2/3})_{0.25}O_3$-based microwave dielectric ceramics with low sintering temperature and ultra-low dielectric loss for dielectric resonator antenna applications. *Journal of Materials Chemistry. C, Materials for Optical and Electronic Devices*, 8(14), 4690–4700. DOI: 10.1039/D0TC00326C

Gupta, A., Chaithra, N., Jha, J., Sayal, A., Gupta, V., & Memoria, M. (2023, May). Machine Learning Algorithms for Disease Diagnosis using Medical Records: A Comparative Analysis. In *2023 4th International Conference on Intelligent Engineering and Management (ICIEM)* (pp. 1-6). IEEE. DOI: 10.1109/ICIEM59379.2023.10165850

Gupta, A., Gupta, S., Memoria, M., Kumar, R., Kumar, S., Singh, D., . . . Ansari, N. (2022, May). Artificial intelligence and Smart Cities: A bibliometric analysis. In *2022 international conference on machine learning, big data, cloud and parallel computing (COM-IT-CON)* (Vol. 1, pp. 540-544). IEEE. DOI: 10.1109/COM-IT-CON54601.2022.9850656

Gupta, C., Jindal, P., & Malhotra, R. K. (2022). A Study of Increasing Adoption Trends of Digital Technologies - An Evidence from Indian Banking. In D. N. & C. A. (Eds.), *AIP Conference Proceedings* (Vol. 2481). American Institute of Physics Inc. DOI: 10.1063/5.0104572

Gupta, S., Kumar, V., & Patil, P. (2022). A Study on Recycling of Waste Solid Garbage in a City. In D. N. & C. A. (Eds.), *AIP Conference Proceedings* (Vol. 2481). American Institute of Physics Inc. DOI: 10.1063/5.0104563

Gupta, S., Kushwaha, P., Chauhan, A. S., Yadav, A., & Badhotiya, G. K. (2023). A study on glazing to optimize daylight for improving lighting ergonomics and energy efficiency of a building. In S. Y., S. G., & B. G.K. (Eds.), *AIP Conference Proceedings* (Vol. 2521). American Institute of Physics Inc. DOI: 10.1063/5.0114766

Gupta, S., Singh, P., Gupta, A. M., & Chauhan, A. (2024). The bridging the gap between technology and social welfare: An IoT cloud-based model for developing countries. In S. S., K. S., & J. P.K. (Eds.), *AIP Conference Proceedings* (Vol. 3121, Issue 1). American Institute of Physics. DOI: 10.1063/5.0221598

Gupta, A., Dixit, A. K., Kumar, K. S., Lavanya, C., Chakravarthi, M. K., & Gangodkar, D. (2022). Analyzing Robotics and Computer Integrated Manufacturing of Key Areas Using Cloud Computing. *Proceedings of 5th International Conference on Contemporary Computing and Informatics, IC3I 2022*, 194 – 199. DOI: 10.1109/IC3I56241.2022.10072581

Gupta, A., & Kumar, H. (2022). Multi-dimensional perspectives on electric vehicles design: A mind map approach. *Cleaner Engineering and Technology*, 8, 100483. Advance online publication. DOI: 10.1016/j.clet.2022.100483

Gupta, A., & Sharma, N. (2020). FinTech in the banking sector: A systematic literature review. *Journal of Corporate Finance*, 60, 101638.

Gupta, H., Taluja, R., Shaw, S., Chari, S. L., Deepak, A., & Rana, A. (2023). Internet of Things Based Reduction of Electricity Theft in Urban Areas. *Proceedings of International Conference on Contemporary Computing and Informatics, IC3I 2023*, 2642 – 2645. https://doi.org/DOI: 10.1109/IC3I59117.2023.10397868

Gupta, M., Arora, K., & Taneja, S. (2023). Bibliometric analysis on employee engagement and human resource management. In *Enhancing Customer Engagement Through Location-Based Marketing*. IGI Global., DOI: 10.4018/978-1-6684-8177-6.ch013

Gupta, M., Kumari, I., & Singh, A. K. (2024). Impact of human capital on SDG1 in selected G20 countries. In *Interlinking SDGs and the Bottom-of-the-Pyramid Through Tourism*. IGI Global., DOI: 10.4018/979-8-3693-3166-8.ch002

Gupta, M., Verma, P. K., Verma, R., & Upadhyay, D. K. (2023). Applications of Computational Intelligence Techniques in Communications. In *Applications of Computational Intelligence Techniques in Communications*. CRC Press., DOI: 10.1201/9781003452645

Gupta, P., Gopal, S., Sharma, M., Joshi, S., Sahani, C., & Ahalawat, K. (2023). Agriculture Informatics and Communication: Paradigm of E-Governance and Drone Technology for Crop Monitoring. *9th International Conference on Smart Computing and Communications: Intelligent Technologies and Applications, ICSCC 2023*, 113 – 118. DOI: 10.1109/ICSCC59169.2023.10335058

Gupta, S., Modgil, S., Bhatt, P. C., Jabbour, C. J. C., & Kamble, S. (2023). Quantum computing led innovation for achieving a more sustainable Covid-19 healthcare industry. *Technovation*, 120, 102544. DOI: 10.1016/j.technovation.2022.102544

Gururani, P., Bhatnagar, P., Bisht, B., Jaiswal, K. K., Kumar, V., Kumar, S., Vlaskin, M. S., Grigorenko, A. V., & Rindin, K. G. (2022). Recent advances and viability in sustainable thermochemical conversion of sludge to bio-fuel production. *Fuel*, 316, 123351. Advance online publication. DOI: 10.1016/j.fuel.2022.123351

Gusain, I., Sharma, S., Debarma, S., Kumar Sharma, A., Mishra, N., & Prakashrao Dahale, P. (2023). Study of concrete mix by adding Dolomite in conventional concrete as partial replacement with cement. *Materials Today: Proceedings*, 73, 163–166. DOI: 10.1016/j.matpr.2022.09.583

Gwak, J., Garg, H., & Jan, N. (2023). Investigation of Robotics Technology Based on Bipolar Complex Intuitionistic Fuzzy Soft Relation. *International Journal of Fuzzy Systems*, 25(5), 1834–1852. DOI: 10.1007/s40815-023-01487-0

Hajoary, P. K., Balachandra, P., & Garza-Reyes, J. A. (2023). Industry 4.0 maturity and readiness assessment: An empirical validation using Confirmatory Composite Analysis. *Production Planning and Control*. Advance online publication. DOI: 10.1080/09537287.2023.2210545

Haldhar, R., Prasad, D., & Saxena, A. (2018). Myristica fragrans extract as an eco-friendly corrosion inhibitor for mild steel in 0.5 M H2SO4 solution. *Journal of Environmental Chemical Engineering*, 6(2), 2290–2301. DOI: 10.1016/j.jece.2018.03.023

Hamad, R. S., Shamsi, A. L., Ameen, A. A., Isaac, O., Al-Shibami, A. H., & Sayed Khalifa, G. (2018). The impact of Innovation and smart government on happiness: Proposing conceptual framework. *International Journal of Management and Human Science*, 2(2).

Hardy, M., & Harvey, H. (2020). Artificial intelligence in diagnostic imaging: Impact on the radiography profession. *The British Journal of Radiology*, 93(1108), 20190840. DOI: 10.1259/bjr.20190840 PMID: 31821024

Heerdegen, Anne & Cellini, Carlotta & Wirtz, Veronika & Rockers, Peter. (2022). Digital Health Technologies Applied by the Pharmaceutical Industry to Improve Access to Noncommunicable Disease Care in Low- and Middle-Income Countries. *Global Health: Science and Practice*. 10. . DOI:DOI: 10.9745/GHSP-D-22-00072

Henrique, K. P., & Tschakert, P. (2021). Pathways to urban transformation: From dispossession to climate justice. *Progress in Human Geography*, 45(5), 1169–1191. DOI: 10.1177/0309132520962856

Ho, M. N., Abhayawansa, S., & Adams, C. A. (2024). Sustainable finance. In *Elgar Encyclopedia of Corporate Communication*. Edward Elgar Publishing Ltd., DOI: 10.4337/9781802200874.ch32

Hoosain, M. S., Paul, B. S., & Ramakrishna, S. (2020). The impact of digital technologies and circular thinking on the United Nations sustainable development goals. *Sustainability (Basel)*, 12(23), 1–16. DOI: 10.3390/su122310143

Hovorushchenko, T., Moskalenko, A., & Osyadlyi, V. (2023). Methods of medical data management based on blockchain technologies. *Journal of Reliable Intelligent Environments*, 9(1), 5–16. DOI: 10.1007/s40860-022-00178-1 PMID: 35646514

How are Intelligent Healthcare Chatbots being used? [new uses for 2022] (2022). Engati. Retrieved October 20, 2022, from https://www.engati.com/blog/chatbots-for-healthcare

Huang, Y., Mian, Q., Conradi, N., Opoka, R. O., Conroy, A. L., Namasopo, S., & Hawkes, M. T. (2021). Estimated Cost-effectiveness of Solar-Powered Oxygen Delivery for Pneumonia in Young Children in Low-Resource Settings. *JAMA Network Open*, 4(6), e2114686. DOI: 10.1001/jamanetworkopen.2021.14686 PMID: 34165579

Husen, A., Bachheti, R. K., & Bachheti, A. (2021). Non-Timber Forest Products: Food, Healthcare and Industrial Applications. In *Non-Timber Forest Products: Food, Healthcare and Industrial Applications*. Springer International Publishing., DOI: 10.1007/978-3-030-73077-2

Ifeanyichi, M., Mosso Lara, J. L., Tenkorang, P., Kebede, M. A., Bognini, M., Abdelhabeeb, A. N., Amaechina, U., Ambreen, F., Sarabu, S., Oladimeji, T., Toguchi, A. C., Hargest, R., & Friebel, R. (2024). Cost-effectiveness of surgical interventions in low-income and middle-income countries: A systematic review and critical analysis of recent evidence. *BMJ Global Health*, 9(10), e016439. DOI: 10.1136/bmjgh-2024-016439 PMID: 39362787

Indu, R., Dimri, S. C., & Kumar, B. (2023). Identification of Location for Police Headquarters to Deal with Crime Against Women in India Using Clustering Based on K-Means Algorithm. *International Journal of Computing and Digital Systems*, 14(1), 965–974. DOI: 10.12785/ijcds/140175

Ingale, N. V., Saravana Kumar, G., Panduro-Ramirez, J., Raj, M., Vaseem Akram, S., & Rawat, R. (2023). Role of IOT in managing education management tools: A technical review. *2023 3rd International Conference on Advance Computing and Innovative Technologies in Engineering, ICACITE 2023*, 2056 – 2061. DOI: 10.1109/ICACITE57410.2023.10182953

Ishengoma, F. R., Shao, D., Alexopoulos, C., Saxena, S., & Nikiforova, A. (2022). Integration of artificial intelligence of things (AIoT) in the public sector: Drivers, barriers and future research agenda. *Digital Policy. Regulation & Governance*, 24(5), 449–462. DOI: 10.1108/DPRG-06-2022-0067

Jacob, L., Thomas, K. T., & Shukla, S. (2023). Potential Applications of AI and IoT Collaborative Framework for Health Care. *The Role of AI. IoT and Blockchain in Mitigating the Impact of COVID*, 19, 69.

Jain, P., Gupta, V. K., Tiwari, H., Shukla, A., Pandey, P., & Gupta, A. (2023). Human-Computer Interaction: A Systematic Review. In M. H.K. & S. S. (Eds.), *Proceedings - 2023 International Conference on Advanced Computing and Communication Technologies, ICACCTech 2023* (pp. 31 – 36). Institute of Electrical and Electronics Engineers Inc. DOI: 10.1109/ICACCTech61146.2023.00015

Jain, S., & Jain, S. S. (2021). Development of Intelligent Transportation System and Its Applications for an Urban Corridor During COVID-19. *Journal of The Institution of Engineers (India): Series B*, 102(6), 1191 – 1200. DOI: 10.1007/s40031-021-00556-y

Jain, V., Tiwari, R., Mehrotra, R., Bohra, N. S., Misra, A., & Pandey, D. C. (2023). Role of Technology for Credit Risk Management: A Bibliometric Review. *2023 IEEE International Conference on Blockchain and Distributed Systems Security, ICBDS 2023*. DOI: 10.1109/ICBDS58040.2023.10346300

Jaiswal, K. K., Dutta, S., Banerjee, I., Pohrmen, C. B., & Kumar, V. (2023). Photosynthetic microalgae–based carbon sequestration and generation of biomass in biorefinery approach for renewable biofuels for a cleaner environment. *Biomass Conversion and Biorefinery*, 13(9), 7403–7421. DOI: 10.1007/s13399-021-01504-y

Jaswal, N., Kukreja, V., Sharma, R., Chaudhary, P., & Garg, A. (2023). Citrus Leaf Scab Multi-Class Classification: A Hybrid Deep Learning Model for Precision Agriculture. *2023 4th IEEE Global Conference for Advancement in Technology, GCAT 2023*. DOI: 10.1109/GCAT59970.2023.10353507

Javaid, M., Haleem, A., Singh, R. P., & Suman, R. (2022). Artificial intelligence applications for industry 4.0: A literature-based study. *Journal of Industrial Integration and Management*, 7(01), 83–111. DOI: 10.1142/S2424862221300040

Jayadeva, S. M., Prasad Krishnam, N., Raja Mannar, B., Prakash Dabral, A., Buddhi, D., & Garg, N. (2023). An Investigation of IOT-Based Consumer Analytics to Assist Consumer Engagement Strategies in Evolving Markets. *2023 3rd International Conference on Advance Computing and Innovative Technologies in Engineering, ICACITE 2023*, 487 – 491. DOI: 10.1109/ICACITE57410.2023.10183310

Jena, L. K., & Pradhan, S. (2020). Digital Transformation in Healthcare and its Impact on Workforce: An Organizational Perspective. *Journal of Organizational Change Management*, 33(5), 715–733.

Jena, S., Cao, S., & Gairola, A. (2024). Cyclonic wind loads and structural mitigation measures – vulnerability assessment of traditional housings in Odisha. *Journal of Earth System Science*, 133(2), 52. Advance online publication. DOI: 10.1007/s12040-024-02255-w

Jena, S., & Gairola, A. (2022). Numerical Method to Generate and Evaluate Environmental Wind Over Hills: Comparison of Pedestrian Winds Over Hills and Plains. *CFD Letters*, 14(10), 56–67. DOI: 10.37934/cfdl.14.10.5667

Jha, J., Vishwakarma, A. K., Chaithra, N., Nithin, A., Sayal, A., Gupta, A., & Kumar, R. (2023, February). Artificial intelligence and applications. In *2023 1st International Conference on Intelligent Computing and Research Trends (ICRT)* (pp. 1-4). IEEE.

Ji, M., Chen, X., Genchev, G. Z., Wei, M., & Yu, G. (2021). Status of AI-enabled clinical decision support systems implementations in China. *Methods of Information in Medicine, 60*(05/06), 123-132.

Jilte, R. D., Kumar, R., & Ahmadi, M. H. (2019). Cooling performance of nanofluid submerged vs. nanofluid circulated battery thermal management systems. *Journal of Cleaner Production*, 240, 118131. Advance online publication. DOI: 10.1016/j.jclepro.2019.118131

Jindal, G., Tiwari, V., Mahomad, R., Gehlot, A., Jindal, M., & Bordoloi, D. (2023). Predictive Design for Quality Assessment Employing Cloud Computing And Machine Learning. *2023 3rd International Conference on Advance Computing and Innovative Technologies in Engineering, ICACITE 2023*, 461 – 465. DOI: 10.1109/ICACITE57410.2023.10182915

Jindal, M., Bajal, E., Singh, P., Diwakar, M., Arya, C., & Sharma, K. (2022). Online education in Covid-19: Limitations and improvements. *2021 IEEE 8th Uttar Pradesh Section International Conference on Electrical, Electronics and Computer Engineering, UPCON 2021*. DOI: 10.1109/UPCON52273.2021.9667605

Jindal, T., Sheoliha, N., Kishore, K., Uike, D., Khurana, S., & Verma, D. (2022). A Conceptual Analysis on the Impact of Internet of Things (IOT) Towards on Digital Marketing Transformation. *2022 2nd International Conference on Advance Computing and Innovative Technologies in Engineering, ICACITE 2022*, 1943 – 1947. DOI: 10.1109/ICACITE53722.2022.9823714

Jindal, V., Kukreja, V., Mehta, S., Chauhan, R., & Verma, G. (2023). Towards Sustainable Agriculture: Federated CNN Models for Cucurbit Leaf Disease Detection. *2023 10th IEEE Uttar Pradesh Section International Conference on Electrical, Electronics and Computer Engineering, UPCON 2023*, 561 – 566. DOI: 10.1109/UPCON59197.2023.10434321

Jindal, V., Kukreja, V., Mehta, S., Srivastava, P., & Garg, N. (2023). Adopting Federated Learning and CNN for Advanced Plant Pathology: A Case of Red Globe Grape Leaf Diseases Dissecting Severity. *2023 3rd Asian Conference on Innovation in Technology, ASIANCON 2023*. DOI: 10.1109/ASIANCON58793.2023.10270034

Jnawali, P., Kumar, V., & Tanwar, B. (2016). Celiac disease: Overview and considerations for development of gluten-free foods. *Food Science and Human Wellness*, 5(4), 169–176. DOI: 10.1016/j.fshw.2016.09.003

Johnson, K. B., Wei, W. Q., Weeraratne, D., Frisse, M. E., Misulis, K., Rhee, K., Zhao, J., & Snowdon, J. L. (2020). Precision Medicine, AI, and the future of Personalized Health Care. *Clinical and Translational Science*, 14(1), 86–93. DOI: 10.1111/cts.12884 PMID: 32961010

Johnson, K. W., Torres Soto, J., Glicksberg, B. S., Shameer, K., Miotto, R., Ali, M., Ashley, E., & Dudley, J. T. (2018). Artificial Intelligence in Cardiology. *Journal of the American College of Cardiology*, 71(23), 2668–2679. DOI: 10.1016/j.jacc.2018.03.521 PMID: 29880128

Johnson, M., Albizri, A., & Harfouche, A. (2023). Responsible artificial intelligence in healthcare: Predicting and preventing insurance claim denials for economic and social wellbeing. *Information Systems Frontiers*, 25(6), 2179–2195. DOI: 10.1007/s10796-021-10137-5

Johnson, M., Anderson, K., & Lee, S. (2019). Smart Card Security: A Comprehensive Review. *Journal of Computer Information Systems*, 59(1), 1–10.

Johnson, M., Anderson, K., & Lee, S. (2020). Cybersecurity Threats in FinTech: A Comprehensive Review. *Journal of Cybersecurity*, 5(1), 1–15.

Johri, S., Singh Sidhu, K., Jafersadhiq, A., Mannar, B. R., Gehlot, A., & Goyal, H. R. (2023). An investigation of the effects of the global epidemic on Crypto Currency returns and volatility. *2023 3rd International Conference on Advance Computing and Innovative Technologies in Engineering, ICACITE 2023*, 345 – 348. DOI: 10.1109/ICACITE57410.2023.10182988

Johri, A., Sayal, A., Chaithra, N., Jha, J., Aggarwal, N., Pawar, D., & Gupta, A. (2024). Crafting the techno-functional blocks for Metaverse-A review and research agenda. *International Journal of Information Management Data Insights*, 4(1), 100213. DOI: 10.1016/j.jjimei.2024.100213

Jones, R., Smith, L., & Davis, M. (2018). Ethical considerations in the integration of Smart Cards and FinTech. *Journal of Business Ethics*, 147(3), 639–654.

Joshi, S., Balakrishnan, S., Rawat, P., Deshpande, D., Chakravarthi, M. K., & Verma, D. (2022). A Framework of Internet of Things (Iot) for the Manufacturing and Image Classification System. In D. R.K., S. A.Kr., K. G., & B. S. (Eds.), *Proceedings of the 2022 11th International Conference on System Modeling and Advancement in Research Trends, SMART 2022* (pp. 371 – 375). Institute of Electrical and Electronics Engineers Inc. DOI: 10.1109/SMART55829.2022.10046756

Joshi, S., Sharma, M., & Barve, A. (2023). Implementation challenges of blockchain technology in closed-loop supply chain: A Waste Electrical and Electronic Equipment (WEEE) management perspective in developing countries. *Supply Chain Forum*, 24(1), 59 – 80. DOI: 10.1080/16258312.2022.2135972

Joshi, K., Patil, S., Gupta, S., & Khanna, R. (2022). Role of Pranayma in emotional maturity for improving health. *Journal of Medical Pharmaceutical and Allied Sciences*, 11(2), 4569–4573. DOI: 10.55522/jmpas.V11I2.2033

Joshi, K., Sharma, R., Singh, N., & Sharma, B. (2023). Digital World of Cloud Computing and Wireless Networking: Challenges and Risks. In *Applications of Artificial Intelligence in Wireless Communication Systems*. IGI Global., DOI: 10.4018/978-1-6684-7348-1.ch003

Joshi, N. C., & Gururani, P. (2022). Advances of graphene oxide based nanocomposite materials in the treatment of wastewater containing heavy metal ions and dyes. *Current Research in Green and Sustainable Chemistry*, 5. Advance online publication. DOI: 10.1016/j.crgsc.2022.100306

Joshi, S., Gangola, S., Bhandari, G., Bhandari, N. S., Nainwal, D., Rani, A., Malik, S., & Slama, P. (2023). Rhizospheric bacteria: The key to sustainable heavy metal detoxification strategies. *Frontiers in Microbiology*, 14, 1229828. Advance online publication. DOI: 10.3389/fmicb.2023.1229828 PMID: 37555069

Joshi, S., & Sharma, M. (2022). Sustainable Performance through Digital Supply Chains in Industry 4.0 Era: Amidst the Pandemic Experience. *Sustainability (Basel)*, 14(24), 16726. Advance online publication. DOI: 10.3390/su142416726

Joshi, S., & Sharma, M. (2023). Strategic challenges of deploying LARG approach for sustainable manufacturing: Research implications from Indian SMEs. *International Journal of Internet Manufacturing and Services*, 9(2–3), 373–397. DOI: 10.1504/IJIMS.2023.132791

Josphineleela, R., Gupta, R., Misra, N., Malik, M., Somasundaram, K., & Gangodkar, D. (2023). Blockchain Based Multi-Layer Security Network Authentication System for Uncertain Attack in the Wireless Communication System. *2023 3rd International Conference on Advance Computing and Innovative Technologies in Engineering, ICACITE 2023*, 877–881. DOI: 10.1109/ICACITE57410.2023.10182747

Josphineleela, R., Jyothi, M., Natrayan, L., Kaviarasu, A., & Sharma, M. (2023). Development of IoT based Health Monitoring System for Disables using Microcontroller. *Proceedings - 7th International Conference on Computing Methodologies and Communication, ICCMC 2023*, 1380–1384. DOI: 10.1109/ICCMC56507.2023.10084026

Josphineleela, R., Kaliappan, S., Natrayan, L., & Bhatt, U. M. (2023). Intelligent Virtual Laboratory Development and Implementation using the RASA Framework. *Proceedings - 7th International Conference on Computing Methodologies and Communication, ICCMC 2023*, 1172–1176. DOI: 10.1109/ICCMC56507.2023.10083701

Josphineleela, R., Siva Reddy, K. V., Reddy, M. V. S. S., & Rawat, R. S. (2023). Design and Development of a Smart Sprinkler Device for IoT-Integrated Plants Irrigation. *Proceedings of the 2023 2nd International Conference on Electronics and Renewable Systems, ICEARS 2023*, 498–501. DOI: 10.1109/ICEARS56392.2023.10084960

Juneja, P. J., Sunori, S., Sharma, A., Sharma, A., & Joshi, V. (2020). Modeling, Control and Instrumentation of Lime Kiln Process: A Review. In S. S. & D. P. (Eds.), *Proceedings - 2020 International Conference on Advances in Computing, Communication and Materials, ICACCM 2020* (pp. 399–403). Institute of Electrical and Electronics Engineers Inc. https://doi.org/DOI: 10.1109/ICACCM50413.2020.9212948

Juneja, P. K., Sunori, S. K., Sharma, A., Sharma, A., Pathak, H., Joshi, V., & Bhasin, P. (2021). A review on control system applications in industrial processes. In K. A., G. D., M. A.K., & K. A. (Eds.), *IOP Conference Series: Materials Science and Engineering* (Vol. 1022, Issue 1). IOP Publishing Ltd. DOI: 10.1088/1757-899X/1022/1/012010

Juneja, P. K., Kumar Sunori, S., Manu, M., Joshi, P., Sharma, S., Garia, P., & Mittal, A. (2022). Potential Applications of Fuzzy Logic Controller in the Pulp and Paper Industry - A Review. *5th International Conference on Inventive Computation Technologies, ICICT 2022 - Proceedings*, 399–401. https://doi.org/DOI: 10.1109/ICICT54344.2022.9850626

Juyal, P., & Sharma, S. (2020). Estimation of Tree Volume Using Mask R-CNN based Deep Learning. *2020 11th International Conference on Computing, Communication and Networking Technologies, ICCCNT 2020*. DOI: 10.1109/ICCCNT49239.2020.9225509

Kaihlanen, Anu-Marja & Virtanen, Lotta & Kainiemi, Emma & Heponiemi, T. (2023). Patients' suitability for digital health - what should be evaluated by health care professionals? *European Journal of Public Health*. 33. . DOI:DOI: 10.1093/eurpub/ckad160.1208

Kakkar, V., Pandey, D. C., Verma, V., Mehrotra, R., Singh, P., & Tiwari, R. (2024, April). Artificial Intelligence for Stock Prediction: A Bibliometric Review. In *2024 1st International Conference on Innovative Sustainable Technologies for Energy, Mechatronics, and Smart Systems (ISTEMS)* (pp. 1-5). IEEE. DOI: 10.1109/ISTEMS60181.2024.10560228

Kaliappan, S., Natrayan, L., & Garg, N. (2023). Checking and Supervisory System for Calculation of Industrial Constraints using Embedded System. *Proceedings of the 4th International Conference on Smart Electronics and Communication, ICOSEC 2023*, 87–90. DOI: 10.1109/ICOSEC58147.2023.10275952

Kalinin, K. (2022, October 10). *Healthcare Chatbots: Role of AI, benefits, future, use cases, development.* Topflight. Retrieved October 16, 2022, from https://topflightapps.com/ideas/chatbots-in-healthcare/

Kalkal, A., Kumar, S., Kumar, P., Pradhan, R., Willander, M., Packirisamy, G., Kumar, S., & Malhotra, B. D. (2021). Recent advances in 3D printing technologies for wearable (bio)sensors. *Additive Manufacturing*, 46, 102088. Advance online publication. DOI: 10.1016/j.addma.2021.102088

Kamra, J., Mani, A. P., & Tripathi, V. M. (2023). Decarbonization Trajectory in Cement Industry. In S. P., N. S., R. J.J.P.C., R. J.J.P.C., R. J.J.P.C., L.-I. G.-A. D., P. T., C. L., & P. L. (Eds.), *2023 8th International Conference on Smart and Sustainable Technologies, SpliTech 2023*. Institute of Electrical and Electronics Engineers Inc. DOI: 10.23919/SpliTech58164.2023.10193682

Kannan, P. R., Periasamy, K., Pravin, P., & Vinod Kumaar, J. R. (2022). An experimental investigation of wire breakage and performance optimisation of WEDM process on machining of recycled aluminium alloy metal matrix composite. *Materials Science Poland*, 40(3), 12–26. DOI: 10.2478/msp-2022-0030

Kanojia, P., Malhotra, R. K., & Uniyal, A. K. (2022). Impact of Organizational Commitment Components on the Teachers of Higher Education in Uttarakhand: An Emperical Analysis. *Proceedings - 2022 International Conference on Recent Trends in Microelectronics, Automation, Computing and Communications Systems, ICMACC 2022*, 360–364. DOI: 10.1109/ICMACC54824.2022.10093606

Kanojia, P., Malhotra, R. K., & Uniyal, A. K. (2022). Organizational Commitment and the Academic Staff in HEI's in North West India. *Proceedings - 2022 International Conference on Recent Trends in Microelectronics, Automation, Computing and Communications Systems, ICMACC 2022*, 365–370. DOI: 10.1109/ICMACC54824.2022.10093347

Kapadiya, K., Patel, U., Gupta, R., Alshehri, M. D., Tanwar, S., Sharma, G., & Bokoro, P. N. (2022). Blockchain and AI-empowered healthcare insurance fraud detection: An analysis, architecture, and future prospects. *IEEE Access : Practical Innovations, Open Solutions*, 10, 79606–79627. DOI: 10.1109/ACCESS.2022.3194569

Kapoor, B., Kapoor, D., Gautam, S., Singh, R., & Bhardwaj, S. (2021). Dietary Polyunsaturated Fatty Acids (PUFAs): Uses and Potential Health Benefits. *Current Nutrition Reports*, 10(3), 232–242. DOI: 10.1007/s13668-021-00363-3 PMID: 34255301

Karani, D. (n.d.). *Dhruvilkarani/malaria-detection-using-pytorch: Pytorch implementation of CNN to Detect malaria*. GitHub. Retrieved November 12, 2022, from https://github.com/DhruvilKarani/Malaria-Detection-using-pytorch

Karimian, G., Petelos, E., & Evers, S. M. (2022). The ethical issues of the application of artificial intelligence in healthcare: A systematic scoping review. *AI and Ethics*, 2(4), 539–551. DOI: 10.1007/s43681-021-00131-7

Kashif, M., Garg, H., Weqar, F., & David, A. (2024). Regulatory Strategies and Innovative Solutions for Deepfake Technology. In Navigating the World of Deepfake Technology (pp. 262–282). IGIGlobal. DOI: 10.4018/979-8-3693-5298-4.ch013

Kashif, M., Shajar, S. N., Singhal, N., & Kumar, P. (2023). Achieving sustainable investment practices through green finance: Challenges and opportunities. In Sustainable Investments in Green Finance (pp. 234–244).

Kashif, M., Kumar, P., Ghai, S., & Kumar, S. (2023). Disruptive technologies in computational finance. In *Algorithmic Approaches to Financial Technology* (pp. 46–60). Forecasting, Trading, and Optimization.

Kashif, M., Singhal, N., Goyal, S., & Singh, S. K. (2024). Foreign Exchange Reserves and Economic Growth of Brazil: A Nonlinear Approach. Finance. *Theory into Practice*, 28(1), 145–154. DOI: 10.26794/2587-5671-2024-28-1-145-154

Kasinathan, P., Pugazhendhi, R., Elavarasan, R. M., Ramachandaramurthy, V. K., Ramanathan, V., Subramanian, S., Kumar, S., Nandhagopal, K., Raghavan, R. R. V., Rangasamy, S., Devendiran, R., & Alsharif, M. H. (2022). Realization of sustainable development goals with disruptive technologies by integrating industry 5.0, Society 5.0, Smart Cities, and Villages. *Sustainability (Basel)*, 14(22), 15258. Advance online publication. DOI: 10.3390/su142215258

Kaswan, M. S., & Rathi, R. (2019). Analysis and modeling the enablers of Green Lean Six Sigma implementation using Interpretive Structural Modeling. *Journal of Cleaner Production*, 231, 1182–1191. DOI: 10.1016/j.jclepro.2019.05.253

Kathir, I., Haribabu, K., Kumar, A., Kaliappan, S., Patil, P. P., Dhanalakshmi, C. S., Madhu, P., & Birhanu, H. A. (2022). Utilization of Tea Industrial Waste for Low-Grade Energy Recovery: Optimization of Liquid Oil Production and Its Characterization. *Advances in Materials Science and Engineering*, 2022, 1–9. Advance online publication. DOI: 10.1155/2022/7852046

Kaur, A., Kukreja, V., Chamoli, S., Thapliyal, S., & Sharma, R. (2023b). Advanced Multi-Scale Classification of Onion Smut Disease Using a Hybrid CNN-RF Ensemble Model for Precision Agriculture. In G. R., H. K., P. R., G. S., T. A. J.V., V. R., M. R., & K. T. (Eds.), *Proceedings of the 2023 6th International Conference on Recent Trends in Advance Computing, ICRTAC 2023* (pp. 553 – 556). Institute of Electrical and Electronics Engineers Inc. DOI: 10.1109/ICRTAC59277.2023.10480840

Kaur, A., Kukreja, V., Nisha Chandran, S., Garg, N., & Sharma, R. (2023). Automated Mango Rust Severity Classification: A CNN-SVM Ensemble Approach for Accurate and Granular Disease Assessment in Mango Cultivation. In G. R., H. K., P. R., G. S., T. A. J.V., V. R., M. R., & K. T. (Eds.), *Proceedings of the 2023 6th International Conference on Recent Trends in Advance Computing, ICRTAC 2023* (pp. 486–490). Institute of Electrical and Electronics Engineers Inc. DOI: 10.1109/ICRTAC59277.2023.10480836

Kaur, G., Sharma, N., Chauhan, R., Singh, P., & Gupta, R. (2023). An Automated Approach for Detection and Classification of Plant Diseases. *2023 2nd International Conference on Futuristic Technologies, INCOFT 2023*. DOI: 10.1109/INCOFT60753.2023.10425170

Kaur, J., Khanna, R., Kumar, R., & Sunil, G. (2024). Role of Blockchain Technologies in Goods and Services Tax. *Proceedings - 2024 3rd International Conference on Sentiment Analysis and Deep Learning, ICSADL 2024*, 607–612. https://doi.org/DOI: 10.1109/ICSADL61749.2024.00104

Kaur, A., Kukreja, V., Chamoli, S., Thapliyal, S., & Sharma, R. (2023a). Advanced Disease Management: An Encoder-Decoder Approach for Tomato Black Mold Detection. *2023 IEEE Pune Section International Conference, PuneCon 2023*. DOI: 10.1109/PuneCon58714.2023.10450088

Kaur, A., Kumar, P., Taneja, S., & Ozen, E. (2023). Fintech emergence – an opportunity or threat to banking. *International Journal of Electronic Finance*, 13(1), 1–19. DOI: 10.1504/IJEF.2024.135163

Kaur, H., Thacker, C., Singh, V. K., Sivashankar, D., Patil, P. P., & Gill, K. S. (2023). An implementation of virtual instruments for industries for the standardization. *2023 International Conference on Artificial Intelligence and Smart Communication, AISC 2023*, 1110–1113. DOI: 10.1109/AISC56616.2023.10085547

Kaur, T., Kaur, B., Bhat, B. H., Kumar, S., & Srivastava, A. K. (2015). Effect of calcination temperature on microstructure, dielectric, magnetic and optical properties of $Ba_{0.7}La_{0.3}Fe_{11.7}Co_{0.3}O_{19}$ hexaferrites. *Physica B, Condensed Matter*, 456, 206–212. DOI: 10.1016/j.physb.2014.09.003

Kaushal, D., Kumar, S., Raj, R., & Negi, A. (2022). Understanding the effect of entrepreneurial orientation, innovation capability and differentiation strategy on firm performance: A study on small and medium enterprises. *International Journal of Business and Globalisation*, 30(1), 57–80. DOI: 10.1504/IJBG.2022.122280

Khalid, A., & Syed, J. (2024). Mental health and well-being at work: A systematic review of literature and directions for future research. *Human Resource Management Review*, 34(1), 100998. DOI: 10.1016/j.hrmr.2023.100998

Khamparia, A., Bharati, S., Podder, P., Gupta, D., Khanna, A., Phung, T. K., & Thanh, D. N. H. (2021). Diagnosis of breast cancer based on modern mammography using hybrid transfer learning. *Multidimensional Systems and Signal Processing*, 32(2), 747–765. DOI: 10.1007/s11045-020-00756-7 PMID: 33456204

Khamparia, A., Gupta, D., de Albuquerque, V. H. C., Sangaiah, A. K., & Jhaveri, R. H. (2020). Internet of health things-driven deep learning system for detection and classification of cervical cells using transfer learning. *The Journal of Supercomputing*, 76(11), 8590–8608. DOI: 10.1007/s11227-020-03159-4

Khamparia, A., Gupta, D., Nguyen, N. G., Khanna, A., Pandey, B., & Tiwari, P. (2019). Sound classification using convolutional neural network and tensor deep stacking network. *IEEE Access : Practical Innovations, Open Solutions*, 7, 7717–7727. DOI: 10.1109/ACCESS.2018.2888882

Khamparia, A., Saini, G., Gupta, D., Khanna, A., Tiwari, S., & de Albuquerque, V. H. C. (2020). Seasonal Crops Disease Prediction and Classification Using Deep Convolutional Encoder Network. *Circuits, Systems, and Signal Processing*, 39(2), 818–836. DOI: 10.1007/s00034-019-01041-0

Khandelwal, C., Kumar, S., Tripathi, V., & Madhavan, V. (2023). Joint impact of corporate governance and risk disclosures on firm value: Evidence from emerging markets. *Research in International Business and Finance*, 66, 102022. Advance online publication. DOI: 10.1016/j.ribaf.2023.102022

Khanna, L. S., Yadav, P. S., Maurya, S., & Vimal, V. (2023). Integral Role of Data Science in Startup Evolution. *Proceedings - 2023 15th IEEE International Conference on Computational Intelligence and Communication Networks, CICN 2023*, 720–726. https://doi.org/DOI: 10.1109/CICN59264.2023.10402129

Khanna, R., Jindal, P., & Noja, G. G. (2023). Blockchain technologies, a catalyst for insurance sector. In *The Application of Emerging Technology and Blockchain in the Insurance Industry*.

Khanna, R., Jindal, P., & Noja, G. G. (2023). Blockchain technologies, a catalyst for insurance sector. In *The Application of Emerging Technology and Blockchain in the Insurance Industry*. DOI: 10.1201/9781032630946-19

Khan, S. A., Alam, T., Khan, M. S., Blecich, P., Kamal, M. A., Gupta, N. K., & Yadav, A. S. (2022). Life Cycle Assessment of Embodied Carbon in Buildings: Background, Approaches and Advancements. *Buildings*, 12(11), 1944. Advance online publication. DOI: 10.3390/buildings12111944

Khan, S., Ambika, , Rani, K., Sharma, S., Kumar, A., Singh, S., Thapliyal, M., Rawat, P., Thakur, A., Pandey, S., Thapliyal, A., Pal, M., & Singh, Y. (2023). Rhizobacterial mediated interactions in Curcuma longa for plant growth and enhanced crop productivity: A systematic review. *Frontiers in Plant Science*, 14, 1231676. Advance online publication. DOI: 10.3389/fpls.2023.1231676 PMID: 37692412

Khan, T., Singh, K., & Purohit, K. C. (2020). Icma: An efficient integrated congestion control approach. *Recent Patents on Engineering*, 14(3), 294–309. DOI: 10.2174/1872212114666191231150916

Khaudiyal, S., Rawat, A., Das, S. K., & Garg, N. (2022). Bacterial concrete: A review on self-healing properties in the light of sustainability. *Materials Today: Proceedings*, 60, 136–143. DOI: 10.1016/j.matpr.2021.12.277

Kholiya, D., Mishra, A. K., Pandey, N. K., & Tripathi, N. (2023). Plant Detection and Counting using Yolo based Technique. *2023 3rd Asian Conference on Innovation in Technology, ASIANCON 2023*. DOI: 10.1109/ASIANCON58793.2023.10270530

Khursheed, R., Singh, S. K., Wadhwa, S., Kapoor, B., Gulati, M., Kumar, R., Ramanunny, A. K., Awasthi, A., & Dua, K. (2019). Treatment strategies against diabetes: Success so far and challenges ahead. *European Journal of Pharmacology*, 862, 172625. Advance online publication. DOI: 10.1016/j.ejphar.2019.172625 PMID: 31449807

Kickbusch, I., Piselli, D., Agrawal, A., Balicer, R., Banner, O., Adelhardt, M., Capobianco, E., Fabian, C., Singh Gill, A., Lupton, D., Medhora, R. P., Ndili, N., Ryś, A., Sambuli, N., Settle, D., Swaminathan, S., Morales, J. V., Wolpert, M., Wyckoff, A. W., & Wong, B. L. H. (2021). The Lancet and Financial Times Commission on governing health futures 2030: growing up in a digital world. *The Lancet, 398* (10312). 1727–1776. DOI: 10.1016/S0140-6736(21)01824-9

Kirola, M., Joshi, K., Chaudhary, S., Singh, N., Anandaram, H., & Gupta, A. (2022, June). Plants diseases prediction framework: A image-based system using deep learning. In *2022 IEEE World Conference on Applied Intelligence and Computing (AIC)* (pp. 307-313). IEEE. DOI: 10.1109/AIC55036.2022.9848899

Kohli, P., Sharma, S., & Matta, P. (2022). Secured Authentication Schemes of 6G Driven Vehicular Communication Network in Industry 5.0 Internet-of-Everything (IoE) Applications: Challenges and Opportunities. *2022 IEEE 2nd International Conference on Mobile Networks and Wireless Communications, ICMNWC 2022*. DOI: 10.1109/ICMNWC56175.2022.10031781

Kohli, P., Sharma, S., & Matta, P. (2022). Secured Privacy Preserving Techniques Analysis of 6G Driven Vehicular Communication Network in Industry 5.0 Internet-of-Everything (IoE) Applications. *2022 International Conference on Smart Generation Computing, Communication and Networking, SMART GENCON 2022*. DOI: 10.1109/SMARTGENCON56628.2022.10084289

Kollipara, V. N. H., Kalakota, S. K., Chamarthi, S., Ramani, S., Malik, P., & Karuppiah, M. (2023). Timestamp Based OTP and Enhanced RSA Key Exchange Scheme with SIT Encryption to Secure IoT Devices. *Journal of Cyber Security and Mobility*, 12(1), 77–102. DOI: 10.13052/jcsm2245-1439.1214

Komkowski, T., Antony, J., Garza-Reyes, J. A., Tortorella, G. L., & Pongboonchai-Empl, T. (2023a). A systematic review of the integration of Industry 4.0 with quality-related operational excellence methodologies. *The Quality Management Journal*, 30(1), 3–15. DOI: 10.1080/10686967.2022.2144783

Komkowski, T., Antony, J., Garza-Reyes, J. A., Tortorella, G. L., & Pongboonchai-Empl, T. (2023b). Integrating Lean Management with Industry 4.0: An explorative Dynamic Capabilities theory perspective. *Production Planning and Control*, 1–19. Advance online publication. DOI: 10.1080/09537287.2023.2294297

Korotkov, K., & Garcia, R. (2012). Computerized analysis of pigmented skin lesions: A review. *Artificial Intelligence in Medicine*, 56(2), 69–90. DOI: 10.1016/j.artmed.2012.08.002 PMID: 23063256

Kostoska, O., & Kocarev, L. (2019). A novel ICT framework for sustainable development goals. *Sustainability (Basel)*, 11(7), 1961. Advance online publication. DOI: 10.3390/su11071961

Kour, D., Kaur, T., Devi, R., Yadav, A., Singh, M., Joshi, D., Singh, J., Suyal, D. C., Kumar, A., Rajput, V. D., Yadav, A. N., Singh, K., Singh, J., Sayyed, R. Z., Arora, N. K., & Saxena, A. K. (2021). Beneficial microbiomes for bioremediation of diverse contaminated environments for environmental sustainability: Present status and future challenges. *Environmental Science and Pollution Research International*, 28(20), 24917–24939. DOI: 10.1007/s11356-021-13252-7 PMID: 33768457

Kowsalya, K., & Rani, R. P. J. Ritu, Bhiyana, M., Saini, M., & Patil, P. P. (2023). Blockchain-Internet of things-Machine Learning: Development of Traceable System for Multi Purposes. *2023 3rd International Conference on Advance Computing and Innovative Technologies in Engineering, ICACITE 2023*, 1112 – 1115. DOI: 10.1109/ICACITE57410.2023.10183065

Krishna, S. H., Upadhyay, A., Tewari, M., Gehlot, A., Girimurugan, B., & Pundir, S. (2022). Empirical investigation of the key machine learning elements promoting e-business using an SEM framework. *Proceedings of 5th International Conference on Contemporary Computing and Informatics, IC3I 2022*, 1960 – 1964. DOI: 10.1109/IC3I56241.2022.10072712

Krittanawong, C., Zhang, H., Wang, Z., Aydar, M., & Kitai, T. (2017). Artificial Intelligence in Precision Cardiovascular Medicine. *Journal of the American College of Cardiology*, 69(21), 2657–2664. DOI: 10.1016/j.jacc.2017.03.571 PMID: 28545640

Kroll, C., Warchold, A., & Pradhan, P. (2019). Sustainable Development Goals (SDGs): Are we successful in turning trade-offs into synergies? *Palgrave Communications*, 5(1), 140. Advance online publication. DOI: 10.1057/s41599-019-0335-5

Kufel, J., Bargieł-Łączek, K., Kocot, S., Koźlik, M., Bartnikowska, W., Janik, M., Czogalik, Ł., Dudek, P., Magiera, M., Lis, A., Paszkiewicz, I., Nawrat, Z., Cebula, M., & Gruszczyńska, K. (2023). What is machine learning, artificial neural networks and deep learning?—Examples of practical applications in medicine. *Diagnostics (Basel)*, 13(15), 2582. DOI: 10.3390/diagnostics13152582 PMID: 37568945

Kukreti, A., Shriyal, A., Sharma, S., & Bhadula, S. (2023). Internet-of-Things Enabled Smart and Portable Terrace Garden Protection Shed. *2023 4th IEEE Global Conference for Advancement in Technology, GCAT 2023*. DOI: 10.1109/GCAT59970.2023.10353281

Kulkov, I., Kulkova, J., Rohrbeck, R., Menvielle, L., Kaartemo, V., & Makkonen, H. (2024). Artificial intelligence-driven sustainable development: Examining organizational, technical, and processing approaches to achieving global goals. *Sustainable Development (Bradford)*, 32(3), 2253–2267. DOI: 10.1002/sd.2773

Kulski, J. K. (2016) Next-generation sequencing — an overview of the history, tools, and "omic" applications. In: Kulski JK (ed) Next generation sequencing - advances, applications and challenges. INTECH, London, eBook (PDF) ISBN: 978-953-51-5419-8

Kumar, A. S., & Desi, A. B. (2023). Collaborative logistics, tools of machine and supply chain services in the world wide industry 4.0 framework. In *Artificial Intelligence, Blockchain, Computing and Security: Volume 2* (Vol. 2). CRC Press. DOI: 10.1201/9781032684994-15

Kumar, A., & Ram, M. (2021). Systems Reliability Engineering: Modeling and Performance Improvement. In *Systems Reliability Engineering: Modeling and Performance Improvement*. De Gruyter. DOI: 10.1515/9783110617375

Kumar, A., Goyal, H. R., & Sharma, S. (2023). Sustainable Intelligent Information System for Tourism Industry. *2023 IEEE 8th International Conference for Convergence in Technology, I2CT 2023*. DOI: 10.1109/I2CT57861.2023.10126400

Kumar, K., Chaudhary, S., Anandaram, H., Kumar, R., Gupta, A., & Joshi, K. (2023). Industry 4.0 and Health Care System with special reference to Mental Health. *2023 1st International Conference on Intelligent Computing and Research Trends, ICRT 2023*. https://doi.org/DOI: 10.1109/ICRT57042.2023.10146640

Kumar, M. A., Prasad, M. S. G., More, P., & Christa, S. (2022). Artificial intelligence-based personal health monitoring devices. In *Mobile Health: Advances in Research and Applications - Volume II*. Nova Science Publishers, Inc.

Kumar, P., Obaidat, M. S., Pandey, P., Wazid, M., Das, A. K., & Singh, D. P. (2023). Design of a Secure Machine Learning-Based Malware Detection and Analysis Scheme. In O. M.S., N. Z., H. K.-F., N. P., & G. Y. (Eds.), *Proceedings of the 2023 IEEE International Conference on Communications, Computing, Cybersecurity and Informatics, CCCI 2023.* Institute of Electrical and Electronics Engineers Inc. DOI: 10.1109/CCCI58712.2023.10290761

Kumar, P., Reepu, & Kaur, R. (2024). Economic and Urban Dynamics: Investigating Socioeconomic Status and Urban Density as Moderators of Mobile Wallet Adoption in Smart Cities. *Lecture Notes in Networks and Systems, 948 LNNS*, 409–417. DOI: 10.1007/978-981-97-1329-5_33

Kumar, P., Taneja, S., & Ozen, E. (2024). Exploring the influence of green bonds on sustainable development through low-carbon financing mobilization. *International Journal of Law and Management.* DOI: 10.1108/IJLMA-01-2024-0030

Kumar, R., Lande, A., Kumar, D., Malhotra, R. K., & Sharma, A. (2023). Technology Bridging -in Entrepreneurs and Consumers in Product Development. *ISED 2023 - International Conference on Intelligent Systems and Embedded Design.* DOI: 10.1109/ISED59382.2023.10444599

Kumar, R., Malhotra, R. K., Pandey, S., Gehlot, A., Gautam, I., & Chamola, S. (2023). Role of Artificial Intelligence in Input Tax Credit Reconciliation. *Proceedings - 2023 3rd International Conference on Pervasive Computing and Social Networking, ICPCSN 2023*, 497–501. DOI: 10.1109/ICPCSN58827.2023.00086

Kumar, V., & Korovin, G. (2023). A Comparision of Digital Transformation of Industry in the Russian Federation with the European Union. In K. V., K. G.L., A. V., & K. E. (Eds.), *Lecture Notes in Information Systems and Organisation: Vol. 61 LNISO* (pp. 45 – 57). Springer Science and Business Media Deutschland GmbH. DOI: 10.1007/978-3-031-30351-7_5

Kumar, V., Sharma, N. K., Mittal, A., & Verma, P. (2023). The Role of IoT and IIoT in Supplier and Customer Continuous Improvement Interface. *EAI/Springer Innovations in Communication and Computing*, 161 – 174. DOI: 10.1007/978-3-031-19711-6_7

Kumar, A., Mani, V., Jain, V., Gupta, H., & Venkatesh, V. G. (2023). Managing healthcare supply chain through artificial intelligence (AI): A study of critical success factors. *Computers & Industrial Engineering*, 175, 108815. DOI: 10.1016/j.cie.2022.108815 PMID: 36405396

Kumar, A., Nirala, A., Singh, V. P., Sahoo, B. K., Singh, R. C., Chaudhary, R., Dewangan, A. K., Gaurav, G. K., Klemeš, J. J., & Liu, X. (2023). The utilisation of coconut shell ash in production of hybrid composite: Microstructural characterisation and performance analysis. *Journal of Cleaner Production*, 398, 136494. Advance online publication. DOI: 10.1016/j.jclepro.2023.136494

Kumar, A., Pant, S., & Ram, M. (2023). Cost Optimization and Reliability Parameter Extraction of a Complex Engineering System. *Journal of Reliability and Statistical Studies*, 16(1), 99–116. DOI: 10.13052/jrss0974-8024.1615

Kumar, A., Saxena, M., Sastry, R. V. L. S. N., Chaudhari, A., Singh, R., & Malathy, V. (2023). Internet of Things and Blockchain Data Supplier for Intelligent Applications. *Proceedings of International Conference on Contemporary Computing and Informatics, IC3I 2023*, 2218 – 2223. DOI: 10.1109/IC3I59117.2023.10397630

Kumar, A., Sharma, N., Chauhan, R., & Sharma, M. (2023). Anomaly Detection in Bitcoin Blockchain: Exploring Trends and Algorithms. *2023 Global Conference on Information Technologies and Communications, GCITC 2023*. DOI: 10.1109/GCITC60406.2023.10426011

Kumar, A., Singh, V. P., Nirala, A., Singh, R. C., Chaudhary, R., Mourad, A.-H. I., Sahoo, B. K., & Kumar, D. (2023). Influence of tool rotational speed on mechanical and corrosion behaviour of friction stir processed AZ31/Al2O3 nanocomposite. *Journal of Magnesium and Alloys*, 11(7), 2585–2599. DOI: 10.1016/j.jma.2023.06.012

Kumar, G., Kumar, A., Singhal, M., Singh, K. U., Kumar, L., & Singh, T. (2023). Revolutionizing Plant Disease Management Through Image Processing Technology. *Proceedings of International Conference on Computational Intelligence and Sustainable Engineering Solution, CISES 2023*, 521 – 528. DOI: 10.1109/CISES58720.2023.10183408

Kumar, G., Saha, R., Rai, M. K., Thomas, R., & Kim, T.-H. (2019). Proof-of-Work Consensus Approach in Blockchain Technology for Cloud and Fog Computing Using Maximization-Factorization Statistics. *IEEE Internet of Things Journal*, 6(4), 6835–6842. DOI: 10.1109/JIOT.2019.2911969

Kumar, H., Bhardwaj, K., Nepovimova, E., Kuča, K., Dhanjal, D. S., Bhardwaj, S., Bhatia, S. K., Verma, R., & Kumar, D. (2020). Antioxidant functionalized nanoparticles: A combat against oxidative stress. *Nanomaterials (Basel, Switzerland)*, 10(7), 1–31. DOI: 10.3390/nano10071334 PMID: 32650608

Kumar, H., Bhardwaj, K., Sharma, R., Nepovimova, E., Kuča, K., Dhanjal, D. S., Verma, R., Bhardwaj, P., Sharma, S., & Kumar, D. (2020). Fruit and Vegetable Peels: Utilization of High Value Horticultural Waste in Novel Industrial Applications. *Molecules (Basel, Switzerland)*, 25(12), 2812. Advance online publication. DOI: 10.3390/molecules25122812 PMID: 32570836

Kumar, I., Rawat, J., Mohd, N., & Husain, S. (2021). Opportunities of Artificial Intelligence and Machine Learning in the Food Industry. *Journal of Food Quality*, 2021. Advance online publication. DOI: 10.1155/2021/4535567

Kumari, J., Singh, P., Mishra, A. K., Singh Meena, B. P., Singh, A., & Ojha, M. (2024). Challenges Hindering Women's Involvement in the Hospitality Industry as Entrepreneurs in the Era of Digital Economy. In *Revolutionizing the AI-Digital Landscape: A Guide to Sustainable Emerging Technologies for Marketing Professionals*. Taylor and Francis., DOI: 10.4324/9781032688305-9

Kumari, N., Alam, T., Ali, M. A., Yadav, A. S., Gupta, N. K., Siddiqui, M. I. H., Dobrotă, D., Rotaru, I. M., & Sharma, A. (2022). A Numerical Investigation on Hydrothermal Performance of Micro Channel Heat Sink with Periodic Spatial Modification on Sidewalls. *Micromachines*, 13(11), 1986. Advance online publication. DOI: 10.3390/mi13111986 PMID: 36422415

Kumar, K. S., Yadav, D., Joshi, S. K., Chakravarthi, M. K., Jain, A. K., & Tripathi, V. (2022). Blockchain Technology with Applications to Distributed Control and Cooperative Robotics. *Proceedings of 5th International Conference on Contemporary Computing and Informatics, IC3I 2022*, 206 – 211. DOI: 10.1109/IC3I56241.2022.10073275

Kumar, K., Singh, V., Mishra, G., Ravindra Babu, B., Tripathi, N., & Kumar, P. (2022). Power-Efficient Secured Hardware Design of AES Algorithm on High Performance FPGA. *Proceedings of 5th International Conference on Contemporary Computing and Informatics, IC3I 2022*, 1634 – 1637. DOI: 10.1109/IC3I56241.2022.10073148

Kumar, K., Veena, N., Aravind, T., Bhatt, C., Kuppusamy, U., & Jain, P. (2025). Game-changing intelligence: Unveiling the societal impact of artificial intelligence in game software. *Entertainment Computing*, 52, 100862. Advance online publication. DOI: 10.1016/j.entcom.2024.100862

Kumar, M., Ansari, N. A., Sharma, A., Singh, V. K., Gautam, R., & Singh, Y. (2021). Prediction of an optimum engine response based on di erent input parameters on common rail direct injection diesel engine: A response surface methodology approach. *Scientia Iranica*, 28(6), 3181–3200. DOI: 10.24200/sci.2021.56745.4885

Kumar, N. M., Islam, S., Podder, A. K., Selim, A., Bajaj, M., & Kamel, S. (2023). Lifecycle-based feasibility indicators for floating solar photovoltaic plants along with implementable energy enhancement strategies and framework-driven assessment approaches leading to advancements in the simulation tool. *Frontiers in Energy Research*, 11. Advance online publication. DOI: 10.3389/fenrg.2023.1075384

Kumar, P., Bhatnagar, M., & Taneja, S. (2023). Investigation of the time pattern of Bit Green Crypto: An Arma modeling approach to unrave volatility. In *Algorithmic Approaches to Financial Technology: Forecasting, Trading, and Optimization*. IGI Global., DOI: 10.4018/979-8-3693-1746-4.ch001

Kumar, P., Taneja, S., Bhatnagar, M., & Kaur, A. K. (2024). Navigating the digital paradigm shift: Designing CBDCs for a transformative financial landscape. In *Exploring Central Bank Digital Currencies: Concepts, Frameworks, Models, and Challenges*. IGI Global., DOI: 10.4018/979-8-3693-1882-9.ch006

Kumar, P., Verma, P., Bhatnagar, M., Taneja, S., Seychel, S., Todorović, I., & Grim, S. (2023). The Financial Performance and Solvency Status of the Indian Public Sector Banks: A CAMELS Rating and Z Index Approach. *International Journal of Sustainable Development and Planning*, 18(2), 367–376. DOI: 10.18280/ijsdp.180204

Kumar, R., Dwivedi, R. K., Arya, R. K., Sonia, P., Yadav, A. S., Saxena, K. K., Khan, M. I., & Ben Moussa, S. (2023). Current development of carbide free bainitic and retained austenite on wear resistance in high silicon steel. *Journal of Materials Research and Technology*, 24, 9171–9202. DOI: 10.1016/j.jmrt.2023.05.067

Kumar, R., Goel, R., Singh, T., Mohanty, S. M., Gupta, D., Alkhayyat, A., & Khanna, R. (2024). Sustainable Finance Factors in Indian Economy: Analysis on Policy of Climate Change and Energy Sector. *Fluctuation and Noise Letters*, 23(2), 2440004. Advance online publication. DOI: 10.1142/S0219477524400042

Kumar, R., Kandpal, B., & Ahmad, V. (2023). Industrial IoT (IIOT): Security Threats and Countermeasures. *International Conference on Innovative Data Communication Technologies and Application, ICIDCA 2023 - Proceedings*, 829 – 833. DOI: 10.1109/ICIDCA56705.2023.10100145

Kumar, R., Kathuria, S., Malholtra, R. K., Kumar, A., Gehlot, A., & Joshi, K. (2023). Role of Cloud Computing in Goods and Services Tax(GST) and Future Application. *2nd International Conference on Sustainable Computing and Data Communication Systems, ICSCDS 2023 - Proceedings*, 1443–1447. DOI: 10.1109/ICSCDS56580.2023.10104597

Kumar, R., & Khanna, R. (2023). RPA (Robotic Process Automation) in Finance & Accounting and Future Scope. *Proceedings of the 2023 2nd International Conference on Augmented Intelligence and Sustainable Systems, ICAISS 2023*, 1640–1645. DOI: 10.1109/ICAISS58487.2023.10250496

Kumar, R., & Khanna, R. (2023a). Role of Artificial Intelligence in Digital Currency and Future Applications. *Proceedings of the 2023 2nd International Conference on Augmented Intelligence and Sustainable Systems, ICAISS 2023*, 42–46. DOI: 10.1109/ICAISS58487.2023.10250480

Kumar, R., Khannna Malholtra, R., & Grover, C. A. N. (2023). Review on Artificial Intelligence Role in Implementation of Goods and Services Tax(GST) and Future Scope. *2023 International Conference on Artificial Intelligence and Smart Communication, AISC 2023*, 348–351. DOI: 10.1109/AISC56616.2023.10085030

Kumar, R., Lamba, A. K., Mohammed, S., Asokan, A., Aswal, U. S., & Kolavennu, S. (2023). Fake Currency Note Recognition using Extreme Learning Machine. *Proceedings of the 2nd International Conference on Applied Artificial Intelligence and Computing, ICAAIC 2023*, 333 – 339. DOI: 10.1109/ICAAIC56838.2023.10140824

Kumar, R., Malholtra, R. K., Singh, R., Kathuria, S., Balyan, R., & Pal, P. (2023). Artificial Intelligence Role in Electronic Invoice Under Goods and Services Tax. *2023 International Conference on Computational Intelligence, Communication Technology and Networking, CICTN 2023*, 140–143. https://doi.org/DOI: 10.1109/CICTN57981.2023.10140870

Kumar, R., Malhotra, R. K., & Grover, N. (2023). Data Mining in Credit Scoring and Future Application. *International Conference on Innovative Data Communication Technologies and Application, ICIDCA 2023 - Proceedings*, 1096–1100. DOI: 10.1109/ICIDCA56705.2023.10100032

Kumar, R., Saxena, A., & Singh, R. (2023). Robotic Process Automation Bridge -in Banking Institute and Consumers. *2023 International Conference on Disruptive Technologies, ICDT 2023*, 428 – 431. https://doi.org/DOI: 10.1109/ICDT57929.2023.10150500

Kumar, R., Sexena, A., & Gehlot, A. (2023). Artificial Intelligence in Smart Education and Futuristic Challenges. *2023 International Conference on Disruptive Technologies, ICDT 2023*, 432 – 435. DOI: 10.1109/ICDT57929.2023.10151129

Kumar, R., Singh, T., Mohanty, S. N., Goel, R., Gupta, D., Alharbi, M., & Khanna, R. (2023). Study on online payments and e-commerce with SOR model. *International Journal of Retail & Distribution Management*. Advance online publication. DOI: 10.1108/IJRDM-03-2023-0137

Kumar, V., Gupta, S., & Khanna, R. (2021). Dengue fever-a worldwide study. *Journal of Medical Pharmaceutical and Allied Sciences*, 10, 102–108. DOI: 10.22270/jmpas.VIC2I1.2014

Kumar, V., Mitra, D., Rani, A., Suyal, D. C., Singh Gautam, B. P., Jain, L., Gondwal, M., Raj, K. K., Singh, A. K., & Soni, R. (2021). Bio-inoculants for Biodegradation and Bioconversion of Agrowaste: Status and Prospects. In *Bioremediation of Environmental Pollutants: Emerging Trends and Strategies*. Springer International Publishing., DOI: 10.1007/978-3-030-86169-8_16

Kumar, V., Pant, B., Elkady, G., Kaur, C., Suhashini, J., & Hassen, S. M. (2022). Examining the Role of Block Chain to Secure Identity in IOT for Industry 4.0. *Proceedings of 5th International Conference on Contemporary Computing and Informatics, IC3I 2022*, 256 – 259. https://doi.org/DOI: 10.1109/IC3I56241.2022.10072516

Kumar, V., Singh, S., Srivastava, B., Bhadouria, R., & Singh, R. (2019). Green synthesis of silver nanoparticles using leaf extract of Holoptelea integrifolia and preliminary investigation of its antioxidant, anti-inflammatory, antidiabetic and antibacterial activities. *Journal of Environmental Chemical Engineering*, 7(3), 103094. Advance online publication. DOI: 10.1016/j.jece.2019.103094

Kunwar, S., Joshi, A., Gururani, P., Pandey, D., & Pandey, N. (2023). Physiological and AI-based study of endophytes on medicina A mini review. *Plant Science Today*, 10, 53–60. DOI: 10.14719/pst.2555

Kushwaha, A. D., Patel, B., Khan, I. A., & Agrawal, A. (2023). Fabrication and characterization of hexagonal boron nitride/polyester composites to study the effect of filler loading and surface modification for microelectronic applications. *Polymer Composites*, 44(8), 4579–4593. DOI: 10.1002/pc.27421

Kutty, A. A., Abdella, G. M., Kucukvar, M., Onat, N. C., & Bulu, M. (2020). A system thinking approach for harmonizing smart and sustainable city initiatives with United Nations sustainable development goals. *Sustainable Development (Bradford)*, 28(5), 1347–1365. DOI: 10.1002/sd.2088

Kyaw, T. L., Ng, N., Theocharaki, M., Wennberg, P., & Sahlen, K. G. (2023). Cost-effectiveness of Digital Tools for Behavior Change Interventions Among People With Chronic Diseases: Systematic Review. *Interactive Journal of Medical Research*, 12, e42396. DOI: 10.2196/42396 PMID: 36795470

Lade, J., Mohammed, K. A., Singh, D., Prasad Verma, R., Math, P., Saraswat, M., & Raj Gupta, L. (2023). A critical review of fabrication routes and their effects on mechanical properties of AMMCs. *Materials Today: Proceedings*. Advance online publication. DOI: 10.1016/j.matpr.2023.03.041

Laka, M., Carter, D., Milazzo, A., & Merlin, T. (2022). Challenges and opportunities in implementing clinical decision support systems (CDSS) at scale: Interviews with Australian policymakers. *Health Policy and Technology*, 11(3), 100652. DOI: 10.1016/j.hlpt.2022.100652

Lange, O. (2023). Health economic evaluation of preventive digital public health interventions using decision-analytic modelling: A systematized review. *BMC Health Services Research*, 23(1), 268. DOI: 10.1186/s12913-023-09280-3 PMID: 36932436

Latif, S., Qadir, J., Farooq, S., & Imran, M. A. (2017). How 5G Wireless and Concomitant Technologies will revolutionize healthcare. *Future Internet*, 9(4), 93. Advance online publication. DOI: 10.3390/fi9040093

Lauesen, L. M. (2016). The landscape and scale of social and sustainable finance. In *Routledge Handbook of Social and Sustainable Finance*. Taylor and Francis., DOI: 10.4324/9781315772578

Leal Filho, W., Trevisan, L. V., Eustachio, J. H. P. P., Dibbern, T., Apraiz, J. C., Rampasso, I., ... & Lambrechts, W. (2023). Sustainable supply chain management and the UN sustainable development goals: Exploring synergies towards sustainable development. *The TQM journal*, (ahead-of-print).

Ledziński, Ł., & Grześk, G. (2023). Artificial intelligence technologies in cardiology. *Journal of Cardiovascular Development and Disease*, 10(5), 202. DOI: 10.3390/jcdd10050202 PMID: 37233169

Lehmann, U., Dieleman, M., & Martineau, T. (2008). Staffing remote rural areas in middle-and low-income countries: A literature review of attraction and retention. *BMC Health Services Research*, 8(1), 1–10. DOI: 10.1186/1472-6963-8-19 PMID: 18215313

Levänen, J., Hossain, M., Lyytinen, T., Hyvärinen, A., Numminen, S., & Halme, M. (2016). Implications of frugal innovations on sustainable development: Evaluating water and energy innovations. *Sustainability (Basel)*, 8(1), 4. Advance online publication. DOI: 10.3390/su8010004

Li, W., Yigitcanlar, T., Browne, W., & Nili, A. (2023). The Making of Responsible Innovation and Technology: An Overview and Framework. In *Smart Cities,* 6(4). 1996–2034. https://doi.org/DOI: 10.3390/smartcities6040093

Liao, J., Li, X., Gan, Y., Han, S., Rong, P., Wang, W., Li, W., & Zhou, L. (2023). Artificial intelligence assists precision medicine in cancer treatment. *Frontiers in Oncology*, 12, 998222. DOI: 10.3389/fonc.2022.998222 PMID: 36686757

Liao, N., Cai, Q., Garg, H., Wei, G., & Xu, X. (2023). Novel Gained and Lost Dominance Score Method Based on Cumulative Prospect Theory for Group Decision-Making Problems in Probabilistic Hesitant Fuzzy Environment. *International Journal of Fuzzy Systems*, 25(4), 1414–1428. DOI: 10.1007/s40815-022-01440-7

Liao, Y., Bang, D., Cosgrove, S., Dulin, R., Harris, Z., Taylor, A., & Giles, W. (2011). Surveillance of health status in minority communities-racial and ethnic approaches to community health across the US (REACH US) risk factor survey, United States, 2009. *MMWR. Surveillance Summaries*, 60(6), 1–44. PMID: 21597458

Lindahl, B., Lidén, E., & Lindblad, B. M. (2011). A meta-synthesis describing the relationships between patients, informal caregivers and health professionals in home-care settings. *Journal of Clinical Nursing*, 20(3-4), 454–463. DOI: 10.1111/j.1365-2702.2009.03008.x PMID: 20412357

Listek, V. (2021, October 18). *Ai driven bioprinting speeds up tissue engineering - 3dprint.com: The Voice of 3D printing / Additive Manufacturing.* 3DPrint.com | The Voice of 3D Printing / Additive Manufacturing. Retrieved November 11, 2022, from https://3dprint.com/273254/ai-driven-bioprinting-speeds-up-tissue-engineering/

Liu, H. Y., Jay, M., & Chen, X. (2021). The role of nature-based solutions for improving environmental quality, health, and well-being. *Sustainability (Basel)*, 13(19), 10950. Advance online publication. DOI: 10.3390/su131910950

Liu, N., Zhang, Z., Wah Ho, A. F., & Ong, M. E. (2018). Artificial Intelligence in emergency medicine. *Journal of Emergency and Critical Care Medicine*, 2, 82–82. DOI: 10.21037/jeccm.2018.10.08

Liu, Z., Han, G., Yan, J., Liu, Z., & Osmani, M. (2022). The relationship between social mentality and health in promoting well-being and sustainable City. *International Journal of Environmental Research and Public Health*, 19(18), 11529. Advance online publication. DOI: 10.3390/ijerph191811529 PMID: 36141799

Lokanadham, D., Sharma, R. C., Palli, S., & Bhardawaj, S. (2022). Wear Rate Modelling and Analysis of Limestone Slurry Particulate Composites Using the Fuzzy Method. *International Journal on Recent and Innovation Trends in Computing and Communication*, 10(1), 133–143. DOI: 10.17762/ijritcc.v10i1s.5818

López-Del-Hoyo, Y., Fernández-Martínez, S., Pérez-Aranda, A., Barceló-Soler, A., Bani, M., Russo, S., Urcola-Pardo, F., Strepparava, M. G., & García-Campayo, J. (2023). Effects of e Health interventions on stress reduction and mental health promotion in healthcare professionals: A systematic review. *Journal of Clinical Nursing*, 32(17-18), 5514–5533. DOI: 10.1111/jocn.16634 PMID: 36703266

Lourens, M., Krishna, S. H., Singh, A., Dey, S. K., Pant, B., & Sharma, T. (2022). Role of Artificial Intelligence in Formative Employee Engagement. In D. R.K., S. A.Kr., K. G., & B. S. (Eds.), *Proceedings of the 2022 11th International Conference on System Modeling and Advancement in Research Trends, SMART 2022* (pp. 936 – 941). Institute of Electrical and Electronics Engineers Inc. DOI: 10.1109/SMART55829.2022.10047422

Lourens, M., Tamizhselvi, A., Goswami, B., Alanya-Beltran, J., Aarif, M., & Gangodkar, D. (2022). Database Management Difficulties in the Internet of Things. *Proceedings of 5th International Conference on Contemporary Computing and Informatics, IC3I 2022*, 322–326. DOI: 10.1109/IC3I56241.2022.10072614

Luthra, S., Sharma, M., Kumar, A., Joshi, S., Collins, E., & Mangla, S. (2022). Overcoming barriers to cross-sector collaboration in circular supply chain management: A multi-method approach. *Transportation Research Part E, Logistics and Transportation Review*, 157. Advance online publication. DOI: 10.1016/j.tre.2021.102582

Luxton, D. D. (2014). Recommendations for the ethical use and design of artificial intelligent care providers. *Artificial Intelligence in Medicine*, 62(1), 1–10. DOI: 10.1016/j.artmed.2014.06.004 PMID: 25059820

M, M., R, S., & Rashmi. (2018, November 20*). Artificial intelligence based skin classification using GMM. Journal of medical systems.* Retrieved November 1, 2022, from https://pubmed.ncbi.nlm.nih.gov/30460413/

Magesh, S., John, D., Li, W. T., Li, Y., Mattingly-App, A., Jain, S., Chang, E. Y., & Ongkeko, W. M. (2021). Disparities in COVID-19 outcomes by race, ethnicity, and socioeconomic status: A systematic review and meta-analysis. *JAMA Network Open*, 4(11), e2134147–e2134147. DOI: 10.1001/jamanetworkopen.2021.34147 PMID: 34762110

Mahesh, K. V., Singh, S. K., & Gulati, M. (2014). A comparative study of top-down and bottom-up approaches for the preparation of nanosuspensions of glipizide. *Powder Technology*, 256, 436–449. DOI: 10.1016/j.powtec.2014.02.011

Mahla, S. K., Goyal, T., Goyal, D., Sharma, H., Dhir, A., & Goga, G. (2022). Optimization of engine operating variables on performance and emissions characteristics of biogas fuelled CI engine by the design of experiments: Taguchi approach. *Environmental Progress & Sustainable Energy*, 41(2), e13736. Advance online publication. DOI: 10.1002/ep.13736

Mahor, V., Bijrothiya, S., Mishra, R., & Rawat, R. (2022). ML techniques for attack and anomaly detection in internet of things networks. In *Autonomous Vehicles* (Vol. 1). wiley. DOI: 10.1002/9781119871989.ch13

Mahor, V., Bijrothiya, S., Mishra, R., Rawat, R., & Soni, A. (2022). The smart city based on AI and infrastructure: A new mobility concepts and realities. In *Autonomous Vehicles* (Vol. 1). wiley. DOI: 10.1002/9781119871989.ch15

Mahor, V., Garg, B., Telang, S., Pachlasiya, K., Chouhan, M., & Rawat, R. (2022). Cyber Threat Phylogeny Assessment and Vulnerabilities Representation at Thermal Power Station. *Lecture Notes in Networks and Systems, 481 LNNS*, 28 – 39. DOI: 10.1007/978-981-19-3182-6_3

Mahor, V., Pachlasiya, K., Garg, B., Chouhan, M., Telang, S., & Rawat, R. (2022). Mobile Operating System (Android) Vulnerability Analysis Using Machine Learning. *Lecture Notes in Networks and Systems, 481 LNNS*, 159 – 169. DOI: 10.1007/978-981-19-3182-6_13

Malhotra, R. K., Gupta, C., & Jindal, P. (2022). Blockchain and Smart Contracts for Insurance Industry. In *Blockchain Technology in Corporate Governance*. Transforming Business and Industries., DOI: 10.1002/9781119865247.ch11

Malhotra, R. K., & Gupta, S. (2021). Tele health in the digital era during covid -19 a case study of Uttarakhand. *Journal of Medical Pharmaceutical and Allied Sciences*, 10, 109–112. DOI: 10.22270/jmpas.VIC2I1.2016

Malhotra, R. K., Ojha, M. K., & Gupta, S. (2021). A study of assessment of knowledge, perception and attitude of using tele health services among college going students of Uttarakhand. *Journal of Medical Pharmaceutical and Allied Sciences*, 10, 113–116. DOI: 10.22270/jmpas.VIC2I1.2020

Malik, D., Kukreja, V., Mehta, S., Gupta, A., & Singh, V. (2023). Mitigating the Impact of Guava Leaf Diseases Using CNNs and Federated Learning. *2023 3rd Asian Conference on Innovation in Technology, ASIANCON 2023*. DOI: 10.1109/ASIANCON58793.2023.10270236

Malik, P., Singh, A. K., Nautiyal, R., & Rawat, S. (2022). Mapping AICTE cybersecurity curriculum onto CyBOK: A case study. In *Machine Learning for Cyber Security*. De Gruyter., DOI: 10.1515/9783110766745-007

Mandalapu, S. R., Sivamuni, K., Chitra Devi, D., Aswal, U. S., Sherly, S. I., & Balaji, N. A. (2023). An Architecture-based Self-Typing Service for Cloud Native Applications. *Proceedings of the 4th International Conference on Smart Electronics and Communication, ICOSEC 2023*, 562 – 566. DOI: 10.1109/ICOSEC58147.2023.10276313

Manero, A., Smith, P., Koontz, A., Dombrowski, M., Sparkman, J., Courbin, D., & Chi, A. (2020). Leveraging 3D printing capacity in times of crisis: Recommendations for COVID-19 distributed manufacturing for medical equipment rapid response. *International Journal of Environmental Research and Public Health*, 17(13), 4634. DOI: 10.3390/ijerph17134634 PMID: 32605098

Mangla, S. K., & Ram, M. (2020). Supply chain sustainability: Modeling and innovative research frameworks. In *Supply Chain Sustainability: Modeling and Innovative Research Frameworks*. De Gruyter. https://doi.org/DOI: 10.1515/9783110628593

Mangla, S. K., Luthra, S., Mishra, N., Singh, A., Rana, N. P., Dora, M., & Dwivedi, Y. (2018). Barriers to effective circular supply chain management in a developing country context. *Production Planning and Control*, 29(6), 551–569. DOI: 10.1080/09537287.2018.1449265

Manjunatha, B. N., Chandan, M., Kottu, S., Rappai, S., Hema, P. K., Singh Rawat, K., & Sarkar, S. (2023). A Successful Spam Detection Technique for Industrial IoT Devices based on Machine Learning Techniques. *Proceedings of the 2nd International Conference on Applied Artificial Intelligence and Computing, ICAAIC 2023*, 363 – 369. DOI: 10.1109/ICAAIC56838.2023.10141275

Mansour, H., & Sharour, L. A. (2021). Results of survey on perception of patient safety culture among emergency nurses in Jordan: Influence of burnout, job satisfaction, turnover intention, and workload. *Journal of Healthcare Quality Research*, 36(6), 370–377. DOI: 10.1016/j.jhqr.2021.05.001 PMID: 34187762

Manzoor, S. I., & Singla, J., & Nikita. (2019). Fake news detection using machine learning approaches: A systematic review. *Proceedings of the International Conference on Trends in Electronics and Informatics, ICOEI 2019*, 230 – 234. DOI: 10.1109/ICOEI.2019.8862770

Marsch, L. A., & Ben-Zeev, D. (2012). Technology-Based Assessments and Interventions Targeting Psychiatric and Substance Use Disorders: Innovations and Opportunities. *Journal of Dual Diagnosis*, 8(4), 259–261. DOI: 10.1080/15504263.2012.723308

Mary Joshitta, S., & Sunil, M. P. Badriasulaimanalfurhood, Bodhankar, A., Ch.Sreedevi, & Khanna, R. (2023). The Integration of Machine Learning Technique with the Existing System to Predict the Flight Prices. *2023 3rd International Conference on Advance Computing and Innovative Technologies in Engineering, ICACITE 2023*, 398–402. DOI: 10.1109/ICACITE57410.2023.10182539

Masal, V., Pavithra, P., Tiwari, S. K., Singh, R., Panduro-Ramirez, J., & Gangodkar, D. (2022). Deep Learning Applications for Blockchain in Industrial IoT. *Proceedings of 5th International Conference on Contemporary Computing and Informatics, IC3I 2022*, 276 – 281. DOI: 10.1109/IC3I56241.2022.10073357

Masood, A., & Al-Jumaily, A. A. (2013). Computer aided diagnostic support system for skin cancer: A review of techniques and algorithms. *International Journal of Biomedical Imaging*, 323268, 1–22. Advance online publication. DOI: 10.1155/2013/323268 PMID: 24575126

Masud, M., Gaba, G. S., Alqahtani, S., Muhammad, G., Gupta, B. B., Kumar, P., & Ghoneim, A. (2021). A Lightweight and Robust Secure Key Establishment Protocol for Internet of Medical Things in COVID-19 Patients Care. *IEEE Internet of Things Journal*, 8(21), 15694–15703. DOI: 10.1109/JIOT.2020.3047662 PMID: 35782176

Mathkor, D. M., Mathkor, N., Bassfar, Z., Bantun, F., Slama, P., Ahmad, F., & Haque, S. (2024). Multirole of the internet of medical things (IoMT) in biomedical systems for managing smart healthcare systems: An overview of current and future innovative trends. *Journal of Infection and Public Health*, 17(4), 559–572. DOI: 10.1016/j.jiph.2024.01.013 PMID: 38367570

Matt, iacolippoiacolippo 3, kHarshitkHarshit, et al. (1965, October 1). *Where do I get a CPU-only version of pytorch?* Stack Overflow. Retrieved November 12, 2022, from https://stackoverflow.com/questions/51730880/where-do-i-get-a-cpu-only-version-of-pytorch

Matta, P., & Pant, B. (2020). TCpC: A graphical password scheme ensuring authentication for IoT resources. *International Journal of Information Technology (Singapore)*, 12(3), 699–709. DOI: 10.1007/s41870-018-0142-z

Maurya, S. K., Ghosal, A., & Manna, A. (2022). Experimental investigations during fabrication and electrical discharge machining of hybrid Al/(SiC+ZrO2+NiTi) MMC. *International Journal of Machining and Machinability of Materials*, 24(3–4), 215–230. DOI: 10.1504/ijmmm.2022.125195

McCool, J., Dobson, R., Muinga, N., Paton, C., Pagliari, C., Agawal, S., Labrique, A., Tanielu, H., & Whittaker, R. (2020). Factors influencing the sustainability of digital health interventions in low-resource settings: Lessons from five countries. *Journal of Global Health*, 10(2), 020396. Advance online publication. DOI: 10.7189/jogh.10.020396 PMID: 33274059

McGuigan, N., Sin, S., & Kern, T. (2017). Sourcing sustainable finance in a globally competitive market: An instructional case. *Issues in Accounting Education*, 32(1), 43–58. DOI: 10.2308/iace-51304

Medhi, M. K., Ambust, S., Kumar, R., & Das, A. J. (2023). Characterization and Purification of Biosurfactants. In *Advancements in Biosurfactants Research*. Springer International Publishing., DOI: 10.1007/978-3-031-21682-4_4

Medical chatbots - use cases, examples and case studies of Conversational AI in Medicine and Health (2020) senseforth.ai. Retrieved November 5, 2022, from https://www.senseforth.ai/conversational-ai/medical-chatbots/

Mehbodniya, A., Alam, I., Pande, S., Neware, R., Rane, K. P., Shabaz, M., & Madhavan, M. V. (2021, September 11). *Financial fraud detection in healthcare using machine learning and Deep Learning Techniques*. Security and Communication Networks. Retrieved November 2, 2022, from https://www.hindawi.com/journals/scn/2021/9293877/

Mehershilpa, G., Prasad, D., Sai Kiran, C., Shaikh, A., Jayashree, K., & Socrates, S. (2023). EDM machining of Ti6Al4V alloy using colloidal biosilica. *Materials Today: Proceedings*. Advance online publication. DOI: 10.1016/j.matpr.2023.02.443

Mehta, K., Sharma, S., & Mishra, D. (2021). Internet-of-Things Enabled Forest Fire Detection System. *Proceedings of the 5th International Conference on I-SMAC (IoT in Social, Mobile, Analytics and Cloud), I-SMAC 2021*, 20 – 23. DOI: 10.1109/I-SMAC52330.2021.9640900

Mekala, K., Laxmi, V., Jagruthi, H., Dhondiyal, S. A., Sridevi, R., & Dabral, A. P. (2023). Coffee Price Prediction: An Application of CNN-BLSTM Neural Networks. *Proceedings of the 2nd IEEE International Conference on Advances in Computing, Communication and Applied Informatics, ACCAI 2023*. DOI: 10.1109/ACCAI58221.2023.10199369

Mensah, G. A., Habtegiorgis Abate, Y., Abbasian, M., Abd-Allah, F., Abdollahi, A., Abdollahi, M., Morad Abdulah, D., Abdullahi, A., Abebe, A. M., Abedi, A., Abedi, A., Olusola Abiodun, O., Ali, H. A., Abu-Gharbieh, E., Abu-Rmeileh, N. M. E., Aburuz, S., Abushouk, A. I., Abu-Zaid, A., Adane, T. D., & Roth, G. A. (2023). Global Burden of Cardiovascular Diseases and Risks, 1990-2022. *Journal of the American College of Cardiology*, 82(25), 2350–2473. DOI: 10.1016/j.jacc.2023.11.007 PMID: 38092509

Mesko, B. (2017). The role of artificial intelligence in precision medicine. *Expert Review of Precision Medicine and Drug Development*, 2(5), 239–241. DOI: 10.1080/23808993.2017.1380516

Meskó, B., & Topol, E. J. (2023). The imperative for regulatory oversight of large language models (or generative AI) in healthcare. *NPJ Digital Medicine*, 6(1), 120. DOI: 10.1038/s41746-023-00873-0 PMID: 37414860

Mettler, M. (2016). Blockchain technology in healthcare: The revolution starts here. *IEEE 18th International Conference on e-Health Networking, Applications and Services (Healthcom)*, Munich, Germany, 1 https://doi.org/DOI: 10.1109/HealthCom.2016.7749510

Mia, M., Singh, G., Gupta, M. K., & Sharma, V. S. (2018). Influence of Ranque-Hilsch vortex tube and nitrogen gas assisted MQL in precision turning of Al 6061-T6. *Precision Engineering*, 53, 289–299. DOI: 10.1016/j.precisioneng.2018.04.011

Millard, J. (2017). Technology innovations in public service delivery for sustainable development. *Public Administration and Information Technology*, 32, 241–282. DOI: 10.1007/978-3-319-63743-3_10

Mishra, A. K., & Wazid, M. (2023). Design of a cloud-based security mechanism for Industry 4.0 communication. *ICSCCC 2023 - 3rd International Conference on Secure Cyber Computing and Communications*, 337–343. DOI: 10.1109/ICSCCC58608.2023.10176702

Mishra, A. K., Singh, S., & Upadhyay, R. K. (2023). Organization citizenship behaviour among indian nurses during SARS-COV-2: A direct effect moderation model. *Quality & Quantity*, 57(1), 541–559. DOI: 10.1007/s11135-022-01325-9

Mishra, A., Shah, J. K., Sharma, R., Sharma, M., Joshi, S., & Kaushal, D. (2023). Enhancing Efficiency in Industrial Environments through IoT Connected Worker Solutions: Smart Wearable Technologies for the Workplace. *2023 International Conference on Advances in Computation, Communication and Information Technology, ICAICCIT 2023*, 1175–1179. DOI: 10.1109/ICAICCIT60255.2023.10466100

Mishra, D., Kandpal, V., Agarwal, N., & Srivastava, B. (2024). Financial Inclusion and Its Ripple Effects on Socio-Economic Development: A Comprehensive Review. *Journal of Risk and Financial Management*, 17(3), 105. Advance online publication. DOI: 10.3390/jrfm17030105

Mishra, P., Aggarwal, P., Vidyarthi, A., Singh, P., Khan, B., Alhelou, H. H., & Siano, P. (2021). VMShield: Memory Introspection-Based Malware Detection to Secure Cloud-Based Services against Stealthy Attacks. *IEEE Transactions on Industrial Informatics*, 17(10), 6754–6764. DOI: 10.1109/TII.2020.3048791

Mishra, V., Thakur, S., Patil, A., & Shukla, A. (2018). Quality by design (QbD) approaches in current pharmaceutical set-up. *Expert Opinion on Drug Delivery*, 15(8), 737–758. DOI: 10.1080/17425247.2018.1504768 PMID: 30044646

Mitra, D., Mondal, R., Khoshru, B., Senapati, A., Radha, T. K., Mahakur, B., Uniyal, N., Myo, E. M., Boutaj, H., Sierra, B. E. G. U. E. R. R. A., Panneerselvam, P., Ganeshamurthy, A. N., Elković, S. A. N. Đ. J., Vasić, T., Rani, A., Dutta, S., & Mohapatra, P. K. D. A. S.MITRA. (2022). Actinobacteria-enhanced plant growth, nutrient acquisition, and crop protection: Advances in soil, plant, and microbial multifactorial interactions. *Pedosphere*, 32(1), 149–170. DOI: 10.1016/S1002-0160(21)60042-5

Mitra, D., Saritha, B., Janeeshma, E., Gusain, P., Khoshru, B., Abo Nouh, F. A., Rani, A., Olatunbosun, A. N., Ruparelia, J., Rabari, A., Mosquera-Sánchez, L. P., Mondal, R., Verma, D., Panneerselvam, P., Das Mohapatra, P. K., & Guerra Sierra, B. E. (2022). Arbuscular mycorrhizal fungal association boosted the arsenic resistance in crops with special responsiveness to rice plant. *Environmental and Experimental Botany*, 193. Advance online publication. DOI: 10.1016/j.envexpbot.2021.104681

Modgil, S., Gupta, S., Stekelorum, R., & Laguir, I. (2022). AI technologies and their impact on supply chain resilience during COVID-19. *International Journal of Physical Distribution & Logistics Management*, 52(2), 130–149. DOI: 10.1108/IJPDLM-12-2020-0434

Mohamed, N., Sridhara Rao, L., & Sharma, M. Sureshbaburajasekaranl, Badriasulaimanalfurhood, & Kumar Shukla, S. (2023). In-depth review of integration of AI in cloud computing. *2023 3rd International Conference on Advance Computing and Innovative Technologies in Engineering, ICACITE 2023*, 1431 – 1434. DOI: 10.1109/ICACITE57410.2023.10182738

Mohd, N., Kumar, I., & Khurshid, A. A. (2023). Changing Roles of Intelligent Robotics and Machinery Control Systems as Cyber-Physical Systems (CPS) in the Industry 4.0 Framework. *2023 International Conference on Communication, Security and Artificial Intelligence, ICCSAI 2023*, 647 – 651. DOI: 10.1109/ICCSAI59793.2023.10421085

Molli, V. L. P. (2023). Blockchain Technology for Secure and Transparent Health Data Management: Opportunities and Challenges. *Journal of Healthcare AI and ML*, 10(10), 1–15.

Moneva, J. M., Scarpellini, S., Aranda-Usón, A., & Alvarez Etxeberria, I. (2023). Sustainability reporting in view of the European sustainable finance taxonomy: Is the financial sector ready to disclose circular economy? *Corporate Social Responsibility and Environmental Management*, 30(3), 1336–1347. DOI: 10.1002/csr.2423

Morley, J., Murphy, L., Mishra, A., Joshi, I., & Karpathakis, K. (2022). Governing data and artificial intelligence for health care: Developing an international understanding. *JMIR Formative Research*, 6(1), e31623. DOI: 10.2196/31623 PMID: 35099403

Motwani, A., Shukla, P. K., & Pawar, M. (2022). Ubiquitous and smart healthcare monitoring frameworks based on machine learning: A comprehensive review. *Artificial Intelligence in Medicine*, 134, 102431. DOI: 10.1016/j.artmed.2022.102431 PMID: 36462891

Muheidat, F., & Tawalbeh, L. A. (2023). AIoMT artificial intelligence (AI) and Internet of Medical Things (IoMT): applications, challenges, and future trends. In Computational Intelligence for Medical Internet of Things (MIoT) Applications (pp. 33-54). Academic Press.

Mukul, T., Taneja, S., Özen, E., & Bansal, N. (2024). CHALLENGES AND OPPORTUNITIES FOR SKILL DEVELOPMENT IN DEVELOPING ECONOMIES. *Contemporary Studies in Economic and Financial Analysis*, 112B, 1–22. DOI: 10.1108/S1569-37592024000112B001

Munir, M., Jajja, M. S. S., & Chatha, K. A. (2022). Capabilities for enhancing supply chain resilience and responsiveness in the COVID-19 pandemic: Exploring the role of improvisation, anticipation, and data analytics capabilities. *International Journal of Operations & Production Management*, 42(10), 1576–1604. DOI: 10.1108/IJOPM-11-2021-0677

Murphy, K., Di Ruggiero, E., Upshur, R., Willison, D. J., Malhotra, N., Cai, J. C., Malhotra, N., Lui, V., & Gibson, J. (2021). Artificial intelligence for good health: A scoping review of the ethics literature. *BMC Medical Ethics*, 22(1), 1–17. DOI: 10.1186/s12910-021-00577-8 PMID: 33588803

Nadarzynski, T., Miles, O., Cowie, A., & Ridge, D. (2019). Acceptability of Artificial Intelligence (ai)-led chatbot services in Healthcare: A mixed-methods study. *Digital Health*, 5, 1–7. DOI: 10.1177/2055207619871808 PMID: 31467682

Nadeem, S. P., Garza-Reyes, J. A., & Anosike, A. I. (2023). A C-Lean framework for deploying Circular Economy in manufacturing SMEs. *Production Planning and Control*, 1–21. Advance online publication. DOI: 10.1080/09537287.2023.2294307

Nagaraju, M., & Chawla, P. (2020). Systematic review of deep learning techniques in plant disease detection. *International Journal of System Assurance Engineering and Management*, 11(3), 547–560. DOI: 10.1007/s13198-020-00972-1

Nagila, A., Saravanakumar, P., Pranavan, S., Goutam, R., Dobhal, D. C., & Singh, G. (2023). An Innovative Approach of CNN-BiGRU Based Post-Earthquake Damage Detection of Reinforced Concrete for Frame Buildings. *International Conference on Self Sustainable Artificial Intelligence Systems, ICSSAS 2023 - Proceedings*, 56 – 61. DOI: 10.1109/ICSSAS57918.2023.10331894

Naim, A., & Khan, F. (2024). The utilization of AI in advancing green supply chain management focusing healthcare sector in Saudi Arabia. *Journal of Information and Optimization Sciences*, 45(3), 747–763. DOI: 10.47974/JIOS-1510

Nainwal, P., Lall, S., & Nawaz, A. (2022). Physiochemical characterization of silver nanoparticles using rhizome extract of Alpinia galanga and its antimicrobial activity. *Journal of Medical Pharmaceutical and Allied Sciences. Int. Confe*, (2), 219–223. DOI: 10.22270/jmpas.VIC2I2.1830

Naithani, D., Khandelwal, R. R., & Garg, N. (2023). Development of an Automobile Hardware-in-the-Loop Test System with CAN Communication. *Proceedings of the 2023 2nd International Conference on Augmented Intelligence and Sustainable Systems, ICAISS 2023*, 1653 – 1656. DOI: 10.1109/ICAISS58487.2023.10250529

Naveen, Y., Lokanadham, D., Naidu, D. R., Sharma, R. C., Palli, S., & Lila, M. K. (2023). An Experimental Study on the Influence of Blended Karanja Biodiesel on Diesel Engine Characteristics. *International Journal of Vehicle Structures and Systems*, 15(2), 154–160. DOI: 10.4273/ijvss.15.2.02

Nedeljko, M., Gu, Y., & Bostan, C. M. (2024). The dual impact of technological tools on health and technostress among older workers: An integrative literature review. *Cognition Technology and Work*, 26(1), 47–61. DOI: 10.1007/s10111-023-00741-7

Negi, D., Sah, A., Rawat, S., Choudhury, T., & Khanna, A. (2021). Block Chain Platforms and Smart Contracts. *EAI/Springer Innovations in Communication and Computing*, 65 – 76. DOI: 10.1007/978-3-030-65691-1_5

Negi, S. S., Memoria, M., Kumar, R., Joshi, K., Pandey, S. D., & Gupta, A. (2022, November). Machine learning based hybrid technique for heart disease prediction. In *2022 International Conference on Advances in Computing, Communication and Materials (ICACCM)* (pp. 1-6). IEEE. DOI: 10.1109/ICACCM56405.2022.10009219

Neha, M., S., Alfurhood, B. S., Bakhare, R., Poongavanam, S., & Khanna, R. (2023). The Role and Impact of Artificial Intelligence on Retail Business and its Developments. *2023 International Conference on Artificial Intelligence and Smart Communication, AISC 2023*, 1098–1101. DOI: 10.1109/AISC56616.2023.10085624

Nethravathi, K., Tiwari, A., Uike, D., Jaiswal, R., & Pant, K. (2022). Applications of Artificial Intelligence and Blockchain Technology in Improved Supply Chain Financial Risk Management. *Proceedings of 5th International Conference on Contemporary Computing and Informatics, IC3I 2022*, 242 – 246. DOI: 10.1109/IC3I56241.2022.10072787

Ngwenya, M., Muthelo, L., Oupa Mbombi, M., Adelaide Bopape, M., & Maria Mothiba, T. (2022). Utilisation of Digital Health in Early Detection and Treatment of Pre-Eclampsia in Primary Health Care Facilities South Africa: Literature Review. DOI:DOI: 10.5772/intechopen.101228

Nikolaidis, P., Ismail, M., Shuib, L., Khan, S., & Dhiman, G. (2022). Predicting Student Attrition in Higher Education through the Determinants of Learning Progress: A Structural Equation Modelling Approach. *Sustainability (Basel)*, 14(20), 13584. Advance online publication. DOI: 10.3390/su142013584

Nimrod, G. (2020). Technostress: Measuring a New Threat to Well-being in Later Life. *Aging & Mental Health*, 24(10), 1503–1508. PMID: 28562064

Niu, S., Ma, J., Yin, Q., Wang, Z., Bai, L., & Yang, X. (2024). Modelling Patient Longitudinal Data for Clinical Decision Support: A Case Study on Emerging AI Healthcare Technologies. *Information Systems Frontiers*, •••, 1–19. DOI: 10.1007/s10796-024-10513-x

Nkwanyana, N. (2022). Key barriers to digital health interventions in South Africa: Systematic scoping review. *2022 IEEE 20th Jubilee International Symposium on Intelligent Systems and Informatics (SISY)*, pp. 000019-000024, DOI:DOI: 10.1109/SISY56759.2022.10036322

Nyambuu, U., & Semmler, W. (2023). Climate Risks, Sustainable Finance, and Climate Policy. *Contributions to Economics*, (Part F32), 171–190. DOI: 10.1007/978-3-031-27982-9_11

Onyema, E. M., Almuzaini, K. K., Onu, F. U., Verma, D., Gregory, U. S., Puttaramaiah, M., & Afriyie, R. K. (2022). Prospects and Challenges of Using Machine Learning for Academic Forecasting. *Computational Intelligence and Neuroscience*, 2022, 1–7. Advance online publication. DOI: 10.1155/2022/5624475 PMID: 35909823

Oren, O., Gersh, B. J., & Bhatt, D. L. (2020). Artificial intelligence in medical imaging: Switching from radiographic pathological data to clinically meaningful endpoints. *The Lancet. Digital Health*, 2(9), e486–e488. DOI: 10.1016/S2589-7500(20)30160-6 PMID: 33328116

Osama, M., Ateya, A. A., Sayed, M. S., Hammad, M., Pławiak, P., Abd El-Latif, A. A., & Elsayed, R. A. (2023). Internet of medical things and healthcare 4.0: Trends, requirements, challenges, and research directions. *Sensors (Basel)*, 23(17), 7435. DOI: 10.3390/s23177435 PMID: 37687891

Overview of Precision Medicine.(n.d) Thermo Fisher Scientific - US. Retrieved November 1, 2022, from https://www.thermofisher.com/us/en/home/clinical/precision-medicine/precision-medicine-learning-center/precision-medicine-resource-library/precision-medicine-articles/overview-precision-medicine.html

Padhi, B. K., Singh, S., Gaidhane, A. M., Abu Serhan, H., Khatib, M. N., Zahiruddin, Q. S., Rustagi, S., Sharma, R. K., Sharma, D., Arora, M., & Satapathy, P. (2024). Inequalities in cardiovascular disease among elderly Indians: A gender perspective analysis using LASI wave-I (2017-18). *Current Problems in Cardiology*, 49(7), 102605. Advance online publication. DOI: 10.1016/j.cpcardiol.2024.102605 PMID: 38692448

Pai, H. A., Almuzaini, K. K., Ali, L., Javeed, A., Pant, B., Pareek, P. K., & Akwafo, R. (2022). Delay-Driven Opportunistic Routing with Multichannel Cooperative Neighbor Discovery for Industry 4.0 Wireless Networks Based on Power and Load Awareness. *Wireless Communications and Mobile Computing*, 2022, 1–12. Advance online publication. DOI: 10.1155/2022/5256133

Pai, V. V., & Pai, R. B. (2021). Artificial intelligence in dermatology and healthcare: An overview. *Indian Journal of Dermatology, Venereology and Leprology*, 87(4), 457–467. DOI: 10.25259/IJDVL_518_19 PMID: 34114421

Pallavi, B., Othman, B., Trivedi, G., Manan, N., Pawar, R. S., & Singh, D. P. (2022). The Application of the Internet of Things (IoT) to establish a technologically advanced Industry 4.0 for long-term growth and development. *2022 2nd International Conference on Advance Computing and Innovative Technologies in Engineering, ICACITE 2022*, 1927 – 1932. DOI: 10.1109/ICACITE53722.2022.9823481

Panda, S. K., Aggarwal, I., Kumar, H., Prasad, L., Kumar, A., Sharma, A., Vo, D.-V. N., Van Thuan, D., & Mishra, V. (2021). Magnetite nanoparticles as sorbents for dye removal: A review. *Environmental Chemistry Letters*, 19(3), 2487–2525. DOI: 10.1007/s10311-020-01173-9

Pande, S. D., Bhatt, A., Chamoli, S., Saini, D. K. J. B., Kute, U. T., & Ahammad, S. H. (2023). Design of Atmel PLC and its Application as Automation of Coal Handling Plant. *2023 International Conference on Sustainable Emerging Innovations in Engineering and Technology, ICSEIET 2023*, 178 – 183. https://doi.org/DOI: 10.1109/ICSEIET58677.2023.10303627

Pandey, N. K., Kashyap, S., Sharma, A., & Diwakar, M. (2023). Contribution of Cloud-Based Services in Post-Pandemic Technology Sustainability and Challenges: A Future Direction. In *Evolving Networking Technologies: Developments and Future Directions*. wiley. DOI: 10.1002/9781119836667.ch4

Pandey, P., Mayank, K., & Sharma, S. (2023). Recommendation System for Adventure Tourism. *2023 4th IEEE Global Conference for Advancement in Technology, GCAT 2023*. DOI: 10.1109/GCAT59970.2023.10353339

Pandey, T., Batra, A., Chaudhary, M., Ranakoti, A., Kumar, A., & Ram, M. (2023). Computation Signature Reliability of Computer Numerical Control System Using Universal Generating Function. *Springer Series in Reliability Engineering*, 149 – 158. https://doi.org/DOI: 10.1007/978-3-031-05347-4_10

Pandey, K., Joshi, H., Paliwal, S., Pawar, S., & Kumar, N. (2020). Technology transfer: An overview of process transfer from development to commercialization. *International Journal of Current Research and Review*, 12(19), 188–192. DOI: 10.31782/IJCRR.2020.121913

Pandey, K., Paliwal, S., Joshi, H., Bisht, N., & Kumar, N. (2022). A review on change control: A critical process of the pharmaceutical industry. *Journal of Medical Pharmaceutical and Allied Sciences*, 11(2), 4588–4592. DOI: 10.55522/jmpas.V11I2.2077

Pandey, R. P., Bansal, S., Awasthi, P., Dixit, V., Singh, R., & Yadava, V. (2023). Attitude and Myths Related to Stalking among Early and Middle Age Adults. *Psychology Hub*, 40(3), 85 – 94. DOI: 10.13133/2724-2943/17960

Pandya, D. J., Kumar, Y., Singh, D. P., Vairavel, D. K., Deepak, A., Rao, A. K., & Rana, A. (2023). Automatic Power Factor Compensation for Industrial Use to Minimize Penalty. *Proceedings of International Conference on Contemporary Computing and Informatics, IC3I 2023*, 2499 – 2504. DOI: 10.1109/IC3I59117.2023.10398095

Pant, R., Gupta, A., Pant, G., Chaubey, K. K., Kumar, G., & Patrick, N. (2022). Second-generation biofuels: Facts and future. In *Relationship between Microbes and the Environment for Sustainable Ecosystem Services: Microbial Tools for Sustainable Ecosystem Services: Volume 3* (Vol. 3). Elsevier. DOI: 10.1016/B978-0-323-89936-9.00011-4

Pant, V., Bhasin, S., & Jain, S. (2017). Self-Learning system for personalized E-Learning. *2017 International Conference on Emerging Trends in Computing and Communication Technologies, ICETCCT 2017*, 2018-Janua, 1 – 6. DOI: 10.1109/ICETCCT.2017.8280344

Papageorgiou, G., Loukis, E., Pappas, G., Rizun, N., Saxena, S., Charalabidis, Y., & Alexopoulos, C. (2023). Open Government Data in Educational Programs Curriculum: Current State and Prospects. *Lecture Notes in Business Information Processing*, 493 LNBIP, 311 – 326. DOI: 10.1007/978-3-031-43126-5_22

Park, T., Kim, H., Song, S., & Griggs, S. K. (2022). Economic Evaluation of Pharmacist-Led Digital Health Interventions: A Systematic Review. *International Journal of Environmental Research and Public Health*, 19(19), 11996. DOI: 10.3390/ijerph191911996 PMID: 36231307

Partiti, E. (2024). Addressing the Flaws of the Sustainable Finance Disclosure Regulation: Moving from Disclosures to Labelling and Sustainability Due Diligence. *European Business Organization Law Review*, 25(2), 299–332. DOI: 10.1007/s40804-024-00317-6

Patel, S. (2011). Harmful and beneficial aspects of Parthenium hysterophorus: An update. *3 Biotech*, 1(1), 1 – 9. DOI: 10.1007/s13205-011-0007-7

Pathak, P., Singh, M. P., Badhotiya, G. K., & Chauhan, A. S. (2021). Identification of Drivers and Barriers of Sustainable Manufacturing. *Lecture Notes on Multidisciplinary Industrial Engineering*, (Part F254), 227–243. DOI: 10.1007/978-981-15-4550-4_14

Patil, S. (2021, May 28). *TOP 5 USE CASES OF ARTIFICIAL INTELLIGENCE IN MEDICAL IMAGING*. Analytics Insight. Retrieved November 3, 2022, from https://www.analyticsinsight.net/top-5-use-cases-of-artificial-intelligence-in-medical-imaging/

Patil, S. P., Singh, B., Bisht, J., Gupta, S., & Khanna, R. (2021). Yoga for holistic treatment of polycystic ovarian syndrome. *Journal of Medical Pharmaceutical and Allied Sciences*, 10, 120–125. DOI: 10.22270/jmpas.VIC2I1.2035

Patrick, M. T., Stuart, P. E., Raja, K., Gudjonsson, J. E., Tejasvi, T., Yang, J., Chandran, V., Das, S., Callis-Duffin, K., Ellinghaus, E., Enerbäck, C., Esko, T., Franke, A., Kang, H. M., Krueger, G. G., Lim, H. W., Rahman, P., Rosen, C. F., Weidinger, S., & Tsoi, L. C. (2018). Genetic signature to provide robust risk assessment of psoriatic arthritis development in psoriasis patients. *Nature Communications*, 9(1), 4178. DOI: 10.1038/s41467-018-06672-6 PMID: 30301895

Pattanshetti, M. K., Jasola, S., Rajput, A., & Pant, V. (2021). Proposed eLearning framework using open corpus web resources. *Proceedings of the 2021 1st International Conference on Advances in Electrical, Computing, Communications and Sustainable Technologies, ICAECT 2021*. DOI: 10.1109/ICAECT49130.2021.9392591

Paul, S. N., Mishra, A. K., & Upadhyay, R. K. (2022). Locus of control and investment decision: An investor's perspective. *International Journal of Services. Economics and Management*, 13(2), 93–107. DOI: 10.1504/IJSEM.2022.122736

Pimenta, S., Hansen, H., Demeyer, H., Slevin, P., & Cruz, J. (2023). Role of digital health in pulmonary rehabilitation and beyond: Shaping the future. *ERJ Open Research*, 9(2), 00212–02022. DOI: 10.1183/23120541.00212-2022 PMID: 36923569

Pithode, K., Singh, D., Chaturvedi, R., Goyal, B., Dogra, A., Hasoon, A., & Lepcha, D. C. (2023). Evaluation of the Solar Heat Pipe with Aluminium Tube Collector in different Environmental Conditions. *2023 3rd Asian Conference on Innovation in Technology, ASIANCON 2023*. DOI: 10.1109/ASIANCON58793.2023.10269867

Pokrajac, L., Abbas, A., Chrzanowski, W., Dias, G. M., Eggleton, B. J., Maguire, S., Maine, E., Malloy, T., Nathwani, J., Nazar, L., Sips, A., Sone, J., Van Den Berg, A., Weiss, P. S., & Mitra, S. (2021). Nanotechnology for a Sustainable Future: Addressing global challenges with the international network4 sustainable nanotechnology. *ACS Nano*, 15(12), 18608–18623. DOI: 10.1021/acsnano.1c10919 PMID: 34910476

Poswal, P., Chauhan, A., Aarya, D. D., Boadh, R., Rajoria, Y. K., & Gaiola, S. U. (2022). Optimal strategy for remanufacturing system of sustainable products with trade credit under uncertain scenario. *Materials Today: Proceedings*, 69, 165–173. DOI: 10.1016/j.matpr.2022.08.303

Prabhakar, P. K., Prasad, R., Ali, S., & Doble, M. (2013). Synergistic interaction of ferulic acid with commercial hypoglycemic drugs in streptozotocin induced diabetic rats. *Phytomedicine*, 20(6), 488–494. DOI: 10.1016/j.phymed.2012.12.004 PMID: 23490007

Praet, J., Anderhalten, L., Comi, G., Horakova, D., Ziemssen, T., Vermersch, P., Lukas, C., van Leemput, K., Steppe, M., Aguilera, C., Kadas, E. M., Bertrand, A., van Rampelbergh, J., de Boer, E., Zingler, V., Smeets, D., Ribbens, A., & Paul, F. (2024). A future of AI-driven personalized care for people with multiple sclerosis. *Frontiers in Immunology*, 15, 1446748. DOI: 10.3389/fimmu.2024.1446748 PMID: 39224590

Prakash, C., & Uddin, M. S. (2017). Surface modification of β-phase Ti implant by hydroaxyapatite mixed electric discharge machining to enhance the corrosion resistance and in-vitro bioactivity. *Surface and Coatings Technology*, 326, 134–145. DOI: 10.1016/j.surfcoat.2017.07.040

Prakash, S., Balaji, J. N., Joshi, A., & Surapaneni, K. M. (2022). Ethical Conundrums in the application of artificial intelligence (AI) in healthcare—A scoping review of reviews. *Journal of Personalized Medicine*, 12(11), 1914. DOI: 10.3390/jpm12111914 PMID: 36422090

Prasad, A. O., Mishra, P., Jain, U., Pandey, A., Sinha, A., Yadav, A. S., Kumar, R., Sharma, A., Kumar, G., Hazim Salem, K., Sharma, A., & Dixit, A. K. (2023). Design and development of software stack of an autonomous vehicle using robot operating system. *Robotics and Autonomous Systems*, 161, 104340. Advance online publication. DOI: 10.1016/j.robot.2022.104340

Prashar, D., Jha, N., Jha, S., Lee, Y., & Joshi, G. P. (2020). Blockchain-based traceability and visibility for agricultural products: A decentralizedway of ensuring food safety in India. *Sustainability (Basel)*, 12(8), 3497. Advance online publication. DOI: 10.3390/su12083497

Praveenchandar, J., Vetrithangam, D., Kaliappan, S., Karthick, M., Pegada, N. K., Patil, P. P., Rao, S. G., & Umar, S. (2022). IoT-Based Harmful Toxic Gases Monitoring and Fault Detection on the Sensor Dataset Using Deep Learning Techniques. *Scientific Programming*, 2022, 1–11. Advance online publication. DOI: 10.1155/2022/7516328

Prikshat, V., Kumar, S., & Nankervis, A. (2019). Work-readiness integrated competence model: Conceptualisation and scale development. *Education + Training*, 61(5), 568–589. DOI: 10.1108/ET-05-2018-0114

Prikshat, V., Kumar, S., & Raje, P. (2017). Antecedents, consequences and strategic responses to graduate work-readiness: Challenges in India. In *Transitions from Education to Work: Workforce Ready Challenges in the Asia Pacific*. Taylor and Francis., DOI: 10.4324/9781315533971-8

Qureshi, A. S., & Roos, T. (2023). Transfer learning with ensembles of deep neural networks for skin cancer detection in imbalanced data sets. *Neural Processing Letters*, 55(4), 4461–4479. DOI: 10.1007/s11063-022-11049-4

Radiation-emitting products(2020). Center for Devices and Radiological Health. U.S. Food and Drug Administration. Retrieved November 2, 2022, from https://www.fda.gov/radiation-emitting-products

Ragu-Nathan, T. S., Tarafdar, M., Ragu-Nathan, B. S., & Tu, Q. (2008). The consequences of technostress for end-users in organizations: Conceptual development and empirical validation. *Information Systems Research*, 19(4), 417–433. DOI: 10.1287/isre.1070.0165

Rai, K., Mishra, N., & Mishra, S. (2022). Forest Fire Risk Zonation Mapping using Fuzzy Overlay Analysis of Nainital District. *2022 International Mobile and Embedded Technology Conference, MECON 2022*, 522 – 526. DOI: 10.1109/MECON53876.2022.9751812

Raja, S., Agrawal, A. P. P., Patil, P., Thimothy, P., Capangpangan, R. Y., Singhal, P., & Wotango, M. T. (2022). Optimization of 3D Printing Process Parameters of Polylactic Acid Filament Based on the Mechanical Test. *International Journal of Chemical Engineering*, 2022, 1–7. Advance online publication. DOI: 10.1155/2022/5830869

Rajawat, A. S., Singh, S., Gangil, B., Ranakoti, L., Sharma, S., Asyraf, M. R. M., & Razman, M. R. (2022). Effect of Marble Dust on the Mechanical, Morphological, and Wear Performance of Basalt Fibre-Reinforced Epoxy Composites for Structural Applications. *Polymers*, 14(7), 1325. Advance online publication. DOI: 10.3390/polym14071325 PMID: 35406199

Rajbalaji, S., Raman, R., Pant, B., Rathour, N., Rajagopa, B. R., & Prasad, C. R. (2023). Design of deep learning models for the identifications of harmful attack activities in IIOT. *2023 International Conference on Artificial Intelligence and Smart Communication, AISC 2023*, 609 – 613. DOI: 10.1109/AISC56616.2023.10085088

Rajeswari, M., Kumar, N., Raman, P., Patjoshi, P. K., Singh, V., & Pundir, S. (2022). Optimal Analysis for Enterprise Financial Management Based on Artificial Intelligence and Parallel Computing Method. *Proceedings of 5th International Conference on Contemporary Computing and Informatics, IC3I 2022*, 2081 – 2086. DOI: 10.1109/IC3I56241.2022.10072851

Raju, K., Balakrishnan, M., Prasad, D. V. S. S. S. V., Nagalakshmi, V., Patil, P. P., Kaliappan, S., Arulmurugan, B., Radhakrishnan, K., Velusamy, B., Paramasivam, P., & El-Denglawey, A. (2022). Optimization of WEDM Process Parameters in Al2024-Li-Si3N4MMC. *Journal of Nanomaterials*, 2022(1), 2903385. Advance online publication. DOI: 10.1155/2022/2903385

Rakhra, M., Bhargava, A., Bhargava, D., Singh, R., Bhanot, A., & Rahmani, A. W. (2022). Implementing Machine Learning for Supply-Demand Shifts and Price Impacts in Farmer Market for Tool and Equipment Sharing. *Journal of Food Quality*, 2022, 1–19. Advance online publication. DOI: 10.1155/2022/4496449

Ramachandran, K. K., Lamba, F. L. R., Rawat, R., Gehlot, A., Raju, A. M., & Ponnusamy, R. (2023). An Investigation of Block Chains for Attaining Sustainable Society. *2023 3rd International Conference on Advance Computing and Innovative Technologies in Engineering, ICACITE 2023*, 1069 – 1076. DOI: 10.1109/ICACITE57410.2023.10182462

Ramakrishnan, T., Mohan Gift, M. D., Chitradevi, S., Jegan, R., Subha Hency Jose, P., Nagaraja, H. N., Sharma, R., Selvakumar, P., & Hailegiorgis, S. M. (2022). Study of Numerous Resins Used in Polymer Matrix Composite Materials. *Advances in Materials Science and Engineering*, 2022, 1–8. Advance online publication. DOI: 10.1155/2022/1088926

Raman, R., Kumar, R., Ghai, S., Gehlot, A., Raju, A. M., & Barve, A. (2023). A New Method of Optical Spectrum Analysis for Advanced Wireless Communications. *2023 3rd International Conference on Advance Computing and Innovative Technologies in Engineering, ICACITE 2023*, 1719 – 1723. DOI: 10.1109/ICACITE57410.2023.10182414

Raman, R., Buddhi, D., Lakhera, G., Gupta, Z., Joshi, A., & Saini, D. (2023). An investigation on the role of artificial intelligence in scalable visual data analytics. *2023 International Conference on Artificial Intelligence and Smart Communication, AISC 2023*, 666–670. DOI: 10.1109/AISC56616.2023.10085495

Ramesh, S. M., Rajeshkannan, S., Pundir, S., Dhaliwal, N., Mishra, S., & Saravana, B. S. (2023). Design and Development of Embedded Controller with Wireless Sensor for Power Monitoring through Smart Interface Design Models. *Proceedings of the 2023 2nd International Conference on Augmented Intelligence and Sustainable Systems, ICAISS 2023*, 1817–1821. DOI: 10.1109/ICAISS58487.2023.10250506

Ram, M., Bhandari, A. S., & Kumar, A. (2022). Reliability Evaluation and Cost Optimization of Solar Road Studs. *International Journal of Reliability Quality and Safety Engineering*, 29(1), 2150041. Advance online publication. DOI: 10.1142/S0218539321500418

Ram, M., Bisht, D. C. S., Goyal, N., Kazancoglu, Y., & Mathirajan, M. (2022). Newly developed mathematical methodologies and advancements in a variety of engineering and management domains. *Mathematics in Engineering. Science and Aerospace*, 13(3), 559–562.

Ram, M., Negi, G., Goyal, N., & Kumar, A. (2022). Analysis of a Stochastic Model with Rework System. *Journal of Reliability and Statistical Studies*, 15(2), 553–582. DOI: 10.13052/jrss0974-8024.1527

Ram, M., & Xing, L. (2023). Reliability Modeling in Industry 4.0. In *Reliability Modeling in Industry 4.0*. Elsevier., DOI: 10.1016/C2021-0-01679-5

Rana, M. S., Cavaliere, L. P. L., Mishra, A. B., Padhye, P., Singh, R. R., & Khanna, R. (2022). Internet of Things (IOT) Based Assessment for Effective Monitoring Data Against Malicious Attacks on Financial Collectors. *2022 2nd International Conference on Advance Computing and Innovative Technologies in Engineering, ICACITE 2022*, 177–181. DOI: 10.1109/ICACITE53722.2022.9823612

Rana, M. S., Dixit, A. K., Rajan, M. S., Malhotra, S., Radhika, S., & Pant, B. (2022). An Empirical Investigation in Applying Reliable Industry 4.0 Based Machine Learning (ML) Approaches in Analysing and Monitoring Smart Meters using Multivariate Analysis of Variance (Manova). *2022 2nd International Conference on Advance Computing and Innovative Technologies in Engineering, ICACITE 2022*, 603–607. https://doi.org/DOI: 10.1109/ICACITE53722.2022.9823597

Rana, D. S., Dimri, S. C., Malik, P., & Dhondiyal, S. A. (2022). Impact of Computational Thinking in Engineering and K12 Education. *4th International Conference on Inventive Research in Computing Applications, ICIRCA 2022 - Proceedings*, 697–701. DOI: 10.1109/ICIRCA54612.2022.9985593

Ranakoti, L., Gangil, B., Mishra, S. K., Singh, T., Sharma, S., Ilyas, R. A., & El-Khatib, S. (2022). Critical Review on Polylactic Acid: Properties, Structure, Processing, Biocomposites, and Nanocomposites. *Materials (Basel)*, 15(12), 4312. Advance online publication. DOI: 10.3390/ma15124312 PMID: 35744371

Rao, K. V. G., Kumar, M. K., Goud, B. S., Krishna, D., Bajaj, M., Saini, P., & Choudhury, S. (2023). IOT-Powered Crop Shield System for Surveillance and Auto Transversum. *2023 IEEE 3rd International Conference on Sustainable Energy and Future Electric Transportation, SeFet 2023*. DOI: 10.1109/SeFeT57834.2023.10245773

Rathert, C., Mittler, J. N., Banerjee, S., & McDaniel, J. (2017). Patient-centered communication in the era of electronic health records: What does the evidence say? *Patient Education and Counseling*, 100(1), 50–64. DOI: 10.1016/j.pec.2016.07.031 PMID: 27477917

Rathod, N. J., Chopra, M. K., Shelke, S. N., Chaurasiya, P. K., Kumar, R., Saxena, K. K., & Prakash, C. (2024). Investigations on hard turning using SS304 sheet metal component grey based Taguchi and regression methodology. *International Journal on Interactive Design and Manufacturing*, 18(5), 2653–2664. DOI: 10.1007/s12008-023-01244-5

Rathore, R., & Goudar, R. H. (2015). SPARQL-based personalised E-Learning system designed using ontology (SPELSO): An architecture. *International Journal of Knowledge and Learning*, 10(4), 384–416. DOI: 10.1504/IJKL.2015.077554

Rawat, R., Goyal, H. R., & Sharma, S. (2023). Artificial Narrow Intelligence Techniques in Intelligent Digital Financial Inclusion System for Digital Society. *2023 6th International Conference on Information Systems and Computer Networks, ISCON 2023*. DOI: 10.1109/ISCON57294.2023.10112133

Rawat, R., Mahor, V., Chouhan, M., Pachlasiya, K., Telang, S., & Garg, B. (2022). Systematic Literature Review (SLR) on Social Media and the Digital Transformation of Drug Trafficking on Darkweb. *Lecture Notes in Networks and Systems, 481 LNNS*, 181 – 205. DOI: 10.1007/978-981-19-3182-6_15

Rawat, B., Rawat, J. M., Purohit, S., Singh, G., Sharma, P. K., Chandra, A., Shabaaz Begum, J. P., Venugopal, D., Jaremko, M., & Qureshi, K. A. (2022). A comprehensive review of Quercus semecarpifolia Sm.: An ecologically and commercially important Himalayan tree. *Frontiers in Ecology and Evolution*, 10, 961345. Advance online publication. DOI: 10.3389/fevo.2022.961345

Rawat, D., Kumar, V., Gautam, G., Sharma, M., & Sonsare, P. K. (2023). Watershed Management and Sustainability. *2023 International Conference on Communication, Security and Artificial Intelligence, ICCSAI 2023*, 676 – 679. DOI: 10.1109/ICCSAI59793.2023.10421450

Rawat, R. S., Singh, V., & Dumka, A. (2022). Complaint Management in Ethiopian Vocational and Technical Education Institutions: A Framework and Implementation of a Decision Support System. *2022 International Conference on 4th Industrial Revolution Based Technology and Practices, ICFIRTP 2022*, 73 – 79. DOI: 10.1109/ICFIRTP56122.2022.10063207

Rawat, R., Sharma, S., & Goyal, H. R. (2023). Intelligent Digital Financial Inclusion System Architectures for Industry 5.0 Enabled Digital Society. *Winter Summit on Smart Computing and Networks. WiSSCoN*, 2023, 1–5. Advance online publication. DOI: 10.1109/WiSSCoN56857.2023.10133858

Rawat, S. S., Pant, S., Kumar, A., Ram, M., Sharma, H. K., & Kumar, A. (2022). A State-of-the-Art Survey on Analytical Hierarchy Process Applications in Sustainable Development. *International Journal of Mathematical. Engineering and Management Sciences*, 7(6), 883–917. DOI: 10.33889/IJMEMS.2022.7.6.056

Rawstorn, J. C., Subedi, N., Koorts, H., Evans, L., Cartledge, S., Wallen, M. P., Grace, F. M., Islam, S. M. S., & Maddison, R. (2024). Stakeholder perceptions of factors contributing to effective implementation of exercise cardiac telerehabilitation in clinical practice. *European Journal of Cardiovascular Nursing*, •••, zvae127. Advance online publication. DOI: 10.1093/eurjcn/zvae127 PMID: 39352400

Raza, K., Thotakura, N., Kumar, P., Joshi, M., Bhushan, S., Bhatia, A., Kumar, V., Malik, R., Sharma, G., Guru, S. K., & Katare, O. P. (2015). C60-fullerenes for delivery of docetaxel to breast cancer cells: A promising approach for enhanced efficacy and better pharmacokinetic profile. *International Journal of Pharmaceutics*, 495(1), 551–559. DOI: 10.1016/j.ijpharm.2015.09.016 PMID: 26383841

Reddy, P. N., Umaeswari, P., Natrayan, L., & Choudhary, A. (2023). Development of Programmed Autonomous Electric Heavy Vehicle: An Application of IoT. *Proceedings of the 2023 2nd International Conference on Electronics and Renewable Systems, ICEARS 2023*, 506 – 510. https://doi.org/DOI: 10.1109/ICEARS56392.2023.10085492

Reepu, R., Taneja, S., Ozen, E., & Singh, A. (2023). A globetrotter to the future of marketing: Metaverse. In *Cultural Marketing and Metaverse for Consumer Engagement*. IGI Global., DOI: 10.4018/978-1-6684-8312-1.ch001

Rejeb, A., Rejeb, K., Treiblmaier, H., Appolloni, A., Alghamdi, S., Alhasawi, Y., & Iranmanesh, M. (2023). The Internet of Things (IoT) in healthcare: Taking stock and moving forward. *Internet of Things : Engineering Cyber Physical Human Systems*, 22, 100721. DOI: 10.1016/j.iot.2023.100721

Ren, X., Li, C., Ma, X., Chen, F., Wang, H., Sharma, A., Gaba, G. S., & Masud, M. (2021). Design of multi-information fusion based intelligent electrical fire detection system for green buildings. *Sustainability (Basel)*, 13(6), 3405. Advance online publication. DOI: 10.3390/su13063405

Ritika, B., Bora, B., Ismail, B. B., Garba, U., Mishra, S., Jha, A. K., Naik, B., Kumar, V., Rather, M. A., Rizwana, , Preet, M. S., Rustagi, S., Kumar, H., & Gupta, A. K. (2024). Himalayan fruit and circular economy: Nutraceutical potential, traditional uses, challenges and opportunities. *Food Production. Processing and Nutrition*, 6(1), 71. Advance online publication. DOI: 10.1186/s43014-023-00220-6

Robotic surgery: The role of AI and Collaborative Robots(2019). *Robotics Online Marketing Team. Automate*. Retrieved November 2, 2022, from https://www.automate.org/blogs/robotic-surgery-the-role-of-ai-and-collaborative-robots

Rojas, Graciela & Martínez, Vania & Martínez, Pablo & Franco, Pamela & Jiménez, Álvaro. (2019). Improving Mental Health Care in Developing Countries Through Digital Technologies: A Mini Narrative Review of the Chilean Case. Frontiers in Public Health. 7. . DOI:DOI: 10.3389/fpubh.2019.00391

Rosenberg, L. (2012). Are healthcare leaders ready for the real revolution? *The Journal of Behavioral Health Services & Research*, 39(3), 215–219. DOI: 10.1007/s11414-012-9285-z PMID: 22736047

Rosen, J. M., Adams, L. V., Geiling, J., Curtis, K. M., Mosher, R. E., Ball, P. A., Grigg, E. B., Hebert, K. A., Grodan, J. R., Jurmain, J. C., Loucks, C., Macedonia, C. R., & Kun, L. (2021). Telehealth's new horizon: Providing smart hospital-level care in the home. *Telemedicine Journal and e-Health*, 27(11), 1215–1224. DOI: 10.1089/tmj.2020.0448 PMID: 33656918

Rosman, R., Redzuan, N. H., & Shaharuddin, S. S. a'. (2024). Instruments of Islamic Sustainable Finance. In *Islamic Finance and Sustainable Development: A Global Framework for Achieving Sustainable Impact Finance*. Taylor and Francis. DOI: 10.4324/9781003468653-9

Roy, S., & Mitra, M. (2021). Enhancing Efficiency in Healthcare Supply Chains: Leveraging Machine Learning for Optimized Operations. *International Journal For Multidisciplinary Research*, 3(2), 10–36948.

Ryan, M., Antoniou, J., Brooks, L., Jiya, T., Macnish, K., & Stahl, B. (2020). The ethical balance of using smart information systems for promoting the United Nations' sustainable development goals. *Sustainability (Basel)*, 12(12), 4826. Advance online publication. DOI: 10.3390/su12124826

Sachs, J. D., Schmidt-Traub, G., Mazzucato, M., Messner, D., Nakicenovic, N., & Rockström, J. (2019). Six transformations to achieve the Sustainable development goals. *Nature Sustainability*, 2(9), 805–814. DOI: 10.1038/s41893-019-0352-9

Sætra, H. S. (2021). Ai in context and the sustainable development goals: Factoring in the unsustainability of the sociotechnical system. *Sustainability (Basel)*, 13(4), 1–19. DOI: 10.3390/su13041738

Saggu, S., Sakeran, M. I., Zidan, N., Tousson, E., Mohan, A., & Rehman, H. (2014). Ameliorating effect of chicory (Chichorium intybus L.) fruit extract against 4-tert-octylphenol induced liver injury and oxidative stress in male rats. *Food and Chemical Toxicology*, 72, 138–146. DOI: 10.1016/j.fct.2014.06.029 PMID: 25010453

Sahni, N., Stein, G., Zemmel, R., & Cutler, D. M. (2023). *The potential impact of artificial intelligence on healthcare spending* (No. w30857). Cambridge, MA, USA: National Bureau of Economic Research.

Sahu, S. R., & Rawat, K. S. (2023). Analysis of Land subsidencein coastal and urban areas by using various techniques– Literature Review. *The Indonesian Journal of Geography*, 55(3), 488–495. DOI: 10.22146/ijg.83675

Saini, S., Sachdeva, L., & Badhotiya, G. K. (2022). Sustainable Human Resource Management: A Conceptual Framework. *ECS Transactions*, 107(1), 6455–6463. DOI: 10.1149/10701.6455ecst

Sajedi, H., & Mohammadipanah, F. (2024). Global data sharing of SARS-CoV-2 based on blockchain. *International Journal of Information Technology : an Official Journal of Bharati Vidyapeeth's Institute of Computer Applications and Management*, 16(3), 1559–1567. DOI: 10.1007/s41870-023-01431-3

Salama, R., Al-Turjman, F., Bordoloi, D., & Yadav, S. P. (2023). Wireless Sensor Networks and Green Networking for 6G communication- An Overview. *2023 International Conference on Computational Intelligence, Communication Technology and Networking, CICTN 2023*, 830 – 834. DOI: 10.1109/CICTN57981.2023.10141262

Sam. (2022, October 30). *17 pros and cons of Artificial Intelligence in Healthcare*. Techemergent. Retrieved November 13, 2022, from https://techemergent.com/pros-and-cons-of-artificial-intelligence-in-healthcare/

Samsudin, R., Khan, N., Subbarao, A., & Taralunga, D.D. (2024). Technological Innovations in Enhancing Digital Mental Health Engagement for Low-Income Groups. *Journal of Advanced Research in Applied Sciences and Engineering Technology*. DOI:DOI: 10.37934/araset.59.1.209226

Sánchez-Segura, M. I., Dugarte-Peña, G. L., De Amescua, A., Medina-Domínguez, F., López-Almansa, E., & Reyes, E. B. (2021). Smart occupational health and safety for a digital era and its place in smart and sustainable cities. *Mathematical Biosciences and Engineering*, 18(6), 8831–8856. DOI: 10.3934/mbe.2021436 PMID: 34814325

Sapna, Chand, K., Tiwari, R., & Bhardwaj, K. (2023). Impact of Welfare Measures on Job Satisfaction of Employees in the Industrial Sector of Northern India. *Finance India*, 37(2), 613–626.

Sathyapriya, G., Natarajan, U., Sureshkumar, B., Navaneethakrishnan, G., Palanisamy, R., Bajaj, M., & Sharma, N. K., & Kitmo. (2022). Quality and Tool Stability Improvement in Turning Operation Using Plastic Compliant Damper. *Journal of Nanomaterials*, 2022. Advance online publication. DOI: 10.1155/2022/8654603

Sathyaseelan, K., Vyas, T., Madala, R., Chamundeeswari, V., Rai Goyal, H., & Jayaraman, R. (2023). Blockchain Enabled Intelligent Surveillance System Model with AI and IoT. *Proceedings of 8th IEEE International Conference on Science, Technology, Engineering and Mathematics, ICONSTEM 2023*. DOI: 10.1109/ICONSTEM56934.2023.10142303

Sati, P., Sharma, E., Soni, R., Dhyani, P., Solanki, A. C., Solanki, M. K., Rai, S., & Malviya, M. K. (2022). Bacterial endophytes as bioinoculant: microbial functions and applications toward sustainable farming. In *Microbial Endophytes and Plant Growth: Beneficial Interactions and Applications*. Elsevier., DOI: 10.1016/B978-0-323-90620-3.00008-8

Saxena, A., Chaturvedi, S., & Kumar, P. (2021). Remote Working, Hybrid Workforce, and the Future of Healthcare: Trends and Challenges in the Digital Age. *Health Informatics Journal*, 27(4), 1450–1462.

Saxena, A., Pant, B., Alanya-Beltran, J., Akram, S. V., Bhaskar, B., & Bansal, R. (2022). A Detailed Review of Implementation of Deep Learning Approaches for Industrial Internet of Things with the Different Opportunities and Challenges. *Proceedings of 5th International Conference on Contemporary Computing and Informatics, IC3I 2022*, 1370 – 1375. DOI: 10.1109/IC3I56241.2022.10072499

Saxena, A., Prasad, D., & Haldhar, R. (2018). Investigation of corrosion inhibition effect and adsorption activities of Cuscuta reflexa extract for mild steel in 0.5 M H2SO4. *Bioelectrochemistry (Amsterdam, Netherlands)*, 124, 156–164. DOI: 10.1016/j.bioelechem.2018.07.006 PMID: 30059849

Saxena, A., Prasad, D., Haldhar, R., Singh, G., & Kumar, A. (2018). Use of Sida cordifolia extract as green corrosion inhibitor for mild steel in 0.5 M H2SO4. *Journal of Environmental Chemical Engineering*, 6(1), 694–700. DOI: 10.1016/j.jece.2017.12.064

Schötteler, S., Laumer, S., & Schuhbauer, H. (2023). Consequences of Enterprise Social Media Network Positions for Employees: A Literature Review and Research Agenda. *Business & Information Systems Engineering*, 65(4), 425–440. DOI: 10.1007/s12599-023-00803-0

Sedjo, R. L., & Devine, S. (2011). Predictors of non-adherence to aromatase inhibitors among commercially insured women with breast cancer. *Breast Cancer Research and Treatment*, 125(1), 191–200. DOI: 10.1007/s10549-010-0952-6 PMID: 20495864

Segovia-Vargas, M. J., Miranda-García, I. M., & Oquendo-Torres, F. A. (2023). Sustainable finance: The role of savings and credit cooperatives in Ecuador. *Annals of Public and Cooperative Economics*, 94(3), 951–980. DOI: 10.1111/apce.12428

Sen Thapa, B., Pandit, S., Patwardhan, S. B., Tripathi, S., Mathuriya, A. S., Gupta, P. K., Lal, R. B., & Tusher, T. R. (2022). Application of Microbial Fuel Cell (MFC) for Pharmaceutical Wastewater Treatment: An Overview and Future Perspectives. *Sustainability (Basel)*, 14(14), 8379. Advance online publication. DOI: 10.3390/su14148379

Shabbiruddin, Kanwar, N., Jadoun, V. K., Jayalakshmi, N. S. J., Afthanorhan, A., Fatema, N., Malik, H., & Hossaini, M. A. (. (2023). Industry - Challenge to Pro-Environmental Manufacturing of Goods Replacing Single-Use Plastic by Indian Industry: A Study Toward Failing Ban on Single-Use Plastic Access. *IEEE Access : Practical Innovations, Open Solutions*, 11, 77336–77346. DOI: 10.1109/ACCESS.2023.3296097

Shah, J. K., Sharma, R., Misra, A., Sharma, M., Joshi, S., Kaushal, D., & Bafila, S. (2023). Industry 4.0 Enabled Smart Manufacturing: Unleashing the Power of Artificial Intelligence and Blockchain. *2023 1st DMIHER International Conference on Artificial Intelligence in Education and Industry 4.0, IDICAIEI 2023*. DOI: 10.1109/IDICAIEI58380.2023.10406671

Shajar, S. N., Kashif, M., George, J., & Nasir, S. (2024). The future of green finance: Artificial intelligence-enabled solutions for a more sustainable world. In Harnessing Blockchain-Digital Twin Fusion for Sustainable Investments. https://doi.org/DOI: 10.4018/9798369318782.ch013

Shajar, S. N., Beg, K., Kashif, M., Khan, M., Saleem, S., & Usmani, F. (2024). Enhancing Firm Performance Through Effective Working Capital Management: A Study of Indian Manufacturing Firms Listed at S&P BSE 500. *International Research Journal of Multidisciplinary Scope*, 05(03), 661–669. DOI: 10.47857/irjms.2024.v05i03.0806

Sharahiley, S. M., & Kandpal, V. (2023). The impact of monetary and non-monetary reward systems upon creativity: How rational are Saudi professional employees? *International Journal of Work Organisation and Emotion*, 14(4), 339–358. DOI: 10.1504/IJWOE.2023.136599

Sharma, A., Mohan, A., & Johri, A. (2024). Impact of Financial Technology (Fin-Tech) on the Restructuring of the Agrarian Economy: A Comprehensive Systematic Review. In M. H. (Ed.), *Proceedings - 2024 6th International Conference on Computational Intelligence and Communication Technologies, CCICT 2024* (pp. 249 – 252). Institute of Electrical and Electronics Engineers Inc. DOI: 10.1109/CCICT62777.2024.00049

Sharma, A., Sharma, A., Juneja, P. K., & Jain, V. (2020). Spectral Features based Speech Recognition for Speech Interfacing to Control PC Windows. In S. S. & D. P. (Eds.), *Proceedings - 2020 International Conference on Advances in Computing, Communication and Materials, ICACCM 2020* (pp. 341 – 345). Institute of Electrical and Electronics Engineers Inc. https://doi.org/DOI: 10.1109/ICACCM50413.2020.9212827

Sharma, H. R., Bhardwaj, B., Sharma, B., & Kaushik, C. P. (2021). Sustainable Solid Waste Management in India: Practices, Challenges and the Way Forward. In *Climate Resilience and Environmental Sustainability Approaches: Global Lessons and Local Challenges*. Springer Nature. DOI: 10.1007/978-981-16-0902-2_17

Sharma, M., Hagar, A. A., Krishna Murthy, G. R., Beyane, K., Gawali, B. W., & Pant, B. (2022). A Study on Recognising the Application of Multiple Big Data Technologies and its Related Issues, Difficulties and Opportunities. *2022 2nd International Conference on Advance Computing and Innovative Technologies in Engineering, ICACITE 2022*, 341 – 344. DOI: 10.1109/ICACITE53722.2022.9823623

Sharma, R., Sharma, M., Singh, M., & Bhatnagar, M. (2024). Facades and Fortunes : Intellectual Capital ' s Influence on Firm Dynamics in the Deepfake Epoch. In *Navigating the World of Deepfake Technology* (pp. 1–6). DOI: 10.4018/979-8-3693-5298-4.ch009

Sharma, S., Gupta, A., & Tyagi, R. (2023). Artificial Intelligence Enabled Sustainable Education System Using Vedic Scripture and Cyber Security. *2023 2nd International Conference on Advances in Computational Intelligence and Communication, ICACIC 2023*. DOI: 10.1109/ICACIC59454.2023.10435133

Sharma, S., Gupta, A., & Tyagi, R. (2023). Sustainable Natural Resources Utilization Decision System for Better Society Using Vedic Scripture, Cloud Computing, and IoT. In B. R.C., S. K.M., & D. M. (Eds.), *Proceedings of IEEE 2023 5th International Conference on Advances in Electronics, Computers and Communications, ICAECC 2023*. Institute of Electrical and Electronics Engineers Inc. https://doi.org/DOI: 10.1109/ICAECC59324.2023.10560335

Sharma, S., Kadayat, Y., & Tyagi, R. (2023a). Artificial Intelligence Enabled Sustainable Life Cycle System Using Vedic Scripture and Quantum Computing. *2023 3rd International Conference on Intelligent Technologies, CONIT 2023*. DOI: 10.1109/CONIT59222.2023.10205771

Sharma, S., Mishra, R. R., Joshi, V., & Kour, K. (2020). Analysis and Interpretation of Global Air Quality. *2020 11th International Conference on Computing, Communication and Networking Technologies, ICCCNT 2020*. https://doi.org/DOI: 10.1109/ICCCNT49239.2020.9225532

Sharma, S., Singh, V., & Sarkar, D. (2023). Machine Vision Enabled Fall Detection System for Specially Abled People in Limited Visibility Environment. *2023 3rd Asian Conference on Innovation in Technology, ASIANCON 2023*. DOI: 10.1109/ASIANCON58793.2023.10270769

Sharma, A. K., Sharma, A., Singh, Y., & Chen, W.-H. (2021). Production of a sustainable fuel from microalgae Chlorella minutissima grown in a 1500 L open raceway ponds. *Biomass and Bioenergy*, 149. Advance online publication. DOI: 10.1016/j.biombioe.2021.106073

Sharma, E., Rana, S., Sharma, I., Sati, P., & Dhyani, P. (2023). Organic polymers for CO_2 capture and conversion. In *CO_2-Philic Polymers, Nanocomposites and Solvents: Capture, Conversion and Industrial Products*. Elsevier., DOI: 10.1016/B978-0-323-85777-2.00002-0

Sharma, H., Rana, A., Singh, R. P., Goyal, B., Dogra, A., & Lepcha, D. C. (2023). Improving Efficiency of Panel Using Solar Tracker Controlled Through Fuzzy Logic. *2023 International Conference on Sustainable Emerging Innovations in Engineering and Technology, ICSEIET 2023*, 286 – 289. DOI: 10.1109/ICSEIET58677.2023.10303639

Sharma, H., Verma, D., Rana, A., Chari, S. L., Kumar, R., & Kumar, N. (2023). Enhancing Network Security in IoT Using Machine Learning- Based Anomaly Detection. *Proceedings of International Conference on Contemporary Computing and Informatics, IC3I 2023*, 2650 – 2654. DOI: 10.1109/IC3I59117.2023.10397636

Sharma, K., Pandit, S., Sen Thapa, B., & Pant, M. (2022). Biodegradation of Congo Red Using Co-Culture Anode Inoculum in a Microbial Fuel Cell. *Catalysts*, 12(10), 1219. Advance online publication. DOI: 10.3390/catal12101219

Sharma, M., Kumar, A., Luthra, S., Joshi, S., & Upadhyay, A. (2022). The impact of environmental dynamism on low-carbon practices and digital supply chain networks to enhance sustainable performance: An empirical analysis. *Business Strategy and the Environment*, 31(4), 1776–1788. DOI: 10.1002/bse.2983

Sharma, M., Luthra, S., Joshi, S., & Joshi, H. (2022). Challenges to agile project management during COVID-19 pandemic: An emerging economy perspective. *Operations Management Research*, 15(1–2), 461–474. DOI: 10.1007/s12063-021-00249-1

Sharma, M., Luthra, S., Joshi, S., & Kumar, A. (2022). Analysing the impact of sustainable human resource management practices and industry 4.0 technologies adoption on employability skills. *International Journal of Manpower*, 43(2), 463–485. DOI: 10.1108/IJM-02-2021-0085

Sharma, M., & Singh, P. (2023). Newly engineered nanoparticles as potential therapeutic agents for plants to ameliorate abiotic and biotic stress. *Journal of Applied and Natural Science*, 15(2), 720–731. DOI: 10.31018/jans.v15i2.4603

Sharma, N. K., Kumar, V., Verma, P., & Luthra, S. (2021). Sustainable reverse logistics practices and performance evaluation with fuzzy TOPSIS: A study on Indian retailers. *Cleaner Logistics and Supply Chain*, 1, 100007. Advance online publication. DOI: 10.1016/j.clscn.2021.100007

Sharma, N., Agrawal, R., & Silmana, A. (2021). Analyzing The Role Of Public Transportation On Environmental Air Pollution In Select Cities. *Indian Journal of Environmental Protection*, 41(5), 536–541.

Sharma, P., Malhotra, R. K., Ojha, M. K., & Gupta, S. (2022). Impact of meditation on mental & physical health and thereby on academic performance of students: A study of higher educational institutions of Uttarakhand. *Journal of Medical Pharmaceutical and Allied Sciences*, 11(2), 4641–4644. DOI: 10.55522/jmpas.V11I2.2309

Sharma, P., Taneja, S., Kumar, P., Özen, E., & Singh, A. (2024). Application of the UTAUT model toward individual acceptance: Emerging trends in artificial intelligence-based banking services. *International Journal of Electronic Finance*, 13(3), 352–366. DOI: 10.1504/IJEF.2024.139584

Sharma, R. C., Palli, S., & Sharma, S. K. (2023). Ride analysis of railway vehicle considering rigidity and flexibility of the carbody. *Zhongguo Gongcheng Xuekan*, 46(4), 355–366. DOI: 10.1080/02533839.2023.2194918

Sharma, R., Jasrotia, K., Singh, N., Ghosh, P., srivastava, S., Sharma, N. R., Singh, J., Kanwar, R., & Kumar, A. (2020). A Comprehensive Review on Hydrothermal Carbonization of Biomass and its Applications. *Chemistry Africa*, 3(1), 1–19. Advance online publication. DOI: 10.1007/s42250-019-00098-3

Sharma, R., Shishodia, A., Gunasekaran, A., Min, H., & Munim, Z. H. (2022). The role of artificial intelligence in supply chain management: Mapping the territory. *International Journal of Production Research*, 60(24), 7527–7550. DOI: 10.1080/00207543.2022.2029611

Sharma, S., & Bhadula, S. (2023). Secure Federated Learning for Intelligent Industry 4.0 IoT Enabled Self Skin Care Application System. *Proceedings of the 2nd International Conference on Applied Artificial Intelligence and Computing, ICAAIC 2023*, 1164–1170. DOI: 10.1109/ICAAIC56838.2023.10141028

Sharma, S., Kadayat, Y., & Tyagi, R. (2023b). Sustainable Global Democratic e-Governance System Using Vedic Scripture, Artificial Intelligence, Cloud Computing and Augmented Reality. *Proceedings of the International Conference on Circuit Power and Computing Technologies, ICCPCT 2023*, 113–118. DOI: 10.1109/ICCPCT58313.2023.10245405

Sharma, S., Kandpal, V., Choudhury, T., Santibanez Gonzalez, E. D. R., & Agarwal, N. (2023). Assessment of the implications of energy-efficient technologies on the environmental sustainability of rail operation. *AIMS Environmental Science*, 10(5), 709–731. DOI: 10.3934/environsci.2023039

Sharma, S., & Kumar, S. (2023). Sustainable finance: A way towards climate neutral economies. In *Perspectives on the Transition Toward Green and Climate Neutral Economies in Asia*. IGI Global., DOI: 10.4018/978-1-6684-8613-9.ch001

Sharma, S., Singh Rawal, R., Pandey, D., & Pandey, N. (2021). Microbial World for Sustainable Development. In *Microbial Technology for Sustainable Environment*. Springer Nature., DOI: 10.1007/978-981-16-3840-4_1

Sharma, S., & Tyagi, R. (2023). Digitalization of Farming Knowledge Using Artificial Intelligence and Vedic Scripture. *3rd IEEE International Conference on ICT in Business Industry and Government, ICTBIG 2023*. DOI: 10.1109/ICTBIG59752.2023.10456219

Sharma, V., & Jain, S. (2020). Managers Training Programs Effectiveness Evaluation by using different Machine Learning Approaches. *Proceedings of the 4th International Conference on Electronics, Communication and Aerospace Technology, ICECA 2020*, 1453–1457. DOI: 10.1109/ICECA49313.2020.9297556

Sharma, V., Kumar, V., & Bist, A. (2020). Investigations on morphology and material removal rate of various MMCs using CO2 laser technique. *Journal of the Brazilian Society of Mechanical Sciences and Engineering*, 42(10), 542. Advance online publication. DOI: 10.1007/s40430-020-02635-5

Sharma, V., Taneja, S., Gupta, M., Jangir, K., & Ozen, E. (2023). Impact of Service Quality on Behavioural Intention to Use Fin Tech Payment Services: An Extension of SERVEQUAL Model. *Asia Pacific Journal of Information Systems*, 33(4), 1093–1117. DOI: 10.14329/apjis.2023.33.4.1093

Sharma, Y. K., Mangla, S. K., Patil, P. P., & Uniyal, S. (2020). Analyzing sustainable food supply chain management challenges in India. In *Research Anthology on Food Waste Reduction and Alternative Diets for Food and Nutrition Security*. IGI Global., DOI: 10.4018/978-1-7998-5354-1.ch023

Sharun, V., Rajasekaran, M., Kumar, S. S., Tripathi, V., Sharma, R., Puthilibai, G., Sudhakar, M., & Negash, K. (2022). Study on Developments in Protection Coating Techniques for Steel. *Advances in Materials Science and Engineering*, 2022, 1–10. Advance online publication. DOI: 10.1155/2022/2843043

Shashikala, R., Singh, B. P., Azam, M., & Magesh, C. R. Rajat, & Singh, D. P. (2022). IoT Engineering Nanomaterial's Approach To Sustainable Advance Crop Production Management. *2022 2nd International Conference on Advance Computing and Innovative Technologies in Engineering, ICACITE 2022*, 2284–2288. DOI: 10.1109/ICACITE53722.2022.9823573

Shekhar, S., Gusain, R., Vidhyarthi, A., & Prakash, R. (2022). Role of Remote Sensing and GIS Strategies to Increase Crop Yield. In S. S. & J. T. (Eds.), *2022 International Conference on Advances in Computing, Communication and Materials, ICACCM 2022*. Institute of Electrical and Electronics Engineers Inc. DOI: 10.1109/ICACCM56405.2022.10009217

Shekhawat, R. S., & Uniyal, D. (2021). Smart-Bin: IoT-Based Real-Time Garbage Monitoring System for Smart Cities. *Lecture Notes in Networks and Systems*, 190, 871–879. DOI: 10.1007/978-981-16-0882-7_78

Shrivastava, A., Usha, R., Kukreti, R., Sharma, G., Srivastava, A. P., & Khan, A. K. (2023). Women Safety Precaution. *2023 1st International Conference on Circuits, Power, and Intelligent Systems, CCPIS 2023*. DOI: 10.1109/CCPIS59145.2023.10291594

Shrivastava, V., Yadav, A. S., Sharma, A. K., Singh, P., Alam, T., & Sharma, A. (2022). Performance Comparison of Solar Air Heater with Extended Surfaces and Iron Filling. *International Journal of Vehicle Structures and Systems*, 14(5), 607–610. DOI: 10.4273/ijvss.14.5.10

Shukla, A., Sharma, M., Tiwari, K., Vani, V. D., & Kumar, N., & Pooja. (2023). Predicting Rainfall Using an Artificial Neural Network-Based Model. *Proceedings of International Conference on Contemporary Computing and Informatics, IC3I 2023*, 2700 – 2704. DOI: 10.1109/IC3I59117.2023.10397714

Shukla, S. K., Pant, B., Viriyasitavat, W., Verma, D., Kautish, S., Dhiman, G., Kaur, A., Srihari, K., & Mohanty, S. N. (2022). An integration of autonomic computing with multicore systems for performance optimization in Industrial Internet of Things. *IET Communications*. Advance online publication. DOI: 10.1049/cmu2.12505

Siddique, A., Kandpal, G., & Kumar, P. (2018). Proline accumulation and its defensive role under diverse stress condition in plants: An overview. *Journal of Pure & Applied Microbiology*, 12(3), 1655–1659. DOI: 10.22207/JPAM.12.3.73

Singamaneni, K. K., Dhiman, G., Juneja, S., Muhammad, G., AlQahtani, S. A., & Zaki, J. (2022). A Novel QKD Approach to Enhance IIOT Privacy and Computational Knacks. *Sensors (Basel)*, 22(18), 6741. Advance online publication. DOI: 10.3390/s22186741 PMID: 36146089

Singh, H., Singh, J. I. P., Singh, S., Dhawan, V., & Tiwari, S. K. (2018). A Brief Review of Jute Fibre and Its Composites. In S. S., D. R.S., & S. M. (Eds.), *Materials Today: Proceedings* (Vol. 5, Issue 14, pp. 28427 – 28437). Elsevier Ltd. DOI: 10.1016/j.matpr.2018.10.129

Singh, K. D., & Singh, P. (2023). A Novel Cloud-based Framework to Predict the Employability of Students. In K. R., K. R., G. M., G. M., S. R., & S. R. (Eds.), *2023 International Conference on Advancement in Computation and Computer Technologies, InCACCT 2023* (pp. 528 – 532). Institute of Electrical and Electronics Engineers Inc. DOI: 10.1109/InCACCT57535.2023.10141760

Singh, K. D., Deep Singh, P., Bansal, A., Kaur, G., Khullar, V., & Tripathi, V. (2023). Exploratory Data Analysis and Customer Churn Prediction for the Telecommunication Industry. *ACCESS 2023 - 2023 3rd International Conference on Advances in Computing, Communication, Embedded and Secure Systems*, 197 – 201. DOI: 10.1109/ACCESS57397.2023.10199700

Singh, K. D., Singh, P., Chhabra, R., Kaur, G., Bansal, A., & Tripathi, V. (2023). Cyber-Physical Systems for Smart City Applications: A Comparative Study. In K. R., K. R., G. M., G. M., S. R., & S. R. (Eds.), *2023 International Conference on Advancement in Computation and Computer Technologies, InCACCT 2023* (pp. 871 – 876). Institute of Electrical and Electronics Engineers Inc. DOI: 10.1109/InCACCT57535.2023.10141719

Singh, K. D., Singh, P., Tripathi, V., & Khullar, V. (2022). A Novel and Secure Framework to Detect Unauthorized Access to an Optical Fog-Cloud Computing Network. In R. H.S., B. R., G. P.K., & S. V.K. (Eds.), *PDGC 2022 - 2022 7th International Conference on Parallel, Distributed and Grid Computing* (pp. 618 – 622). Institute of Electrical and Electronics Engineers Inc. DOI: 10.1109/PDGC56933.2022.10053223

Singh, K. K., Vats, C., & Singh, M. P. (2023). An Empirical Study of the Impact of Organizational, Social, and Psychological Factors on the Performance of Employees. In M. P., M. P., S. A., K. S., K. S.K., & M. S.K. (Eds.), *Springer Proceedings in Business and Economics* (pp. 621 – 636). Springer Nature. DOI: 10.1007/978-981-99-0197-5_39

Singh, N. K., Singh, Y., & Sharma, A. (2020). Experimental investigation on electric discharge drilling of titanium alloy (Ti–6Al–4V) with a gas-aided rotary tool. *Sadhana - Academy Proceedings in Engineering Sciences, 45*(1). DOI: 10.1007/s12046-020-01497-w

Singh, N., Rana, A., & Badhotiya, G. K. (2021). Manufacturing processes for the development of engineered wood - A mini-review. In S. Y. (Ed.), *Materials Today: Proceedings* (Vol. 46, pp. 11235 – 11238). Elsevier Ltd. DOI: 10.1016/j.matpr.2021.02.612

Singh, P., & Singh, K. D. (2023). Fog-Centric Intelligent Surveillance System: A Novel Approach for Effective and Efficient Surveillance. In K. R., K. R., G. M., G. M., S. R., & S. R. (Eds.), *2023 International Conference on Advancement in Computation and Computer Technologies, InCACCT 2023* (pp. 762 – 766). Institute of Electrical and Electronics Engineers Inc. DOI: 10.1109/InCACCT57535.2023.10141802

Singh, Y., Singh, N. K., & Sharma, A. (2023). Biodiesel as an alternative fuel employed in CI engine to meet the sustainability criteria: A review. In S. Y., S. G., & B. G.K. (Eds.), *AIP Conference Proceedings* (Vol. 2521). American Institute of Physics Inc. DOI: 10.1063/5.0113825

Singh, A. B., Meena, H. K., Khandelwal, C., & Dangayach, G. S. (2023). Sustainability Assessment of Higher Education Institutions: A Systematic Literature Review †. *Engineering Proceedings*, 37(1), 23. Advance online publication. DOI: 10.3390/ECP2023-14728

Singh, A. K., Singh, R., & Singh, S. (2024). A review on factors affecting and performance of nutritional security of women and children in India. In *Impact of Women in Food and Agricultural Development*. IGI Global., DOI: 10.4018/979-8-3693-3037-1.ch019

Singh, A. P., Pradhan, N. R., Luhach, A. K., Agnihotri, S., Jhanjhi, N. Z., Verma, S., Kavita, , Ghosh, U., & Roy, D. S. (2020). A novel patient-centric architectural framework for blockchain-enabled healthcare applications. *IEEE Transactions on Industrial Informatics*, 17(8), 5779–5789. DOI: 10.1109/TII.2020.3037889

Singh, A., Lin, Y., Ebenso, E. E., Liu, W., Pan, J., & Huang, B. (2015). Gingko biloba fruit extract as an eco-friendly corrosion inhibitor for J55 steel in CO2 saturated 3.5% NaCl solution. *Journal of Industrial and Engineering Chemistry*, 24, 219–228. DOI: 10.1016/j.jiec.2014.09.034

Singh, A., Sharma, S., Purohit, K. C., & Nithin Kumar, K. C. (2021). Artificial Intelligence based Framework for Effective Performance of Traffic Light Control System. *Proceedings of the 2021 IEEE International Conference on Innovative Computing, Intelligent Communication and Smart Electrical Systems, ICSES 2021*. DOI: 10.1109/ICSES52305.2021.9633913

Singhal, P., Sharma, S., Saha, S., Mishra, I., Alfurhood, B. S., & Singh, P. (2023). Smart security system using Hybrid System with IoT and Blockchain: A security system Human sased Detection. *2023 3rd International Conference on Advance Computing and Innovative Technologies in Engineering, ICACITE 2023*, 1032 – 1036. DOI: 10.1109/ICACITE57410.2023.10182383

Singh, G., & Arya, S. K. (2019). Utility of laccase in pulp and paper industry: A progressive step towards the green technology. *International Journal of Biological Macromolecules*, 134, 1070–1084. DOI: 10.1016/j.ijbiomac.2019.05.168 PMID: 31129205

Singh, G., Gupta, M. K., Mia, M., & Sharma, V. S. (2018). Modeling and optimization of tool wear in MQL-assisted milling of Inconel 718 superalloy using evolutionary techniques. *International Journal of Advanced Manufacturing Technology*, 97(1–4), 481–494. DOI: 10.1007/s00170-018-1911-3

Singh, G., Pruncu, C. I., Gupta, M. K., Mia, M., Khan, A. M., Jamil, M., Pimenov, D. Y., Sen, B., & Sharma, V. S. (2019). Investigations of machining characteristics in the upgraded MQL-assisted turning of pure titanium alloys using evolutionary algorithms. *Materials (Basel)*, 12(6), 999. Advance online publication. DOI: 10.3390/ma12060999 PMID: 30917617

Singh, K. D., Singh, P., Kaur, G., Khullar, V., Chhabra, R., & Tripathi, V. (2023). Education 4.0: Exploring the Potential of Disruptive Technologies in Transforming Learning. *Proceedings of International Conference on Computational Intelligence and Sustainable Engineering Solution, CISES 2023*, 586 – 591. DOI: 10.1109/CISES58720.2023.10183547

Singh, K. U., Chaudhary, V., Sharma, P. K., Kumar, P., Varshney, N., & Singh, T. (2024). Integrating GPS and GSM Technologies for Enhanced Women's Safety: A Fingerprint-Activated Device Approach. *2024 International Conference on Automation and Computation, AUTOCOM 2024*, 657 – 662. DOI: 10.1109/AUTOCOM60220.2024.10486120

Singh, N. K., Singh, Y., Rahim, E. A., Senthil Siva Subramanian, T., & Sharma, A. (2023). Electric discharge machining of hybrid composite with bio-dielectrics for sustainable developments. *Australian Journal of Mechanical Engineering*, 1–18. Advance online publication. DOI: 10.1080/14484846.2023.2249577

Singh, N. K., Singh, Y., Sharma, A., Paswan, M. K., Singh, V. K., Upadhyay, A. K., & Mishra, V. R. (2021). Performance of CuO nanoparticles as an additive to the chemically modified Nicotiana Tabacum as a sustainable coolant-lubricant during turning EN19 steel. *Wear*, 486–487, 204057. Advance online publication. DOI: 10.1016/j.wear.2021.204057

Singh, N. K., Singh, Y., Sharma, A., Singla, A., & Negi, P. (2021). An environmental-friendly electrical discharge machining using different sustainable techniques: A review. *Advances in Materials and Processing Technologies*, 7(4), 537–566. DOI: 10.1080/2374068X.2020.1785210

Singh, P., Nayyar, A., Kaur, A., & Ghosh, U. (2020). Blockchain and fog based architecture for internet of everything in smart cities. *Future Internet*, 12(4), 61. Advance online publication. DOI: 10.3390/fi12040061

Singh, R., Chandra, A. S., Bbhagat, B., Panduro-Ramirez, J., Gaikwad, A. P., & Pant, B. (2022). Cloud Computing, Machine Learning, and Secure Data Sharing enabled through Blockchain. *Proceedings of 5th International Conference on Contemporary Computing and Informatics, IC3I 2022*, 282 – 286. DOI: 10.1109/IC3I56241.2022.10072925

Singh, S. K., Chauhan, A., & Sarkar, B. (2023). Sustainable biodiesel supply chain model based on waste animal fat with subsidy and advertisement. *Journal of Cleaner Production*, 382, 134806. Advance online publication. DOI: 10.1016/j.jclepro.2022.134806

Singh, S. P., Piras, G., Viriyasitavat, W., Kariri, E., Yadav, K., Dhiman, G., Vimal, S., & Khan, S. B. (2023). Cyber Security and 5G-assisted Industrial Internet of Things using Novel Artificial Adaption based Evolutionary Algorithm. *Mobile Networks and Applications*. Advance online publication. DOI: 10.1007/s11036-023-02230-7

Singh, S., Anil, A. G., Khasnabis, S., Kumar, V., Nath, B., Adiga, V., Kumar Naik, T. S. S., Subramanian, S., Kumar, V., Singh, J., & Ramamurthy, P. C. (2022). Sustainable removal of Cr(VI) using graphene oxide-zinc oxide nanohybrid: Adsorption kinetics, isotherms and thermodynamics. *Environmental Research*, 203, 111891. Advance online publication. DOI: 10.1016/j.envres.2021.111891 PMID: 34419468

Singh, S., Kumar, V., Datta, S., Wani, A. B., Dhanjal, D. S., Romero, R., & Singh, J. (2020). Glyphosate uptake, translocation, resistance emergence in crops, analytical monitoring, toxicity and degradation: A review. *Environmental Chemistry Letters*, 18(3), 663–702. DOI: 10.1007/s10311-020-00969-z

Singh, S., Kumar, V., Dhanjal, D. S., Datta, S., Bhatia, D., Dhiman, J., Samuel, J., Prasad, R., & Singh, J. (2020). A sustainable paradigm of sewage sludge biochar: Valorization, opportunities, challenges and future prospects. *Journal of Cleaner Production*, 269, 122259. Advance online publication. DOI: 10.1016/j.jclepro.2020.122259

Singh, S., Prakash, C., & Ramakrishna, S. (2019). 3D printing of polyether-ether-ketone for biomedical applications. *European Polymer Journal*, 114, 234–248. DOI: 10.1016/j.eurpolymj.2019.02.035

Singh, V. P., Kumar, R., Kumar, A., & Dewangan, A. K. (2023). Automotive light weight multi-materials sheets joining through friction stir welding technique: An overview. *Materials Today: Proceedings*. Advance online publication. DOI: 10.1016/j.matpr.2023.02.171

Singh, Y., Rahim, E. A., Singh, N. K., Sharma, A., Singla, A., & Palamanit, A. (2022). Friction and wear characteristics of chemically modified mahua (madhuca indica) oil based lubricant with SiO_2 nanoparticles as additives. *Wear*, 508–509, 204463. Advance online publication. DOI: 10.1016/j.wear.2022.204463

Singla, A., Singh, Y., Singh, Y., Rahim, E. A., Singh, N. K., & Sharma, A. (2023). Challenges and Future Prospects of Biofuel Generations: An Overview. In *Biowaste and Biomass in Biofuel Applications*. CRC Press., DOI: 10.1201/9781003265597-4

Singla, R. K., De, R., Efferth, T., Mezzetti, B., Sahab Uddin, M., Sanusi, , Ntie-Kang, F., Wang, D., Schultz, F., Kharat, K. R., Devkota, H. P., Battino, M., Sur, D., Lordan, R., Patnaik, S. S., Tsagkaris, C., Sai, C. S., Tripathi, S. K., Găman, M.-A., & Shen, B. (2023). The International Natural Product Sciences Taskforce (INPST) and the power of Twitter networking exemplified through #INPST hashtag analysis. *Phytomedicine*, 108, 154520. Advance online publication. DOI: 10.1016/j.phymed.2022.154520 PMID: 36334386

Širić, I., Eid, E. M., Taher, M. A., El-Morsy, M. H. E., Osman, H. E. M., Kumar, P., Adelodun, B., Abou Fayssal, S., Mioč, B., Andabaka, Ž., Goala, M., Kumari, S., Bachheti, A., Choi, K. S., & Kumar, V. (2022). Combined Use of Spent Mushroom Substrate Biochar and PGPR Improves Growth, Yield, and Biochemical Response of Cauliflower (Brassica oleracea var. botrytis): A Preliminary Study on Greenhouse Cultivation. *Horticulturae*, 8(9), 830. Advance online publication. DOI: 10.3390/horticulturae8090830

Slowik, C. (2022, November 3). *Benefits of AI in Healthcare - usage, advantages. Neoteric*. Retrieved November 12, 2022, from https://neoteric.eu/blog/benefits-of-ai-in-healthcare/

Smith, A. (2017). The Evolution of Smart Cards in Financial Services. *Journal of Financial Services Marketing*, 22(2), 83–93.

Smith, J., & Brown, M. (2021). Smart Cards and FinTech Integration: A Case Study Approach. *International Journal of Finance & Economics*, 26(3), 4057–4074.

Smith, J., & Brown, M. (2022). Collaborative Approaches in Addressing Ethical Challenges in FinTech Integration. *Journal of Business Ethics*, 160(4), 1015–1030.

Sonnad, S., Awasthy, M., Rane, K., Banerjee, M., Buddhi, D., & Pant, B. (2022). Blockchain-Based Secure Mengers Authentication for Industrial IoT. In D. R.K., S. A.Kr., K. G., & B. S. (Eds.), *Proceedings of the 2022 11th International Conference on System Modeling and Advancement in Research Trends, SMART 2022* (pp. 853 – 858). Institute of Electrical and Electronics Engineers Inc. DOI: 10.1109/SMART55829.2022.10046934

Spencer, M. (2015). Brittleness and Bureaucracy: Software as a Material for Science. *Perspectives on Science*, 23(4), 466–484. DOI: 10.1162/POSC_a_00184

Srinivasan, R., & Swink, M. (2018). An investigation of visibility and flexibility as complements to supply chain analytics: An organizational information processing theory perspective. *Production and Operations Management*, 27(10), 1849–1867. DOI: 10.1111/poms.12746

Srivastava, A., Hassan, M., & Gangwar, R. (2023). Improving Railway Track System Using Soil Nails for Heavy Axle Load. *Lecture Notes in Civil Engineering, 338 LNCE*, 1 – 13. DOI: 10.1007/978-981-99-1886-7_1

Srivastava, A., Jawaid, S., Singh, R., Gehlot, A., Akram, S. V., Priyadarshi, N., & Khan, B. (2022). Imperative Role of Technology Intervention and Implementation for Automation in the Construction Industry. *Advances in Civil Engineering*, 2022(1), 6716987. Advance online publication. DOI: 10.1155/2022/6716987

Srivastava, B., Kandpal, V., & Jain, A. K. (2024). Financial well-being of women self-help group members: A qualitative study. *Environment, Development and Sustainability*. Advance online publication. DOI: 10.1007/s10668-024-04879-w

Starks, L. T. (2023). Presidential Address: Sustainable Finance and ESG Issues—Value versus Values. *The Journal of Finance*, 78(4), 1837–1872. DOI: 10.1111/jofi.13255

Steele, C. B., Cardinez, C. J., Richardson, L. C., Tom-Orme, L., & Shaw, K. M. (2008). Surveillance for health behaviors of American Indians and Alaska Natives—Findings from the behavioral risk factor surveillance system, 2000–2006. *Cancer*, 113(S5), 1131–1141. DOI: 10.1002/cncr.23727 PMID: 18720374

Streimikiene, D., Mikalauskiene, A., & Burbaite, G. (2023). THE ROLE OF SUSTAINABLE FINANCE IN ACHIEVING SUSTAINABLE DEVELOPMENT GOALS. *Economics & Sociology (Ternopil)*, 16(1), 256–283. DOI: 10.14254/2071-789X.2023/16-1/17

Subramani, R., Kaliappan, S., Kumar, P. V. A., Sekar, S., De Poures, M. V., Patil, P. P., & Raj, E. S. E. (2022). A Recent Trend on Additive Manufacturing Sustainability with Supply Chain Management Concept, Multicriteria Decision Making Techniques. *Advances in Materials Science and Engineering*, 2022. Advance online publication. DOI: 10.1155/2022/9151839

Subramani, R., Kaliappan, S., Sekar, S., Patil, P. P., Usha, R., Manasa, N., & Esakkiraj, E. S. (2022). Polymer Filament Process Parameter Optimization with Mechanical Test and Morphology Analysis. *Advances in Materials Science and Engineering*, 2022, 1–8. Advance online publication. DOI: 10.1155/2022/8259804

Sui, A., Sui, W., Liu, S., & Rhodes, R. (2023). Ethical considerations for the use of consumer wearables in health research. *Digital Health*, 9, 20552076231153740. DOI: 10.1177/20552076231153740 PMID: 36756643

Sunori, S. K., Kant, S., Agarwal, P., & Juneja, P. (2023). Development of Rainfall Prediction Models using Linear and Non-linear Regression Techniques. *2023 4th IEEE Global Conference for Advancement in Technology, GCAT 2023*. DOI: 10.1109/GCAT59970.2023.10353508

Sunori, S. K., Mohan, L., Pant, M., & Juneja, P. (2023). Classification of Soil Fertility using LVQ and PNN Techniques. *Proceedings of the 8th International Conference on Communication and Electronics Systems, ICCES 2023*, 1441–1446. DOI: 10.1109/ICCES57224.2023.10192793

Suresh, M., Antony, J., Nair, G., & Garza-Reyes, J. A. (2023). Lean-sustainability assessment framework development: Evidence from the construction industry. *Total Quality Management & Business Excellence*, 34(15–16), 2046–2081. DOI: 10.1080/14783363.2023.2222088

Suryavanshi, A., Kukreja, V., Bordoloi, D., Mehta, S., & Choudhary, A. (2023). Agricultural Insights Through Federated Learning CNN: A Case Study on Jackfruit Leaf Disease. In D. R.K., S. A.Kr., S. R., B. S., & K. V. (Eds.), *Proceedings of the 2023 12th International Conference on System Modeling and Advancement in Research Trends, SMART 2023* (pp. 36 – 42). Institute of Electrical and Electronics Engineers Inc. DOI: 10.1109/SMART59791.2023.10428321

Suryavanshi, A., Tanwar, S., Kukreja, V., Choudhary, A., & Chamoli, S. (2023). An Integrated Approach to Potato Leaf Disease Detection Using Convolutional Neural Networks and Random Forest. *Proceedings of the 2023 International Conference on Innovative Computing, Intelligent Communication and Smart Electrical Systems, ICSES 2023*. DOI: 10.1109/ICSES60034.2023.10465557

Syed, F. A., Bargavi, N., Sharma, A., Mishra, A., Nagpal, P., & Srivastava, A. (2022). Recent Management Trends Involved with the Internet of Things in Indian Automotive Components Manufacturing Industries. *Proceedings of 5th International Conference on Contemporary Computing and Informatics, IC3I 2022*, 1035 – 1041. DOI: 10.1109/IC3I56241.2022.10072565

Talaat, F. M., & El-Balka, R. M. (2023). Stress monitoring using wearable sensors: IoT techniques in medical field. *Neural Computing & Applications*, 35(25), 18571–18584. DOI: 10.1007/s00521-023-08681-z PMID: 37362562

Tamilmani, S., Mohan, T., Jeyalakshmi, S., Shukla, G. P., Gehlot, A., & Shukla, S. K. (2023). Blockchain Integrated with Industrial IOT Towards Industry 4.0. *2023 International Conference on Artificial Intelligence and Smart Communication, AISC 2023*, 575 – 581. DOI: 10.1109/AISC56616.2023.10085226

Taneja, S., Bhatnagar, M., Kumar, P., & Grima, S. (2023). A Panel Analysis of the Effectiveness of the Asset Management in Indian Agricultural Companies. *International Journal of Sustainable Development and Planning*, 18(3), 653–660. DOI: 10.18280/ijsdp.180301

Taneja, S., Bhatnagar, M., Kumar, P., & Rupeika-apoga, R. (2023). India ' s Total Natural Resource Rents (NRR) and GDP : An Augmented Autoregressive Distributed Lag (ARDL) Bound Test. *Journal of Risk and Financial Management*, 16(2), 91. https://doi.org/doi.org/10.3390/jrfm16020091. DOI: 10.3390/jrfm16020091

Taneja, S., & Özen, E. (2023). To analyse the relationship between bank's green financing and environmental performance. *International Journal of Electronic Finance*, 12(2), 163–175. DOI: 10.1504/IJEF.2023.129919

Tang, V. (2020). Development of a knowledge-based decision support system for long-term geriatric care management.

Tanwar, V., Anand, V., Chauhan, R., & Rawat, D. (2023). A Deep Learning for Early Tomato Leaf Disease Detection: A CNN Approach. *2023 2nd International Conference on Futuristic Technologies, INCOFT 2023*. DOI: 10.1109/INCOFT60753.2023.10425552

Tarafdar, M., Cooper, C. L., & Stich, J.-F. (2020). The Technostress Trifecta—Techno Eustress, Techno Distress, and Design: Theoretical Directions and an Agenda for Research. *Information Systems Journal*, 30(1), 83–114.

Tarafdar, M., Tu, Q., & Ragu-Nathan, T. S. (2020). Examining Factors Affecting Online Technostress in a Work Environment. *Computers in Human Behavior*, 46, 163–172. DOI: 10.1016/j.chb.2014.10.046

Temsah, M. H., Aljamaan, F., Malki, K. H., Alhasan, K., Altamimi, I., Aljarbou, R., . . . Al-Eyadhy, A. (2023, June). Chatgpt and the future of digital health: a study on healthcare workers' perceptions and expectations. In Healthcare (Vol. 11, No. 13, p. 1812). MDPI.

Ter Horst, R., Jaeger, M., Smeekens, S. P., Oosting, M., Swertz, M. A., Li, Y., Kumar, V., Diavatopoulos, D. A., Jansen, A. F. M., Lemmers, H., Toenhake-Dijkstra, H., van Herwaarden, A. E., Janssen, M., van der Molen, R. G., Joosten, I., Sweep, F. C. G. J., Smit, J. W., Netea-Maier, R. T., Koenders, M. M. J. F., & Netea, M. G. (2016). Host and environmental factors influencing individual human cytokine responses. *Cell*, 167(4), 1111–1124.e13. DOI: 10.1016/j.cell.2016.10.018 PMID: 27814508

Thakur, A., & Kumar, A. (2021). Sustainable Inhibitors for Corrosion Mitigation in Aggressive Corrosive Media: A Comprehensive Study. *Journal of Bio- and Tribo-Corrosion*, 7(2), 67. Advance online publication. DOI: 10.1007/s40735-021-00501-y

Thakur, S., Malik, D., Kukreja, V., Sharma, R., Yadav, R., & Joshi, K. (2023). Multi-Stage Classification of Pomegranate Anthracnose Disease Severity Levels with CNN and SVM. *Proceedings of the 4th International Conference on Smart Electronics and Communication, ICOSEC 2023*, 1117–1121. DOI: 10.1109/ICOSEC58147.2023.10276047

Thentral, T. M. T., Usha, S., Palanisamy, R., Geetha, A., Alkhudaydi, A. M., Sharma, N. K., Bajaj, M., Ghoneim, S. S. M., Shouran, M., & Kamel, S. (2022). An energy efficient modified passive power filter for power quality enhancement in electric drives. *Frontiers in Energy Research*, 10. Advance online publication. DOI: 10.3389/fenrg.2022.989857

Thesmar, D., Sraer, D., Pinheiro, L., Dadson, N., Veliche, R., & Greenberg, P. (2019). Combining the power of artificial intelligence with the richness of healthcare claims data: Opportunities and challenges. *PharmacoEconomics*, 37(6), 745–752. DOI: 10.1007/s40273-019-00777-6 PMID: 30848452

Thomas, R. (2019, September 2). *AI for Medical Imaging — now?* tds. Retrieved November 1, 2022, from https://towardsdatascience.com/ai-for-medical-imaging-now-8fad32c4c96b /

Tiwari, K., Bafila, P., Negi, P., & Singh, R. (2023). The applications of nanotechnology in nutraceuticals: A review. In S. Y., S. G., & B. G.K. (Eds.), *AIP Conference Proceedings* (Vol. 2521). American Institute of Physics Inc. DOI: 10.1063/5.0129695

Tiwari, R., Agrawal, P., Singh, P., Bajaj, S., Verma, V., & Chauhan, A. S. (2023). Technology Enabled Integrated Fusion Teaching for Enhancing Learning Outcomes in Higher Education. *International Journal of Emerging Technologies in Learning*, 18(7), 243–249. DOI: 10.3991/ijet.v18i07.36799

Tiwari, R., Kaur, H., Sharma, S., Kargeti, H., Prakash, N., & Sharma, S. (2023, December). Artificial Intelligence in Health Insurance: A Bibliometric Review. In *2023 International Conference on Advanced Computing & Communication Technologies (ICACCTech)* (pp. 14-18). IEEE DOI: 10.1109/ICACCTech61146.2023.00012

Tiwari, R., Rautela, S., Sharma, S., Choudhary, B. P., Tripathi, R., & Singh, P. (2023, December). Role of AI for Fraud Detection in Banks: A Bibliometric Analysis. In *2023 International Conference on Advanced Computing & Communication Technologies (ICACCTech)* (pp. 66-71). IEEE. DOI: 10.1109/ICACCTech61146.2023.00020

Tomar, S., & Sharma, N. (2021). A systematic review of agricultural policies in terms of drivers, enablers, and bottlenecks: Comparison of three Indian states and a model bio-energy village located in different agro climatic regions. *Groundwater for Sustainable Development*, 15, 100683. Advance online publication. DOI: 10.1016/j.gsd.2021.100683

Tomar, S., Sharma, N., & Nehra, N. S. (2023). A sustainable rural entrepreneurship model developed by the organic farmers of India. *Emerald Emerging Markets Case Studies*, 13(2), 1–17. DOI: 10.1108/EEMCS-09-2022-0329

Topol, E. J. (2019). High-performance medicine: The convergence of human and artificial intelligence. *Nature Medicine*, 25(1), 44–56. DOI: 10.1038/s41591-018-0300-7 PMID: 30617339

Trache, D., Tarchoun, A. F., Abdelaziz, A., Bessa, W., Hussin, M. H., Brosse, N., & Thakur, V. K. (2022). Cellulose nanofibrils-graphene hybrids: Recent advances in fabrication, properties, and applications. *Nanoscale*, 14(35), 12515–12546. DOI: 10.1039/D2NR01967A PMID: 35983896

Tripathi, V. M., & Mohan, A. (2016). Microfinance and empowering rural women in the Terai, Uttarakhand, India. *International Journal of Agricultural and Statistics Sciences*, 12(2), 523–530.

Tripathy, S., Verma, D. K., Thakur, M., Patel, A. R., Srivastav, P. P., Singh, S., Chávez-González, M. L., & Aguilar, C. N. (2021). Encapsulated Food Products as a Strategy to Strengthen Immunity Against COVID-19. *Frontiers in Nutrition*, 8. Advance online publication. DOI: 10.3389/fnut.2021.673174

Tyagi, S., Krishna, K. H., Joshi, K., Ghodke, T. A., Kumar, A., & Gupta, A. (2023). Integration of PLCC modem and Wi-Fi for Campus Street Light Monitoring. In N. P., S. M., K. M., J. V., & G. K. (Eds.), *Proceedings - 4th IEEE 2023 International Conference on Computing, Communication, and Intelligent Systems, ICCCIS 2023* (pp. 1113 – 1116). Institute of Electrical and Electronics Engineers Inc. DOI: 10.1109/ICCCIS60361.2023.10425715

Tyagi, S., Mathur, K., Gupta, T., Khantwal, S., & Tripathi, V. (2023). The Effectiveness of Augmented Reality in Developing Pre-Primary Student's Cognitive Skills. *IEEE Region 10 Humanitarian Technology Conference, R10-HTC*, 997 – 1002. DOI: 10.1109/R10-HTC57504.2023.10461754

Tyagi, S., Jindal, T., Krishna, S. H., Hassen, S. M., Shukla, S. K., & Kaur, C. (2022). Comparative Analysis of Artificial Intelligence and its Powered Technologies Applications in the Finance Sector. *Proceedings of 5th International Conference on Contemporary Computing and Informatics, IC3I 2022*, 260 – 264. DOI: 10.1109/IC3I56241.2022.10073077

Uike, D., Agarwalla, S., Bansal, V., Chakravarthi, M. K., Singh, R., & Singh, P. (2022). Investigating the Role of Block Chain to Secure Identity in IoT for Industrial Automation. In D. R.K., S. A.Kr., K. G., & B. S. (Eds.), *Proceedings of the 2022 11th International Conference on System Modeling and Advancement in Research Trends, SMART 2022* (pp. 837 – 841). Institute of Electrical and Electronics Engineers Inc. https://doi.org/DOI: 10.1109/SMART55829.2022.10047385

Umamaheswaran, S. K., Singh, G., Dixit, A. K., Mc, S. C., Chakravarthi, M. K., & Singh, D. P. (2023). IOT-Based Analysis for Effective Continuous Monitoring Prevent Fraudulent Intrusions in Finance and Banking. *2023 International Conference on Artificial Intelligence and Smart Communication, AISC 2023*, 548–552. DOI: 10.1109/AISC56616.2023.10084920

Unhelkar, B., Joshi, S., Sharma, M., Prakash, S., Mani, A. K., & Prasad, M. (2022). Enhancing supply chain performance using RFID technology and decision support systems in the industry 4.0–A systematic literature review. *International Journal of Information Management Data Insights*, 2(2), 100084. Advance online publication. DOI: 10.1016/j.jjimei.2022.100084

United Nations. (2021). Transforming our world: the 2030 Agenda for Sustainable Development. Available at: https://sdgs.un.org/2030agenda

Uniyal, A. K., Kanojia, P., Khanna, R., & Dixit, A. K. (2022). Quantitative Analysis of the Impact of Demography and Job Profile on the Organizational Commitment of the Faculty Members in the HEI'S of Uttarakhand. *Communications in Computer and Information Science, 1742 CCIS*, 24–35. DOI: 10.1007/978-3-031-23647-1_3

Uniyal, S., Sarma, P. R. S., Kumar Mangla, S., Tseng, M.-L., & Patil, P. (2022). ICT as "Knowledge Management" for Assessing Sustainable Consumption and Production in Supply Chains. In *Research Anthology on Measuring and Achieving Sustainable Development Goals* (Vol. 3). IGI Global. DOI: 10.4018/978-1-6684-3885-5.ch048

Uniyal, A., Prajapati, Y. K., Ranakoti, L., Bhandari, P., Singh, T., Gangil, B., Sharma, S., Upadhyay, V. V., & Eldin, S. M. (2022). Recent Advancements in Evacuated Tube Solar Water Heaters: A Critical Review of the Integration of Phase Change Materials and Nanofluids with ETCs. *Energies*, 15(23). Advance online publication. DOI: 10.3390/en15238999

Uniyal, S., Mangla, S. K., & Patil, P. (2020). When practices count: Implementation of sustainable consumption and production in automotive supply chains. *Management of Environmental Quality*, 31(5), 1207–1222. DOI: 10.1108/MEQ-03-2019-0075

Uniyal, S., Mangla, S. K., Sarma, P. R. S., Tseng, M.-L., & Patil, P. (2021). ICT as "Knowledge management" for assessing sustainable consumption and production in supply chains. *Journal of Global Information Management*, 29(1), 164–198. DOI: 10.4018/JGIM.2021010109

Upreti, H., & Malhotra, R. K. (2024). Bridging The Urban-Rural Education Gap In India Through CSR (Corporate Social Responsibility) Initiatives: A Conceptual Study With Special Reference To Sustainable Development Goal 4 (Quality Education). In P. P.K. (Ed.), *E3S Web of Conferences* (Vol. 556). EDP Sciences. https://doi.org/DOI: 10.1051/e3sconf/202455601032

Upreti, H., Uddin, Z., Pandey, A. K., & Joshi, N. (2023). Particle swarm optimization based numerical study for pressure, flow, and heat transfer over a rotating disk with temperature dependent nanofluid properties. *Numerical Heat Transfer Part A*, 83(8), 815–844. DOI: 10.1080/10407782.2022.2156412

Using artificial intelligence to diagnose rare genetic diseases (2022, March 24). National Gaucher Foundation. Retrieved November 1, 2022, from https://www.gaucherdisease.org/blog/ai-and-rare-disease-diagnosis-national-gaucher-foundation/

Vaid, S. K., Kumar, B., Sharma, A., Shukla, A. K., & Srivastava, P. C. (2014). Effect of zinc solubilizing bacteria on growth promotion and zinc nutrition of rice. *Journal of Soil Science and Plant Nutrition*, 14(4), 889–910.

Valentijn, P., Tymchenko, L., Jacobson, T., Kromann, J., Biermann, C., AlMoslemany, M. A., & Arends, R. (2022). Digital health interventions for musculoskeletal pain conditions: Systematic review and meta-analysis of randomized controlled trials. *Journal of Medical Internet Research*, 24(9), e37869. DOI: 10.2196/37869 PMID: 36066943

Vasanthan, L., Natarajan, S. K., Babu, A., Kamath, M. S., & Kamalakannan, S. (2024). Digital health interventions for improving access to primary care in India: A scoping review. *PLOS Global Public Health*, 4(5), e0002645. Advance online publication. DOI: 10.1371/journal.pgph.0002645 PMID: 38743672

Vekariya, D., Rastogi, A., Priyadarshini, R., Patil, M., Kumar, M. S., & Pant, B. (2023). Mengers Authentication for efficient security system using Blockchain technology for Industrial IoT(IIOT) systems. *2023 3rd International Conference on Advance Computing and Innovative Technologies in Engineering, ICACITE 2023*, 894 – 896. https://doi.org/DOI: 10.1109/ICACITE57410.2023.10182454

Venkatesh, J., Shukla, P. K., Ahanger, T. A., Maheshwari, M., Pant, B., Hemamalini, R. R., & Halifa, A. (2023). A Complex Brain Learning Skeleton Comprising Enriched Pattern Neural Network System for Next Era Internet of Things. *Journal of Healthcare Engineering*, 2023. Advance online publication. DOI: 10.1155/2023/2506144

Vennila, H., Giri, N. C., Nallapaneni, M. K., Sinha, P., Bajaj, M., Abou Houran, M., & Kamel, S. (2022). Static and dynamic environmental economic dispatch using tournament selection based ant lion optimization algorithm. *Frontiers in Energy Research*, 10, 972069. Advance online publication. DOI: 10.3389/fenrg.2022.972069

Verma, M., Ahmad, W., Park, J.-H., Kumar, V., Vlaskin, M. S., Vaya, D., & Kim, H. (2022). One-step functionalization of chitosan using EDTA: Kinetics and isotherms modeling for multiple heavy metals adsorption and their mechanism. *Journal of Water Process Engineering*, 49, 102989. Advance online publication. DOI: 10.1016/j.jwpe.2022.102989

Verma, M., Sharma, S., Kumar, A., Kumar, V., Kim, M., Hong, Y., Lee, I., & Kim, H. (2021). Application of green nanomaterials in catalysis industry. In *Green Nanomaterials for Industrial Applications*. Elsevier., DOI: 10.1016/B978-0-12-823296-5.00013-7

Verma, P. K., Agrawal, P., Amorim, I., & Prodan, R. (2021). WELFake: Word Embedding over Linguistic Features for Fake News Detection. *IEEE Transactions on Computational Social Systems*, 8(4), 881–893. DOI: 10.1109/TCSS.2021.3068519

Verma, P., Chaudhari, V., Dumka, A., & Singh, R. P. (2022). A Meta-Analytical Review of Deep Learning Prediction Models for Big Data. In *Encyclopedia of Data Science and Machine Learning*. IGI Global., DOI: 10.4018/978-1-7998-9220-5.ch023

Verma, P., Kumar, V., Daim, T., Sharma, N. K., & Mittal, A. (2022). Identifying and prioritizing impediments of industry 4.0 to sustainable digital manufacturing: A mixed method approach. *Journal of Cleaner Production*, 356, 131639. Advance online publication. DOI: 10.1016/j.jclepro.2022.131639

Vijayalakshmi, S., Hasan, F., Priyadarshini, S. M., Durga, S., Verma, V., & Podile, V. (2022). Strategic Evaluation of Implementing Artificial Intelligence Towards Shaping Entrepreneurial Development During Covid- 19 Outbreaks. *2022 2nd International Conference on Advance Computing and Innovative Technologies in Engineering, ICACITE 2022*, 2570 – 2573. DOI: 10.1109/ICACITE53722.2022.9823894

Vogt, F., Wallwiener, M., & Fischer, J. M. (2021). The role of digital platforms in preventive healthcare: A systematic review. *Journal of Medical Internet Research*, 23(2), e24573. https://doi.org/10

von Humboldt, S., Mendoza-Ruvalcaba, N. M., Arias-Merino, E. D., Costa, A., Cabras, E., Low, G., & Leal, I. (2020). Smart technology and the meaning in life of older adults during the Covid-19 public health emergency period: A cross-cultural qualitative study. *International Review of Psychiatry (Abingdon, England)*, 32(7–8), 713–722. DOI: 10.1080/09540261.2020.1810643 PMID: 33016790

Wang, D., Wang, L., Zhang, Z., Wang, D., Zhu, H., Gao, Y., . . . Tian, F. (2021, May). "Brilliant AI doctor" in rural clinics: Challenges in AI-powered clinical decision support system deployment. In *Proceedings of the 2021 CHI conference on human factors in computing systems* (pp. 1-18).

Wang, Y., Fekadu, G., & You, J. H. (2023). Cost-Effectiveness Analyses of Digital Health Technology for Improving the Uptake of Vaccination Programs: Systematic Review. *Journal of Medical Internet Research*, 25, e45493. DOI: 10.2196/45493 PMID: 37184916

Wang, Y., Kung, L., & Byrd, T. A. (2018). Big data analytics: Understanding its capabilities and potential benefits for healthcare organizations. *Technological Forecasting and Social Change*, 126, 3–13. DOI: 10.1016/j.techfore.2015.12.019

Wazid, M., Das, A. K., & Park, Y. (2021). Blockchain-Envisioned Secure Authentication Approach in AIoT: Applications, Challenges, and Future Research. *Wireless Communications and Mobile Computing*, 2021(1), 3866006. Advance online publication. DOI: 10.1155/2021/3866006

Webster, M. (2021). *Do No Harm: protecting connected medical devices, healthcare, and data from hackers and adversarial nation states*. John Wiley & Sons.

William, P., Ramu, G., Kansal, L., Patil, P. P., Alkhayyat, A., & Rao, A. K. (2023). Artificial Intelligence Based Air Quality Monitoring System with Modernized Environmental Safety of Sustainable Development. *Proceedings - 2023 3rd International Conference on Pervasive Computing and Social Networking, ICPCSN 2023*, 756 – 761. DOI: 10.1109/ICPCSN58827.2023.00130

Wilson, E., Gannon, H., Chimhini, G., Fitzgerald, F., Khan, N., Lorencatto, F., Kesler, E., Nkhoma, D., Chiyaka, T., Haghparast-Bidgoli, H., Lakhanpaul, M., Cortina Borja, M., Stevenson, A. G., Crehan, C., Sassoon, Y., Hull-Bailey, T., Curtis, K., Chiume, M., Chimhuya, S., & Heys, M. (2022). Protocol for an intervention development and pilot implementation evaluation study of an e-health solution to improve newborn care quality and survival in two low-resource settings, Malawi and Zimbabwe: Neotree. *BMJ Open*, 12(7), e056605. DOI: 10.1136/bmjopen-2021-056605 PMID: 35790332

Wongchai, A., Shukla, S. K., Ahmed, M. A., Sakthi, U., Jagdish, M., & kumar, R. (2022). Artificial intelligence - enabled soft sensor and internet of things for sustainable agriculture using ensemble deep learning architecture. *Computers & Electrical Engineering*, 102, 108128. Advance online publication. DOI: 10.1016/j.compeleceng.2022.108128

Wong, L. W., Tan, G. W. H., Ooi, K. B., Lin, B., & Dwivedi, Y. K. (2024). Artificial intelligence-driven risk management for enhancing supply chain agility: A deep-learning-based dual-stage PLS-SEM-ANN analysis. *International Journal of Production Research*, 62(15), 5535–5555. DOI: 10.1080/00207543.2022.2063089

Xu, F., Sepúlveda, M. J., Jiang, Z., Wang, H., Li, J., Liu, Z., Yin, Y., Roebuck, M. C., Shortliffe, E. H., Yan, M., Song, Y., Geng, C., Tang, J., Purcell Jackson, G., Preininger, A. M., & Rhee, K. (2020). Effect of an artificial intelligence clinical decision support system on treatment decisions for complex breast cancer. *JCO Clinical Cancer Informatics*, 4(4), 824–838. DOI: 10.1200/CCI.20.00018 PMID: 32970484

Yadav, A., Singh, Y., Singh, S., & Negi, P. (2021). Sustainability of vegetable oil based bio-diesel as dielectric fluid during EDM process - A review. In S. Y. (Ed.), *Materials Today: Proceedings* (Vol. 46, pp. 11155 – 11158). Elsevier Ltd. DOI: 10.1016/j.matpr.2021.01.967

Yadav, P. M., Patra, I., Mittal, V., Nagorao, C. G., Udhayanila, R., & Saranya, A. (2023). Implementation of IOT on English Language Classroom Management. *2023 3rd International Conference on Advance Computing and Innovative Technologies in Engineering, ICACITE 2023*, 1686 – 1690. DOI: 10.1109/ICACITE57410.2023.10182984

Yadav, V. (2022). AI-Driven Predictive Models for Healthcare Supply Chains: Developing AI Models to Predict and Optimize Healthcare Supply Chains, especially during Global Health Emergencies. Progress in Medical Sciences. PMS-1127. *Prog Med Sci*, 6(1).

Yadav, A. R., Shekhar, S., Vidyarthi, A., Prakash, R., & Gowri, R. (2023). Hyper-Parameter Tuning with Grid and Randomized Search Techniques for Predictive Models of Hotel Booking. *IEEE International Conference on Electrical, Electronics, Communication and Computers, ELEXCOM 2023*. DOI: 10.1109/ELEXCOM58812.2023.10370718

Yadav, A. S., Alam, T., Gupta, G., Saxena, R., Gupta, N. K., Allamraju, K. V., Kumar, R., Sharma, N., Sharma, A., Pandey, U., & Agrawal, Y. (2022). A Numerical Investigation of an Artificially Roughened Solar Air Heater. *Energies*, 15(21), 8045. Advance online publication. DOI: 10.3390/en15218045

Yadav, A. S., Mishra, A., Dwivedi, K., Agrawal, A., Galphat, A., & Sharma, N. (2022). Investigation on performance enhancement due to rib roughened solar air heater. *Materials Today: Proceedings*, 63, 726–730. DOI: 10.1016/j.matpr.2022.05.071

Yadav, S., Samadhiya, A., Kumar, A., Luthra, S., & Pandey, K. K. (2024). Nexus between fintech, green finance and natural resources management: Transition of BRICS nation industries from resource curse to resource blessed sustainable economies. *Resources Policy*, 91, 104903. Advance online publication. DOI: 10.1016/j.resourpol.2024.104903

Yang, L., Ene, I. C., Arabi Belaghi, R., Koff, D., Stein, N., & Santaguida, P. (2022). Stakeholders' perspectives on the future of artificial intelligence in radiology: A scoping review. *European Radiology*, 32(3), 1477–1495. DOI: 10.1007/s00330-021-08214-z PMID: 34545445

Yeruva, A. R., Vijaya Durga, C. S. L., Gokulavasan, B., Pant, K., Chaturvedi, P., & Srivastava, A. P. (2022). A Smart Healthcare Monitoring System Based on Fog Computing Architecture. *Proceedings of International Conference on Technological Advancements in Computational Sciences, ICTACS 2022*, 904 – 909. DOI: 10.1109/ICTACS56270.2022.9987881

Yuan, W. X., Yan, B., Li, W., Hao, L. Y., & Yang, H. M. (2023). Blockchain-based medical health record access control scheme with efficient protection mechanism and patient control. *Multimedia Tools and Applications*, 82(11), 16279–16300. DOI: 10.1007/s11042-022-14023-3 PMID: 36404935

Yu, R., Lee, S., Xie, J., Billah, S. M., & Carroll, J. M. (2024). Human–AI Collaboration for Remote Sighted Assistance: Perspectives from the LLM Era. *Future Internet*, 16(7), 254. DOI: 10.3390/fi16070254

Yuri, Y. M. (2021, September). The promise of artificial intelligence: A review of the opportunities and challenges of artificial intelligence in healthcare. *British Medical Bulletin*, 139(1), 4–15. DOI: 10.1093/bmb/ldab016 PMID: 34405854

Yuvaraj, N., Srihari, K., Dhiman, G., Somasundaram, K., Sharma, A., Rajeskannan, S., Soni, M., Gaba, G. S., Alzain, M. A., & Masud, M. (2021). Nature-Inspired-Based Approach for Automated Cyberbullying Classification on Multimedia Social Networking. *Mathematical Problems in Engineering*, 2021, 1–12. Advance online publication. DOI: 10.1155/2021/6644652

Yu, W., Zhao, G., Liu, Q., & Song, Y. (2021). Role of big data analytics capability in developing integrated hospital supply chains and operational flexibility: An organizational information processing theory perspective. *Technological Forecasting and Social Change*, 163, 120417. DOI: 10.1016/j.techfore.2020.120417

Zaki, W. M., Shakhih, M. F., Ramlee, M. H., & Wahab, A. A. (2019). Smart Medical Chatbot with integrated contactless vital sign monitor. *Journal of Physics: Conference Series*, 1372(1), 012025. DOI: 10.1088/1742-6596/1372/1/012025

Zamiela, C., Hossain, N. U. I., & Jaradat, R. (2022). Enablers of resilience in the healthcare supply chain: A case study of US healthcare industry during COVID-19 pandemic. *Research in Transportation Economics*, 93, 101174. DOI: 10.1016/j.retrec.2021.101174

Zarifis, A., Kawalek, P., & Azadegan, A. (2021). Evaluating if trust and personal information privacy concerns are barriers to using health insurance that explicitly utilizes AI. *Journal of Internet Commerce*, 20(1), 66–83. DOI: 10.1080/15332861.2020.1832817

Zeidan, R. (2022). Obstacles to sustainable finance and the covid19 crisis. *Journal of Sustainable Finance & Investment*, 12(2), 525–528. DOI: 10.1080/20430795.2020.1783152

Zengin, Y., Naktiyok, S., Kaygın, E., Kavak, O., & Topçuoğlu, E. (2021). An investigation of industry 4.0 and Society 5.0 within the context of sustainable development goals. *Sustainability (Basel)*, 13(5), 1–16. DOI: 10.3390/su13052682

Zhang, J., Luximon, Y., & Li, Q. (2022). Seeking medical advice in mobile applications: How social cue design and privacy concerns influence trust and behavioral intention in impersonal patient–physician interactions. *Computers in Human Behavior*, 130, 107178. DOI: 10.1016/j.chb.2021.107178

Zhang, Y., Cao, C., Gu, J., & Garg, H. (2023). The Impact of Top Management Team Characteristics on the Risk Taking of Chinese Private Construction Enterprises. *Systems*, 11(2), 67. Advance online publication. DOI: 10.3390/systems11020067

Zingg, A., Franklin, A., Ross, A., & Myneni, S. (2024). A pilot acceptability evaluation of MomMind: A digital health intervention for Peripartum Depression prevention and management focused on health disparities. *PLOS Digital Health*, 3(5), e0000508. DOI: 10.1371/journal.pdig.0000508 PMID: 38776283

Žižek, S. Š., Mulej, M., & Potočnik, A. (2021). The sustainable socially responsible society: Well-being society 6.0. *Sustainability (Basel)*, 13(16), 9186. Advance online publication. DOI: 10.3390/su13169186

About the Contributors

Mohit Kukreti holds a Ph.D. in Human Resource Development (HRD), with over 25 years of international expertise in roles such as higher education administration, academic quality assurance, and strategic planning for higher education institutions (HEIs). With a rich career, he has held academic leadership positions in Nepal, Ethiopia, and Sultanate of Oman. He had served as the Head of Departments, Program Director for the IBA Program at the Directorate General of 6 CAS Colleges in the Ministry of Higher Education in the Sultanate of Oman. He is presently associated with the recently established government's University of Technology and Applied Sciences (College of Economics and Business Administration - Ibri). Dr. Kukreti's academic contributions extend to numerous articles and chapters published in peer-reviewed, ABDC and Scopus-indexed international Q1 journals and international books. His has participated and presented at conferences in the various countries .He has conducted various workshops, served as a session chair in conferences, undertaken editorial roles, and presently working as a reviewer for esteemed journals publishers such as Emerald, Routledge, IGI, and Inderscience. He has delivered talks at various universities, colleges and to the Ministry of Tourism officials, Government of India. His expertise extends to HEI quality assurance, HEI strategic Management, curriculum and courses designing at both undergraduate and postgraduate levels. He has lent his expertise as a Ph.D. examiner at several universities in India. His research areas span HRD, Business Management, HEI's strategy development and quality assurance, entrepreneurship, and tourism.

Sabina Sehapal is a dedicated and self-driven nursing professional with over 10 years of experience. She currently serves as an Associate Professor at the University Institute of Nursing, Chandigarh University, where she is the Single Point of Contact (SPOC) for both the advanced credit programme and a value-added course on the Prevention of Hospital-Acquired Infections. Sabina is recognized for her leadership, communication, and organizational skills, consistently raising the bar for achieving professional goals. Her extensive experience includes attending various workshops such as radiation therapy at Christian Medical College and Hospital, Ludhiana, maternal care at Civil Hospital, Mohali, and cardiac health at Fortis Mohali. She has also participated in key conferences and workshops on AIDS, tuberculosis, and evidence-based medicine. Sabina has spoken at panel discussions and remains actively engaged in professional development through national and international forums.

Rajesh Tiwari is working as Professor, Academic Coordinator and Chair Head-Finance in Graphic Era (Deemed to be University), Dehradun. He has over twenty years of rich experience in academics and industry. He is MBA (Finance), Chartered Financial Analyst (CFA), UGC-NET, PhD in Management. He has previously worked as Director in Indus University, Ahmedabad, United Group-Greater Noida (Affiliated to Guru Gobind Singh Indraprastha University, New Delhi), Sai Balaji Group-Pune. He has been academic coordinator for Management Programmes of Staffordshire University, UK and other reputed B Schools. He has won best paper award two times. He has published research papers in reputed journals indexed in Scopus, Web of Science and presented papers in national and international journals. He is actively involved in Faculty Development Programme and Management Development Programme. He has been engaged in social initiatives through plantation, blood donation, cleanliness drive and functional literacy programmes. He has been associated with Ministry of MSME, Government of India for Management Development Programmes and Entrepreneurship Development Programmes. He has 5 patents under his credit.

Kiran Sood is a Professor at Chitkara Business School, Chitkara University, Punjab, India. She received her Undergraduate and PG degrees in commerce from Panjab University, respectively, in 2002 and 2004. She earned her Master of Philosophy degree in 2008 and Doctor of Philosophy in Commerce with a concentration on Product Portfolio Performance of General Insurance Companies in 2017 from Panjabi University, Patiala, India. Before joining Chitkara University in July 2019, Kiran had served four organisations with a total experience of 18 yrs. She has published various articles in various journals and presented papers at various international conferences. She serves as an Editor of the refereed journal, particularly the IJBST International Journal of BioSciences and Technology and International Journal of Research Culture Society and The Journal of Corporate Governance, Insurance, and Risk Management (JCGIRM). 2021. Her research mainly focuses on regulations, marketing and Finance in insurance, insurance management, economics and management of innovation in insurance. She has edited more than ten books with various international publishers such as emerald, CRC, Taylors & Francis, AAP, WILEY scrivener, IET, Rivers Publishers, and IEEE.

* * *

Anamika Ahirwar, PhD, is a Professor in the Department of Computer Science and Engineering at Compucom Institute of Technology & Management, Jaipur, Rajasthan, India. With over 20 years of experience in teaching and research, Dr. Ahirwar has published five patents and contributed to more than 70 research papers and book chapters in prestigious national and international journals, conferences, and edited volumes. She has also authored and reviewed numerous books published by both national and international publishers. Additionally, she has edited more than four books with renowned international publishers, including CRC Press, Taylor & Francis, AAP, Wiley-Scrivener, and Nova Science. Dr. Ahirwar earned her PhD in Computer Applications from Rajiv Gandhi Proudyogiki Vishwavidyalaya (RGPV), Bhopal, India. Her research interests include medical imaging, data mining, celestial sound, the Internet of Things (IoT), and machine learning. She has delivered numerous expert and guest lectures, participated in seminars, and chaired sessions at various IEEE and other international conferences. Furthermore, she actively serves as a reviewer for esteemed journals published by IEEE, Springer, and John Wiley and is a member of the editorial board for IEEE conferences and other reputed international journals and conferences.

Bhumika Bansal is working as Associate Professor, General Management, NDIM, Delhi, India.

Vishwajit K. Barbudhe is a professor in the Artificial Intelligence and Data Science Department at Sandip Institute of Technology and Research Center (SITRC), Nashik. With over 14 years of academic experience, he has published more than 50 papers in international journals. Prof. Barbudhe has served as an expert at various international conferences and is a member of the editorial boards of over 15 international journals. He has reviewed for more than 40 journals and conferences and has guided more than 10 PG and 30 UG students. Additionally, he has authored over 40 books on Artificial Intelligence, Electronics, and Computer Engineering.

Santi Behera is working as an Assistant Professor in the Department of Computer Science and Engineering at VSSUT, Burla. She has 15 years of teaching and research experience and has published more than 60 research papers. Her area of expertise is image processing, particularly in medical imaging and agricultural applications.

Padam Bhushan is working as Associate professor, USB- BBA, Chandigarh University, India.

Khem Chand is working as Associate Professor, Mittal School of Business, Lovely Professional University, India.

Tripti Desai is a Professor in Management, New Delhi Institute of Management, India.

Sandip Dey was an Associate Professor and the HOD with the Department of Computer Science and Engineering, Global Institute of Management and Technology, India. He worked as an Assistant Professor in OmDayal Group of Institution and Camellia Institute of Technology for several years. Before that he worked as a Lecturer in Narula Institute of Technology. He is currently an Assistant Professor in the Department of Computer Science, Sukanta Mahavidyalaya, Jalpaiguri. He has coauthored one book titled "Quantum-Inspired Metaheuristics for Image Analysis"; Publisher: John Wiley & Sons, UK, coedited three books, and authored or coauthored about 60 research publications in international journals, book chapters, and conference proceedings. His research interests include soft computing, hybrid intelligence, quantum computing, and image analysis. Dey reviewed several international peer-reviewed journals like Applied Soft Computing, Swarm and Evolutionary Computation, Information Sciences, Journal of Computational Science, Engineering Applications of Artificial Intelligence, Expert Systems With Applications, Advanced Engineering Informatics, IEEE Transactions on Signal Processing and so on.

Harshi Garg is a dedicated PhD scholar, is recognized for her expertise as a market and user researcher & consultant, with a particular focus on digital and social media analysis. Her contributions to the field are marked by a series of notable achievements. Not only has she presented her research findings at international conferences, but she has also authored research papers in prestigious journals and contributed chapters to esteemed Scopus indexed books. Harshi's commitment to rigorous inquiry and her diligent approach to research underscore her standing as a respected figure in her field.

Ridhima Goel is a distinguished research scholar at the Institute of Management Studies and Research, Maharshi Dayanand University, India. She brings a rich interdisciplinary approach to her research, combining her business administration and English literature expertise with an M.B.A. and an M.A. in English from the same institution. As an educator, she imparts knowledge to postgraduate students, teaching open elective subjects such as Fundamentals of Management, Information Technology, and Fundamentals of Marketing. Ridhima has published several research articles in Scopus-indexed and Web of Science journals. Additionally, she has contributed to Scopus-indexed book chapters published by IGI Global and Emerald Publishing. Her research interests encompass human resource management, human-computer interaction, organizational behavior, and occupational health.

Ashulekha Gupta is a Professor of Data Analytics and Economics in the Department of Management Studies at Graphic Era (Deemed to be University), Dehradun, Uttarakhand, India. She is an avid researcher in the diverse field of Artificial Intelligence, Deep Learning, Big Data, Block Chain, Industry 4.0, Circular Economy, and Behavioural Economics. She has a distinguished academic record and holds a Doctorate and a Post-Graduation in International Economics. In addition, She is also a Post Graduate in Marketing Management and International Business. Dr. Gupta has more than 22 years of rich experience in teaching, research and Industry. Beside academics she also holds different Administrative positions in Academic Institutions and Corporate. Dr. Gupta's has published more than 66 research papers Scopus and SCI indexed journals, presented in national and international conferences which includes Bangkok, Thailand and contributed various Chapters in edited books. She had published research papers in ABDC- A, B and C and ABS Category Journals. Few Journal names are IEEE Transactions on Engineering Management, Cleaner Engineering Technology, Journal of Modelling in Management, Journal of Financial Service Marketing, Sustainable Futures, International Journal of Information Management Data Insights, Journal of Applied Research in Higher Education and Journal of Water Process Engineering. Dr. Gupta received research grant for a socio economic development project from UCOST.

Priyanka Gupta is an Assistant professor at Graphic Era Deemed to be University. For the last 4 years, she has been contributing in teaching and research. She has developed skills in qualitative and quantitative research methods. Her current research areas are Sustainable Human Resource Management, Artificial Intelligence, Digital Stress, Internet of Things (IoT).

Swati Gupta specializes in teaching subjects such as Consumer Behavior, Market Research, Marketing Management, Organizational Behavior, Sales and Distribution Management, Services Marketing and Retail Management. Known for her energy and dedication, she possesses excellent analytical, problem-solving and decision-making skills. Currently, she is working as an Assistant Professor at Chitkara Business School, Chitkara University, Punjab, India. Having served as the editor for various books under renowned publishing houses including NOVA, Emerald, IGI Global and AAP, she has contributed significantly to the academic field. Additionally, she has undertaken the role of a reviewer for IGI Global and has chapters indexed in Scopus covering topics in marketing, Digital Marketing, Green Business Management, Consumer Behavior among others. Furthermore, she holds patent and copyrights in her name.

Anuradha Jain is working as a Professor, Vivekananda Institute of Professional Studies, India.

Vibhuti Jain is working as Assistant Professor in the Department of Management Studies, Graphic Era (Deemed to be University).

Sudhanshu Joshi is currently working in Operations & Supply Chain Management Area, Doon University, INDIA. His research interest anchored within Digital-Twin, Cyber Supply Chain Management with special focus on green supply chain network design, sustainable supply chain design, and coordination in humanitarian supply chain network, application of big data analytics in sustainable and humanitarian supply chains, emerging technologies (Including Industry 4.0), Circular Economy, Agriculture Supply Chain and Soft-computing Applications in Supply Chain Management. He is member with leading Societies including CSI, IEEE, POMS, INFORMS. He is a series editor of research note series CRC press, Taylor & Francis.

Sudhanshu Joshi is currently working in Operations & Supply Chain Management Area, Doon University, India. His research interest anchored within Digital-Twin, Cyber Supply Chain Management with special focus on green supply chain network design, sustainable supply chain design, and coordination in humanitarian supply chain network, application of big data analytics in sustainable and humanitarian supply chains, emerging technologies (Including Industry 4.0), Circular Economy, Agriculture Supply Chain and Soft-computing Applications in Supply Chain Management. He is member with leading Societies including CSI, IEEE, POMS, INFORMS. He is a series editor of research note series CRC press, Taylor & Francis.

Vanshika Kakkar is a student of MBA at the Department of Management Studies, Graphic Era (Deemed to be University).

Narendra Kumar Kamila is presently working as Professor and Head, Department of Computer Science and Engineering, C V Raman College of Engineering, Bhubaneswar, Odisha, India. He received his master degree from Indian Institute of Technology, Kharagpur and subsequently obtained his Ph. D. degree from Utkal University, Bhubaneswar in the year 2000. Prof. Kamila was also post doctoral fellow to University of Arkansas, USA. He has published several research papers in the national/international journal of repute in the field of wireless sensor networking, Adhoc-networking, Image processing, meta cognition, data privacy/security. He has served as program committee members in many international conferences. He has also conducted staff development programs under the financial support of All Indian Council for Technical Education as chief-coordinator. However, he had organized "International Conference on Computer Technology (ICCT-2010)" from 3rd Dec. to 5th Dec. 2010 at C V Raman College of Engineering successfully as General/Local Organizing Chair with financial assistance from AICTE, CSIR and Biju Patnaik University of Technology. He was also Guest Editor of International Journal of Computer and Communication Technology, Vol. 2, Issues 2, 3 and 4, 2010. He has completed many projects sponsored by various sponsoring agencies. He has guided many M.Tech. and Ph.D. students under different universities. However Dr. Kamila has been appointed as DSC member of Biju Patnaik University of Technology, Dr. Kamila has been rendering his best services as editorial board member to American Journal of Intelligent System, American Journal of Advances in Networks, American journal of Networks and Communications, Reviewer of International journal of Intelligent Information System(USA), Reviewer of International journal of Automation Control and Intelligent Systems(USA), Reviewer of Elsevier Publication, Reviewer of AMSE, modelling simulation(France), editor-in-chief of International Journal of Advanced Computer Engineering and Communication Technology, former editor-in-chief of International Journal of Communication Network and Security(IJCNS) and editor-in-chief of many international conference proceedings.

Bhavana S. Karmore is working as Assistant Professor and Head of Department at BCA and MCA Department of G. H. Raisoni University, Amravati for U.G. and P. G. Department . Total Years of Experience 15+. She publish more than 20+ Papers in International Journals . She work as International

Expert at International Conferences. She worked as a Editorial Board Members in 5+ International Journals and Reviewer in 10+ International Journals and International Conferences . Project Guided 10+ PG students and 10+ UG Students . She publish more than 10+ books of Electronics and Computer Engg. subjects. 3 Design patent, 2 copyright . Dr. Bhavana S. Karmore is an esteemed academician currently serving as an Assistant Professor and Head of the Department at G. H. Raisoni University in Amravati, overseeing the Bachelor of Computer Applications (BCA) and Master of Computer Applications (MCA) programs. With over 15 years of experience in the field, she has made significant contributions to both undergraduate and postgraduate education. Dr. Karmore's research prowess is evident through her extensive publication record, with more than 20 papers published in reputable international journals. Furthermore, she has showcased her expertise as an international expert at various conferences, enriching the academic discourse with her insights and knowledge. Her commitment to academic excellence extends beyond research and teaching roles. Dr. Karmore has served as an editorial board member for more than 5 international journals, contributing to the dissemination of scholarly work and fostering academic collaboration. Additionally, her role as a reviewer for over 10 international journals and conferences highlights her dedication to maintaining the quality and rigor of academic publications. In the realm of student mentorship, Dr. Karmore has guided the research endeavors of more than 10 postgraduate and undergraduate students, nurturing the next generation of scholars and professionals in the field of electronics and computer engineering. Her scholarly contributions also include authoring more than 10 books on subjects related to electronics and computer engineering, further solidifying her status as a thought leader in her field. Moreover, her innovative ideas have been recognized through the acquisition of 3 design patents and 2 copyrights, showcasing her ability to translate theoretical knowledge into tangible innovations. Overall, Dr. Bhavana S. Karmore's multifaceted contributions to academia encompass research, teaching, mentoring, and innovation, making her a highly respected figure in the field of computer science and engineering.

Mohammad Kashif is a distinguished academician and researcher in the area of finance, financial technology, Sustainability, green finance economics and international business at Graphic Era Deemed to be University, Dehradun, India . He has several publications indexed in WoS, Scopus and ABDC. He authored a text book titled Financial Management for undergraduate students. He is the editor in upcoming edited books under Emerald Publishers and Bentham Science Publishers. He is guiding PhD scholars in his area of expertise. Besides he is a member of several professional bodies at university level. He has been awarded many academic and research awards by reputed organizations.

Sanjeet Kumar is working as Chairperson and Professor, Department of Business Administration, CDLU, Sirsa, India.

Jyoti Kumari is a Research Scholar at VSSUT, Burla. She is pursuing her Ph.D. in Neurological Disorder Diagnosis using Image Processing. She has published 5 research papers.

Geetha Manoharan is currently working in Telangana as an assistant professor at SR University. She is the university-level PhD program coordinator and has also been given the additional responsibility of In Charge Director of Publications and Patents under the Research Division at SR University.

Nilamadhab Mishra is an Associate Professor in the School of Computer Science and Engineering, AI-ML Division, at VIT Bhopal University, India. He received his Doctor of Philosophy (Ph.D.) in Computer Science and Information Engineering with a specialization in AI-data science and machine learning from Chang Gung University, Taiwan. He has over 23 years of national and international involvement in academic teaching and research at recognized Indian, Taiwanese, and African universities. He has over 100 publications in SCI/SCIE and SCOPUS-indexed journals, ISBN books and chapters, Indian and Australian patents, IEEE conference proceedings, etc. He has been a reviewer, associate editor, and editorial board member for SCI/SCIE-indexed journals and conferences. He has been involved with several professional bodies: "Fellow Member of "ISROSET"; Fellow Member of "ISRD"; Senior Member of "ASR" (Hong Kong); Senior Member of "IEDRC" (Hong Kong); and Member of "IEEE Collabratec". He is currently an Associate Editor for two SCOPUS-indexed journals, and his research interests span the areas of AI, Data Science, Machine Learning, and Cognitive Analytics & Applications.

Laris Mistrean is an associate Professor, The Academy of Economic Studies of Moldova, Moldova.

Reepu, a distinguished educator and researcher from Chandigarh University, not only imparts knowledge to MBA students but actively contributes to the academic discourse. Holding a PhD in Finance, Dr Reepu has showcased her research prowess at numerous national and international conferences, enriching her perspectives and staying at the forefront of business trends. Her dynamic teaching style and participation in academic forums reflect her dedication to shaping future business leaders with a global perspective.

Latika Sahni is working as Professor, Department general Management, NDIM, New Delhi, India.

P.K. Sethy is an esteemed Associate Professor in the Department of Electronics and Communication Engineering at Guru Ghasidas Vishwavidyalaya (Central University, Govt. of India), Bilaspur, Chhattisgarh, India, a position he has held since December 2023. Prior to this, he served at Sambalpur University (State University, Govt. of Odisha) from February 2013 to December 2023 and worked as an Engineer in Doordarshan, Ministry of Broadcasting, Govt. of India, between August 2009 and February 2013. Dr. Sethy holds a Ph.D. from Sambalpur University, an M. Tech. from IIT Dhanbad, and a B.E. from BPUT Odisha. He hails from the small village of Kapundi, located on the banks of the Baitarani River in Keonjhar District, Odisha. His early education, including primary and intermediate studies, took place in Keonjhar, Odisha. Dr. Sethy serves as an editor of three reputable journals and is an editorial board member for the International Journal of Electrical and Computer Engineering and Ingénierie des Systèmes d'Information (IIETA). He is also an editorial member for Automation, Control and Intelligent Systems (Science Publishing Group) and PriMera Scientific Engineering (ISSN: 2834-2550), and holds the position of Associate Editor of Onkologia I Radioterapia. With two patents and one copyright to his name, Dr. Sethy has been recognized for his outstanding contributions. In 2020, he received the "InSc Young Achiever Award" for his research paper on "Detection of coronavirus (COVID-19) based on Deep Features and Support Vector Machine," organized by the Institute of Scholars, Ministry of MSME, Government of India. A Senior Member of IEEE, he actively engages as a reviewer for various journals and serves as a session chair at international conferences. He has also been recognized as one of the World's Top 2% Scientists by Stanford University in both 2023 and 2024.

Janmejai Shah is an Assistant professor at Graphic Era Deemed to be University, India. He is pursuing his PhD in the area of supply chains and innovation from Graphic Era Deemed to be University. His area of interest includes SCM, Circular Economy and Industry 4.0 technologies.

Gajendra Sharma is working as a Professor, Management, New Delhi Institute of Management, India.

Manu Sharma is an Associate professor at Graphic Era Deemed to be University. She has received her Post-Doctoral Fellowship sponsored by Indian Council of Social Science Research (ICSSR), Ministry of Human Resource Development, Government of India, from Doon University, INDIA. For the last ten years, she has been contributing in teaching and research. She has developed skills in qualitative and quantitative research methods such as Multi-Criteria Decision Making, Fuzzy Theory, Multivariate analysis etc. Her current research areas are Digital supply chains, Digital Marketing, Circular economy, Sustainability, Waste management, Internet of Things (IoT). She is serving various journals as an editorial board member in the area of Digital Technologies, Sustainable development, Waste Management, Supply Chains published by Emerald, Springer, Elsevier and IGI.

Rishi Prakash Shukla is working as Professor (Marketing) at Jaipuria Institute of Management, Jaipur. He has about 15 years of experience in academics. With 15 years of comprehensive experience, he has made significant contributions through extensive research and development. Dr. Shukla holds 6 patents and has authored 20 research papers, showcasing his deep expertise in Marketing. His industry journey spans prestigious institutions such as Symbiosis Institute of Business Management, Symbiosis Centre for Management Studies, Chandigarh University and projects at the Indian Institute of Management Ahmedabad. Dr. Shukla's scholarly interests include cutting-edge technologies, particularly in the field of neuromarketing. He is certified by IBM and SAS in advanced predictive modeling and has authored 5 books on futuristic technologies. Beyond academia, Dr. Shukla is known for his affable nature, passion for travel, and innovative social experiments using technology.

Malkeet Singh is working as an Assistant Professor, JCDV - Jan Nayak Choudhary Devi Lal Vidyapeeth, Sirsa.

Azad Singh, JRF/SRF, MBA, Ph.D. from Chaudhary Devi Lal University, Sirsa, Haryana, India. He is a reviewer in various Journal. He has specialized in Human Resource Management, Marketing Management, and General Management. He has published more than 15 research papers, and book chapters in edited books and attended various conferences regarding Human Resource Management and other management areas, and invited talks on a wide variety of management subjects. With 8+ years of blended experience (Industry & Academia) presently working as an Assistant Professor position at, Geeta University, Panipat (Haryana).

Gurinderpal Singh is working as an associate professor, University School of Business, Chandigarh University, India.

Mandeep Singh is working as Associate Professor, AIT-APEX, Chandigarh University, India.

Raj Kumar Singh (Ph. D., UGC-NET, MBA, and M.A.-Eco), an alumnus of IIM Indore, is an Associate Professor of Marketing in the SoM-MBA, Graphic Era Hill University, Dehradun, India. He has contributed over seventeen years in teaching and corporate. His leading publications are in national and international Scopus (Q1 & Q2), ABDC, and Thomson Reuters indexed journals. His research domains are marketing, digital marketing, entrepreneurship, and bibliometric analysis. He is the guest reviewer of various Scopus, ABDC, and Thomson Reuters-indexed journals. He has delivered several lectures at All India Radio and the Ministry of Agriculture in association with NABARD. He is running an NGO, Manav Utthan Society, India, and has conducted hundreds of programs for social upliftment across India.

Nikita Singhal is currently working as an Associate Professor at IIMT University. Her area of specialization is Taxation, Insurance and Banking. She has published around 31 research papers in ABDC listed, Web of Science and SCOPUS index journals including Journals of Taylor and Francis and conferences of national and international repute. She also has books on accountancy and three chapters in Edited book. Dr. Nikita Singhal has also received a special mention paper award for her manuscript in the 7th PAN IIM world management conference organized by IIM Rohtak. She has been speaker and organizer of various faculty development programs and conferences. She has been appointed as reviewer of research papers for journals of Emerald Publishing House, Springer, Sage and Taylor and Francis. She is also a managing editor of IJAST Journal of IIMT University. She has completed her Ph.D. from Department of Commerce, Aligarh Muslim University and awarded JRF (Commerce) in 2013 and JRF (Management) in 2012. Dr. Nikita Singhal is also an awardee of Major Research project on the title, "Insurance claim settlement during Covid-19: A new challenge for Indian insurance sector" sponsored by Indian Council of Social Science Research.

Jagdeep Singla is presently employed as an Associate Professor at the Institute of Management Studies and Research, Maharshi Dayanand University, India. He had also served as a Professor at HPKV Business School, CUHP, Dharamshala. He has more than 28 years of teaching and industry experience after completing his post-graduation. He has more than 35 research papers/articles to his credit, published in national and international journals of repute. He has supervised 11 Ph.D. His areas of Specialization are Production and Operations Management, Supply Chain Management, Marketing Management, Human Resource Management, and Brand Management.

Sanjay Taneja is working as Associate Professor, DOMS, Graphic Era Deemed to be University, India.

Luan Vardari is Vice-Rector for Teaching, Student Affairs and Scientific Research, University "Ukshin Hoti" Rruga e Shkronjave Nr. 1, Kosova.

Vivek Verma is working as Assistant Professor in Department of Management Studies, Graphic Era (Deemed to be University).

Shraddha N. Zanjat currently serves as an Assistant Professor in the EEE Department at the School of Engineering and Technology (SOET), Sandip University, Nashik. With 10 years of teaching experience and 2 years of industry exposure, she brings a wealth of knowledge to her role. She holds a post-graduation degree, a Master of Technology in Electronics and Communication, from RTMN

University. Additionally, she is pursuing her PhD at Sandip University, Nashik. Prof. Shraddha N. Zanjat has presented ten conference papers at both national and international levels and has published five papers in esteemed international journals such as IEEE, UGC, and others. Furthermore, she has obtained five Indian design patents. She is also a member of two technical association bodies. Prof. Shraddha N. Zanjat has registered four copyrights under her name and has published two book chapters in Scopus-indexed publications. Additionally, she has authored more than 50 books with international publications and has received royalties of about 20k.

Index

A

accountability 19, 44, 48, 49, 60, 84, 85, 86, 87, 88, 89, 90, 92, 169, 171, 173, 185, 187, 189, 191, 193, 270, 272, 273, 276, 282, 284, 285, 286, 318, 320, 351, 371, 374, 377, 379, 380, 453, 456, 459, 461, 462, 464, 523, 528, 530, 546
Anthropometrics 394
Application 1, 2, 7, 12, 20, 27, 32, 47, 49, 57, 69, 72, 73, 74, 107, 110, 115, 125, 129, 149, 156, 158, 159, 164, 165, 166, 171, 183, 195, 205, 206, 208, 209, 223, 224, 230, 232, 233, 235, 236, 239, 247, 262, 269, 275, 281, 282, 291, 297, 298, 302, 321, 324, 329, 330, 333, 356, 360, 362, 371, 383, 385, 386, 387, 391, 397, 402, 403, 404, 406, 411, 414, 434, 437, 444, 459, 461, 463, 468, 470, 479, 486, 487, 494, 495, 506, 510, 520, 542

B

Bioinformatics 56, 393, 399
Biomechanics 390, 391, 394, 395, 396, 397
Bioprinting 28, 115, 116, 126, 134, 136
Block chain 163, 176, 206, 232, 238, 247, 248, 251, 254, 294, 301, 388, 436

C

chatbots 28, 116, 117, 118, 119, 135, 136, 181, 182, 183, 185, 186, 187, 188, 189, 190, 191, 192, 193, 194, 197, 463, 475, 523, 526
Classification 32, 42, 46, 68, 72, 80, 136, 139, 140, 142, 143, 144, 145, 146, 147, 149, 150, 151, 152, 153, 172, 203, 215, 216, 217, 218, 219, 220, 221, 222, 223, 230, 262, 291, 292, 323, 327, 335, 336, 355, 358, 364, 382, 414, 421, 422, 434, 441, 459, 505, 551, 555
cost-effectiveness 1, 2, 3, 4, 5, 6, 7, 8, 9, 10, 23, 52, 83, 86, 87, 89, 90, 91, 109, 243, 283, 303, 304, 313, 367, 378, 499, 501, 503, 534, 536
cost efficiency 23, 37, 63, 65, 100, 104, 121, 241
cost management 367
cost reduction 2, 52, 86, 107, 254, 495
COVID-19 18, 19, 22, 32, 35, 44, 47, 68, 70, 71, 100, 103, 108, 110, 111, 113, 149, 167, 175, 177, 178, 197, 236, 238, 250, 251, 252, 260, 262, 270, 275, 278, 298, 301, 304, 305, 306, 326, 339, 340, 341, 343, 344, 346, 347, 348, 349, 350, 351, 352, 353, 357, 375, 378, 386, 388, 400, 401, 403, 411, 412, 413, 414, 415, 416, 417, 418, 419, 420, 423, 424, 425, 426, 427, 428, 429, 440, 441, 466, 467, 474, 475, 496, 510, 519, 521, 525, 527, 537, 544, 545, 552

D

data analysis 22, 42, 45, 47, 118, 120, 134, 139, 140, 141, 142, 143, 149, 153, 159, 209, 250, 334, 339, 363, 422, 455, 488, 497, 499
Data Analytics 11, 39, 40, 41, 55, 56, 58, 59, 63, 65, 66, 68, 83, 101, 108, 110, 111, 113, 121, 140, 177, 250, 269, 270, 284, 286, 288, 297, 308, 319, 321, 342, 343, 346, 348, 349, 352, 368, 372, 389, 392, 395, 400, 433, 448, 457, 466, 474, 475, 476, 478, 479, 493, 500, 504
data governance 60, 196, 367, 368, 370, 371, 377, 459
Data Mining 40, 135, 140, 141, 142, 147, 148, 158, 329, 343, 404, 506
Decision Tree 142, 144, 147, 148, 149, 150, 151, 152, 153, 411, 422, 423, 429
Detection 3, 9, 22, 28, 38, 39, 40, 42, 45, 46, 58, 68, 69, 70, 71, 72, 75, 78, 79, 80, 116, 122, 130, 136, 137, 148, 151, 166, 177, 178, 179, 197, 205, 206, 208, 213, 216, 218, 219, 220, 221, 222, 223, 224, 233, 236, 250, 264, 291, 294, 295, 296, 324, 325, 326, 327, 328, 334, 335, 339, 342, 343, 344, 348, 349, 355, 356, 357, 358, 359, 360, 362, 363, 364, 382, 386, 389, 392, 394, 400, 414, 415, 416, 436, 461, 466, 469, 470, 487, 492, 505, 506, 509, 510, 518, 519, 520, 541, 551, 552, 553, 555
Digital Health 1, 2, 3, 4, 5, 6, 7, 8, 9, 10, 13, 27, 30, 32, 101, 108, 137, 148, 169, 171, 175, 176, 241, 242, 243, 248, 249, 250, 251, 254, 259, 260, 261, 263, 264, 265, 267, 268, 269, 270, 272, 275, 276, 277, 278, 281, 283, 284, 285, 286, 307, 308, 310, 312, 317, 339, 341, 346, 349, 350, 351, 352, 353, 369, 370, 371, 374, 375, 376, 377, 378, 379, 380, 475, 476, 477, 479, 513, 529, 530, 531, 532, 533, 534, 544
Digital healthcare 2, 3, 4, 6, 7, 171, 318, 319, 320, 321, 532, 534
Digital Health Technology 7, 10, 101, 175, 261
digital interventions 1, 3, 4, 5, 6, 346
Digital Stress 241, 242, 243, 252, 253, 254, 255, 256, 257, 258, 259, 261
Digital Transformation 32, 73, 165, 205, 232, 241, 242, 252, 255, 256, 259, 263, 329, 347, 359, 384, 440, 441, 453, 482, 541

E

efficiency 1, 2, 3, 4, 7, 13, 23, 24, 27, 28, 29, 37, 38, 44, 52, 53, 54, 63, 65, 66, 70, 74, 83, 89, 91, 100, 101, 104, 105, 106, 107, 112, 115, 121, 128, 129, 133, 153, 161, 165, 166, 167, 176, 181, 185, 187, 189, 190, 192, 194, 196, 241, 247, 252, 254, 255, 265, 268, 272, 273, 274, 275, 277, 280, 281, 282, 284, 285, 286, 307, 314, 315, 326, 330, 344, 345, 346, 351, 357, 360, 368, 372, 377, 391, 392, 393, 394, 395, 397, 420, 440, 442, 445, 448, 450, 454, 455, 456, 458, 459, 460, 462, 464, 465, 477, 478, 480, 482, 483, 491, 492, 494, 495, 497, 498, 499, 500, 501, 502, 509, 511, 518, 521, 525, 529, 533, 536, 542, 545, 549

empathy 61, 117, 119, 184, 453, 455, 456, 458, 460, 463, 465

Environment 14, 16, 24, 42, 43, 55, 57, 71, 74, 77, 78, 91, 96, 100, 101, 130, 159, 165, 168, 179, 237, 248, 256, 259, 265, 268, 274, 277, 278, 281, 288, 296, 298, 299, 300, 316, 317, 319, 324, 331, 333, 335, 349, 351, 352, 353, 356, 361, 362, 372, 373, 386, 387, 409, 437, 442, 443, 457, 458, 459, 460, 462, 470, 479, 480, 482, 500, 503, 507, 524, 535, 539

equitable access 4, 90, 91, 267, 270, 272, 274, 278, 287, 319, 322, 343, 346, 348, 352, 367, 370, 371, 373, 374, 375, 378, 458

Equity 30, 60, 86, 171, 172, 174, 242, 268, 271, 275, 278, 279, 280, 282, 283, 285, 305, 315, 341, 351, 367, 368, 369, 370, 372, 373, 374, 376, 380, 480, 483, 497, 500, 524, 534, 546

Ergonomics 70, 326, 357, 391, 394, 395

ethical considerations 37, 44, 48, 58, 90, 91, 106, 172, 185, 189, 190, 193, 264, 284, 339, 353, 368, 375, 376, 378, 394, 443, 447, 450, 452, 457, 460, 463, 494, 497, 501, 516

Ethics 30, 84, 86, 89, 90, 110, 112, 171, 182, 259, 318, 347, 379, 448, 452, 461, 483, 513, 519

F

Feature Selection 144, 147, 215

Fintech 157, 203, 327, 337, 358, 403, 439, 440, 441, 442, 443, 444, 445, 446, 447, 448, 449, 450, 451, 452, 467, 540

Fraud 85, 116, 122, 137, 247, 254, 285, 441, 448, 509, 510, 518, 519, 520, 530

funding strategies 282, 285, 286, 367

G

genomics 28, 39, 42, 57, 64, 66, 115, 127, 134, 176, 250, 375, 377, 393, 473

Global Health 8, 9, 11, 12, 13, 20, 26, 27, 30, 57, 113, 197, 242, 243, 248, 308, 339, 340, 341, 342, 343, 348, 367, 368, 369, 370, 371, 372, 373, 374, 375, 376, 378, 380, 392, 411, 412, 413, 473, 474, 475, 476, 480, 481, 482, 483, 484, 521, 522, 524, 527, 532, 534

global health outcomes 473, 475, 480, 521, 534

H

Health 1, 2, 3, 4, 5, 6, 7, 8, 9, 10, 11, 12, 13, 16, 18, 19, 20, 21, 22, 23, 24, 25, 26, 27, 28, 30, 32, 33, 34, 35, 38, 39, 40, 42, 43, 44, 47, 48, 49, 50, 51, 53, 55, 56, 57, 58, 59, 60, 62, 63, 64, 65, 66, 68, 74, 83, 85, 87, 88, 89, 90, 91, 95, 96, 99, 100, 101, 102, 103, 104, 106, 107, 108, 109, 110, 111, 112, 113, 115, 116, 117, 118, 122, 127, 128, 129, 133, 135, 136, 137, 140, 141, 142, 147, 148, 152, 156, 161, 162, 163, 164, 165, 166, 167, 168, 169, 170, 171, 172, 173, 174, 175, 176, 177, 181, 182, 183, 184, 185, 186, 187, 188, 189, 190, 191, 192, 193, 194, 195, 196, 197, 198, 205, 214, 231, 236, 241, 242, 243, 245, 246, 247, 248, 249, 250, 251, 252, 254, 255, 256, 257, 258, 259, 260, 261, 262, 263, 264, 265, 267, 268, 269, 270, 271, 272, 273, 274, 275, 276, 277, 278, 279, 280, 281, 282, 283, 284, 285, 286, 287, 288, 292, 293, 304, 305, 306, 307, 308, 309, 310, 311, 312, 313, 314, 315, 316, 317, 318, 319, 320, 321, 327, 329, 333, 339, 340, 341, 342, 343, 344, 345, 346, 347, 348, 349, 350, 351, 352, 353, 367, 368, 369, 370, 371, 372, 373, 374, 375, 376, 377, 378, 379, 380, 389, 391, 392, 393, 396, 398, 399, 400, 401, 403, 405, 408, 411, 412, 413, 415, 416, 417, 418, 419, 420, 423, 424, 425, 426, 427, 428, 429, 433, 434, 456, 457, 458, 459, 460, 461, 462, 463, 466, 468, 473, 474, 475, 476, 477, 478, 479, 480, 481, 482, 483, 484, 488, 492, 495, 496, 504, 509, 510, 511, 512, 513, 516, 517, 518, 519, 520, 521, 522, 523, 524, 525, 526, 527, 528, 529, 530, 531, 532, 533, 534, 535, 536, 537, 544, 550, 551

Healthcare 1, 2, 3, 4, 5, 6, 7, 9, 11, 13, 20, 22, 23, 25, 26, 27, 28, 29, 30, 31, 34, 37, 38, 39, 40, 41, 42, 43, 44, 45, 46, 48, 49, 50, 51, 52, 53, 54, 55, 56, 57, 58, 59, 60, 61, 62, 63, 64, 65, 66, 83, 84, 85, 86, 87, 88, 89, 90, 91, 92, 99, 100, 101, 102, 103, 104, 105, 106, 107, 108, 109, 110, 111, 112, 113,

115, 116, 117, 118, 119, 120, 122, 124, 127, 128, 129, 130, 133, 134, 135, 136, 137, 138, 139, 140, 141, 142, 143, 147, 148, 149, 153, 154, 161, 162, 163, 164, 165, 166, 167, 168, 169, 170, 171, 172, 173, 174, 175, 176, 181, 182, 183, 184, 185, 186, 187, 188, 189, 190, 191, 192, 193, 194, 195, 196, 197, 198, 200, 212, 228, 239, 241, 242, 243, 244, 245, 246, 247, 249, 251, 254, 255, 256, 258, 259, 260, 261, 262, 263, 264, 265, 267, 268, 269, 270, 271, 272, 273, 274, 275, 276, 277, 278, 279, 280, 281, 282, 283, 284, 285, 286, 287, 292, 302, 303, 304, 305, 306, 307, 308, 309, 310, 311, 312, 313, 314, 315, 316, 317, 318, 319, 320, 321, 322, 340, 341, 343, 344, 345, 346, 347, 348, 349, 352, 353, 367, 368, 369, 370, 371, 372, 373, 374, 375, 376, 377, 378, 379, 380, 389, 390, 391, 392, 394, 396, 398, 399, 411, 412, 413, 414, 415, 416, 417, 419, 423, 424, 426, 453, 454, 455, 456, 457, 458, 459, 460, 461, 462, 463, 464, 465, 473, 474, 475, 476, 477, 478, 479, 480, 481, 482, 483, 491, 492, 493, 494, 495, 496, 497, 498, 499, 500, 501, 502, 503, 505, 509, 510, 516, 518, 519, 520, 521, 522, 523, 524, 525, 526, 527, 528, 529, 530, 531, 532, 533, 534, 535, 536, 537, 544, 546, 554

Healthcare accessibility 1, 176, 186, 191, 249, 308, 374

healthcare innovation 256, 267, 268, 271, 274, 275, 276, 286, 287, 370

Healthcare sector 7, 102, 112, 115, 124, 140, 153, 166, 167, 176, 261, 268, 272, 279, 280, 281, 413, 453, 454, 463, 465, 474, 477, 478, 479, 498, 521

Healthcare Supply Chains 99, 100, 101, 102, 104, 106, 110, 112, 113, 492, 500

health communication 182, 183, 184, 185, 194, 195, 196, 197, 349

health disparities 10, 56, 60, 99, 272, 278, 283, 307, 341, 351, 373, 461, 462, 484, 510

health equity 278, 282, 283, 285, 367, 369, 370, 372, 373, 374, 376, 380, 480, 524, 534

Health Insurance 24, 44, 48, 60, 85, 87, 270, 271, 276, 312, 318, 320, 371, 459, 509, 510, 511, 517, 518, 520, 528, 530

health tech 23, 279, 306

health technology 7, 10, 101, 175, 195, 261, 308, 339, 351, 352, 369, 370, 371, 372, 373

I

Image Processing 73, 115, 116, 213, 328, 359

impact 1, 2, 3, 4, 6, 7, 14, 18, 26, 31, 33, 50, 51, 61, 62, 65, 66, 69, 70, 71, 74, 76, 77, 78, 79, 87, 90, 94, 95, 96, 97, 100, 104, 106, 107, 109, 110, 111, 112, 133, 135, 155, 156, 157, 158, 159, 160, 165, 177, 179, 188, 192, 197, 201, 202, 222, 224, 227, 228, 236, 241, 255, 256, 260, 261, 263, 264, 267, 271, 272, 273, 275, 277, 281, 282, 283, 284, 285, 286, 288, 289, 290, 291, 293, 298, 299, 302, 303, 304, 314, 316, 324, 325, 326, 328, 330, 331, 332, 333, 334, 336, 339, 340, 341, 344, 346, 347, 349, 355, 360, 362, 363, 373, 378, 386, 391, 394, 395, 396, 397, 400, 401, 402, 403, 406, 407, 408, 410, 411, 412, 416, 417, 425, 426, 427, 429, 437, 441, 443, 444, 445, 447, 449, 450, 457, 458, 459, 461, 462, 466, 467, 469, 473, 477, 479, 480, 483, 488, 493, 494, 495, 496, 497, 498, 499, 501, 502, 504, 505, 511, 513, 514, 523, 527, 530, 535, 539, 543, 547

India 1, 10, 11, 20, 22, 23, 24, 25, 29, 31, 37, 69, 70, 71, 76, 77, 79, 83, 94, 95, 96, 97, 99, 115, 128, 139, 155, 156, 157, 159, 160, 161, 181, 200, 211, 213, 227, 237, 238, 239, 241, 267, 275, 288, 292, 299, 301, 303, 311, 312, 324, 325, 326, 327, 333, 335, 336, 339, 356, 357, 362, 364, 367, 387, 389, 400, 402, 403, 407, 408, 409, 410, 411, 414, 415, 435, 439, 453, 469, 470, 473, 488, 491, 507, 509, 511, 515, 518, 521, 527, 542, 543, 544, 545, 546, 548, 553

Industry 5.0 33, 204, 208, 231, 234, 332, 383, 403, 435, 474, 478, 479, 480, 482, 483

innovation 13, 16, 23, 27, 28, 31, 32, 33, 34, 38, 45, 55, 57, 58, 61, 69, 71, 72, 74, 78, 94, 102, 110, 156, 164, 165, 169, 170, 179, 197, 203, 230, 241, 256, 267, 268, 270, 271, 272, 273, 274, 275, 276, 277, 280, 284, 285, 286, 287, 291, 294, 303, 305, 308, 316, 317, 318, 319, 326, 327, 330, 351, 352, 353, 358, 360, 362, 370, 371, 374, 376, 377, 378, 380, 394, 397, 398, 402, 436, 439, 440, 442, 443, 444, 445, 450, 465, 470, 474, 476, 477, 478, 479, 480, 481, 482, 491, 494, 502, 503, 519, 529, 531, 534, 536, 537, 541, 545

intelligent cards 440, 441, 442, 448

intelligent technologies 77, 202, 333, 339, 362, 473, 474, 475, 476, 477, 480, 481, 482, 483, 484

international collaboration 88, 89, 92

interoperability 55, 161, 163, 164, 165, 166, 169, 269, 270, 319, 346, 351, 367, 368, 369, 370, 371, 373, 375, 377, 379, 494, 497, 500

Investor 75, 273, 331, 361

K

Kinetic Profiling 393

KNN 143, 147, 148, 215, 217, 422

L

language barriers 181, 182, 196
Logistic Regression 128, 142, 145, 147, 148, 150, 151, 152, 153, 221, 223, 224, 411, 414, 419, 422, 423

M

Machine Learning 20, 26, 28, 38, 39, 42, 43, 44, 45, 46, 47, 48, 49, 53, 56, 57, 58, 63, 65, 68, 74, 75, 78, 83, 104, 108, 111, 112, 118, 120, 123, 126, 127, 128, 134, 135, 137, 139, 140, 141, 142, 143, 144, 145, 146, 147, 149, 153, 154, 162, 166, 175, 177, 178, 179, 182, 185, 190, 194, 197, 199, 204, 205, 206, 207, 208, 210, 213, 215, 219, 220, 221, 223, 224, 226, 231, 234, 236, 239, 263, 269, 292, 293, 294, 297, 302, 304, 306, 308, 321, 323, 342, 344, 345, 346, 355, 381, 383, 385, 386, 389, 392, 393, 394, 399, 405, 406, 408, 411, 412, 413, 414, 415, 416, 417, 418, 419, 420, 421, 422, 423, 424, 425, 426, 428, 429, 434, 435, 436, 440, 442, 456, 457, 461, 466, 468, 469, 470, 479, 487, 494, 506, 517, 518, 541, 546, 552
MRI 29, 125, 147, 150, 213, 215, 216, 217, 218, 219, 220, 222, 223, 224

N

Naïve-Bayes 422
National Stock Exchange 543, 547
Natural Language Processing 117, 181, 182, 184, 185, 190, 413
Neurological Disorder 213
Neuroplasticity 393

O

outcome-based financing 267

P

Parkinson's Diseases 213, 214, 224
Patient care 2, 45, 49, 57, 59, 63, 65, 83, 84, 85, 86, 89, 90, 92, 100, 104, 105, 108, 116, 121, 130, 140, 161, 162, 165, 166, 169, 170, 171, 173, 176, 185, 187, 190, 192, 245, 246, 247, 251, 260, 261, 267, 268, 276, 277, 282, 283, 321, 344, 353, 372, 378, 413, 453, 454, 455, 457, 458, 460, 461, 462, 464, 465, 475, 476, 479, 491, 492, 493, 494, 496, 498, 500, 502, 523, 524, 525, 526, 531, 533, 535
patient-centered 28, 57, 62, 107, 112, 165, 166, 167, 171, 190, 194, 278, 285, 380, 453, 461, 494, 495, 496, 497, 499, 500, 501, 502, 536
patient engagement 37, 64, 66, 100, 101, 181, 185, 187, 189, 190, 191, 194, 197, 268, 269, 278, 285, 308, 317, 460, 494, 496, 497, 499, 502, 503, 526, 528
patient outcomes 26, 29, 37, 38, 39, 41, 43, 44, 48, 52, 53, 54, 55, 58, 62, 63, 65, 66, 83, 84, 86, 87, 89, 91, 106, 123, 153, 154, 166, 170, 224, 246, 267, 268, 269, 272, 277, 283, 284, 286, 368, 371, 372, 377, 378, 412, 414, 417, 429, 454, 458, 459, 460, 464, 465, 479, 482, 493, 495, 500, 522, 523, 524, 531, 533
personalized healthcare 37, 38, 42, 45, 48, 57, 59, 63, 64, 65, 66
PET 46, 213, 216, 218, 219, 220, 224
Pharmaceutical 8, 74, 75, 95, 96, 108, 116, 117, 156, 164, 175, 206, 208, 226, 233, 235, 236, 247, 289, 295, 327, 329, 333, 373, 384, 403, 405, 407, 408, 436, 464, 468, 481, 487, 488, 510, 543, 544, 545, 546, 548, 550, 553
precision medicine 37, 38, 39, 40, 41, 42, 44, 52, 53, 54, 55, 56, 57, 59, 62, 64, 65, 66, 116, 119, 120, 121, 127, 134, 135, 137, 175, 245, 262, 263, 375, 378, 389, 399, 462, 478, 482
Predictive Analytics 28, 38, 39, 40, 42, 43, 47, 49, 50, 51, 53, 60, 62, 63, 65, 66, 86, 89, 106, 162, 164, 165, 167, 175, 189, 194, 195, 197, 246, 250, 284, 317, 321, 339, 341, 344, 345, 346, 347, 375, 390, 417, 418, 454, 457, 462, 463, 493, 496, 533, 537
Privacy 30, 37, 44, 48, 55, 59, 60, 83, 84, 85, 87, 88, 89, 90, 91, 92, 100, 104, 106, 107, 113, 116, 130, 161, 163, 165, 166, 168, 169, 173, 175, 182, 185, 188, 189, 193, 194, 196, 197, 198, 209, 247, 270, 276, 285, 305, 313, 318, 319, 320, 339, 343, 344, 346, 347, 349, 350, 351, 352, 367, 368, 369, 370, 371, 373, 375, 376, 377, 383, 391, 394, 398, 403, 412, 413, 426, 435, 441, 442, 443, 446, 447, 448, 450, 452, 457, 463, 464, 481, 483, 488, 497, 500, 501, 510, 520, 522, 523, 528, 529, 530, 531, 532, 534, 537
public-private partnerships 59, 267, 272, 273, 274, 276, 277, 282, 284, 285, 286, 316, 318, 346, 369, 370, 371, 374, 380, 481, 535

R

Random Forest 46, 79, 147, 148, 149, 150, 151, 152, 153, 215, 217, 335, 364, 411, 414, 419, 422, 423, 429
regulatory frameworks 45, 49, 55, 58, 61, 88, 89, 90, 91, 92, 106, 165, 166, 278, 285, 286, 304, 313,

316, 319, 347, 352, 353, 367, 368, 369, 371, 375, 377, 378, 379, 391, 394, 450, 453, 459, 465, 497, 534, 537
remote care delivery 270
resilience 16, 77, 108, 109, 111, 113, 201, 256, 258, 259, 333, 339, 340, 341, 343, 344, 345, 347, 348, 349, 352, 353, 362, 378, 389, 390, 392, 395, 396, 397, 399, 475, 477, 480, 485, 492, 493, 494, 496, 497, 498, 499, 500, 501, 502, 537, 546
reskilling 369, 370, 372, 379, 453, 455, 456
resource allocation 38, 49, 58, 63, 66, 89, 91, 170, 281, 282, 286, 321, 340, 344, 345, 352, 371, 413, 416, 417, 479, 480, 491, 495, 496, 497, 499, 500, 531, 537
resource management 53, 54, 95, 156, 202, 229, 235, 263, 291, 297, 298, 326, 339, 347, 382, 386, 402, 476, 480, 496
Returns 203, 229, 272, 543, 547, 548
Russia-Ukraine War 544, 545, 547, 548

S

scalability 6, 7, 170, 268, 284, 304, 308, 310, 316, 317, 345, 346, 348, 352, 368, 371, 379, 502, 503, 535
Scopus 3, 94, 103, 104, 105, 156, 201, 290, 325, 401, 467, 509, 511, 512, 513, 514, 518
SDG 3 16, 20, 21, 22, 23, 24, 25, 26, 102, 242, 243, 249, 250, 367, 369, 370, 372, 373, 374, 380, 473, 474, 476, 480, 481, 521, 522, 524, 527, 529, 531, 534, 535, 536, 537
SDG framework 475, 480, 482
Security 2, 19, 44, 48, 55, 71, 74, 76, 77, 79, 83, 84, 85, 87, 88, 89, 90, 91, 92, 96, 103, 104, 106, 107, 109, 116, 130, 137, 156, 158, 159, 162, 163, 164, 165, 166, 167, 168, 169, 171, 175, 178, 179, 185, 188, 193, 201, 204, 205, 208, 228, 231, 232, 236, 237, 239, 247, 265, 269, 270, 276, 285, 286, 290, 291, 293, 295, 299, 300, 302, 313, 317, 318, 319, 320, 325, 326, 334, 341, 348, 349, 352, 357, 362, 363, 371, 375, 376, 377, 379, 382, 383, 384, 386, 402, 404, 405, 408, 433, 434, 436, 440, 441, 442, 445, 448, 449, 450, 451, 452, 458, 467, 468, 470, 481, 483, 486, 487, 494, 502, 505, 506, 507, 509, 519, 523, 528, 530, 532, 535
smart cities 33, 34, 135, 157, 205, 237, 299, 359, 403, 467, 474, 483, 486, 540, 554
Society 5.0 33, 35, 474, 480, 482, 483
supply chain automation 108
surveillance 27, 28, 54, 76, 96, 159, 208, 235, 300, 331, 334, 341, 342, 343, 344, 346, 347, 348, 350, 351, 352, 361, 363, 409, 463, 464, 488, 520

Sustainability 4, 9, 14, 15, 18, 19, 32, 33, 34, 35, 38, 63, 65, 68, 70, 75, 76, 77, 78, 79, 96, 104, 106, 107, 109, 156, 159, 165, 172, 174, 177, 178, 179, 199, 206, 208, 210, 212, 232, 235, 237, 241, 242, 243, 254, 255, 260, 267, 268, 274, 277, 282, 284, 285, 288, 292, 293, 294, 300, 314, 315, 316, 323, 325, 330, 331, 333, 334, 335, 341, 345, 355, 357, 360, 362, 363, 372, 376, 379, 380, 383, 385, 400, 408, 409, 435, 438, 458, 466, 469, 470, 477, 479, 480, 481, 482, 483, 486, 494, 500, 502, 504, 506, 524, 529, 535, 537, 546, 552, 553
Sustainable Development 11, 12, 14, 15, 16, 17, 18, 19, 20, 21, 22, 24, 25, 30, 32, 33, 34, 35, 73, 77, 78, 79, 80, 94, 95, 102, 109, 110, 155, 157, 159, 165, 179, 211, 229, 235, 237, 239, 241, 242, 243, 248, 265, 288, 291, 294, 297, 299, 325, 332, 335, 336, 337, 359, 361, 362, 364, 365, 368, 370, 373, 374, 383, 387, 400, 409, 410, 435, 438, 468, 470, 473, 474, 477, 479, 480, 481, 486, 507, 521, 522, 531, 534, 535, 540, 542
SVM 46, 68, 69, 72, 80, 142, 143, 144, 145, 147, 148, 149, 150, 152, 153, 165, 215, 217, 219, 222, 223, 323, 327, 336, 355, 358, 364, 413, 422

T

Techno Invasion 241, 242, 243, 254, 255
technological integration 241, 535
technology 1, 2, 4, 6, 7, 9, 10, 11, 20, 21, 22, 23, 26, 27, 28, 29, 30, 31, 32, 33, 34, 35, 56, 58, 61, 69, 70, 71, 72, 73, 74, 75, 76, 77, 78, 79, 80, 83, 86, 88, 90, 92, 94, 101, 106, 107, 109, 110, 117, 119, 124, 126, 128, 130, 133, 134, 140, 141, 143, 144, 155, 156, 157, 159, 160, 161, 163, 164, 165, 166, 167, 168, 169, 170, 171, 172, 173, 174, 175, 176, 179, 180, 183, 189, 190, 194, 195, 201, 202, 203, 204, 206, 208, 210, 211, 213, 219, 224, 226, 228, 229, 230, 231, 232, 233, 235, 237, 238, 239, 241, 242, 243, 244, 246, 247, 249, 250, 252, 253, 254, 255, 256, 257, 258, 259, 260, 261, 262, 264, 265, 268, 269, 270, 275, 276, 277, 278, 284, 285, 286, 289, 290, 291, 292, 293, 294, 297, 299, 301, 302, 303, 305, 306, 308, 309, 310, 311, 312, 315, 316, 317, 319, 320, 323, 324, 325, 326, 327, 328, 329, 330, 331, 332, 335, 339, 340, 343, 346, 347, 348, 351, 352, 353, 355, 356, 357, 358, 359, 360, 361, 362, 364, 365, 367, 368, 369, 370, 371, 372, 373, 374, 375, 376, 377, 378, 379, 380, 382, 383, 384, 385, 386, 387, 394, 395, 396, 398, 400, 401, 402, 403, 404, 405, 406, 407, 408, 409, 411, 413, 415, 416, 433, 434, 435, 438, 439, 440, 441, 442, 443,

444, 445, 447, 448, 449, 450, 451, 453, 454, 457, 458, 460, 461, 464, 466, 467, 468, 469, 470, 471, 473, 474, 475, 476, 477, 478, 479, 480, 481, 482, 483, 485, 486, 488, 489, 491, 494, 504, 505, 506, 507, 509, 510, 512, 513, 517, 519, 521, 522, 524, 525, 526, 528, 529, 530, 531, 532, 534, 535, 536, 537, 540, 541, 542, 544, 546, 550, 552, 553, 554

Telemedicine 1, 2, 3, 11, 20, 22, 23, 27, 29, 30, 51, 57, 58, 110, 112, 161, 165, 167, 175, 188, 192, 195, 222, 245, 248, 249, 251, 256, 262, 267, 268, 269, 275, 303, 304, 305, 306, 307, 308, 309, 310, 311, 312, 313, 314, 315, 316, 317, 318, 319, 320, 321, 322, 347, 348, 349, 351, 352, 353, 374, 375, 378, 380, 393, 395, 474, 475, 477, 478, 521, 522, 524, 525, 526, 527, 528, 529, 530, 531, 532, 533, 534, 535, 536, 537

traditional methods 5, 116, 245, 442, 457

Transparency 28, 45, 48, 49, 51, 60, 84, 85, 86, 88, 89, 90, 92, 102, 144, 164, 166, 168, 171, 173, 176, 185, 189, 193, 196, 197, 224, 247, 254, 269, 273, 284, 285, 286, 343, 348, 349, 352, 368, 371, 374, 375, 378, 380, 398, 428, 429, 456, 459, 462, 463, 483, 494, 499, 500, 501, 509, 518, 523, 546

V

voice assistants 181, 182, 183, 184, 197

W

wellness management 181

Printed in the United States
by Baker & Taylor Publisher Services